TABLE B MEASURES OF U.S. INCOME, PRICES, AND FEDER[illegible]

Year	Net National Product	National Income	Personal Income	Disposable Income	GDP Deflator (1987=100) Index Number	GDP Deflator Percent Change	CPI (1982–1984=100) Index Number	CPI Percent Change	Federal Budget Deficit	Federal Debt
	Billions of Dollars								Billions of Dollars	
1929	94.0	84.7	84.3	81.7	12.5	—	—	—	0.7	16.9
1933	48.4	39.4	46.3	44.9	9.5	-4.1%	—	-5.1%	-2.6	22.5
1940	91.1	79.6	77.6	75.0	11.0	10.2%	14.0	0.7%	-2.9	50.7
1945	201.0	181.6	170.0	149.2	1.0	-4.0%	18.0	2.3%	-47.6	260.1
1950	264.6	239.8	228.1	207.5	20.2	1.5%	24.1	1.3%	-3.1	256.9
1951	306.2	277.3	256.5	227.6	21.3	5.4%	26.0	7.9%	6.1	255.3
1952	322.5	291.6	273.8	239.8	21.5	0.9%	26.5	1.9%	-1.5	259.1
1953	340.7	306.6	290.5	255.1	22.0	2.3%	26.7	0.8%	-6.5	266.0
1954	340.0	306.3	293.0	260.5	22.2	0.9%	26.9	0.7%	-1.2	270.8
1955	371.5	336.3	314.2	278.8	22.9	3.2%	26.8	-0.4%	-3.0	274.4
1956	390.1	356.3	337.2	297.5	23.6	3.1%	27.2	1.5%	3.9	272.7
1957	409.9	372.8	356.3	313.9	24.4	3.4%	28.1	3.3%	3.4	272.3
1958	414.0	375.0	367.1	324.9	24.9	2.0%	28.9	2.8%	-2.8	279.7
1959	452.5	410.1	391.2	346.7	25.6	2.8%	29.1	0.7%	-12.8	287.5
1960	470.2	425.7	409.2	360.5	26.0	1.6%	29.6	1.7%	0.3	290.5
1961	487.7	440.5	426.5	376.2	26.3	1.2%	29.9	1.0%	-3.3	292.6
1962	526.5	474.5	453.4	398.7	26.8	1.9%	30.2	1.0%	-7.1	302.9
1963	556.4	501.5	476.4	418.4	27.2	1.5%	30.6	1.3%	-4.8	310.3
1964	599.2	539.1	510.7	454.7	27.7	1.8%	31.0	1.3%	-5.9	316.1
1965	650.7	586.9	552.9	491.0	28.4	2.5%	31.5	1.6%	-1.4	322.3
1966	712.8	643.7	601.7	530.7	29.4	3.5%	32.4	2.9%	-3.7	328.5
1967	752.4	679.9	646.5	568.6	30.3	3.1%	33.4	3.1%	-8.6	340.4
1968	821.5	741.0	709.9	617.8	31.7	4.6%	34.8	4.2%	-25.2	368.7
1969	884.2	786.9	773.7	663.8	33.3	5.0%	36.7	5.5%	3.2	365.8
1970	928.3	833.5	831.0	722.0	35.1	5.4%	38.8	5.7%	-2.8	380.9
1971	1,007.3	899.5	893.5	784.9	37.0	5.4%	40.5	4.4%	-23.0	408.2
1972	1,105.7	992.9	980.5	848.5	38.8	4.9%	41.8	3.2%	-23.4	435.9
1973	1,241.9	1,119.5	1,098.7	958.1	41.3	6.4%	44.4	6.2%	-14.9	466.3
1974	1,334.1	1,198.8	1,205.7	1,046.5	44.9	8.7%	49.3	11.0%	-6.1	483.9
1975	1,433.9	1,285.3	1,307.3	1,150.9	49.2	9.6%	53.8	9.1%	-53.2	541.9
1976	1,602.7	1,435.5	1,446.3	1,264.0	52.3	6.3%	56.9	5.8%	-73.7	629.0
1977	1,789.4	1,609.1	1,601.3	1,391.3	55.9	6.9%	60.6	6.5%	-53.7	706.4
1978	2,019.8	1,829.8	1,807.9	1,567.8	60.3	7.9%	65.2	7.6%	-59.2	776.6
1979	2,248.4	2,038.9	2,033.1	1,753.0	65.5	8.6%	72.6	11.3%	-40.2	828.9
1980	2,430.2	2,198.2	2,265.4	1,952.9	71.7	9.5%	82.4	13.5%	-73.8	908.5
1981	2,701.4	2,432.5	2,534.7	2,174.5	78.9	10.0%	90.9	10.3%	-79.0	994.3
1982	2,780.8	2,522.5	2,690.9	2,319.6	83.8	6.2%	96.5	6.2%	-128.0	1,136.8
1983	3,016.0	2,720.8	2,862.5	2,493.7	87.2	4.1%	99.6	3.2%	-207.8	1,371.2
1984	3,368.3	3,058.3	3,154.6	2,759.5	91.0	4.4%	103.9	4.3%	-185.4	1,564.1
1985	3,599.1	3,268.4	3,379.8	2,943.0	94.4	3.7%	107.6	3.6%	-212.3	1,817.0
1986	3,799.1	3,437.9	3,590.4	3,131.5	96.9	2.6%	109.6	1.9%	-221.2	2,120.1
1987	4,042.4	3,692.3	3,802.0	3,289.5	100.0	3.2%	113.6	3.6%	-149.8	2,345.6
1988	4,374.2	4,002.6	4,075.9	3,548.2	103.9	3.9%	118.3	4.1%	-155.2	2,600.8
1989	4,686.4	4,249.5	4,380.3	3,787.0	108.5	4.4%	124.0	4.8%	-152.5	2,867.5
1990	4,940.1	4,468.3	4,664.2	4,042.0	113.2	4.3%	130.7	5.4%	-221.4	3,206.3
1991	5,068.8	4,544.2	4,828.3	4,209.6	117.8	4.1%	136.2	4.2%	-269.5	3,599.0
1992	5,294.3	4,743.4	5,058.1	4,430.8	120.9	2.6%	140.3	3.0%	-290.4	4,002.7

SOURCE: *Economic Report of the President,* January, 1993.

William A. McEachern

William A. McEachern is a professor of economics at the University of Connecticut. Since 1973 he has taught principles of economics, and in 1980 he developed a series of annual workshops for teaching assistants. He has given teaching workshops around the country. He earned an undergraduate degree *cum laude* in the honors program from Holy Cross College and an M.A. and a Ph.D. from the University of Virginia. He has published several books and monographs in public finance, public policy, and industrial organizations. His research has appeared in a variety of journals including *Economic Inquiry, National Tax Journal, Journal of Industrial Economics, Kyklos, The Quarterly Review of Economics and Business, Challenge,* and *Public Choice.* He has been quoted in publications such as the *Wall Street Journal, New York Times, Christian Science Monitor,* and *USA Today.* Professor McEachern has advised federal, state, and local governments on policy matters and directed a bipartisan commission examining Connecticut's finances. He has received the University of Connecticut's Faculty Award for Distinguished Public Service.

3RD EDITION

ECONOMICS

3RD EDITION

ECONOMICS

A CONTEMPORARY INTRODUCTION

William A. McEachern
Professor of Economics
University of Connecticut

COLLEGE DIVISION South-Western Publishing Co.
Cincinnati Ohio

Sponsoring Editor: James M. Keefe
Developmental Editor: Alice C. Denny
Production Editor: Rebecca Roby
Production House: Lifland et al., Bookmakers
Cover Design: Dolores Fairman
Interior Design: Joseph M. Devine
Senior Marketing Manager: James M. Keefe

HB83CA

ISBN: 0-538-82849-8

1 2 3 4 5 6 7 8 9 0 KI 2 1 0 9 8 7 6 5 4 3

Printed in the United States of America

Library of Congress Cataloging-in-Publication Data
McEachern, William A.
Economics : a contemporary introduction / William A. McEachern. — 3rd ed.
p. cm.
Includes bibliographical references and index.
ISBN 0-538-82849-8
1. Economics. I. Title.
HB171.5.M475 1994
330—dc20 93-10939
CIP

I(T)P South-Western is a subsidiary of ITP (International Thomson Publishing). The trademark ITP is used under license.

To Pat

PREFACE

Economics has a short history but a long past. As a distinct discipline, economics has been studied for only a few hundred years, but civilizations have confronted the economic problem of scarce resources and unlimited wants for thousands of years. Economics may be centuries old, but it is new every day. Each day offers fresh evidence that can be used to support or to reshape evolving economic theory. In *Economics: A Contemporary Introduction*, I draw on my twenty years of teaching principles of economics to convey the vitality and timeliness of the discipline. I believe that I am new enough to the task to keep the discussion fresh but experienced enough to get it right.

Remember the last time you were in an unfamiliar neighborhood and had to ask for directions? Along with the directions came the standard comment "You can't miss it!" So how come you missed it? Because the "landmark" that was obvious to the neighborhood resident who gave the directions might as well have been invisible to you, a stranger. Writing a principles text is much like giving directions. The author's familiarity with the material can be both a strength and a weakness. Knowing the material is obviously essential to the task. But familiarity can dull one's perceptions: those who have taught economic principles for years may have trouble seeing them with fresh eyes. As a result, principles authors sometimes have difficulty describing an economic point to newcomers. Some authors try to compensate by telling all they know, in the process overwhelming the student with so much detail that the central point gets lost. Other authors take a minimalist approach by offering little of what students may already know intuitively and instead talking about abstracts—good *x* and good *y*, units of labor and units of capital, or the proverbial widget. This turns economics into a foreign language—an approach that may work with advanced undergraduates and with graduate students but not with students in a principles course.

Students typically arrive the first day of class with a lifetime of experience with economic institutions, economic events, and economic choices. Each student grew up in a household—the central economic institution. As consumers, students are familiar with fast food restaurants, movie theaters, car dealers, and dozens of stores at the mall. Most students have also been resource suppliers—more than half held jobs while in high school. Students also have experience with government: they know about sales taxes, drivers licenses, speed limits, and public education. And they have a growing awareness of the rest of the world: they buy all sorts of imported goods, and the nightly news tells them about trade deficits, famines in Africa, and emerging market economies around the globe.

Thus, students have abundant experience with economic institutions, economic events, and economic choices. But many principles authors neglect this rich lode of student experience, believing instead they must create for the student a new world based on economics as a foreign language. These authors miss the chance to make the connection between economics and what Alfred Marshall called "the ordinary business of life." If examples fail to connect with student experience, the point is lost. Examples should be self-explanatory; they should convey the point quickly and directly. Having to explain an example is like having to explain a joke. As Edmund Burke noted, "Example is the school of mankind, and they will learn at no other."

Good directions rely on landmarks familiar to us all: a stop light, a fork in the road, a white picket fence. Likewise, a good textbook builds bridges from the familiar to the unknown. In this book I draw on common experience to convey economic points. I try to create graphic pictures in the students' minds by using examples that need little explanation. I try to elicit from the reader that light of recognition, that "aha!" Clear and palpable examples allow me to push the analysis further than is possible in textbooks that rely on less obvious or more abstract examples. Throughout, I provide just enough intuitive information and institutional detail to get the point across without overwhelming the student. My approach is to start where students are, not where we would like them to be. For example, to explain the division of labor, rather than refer to Adam Smith's pin factory, I call attention to the division of labor at McDonald's. Similarly, I explain resource substitution by talking about specific examples of alternative labor–capital mixes—for example, a drive-through car wash versus a Saturday morning send-the-band-to-Disney-World charity car wash—rather than by referring to abstract units of labor and capital.

Since instructors can cover only a fraction of the textbook material in class, principles texts should, to the extent possible, be self-explanatory, thereby providing instructors with greater flexibility to emphasize topics of special interest. Because my examples are so contemporary, instructors can draw on more traditional examples to provide students with additional insight.

Introductory Chapters

Topics common to both macroeconomics and microeconomics are covered in the first four chapters. Limiting the introductory material to four chapters saves precious class time, particularly at institutions where students can take macro and micro courses in either order (and hence where students are likely to end up repeating the introductory chapters).

Growing Significance of the World Economy

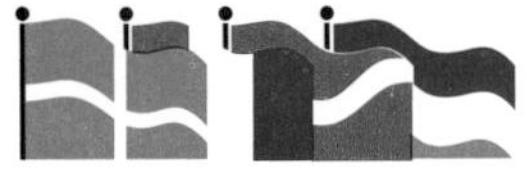

This edition reflects the growing impact of the world economy on U.S. economic welfare. The book stresses the interdependence between the U.S. economy and the rest of the world. International issues are introduced early and are discussed often. For example, the rest of the world is introduced as an economic actor in Chapter 1, and comparative advantage and the production possibilities frontier are each discussed from a global perspective in Chapter 2.

The international coverage is not simply added as an afterthought; it is woven into the text to enhance the entire presentation. For example, students gain greater perspective about such topics as economic growth, unemployment, inflation, federal deficits and debt, central banks, unionization trends, environmental laws, tax rates, and the distribution of income if the U.S. experience is compared with that in other countries around the world. Likewise, students can better understand how free markets allocate resources when problems confronting the transitional economies around the world are examined. And recent trends in the competitive structure of the U.S. economy cannot be understood without examining the role of imports, trade barriers, and trade pacts such as the North American Free Trade Agreement. The flag icon that appears in the margin calls attention to international coverage.

Macroeconomics

Since there is no consensus about which macroeconomic model explains the economy best, some textbooks present a smorgasbord of alternative macroeconomic approaches, leaving it to the student to choose among them. Students, however, lack sufficient background to evaluate the alternatives, so competing theories often seem unrelated and confusing. Rather than dwell on the differences among competing schools of thought, I use the aggregate demand and aggregate supply model to focus on the fundamental distinction between those economists who believe that the economy is essentially stable and self-correcting and those who believe that the economy is unstable and in need of government intervention. This approach allows for a discussion of the policy prescriptions that flow from these differences between activists and nonactivists.

Wherever possible, I rely on the students' experience and intuition to explain the theory behind macroeconomic abstractions such as aggregate demand and aggregate supply. For example, to explain how employment can temporarily exceed its natural rate, I note how students, as the term draws to a close, can temporarily shift into high gear to study for final exams and finish term papers.

In light of changes in the national income accounts, this edition uses gross domestic product, or GDP, rather than gross national product, or GNP. I have made the graphs more readable and more intuitively obvious by using numbers rather than letters. And to convey a feel for the size of the U.S. economy, I use trillions of dollars rather than billions of dollars. For example, students have an easier time grasping a change in real GDP expressed as an increase from \$5.0 trillion to \$5.2 trillion rather than as an increase from Y to Y'.

Emerging issues of macroeconomics that receive special scrutiny in this edition include asymmetric information in banking, the time inconsistency problem in macroeconomic policy, cold turkey and inflation, President Clinton's fiscal policies, and the convergence of national economies. Some other timely issues are discussed in new case studies on hysteresis and the problem of high unemployment in Great Britain and France, Clinton's industrial policy, the link between central bank independence and inflation around the world, and the connection between easy bank credit and overbuilding in commercial real estate.

Microeconomics

My approach to microeconomics underscores the role of time and information in production and consumption. For example, Chapter 4 has a new case study on how the microchip has fueled the information revolution, making information processing a modern-day cottage industry. Chapter 28 reflects the growing literature on problems of imperfect information; the chapter addresses informational issues such as optimal search theory, the lemon problem, the winner's curse, adverse selection, signaling, screening, moral hazard, principal–agent problems, and reputation as hostage. The microeconomic presentation also reflects the growing interest in economic institutions, particularly the internal organization of firms and governments. More generally, I try to convey the intuitive notion that most microeconomic principles operate like gravity: market forces work whether or not individual economic actors understand them.

In Chapter 27 I discuss recent developments in financial markets, such as the market for corporate control, leveraged buyouts, and S corporations. Chapter 31 examines the economic implications of current, though controversial, issues such as global warming, the destruction of the tropical rain forests, and the market for pollution rights. Chapter 32 includes additional information about poverty among those of Hispanic origin and focuses more on female householders, the underclass, and why the overall poverty rate has not improved since 1969. Some other timely issues include new case studies about entry barriers in the airline industry, pollution in Mexico City, the demand for architects as a reflection of derived demand, and U.S. Postal Service productivity.

Use of Color

Color is used systematically to enhance student understanding of graphs and charts. For example, notice how color shading highlights the underlying data in the following exhibit drawn from Chapter 4, which displays federal spending by major category since 1940. Throughout the book, demand curves are blue and supply curves are red. In comparative statics, the curves determining the final equilibrium point are darker than the initial curves.

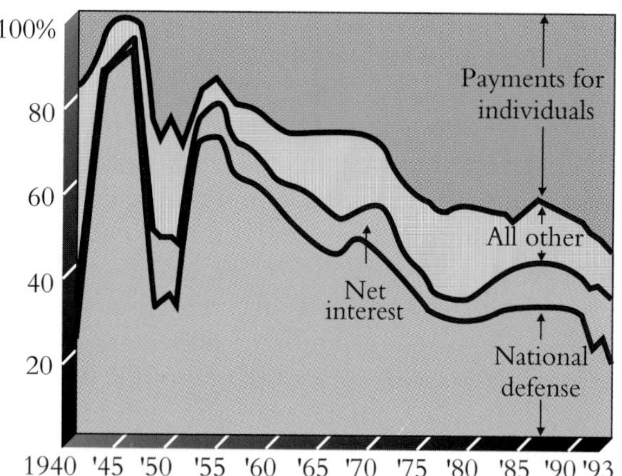

Color shading also identifies areas in graphs reflecting such measures as tax incidence, economic profit or loss, consumer surplus, producer surplus, the welfare effects of tariffs and quotas, and aggregate output below and above the economy's potential. For example, in the following exhibit, drawn from Chapter 11, red shading identifies real GDP levels below the economy's potential and blue shading identifies levels exceeding the economy's potential. Note that the initial aggregate demand curve is the lighter blue *AD* and the resulting aggregate demand curve is the darker blue AD^*. Note also that magnitudes along the axes are measured in trillions of dollars rather than identified by letter symbols. Graphs are accompanied by captions (omitted here) that explain the key features.

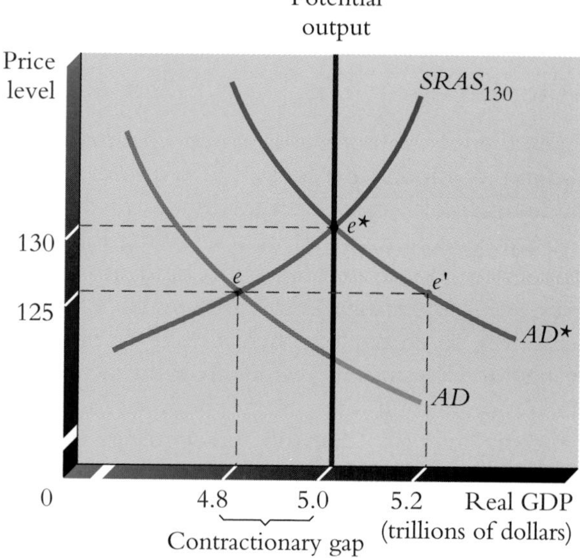

As another example of the use of color, consider this exhibit drawn from Chapter 21. Notice

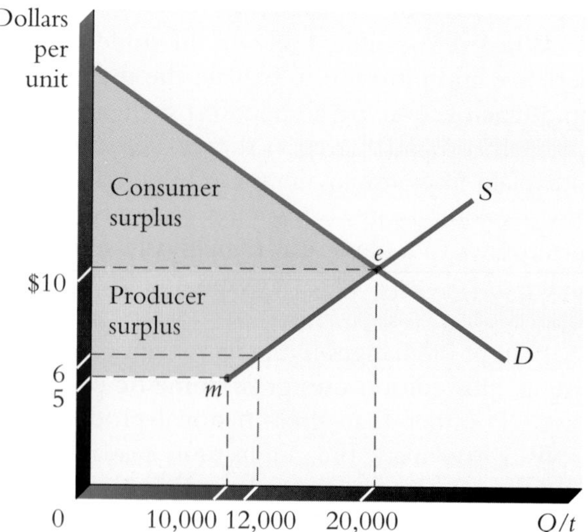

how easily color allows the student to identify the consumer surplus and producer surplus. If it were not for the color shading, the student would have to be guided by a series of points identifying each triangle. In short, color is employed consistently and with forethought as a pedagogical aid; color is more than mere face entertainment.

Organization

In many principles textbooks, chapters are interrupted by boxed material, parenthetical explanations, qualifying footnotes, and other distractions that disrupt the flow. Segregating material from the mainstream of a chapter leaves students uncertain about when or if this material should be read. In contrast, this book has a natural flow. Each chapter opens with a motivating paragraph and a list of key ideas, then tells a compelling story, using logical sections and subsections. Qualifying footnotes are used sparingly and parenthetical explanations are used hardly at all. Moreover, case studies appear in the natural sequence of the chapter. Students can thus read each chapter smoothly from beginning to end, without a hitch. The text includes the following features:

A CLOSER LOOK. Some otherwise complicated diagrams, such as the circular flow, are introduced as a series of transparency overlays. Called "A Closer Look," these overlays allow students to learn the material in a step-by-step manner.

CASE STUDIES. Each chapter contains a minimum of one case study, which draws out the economic implications of a contemporary event. These self-contained features show the link between economic theory and everyday life. There are two end-of-chapter questions based on each case study; these questions are color coded with a bar that matches the marginal shading of the case studies.

END-OF-CHAPTER MATERIALS. Each chapter contains both a *Conclusion* and a *Summary.* The conclusion draws the discussion to a close; the summary reviews the key points. The number of end-of-chapter questions has been increased. Many questions are analytical, requiring the student to perform calculations or to draw graphs. Suggested answers to the questions and problems are provided in the *Instructor's Manual.*

MARGINAL DEFINITIONS. Important economic terms appear in boldface in the body of the text. These terms are defined in the margins and are also listed in the Glossary.

APPENDIXES. Several end-of-chapter appendixes provide more detailed treatment of various topics. The appendix to Chapter 1 is recommended for all students unfamiliar with variables, graphs, slopes, and the like. Other appendixes are optional in the sense that subsequent material does not rely on them. Including additional material in this way offers the instructor greater flexibility of coverage with no loss of continuity.

GLOSSARY. Key terms are listed alphabetically in the glossary, which appears at the end of the book, just before the index.

Student Ancillaries

STUDY GUIDE. Chapters of the student *Study Guide* correspond to the chapters in the text. Each chapter includes (1) an introduction; (2) a chapter outline, with definitions of all terms; (3) a discussion of the chapter's main points; (4) a "lagniappe," or bonus, which supplements the material in the chapter and is accompanied by a "Question to Think About"; (5) a list of key terms; (6) a variety of questions, including completion, true/false, multiple choice, and discussion questions; and (7) answers to all these questions. The *Study Guide* may be purchased at your bookstore.

CD-ROM DISC. South-Western's multimedia CD-ROM disc combines text, audio, video, still images, and animated figures in an interactive format ideal for student-controlled learning as well as instructor-led presentations. The CD-ROM disc for McEachern's *Economics: A Contemporary Introduction* contains the entire textbook, the accompanying *Study Guide*, over two-hundred animated exhibits, and video and audio explanations of key exhibits. All of this information can be randomly accessed and displayed through an MPC-compatible computer system employing a CD-ROM disc drive. The accompanying *CD-ROM User's Guide* describes how to operate this technology. The CD-ROM disc may also be purchased at your bookstore.

McEachern Support Package

ANNOTATED INSTRUCTOR'S EDITION. The *Annotated Instructor's Edition* includes additional information in the margins to support the instructor's classroom presentation. Three types of marginal comments are provided: (1) *points to stress* underscore economic concepts that may need emphasis; (2) *examples* reinforce economic concepts; and (3) *teaching tips* suggest alternative ways to convey key ideas. In all, there are more than one thousand marginal comments in the *Annotated Instructor's Edition.*

Point to Stress The law of demand refers to the *direction* of the relationship between quantity demanded and price; price elasticity of demand refers to the *relative size* of the relationship.

VIDEODISC. Videodisc technology is the ultimate multimedia approach to classroom presentations. Its flexibility and ease of use make it a dynamic tool for instructors. The videodisc for *Economics: A Contemporary Introduction* contains text-related video, definitions, transparencies, and animated illustrations for classroom projection. The videos and other segments can be viewed in any order, and, with an optional computer and South-Western software, the instructor can prepare a complete video presentation ahead of time. An accompanying *Videodisc Instructor's Guide* describes how to integrate this technology in the classroom. A compatible "CAV-type" videodisc player is required to use this ancillary.

HYPERMEDIA SOFTWARE FOR WINDOWS AND MACINTOSH. This cutting-edge software is a valuable resource for the classroom and for student computer laboratories. For each chapter, the software includes (1) all exhibits, on which the instructor can shift curves, identify points and shaded areas on graphs, and carry out what-if calculations; (2) all marginal definitions, along with the ability to enter notes or examples for each definition; (3) a scrolling field that contains the chapter's key points and that may be modified by the user; and (4) for the Windows version, a series of questions about each exhibit, along with answers and explanations. The Windows version is in color; the Macintosh version in monochrome and runs on virtually all Macintosh computers. The computer disk for this program is provided free to adopters of this textbook; the disk may be copied and distributed to students. This software was written by John Pisciotta of the Baylor University Department of Economics.

LECTURE PRESENTATION MANAGER. The *Lecture Presentation Manager* integrates instructor resource materials provided by South-Western with the instructor's own text files, graphics, and support software and formats them for effective classroom display using any standard computer projection device. This software runs on any computer running MS-DOS with a graphics display and one disk drive, although a hard disk is recommended.

INNOVATIVE TEACHING TRANSPARENCIES. There are 100 transparencies of exhibits in the text. Most are in multiple colors and more than one-third are Innovative Teaching Transparencies: hinged overlays allowing for a step-by-step exposition of complicated diagrams.

TEST BANK. The *Test Bank* has been thoroughly revised since the second edition, and the number of questions has been increased to over seven thousand. Included in each chapter of the the test bank are multiple choice, true/false, and short-answer questions. *None of the questions duplicates those in the Study Guide and most are new or revised since the previous edition.* The *Test Bank* comes in two volumes—macro and micro—and is also available on a computer disk that can be used with either IBM-compatible or Macintosh computers. The software allows instructors to edit questions and to print graphs in the body of the test.

INSTRUCTOR'S MANUAL. The *Instructor's Manual* includes (1) an outline and brief overview of each chapter; (2) a summary of each chapter's main points; (3) pedagogical tips that expand on points raised in the chapter; (4) a list of additional readings; and (5) suggested answers to the end-of-chapter questions and problems.

TEACHING ASSISTANCE MANUAL. The *Teaching Assistance Manual* provides additional support beyond the *Instructor's Manual* and may be especially useful to new instructors, graduate students, and teachers who would like to generate more class discussion. This manual offers (1) overviews and outlines of each chapter; (2) chapter objectives and quiz material; (3) material for class discussion; (4) topics warranting special attention; (5) supplementary examples; and (6) "What if?" discussion questions. Four appendixes provide guidance on (a) presenting material; (b) generating and sustaining class discussions; (c) preparing, administering, and grading quizzes; and (d) coping with the special problems confronting foreign graduate assistants.

THE TEACHING ECONOMIST. Since 1990 I have edited the *The Teaching Economist*, which is a newsletter aimed at making teaching more interesting and more fun. The newsletter discusses new and imaginative ways to present topics—for example, how to integrate international topics or how to generate and sustain class discussion. A regular feature of *The Teaching Economist* is "The Grapevine," which offers teaching ideas suggested by colleagues from across the country. (The first six issues of *The Teaching Economist* are reprinted at the end of the *Teaching Assistance Manual.*) Contact your South-Western representative for more information.

Acknowledgments

Many people contributed to this book's development. I would like to thank my colleagues at the University of Connecticut who provided helpful feedback for the third edition, especially Francis Ahking, William Alpert, Peter Barth, Alpha Chiang, Dennis Heffley, Stephen Miller, William Lott, Stephen Sacks, and Imanuel Wexler. I also gratefully acknowledge the insightful comments of those who reviewed material for this edition:

Ted Amato, *University of North Carolina at Charlotte*

Thomas Andrews, *Temple University*

Dale G. Bails, *Iowa Wesleyan College*

Maurice Ballabon, *CUNY Bernard M. Baruch College*

Andy Barnett, *Auburn University*

Richard Barnett, *SUNY at Buffalo*

Jurgen Brauer, *Augusta College*

Gardner Brown Jr., *University of Washington*

Robert K. Brown, *Texas Tech University*

Judy C. Butler, *Baylor University*

Giorgio Canarella, *California State University at Los Angeles*

Richard J. Cebula, *Georgia Institute of Technology*

James Peery Cover, *University of Alabama*

Joseph Daniels, *Marquette University*

Elynor G. Davis, *Georgia Southern University*

Susan M. Davis, *SUNY College at Buffalo*

A. Edward Day, *University of Central Florida*

Janet S. Deans, *Chestnut Hill College*

David A. Denslow, *University of Florida*

Donald S. Elliott Jr., *Southern Illinois University at Edwardsville*

Gisela Meyer Escoe, *University of Cincinnati*

Mark Evans, *California State University at Bakersfield*

Eleanor R. Fapohunda, *SUNY College of Technology at Farmingdale*

Mohsen Fardmanesh, *Temple University*

Rudy Fichtenbaum, *Wright State University*

Rodney Fort, *Washington State University*

Michael P. Gallaway, *University of Texas at Austin*

Grant W. Gardner, *Southern Methodist University*

Adam Gifford, *California State University at Northridge*

J. Robert Gillette, *Texas A&M University*

Daniel M. Gropper, *Auburn University*

Robert Halvorsen, *University of Washington*

Nathan Hampton, *St. Cloud State University*

William T. Harris, *University of Delaware*

Baban Hasnat, *SUNY College at Brockport*

Jane Smith Himarios, *University of Texas at Arlington*

Bruce C. Horning, *Vanderbilt University*

Calvin Hoy, *County College of Morris*

Shane Hunt, *Boston University*

Beth Ingram, *University of Iowa*

David D. Jaques, *California State Polytechnic University at Pomona*

Nancy Jianakoplos, *Colorado State University*

John Kane, *SUNY College at Oswego*

Walter H. Kemmsies, *Memphis State University*

D. Mark Kennet, *Tulane University*

Faik Koray, *Louisiana State University*

Joseph D. Kotaska, *Monroe Community College*

Laraine Lomax, *Northeastern University*

Ana Maria Lomperis, *North Carolina State University*

Richard Long, *Georgia State University*

Gabriel Manrique, *Winona State University*

Robert A. Margo, *Vanderbilt University*

Wolfgang Mayer, *University of Cincinnati*

J. Harold McClure Jr., *Villanova University*

John M. McDowell, *Arizona State University*

James McLain, *University of New Orleans*

Milton G. Mitchell, *University of Wisconsin at Oshkosh*

Kellie Poyas, *Colorado State University*

Reza Ramazani, *St. Michaels College*

Carol H. Rankin, *Xavier University*

John J. Reid, *Memphis State University*

Diane Lim Rogers, *Pennsylvania State University*

Mark Rush, *University of Florida*

Richard Saba, *Auburn University*

Peter M. Schwarz, *University of North Carolina at Charlotte*

Lee J. Van Scyoc, *University of Wisconsin at Oshkosh*

Donna E. Shea, *Bentley College*

William F. Shughart II, *University of Mississippi*

Philip A. Smith, *DeKalb College*

V. Kerry Smith, *North Carolina State University*

Janet Speyrer, *University of New Orleans at Lakefront*

George Spiva, *University of Tennessee*

Stuart E. Theil, *Washington State University*

Jin Wang, *University of Wisconsin at Stevens Point*

William Weber, *Eastern Illinois University*

David R. Weinberg, *Xavier University*

Michael D. White, *St. Cloud State University*

Peter Wyman, *Spokane Falls Community College*

William Zeis, *Bucks Community College*

I also thank the following, who reviewed material for the second edition:

David W. Brasfield, *Murray State University*

Charles Callahan III, *SUNY College at Brockport*

Larry A. Chenault, late of *Miami University*

Curtis R. Clarke, *Brookhaven College*

Steven A. Cobb, *Xavier University*

James M. Cox, *DeKalb College*

Jerry L. Crawford, T. *Arkansas State University*

Joseph P. Daniels, *Marquette University*

David H. Dean, *University of Richmond*

G. Rod Erfani, *Transylvania University*

T. Windsor Fields, *James Madison University*

Gary M. Galles, *Pepperdine University*

James R. Hill, *Central Michigan University*

Janice Holtkamp, *Iowa State University*

Joseph M. Lammert, *Raymond Walters College*

Thomas M. Maloy, *Muskegon Community College*

Wolfgang Mayer, *University of Cincinnati*

Floyd B. McFarland, *Oregon State University*

Martin I. Milkman, *Murray State University*

Kathryn A. Nantz, *Fairfield University*

Mitch Redlo, *Monroe Community College*

Rexford Santerre, *Bentley College*

Robert J. Stonebreaker, *Indiana University of Pennsylvania*

Thomas TenHoeve III, *Iowa State University*

David R. Weinberg, *Xavier University*

Richard D. Winkelman, *Arizona State University*

Mesghena Yasin, *Morehead State University*

Finally, I thank the following reviewers of the first edition:

Polly Reynolds Allen, *University of Connecticut*

Jacquelene M. Browning, late of *Texas A&M University*

Art Goldsmith, *Washington and Lee University*

William R. Hart, *Miami University*

Andrew J. Policano, *University of Wisconsin-Madison*

Steven M. Sheffrin, *University of California, Davis*

Roger Sherman, *University of Virginia*

Houston H. Stokes, *University of Illinois at Chicago*

Gregory H. Wassall, *Northeastern University*

Leland B. Yeager, *Auburn University*

I relied on the division of labor based on comparative advantage to prepare the most complete teaching package on the market today. As noted already, John Pisciotta of Baylor University wrote the Hypermedia software. John Lunn of Hope College wrote the *Study Guide*. Steven Cobb of Xavier University authored the *Instructor's Manual* and coauthored the *Test Bank*. Other *Test Bank* coauthors include Elynor Davis of Georgia Southern University, Charles Martie of Quinnipiac College, and Paul Natke of Central Michigan University. Brigid Harmon, who was closely involved with the previous edition as Developmental Editor, wrote the marginal annotations for the *Annotated Instructor's Edition*. I thank all of my colleagues for their contributions to the project.

The talented staff at South-Western Publishing provided invaluable editorial, administrative, and sales support. I would especially like to acknowledge the help of Alice Denny, Developmental Editor, Rebecca Roby, Production Editor, and the creative efforts of the advertising staff. I am deeply indebted to Jim Keefe, who, first as Acquisitions Editor and now as Senior Marketing Manager, has had overall responsibility for the project, beginning with the first edition. I also gratefully acknowledge the support of South-Western's dedicated customer service and sales force, for they contributed in a significant way to the gratifying success of the second edition, which made the third edition possible. In addition, the support of the following Sales Specialists is much appreciated: Peter Adams, Rob Jared, Pamela Killingsworth, Tim Meekma, Dave Phanco, and Jim Simpson. Finally, I owe a profound debt to my wife, Pat, who not only offered encouragement and support but read the entire manuscript, providing helpful comments and insights along the way.

William A. McEachern

Three Suggested Outlines for One-Term Courses

	Emphasis		
	Macroeconomics	*Microeconomics*	*Balanced Macro/Micro*
1 The Art and Science of Economic Analysis	R	R	R
2 Some Tools of Economic Analysis	R	R	R
3 The Market System	R	R	R
4 The Economic Actors	R	R	R
5 Introduction to Macroeconomics	R		R
6 Measuring Economic Aggregates and the Circular Flow of Income	R		R
7 Unemployment and Inflation	R		R
8 Aggregate Demand: Consumption, Investment, and Net Exports	R		R
9 Aggregate Expenditure and Demand-Side Equilibrium	R		R
10 Aggregate Supply	R		O
11 Fiscal Policy, Aggregate Demand, and Equilibrium Output	R		O
12 Money and the Financial System	R		R
13 Banking and the Money Supply	R		R
14 Monetary Theory and Policy	R		
15 The Policy Debate: Activism Versus Nonactivism	R		
16 Budgets, Deficits, and Public Policy	R		
17 Productivity and Growth	R		
18 Elasticity of Demand and Supply		R	R
19 Consumer Choice and Demand		R	
20 Cost and Production in the Firm		R	R
21 Perfect Competition		R	R
22 Monopoly		R	R
23 Monopolistic Competition and Oligopoly		R	R
24 Resource Markets		R	R
25 Human Resources: Labor and Entrepreneurial Activity		R	O
26 Unions and Collective Bargaining		O	
27 Capital, Interest, and Corporate Finance		O	
28 Imperfect Information, Transaction Costs, and Market Behavior		O	
29 Regulation, Deregulation, and Antitrust Activity		O	
30 Public Choice	O	O	O
31 Externalities and the Environment		O	
32 Income Distribution and Poverty		O	O
33 International Trade	O	R	R
34 International Finance	R	O	O
35 Problems of Developing Countries	O		O
36 Economies in Transition: From Central Planning to Competitive Markets		O	O

R = Recommended; O = Optional.

CONTENTS IN BRIEF

Part 3
Fiscal and Monetary Policy

Part 4
Introduction to the Market System

Part 5
Market Structure and Pricing

Part 6
Resource Markets

Part 7
Market Failure and Public Policy

Part 8
The International Setting

CONTENTS

PART 1
INTRODUCTION TO ECONOMICS 1

PART 3 FISCAL AND MONETARY POLICY 255

3RD EDITION

ECONOMICS

PART 1

Introduction to Economics

CHAPTER 1

THE ART AND SCIENCE OF ECONOMIC ANALYSIS

You have been reading and hearing about economic issues for years—unemployment, inflation, oil prices, the federal deficit, college tuition, housing prices. When the explanations of these issues go into any depth, your eyes probably glaze over, and you tune out the same way you do when the weather forecaster tries to provide an in-depth analysis of high-pressure fronts colliding with moisture carried in from the coast. Because of a negative experience with economics, some of you may have been dreading this course. Some of you may have had to work up your courage just to open this book.

What many people fail to realize is that economics is much more alive than the dry accounts offered by the news media. Economics is about making choices, and you make economic choices every day—choices about whether to get a part-time job or focus entirely on your studies, live in a dorm or off-campus, take a course in accounting or one in history, pack a lunch or buy a Big Mac. Because you, as an economic decision maker, are the subject of this book, you already know much more about economics than you realize. You bring to the subject a rich personal experience, an experience that will be tapped throughout the book to reinforce your understanding of the basic ideas. This chapter will introduce you to the art and science of economic analysis. Topics discussed in this chapter include

- Scarce resources
- Unlimited wants
- Marginal analysis
- Rational self-interest
- Scientific method
- Normative versus positive analysis
- Pitfalls of economic thinking

The Economic Problem: Scarce Resources but Unlimited Wants

Would you like a new car, a nicer home, better meals, more free time, a more interesting social life, more spending money, more sleep? Yes, you say? Even if you are able to satisfy some of these desires, others will keep popping up. *The problem is that although your wants, or desires, are virtually unlimited, your resources are scarce.* A resource is *scarce* when there is not enough of it to satisfy people's wants. Because of scarce resources, you must choose from among your many wants and, whenever you choose, you must forgo satisfying some wants.

Point to Stress Resources are scarce in a relative sense even if they appear abundant in an absolute sense. Because of relative scarcity, they command a price.

This problem of scarce resources but unlimited wants is faced to a greater or lesser extent by each of the more than five billion people around the world. It is faced by taxicab drivers, by farmers, by students, by politicians, by shepherds, by everybody. The taxicab driver uses the cab and other scarce resources—knowledge of the city, driving skills, time—to earn income, which can be exchanged for housing, groceries, clothing, trips to Disney World, and other goods and services aimed at satisfying the driver's unlimited wants. **Economics** is the study of how people choose to allocate their scarce resources in order to produce, exchange, and consume goods and services in an attempt to satisfy their unlimited wants. We shall first consider what we mean by resources, next examine goods and services, and finally focus on the heart of the matter: economic choice, which arises from scarcity.

Economics The study of how people choose to use their scarce resources in an attempt to satisfy unlimited wants

Resources

Resources are divided into four broad categories: land, labor, capital, and entrepreneurial ability. These resources are combined in various ways to produce goods and services. **Land** represents not only land in the conventional sense of plots of ground but all other natural resources—all so-called gifts of nature, including bodies of water, trees, minerals, and even animals. **Labor** comprises the broad category of human effort, both physical and mental. Labor includes the effort of both the cab driver and the brain surgeon. Note that labor itself is derived from a more fundamental scarce resource: *time*. Time is really the ultimate raw material of life. Without it we can accomplish nothing. Our time can be put to alternative uses: we can *sell* our time as labor, or we can *spend* our time doing other things such as sleeping, listening to music, or watching TV.

Land Plots of ground and other natural resources used in the production of goods and services

Labor The physical and mental effort of humans

Capital represents human creations that are used to produce goods and services. We often distinguish between human capital and physical capital. *Human capital* consists of the knowledge and skills people acquire to enhance their productivity, such as the taxi driver's knowledge of the city's streets or the surgeon's knowledge of the human body. *Physical capital* consists of roads, airports, buildings, machinery, tools, and other manufactured items that are used to produce goods and services. Physical capital includes the driver's cab,

Capital All buildings, equipment, and human skill used to produce goods and services

Entrepreneurial ability Managerial and organization skills combined with the willingness to take risks

Rent The payment resource owners receive for the use of their land

Wages The payment resource owners receive for their labor

Interest The payment resource owners receive for the use of their capital

Profit The return resource owners receive for their entrepreneurial ability

the surgeon's scalpel, the ten-ton press used to print *Newsweek*, the interstate highway system, and the building where your economics class meets.

A special kind of human skill is called **entrepreneurial ability**—that rare talent required to build a better mousetrap. The entrepreneur identifies the need for a new product or finds a better way to produce an existing product. The entrepreneur tries to discover and act on profitable opportunities by hiring resources and assuming the risk of success or failure. The largest firms in the world today, such as Ford, IBM, and Microsoft, each began as an idea in the mind of an individual entrepreneur.

Resource owners are paid for the *time* their resources are employed by entrepreneurs, so resource payment has a time dimension, as in a wage of $10 per hour or rent of $600 per month. Resource owners are paid **rent** for their land, **wages** for their labor, and **interest** for their capital. The entrepreneur's effort is rewarded by **profit**, which is the difference between sales revenue and the cost of other resources employed. Put another way, the entrepreneur is the *residual claimant*, who *claims* the *residual*—what's left over—after all other resource suppliers are paid. Sometimes the entrepreneur ends up in the hole.

Teaching Tip If you want to provide more detail about entrepreneurial ability, incorporate some of the material found in Chapter 25.

Goods and Services

Good A tangible item that is used to satisfy wants

Service An intangible activity that is used to satisfy wants

Scarce The amount people desire exceeds the amount that is freely available

Resources are combined in a variety of ways to produce goods and services to satisfy human wants. A farmer, a tractor, 50 acres of land, plus seeds and fertilizer produce a good: corn. One hundred musicians, musical instruments, some chairs, a conductor, a musical score, and a music hall combine to produce a service: Beethoven's Fifth Symphony. Corn is a **good** because it is something we can see, feel, and touch that requires scarce resources to produce and is used to satisfy human wants. The book you now hold, the chair you are sitting in, your next meal, and the clothes you have on are all goods. The rendition of the Fifth Symphony is a **service** because it is not something tangible, yet it uses scarce resources to satisfy human wants. Lectures, movies, phone calls, dry cleaning, and haircuts are all services.

Because goods and services require scarce resources, they are themselves scarce. A good or service is **scarce** if the amount people desire exceeds the amount that is freely available. Since we cannot have all the goods and services we would like, we must continually choose among them. We must choose among better living quarters, better meals, nicer clothes, higher-quality entertainment, more late-night pizza, and so on. Making choices in a world of scarcity means that some goods and services must be passed up.

Point to Stress Making choices is often necessary because time is scarce.

A few goods and services are considered *free* because the amount freely available exceeds the amount people desire. For example, air and seawater are often considered free because we can breathe all the air we want and have all the seawater we can haul away. Yet, despite the old saying that "The best things in life are free," most goods and services are scarce, not free, and even those that seem to be free come with strings attached. For example, *clean* air and *clean* seawater have become increasingly scarce because the atmosphere is used as a gas dump and the ocean as a sewer. *Without scarcity, there would be no*

Example Competing uses: Trees in a rain forest in Western Samoa have been found to contain a compound that, in laboratory experiments, protects cells against the AIDS virus. In 1987, those same trees were to be sold for lumber to provide funds for a village school. The sale was stopped, and the forest declared a national preserve.

economic problem. Goods and services that are truly free are not the subject matter of economics.

Sometimes we mistakenly think of certain goods as free because they involve no apparent cost to us. Those subscription cards that keep falling out of magazines appear to be free. At least it seems we would have little difficulty rounding up about three thousand if necessary! Their production, however, uses up scarce economic resources, resources drawn away from competing uses, such as producing higher-quality magazines perhaps. You may have heard the expression "There is no such thing as a free lunch." The lunch may appear to be free to us, but it draws scarce resources away from the production of other goods and services. A Russian saying makes a similar point but with more bite: "The only place you find free cheese is in a mousetrap."

Economic Actors

Point to Stress The interaction of these economic actors determines how an economy's resources are allocated.

There are four types of actors in the U.S. economy: households, firms, governments, and the rest of the world. *Households* play the leading role. As consumers, households demand the goods and services produced, and as resource owners, households supply the land, labor, capital, and entrepreneurial ability to firms and to governments. *Firms* and *governments* are supporting actors because they supply the goods and services demanded by households. The *rest of the world* includes foreign households, firms, and governments, which supply products to U.S. markets and demand U.S. products.

Market A set of arrangements through which buyers and sellers carry out exchange at mutually agreeable terms

Product market A market in which goods and services are exchanged

Resource market A market in which resources are exchanged

Markets are the means by which buyers and sellers carry out exchange. Markets are often physical places, such as a supermarket, department store, or shopping mall. Markets also include the mechanisms by which buyers and sellers communicate their intentions, such as letters, phone calls, classified ads, radio and television ads, and face-to-face bargaining. These market mechanisms provide information about the quantity, quality, and price of products offered for sale. Goods and services are bought and sold in **product markets**; resources are bought and sold in **resource markets**. The most important resource market is the labor market, or job market. Think of your experience looking for a job, and you get some idea of this market.

Microeconomics and Macroeconomics

Microeconomics The study of the economic behavior of decision makers

Although you have made thousands of economic choices, if you are like most people, you have seldom reflected on your own economic behavior. For example, why did you choose to spend your scarce resource—time—reading this book right now rather than doing something else? **Microeconomics** is the study of your economic behavior and the economic behavior of other economic actors making choices about such matters as what to buy and what to sell, how much to work and how much to play, how much to borrow and how much to save. Microeconomics examines the factors that affect individual economic choices, how changes in these factors affect such choices, and how the choices of various decision makers are coordinated by markets. For example, microeconomics focuses on the determination of price and output in individual markets, such as the market for breakfast cereal or the market for sports equipment.

You have perhaps given little thought to the factors influencing your own economic behavior. You have probably given even less thought to the way your choices link up with the billions of choices made by hundreds of millions of other individuals to bring about changes in economy-wide aggregate variables such as inflation, unemployment, and economic growth. **Macroeconomics** studies the performance of the economy as a whole. Whereas microeconomics is a study of the individual pieces of the economic puzzle, as reflected, for example, by particular markets, macroeconomics puts all the pieces together to focus on the big picture. Macroeconomics considers the combined effects of billions of individual choices on the overall performance of the economy as reflected by such measures as the nation's general price level, total production, level of employment, and economic growth.

Macroeconomics The study of the behavior of entire economies

Just as the whole consists of the sum of its parts, the economy is ultimately driven by the individual choices made by people like you in responding to changes in the economic environment. Thus, a study of the big picture—of economic aggregates such as unemployment, inflation, and growth—must be based on an understanding of the individual choices behind those aggregates.

THE ART OF ECONOMIC ANALYSIS

Our economy results from the choices of millions of individuals attempting to satisfy their unlimited wants. Because these choices lie at the very heart of the economic problem—the problem of scarce resources but unlimited wants—they deserve closer scrutiny. Developing an understanding of the factors that shape economic choices is the first step toward mastering the art of economic analysis.

Rational Self-Interest

A key economic assumption is that individuals, in making choices, rationally select alternatives they perceive to be in their best interests. By *rational* we mean simply that people try to make the best choices they can under the circumstances. People may not know with certainty which alternative will turn out to be the best. They simply select the alternatives they *expect* will yield them the most satisfaction and happiness.

Point to Stress The rational self-interest assumption implies that individuals do not *consciously* make themselves worse off, but it does not imply that individuals cannot make bad choices.

This reliance on *rational self-interest* should not be viewed as blind materialism, pure selfishness, or greed. We all know people whose favorite radio station is WIIFM (What's In It For Me?), but for most of us self-interest often includes the welfare of our family, our friends, and perhaps the poor of the world. But our concern for others is influenced by economic considerations. We are more likely to donate our old clothes than our new ones to organizations such as Goodwill Industries. We may volunteer to drive a friend to the airport on Saturday afternoon, but we are less likely to offer a ride if our friend's plane leaves at 6:00 A.M. People are more inclined to give to their favorite charities if their contributions are tax deductible. *The point is that the notion of self-interest does not rule out concern for others; it simply means that concern for others is to some extent influenced by the same economic factors that affect other economic choices.* The lower the personal cost of helping others, the more help will be offered.

Teaching Tip In general, rational self-interest means that individuals try to minimize the cost of achieving a given benefit or maximize the benefit achieved with a given cost.

Economic Analysis Is Marginal Analysis

Economic choice usually involves some adjustment to the existing situation, or to the status quo. The software producer must decide whether to revise or discontinue one of the company's word processing programs. The town manager must decide whether to hire another worker for street maintenance. Your favorite jeans are on sale, and you must decide whether to buy another pair. You are wondering whether you should carry an extra course next term. You have just finished dinner and must decide whether to have dessert.

Economic choices may involve working a little more or a little less, studying a little more or a little less, buying a little more or a little less, selling a little more or a little less. Economic choices are based on a comparison of the expected marginal costs and the expected marginal benefits of the change under consideration. **Marginal** means "incremental" or "decremental"; it refers to a change in an economic variable, a change in the status quo. *You, as a rational decision maker, will change the status quo as long as your expected marginal benefit from the change exceeds your expected marginal cost.* Thus, you compare the marginal benefit you expect from the dessert—your additional enjoyment from consuming it—with its marginal cost—the extra money, extra time, and extra calories.

Marginal A term meaning "incremental" or "decremental," used to describe a change in an economic variable

Typically the change under consideration is small, but marginal choices can involve what appear to be major economic adjustments, as in the decision to quit school and get a job. For a firm, a marginal choice might mean producing a new product, building a plant in Taiwan, or even filing for bankruptcy. By focusing on the effects of marginal adjustments to the status quo, the economist is able to cut the analysis of economic choice down to manageable size. Rather than confront head-on a bewildering economic reality, the economist can begin with marginal choices, then see how these marginal choices affect particular markets and help shape the economic system as a whole.

Example In 1992, General Motors was unable to produce Saturns quickly enough to maintain stock at the dealerships. Auto analysts concluded that General Motors should consider building another Saturn plant in Tennessee at a cost of $500 million to $1 billion.

Choice Requires Time and Information

Rational choice takes time and requires information. But both time and information are scarce and valuable, so we seldom know all we would like to know prior to making choices. If you have any doubts about the time and information required to make choices, talk to someone who recently purchased a house, a car, or a personal computer. Talk to a corporate official deciding whether to introduce a new product or where to locate a new factory.

Teaching Tip Explain that rational decision makers will continue to acquire information only as long as the expected additional benefit exceeds the expected additional cost of the information.

Example Households are more likely to do a lot of comparison shopping before buying a car than before buying laundry detergent.

Consider your own experience in selecting a college. You probably talked to friends, relatives, teachers, and guidance counselors; very likely you looked at school catalogs and various college guides; you may have visited a few campuses to meet with the admissions staff and with anyone else who was willing to talk. The decision took time and money, not to mention creating aggravation and anxiety.

Because information is costly to acquire, we are often willing to pay others to gather and digest it for us. The market for stock analysts, travel agents, real estate brokers, career counselors, restaurant guidebooks, college guidebooks, and *Consumer Reports* magazine indicates our willingness to pay for information that will improve our economic choices.

To review: The art of economic analysis focuses on how individuals use their scarce resources in an attempt to satisfy their unlimited wants. Rational self-interest guides individual choice. Choice involves a comparison of the marginal costs and marginal benefits of alternative actions, a comparison that requires time and information. To understand when and why marginal changes occur, we must examine the impact of economic events on individual choices. The economist studies such impacts in a systematic manner called the scientific method. We examine the science of economic analysis next.

THE SCIENCE OF ECONOMIC ANALYSIS

Economic theory, economic model A simplification of reality designed to capture the important elements of the relationship under consideration

Teaching Tip Provide an example of an economic theory, such as "An increase in households' disposable income, other things constant, will cause an increase in consumption spending."

Economists use the science of economic analysis to develop theories, or models, to explain how some aspect of the economy works. An **economic theory**, or **economic model**, is a simplification of economic reality that captures only the important elements of the situation under study. Theories, or models, *are used to make predictions about the real world.* Economic theories need not contain every detail and interrelation. In fact, the more details a theory contains, the more unwieldy it becomes and the less useful it is. The world we confront is so complex that we must simplify if we want to make any sense of things. A theory can be presented verbally, graphically, or mathematically.

The Role of Theory

The role of theory is usually not well understood by most people. Perhaps you have heard someone say "Oh, that's fine in theory, but in practice it's another matter." The implication is that the theory provides little aid in practical matters. People who say this fail to realize that what they are actually doing is substituting their own theory for a theory they either do not believe or do not understand. In effect, they are saying "I have my own theory, which works better."

All of us employ theories, however poorly defined or understood. Someone who pounds on the Pepsi machine that just ate his quarter has a crude theory about how that machine works and what just went wrong. One version of that theory might go: "The quarter drops through a series of whatchamacallits, but sometimes the quarter gets stuck. *If* I pound on the machine, *then* I can free up the quarter and send it on its way." Evidently this theory works well enough that many individuals continue to pound on machines that fail to perform (a real problem for the vending machine industry). Yet if you asked this mad pounder to explain his "theory" about how the machine operates, he would look at you as if you were crazy.

Point to Stress Economics is a *social* science dealing with the structure of society and the activities of its members. As such, the study of economics overlaps with other social sciences such as psychology and political science.

The Scientific Method

To study economic problems, economists employ a process of theoretical investigation called the *scientific method*. This method can be understood most easily by breaking it down into four steps.

Variable A measure, such as price or quantity, that can take on different possible values

STEP ONE. The first step is to identify and define the key variables that are relevant to the economic problem under consideration. A **variable** is a measure, such as the *price* of Pepsi or the *quantity* of Pepsi, that can take on different possible values. The variables of concern become the basic elements of the theory, so they must be selected with care.

Other-things-constant assumption The assumption, when focusing on key economic variables, that other variables remain unchanged

STEP TWO. The second step is to specify the assumptions about the conditions under which the theory is to apply. Assumptions lay out the framework for the theory. One major category of assumptions is the **other-things-constant assumption**—in Latin, the *ceteris paribus* assumption. The idea is to identify the variables of interest, then to focus exclusively on the relation among them, assuming that nothing else of importance will change. For example, suppose that we are interested in how the quantity of Pepsi purchased per week is influenced by changes in its price. Since we wish to isolate the relation between the price of Pepsi and the quantity purchased, we assume that there will be no changes in other important variables such as consumer income, the price of Coke, and the average temperature.

Behavioral assumption An assumption that describes the expected behavior of economic actors

We also make assumptions about individual behavior; these are called **behavioral assumptions**. Perhaps the most fundamental behavioral assumption is that of rational self-interest. As noted earlier, we assume that individual decision makers rationally pursue their self-interest and make choices accordingly. Rationality implies that each consumer buys the products expected to maximize his or her level of satisfaction. Rationality also implies that each producer supplies the products expected to maximize the firm's profit. These kinds of assumptions are known as behavioral assumptions because they specify how economic actors are expected to behave—what makes them tick, so to speak.

Hypothesis A statement about relationships among key variables

STEP THREE. The third step of the scientific method is to formulate a **hypothesis**, which is a theory about how key variables relate. For example, one hypothesis holds that *if* the price of Pepsi goes up, other things constant, *then* the quantity purchased will go down. Thus, the hypothesis becomes a prediction of what will happen to the quantity purchased if the price goes up. The purpose of this theory, like that of any theory, is to make predictions about the real world.

Point to Stress Economic theories cannot be proved, only rejected or not rejected.

STEP FOUR. The validity of the theory must be tested by confronting its predictions with evidence. Testing hypotheses, the fourth step, is perhaps the most difficult because data must be collected in a way that focuses attention on the variables in question, while at the same time carefully controlling for other effects. The test will lead us either to reject the theory as inconsistent with the evidence or to continue using the theory until another one comes along that predicts even better. It may be that a theory is not a good predictor at all times, yet still does a better job of predicting than competing theories.

Economists Tell Stories

Despite economists' reliance on the scientific method for developing and evaluating theories, economic analysis is perhaps as much art as science. Observing some phenomenon in the real world, isolating the key variables, formulating a theory to predict how these variables relate, and devising an unambiguous way to test the predictions all involve more than simply an understanding of economics and the scientific method. Carrying out these steps requires a good intuition for identifying, relating, measuring, and testing theories.

Economic analysis also calls for the imagination of a storyteller. Economists tell stories about how they think the world works. Although these are technically called theories or models, they are stories nonetheless. To tell a compelling story, the economist relies on case studies, anecdotes, parables, and the personal experience of the listener. Throughout this book you will hear stories that bring you closer to the ideas under consideration. These stories help breathe life into economic theory and allow you to personalize abstract ideas. For example, here is a case study about the popular use of vending machines in Japan.

CASE STUDY

A Yen for Vending Machines

The rate of unemployment in Japan is usually less than half the rate in the United States. For example, in 1992 Japan's unemployment rate was about 2 percent, compared to about 7 percent in the United States. A low Japanese birth rate and tight controls on immigration have reduced the availability of even unskilled workers in Japan. Because labor there is relatively scarce, Japanese retailers rely extensively on vending machines as a way of reducing the labor required to sell goods. Vending machines obviously eliminate the need for a sales clerk. Japan has more vending machines per capita than any other country in the world—more than twice as many as the United States and nearly ten times as many as Europe.

A low unemployment rate is not the only reason vending machines are more popular in Japan than in the United States. As noted earlier, in the

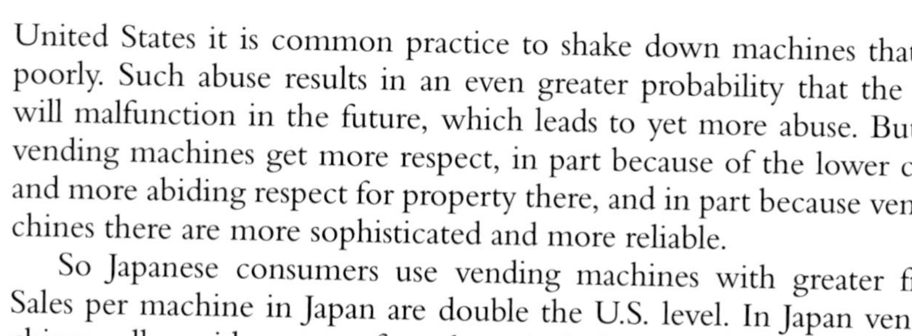

United States it is common practice to shake down machines that perform poorly. Such abuse results in an even greater probability that the machines will malfunction in the future, which leads to yet more abuse. But in Japan vending machines get more respect, in part because of the lower crime rate and more abiding respect for property there, and in part because vending machines there are more sophisticated and more reliable.

So Japanese consumers use vending machines with greater frequency. Sales per machine in Japan are double the U.S. level. In Japan vending machines sell a wide range of products including video cassettes, whisky, hot pizza, and even dating services. Despite the relative abundance of vending machines in Japan, they are expected to continue to multiply.

Source: See "Push-button Lover," *The Economist*, 16 November 1991.

The case study conveys two points. First, producers combine resources in a way that conserves the resource that is relatively more costly, in this case labor. Second, the customs and conventions of the marketplace may differ across countries and this may result in different types of economic arrangements, such as the more extensive use of vending machines in Japan.

Predictions Versus Forecasts

A prediction of a theory is not the same as an economic forecast. Economic theory might predict that *if* consumer spending increases, *then* employment will increase, other things constant. A theory is usually offered as a *conditional* statement—that is, a statement in the form of *if-then*. In contrast, an *economic forecast* might state simply that employment will increase next year. The forecast is not offered as a conditional statement but more as a guess about what will happen to employment. If the forecast turns out to be wrong, this says nothing about the validity of the theory linking consumer spending and employment because the forecast was not offered as a prediction of a theory.

Remember this distinction between the predictions of economic theories and the forecasts of economists. Predictions are conditional statements of the *if-then* variety, whereas forecasts are more like guesses about what will actually occur. It is the forecaster you hear from most in the media. It's been said that economists make forecasts not necessarily because they know but because they are asked. *Although the economist may be the most informed forecaster, keep in mind that forecasts are nothing more than educated guesses.*

Example If the federal government cuts personal income taxes across the board, certain households may choose to save all of their increase in disposable income. On average, however, household spending will rise.

Predicting Average Behavior

The task of an economic theory, then, is to predict the effect of an economic change on economic choices and, in turn, the effect of these choices on particular markets and on the economy as a whole. Does this mean that economists try to predict the behavior of particular consumers or producers? No, because any particular individual may behave in an unpredictable way. But the unpredictable actions of numerous individuals tend to cancel one another out, so the *average behavior* of groups can be predicted with more accuracy. For example, the instructor cannot predict very well which particular students will be absent on a given day but can predict fairly accurately what percentage of the class will be absent. Likewise, if the price of a Whopper is cut in half, the manager of Burger King can better predict how total Whopper sales will increase than how a particular customer will respond. *The random actions of individuals tend to offset one another so that the average behavior of a large group can be predicted more accurately than can the behavior of a particular individual.* Consequently, economists focus on the average behavior of people in groups—for example, as Whopper consumers—rather than on the specific behavior of a particular economic actor.

Example Positive statement: According to the Census Bureau, the percentage of the U.S. population living in poverty increased from 13.5 percent in 1990 to 14.2 percent in 1991. Normative statement: The federal government should allocate more money to programs designed to reduce poverty.

Normative Versus Positive Analysis

Positive economic statement A statement that can be proved or disproved by reference to facts

Normative economic statement A statement that represents an opinion, which cannot be proved or disproved

Economists, through their simplifying models, try to explain how the world works. But sometimes economists concern themselves not with how the world works but with how it *should* work. Compare these two statements: "The U.S. unemployment rate is 7 percent" and "The U.S. unemployment rate should be lower." The first is called a **positive economic statement** because it is an assertion about economic reality that can be supported or rejected by reference to the facts. The second statement is called a **normative economic statement** because it reflects an opinion, and an opinion is merely that—it cannot be shown to be true or false by reference to the facts. Positive statements concern what *is*; normative statements concern what, in someone's opinion, *should be*. Positive statements do not have to be true, but they must be subject to verification or refutation by reference to the facts.

Theories are expressed as positive statements, such as "If the price increases, the quantity demanded will decrease." Most of the disagreement among economists involves questions about normative policy rather than statements of positive analysis. To be sure, many theoretical issues still are unresolved, but there is broad consensus in the economics profession about most fundamental theoretical principles—that is, there is much agreement about positive economic analysis. For example, in a survey of two hundred U.S. economists,[1] 90 percent agreed with the statement "A minimum wage increases unemployment among young and unskilled workers"; 98 percent agreed with the statement "A ceiling on rents reduces the quantity and quality of housing available." Both of these are positive statements because they can be shown to be consistent or inconsistent with the evidence. In contrast, there was much less agreement on normative statements, such as "The government should be an employer of last resort and initiate a guaranteed job program." Only 53 percent of the economists surveyed agreed with that statement.

Point to Stress Economic hypotheses that are generally accepted in one country may not be generally accepted in another country. For example, a survey reported in the *American Economic Review* in December, 1984 indicated that 79.2 percent of U.S. economists agreed that tariffs and import quotas reduce general economic welfare, but only 26.5 percent of French economists agreed.

1. J. Kearl et al., "A Confusion of Economists," *American Economic Review* 69 (May 1979): Table 1.

Example Hurricane Andrew hit south Florida and Louisiana in August, 1992. The U.S. dollar reached historic lows against the German mark in September. But the statement "The hurricane caused the international value of the U.S. dollar to fall" is false.

Some Pitfalls of Faulty Economic Analysis

Economic investigation, like other forms of scientific inquiry, is subject to common mistakes in reasoning that can cause the unwary to draw faulty conclusions. We will discuss three possible sources of confusion.

Association-causation fallacy The incorrect idea that if two variables are associated in time, one must necessarily cause the other

THE FALLACY THAT ASSOCIATION IS CAUSATION. Does this sound familiar: "The stock market was up today as traders reacted favorably to higher profits reported by General Motors"? Although stock-market analysts typically claim that millions of stock market transactions spring from a single event, such simplifications are often misleading and even wrong. To assume that event B was caused by event A simply because B and A were associated in time is to fall into the **fallacy that association is causation**, a common error. The fact that one event follows another or that one event occurs with another does not necessarily imply that one causes the other. Do not confuse subsequence with consequence. Remember: *Association is not necessarily causation.*

Fallacy of composition The incorrect belief that what is true for the individual or part must necessarily be true for the group or whole

THE FALLACY OF COMPOSITION. Suppose a farmer with an abundant harvest anticipates a financially successful year. But other farmers also have abundant harvests so the increase in supply depresses farm prices enough to *reduce* total farm revenue. The farmer has committed the **fallacy of composition**, which is an erroneous belief that what is true for the individual or for the part is also true for the group or the whole. Similarly, standing up at a football game to get a better view doesn't work if others stand as well. And arriving early to get in line for the rock-concert tickets doesn't work if many others arrive early as well.

Example A gas station at an intersection with two or three competing stations will not take customers away from its competitors by lowering its price if the competing stations match the price cut. All stations will lose revenues.

THE MISTAKE OF IGNORING THE SECONDARY EFFECTS. In many cities, public officials, because of concern about escalating rents, have imposed rent controls on housing. The *primary effect* of this policy, the effect on which policy makers focus, is to keep rents from rising. Over time, however, fewer new units are built because the rental business becomes less profitable. Moreover, existing rental units deteriorate because owners cannot recover rising maintenance costs through higher rents. Thus, the quantity and quality of housing may well decline as a result of what appeared to be a reasonable public policy of keeping rents from going up. The policy makers' mistake was to ignore the **secondary effects** of their policy. Economic actions have secondary effects that often turn out to be more important than the primary effects. Secondary effects may develop more slowly and may not always be obvious, but good economic analysis takes them into account.

Secondary effects Unintended consequences of economic actions that develop slowly over time as people react to events

If Economists Are So Smart, Why Aren't They Rich?

Example The current structure of the U.S. welfare system has the secondary effect of lowering incentives to work.

Why aren't economists rich? Well, some of them are. Taikichiro Mori of Japan, a former economics professor, is reportedly the richest person in the world.[2] Some economists earn as much as $20,000 per appearance on the

2. This ranking is found in "The World's Billionaires," *Forbes,* 20 July 1992, p. 164.

lecture circuit. Others earn thousands a day as consultants. Economists have been appointed to many high-level government positions, including not only positions for which they have clear expertise, such as Chairman of the Federal Reserve Bank, Director of the Office of Management and Budget, Chairman of the President's Council of Economic Advisers, Secretary of Commerce, Secretary of the Treasury, and Secretary of Labor, but also other positions where the connection is less obvious, such as Secretary of State and Secretary of Defense. Both Presidents Reagan and Bush majored in economics. Economics is the only social science and the only business discipline for which the prestigious Nobel Prize is awarded, and pronouncements by economists are reported in the media daily.

Leonard Silk, an economic columnist for the *New York Times*, writes: "Businessmen employ economists in large numbers or consult them at high fees, believing that their cracked crystal balls are better than none at all. The press pursues the best-known seers. While many laymen may be annoyed by economists, other social scientists *hate* them—for their fame, Nobel Prizes, and ready access to political power."[3] Despite its critics, the economics profession thrives because its models usually do a better job of making economic sense out of a confusing world than do alternative approaches. In the land of the blind, the one-eyed man is king.

But not all economists are rich, nor is personal wealth the objective of the discipline. In a similar vein, not all doctors are healthy (some of them even smoke); not all carpenters live in perfectly built homes; not all marriage counselors are happily married; and not all child psychologists have well-adjusted children.

CONCLUSION

This textbook describes how economic factors affect individual choices and how all these choices come together to shape the economic system. Economics is not the whole story, and economic factors are not always the most important. But economic factors have important and predictable effects on individual choices, and these choices affect the way we live. Economics is a challenging discipline, but it is also an exciting and rewarding one. The good news is that you already know a great deal about economics. But to use this knowledge, you must cultivate the art and science of economic analysis. You must be able to simplify the real world to isolate the key variables and then tell a persuasive story about how these variables relate.

An economic relation can be stated in words, represented as a schedule of quantities, described by a mathematical equation, or illustrated as a graph. The appendix to this chapter provides an introduction to the use of graphs. Some of you may find the appendix unnecessary. If you are already familiar

3. Leonard Silk, *Economics in Plain English* (New York: Simon and Schuster, 1978), p. 17 (emphasis in original).

with relations among variables, slopes, tangents, and the like, you can probably just browse. Those of you with little recent experience with graphs, however, will benefit from a more careful reading, with pencil and paper in hand. In the next chapter we will introduce some key ideas of economic analysis. Subsequent chapters will use these ideas to explore economic problems and to explain economic behavior that may otherwise appear puzzling. You must walk before you can run, however, and in the next chapter you will take those first wobbly steps.

SUMMARY

1. Economics is the study of how people choose to use their scarce and limited resources to produce, exchange, and consume goods and services in an attempt to satisfy their unlimited wants. The economic problem arises from the conflict between scarce resources and unlimited wants. If wants were limited or if resources were not scarce, there would be less need to study economics.

2. Economic resources are combined in a variety of ways to produce goods and services. Major categories of resources include (1) land, representing all natural resources, (2) labor, (3) capital, and (4) entrepreneurial ability. Because economic resources are scarce, only a limited amount of goods and services can be produced with them; hence, choices must be made.

3. Microeconomics focuses on choices in households, in firms, and in governments and how these choices affect particular markets such as the market for stereo equipment. Each choice is assumed to be guided by rational self-interest. Choice typically requires time and information, both of which are scarce and valuable. Whereas microeconomics examines the individual pieces of the puzzle, macroeconomics steps back to consider the big picture—the performance of the economy as a whole.

4. Economists use theories, or models, to help predict the effects that changes in economic factors will have on choices and, in turn, the effects these choices will have on particular markets and on the economy as a whole. Economists employ the scientific method to study economic problems by (1) isolating the key variables, (2) specifying the assumptions under which the theory operates, (3) deriving predictions about how, according to the theory, the variables relate, and (4) testing the theory by comparing these predictions with the evidence. Some theories may not work perfectly, but they will continue to be used as long as they predict better than competing theories.

5. Positive economic analysis is aimed at discovering how the world works. Normative economic analysis is concerned more with how, in someone's opinion, the world should work. Economic analysis, if not pursued carefully, can result in inaccurate conclusions arising from the fallacy that association is causation, the fallacy of composition, and ignorance of the secondary effects.

QUESTIONS AND PROBLEMS

1. (Definition of Economics) Recently some economists have conducted controlled experiments on animals. They claim that some animals act according to basic economic theory. That is, when animals are faced with external constraints, they act as though they are seeking to satisfy goals. If the researcher changes the constraints, the animals exhibit predictable behavioral changes. How does such constrained goal seeking conform to the definition of economics given in the text? Are animals different from humans when it comes to economic behavior?

2. (Resources) Determine which category of resources each of the following belongs in:
   a. A taxicab
   b. Computer software
   c. One hour of legal counsel
   d. A parking lot
   e. A forest
   f. The Mississippi River
   g. A prison

3. (Goods and Services) Explain why each of the following should *not* be considered a "free lunch" for the economy as a whole:
   a. Food stamps
   b. U. S. aid to developing countries
   c. Corporate charitable contributions
   d. Noncable television programs
   e. High school education

4. (Resources) California, New York, and Michigan have high per-capita incomes; some other states have low per-capita incomes. Can these differences be explained by scarcity of resources?

5. (Resources and Scarcity) "The only real resource that the human race has is the human mind." This line is often used to counter arguments that society is running out of its scarce resources. Is there truth in the statement? Are the resources of land, labor, and capital being depleted faster than they can be replaced?

6. (Micro Versus Macro) Some economists believe that in order to really understand macroeconomics, one must fully understand microeconomics. How does microeconomics relate to macroeconomics?

7. (Rational Self-Interest) Classical economists maintained that society would be optimally arranged if individual members of society pursued their own self-interest. Is such a sweeping generalization valid? What about such problems as traffic jams, litter, and runs on banks? Doesn't self-interest need to be considered in the context of the aggregation of individual goals and their feasibility?

8. (Marginal Analysis) A small pizza store must decide whether to increase the radius of its delivery area by a mile. What considerations must be taken into account if such a decision is to contribute to profitability?

9. (The Value of Time) Economists often attempt to measure the value of time by using wage rates or average salary levels. According to these measures, the value of time in growing economies is always rising. How does the growing value of time affect the types of products and services being introduced into the economy? How might this increase in the value of time be related to the widespread use of microwave ovens, video cassette recorders, McDonald's, and automatic tellers at banks?

10. (Pitfalls of Economic Thinking) Using the discussion of pitfalls in economic thinking, identify the fallacy or mistake in thinking in each of the following statements:
    a. Raising taxes will always increase government revenues.
    b. Whenever there is a recession, imports tend to decrease. Thus, to stop a recession, we should increase imports.
    c. Thriftiness is a sound virtue for the family and for the nation as a whole.
    d. Capitalist economies do well in wartime because war promotes full employment and growing incomes. Hence, an economic boom can lead to conditions favorable to war.
    e. Air bags in automobiles can reduce accidental death from collision. Therefore, air bags in cars make good economic sense.
    f. Gold sells for about $400 per ounce. Therefore, the U. S. government could sell all of the gold in Fort Knox at $400 per ounce and eliminate the national debt.

11. (Role of Theory) What good is economic theory if it can't predict anybody's behavior?

12. (Rational Self-Interest) If behavior is governed by rational self-interest, why do people give to charitable institutions?

13. (Rational Decision Making) Information necessary to make good decisions is often costly to obtain. Yet your own interests can best be served by rationally weighing all options available to you, which therefore requires completely informed decision making. Does this mean that making uninformed decisions is irrational? How do you determine what amount of information is the right amount of information?

14. (Prediction Versus Forecast) An old joke goes as follows: If you take all the economists in the world and lay them end-to-end, you'll never reach a conclusion. Why do you suppose that if you ask the members of a group of economists what will happen to the economy over the next six months, they will give widely varying answers—even if they all believe in the same model of the economy?

15. (Association Versus Causation) Suppose that I observe that communities with lots of doctors tend to have relative high rates of illness. I conclude, therefore, that doctors cause illness. What's wrong with this reasoning?

16. (Marginal Analysis) Suppose that I am taking a trip that takes 8 hours by automobile or 1 hour by plane. In what sense is my transportation decision an example of marginal analysis, and what factors should I consider in making my decision?

17. (A Yen for Vending Machines) Do vending machines conserve on any other resources besides labor? Does your answer offer any additional insight into the widespread use of vending machines in Japan?

18. (A Yen for Vending Machines) Suppose you had the choice of purchasing identically priced lunches at an automat (vending machines only) or a cafeteria. Which would you typically prefer to do? Why?

APPENDIX
UNDERSTANDING GRAPHS

Take out a pencil and a blank piece of paper. Go ahead, do it. Put a point in the middle of the paper. That will be the point of departure, called the **origin**. With your pencil at the origin, draw a straight line off to the right; this line is called the **horizontal axis**. The value of the variable *x* measured along the horizontal axis increases as you move to the right of the origin. Now mark off this line into increments of, say, 5 units each from 0 to 20. Returning to the origin, draw another line up, or north; this line is called the **vertical axis**. Similarly, the value of the variable *y* measured along the vertical axis increases as you move upward. Again, mark off this line into increments of 5 units each from 0 to 20. Within the space framed by the axes, you can plot possible combinations of the variables measured along each axis. For example, place point *a* in your graph to reflect the combination where *x* equals 5 units and *y* equals 15 units. Likewise, place point *b* in your graph to reflect 10 units of *x* and 5 units of *y*. Now compare your results with those in Exhibit 1.

EXHIBIT 1

Basics of a Graph

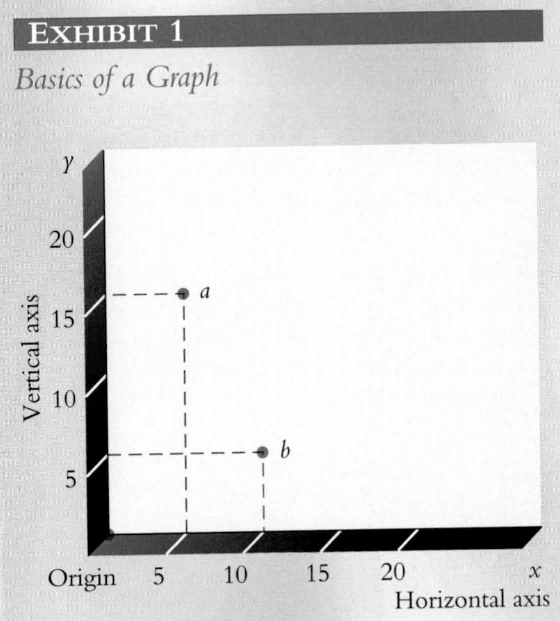

Any point on a graph represents a combination of particular values of two variables. Here point *a* represents the combination of 5 units of variable *x* (measured on the horizontal axis) and 15 units of variable *y* (measured on the vertical axis). Point *b* represents 10 units of *x* and 5 units of *y*.

A **graph** is a picture showing how variables relate, and a picture can be worth a thousand words. Consider Exhibit 2, which shows the U.S. unemployment rate for each year since 1900. As you can see, the year is measured along the horizontal axis, and the unemployment rate along the vertical axis. Exhibit 2 is a **time-series graph** because it shows the value of a variable over time, in this case the unemployment rate. If you had to describe the information presented in Exhibit 2 in words, the explanation would take pages and would be numbing. The picture shows not only how one year compares to the next but also how one decade compares to another and what the trend has been over time. The eye can wander over the hills and valleys to observe patterns that would be hard to convey in words. The sharply higher unemployment rate during the Great Depression of the 1930s is unmistakable. The graph also shows that the average unemployment rate has drifted upward since the 1940s. *Graphs convey information in a compact and efficient way.*

This appendix shows how graphs are used to express a variety of relations among variables. Most of the graphs of interest in this book reflect the relation between two economic variables, such as the year and the unemployment rate, the price of a product and the quantity demanded, or the cost of production and the quantity supplied. Because we focus on just two variables at a time, we must abstract from other details in the economy.

We often observe that one thing appears to depend on another. The time it takes you to drive home depends on your average speed. Your weight depends on how much you eat. The amount of Pepsi purchased depends on its price.

EXHIBIT 2

U.S. Unemployment Rate Since 1900

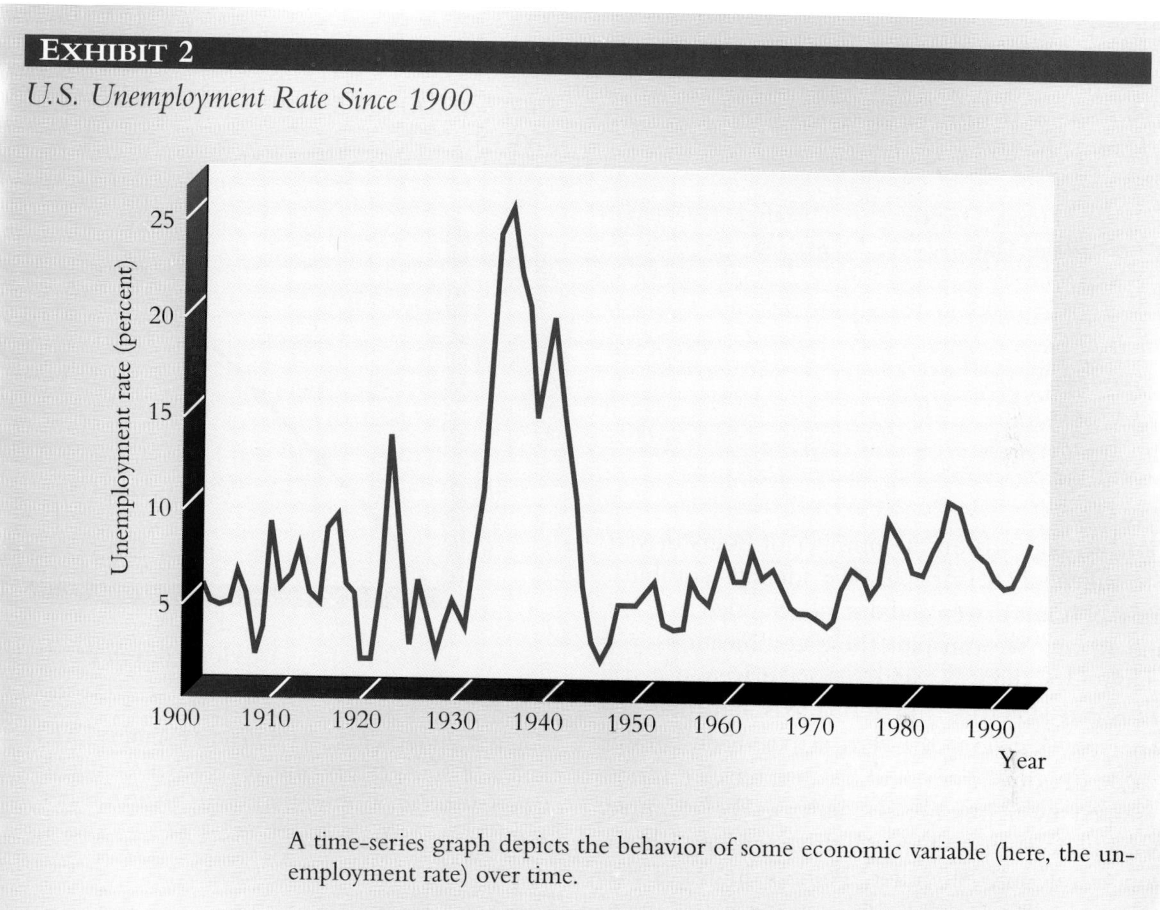

A time-series graph depicts the behavior of some economic variable (here, the unemployment rate) over time.

Sources: *Historical Statistics of the United States*, 1970, and *Economic Report of the President*, 1993.

A **functional relation** exists between two variables when the value of one variable *depends* on the value of another variable. The value of the **independent variable** determines the value of the **dependent variable**. How much you eat, the independent variable, determines your weight, the dependent variable. This is not to say that other factors, such as exercise, age, and metabolism, do not affect your weight, but we typically focus on the relation between the two key variables, assuming other factors constant. The task of the economist is to isolate economic relations and determine the direction of causality, if any. Recall that one of the pitfalls of economic thinking is the erroneous belief that association is causation. We cannot conclude that, simply because two events are related in time, the first event is the independent variable. There may be no relation between the two events.

Drawing Graphs

Consider a very simple relation. Suppose you are planning to drive across country and want to determine how far you will travel each day. You estimate that your average speed will be 50 miles per hour. Possible combinations of driving time and distance traveled are presented in Exhibit 3. One column lists the hours driven per day, and the next column gives the number of miles traveled per day, assuming an average speed of 50 miles per hour. The distance traveled, the dependent

EXHIBIT 3

Schedule Relating Distance Traveled to Hours Driven

	Hours Driven per Day	Distance Traveled per Day
a	1	50
b	2	100
c	3	150
d	4	200
e	5	250

EXHIBIT 4

Graph Relating Distance Traveled to Hours Driven

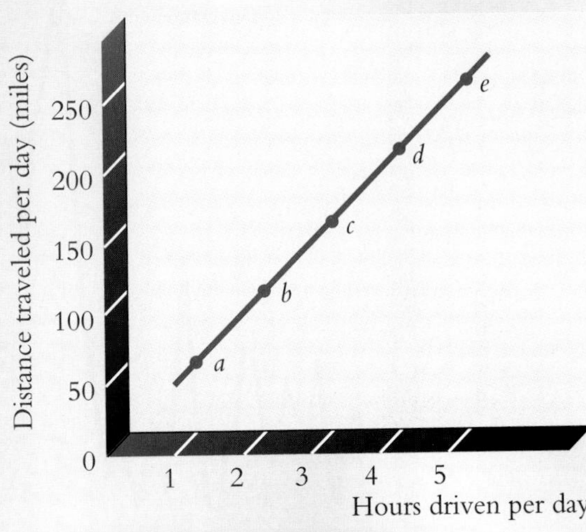

Points *a* through *e* depict different combinations of hours driven per day and the corresponding distances traveled. Connecting these points creates a graph.

variable, depends on the number of hours driven, the independent variable. We identify combinations of hours driven and distance traveled as *a*, *b*, *c*, and so on. We can plot these combinations as a graph in Exhibit 4, with hours driven per day measured along the horizontal axis and total distance traveled along the vertical axis. Each combination of hours driven and distance traveled is represented by a point in Exhibit 4. For example, point *a* shows that when you drive for only 1 hour, you travel only 50 miles. Point *b* indicates that when you drive for 2 hours, you travel 100 miles. By connecting the points, or combinations, we create a line running upward and to the right.

Three types of relations between variables are possible: (1) as one variable increases, the other increases as well, as in Exhibit 4, in which case there is a **positive**, or **direct**, **relation** between the variables; (2) as one variable increases, the other decreases, in which case there is a **negative**, or **inverse**, **relation**; and (3) as one variable increases, the other remains unchanged, in which case the two variables are said to be *independent*, or *unrelated*.

In later chapters we will consider demand, a key economic idea. The *demand curve* shows the relation between the quantity of a product demanded and the price of that product. Exhibit 5 depicts the relation between the price of Pepsi and the quantity of Pepsi demanded per week. This demand curve is identified simply as *D*. As you can see, more Pepsi is demanded at lower prices than at higher prices: there is an inverse, or negative, relation between price and quantity demanded. Inverse relations are expressed by downward-sloping curves. One of the advantages of graphs is that they easily convey the relation between variables. We need not examine the particular combinations of numbers; we need only focus on the shape of the curve.

Economists usually measure price, the independent variable, along the vertical axis, and quantity demanded, the dependent variable, along the horizontal axis. This arrangement appears odd to mathematicians, who usually put the independent variable on the horizontal axis and the dependent variable on the vertical axis. In another context, however, the cost of production is the dependent variable and quantity produced the independent variable, so for consistency economists measure dollar amounts on the vertical axis and quantity on the horizontal axis.

EXHIBIT 5

Hypothetical Demand Curve for Pepsi

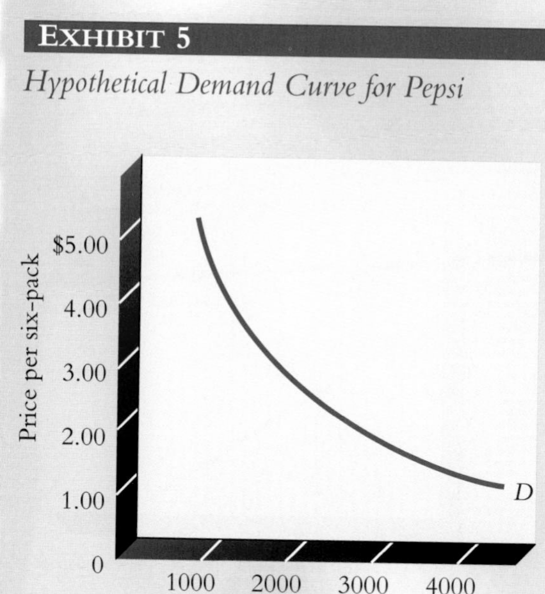

The demand curve shows an inverse, or negative, relation between price and quantity demanded. The curve slopes downward from left to right, indicating that the quantity demanded increases as the price falls.

The Slopes of Straight Lines

A more precise way to describe the shape of a curve is to measure its slope. The **slope** of a line indicates how much the vertical variable changes for a given increase in the horizontal variable. Specifically, the slope between any two points along any straight line is the vertical change between these two points divided by the horizontal change, or

$$\textbf{Slope} = \frac{\textbf{Change in the vertical distance}}{\textbf{Change in the horizontal distance}}$$

For short, we refer to the slope as the *rise over the run*, where the *rise* is the vertical change and the *run* is the horizontal change.

The four panels in Exhibit 6 each indicate the vertical change, given a 10-unit increase in the horizontal variable. In panel (a), the vertical distance increases by 5 units when the horizontal distance increases by 10 units. The slope of the line in panel (a) is therefore 5/10, or 0.5. Notice that the slope in this case is a positive number because the relation between the two variables is positive, or direct. This slope indicates that for every 1-unit increase in the horizontal variable, the vertical variable increases by 0.5 unit. The slope, incidentally, does not imply causality—the increase in the horizontal variable does not necessarily cause the increase in the vertical variable. The slope simply indicates in a uniform way the relation between an increase in the horizontal variable and the associated change in the vertical variable.

In panel (b), the vertical distance declines by 7 units when the horizontal distance increases by 10 units, so the slope equals –7/10, or –0.7. The slope in this case is a negative number because the two variables have a negative, or inverse, relation. In panel (c), the vertical variable remains unchanged as the horizontal variable increases by 10, so the slope equals 0/10, or 0. These two variables are unrelated. Finally, in panel (d), the vertical variable can take on any value, though the horizontal variable remains unchanged. In this case any change in the vertical measure, for example a 10-unit change, is divided by 0, since the horizontal value does not change. Any change divided by 0 is infinitely large, so we say that the slope of a vertical line is infinite. Again, the two variables are unrelated.

The Slope Depends on How Units Are Measured

The mathematical value of the slope depends on the units of measurement on the graph. For example, suppose copper tubing costs $1 per foot to produce. Graphs depicting the relation between output and total cost are shown in Exhibit 7. In panel (a), total cost increases by $1 for each 1-foot increase in the amount of tubing produced. Thus, the slope in panel (a) equals 1/1, or 1. If the cost of production remains the same but the unit of measurement is not *feet* but *yards*, the relation between output and total cost is as depicted in panel (b). Now total cost

Exhibit 6

Alternative Slopes for Straight Lines

(a) Positive relation

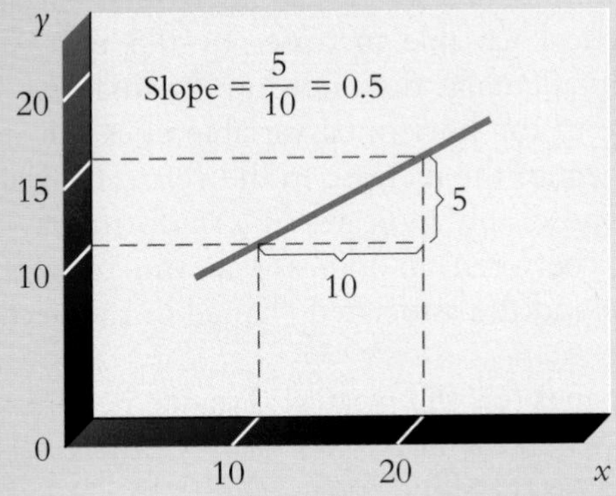

(b) Negative relation

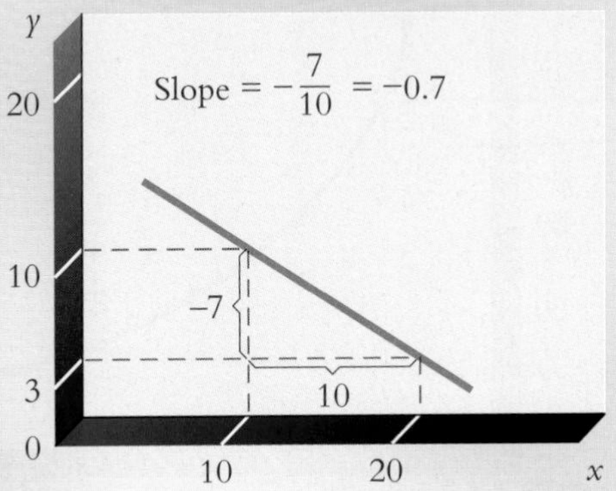

(c) No relation: zero slope

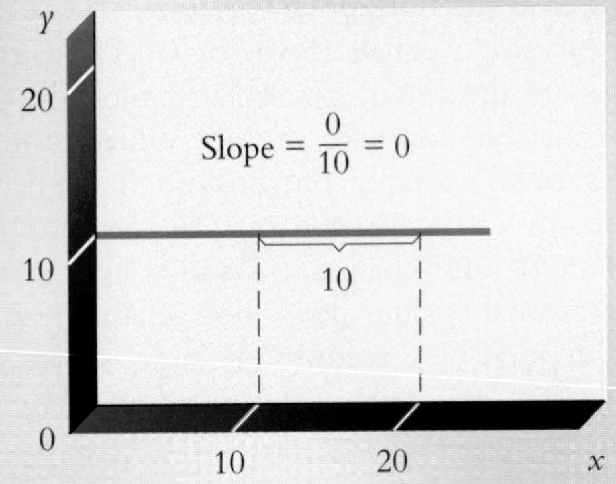

(d) No relation: infinite slope

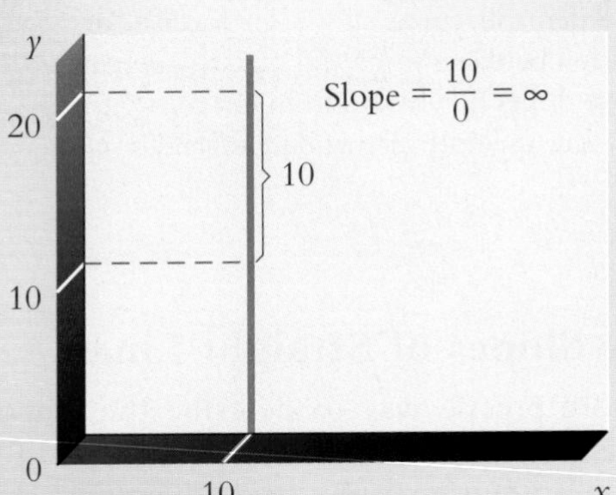

The slope of a line indicates how much the vertically measured variable changes for a given increase in the variable measured on the horizontal axis. Panel (a) shows a positive relation between two variables; the slope is 0.5, a positive number. Panel (b) depicts a negative, or inverse, relation. When the x variable increases, the y variable decreases; the slope is –0.7, a negative number. Panels (c) and (d) represent situations in which two variables are unrelated. In panel (c), the y variable always takes on the same value; the slope is 0. In panel (d), the x variable always takes on the same value; the slope is infinite.

EXHIBIT 7

Slope Depends on the Unit of Measure

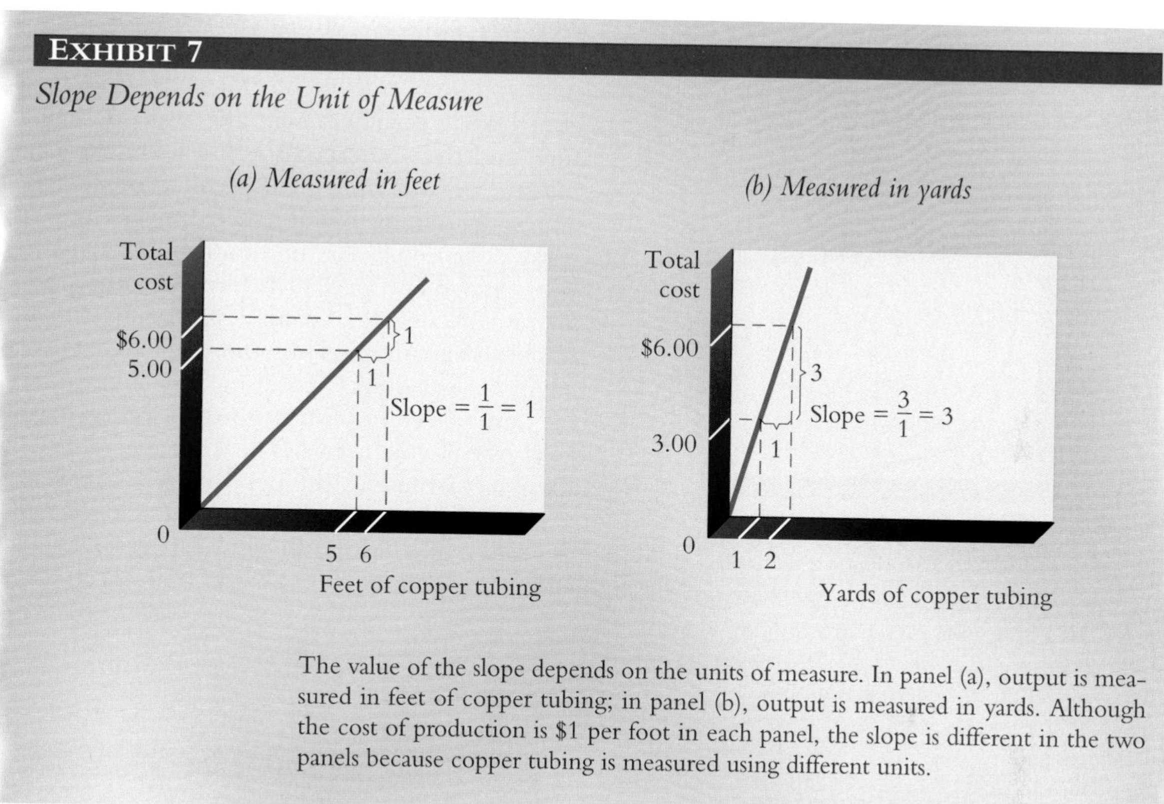

The value of the slope depends on the units of measure. In panel (a), output is measured in feet of copper tubing; in panel (b), output is measured in yards. Although the cost of production is $1 per foot in each panel, the slope is different in the two panels because copper tubing is measured using different units.

increases by $3 for each 1-yard increase in output, so the slope equals 3/1, or 3. Because of differences in the units used to measure copper tubing, the two panels reflect different slopes, even though the cost of tubing is $1 per foot in each panel. So keep in mind that *the slope will depend in part on the unit of measurement.*

As noted earlier, economic analysis usually involves *marginal analysis,* such as the marginal cost of producing one more unit of output. The slope is a convenient device for measuring marginal effects because it reflects the change in total cost along the vertical axis for each 1-unit change along the horizontal axis. For example, in panel (a) of Exhibit 7, the marginal cost of another *foot* of copper tubing is $1, which also equals the slope of the line. In panel (b), the marginal cost of another *yard* of tubing is $3, which, again, is the slope of that line. Because of its applicability to marginal analysis, the slope has special significance in economics.

The Slopes of Curved Lines

The slope of a straight line is the same everywhere along the line, but the slope of a curved line usually varies at every point along the curve. Consider the curve in Exhibit 8. To find the slope of that curved line at a particular point, draw a straight line that just touches the curve at that point but does not cut or cross the curve. Such a line is called a *tangent* to the curve at that point. The slope of the tangent is the slope of the curve at that point. Consider the line *AA*, which is tangent to the curve at point *a*. As the horizontal value increases from 0 to 10 along *AA*, the vertical value drops from 40 to 0. Thus, the vertical change divided by the horizontal change equals −40/10, or −4, which is the slope of the curve at point *a*. This slope is negative because the curve slopes downward, reflecting a negative, or inverse, relation between the two variables (as one declines, the other increases). Alternatively,

EXHIBIT 8

Slopes at Different Points on a Curved Line

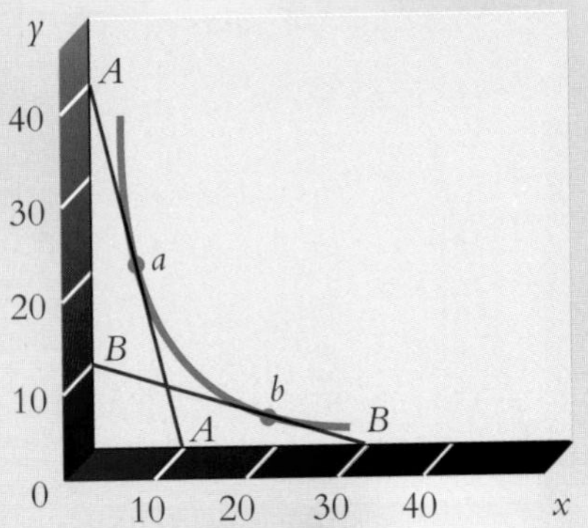

The slope of a curved line varies from point to point. At a given point, such as *a* or *b*, the slope of the curve is equal to the slope of the straight line that is tangent to the curve at that point.

consider *BB*, a line drawn tangent to the curve at point *b*. The slope of *BB* is the change in the vertical divided by the change in the horizontal, or −10/30, which equals −0.33. As you can see, the curve depicted in Exhibit 8 gets flatter as the horizontal variable increases, so the value of its slope approaches zero.

Other curves, of course, will reflect different slopes as well as different changes in the slope along the curve. Downward-sloping curves have a negative slope, and upward-sloping curves, a positive slope. Sometimes curves are more complex, having both positive and negative ranges. For example, consider the hill-shaped curve in Exhibit 9. For relatively small values of x, there is a positive relation between x and y. As the value of x increases, however, its positive relation with y diminishes, eventually becoming negative. We can divide the curve into two segments: (1) the segment between the origin and point *a*, where the slope is positive, and (2) the segment of the curve to the right of point *a*, where the slope is negative. The slope of the curve at point *a* is 0. This type of curve could be used to show the relation between the temperature of a swimming pool and your enjoyment of a swim. The horizontal axis could represent the water temperature, and the vertical axis could represent some measure of your enjoyment. At very low temperatures, swimming is not much fun because the water is too cold. As the temperature increases, your enjoyment level increases. At some point, say at 85 degrees, your level of enjoyment reaches a maximum. Thus, the value of x at point *a* equals 85 degrees. At still higher temperatures, the water becomes uncomfortably hot, so your level of enjoyment falls. The U-shaped curve in Exhibit 9 represents the opposite relation: x and y are negatively related until point *b* is reached; thereafter they are positively related. The slope equals 0 at point *b*.

EXHIBIT 9

Curves with Both Positive and Negative Ranges

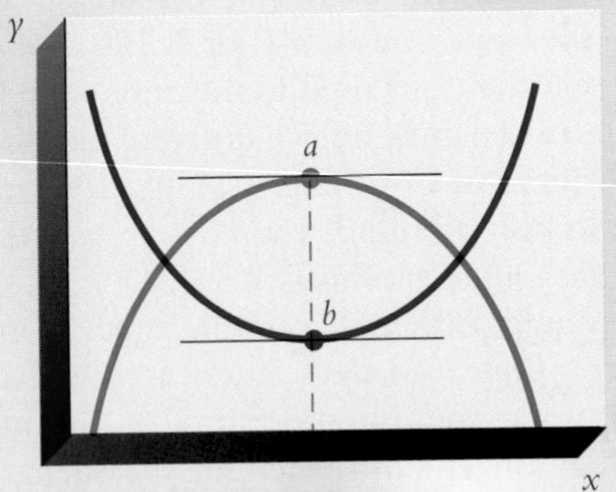

Some curves have both positive and negative slopes. The hill-shaped curve has a positive slope to the left of point *a*, a slope of 0 at point *a*, and a negative slope to the right of that point. The U-shaped curve starts off with a negative slope, has a slope of 0 at point *b*, and has a positive slope to the right of that point.

Curve Shifts

Now that you have some feel for curves, you should know that economic analysis often involves shifts in the curves under consideration. Exhibit 10 depicts a hypothetical demand curve, *D*, for Pepsi, first presented as Exhibit 5. The curve reflects the inverse relation between the price of Pepsi and the quantity demanded per week, other things constant. Suppose an increase in consumer income makes consumers demand more Pepsi at each price level. As a result, the demand curve for Pepsi shifts to the right, from *D* to *D′*, indicating that more Pepsi is demanded at each price. For example, the original demand curve indicates at point *a* that 1500 six-packs of Pepsi were demanded per week when the price was $3 per six-pack. With the increase in demand, the quantity demanded at that price increases to 2500 six-packs per week, as reflected by point *b*. Conversely, we could trace the effects of a decrease in consumer income on the demand for Pepsi. A decrease in income would shift the demand for Pepsi to the left, so less Pepsi would be demanded at each price level.

EXHIBIT 10

Shift in the Demand Curve for Pepsi

The demand curve *D* shifts to the right to *D′* because higher consumer income increases the demand for Pepsi. After the shift in the demand curve, more Pepsi is demanded at each price. For example, at a price of $3 per six-pack, the quantity demanded per week increases from 1500 to 2500.

Of Mice and Fleas: The 45-Degree Line from the Origin

As noted earlier, economists tell stories to convey concepts. Picture a family of mice living in the belfry of a country church. Because the belfry is unheated and drafty, the temperature inside is always the same as the temperature outside. Thus, when it is 0 degrees outside, it is 0 degrees in the belfry. The outside temperature is the independent variable, and the inside temperature, the dependent variable.

The relation between the inside and outside temperatures is shown by the line on the graph in Exhibit 11, where the external temperature is

EXHIBIT 11

The 45-degree Line from the Origin

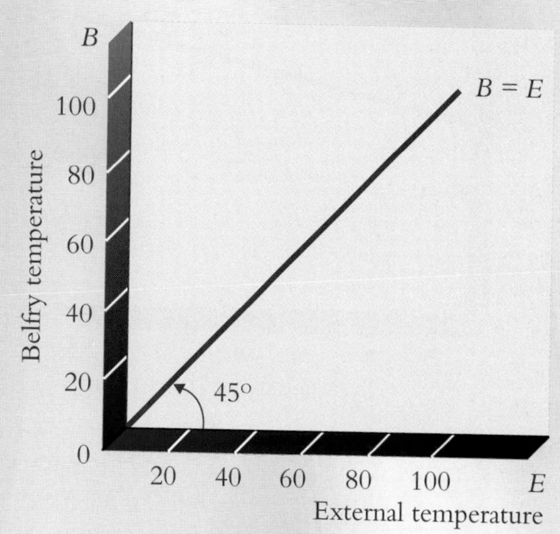

The 45-degree line extending from the origin has a slope equal to 1. At each point along the line, the value of what is measured on the horizontal axis (here, the external temperature) is equal to the value of what is measured on the vertical axis (the internal temperature of the belfry).

measured along the horizontal axis and the belfry temperature along the vertical axis. Since the belfry temperature increases by 1 degree each time the outside temperature increases by 1 degree, the slope of the line is equal to 1. The line bisects, or cuts in half, the angle formed by the two axes so that every point on the line is of equal distance from both axes. We say that the line is a **ray** drawn from the origin, forming a 45-degree angle with the horizontal axis. (By the way, the degrees measuring an angle have nothing to do with the temperature degrees in our example.) Many different rays can be drawn from the origin, but only a 45-degree line exactly bisects the 90-degree angle formed by the right angle connecting the two axes. This line reflects the equation $B = E$, where B is the belfry temperature and E the external temperature.

Although the church belfry is unheated, the main hall of the church is heated with a furnace in winter and cooled with air conditioning in summer. The parishioners might prefer to maintain the temperature of the hall at 72 degrees all year round, but keeping this drafty building at

EXHIBIT 12

The 45-degree Line as a Reference Line

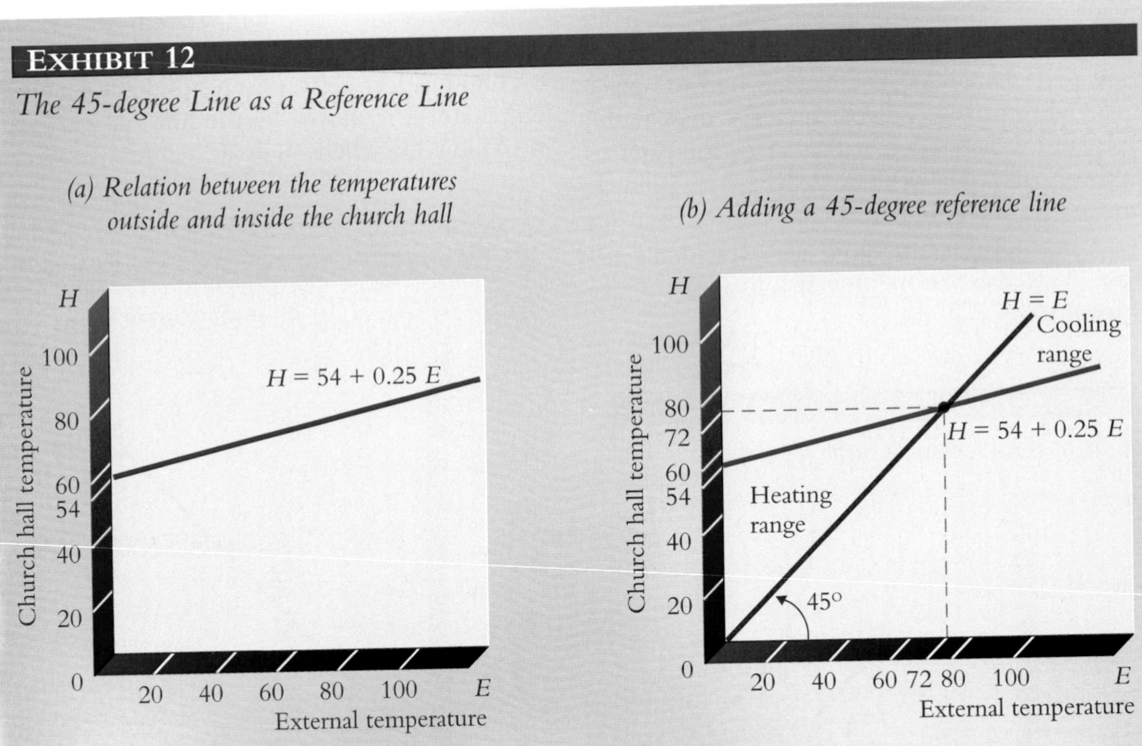

Panel (a) is a graph showing the relation between the external temperature and the church hall temperature. When the external temperature, E, is 0, the hall temperature is 54 degrees. For each 4-degree increase in external temperature, the hall temperature increases by 1 degree. The slope of the line is 0.25. Panel (b) introduces a 45-degree reference line showing all points at which external temperature and hall temperature are equal. The two lines intersect at a temperature of 72 degrees. At external temperatures below 72 degrees, the hall temperature exceeds the external temperature because the heating system is operating. At external temperatures above 72 degrees, the external temperature exceeds the hall temperature because the air conditioning is on.

such a constant temperature would cost more than the parish can afford. Consequently, the temperature in the church hall varies, depending on the external temperature, as shown by the upward-sloping line in Exhibit 12(a). As you can see, even when it is 0 degrees outside, it is still 54 degrees in the church hall. As the outside temperature gets warmer, the inside temperature increases too, but not by as much. Specifically, each 4-degree increase in the external temperature raises the inside temperature by 1 degree. Thus, the slope of this temperature function equals 1 divided by 4, or 0.25. This line can be expressed algebraically as $H = 54 + 0.25E$, where H represents the temperature in the church hall and E the external temperature. Notice again that when E is 0, H equals 54 degrees. This point, where the line cuts the vertical axis, is called the vertical **intercept**. When E equals 100, H equals 54 plus 25, or 79.

In Exhibit 12(b) we again present the temperature function for the church hall, but to add perspective we borrow the 45-degree ray developed in the belfry and use it here simply as a reference line. The intersection of our temperature function for the church hall with the 45-degree reference line provides an easy way to determine when the external temperature exactly equals the temperature in the church hall. The two lines intersect at 72 degrees. When the outside temperature is less than 72 degrees, the heat is on in the church hall. When the outside temperature is above 72 degrees, air conditioning keeps the hall from heating up as much as the outside temperature. When it is exactly 72 degrees outside, neither heating nor cooling is required.

To finish the story, why haven't the mice migrated south to the balmy church hall? Because of the cat—a restless cat that patrols the hall, ever vigilant to the stirrings of creatures, especially mice. Why is the cat so restless? Because of the fleas—fleas that live in the cat's thick fur. The fleas' environment is maintained by the cat's body heat at a constant 101.8 degrees, regardless of the temperature outside. The fleas never eat out. The relation between the temperature on the cat's back and the external temperature is a horizontal line drawn at 101.8 degrees, as shown in Exhibit 13. We can express the relation as simply $C = 101.8$, where C is the temperature in the cat's fur. Thus, the temperature in the snug little world of the fleas is independent of the outside temperature.

EXHIBIT 13

Temperature in the Cat's Fur

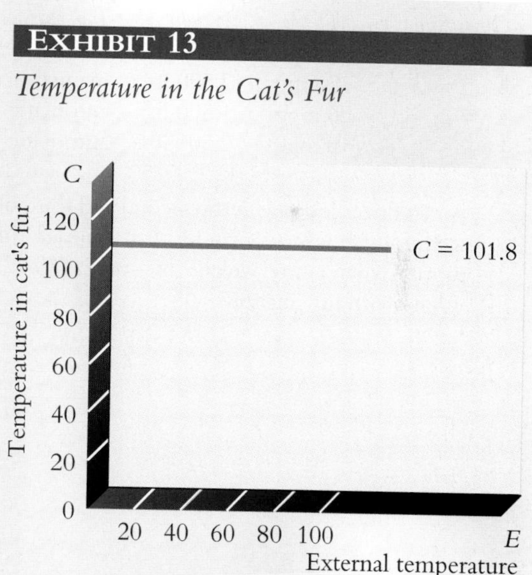

The temperature in the cat's fur is independent of the external temperature. This is illustrated by a horizontal line with a height equal to 101.8 degrees, the temperature in the cat's fur. The line has a slope of 0, indicating that the value of the variable measured on the vertical axis is independent of the value of the variable measured on the horizontal axis.

Appendix Questions

1. (Use of Graphs) Graph the relationship $TC = 10 + 12Q$, where TC = total cost (in dollars) and Q = dozens of eggs.
   a. What is the intercept?
   b. What is the slope?
   c. How would the slope change if you graphed total cost against single eggs rather than dozens of eggs?
   d. What is the marginal cost of an egg?

2. (Use of Graphs) Suppose you have collected the following data on automobiles:

Observation	*Mileage*	*Weight*	*Transmission*
1	40 mpg	1,500 lb	manual
2	30 mpg	2,500 lb	manual
3	20 mpg	1,500 lb	automatic
4	10 mpg	2,500 lb	automatic

   a. An engineer looking at the second and third observations might conclude that mileage improves when auto weight increases. What is wrong with this analysis?
   b. Draw a graph relating auto weight (on the horizontal axis) to mileage (on the vertical axis) for cars with manual transmissions.
   c. How would changing the transmission influence your graph?

3. (Use of Graphs) A demand curve shows a relation between the price of an item and the quantity demanded.
   a. Construct a demand curve based on the following data:

Quantity Demanded	*Price*	*Income of Demander*
0	$50	$100
10	$40	$150
15	$20	$100
20	$10	$100

   b. What is the vertical intercept?
   c. What is the slope?

CHAPTER 2

Some Tools of Economic Analysis

In the first chapter we learned that because of scarcity, we must make choices. And whenever we choose, we must pass up some alternative. In the first chapter we also learned that choices are guided by rational self-interest and require both time and information. But the first chapter said little about how to analyze economic choices. In this chapter we develop a framework to evaluate economic alternatives. First we consider the cost involved in selecting one alternative over others. We then develop tools to explore the production choices available to individuals and to the economy as a whole. Finally, we consider how different economies address the economic choices they confront—choices about what goods and services are produced, how they are produced, and for whom they are produced. Topics discussed in this chapter include

- Opportunity cost
- Division of labor
- Comparative advantage
- Specialization
- Production possibilities frontier
- Three economic questions
- Economic systems

Choice and Opportunity Cost

In Chapter 1 we noted that human wants are unlimited but resources are scarce. Because resources are scarce, not all wants can be satisfied. Therefore, we must choose from among our many wants. But in choosing, we must forgo satisfying other wants.

Point to Stress The opportunity cost of a choice refers to the sacrifice of the *single best alternative,* not the sum of all sacrificed alternatives. *Every* choice has an opportunity cost.

Opportunity Cost

Opportunity cost The benefit expected from the best alternative forgone when an item or activity is chosen

Suppose you spend $300 on a compact-disk player. Let's say your best alternative to spending that money on a CD player is spending it on your wardrobe. So to buy the CD player, you had to forgo buying some more stylish clothes. Or consider an actual decision you just made: the decision to read this chapter now rather than use the time to study for another course, sleep, watch TV, or do something else. Suppose your best alternative to reading now is getting some sleep, so the cost of reading is passing up the opportunity to sleep. Because of scarcity, whenever you make a choice, you must pass up other opportunities; you must incur an opportunity cost. The **opportunity cost** of the chosen item or the chosen activity is the benefit expected from the *best alternative* that is forgone. You might think of opportunity cost as the *opportunity lost.* Sometimes opportunity cost can be measured in terms of money, though as we shall see money is usually only part of the cost.

How many times have you heard people say they did something because they "had nothing better to do"? They actually mean they had no attractive alternatives, so they were sacrificing very little to undertake the chosen activity. But according to the idea of opportunity cost, people always do what they do because they have nothing better to do. The choice selected seems, at the time, preferable to all other possible choices. You are reading this chapter right now because you have nothing better to do. In fact, you are attending college for the same reason: college appears more attractive than your best alternative. Consider the opportunity cost of attending college in the following case study.

CASE STUDY

The Opportunity Cost of College

What is your opportunity cost of attending college this year—that is, what does it cost you this year to attend college? What was the best alternative you gave up to attend college? It was probably a full-time job. Based on the experiences of acquaintances who took jobs right out of high school, you likely had some idea of your employment prospects. Suppose you expected to land a job paying $13,000 a year. Even as a college student, you still could work part time during the school year and full time during the summer. Suppose you earn a total of $6,000 during the year. Thus, by attending college this year you are giving up earnings of $7,000 ($13,000 – $6,000) per year.

There is also the direct cost of college itself. Suppose you pay $8,000 per year for tuition, fees, and books. This income is therefore unavailable to you (or your family) to spend elsewhere. Hence, the opportunity cost of paying for tuition, fees, and books is the forgone benefit you expected from the alternative goods and services that money could have purchased. The cost of room and board must be considered more carefully because even if you had not gone to college, you would still have to live somewhere and eat something. In fact, whether or not you attended college, you would still face outlays for items such as entertainment, clothes, and laundry. Such expenses do not represent an opportunity cost of attending college. They are the personal upkeep costs that arise regardless of what you are doing. For simplicity, let's assume that these outlays are the same whether or not you attend college, so we can ignore them. Thus, the forgone earnings of $7,000 per year plus the $8,000 per year in direct costs yield an opportunity cost of attending college of $15,000 this year.

This analysis assumes that other things are constant. If, in your view, attending college is "more of a pain" than you expected the best alternative to be, the opportunity cost of attending college is even higher. That is, if you are one of those people who find college difficult, often boring, and in most ways more unpleasant than a full-time job right out of high school would have been, then the cost in money terms understates your true opportunity cost. Not only are you incurring the added expense of college, you are also forgoing a more pleasant quality of life. If, on the contrary, you think the wild and crazy life of a college student is more enjoyable on balance than a full-time job, then $15,000 overstates your true opportunity cost because the best alternative involves a less satisfying quality of life.

Example According to Lawrence Katz of Harvard University, an individual can expect to increase his or her cumulative future income by 10 percent to 16 percent for each additional year of schooling.

Note that our analysis of opportunity cost focuses primarily on the forgone value of your best alternative; the analysis ignores the benefits you expect to derive from a college education. Thus, the focus is on the cost of your choice, not its benefit. Evidently, you view college as a wise investment in your future even though it is costly and perhaps even painful. For you, the net benefits expected from college—that is, the total benefits minus the total costs—exceed those expected from the best alternative, and that is why you as a rational decision maker selected the college option.

Opportunity Cost Is Subjective

Opportunity cost is a subjective idea. Only the individual chooser can estimate the expected value of the best alternative. In fact, we seldom know the actual value of the forgone alternative, because by definition that opportunity lost is "the road not taken"—the alternative passed up in favor of the preferred option. Thus, if you gave up an evening of pizza and conversation with friends to work on a term paper, you will never know the exact value of what you gave up. You know only what you *expected*. Evidently, you considered the marginal benefit of working on that paper to be greater than your best alternative. Incidentally, focusing on the *best* alternative forgone makes all other alternatives irrelevant.

Point to Stress Choices are based on *expected* opportunity costs, not on actual opportunity costs.

CALCULATING OPPORTUNITY COST REQUIRES TIME AND INFORMATION. People, in employing their scarce resources, rationally choose the use that promises the highest expected net benefit. This does not mean that people exhaustively calculate costs and benefits for all possible alternatives. Since acquiring information about alternatives is often costly and time-consuming, people usually make choices based on limited or even wrong information about their alternative. Indeed, some choices may turn out to be poor ones (for example, you went on a picnic and it rained; the videotape you rented was boring; the shoes you bought gave you blisters). At the time you made the choice, however, you thought you were making the best use of all your scarce resources, including the time required to gather and evaluate information about your alternatives. In that old movie *Animal House*, Bluto, after hearing the news that he had just flunked out of college, wails, "Seven years of college down the drain!" College represented a poor use of his time.

Time Is the Ultimate Constraint. The sultan of Brunei is among the world's richest people, based on the huge oil revenues that flow into his tiny country. Supported by such wealth, he would appear to have resolved the economic problem caused by scarce resources but unlimited wants. He owns 153 cars and has a palace with 1,788 rooms. But even though the sultan can buy whatever he wants, he has limited *time* in which to enjoy his acquisitions. If he pursues one activity, he cannot at the same time do something else, so each activity he undertakes has an opportunity cost. Consequently, the sultan must choose from among the competing uses of his scarcest resource, time. Though your alternatives may not be as exotic as the sultan's, you too face a time constraint.

Example The Sultan cannot drive one of his cars and relax in one of his rooms at the same time.

Opportunity Cost May Vary with Circumstance. Since opportunity cost depends on the alternatives, the opportunity cost of consuming a particular good or undertaking a certain activity will vary with circumstance. This is why you are less likely to study on a Saturday night than on a Tuesday night. On a Saturday night the opportunity cost of studying is greater because you have more alternatives, and usually the expected benefit of at least one of these alternatives exceeds the expected benefit from studying. Suppose you decide on a movie for Saturday night. The opportunity cost of the movie is your best alternative, which might be attending a sporting event. For some of you, studying on Saturday night may be well down the list of alternatives—perhaps ahead of reorganizing your closet but behind watching trucks being unloaded at the supermarket.

Although opportunity cost is subjective, in some circumstances money paid for goods and services becomes a reasonably good approximation of their opportunity cost. But the monetary cost definition may leave out some important elements, particularly the time involved. Watching a video costs you not only the rental fee but the time and travel expense to get it, watch it, and return it.

Example You pay \$6.50 to see a new movie and find it very boring. The \$6.50 is irrelevant to a decision on whether to watch the movie to its end.

Sunk Costs and Choice

Suppose you have just finished shopping for groceries and are wheeling your basket up to a row of checkout counters. How do you decide which line to join? You pick the line you think will involve the least time. Suppose that after waiting in line for 10 minutes, you realize that another line has moved much more quickly and has in fact disappeared. Do you switch to the open cashier? Or do you think, "Since I have already spent 10 minutes in this line, I'm going to stay in this line." The 10 minutes you already waited in line represents a **sunk cost**, which is a cost that cannot be recovered regardless of what you do. Such costs should be ignored in making economic choices. So

Sunk cost A cost that cannot be recovered and that is therefore irrelevant when an economic choice is being made

you should switch to the open cashier. *Economic decision makers should consider only those costs that are affected by the choice. Sunk costs are by definition not affected by your choice and are therefore irrelevant.* As Shakespeare's Lady Macbeth advised, "Things without all remedy should be without regard: what's done is done."

Specialization, Comparative Advantage, and Exchange

Suppose you live in the dormitory, where your meals and chores are taken care of. You and your roommate have such busy social and academic schedules that you each can spare only about an hour per week for such mundane tasks as typing and ironing. Each of you must turn in a three-page typewritten paper every week, and you each prefer to have your shirts ironed if you have the time. Let's say you take 10 minutes to type one page, or half an hour to type a three-page paper. Your roommate is from the hunt-and-peck school and takes about 20 minutes per page, or an hour for the three pages. But your roommate is talented at ironing and can iron a shirt in 5 minutes flat (or should that be iron it flat in 5 minutes?). You take about twice as long, or 10 minutes, to iron a shirt.

The typing takes priority during the hour available for typing and ironing. If you and your roommate each do your own typing and ironing every week, it takes you half an hour to type the paper; in the remaining half hour you iron three shirts. Your roommate takes the entire hour to type the paper and so has no time left for ironing. Thus, with each of you performing your own tasks, the combined output is two papers and three ironed shirts.

Point to Stress A producer has the comparative advantage when his or her opportunity cost is lower than the opportunity cost of alternative producers. In Case 1 (in Exhibit 1), your opportunity costs of typing and ironing both equal 1. Your roommate's opportunity costs are 1/4 for ironing and 4 for typing. Thus, you should specialize in typing.

The Law of Comparative Advantage

Before long, you both realize that combined output would increase if you did all the typing and your roommate did all the ironing. In the hour available for these tasks, you type both papers and your roommate irons twelve shirts. Total output has increased by nine shirts as a result of specialization. You strike a deal to exchange your typing for your roommate's ironing, so that each of you ends up with a typed paper and six ironed shirts. Thus, *each of you is better off as a result of specialization.*

By specializing in the tasks that you each do best, you and your roommate are applying the **law of comparative advantage**, which states that the individual with the lower opportunity cost for producing a particular output should specialize in producing that output. In this example it is clear that you are the better typist and your roommate the better ironer, and we need no economic law to figure out that there are gains from specialization. In a more complicated situation the law of comparative advantage is not quite so obvious, yet there are still gains from specialization, as we shall now see.

Law of comparative advantage The individual or country with the lowest opportunity cost of producing a particular good should specialize in producing that good

Point to Stress In Case 1 (in Exhibit 1), you take twice as long as your roommate to iron a shirt, and your roommate takes twice as long as you do to type a page. Thus you have an absolute advantage in typing; your roommate has the absolute advantage in ironing.

Absolute advantage The ability to produce something with fewer resources than other producers use

Teaching Tip When measuring labor input in terms of the time required to produce a good or service, the opportunity cost of an activity is the time needed for the chosen task divided by the time needed for the alternative task.

Comparative advantage The ability to produce something at a lower opportunity cost than other producers face

Example If Carl can mow the lawn in 1 hour and wash the family car in 50 minutes, and his wife Kelley mows the lawn in 40 minutes and washes the car in 30 minutes, Kelley has an absolute advantage in both activities. Carl has a comparative advantage in mowing the lawn (60/50 < 40/30); Kelley has a comparative advantage in washing the car (30/40 < 50/60).

Absolute and Comparative Advantage

The gains from specialization and exchange in the example above are intuitively obvious. A more interesting case arises if we change the example so that you are not only a faster typist than your roommate but also a faster ironer. Suppose your roommate takes 12 minutes to iron a shirt, compared to your 10 minutes. You now have an absolute advantage in performing both tasks because you can do each task in less time than your roommate can. More generally, having an **absolute advantage** means having the ability to produce the output with fewer resources than other producers use.

Does your absolute advantage in both activities mean specialization is no longer a good idea? Recall that the law of comparative advantage states that the individual with *the lower opportunity cost* of producing a particular good should specialize in producing that good. You still need 10 minutes to type a page and 10 minutes to iron a shirt, so in the time it takes you to type one page you could iron one shirt. Therefore, your opportunity cost per page of typing is not ironing one shirt. Your roommate takes 20 minutes to type a page and 12 minutes to iron a shirt, so your roommate could iron 20/12, or $1\frac{2}{3}$, shirts instead of typing one page. Therefore, your roommate's opportunity cost per page of typing is not ironing $1\frac{2}{3}$ shirts. Because your opportunity cost of typing is lower than your roommate's, you have a comparative advantage in typing.

And if you have a comparative advantage in typing, we can easily show that your roommate has a comparative advantage in ironing. Your opportunity cost of ironing a shirt is not typing one page; your roommate's opportunity cost of ironing a shirt is not typing 12/20, or $\frac{3}{5}$, of a page. Since your roommate's opportunity cost of ironing is lower than yours, your roommate has a comparative advantage in ironing. Hence you should do all the typing, and your roommate, all the ironing.

Although you have an absolute advantage in both tasks, your **comparative advantage** calls for specializing in the task for which you have the lower opportunity cost—in this case, typing. If you did not specialize, you could type one paper *and* iron three shirts in an hour; your roommate could still type just one paper. So the combined output would remain at two papers and three shirts. But if you each specialized according to the law of comparative advantage, you could type both papers in an hour and your roommate could iron five shirts. Thus, specialization increases total output by two ironed shirts. Exhibit 1 summarizes the example. Even though you are better at both tasks than your roommate, you are comparatively better at typing. Put another way, your roommate, although worse at both tasks, is not quite as poor at ironing as at typing. And don't think this is simply common sense. Common sense would lead you to do your own ironing and typing, since you are more skilled at both tasks than your roommate. Spend a little time reviewing Exhibit 1.

Absolute advantage focuses on who produces a given amount of output using the fewest resources, but comparative advantage focuses on what else those resources could have been used to produce—that is, on the opportunity cost of those resources in terms of other output forgone. Comparative

EXHIBIT 1

Comparative Advantage: Maximizing Output

CASE 1: You are a faster typist and your roommate is a faster ironer.

	Output per Hour			
	Each Does Own		Each Specializes	
	Typed Pages	Ironed Shirts	Typed Pages	Ironed Shirts
You	3	3	6	0
Roommate	3	0	0	12
Total	6	3	6	12

CASE 2: You are a faster typist and a faster ironer, but you are a comparatively faster typist.

	Output per Hour			
	Each Does Own		Each Specializes	
	Type	Iron	Type	Iron
You	3	3	6	0
Roommate	3	0	0	5
Total	6	3	6	5

Cases 1 and 2 both show gains from specialization and exchange for you and your roommate. In both cases it takes you half an hour to type the paper and 10 minutes to iron one shirt. In both cases your roommate takes 1 hour to type the paper. But, whereas in Case 1 it takes your roommate only 5 minutes to iron a shirt, in Case 2 it takes 12 minutes to iron a shirt. In Case 1 you have an absolute advantage and a comparative advantage in typing, so total output is greater if you do all the typing and your roommate does all the ironing. In Case 2 you have an absolute advantage in both typing and ironing. But you have a comparative advantage only in typing because you have a lower opportunity cost of typing than does your roommate. So in Case 2 output is maximized if you do all the typing and your roommate does all the ironing.

Example Assume that the United States can produce a unit of food with a labor input of 10 minutes and a unit of clothing with a labor input of 30 minutes. The required labor input in Europe is 1 hour for either food or clothing. The opportunity cost of a unit of clothing is 3 units of food in the United States and 1 unit of food in Europe. Europe has the comparative advantage in clothing; the United States has the comparative advantage in food.

advantage is more important than absolute advantage because the focus of comparative advantage is on opportunity cost.

The law of comparative advantage applies not only to individuals but to firms, to regions of a country, and to countries. Those individuals, firms, regions, or countries with the lowest opportunity cost of producing a particular good should specialize in producing that good. Because of such factors as climate, the skills of the work force, and the capital or natural resources available, certain parts of the country or certain parts of the world have a comparative advantage in producing particular goods. Regardless of what is being produced—from Apple computers in California's "Silicon Valley" to oranges in Florida, from VCRs in Korea to bananas in Honduras—*resources are allocated most efficiently across the country and around the world when production and trade conform to the law of comparative advantage.*

Specialization and Exchange

Barter The direct exchange of one good for another without the use of money

In the previous example you specialized in typing and your roommate specialized in ironing, and you each exchanged your output. No money was involved. In other words, you engaged in barter. **Barter** is a system of exchange in which products are traded directly for other products. Barter works satisfactorily in very simple economies where there is little specialization and few different goods to trade, but for economies with greater specialization, *money* plays an important role in facilitating exchange. Money serves as a *medium of exchange* because it is the one thing that everyone is willing to accept in return for all goods and services.

Because of specialization and comparative advantage, most people consume little of what they produce and produce little of what they consume. People specialize in particular activities, such as plumbing or carpentry, and exchange their products for money, which, in turn, is exchanged for output produced by others. Thus, people sell their specialized products in one market and buy the products of others in another market. Did you make a single article of clothing you are now wearing? Probably not. Consider the degree of specialization that went into your cotton shirt or blouse. Some farmer in a warm climate grew the cotton and sold it to someone who spun it into thread, who sold it to someone who wove it into fabric, who sold it to someone who made the shirt, who sold it to a wholesaler, who sold it to a retailer, who sold it to you. Your shirt or blouse was produced by many specialists.

Division of Labor and Gains from Specialization

Picture a visit to McDonald's: "Let's see, I'll have a Big Mac, an order of fries, and a chocolate shake." About 30 seconds later your order is ready. In contrast, consider how long it would take you to prepare the same meal yourself. It would take at least 15 minutes to make a homemade version of the Big Mac with all its special ingredients. Peeling, slicing, and frying the potatoes would take another 15 minutes. With the ice cream on hand, you should be able to make the shake in 5 minutes. In all, it would take you at least an hour to buy the ingredients, prepare the meal, and clean up afterward.

Division of labor The organization of production of a single good into separate tasks in which people specialize

Why is the McDonald's meal faster, cheaper, and, for some people, better than one you could make yourself? Why is fast food so fast? The manager of McDonald's is taking advantage of the gains resulting from the **division of labor**. Rather than have each worker prepare an entire individual meal, McDonald's separates meal preparation into various tasks and assigns individuals to specialize in these separate tasks. This division of labor allows the group to produce much more than it could if each person tried to prepare an entire meal. Instead of one worker doing it all and making twenty complete meals in an hour, the ten employees specialize and thereby produce more than two hundred meals per hour.

How is this increase in productivity possible? First, the manager can assign tasks according to individual preferences and abilities. The employee with the toothy smile and pleasant personality can handle the customers up front; the employee with the strong back but few social graces can handle the 50-pound sacks of potatoes out back. Second, a worker who performs the same task again and again gets better at it. Experience is a good teacher. The employee operating the cash register, for example, becomes better at handling the special problems that arise in dealing with customers. Third, there is no time lost in moving from one task to another. Finally, and perhaps most importantly, the **specialization of labor** allows for the introduction of more sophisticated production techniques, which would not make economic sense on a smaller scale. For example, McDonald's does not prepare each milkshake separately but mixes ingredients in a machine that shakes gallons at a time. Such machines would be impractical in the home. The specialization of labor allows for the introduction of specialized machines, and these machines make each worker more productive.

Specialization of labor Focusing an individual's efforts on a particular product or a single task

The specialization of labor takes advantage of individual preferences and natural abilities, allows workers to develop more experience at a particular task, reduces the time required to shift between different tasks, and permits the introduction of labor-saving machinery. Specialization and the division of labor occur not only among individuals, but also within firms, regions, and indeed entire countries. As mentioned earlier, clothing production often involves growing cotton in one country, turning the cotton into cloth in another, making the clothing in a third country, and marketing that clothing in a fourth country.

We should note that specialization can create problems, since doing the same thing 8 hours a day often becomes tedious. Consider, for example, the assembly line worker whose task is to tighten a particular bolt on each product. Such a job could drive that worker crazy. Repetitive motion can also be unhealthy. Thus, the gains from breaking production down into individual tasks must be weighed against the problems caused by assigning workers to repetitive and tedious jobs.

THE ECONOMY'S PRODUCTION POSSIBILITIES

The focus to this point has been on how individuals choose to use their scarce resources to satisfy their unlimited wants—more specifically, how they specialize based on comparative advantage. This emphasis on the individual has been appropriate because the world of economics is driven by the choices of individual decision makers, whether they are consumers, producers, or public officials. Just as resources are scarce for the individual, they are scarce for the economy as a whole. An economy has millions of different resources, which can be combined in all kinds of ways to produce millions of possible goods and services. In this section we abstract from the immense complexity

Point to Stress The PPF connects the points showing the *maximum* possible combinations of two goods that can be produced. Other possible production combinations are inside the frontier.

of the real economy to develop a simple model that presents the economy's production options.

Efficiency and the Production Possibilities Frontier

Here are the model's simplifying assumptions: (1) To reduce the analysis to manageable proportions, we limit the output of the hypothetical economy to just two products; in our example they are food and education. (2) The focus is on a given time period—in this case, a year. (3) The resources available in the economy are fixed during the time period. And (4) society's knowledge about how these resources can be combined to produce output—that is, society's available *technology*—does not change during the year. The point of these assumptions is to freeze the economy in time to focus on the economy's production alternatives during that time.

Production possibilities frontier A curve showing all alternative combinations of goods that can be produced when available resources are used fully and efficiently

Efficiency The condition that exists when there is no way resources can be reallocated to increase the production of one good without decreasing the production of another

Given the resources and the technology available in the economy, the **production possibilities frontier**, or **PPF**, reveals the various possible combinations of the two goods that can be produced when all available resources are employed efficiently. The economy's PPF for food and education is shown by the curve *FE* in Exhibit 2, where *F* represents the amount of food produced per year if all the economy's resources are used efficiently to produce food, and *E* represents the amount of education produced per year if all the economy's resources are used efficiently to produce education. Points along the curve between *F* and *E* represent the possible combinations of food and education that can be produced when all the economy's resources are used efficiently to produce both goods. Resources are employed with **efficiency** when no change in the way the resources are combined could increase the production of one good without decreasing the production of the other good. *Efficiency involves getting the maximum possible output from available resources.*

Inefficient and Unattainable Production

Points along the production possibilities frontier indicate the various possible combinations of output that can be produced when all available resources are employed efficiently. Points outside the PPF, such as *K* in Exhibit 2, represent unattainable combinations of food and education given the resources and the technology available. Points inside the PPF, such as *J*, represent combinations of food and education that do not employ resources fully or that employ them inefficiently. Notice that if you start from any point inside the PPF, such as *J*, it is always possible to increase the production of one good without reducing the production of the other good. For example, from point *J* it is possible, by combining resources more efficiently or by employing previously idle resources, to move to point *B* and produce more food without reducing the amount of education produced. Alternatively, it is possible, by using resources more efficiently or by employing previously idle resources, to move from point *J* to point *D* and thereby increase the amount of education produced without reducing the production of food. Indeed, as you can see, it is

EXHIBIT 2

The Economy's Production Possibilities Frontier

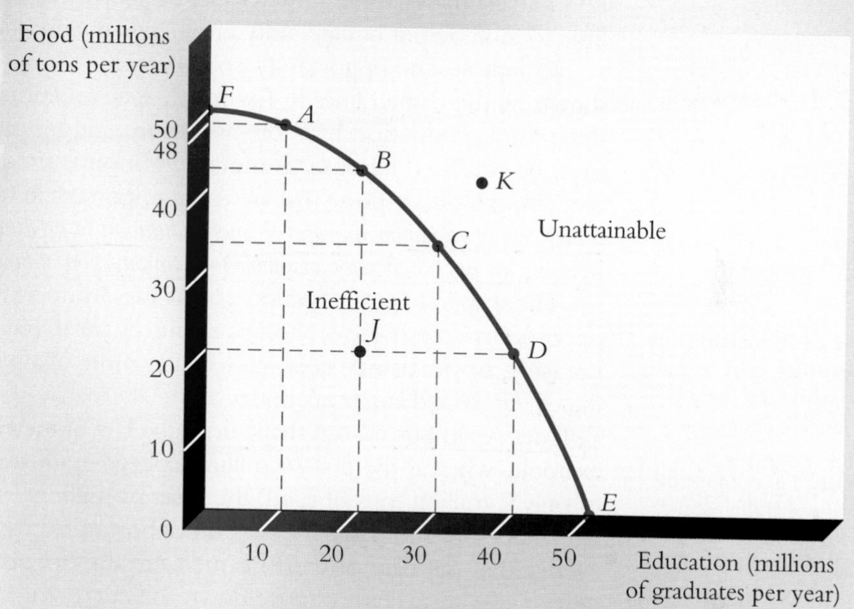

If the economy uses its available resources and technology fully and efficiently in producing food and education, it will be on its production possibilities frontier, curve *FE*. The PPF is bowed out to illustrate the law of increasing opportunity cost: additional units of education require the economy to sacrifice more and more units of food. Note that more food must be given up in moving from *D* to *E* than in moving from *F* to *A*, though in each case the gain in education is 10 million graduates. Points inside the PPF, such as *J*, represent inefficient use of resources. Points outside the PPF, such as *K*, represent unattainable combinations.

Example If the United States is growing oranges in Alaska and pumping oil in Florida, production of both items could be increased by switching orange production to Florida and oil production to Alaska.

possible to move from point *J* to any point between *B* and *D* along the PPF, such as point *C*, and thereby increase the production of both food and education. Thus *the PPF not only reflects efficient combinations of production but also serves as a border between inefficient combinations inside the frontier and unattainable combinations outside the frontier.*

Shape of the Production Possibilities Frontier

Focus again on point *F* in Exhibit 2. Although all resources are used efficiently at point *F*, certain resources contribute little to the production of food, as some economics professors make terrible farmers and school buildings are not easily adapted to food production. Any movement along the PPF involves giving up some units of one good to get units of the other. Movements down the curve indicate that the opportunity cost of more education is less food. For example, moving from point *F* to point *A* increases the number of graduates per year from none to 10 million and reduces food production by only 2 million tons, from 50 million to 48 million tons. Increasing the number of graduates to 10 million causes food production to fall little because education production initially draws upon those resources, such as classrooms and teachers, that add little to food output but are quite productive in education.

To repeat: The opportunity cost of more education is the forgone food. As shown by the dashed lines in Exhibit 2, each additional 10 million graduates reduce food production by more and more. Larger and larger amounts of food must be sacrificed because, as more education is produced, the resources drawn away from food are those that are more important in food production. *The opportunity cost of education increases as more education is produced because the resources in the economy are not all perfectly adaptable to the production of both food and education.*

Law of increasing opportunity cost As more of a particular good is produced, larger and larger quantities of an alternative good must be sacrificed if the economy's resources are already being used fully and efficiently

The shape of the production possibilities frontier reflects the law of increasing opportunity cost. If the economy's resources are all used efficiently, the **law of increasing opportunity cost** states that as more of a particular commodity is produced, larger and larger quantities of the alternative good must be sacrificed. The PPF derives its bowed-out shape from the law of increasing opportunity cost. For example, whereas the first 10 million college graduates have an opportunity cost of only 2 million tons of food, the final 10 million—that is, those produced between point *D* and point *E*—have an opportunity cost of 20 million tons of food. Notice that the *slope* of the PPF indicates the opportunity cost of an additional unit of education. As we move down the curve, the slope gets steeper, reflecting the higher opportunity cost of education in terms of food.

Point to Stress Opportunity costs increase only when the economy's resources are already used fully and efficiently and the resources are not perfectly adaptable to either industry.

The law of increasing opportunity cost also applies when moving from the production of education to the production of food. When all resources in society are concentrated on education, as at point *E*, certain resources, such as tractors and cows, contribute little to output. (In fact, the cows foul the sidewalks and block the hallways if they are allowed to hang around the schools.) Thus, in shifting resources into the production of food, little education must be surrendered initially. As more food is produced, however, resources that are of greater value in the production of education must be used, reflecting the law of increasing opportunity cost. Incidentally, if resources were perfectly adaptable to alternative uses, the PPF would be a straight line, reflecting a constant opportunity cost along the PPF.

What Shifts the Production Possibilities Frontier?

Teaching Tip Ask students to describe the likely impact on the PPF of an increase in average vacation time, a drop in the average age of retirement, an increase in immigration of skilled labor, or an increase in the emigration of skilled labor.

When we construct the production possibilities frontier, we assume that the amount of resources available in the economy and the level of technology are constant. Over time, however, the PPF may shift as a result of changes in resource availability or in technology.

CHANGES IN RESOURCE AVAILABILITY. For example, if individuals in the economy decided to work longer hours, this would shift the PPF out so that more of both goods could be produced, as depicted in Exhibit 3(a). An increase in the size or health of the labor force, an increase in the skills of the labor force, or an increase in the availability of other resources, such as new

Exhibit 3

Shifts in the Economy's Production Possibilities Frontier

(a) Increase in available resources

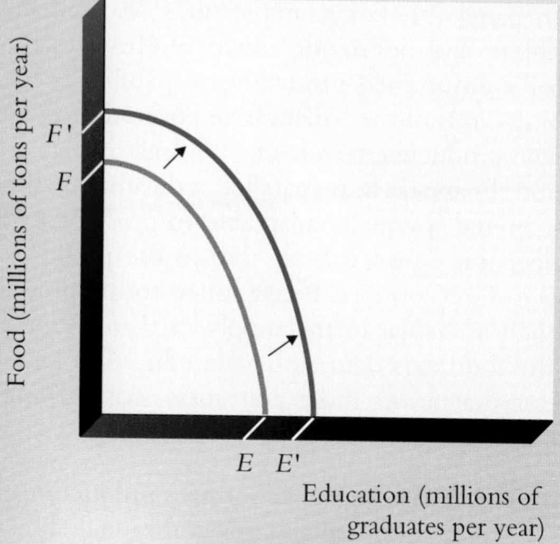

(b) Decrease in available resources

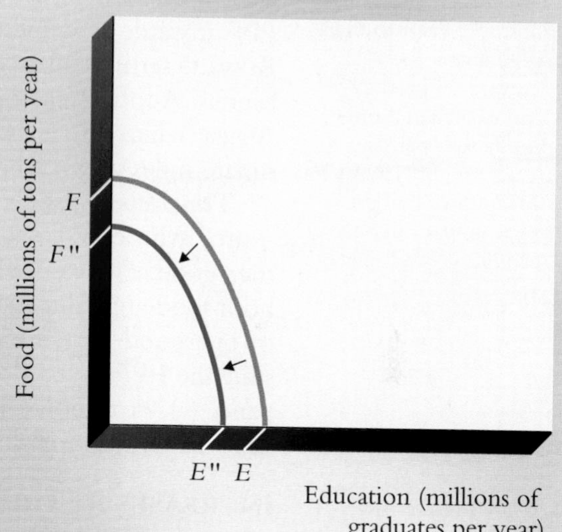

(c) Technological advance in food production

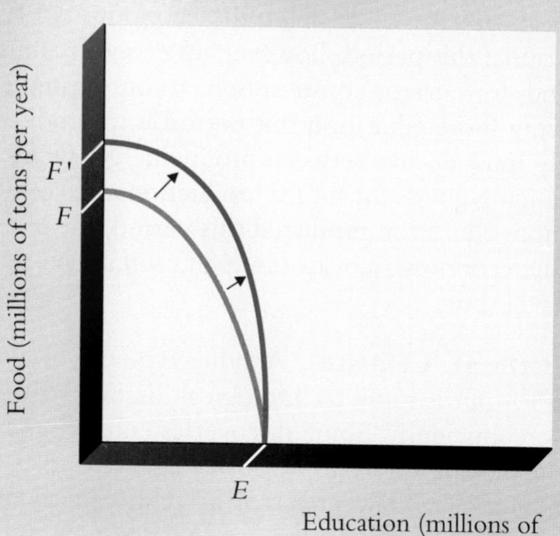

(d) Technological advance in education production

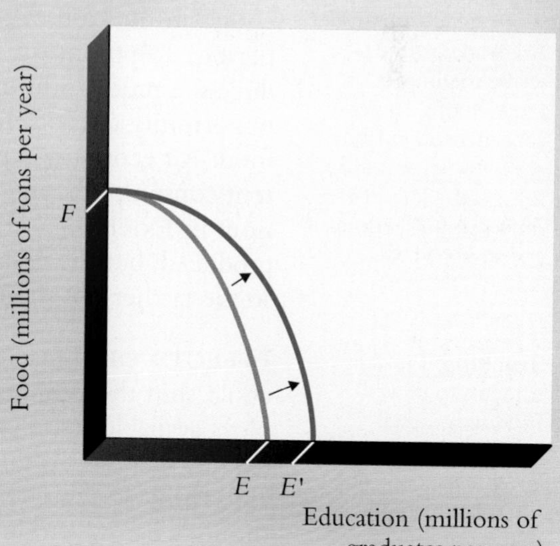

When the resources available to an economy change, the PPF shifts. If more resources become available, the PPF shifts outward, as in panel (a), indicating that more output can be produced. A decrease in available resources causes the PPF to shift inward, as in panel (b). Technological changes also shift the PPF. Panel (c) shows the effect of a technological improvement in food production. More food can now be produced for any given level of education. Panel (d) shows the effect of a technological advance in the production of education.

Example Kuwait sustained $160 billion of damage to its capital stock. Prior to the 1990 invasion, Kuwaiti oil production exceeded 2 million barrels per day. As of August, 1992, the country's oil production was still only 1 million barrels per day.

oil discoveries, would also shift the PPF outward. The health of the labor force may increase from improved nutrition and better health care. In contrast, a decrease in the availability or the quality of resources would shift the PPF inward, as depicted in panel (b). For example, in 1990 Iraq invaded Kuwait, setting oil fields ablaze and destroying much of Kuwait's physical capital. Another example of a diminished production capability is in West Africa, where the encroaching sands of the Sahara have covered thousands of square miles of what had been productive farmland.

The shifts in panels (a) and (b) appear to be parallel, indicating that the resource whose availability is altered is equally adaptable to production of either good. For example, electrical power can be used in the production of both food and education. But if a resource is better suited to the production of one good—say, food—then a change in the supply of that resource will shift the PPF more along the food axis than along the education axis, as in panel (c). A resource increase that favors more education would result in a shift that looks more like the one in panel (d).

Example Assume two industries: clothing and wheat. The clothing industry is very labor-intensive; the wheat industry is very capital-intensive. Ask students to describe the impact on the PPF of a 10 percent increase in labor and a 10 percent drop in capital. (The PPF shifts out for clothing and in for wheat.)

INCREASES IN THE CAPITAL STOCK. An economy's production possibilities frontier depends on its stock of human and physical capital. The more capital an economy produces in one period, the more output can be produced in the next period. Thus, increased production of capital this period (for example, by more education in the case of human capital or more machines in the case of physical capital) will increase the economy's PPF next period. To produce more capital this period, however, an economy must reduce the production of goods for current consumption. In our example, the opportunity cost of producing more education this period is to produce less food. An economy typically must decide between producing goods for current consumption and producing goods for future production and consumption. In Exhibit 3(a), the more education produced this period, the less food produced, but the greater the economy's stock of human capital next period, so the farther out the PPF will shift.

Teaching Tip Ask students to draw a PPF with capital goods on one axis and consumer goods on the other axis. Then select two different combinations of capital and consumer goods on the PPF and illustrate the different impact of each combination on the economy's future PPF.

EFFECTS OF TECHNOLOGICAL CHANGE. Another type of change that could shift the economy's PPF out is some technological discovery that employs available resources more efficiently. Some discoveries enhance the production of both products, such as an innovation that manages resources more efficiently, as shown in Exhibit 3(a). The effect of a technological breakthrough in the production of food, such as a more bug-resistant strain of crops, is reflected by an outward shift in the PPF along the food axis, as shown in Exhibit 3(c). As you can see, such a development primarily increases the production of food. Exhibit 3(d) shows the result of a technological breakthrough in the production of education, such as the development of a computer program for self-instruction.

What We Can Learn from the PPF

The production possibilities frontier demonstrates several ideas introduced so far. The first is *efficiency*: the PPF describes the maximum combinations of

Example A 1982 study by the World Bank investigated the impact of increased military expenditures in sixty-nine less developed countries in the 1950s and 1960s. The study concluded that increased military spending led to reductions in agricultural production, total investment, and economic growth.

output that are possible, given the economy's resources and technology. The second is *scarcity*: since resources and technology are fixed during the period, the economy can produce only so much. The PPF slopes downward, indicating that as more of one good is produced, less of the other good is produced. This tradeoff demonstrates *opportunity cost.* The bowed-out shape of the PPF reflects the *law of increasing opportunity cost*, which arises because not all resources are perfectly adaptable to the production of all goods. Society must somehow choose a specific combination of output—a single point—along the PPF, so the PPF also underscores the need for *choice*. That choice will determine not only what can be consumed this period but the size of the capital stock available next period. How society goes about choosing a particular combination will depend upon the nature of the economic system, as we will see in the next section. Finally, a shift outward in the PPF reflects *economic growth*.

Point to Stress *All* economies face these economic questions—regardless of their level of development and regardless of the type of economic system they have.

Three Questions Each Economic System Must Answer

Economic system The set of mechanisms and institutions that resolve the what, how, and for whom questions

Every point along the economy's production possibilities frontier is an efficient combination of output. Whether the economy produces efficiently and how the most preferred combination is selected will depend on the decision-making rules operating in the economy. Regardless of how decisions are made, each economy must answer three fundamental questions: What goods and services will be produced? How will they be produced? And for whom will they be produced? An **economic system** is the set of mechanisms and institutions that resolve the what, how, and for whom questions. Several criteria are used to distinguish among economic systems: who owns the resources, what decision-making process is used to allocate resources and products, and what types of incentives guide economic actors.

WHAT GOODS AND SERVICES WILL BE PRODUCED? As you observe the economy around you, you take for granted the incredible number of choices that go into deciding what gets produced. From the thousands of aspiring novelists, which ones will get their novels published? Which new kitchen appliances will be introduced? Which new roads will be built? Although different economies resolve these and millions of other questions using different decision-making rules and mechanisms, all economies must attempt to satisfy unlimited wants in the face of scarce resources.

HOW WILL GOODS AND SERVICES BE PRODUCED? The economic system—or, more specifically, individual decision makers in the economic system—must determine how output is to be produced. Which resources should be used, and how should they be combined to produce each product? How much labor should be used and at what skill level? What kinds of machines should be used? How much fertilizer should be used to grow the best strawberries? Should the factory be built in the city or closer to the interstate highway? Again, billions of individual decisions must be made to determine which resources are to be employed and how these resources are to be combined.

For Whom Will Goods and Services Be Produced? Finally, who will actually consume the goods and services produced? The economic system must determine how to allocate the fruits of production among the population. Should equal amounts of the good be provided to everyone? Should the weak and the sick receive more? Should those willing to wait in line the longest receive more? Should goods be allocated according to height? Weight? Religion? Age? Gender? Race? The value of resources supplied? Political connections? The question "For whom will goods and services be produced?" is often referred to as the *distribution question*.

Although the three economic questions have been discussed separately, they are closely interwoven. The answer to one depends very much on the answers to the others. For example, an economy that distributes goods and services in uniform amounts to all will, no doubt, answer the what-is-to-be-produced question differently than an economy that somehow allows each person to choose a unique bundle. The laws about resource ownership and the extent to which the government attempts to coordinate economic activity determine the "rules of the game"—the set of conditions that shape individual incentives and constraints. Along a spectrum ranging from the most free to the most regimented type of economic system, *pure capitalism* would be at one end and the *command economy* would be at the opposite end.

Pure Capitalism

Pure capitalism An economic system characterized by private ownership of resources and the use of prices to coordinate economic activity in free, competitive markets

Under **pure capitalism**, the rules of the game include the private ownership of all resources and the coordination of economic activity by the price signals generated in free, unrestricted markets. Any income derived from the use of land, labor, capital, or entrepreneurial ability goes exclusively to the individual owners of those resources. Owners have *property rights* to the use of their resources and are therefore free to sell their resources to the highest bidder. Producers are free to make and sell whatever output they think will be profitable. Consumers are free to buy whatever goods they can afford. All this voluntary buying and selling is coordinated by unrestricted markets, where buyers and sellers make their wishes known. Market prices guide resources to their highest-valued use and direct goods and services to consumers who value them the most.

Point to Stress
Under pure capitalism, there is no government intervention in the marketplace. The U.S. government intervenes through activities such as regulating prices in some industries, supplying some goods and services (national defense, public education), redistributing income, and so forth.

Under pure capitalism, markets direct the what, how, and for whom of production. Markets transmit information about relative scarcity, provide individual incentives, and distribute income among resource suppliers. No single individual or small group coordinates these activities. Rather, it is the voluntary choices of many buyers and sellers responding only to their individual incentives and constraints that direct resources and products to those who value them the most. According to Adam Smith (1723–1790), one of the first to explain the allocative role of markets, market forces coordinate as if by an "invisible hand"—an unseen force that harnesses the pursuit of self-interest to direct resources where they earn the greatest return. According to Smith, *although each individual pursues his or her self-interest, the invisible hand promotes the general welfare*. Pure capitalism is sometimes called *laissez-faire* capitalism; translated from the French, this phrase means "to let do," or to let people do as they choose without government intervention. Thus, *under pure capitalism, voluntary choices based on rational self-interest are made in unrestricted markets to answer the questions what, how, and for whom.*

As we shall see in later chapters, pure capitalism has its flaws. Most notably, (1) there is no central authority that can protect property rights, enforce contracts, and otherwise ensure that the "rules of the game" are followed; (2) people with no resources to sell may starve; (3) producers may try to monopolize markets by eliminating the competition; and (4) so-called public goods, such as national defense, will not be produced by private firms because private firms cannot prevent those who fail to pay from enjoying the benefits of public goods.

Command Economy

Command economy An economic system characterized by centralized economic planning and public ownership of resources

Point to Stress Even before the movement away from communism in the former Soviet Union, certain sectors of the economy had elements of capitalism. For example, some farming occurred on privately owned plots and the owners were permitted to sell their output on the open market.

In a **command economy**, resources are allocated based on the "command" of some central authority. At least in theory, there is public, or communal, ownership of property. Resources are directed and production coordinated through some form of *central planning* rather than by markets. These planners, as representatives of all the people, determine, for example, how much steel, how many cars, how many tubes of toothpaste, and how many personal computers are to be produced. The central planners also determine how these goods are to be produced and who will receive the goods. In theory, the command economy incorporates individual choices into collective choices, which, in turn, are reflected in central planning decisions. In practice, command economies also have flaws. Most notably, (1) running an economy may be too complicated a task for central planners so that resources are used inefficiently; (2) since nobody in particular owns resources, there is less incentive to employ them in their highest valued use; (3) central plans may reflect more the preferences of central planners than those of society; and (4) each individual has less personal freedom in making economic choices.

Mixed and Transitional Economies

No country on earth exemplifies either type of economic system in its pure form. The United States represents a *mixed capitalist economy*, with government directly accounting for a little more than one-third of all economic activity. But even the economic activity carried out by the private sector is often regulated by government in a variety of ways. Most other advanced industrial nations, such as Germany, Japan, Great Britain, and Canada, also have mixed capitalist economies.

Economic systems have been growing more alike over time, with the role of government increasing in capitalist economies and the role of markets increasing in command economies. Most countries that could have been described as having command economies are currently introducing more market incentives. Prior to recent market reforms, these command economies had several features in common: prices were fixed by central planners rather than by markets; their economies were largely isolated from global markets; private property rights to resources other than labor did not exist or were poorly defined; and production was carried out by state-owned enterprises, which had little experience with the need to satisfy the consumer. The result of these common characteristics was a poor allocation of resources, obsolete capital equipment, low worker productivity, and severe environmental problems.

Among economies that had been centrally planned, from East Germany to Mongolia, from Hungary to China, markets are playing a growing role in allocating resources. For example, about 20 percent of the world's population live in the People's Republic of China, which grows more decentralized, or market oriented, each year. The former Soviet Union has dissolved into fifteen independent republics, and most of these are trying to privatize what had been state-owned enterprises to turn production decisions over to market forces. What had been centrally planned East Germany has merged with capitalist West Germany to form capitalist Germany. The transitions to market economies now underway will shape the world economy in the twenty-first century.[1]

Example One country that has been resisting the movement away from central planning is Cuba.

Economies Based on Custom or Religion

Finally, some economic systems are directed largely by custom or religion. Laws of the Muslim religion set limits on the rate of interest that can be earned on certain investments. The caste system in India and elsewhere often restricts one's choice of occupation. Hence, religion, custom, and family relations play important roles in the organization and coordination of economic activity. Your own pattern of consumption and choice of occupation may be influenced by some of these factors.

CONCLUSION

Although economies can answer the three economic questions in a variety of ways, this text will focus primarily on the mixed form of capitalism found in the United States. This type of economy blends private choice, guided by the price system in competitive markets, with public choice, guided by democracy in political markets. The study of mixed capitalism grows more relevant as capitalist economies and command economies grow more alike.

If you were to quit right now, you would already know more about economics than most people do. But to understand market economies, we must learn how markets work, as we do in the next chapter, which introduces the market interaction of supply and demand.

1. A full discussion of transitional economies can be found in the final chapter of this book.

Summary

1. Resources are scarce but human wants are unlimited. Since we cannot satisfy all wants, we must make choices, and choice involves an opportunity cost. The opportunity cost of the preferred option is the forgone benefit from the best alternative.

2. The law of comparative advantage states that the individual, firm, region, or country with the lowest opportunity cost of producing a particular good should specialize in the production of that good. Specialization according to the law of comparative advantage promotes the most efficient use of resources.

3. The specialization of labor increases efficiency by (1) taking advantage of individual preferences and natural abilities, (2) allowing workers to develop more experience at a particular task, (3) reducing the time required to shift between different tasks, and (4) introducing labor-saving machinery.

4. The production possibilities frontier shows the productive capabilities of the economy during a particular time period, assuming all resources are used efficiently. The frontier's bowed-out shape reflects the law of increasing opportunity cost, which arises because resources are not perfectly adaptable to the production of all goods. Over time, the frontier can shift in or out as a result of changes in the availability of resources or in technology. The frontier demonstrates several economic concepts, including efficiency, scarcity, the law of increasing opportunity cost, choice, and economic growth.

5. All economic systems, regardless of their decision-making process, must answer three fundamental questions: What is to be produced? How is it to be produced? And for whom is it to be produced? Nations answer the questions differently, depending on who owns their resources and how economic activity is coordinated.

Questions and Problems

1. (Opportunity Costs) Discuss the ways in which the following conditions might affect the opportunity cost of going to a movie.
   a. You have a final exam the next day.
   b. School will be out for one month starting today.
   c. The same movie will be shown on TV tomorrow night.
   d. The school dance or concert is the same night as the movie.

2. (Opportunity Costs) "You should never buy precooked frozen foods because you are paying for the labor costs of preparing the food." Is this statement always true, or can it be invalidated by the principle of comparative advantage?

3. (Production Possibilities) During the late 1960s and early 1970s, Mao Zedong and the leaders of the Great Proletarian Cultural Revolution forced highly educated professionals in China to move to farms and work as peasants. The action was justified by arguing that such professionals, by becoming acquainted with honest labor, would learn to respect the common laborer. This policy created a massive reduction in productivity, incentives, and economic growth, and it was later abandoned. How does such a policy relate to the production possibilities frontier?

4. (Production Possibilities) In response to what seemed to be a flood of illegal aliens, Congress made it a federal offense to hire illegal aliens. How will the measure affect the U.S. production possibilities frontier? Will all industries be affected equally? Which individuals in society will be helped, and which will be hurt?

5. (Production Possibilities) "If society decides, by way of the marketplace, to use its resources fully (that is, to keep the economy on the production possibilities frontier), then future generations will be worse off because they will not be able to use these resources." If this assertion is true, full employment of resources may not be a good thing. Comment on the validity of the assertion.

6. (Production Possibilities) People are often confused about what will shift the production possibilities frontier. For example, someone might think that a reduction in the unemployment rate would shift the PPF outward. Explain why this is *not* the case.

7. (Specialization) Discuss the strengths and weaknesses of the practice at universities of having each subject taught by a different professor. Why not have one professor teach history, economics, physics, mathematics, and so on?

8. (Comparative and Absolute Advantage) In the United States some states specialize in the production of certain products. For example, over 50 percent of the apples consumed in the United States come from the Pacific Northwest. Identify states that have absolute advantages in the production of their goods and states that have comparative advantages in the production of their goods.

9. (Comparative Advantage) Corporate executives often use limousines, even though the executives are perfectly good drivers. Suppose that a certain executive is a better driver than her chauffeur. Use the principle of comparative advantage to show that the executive should still employ the driver rather than drive the car herself.

10. (Opportunity Cost) Frick can pick 12 bushels of corn in one hour; Frack can pick 20 bushels. If Frick spends his hour fishing, he can catch three fish; Frack can catch four fish in the same amount of time.
    a. What is the (opportunity) cost of a fish for Frick? For Frack?
    b. What is the (opportunity) cost of a bushel of corn for Frick? For Frack?
    c. What is the greatest number of fish the two can catch together if they also pick 20 bushels of corn? Explain.

11. (Production Possibilities) Suppose a production possibilities frontier includes the following data points:

Cars	*Washing Machines*
0	1,000
100	600
200	0

    a. Graph the production possibilities frontier, assuming that it has no curved segments.
    b. What is the cost of a car when 50 cars are produced?
    c. What is the cost of a car when 150 cars are produced?
    d. What is the cost of a washing machine when 50 cars are produced? 150 cars?
    e. What do your answers tell you about opportunity costs?

12. (Sunk Cost) You go to a restaurant and buy an expensive meal. Halfway through, in spite of feeling stuffed, you decide to clean your plate. After all, you think, you paid for the meal, so you are going to eat all of it. What's wrong with this thinking?

13. (Opportunity Cost) You win a full scholarship to go to graduate school. You aren't sure that you will benefit much from going, but you decide to go because it is free. What's wrong with this thinking?

14. (Opportunity Cost) Suppose you wait in line all night in order to purchase a ticket for a concert. The ticket price is $20.
    a. What is the true cost of this ticket?
    b. If, at the concert door, someone offers you $100 for your ticket, what is the opportunity cost at that point?

15. (Production Possibilities Frontier) Suppose that in an hour George can either write one poem or mow two lawns, and Martha can either write two poems or mow three lawns. Construct a daily production possibility frontier for George *and* Martha assuming each works an 8-hour day.

16. (Production Possibilities Frontier) Consider two possible output combinations. Combination A is on the production possibility frontier, and combination B, which lies below and to the right of A, is inside the production possibility frontier. Which is better? Explain your answer.

17. (Comparative Advantage) Suppose that you are a doctor and also a good car mechanic. Why should you pay someone to repair your car?

18. (Production Possibilities Frontier) Suppose that government deficits drive up the cost of borrowing money so that businesses no longer can afford to fund research and development. How might this affect the production possibilities frontier?

19. (The Opportunity Cost of College) During the Vietnam War period, colleges and universities were literally overflowing with students. Was this bumper crop of undergraduates caused by a greater expected return on a college education or by a change in the opportunity cost of attending college? Explain.

20. (The Opportunity Cost of College) Suppose that the minimum wage was increased to $10 per hour. What impact, if any, would you think this would have on the opportunity cost of attending college?

CHAPTER 3

THE MARKET SYSTEM

Why are vine-ripened tomatoes cheaper in August than in January? Supply and demand. Why are hotel rooms in Phoenix, Arizona, cheaper in the summer, when the temperature is 110 degrees, than in the winter, when the temperature is 70 degrees? Supply and demand. Why is the designer-original dress from Paris more expensive than a dress off the rack from Wal-Mart? You guessed it: supply and demand.

It seems that many economic questions boil down to the workings of supply and demand. Indeed, some people believe that if you programmed a computer to respond "supply and demand" to economic questions, you could put many economists out of work. *The concepts of supply and demand are the most fundamental and the most powerful of all economic tools.* An understanding of the two will take you far in developing your skills in the art and science of economic analysis. This chapter will introduce the underpinnings of supply and demand and show how the two interact in competitive markets. As you will see, the correct analysis of supply and demand takes skill and care. The chapter uses graphs extensively, so you may want to refer back to the appendix of Chapter 1 for a refresher. Topics discussed in this chapter include

- Demand and quantity demanded
- Supply and quantity supplied
- Markets
- Transaction costs
- Equilibrium price and quantity
- Disequilibrium

DEMAND

If the price of Pepsi is $3 a six-pack, how many six-packs will consumers demand each week? How many will be demanded if the price is $2? If the price is $1? The answers to these questions provide a schedule conveying the relation between the price of Pepsi and the quantity demanded. This schedule is called the demand for Pepsi. More generally, **demand** is a relation indicating the quantity of a well-defined commodity that consumers are both *willing* and *able* to buy at each possible price during a given period of time, other things constant. Because demand is calculated for a specific period of time, such as a day, a week, or a month, demand is best thought of as the desired *rate* of purchase at each possible price. Note that demand reflects the quantity that consumers are both *willing* and *able* to buy at each alternative price. For example, you may be *able* to buy a motorcycle at a price of $2,000 because you have enough money to pay for it, but you may not be *willing* to buy one if motorcycles do not interest you.

Demand A relation showing how much of a good consumers are willing and able to buy at each possible price during a given period of time, other things constant

Point to Stress Emphasize from the beginning the importance of the "other things constant" assumption—the demand schedule is designed to highlight the impact of changes in a product's price.

The Law of Demand

In a remote region of western Pennsylvania is a poorly lit, run-down yellow building known as Pechin's Mart. The aisles are unmarked and strewn with half-empty boxes arranged in no apparent design. The sagging roof leaks when it rains. Why do shoppers come from as far away as Maryland and put up with the chaos and the grubbiness to buy as many groceries as they can haul away? The store has violated nearly all the rules of retailing, yet it thrives, with annual sales more than four times the average for supermarkets around the country. The store thrives because it follows a rule merchants have known for thousands of years—its prices are the lowest around.

You as a consumer have little trouble grasping the notion that people will buy more of a particular good at a lower price than at a higher price. Sell the product for less, and the world will beat a path to your door. In fact, the relation between the price of a good and the quantity demanded has been elevated to the status of an economic law. The **law of demand** states that the quantity of a product demanded in a given time period is inversely related to its price, other things constant. Thus, the higher the price, the smaller the quantity demanded; the lower the price, the greater the quantity demanded.

Teaching Tip Consider briefly explaining that there are some exceptions to the law of demand.

Law of demand The quantity of a good demanded is inversely related to its price, other things constant

DEMAND, WANTS, AND NEEDS. Consumer *demand* and consumer *wants* are not the same thing. As we have seen, wants are unlimited. You may *want* a Mercedes-Benz 300, but at a price of $70,000, it is likely beyond your budget (that is, the quantity you demand at that price is zero). Nor is *demand* the same as *need*. You may *need* a new muffler for your car, but if the price is $200, you may decide "I am not going to pay a lot for this muffler." Evidently, you believe you have better ways to spend your money. If, however, the price of mufflers drops enough—say, to $60—then you will be both willing and able to buy one.

Point to Stress The substitution effect is always negative—the quantity demanded of the relatively cheaper product always rises.

THE SUBSTITUTION EFFECT OF A PRICE CHANGE. What explains the law of demand? Why, for example, is less demanded when the price is higher? The explanation begins with scarce resources meeting unlimited wants. Many goods and services are capable of satisfying particular wants. For example, your hunger can be satisfied by pizza, tacos, burgers, or fried chicken. Similarly, your desire for warmth in the winter can be met by warm clothing, home insulation, heating oil, or a trip to Hawaii. Clearly, some ways of satisfying your wants will be more appealing to you than others—a trip to Hawaii is more enjoyable than warmer clothing. In a world without scarcity, there would be no prices, so you would always choose the most appealing alternative. Scarcity, however, is an overriding reality, and the degree of scarcity of one good relative to another determines each good's *relative* price.

Notice that the definition of demand includes the "other-things-constant" assumption. Among things held constant are the prices of other goods. When the price of one good goes up and other prices do not change, this good becomes relatively more costly. Consumers therefore tend to substitute other goods for the higher-priced good. For example, if the price of pizza goes up, you tend to eat less pizza and more of other foods. This phenomenon is called the **substitution effect** of a price change. On the other hand, a decrease in the price of one good causes consumers to substitute that good for other goods, which are now relatively more expensive. Consumers are more *willing* to purchase the good when its relative price falls. Remember, it is the change in the *relative* price—the price of one good relative to the prices of other goods—that causes the substitution effect. If all prices rise by the same percentage, there is no change in relative prices, so there is no substitution effect.

Substitution effect When the price of a good falls, consumers will substitute it for other goods, which are now relatively more expensive

Teaching Tip The discussion of the income effect talks about the "typical" response to a change in real income because the effect would be negative for inferior goods.

THE INCOME EFFECT OF A PRICE CHANGE. A rise in price causes a decline in the quantity demanded for another reason. Suppose you earn $30 a week from a part-time job. You spend all your income on pizza, buying six a week at $5 per pizza. What will happen to the quantity of pizza you demand if its price doubles to $10? At that price you can buy at most three pizzas a week with your income. The increase in the price of pizza has reduced your **real income**—that is, your income measured in terms of the goods and services it can buy. The price increase reduces the *purchasing power* of your income. The quantity of pizza you demand is reduced because of this **income effect** of a price increase. More generally, as the price of a particular good goes up, other things constant, your *ability* to purchase this good declines. Because of the resulting decline in real income, you typically reduce the quantity demanded. Conversely, as the price of a particular good declines, other things constant, your real income increases, so you typically increase the quantity demanded.

Real income Income measured in terms of the goods and services it can buy

Income effect A fall in the price of a good increases consumers' real income, making them more able to purchase all normal goods, so the quantity demanded increases

The Demand Schedule and Demand Curve

Demand can be expressed as a *demand schedule* or as a *demand curve*. Panel (a) of Exhibit 1 shows a hypothetical demand schedule for milk. When we describe demand, we must be specific about the units being measured and the

EXHIBIT 1

The Demand Schedule and Demand Curve for Milk

(a) Demand schedule

	Price per Quart	Quantity Demanded per Month (millions of quarts)
a	$1.25	8
b	1.00	14
c	0.75	20
d	0.50	26
e	0.25	32

(b) Demand curve

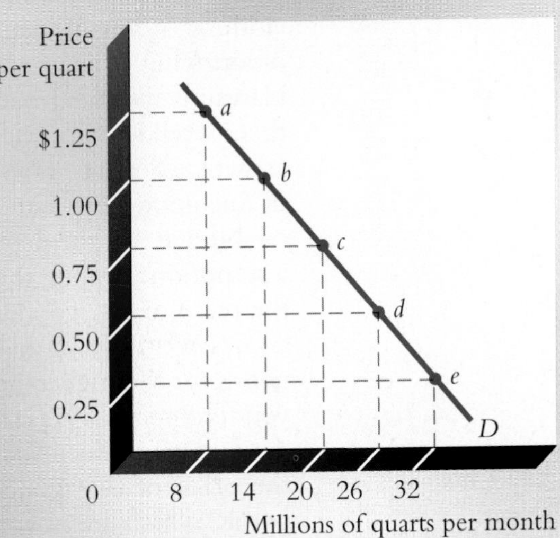

The market demand curve, *D*, shows the quantity of milk demanded, at various prices, by all consumers.

time period under consideration. In our example, the price is for a quart of milk, and the period is a month. The milk is of uniform quality, in this case grade A. The schedule lists alternative prices, along with the quantity demanded at each price. At a price of $1.25 per quart, for example, consumers will demand 8 million quarts per month. As you can see, the lower the price, the greater the quantity demanded: if the price drops as low as $0.25, 32 million quarts will be demanded per month. As the price of milk falls, milk becomes relatively cheaper so consumers substitute milk for other goods. And as the price of milk falls, the income effect also increases the quantity of milk demanded.

Demand curve A curve showing the quantity of a commodity demanded at various possible prices, other things constant

The demand schedule in panel (a) is presented as a **demand curve** in panel (b). Price is measured on the vertical axis and the quantity demanded is measured on the horizontal axis. Each combination of price and quantity demanded listed in the demand schedule in panel (a) is represented by a point in panel (b). Point *a*, for example, indicates that at a price of $1.25, 8 million quarts will be demanded per month. These points are connected to form the demand curve for milk, which is labeled *D*. Note that the demand curve slopes downward, reflecting the *law of demand:* price and quantity demanded are inversely related, other things constant. Assumed to be constant along the demand curve are the prices of other goods. Thus along the demand curve for milk, the price of milk changes *relative to the prices of other goods*. Therefore, the demand curve shows the effects of a change in the *relative price* of milk—that is, relative to other prices, which are assumed to remain unchanged.

Take care to distinguish between the *demand* for milk and the *quantity demanded*. The demand for milk is not a specific quantity but the entire relation indicating the quantity demanded at each price. *Demand* is represented by the complete demand schedule or demand curve. But an individual point on the demand curve shows the *quantity demanded* at a particular price. For example, at a price of $0.75 per quart, the quantity demanded is 20 million quarts. When the price of milk changes, say from $0.75 to $1.00, this change is expressed in Exhibit 1 by a movement along the demand curve—in this case from point *c* to point *b*. Any movement along a demand curve reflects a *change in quantity demanded*, not a change in demand.

Point to Stress A change in quantity demanded of good X occurs when only the price of X changes—all other factors affecting the quantity demanded are constant.

The law of demand applies to the millions of products found in grocery stores, department stores, clothing stores, drug stores, music stores, book stores, travel agencies, restaurants, yellow pages, classified ads, stock markets, housing markets, and all other markets. The law of demand applies even to choices that seem more personal than economic, such as whether or not to own a pet. For example, after New York City passed a dog-litter law, owners had to follow their dogs around the city's sidewalks with scoopers, plastic bags, or whatever else would do the job. Because the law raised the price of owning a dog, the quantity demanded decreased. The number of dogs left at animal shelters doubled. Many other dogs were simply abandoned by their owners, raising the number of strays in the city. Such behavior could have been predicted based on the law of demand.

Teaching Tip Explain that market demand is found by totalling the quantities demanded by all consumers in the market at each possible price.

At times it is useful to distinguish between *individual demand*, which is the demand of an individual consumer, and *market demand*, which is the sum of the individual demands of *all* consumers in the market. Market demand conveys the relation between the price of a good and the quantity that all consumers in the market are willing and able to buy. In most markets there are many consumers, sometimes millions. Unless otherwise noted, when we talk about demand, we will be referring to market demand, as in Exhibit 1.

CHANGES IN DEMAND

A given demand curve isolates the relation between the price of a good and the quantity demanded when other factors that could affect demand remain unchanged. What we will consider next is what happens to the demand curve when other factors *do* change. What are these other factors and how do changes in these other factors affect demand? Variables that can affect market demand are (1) consumer income, (2) the prices of other goods, (3) consumer expectations, (4) the number of consumers in the market, and (5) consumer tastes.

Teaching Tip Some students may confuse the impact of a change in consumer income with the income effect discussed earlier in the chapter. Emphasize that the income effect refers to a situation in which the price of a good changes; the consumer's money income is unchanged. You might note that inferior goods have a negative income effect as well.

Example The percentage of black families in the United States with incomes over $50,000 per year (in constant 1990 dollars) increased from 9.9 percent in 1970 to 14.5 percent in 1990. Sales of Estee Lauder cosmetics for black women increased 50 percent in the last few years.

Changes in Consumer Income

Exhibit 2 shows *D*, the market demand curve for milk. This demand curve assumes a given level of consumer income. Suppose consumer incomes increase. Consumers will then be willing and able to purchase more milk at each price level, so the demand curve for milk will shift to the right, as reflected by the movement from *D* to *D′*. For example, at a price of $1, the quantity demanded increases from 14 million to 20 million quarts per month, as indicated by the movement from point *b* on *D* to point *g* on *D′*. But an increase in the demand for milk also means that consumers are willing and able to pay a higher price for each *quantity* of milk. For example, consumers were initially willing and able to pay $1 per quart for 14 million quarts, as reflected by point *b*. After the increase in demand, consumers are willing and able to pay $1.25 per quart for 14 million quarts, as reflected by point *f* on the new demand curve, which is directly above point *b* on the original demand curve. In short, *an increase in demand—that is, a shift to the right in the demand curve—means that consumers are willing and able to buy more units at each price level and to pay more per unit at each quantity level.*

EXHIBIT 2

An Increase in the Market Demand for Milk

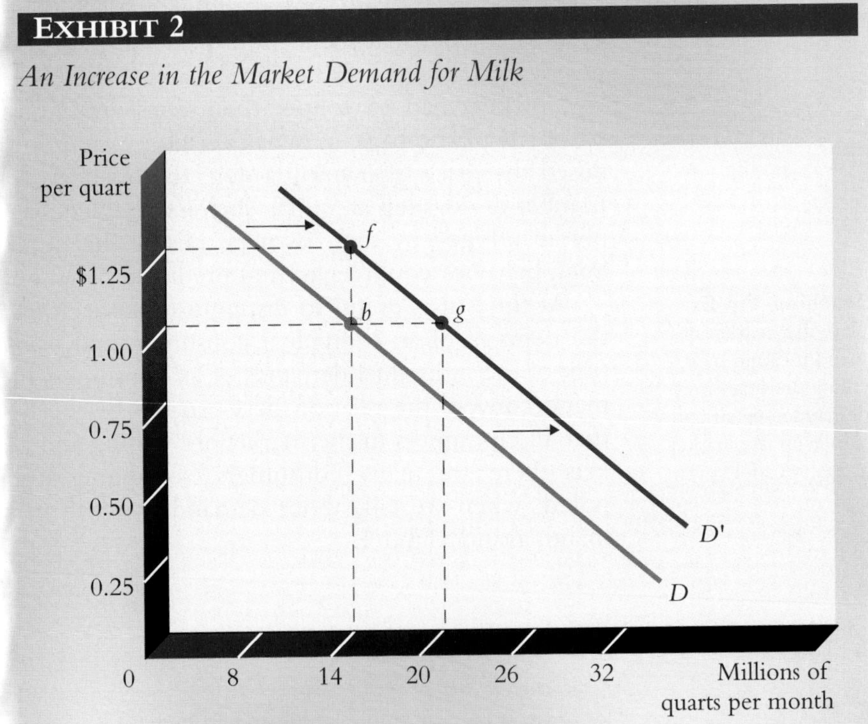

An increase in the demand for milk is reflected by an outward shift in the demand curve. After the increase in demand, the quantity of milk demanded at a price of $1 per quart increases from 14 million quarts (point *b*) to 20 million quarts (point *g*). Another way to interpret the shift is to say that the maximum price consumers are willing to pay for 14 million quarts has increased from $1 per unit (at point *b*) to $1.25 per unit (at point *f*).

Normal good A good for which demand increases as consumer income rises

Inferior good A good for which demand decreases as consumer income rises

We classify goods into two broad groupings depending on how demand for the good responds to changes in income. The demand for **normal goods** increases as income increases. Because the demand for milk increases when consumer income increases, milk is considered to be a normal good. Most goods are normal goods. In contrast, the demand for **inferior goods** actually declines as income increases. Examples of inferior goods include ground chuck, trips to the laundromat, bus rides, and powdered milk. As income increases, consumers tend to switch from consuming these inferior goods to consuming normal goods (steak, their own washers and dryers, automobile or plane rides, and whole milk), so the demand curve for inferior goods shifts to the left.

Teaching Tip Some students may confuse the impact of a change in the price of a substitute good with the substitution effect discussed earlier in the chapter. Emphasize that the substitution effect refers to the impact of a change in a good's own price, not the impact of a change in a substitute good's price.

Changes in the Prices of Other Goods

Substitutes Goods that are related in such a way that an increase in the price of one leads to an increase in demand for the other

The demand curve isolates the relation between the price of a product and the quantity demanded, other things constant. One thing held constant is the prices of other goods, especially goods that are closely related to the good in question. As noted earlier, there are alternative ways of trying to satisfy any particular want. For example, thirst can be quenched not only by milk but also by soft drinks, fruit juices, or water. These goods are, to a certain extent, substitutes in satisfying thirst. Consumers choose among substitutes partly on the basis of their relative prices. Consider two substitutes, milk and juice. Obviously, they are not perfect substitutes (you wouldn't pour juice on cereal or use it to make hot chocolate), but an increase in the price of juice, other things constant, will encourage some consumers to buy less juice and more milk. Two goods are **substitutes** if an increase in the price of one leads to an increase in the demand for the other, and conversely, if a decrease in the price of one leads to a decrease in the demand for the other.

Complements Goods that are related in such a way that an increase in the price of one leads to a decrease in the demand for the other

Two goods are complements if they are used in combination to satisfy some particular want. Milk and chocolate chip cookies, computer hardware and software, popcorn and movies, and airline tickets and rental cars are considered complements because they are often used in combination. For example, a 1992 decline in airfares increased the demand for rental cars. Two goods are **complements** if a decrease in the price of one leads to an increase in the demand for the other, and conversely, if an increase in the price of one leads to a decrease in the demand for the other.

Most pairs of goods selected at random are *unrelated*—for example, milk and housing, pizza and socks, and dental floss and golf equipment. Usually, there is no relation between the demand of one good and the price of an unrelated good. However, because of the income effect of a price change, there may be a relation between the demand for a good and the price of a seemingly unrelated good. For example, an increase in the price of housing may reduce the consumer's real income enough to reduce the demand for milk.

Changes in Consumer Expectations

Another factor that can shift the demand curve is a change in consumer expectations about factors that influence demand, such as future income and the future

Example The average prices of a Honda Accord and a Ford Taurus differed by only $600 in 1991. Ask students to consider the impact of an increase in the price of the Accord.

Example Immigrant workers in south Florida normally earn $20 to $30 per day picking crops during the harvest season. The destruction of mango, avocado, and lime orchards by Hurricane Andrew in August, 1992 reduced their income expectations.

price of a good. A consumer who expects a pay increase may increase current demand in anticipation of that pay increase. For example, a college senior who lands that first job may buy a new car even before graduation in anticipation of a steady paycheck. Demand in this case is based not on current income but on expected income. Changes in price expectations can also affect demand. For example, if consumers expect the price of new housing to jump next year, they will probably increase their demand for new housing this year. On the other hand, expectations of a lower price in the future will encourage consumers to postpone purchases, or reduce current demand.

Changes in the Number of Consumers

We mentioned earlier that market demand is the sum of the individual demands of all consumers in the market. If the number of consumers in the market changes, demand will change. For example, if the population grows, the demand for food will increase. Even if the total population remains the same, demand could change as a result of a change in the composition of the population. For example, if the number of retired couples increases, the demand for recreational vehicles will probably increase. If the baby population declines, the demand for baby food will decrease.

Changes in Consumer Tastes

Do you like anchovies on your pizza? How about sauerkraut on your hot dog? Is music to your ears more likely to be new wave, heavy metal, rap, reggae, or country and western? Choices in food, clothing, movies, music, reading—indeed, all consumption choices—are influenced by consumer tastes. *Tastes* are nothing more than your likes and dislikes as a consumer. What determines tastes? Who knows? Economists certainly don't, nor do they spend much time worrying about it. Economists do recognize, however, that tastes are very important in shaping demand, and that a change in tastes can change demand.

Example L. G. Balfour Co., a large manufacturer of high school class rings, has found that it is now much harder to sell class rings in U.S. high schools than in the past. In 1992, the company announced the introduction of class rings from the fictional West Beverly High School of the television series "Beverly Hills 90210." The company expected first-year sales of at least 100,000 rings.

Because a change in tastes is so difficult to isolate from other economic changes, we should be reluctant to attribute a change in demand to a change in tastes. In our analysis of consumer demand, we will assume that tastes are given and are relatively stable over time. We know, for example, that younger people tend to prefer rock music, whereas older people tend to prefer other kinds of music. In fact, the music piped into shopping malls tends to be so-called easy listening music, a choice designed to discourage younger people from hanging around the mall any longer than required to do their shopping.

If we could not assume that tastes are relatively stable, there would be a temptation to explain any shift in demand as a change in tastes. For example, the question "Why did the demand for milk change?" could be answered by saying "Obviously, the taste for milk changed." But since it is usually difficult to verify such an assertion, we use the change-in-tastes explanation sparingly and only after other possible changes have been ruled out. At times, a change in tastes may be traced to a specific event. For example, after the American

Change in quantity demanded A movement along the demand curve for a good in response to a change in the price of the good

Change in demand A shift in a given demand curve caused by a change in one of the determinants of demand for the good

Heart Association linked cholesterol to heart disease, the sales of eggs, which are loaded with cholesterol, fell by 25 percent. As another example, the demand for fur coats has dropped sharply because animal-rights activists have campaigned against wearing fur. The price of a raccoon pelt has dropped from $25 fifteen years ago to less than $1 today.

Remember that a **change in quantity demanded** results from a change in price, other things constant. A **change in demand** results from a change in one of the determinants of demand that causes a shift in the entire demand curve. A movement along a given demand curve is called a change in quantity demanded; a shift in that curve is called a change in demand. The distinction between a change in demand and a change in the quantity demanded may be confusing at first, so be careful.

SUPPLY

Supply A relation showing how much of a good producers are willing and able to sell at various prices during a given time period, other things constant

Law of supply The quantity of product supplied in a given time period is usually directly related to its price, other things constant

Supply curve A curve showing the quantity of a good supplied at various prices, other things constant

Teaching Tip Note the statement that the relationship between price and quantity supplied is "normally" direct. In special circumstances, such as within a decreasing-cost, perfectly competitive industry in the long run, an inverse relationship might develop between price and quantity supplied.

Just as demand is the relation between price and quantity demanded, supply is the relation between price and quantity supplied. Specifically, **supply** indicates how much of the good producers are both *willing* and *able* to offer for sale in a given time period at each possible price, other things constant. The relation between price and quantity supplied is normally a direct one; that is, more is supplied at a higher price than at a lower price, other things constant. The **law of supply** states that the quantity of product supplied in a given time period is usually directly related to its price, other things constant. Thus, the higher the price, the greater the quantity supplied; the lower the price, the smaller the quantity supplied.

The Supply Schedule and Supply Curve

Exhibit 3 presents the market *supply schedule* and market **supply curve**, *S*, for milk, showing the quantity of milk supplied at various possible prices by thousands of dairy farmers. As you can see, price and quantity supplied are directly, or positively, related. More is offered for sale at a higher price than at a lower price, so the supply curve slopes upward. There are two reasons producers tend to offer more goods for sale when prices are higher. The first has to do with a *willingness* to offer more for sale at a higher price than at a lower price. An increase in the price of milk provides farmers with a profit incentive to shift some resources out of the production of other goods, such as corn, for which the price is now relatively lower, and into milk, for which the price is now relatively higher. Prices act as signals to existing and potential suppliers about the relative rewards for producing various goods. *A higher milk price attracts resources from lower-valued uses to the higher-valued use.* As the price of a good increases, other things constant, a producer is more *willing* to supply the good.

A second reason the supply curve tends to slope upward is that higher prices increase the *ability* to supply the good. The law of increasing opportu-

EXHIBIT 3

The Supply Schedule and Supply Curve for Milk

(a) Supply schedule

Price per Quart	Quantity Supplied per Month (millions of quarts)
$1.25	28
1.00	24
0.75	20
0.50	16
0.25	12

(b) Supply curve

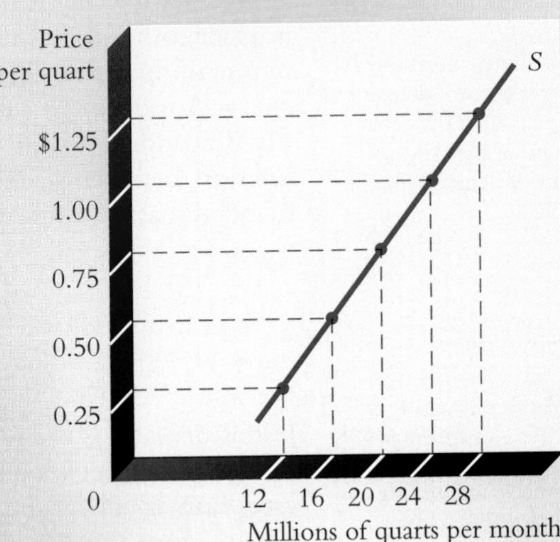

The market supply curve, *S*, shows the quantity of milk supplied, at various prices, by all farmers.

Example After the oil embargo of the mid-1970s, the price of oil rose high enough to justify recovering oil from high-cost locations such as the North Sea or Alaska.

nity cost states that as more of a particular good is produced, the opportunity cost of additional output rises—that is, the *marginal cost* increases. Since producers face a higher marginal cost for additional output, they must receive a higher price for that output to be *able* to increase the quantity supplied. For example, when milk production is low, farmers are able to employ resources that are well suited to the task. As output increases, however, producing the additional increments of milk requires resources that may be better suited to the production of other goods. To feed additional cows, for example, a farmer may have to convert a productive wheat field into grazing land. Therefore, additional output has a higher opportunity cost. *Higher milk prices make farmers more able to draw resources away from alternative uses.*

Thus, a higher price makes producers more *willing* and more *able* to increase the quantity of goods offered for sale. Producers are more *willing* because production of the higher-priced good is now relatively more attractive than the alternative uses of the resources involved. Producers are more *able* because the higher price allows them to cover the higher marginal costs typically involved with higher rates of production.

As with demand, we distinguish between *individual* supply and *market* supply. Market supply is the sum of the amount supplied at each price by all the individual suppliers. Unless otherwise noted, when we talk about supply, we will be referring to market supply. We also distinguish between *supply* and *quantity supplied*. Supply is the relation between the price and quantity supplied, as reflected by the entire supply schedule or supply curve. Quantity supplied refers to a particular amount offered for sale at a particular price, as reflected by a point on a given supply curve.

CHANGES IN SUPPLY

Teaching Tip Students may also be interested in the impact of supply shocks. For example, Iraq's invasion of Kuwait in 1990 and the resulting Persian Gulf war destroyed many oil wells, pipelines, telecommunications, roads, buildings, and factories. Damages totalled $160 billion in Kuwait and $190 billion in Iraq.

The supply curve expresses the relation between the price of a good and the quantity supplied, other things constant. So the supply curve is drawn under the assumption that no changes occur in other factors that determine supply. Such factors include (1) the state of technology, (2) the prices of relevant resources, (3) the prices of alternative goods, (4) producer expectations, and (5) the number of producers in the market. We will consider how a change in each of these determinants of supply will affect the supply curve.

Changes in Technology

Example In the early 1990s, Cincinnati Gas & Electric encouraged major customers to install a new air conditioning system that uses machines called thermal-energy storage units. The machines make ice overnight when utility rates are lower and store the ice in a 330-ton tank. During the day, the ice melts to cool the building. Estimated savings per machine were as high as $100,000 per year.

Recall from Chapter 2 that the state of technology represents the economy's stock of knowledge about how resources can be combined most efficiently. Along a given supply curve, the technology—the knowledge of how to most efficiently produce this good—is assumed to remain unchanged. If a more efficient method is discovered to produce the good, production costs will fall, so suppliers will be more willing and more able to supply the good at each price. Supply will increase, as reflected by a shift to the right in the supply curve. For example, suppose a new milking machine called The Invisible Hand has a very soothing effect on cows; cows find the new machine so udderly delightful that they produce more milk. Such a technological advance is reflected by a shift to the right in the market supply curve for milk, as shown by the shift from S to S' in Exhibit 4.

Notice that just as a change in demand can be interpreted in two different ways, so can a change in supply. First, an increase in supply means dairy farmers supply more milk at each possible price. For example, when the price is $1.00 per quart, the amount of milk supplied increases from 24 million to 28 million quarts per month, as shown by the movement from point *h* to point *i* in Exhibit 4. Second, an increase in supply means that farmers are willing and able to supply the same quantity at a lower price. For example, farmers originally supplied 24 million quarts when the price was $1.00 per quart; on the new supply curve, that same quantity is supplied for only $0.75 per quart, as shown by the movement from point *h* to point *j*.

Changes in the Prices of Relevant Resources

Relevant resources Resources used to produce the good in question

Relevant resources are those resources employed in the production of the good in question. For example, suppose the price of feed falls. This lower resource price reduces the cost of milk production. Dairy farmers are therefore more willing and able to supply milk, and the supply curve for milk shifts to

EXHIBIT 4

An Increase in the Supply of Milk

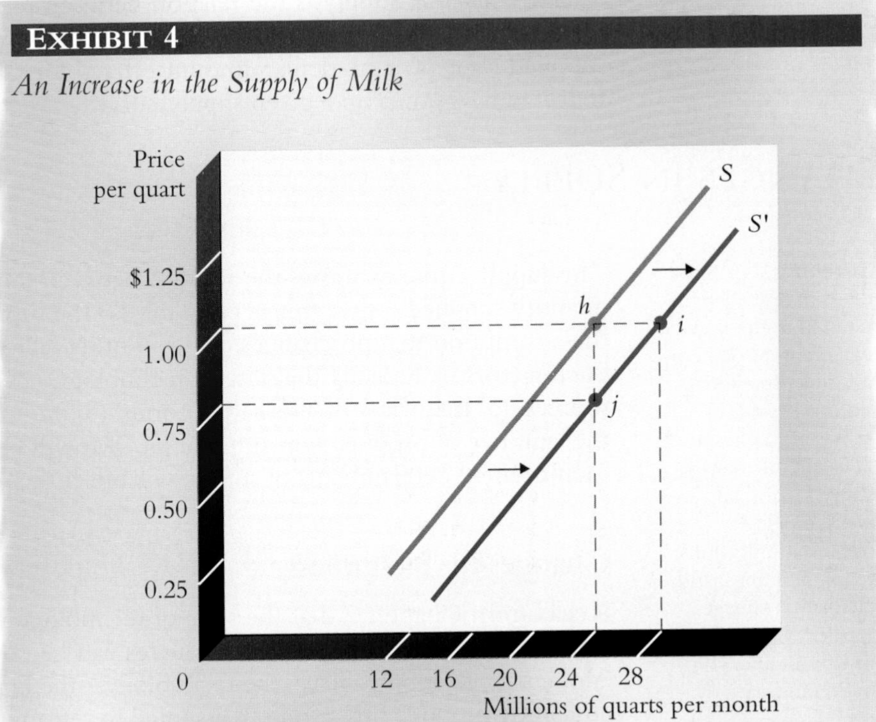

An increase in the supply of milk is reflected by a shift to the right in the supply curve, from *S* to *S'*. After the increase in supply, the quantity of milk supplied at a price of $1 per quart increases from 24 million quarts (point *h*) to 28 million quarts (point *i*). Another way to interpret the shift is to say that it shows a reduction in the minimum price suppliers require in order to produce 24 million quarts. Previously, a price of $1 per quart was required (point *h*); after the increase in supply, suppliers require a price of only $0.75 per quart (point *j*).

Example Health insurance costs for General Motors' employees rose 12 percent annually between 1965 and 1991. By 1991, increases in health insurance costs for General Motors (see earlier annotation) added $900 to the cost of each GM vehicle.

Example In 1992, Coca-Cola Co. launched a flavored sparkling water beverage called Nordic Mist. The flavored-water segment of the market was growing 8 percent per year while sales growth for traditional soft drinks had slowed to 1.3 percent per year.

the right, as shown in Exhibit 4. On the other hand, an increase in the price of a relevant resource will reduce supply. For example, higher electricity rates would increase the cost of lighting the barn and operating the milking machines. These higher production costs would be reflected by a shift to the left in the supply curve.

Changes in the Prices of Alternative Goods

Alternative goods Other goods that use some of the same type of resources used to produce the good in question

Nearly all resources have alternative uses. The farmer's field, tractor, barn, and labor could be used to produce a variety of crops. **Alternative goods** are goods that use some of the same resources as are used to produce the good under consideration. For example, if the price of beef increases enough, dairy cows may be worth more dead than alive. Higher beef prices raise the opportunity cost of producing milk. Some farmers will shift from supplying milk to supplying beef, so the supply of milk will decrease, or shift to the left. On the other hand, a fall in the price of an alternative good will make milk production relatively more attractive. As resources shift into milk production, the supply of milk will increase, or shift to the right.

Example After Hurricane Andrew, analysts considered the possibility of an oversupply of winter vegetables in the United States. They thought it likely that farmers elsewhere in Florida and in Mexico would increase production substantially in anticipation of a weak crop in South Florida and higher prices.

Changes in Producer Expectations

Changes in producer expectations about market factors that influence supply can result in a shift of the supply curve. For example, a farmer expecting higher prices for milk in the future may begin to expand the dairy today, thereby increasing the supply of milk. When a good can be easily stored (crude oil, for example, can be left in the ground), an expectation of a higher price in the future will prompt producers to reduce their current supply and await the higher price. Their reduction in supply is reflected by a shift to the left in the supply curve. Thus, an expectation of higher prices in the future could either increase or decrease the current supply, depending on the nature of the good under consideration. More generally, any change expected to affect future profitability in a market, such as a change in business taxes, will influence supply.

Example In 1992, Nissan Motor Corporation introduced a new car, the Altima, to the U.S. mid-size family sedan market. The company spent $475 million to double capacity at its Tennessee plant in order to produce the car.

Changes in the Number of Producers

Since the market supply is the sum of the amount supplied by all producers, market supply depends on the number of producers in the market. If the number of producers increases, supply will shift to the right; if the number decreases, supply will shift to the left. For example, during the 1980s the number of stores renting movie videos mushroomed, so the supply of videos available for rent increased sharply, shifting the supply curve to the right.

Change in quantity supplied A movement along the supply curve for a good in response to a change in the price of the good

Change in supply A shift in a given supply curve caused by a change in one of the determinants of the supply of the good

Before leaving this section on supply, notice that supply and demand have some similar determinants. Both depend on the prices of other goods, expectations, and the number of participants in the market. Note also that we distinguish between (1) a **change in quantity supplied**, which is the response to a change in the price of the good, other things constant, and is represented as a movement between points along a given supply curve, and (2) a **change in supply**, which is the response to a change in one of the determinants of supply, and is represented as a shift in the entire supply curve. We are now ready to bring supply and demand together.

Putting It All Together: Supply, Demand, and Equilibrium

Suppliers and demanders have different views of price because demanders *pay* the price and suppliers *receive* the price. Thus, a higher price tends to be bad news for consumers but good news for producers. As the price rises, consumers reduce their quantity demanded and producers increase their quantity supplied. How is this ongoing conflict between producers and consumers resolved?

Markets

The differing views of price held by suppliers and demanders are sorted out by the market for the product. A *market*, a term first introduced in Chapter 1, is an impersonal mechanism that coordinates the independent decisions of buyers and sellers. A market represents all the arrangements used to buy and sell a particular good or service. Markets reduce the cost of bringing buyers and sellers together and allow them to find out what's for sale, at what price, and of what quality. Thus, we say that markets reduce the **transaction costs** of exchange—the cost of time and information required for exchange. For example, suppose you are looking for a summer job. One approach would be to go from employer to employer seeing if there are any openings. But this would be time-consuming and could involve extensive travel. Alternatively, you could pick up a copy of the local newspaper and let your fingers do the walking through the help-wanted ads. These ads, which are one element of the job market, reduce the transaction costs required to bring workers and employers together.

Transaction costs The costs of time and information required to carry out an exchange

Teaching Tip Refer to Chapter 4 for additional discussion of specialization and reduced transaction costs.

The coordination that occurs through markets takes place not because of some central plan but because of Adam Smith's "invisible hand." For example, most of the auto dealers in your community tend to locate together, usually on the outskirts of town, where land is cheaper. The dealers congregate not because they like one another's company but because each dealer wants to be where customers shop for cars—that is, near other dealers. Similarly, stores group together downtown and in shopping malls, and Disney World, Sea World, and Universal Studios have located together in Orlando, Florida. On the West Coast, similar theme parks have located in the Los Angeles area.

Specialized Markets

Markets can encompass the entire world, such as the market for crude oil, or they can be as narrow as the competing gas stations at an intersection. Some markets are very specialized; others are more general. In Quincy Market, a shopping center in Boston, one store sells nothing but kites. In a rural community outside of Boston, there is a general store that sells goods ranging from a monkey wrench to a pound of lamb chops. Why do some stores sell many different products while others specialize?

Adam Smith gave us the answer more than two hundred years ago when he noted that *the degree of specialization is limited by the extent of the market*. The larger the market—that is, the greater the potential number of customers—the greater the degree of specialization. The shopping complex in Boston attracts millions of shoppers each year. Even if just a tiny fraction of them buy kites, the store can thrive. The general store, however, relies on a much smaller market—the several dozen homes scattered across the surrounding countryside—so it must offer a wider range of goods to make a profit. Thus, specialty stores are more likely to locate in major population areas than in rural communities.

Similarly, some magazines, such as *Time* and *People*, are aimed at a general readership, so their subject matter and advertisements reflect this general interest. Specialized periodicals, such as the *American Economic Review* and *Cigar*, contain subject matter and advertising reflecting the narrow interests of their readers. Restaurants specialize, too, to suit a range of tastes—French, Italian, Mexican, Chinese, Indian, homestyle, barbecue, pizza, and so on. In Greenville, Mississippi a restaurant called "Hello I'm Jello" sells nothing but Jell-O.

Point to Stress Students should be careful not to measure surpluses as the difference between quantity supplied and the equilibrium quantity and shortages as the difference between the quantity demanded and the equilibrium quantity.

Market Equilibrium

To see how a market works, let's bring together market supply and market demand. Exhibit 5 shows the supply and demand for milk, using schedules in panel (a) and curves in panel (b). To get things started, suppose the price initially is $1 per quart. At that price producers supply 24 million quarts per month, but consumers demand only 14 million quarts per month. So when the price is $1 per quart, the quantity supplied exceeds the quantity demanded, resulting in an *excess quantity supplied*, or a **surplus**, of 10 million quarts per month. The 10 million quarts of unsold milk signals producers that the price is too high. Unless the price falls, the surplus will continue and milk will sour on store shelves. How can the surplus be eliminated? By lowering the price. Thus, the suppliers' desire to eliminate the surplus puts downward pressure on the price, as reflected by the arrow pointing downward in panel (b). As the price falls, producers reduce their quantity supplied and consumers increase their quantity demanded. As long as quantity supplied exceeds quantity demanded, the resulting surplus will exert pressure for a lower price.

Surplus An excess of quantity supplied over quantity demanded at a given price

Alternatively, suppose the price is initially $0.50 per quart. You can see from Exhibit 5 that at that price consumers demand 26 million quarts per month but producers supply only 16 million quarts per month, resulting in an *excess quantity demanded*, or a **shortage**, of 10 million quarts per month. Producers notice that the quantity supplied has quickly sold out and customers are grumbling because milk is no longer available. Empty store shelves, frustrated consumers, and profit-seeking producers create market pressure for a higher price, as reflected by the arrow pointing upward in panel (b). As the price rises, producers increase the quantity supplied and consumers reduce the quantity demanded. The price will continue to rise as long as quantity demanded exceeds quantity supplied.

Shortage An excess of quantity demanded over quantity supplied at a given price

Thus, a surplus creates downward pressure on the price, and a shortage creates upward pressure on the price. As long as quantity demanded and quantity supplied differ, market forces will exert pressure for a price change, which in turn will affect quantity demanded and quantity supplied. When the quantity consumers are willing and able to buy equals the quantity producers are willing and able to sell, the market is said to be in equilibrium. In **equilibrium**, the independent plans of both buyers and sellers exactly match, so market forces will exert no pressure for a change in price or quantity.

Equilibrium The condition that exists in a market when the plans of buyers match the plans of sellers

In panel (b) of Exhibit 5, the eye is drawn to the intersection of the demand and supply curves, identified as point *c*. At this *equilibrium point*, the *equilibrium price* is $0.75 per quart and the *equilibrium quantity* is 20 million

EXHIBIT 5

Equilibrium in the Milk Market

(a) Market schedules

	Millions of Quarts per Month			
Price per Quart	**Quantity Demanded**	**Quantity Supplied**	**Surplus or Shortage**	**Price Will**
$1.25	8	28	Surplus of 20	Fall
1.00	14	24	Surplus of 10	Fall
0.75	20	20	Equilibrium	Remain the same
0.50	26	16	Shortage of 10	Rise
0.25	32	12	Shortage of 20	Rise

(b) Market curves

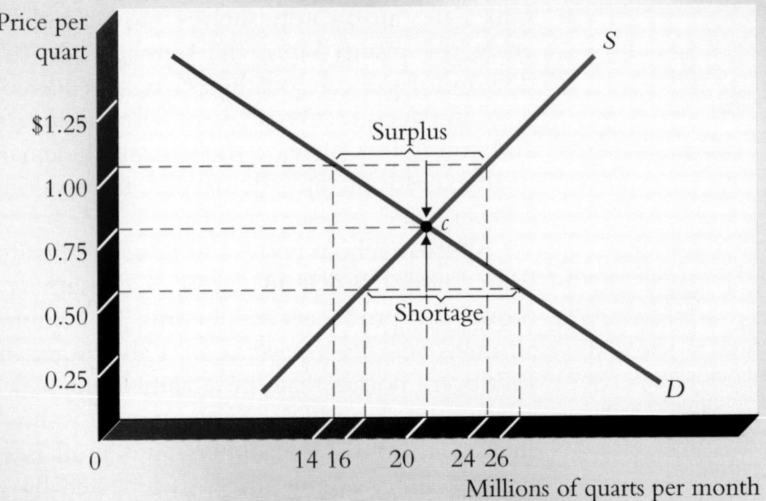

Market equilibrium occurs at a price at which the quantity demanded by consumers is equal to the quantity supplied by producers. This is shown at point *c*. At prices above the equilibrium price, the quantity supplied exceeds the quantity demanded; at these prices there is a surplus, and there is downward pressure on the price. At prices below equilibrium, quantity demanded exceeds quantity supplied; the resulting shortage puts upward pressure on the price.

quarts per month. At the equilibrium price and quantity, the market *clears*; there is no shortage or surplus. Once equilibrium is achieved, there will be no tendency for price or quantity to change as long as demand and supply remain unchanged.

Teaching Tip When a shortage occurs and prices are not permitted to rise to equilibrium, goods must be rationed in some other way—such as when customers end up standing in long lines.

Markets Have a Mind of Their Own

Note that market equilibrium is achieved through the independent actions of thousands, or even millions, of buyers and sellers. Prices are signals of relative scarcity. The equilibrium price rations the product to those consumers most willing and able to pay that price. In one sense the market is very personal because each consumer and each producer makes a personal decision regarding how much to buy or sell at a given price. In another sense the market is very impersonal because it requires no conscious coordination among consumers or producers. *Impersonal market forces synchronize the personal and independent decisions of many individual buyers and many individual sellers to determine equilibrium price and quantity.*

Markets are efficient devices for allocating scarce resources to their highest-valued use. The measure of value is consumers' willingness and ability to pay. In a market economy, those who are unable to pay go without. Many people view this feature of the market system as a flaw. Some observers are troubled, for example, that U.S. consumers spend more than $20 billion each year on pet food at a time when thousands of homeless people are sleeping on the nation's streets. On your next trip to the supermarket, notice how much shelf space is devoted to pet products—often an entire aisle.

Changes in Equilibrium Price and Quantity

Point to Stress Throughout the discussion of changes in equilibrium, demand curves are assumed to have their "normal" downward slope and supply curves are assumed to have their "normal" upward slope.

Equilibrium is that combination of price and quantity at which the desires of demanders and suppliers exactly match. Once equilibrium is achieved, that price and quantity will prevail unless one of the determinants of supply or demand changes. A change in any one of these factors will change equilibrium price and quantity in a predictable way, as we shall see.

Impact of Changes in Demand on Equilibrium Price and Quantity

Teaching Tip Throughout the discussion of changes in equilibrium, make sure that students can clearly distinguish a change in quantity demanded from a change in demand and a change in quantity supplied from a change in supply.

In Exhibit 6 the initial equilibrium price and quantity of milk are as depicted earlier with demand curve *D* and supply curve *S*. The price is $0.75 per quart and the quantity is 20 million quarts per month. Suppose that one of the determinants of demand changes in a way that increases demand, shifting the demand curve to the right from *D* to *D′*. Any of the following changes could increase demand: (1) an increase in consumer income (as long as milk is a normal good); (2) an increase in the price of a substitute, such as juice, or a decrease in the price of a complement, such as cereal; (3) a change in consumers' expectations that encourages them to buy more milk now; (4) an increase in the number of consumers; (5) a change in consumer tastes—based, for example, on a growing awareness that the calcium in milk builds stronger bones.

EXHIBIT 6

Effects of an Increase in Demand

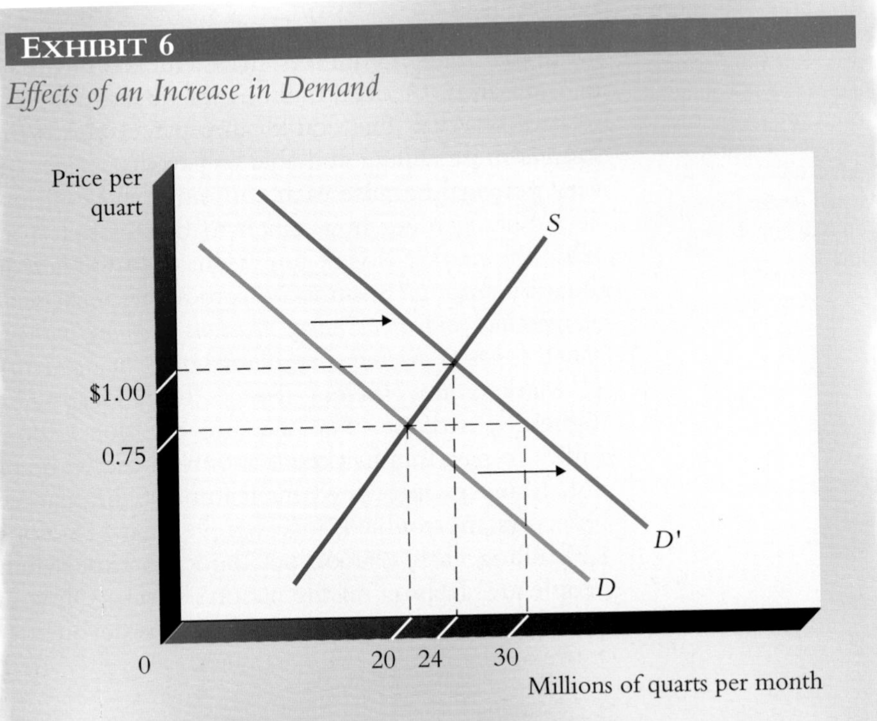

After an increase in demand shifts the demand curve from *D* to *D′*, quantity demanded exceeds quantity supplied at the old price of $0.75 per quart. As the price rises, quantity supplied increases along supply curve *S*, and quantity demanded falls along demand curve *D′*. When the new equilibrium price of $1 per quart is reached, the quantity demanded will once again equal the quantity supplied. Both price and quantity are higher following the increase in demand.

Example The prices of plywood and roofing materials increased throughout the United States as a result of the repairs being undertaken in south Florida after Hurricane Andrew.

After the increase in demand, as reflected in Exhibit 6, the quantity demanded at the original price of $0.75 is 30 million quarts, which obviously exceeds the quantity supplied of 20 million quarts. Thus the quantity demanded exceeds the quantity supplied by 10 million quarts. This shortage puts upward pressure on the price. As the price increases, the quantity demanded decreases along the new demand curve, *D′*, and the quantity supplied increases along *S* until the two quantities are in equilibrium once again. The new equilibrium price is $1 per quart, and the new equilibrium quantity is 24 million quarts per month. Thus, given an upward-sloping supply curve, an increase in demand increases both the equilibrium price and the equilibrium quantity. In contrast, a decrease in demand would result in a lower equilibrium price and quantity. We can summarize these results as follows: *any increase or decrease in demand, with the supply curve held constant, will change equilibrium price and quantity in the* ***same*** *direction as the change in demand.*

Impact of Changes in Supply on Equilibrium Price and Quantity

In Exhibit 7 the initial equilibrium price is $0.75 per quart and the initial equilibrium quantity is 20 million quarts. Suppose one of the determinants of supply changes, resulting in a supply increase from *S* to *S′*. Consider the kinds of changes that could shift the supply curve to the right: (1) a breakthrough in biotechnology that increases the milk yield per cow; (2) a reduction in the price of a resource, such as feed; (3) a reduction in the price of an alternative good, such as beef or cheese; (4) a change in expectations that encourages farmers to supply more milk now; or (5) an increase in the number of dairy farmers.

After the increase in supply in Exhibit 7, the amount supplied at the initial equilibrium price of $0.75 increases to 30 million quarts, resulting in a 10-million-quart surplus at the initial price. This surplus forces the price down. As the price falls, the quantity supplied declines along the new supply curve and the quantity demanded increases until a new equilibrium point is established. The new equilibrium price is $0.50 per quart, and the new equilibrium quantity is 26 million quarts. As a result of the increase in supply, the equilibrium price falls and the equilibrium quantity rises.

Alternatively, a reduction in supply—that is, a shift to the left in the supply curve—will cause the equilibrium quantity to fall but the equilibrium price to rise. Thus, *a shift in the supply curve, with the demand curve held constant, will cause the equilibrium quantity to change in the same direction as the change in sup-*

EXHIBIT 7

Effects of an Increase in Supply

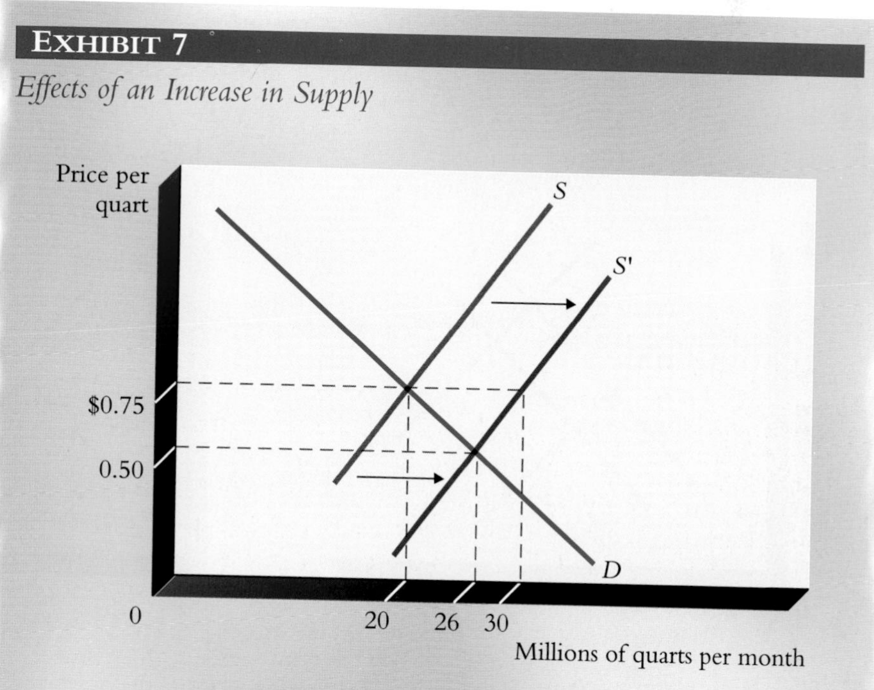

An increase in supply is depicted as a shift to the right in the supply curve, from *S* to *S′*. At the new equilibrium, quantity is greater and price is lower than before the increase in supply.

ply but will cause the equilibrium price to change in the opposite direction. An easy way to remember this is to picture the supply curve moving along a given downward-sloping demand curve. As the supply curve shifts to the left, price increases but quantity decreases; as the supply curve shifts to the right, price decreases but quantity increases.

Simultaneous Changes in Supply and Demand

As long as only one curve shifts at a time, we can say for sure what will happen to the equilibrium price and quantity. But if both curves shift simultaneously, the outcome is less obvious. For example, suppose both demand and supply increase. As we shall see, such shifts increase the equilibrium quantity, but the effect on the equilibrium price depends on which shifts more, supply or demand. Notice what happens in Exhibit 8 (again, price is measured on the vertical axis and the horizontal axis measures Q/t, shorthand for quantity per period of time). In panel (a) the demand curve shifts more than the supply curve, and in panel (b) the supply curve shifts more than the demand curve. In both panels, the equilibrium quantity increases; the equilibrium price, however, rises in panel (a) and falls in panel (b). The effect on the equilibrium price depends on the size of the shift in demand *relative* to the shift in supply. If the shift in demand is greater, as in panel (a), the equilibrium price increases. If the shift in supply is greater, as in panel (b), the equilibrium price decreases.

EXHIBIT 8

Indeterminate Effect of an Increase in Both Supply and Demand

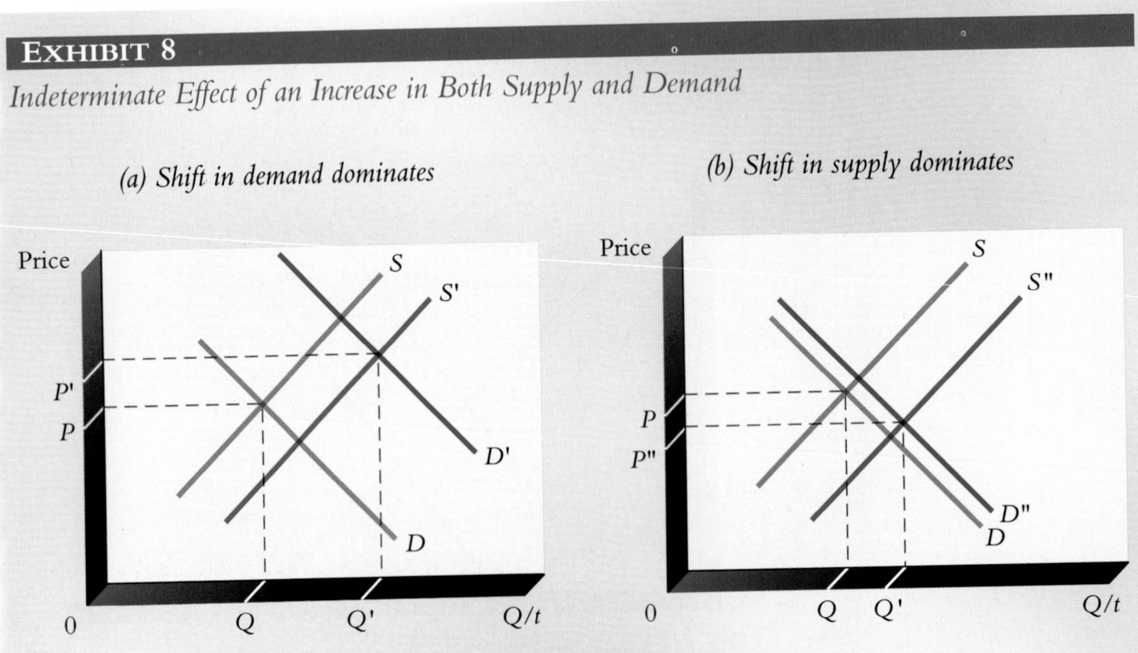

When both supply and demand increase, the quantity exchanged—the equilibrium quantity—also increases. The effect on price depends on which curve shifts farther. In panel (a), the shift in demand is greater than the shift in supply; as a result, the price rises. In panel (b), the shift in supply is greater, so the price falls.

Conversely, if both curves decrease, the equilibrium quantity decreases, but again we cannot say what will happen to the equilibrium price unless we examine the relative shifts. (You can imagine reductions in supply and demand in Exhibit 8 by supposing that D' and S' are the initial curves.) If the reduction in demand exceeds the reduction in supply, the price will fall. If the reduction in supply exceeds the reduction in demand, the price will rise. What will happen to equilibrium price when both curves shift in the same direction can be summarized as follows: *If the shift in demand is greater, the equilibrium price will increase when both curves shift to the right and will decrease when both curves shift to the left.*

If supply and demand move in opposite directions, without reference to particular shifts we cannot say what will happen to the equilibrium quantity, but we can say what will happen to the equilibrium price: the equilibrium price will increase if demand increases and supply decreases, and the equilibrium price will decrease if demand decreases and supply increases. These results are probably somewhat confusing to you, but Exhibit 9 summarizes the four possible combinations. Take time now to work through some hypothetical shifts in supply and demand to develop an understanding of the results.

EXHIBIT 9

Effects of Changes in Both Supply and Demand

Change in Supply	Change in Demand: Demand increases	Change in Demand: Demand decreases
Supply increases	Equilibrium price change is indeterminate. Equilibrium quantity increases.	Equilibrium price falls. Equilibrium quantity change is indeterminate.
Supply decreases	Equilibrium price rises. Equilibrium quantity change is indeterminate.	Equilibrium price change is indeterminate. Equilibrium quantity decreases.

When the supply and demand curves shift in the same direction, equilibrium quantity also shifts in that direction; the effect on equilibrium price depends on which curve shifts more. If the curves shift in opposite directions, equilibrium price will move in the same direction as demand; the effect on equilibrium quantity depends on which curve shifts more.

Disequilibrium Prices

A surplus triggers market forces that exert downward pressure on the price; a shortage exerts upward pressure on the price. Markets, however, do not always attain equilibrium quickly. During the time it takes to adjust, the market is said to be in disequilibrium. For example, popular toys, best-selling books, and chart-busting compact disks are often sold out and unavailable, at least temporarily. On the other hand, items that bomb in the market stack up unsold on store shelves. *Disequilibrium* is usually a temporary phase while the market gropes for equilibrium. But sometimes, often as a result of government intervention in markets, disequilibrium can last a long time, as we will see next.

Example Have students analyze the impact of minimum wage laws if the minimum wage is set above the equilibrium wage.

Price Floors

Price floor A minimum legal price below which a good or service cannot be sold

Prices are sometimes fixed at a level above the equilibrium value. For example, the federal government often regulates the prices of agricultural commodities in an attempt to ensure farmers a higher and more stable income than they would otherwise earn. To achieve higher prices, the federal government sets a *minimum*, or a **price floor**, on the price at which certain farm products can be sold. The effect of this floor on the milk market is shown in panel (a) of Exhibit 10, where we assume that a minimum price of $1 per quart has been established. At that price farmers supply 24 million quarts per month, but consumers demand only 14 million quarts. Thus the price floor results in a surplus of 10 million quarts.

Unless this surplus is somehow eliminated, it will create downward pressure on the price of milk. So, as part of the price support program, the government agrees to buy the surplus milk to take it off the market. The federal government, in fact, spends billions of dollars each year on surplus agricultural products. The government tries on occasion to distribute this surplus to the poor here and abroad, but the government must be careful not to reduce market demand since a drop in demand would increase the surplus even more. Consequently, the government simply stores much of the surplus.

Price Ceilings

Price ceiling A maximum legal price above which a good or service cannot be sold

Sometimes public officials try to keep prices below their equilibrium values by establishing a *maximum*, or a **price ceiling**, on the price that can be charged. For example, concern about the rising cost of rental housing in some cities prompted legislation to impose rent ceilings. Panel (b) depicts the supply and demand for rental housing in a hypothetical city; the number of rental units is measured on the horizontal axis, and the monthly rent on the vertical axis. The equilibrium, or market-clearing, price is $600 per month, and the equilibrium quantity is 50 thousand housing units.

Suppose the government sets a maximum price of $400 per month. At that price ceiling, 60 thousand rental units are demanded, but only 40 thou-

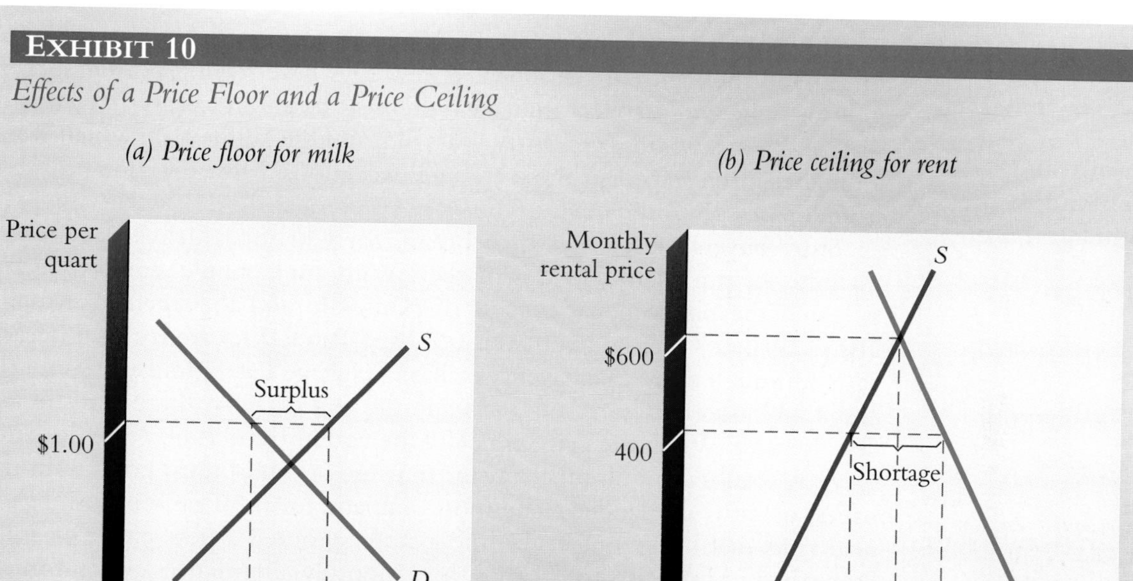

If a price floor is established above the equilibrium price, a permanent surplus will result. A price floor established at or below the equilibrium price will have no effect. If a price ceiling is established below the equilibrium price, a permanent shortage will result. A price ceiling established at or above the equilibrium price will have no effect.

sand are supplied, resulting in a housing shortage of 20 thousand units. Because of such excess demand, price no longer rations housing units to those who value the housing most highly. Consequently, other rationing devices emerge, such as waiting lists, political connections, and the willingness to pay under-the-table charges, such as "key fees," "finder's fees," excessive security deposits, and the like. Advocates of rent control often ignore the secondary effects that price ceilings have on the quantity of housing supplied and demanded. And the rentals that are available do not necessarily go to those who are most needy. Many of the rich and famous who live at fancy addresses in New York City reportedly pay only about 20 percent of the market value for their rent-controlled apartments.

Government restrictions distort market forces. Artificially high prices encourage too much production, and artificially low prices discourage sufficient production and encourage consumption. These restrictions will give rise to various nonprice allocation devices to cope with the surpluses or shortages produced by the market interference. Disequilibrium cannot always be blamed on government, however, as shown in the following case study.

CASE STUDY

Supply and Demand in the Cabbage Patch

The toy business is not much fun. Each year thousands of new toys are introduced and thousands are dropped. A few toys have staying power, such as G.I. Joe, who could collect military retirement based on twenty-five years of service, Barbie, who is over thirty years old, and the Wiffle Ball, which is still a hit after forty years. But these are rare exceptions. Most toys don't make it from one season to the next.

Store buyers must order in February for Christmas delivery. Can you imagine the uncertainty of this market? Who, for example, could have anticipated the phenomenal success of Nintendo and the Teenage Mutant Ninja Turtles? Or how about the Cabbage-Patch-Kids frenzy of a decade ago? Although more than twenty million Cabbage Patch dolls were sold for about $30 each between mid-1983 and the end of 1984, there was still excess demand. When the price is below the equilibrium level, price does not serve as a full rationing mechanism, so other schemes must cope with the excess quantity demanded. The most dramatic forms of rationing were the near riots that broke out each time a store sprouted a new patch of dolls. Stores had waiting lists to allocate their monthly allotments, and customers sometimes had to wait for up to eight months. Classified ads also appeared, offering dolls for as much as $250. Some car dealers and furniture stores promised a free doll to those making a major purchase. The shortage attracted boatloads of counterfeit dolls from overseas. Some of these illegal aliens were detained at the border, but many more made it through.

Why didn't Coleco, the doll's manufacturer, simply allow the price to seek its market level? Suppose, for example, that the market-clearing price had been $60, twice the established price. Consumers might have resented paying such a high price for a doll, and Coleco, a producer of a variety of toys, may not have wanted to risk criticism for being an opportunist, or a "price gouger." After all, a firm's reputation is important. Suppliers who hope to retain customers for a long time often avoid appearing greedy. That's why the local hardware store doesn't raise the price of snow shovels after the first winter storm, and why Wal-Mart doesn't jack up the price of air conditioners during the dog days of summer. But perhaps the doll manufacturer should have charged a higher price. Once the Cabbage Patch craze quieted down, the company lost its fizz. Coleco filed for bankruptcy in 1988.

Example Although General Motors could not manufacture Saturns fast enough to keep its dealerships in stock in 1992, GM maintained an average sales price of only $10,000, well below the $17,200 average sales price of the Honda Accord.

Conclusion

Although markets usually involve the interaction of many buyers and sellers, markets are seldom consciously designed by any individual or group. Just as the law of gravity works whether or not we understand Newton's principles, market forces operate whether or not market participants understand supply and demand. These forces arise naturally, much the way car dealers congregate on the outskirts of town.

Supply and demand are the foundation of a market economy. To build on that foundation, we need to take a closer look at key economic decision makers in the economy. In the next chapter we focus on the four economic actors: households, firms, governments, and the rest of the world.

Summary

1. Demand is a relation between the price of a good and the quantity consumers are willing and able to buy per period, other things constant. According to the law of demand, the price of a good is inversely related to the quantity demanded during a given time period, other things constant. This inverse relation between price and quantity is expressed graphically by a downward-sloping demand curve.

2. A demand curve slopes downward for two reasons. A decrease in the price of a good makes consumers more willing to substitute this good for other goods. And a decrease in the price of a good increases the real income of consumers, making them more able to buy the good.

3. The factors that can affect the demand for a product are (1) consumer income, (2) the prices of other goods, (3) consumer expectations, (4) the number of consumers in the market, and (5) consumer tastes.

4. Supply is a relation between the price of a good and the quantity producers are willing and able to sell per period, other things constant. According to the law of supply, price and quantity supplied are usually directly, or positively, related, so the supply curve typically slopes upward. Supply curves slope upward because higher prices make producers more willing to supply this good than alternative goods and higher prices make producers more able to cover the higher marginal cost associated with greater output rates.

5. The factors that can affect the supply of a product are (1) the state of technology, (2) the prices of relevant resources, (3) the prices of alternative goods, (4) producer expectations, and (5) the number of producers.

6. Demand and supply come together in a market for a given product. Markets provide information about the price, quantity, and quality of the product for sale. Markets reduce the transaction costs of exchange—the costs of time and information required to undertake exchange. The interaction of supply and demand guides resources and products to their highest-valued use.

7. The market equilibrium reconciles the independent wishes of buyers and sellers. Equilibrium will continue unless there is a change in one of the determinants of supply or demand. Disequilibrium is usually a temporary phase while markets seek equilibrium, but sometimes it lasts longer.

Questions and Problems

1. (Demand and Quantity Demanded) According to the text, what variables increase the demand for normal goods? Explain why a reduction in the price of a normal good does *not* increase the demand for the good.

2. (Income Effects) Often economists use the size of the income effect to classify a good or service as a luxury or necessity. What do people commonly mean by *luxuries*, and how would income effects be related to this meaning of *luxuries*?

3. (Shifting Demand) Using supply and demand curves, show the effect of each of the following events on the market for cigarettes:
   a. A cure for lung cancer is found.
   b. There is an increase in the price of cigars and pipes.
   c. There is a substantial increase in wages in states that grow tobacco.
   d. A fertilizer that increases the yield per acre of tobacco is discovered.

e. There is a substantial rise in the price of matches and cigarette lighters.
f. An embargo is placed on foreign tobacco products.

4. (Substitutes) During 1973 and 1974, there was a sharp rise in the price of oil. How might this event be related to the subsequent rise in Cadillac sales in Eastern Kentucky and West Virginia?

5. (Equilibrium) Determine whether each of the following statements is true or false. Then provide a short explanation for your answer.
   a. At equilibrium, all sellers can find buyers.
   b. At equilibrium, no buyer is willing and able to buy more than that buyer is being sold.
   c. At equilibrium, there is no pressure on the market to produce or to consume more than is being sold.
   d. At prices *above* equilibrium, the quantity exchanged is larger than the quantity demanded.
   e. At prices *below* equilibrium, the quantity exchanged is equal to the quantity supplied.

6. (Demand) Water is essential for life, whereas diamonds are not essential for life. Yet a bucket of diamonds is worth far more (in dollars) than a bucket of water. Explain why.

7. (Supply and Demand) How did each of the following affect the world price of oil? (Use basic supply and demand analysis.)
   a. Tax credits for home insulation
   b. Completion of the Alaskan oil pipeline
   c. Decontrol of oil price ceilings
   d. Discovery of oil in Mexico and the North Sea
   e. Mass production of smaller rather than larger automobiles
   f. Increased use of nuclear power

8. (Price Floor) There is considerable interest in whether the minimum wage rate contributes to teenage unemployment. Draw a supply and demand diagram for the unskilled labor market and discuss the effects of a minimum wage. Who is helped, and who is hurt? Does the minimum wage make society worse off?

9. (Price Ceiling) Often a sick person will have to wait a considerable amount of time to see a doctor. How is the value of the time spent in the office, along with the price of the doctor's service, related to the market-clearing price of the office visit?

10. (Supply and Demand) Tuition at many U. S. universities is rising each year. At some places the cost of attending school exceeds $20,000 per year. Using supply and demand analysis, explain why this is happening. Do you think this trend will continue?

11. (Equilibrium) If a price is not an equilibrium price, there will be a tendency for it to move to its equilibrium value. Regardless of whether the price was too high or too low to begin with, the adjustment process will increase the quantity of the good purchased. Explain, using a supply-demand diagram.

12. (Income Effects) When you move along the demand curve, you must hold income constant. Yet one factor that can cause a change in the quantity demanded is an "income effect." Explain.

13. (Equilibrium) We have all observed that in December there is an increase in both the price of evergreen trees and the quantity purchased. In January, price and quantity both fall. In the case of apples, the price is lower in the fall than in the spring, and the quantity purchased is higher. How can we explain these apparently contradictory phenomena with the same theory of supply and demand?

14. (Price Ceiling) Suppose the supply and demand curves for rental housing units have the typical slopes, and that rent control establishes a rent level below the equilibrium level.
    a. What happens to the quantity of housing consumed?
    b. Who gains from rent control?
    c. Who loses from rent control?

15. (Demand and Supply) What happens to the equilibrium price and quantity of ice cream in response to each of the following? Explain your answers.
    a. An increase in the price of grain
    b. A decrease in the price of beef
    c. New concerns about the fat content of ice cream and an increase in the price of sugar used to produce ice cream

16. (Income and Substitution Effects) The income and substitution effects tend to cause the quantity demanded to decrease when the price of the good

increases. What factors might be important in determining the size of these effects?

17. (Demand) Construct an example in which an increase in the price of a good causes total spending on that good to *increase*. What happens to the demand curves for other goods in this situation?

18. (Supply) A positively sloped supply curve means that a firm requires a higher price to induce it to produce more of a product. What factors can you suggest that might determine how steep (or flat) the supply curve will be?

19. (Supply and Demand in the Cabbage Patch) In an equilibrium price situation, everyone who is willing and able to pay the market price can purchase the item. In a shortage situation, as in the case of the Cabbage Patch dolls, this is not true. Is there any reason to believe that those who were willing to pay the most for these dolls actually got them? Should they have been able to?

20. (Supply and Demand in the Cabbage Patch) How, besides increasing the price, might Coleco have been able to ration the Cabbage Patch dolls to its advantage?

CHAPTER 4

THE ECONOMIC ACTORS: HOUSEHOLDS, FIRMS, GOVERNMENTS, AND THE REST OF THE WORLD

To develop a better understanding of how the economy works, we must become more acquainted with key players in the economy. In this chapter we examine the four main actors: households, firms, governments, and the rest of the world. We consider their structure, organization, and objectives. At the end of the chapter, a section entitled "A Closer Look" lays out the interconnections among the four economic actors. You already know more than you realize about these actors; this chapter will remind you of the abundant personal experience you bring to the material. Topics discussed in this chapter include

- Evolution of the household
- Evolution of the firm
- Household production versus firm production
- Role of government
- Government spending and taxation
- International trade and finance
- Trade restrictions
- Circular flow model

STARRING: THE HOUSEHOLD

Households play the starring role in the economy, for they are suppliers of resources and demanders of goods and services. Households supply land, labor, capital, and entrepreneurial ability to resource markets. And from product markets, households, as consumers, demand goods, such as notebooks, and services, such as medical care. As suppliers of resources and demanders of goods and services, households make all kinds of choices, such as

Teaching Tip The discussion of households as resource suppliers and demanders of goods and services can be easily related to the circular flow developed in "A Closer Look," which appears at the end of this chapter.

where to live, where to work, what to buy, and how much to save. Consumer demand for goods and services ultimately determines what's produced. Although a household usually consists of several individuals, each household is often viewed as acting as a single decision-making unit.

The Evolution of the Household

In earlier times, when the economy was primarily agricultural, roles for each individual family member reflected the division of labor and specialization of tasks on the farm. Parents were assisted in these tasks by their many children, who often specialized in specific chores. The household as an economic unit was much more self-sufficient than is the modern household. But with the introduction of new seed varieties, fertilizers, and labor-saving machinery, farm productivity increased sharply. The invention of the reaper, for example, allowed one farmer to accomplish what previously had taken many to do. Therefore, not as many farmers were needed to grow enough food to feed a nation. Simultaneously, the growth of factories in the cities created an increased demand for labor in urban areas. As a result, more people moved from farms to the cities, where they were far less self-sufficient.

Since World War II, the household has continued to change in important ways. Perhaps most significant has been the dramatic increase in the number of married women in the U.S. labor force. In 1950 only about 15 percent of married women with children under eighteen years of age were in the labor force, compared with more than 50 percent today. Economists who have studied the matter argue that an increased level of education among married women and an increased demand for labor, particularly for service workers, were the primary reasons for the rising tide of married women in the work force.[1] Rising wages and expanded job possibilities increased the opportunity cost of working in the home.

Example In 1991, 58 percent of U.S. households with children had two wage earners; only 18.6 percent of households with children had two wage earners in 1960.

The rise of the two-earner household has affected the family as an economic unit. Less production takes place in the home, and more goods and services are demanded in the market. For example, child-care services, fast food, and microwave meals have displaced some household production. The rise of the two-worker family therefore reduced the advantages of specialization within the household—a central feature of the farm family. Nonetheless, some production still occurs in the home, as we will explore in a later section.

Example In 1991, 30 percent of U.S. households were classified as *nonfamily:* persons who live alone or with unrelated people. Fifteen percent were single-parent households; 55 percent were married-couple households.

Households Maximize Utility

There are about ninety-five million households in the United States. All those who live under one roof are considered part of the same household. What exactly do householders attempt to accomplish in making decisions? Economists assume that people attempt to maximize their level of satisfaction, sense of well-being, or overall welfare. For short, we say that householders attempt to maximize **utility**. Householders, like other economic

Utility The satisfaction received from consuming a good or service

1. See, for example, Claudia D. Goldin, "The Role of World War II in the Rise of Women's Employment," *American Economic Review 81* (September 1991): 741–756.

Teaching Tip Utility maximization also involves decisions about allocating time among work outside the home, work at home, and leisure. Such decisions affect the flow of labor resources to the firms in the circular flow.

actors, are viewed as rational decision makers, meaning that they act in their own best interests and would not deliberately select an option expected to make them worse off than they could be. Utility maximization is based on each household's subjective goals, not on some objective standard. The subjectivity of utility allows for a wide range of behavior, all consistent with utility maximization. Some households are large; others are small. Some households maintain a neat home with a well-groomed lawn; others pay no attention to their home and use the lawn as a junkyard.

Households as Resource Suppliers

Example In 1991, 10 percent of U.S. households consisted of a single female with children; 2 percent consisted of a single male with children. One out of every four children lived with a single parent—double the percentage in 1970.

Householders use their limited resources in an attempt to satisfy their unlimited wants. They can use these resources to produce goods and services in their homes—they can prepare their own meals or fix that leaky roof, for example. Or they can sell these resources in the resource market and use the income to buy goods and services in the product market.

Labor is the most valuable resource sold by most households. But because of poor education, disability, or bad luck, some households have few valuable resources to sell. Also, female-headed households are a growing share of all households, and many single mothers remain at home to care for small children. Society has made the political decision that individuals in such circumstances are entitled to some form of public assistance. Consequently, some households receive **transfer payments** from the government. *Cash transfers* are monetary payments, such as Aid to Families with Dependent Children or Social Security benefits. *In-kind transfers*, such as food stamps and free medical care, fund specific goods and services.

Transfer payments Cash or in-kind benefits given to individuals as outright grants from the government

Exhibit 1 shows the various sources of personal income received by U.S. households in 1992. Personal income that year totaled $5.0 trillion. As you can see, about two-thirds of personal income comes from wages and salaries. Tied for second place are interest earnings and cash transfer payments, followed by proprietors' income. *Proprietors* are people who work for themselves rather than for employers—farmers, plumbers, and doctors are examples. Only a tiny fraction of personal income is received in the form of rents and dividends. *The majority of personal income in the United States is derived from labor earnings rather than from the ownership of other resources such as capital and land.*

Teaching Tip Since the self-employed typically provide labor, land, capital, and entrepreneurial ability to their businesses, proprietors' income contains elements of wages, rent, interest, and profit.

Households as Demanders of Goods and Services

What happens to personal income once it comes into the household? Households can allocate their income in three ways. They can spend it on privately provided goods and services such as food and housing; this household spending is called *personal consumption*. About 80 percent of U.S. personal income goes to such expenditures. Households can save their income; about 5 percent is usually saved. And they must pay some to the government as taxes to support publicly provided goods and services. About 15 percent of U.S. personal income goes to taxes. Because decisions about government are made by all voters collectively through some sort of public choice, each household has little individual say about the percentage of income paid as taxes.

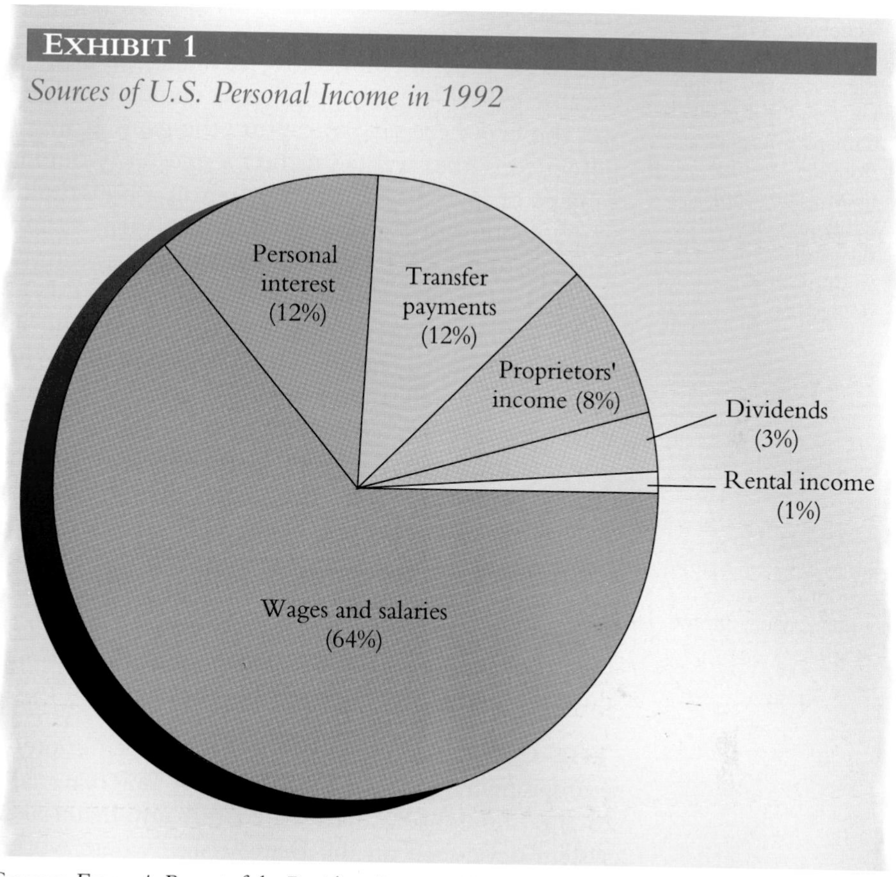

Source: *Economic Report of the President,* January 1993.

Personal consumption is divided into three broad categories: (1) consumption of *durable goods*, such as refrigerators and cars, (2) consumption of *nondurable goods*, such as potato chips and soap, and (3) consumption of *services*, such as phone calls and bus rides. Over half of personal consumption is for services and about one-third is for nondurable goods. The services sector is the fastest-growing area of personal consumption because many activities, such as meal preparation and child care, which had been produced in the household are now often purchased in the market.

SUPPORTING ACTOR: THE FIRM

Members of households once built their own homes, made their own clothes and furniture, grew their own food, and amused themselves. Over time, however, the efficiency gains from comparative advantage resulted in a greater specialization among resource suppliers. What we explore in this section is why *firms* evolved to promote this greater specialization.

Teaching Tip The circular flow model at the end of this chapter shows that firms demand resources from the resource market and supply goods and services to the product market.

Transaction Costs and Evolution of the Firm

Specialization and comparative advantage explain why households gradually became less self-sufficient, but why couldn't each household specialize? Why was the firm necessary to capture the gains arising from specialization? Suppose a consumer wanted to buy a sweater. Couldn't that consumer take advantage of specialization by relying on a household that raised sheep for the wool, another that spun the wool into yarn, a third that dyed the yarn, and finally a fourth that knit the yarn into a sweater? Production could occur through such household specialization, but the consumer would have to reach separate agreements with each specializing household about quantity, quality, and price. How much wool would be needed? How much time would be required to spin the wool into yarn? How much yarn of each color would be necessary? Transacting each contract would require much information and involve much time. These *transaction costs* could easily erase the efficiency gains arising from the greater specialization of labor.

Teaching Tip A more detailed discussion of the role of the entrepreneur is found in Chapter 25.

Instead of negotiating with each specialist, the consumer could simply purchase the sweater from someone who would do all that bargaining. The consumer could buy the sweater from an *entrepreneur* who contracted for all the resources necessary to knit a sweater. The entrepreneur, by arranging for the production of many sweaters rather than just one, was thereby able to reduce the transaction costs per sweater.

THE COTTAGE INDUSTRY ERA. For hundreds of years, profit-seeking entrepreneurs relied on "putting out" raw material such as wool and cotton to rural households that turned this raw material into finished goods. The system developed on the British Isles, where workers' simple thatched cottages served as tiny factories specializing in one stage of production. This approach to production, which came to be known as the *cottage industry* system, still exists in some parts of the world today.

THE INDUSTRIAL REVOLUTION. As the economy began to expand in the eighteenth century, entrepreneurs organized the various stages of production under one roof. Technological developments increased the productivity of each worker and contributed to the shift of employment from the farm to the factory. *Work therefore became organized in large, centrally powered factories, which promoted a more efficient division of labor, the direct supervision of production, reduced transportation costs, and the use of machines far bigger than anything that had been used in the home.* The development of large-scale factory production came to be known as the *Industrial Revolution*, which began in Great Britain around 1750 and spread to other parts of the world.

THE FIRM. So production has evolved from self-sufficient, rural households through the cottage industry system to the current system of handling much production under one roof. Today, entrepreneurs combine resources in firms such as factories, mills, offices, stores, and restaurants. **Firms** are therefore economic units formed by profit-seeking entrepreneurs, who combine the other resources—land, labor, and capital—to produce goods and services. *Firms that operate on a large scale not only achieve lower production costs per unit,*

Firms Economic units, formed by profit-seeking entrepreneurs, that hire resources to produce goods and services for sale

they achieve lower transaction costs in hiring and directing a variety of resources. Just as we assume that householders attempt to maximize utility, we assume that firm owners attempt to *maximize profit.*

Why Do Firms Specialize?

If the firm is such an efficient device for combining resources under one roof, why aren't all phases of production combined within a single firm? For example, why do sweater companies purchase wool from other firms rather than raise their own sheep? Or why do sweater producers sell their finished products to retailers rather than directly to households? To answer these questions, we must consider the costs and benefits of coordinating activity within the firm versus coordinating activity through markets.

Teaching Tip Coordinating activity within a firm (which requires conscious direction by management) is an alternative to coordinating activity through markets. A firm should not undertake activities that are more efficiently coordinated through a market.

Although firms are convenient devices for assembling and coordinating specialized factors of production under one roof, the gains from this coordination are limited. Like other people, entrepreneurs have *bounded rationality*, which means that they face limits on their ability to monitor all the specialists, exercise quality control at each stage, and keep track of the entire process. As the entrepreneur brings together more and more specialized resources, the cost of all this internal coordination grows. At some point the cost of adding one more activity exceeds the benefit, so things start to go wrong. The entrepreneur tries to become a jack-of-all-trades, but ends up a master of none. Thus, entrepreneurs, and the firms they create, become more efficient by purchasing certain specialized inputs from other firms. The market, relying only on the profit-maximizing motives of each entrepreneur, guides resources through the intermediate steps "as if by an invisible hand," coordinating the task of linking one firm's output with another firm's input to produce the final good.

Consequently, a firm is often more efficient if it specializes in a single product or in a limited range of products. For instance, many seasoned travelers are wary of eating at a hotel's restaurant, despite its convenience, because of the difficulty of operating both a nice hotel and a fine restaurant. Different entrepreneurs have different opinions about their abilities to coordinate production in the firm, so some hotels have restaurants and some do not.

Example According to the International Labor Organization, because of cultural and legal restrictions, Algerian women constitute only 8 percent of that country's formal work force. Worldwide, women make up 36 percent of the formal work force. Thus, the opportunity cost of performing tasks such as child care at home would be lower in Algeria.

Why Does Household Production Still Exist?

If firms are such convenient units for reducing the production and transaction costs of bringing together specialized resources, why doesn't all production occur within firms? Why are activities such as house cleaning, laundry, and meal preparation still undertaken primarily by households and not by firms? Indeed, some people repair their own cars, paint their own homes, and perform many other tasks that are also performed by firms. Why hasn't all productive activity shifted to the market? In general, *if a household's opportunity cost of performing a task is less than the market price, the task will usually be performed by the household.* Households with the lowest opportunity cost of time will tend to do more for themselves. For example, janitors typically mow their own lawns; physicians don't. Consider some reasons for household production.

SOME HOUSEHOLD PRODUCTION REQUIRES FEW SPECIALIZED RESOURCES. Some activities require so few specialized resources that households may find it cheaper to do these jobs themselves. Sweeping the floor requires only a broom and some time and is usually performed by household members. Sanding the floor, however, involves costly machinery and special skills, so this service is usually purchased in the market. Similarly, although you would not hire someone to brush your teeth, repairing a tooth is another matter. Household tasks that demand neither particular skills nor specialized machinery are often performed by household members.

HOUSEHOLD PRODUCTION AVOIDS TAXES. Income taxes, sales taxes, and other taxes are usually based on market transactions. Suppose you are trying to decide whether to hire a painting contractor or to paint the house yourself. If the income tax rate is one-third, a painter who charges you $3,000 for the job will net only $2,000 after paying $1,000 in taxes. In order to have the $3,000 in after-tax income to pay the painter, you must earn $4,500 before taxes. Thus, you must earn $4,500 so that the painter can net $2,000 after taxes. If you paint the house yourself, however, no taxes need be paid. The tax-free nature of do-it-yourself activity favors household production over market purchases.

HOUSEHOLD PRODUCTION REDUCES TRANSACTION COSTS. Lining up bids from painting contractors, hiring a contractor, negotiating terms, and monitoring job performance all take time and require information. Doing the job yourself reduces these transaction costs. Household production also allows for more personal control over the final product than is available through a market transaction. For example, some people prefer home-cooked meals to restaurant food, in part because home-cooked meals can be prepared according to individual tastes. In fact, some market products are promoted as "just like homemade."

Example According to the Urban Institute, 16 percent of workers in upper-income families were given the option by their employers of working at home in 1992, but only 4 percent of workers from low-income families were given this option.

TECHNOLOGICAL ADVANCES HAVE INCREASED HOUSEHOLD PRODUCTIVITY. Technological breakthroughs have not been confined to firms. Vacuum cleaners, dishwashers, microwave ovens, and other inventions reduce the time and often the skill required to perform household tasks. For example, automatic washers and dryers and wrinkle-resistant clothing have reduced the demand for professional laundry service. Also, such new technologies as VCRs, cable TV, and video games offer more fun at home. In fact, microchip-based technologies have shifted some market production from the firm to the household, as shown in the following case study.

CASE STUDY

Bringing Home the Business

The Industrial Revolution shifted production from rural cottages to urban factories. But the information revolution spawned by the invention of the microchip has begun to shift some specialized production back to the household. These days some people who say they work at the home office are not referring to corporate headquarters but to the room just off their kitchen. And the walk to work is only ten steps from their breakfast table.

People sitting at home with a personal computer, a modem, a fax machine, and a phone line are ready for business. They can send a memo via fax or electronic mail to colleagues around town, around the country, or around the world. They can buy gold in Zurich or sell oil in London. They can use a spreadsheet to evaluate the coffee crop in Colombia and then buy coffee beans for delivery next year. And they can do all this without leaving home. If they do leave home, they can keep business rolling with their cellular phone and fax.

The machines that fueled the Industrial Revolution were usually operated by many workers in large centrally powered factories. But the microchip has reduced the efficient scale of production, so the machines that fuel the information revolution require only one person at a home office. The production, analysis, and transmission of information are becoming a modern-day cottage industry.

Kinds of Firms

There are about twenty million businesses in the United States. Two-thirds of these are small farms, small retail businesses, or small services, with many people working out of their homes. Each year nearly a million new firms are started, many of which fail. In fact, three of five new businesses go "belly up" before their third year of operation. A firm can be organized in one of three ways: as a sole proprietorship, as a partnership, or as a corporation. The advantages and disadvantages of each structure will be examined next.

Sole proprietorship A firm with a single owner who has the right to all profits and who bears unlimited liability for the firm's debts

SOLE PROPRIETORSHIPS. The simplest form of organization is the **sole proprietorship**, a single-owner firm: Old MacDonald's farm, Momma's Pizza Palace, the family physician. A sole proprietorship is easy to organize, and the owner is in complete control. No special legal requirements are involved; the proprietor simply opens for business. But the owner has *unlimited liability* for any debts the business incurs, so the owner could lose everything. Also, since the sole proprietor has no partners or other financial backers, raising enough money to get the business up and running can be difficult. One final disadvantage is that sole proprietorships usually go out of business upon the death of the proprietor. Sole proprietorships are the most common form of business organization, accounting most recently for 72 percent of all businesses. Because this type of firm is typically small, however, proprietorships generate only a small portion of all business sales—only 6 percent.

Partnership A firm with multiple owners who share the firm's profits and who each bear unlimited liability for the firm's debts

PARTNERSHIPS. A more complicated form of business organization is the **partnership**, which involves two or more individuals who agree to contribute some of their own resources to the business in return for a share of the profit or loss. Law, accounting, and medical partnerships typify this business form. To organize, the partners must reach some agreement about the division of responsibilities and rewards. Partners have strength in numbers and often find it easier than the sole proprietor to raise enough funds to get the business going. But partnerships also have disadvantages. The partners may not always agree. Also, each partner usually faces unlimited liability for all the debts and claims against the partnership, so one partner could lose everything because of another's mistake. Finally, the death or departure of one partner may disrupt the firm's continuity and could require a complete reorganization. The partnership is the least common form of business organization, making up only 9 percent of all firms and accounting for only 4 percent of all firm sales.

Corporation A legal entity owned by stockholders whose liability is limited to the value of their stock

Teaching Tip Greater detail about corporate finance is provided in Chapter 27.

Teaching Tip Chapter 7 provides a brief discussion of the further reduction in after-tax capital gains if the tax system does not take inflation into account by indexing the capital gains.

CORPORATIONS. By far the most complicated form of business organization is the corporation. The **corporation** is a legal entity established through articles of incorporation. The owners of the corporation are issued shares of stock entitling them to corporate profits in proportion to their stock ownership. A major advantage of the corporate form is that many individuals—hundreds or even thousands—can pool their money to finance the firm, so incorporating represents the easiest way to amass large sums of financing. Also, stockholders have *limited liability*, meaning their liability for the firm's losses is limited to the value of their stock. A final advantage of this form is that the corporation has a life separate and apart from those of the owners; it can be taxed and sued as if it were a person, and it continues to exist even if ownership of the firm changes hands.

The corporate form has some disadvantages as well. A stockholder's ability to influence corporate policies is limited to voting for a board of directors, which oversees the operation of the firm. Each share of stock usually carries with it one vote; the typical stockholder of a large corporation owns only a tiny fraction of the shares and thus has little say. Whereas the income from sole proprietorships and partnerships is taxed only once, corporate income is taxed twice: first as corporate profits and second as stockholder income, either as corporate dividends or as realized capital gains. A *realized capital gain* is any increase in the market value of a share that occurs between the time the share is bought and the time it is sold.

A hybrid type of corporation has evolved to take advantage of the limited liability feature of the corporate structure, while reducing the impact of double taxation. The *S corporation* has limited liability, but corporate profits are taxed only once—as income on each shareholder's personal income tax return. To qualify as an S corporation, a firm must have no more than thirty-five stockholders and must have no foreign or corporate stockholders.

Corporations make up only 19 percent of all businesses, but because they tend to be much larger than the other two forms of business, corporate sales represent 90 percent of all business sales. Exhibit 2 summarizes the share of each kind of business in terms of total numbers and total sales. As we have said, *the sole proprietorship is the most important in terms of total numbers, but the corporation is the most important in terms of total sales.*

EXHIBIT 2

Number and Sales of Each Type of Firm

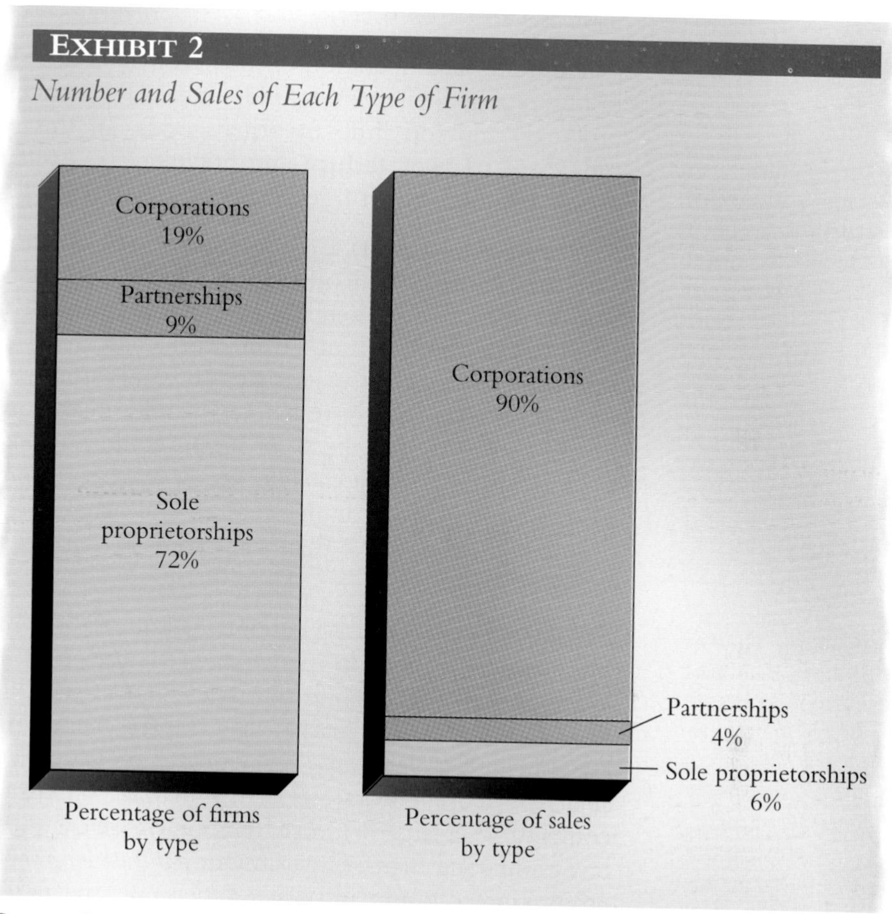

Source: *Statistical Abstract of the United States,* 1992, U.S. Bureau of the Census, 1992.

Nonprofit Institutions

To this point we have considered firms that maximize profit. But some institutions, such as nonprofit hospitals, the Red Cross, the Salvation Army, churches and synagogues, and perhaps the college you are attending, do not have profit as an explicit objective. But even nonprofit institutions must somehow pay for the resources they employ. Revenue sources typically include some combination of voluntary contributions and service charges, such as college tuition and hospital bills. Although there are millions of nonprofit institutions, when we talk about firms in this book, we will be referring to for-profit firms.

SUPPORTING ACTOR: THE GOVERNMENT

Since firms maximize profit by attempting to satisfy consumer demands, why aren't all consumer demands satisfied by firms? Why is it necessary for yet another economic institution to get into the act? For reasons that will be examined next, voluntary exchange through private markets does not necessarily guarantee a socially desirable outcome.

The Role of Government

Market failure A condition that arises when unrestrained operation of markets yields socially undesirable results

The unrestrained operation of markets may at times result in an allocation of resources that society finds undesirable. Too much of some goods may be produced and too little of other goods. In this section we consider the sources of **market failure** and how society's welfare may at times be improved by government intervention.

ESTABLISHING AND ENFORCING THE RULES OF THE GAME. Private markets are based on people like you voluntarily employing their resources to maximize their utility. What if you were regularly robbed of your paycheck on the way home from work each week, or what if your employer told you after a week's work that you would not be paid? Why bother working? The system of private markets would break down if you could not safeguard your private property or if you could not enforce contracts. Governments play a role in *safeguarding private property* through police protection and in *enforcing contracts* through a judicial and penal system. More generally, governments attempt to see that participants in markets play fair and abide by the "rules of the game."

Teaching Tip Antitrust laws and natural monopolies are covered in detail in Chapter 29.

PROMOTING COMPETITION. Although the "invisible hand" of competition generally promotes an efficient allocation of resources, some firms try to avoid market discipline through *collusion*, which is an agreement among firms to divvy up the market or to fix the market price. Or individual firms may pursue *anticompetitive* behavior, which is unfair business practices aimed at driving competitors out of the market. For example, to eliminate local competitors, a large firm may temporarily sell at a price below its cost or may buy competing firms. Government *antitrust laws* try to *promote competition* by prohibiting collusion and other anticompetitive practices.

Monopoly A sole producer of a product for which there are no good substitutes

Natural monopoly When one firm can serve a market more cheaply than two or more firms can, the firm is called a natural monopoly

REGULATING NATURAL MONOPOLIES. Typically, when a number of firms compete, resources are employed more efficiently than when only one firm, a **monopoly**, is the sole supplier in a market. Certain goods and services, however, are provided more efficiently by one firm than by several firms. For example, electricity is provided more efficiently by a single firm that wires the community than by many firms running their own wires. When it is cheaper for one firm to serve the market than for two or more firms to do so, that firm is called a **natural monopoly**. Since a natural monopoly faces no competition, such a firm tends to charge a higher price than is optimal from society's point of view. Therefore the government usually regulates the monopoly, forcing it to lower the price.

Point to Stress Not all public goods are provided by the government. Radio and network TV broadcasts are examples of public goods provided by private firms.

PROVIDING PUBLIC GOODS. Governments provide certain goods such as national defense, a legal system, public education, and public health service. Why aren't such goods provided by IBM, General Motors, General Electric, or some other for-profit firm? The answer lies in the distinction between *private* goods and *public* goods. So far in this book we have been talking about private goods, which have two important features. First, private goods are *rival* in consumption, meaning that the amount consumed by one person is unavailable for others to consume. For example, when you and some friends share a pizza, each slice you eat is one less slice available for the others. Second, the supplier of a private good can easily *exclude* those who fail to pay. Only paying customers get a pizza. Thus private goods have a feature called *excludability*. In contrast, **public goods**, such as national defense and a system of justice, are *nonrival* in consumption. They are available to all, and one person's consumption of them does not diminish the amount available to others. What's more, suppliers cannot easily prevent those who neglect to pay from consuming public goods. For example, national defense is *nonexcludable*—it is available to all regardless of who pays for it and who doesn't. Thus public goods are nonrival and nonexcludable, so a private firm cannot profitably supply them. The government, however, has the authority to impose taxes for public goods.

Public good A good that is available for all to consume, regardless of who pays and who does not

Teaching Tip Externalities are discussed in detail in Chapter 31.

DEALING WITH EXTERNALITIES. Market prices reflect the *private* costs and benefits of producers and consumers. But sometimes production or consumption imposes a cost or a benefit on a third party—someone who is not directly involved in the market transaction. For example, a paper mill fouls the air breathed by nearby residents, but the price of paper as determined in the private market fails to reflect the cost of such pollution on society. On the other hand, your decision on whether to get a flu shot likely ignores the benefit of your flu shot on others who will be less likely to catch the flu from you. Pollution costs and the flu-shot benefits are outside, or *external* to, the market activity and are therefore referred to as externalities. An **externality** is a cost or a benefit that falls on a third party and is therefore ignored by those who take part in the transaction. A *negative externality* imposes an external cost on a third party, such as factory pollution or jet noise. A *positive externality* confers an external benefit on a third party, such as the effects on others of your good health or your safe driving. Because market prices do not reflect externalities, governments often employ taxes, subsidies, and regulations to discourage negative externalities and to encourage positive externalities.

Externality A cost or a benefit that falls on a third party and is therefore ignored by those who take part in the transaction

Teaching Tip Chapter 32 provides a more detailed explanation of government efforts to redistribute income.

PROVIDING FOR MORE EQUALITY IN THE DISTRIBUTION OF INCOME. As noted earlier, some people, because of a lack of education, mental or physical disabilities, or perhaps the need to care for small children at home, may be unable to earn enough to support themselves. Since resource markets do not necessarily guarantee each household even a minimum level of income, transfer payments reflect an attempt to ensure a basic standard of living. Nearly all citizens agree that, through government, society should alter some of the results of the market by redistributing income to the poor. (Notice the normative aspect of this economic statement.) Where differences of opinion arise is in deciding just how much redistribution should occur and what form it should take.

PROMOTING FULL EMPLOYMENT, PRICE STABILITY, AND ADEQUATE GROWTH. The government, through its ability to tax and spend, and its control of the money supply, attempts to promote full employment, price stability, and an adequate rate of growth in the economy. The government's pursuit of these objectives through its taxing and spending powers is called **fiscal policy**. The government's pursuit of these objectives through the regulation of the money supply is called **monetary policy**. These controversial policies are examined in the study of macroeconomics.

Fiscal policy The use of government purchases, taxes, and borrowing to influence aggregate economic activity

Monetary policy Regulation of the money supply in order to influence macroeconomic activity

Government's Structure and Objectives

The United States has a *federal system* of government, meaning that responsibilities are shared across levels of government. The state government grants some powers to local government and surrenders some powers to the national, or federal, government. As the system has evolved, the federal government has primary responsibility for the security of the nation and the stability of the economy. State governments support higher education, prisons, and, with aid from the federal government, highways and aid to the needy. Local governments' responsibilities include primary and secondary education, plus police and fire protection.

Teaching Tip See Chapter 30 for detailed discussions of government objectives.

Difficulty in Defining Government Objectives. We assume that households maximize utility and firms maximize profit, but what assumptions can we make about government behavior? What do governments—or, more specifically, government decision makers—attempt to maximize? One problem with focusing on the government's objectives is that our federal system consists of not one but many governments—more than eighty thousand separate jurisdictions in all. Also, the federal government was developed under a system of offsetting, or countervailing, powers among the *executive, legislative*, and *judicial* branches, so the federal government does not act as a single, consistent decision maker. Even within the federal executive branch there are so many agencies and bureaus that at times they appear to be working at cross purposes. For example, at the same time the U.S. Surgeon General requires health warnings on cigarettes, the U.S. Department of Agriculture subsidizes tobacco farmers. Given this thicket of jurisdictions, branches, and bureaus of government, one useful theory of government behavior is that elected officials make decisions with the objective of maximizing the number of votes they will receive in the next election. Thus, we can assume that elected officials are *vote maximizers*.

Voluntary Exchange Versus Coercion. Market exchange is based on the voluntary behavior of all buyers and sellers; no coercion is involved. If you don't like tofu, no problem—just don't buy any. But in political markets, only a voting rule requiring unanimous consent ensures that no coercion is involved. Voting rules calling for less than unanimity imply some government coercion. Public choices are enforced by the police power of the state. Those who fail to pay their taxes could go to jail, even if they object to the programs funded by the taxes.

Example The College Board estimated that in-state tuition and fees at four-year, public universities averaged $2,137 in 1992, compared to $10,017 at private universities.

Absence of Market Prices. Another distinguishing feature of governments is that the selling price of public output is usually either zero or some amount below its cost. If you are now attending a state college or university, your tuition probably covers less than half of the total cost of providing your education. (Why are taxpayers willing to subsidize your education?) Since the revenue side of the government budget is usually separate from the expenditure side, there is no necessary link between the cost and benefit of a public program. In private transactions, however, the expected benefit must equal or exceed the cost.

Size and Growth of Government

One way to consider the role of government over time is by measuring government's share of all spending in the economy. The *gross domestic product*, or *GDP*, is the total value of all final goods and services produced in the United States. In 1929, the year the Great Depression began, government spending, mostly state and local, accounted for 10 percent of GDP. The federal government at that time played a minor role. In fact, during the country's first one hundred and fifty years, federal spending, except during times of war, never amounted to more than 3 percent of GDP.

The Great Depression, World War II, and a change in mainstream macroeconomic thinking increased the role of the federal government in the economy. Exhibit 3 shows the big jump in federal spending during World War II and the steady growth in government spending as a percentage of the gross domestic product since 1950. Spending by all levels of government in the United States was about 36 percent of GDP in 1992. In comparison, government spending in 1992 as a percent of GDP was 46 percent in West Germany, Canada, and the United Kingdom; 50 percent in Italy; and 53 percent in France. Among advanced economies, only Japan, with 33 percent, had a level of government spending below the U.S. level.

The federal government accounts for about two-thirds of all government spending. Exhibit 4 provides a detailed view of the composition of federal

EXHIBIT 3

Government Spending Since 1929 as a Percentage of Gross Domestic Product

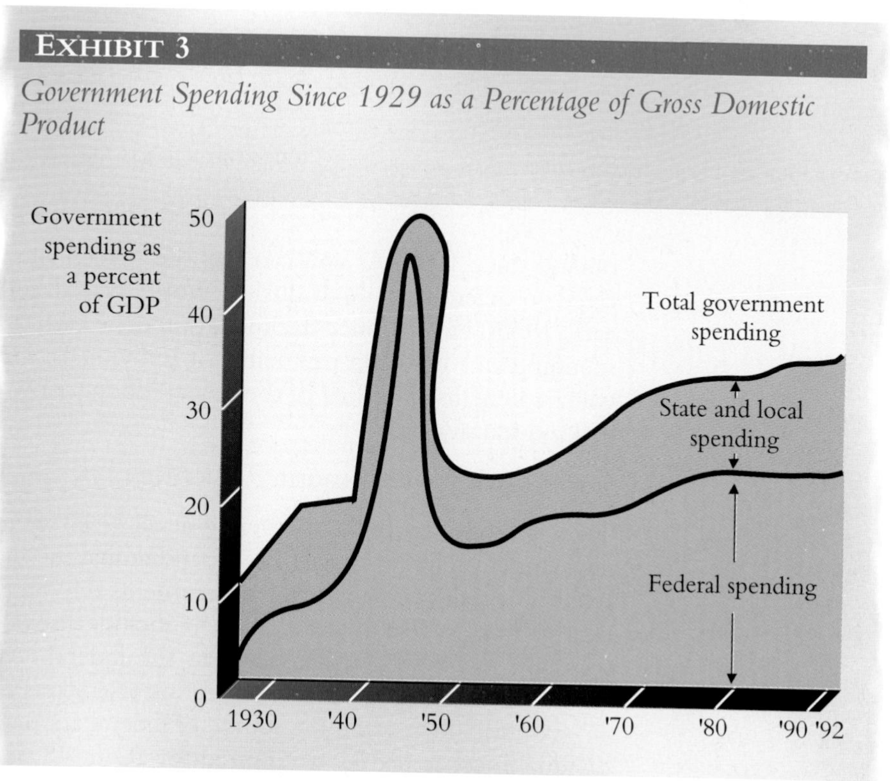

Source: *Economic Report of the President,* January 1993.

EXHIBIT 4

Percentage Composition of Federal Government Outlays Since 1940 (share of total)

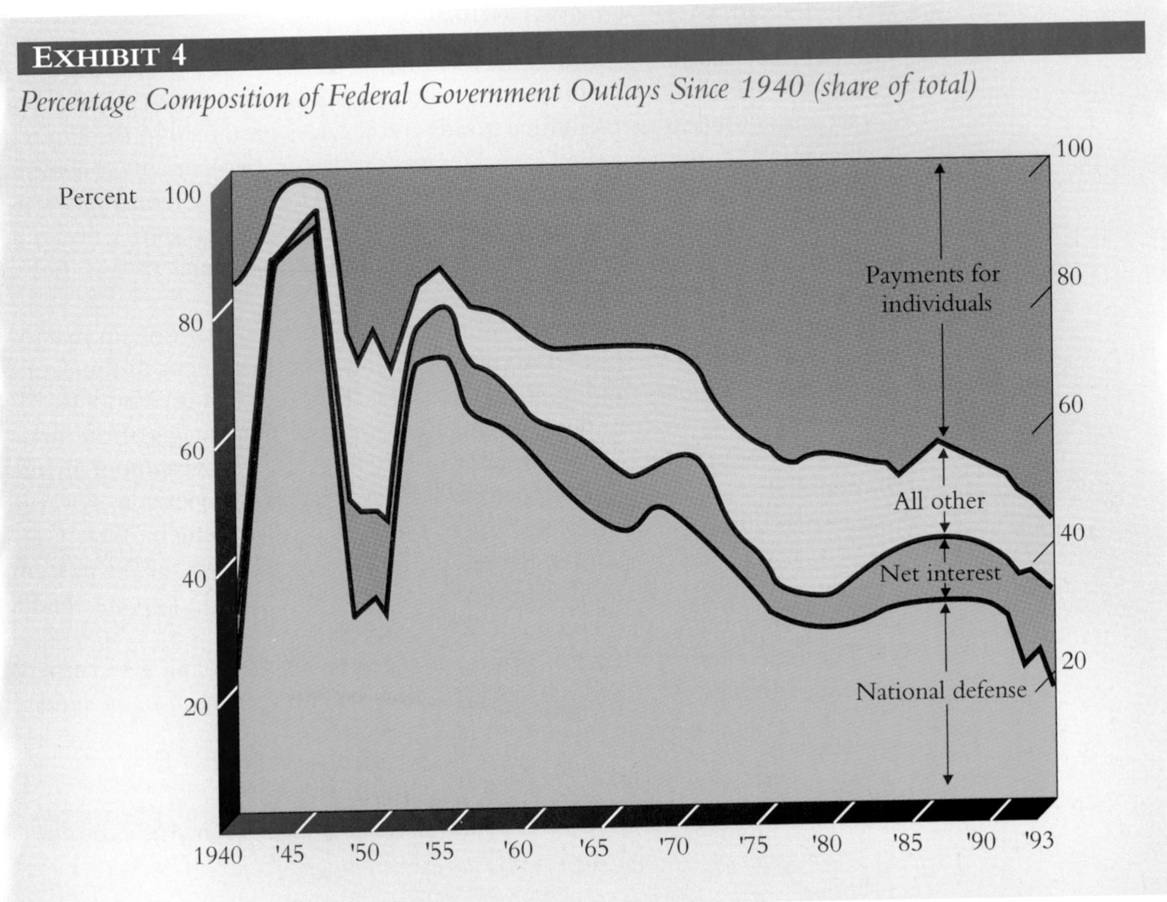

Sources: Historical tables, *Budget of the U.S. Government,* FY 1993, Office of Management and Budget; *Economic Report of the President,* January 1993.

outlays since 1940. As you can see, the percentage of federal spending allocated to defense was high during World War II and the Korean War of the early 1950s, but has since declined. Since the early 1950s, the fastest-growing spending area has been payments for individuals, such as Social Security and welfare benefits; over half of the federal budget now consists of such cash and in-kind transfer programs.

Sources of Government Revenue

Taxes provide the bulk of revenue at all levels of government. The federal government relies primarily on the individual income tax, state governments rely on the sales tax, and local governments rely on the property tax. In addition to taxes, other revenue sources include user charges, such as highway tolls, and borrowing, particularly at the federal level, where recent deficits have been huge. Some states also sell lottery tickets and liquor to raise money.

Exhibit 5 focuses on the source of federal tax receipts since 1940. The individual income tax has accounted for about 45 percent of federal revenues since about 1945. In the early 1950s, payroll taxes accounted for only about

EXHIBIT 5

Percentage Composition of Federal Government Receipts Since 1940 (share of total)

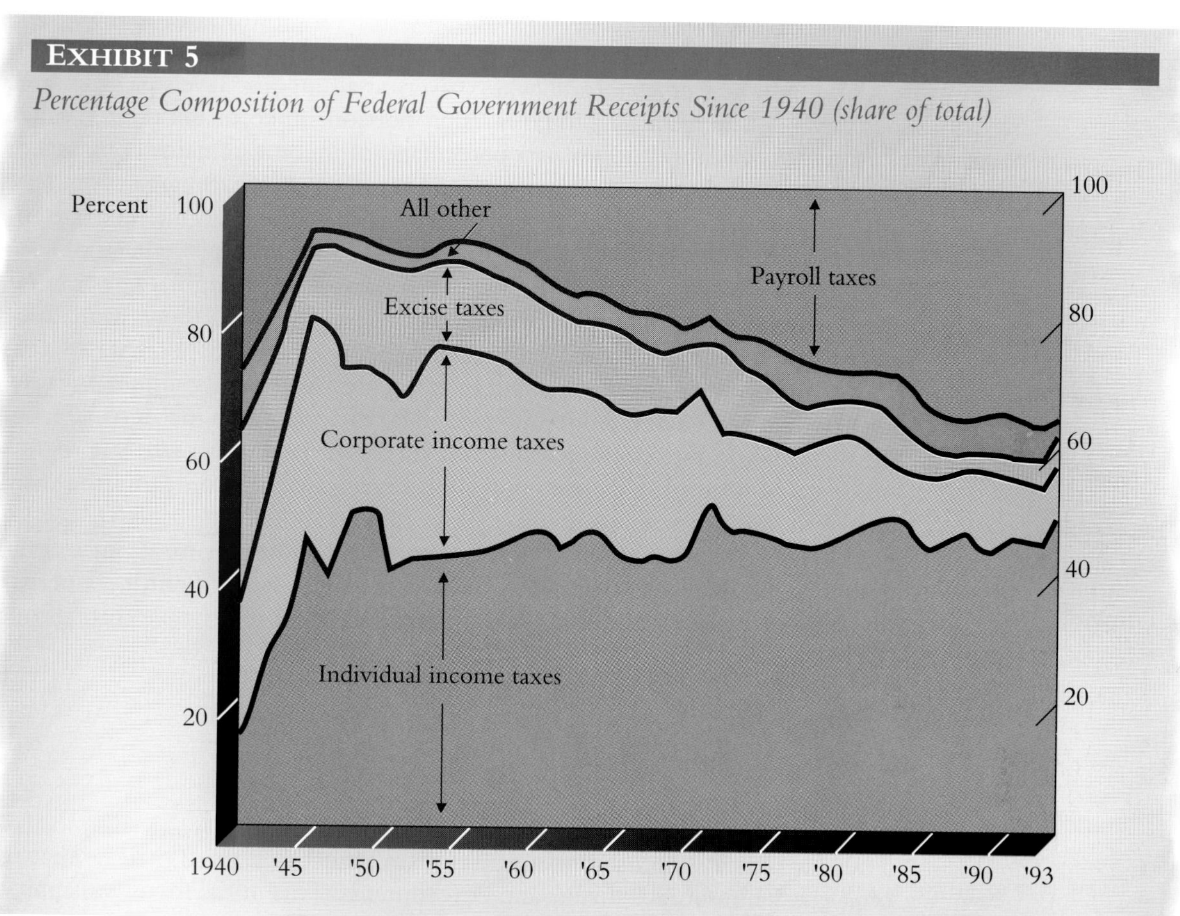

Sources: Historical tables, *Budget of the U.S. Government*, FY 1993, Office of Management and Budget; *Economic Report of the President*, January 1993.

10 percent of federal receipts, compared to nearly 40 percent today. *Payroll taxes* are deducted from paychecks to support Social Security, unemployment benefits, and medical care for the elderly. Corporate income taxes and *excise*, or sales, taxes have generally declined as a share of the total since the 1940s, though the share of corporate income taxes has increased slightly since the mid-1980s.

Tax Principles and Tax Incidence

A tax is often justified on the basis of one of two general principles. The first is that a tax should be related to the individual's *ability to pay* so that those with a greater ability pay more taxes. Income or property taxes are often based on this principle. The second tax principle is that of *benefits received*, which argues that taxes should be related to the benefits the individual receives from the government activity funded by the tax. For example, the tax on gasoline, which is earmarked to fund highway construction and maintenance, links tax payment to road use. The benefits-received principle links the revenue side of the budget with the spending side of the budget.

Tax incidence A description of who actually bears the burden of a tax

Tax incidence indicates who actually bears the burden of the tax. One way of evaluating tax incidence is by measuring the tax as a percentage of income. Under *proportional taxation*, taxpayers at all income levels pay the same percentage of their income in taxes. A proportional income tax is often called a *flat-rate tax* because the tax as a percentage of income remains constant, or flat, as income changes. Under *progressive taxation*, the percentage of income paid in taxes increases as income increases; that is, the marginal tax rate increases with income. The *marginal tax rate* indicates what percentage of each additional dollar of income must be paid in taxes. High marginal rates can reduce people's incentives to work and to invest. In 1992, there were three marginal rates under the federal personal income tax—15 percent, 28 percent, and 31 percent—so the system is progressive. Finally, under *regressive taxation*, the percentage of income paid in taxes decreases as income increases: the marginal tax rate declines as income increases. Payroll tax rates are regressive because they are a flat rate up to a certain level of income and the marginal rate drops to zero on income above that level.

Example A sales tax on food is generally considered to be regressive because low-income householders, who spend a much greater percentage of their income on food, end up paying a greater percentage of their income for the tax.

This discussion of revenue sources brings to a close, for now, our examination of the role of government in the economy. Government has a pervasive influence on the economy, and discussions of its role weave throughout the book.

Supporting Actor: The Rest of the World

Teaching Tip The role of the rest of the world in the economy is woven throughout the textbook. For detailed discussions of international trade and exchange rates, see Chapters 33 and 34.

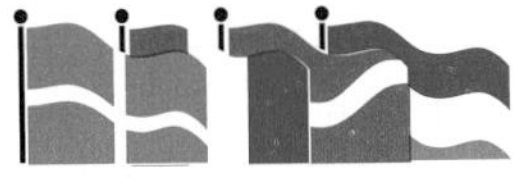

Thus far we have focused on institutions within the United States—that is, on *domestic* households, firms, and governments. This initial focus was appropriate because our primary objective has been to understand the workings of the U.S. economy, and the United States has by far the largest national economy in the world. But the success of the U.S. economy depends in part on the rest of the world. For example, political unrest in the Persian Gulf can interrupt the flow of oil, raising the price Americans pay for energy. Asian economies such as those of Japan and South Korea supply U.S. markets with autos, electronic equipment, and other manufactured goods, affecting U.S. prices, wages, and profits. Foreign actors, therefore, have a profound effect on the U.S. economy—on what is consumed by U.S. households and what is produced by U.S. firms. The *rest of the world* consists of the households, firms, and governments in more than 150 foreign countries.

International Trade

In Chapter 2 you learned about the principle of comparative advantage and the gains from specialization. These gains explain why households stopped trying to do everything for themselves and began to specialize. International trade arises for the same reasons. Production and exchange among countries follow the law of comparative advantage. *International trade occurs because the opportunity cost of producing specific goods differs across countries.* Americans import

Example Canada is the country with which the United States has the largest volume of trade. With approval of the North American Free Trade Agreement, Mexico is expected to replace Japan as the second largest U.S. trading partner. U.S. trade with Mexico had already doubled between 1986 and 1991.

raw materials such as crude oil, diamonds, and coffee beans and finished goods such as cameras, VCRs, and automobiles. U.S. producers export sophisticated products such as computers, aircraft, and movies, as well as agricultural products such as wheat and corn.

International trade between the United States and the rest of the world has been rising in recent decades. In 1970 U.S. imports amounted to only about 6 percent of the gross domestic product. That figure has doubled, primarily because of oil imports, to about 12 percent of GDP. American exports have also grown, from about 7 percent of GDP in 1970 to about 11 percent today. The United States' chief trading partners are Canada, Japan, Mexico, Germany, Great Britain, France, and South Korea.

Merchandise trade balance The value of a country's merchandise exports minus the value of its merchandise imports during a given time period

Balance of payments A record of all economic transactions between residents of one country and residents of the rest of the world during a given time period

The **merchandise trade balance** equals the value of exports minus the value of imports. In recent years the United States has experienced a trade *deficit*, meaning that the value of U.S. imports has exceeded the value of U.S. exports. Just as a household must cover its spending, so too must a nation. A nation's **balance of payments** is the record of transactions between its residents and residents of the rest of the world. The balance of payments is made up of several accounts, such as the merchandise trade balance. Without detailing those accounts here, we can say that a deficit in the merchandise trade balance must be offset by a surplus in one or more of the other balance-of-payments accounts. Since the early 1980s, Americans have been consuming more than they are producing and have been borrowing from abroad to finance the difference.

Exchange Rates

Foreign exchange The currency of another country needed to carry out international transactions

Trade across international borders is complicated by the lack of a common currency. How many U.S. dollars are required to purchase a Mercedes selling for 100,000 marks in Germany? An American customer who purchases the auto cares only about the dollar cost; the German manufacturer cares only about the marks received. To facilitate trade between nations, a market for foreign exchange has developed. **Foreign exchange** is the currency of another country needed to carry out international transactions. The supply and demand for foreign exchange come together in *foreign exchange markets* to yield an equilibrium exchange rate around the world. The *exchange rate* measures the price of one currency in terms of another. For example, the exchange rate between U.S. dollars and German marks might indicate that one mark can be exchanged for 70 cents. The greater the demand for a particular foreign currency or the smaller the supply, the higher its exchange rate will be—that is, the more dollars it will cost. The exchange rate affects the prices of imports and exports and thus influences the flow of foreign trade.

Trade Restrictions

Tariff A tax on imports or exports

Although there are clear gains from international specialization and exchange, nearly all countries impose some restrictions on trade. These restrictions can take the form of (1) **tariffs**, which are taxes on imports or exports;

Quota A legal limit on the quantity of a particular product that can be imported or exported

(2) **quotas**, which are legal limits on the quantity of a particular good that can be imported or exported; and (3) other restrictions, such as the agreement by Japanese car manufacturers to voluntarily limit their exports to the United States during the early 1980s.

If specialization according to comparative advantage is so beneficial, why do most countries restrict trade? Restrictions are introduced primarily to benefit certain domestic producers, although such protection occurs at the expense of domestic consumers. For example, U.S. textile manufacturers have sought and received protective legislation restricting textile imports, thereby raising U.S. textile prices. Such restrictions interfere with the free flow of products across borders and tend to harm the overall economy.

CONCLUSION

In this chapter we examined four economic actors in the economy: households, firms, governments, and the rest of the world. Domestic households are by far the most important actors, for they, along with foreign households, supply all the resources and demand all the goods and services produced. But government spending accounts for a growing share of economic activity. In recent years the U.S. economy has come to depend more on the rest of the world both as a source of products and as a market for U.S. goods. The transaction links among the four actors are examined in "A Closer Look," which appears at the end of the chapter.

This chapter completes our introduction to economics. From now on the discussion will focus primarily on either macroeconomics or microeconomics.

SUMMARY

1. Most household income arises from the sale of labor, and most household income is spent on personal consumption. Personal consumption consists of expenditures on durable goods, nondurable goods, and services—the fastest-growing portion of personal consumption. Income not spent on personal consumption is either saved or paid as taxes.

2. Firms are convenient devices for bringing together specialized resources. But when the net benefits of organizing production within the firm are exhausted, market exchange becomes a more efficient way to coordinate production. The market, relying only on the profit motives of each firm, guides resources through the intermediate stages required to produce the final good.

3. Firms can be organized in three different ways: as sole proprietorships, partnerships, or corporations. Because the corporation is typically large, corporations account for the bulk of all sales by firms.

4. When private markets yield socially undesirable results, government may intervene to correct these market failures. Government programs are designed to (1) protect private property and enforce contracts; (2) promote competition; (3) regulate natural monopolies; (4) provide public goods; (5) discourage negative externalities and encourage positive externalities; (6) provide for greater equality in the distribution of income; and (7) promote full employment, price stability, and growth.

5. In the United States, the federal government relies primarily on the personal income tax, states on the sales tax, and localities on the property tax. A tax is usually based either on the individual's ability to pay the tax or on the benefits the taxpayer receives from those activities financed by the tax.

6. The rest of the world is also populated by households, firms, and governments. Since international trade involves different currencies, a rate of exchange between these currencies is established in foreign exchange markets. The transactions between the residents of one country and the residents of the rest of the world are summarized in the balance of payments. Despite the benefits from comparative advantage that arise from international trade, nearly all countries impose trade restrictions to protect specific industries.

7. The movement of resources, products, income, and expenditures through the economy can be depicted by the circular flow model, which is described right after this summary. As you will see, this model shows that the prices of goods and services are determined in the product markets and the prices of resources are determined in the resource markets.

QUESTIONS AND PROBLEMS

1. (Consumption) It is now well known that the service sector of the U.S. economy has been growing very fast. Many economists claim that this sector will provide most new jobs in the future. What services will be important in the future, and what skills, if any, will be needed by the workers in those industries?

2. (Consumption) What factors come into play when a consumer considers buying a durable good such as an automobile or a refrigerator?

3. (Household Production) Technological breakthroughs have made household production possible in some cases. What are some technological advances that have made household production of entertainment possible? How has the entertainment industry reacted to such devices?

4. (Household Production) Many households supplement their food budget by cultivating small vegetable gardens. Explain how each of the following might affect this kind of household production:
   a. Both husband and wife are professionals earning high salaries.
   b. The household is located in the city rather than in the country.
   c. The household is located in the South rather than in the North.
   d. The household is located in a region where there is a high sales tax on food.
   e. The household is located in a region that has a high property tax rate.

5. (Specialization) Why did the institution of the firm appear after the advent of the Industrial Revolution in the nineteenth century? What type of business organization existed before this?

6. (Corporations) Why do most large businesses organize as corporations rather than as partnerships or sole proprietorships? Must corporations always be large in terms of sales and production?

7. (Government) Economists sometimes argue over whether the government should provide a particular service. However, even when everyone agrees that the government should provide the service, it must still be decided whether the government service is best provided by the local, state, or federal government. What factors are important in determining which level of government should provide the service?

8. (Government) One of the most important government services is provided by the National Weather Service. Why isn't it possible for a private weather service to provide information and predictions about the weather? Why is it necessary to have a National Weather Service?

9. (Government) Often it is said that government is necessary when private markets fail to work effectively and fairly. Based on your reading of the text, discuss how private markets might break down.

10. (Government) How is each of the following related to the various services that government is responsible for providing?
    a. The Food and Drug Administration
    b. The Pentagon
    c. The Supreme Court of the United States
    d. The progressive income tax system
    e. State-supported universities
    f. State utility rate commissions

11. (Tax Rates) Suppose taxes are related to income level as follows:

Income	*Taxes*
$1000	$200
2000	350
3000	450

    a. What percentage of income is paid in taxes at each level?
    b. Is the tax progressive, proportional, or regressive?
    c. What is the marginal tax rate on the first $1000 of income? The second $1000? The third $1000?

12. (Externality) Suppose a good has an external cost associated with its production. What's wrong with letting the market decide how much should be produced?

13. (International Trade) Suppose a VCR costs 100,000 yen in Japan. If the exchange rate is $1 = Y200, how much will a Japanese VCR cost here? What would the cost be if the dollar strengthened to $1 = Y250? If a bushel of wheat costs $10 in the United States, how much will it cost in Japan under each of these two exchange rates?

14. (Household Productivity) Although technology has enhanced the ability of households to increase home production of many forms of activities, the more traditional forms of household production (e.g., meal preparation, laundry) have increasingly been handled outside the household unit. Can you explain this phenomenon?

15. (Tax Principles) Taxation according to ability to pay would seem, on the surface, to be a reasonable idea. What problems can you envision with trying to structure a tax system based on this concept?

16. (International Trade) The conventional wisdom is that running a merchandise trade surplus, whereby exports exceed imports, is good. In what sense might such a surplus make us as a nation worse off?

17. (Government) According to the text, public goods are nonrival in consumption and nonexcludable to consumers. Can you think of any goods that are nonrival yet excludable? Who should produce such goods?

18. (Taxation) One form of tax often discussed in Washington is an expenditure tax, whereby taxes are paid on total annual expenditures. Although such a tax encourages saving, critics argue that it is a regressive tax. Why do you suppose that they make this argument?

19. (Bringing Home the Business) Can you think of any other kinds of goods that may return to "cottage industry" production because of technological or demographic trends?

20. (Bringing Home the Business) Is the product of the information industry, in any sense, a public good? From this perspective, do you think that the trend toward home production is a good thing?

A CLOSER LOOK

THE CIRCULAR FLOW MODEL

Now that we have examined the economic actors, we can take "A Closer Look" at how they interact. Their interaction is conveyed by the **circular flow model**, which describes the flow of resources, products, income, and revenue among households, firms, governments, and the rest of the world. We begin with the interaction of households and firms; we then add government and the rest of the world to the picture. A step-by-step approach is developed through the series of transparency overlays presented as part of Exhibit 6. When you turn the page, you will find Exhibit 6 on the right-hand page and an explanation on the left-hand page. Please turn the page.

FLOW OF RESOURCES AND PRODUCTS BETWEEN HOUSEHOLDS AND FIRMS We begin with the most fundamental interaction in a market economy—that between households and firms. The Base Page of Exhibit 6 shows households on the left and firms on the right. (To see the Base Page clearly, you must lift the transparencies and keep them in your hand.) Households supply land, labor, capital, and entrepreneurial ability to firms through *resource markets*, shown on the lower portion of the exhibit. In return, households demand goods and services from firms through *product markets,* shown at the top of the exhibit. Viewed from the business end, firms supply goods and services to households through product markets and demand land, labor, capital, and entrepreneurial ability from households through resource markets. Resources and products flow in a counterclockwise direction.

FLOW OF INCOME AND REVENUE BETWEEN HOUSEHOLDS AND FIRMS The base page shows the flows of resources and products between households and firms. In a barter economy, exchange is limited to real flows—that is, to flows of resources and products. But in nearly all economies of the world, the flows of resources and products are supported by flows of income and expenditure—that is, by the flow of money. The First Overlay adds money flows to the picture. (Place the First Overlay over the Base Page.) Supply and demand in resource markets determine equilibrium wages, rents, interest, and profits, which flow as income to households. Supply and demand in product markets determine equilibrium prices for goods and services, which flow as revenue to firms. Note that resources and products flow in a counterclockwise direction, and the corresponding payments for these products and resources flow in a clockwise direction.

GOVERNMENT FLOWS Thus far we have focused on the private sector. But another actor in the United States and most other countries is government. You can bring government into the picture by adding the Second Overlay to the exhibit. Note that governments are linked with all four elements in the circular flow: households, firms, resource markets, and product markets. Let's first examine the real flows. Governments purchase resources, such as labor, from resource markets and purchase goods and services, such as food for the cafeteria at a state university, from product markets; governments convert these into public goods and services, which they provide to households and firms. To finance this public production governments rely on the net revenue received from households and firms. Net government revenue from households equals taxes plus any fees charged minus transfer payments. Net government revenue from firms equals taxes plus charges minus subsidies. So governments finance the production of public goods and services with the net revenue received from households and firms.

FLOWS TO AND FROM THE REST OF THE WORLD The flows pictured so far have been limited to the domestic economy. To complete the picture we must add the flows to and from the rest of the world, as shown by the Third Overlay. (Add the Third Overlay to the exhibit.) The rest of the world both supplies resources to our resource markets and demands resources from those markets. For example, foreigners sell specialized machines to U.S. firms and foreigners buy specialized machines from U.S. producers. Because resources flow in both directions, there is an arrow at both ends of the pipeline. Likewise, foreigners supply goods and services to U.S. product markets and demand goods and services from U.S. product markets; again, to indicate the two-way nature of the flows, the arrows point in both directions. The same goes for the pipelines indicating the resource payments and product prices.

EXHIBIT 6

The Circular Flow of Income and Expenditure

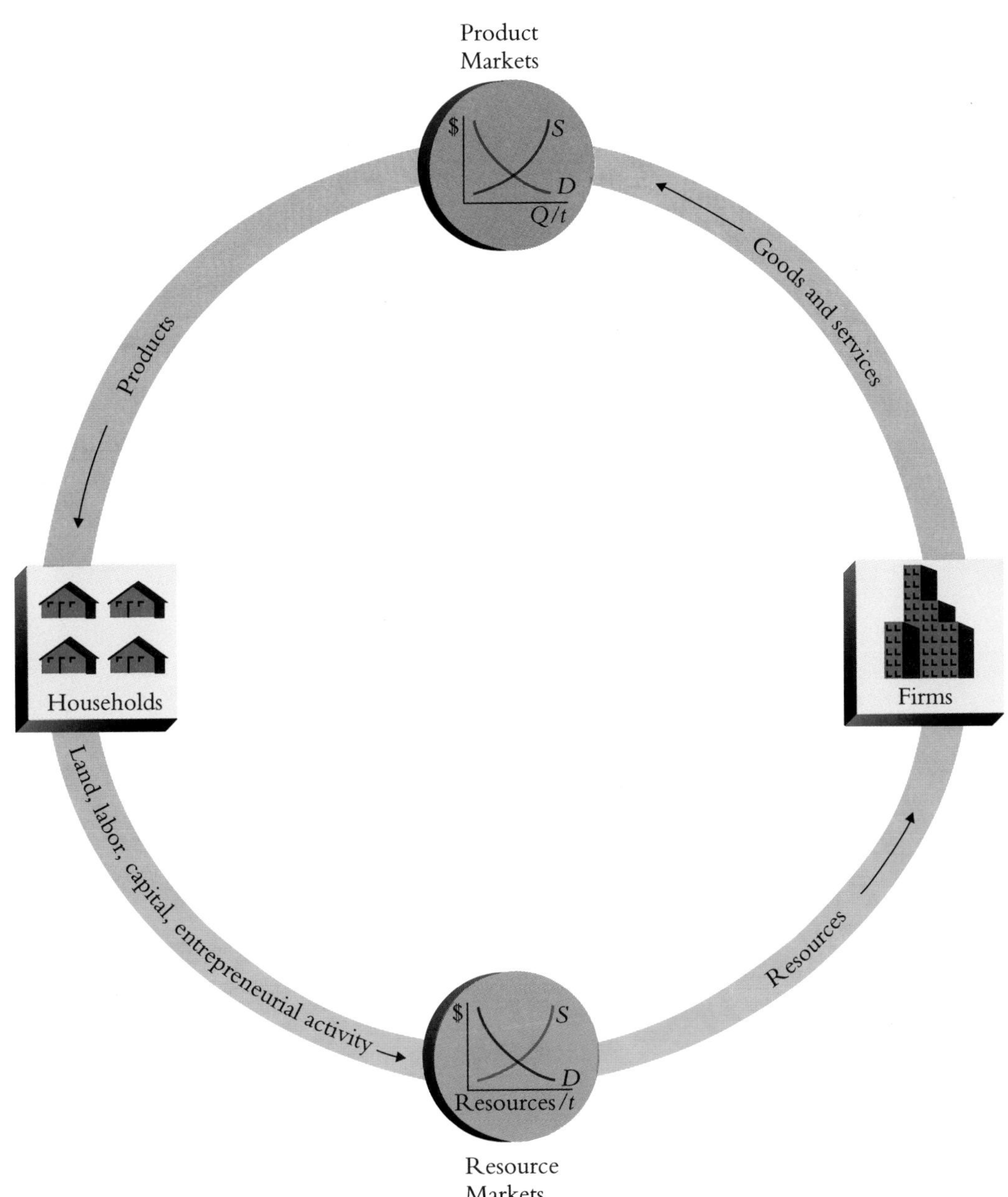

PART 2

Fundamentals of Macroeconomics

CHAPTER 5

INTRODUCTION TO MACROECONOMICS

In macroeconomics we think big—not about the supply and demand for chewing gum but about the supply and demand for everything produced in the economy; not about the price of floppy disks but about the average price level of all products sold in the economy; not about consumption by the Jackson household but about consumption by all households combined; not about the investment by General Motors but about the investment by all firms combined.

We are concerned not only with determining such aggregates as the level of the economy's prices, employment, and output but also with understanding the movements in these aggregates over time. What determines the ability of the economy to use available resources productively, to adapt, to grow? As we shall see, the economy has a certain rhythm of its own. We want to feel the beat. *The ultimate objective of macroeconomics is to develop and test theories about how the economy as a whole works—theories that can be used to predict the consequences of economic events.*

Economists agree less on macroeconomics than on microeconomics. Disagreement centers first on how stable the economy is and second on what should be done when the economy fails to perform as we would like. The first disagreement is over economic theory, the second over economic policy. Theory and policy intertwine more closely in macroeconomics than in microeconomics. Topics discussed in this chapter include

- The national economy
- The analogy between the human body and the economy
- The business cycle
- Aggregate demand and aggregate supply
- A short history of the U.S. economy
- Demand-side and supply-side economics

The National Economy

Macroeconomics concerns the overall performance of the economy. The term *economy* can be defined as the structure of economic life or economic activity in a community, a region, a country, a group of countries, or the world. We could talk about the St. Louis economy, the Missouri economy, the Midwest economy, the U.S. economy, the North American economy, or the world economy. The performance of an economy can be measured in different ways, such as the number of individuals employed, the size and number of producers, or the average earnings of labor. One measure, however, appears to capture the most economic information and is most effective for considering the same economy over time or for comparing different economies at the same time: the gross product. The **gross product** is the market value of final goods and services produced in a particular geographical region during a given time period, usually one year. If the focus is the Missouri economy, we consider the gross *state* product. If the U.S. economy is the object of interest, we consider the gross *domestic* product.

Gross product The market value of final goods and services produced in a particular geographical region during a given time period, usually one year

What Is Special About the National Economy?

Consider the reasons for treating the national economy as a special entity. If you were to drive west on Interstate 10 in Texas, you would hardly notice crossing the state line into New Mexico. If you took the Juarez exit off I-10 south to Mexico, however, you would become quite aware that you were crossing an international border. You would have to present personal identification, provide reasons for your trip, and prepare to be searched. Like other countries of the world, the United States and Mexico typically allow freer movement of people and goods *within* their borders than *across* their borders.

The differences between the United States and Mexico are far greater than the differences between Texas and New Mexico. For example, each country has its own culture and language, its own communication and transportation systems, its own unique mix of economic resources, its own system of government, its own currency, and, most importantly, its own "rules of the game"—that is, its own regulations for conducting economic activity both within and across its borders. More fundamentally, each country answers the three economic questions—what is to be produced, how is it to be produced, and for whom is it to be produced—in different ways.

Point to Stress As the rest of the world has come to play a larger and larger role in national economies, it is increasingly difficult to focus on national economies to the exclusion of international issues. Therefore, the textbook weaves discussion of the world economy throughout the chapters on macroeconomics.

The focus of macroeconomics is the performance of the national and world economies. To gain some notion of the complicated nature of the U.S. economy, consider a profile of households, firms, and governments. There are about ninety-five million households, about twenty million businesses, and about eighty thousand separate governments. And there are more than 150 sovereign countries throughout the world, ranging from Djibouti, a tiny country in East Africa with a population smaller than that of any state in the United States, to the People's Republic of China, with a population of over one billion. Such snapshots convey an idea of the economic actors, but our interest in the economy is not like a coroner's interest in a lifeless body. The

Teaching Tip Money is discussed in detail in Chapters 12 and 13. Here you could briefly explain that money refers to anything generally accepted in payment for goods and services.

economy is dynamic—living, breathing, constantly changing. The economy is too complex to be confronted head on, which is why we use theoretical models to simplify and crystallize the key relations. Perhaps the easiest way to introduce macroeconomics is to compare the national economy to something more familiar. Let's consider the similarities and differences between the human body and the economy.

Similarities Between the Human Body and the Economy

Example Stock: total savings accumulated; flow: amount saved in one year. Stock: number of cars in inventory; flow: car production in one year.

The body is made up of millions of individual cells, each carrying out particular functions yet each linked to the operation of the entire body. Similarly, the economy is composed of millions of individual economic units, each acting with some independence yet each interconnected with the economy as a whole. The economy, like the body, is continually renewing itself, with new households, new businesses, new foreign competitors, and an ever-changing cast of public officials.

Money A medium that circulates throughout the economy, facilitating the exchange of resources and products among individual economic units

Blood is a medium that circulates throughout the body, facilitating the exchange of vital nutrients among cells. Similarly, **money** is a medium that circulates throughout the economy, facilitating the exchange of resources and products among individual economic units. In fact, money is called a *medium of exchange*. As noted in Chapter 4, the pattern traced by the movement of money, products, and resources throughout the economy is a *circular flow*, as is the pattern traced by the movement of blood and nutrients throughout the body.

Stocks and Flows. Just as the same blood is recirculated again and again in the body, the same money recirculates several times during the year to finance many transactions. The same dollars you use to pay for croissants may then be used by the baker to buy butter and then by the dairy farmer to buy radial tires. We often distinguish between stocks and flows. A **stock** variable represents an amount of something at a particular time, such as the amount of blood in your body or the number of dollars in your wallet right now. A **flow** variable represents an amount per unit of time, such as heartbeats per minute or the amount spent in the economy per year. If a time dimension is required to convey meaning (e.g., per hour, per day, per year), the variable is a flow variable.

Stock A variable that measures the amount of something at a particular point in time, such as the amount of money you have right now

Flow A variable that measures the amount of something over an interval of time, such as the amount you spend on food per week

Point to Stress The role of expectations is especially important in the discussion of the appropriate role of government in the macroeconomy.

Role of Expectations. In both medicine and macroeconomics, *expectations* play an important role in the performance of the system. If the patient expects a certain medicine to provide a cure, the body often promotes that cure, even if the medicine is only a sugar pill, or placebo. Doctors don't yet understand how the placebo effect works. A similar mechanism operates in the economy, but economists have a pretty good idea how it works. Consider the extreme situation in which all firms expect greater demand for their products. They will invest in more plant and equipment and hire more labor to produce more output. As more resources are employed, households, as suppliers of those resources, earn greater incomes and therefore increase their demand for goods and services. Thus, when producers expect greater demand for their products, their behavior often fosters the very prosperity they expect. Negative expectations can also be self-fulfilling. If all firms expect the demand for their products

Example The "Index of Consumer Expectations," developed at the University of Michigan, is one of the leading indicators reported monthly by the government.

to fall, they will reduce their investment and cut back on hiring. As the demand for resources falls, household incomes decline, thereby reducing the demand for goods and services.

DIFFERENCES OF OPINION. Both in medicine and in macroeconomics, problems are often seen from varying viewpoints. First, diagnoses of what ails the patient or the economy may differ. Second, even when doctors or economists agree about the nature of the malady, they may disagree about the best remedy. Medicine and the other natural sciences, however, have one major advantage in the development and evaluation of new theories: the ability to test these theories in a laboratory setting.

Testing New Theories

Physicians and other natural scientists can conduct experiments under controlled conditions to test their theories. Macroeconomists, however, have no laboratory and little ability to run experiments of any kind. Granted, they can study the workings of different economies throughout the world. But each economy displays such a unique blend of economic conditions that comparisons across countries are tricky. Testing a drug or medical procedure in a variety of circumstances offers medical researchers something that is typically unavailable to macroeconomists: an opportunity to make the chance, or serendipitous, discovery. With only one patient, the macroeconomist cannot introduce particular policies in a variety of ways. Therefore, the unexpected discovery (such as penicillin) that often characterizes breakthroughs in the natural sciences is unlikely in economics. Cries of "Eureka!" are seldom heard among macroeconomists.

Knowledge and Performance

Throughout history we had little knowledge of how the body works, yet many people enjoyed good health. Not until 1638, for example, did we discover that the blood actually circulates through the body; it took another 150 years to determine why. Similarly, over the millennia various complex economies developed and flourished, though at the time there was little understanding or even concern about how these economies worked.

The economy is much like the body: as long as it functions smoothly, we need not understand its operation. But if a problem develops—high inflation, severe unemployment, or stagnant growth, for example—we need to know how a healthy economy works before we can consider if and how the problem can be corrected. We need not know every detail of the economy, just as we need not know every detail of the body. But we must understand the essential relations among key elements of the economy. For example, we would like to know to what extent the economy is self-organizing and self-adjusting. Does the economy work well enough on its own, or does it generally perform so poorly as to require constant government intervention? If it does perform poorly, are there reliable diagnostic measures to identify the problem and are there reliable public policies to correct the problem, or do corrective efforts ultimately do more harm than good?

Teaching Tip The role of expectations is an important part of this controversy. Chapter 15 provides a detailed discussion of these issues.

When doctors did not understand how the body worked, the cure was often worse than the disease. Much of the history of medicine describes misguided attempts to deal with disease. As recently as the nineteenth century, medical "remedies" included "bleeding, cupping, violent purging, the raising of blisters by vesicant ointments, the immersion of the body in either ice water or intolerably hot water, endless lists of botanical extracts evoked up and mixed together under nothing more than pure whim."[1]

Mercantilism A theory that viewed the accumulation of precious metals as the source of a nation's economic vitality; nations that followed the theory tried to promote exports and restrict imports

Likewise, national policy makers have often implemented the wrong economic prescription because of a flawed theory about how the economy works. At one time, for example, a nation's economic vitality was thought to spring from the stock of precious metals the nation could accumulate in the public treasury. This theory spawned a policy called **mercantilism**, which held that the best way for a nation to accumulate gold and silver was to sell more output to foreigners than it bought from them. To achieve this, nations restricted imports by such devices as tariffs and quotas. But these restrictions reduced international trade, thereby reducing the gains from specialization that arise from trade. Another flawed economic theory prompted President Herbert Hoover to introduce a major tax *increase* when the nation was in the grip of the Great Depression. Policy makers have since learned that such a policy does more harm than good.

We all have some acquaintance with cycles in nature—the changing seasons, the ebb and flow of the tides, the regular movements of celestial bodies, the biorhythms of the body. As we shall see, the economy also has a rhythm of its own.

The Business Cycle

Business cycle The rise and fall of economic activity relative to the long-term growth trend of the economy

Example Even Japan is subject to the business cycle. The Japanese economy slowed substantially in 1992; the stock market fell to less than one-half its peak value in late 1989.

Point to Stress The NBER is a prestigious private research institute, not a government agency.

Economic activity, like cycles in nature, fluctuates in a fairly regular way. The U.S. economy and other industrial market economies historically have experienced alternating periods of expansion and contraction in the level of economic activity. These fluctuations give rise to a roller coaster–like effect called the business cycle. The **business cycle** reflects the rise and fall of economic activity relative to the long-term growth trend of the economy. These fluctuations in the level of economic activity vary a great deal in length and intensity, yet some features appear common to all cycles. First, these ups and downs usually involve the entire nation and often the world, and they affect nearly all dimensions of economic activity, not simply employment and production levels. Second, each full cycle has staying power, spanning on average about four years.

Business Cycle Analysis

Perhaps the easiest way to understand the business cycle is to break it down into its components. During the 1920s and 1930s, Wesley C. Mitchell (1874–1948), Director of the National Bureau of Economic Research (NBER), became famous for his analysis of business cycles. In simplest terms, the economy, accord-

1. As described by Lewis Thomas in *The Youngest Science: Notes of a Medicine Watcher* (New York: Viking Press, 1983), 19.

Depression A severe reduction in an economy's total production accompanied by high unemployment lasting several years

Recession A decline in an economy's total production lasting six months or longer

Teaching Tip The slope of the trend line indicates the rate of long-term growth.

ing to Mitchell, has two phases: periods of expansion and periods of contraction. Before World War II, some periods of contraction were so severe and so prolonged that they were called depressions. Although there is no official definition, a **depression** can be viewed as a severe reduction in the nation's total production accompanied by high unemployment that lasts several years. Since World War II, periods of contraction have taken a milder form called a **recession**. According to the NBER definition, a recession is a decline in the nation's production that lasts at least six months.

Over the long run, the economy's production tends to increase because of (1) increases in the amount and quality of resources, (2) enhanced technology, and (3) improvements in the "rules of the game" that facilitate production and exchange. Exhibit 1 shows this long-term growth trend as an upward-sloping straight line. The business cycle reflects movements around this growth trend. This hypothetical exhibit depicts three full cycles. A recession begins after the previous expansion has reached its *peak* and continues until the economy reaches

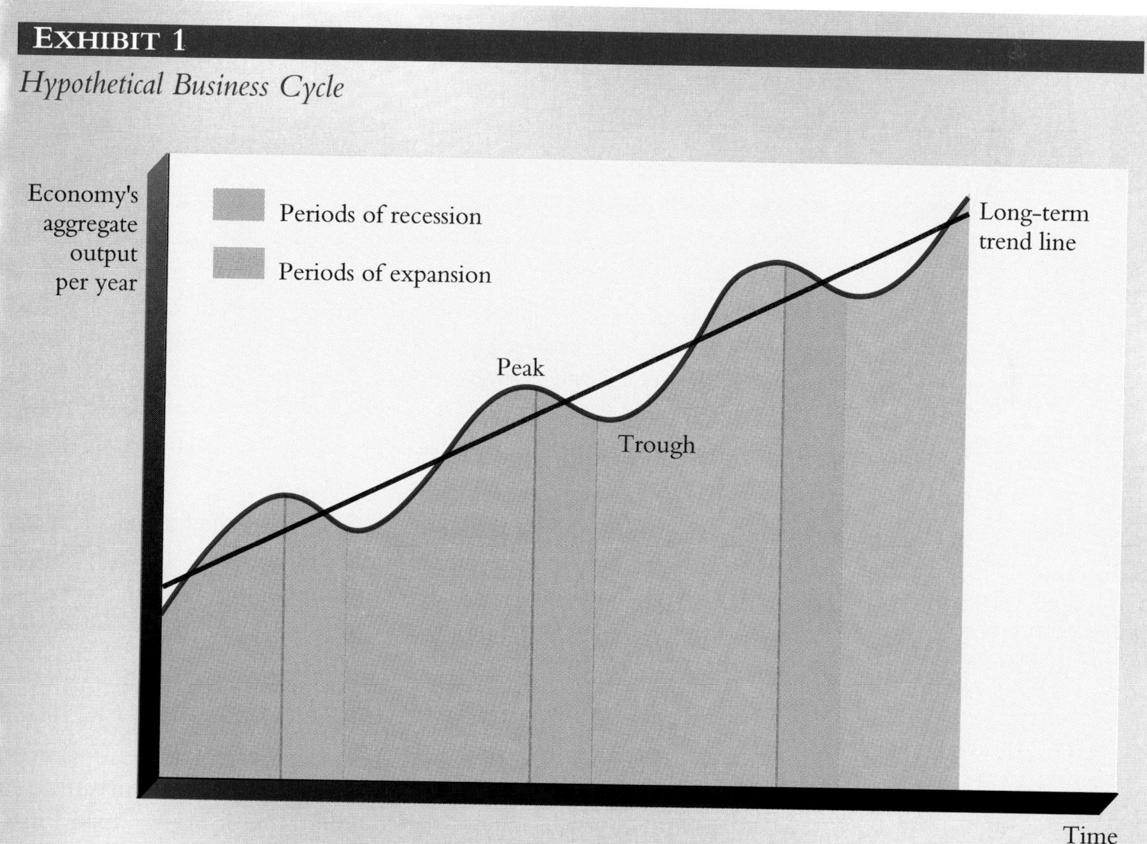

The business cycle reflects movements of economic activity around a trend. A recession (shown in red) begins after a previous expansion (shown in gold) has reached its peak and continues until the economy reaches a trough. An expansion begins when economic activity starts to increase and continues until the economy reaches a peak.

EXHIBIT 2

Historical Business Cycles in the United States

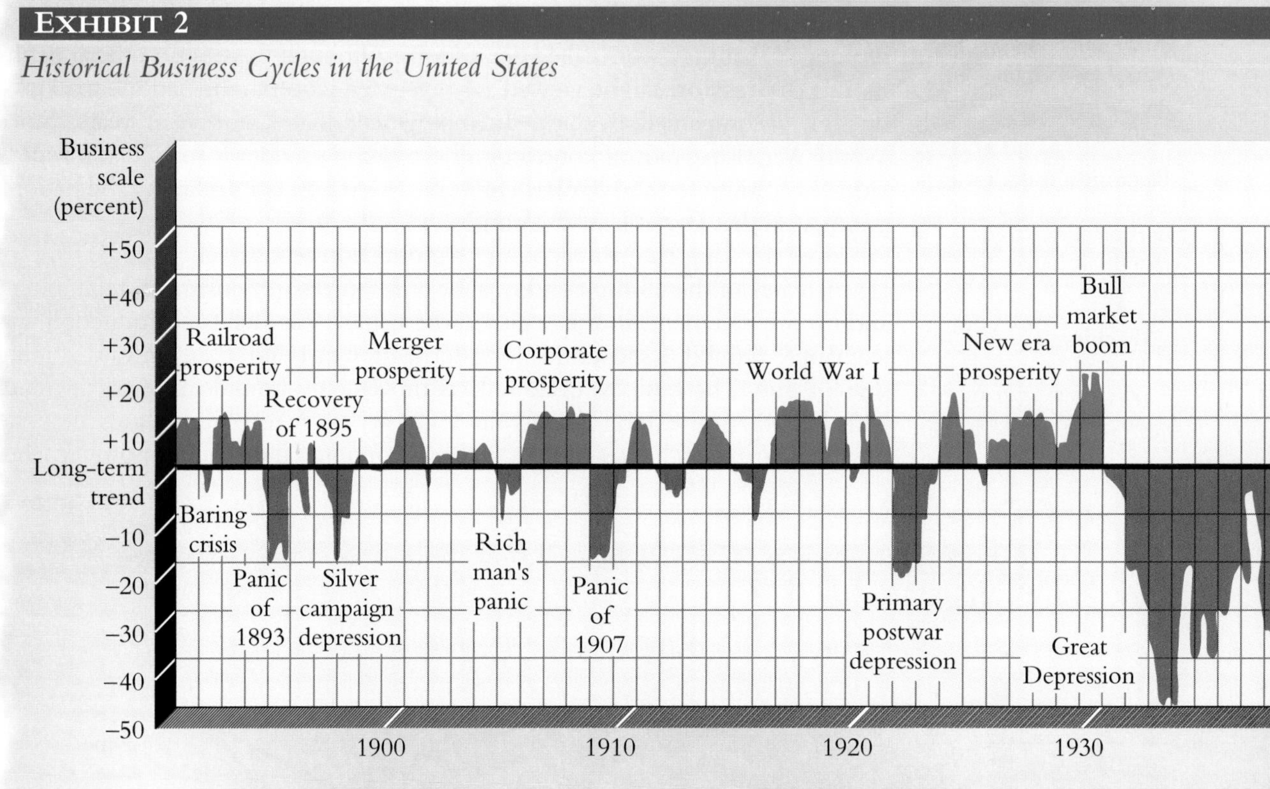

This historical chart shows the phases of the U.S. business cycle since 1890. The vertical scale indicates the percentage by which the level of business activity exceeded or fell short of the long-term trend.

Source: "American Business Activity from 1790 to Today," Ameritrust Corporation, January 1988. Updated by author.

Expansion An increase in the economy's total production lasting six months or longer

a *trough*. The period between the peak and the trough is called a *recession* and the period between the trough and the subsequent peak is called an **expansion**.

The actual experience of the U.S. economy is pictured in Exhibit 2, which shows the percentage change in economic activity relative to the trend line during the last hundred years. As you can see, the phases of the cycle vary widely in duration and in rate of change. The big declines during the Great Depression of the 1930s and the sharp gains during World War II stand in stark contrast. Analysts at NBER have been able to track the U.S. economy back to 1854. Since then the country has gone through thirty-one full business cycles. No two have been exactly alike. The longest expansion on record lasted 106 months, from 1961 to 1969, a stretch that included the Vietnam War. The longest *peacetime* expansion began in November 1982 and continued for nearly eight years until a recession began in August 1990. The longest contraction lasted sixty-five months, from 1873 to 1879.

Point to Stress 1933 was the lowest point of the Great Depression. The unemployment rate of 25 percent during that year is the highest recorded rate in U.S. history.

Since 1933 the U.S. economy has completed eleven business cycles. During this period peacetime expansions averaged about three and one-half years and peacetime contractions about one year; wartime expansions were longer.

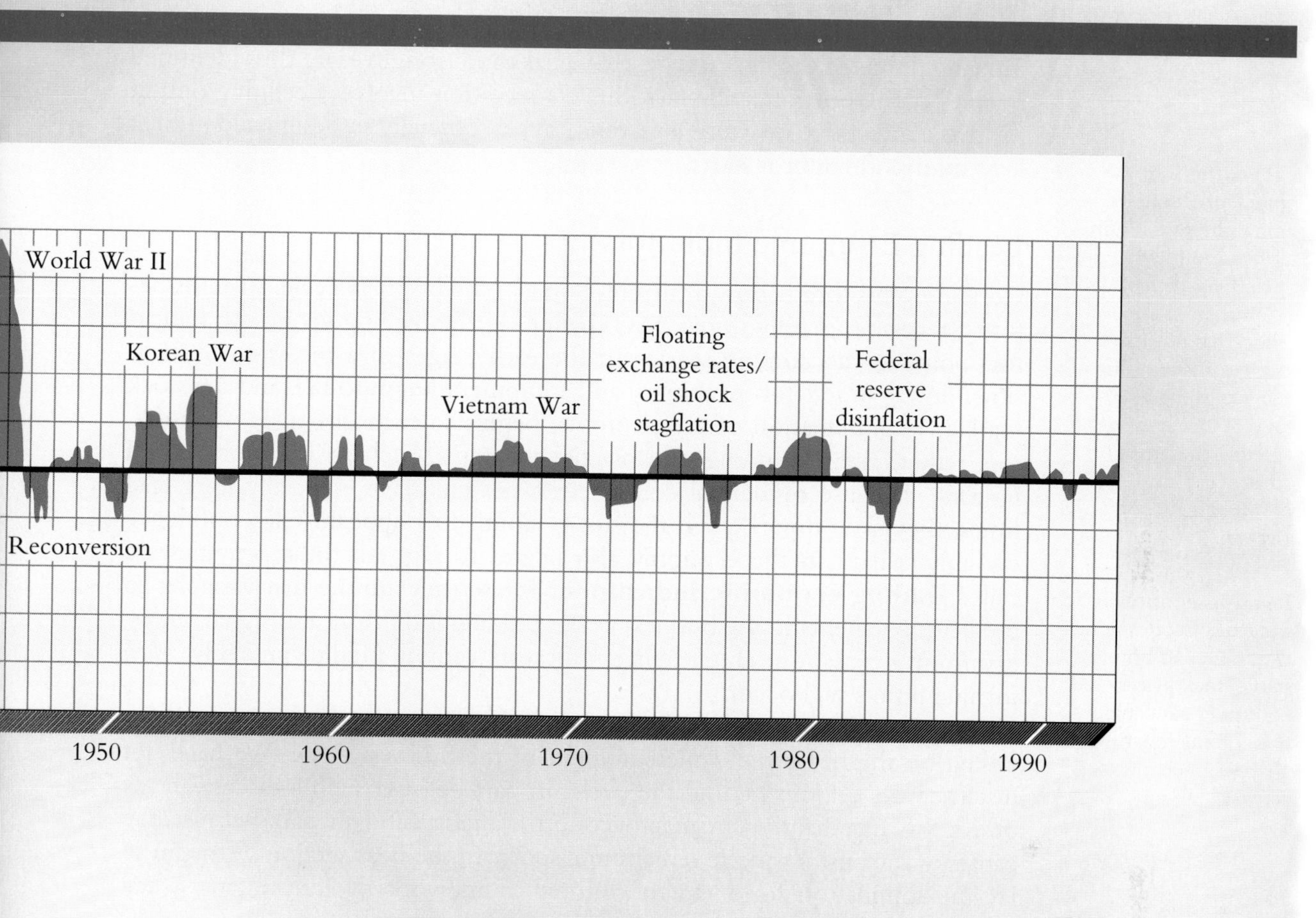

Example In August, 1992, Hurricane Andrew created a random disturbance in the south Florida job market. The Florida Department of Labor estimated the repair work would create 7,000 new construction jobs (expected to last three years) in the area. The area had lost 18,000 construction jobs in the two years before the hurricane.

In contrast, during the peacetime cycles between 1854 and 1933, expansions lasted about two years, and contractions a little less than two years.[2] Not only have the recessions become shorter since 1933, they have also become less severe. Depressions were a common feature of earlier business cycles, but none has occurred since the 1930s. There has been a clear shift toward longer expansions and shorter contractions. The entire cycle lasts about four and one-half years on average. The intensity of the cycles varies from region to region across the United States. For example, a recession hits hardest in those regions that produce durable goods, such as automobiles, major appliances, and computers, since the demand for these items falls sharply with the onset of a recession.

Because of seasonal fluctuations and random disturbances, the economy does not move smoothly through the business cycle. We cannot always distinguish between temporary changes in economic activity and actual turning

2. These averages have been computed based on data found in the *Survey of Current Business*, June 1992, Business Cycle Expansions and Contractions: page C-25.

points in the cycle. The drop in production in a particular period may be the result of a snowstorm or a poor harvest rather than the onset of a recession. Turning points in the business cycles—peaks and troughs—are thus identified by the NBER only after the fact. Since a recession involves declining output for two consecutive quarters, a recession is not officially so designated until at least six months after it starts.

Teaching Tip An index of eleven leading indicators is published monthly by the U.S. Department of Commerce. The index has not worked well as a forecasting device in the 1980s and 1990s. It failed to predict the recession that began in August, 1990 and ended in March, 1991.

Leading Economic Indicators

Leading economic indicators Economic statistics, such as housing starts, stock prices, and consumer expectations, that foreshadow future changes in economic activity

Certain events foreshadow a turning point in the business cycle. Months before a recession is fully under way, changes in the leading economic indicators point to the coming storm. In the early stages of a recession business slows down, orders for machinery and equipment begin to fall, and the stock market, in anticipation of lower profits, begins to turn down. Households, too, reduce their spending on "big-ticket" items, such as automobiles and housing. Because residential construction permits have especially long lead times, they slow down when the storm clouds first appear. The confidence consumers have in the economy also begins to sag. All these activities are called **leading economic indicators** because they are the first variables to predict movements in the business cycle. Leading indicators also signal recovery from a recession. But leading indicators cannot predict precisely *when* turning points will occur.

Our introduction to the business cycle has been largely mechanical, focusing on the history and measurement of the business cycle. We have not discussed the reasons behind the cycle, in part because such a discussion requires a firmer footing in macroeconomic theory and in part because the causes of the business cycle remain in dispute. In the next section we begin to lay the foundation for a macroeconomic framework by introducing a key model of analysis.

AGGREGATE DEMAND AND AGGREGATE SUPPLY

Point to Stress Much of the macroeconomics course will address issues of why the economy expands and contracts and what, if anything, the government should do to control it.

The economy is so complex that we need to simplify or to abstract from the millions of relations in order to capture the important elements under consideration. We must step back from all the individual economic transactions to survey the resulting mosaic. Perhaps the clearest way to characterize the operation of the entire economy is with the familiar tools of demand and supply.

Aggregate Output and the Price Level

Aggregate demand The relation between the price level in the economy and the quantity of aggregate output demanded

The demand for food shows the relation between the average price of food and the quantity of food demanded. When we consider the demand for food, we must take into account a diverse array of products—milk, bread, fruit, vegetables, beef, chicken, and so on. But moving from a specific product, milk, to a general product, food, is not conceptually difficult. **Aggregate demand** is the relation between the quantity of *all* goods and services demanded in the economy and the economy's price level, or the average price of *all* goods and services.

To understand aggregate demand, we must move from the demand for food or housing or clothing or entertainment or medical care to the demand for all output produced in the economy—the demand for aggregate output. **Aggregate output** is the total quantity of goods and services produced in the economy during a given time period. A unit of aggregate output is a composite measure of all output in the same sense that a unit of food is a composite measure of all food. Likewise, the **price level** in the economy is a composite measure reflecting the price on average of housing, food, clothing, entertainment, medical care, and all other aggregate output. In earlier chapters, when we referred to the price we were talking about the price of a particular product, such as milk, *relative to the prices of other products.* But here we are talking about the price, on average, of all goods and services produced in the economy.

Aggregate output The total quantity of final goods and services produced in an economy during a given time period

Price level A composite measure reflecting the prices of all goods and services in the economy

You are more familiar than you think you are with aggregate output and the price level. Reports in the media about economic growth or an economic slowdown are usually referring to changes in the gross domestic product, the most common measure of aggregate output. The *gross domestic product,* or *GDP,* measures the market value of all final goods and services produced in the United States during a given time period, usually a year. And the economy's price level is nothing more than the "cost of living" so often mentioned in news reports. Two common measures of the price level are (1) the *consumer price index,* which tracks changes in the prices of the "basket" of goods and services consumed by the typical family, and (2) the *implicit price deflator,* which tracks the price changes of all items in the gross domestic product. Both measures of the price level express average prices in a particular year, say 1992, relative to the average prices that prevailed in a base year, or a reference year.

In the next chapter, you will learn more about how to compute the price level. All you need know now is that the price level in the base year is set at a benchmark value of 100 and the price levels in other years are expressed relative to the base-year price level. For example, in 1992 the U.S. implicit price deflator was 121, indicating that the price level that year was 21 percent higher than its value of 100 in the base year of 1987.

Point to Stress Real GDP is valued using prices in the base year. If the nominal GDP value in 1992 exceeded the base year GDP by 21 percent, and 1992 prices were also 21 percent above 1987 prices, then there has been no change in real output since 1987.

The implicit price deflator is used to "deflate" the gross domestic product—that is, to eliminate any year-to-year growth in GDP due solely to inflation, or increases in the price level. Remaining changes are thus changes in real output. After deflating GDP for price changes, we end up with what is called the *real* gross domestic product—that is, GDP measured in terms of dollars of constant purchasing power. The GDP values reported in this chapter will measure real GDP.

Aggregate demand curve A curve representing the relation between the economy's price level and the amount of aggregate output demanded per period of time, other things held constant

Aggregate Demand Curve

The **aggregate demand curve** shows the relation between the price level in the economy and the aggregate output demanded, other things constant. Exhibit 3 presents a hypothetical aggregate demand curve, *AD.* You might think of

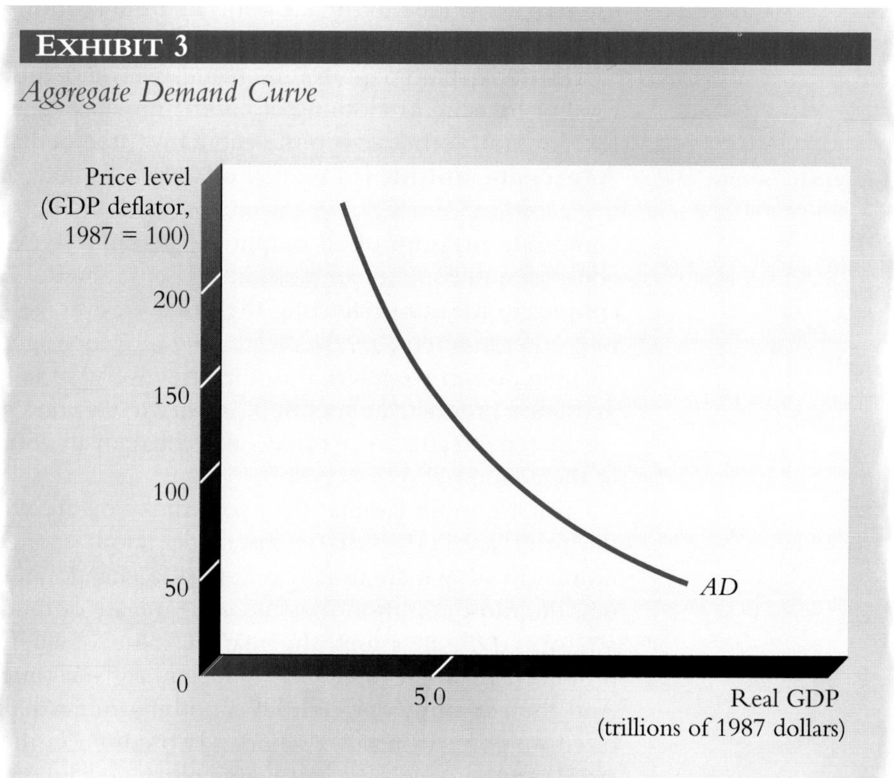

EXHIBIT 3

Aggregate Demand Curve

this as the aggregate demand curve for the year 1992. Aggregate output is measured along the horizontal axis by real GDP, or real gross domestic product (using 1987 dollars); the economy's price level is measured along the vertical axis by the implicit price deflator (using 1987 as a base year).

The aggregate demand curve in Exhibit 3 reflects an inverse relation between the price level in the economy and the quantity of aggregate output demanded. The inverse relation indicates that as the price level in the United States falls, other things constant, households demand more washers and Wheaties, firms demand more trucks and typewriters, governments demand more computer software and military hardware, and the rest of the world demands more U.S. grain and U.S. aircraft.

The reasons behind this inverse relation will be examined more in later chapters. Here we provide some quick intuitive explanations. The quantity of aggregate output demanded depends in part on household *wealth*. Some wealth is held in dollar amounts, such as money in a savings account. A reduction in the price level, other things constant, increases the amount of goods and services that can be purchased with a given amount of savings. Therefore, households feel richer with a decrease in the price level, so they increase the quantity of aggregate output demanded. Conversely, an increase in the price level decreases the amount of goods and services that can be purchased with a given amount of money. Households feel poorer when there is

Teaching Tip Some factors held constant are the level of nominal wealth, expectations, and the level of the money supply.

an increase in the price level, so they decrease the quantity of aggregate output demanded.

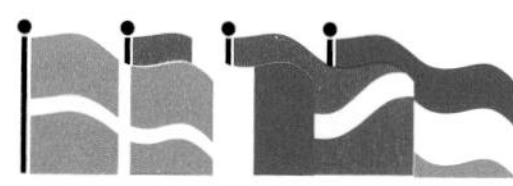

The aggregate demand curve reflects both domestic and foreign demand for U.S. output. So another reason for the negative slope of the aggregate demand curve involves the relation between the *domestic* price level and the *foreign* price level. Among the factors held constant along a given aggregate demand curve is the price level in other countries, as well as the exchange rate between the dollar and foreign currencies. When the price level in the United States falls, the average price of U.S. products falls relative to the price of foreign products. Consequently, Americans increase the quantity they demand of now relatively cheaper U.S. goods and decrease their demand for foreign goods. Foreigners also find U.S. goods relatively cheaper, so they increase their quantity demanded of U.S. exports. Conversely, a rise in the price level reduces the quantity of U.S. output demanded by both Americans and foreigners.

Aggregate Supply Curve

Aggregate supply curve A curve representing the relation between the economy's price level and the amount of aggregate output supplied per period of time, other things held constant

Example Patent and copyright laws are part of the "rules of the game."

Teaching Tip The shape of the aggregate supply curve is explained in detail in Chapter 10.

The **aggregate supply curve** indicates the quantity of aggregate output that producers in the aggregate are willing and able to supply at each price level, other things constant. How does quantity supplied respond to changes in the price level? The upward-sloping supply curve, *AS*, in Exhibit 4 depicts a positive relation between the price level and the quantity of aggregate output producers supply, other factors that affect supply held constant. Held constant along an aggregate supply curve are the supply of resources, the state of technology, and the "rules of the game" in the economy, which provide production incentives. Since the cost per unit of resource remains fairly constant along an aggregate supply curve, higher product prices encourage producers to increase the quantity supplied. *As long as the prices producers receive for their output rises more than the cost of producing that output, producers find it profitable to expand output as the price level increases.*

Equilibrium

The intersection of the aggregate demand and aggregate supply curves determines the equilibrium levels of price and aggregate output in the economy. Only at the equilibrium level will the desires of buyers and sellers match. If for some reason the price level is initially higher than the market-clearing, or equilibrium, level, the resulting excess quantity supplied will force the price level down until quantity demanded and quantity supplied are equal. If the price level is initially below the equilibrium level, the resulting shortage of goods and services will put upward pressure on the price level until the shortage is eliminated. Exhibit 4 is a rough depiction of aggregate demand and supply in 1992; the equilibrium price level that year was 121 and the equilibrium real GDP was about $5.0 trillion, measured in dollars of 1987 purchasing power.

Although employment is not measured directly along the horizontal axis, firms must hire additional workers to produce more goods and services.

EXHIBIT 4

Aggregate Demand and Supply

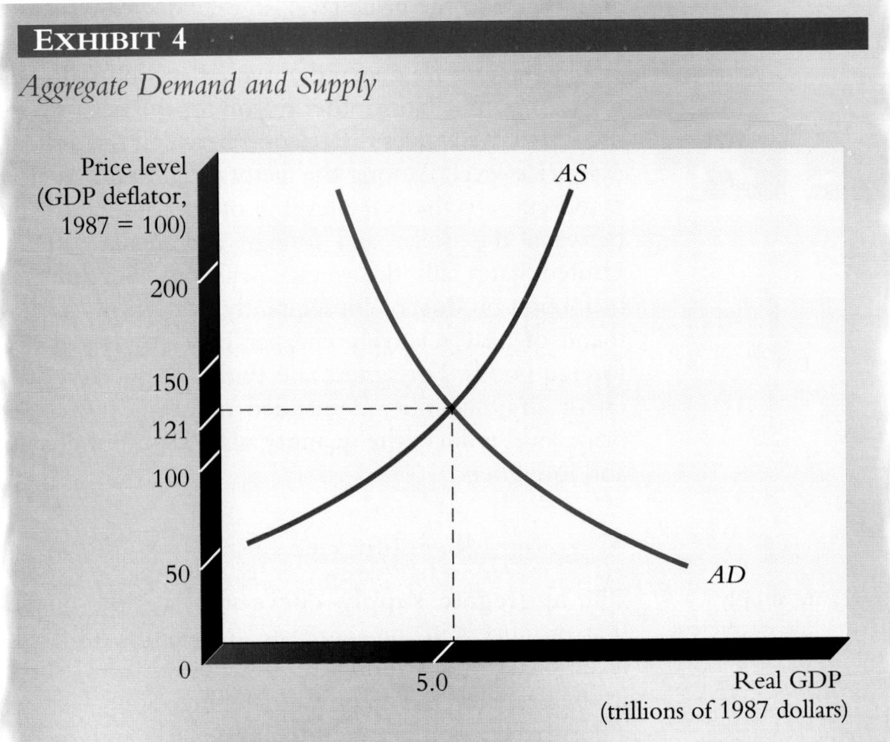

The total output of the economy and its price level are determined at the intersection of the aggregate demand and aggregate supply curves.

Thus, higher levels of aggregate output reflect higher levels of employment. In terms of economic policy, greater aggregate output seems desirable for two reasons. First, greater output means that more goods and services are available in the economy. Second, greater output means that more people in the economy are employed and fewer are unemployed. For a given aggregate supply curve, such as in Exhibit 4, more aggregate output will usually be supplied only if the price level increases. As we shall see later, however, a rising price level may create another set of problems, so greater output is not always the only goal of the economy.

Perhaps the best way to convey an understanding of aggregate demand and supply is to apply these tools to changes in the U.S. economy. In the next section we greatly simplify U.S. economic history to show how the price level and the level of aggregate output have been related over time.

A Short History of the U.S. Economy

The history of the U.S. economy can be crudely divided into three economic eras: (1) before World War II, (2) between World War II and the early

1970s, and (3) since the early 1970s. The first era was marked by a series of economic depressions, culminating in the Great Depression of the 1930s. These depressions were often accompanied by a falling price level. The second era was one of generally strong economic growth, with only moderate increases in the price level. The third era was characterized by problems with both unemployment and inflation, which is a sustained and continuous increase in the price level.

Before World War II

Teaching Tip Refer to the first half (pre-1940) of Exhibit 2.

As we have mentioned, U.S. economic history records alternating periods of prosperity and sharp economic decline before World War II. There was the depression of the 1820s and "panics" in 1837 and in 1857. Depression hit again between 1873 and 1879, when eighty railroads went bankrupt and most of the steel industry was shut down. During the depression of the 1890s, the unemployment rate topped 18 percent. The stock market crash of October, 1929 occurred at the beginning of what was to become the most severe economic contraction in our nation's history, the Great Depression of the 1930s.

In terms of aggregate demand and aggregate supply, the Great Depression can be viewed as a shift to the left in the aggregate demand curve, as shown in Exhibit 5. AD_{1929} is the aggregate demand curve in 1929, before the onset

EXHIBIT 5

The Decrease in Aggregate Demand Between 1929 and 1933

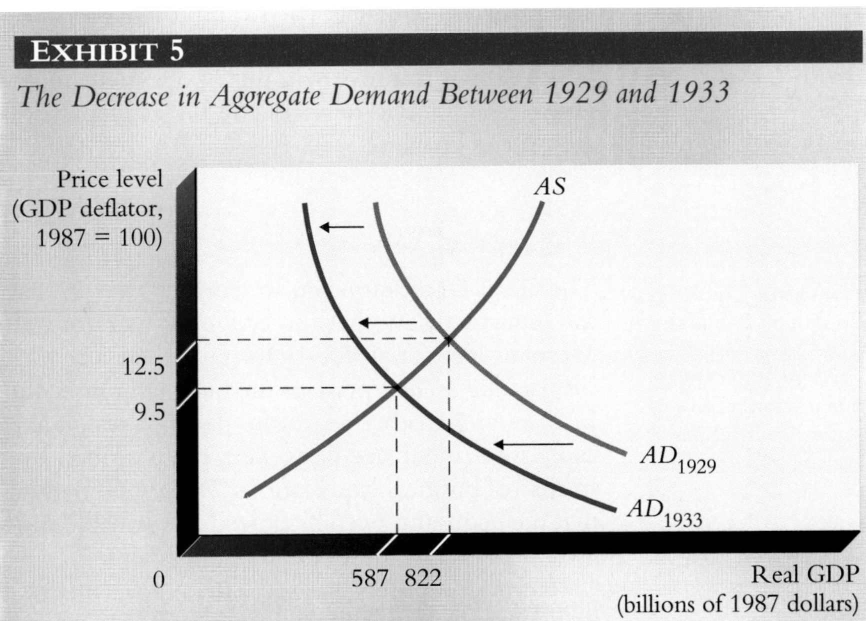

The Great Depression of the 1930s can be represented by a shift to the left of the aggregate demand curve, from AD_{1929} to AD_{1933}. As a result of the depression, real GDP fell from \$822 billion to \$587 billion, and the price level dropped from 12.5 to 9.5.

of the depression. At that time real GDP was about $822 billion (measured in 1987 dollars) and the price level was 12.5 (relative to a 1987 price level of 100). Thus the average price level in 1929 was only 12.5 percent of the level in 1987. By 1933 the aggregate demand curve had decreased to AD_{1933}.[3] With this decline in aggregate demand, both the price level and real GDP declined. Between 1929 and 1933, the price level decreased by 24 percent, from 12.5 to 9.5. And real GDP fell by about 29 percent, from $822 billion to $587 billion. As aggregate output declined, the unemployment rate shot up, climbing from about 3 percent in 1929 to 25 percent in 1933, the highest ever recorded in the United States.

Why did aggregate demand fall so dramatically? Though the causes are still subject to debate, grim business expectations and a sharp decline in the nation's money supply each contributed to the drop in aggregate demand. Before the Great Depression, public policy was based primarily on the laissez-faire philosophy of Adam Smith. Recall that Smith argued in his book *The Wealth of Nations* that if people were allowed to pursue their self-interest in a free market, resources would be guided as if by an "invisible hand" to produce the greatest, most efficient level of aggregate output. The policy pursued by governments before the Great Depression was based on the theory that the economy would perform better if left alone than if government intervened. Though the U.S. economy had suffered through at least six major depressions since the beginning of the nineteenth century, the common view each time was that these contractions were unfortunate but essentially *self-correcting*. Each economic crisis and subsequent depression was viewed by most economists of the day as a natural phase of the economy, which would improve without government intervention. President Herbert Hoover said at the onset of the Great Depression that prosperity was "just around the corner."

The Age of Keynes

Teaching Tip Refer to Exhibit 2 to illustrate the length and severity of the Great Depression relative to earlier contractions.

The Great Depression was so severe, however, that it gave more credibility to the minority view that the economy was not self-correcting. In 1936, John Maynard Keynes (1883–1946) published *The General Theory of Employment, Interest, and Money*, perhaps the most famous economics book of this century. In it he argued that aggregate demand was inherently unstable, in part because investment decisions were often guided by the unpredictable "animal spirits" of business expectations. He saw no natural forces operating to ensure that the economy, even if allowed a reasonable time, would return to a higher level of aggregate output and employment.

Keynes proposed that the federal government shock the economy out of its depression by increasing aggregate demand. This could be done directly,

3. The aggregate supply curve probably also shifted somewhat during the period, but for simplicity we assume it was unchanged. Most economists agree that the shift in the aggregate demand curve was the dominant factor.

by increasing government spending, or indirectly, by cutting taxes to stimulate the primary components of private-sector demand, consumption, and investment. Either way, government spending would likely exceed government revenues, resulting in a *federal budget deficit*. Thus, Keynes recommended an *expansionary fiscal policy* and called for a federal budget deficit. If this policy worked as Keynes expected, aggregate demand would increase. To see what Keynes had in mind, imagine the aggregate demand curve in Exhibit 5 shifting back to its original position. Most importantly, such a shift would raise the equilibrium level of aggregate output and employment. This change would also raise the price level, but changes in the price level were of less concern to Keynes.

According to the Keynesian prescription, the miracle drug of government fiscal policy—changes in government spending and taxes—was needed to compensate for what Keynes viewed as the inherent instability of private spending, especially investment. If demand in the private sector declined, it became the government's responsibility to pick up the slack. We can think of the Keynesian approach as **demand-side economics** because it focused on how increases in aggregate demand could promote full employment. Keynes argued that government spending, if injected into the circular flow at the right time and in the proper dose, could be just the tonic to stimulate the economy out of its depression and back to health.

Demand-side economics Macroeconomic policy that focuses on changes in aggregate demand as a way of promoting full employment and price stability

The U.S. economy languished during the 1930s, but World War II broke out, and huge federal budget deficits were created to finance the war. The additional demand stimulated output and employment and seemed to confirm the powerful role that government spending could play in stimulating the economy. After the war, memories of the depression were still vivid, and everyone wanted to avoid a recurrence. Congress, therefore, approved the *Employment Act of 1946,* which imposed a clear responsibility on the federal government to foster, in the language of the act, "maximum employment, production, and purchasing power." One provision of the act set up the *Council of Economic Advisers* and required the President to report annually on the state of the economy. In his first *Economic Report*, President Harry Truman wrote: "The job at hand is to see to it that America is not ravaged by recurring depressions and long periods of unemployment, but that instead we build an economy so fruitful, so dynamic, so progressive that each citizen can count upon opportunity and security for himself and his family."[4]

The economy seemed to prosper during the 1950s largely without the help of expansionary fiscal policies. The decade of the 1960s, however, proved to be the *Golden Age of Keynesian economics*, a period when policy makers believed that by manipulating government taxation and spending, they could "fine-tune" the economy to avoid the recessionary phase of the business cycle. During the 1960s nearly all developed economies of the world enjoyed low unemployment and healthy growth in output with only modest increases in the average level of prices. The value of U.S. exports ex-

Teaching Tip Refer to Exhibit 2 to indicate the longest expansion in U.S. history: from 1961 to 1969. Inflation was as low as 1.0 percent and the unemployment rate remained below 4.0 percent.

4. *Economic Report of the President* (Washington, DC: U.S. Government Printing Office, 1947), 7.

ceeded that of U.S. imports, and income flowed into the country from extensive U.S. investments in foreign countries. The U.S. economy boomed.

The economy was on such a roll that toward the end of the 1960s, some economists were beginning to speak of the obsolescence of the business cycle. As a sign of the times, the federal government changed the name of a publication called *Business Cycle Developments* to *Business Conditions Digest*. As it turned out, reports of the death of the business cycle were premature. In the early 1970s, the cycle returned with a fury. Prior to 1970 the problem of inflation occurred primarily during expansions, but inflation increased during the two recessions in the middle and late 1970s. The confidence economists had in demand-side policies was shaken, and the expression "fine-tuning" passed from economists' vocabularies. What happened in the short span of a few years to end the Golden Age of Keynesian economics?

The Great Stagflation

Inflation rate The annual percentage change in the price level

Teaching Tip Refer to Exhibit 2 to indicate the recessions in 1970 and 1974–1975.

During the late 1960s, the federal government stepped up the war in Vietnam and increased spending on social programs at home. These simultaneous efforts increased aggregate demand enough that in 1968 the **inflation rate**, the annual percentage increase in the price level, climbed to 4.2 percent—the first time it had risen above 4.0 percent since 1951. Inflation drifted to 5.5 percent in 1969, and to 5.7 percent in 1970. These rates, which appear normal by today's standards, were so alarming at the time that in August of 1971 President Richard Nixon introduced measures to freeze prices and wages. The initial three-month freeze was followed by several "phases" of controls that imposed varying wage and price restrictions during 1972 and 1973.

These freezes were eliminated about the time that grain prices were driven up by crop failures in several key grain-producing regions around the world. To compound these problems, huge increases in oil prices were pushed through by the suddenly powerful Organization of Petroleum Exporting Countries (OPEC). All of these shocks in resource supplies hit the economy hard. In part because of the higher price of imported oil, Americans for the first time in decades were spending more on imports than they received for their exports. The result was a deficit in our merchandise trade balance. This trend, which was to worsen during the 1980s, showed how vulnerable the U.S. economy had become to economic forces around the world.

Whereas macroeconomic fluctuations during the 1960s seemed to be dominated by movements in the aggregate demand curve, the shocks of the 1970s reduced aggregate supply. A reduction in aggregate supply—a shift to the left in the aggregate supply curve—touched off the so-called *Great Stagflation* of the 1970s. This reduction in aggregate supply, shown in Exhibit 6 by the shift to the left in the aggregate supply curve, from AS_{1973} to AS_{1975}, resulted in the double trouble of a lower level of real GDP and employment and a higher price level. Between 1973 and 1975, real GDP declined from \$3.27 trillion to \$3.22 trillion, or by \$50 billion, while the price level increased from 41.3 to 49.2. The unemployment rate climbed from 4.9 percent in 1973 to

EXHIBIT 6

Stagflation Between 1973 and 1975

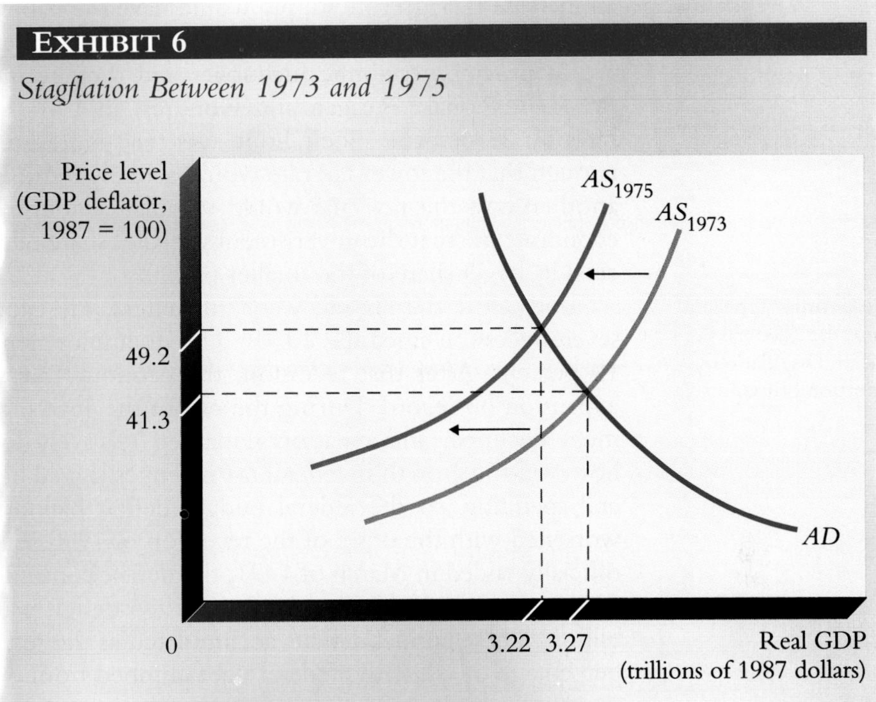

The stagflation of the 1970s can be represented as a reduction in aggregate supply from AS_{1973} to AS_{1975}. Aggregate output fell from \$3.27 trillion to \$3.22 trillion (stagnation), and the price level rose from 41.3 to 49.2 (inflation).

Stagflation A contraction of a nation's output accompanied by inflation

8.5 percent in 1975. **Stagflation** means **stag**nation, or contraction, in the economy's aggregate output and in**flation**, or an increase, in the price level.

Since the problem was primarily on the supply side, not on the demand side, the demand-management prescriptions of Keynes seemed less effective in the 1970s. A government-induced increase in aggregate demand would worsen inflation. Stagflation appeared again at the end of the decade, partly as a result of another boost in oil prices. Between 1979 and 1980 real GDP declined at the same time the price level increased by 9.5 percent. Macroeconomics has not been the same since.

Teaching Tip To illustrate the impact of increased *AS*, use Exhibit 6 and assume that the *AS* curve moves from left to right.

Experience Since 1980

Supply-side economics Macroeconomic policy that focuses on use of tax cuts to stimulate production so as to increase aggregate supply

Increasing aggregate supply seemed an appropriate way to combat stagflation, for such a move would both lower inflation and increase output and employment. Attention therefore turned from aggregate demand to aggregate supply. A key idea behind so-called **supply-side economics** was that the federal government, by lowering tax rates, would increase the after-tax wage and thereby provide greater incentives to supply labor and other resources. This greater resource supply would increase aggregate supply. Theoretically, an increase in aggregate supply would have the happy result of increasing real GDP and reducing the price level. But this was easier said than done.

To provide economic incentives and thereby increase aggregate supply, President Ronald Reagan and Congress in 1981 cut personal income tax rates by 23 percent. Their hope was that aggregate output would increase enough that the lower tax rate would actually result in more tax revenue. Put another way, the tax cuts would stimulate enough of an expansion of the economic pie that the government's smaller share of the bigger pie would exceed its larger share of the smaller pie.

Teaching Tip Point out the "Federal Reserve Disinflation" portion of Exhibit 2.

But before the tax cut went into effect, the economy suffered the most severe recession since the 1930s. The unemployment rate climbed to nearly 10 percent. After that recession, the economy began its longest peacetime expansion on record. During the rest of the 1980s, output grew, unemployment declined, and inflation remained relatively low. During this period, however, the growth in federal tax revenues lagged behind the growth in federal spending, so the federal budget deficit ballooned. The federal deficit worsened with the onset of the recession of 1990. Even though the recession officially ended in March of 1991, the deficit continued to grow. By 1992 the deficit topped $290 billion, and the 1993 deficit was projected to top $325 billion. These annual deficits accumulated as the federal debt. Measured as a percentage of GDP, the federal debt climbed from 34 percent in 1980 to 68 percent by 1992.

The Twin Deficits

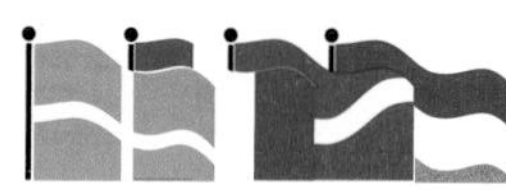

Point to Stress The twin deficits problem is an example of the difficulty of discussing the national economy without considering the world economy. (See the first annotation in this chapter.)

On the international scene, the U.S. trade balance deteriorated during the 1980s, with the trade deficit exceeding $140 billion in 1987. These annual trade deficits meant that foreigners were accumulating dollars from their net sales to the United States. Foreigners used these dollars to invest in U.S. firms, to buy U.S. stocks and bonds, and to buy other U.S. assets such as real estate. Thus there were twin deficits during the 1980s and early 1990s—the federal budget deficit and the balance-of-trade deficit—and the two were related. The rest of the world took the dollars accumulated because of our trade deficits and lent them back to us, thereby helping us finance the federal budget deficits. But in the process Americans were growing more indebted, both because of the federal debt and because of what we owed to foreigners. We will learn more about these deficits and these debts in later chapters.

We close with a case study that summarizes the price and output levels of the U.S. economy during the last half century.

CASE STUDY

A Half Century of Price Levels and Real GDP

In Exhibit 7 we trace the combination of the price level and real GDP since 1940. Only points for 1940 and 1992 show the aggregate demand and aggregate supply curves, but all the points in the series are derived from the intersection of such curves. Years of growing real GDP are indicated as blue points and years of declining real GDP as red points. Despite the recessions over the years, the upward long-term trend in the economy is unmistakable: real GDP during the period climbed from $0.9 trillion in 1940 to $4.9 trillion in 1992—more than a fivefold increase in production. The price level, as

EXHIBIT 7

Tracking the U.S. Real GDP and Price Level Since 1940

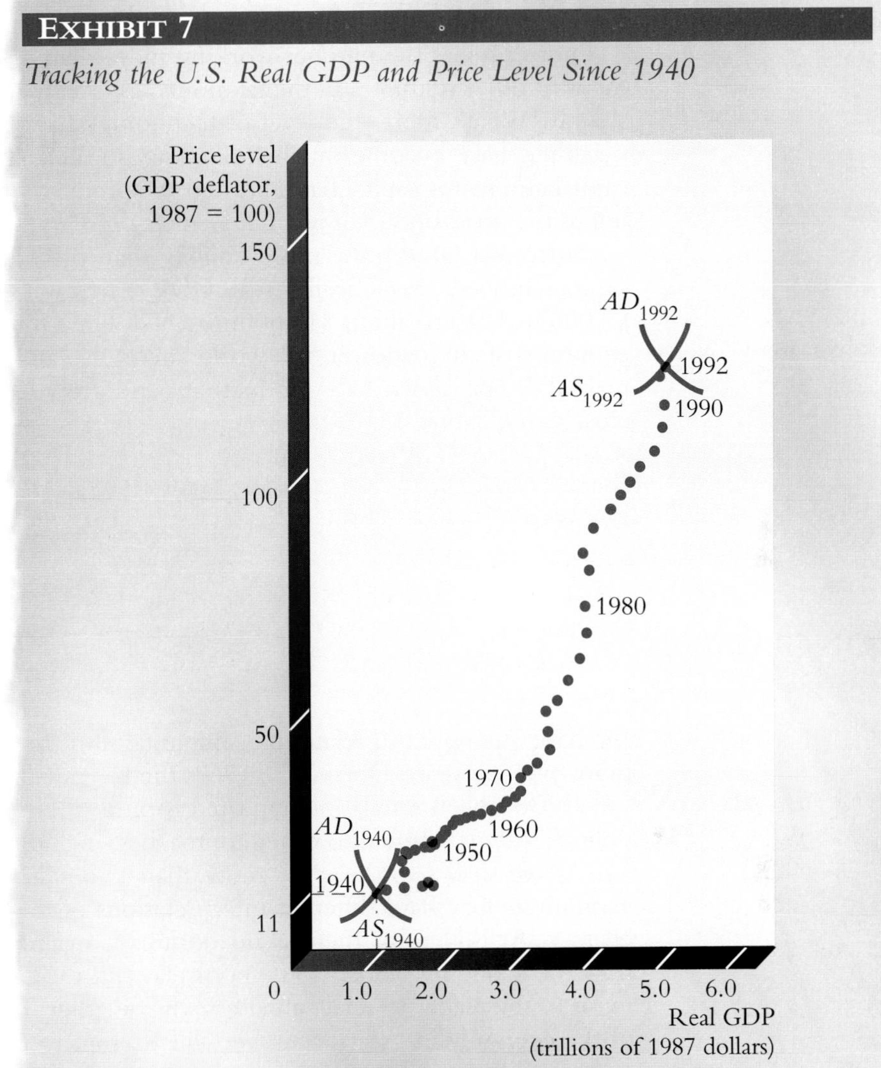

As you can see, both the price level and real GDP increased sharply since 1940. The blue points indicate years of growing real GDP and the red points are years of declining real GDP. Real GDP was about 5.5 times higher in 1992 than in 1940, and the price level was eleven times higher.

reflected by the implicit price deflator, climbed even more, rising from only 11 in 1940 to 121 in 1992—an elevenfold increase.

Because the population is growing all the time, the economy must generate new jobs each year just to employ the additional people entering the labor force. For example, the U.S. population nearly doubled from 132 million in 1940 to about 255 million in 1992. During that same period the number of people employed in the economy more than doubled from 47.5

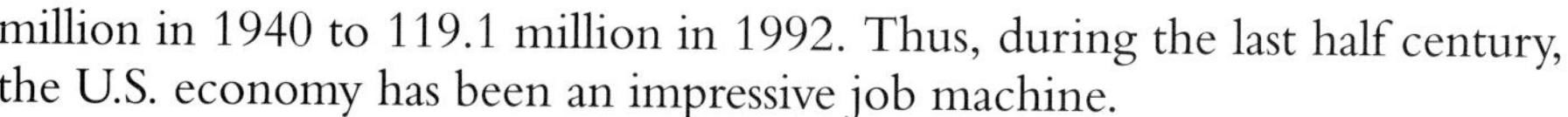

million in 1940 to 119.1 million in 1992. Thus, during the last half century, the U.S. economy has been an impressive job machine.

Not only has the number working more than doubled, but the employment of other resources in the economy, especially capital, has also increased sharply. What's more, the level of technology has improved steadily so that machines have become much more sophisticated. The availability of more capital and better capital has increased the productivity of each worker, leading to the quadrupling of real GDP since 1940.

Since real GDP grew more quickly than the population, real GDP per capita climbed. Specifically, real GDP per capita increased from about $7,000 in 1940 to about $19,600 in 1992. The United States has the largest economy of any nation in the world and is also among the world leaders in real GDP per capita. U.S. productivity and growth will be examined more closely in Chapter 17.

Sources: *Economic Report of the President*, January 1993 and *Economic Report of the President*, February 1991.

Conclusion

We have attempted to relate in a simple fashion the course of economic activity over the years. During the 1960s the Keynesian demand-side view prevailed. But when stagflation appeared to limit the relevance of demand-side policies, interest shifted to other approaches, including supply-side economics. As we shall see, there are more than two sides to this story. Different economists may have different interpretations of the events discussed in this chapter. At this point there is no dominant macroeconomic theory about how the economy works. Some books lay out the competing theories, leaving it to the reader to select an alternative. Rather than describe each theory of the economy in great detail, we will attempt to integrate theories whenever possible to find the common ground among them.

Because macroeconomists have no test subjects and cannot rely on luck, they hone their craft by developing models of the economy and closely observing the economy's performance for evidence to support or refute these models. In this sense macroeconomics is largely retrospective, always looking at recent history for hints about which model works best. The macroeconomist is like a traveler who has a view of only the road behind, not the road ahead, and must find the way using a collection of poorly drawn maps. The traveler must continually check each map (or model) against the landmarks passed, to see if one map appears more consistent with the terrain than the others. Hence, each new batch of information about the economy's performance causes macroeconomists to shuffle through their "maps" of the economy to reevaluate their models.

In macroeconomics there is often an emphasis on what can go wrong with the economy. Problems associated with unemployment, inflation, and faltering economic growth capture much of the attention in macroeconomic theory and policy. We should not forget, however, that we must understand how a healthy economy operates before we can consider remedial policies when the economy fails in some important way. As a first step we must learn how to keep track of the economy. In the next chapter we will begin to "get the lay of the land" by learning how to measure economic activity.

SUMMARY

1. Because each country has a unique economic setting, the focus of macroeconomics is on the national economy. A standard way of gauging an economy's performance is by measuring its gross domestic product, or GDP, the value of final goods and services produced during a year.

2. The business cycle reflects the rise and fall of economic activity relative to the long-term growth trend of the economy. The economy has two phases: periods of expansion and periods of contraction. Although business cycles differ, contractions last about a year on average, and expansions average about three and one-half years.

3. The aggregate demand curve slopes downward, reflecting a negative, or inverse, relation between the price level and the quantity of aggregate output demanded. The aggregate supply curve slopes upward, reflecting a positive, or direct, relation between the quantity of aggregate output supplied and the price level. The intersection of the two curves determines the economy's equilibrium price and output levels.

4. The Great Depression prompted Keynes to argue that the economy was inherently unstable, largely because the components of private spending, particularly business investment, were erratic. Keynes did not believe that depressions were self-correcting. He argued that whenever aggregate demand declined, the federal government should spend more or tax less. Keynes's demand-side policies dominated macroeconomics between World War II and the late 1960s.

5. During the 1970s supply shocks caused by higher energy prices and global crop failures reduced aggregate supply. The result was stagflation, the troublesome combination of slumping production and a higher rate of inflation. Demand-side policies appeared less effective in an economy suffering from a reduction in aggregate supply.

6. Supply-side tax cuts in the early 1980s were supposed to increase aggregate supply, thereby increasing output while dampening inflation. But federal spending increased faster than federal revenues, resulting in huge federal deficits, which continued through the 1980s and into the 1990s.

QUESTIONS AND PROBLEMS

1. (Stocks and Flows) Wages and profits are considered flows; the money supply and the federal debt are considered stocks. Explain why this is the case. What is the relationship between the federal budget deficit and the federal debt and between annual investment and the value of the capital stock?

2. (Business Cycles) Some businesses do well during a recession and tend to experience a drop in sales when the economy is recovering. Give some examples of such countercyclical businesses.

3. (Business Cycles) Explain why each of the following is used by the Commerce Department as a component in the index of leading economic indicators:
   a. Average work week
   b. Number of unemployment claims
   c. Orders for consumer goods
   d. New building permits
   e. Inventories
   f. Stock prices
   g. The money supply

4. (U.S. Economic History) During the Vietnam War there was a considerable increase in government spending without much additional taxation. How can the government spend without taking in sufficient tax revenues?

5. (Aggregate Demand and Supply) Explain why a decrease in the aggregate demand curve results in a lower level of employment, given a fixed aggregate supply.

6. (Stagflation) Discuss some causes of the stagflations of 1973 and 1979. What differences are there between these episodes of stagflation and the Great Depression of the 1930s?

7. (Aggregate Demand and Supply) Is it possible for prices to be falling while production and employment are rising? How might this happen?

8. (The Macroeconomy) When someone gets sick, doctors often claim that the body will cure itself. Is it reasonable to believe that the economy also will return to normal business conditions after experiencing a recession, assuming that government takes no action? Why or why not?

9. (Aggregate Demand and Supply) Use an aggregate demand-supply diagram to predict the change in aggregate output and price under the following conditions:
   a. A decrease in wealth
   b. An increase in the resource base
   c. An increase in the price of OPEC oil
   d. An increase in foreign price levels
   e. An increase in the value of the dollar against foreign currencies

10. (Business Cycles) Using the constant (1987) dollar GDP figures from Table A on the inside front cover, identify peak years, trough years, and recession years for the U.S. economy.

11. (Supply-Side Economics) One supply-side measure pushed by the Reagan administration was a cut in income tax rates. Use an aggregate demand-supply diagram to show what the effect was intended to be. Show what might happen if such tax cuts also generated an increase in aggregate spending.

12. (Trade Deficit) Explain how a desire by foreigners to invest in this country (e.g., to buy real estate, Treasury bills, and factories) could foster a trade deficit.

13. (Aggregate Demand) In Chapter 3 we learned that demand curves have a negative slope because of, among other things, a "substitution effect." Does the same kind of "substitution effect" influence the slope of the aggregate demand curve? Explain your answer.

14. (Aggregate Supply) In Chapter 3 we also learned that supply curves have a positive slope because higher prices attract more resources into production of the good whose price has risen. Is there anything about the aggregate supply curve that suggests that such an analysis may be less appropriate in explaining the slope of the aggregate supply curve?

15. (Aggregate Supply) In Chapter 2 we learned about the production possibilities frontier, which shows what the economy is capable of producing. Do you think that aggregate supply and the production possibilities frontier are related? What causes these curves to shift?

16. (Business Cycles) Using the data shown in Exhibit 7, can you decide what changes in output were caused by supply shifts as opposed to demand shifts? What should you look at to answer this question?

17. (Real GDP) Given the information in the case study, what has been the increase in the undeflated value of GDP?

18. (Real GDP) Productivity is usually interpreted as output per unit of labor. What is your estimate of the productivity change between 1940 and 1992?

CHAPTER 6

MEASURING ECONOMIC AGGREGATES AND THE CIRCULAR FLOW OF INCOME

Although Americans account for only 5 percent of the world's population, U.S. output accounts for one-quarter of the world's production. In this chapter you will learn how to keep track of the billions of economic transactions that underpin the U.S. economy—the largest and most complex economy in the history of the world. The scorecard is the national income accounting system, which reflects the performance of the economy as a whole by reducing a huge network of economic activity to a few aggregate measures. This chapter focuses on one of the most important aggregate measures of economic activity: the gross domestic product, or GDP—a term already introduced in the last chapter.

As we shall see, total output can be calculated either from the total spending on output or from the total income generated by producing that output. We examine each approach, show how they are equivalent, and discuss how to adjust for the effects of changes in the price level over time. To help clarify the equalities of the national income accounts, we develop a more sophisticated version of the circular flow model first introduced in Chapter 3.

The major components and important equalities built into the national income accounts are presented as another way of understanding how the economy works—not as a foreign language to be mastered before the next exam. The emphasis is more on economic intuition than on accounting precision. The main part of this chapter provides the background needed for later chapters, but it only scratches the surface. More detail about the national income accounts is offered in the appendix to this chapter. Topics discussed in this chapter include

- Gross national product and gross domestic product
- Expenditure and income approaches
- Disposable income
- Circular flow of income and spending
- Limitations of national income accounting
- Implicit price deflator
- Consumer price index

THE PRODUCT OF A NATION

How do we measure the economy's performance? During much of the seventeenth and eighteenth centuries, when the dominant economic policy was mercantilism, many thought that economic prosperity was best measured by the *stock* of precious metals a nation accumulated. Francois Quesnay (1694–1774) was the first to measure economic activity as a *flow*. In 1758 he published his *Tableau Économique*, a book that described the circular flow of goods and income among different sectors of the economy. His insight was probably inspired by his knowledge of the circular flow of blood in the body—Quesnay was the court physician to King Louis XV of France.

Teaching Tip The federal government provides quarterly estimates of GDP. Figures are annualized assuming that the rate of production in the quarter would continue over twelve months.

Rough measures of national income were developed in England more than two hundred years ago, but detailed calculations built up from microeconomic data were first worked out by Simon Kuznets during the Great Depression. The resulting *national income accounting system* organized tremendous quantities of data collected from a variety of sources around the country. These data are summarized, assembled into a coherent framework, and reported periodically by the federal government. The U.S. national income accounts are the most widely reported and the most highly regarded in the world and have earned their developers Nobel Prizes.

Teaching Tip An exception to the "market value" approach to measuring GDP is government services, which are evaluated at the cost of the resources.

Gross National Product and Gross Domestic Product

Gross national product, or **GNP** The market value of all final goods and services produced by resources supplied by U.S. residents and firms, regardless of location

Gross domestic product, or **GDP**. The market value of all final goods and services produced by resources located in the United States, regardless of who owns those resources

How do the national income accounts keep track of the incredible variety of goods and services produced, from phone service to wedding rings? Between 1941 and 1991, the federal government's broadest measure of production was the **gross national product**, or **GNP**, which measures the market value of all final goods and services produced by resources supplied by U.S. residents and firms, regardless of location of the resources. For example, GNP includes profit earned by a Ford plant in Great Britain but excludes profit earned by a Toyota factory in the United States. Beginning in November of 1991, the federal government began reporting the **gross domestic product**, or **GDP**, which measures the market value of all final goods and services produced by resources located in the United States, regardless of who owns those resources. Thus, for example, GDP would exclude a U.S. firm's overseas profit, but would include profit earned in the United States by foreign companies.

The quantitative differences between GNP and GDP are relatively minor (typically less than 1 percent) for a country such as the United States, because income from foreign ownership of resources located in the United States tends to be offset by income from U.S. resource holdings abroad. Differences between GNP and GDP are more important for countries such as Egypt and Turkey, many of whose citizens work abroad. For example, the income of Turkish citizens working abroad would be included in Turkey's GNP but not in its GDP. Thus, Turkey's GNP is much higher than its GDP. In keeping with the federal government's current reporting policy, this book will refer primarily to GDP.

National Income Accounts

The national income accounts are based on a double-entry bookkeeping system in which sales of aggregate output are recorded on one side and resource payments are recorded on the other side. Therefore, GDP can be measured either by looking at total spending on U.S. production or by looking at total income received from that production. The **expenditure approach** involves adding up the aggregate expenditure on all final goods and services produced during the year. The **income approach** involves adding up the aggregate income earned during the year by those who produce that output.

Expenditure approach A method of calculating GDP that involves adding up expenditures on all final goods and services produced during the year

Income approach A method of calculating GDP that involves adding up all payments to owners of resources used to produce output during the year

The gross domestic product includes only **final goods and services**, which are goods and services sold to the final, or ultimate, user. A toothbrush, a pair of contact lenses, and a bus ride are examples of final goods and services. Whether a sale is to the final user often depends on who buys the product. Your purchase of a chicken from the grocer is reflected in GDP. When a Kentucky Fried Chicken franchise purchases chicken, this transaction is not directly recorded in GDP because the franchise is not the final consumer; only when the chicken is fried and sold to consumers is a sale recorded as part of GDP.

Final goods and services Goods and services sold to final, or ultimate, users

Intermediate goods and services Goods and services purchased for further reprocessing and resale

Intermediate goods and services are those purchased for additional processing and resale, such as the chicken purchased by a franchise. This additional processing may be imperceptible, as when the corner grocer buys canned goods to stock the shelves. Or the intermediate goods can be dramatically altered, as when paint and canvas are transformed into a work of art. Sales of intermediate goods and services are excluded from GDP to avoid the problem of *double counting*, which is counting an item's value more than once. For example, suppose the grocer buys a can of tuna for $0.60 and sells it for $1. If GDP included both the intermediate transaction of $0.60 and the final transaction of $1, that same can of tuna would be counted twice in GDP, and the recorded value of $1.60 would be $0.60 more than the final value of the good. Hence, the gross domestic product counts only the final value of the product. The GDP also ignores secondhand sales, such as used cars, previously owned homes, and used textbooks. These goods were counted as part of GDP when they were initially produced.

Point to Stress Intermediate goods produced in the year but not yet reprocessed or resold are included in inventory figures that count in GDP calculations.

Teaching Tip The *Federal Reserve Bulletin* and the *Survey of Current Business* are good sources of updated data for the expenditure approach. The *Wall Street Journal* also provides expenditure figures when the government releases its quarterly estimates.

Consumption All household purchases of final goods and services

Investment Purchases of output produced during a year but not used for current consumption

Physical capital Manufactured items used to produce goods and services

Inventories Producers' stocks of finished or in-process goods

Point to Stress Consumption is also a very stable component of GDP, whereas investment is relatively unstable.

Point to Stress Financial transactions, such as purchases of newly issued stocks and bonds, provide the funds used for investment. They themselves are not investments.

Government purchases Spending for goods and services by all levels of government

GDP Based on the Expenditure Approach

As we have said, one way to measure the value of GDP is by keeping track of the aggregate expenditure on final goods and services produced in the economy during the year. Perhaps the easiest way to grasp the notion of aggregate expenditure is to divide it into its four components: consumption, investment, government purchases, and net exports. We will discuss each in turn.

Consumption, or more specifically, *personal consumption expenditures*, consist of purchases of final goods and services by households during the year. Consumption is the largest spending category but also the easiest to understand. Along with services, such as dry cleaning and hair cuts, consumption includes purchases of nondurable goods, such as soap and soup, and durable goods, such as stereos and station wagons. Durable goods are those expected to last for more than a year. Consumption accounts for about two-thirds of the total amount spent on final goods and services.

Investment, or more specifically, *gross private domestic investment*, consists of spending during the year on output that is not used for present consumption. Investment in the United States accounts for about 15 percent of the gross domestic product. The most important category of investment is new **physical capital**, such as new buildings, new machinery, and other new manufactured items purchased by firms and used to produce goods and services. Investment also includes new residential construction. Physical capital can range from the smallest screwdriver to the largest steam shovel, from the Dumpster behind your local convenience store to the Sears Tower in Chicago. Investment excludes purchases both of used physical assets, such as existing buildings, and of financial assets, such as stocks and bonds.

Firm inventories are another category of investment. Firm **inventories** are stocks of final goods and goods in process. Inventories could be thought of as buffer stocks, which help insulate the firm against unanticipated changes in the supply of its resources or in the demand for its product. For example, an auto manufacturer maintains stocks of both auto components and finished autos. A *net* increase in inventories during the year is counted as investment, since production added to inventories is not used for current consumption. For example, suppose General Motors sells one hundred thousand fewer cars than expected, so dealer inventories grow by that amount during the year. The gross domestic product will increase by the value of net inventory increases. Using the expenditure approach, you can think of the car dealers as buying this inventory from General Motors. Conversely, a net inventory reduction during the year is counted as negative investment, or *disinvestment*, since inventory reductions represent the sale of output already credited to a prior year's GDP.

Government purchases include spending by all levels of government for goods and services—from clearing snow to clearing court dockets, from library books to the librarian's pay. According to the national income accounts, governments are viewed as the final users of the goods and services they purchase, even though governments presumably function on behalf of the public. Government purchases account for about one-fifth of the total amount spent on final goods and services in the United States. Government

Net exports The value of a country's products purchased by foreigners minus the value of foreign products purchased by a country's residents

Point to Stress Net exports are not the same as the merchandise trade balance (MTB) introduced in Chapter 4. The MTB does not include trade in services.

Aggregate expenditure Total spending on final goods and services at a given price level during a given time period

purchases, and therefore GDP, do not include transfer payments, such as Social Security and welfare benefits. Such payments merely reflect an outright grant from the government to recipients and are not true purchases by the government or true earnings by the recipients.

The final component of aggregate expenditure results from the interaction of the U.S. economy with the rest of the world. **Net exports** equal the value of U.S. exports minus the value of U.S. imports. The net export accounts include not only merchandise trade—that is, commodities—but also so-called *invisibles*, such as earnings from tourism. Prior to 1983 the United States was a net exporter of goods and services, meaning net exports were positive. Since then, net exports have been negative, meaning imports have exceeded exports.

With the expenditure approach, the nation's aggregate expenditure is set equal to GDP. **Aggregate expenditure** is equal to the sum of consumption, C, investment, I, government purchases, G, and net exports, $(X - M)$, which is the value of exports, X, minus the value of imports, M. Summing these spending components yields aggregate expenditure, or GDP:

$$C + I + G + (X - M) = \text{GDP}$$

GDP Based on the Income Approach

Teaching Tip A detailed discussion of the income approach is provided in the appendix.

Aggregate income The sum of all income earned by resource suppliers in an economy during a given time period

Whereas the expenditure approach to GDP involves totaling the aggregate spending on production, the income approach involves adding up the aggregate income arising from that production. The practice of double-entry bookkeeping ensures that the value of aggregate output must equal claims on its value by the individuals who owned the resources used to produce that output: the wages, rent, interest, and profit arising from production. The price of a Hershey Bar represents income to all the resources employed to bring that bar to the grocer's shelf. **Aggregate income** equals the sum of all the income earned by resource suppliers in the economy. Thus, we can say that

Aggregate expenditure = GDP = aggregate income

Value added The difference at each stage of production between the value of a product and the cost of materials needed to make it

Usually a final product is processed by several firms on its way to the consumer. Furniture, for example, starts as raw timber, which is cut by one firm, milled by another, transformed into furniture by a third, wholesaled by a fourth, and retailed by a fifth. Double counting can be avoided either by including only the market value of furniture when sold by a retailer or by carefully *calculating the value added at each stage of production.* The **value added** by each firm equals that firm's selling price minus the amount paid to other firms for materials. The value added at each stage represents income to resource suppliers at that stage. *The sum of the value added at each stage equals the market value of the final good, and the sum of the value added for all final goods and services equals the GDP based on the income approach.* For example, suppose you buy a wooden desk for $200. Because you are the ultimate user of this desk,

EXHIBIT 1

Computation of Value Added for a New Desk

Stage of Production	Sale Value (1)	Cost of Intermediate Goods (2)	Value Added (3)
Logger	$ 20	—	$ 20
Miller	50	20	30
Manufacturer	120	50	70
Retailer	200	120	80
			$200

$200 is the final market value added directly into GDP. Consider the history of that desk. The tree that gave its life for your studies was cut into a log that was sold for $20 to a miller. That log was milled into lumber that sold for $50 to a manufacturer, who built your desk and sold it for $120 to a retailer, who sold the desk to you for $200.

Column (1) of Exhibit 1 lists the selling price at each stage of production. If all of these transactions were added together, the desk would add a total of $390 to GDP. To avoid double counting, we include as part of GDP only the value added at each stage of production, listed in column (3) as the difference between the purchase price and the selling price. The value added at the logging stage was $20. The miller paid $20 for the log and sold the finished lumber for $50, in the process adding $30 to the value. The manufacturer added $70, and the retailer added $80 to the value. The value added at each stage equals the income to all who supplied resources at that stage. For example, the $80 in value added by the retailer represents income to all who contributed resources at that final stage, from the newspaper that carried the retailer's advertising to the driver who provided the so-called free delivery of your desk. The sum of this value added at all stages equals $200, the final market value of the desk and the total income earned by all resource suppliers along the way.

THE CIRCULAR FLOW OF INCOME AND EXPENDITURE

The equalities among GDP, aggregate expenditure, and aggregate income can be clarified by examining the circular flow diagram. The leading actors in the circular flow are domestic *households*, which make the key decisions about how much to consume and how much to save. The supporting actors are *governments*, which make decisions about government purchases, transfers,

Point to Stress Leakages reduce spending on domestically produced goods and services. Injections increase spending on domestically produced goods and services.

Leakage Any diversion of aggregate income from the domestic spending stream; includes saving, taxes, and imports

Injection Any payment of income other than by firms or any spending other than by domestic households; includes investment, government purchases, transfer payments, and exports

and taxes; domestic *firms*, which make production and investment decisions; and those in *the rest of the world* who demand U.S. exports and supply U.S. imports. Whereas the circular flow presented in Chapter 4 included the flow of products and resources, Exhibit 2 concentrates on the flow of income and spending—a flow reflected in dollar amounts.

Income flows through the bottom half of the diagram, and spending flows through the top half. The mainstream flows clockwise around the ring, first as income from firms to households, then as spending from households back to firms. At various points around the loop, the flow is diverted from the mainstream. Any diversion from the mainstream is called a **leakage** from the circular flow. In the lower portion of the loop, taxes paid to governments represent a leakage from the income stream. In the upper portion of the loop, spending on imports and saving represent leakages from the domestic spending stream.

Leakages from the circular flow are offset by injections into the mainstream. Any payment of income made into the income stream other than by firms or any expenditure made into the spending stream other than by domestic households is called an **injection**. In the bottom half of the circular flow, transfer payments are injections into the income stream. In the upper half of the diagram, investment, government purchases, and receipts from exports are injections into the expenditure stream. As we shall see, the sum of the leakages must equal the sum of the injections.

The Income Half of the Circular Flow

Although we could pick up the flow at any point around the ring, the logic of the model is clearest if we begin at juncture (1), where U.S. firms make their production and investment decisions. The circular flow is a continuous process, but production usually must occur before income is earned and output can be sold. For example, General Motors must build autos before autos can be sold. Therefore, firms must decide how much to produce before spending actually takes place, so they must estimate the amount of output that will be sold and then produce accordingly.

Teaching Tip See the appendix for an explanation of the calculation of disposable income in the national income accounts.

Aggregate output, or GDP, gives rise to an equal amount of aggregate income. Households supply their land, labor, capital, and entrepreneurial ability to firms and receive rent, wages, interest, and profit. Here we make a simplifying assumption that firms pay out all profits to firm owners and retain no earnings. We can therefore say that at juncture (1) GDP equals aggregate income. Not all that income becomes available to households. At juncture (2) governments collect taxes, T, which are used to purchase goods and services and make transfer payments. In reality the government imposes many kinds of taxes, such as personal and corporate income taxes and sales taxes. But for simplicity we lump all those taxes together as T. Some of these tax dollars are returned to the income stream as transfer payments, R, at point (3). Consequently, aggregate income has been reduced by taxes but increased by transfer payments. By subtracting taxes and adding

EXHIBIT 2

The Circular Flow of Income and Expenditure

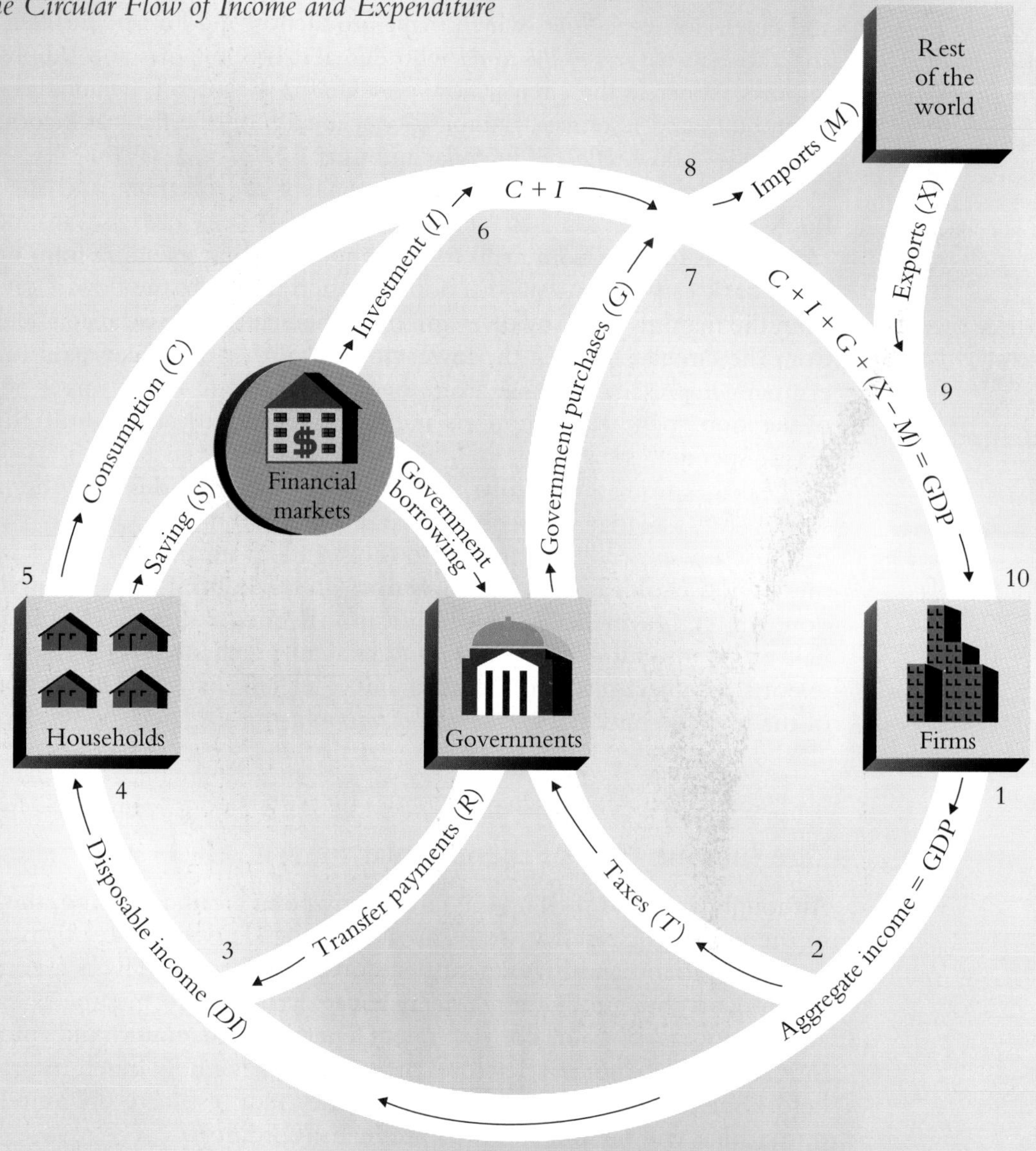

The circular flow diagram captures important relationships in the economy. The bottom half of the diagram depicts the income flow arising from production. At juncture (1) GDP equals aggregate income. Taxes leak out of the flow at point (2), but transfer payments augment the flow at point (3). Aggregate income minus taxes plus transfer payments equals disposable income, which flows to households at juncture (4).

The top half of the diagram shows the flow of expenditures on GDP. At juncture (5) households split their disposable income between consumption and saving. The saving stream flows into financial markets, where it is channeled to government borrowing and to business investment. At point (6) the injection of investment augments the spending stream. At juncture (7) government purchases represent another injection into the circular flow. At point (8) imports are a leakage of spending, and at point (9) exports are an injection of spending into the circular flow. Consumption plus investment plus government purchases plus exports minus imports equals the aggregate expenditure on GDP faced by firms at point (10).

Disposable income The income households have available to spend or save after paying taxes and receiving transfer payments

Point to Stress *NT* will be negative if transfer payments exceed tax revenues.

transfers, we transform aggregate income into **disposable income**, ***DI***, which flows to households at juncture (4).[1] Disposable income is the take-home pay, which households can spend or save.

The bottom half of this circular flow can be viewed as the *income half* because it focuses on the income stemming from production. Two measures of income are identified: (1) aggregate income, which is the total income arising from producing GDP, and (2) disposable income, *DI*, which is the income that remains after taxes have been subtracted and transfers added. To streamline the discussion, we will define *net taxes* as taxes, *T*, minus transfer payments, *R*, or $(T - R)$. Net taxes can be represented more simply as *NT*. So disposable income equals GDP minus net taxes. Put another way, we can say that aggregate income equals disposable income plus net taxes:

$$\textbf{GDP} = \textbf{Aggregate income} = DI + NT$$

To review: At juncture (4) firms have produced output and have paid resource suppliers; governments have collected taxes and distributed transfers; households have received their disposable income and must now decide how much to spend and how much to save. Firms in particular are eager to see how much consumers and others plan to spend, since firms have already produced the output and have paid resource suppliers. Should any output go unsold, suppliers are stuck with it; unsold goods must become part of inventories.

The Expenditure Half of the Circular Flow

We are most interested in how disposable income is actually allocated, or *disposed* of. Households have only two choices in allocating disposable income; they can spend it or save it. More precisely, the stream of disposable income splits in two at juncture (5): part flows to consumption, *C*, and the remainder to saving, *S*. Thus,

$$DI = C + S$$

Financial markets Banks and other institutions that facilitate the flow of funds from savers to borrowers

Spending on consumption remains in the circular flow and represents the most important component of aggregate expenditure, about two-thirds of the total. Household saving flows to financial markets, identified by the small circle. **Financial markets** consist of banks and other institutions that provide a link between savers and borrowers. For simplicity, we show households as the only savers, although governments, firms, and the rest of the world could be savers, too. The primary borrowers are firms and governments, but households borrow as well, particularly for new homes, and the rest of the world also borrows. In reality, financial markets should be connected to all four economic actors, but we have simplified the exhibit to keep it from looking like a plate of spaghetti.

1. This is a rough definition of disposable income. A more precise definition, based on a fuller examination of the national income accounts, is provided in the appendix.

Since firms in our simplified model pay resource suppliers an amount equal to the entire value of output, firms have no revenue left for investment. Thus, if firms want to invest, they must go through financial markets to borrow from households that save. Firms must borrow to finance purchases of physical capital plus any increases in their inventories. Households also borrow from financial markets to purchase new homes. Therefore, investment, I, consists of spending on capital investment by firms including inventory increases and spending on residential construction. Investment represents the second injection of spending into the circular flow, shown at juncture (6), and brings aggregate spending at that point to $C + I$.

Example The last U.S. federal budget surplus occurred in 1969.

Governments must borrow whenever their total outlays—transfer payments plus purchases of goods and services—exceed their revenues. Simply put, governments must borrow whenever they incur deficits. A **government budget deficit** is a flow variable that measures for a particular period the amount by which one flow, total government outlays, exceeds another flow, total government revenues. In contrast, **government debt** is a stock variable that measures the net accumulation of all prior deficits. For example, in 1992 federal outlays exceeded federal revenues by over $300 billion, resulting in a deficit that raised the federal debt that year to $4 trillion. Government outlays consist of transfer payments and purchases of goods and services. Transfer payments were shown as an injection to the income stream in the lower half of the circular flow. Government purchases of goods and services, represented by G at juncture (7), are an injection of spending into the circular flow.

Government budget deficit A flow variable measuring, for a particular time period, the amount by which one flow variable, total government outlays, exceeds another flow variable, total government revenues

Government debt A stock variable measuring, at a particular point in time, the net accumulation of all prior budget deficits

Some spending on consumption, investment, and government purchases goes for imports. Since spending on imports does not flow to U.S. producers, imports are a leakage from the circular flow, reflected by M at juncture (8). But the rest of the world also buys U.S. products, so foreign spending on our exports is an injection into the circular flow, reflected by X at juncture (9). The net impact of *the rest of the world* on aggregate expenditure equals exports minus imports, $(X - M)$, or net exports.

Point to Stress $(X - M)$ can be either positive or negative.

The upper half of the circular flow can be viewed as the expenditure half because it focuses on the components that make up aggregate expenditure: consumption, C, investment, I, government purchases, G, and net exports, $(X - M)$. Aggregate expenditure flows into firms at juncture (10). The amount spent in the economy equals the market value of aggregate output in the economy, or GDP. In other words,

$$\textbf{GDP} = \textbf{aggregate expenditure} = C + I + G + (X - M)$$

Leakages and Injections

Let's step back now and consider the big picture. In the lower half of the circular flow, aggregate income equals disposable income plus net taxes. In the upper half, aggregate expenditure equals the sum of the spending on U.S. output by each sector. As noted earlier, *the aggregate expenditure on output equals the aggregate income arising from that output.* Thus, aggregate income (disposable income plus net taxes) equals aggregate expenditure (spending by each sector), or

$$\underbrace{DI + NT}_{\text{Aggregate income}} = \underbrace{C + I + G + (X - M)}_{\text{Aggregate expenditure}}$$

We know, however, that disposable income equals consumption plus saving. If we substitute $C + S$ for DI in the above equation, then add M to both sides and subtract C from both sides, we get

$$S + NT + M = I + G + X$$

Point to Stress Calling *NT* a leakage assumes that tax revenues exceed transfer payments. If transfer payments exceed tax revenues, *NT* is an injection.

On the left-hand side, saving plus net taxes plus imports represent the leakages from the circular flow. On the right-hand side, investment plus government purchases plus exports represent the injections into the circular flow. This leakages-injections equation demonstrates a second accounting identity: according to the principles of double-entry bookkeeping, *the leakages from the circular flow must equal the injections into that flow.*

Planned Investment Versus Actual Investment

Point to Stress The distinction between planned and actual investment is an important component of discussions of macroeconomic equilibrium in later chapters.

Planned investment The amount of investment firms plan to undertake during a year

Actual investment The amount of investment actually undertaken during a year; equals planned investment plus unplanned changes in inventories

As we have said, at juncture (1) in the circular flow, firms make production decisions plus decisions about how much they plan to invest. Their investment plans may go awry, however, if aggregate expenditure does not match their expectations. Suppose, for example, that firms produce \$5.0 trillion in output, but the spending components add up to only \$4.8 trillion. Firms will end up with \$200 billion in unsold products, which must be added to their inventories. Since increases in inventories are counted as investment, *actual* investment is \$200 billion greater than firms had *planned*. Note the distinction between **planned investment**, the amount firms plan to invest before they know how much will be sold, and **actual investment**, which includes both planned investment and unplanned changes in inventories. Unplanned increases in inventories will cause firms to decrease their production and unplanned decreases will cause firms to increase their production. Only when there are no unplanned changes in inventories will the level of GDP be at what we will call an equilibrium level—that is, a level that can be sustained. Only in equilibrium will the planned investment equal the actual investment.

The relation between actual and planned investment will be examined more closely in Chapter 9; for now, you need only understand that the national income accounting system reflects *actual* investment, not necessarily *planned* investment. *The national income accounts always look at economic activity after transactions have occurred—after the dust has settled.* The actual leakages must always equal the actual injections.

In summary, the practice of double-entry bookkeeping provides the underpinnings for national income accounting. Economic activity can be measured in two fundamental ways: by determining the market value of spending on all final goods and services produced in the economy during the year or by totaling the income arising from that production. The national income accounting system was developed over the years to trace economic activity consisting of billions of individual transactions. Such an all-purpose system is bound to have limitations, as we shall see next.

Limitations of National Income Accounting

Teaching Tip The national income accounts also ignore other measures of welfare such as life expectancy and infant mortality rates. Welfare measures should also consider the distribution of income, not just total national income.

Imagine the difficulty of developing an accounting system that must capture the subtleties of such a complex and dynamic economy. In the interest of clarity and simplicity, some features of the economy are neglected; others receive perhaps inordinate weight. In this section we examine some limitations of the national income accounting system, beginning with productive activity that is not captured by GDP.

Some Production Is Not Included in GDP

With some minor exceptions, GDP includes only those products that are sold in formal markets. It thus misses all household production. Child care, meal preparation, laundry, house cleaning, leaf raking—all household services not purchased in the market—are excluded from GDP. Thus an economy in which households are largely self-sufficient will have a much lower GDP than will an economy in which households specialize and sell goods and services to one another through markets.

This irregularity of the national income accounts has influenced the recorded growth of GDP in recent years. During the 1950s more than 80 percent of mothers with small children stayed at home caring for the family, but all this care counted not one whit toward GDP. Today more than half the mothers with small children are in the work force, where their labor services are reflected in GDP. Moreover, with more mothers working, households are more likely to purchase goods and services that formerly were produced by the household, such as meals and child-care services. Consequently, the measured GDP has increased, both because more mothers are in the work force and because activities that had been carried out within the household are now more frequently recorded as market transactions. Typically, the less developed the economy, the more economic activity is "do-it-yourself." Because official GDP figures ignore most home production, these figures tend to understate the quantity of goods and services actually available to households in less developed countries.

Underground economy An expression used to describe all market exchange that goes unreported either because it is illegal or because those involved want to evade taxes

Estimates of GDP also fail to capture transactions when no official records are kept. The **underground economy** is an expression used to describe all market exchange that goes unreported either because the activity itself is illegal or because those involved want to evade taxes on otherwise legal activity. Although there are no official estimates on the extent of the underground economy, most economists agree that it is substantial. One Census Bureau

sonous gas leaks. These negative externalities—costs that fall on those not directly involved in the transactions—are largely ignored in GDP accounting, even though they diminish the quality of life and may limit future production. To the extent that growth in GDP also involves growth in such negative externalities, a rising GDP may not be as attractive as it would first appear.

Gross Domestic Product Is Really Gross

Depreciation The value of capital stock used up during a year in producing GDP

As GDP is produced, some capital wears out, such as the delivery truck that finally dies, and some capital becomes obsolete, such as an outmoded computer. **Depreciation** measures the value of the capital stock used up in the production process. The gross domestic product is called "gross" because it fails to take into account this depreciation. A measure of output that nets out depreciation is discussed in the appendix to this chapter.

GDP Values All Output Equally

In GDP, the market price of output is used as the measure of its value. Therefore, each dollar spent purchasing hand guns is counted in GDP the same as each dollar spent purchasing Bibles. Positive economic analysis tries to avoid making value judgments about how people choose to spend their money. Because the level of GDP provides no information about its composition, some economists question whether GDP is a good measure of the country's economic welfare. For example, at a time when many people in the nation are hungry and homeless, Americans spend billions of dollars on tobacco products, even though these products are linked to illness and death.

GDP Comparisons Across Countries Are Tricky

Teaching Tip GDP comparisons also are difficult because each country has a different currency. Changes in exchange rates can change the dollar value of a country's GDP even if real GDP remains unchanged.

Observers are tempted to make much of international differences in various economic measures, particularly when something like GDP per capita is measured, but such comparisons are fraught with complications. The United States has perhaps the most thorough and systematic national income accounting system in the world. Some less developed countries, however, are simply too poor to support the sophisticated surveys required to monitor economic activity. Also, poor countries rely more on household production, which does not get counted in GDP. Thus, the national income statistics generated in poor countries tend to be unreliable, and international comparisons of GDP data should be viewed with caution.

Despite the limitations and inaccuracies associated with official GDP estimates, the trend of GDP over time provides a fairly accurate picture of the overall movement of the U.S. economy. Inflation, however, distorts the direct comparability of dollar amounts from one year to the next. In the next section we examine ways of adjusting GDP for changes in the economy's price level.

Accounting for Price Changes

Current dollar value The value of dollars that are actually paid or received at the time of a transaction; nominal dollar values of national output

Nominal value Value measured in current-year dollars

Real GDP The value of GDP measured in terms of dollars of fixed purchasing power

Teaching Tip Explain that the percentage change in real GDP is approximately equal to the percentage change in nominal GDP minus the percentage change in the price level (as measured by the implicit price deflator).

Base year A reference year against which other years are measured

As noted earlier, the national income accounts are based on the market values of the goods and services produced in a particular year. The gross domestic product is therefore computed in **current dollar values**—that is, in the dollars actually paid or received at the time of the transaction. If GDP is based on current dollars, then the national income accounts measure the **nominal value** of national output. Hence, the current-dollar GDP, or nominal GDP, is based on the prices prevailing at the time of the transaction.

The system of national income accounting based on current, or nominal, dollars allows us to make comparisons among income or expenditure components in a particular year. But the economy's price level tends to change over time, making current-dollar comparisons across years less meaningful. For example, between 1979 and 1980, nominal GDP increased by about 9 percent. That sounds like an impressive growth in production for one year, but the economy's price level grew at about the same rate. Thus, the growth in nominal GDP between 1979 and 1980 was the result of inflation. **Real GDP**—that is, GDP measured in terms of the actual amount produced—was unchanged. You were already introduced to this general idea in the last chapter.

To make meaningful comparisons of GDP across years, we must adjust GDP for changes in the price level, so that we focus only on *real* changes in production, or changes measured in dollars of constant purchasing power. To do this, we must devise a way to compare the price level in one year with the price level in another year.

The Price Index

To compare the price level over time, we must first select a reference point that can be used to construct index numbers. An *index number* compares the value of some variable in a particular year to its value in some base, or reference, year. To see how index numbers are used, consider the simplest case imaginable. Suppose bread is the only good produced in the economy. As a reference point against which to measure price changes, we choose the price of bread in some specified year. The year selected is called the **base year**; prices in other years are expressed in terms of the base-year price.

Suppose the base year chosen is 1991, when a loaf of bread in our simple economy sold for \$1.25. Let's say the price of bread increased to \$1.30 in 1992, and to \$1.40 in 1993. We construct a *price index* by dividing each year's price by the price in the base year and then multiplying by 100, as shown in Exhibit 3. For 1991, the base year, we divide the base price of bread by itself, \$1.25/\$1.25, so the price index in the base year equals $1 \times 100 = 100$. *In the base period the index is always 100.* The index in 1992 is \$1.30/\$1.25, which equals 1.04, which when multiplied by 100 equals 104. In 1993 the index is \$1.40/\$1.25, or 1.12, which when multiplied by 100 equals 112. Thus, the index in 1992 is 4 percent higher than in the base year; in 1993 it is 12 percent higher than in the base year.

EXHIBIT 3

Hypothetical Example of a Price Index (base year = 1991)

Year	Price of Bread in Current Year (1)	Price of Bread in Base Year (2)	Price Index (3) = (1)/(2) × 100
1991	$1.25	$1.25	100
1992	1.30	1.25	104
1993	1.40	1.25	112

The price index not only permits comparisons between the base year and any other year but also allows for comparisons between any two years. For example, what if you were presented with the indexes for 1992 and 1993 and asked to determine what happened to the price level between the two years? By dividing the 1993 price index by the 1992 price index, 112/104, you would find that the price level increased by 7.7 percent.

This section has shown how to develop a price index assuming we already know the price level each year. Determining the price level is a bit more involved, as we now see.

Consumer Price Index

Consumer price index (CPI) A measure over time of the cost of a fixed "market basket" of consumer goods and services

Teaching Tip The "market basket" is based on data from the government's Consumer Expenditure Survey and is updated every ten years.

Perhaps the price index most familiar to you is the **consumer price index**, or **CPI**, which measures changes over time in the cost of buying the "market basket" of goods and services purchased by a typical family. The cost of buying this same basket each year is computed based on the prices prevailing each year. Changes in the cost of this basket are often referred to as changes in the "cost of living." To show how the CPI is calculated for a simple case, we will develop a hypothetical market basket. For simplicity, suppose a typical family's market basket for the year includes 365 packages of Twinkies, 500 gallons of fuel oil, and 12 months of cable TV service. Prices in the base year are listed in column (2) of Exhibit 4. The annual cost of each product in the base year is found by multiplying price times quantity, as shown in column (3). The total cost of such a market basket in the base year is shown at the bottom of column (3) to be $918.85.

Current-year prices are listed in column (4). Notice that not all prices changed by the same amount. The price of fuel oil increased by 50 percent, but the price of Twinkies actually declined. The cost of purchasing that same basket in the current year is $1,214.25, shown as the total of column (5). To compute the consumer price index, we simply divide the total cost in the current year by the total cost of that same basket in the base year, $1,214.25/$918.85, then multiply by 100. This calculation yields 132.1. We could say that the "cost of living" has increased by 32.1 percent, although not all prices increased by the same percentage.

EXHIBIT 4

Hypothetical Market Basket Used to Develop the Consumer Price Index

Good or Service	Quantity in Market Basket (1)	Prices in Base Year (2)	Cost of Basket in Base Year (3) = (1) × (2)	Prices in Current Year (4)	Cost of Basket in Current Year (5) = (1) × (4)
Twinkies	365 packages	$ 0.49/package	$178.85	$ 0.45	$ 164.25
Fuel Oil	500 gallons	1.00/gallon	500.00	1.50	750.00
Cable TV	12 months	20.00/month	240.00	25.00	300.00
			$918.85		$1,214.25

Point to Stress
Changes in the CPI are used to adjust social security benefits and food stamp benefits. Some collective bargaining agreements tie wage adjustments to the CPI.

The federal government uses the average price level between 1982 and 1984 as the base value to calculate the CPI for about four hundred items. These items are chosen as representative of the bundle purchased by a typical urban household. The CPI is reported each month based on price data collected from about eighteen thousand sellers in fifty-six localities across the country. In reality, of course, each household consumes a unique bundle of goods, so we could develop ninety-five million CPIs—one for each household.

GDP Price Deflator

GDP implicit price deflator A comprehensive price index of all goods and services included in the gross domestic product

The consumer price index reflects the average change in the price of a representative basket of consumer goods. A more comprehensive index, the **GDP implicit price deflator**, introduced in the previous chapter, keeps track of price changes for *all production* in the economy. Exhibit 5 illustrates how to compute this price index. Again, for simplicity, we assume that the economy produces only three outputs—Twinkies, fuel oil, and cable TV service—but in fact the GDP implicit price deflator captures price changes for the thousands of goods and services produced. Total output in the current year is listed in column (1). Current prices are listed in column (2), and current expenditures in column (3). Current expenditures on each item equal the output in the current year multiplied by the price in the current year.

The current-year GDP is simply the sum of expenditures on all items, which equals $51,750 for this hypothetical economy. What would the value of this same output be if, instead of using current-year prices, we used the prices prevailing in the base year? All we need do is substitute the base-year prices for the current-year prices and recompute total expenditures. Column (4) lists the base-year prices. Multiplying these prices by the quantities listed in column (1) yields the base-year equivalent expenditures in column (5).

Whereas GDP in current prices, or nominal GDP, is $51,750, GDP computed in base-year prices, or real GDP, is $41,350. The price index, in this case called the GDP implicit price deflator, is found by dividing expenditures in current-year prices by expenditures on that same output using base-year

EXHIBIT 5

Hypothetical Data Used to Develop the GDP Implicit Price Deflator

Good or Service	Output in Current Year (1)	Prices in Current Year (2)	Expenditures in Current Year (3) = (1) × (2)	Base-Year Prices (4)	Base-Year Equivalent Expenditure (5) = (1) × (4)
Twinkies	15,000 packages	$ 0.45/package	$ 6,750	$ 0.49	$ 7,350
Fuel Oil	10,000 gallons	1.50/gallon	15,000	1.00	10,000
Cable TV	1,200 months	25.00/month	30,000	20.00	24,000
			$51,750		$41,350

Teaching Tip Explain that this method is used to calculate the overall implicit price deflator because the government actually deflates each component of GDP with a separate deflator and then sums the results to find real GDP.

prices, then multiplying by 100. In our example the implicit price deflator equals 125.2 ($51,750/$41,350 × 100). This deflator says that, on average, prices in the current year are 25.2 percent higher than prices in the base year. *We can find the GDP implicit price deflator for any year by dividing nominal GDP in that year by real GDP in that year, then multiplying by 100.* Thus,

GDP implicit price deflator = (nominal GDP/real GDP) × 100

Suppose nominal GDP increases in a given year. Part of this increase may simply be the result of inflation—pure hot air. To *deflate* GDP—that is, to take out the hot air—we hold prices constant, thereby eliminating increases due solely to increases in the price level. The calculations required to develop real GDP for the U.S. economy involve thousands of prices, but the principle is the same as in our simple example. The federal government has deflated GDP over time by applying 1987 prices to the output produced each year. The record of the U.S. GDP since 1960 is presented in Exhibit 6. The blue line indicates nominal GDP, or GDP measured in the prices that prevailed each year. The red line indicates real GDP, or GDP measured in 1987 prices. Notice that for years prior to 1987, real GDP exceeds nominal GDP because the 1987 prices used to compute real GDP on average exceed the prices that prevailed prior to 1987. After 1987, however, real GDP is below nominal GDP because 1987 prices on average are below the prices since 1987. Real GDP and nominal GDP are identical in the base year, 1987, since for that year 1987 prices are used to compute both measures of GDP. The GDP implicit price deflator is reported every three months, or every quarter, along with reports of GDP growth.

Point to Stress The GDP implicit price deflator uses a different basket of goods each year. The CPI uses the same basket of goods each year.

Price indexes are weighted averages of various prices. Whereas the implicit price deflator includes the prices of *all* final domestic production in a year, including capital goods, the CPI focuses on the prices of a market basket of specific items consumed by a typical household—just a sample of current production. Since consumers buy imported goods as well as domestically produced goods, a sample of imported goods is included in the CPI market basket. Two other indexes computed by the U.S. government are the producer price index and the export price index.

EXHIBIT 6

Comparison of GDP Using Current and Base-Year Prices Since 1960

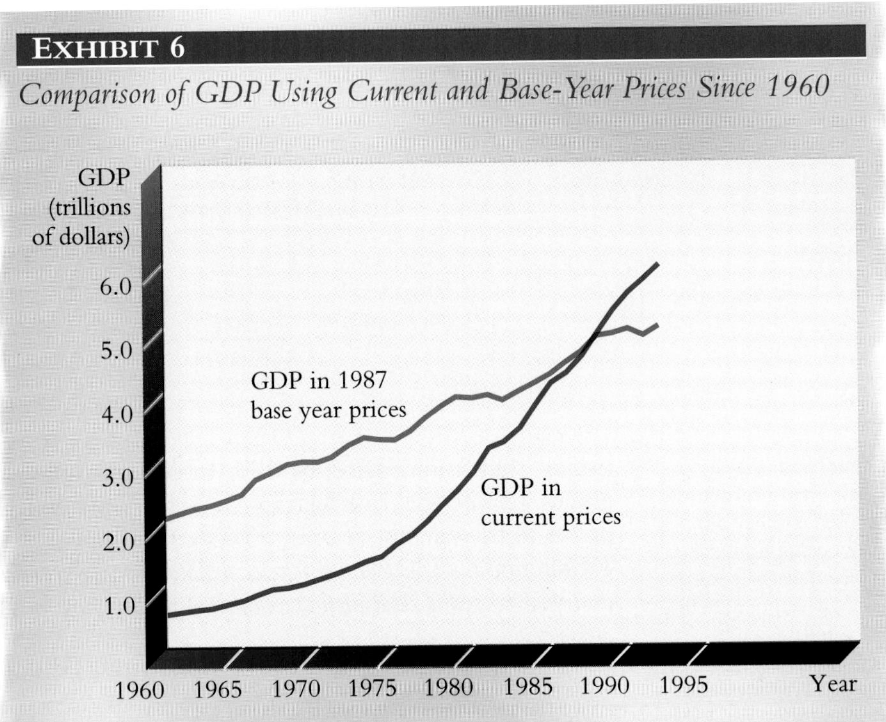

Since 1960 GDP measured in current prices has increased every year. Much of that increase, however, has been due to price changes. Real GDP, measured in 1987 prices, has increased more slowly and has fallen during some years.

Source: *Economic Report of the President,* January 1993.

Problems with Inflation Measures

Teaching Tip Inflation is discussed in detail in Chapter 7.

There is no perfect way to measure changes in the price level. All price indexes involve certain distortions or biases. As already noted, the quality and variety of products are, on average, improving all the time, so some price increases may be as much a reflection of quality improvements as of inflation. For example, the computing power per dollar cost of personal computers has increased sharply in the last decade. There have been some attempts to account for quality differences over time in calculating changes in the price level, but these efforts fail to reflect all quality changes. Thus we say there is a *quality bias,* since each price index assumes that quality remains relatively constant over time even though quality has generally improved. As a result, *the true extent of inflation tends to be overstated.*

With the CPI, inflation tends to be overstated for another reason. Recall that the CPI, in order to focus on the pure effect of price changes, holds constant the kind and amount of goods and services in the typical market basket. But not all prices change by the same percentage. And a family would probably respond to changes in relative prices by consuming more of the relatively cheaper goods and less of the relatively more expensive goods.

Because the CPI calculations hold constant the bundle of commodities consumed over time, this approach does not recognize that consumers adjust to changes in relative prices. The CPI calculations thus imply uneconomical consumer behavior, thereby *overstating the true extent of inflation experienced by the typical family.* The implicit price deflator calculates the effects of inflation based on the quantities of goods actually produced each year. In the next chapter we will take a closer look at inflation.

CONCLUSION

Necessity was the mother of invention in the development of the national income accounts. The Great Depression created the demand for more information about the economy. The national income accounts are not perfect, but they do offer a reasonably accurate measure of year-to-year movements in the economy. The national income accounts are published in much greater detail than the preceding discussion suggests. The appendix to this chapter provides some of that detail.

This chapter explained how to adjust GDP for changes in the economy's price level. In the following chapters we will often refer to distinctions between real and nominal values. Though no price index is perfect, the price indexes now in use provide reasonably good measures of the trend in price levels over time.

SUMMARY

1. The gross domestic product measures the market value of all final goods and services produced during the year by resources located in the United States, regardless of who owns those resources. There are two ways of measuring gross domestic product: the expenditure approach and the income approach. The expenditure approach involves adding up the market value of all final goods and services produced in the economy during the year. The income approach involves adding up all the income generated as a result of production during the year.

2. The circular flow of income summarizes the flow of income and spending through the economy. Disposable income is either spent or saved. Saving and net taxes represent leakages from the circular flow. These leakages must equal the injections into the circular flow: investment, government purchases, and net exports.

3. GDP reflects mostly recorded market exchanges; household production and the underground economy are not included. Improvements in the quality and variety of goods are generally not reflected in GDP either. In other ways GDP may overstate the true amount of production that occurs. GDP fails to account for depreciation of the capital stock or for any externalities arising from production.

4. Nominal GDP in a particular year values output based on market prices prevailing that year. To examine real GDP over time, nominal GDP must be adjusted to filter out the effects of changes in the price level. Two price indexes used to convert nominal GDP to real GDP are the consumer price index and the implicit price deflator. Although no adjustment for changes in the price level is perfect, an examination of real GDP over time provides a useful picture of the trend in economic activity.

Questions and Problems

1. (National Income Accounting) Identify the component of aggregate expenditure to which each of the following belongs:
   a. Purchase of a new Japanese automobile
   b. Purchase of one hour of legal counsel by a household
   c. Construction of a new house
   d. An increase in semiconductor inventories over last year's level
   e. Acquisition of ten new police cars for a city

2. (Circular Flow) Suppose that consumers decide to cut spending by 20 percent. This will cause a rise in firms' inventories. How will such inventories, which have accumulated unexpectedly, be financed by the firms?

3. (Injections and Leakages) Explain why injections must equal leakages if aggregate expenditure is equal to aggregate income.

4. (Leakages and Injections) Japan has one of the highest saving rates in the world. Some economists say it is because Japan has a policy of forced early retirement; others say it is because the country lacks a social security system such as the one in the United States; and still others say it is because of the extraordinary cost of buying living space. Expand the equation of leakages and injections found in this chapter to include net exports, and discuss the Japanese situation.

5. (Investment) In the national income accounts, one part of measured investment is net changes in inventories. Last year's inventories are subtracted from this year's inventories to obtain a net change. Explain why this variable is considered part of the national income. Also, discuss why it is not sufficient to measure inventories only for the current year. (Remember the difference between stocks and flows.)

6. (Underground Economy) Many underdeveloped countries do not use checking accounts. If such countries placed high income taxes on the working population, what do you expect would happen to their underground economies? Why is the use of currency so essential to the underground economy?

7. (Price Index) Home computers and video cassette recorders have not been part of the U.S. economy for very long, and both goods have been decreasing in price and improving in quality. What problems does this situation pose for people who are responsible for computing a price index?

8. (Price Index) Compute a new price index for the data in Exhibit 5 in this chapter, given that the current price of fuel oil is \$0.46 per gallon. Is the current price level higher or lower than that of the base year?

9. (Price Index) The health expenditure component of the price index has been steadily rising. How might this index be biased by quality and substitution effects? Are there any substitutes for health care?

10. (Inflation) Inflation is a continuous and prolonged rise in the level of prices. Hyperinflation is unusually high rates of inflation—for example, 40 percent per month. Who would be hurt by hyperinflation? How would a government cope with the increased demand for currency?

11. (National Income Accounting) Suppose a company produces something nobody wants. Since production of the good generates income to the resources employed, it is included in GDP on the income side. How would it be counted on the expenditure side?

12. (Circular Flow) Using the national income identity in which aggregate income equals aggregate expenditure, show how government budget deficits must be financed from a combination of imbalances between (a) exports and imports and (b) saving and investment.

13. (Price Index) Consider the following data.

Good	*Current Output Level (units)*	*Typical Household Consumption Level (units)*	*Base Price (per unit)*	*Current Price (per unit)*
Clothing	100,000	2	$10	$12
Food	120,000	3	2	4
Durables	6,000	1	50	40

   a. Calculate the rate of price increase from the base period to the current period, using both the implicit GDP deflator and the consumer price index methods.
   b. Explain why the two measures are different.
   c. Which is better?

14. (Gross Domestic Product) Explain why each of the following should be taken into account when GDP data are used to compare the "level of well-being" in different countries.
   a. Population levels
   b. Distribution of income
   c. The amount of production that takes place *outside* of markets (e.g., housekeeping by a family member)
   d. The length of the average work week
   e. The degree of pollution in the environment

15. (National Income Accounting) Much of nontransfer government spending is for salaries of civil servants rather than the purchase of goods and services produced in the private sector. How is such production measured in the national accounts? What alternatives to this method can you suggest?

16. (Leakages and Injections) Explain the significance of distinguishing between *ex ante* (planned) and *ex post* (actual) leakages and injections. Which is of more importance for analyzing the stability of aggregate GDP?

17. (GDP Deflator) At the end of 1991 the government changed the base year used for calculating real GDP from 1982 to 1987. This change created an unusual situation: during the second quarter of 1991 the real GDP grew using 1987 prices but fell using 1982 prices. How could this happen?

18. (Consumer Price Index) One form of the CPI that has been advocated by lobbying groups is a "CPI for the elderly." The Bureau of Labor Statistics currently produces only indexes for "all urban households" and "urban wage earners and clerical workers." Should the BLS produce such an index for the elderly?

19. (Tracking a $6 Trillion Economy) Measuring aggregate GDP in real terms requires using "constant dollars" for prices. If a good has improved in quality, how could the "constant dollar prices" be adjusted to reflect this?

20. (Tracking a $6 Trillion Economy) As the case study suggests, measuring services in the national accounts tends to be more difficult than measuring manufacturing output. Discuss the kinds of problems one would face in measuring the service output of a car insurance firm.

APPENDIX
A Closer Look at the National Income Accounts

This chapter has focused on two key definitions of output and income: gross domestic product and disposable income. Although these two measures will be of most interest in subsequent chapters, other economic aggregates also convey useful information and receive media attention. In this appendix we examine these other aggregate measures.

Recall that the *gross domestic product*, or *GDP*, measures the market value of all final goods and services produced by resources located in the United States, regardless of who owns those resources. The *gross national product*, or *GNP*, measures the market value of all final goods and services produced by resources supplied by U.S. residents and firms, regardless of the location of those resources. GNP equals GDP plus receipts from resource income from the rest of the world minus payments of resource income to the rest of the world. Actual differences between the two measures for a country such as the United States are tiny. For example, the GDP was $5.95 trillion in 1992: by adding resource income from the rest of the world and subtracting resource payments to the rest of the world, we convert GDP of $5.95 trillion into GNP of $5.96 trillion. Throughout this appendix, GNP will serve as basis for a more detailed breakdown of the national income accounts. We begin by accounting for capital depreciation.

Net National Product

In the course of producing GNP, some capital stock becomes worn out, grows obsolete, or is damaged during the year. For example, a new truck that logs a hundred thousand miles its first year has been subject to wear and tear and therefore has a diminished value as a resource. A truer picture of the *net* production that actually occurs during the year is found by subtracting this *depreciation* from GNP. The **net national product** equals GNP minus depreciation—the value of the capital stock used up in the production process.

We can now distinguish between two definitions of investment. **Gross investment** measures the value of all investment during the period, including investment required to replace capital used up during the production process. Gross investment is used in computing GNP. **Net investment** equals gross investment minus depreciation. The economy's productive abilities depend on what happens to net investment. If net investment is negative—that is, if depreciation exceeds gross investment—the capital stock declines, so its contribution to output declines as well.[3] If net investment is zero, the capital stock remains constant, as does its contribution to output. And if net investment is positive, the capital stock grows, as does its contribution to the economy's ability to produce.

As the names imply, the *gross* national product (GNP) includes *gross* investment and the *net* national product (NNP) includes *net* investment. If we let D represent the value of depreciation and I' net investment, then $I - D = I'$ and

$$\mathbf{GNP} - \boldsymbol{D} = \mathbf{NNP} = \boldsymbol{C} + \boldsymbol{I'} + \mathbf{G} + (\boldsymbol{X} - \boldsymbol{M})$$

Exhibit 7 presents an example of calculating net national product by subtracting depreciation from GNP. Developing a figure for depreciation involves much guesswork. For example, what is the appropriate measure of depreciation for the parking lots at Disney World, the metal display shelves at Wal-Mart, or the 5,000-gallon casks used to age wine in the Napa Valley?

3. This discussion assumes there is no major change in inventories during the period. As we have said, changes in inventories are reflected in investment. A major reduction in inventories could result in a negative net investment even when the capital stock has not declined.

EXHIBIT 7

Deriving Net National Product and National Income Using 1992 Data (in trillions of dollars)

Gross national product (GNP)	$5.96
Minus depreciation	−0.66
Net national product	5.30
Minus indirect business taxes (net of subsidies)	−0.58
National income	$4.72

Source: *Economic Report of the President,* January 1993; estimated based on figures from three quarters.

National Income

The value of final goods and services is computed at market prices, but some products sell for less, and others for more, than resource suppliers receive. Because of **government subsidies**, such as payments to suppliers of low-income housing, some products sell for less than resource suppliers receive. Because of **indirect business taxes**, such as sales, excise, and property taxes, some products sell for more than resource suppliers receive. For example, a gallon of gasoline may sell for $1.25, but about $0.25 in taxes must be paid to the government before any resource supplier receives a penny.

Since subsidies are received as income, they should be included in national income, even though they are not part of the selling price. And since indirect business taxes are not received as income by any individual, they should not be included in national income, even though they are part of the selling price. **National income** therefore equals net national product plus government subsidies minus indirect business taxes. Since indirect business taxes are about twenty times greater than government subsidies, we simplify the reporting by computing indirect business taxes net of subsidies. Exhibit 7 shows how to go from net national product to national income.

We have now moved from gross national product to net national product to national income. Next we peel back yet another layer to arrive at personal income, the income people actually receive.

Personal Income

Some of the income received this year was not earned this year, and some of the income earned this year was not actually received this year by those who earned it. By adding to national income the income received but not earned and subtracting the income earned but not received, we convert national income into all income *received* by individuals, which is termed **personal income**. Personal income, a widely reported measure of economic welfare, is computed by the federal government monthly.

The adjustment from national income to personal income is shown in Exhibit 8. Income earned but not received includes (1) the employer's share of Social Security taxes, (2) corporate income taxes, and (3) undistributed corporate profits, which are profits the firm retains rather than pays as dividends. Income received but not earned in the current period includes (1) government transfer payments, (2) receipts from private pension plans, and (3) interest paid by government and by consumers.

EXHIBIT 8

Deriving Personal Income and Disposable Income Using 1992 Data (in trillions of dollars)

National income	$4.72
Minus income earned but not received (Social Security taxes, corporate income taxes, undistributed corporate profits)	−0.80
Plus income received but not earned (government and business transfers, net personal interest income)	1.12
Personal income	5.04
Minus personal tax and nontax charges	−0.62
Disposable income	$4.42

Source: *Economic Report of the President,* January 1993; estimated based on figures for three quarters.

Disposable Income

Although several taxes have been considered so far, we have not yet discussed personal taxes. Personal taxes consist primarily of federal, state, and local personal income tax and the employee's share of the Social Security tax. Subtracting personal taxes and other government charges from personal income yields **disposable income**, which is the amount available for spending or saving—the amount that can be "disposed of" by the household. Think of disposable income as take-home pay. Exhibit 8 shows that personal income minus personal taxes and other government charges yields disposable income.

Summary of National Income Accounts

The income side of national income accounts can be summarized as follows. We begin with *gross national product*, or *GNP*, the market value of final goods and services produced during the year by resources provided by U.S. residents and firms, regardless of the location of the resources. We subtract depreciation from GNP to yield the *net national product*. From net domestic product we subtract indirect business taxes (net of subsidies) to yield *national income*. We obtain *personal income* by subtracting from domestic income all income earned but not received (e.g., undistributed corporate profits) and adding to domestic income all income received but not earned (e.g., transfer payments). By subtracting personal taxes and other government charges from personal income, we arrive at the bottom line: *disposable income*, the amount people are actually free either to save or to spend. The components of the national income accounts are summarized below.

Gross national product = market value of output *produced* in the economy during the year by resources provided by U.S. residents and firms

Net national product = market value of output *available for use* by households, firms, governments, and foreign purchasers

National income = amount of income *earned* by suppliers of resources used to produce GDP

Personal income = amount of income *received* by suppliers of resources before personal taxes have been paid

Disposable income = amount of *spendable* income for saving and consumption after personal taxes have been paid

We now have a more detailed picture of the income side of the national income accounts. As we have said, GNP can be computed either by considering aggregate expenditures on production or by allocating the income arising from that production.

Summary Income Statement of the Economy

Exhibit 9 presents an annual income statement for the entire economy. The upper portion lists aggregate expenditure, which consists of consumption, gross investment, government pur-

EXHIBIT 9

Expenditure and Income Statement for the U.S. Economy Using 1992 Data (in trillions of dollars)

Aggregate Expenditure	
Consumption (*C*)	$4.10
Gross investment (*I*)	0.78
Government purchases (*G*)	1.12
Net exports ($X - M$)	−0.04
GNP	$5.96

Allocation of Income	
Depreciation	$0.66
Net indirect business taxes	0.58
Compensation of employees	3.45
Proprietor's income	0.40
Corporate profits	0.36
Net interest	0.50
Rental income of persons	0.01
GNP	$5.96

Source: *Economic Report of the President,* January 1993; estimated based on figures for three quarters.

chases, and net exports. Because imports exceeded exports, net exports were negative. You might think of aggregate expenditure as the revenue of a giant firm. The income from this expenditure is broken down in the lower portion of Exhibit 9. After depreciation and net indirect business taxes, the remaining allocations equal national income. National income, which represents the sum of all earnings from resources supplied by U.S. residents and firms, can be divided into its five components: employee compensation, proprietors' income, corporate profits, net interest, and rental income of persons.

Employee compensation, which is by far the largest source of income, includes both money wages and employer contributions to cover Social Security taxes, medical insurance, and other fringe benefits. **Proprietors' income** includes the earnings of farmers and other owners of unincorporated businesses. **Corporate profits** are the net revenues received by incorporated businesses before subtraction of corporate income taxes. **Net interest** is the interest received by individuals, excluding interest paid by consumers to businesses and interest paid by government.

Each family that owns its own home is viewed as a tiny firm that rents its home to itself. Since homeowners do not, in fact, rent homes to themselves, an *imputed* rental value must be developed based on what the market rent would be. **Rental income of persons** consists primarily of the imputed rental value of owner-occupied housing minus the cost of owning that property (such as property taxes, insurance, depreciation, and interest paid on the mortgage). From the totals in Exhibit 9, you can see that aggregate spending in the economy equals the income generated by that spending.

APPENDIX QUESTIONS

1. (National Income Accounts) Use the following data to answer the questions below.

Net investment	$100
Depreciation	40
Exports	50
Imports	30
Government spending	150
Consumption	400
Indirect business taxes (net of subsidies)	35
Income earned but not received	60
Income received but not earned	70
Personal income taxes	50
Employee compensation	460
Corporate profits	60
Rental income	20
Net interest	40
Proprietor's income	55

   a. Calculate GNP using the income-based and the expenditure methods.
   b. Calculate gross investment.
   c. Calculate NNP, NI, PI, and DI.
   d. What percent of personal income is employee compensation?
   e. What percent of personal income goes to personal income taxes?

2. (National Income Accounting) According to Exhibit 9, GDP can be calculated either by adding up final goods expenditures or by adding up the allocations of these expenditures to the various resources used to produce these goods. Why do you suppose the portion of final goods expenditures that goes to pay for intermediate goods and/or raw materials is excluded from the allocation of income method of calculation?

CHAPTER 7

UNEMPLOYMENT AND INFLATION

In this chapter we explore the two macroeconomic phenomena that usually pose the greatest problems for the economy: unemployment and inflation. To be sure, these are not the only problems faced by the economy—poverty and huge federal deficits are two others—but low unemployment and low inflation go a long way to help diminish the effects of other economic problems. Although unemployment and inflation are often related, we will initially describe each separately. Our focus will be more on the extent and consequences of these problems than on their causes. The causes of each and the relationship between the two will become clearer as you learn more about the economy.

As this chapter will show, not all unemployment or all inflation harms the economy. Even in a healthy economy, a certain amount of unemployment reflects the voluntary choices of workers seeking their best job opportunities. And inflation that is fully anticipated creates fewer distortions than does unexpected inflation. Topics discussed in this chapter include

- Measuring unemployment
- Frictional, structural, seasonal, and cyclical unemployment
- Meaning of full employment
- Sources and consequences of inflation
- Relative price changes
- Nominal and real interest rates

Unemployment

"They scampered about looking for work. . . . They swarmed on the highways. The movement changed them; the highways, the camps along the road, the fear of hunger and the hunger itself, changed them. The children without dinner changed them, the endless moving changed them."[1]

There is no question that a long stretch of unemployment can have a profound effect on an individual and a family. The most obvious loss is a steady paycheck, but the unemployed often suffer a loss of self-esteem. Moreover, researchers have found that unemployment appears to be linked to a greater incidence of crime and to a variety of afflictions including heart disease, suicide, and mental illness. However much they complain about their jobs, people tend to rely on these jobs not only for income but also for part of their personal identity. So the loss of a job involves some loss of that identity.

In addition to these personal costs, unemployment imposes a cost on the economy as a whole since fewer goods and services are produced. When the economy does not generate enough jobs to employ all those who are willing and able to work, that unemployed labor service is lost forever. *This lost potential output coupled with the economic and psychological damage to unemployed workers and their families represents the real cost of unemployment.* As we begin our analysis of unemployment, keep in mind that unemployment statistics reflect millions of individuals with their own stories. For some, unemployment is inconvenient but brief. For others, unemployment can have a profound effect on their family's stability and economic welfare.

Measuring Unemployment

"Although the unemployment rate increased in September, administration officials predicted the rate would soon fall." So reads a typical news story on the unemployment rate, perhaps the most widely reported measure of the nation's economic condition. What does the unemployment rate measure, what are the sources of unemployment, and how does unemployment change over time? These are some of the questions explored in this section. To start, we will consider how unemployment is measured.

Point to Stress The labor force equals the amount of people employed plus the amount unemployed.

Labor force All noninstitutionalized individuals sixteen years of age and older who are either working or actively looking for work

We will begin with the U.S. noninstitutional adult population, which consists of all persons sixteen years of age and older, except for those in prisons or in mental hospitals. In this chapter when we refer to the *adult population*, we will mean the noninstitutional adult population. The **labor force** consists of those in the adult population who are either working or looking for work. Those looking for work are considered unemployed. More specifically, the Bureau of Labor Statistics counts people as unemployed if they have no job but have looked for work at least once in the

1. John Steinbeck, *The Grapes of Wrath* (New York: Viking Press, 1939), 392.

Unemployment rate The number of unemployed individuals expressed as a percentage of the labor force

preceding four weeks. The unemployment rate measures the percentage of those in the labor force who are unemployed. Thus, the **unemployment rate** equals the number unemployed—that is, those without jobs who are looking for work—divided by the number in the labor force.

Only a fraction of those adults not working are actually considered unemployed. The others may have retired, may have chosen to remain at home to care for small children or perform household tasks, or may be full-time students. The "idle rich" may pursue a life of leisure. Some people may be unable to work because of long-term illness or disability. Finally, some people may have become so discouraged by an unfruitful job search that they have given up their job search in frustration. Since these so-called **discouraged workers** have, in effect, dropped out of the labor force, they are not counted as unemployed. *Because the official unemployment rate does not include discouraged workers, the true extent of unemployment in the economy tends to be understated.*

Discouraged worker A person who has dropped out of the labor force because of lack of success in finding a job

The above definitions are illustrated in Exhibit 1, where circles represent the various groups and subgroups, and the number of individuals in each category and subcategory is listed in parentheses (in millions). The circle on the left depicts the entire U.S. labor force, including both those employed and those unemployed. The circle on the right represents those in the adult population who, for whatever reason, are not working. These

EXHIBIT 1

Composition of Adult Population, 1992 (in millions)

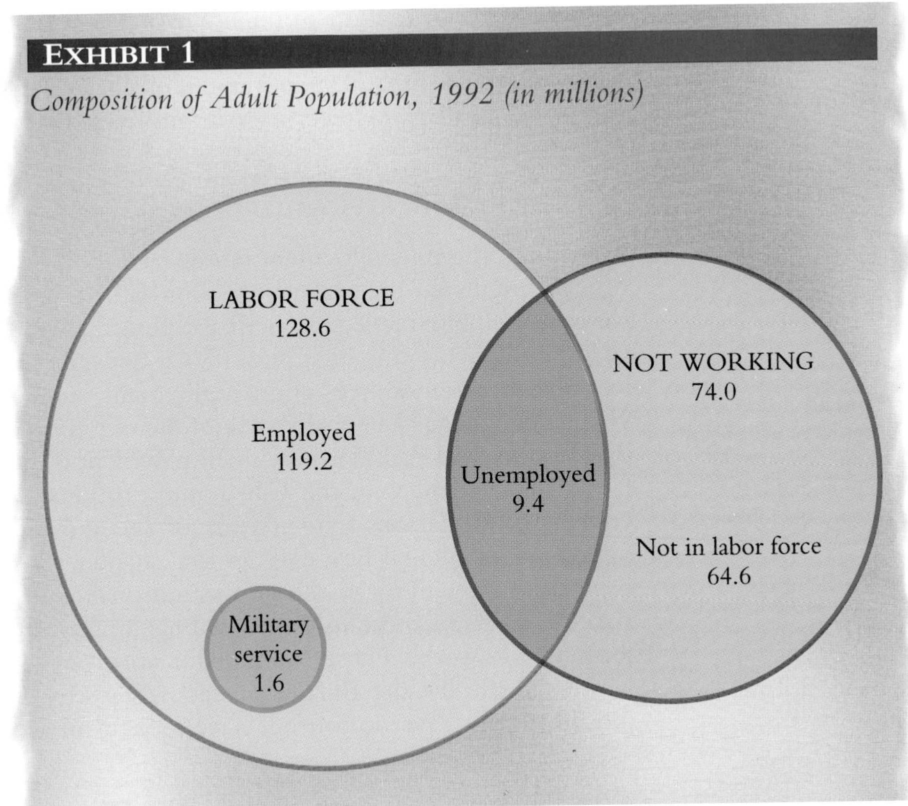

Source: *Economic Report of the President,* January 1993.

two circles reflect the entire adult population.[2] Their intersection identifies the number of *unemployed* workers—that is, the number in the labor force who aren't working.

UNEMPLOYMENT RATE. You can see from the circles in Exhibit 1 that all those who are unemployed are counted as not working, but not all those who are not working are counted as unemployed. The number of individuals in each category and subcategory is listed in parentheses (in millions). Of the 128.6 million in the labor force in 1992, 9.4 million were unemployed. The unemployment rate is found by dividing the number unemployed (9.4 million) by the number in the labor force (128.6 million); in 1992, the unemployment rate averaged 7.3 percent.

LABOR FORCE PARTICIPATION RATE. The labor force participation rate indicates the proportion of the adult population that is in the labor force. In Exhibit 1 the U.S. adult population in 1992 equals those in the labor force (128.6 million) plus those not in the labor force (64.6 million): a total of 193.2 million. The **labor force participation rate** therefore equals the number in the labor force divided by the adult population, or 66.5 percent (128.6/193.2). So two of three adults are in the labor force.

Labor force participation rate The ratio of the number in the labor force to the population of working age

CIVILIAN UNEMPLOYMENT RATE. Those in military service are depicted by the small circle identifying that subset of the labor force. Since all those in the military are considered employed (even those who "only stand and wait"), this small circle does not intersect the "not working" circle. Official unemployment statistics often distinguish between the overall unemployment rate, which was just discussed, and the civilian unemployment rate, which is found by dividing the number unemployed by the civilian labor force. Until the reporting method was changed during the Reagan administration, military personnel were not included in the labor force. Including them lowers the official unemployment rate below the civilian unemployment rate. Recent reductions in the size of the military tend to increase the official unemployment rate.

Example In 1992, the civilian unemployment rate was 7.4 percent, whereas the overall unemployment rate was 7.3 percent.

Changes over Time in Unemployment Statistics

The adult population changes slowly over time. The only way to join that group is to become sixteen years of age, be deinstitutionalized, or immigrate to the United States; the only way to leave the adult population is to die, become institutionalized, or to emigrate to another country. Since 1950 the adult population in the United States has grown by an average of only 1.6 percent per year.

2. Prior to the 1940 census, "workers" could include anyone ten years of age or older. In 1940 age fourteen became the lower limit, and in 1966 the lower limit was raised to sixteen, where it remains.

Example More than one-half of U.S. mothers with preschool children worked outside the home in 1991, compared to only 20 percent in 1960.

Moving in and out of the labor force is easier than moving in and out of the adult population. Thus, the labor force participation rate can change more quickly than the adult population. Since the end of World War II, for example, many more women joined the labor force. Their labor force participation rate climbed from 33 percent in 1948 to 58 percent in 1992. The participation rate among men, however, declined from 87 percent in 1948 to 76 percent in 1992, primarily because of a trend toward early retirement.

What changes even more quickly over time than labor force participation or the adult population is the unemployment rate. Exhibit 2 depicts the U.S. unemployment rate since 1900, with shading to indicate years of recession or depression. As you can see, the rate rose during contractions and fell during expansions. Perhaps the most striking feature of the graph is the dramatic jump that occurred during the Great Depression, when the unemployment rate peaked at 25 percent.

Note that since the end of World War II there has been an upward trend in the unemployment rate (a trend line has been superimposed on

EXHIBIT 2

The U.S. Unemployment Rate Since 1900

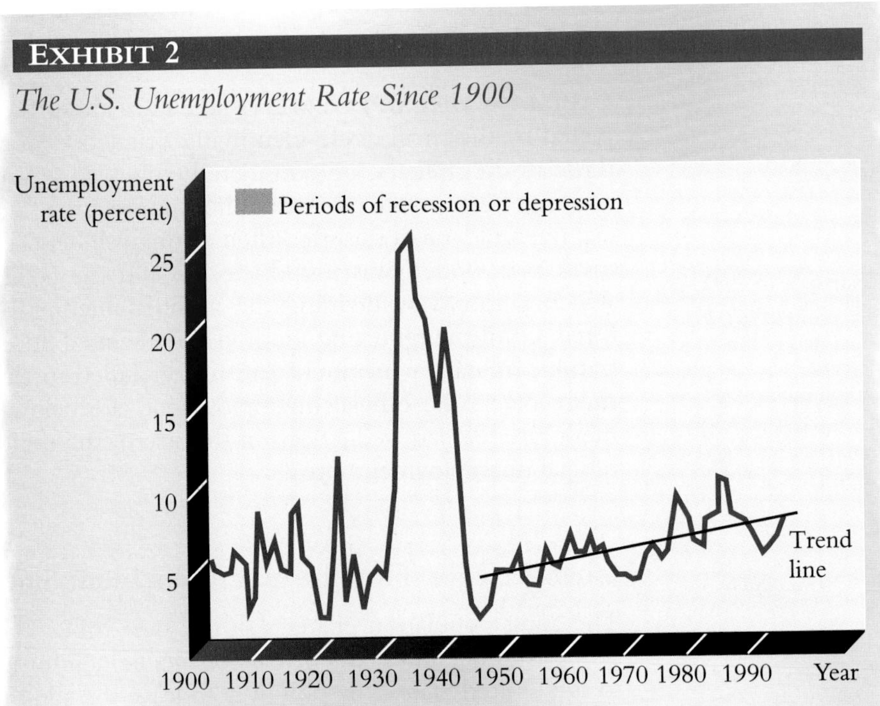

Since 1990 the unemployment rate has fluctuated widely, rising during recessions and falling during expansions. During the Great Depression of the 1930s, the rate rose as high as 25.2 percent. Since 1950 there has been an upward trend in the unemployment rate.

Sources: *Historical Statistics of the United States,* 1970, and *Economic Report of the President,* January 1993.

the data). Between 1947 and 1970, for example, the rate averaged 4.6 percent, never reaching 7.0 percent any year during that stretch. Since 1970, however, the unemployment rate has averaged 7.0 percent, never falling as low as 4.6 percent. These numbers imply that on average since 1970 about 2.5 million more people have been unemployed than was the case between 1947 and 1970. (Later in this section, we examine some possible reasons why the unemployment rate has increased.) We should also note, however, that the labor force grew sharply between these two periods because of a growing population and a rising labor force participation rate. Thus although the number of unemployed increased, the number employed increased as well, growing by about forty million since 1970. In fact, the United States during the 1970s and 1980s was considered an "astounding job machine," and was the envy of the world. At the same time the U.S. economy was creating nearly forty million jobs, the industrialized countries of Western Europe experienced little employment growth.

Unemployment in Various Groups

The overall unemployment rate says nothing about who is unemployed or for how long. Even a low rate of unemployment often belies some wide differences in unemployment rates across ages, races, genders, and geographical areas. Unemployment rates since 1972 for different groups appear in Exhibit 3. Each panel presents the unemployment rate by race and by gender; panel (a) considers those twenty years of age and older, and panel (b) those sixteen to nineteen years old. Years of recession are shaded. As you can see, rates are higher among blacks than among whites, and rates are higher among teenagers than among those age twenty and older. During recessions, the rates of all groups climbed. Unemployment also varies by occupational group. Historically, professional and technical workers have experienced lower unemployment rates than blue-collar workers, especially construction workers.

Duration of Unemployment

Any given unemployment rate says little about how long people have been unemployed—that is, the *average duration of unemployment.* The average duration of unemployment in 1992 was 17.9 weeks. Some people were unemployed longer than others: 35 percent were unemployed fewer than five weeks; 29 percent from five to fourteen weeks; 15 percent from fifteen to twenty-six weeks; and 21 percent twenty-seven weeks or longer. Typically, a rise in the unemployment rate is due to both a larger number of people unemployed and a longer average duration of unemployment.

Unemployment Differences Across the Country

The national unemployment rate masks much variance in rates across the country. For example, during 1988, when the U.S. unemployment rate

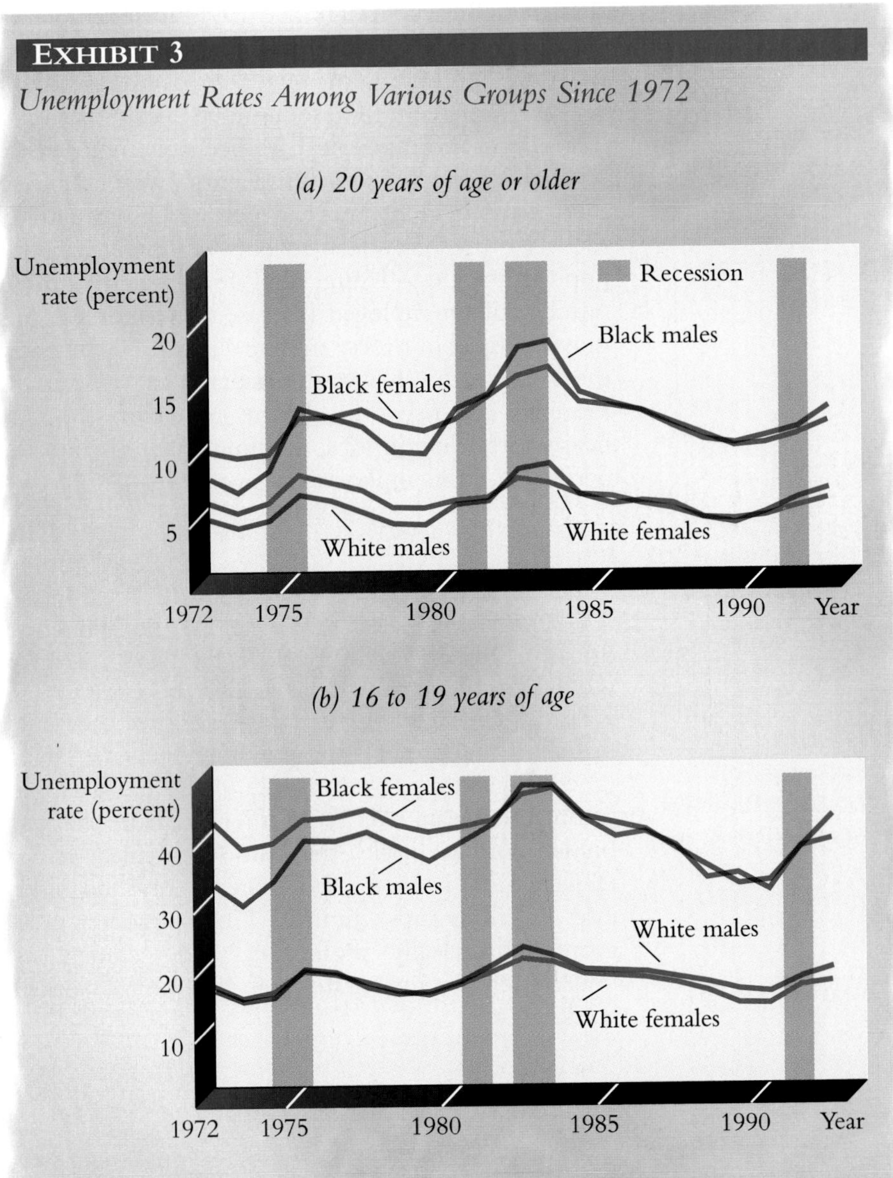

Unemployment affects different groups in different ways. The unemployment rate is higher for blacks than for whites and higher for teenagers than for older persons.

Source: *Economic Report of the President,* January 1993.

averaged only 5.5 percent, more than one hundred counties had unemployment rates exceeding 15 percent and thirty counties had rates exceeding 25 percent. To look behind the numbers, we examine one county's experience with high unemployment in the following case study.

CASE STUDY

Poor King Coal

For decades McDowell County, West Virginia, prospered by supplying the coal that fired the nation's steel mills. Mining jobs were abundant and wages attractive; many miners earned over $40,000 a year in 1980, which in today's dollars would be more than $70,000. Most young people, rather than finishing their educations, became miners. The mining companies dominated the county. They owned most of the property and discouraged other types of economic development.

Then, between 1980 and 1985, the value of the dollar rose relative to foreign currencies, so American steel became more expensive overseas and foreign steel became cheaper in the United States. As the world's demand for U.S. steel fell, so did the demand for the coal needed to produce that steel. Coal mines in McDowell County shut down, and by 1988 the official unemployment rate for the county had reached a whopping 32 percent. Local officials claimed the actual rate was even higher.

The county tried to attract new industry—even a nuclear-waste dump—but met with little success. The county's poor roads and bridges and a labor force trained only for mining scared off potential employers. In short, the county had all its eggs in one basket, but the basket fell.

Source: Alan Murray, "Unemployment Tops 25% in Some Regions Mired in Deep Poverty," *Wall Street Journal*, 21 April 1988.

Sources of Unemployment

Consider all the ways in which people can become unemployed. They may quit or be fired from their jobs. They may be looking for a first job because they just turned sixteen or graduated. Or they may be reentering the labor force after an absence. An examination of the reasons behind unemployment during 1992 indicates that fifty-six percent of those unemployed lost their previous jobs, 10 percent quit their previous jobs, 10 percent were entering the labor market for the first time, and 24 percent were reentering the market. *Thus, 44 percent were unemployed either because they quit their jobs or because they were just joining or rejoining the labor force.*

Pick up any metropolitan newspaper and thumb through the classified pages. The "Help Wanted" section may run more than forty pages and include more than ten thousand jobs, listed alphabetically from accountants to x-ray technicians. Why, when millions are unemployed, are so many jobs unfilled? To understand this paradox, we must take a closer look at the reasons behind unemployment. Based on the source of unemployment, we distinguish among four basic types: frictional, structural, seasonal, and cyclical unemployment.

Point to Stress Frictional unemployment is affected by the efficiency with which information about job openings and prospective employees spreads through the job market.

FRICTIONAL UNEMPLOYMENT. Just as employers do not often hire the first applicant who comes through the door, workers do not always accept their first job offer. Both employers and job applicants need time to explore the job market. Employers need time to find out about the talent available,

Frictional unemployment Unemployment that arises because of the time needed to match qualified job seekers with available job openings

and job seekers need time to find out about openings. The time required to bring together labor suppliers and labor demanders results in **frictional unemployment**. Although unemployment often creates economic and psychological hardships, not all unemployment is necessarily bad. Frictional unemployment does not usually last long and results in a better match-up between workers and jobs, so the entire economy becomes more efficient.

Structural unemployment Unemployment that arises because the skills demanded by employers do not match the skills of the unemployed or because the unemployed do not live where the jobs are located

Example As a result of the increased use of personal computers, Smith-Corona announced the closing of its last typewriter factory in the United States in 1992.

STRUCTURAL UNEMPLOYMENT. A second reason job vacancies and unemployment can occur simultaneously is that unemployed workers often do not have the skills demanded by employers or do not live in the area where their skills are in demand. Unemployment arising from a mismatch of skills or geographic location is called **structural unemployment**. Structural unemployment occurs because changes in taste, technology, taxes, or competition reduce the demand for certain skills and increase the demand for other skills. For example, the introduction of cable TV service reduced the demand for those who install satellite dishes. Likewise, automatic teller machines put many bank tellers out of work. In our dynamic economy, some people are stuck with skills that are no longer demanded. Whereas most frictional unemployment is short term and voluntary, structural unemployment poses more of a problem because workers must seek jobs elsewhere or must develop other skills. For example, unemployed satellite-dish installers, bank tellers, coal miners, and auto workers must seek work in other industries or in other regions. Moving to where the jobs are is easier said than done. People prefer to remain near friends and relatives. Those laid off from high-wage jobs may be reluctant to leave the area because they hope to be rehired. Families in which one spouse is employed may not be willing to give up that partner's job to find work for the other. Finally, the available jobs may be in areas where the cost of living is much higher. So the unemployed often stay put.

Seasonal unemployment Unemployment caused by seasonal shifts in labor supply and demand

Example Unemployment can also be affected by supply shocks. Consider the impact of Hurricane Andrew on unemployment among migrant farm workers in south Florida.

SEASONAL UNEMPLOYMENT. Unemployment caused by seasonal shifts in labor supply and demand during the year is called **seasonal unemployment**. It occurs in industries such as construction, agriculture, and tourism, where the weather affects the demand for labor. Little farming or construction occurs during winter months in regions where the ground freezes. Likewise, the tourist trade in places such as Miami and Phoenix wilts in the summer heat. The Christmas holidays increase the demand for those who can serve as sales clerks, postal carriers, or Santa Clauses. Those employed in seasonal occupations know they will probably be unemployed during particular months. Some may even have purposely chosen a seasonal occupation. To eliminate seasonal unemployment, we might have to outlaw winter and abolish Christmas. Official employment statistics spread out seasonal unemployment over the year and thus mask the bulges that occur in particular months because of seasonal factors.

Cyclical unemployment Unemployment that occurs because of declines in the economy's aggregate output during recessions

CYCLICAL UNEMPLOYMENT. Recall that Exhibits 2 and 3 indicated an increase in the unemployment rate during recessions. Because of the general decline in output during a recession, most firms reduce their demand for inputs, including labor. **Cyclical unemployment** reflects the decline in aggregate output that occurs during the recessionary phase of the business cycle. Between 1932 and 1934, when unemployment averaged about 24 percent, there was clearly much cyclical unemployment. Between 1942 and 1945, when the unemployment rate averaged only 1.6 percent, there was no cyclical unemployment. Government policies that stimulate aggregate demand during recessions are aimed more at reducing cyclical unemployment than other types of unemployment.

The Meaning of Full Employment

Full employment The level of employment when there is no cyclical unemployment

When economists talk about "full employment," they do not mean zero unemployment. In an ever-changing economy such as ours, where entrepreneurs are continually introducing new products, shifts in demand and technology alter the supply and demand for existing products. Consequently, even when the economy is at **full employment,** there will be some frictional, structural, and seasonal unemployment. After all, nearly half of those unemployed have quit their last job or are new entrants or reentrants into the labor force. A large proportion of this group could be counted among the frictionally unemployed.

Point to Stress Discussions in later chapters will indicate that unemployment that is "too low" increases inflationary pressures in the economy. When unemployment fell to very low levels during World War II, the government imposed wage and price controls to dampen the resulting inflation.

Most economists believe that unemployment of the frictional-structural-seasonal variety has risen since the late 1950s, perhaps from 4 percent to 5 or 6 percent; that low an unemployment rate would now constitute full employment. Why did this increase occur? The full employment level may have changed over time primarily because of changes in the composition of the labor force and changes in the institutional structure of the economy. When many new workers flood into the labor market for the first time, unemployment increases, because even a healthy economy needs time to absorb these new workers. Teenagers, for example, tend to have higher unemployment rates because they are new entrants who arrive with no particular skills and no job experience. Since the 1950s the composition of the labor force has shifted. Today, groups that have historically experienced lower unemployment rates comprise a smaller proportion of the labor force. For example, the group that experiences the lowest average unemployment in the labor force—white males twenty years of age and older—made up about two-thirds of all workers in 1955. Now they make up only about half of the labor force.

Unemployment Insurance

As noted earlier, unemployment often imposes an economic and psychological hardship on those who are affected. For a variety of reasons, however, the burden on those who are unemployed may not be as severe today as during the Great Depression. Today, with so many more women in the labor force, households with an unemployed worker are now more likely to have someone else in the household who has a job. When a household has more than one person in the labor force, the economic shock of unemployment is to some extent cushioned. Moreover, workers who lose their jobs usually receive unemployment benefits.

Unemployment insurance Temporary income provided to unemployed workers who actively seek employment and who meet other qualifications

Example Congress extended unemployment benefits in response to the 1990–1991 recession.

In response to the massive unemployment of the Great Depression, Congress passed the Social Security Act of 1935, which provided for an unemployment insurance system financed by a tax on employers. Unemployed workers who meet certain qualifications can receive **unemployment insurance** for up to six months, provided they actively seek employment. During recessions, benefits are often extended beyond six months in states with particularly high unemployment. The insurance is aimed primarily at those who have lost jobs. Not covered are those just entering or reentering the labor force, those who quit their last job, or those fired for just cause such as excessive absenteeism or theft. Because of these restrictions, slightly fewer than half of all unemployed workers receive unemployment benefits.

Unemployment insurance usually replaces more than half of a person's take-home pay. In 1992, for example, an average of $173 per week was paid to the unemployed who received benefits. Because unemployment benefits reduce the opportunity cost of remaining unemployed, they may create disincentives in finding a job while benefits are in effect. For example, if you faced the choice of washing dishes for a take-home pay of $200 per week or collecting $150 per week in unemployment benefits, which would you choose? Evidence suggests that unemployed workers who receive insurance benefits tend to search less actively than those without such benefits, and they tend to find jobs only when their benefits are about to run out. Therefore, although unemployment insurance provides a safety net for the unemployed, it may also reduce the urgency of finding work, thereby contributing to an increase in frictional unemployment. On the plus side, unemployment insurance may allow for a higher-quality search, since the individual has "walking-around" money and need not take the first job available.

International Comparisons of Unemployment

Consider unemployment rates around the world. In December of 1992, when the U.S. unemployment rate was 7.2 percent, it was 11.5 percent in Canada, 7.4 percent in Germany, 10.5 percent in France, 10.5 percent in the United Kingdom, 10.0 percent in Italy, and 2.3 percent in Japan. We should view international comparisons with caution, however, because the definitions of unemployment may differ across countries with respect to age limits, the criteria used to determine whether a person is looking for work, the way layoffs are treated, how those in the military are counted, and in other subtle ways. These differences can affect estimates of unemployment. For example, most countries in North and South America and some European countries base their unemployment estimates on periodic surveys of the labor force. Experts believe that such sample surveys yield the most reliable results. But most other countries, including Germany, Great Britain, and a majority of less developed countries, base official estimates on registrations with government employment offices. Reliance on such self-reporting tends to underestimate the actual level of unemployment, particularly in less developed countries where there are few jobs, no unemployment benefits, and hence no real reason to bother registering as unemployed with the government. Centrally planned economies, such as China and Cuba, do not usually report unemployment rates.

Example Employment in Japan is becoming less secure. In 1992, Nissan Motor Company announced plans to cut its work force by 4,000.

The true extent of unemployment in Japan is higher than official figures indicate because many firms offer an implicit promise to provide employment security for life. As a result, some employees in Japan may do little or no work yet are still carried on the company's payroll. Other employment practices also differ across countries. For example, Germany imposes penalties on firms for "socially unjustified" layoffs, and Swedish law makes it harder to lay off Swedish citizens than foreign workers.

Problems with Official Unemployment Figures

Underemployment A situation in which workers are overqualified for their jobs or work fewer hours than they would prefer

Official unemployment statistics are not without their problems. As we said earlier, not counting discouraged workers in the official labor force understates unemployment. Official employment data also ignore the problem of **underemployment**, which arises because people are counted as employed even if they can find only part-time jobs or even if they are vastly overqualified for the job, as when someone with a Ph.D. can find employment only as a bookstore clerk. Counting part-time workers and the underemployed as employed also tends to understate the actual amount of unemployment.

Example An individual need work only 1 hour per week for pay to be considered by the U.S. government to be employed. Those who work more than 15 hours per week in a family business are also considered employed even if they are not paid.

On the other hand, because unemployment benefits and some welfare programs require recipients to seek employment, some people may act as if they are looking for work just to qualify for such programs. If these people do not in fact want to find a job, their inclusion among the unemployed will tend to overstate the official unemployment figures. *On net, however, most experts believe that official U.S. unemployment figures tend to underestimate the true extent of unemployment because of the exclusion of discouraged workers and because underemployed workers are considered fully employed.* Despite several qualifications and limitations, the unemployment rate is a useful measure of unemployment trends over time.

We turn next to the second major concern in today's economy: inflation.

INFLATION

We begin our discussion of inflation with a case study that highlights the cost of high inflation by focusing on the recent experience of Bolivia.

CASE STUDY

Wild Inflation in Bolivia

In the spring of 1985, the inflation rate in Bolivia was running at 25,000 percent a year, one of the highest in history. That high rate, coupled with high rates for the two previous years, meant that in 1985 it took more than five thousand pesos to equal the purchasing power of one 1982 peso. To put this in perspective, if that rate prevailed in the United States, the price of a gallon of gasoline would have climbed from $1.25 in 1982 to $6,250 in 1985. A pair of jeans that sold for $35 in 1982 would have cost $175,000 in 1985!

Cash registers in Bolivia did not contain enough zeros to ring up even a hamburger. Prices were no longer printed on menus. With the value of the Bolivian peso cheapening by the hour, people understandably did not want to hold pesos. As soon as workers were paid, they tried to get rid of pesos, either by buying goods and services before prices increased further or by exchanging pesos for a more stable currency, such as the U.S. dollar. Prices were rising so fast that the price of a movie ticket often rose while people waited in the ticket line. With such wild inflation, everyone, including merchants, had difficulty keeping track of prices. Price differences among sellers of the same product became greater, prompting shoppers to incur the "shoe-leather cost" of walking around in search of the lowest price.

With the peso worth so little, carrying money for spending was a real burden. Bolivians became accustomed to lugging incredible wads of pesos in sacks or in blankets slung over their shoulders—whatever would do the job. Money was folded in individual packets of one million pesos, and the packets were tied into foot-long bundles. Few people bothered to count the money in each packet—they simply counted the packets.

To focus on the sheer physical effort required to carry money, think again in terms of dollars. Suppose the dollar became so inflated that it took $5,000 in today's dollars to purchase what one dollar had purchased three years ago. To carry the equivalent of $10 in the spending power of three years ago, you would need $50,000 in today's dollars ($10 × 5,000). Can you imagine toting that much around just to pay for a meal or a movie? To carry the equivalent of $200 in preinflated spending power for a shopping trip, you would have to load yourself down with a million dollars. If you carried this amount in dollar bills, it would weigh a ton—literally. Even in $100 bills, it would still weigh more than 20 pounds—that's one fat wallet!

Lugging money around, shopping for the lowest price, and continually attending to money matters all involve a great deal of time and effort—time and effort taken away from production. Thus, the high and unpredictable inflation in Bolivia and more recently in Brazil resulted in much activity that was rational for each individual but unproductive for the economy as a whole. When people are required to pay constant attention to wages, prices, and the value of the currency, the economy's productivity suffers.

Source: "Bolivia Struggles to Curb World's Highest Inflation," *Hartford Courant* (July 21, 1985): A12.

Inflation A sustained and continuous increase in the price level

Hyperinflation A very high rate of inflation

Deflation A sustained and continuous decrease in the price level

We have already discussed inflation in different contexts. **Inflation** is a sustained and continuous increase in the average level of prices. If the price level bounces around—moving up one month, falling back another — any particular increase in the price level would not necessarily be called inflation. A sustained and continuous price increase means that prices rise month after month. Very high inflation, as in Bolivia, is often called **hyperinflation**. **Deflation** is a sustained and continuous decrease in the average level of prices.

Example The rising U.S. inflation in the late 1960s was an example of demand-pull inflation—inflation resulting from increased government expenditures for the Vietnam War and for social programs. The rising inflation in the 1970s that resulted from increased oil prices was an example of cost-push inflation.

Demand-pull inflation A continuous rise in the price level caused by increases in aggregate demand

We typically measure inflation on an *annual* basis. The annual *inflation rate* equals the percentage increase in the average price level from one year to the next. For example, between 1991 and 1992, the consumer price index increased from 136.2 to 140.1, reflecting an annual inflation rate of 2.9 percent; this rate is found by dividing the increase in the index of 3.9 (140.1 - 136.2) by 136.2. In this section we first consider two sources of inflation. We then examine the extent and consequences of inflation in the United States and around the world.

Two Sources of Inflation

Inflation can be depicted as an increase in the economy's price level resulting from an increase in aggregate demand or a decrease in aggregate supply. Panel (a) of Exhibit 4 shows that an increase in aggregate demand raises the price level from P to P'. Inflation that springs from an increase in aggregate demand is often called **demand-pull inflation**. In such cases a rising aggregate demand curve *pulls up* the price level. To generate repeated and continuous price increases, the aggregate demand curve would have to keep shifting out.

EXHIBIT 4

Inflation Caused by Shifts in the Aggregate Demand and Supply Curves

(a) Demand-pull inflation: inflation induced by an increase in aggregate demand

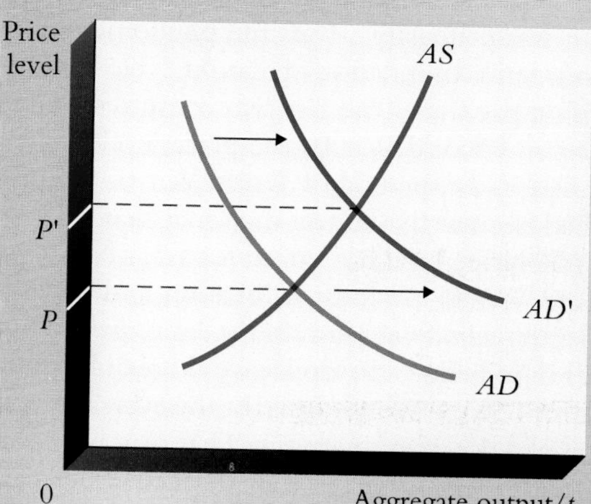

(b) Cost-push inflation: inflation induced by a decrease in aggregate supply

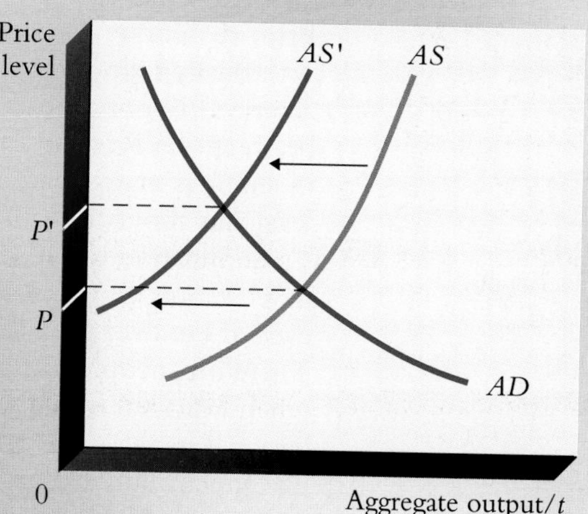

Panel (a) illustrates demand-pull inflation. An outward shift of the aggregate demand to AD' "pulls" the price level up from P to P'. Panel (b) shows cost-push inflation, in which a decrease in aggregate supply to AS' "pushes" the price level up from P to P'.

Cost-push inflation A continuous rise in the price level caused by reductions in aggregate supply

Alternatively, inflation can arise from a reduction in aggregate supply, as shown in panel (b) of Exhibit 4, where a shift to the left in the aggregate supply curve raises the price level. For example, crop failures and reductions in the supply of oil during the 1970s reduced aggregate supply, thereby raising the price level. Inflation stemming from a decrease in aggregate supply is often called **cost-push inflation**, suggesting that an increase in the cost of production has *pushed up* the price level. A decrease in aggregate supply usually leads not only to a higher price level but to a falling level of output, a combination that was identified in Chapter 5 as *stagflation*. Again, to generate sustained and continuous price increases, the aggregate supply curve would have to keep shifting to the left.

A Historical Look at Inflation and the Price Level

In Chapter 5 we traced the relation between the price level, as measured by the implicit price deflator, and real GDP since 1940. The consumer price index is the price level you are likely to encounter most frequently, so we accord it some attention here. Exhibit 5 indicates the movement of the price level in the United States since 1900, as measured by the consumer price index. Panel (a) shows the *level* of prices in each year, which is measured by an index relative to the base period of 1982–1984. As you can see, the price level was not much higher in 1940 than in 1900. Since 1940, however, it has risen steadily, especially during the 1970s.

Of most concern is not the level of prices but changes in that level. Panel (b) shows the annual *rate of change* in the CPI, or the annual rate of *inflation* or *deflation*, since 1900. The decade of the 1970s was not the only period of high inflation during this century. Inflation was also in double digits from 1917 to 1920, in 1942, and in 1947—periods associated with world wars. Prior to World War II, inflation was primarily a wartime phenomenon and was usually followed by deflation. Such an inflation-deflation cycle has characterized war and peace stretching back over the last two centuries. In fact, between the Revolutionary War and World War II, the price level declined in about as many years as it increased. At the end of World War II, the price level was about the same as it had been at the end of the Civil War.

So inflation is nothing new; the price level has varied for as far back as we have records. But prior to World War II, periods of inflation and deflation evened out over the long run, so the *purchasing power of the dollar changed little*. Therefore, people had good reason to believe the dollar would retain its value when averaged over the long term. Since World War II, however, the price level has increased by an average of 4.4 percent per year. That may not sound like much, but it translates into an *eightfold* increase in the consumer price index since 1946. We have not had a year of deflation since 1955. So inflation has reduced confidence in the value of the dollar over the long term.

Anticipated Versus Unanticipated Inflation

What is the effect of inflation on the economy's performance? *Unanticipated inflation* creates more problems for the economy than does *anticipated inflation*.

EXHIBIT 5

Consumer Price Index Since 1900

(a)

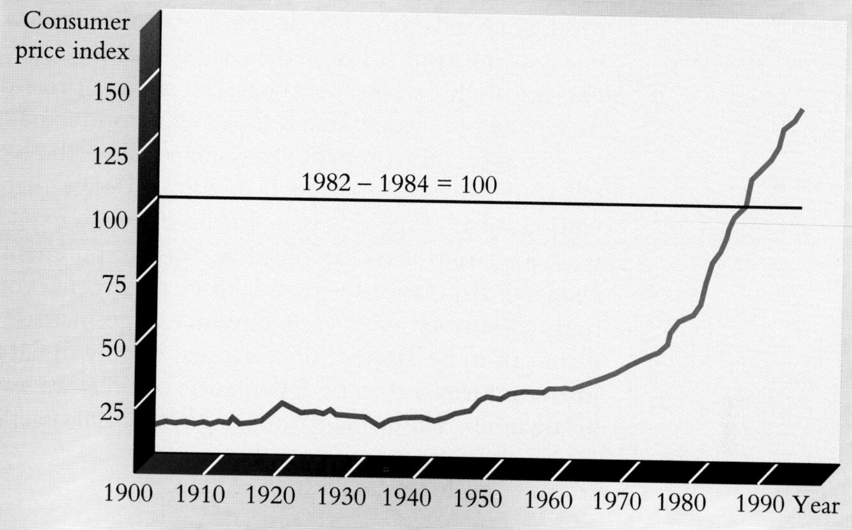

(b)

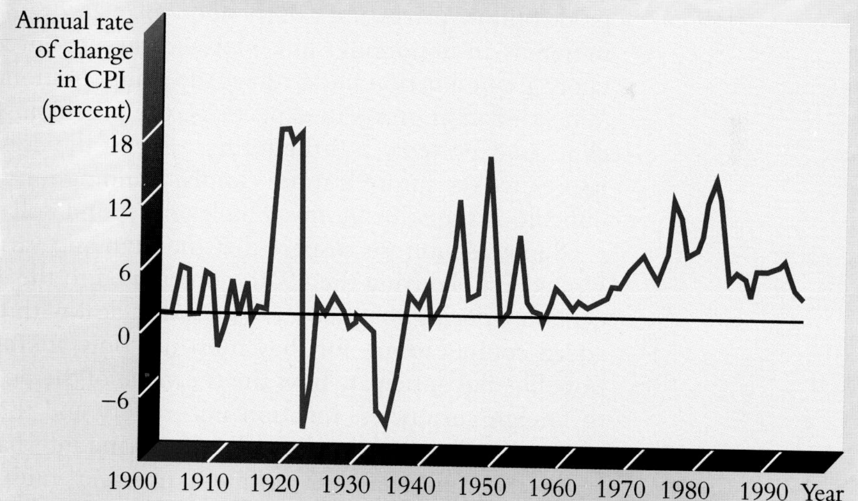

Panel (a) shows that, despite some fluctuations, the price level was not much higher in 1940 than it had been in 1900. Since 1940 the price level has risen almost every year. Panel (b) shows the annual rate of change in the price level. Between 1900 and 1946, the average annual inflation rate was 1.3 percent. Since 1946 the inflation rate has averaged 4.4 percent annually.

Sources: *Historical Statistics of the United States,* 1970, and *Economic Report of the President,* January, 1993.

To the extent that inflation is higher or lower than anticipated, it arbitrarily creates winners and losers. If inflation is higher than expected, the winners are all those who had contracted to buy for a price that did not reflect the higher inflation. The losers are all those who contracted to sell at that price. If inflation is lower than expected, the situation is reversed: the winners are all those who contracted to sell at a price that anticipated higher inflation, and the losers are all those who contracted to buy at that price.

Suppose inflation next year is expected to be 5 percent, and you agree to sell your labor for a *nominal*, or money, wage that is 5 percent higher than your nominal wage this year. In this case you expect your *real* wage—that is, your wage measured in dollars of constant purchasing power—to remain unchanged. If inflation turns out to be 5 percent, you and your employer will both be satisfied with your nominal wage increase of 5 percent. If inflation turns out to be 10 percent, your real wage will fall and you will be a loser. If inflation turns out to be 2 percent, your real wage will increase and you will be a winner. *The arbitrary gains and losses arising from unanticipated inflation is one reason why inflation is so unpopular.*

The Transaction Costs of Variable Inflation

During long periods of price stability, people correctly believe that they can predict future prices and can therefore plan accordingly. As Keynes once said, money is an important "link between the present and the future."[3] Uncertainty about inflation undermines the ability of money to serve as such a link. When inflation grows unexpectedly, the purchasing power of the dollar declines unexpectedly and the future value of the dollar becomes more uncertain. Since the future is more cloudy, planning for that future becomes more difficult. A sound economy is built on a sound dollar.

Some economists suspect that the high and variable inflation rate in the United States during the 1970s contributed to the slower growth rate of the economy during that decade. Firms that deal with the rest of the world face added complications, for they must not only attempt to plan for U.S. inflation, but also anticipate how the the value of the dollar might change relative to foreign currencies. Inflation uncertainty and the resulting exchange-rate uncertainty increase the difficulty of making international business decisions. In this more uncertain environment, managers must shift their attention from worrying about productivity to anticipating the effects of inflation and exchange-rate variations on the firm's finances.

Inflation forces individuals and firms to try to hedge against unexpected changes in the dollar's value. This hedging has taken such forms as including cost-of-living escalators in wage settlements, making adjustments in accounting procedures, and basing investment decisions on expected inflation. During the 1970s, for example, the variable-rate home mortgage began replacing

3. J. M. Keynes, *The General Theory of Employment, Interest, and Money* (London: Macmillan, 1936), 293.

the fixed-rate mortgage typically offered by banks. The interest rate on a variable-rate mortgage varies from year to year, depending on the market rate of interest. There was also a trend toward mortgages that are shorter than the standard thirty-year variety, and the maturity date of corporate bonds was also shortened. Lenders became more apprehensive about inflation over the long term, so they wanted to get their money back sooner. The transaction costs of drawing up contracts, particularly long-term contracts, increased.

Example Between 1985 and 1992, the prices of prescription drugs increased 72 percent, compared to a 30 percent increase in the overall rate of inflation. The CPI for medical care rose 66.5 percent during the same period.

Adapting to Relative Price Changes

Inflation has been defined as a sustained and continuous rise in the price level. This definition, however, misses an important problem with inflation: not all prices change at the same rate. Even with no inflation some prices would go up and some would go down, reflecting the workings of supply and demand for different products. So inflation does not necessarily cause the changes in relative prices, but inflation can obscure them. Consider the changes in relative prices discussed in the following case study.

CASE STUDY

Changes in Relative Prices

As we have seen, inflation does not mean that all prices rise by the same amount or by the same proportion. During the last two decades, for example, the price level in the United States roughly tripled, yet the prices of color televisions, VCRs, pocket calculators, computers, and many other items declined steadily. Because the prices of various goods change by different amounts, *relative prices* change. Whereas the price level describes the terms by which some representative bundle of goods is exchanged for *money*, relative prices describe the terms by which individual goods are exchanged for *one another.*

Let's examine more closely the composition of inflation and the change in inflation between two periods. Exhibit 6 compares the composition of inflation during 1978–1980 with that during 1982–1984. Each major consumer item is listed, along with the weight that item receives in the consumer price index. Keep in mind that the prices of about four hundred individual products are included in the market basket, so we are considering here only summary statistics for the major groupings. Of the major components listed, housing plays the most important role, accounting for 42.7 percent of the budget.

The highest single stretch of inflation since 1947 occurred between 1978 and 1980, when annual inflation averaged 12.4 percent. Notice, however, the difference in price changes across major components. The annual rate of price increase for clothing was less than half the average increase. On the other hand, because of OPEC-related price hikes, the price of motor fuel increased by three times the average increase. The first lesson we learn from the exhibit is that *the rates of price increases can differ sharply among items.*

Disinflation A reduction in the rate of inflation

During the 1982–1984 period, inflation declined to an annual rate of 3.7 percent, less than one-third the rate during 1978–1980. A reduction in the rate of inflation is called **disinflation**. Make no mistake: the price *level* was

EXHIBIT 6

Case Study of Disinflation Between 1978–1980 and 1982–1984

Item	Weight in CPI	Annual Percentage Change in CPI 1978–1980	1982–1984	Contribution of Item to Disinflation (percentage points)
All items	100.0	12.4	3.7	−8.7
Housing	42.7	13.9	3.4	−4.5
Food	19.0	9.6	3.0	−1.3
Clothing	4.5	5.7	2.2	−0.2
Motor Fuel	6.1	37.1	−2.4	−2.4
Electricity and gas	4.0	13.9	6.3	−0.3
New cars	3.1	8.0	2.7	−0.2
Used cars	4.5	5.5	12.6	+0.3
Medical care	4.7	10.1	7.5	−0.1
Entertainment	3.4	7.8	4.0	−0.1
Other goods and services	4.3	7.9	8.8	+0.1

Source: Bureau of Labor Statistics; *Economic Report of the President,* January 1987.

still rising during this disinflation, but the rate of increase in the price level was falling. During the 1982–1984 period, some prices increased faster than the average and some increased slower than the average. The price of used cars went up by more than three times the average rate; the price of motor fuel actually dropped. Hence, not only was the price level changing, but *relative prices* were changing as well. Motor fuel became relatively cheaper compared to other goods, and used cars became relatively more costly.

Based on the data provided in the first three columns of Exhibit 6, we can calculate the contribution each major component made to the disinflation that occurred. For example, the average increase in housing costs dropped from 13.9 percent to 3.4 percent between the two periods, for a difference of 10.5 percent. If we multiply this difference by housing's share of the total budget, we get 4.5 percent (10.5 x 0.427). Thus, of the 8.7 percent average reduction in inflation between the periods 1978–1980 and 1982–1984, 4.5 percent, or about half of the total, can be traced to the lower inflation rate in housing costs. The second leading contributor to disinflation was the drop in the price of motor fuel, which accounted for 2.4 percent of the 8.7 percent drop in the inflation rate. More recently, disinflation occurred when inflation declined from 6.1 percent in 1990 to 3.1 percent in 1991. Most of that drop came from lower energy prices.

Source: This approach to examining inflation was developed by Otto Eckstein in "Disinflation," in *Issues in Contemporary Macroeconomics and Distribution*, G. W. Feiwel, Ed. (Albany, N.Y.: State University of New York Press, 1985), 297–323.

During periods of volatile inflation, there is greater uncertainty about the price of one good relative to another—that is, about relative prices. Milton Friedman, in his Nobel Prize address, noted, "The more volatile the rate of general inflation, the harder it becomes to extract the signal about relative prices from the absolute prices; the broadcast about relative prices is, as it were, being jammed by the noise coming from the inflation broadcast."[4] But relative price changes are important for allocating the economy's resources efficiently. Incidentally, because price changes differ across products and because different households consume different bundles of goods, each household experiences its own rate of inflation.

If all price changes moved together, producers could simply link the selling price of their goods to the overall inflation rate. Since not all prices move in unison, however, tying a particular product's price to the overall inflation rate may result in a price that is too high or too low for market conditions. The same is true of agreements by employers to raise wages in accord with inflation. If the price of an employer's product lags behind the inflation rate, the employer will be hard-pressed to increase wages by the rate of inflation. Consider the problem confronting oil producers who had signed labor contracts agreeing to pay their workers cost-of-living wage increases. In some years those employers had to provide pay increases at a time when the price of oil was falling like a rock.

International Comparisons of Inflation

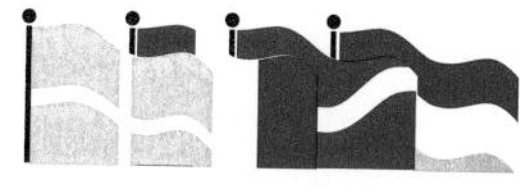

Teaching Tip Different countries tend to have different levels of tolerance for inflation. The 3.8 percent rate of inflation in Germany (a rate considered acceptable in the United States) prompted the German central bank to drive up interest rates in an attempt to lower inflation.

In 1992 the U.S. inflation rate as measured by consumer prices was 2.9 percent, compared to 0.7 percent in Japan, 3.8 percent in Germany, 2.0 percent in France, 2.6 percent in the United Kingdom, 4.7 percent in Italy, and 2.1 percent in Canada. Exhibit 7 presents the trend since 1980 in consumer prices in these seven industrialized countries (known commonly as G-7). Note there was disinflation between the early part of the decade and the middle; the rate of increase in consumer prices declined. Since 1985, inflation has been relatively low except for in the United Kingdom, where the rate climbed above 10 percent during the first half of 1990. Inflation has been much higher in Brazil and in the emerging transitional economies of Eastern Europe and the Commonwealth of Independent States.

As with unemployment statistics, the quantity and quality of data collected to track movements in the price level vary across countries. In less developed countries fewer products are sampled and the geographical region covered is often limited to the capital city. Whereas some four hundred items are sampled in the United States, as few as thirty might be sampled in some less developed countries. In centrally planned economies, reported inflation must be viewed with caution, since most prices in such countries are established and controlled by the government. The fact that inflation is low in centrally planned economies may offer little comfort to consumers who find store shelves bare because of artificially low prices.

4. Milton Friedman, "Nobel Lecture: Inflation and Unemployment," *Journal of Political Economy* 85 (June 1977): 467.

EXHIBIT 7

International Consumer Prices

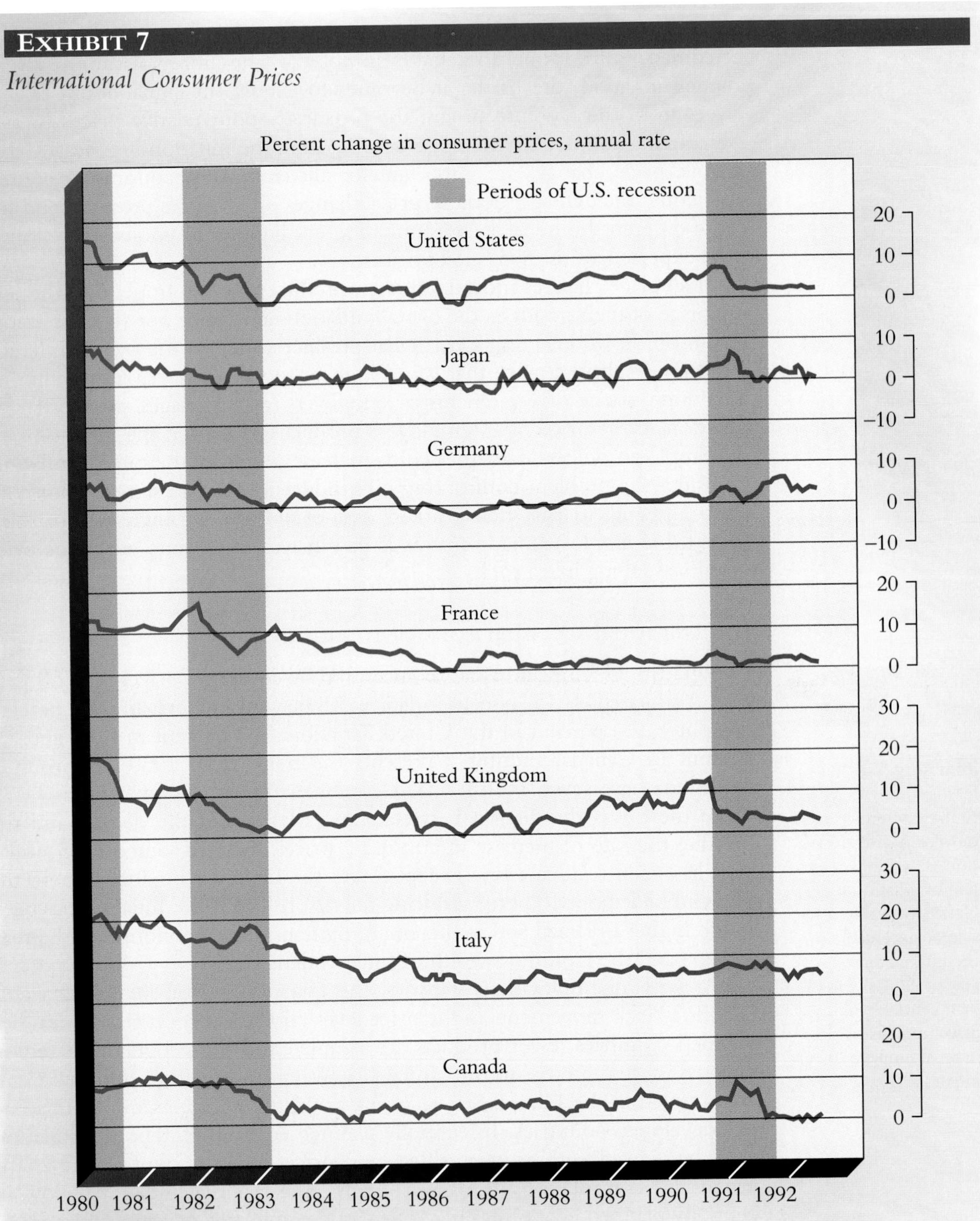

Source: U.S. Department of Commerce, *Survey of Current Business,* Vol. 7 (September 1992), p. C-23.

Point to Stress The CPI tends to overstate inflation during periods of high, rising inflation because it uses a fixed market basket of goods.

Even with market-clearing prices and sophisticated sampling techniques, however, there is still debate over which measure best captures inflation. For example, in the previous chapter we examined how the CPI, by fixing the bundle of goods and services in the consumer basket, does not reflect rational consumption behavior in the face of changes in relative prices. Therefore, the CPI tends to overstate the extent of inflation.

Inflation and Interest Rates

Interest rate The amount of money paid for the use of a dollar for one year

No discussion of inflation would be complete without a consideration of the role of interest. Interest is the reward offered savers, or lenders, to forgo present consumption. Specifically, the **interest rate** can be viewed as the amount of money earned for supplying the use of one dollar for one year. For example, if the interest rate is 5 percent, the lender earns 5 cents per $1 lent per year. The greater the interest rate, other things constant, the greater the reward for lending money. Thus the quantity of money people are willing to lend increases as the interest rate rises, other things constant. The supply of loanable funds therefore slopes upward, as indicated by line *S* in Exhibit 8.

These funds are demanded by firms and individuals who want to finance purchases, such as buildings, machinery, and homes. The lower the interest rate, other things constant, the lower the opportunity cost of borrowing funds.

EXHIBIT 8

The Market for Loanable Funds

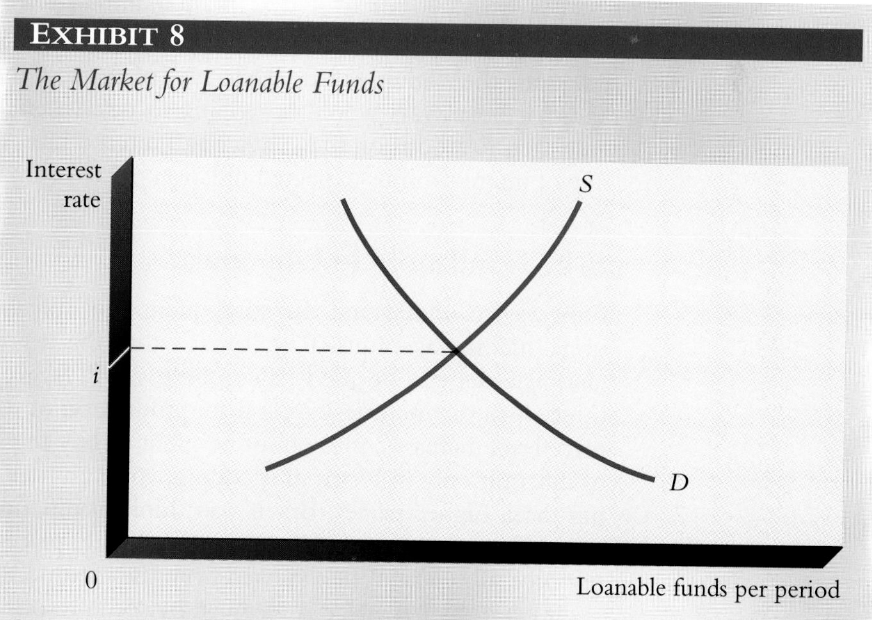

The upward-sloping cupply curve, *S*, shows that more savings are supplied to financial markets at higher interest rates. The downward-sloping demand curve, *D*, shows that the quantity of loanable funds demanded is greater at lower interest rates. The two curves intersect to determine the equilibrium interest rate, *i*.

Hence, the quantity of loanable funds demanded increases as the interest rate falls, other things constant. The demand for loans therefore slopes downward, as indicated by line D in Exhibit 8. The downward-sloping demand for loanable funds and the upward-sloping supply of loanable funds intersect at the equilibrium point to yield the equilibrium rate of interest, i.

Nominal rate of interest The interest rate expressed in current dollars

Real rate of interest The nominal rate of interest minus the inflation rate

The **nominal rate of interest** measures interest in terms of the actual dollars paid even if inflation has eroded the value of those dollars. The nominal rate of interest is the rate that appears on the borrowing agreement; it is the rate discussed in the news media and is often of political significance. The **real rate of interest** is the nominal rate of interest minus the inflation rate:

Real rate = nominal rate − inflation rate

For example, if the nominal rate of interest is 5 percent and the annual rate of inflation is 4 percent, the real rate of interest is only 1 percent. Under these conditions, if you lend $100 for a year you would earn a nominal interest income of $5 per year but a real interest income of only $1 per year. If there were no inflation, the nominal rate of interest and the real rate of interest will be identical. But with inflation, the real rate of interest will be less than the nominal rate of interest. The real rate of interest, however, is known only after the fact—that is, only after inflation actually occurs. The nominal rate of interest is always positive; the real rate could turn out to be negative.

Because the future is uncertain, lenders and borrowers must form expectations about inflation, and base their willingness to lend and to borrow on these expectations. Other things held constant, the higher the *expected* rate of inflation, the higher the nominal rate of interest that lenders would require and that borrowers would be willing to pay. In effect lenders and borrowers base their decisions on the *expected* real interest rate, which equals the nominal rate of interest minus expected inflation.[5]

Why Is Inflation So Unpopular?

One way to understand the consequences of inflation is in terms of the national income accounts. Recall that either the *expenditure approach* or the *income approach* can be used to compute GDP. Aggregate spending on output must equal the income arising from production of that output. Whenever the price level increases, more must be spent to buy the same output. If you think of inflation only in terms of spending, you consider only the problem of paying those higher prices. But if you think of inflation in terms of the higher money incomes that result, you see that higher prices mean higher receipts for resource suppliers. When viewed from the income side, inflation is not so bad.

If every higher price is received by some resource supplier, why are people so troubled by inflation? Presidents Ford and Carter could not control

5. Although the discussion has implied that there is only one rate of interest, a variety of rates can exist simultaneously, depending on differences in such factors as the risk and maturity of different loans.

inflation and were turned out of office. Inflation fell significantly during the Reagan administration, and President Reagan was reelected in a landslide, even though the level of unemployment was higher during his first term than during President Carter's tenure. During the 1988 and 1992 elections, George Bush kept reminding voters what the rate of inflation was the last time a Democrat was president.

INFLATION AFFECTS EVERYONE. One difference between inflation and unemployment is that, at any particular time, unemployment affects only a fraction of the labor force, usually less than 10 percent. In contrast, inflation affects everyone, whether in or out of the labor force, employed or unemployed, buying or selling goods, borrowing or lending money. *People are usually more concerned with inflation than with unemployment because more people are affected by inflation.* Also, whereas people view their higher incomes as the just rewards for their labor, they see inflation as a penalty that unjustly robs them of purchasing power. Most people do not stop to realize that, unless real output per worker increases, higher wages must result in higher prices. Prices and wages are two sides of the same coin. To the extent that nominal wages on average keep up with inflation, most workers do not suffer a loss of real income as a result of inflation. In fact, between 1955 and 1973 the average real wage per hour in the private sector increased by about 40 percent; since 1973, however, the real hourly wage has fallen by about 13 percent. So in the last twenty years inflation has slowly eroded real wages on average; this is another reason why inflation is so unpopular. Although inflation affects everyone, it hits hardest those whose incomes are fixed in nominal terms. For example, retirees who rely on fixed nominal interest income see their incomes eroded by unanticipated inflation.

Example In 1991, a male high school graduate in the United States earned 26.5 percent less than in 1979 after adjusting for inflation.

INFLATION'S EFFECTS ARE TAXED UNFAIRLY. Another reason inflation is so unpopular is that most tax laws ignore distinctions between real and nominal changes. Taxes on capital gains and on interest income are imposed on nominal changes even if there is no real change. A *capital gain*, recall, is any increase in the market value of an asset that occurs between the time the asset is purchased and the time it is sold. For example, suppose you bought a share of stock in 1980 for $100 and sold it in 1990 for $150, for a nominal capital gain of $50. During that period the price level in the economy actually increased by 59 percent, so the $150 you received from selling your stock had a real value of only $94.33 ($150/1.59) in 1980 dollars. Thus, when measured in dollars of constant purchasing power, you actually lost money on the deal. Yet you would still have to pay income taxes on your nominal gain of $50. The same is true of interest income. Suppose you earn 4 percent nominal interest on money in a savings account. If the inflation rate is 5 percent, your real rate of interest is negative, yet you must pay income taxes on your nominal interest earnings. Many observers argue that taxing nominal capital gains and nominal interest discourages incentives to save and to invest, and thereby retards growth. Tax reforms during the Reagan administration indexed personal income tax brackets and tax rates to inflation, but nominal interest income and nominal capital gains are still taxed as before.

Point to Stress Taxation can also turn a positive before-tax real gain into a negative after-tax real gain.

Example In 1992, some advisers to President Bush recommended that he sign an executive order requiring the U.S. Treasury to index capital gains.

Conclusion

To the extent that the level and composition of inflation are fully anticipated by all market participants, inflation is of less concern in macroeconomic analysis. But unanticipated inflation arbitrarily redistributes income and wealth from one group to another and reduces the ability to make long-term plans. The more variable and unpredictable inflation is, the greater the difficulty of negotiating long-term contracts. The overall productivity of the economy falls, because people must spend more time coping with the uncertainty created by inflation and less time producing goods and services.

This chapter has focused on two problems with the economy: unemployment and inflation. Though we have discussed them separately, they are related in a variety of ways, as we will see in later chapters. Politicians sometimes add the unemployment rate to the rate of inflation to come up with what they refer to as the "misery index." For example, in 1980 an unemployment rate of 7.0 percent combined with a CPI increase of 13.5 percent to yield a misery index of 20.5—a number that explains why President Carter was not reelected that year. By 1984 the misery index had dropped to 11.4 and by 1988 to 9.5; Republicans retained the White House in both elections. By 1992 the index had climbed slightly to 10.2 percent, an increase that spelled trouble for President Bush.

In the next chapter we begin building a model of the economy by examining components of aggregate demand. Once we have a better idea of how a healthy economy works, we can consider the policy options in the face of high unemployment or high inflation.

Summary

1. The unemployment rate equals the number of people looking for work divided by the number in the labor force. Since the 1950s women have increased their labor force participation rate, but many older workers have retired earlier. The overall unemployment rate hides rate differences among particular groups. The lowest rate is among adult white males; the highest rate is among black teenagers.

2. There are four types of unemployment. Frictional unemployment arises because job seekers and employers need time to find one another. Structural unemployment arises because changes in taste, technology, taxes, or competition reduce the demand for certain skills. Seasonal unemployment stems from the effects of the weather and the calendar on certain industries, such as construction and agriculture. Cyclical unemployment comes from the decline in production during recessions.

3. Unemployment imposes both an economic and a psychological burden on those who are unemployed. For some people this burden is reduced by unemployment insurance, which typically replaces more than half of take-home pay. Unemployment insurance provides a safety net for people who are unemployed, but it also may reduce their incentive to find work.

4. Inflation is a sustained and continuous rise in the average level of prices. Demand-pull inflation results from an increase in aggregate demand. Cost-push inflation results from a decrease in aggregate supply. Until World War II, both increases and decreases in the price level were common, but since then the price level has steadily increased.

5. Anticipated inflation causes fewer distortions in the economy than does unanticipated inflation.

Unanticipated inflation arbitrarily creates winners and losers, and it forces people to spend more time and energy coping with inflation. The negative effects of high and variable inflation on an economy's productivity can be observed in those countries that have experienced hyperinflation.

6. Because not all prices change by the same amount during inflationary periods, people have difficulty keeping track of relative prices. Uncertainty about relative prices makes economic activity more costly and more risky.

7. The intersection of the supply and demand curves for loanable funds indicates the equilibrium interest rate. The nominal rate of interest equals the real rate of interest plus the rate of inflation. The higher the expected inflation, the higher the nominal rate of interest.

QUESTIONS AND PROBLEMS

1. (Labor Force) Refer to Exhibit 1 in this chapter to determine whether the following are true or false.
   a. Some people who are unemployed are not in the labor force.
   b. Some people in the labor force are not working.
   c. All people who are not unemployed are in the labor force.
   d. Some people who are not working are not unemployed.

2. (Frictional Unemployment) Why might there be less frictional unemployment in a small, developed country than in a large, less developed country? Does the geographic size of a country have anything to do with the amount of frictional unemployment it has?

3. (Unemployment Across Industries) The rate of unemployment in such industries as financial services, transportation, and public utilities is consistently below that in manufacturing, which in turn is below that in construction. Are there any fundamental economic or social reasons why this is so? Explain.

4. (Structural Unemployment) Which industries in the U.S. economy are most likely to develop large-scale structural unemployment? Are colleges preparing students for such structural changes? Are unskilled workers more or less likely to become structurally unemployed than educated and skilled workers are?

5. (Unemployment Insurance) It is commonplace to hear that the average duration of unemployment in the United States is greatly influenced by the fact that this country has unemployment insurance. In Japan companies offer bonuses to workers who accept reduced hours or different jobs rather than continuing to collect unemployment insurance. Some countries in Europe scale down the unemployment benefits the longer an individual collects unemployment insurance. How would such programs work in the United States? What problems are associated with such programs?

6. (Inflation) (See Exhibit 5 in this chapter.) Using the concepts of aggregate supply and demand, explain why inflation usually rises during wartime.

7. (Inflation) If actual inflation is higher than anticipated inflation, who will lose purchasing power and who will gain?

8. (Anticipated Inflation) What are the benefits associated with correctly anticipating inflation? Is such anticipation free, or does it require some of the economy's scarce resources? Why would greater uncertainty about inflation inhibit the undertaking of long-term capital spending by business?

9. (Real Interest Rates) During much of the 1970s, real interest rates in the United States were negative. How can bankers and other lenders conduct business when they are lending at negative interest rates? What caused lenders to lend consistently at rates that were too low?

10. (Nominal Versus Real Interest Rates) Why does a 10 percent tax imposed on nominal interest earned result in more than a 10 percent tax on real interest earned when there is inflation?

11. (Unemployment Rate) Suppose that the U.S. noninstitutional adult population is 180 million and the labor force participation rate is 65 percent.
    a. What is the size of the U.S. labor force?
    b. If 70 million of the adult population are not working, what is the unemployment rate?
    c. If the number of adults in the military is 2 million, what is the civilian unemployment rate?

12. (Unemployment Rate) Suppose that the unemployment rates for population subgroups remain constant as follows:

Teenagers	18%
Young adults (20–39)	9%
Older adults (40–65)	3%

    a. Explain how changes in the composition of the population across these subgroups lead to changes in the overall unemployment rate.
    b. Calculate the overall unemployment rate given the composition of the labor force in the two years shown below.

	1960	*1985*
Teenagers	40%	20%
Young adults	30%	50%
Older adults	30%	30%

13. (Inflation) Explain why steady inflation is likely to be less harmful to an economy than a situation in which inflation rates fluctuate a lot.

14. (Relative Prices) Suppose the elderly poor spend all of their incomes on just three items in the following proportions:

Food	35%
Housing	50%
Medical care	15%

    Using the data in Exhibit 6, calculate the inflation rate for this group for 1978-1980 and 1982-1984, and compare your answer to the CPI figures for all items.

15. (Nominal Versus Real Interest Rates) Using a supply-demand diagram for loanable funds (like Exhibit 8), show what happens to nominal interest rates, real interest rates, and the equilibrium quantity of loans when both borrowers and lenders increase their estimates of the expected inflation rate from 5 percent to 10 percent (assume an initial equilibrium nominal interest rate of 8 percent).

16. (Unemployment) How might each of the following influence the natural rate of unemployment?
    a. An increase in minimum wage
    b. Globalization of national economies
    c. Increasing numbers of two-earner households

17. (Inflation and Interest Rates) For much of 1992, the spread between short- and long-term interest rates on U.S. government debt was at record levels. Could this be explained, at least in part, by anticipated inflation?

18. (Nominal Versus Real Interest Rates) Explain as carefully as you can why borrowers would be willing to pay a higher rate of interest if they expected the inflation rate to increase in the future.

19. (Inflation Costs) Suppose that the rate of inflation is constant and known with certainty so that all time-related contracts can be indexed perfectly for inflation, and therefore no risk from inflation exists. What kinds of problems might still exist if the inflation rate was exceedingly high?

20. (Poor King Coal) In what sense is the unemployment in McDowell County structural? In what sense could it be considered frictional?

21. (Poor King Coal) What are some options to "solve" the McDowell County unemployment problem?

22. (Wild Inflation in Bolivia) In countries like Bolivia that are having massive inflation problems, the increased use of another country's currency (like the U.S. dollar) becomes common. Why do you suppose this happens?

23. (Wild Inflation in Bolivia) Suppose that the exchange rate between Bolivian pesos and the U.S. dollar is fixed (e.g., 1 dollar = 10,000 pesos). What would this policy do to international trade between the two countries?

24. (Changes in Relative Prices) Look at the inflation rates for new and used cars for the two time periods shown in Exhibit 6. What explanation can you offer for this flip-flop?

25. (Changes in Relative Prices) When prices of different goods change at different rates, it means that the consumer price index may not be useful as a cost-of-living indicator for different segments of the population. Discuss.

CHAPTER 8

AGGREGATE DEMAND: CONSUMPTION, INVESTMENT, AND NET EXPORTS

Chapter 5 introduced the aggregate demand and aggregate supply curves. The intersection of these two curves determines the economy's equilibrium price level and the equilibrium quantity of aggregate output. Using these concepts along with the circular flow, we developed a rough idea of how the economy works and considered the problems arising from unemployment and inflation.

In this chapter and the next, we focus on aggregate demand, especially the private-sector components of aggregate demand: consumption, investment, and net exports. In Chapter 10 we will develop aggregate supply and show how it interacts with aggregate demand arising from the private sector to create the economy's equilibrium level of price and output. When the private-sector equilibrium occurs where there is much unemployment, the question is whether self-correcting forces operate in the economy to reduce unemployment or whether government intervention is necessary. Government will get into the act in Chapter 11. Topics discussed in this chapter include

- Say's Law
- Consumption function
- Marginal propensities to consume and to save
- Shifts in the consumption function
- Investment function
- Net export function

EARLY VIEWS OF THE MACROECONOMY

Teaching Tip The changes in views of the macroeconomy can be related to the discussion of the role of theory and the scientific method in Chapter 1.

We first consider some early views of the macroeconomy and discuss the reexamination of these views caused by the Great Depression. In Chapter 6 we mentioned Quesnay's contribution to our understanding of the circular flow of income. He had other insights into the economy's performance that contributed to subsequent developments in macroeconomics. Quesnay argued that even though people were motivated by self-interest, the economy was ruled by natural laws, laws that government intervention would only distort. The phrase "laissez-faire et laissez-passer"—roughly, let it alone and let it flow—came to be associated with the view that unfettered markets best promote national economic prosperity.

The Classical View

Quesnay's notions of a natural economic order and his philosophy of laissez-faire influenced Adam Smith (1723–1790), who wrote *The Wealth of Nations*, the most famous book in economics. Published in 1776, Smith's study argued for a "system of natural liberty." Smith, like Quesnay, had no misconception about individual motives; he too assumed that people pursued their own self-interest. Fortunately for humankind, according to Smith, the "great Director of Nature" led individuals as if "by an invisible hand" to promote the general good.

To understand the revolutionary nature of Smith's declaration of economic independence, you must keep in mind that during the previous two hundred years European countries had followed a mercantilist policy, which carefully regulated international trade in order to accumulate gold and silver in the public treasury. Smith established a school of thought that came to be called classical economics. **Classical economists** criticized mercantilism and advocated laissez-faire. These economists did not deny the existence of depressions and unemployment, but they argued that the sources of such crises lay outside the economic system, in the effects of wars, tax increases, poor growing seasons, and changing tastes. Such external "shocks" could affect output and employment. The resulting disequilibrium, however, was viewed as a short-run phenomenon that would be corrected by natural market forces, such as flexibility of prices, wages, and interest rates. Simply put, classical economists argued that if the price level was too high to sell all that was produced, prices would fall until the quantity supplied equaled the quantity demanded; if wages were too high to employ all workers, wages would fall until the quantity of labor supplied equaled the quantity demanded; and if interest rates were too high to channel the amount saved into the amount invested, the interest rate would fall until the amount saved equaled the amount invested.

Classical economists A group of eighteenth- and nineteenth-century British economists who criticized mercantilism and believed that self-interest and competition promoted economic development

Consumption, Saving, and Investment

Classical economists addressed common fears that the sharp depressions of the period meant that the quantity of goods supplied would exceed the quantity demanded, resulting in a "general glut" of goods. Thus, the important question for the classical economist was "Will the aggregate quantity demanded be sufficient to purchase the aggregate quantity supplied, or will goods be left unsold?" *As long as all output was purchased, firms would continue to employ the labor necessary to supply that output. As long as all earnings were spent, total spending would equal total income. If, however, spending fell short of income, some output might remain unsold. If the excess supply persisted, unemployment would result, since firms would not continue to produce goods they could not sell.*

The income that arises from supplying aggregate output is of sufficient purchasing power to buy that level of output. Smith divided this purchasing power into two flows, consumption and saving; saving represented a potential diversion from the circular flow. For example, if only 80 percent of income was spent on consumption and if consumption represented the only source of spending in the economy, then not all output would be purchased, so output and employment would fall.

Smith, however, believed that people saved only because they wanted to invest—that is, to buy new physical capital. The economy of the day was still primarily agricultural, so savers and investors were often the same people. Thus, saving was not a leakage of purchasing power from the circular flow because it was directly converted into investment demand. To Smith, saving was "the immediate cause of the increase in capital."[1] Moreover, even if not every saver was also an investor, the interest rate would adjust in the market for loanable funds until planned saving equaled planned investment. So saving was actually a virtue because the resulting increase in investment expanded the economy's capital stock, thereby enhancing the economy's ability to produce. (Incidentally, we hear echoes of Smith today when economic observers lament the relatively low rate of saving in the United States.) According to Smith, *the combination of consumption demand and investment demand would always be sufficient to clear the market of total output, so the quantity of aggregate output demanded would always equal the quantity of aggregate output supplied.*

Teaching Tip Refer to Exhibit 8 in Chapter 7 to show that if the quantity of loanable funds supplied (determined by saving) exceeds the quantity of loanable funds demanded (determined by investment), the interest rate will fall.

Say's Law: Quantity Supplied Creates Its Own Quantity Demanded

The classical view of the economy's natural ability to sell all that was produced is perhaps best reflected by **Say's Law**. According to this law, *people supply their resources to the market only because they want to buy something in return, so the quantity supplied creates its own quantity demanded.* Consequently, every supplier is also a demander. Although Say's Law is credited to the French economist Jean Baptiste Say (1767–1832), it is actually a collection of related ideas embellished by a number of economists of the period. According to these classical economists, since the quantity supplied would create an equal quantity demanded, the quantity demanded would always be sufficient to

Say's Law People produce because they want to spend, so the supply of a given quantity of aggregate output generates an equivalent quantity demanded

1. Adam Smith, *The Wealth of Nations*, bks. I–III, with an introduction by Andrew Skinner (Great Britain: Penguin Books, 1970), 437.

clear the market of production, regardless of how fast or how large the economy grew. Although widespread unemployment could arise temporarily because of external shocks to the economy, natural market forces in the form of price and wage adjustments would correct this imbalance and reduce unemployment. Therefore, *classical economists believed that in the long run a high level of output and employment could be sustained naturally with no assistance from government. Production generated the purchasing power required to demand that output. Markets would always clear.*

The history of economic thought reflects the interplay of theory and events. The classical belief in laissez-faire and the self-correcting nature of markets dominated economic thinking through much of the nineteenth and early twentieth centuries. New theories of macroeconomics evolve as existing theories are shaken by economic events, however, and the Great Depression was such a theory-shaking event.

Keynes and the Great Depression

Although classical economists had admitted that capitalistic, market-oriented economies could experience temporary unemployment, the prolonged depression of the 1930s strained belief in the economy's self-correcting ability. As discussed earlier, the Great Depression was marked by severe unemployment and much unused plant capacity. With abundant unemployed resources, output and income fell far short of the economy's potential.

The stark contrast between the natural market adjustments predicted by the classical theory and the years of high unemployment during the Great Depression represented a collision of theory and fact. We should say, however, that to this day there remains some controversy whether the Great Depression was a failure of the market system or whether it was in fact caused by a sharp drop in the supply of money to the economy. If monetary authorities were to blame, or even if they just contributed to the problem, then classical theory would not be called into such question.

In 1936 John Maynard Keynes, of Cambridge University in England, published *The General Theory of Employment, Interest, and Money*, a book that questioned the classical view of the economy and touched off what has come to be called the Keynesian revolution. *Keynesian theory and policy were developed to address the problem of unemployment arising from the Great Depression.* The main quarrel Keynes had with the classical economists was that prices and wages did not appear sufficiently flexible to ensure the full employment of resources. Keynes also argued that saving and investment were carried out by different groups of people for different reasons, and there was no reason to expect these two groups to have identical intentions. Keynes believed that business expectations might at times become so grim that even very low interest rates would not be sufficient to induce firms to invest all that consumers might save.

Once the link between the amount households save and the amount firms plan to invest is broken, it becomes possible for saving to exceed planned investment. Thus the leakage of saving from the circular flow may

Example Let production equal $5 trillion, consumption $4 trillion, and saving $1 trillion. Planned investment of $0.5 trillion would then result in aggregate spending of only $4.5 trillion, so $0.5 trillion of production would go unsold.

Point to Stress In the Keynesian model, the level of aggregate demand is an important factor in determining the level of employment.

exceed the injection of planned investment into the circular flow. *If saving exceeds the amount firms plan to invest, then the quantity of aggregate output demanded will fall short of the quantity of aggregate output supplied. Some goods will remain unsold, causing firms to reduce production, so the levels of aggregate income and employment will fall.* In the classical model, flexible wages, prices, and interest rates would adjust to increase income and employment, returning the economy to its full employment level. According to Keynes, however, prices and wages were relatively inflexible—they were "sticky"—so natural market forces would not return the economy to full employment.

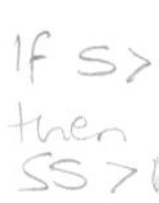

Though Keynes and the classical economists had differing views of how the economy works, there was still much agreement. Both Smith and Keynes focused on the combined effect of consumption and investment in the context of the circular flow. Indeed, Keynes once said that his intent was "to use what we have learned from modern experience and modern analysis, not to defeat but to implement the wisdom of Adam Smith."[2] In the balance of this chapter we shift gears to discuss the private-sector components of aggregate demand: consumption, investment, and net exports. In Chapter 9 we will combine these components and show how to derive the aggregate demand curve for the private sector. Chapter 10 will introduce aggregate supply. Only after we have some idea how the private sector works will we introduce government in Chapter 11.

CONSUMPTION

Suppose a new friend at college invited you home for the weekend. One thing you would learn from your visit is how well off the family is—you would get an impression of their standard of living. Is their home something you might see on "Lifestyles of the Rich and Famous," or is it more modest? Do they drive a new BMW, or do they take the bus? What do they eat? What do they wear? The simple fact is that consumption tends to reflect income. You can usually tell much about a family's economic status by observing their consumption pattern. Although you sometimes come across people who live well beyond their means or who still have the first nickel they ever earned, by and large consumption and income tend to be highly correlated. *The positive and stable relation between consumption and income, both for the household and for the economy as a whole, is the central idea of this chapter.*

An Initial Look at Consumption and Income

Keynes observed that the most important determinant of how much people spend is how much they have available to spend. Although his observation

2. Speech in the House of Lords, December 18, 1945, as quoted in Eric Roll, *A History of Economic Thought*, 3d ed. (Englewood Cliffs, N.J.: Prentice-Hall, 1964), 525.

seems obvious, it is fundamental to an understanding of how the economy works. The red line in Exhibit 1 depicts real disposable income in the United States since 1929, and the blue line depicts real consumer spending. *Disposable income*, remember, is the income actually available for spending or saving. (The use of the term "real" here and later indicates that the data have been adjusted for inflation so that dollars are of constant value.)

Example In 1939, U.S. real consumption spending was equal to 102.1 percent of U.S. real disposable income. In 1944, it was equal to 74.3 percent of real disposable income. More typically, real consumption spending tends to be 90 to 95 percent of real disposable income.

Note in Exhibit 1 that consumer spending and disposable income tend to move together over time. Both are measured along the vertical axis in 1987 dollars. Consumer saving is the difference between disposable income and consumer spending; it is indicated in Exhibit 1 by the vertical distance between the two lines. During the Great Depression, the two lines were nearly identical, indicating that households spent all their income. Because of military demands during World War II, however, few consumer goods were available; many items were rationed. With jobs and income relatively abundant, but little to buy, people saved a lot during the war. Since World War II, the relation between income and consumption has been relatively stable. Both have increased nearly every year.

EXHIBIT 1

Consumer Spending and Disposable Income in the United States Since 1929

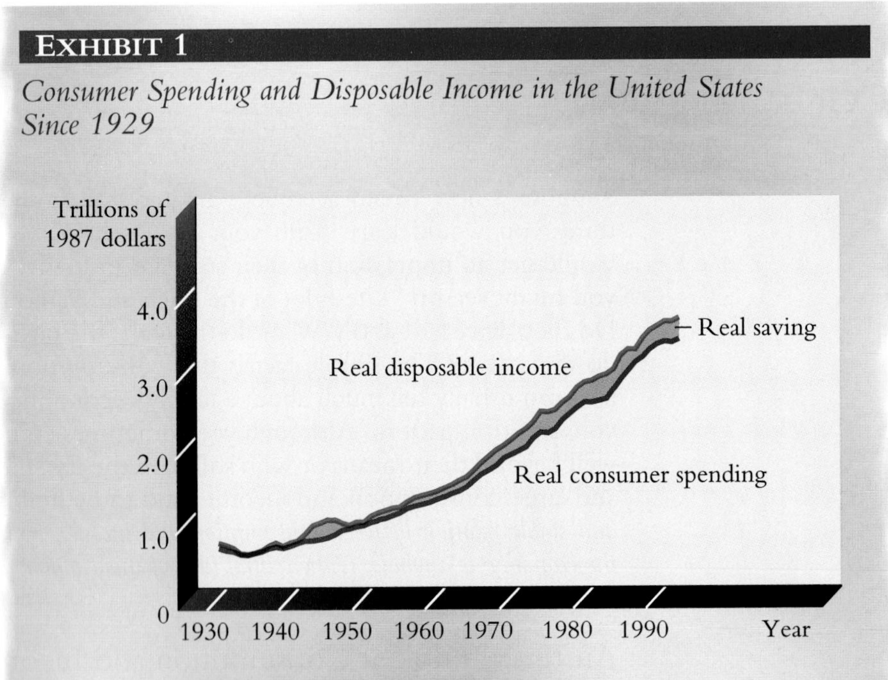

Income and consumer spending move together over time. Consumer saving is the difference between disposable income and consumer spending and is shown by the blue shaded area on the graph. Saving was close to zero during the Great Depression of the 1930s.

Source: *Economic Report of the President,* January 1993.

Another way to graph the relation between income and consumption over time is shown in Exhibit 2, where disposable income is measured along the horizontal axis and personal consumption along the vertical axis. Notice that each axis measures the same units: dollars—in this case dollars of 1987 purchasing power. The exhibit focuses on the relation between income and consumption in the United States since 1950. Each year is depicted by a point that reflects two values: disposable income and consumption. For example, in 1964 disposable income (read from the horizontal axis) was $1.56 trillion, and consumption (read from the vertical axis) was $1.42 trillion.

As you can see, there is a clear and direct relation between consumption and disposable income, a relation that should come as no surprise after Exhibit 1. You need little imagination to see that by connecting the points on the graph in Exhibit 2, you could trace a line relating consumption to income. Such a relation has special significance in macroeconomics.

EXHIBIT 2

Consumer Spending and Disposable Income in the United States Since 1950

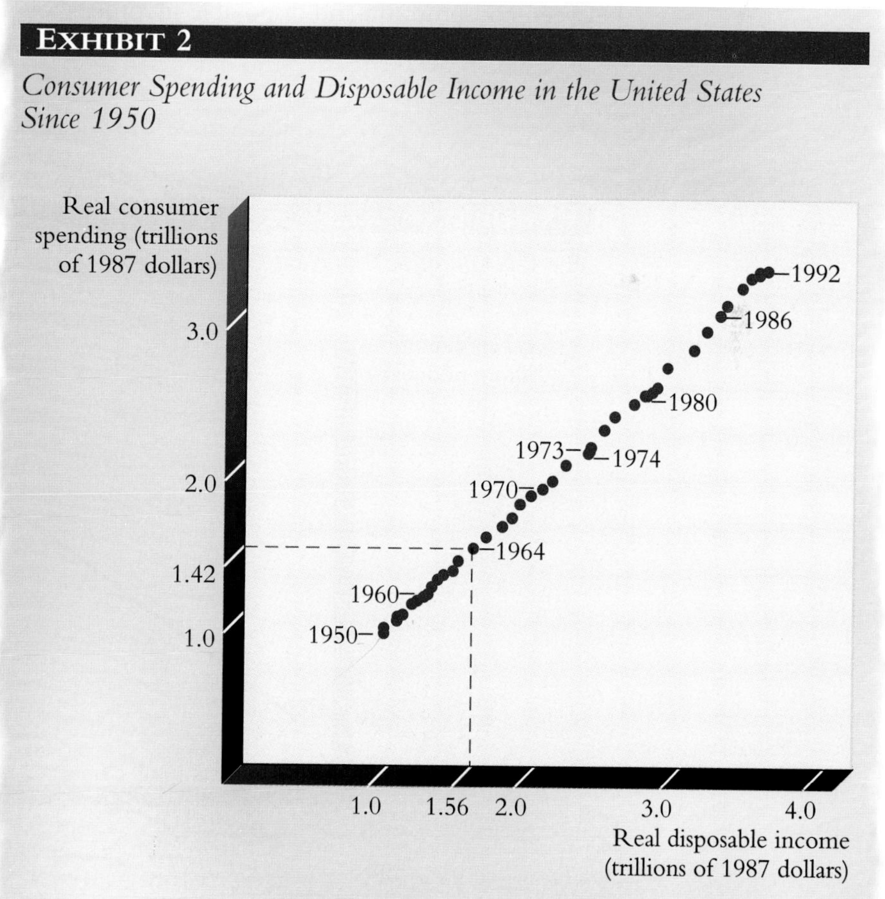

The clear, direct relation between consumption and disposable income is apparent when the two variables are plotted against each other on the same graph.

Source: *Economic Report of the President,* January 1993.

The Consumption Function

We have examined the link between consumption and disposable income and have found it to be quite stable, particularly since World War II. Given their level of disposable income, households decide how much to consume and how much to save. Households save both for unforeseen emergencies, such as medical problems, and for fully anticipated expenses, such as college tuition. So consumption depends on disposable income. *Disposable income is the independent variable, and consumption the dependent variable.*

Consumption function The relation between the level of income in an economy and the amount households spend on consumption, other things constant

Because consumption depends on income, we say that consumption is a *function* of disposable income. Exhibit 3 presents a hypothetical **consumption function**, which shows a positive relation between the amount spent on consumption and the level of disposable income in the economy, other determinants of consumption held constant. Both consumption and disposable income are measured in real terms. Notice that our hypothetical consumption function in Exhibit 3 looks similar to the actual historical relation between consumption and disposable income, shown in Exhibit 2.

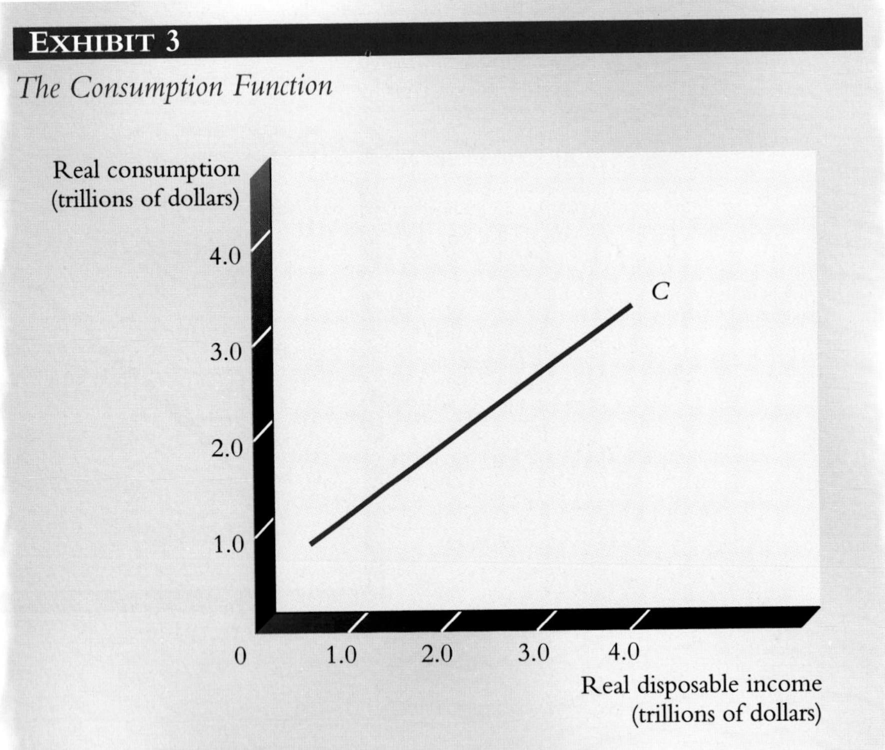

The consumption function, *C*, shows the relation between consumption expenditure and disposable income, other things constant.

Point to Stress It is important to consider marginal changes because the macroeconomy is not static. Rather it is constantly reacting to factors changing the levels of output and prices.

Marginal Propensities to Consume and to Save

In Chapter 1 we noted that economic analysis focuses on activity at the margin. Economists are usually interested in changes from one period to the next. How much did the economy grow this year? What growth rate is expected next year? To focus on such changes, we must apply marginal analysis to the the relation between changes in disposable income and changes in consumption. The effect of a change in disposable income on consumption is of special interest. For example, suppose households receive another billion dollars in disposable income. Some of this additional income is spent on consumption and some will be saved. The fraction, or proportion, of that additional income that is consumed is called the marginal propensity to consume. More precisely, the **marginal propensity to consume** equals the change in consumption divided by the change in income. Likewise, the fraction of that additional income that is saved is called the marginal propensity to save. Again, more precisely, the **marginal propensity to save** equals the change in saving divided by the change in income.

Marginal propensity to consume The fraction of a change in disposable income that is spent on consumption; the change in consumption spending divided by the change in disposable income that caused it

Marginal propensity to save The fraction of a change in disposable income that is saved; the change in saving divided by the change in disposable income that caused it

These propensities can be understood best by reference to Exhibit 4, which presents the hypothetical data underlying the consumption function presented in Exhibit 3. The table shows, for a range of possible incomes, how much consumers would like to spend and how much they would like to save. The first column presents alternative levels of disposable income, *DI*, beginning with $2.8 trillion and ranging up to $5.2 trillion in increments of $0.4 trillion.

EXHIBIT 4

Marginal Propensity to Consume and Marginal Propensity to Save (trillions of dollars)

Income (real *DI*) (*Y*) (1)	Change in Income (Δ*DI*) (2)	Consumption (*C*) (3)	Change in C (Δ*C*) (4)	Saving (*S*) (5)	Change in Saving (Δ*S*) (6)	MPC = (4) ÷ (2) (Δ*C*/Δ*DI*) (7)	MPS = (6) ÷ (2) (Δ*S*/Δ*DI*) (8)
2.8		2.8		0		0.3/0.4 = 3/4	0.1/0.4 = 1/4
	0.4		0.3		0.1		
3.2		3.1		0.1			
	0.4		0.3		0.1	3/4	1/4
3.6		3.4		0.2			
	0.4		0.3		0.1	3/4	1/4
4.0		3.7		0.3			
	0.4		0.3		0.1	3/4	1/4
4.4		4.0		0.4			
	0.4		0.3		0.1	3/4	1/4
4.8		4.3		0.5			
	0.4		0.3		0.1	3/4	1/4
5.2		4.6		0.6			

As you can see from the table, if income increases from \$2.8 trillion to \$3.2 trillion, an increase of 0.4 trillion, consumption increases by \$0.3 trillion and saving increases by \$0.1 trillion. The marginal propensity to consume, or MPC, equals the change in consumption divided by the change in income; in this case the change in consumption is \$0.3 trillion and the change in income is \$0.4 trillion, so the marginal propensity to consume is 0.3/0.4, or 3/4. Notice that each time income increases by \$0.4 trillion, as indicated in column (2), consumption increases by \$0.3 trillion, as indicated in column (4). Therefore, the MPC is 3/4 at all levels of income. The marginal propensity to consume, or MPC, is listed in column (7).

Teaching Tip If you plan later to develop the model with an income tax described in Chapter 11, stress here that this equality holds because the marginal propensities are defined in terms of disposable income.

At each income level, the decision about consumption also determines saving. Notice from column (6) that saving increases by \$0.1 trillion with each \$0.4 trillion increase in disposable income, so the marginal propensity to save, or MPS, equals 0.1/0.4, or 1/4, at all levels of income. The marginal propensity to save is listed in the final column. Since disposable income is either spent or saved, the marginal propensity to consume plus the marginal propensity to save must add up to 1. In our example, 3/4 + 1/4 = 1. We can say more generally that

MPC + MPS = 1

Graphing the MPC and MPS

You may recall from the appendix to Chapter 1 that the slope of a straight line is equal to the vertical distance between any two points divided by the horizontal distance between those points. Consider, for example, the slope between points *a* and *b* on the consumption function in Exhibit 5(a). The vertical distance between these points represents the change in consumption (denoted ΔC), in this case \$0.3 trillion. The horizontal distance represents the change in disposable income (denoted ΔDI), in this case \$0.4 trillion. The slope is therefore equal to 0.3/0.4, or 3/4, which equals the marginal propensity to consume.

Thus, *the marginal propensity to consume is measured graphically by the slope of the consumption function.* After all, the slope is nothing more than the increase in consumption divided by the increase in income. *Because the slope of any straight line is constant everywhere along the line, the MPC for any linear, or straight-line, consumption function will be constant at all levels of income.* Our hypothetical data yield a consumption function that is linear, with a constant marginal propensity to consume. Note, however, that we make this constant-value assumption for simplicity and ease of exposition. In reality, the marginal propensity to consume will not necessarily be constant. The consumption function could be curved so that the MPC was greater at lower levels of income, meaning that the slope of the consumption function would get flatter as income increased.

Saving function The relation between saving and level of income in the economy, other things constant

Panel (b) of Exhibit 5 presents the **saving function**, *S*, which relates saving to the level of income, reflecting the hypothetical data presented in Exhibit 4. The saving function can be subjected to the same sort of graphical analysis as the consumption function. The slope between any two points on the saving

EXHIBIT 5

Marginal Propensities to Consume and to Save

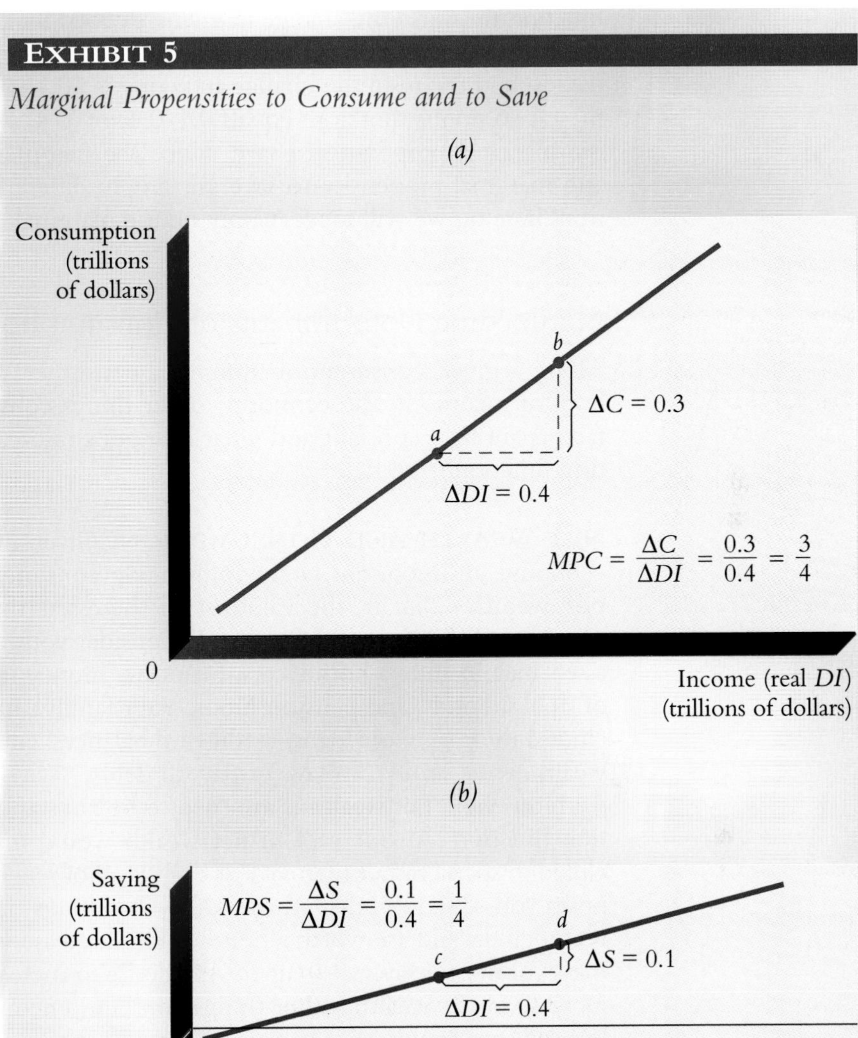

The slope of the consumption function is the marginal propensity to consume. For the straight-line consumption function of panel (a), the slope is the same at all levels of income and is given by the change in consumption divided by the change in disposable income that causes it. Hence, the marginal propensity to consume is $\Delta C/\Delta DI$, or $0.3/0.4 = 3/4$. The slope of the saving function is the marginal propensity to save, $\Delta S/\Delta DI$, or $0.1/0.4 = 1/4$.

function measures the change in saving divided by the change in income. For example, between points *c* and *d* in Exhibit 5(b), the change in income is $0.4 trillion and the resulting change in saving is $0.1 trillion. The slope between these two points therefore equals 0.1/0.4, or 1/4, which by definition equals the marginal propensity to save. Since the marginal propensity to consume and marginal propensity to save are simply different sides of the same coin, from here on we will focus mainly on the marginal propensity to consume.

Nonincome Determinants of Consumption

Along a given consumption function, consumer spending depends on the level of income in the economy, other things constant. Now let's see what factors are held constant and what changes could cause the entire consumption function to shift.

Net wealth The value of a household's assets minus its liabilities

NET WEALTH AND CONSUMPTION. Given the level of income in the economy, an important factor influencing consumption is each household's **net wealth**—that is, the value of all the assets that each household owns minus any liabilities, or debts owed. Consider your own family. Your family's assets may include a home, cars, furniture, money in the bank, and the value of stocks, bonds, and pension funds. Your family's liabilities, or debt, may include a mortgage, car loans, credit card balances, and the like. To increase net wealth, your family can save or pay off debts.

Household net wealth is assumed to be constant along a given consumption function. An increase in net wealth would make consumers more inclined to spend rather than save at each level of real income. To see why, suppose you discover that those dusty paintings in the attic are in fact Rembrandts and are worth a bundle. This increase in wealth reduces the primary motive for saving—namely, the desire to increase net wealth. Hence, an increase in net wealth, other things constant, encourages households to save less and spend more at each level of income. The original consumption function is depicted as line *C* in Exhibit 6. If net wealth increases, the consumption function shifts from *C* up to C', because households are willing and able to spend more at every level of income.

Example Consider the impact on net wealth of falling home prices in the late 1980s and early 1990s.

Conversely, if net wealth decreases, the consumption function shifts from *C* down to C'', reflecting households' desire to spend less and save more at every level of income. For example, when prices fell sharply on the stock market in October of 1987, the decrease in stockholders' net wealth prompted them to reduce consumption. The demand for real estate, expensive cars, and jewelry reportedly declined.

Teaching Tip You can call movements along the consumption function *induced* changes in spending and shifts in the consumption function *autonomous* changes in spending.

Again, *it is a change in net wealth, not a change in income, that shifts the consumption function. Changes in income simply result in a movement along a given consumption function, not a shift in the function.* Be mindful of the difference between a *movement along* the consumption function, which results from a change in income, and a *shift in* the consumption function, which results from a change in one of the nonincome determinants of consumption, such as net wealth.

EXHIBIT 6

Shifts in the Consumption Function

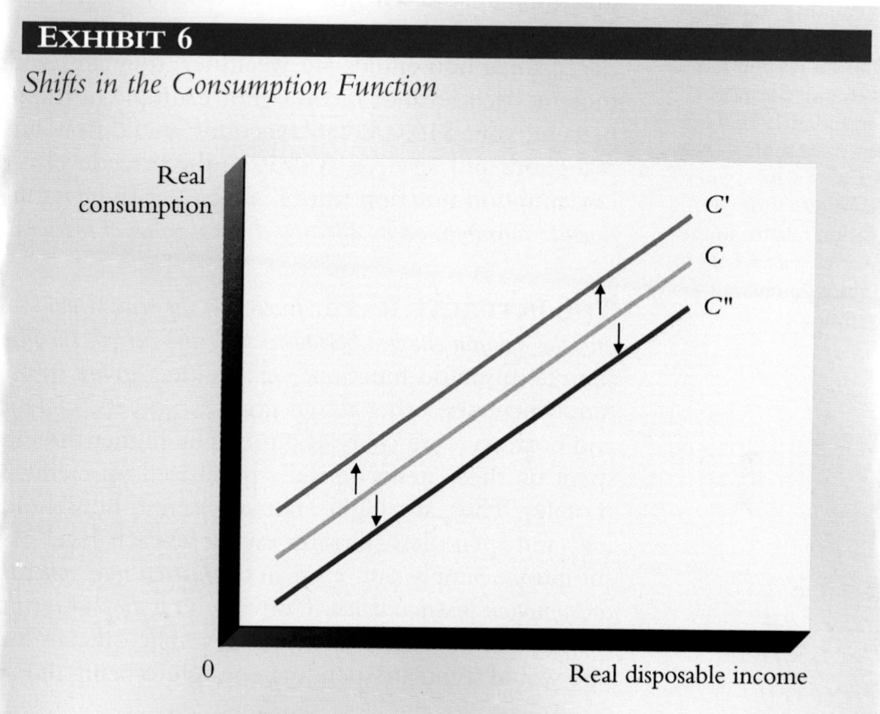

An upward shift in the consumption function, such as from *C* to *C*′, can be caused by an increase in wealth, a decrease in the price level, a favorable change in consumer expectations, or a decrease in the interest rate. A downward shift, such as that from *C* to *C*′′, can be caused by a decrease in wealth, an increase in the price level, an unfavorable change in expectations, or an increase in the interest rate.

THE PRICE LEVEL. Another variable that can affect the consumption function is the price level prevailing in the economy. As we have said, household wealth is an important determinant of consumption. The greater the household wealth, other things constant, the greater consumption will be at each level of income. Much household wealth is held in assets whose values are fixed in dollar terms. The most obvious of these is money itself. The higher the price level, the lower the real value of a given quantity of money in the economy. When the price level changes, so does the real value of bank accounts and other dollar-denominated financial assets.

For example, suppose your wealth consists of $10,000 in a bank account. If the price level increases by 10 percent, your bank account will purchase about 10 percent fewer real goods and services. You feel poorer because you are poorer. The real value of your wealth has declined. To rebuild the real value of your wealth to some desired level, you decide to save more and spend less. An increase in the price level reduces the purchasing power of wealth held in fixed-dollar assets and, as a consequence, causes households to save more and consume less at each level of income. So the consumption

Teaching Tip As measured by the CPI, the last drop in the U.S. price level occurred in 1955. However, for money assets earning a fixed interest rate, a drop in inflation relative to the interest rate would increase purchasing power.

function shifts down from C to C'', as shown in Exhibit 6. Conversely, a drop in the price level increases the real value of dollar-denominated assets; since households are wealthier, they are willing and able to consume more at each level of income. For example, if the price level declined by 10 percent, your $10,000 bank account would now buy about 10 percent more real goods and services. A drop in the price level is reflected by a shift in the consumption function from C up to C'. In effect, *a change in the price level influences consumption by affecting the real value of net wealth.*

THE INTEREST RATE. *Interest is the reward paid to savers to defer consumption and the amount charged borrowers to secure current spending power.* When graphing the consumption function, we assume a given interest rate. If the rate of interest increases, other things constant, savers, or lenders, are rewarded more, and borrowers are charged more. The higher the interest rate, the less will be spent on those items typically purchased on credit, such as homes and automobiles. Thus, at a higher rate of interest, households will save more, borrow less, and spend less. Greater saving at each level of income means less consumption. Simply put, *a rise in the interest rate, other things constant, will shift the consumption function down.* Conversely, *a drop in the interest rate will shift the consumption function up.* During 1991, public officials hoped that a falling interest rate would stimulate spending enough to bring the economy out of recession.

EXPECTATIONS. As noted early in this book, expectations influence economic behavior in a variety of ways. For example, suppose you are a senior in college and you land a high-paying job to start upon graduation. Your consumption will probably jump long before the job actually begins because you anticipate a higher income. You will likely make credit card purchases, borrow for a new car, and draw down whatever savings you had. You will probably spend more than friends who do not yet have a job or who plan to pursue graduate study. More generally, your college years are a period when your consumption usually far outstrips your income, all in anticipation of higher income after graduation. Any change that leads you to expect higher income in the future will shift your consumption function up. Conversely, the worker who receives a "pink slip" announcing a layoff that is to take effect at the end of the year will likely reduce consumption immediately, well before the actual date of the layoff. As households become more uncertain about future employment prospects, such as occurs with the onset of a recession, they reduce the amount consumed at each level of income.

Example Similarly, a part-time student working on an MBA may increase consumption spending during the last school term in anticipation of a raise at work upon receipt of the degree.

Expectations about inflation also affect consumption. An expectation of a higher price level in the future encourages people to buy more now. For example, expectations of a big jump in housing prices or interest rates will prompt households to buy homes now. On the other hand, an expectation of a lower price level or a lower interest rate in the future makes people defer major purchases until after the price level falls. Thus, expectations affect spending at each level of income, and a change in expectations shifts the consumption function. This is why consumer confidence is monitored so closely by those who keep track of the economy.

Again, keep in mind the distinction between *movements along a given consumption function* as a result of a change in income and *shifts in the consumption function* as a result of a change in another variable. We conclude our introduction to consumption with the following case study, which discusses consumption and saving patterns over people's lifetimes.

CASE STUDY

The Life-Cycle Hypothesis

Do rich people save a larger fraction of their incomes than poor people do? Both theory and evidence seem to suggest that they do. The easier it is to make ends meet, the more likely it is that money will be left over for saving. Does it follow from this that richer economies save more than poorer ones—that economies save a larger fraction of total disposable income as they grow? In his famous book *The General Theory*, published in 1936, John Maynard Keynes drew this conclusion. But as later economists studied the data—such as that presented in Exhibit 2—it became clear that Keynes was wrong. For societies, the fraction of total disposable income saved seems to stay constant as income grows.

So how can it be that richer individuals save more than poorer individuals, yet richer countries do not necessarily save more than poorer countries? By the early 1950s several answers had been proposed. One of the most important of these was the *life-cycle model of consumption*. According to this model, people tend to save more when they are younger for financial security in old age. In old age they dissave, or draw down their savings. On net, most individuals save little during their entire life cycle.

The life-cycle hypothesis suggests that the saving rate in an economy depends among other things on the relative number of young savers and old dissavers in the population. Other factors that influence the saving rate across countries include the tax treatments of savings, the market for housing, and the convenience and reliability of saving institutions. For example, in Japan 20,000 post offices nationwide offer savings accounts to more than half the country's population. In fact, Japan's postal savings system is the world's largest financial institution. Also, a homebuyer in Japan must make a down payment that represents a relatively large fraction of the home's purchase price; this calls for substantial savings by young families. Japan has one of the highest saving rates in the world.

Source: Paul Jessup and Mary Bochnak, "A Case for a U.S. Postal Savings System," *Challenge*, November/December 1992: 57–59.

We next consider another component of aggregate expenditure: investment. Our objective is to work up to the relation between the total spending in the economy and the level of income.

INVESTMENT

The second component of aggregate expenditure is investment, or, more precisely, *gross private domestic investment*. By investment we do not mean buy-

Point to Stress The discussion of investment is focused on *planned* investment.

ing stocks, bonds, or other financial assets. Investment consists of spending on (1) the construction of factory plants and equipment, (2) the construction of housing, and (3) net increases in inventories. Just as we assumed that consumption decisions are based on utility-maximization by households, we assume that investment decisions are based on profit-maximization by firms. Thus, investment is undertaken because those who run the firm believe that such spending will increase the firm's profit.

An investment represents a commitment of current resources in expectation of a future stream of profit. Some machines, for example, are expected to last five years, others thirty years. Since the payoff occurs in the future, a potential investor must estimate how much profit a particular investment will yield this year, next year, the year after, and in all future years covered by the productive life of the investment. *Firms buy new capital goods only if they expect this investment to be more profitable than other possible uses of their funds.*

The Demand for Investment

Point to Stress An increase in cost or a decrease in expected earnings reduces the expected rate of return.

Point to Stress A firm should reject any potential investment whose expected rate of return falls below the interest rate at which the firm can borrow or can earn on saved funds.

Teaching Tip If the club purchased four carts, total annual returns would equal $1,000 ($400 + $300 + $200 + $100). If the club purchased three carts and earned $160 by placing $2,000 in a bank account, total annual returns would be higher: $1,060 ($400 + $300 + $200 + $160).

To understand the investment decision, consider a simple example. The operators of the Hacker Haven Golf Club are contemplating buying additional solar-powered golf carts to rent to golfers. The model under consideration, called the Weekend Warrior, sells for $2,000, requires no maintenance or operating expenses, and is expected to last indefinitely. In this simplified example, the *expected rate of return* equals the annual dollar earnings expected from the investment divided by its dollar cost. The first cart purchased is expected to earn a rental income of $400 per year. Dividing this income by the cost of the cart, we find that the first cart purchased can be expected to yield a rate of return of $400/$2,000, or 20 percent per year. Additional carts will be used less. A second cart is expected to generate $300 per year in rental income, yielding a rate of return of $300/$2,000, or 15 percent; a third cart, $200 per year, or 10 percent; and a fourth cart, $100 per year, or 5 percent. A fifth cart would not be used at all, so it has an expected rate of return of 0 percent.

Should the operators of Hacker Haven purchase any carts, and if so, how many? Suppose they plan to borrow the money to buy the carts. The number of Weekend Warriors they should purchase will depend on the rate of interest they must pay to borrow money. If the rate of interest exceeds 20 percent, their cost of borrowing exceeds the expected rate of return on even the first cart, so no carts will be purchased. What if the operators had saved enough money to buy the carts? The market rate of interest also reflects what the club owners could earn by saving money. If the interest rate exceeds 20 percent, they will earn a higher rate of return by saving any funds on hand than by investing these funds in golf carts, so no carts would be purchased. *The market rate of interest represents the opportunity cost of investing in capital.*

Suppose the market rate of interest is 8 percent per year. At that rate of interest, the first three carts, with expected rates of return above 8 percent, would more than pay for themselves. A fourth cart would lose money, since its expected rate of return is only 5 percent. The investment decision is easier to understand if you refer to Exhibit 7, where the expected rate of return and

EXHIBIT 7

Rate of Return on Golf Carts and the Opportunity Cost of Funds

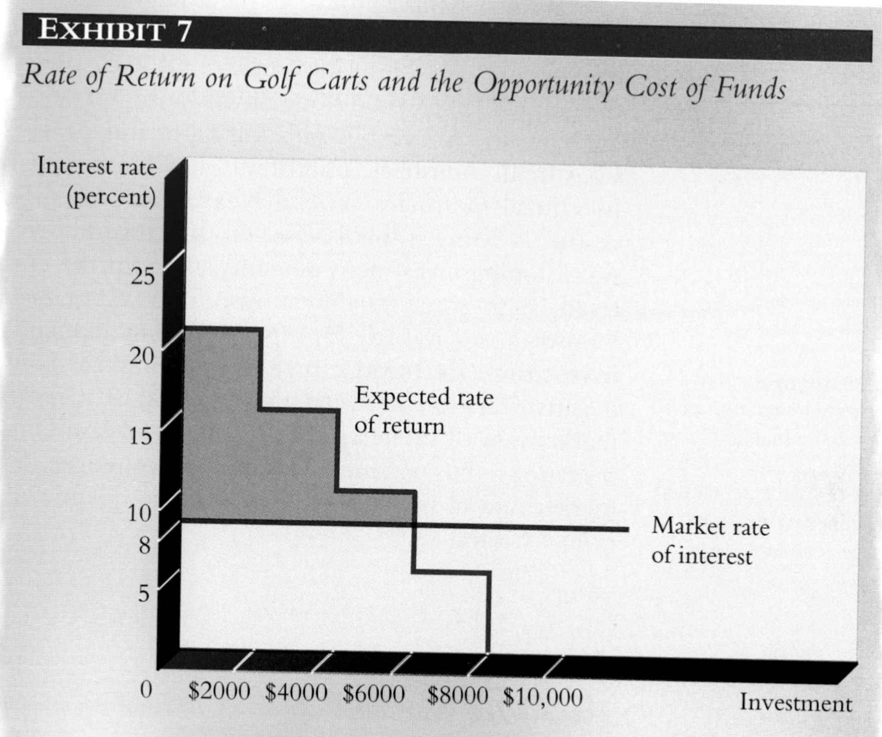

An individual firm will invest in any project whose rate of return exceeds the market interest rate. At an interest rate of 8 percent, Hacker's Haven would purchase three golf carts, which represents investment spending of $6,000.

market rate of interest are measured along the vertical axis, and the amount invested by Hacker Haven in golf carts is measured along the horizontal axis. The steplike relation shows the expected rate of return earned on additional dollars invested in golf carts. This relation also indicates the amount invested in golf carts at each interest rate, so you can view this steplike relation as Hacker Haven's demand for this type of investment.

Teaching Tip Show that total investment would rise to $8,000 if the market interest rate fell to 4 percent—because the club would buy four carts. Total investment would fall to $4,000 if the market interest rate rose to 12 percent—because the club would buy only two carts.

The horizontal line at 8 percent indicates the market rate of interest, which represents the opportunity cost of investment funds to the firm. This line can be viewed as the supply of investment funds available to the course operators. Recall that the course operators' objective is to choose an investment strategy that maximizes profit. Profit is maximized when $6,000 is invested in the carts—that is, when three carts are purchased. The expected return from a fourth cart is below the opportunity cost of funds. Therefore, investing in four or more carts would lower total profit.

From Micro to Macro

So far we have examined the investment decision for a single golf course, but there are over thirteen thousand golf courses in the United States.

The industry demand for investment in golf carts shows the relation between the amount all course operators invest and the rate of return on that type of investment. Like the relation in Exhibit 7, the investment demand curve for the golf industry would slope downward.

Now let's move beyond golf carts and consider the investment decisions in all industries: publishing, fast foods, apparel, and hundreds more. Individual industries generally have a downward-sloping demand for investment. More is invested when the cost of borrowing is lower. A downward sloping investment demand curve for the entire economy can be derived, with some qualifications, from a horizontal summation of each industry's downward sloping investment demand curve. The economy's **investment demand curve** is represented as *D* in Exhibit 8. It shows the negative relation between the quantity of investment demanded and the market rate of interest, other things held constant, including business expectations. For example, in our hypothetical demand curve, when the market rate of interest is 8 percent, the quantity of investment demanded is $0.4 trillion.

Investment demand curve The relation between the market rate of interest and the quantity of investment demanded in the economy, other things constant

EXHIBIT 8

Investment Demand for the Economy

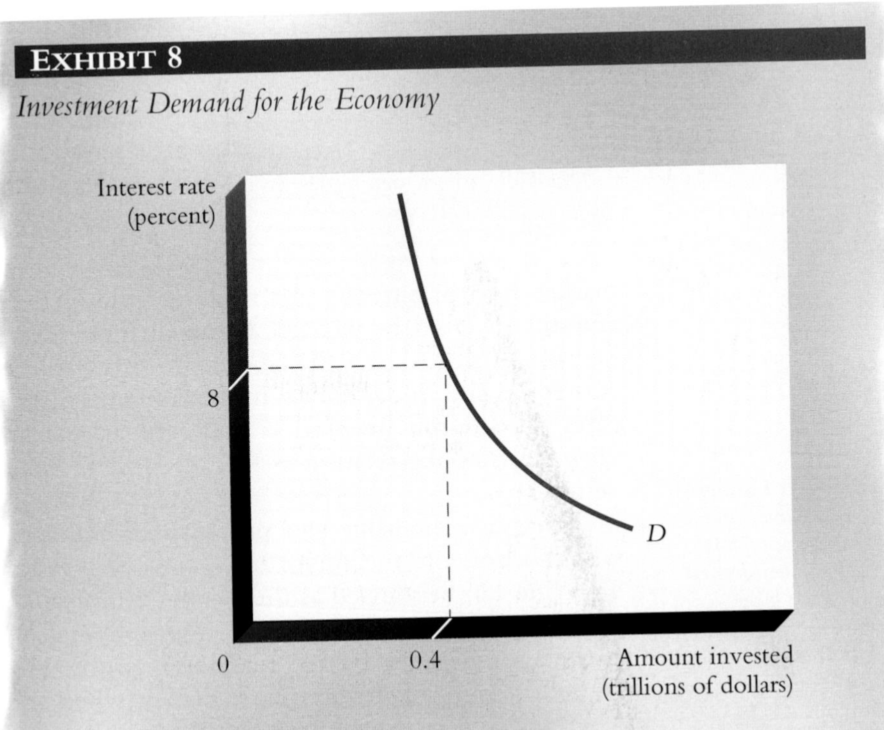

The investment demand curve for the economy is obtained by summing the amount of investment undertaken by each firm for each interest rate. At lower interest rates, more investment projects become profitable for individual firms, so the total investment spending in the economy increases.

Teaching Tip Use Exhibit 8 to illustrate the increase in the amount invested. Explain that if the interest rate falls to 6 percent, for example, firms add investments with expected rates of return of 7.5 percent, 7.0 percent, and so forth to the $0.4 trillion of investment already accepted when the interest rate was 8 percent. Total investment is thus greater than $0.4 trillion.

Point to Stress Any spending component that is autonomous with respect to income in the income-expenditure model is drawn as a flat line.

Investment function The relation between planned investment and the level of income, other things constant

Autonomous A term that means "independent"; autonomous investment is independent of the level of income

Planned Investment and the Economy's Level of Income

To integrate the discussion of investment with our earlier analysis of consumption, we need to know if and how planned investment varies with the level of disposable income in the economy. Whereas we were able to present empirical evidence relating consumption to the level of income over time, there is less of a link between investment and income. *Investment varies greatly from year to year, depending more on business expectations and on interest rates than on the current level of income in the economy.* Some investments may take years to complete, such as a new electric power plant. The investment decision is thus said to be "forward looking," based more on expected profit than on current income levels.

So how does investment relate to the economy's disposable income? The simplest **investment function** assumes that planned investment is unrelated to the current level of disposable income; investment is assumed to be **autonomous** with respect to income. For example, suppose that given current business expectations and prevailing interest rates, firms plan to invest $0.4 trillion a year, regardless of the economy's income level. Exhibit 9 measures disposable income on the horizontal axis and *planned investment* on the vertical

EXHIBIT 9

Autonomous Investment Function

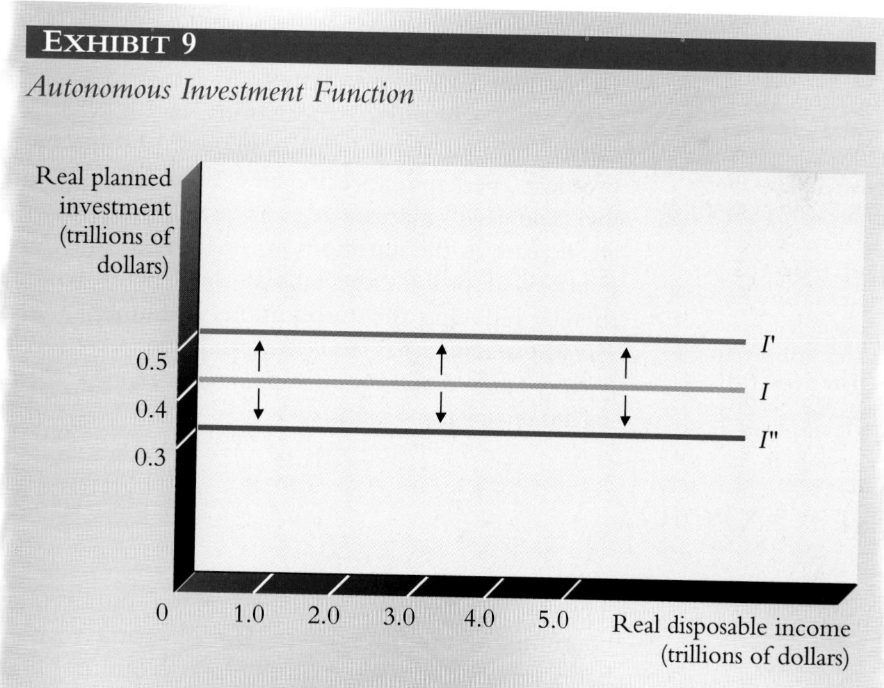

Autonomous investment spending is independent of income, as shown by the horizontal lines. A decrease in the interest rate or improved business expectations can increase autonomous investment, as shown by the upward shift from I to I'. An increase in the interest rate or unfavorable business expectations can shift the investment function down to I''.

axis. Investment of $0.4 trillion is shown by the flat autonomous investment function, *I*. As you can see, along investment function *I*, planned investment does not vary even though disposable income does.

Nonincome Determinants of Investment

The autonomous investment function isolates the relation between the level of income in the economy and the amount decision makers would like to invest, or planned investment, other things constant. We have already mentioned two important components that are held constant: business expectations and the interest rate. Now let's consider the effect of changes in these factors on autonomous investment.

Teaching Tip Use the earlier golf cart example. If the expected rate of return on the fourth cart rises to 9 percent (expected revenues rise from $100 to $180), then the total amount invested when the interest rate is 8 percent will increase from $6,000 to $8,000. Alternatively, if expected revenues on the third cart drop from $200 to $150, its expected rate of return falls to 7.5 percent and the club will now purchase only two carts when the interest rate is 8 percent.

MARKET INTEREST RATE. Autonomous investment, *I*, is based on a given interest rate. If the interest rate falls because of, say, some change in the nation's monetary policy (as happened in 1992), the cost of borrowing falls, and this reduces the opportunity cost of investment. The resulting increase in planned investment is reflected in Exhibit 9 by a shift up in the autonomous investment function from I to I'. Conversely, an increase in the rate of interest, other things constant, will raise the cost of borrowing and will lower the autonomous investment function from I down to I''.

BUSINESS EXPECTATIONS. As noted in Chapter 5, investment depends primarily on business expectations, or on what Keynes called the "animal spirits" of business. If firms in general become more optimistic about profit prospects, perhaps expecting an economic expansion next year, their planned investment will increase at every level of income, as reflected in Exhibit 9 by an increase in the autonomous investment function from I up to I'. On the contrary, if profit expectations sour, firms will be less willing to invest, thereby reducing the autonomous investment function from I down to I''. *Factors that could affect business expectations are wars, political events such as the abolition of tariffs, technological breakthroughs, changes in business taxes, and changes in the cost of capital equipment.*

NET EXPORTS

Thus far this chapter has focused on two important components of spending: consumption and investment. But in recent years, the rest of the world has had a growing influence on the U.S. economy. The rest of the world affects aggregate expenditure through imports and exports.

Example U.S. export sales slowed significantly in 1992 when recession hit the European economies.

Net Exports and Disposable Income

How do imports and exports relate to the level of income in the economy? When their disposable income rises, Americans tend to spend more, and some of this increased spending goes for imported goods. Higher incomes lead to more spending on Japanese automobiles, French wines, Korean VCRs, trips to Europe, and thousands of other foreign products. How does the value of U.S. exports relate to the economy's level of disposable income? The amount of U.S. exports purchased by the rest of the world depends on the income of foreigners, not on the U.S. level of income. The desire of the French to purchase U.S. computers or the desire of Saudi Arabia to purchase U.S. military hardware is not influenced by the level of income in the United States.

Point to Stress The assumption of autonomous net exports is made to simplify the graphical and algebraic models. A more complete model assumes that imports vary with the level of income.

Since our exports are relatively insensitive to the level of U.S. income but imports tend to increase with income, *net exports*, *NX*, which equal exports, *X*, minus imports, *M*, tend to decline as income increases. Such an inverse relation is developed graphically in the appendix to this chapter. For now, we simplify the analysis by assuming that net exports are independent of the level of income, or *autonomous*. If exports exceed imports, net exports are positive; if imports exceed exports, net exports are negative, and if exports equal imports, net exports equal zero. Suppose net exports equal zero, as shown by the net export function *NX* in Exhibit 10; *NX* is a line that coincides with the horizontal axis.

EXHIBIT 10

Autonomous Net Export Function

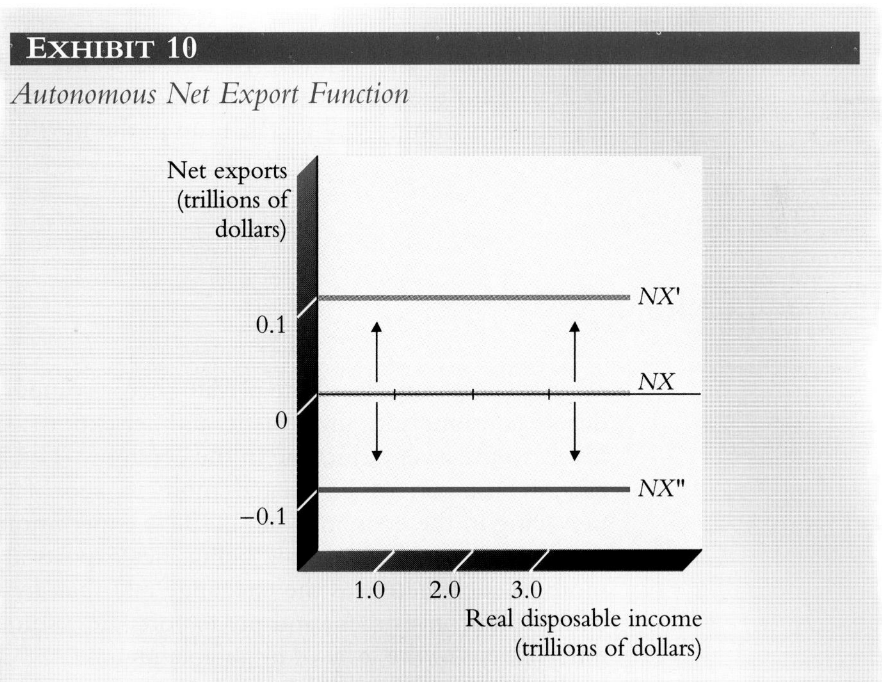

Autonomous net exports are independent of disposable income, as shown by the horizontal lines. *NX* is the net export function if net exports are equal to zero. Note that *NX* coincides with the horizontal axis. A decrease in the value of the dollar relative to other currencies would cause net exports to increase, as shown by the shift up to *NX′*. An increase in the value of the dollar would cause net exports to decrease, as shown by the shift down to *NX″*.

Net export function The relation between net exports and the level of income in the economy, other things constant

Example Assume the value of the dollar falls from \$1 = 1 German mark to \$2 = 1 German mark. A U.S. export priced at \$1,000 would initially cost 1,000 marks, and an import from Germany priced at 1,000 marks would cost \$1,000. After the change in the exchange rate, the buyer's price of the U.S. export would be 500 marks and the buyer's price of the U.S. import would be \$2,000.

Nonincome Determinants of Net Exports

The **net export function** shows the relation between net exports and the level of income in the economy, other things constant. Factors held constant include the U.S. price level, the price levels in other countries, interest rates here and abroad, foreign income levels, and the exchange rate between the dollar and foreign currencies. Consider the effects of a change in one of these factors. Suppose the value of the dollar falls relative to foreign currencies, as it did in 1992. With the dollar worth less on world markets, foreign products become more expensive for Americans and U.S. products become cheaper for foreigners. The impact of a declining dollar is thus an increase in exports but a decrease in imports at each level of income, resulting in an increase in net exports. The hypothetical impact of a decline in the value of the dollar is shown in Exhibit 10 as a parallel shift in the net export function from *NX* up to *NX′*, reflecting autonomous net exports of \$0.1 trillion. Countries often attempt to devalue their currency as a way of increasing their net exports.

A rise in the dollar's value will have the opposite effect, decreasing exports and increasing imports, resulting in a decrease in net exports. An autonomous decline in net exports is shown in our example by a parallel drop in the net export function, from *NX* down to *NX″*, where autonomous net exports equal −\$0.1 trillion. In fact, U.S. net exports have been negative each year for the last decade. The effect of net exports on aggregate spending in the economy will be taken up in the next chapter.

CONCLUSION

We have now considered the private-sector components of aggregate expenditure: consumption, investment, and net exports. Consumption relates positively to the level of income in the economy. The level of investment, however, is assumed to be related more to such factors as the interest rate prevailing in the economy and business expectations than to the level of income. Likewise, for the time being, net exports are assumed to be affected more by such factors as the exchange rate than by the level of domestic income. Thus, investment and net exports are assumed to be autonomous, or independent of the level of disposable income.

In the appendix to this chapter we develop a more realistic but more complicated picture by showing how net exports decline as the level of income increases. In the next chapter we show how consumption, investment, and net exports add up to the aggregate expenditure function, which is then used to derive the equilibrium quantity of aggregate output demanded by the private sector.

SUMMARY

1. Classical economists believed that people produced only because they wanted to spend, so the quantity supplied would equal the quantity demanded. Although external shocks to the economy could temporarily increase unemployment, natural market forces, including adjustments in prices, wages, and interest rates, would reduce unemployment.

2. The Great Depression was so deep and so prolonged that belief in the natural recuperative powers of the economy was seriously challenged. Keynes argued that saving could exceed investment, so some goods would remain unsold. This would cause firms to cut production, creating unemployment. According to Keynes, wages and prices were relatively sticky, so they would not adjust to ensure full employment.

3. One of the most predictable and useful relations in macroeconomics is that between consumption and income. The consumption function indicates that the more income people have, the more they spend on consumption, other things constant.

4. The slope of the consumption function reflects the marginal propensity to consume, which equals the change in consumption divided by the change in income. The slope of the saving function reflects the marginal propensity to save, which equals the change in saving divided by the change in income.

5. Certain factors can cause the consumption function to shift. An increase in net wealth will reduce the need to save and hence increase consumption at every level of income. A higher price level will reduce the value of dollar-denominated assets and will thereby reduce consumption. A reduction in the interest rate will make saving less rewarding and borrowing less costly and hence will increase consumption. Finally, expectations about future income and price levels will also influence consumption.

6. Planned investment depends on the market rate of interest and business expectations. We assume that investment is autonomous, or independent of income.

7. Net exports equal exports minus imports. Exports tend to be unrelated to the level of disposable income in this country. Imports tend to be positively related to disposable income. Thus, net exports tend to decline as disposable income increases. For simplicity, we initially assume that net exports are autonomous, or unrelated to disposable income.

QUESTIONS AND PROBLEMS

1. (Classical Economic Theory) It is sometimes said that the classical economic system assumed flexible prices in all markets. Discuss how flexible prices and wages would eliminate excess production of goods, excess supply of labor, and excess supply of savings, all of which occur during a recession.

2. (Classical Versus Keynesian Economics) Why was the flexibility of wages, prices, and interest rates such an important issue between Keynesian and classical economists?

3. (Consumption) For each of the following cases, discuss which way the consumption function will shift; that is, will it shift up or down, or are you unable to tell?
   a. Wealth increases, and interest rates fall.
   b. Wealth increases, and the price level increases.
   c. Interest rates rise, and people expect a recession.
   d. The price level increases, and people expect prices to rise more in the future.

4. (Consumption Function) How does an *increase* in each of the following variables affect the consumption function? The saving function?
   a. Lump-sum taxes
   b. Interest rates
   c. Consumer optimism, or confidence
   d. Price level
   e. Real wealth
   f. Disposable income

5. (Wealth and Consumption) Two people have the same annual income, but one has a higher level of real wealth. Economists would expect the person with greater wealth to spend a greater fraction of total disposable income. Why?

6. (Investment Spending) One of the most unstable components of investment spending is construction, both residential and commercial. One of the most unstable prices in the economy is the price of borrowing, which is the interest rate. Is there a relationship between the two? What are some possible reasons for the volatility of interest rates?

7. (Autonomous Investment) Some investment projects are relatively insensitive to the *current* level of income in the economy. Give some examples of such investment projects. Why are they so insensitive?

8. (Investment) Consider Exhibit 7 in this chapter. If the owners of the golf course revised their estimates of the revenue from the golf carts so that each cart earned $100 less, how many carts would they buy when the interest rate was 8 percent? How many would they buy when the interest rate was 3 percent?

9. (Investment) Why would the following investment expenditures rise as interest rates fell?
   a. Purchase of a new plant and equipment
   b. Construction of new housing
   c. Accumulation of planned inventories

10. (Keynes) According to the national income accounting rules discussed in Chapter 6, leakages equal injections into the circular flow. In a model containing only households and firms, therefore, $S = I$. Why doesn't this disprove the Keynesian criticism of the classical model—namely, that interest rates need not cause savings and investment to balance?

11. (Consumption) Use the following data to answer the questions below.

Disposable Income	*Consumption*
$100	$150
200	200
300	250
400	300

   a. Graph the consumption function with consumption on the vertical axis and disposable income on the horizontal axis.
   b. If the consumption function is a straight line, what are its intercept and slope?
   c. If investment is equal to $100, what level of disposable income causes savings to equal investment?

12. (Consumption Function) According to the discussion of the consumption function, a number of factors can cause this function to shift. What, if anything, happens to the saving function when the consumption function shifts? Explain.

13. (Savings Function) In Exhibit 5, the savings function crosses the horizontal axis. What does this mean and what can we say about the consumption function at this point?

14. (Classical Theory) In Exhibit 9, the investment function is shown as shifting because of changes in interest rates and/or business expectations. What happens to the saving and consumption functions in response to the shift in investment, according to the classical theory? Explain.

15. (Net Exports) One of the factors that can cause the net export function to shift is the interest rate differential between the United States and the rest of the world. Why do you think this is true?

16. (Consumption and Savings) Suppose that consumption equals $500 billion when disposable income is $0, and each increase of $100 billion in disposable income causes consumption to increase by $70 billion. Draw a graph of the saving function using this information.

17. (MPC and MPS) Why must it always be true that a rise in the MPC will force a fall in the MPS? Why do economists believe that the MPC is a fraction between zero and one?

18. (MPC and MPS) Why would the MPC be different for different countries? For example, how would Japan's MPC compare with that of the United States? How would the MPC of Chad compare with that of the United States?

19. (Life-Cycle Hypothesis) Using the life-cycle hypothesis as the basis for your answer, determine what impact on the savings rate you might expect to see from an income tax cut that was publicized as being temporary.

20. (Life-Cycle Hypothesis) What are people doing to their lifetime consumption patterns relative to income, according to the life-cycle hypothesis?

APPENDIX
Variable Net Exports

In this appendix we examine more closely the relation between net exports and the U.S. level of income. We first look at the individual effects of exports and imports and then consider exports minus imports, or net exports.

Net Exports and Income

As noted in the chapter, the amount purchased by foreigners depends not on the U.S. level of income but on income levels in their own countries. We therefore assume that U.S. exports do not vary with respect to the U.S. income level. Specifically, suppose the rest of the world spends \$0.2 trillion per year on U.S. exports; the export function, *X*, would be as shown in panel (a) of Exhibit 11. On the other hand, when income increases, U.S. consumers tend to spend more on all goods, including imported goods. Thus, the relation between imports and disposable income is positive, as expressed by the upward-sloping import function, *M*, in panel (b) of Exhibit 11. Imports are assumed to be 10 percent of income, so when income is \$2.0 trillion, imports are \$0.2 trillion.

So far we have considered imports and exports as separate functions of income. What matters in terms of total spending on U.S. products are exports, *X*, minus imports, *M*, or net exports, $X - M$. By subtracting the import function depicted in panel (b) from the export function in panel (a), we derive the net export function, depicted as $X - M$ in panel (c) of Exhibit 11. Note that when disposable income is \$2.0 trillion, *imports* in panel (b) equal \$0.2 trillion. Since *exports* in panel (a) equal \$0.2 trillion at all levels of income, net exports equal zero when U.S. income equals \$2.0 trillion. At levels of income below \$2.0 trillion, net exports are positive because exports exceed imports. At levels of income greater than \$2.0 trillion, net exports are negative because imports exceed exports. The United States has experienced negative net exports since 1983.

EXHIBIT 11

Imports, Exports, and Net Exports

(a)

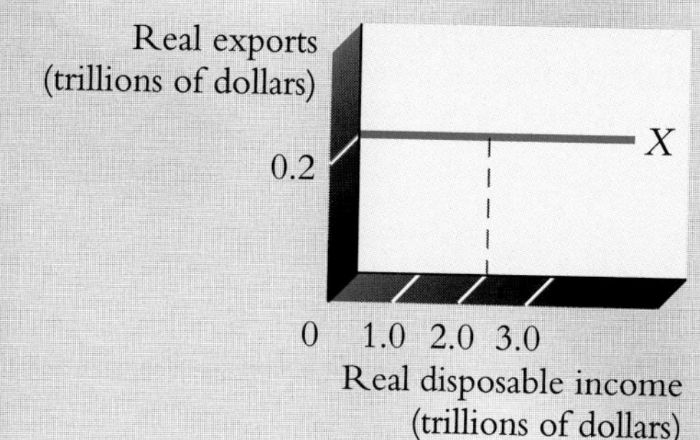

(b)

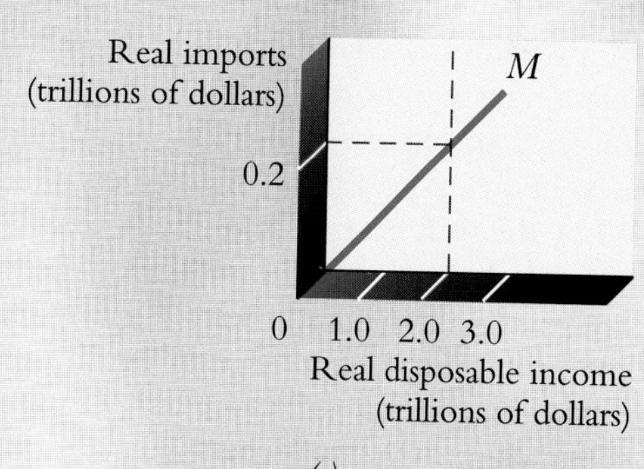

(c)

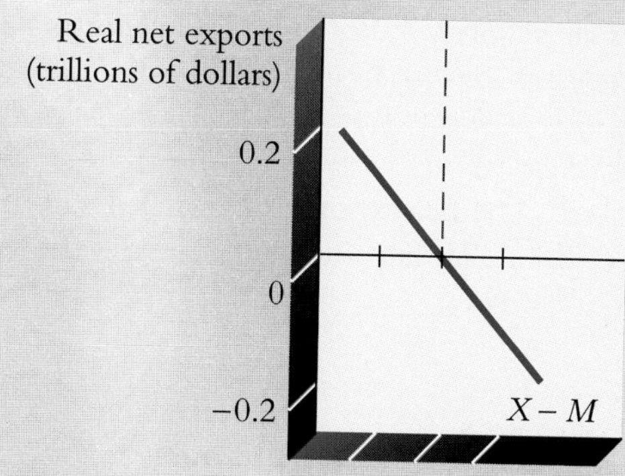

Exports are independent of the level of disposable income, as shown in panel (a). Imports are positively related to disposable income, as shown in panel (b). Net exports equal exports minus imports; net exports are negatively related to disposable income, as shown in panel (c).

Our trade deficit can be traced in part to the healthy level of economic expansion in the United States during the last half of the 1980s. Our trade deficit improved during the economic recession of the early 1990s.

Shifts in Net Exports

The net export function, $X - M$, shows the relation between net exports and real income, other things constant. Suppose the value of the dollar falls relative to foreign currencies. With the dollar worth less on world markets, foreign products become more expensive for Americans and U.S. products become cheaper for foreigners. The impact of a declining dollar value is to increase exports but decrease imports at each level of income. This increase in exports and decrease in imports increases the net export function, as shown in Exhibit 12 by the shift from $X - M$ up to $X' - M'$. A rise in the dollar's value will have the opposite effect, decreasing exports and increasing imports, as reflected in Exhibit 12 by a shift down in the net export function from $X - M$ to $X'' - M''$. Countries often attempt to devalue their currency as a way of increasing their net exports.

In summary, in this appendix we assumed that *imports are positively related to the level of disposable income, whereas exports are independent of the domestic level of income. Net exports, which equal exports minus imports, therefore vary inversely with the level of disposable income.* The net export function shifts up if the value of the dollar falls and shifts down if the value of the dollar rises.

EXHIBIT 12

Shifts in Net Exports

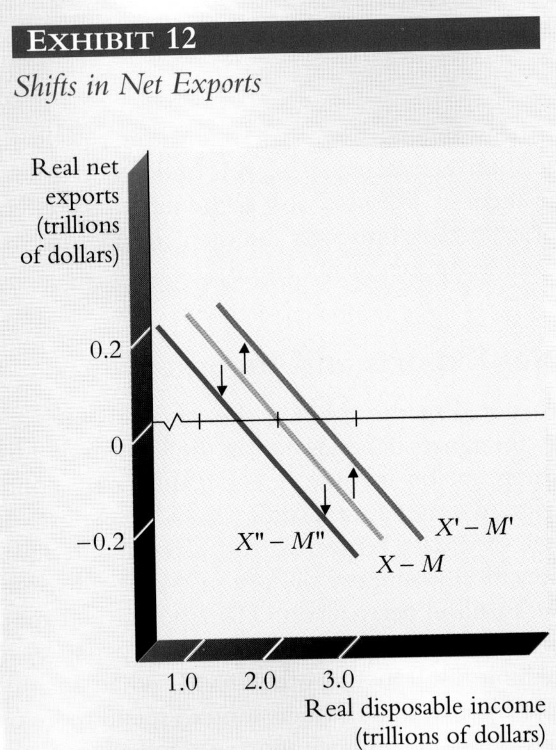

A decline in the value of the dollar, other things constant, will increase exports and reduce imports, thereby contributing to an increase in net exports, as shown by the shift from $X - M$ up to $X' - M'$. A rise in the value of the dollar will reduce exports and increase imports, causing net exports to fall, as shown by the shift from $X - M$ down to $X'' - M''$.

APPENDIX QUESTION

1. (Rest of the World) Using a graph of net exports ($X - M$) against disposable income, show the effects of the following:
   a. An increase in the foreign income level
   b. An increase in the U.S. income level
   c. An increase in U.S. interest rates
   d. An increase in the value of the dollar against foreign currencies

   Explain each of your answers.

CHAPTER 9

AGGREGATE EXPENDITURE AND DEMAND-SIDE EQUILIBRIUM

Thus far we have considered in detail three components of aggregate spending: consumption, investment, and net exports. We showed how each is related to the level of income in the economy. In this chapter we add up these private-sector components of spending to see how total spending, or aggregate expenditure, by the private sector relates to the level of income. We use this information to develop the aggregate demand curve for the private sector; we then examine shifts in that curve.

Throughout most of the chapter we rely on the simplifying assumption that net exports are autonomous, or independent of the level of income. In Appendix A we develop an aggregate expenditure function based on the more realistic assumption that imports tend to increase with income. An algebraic approach to the aggregate expenditure framework is developed in Appendix B. Aggregate supply will be examined in the next chapter, and government will be brought into the picture in Chapter 11. Topics discussed in this chapter include

- Aggregate expenditure function
- Equilibrium aggregate expenditure
- Effect of changes in aggregate expenditure
- Simple multiplier
- Effect of changes in the price level
- Aggregate demand curve

Aggregate Expenditure and Income

We begin developing the aggregate demand curve by asking how much aggregate output would be demanded at a given price level. By finding the quantity demanded at a particular price level, we will identify a single point on the aggregate demand curve. We continue to ignore government, so there are no taxes, transfers, or government purchases. For simplicity, we also assume there is no depreciation and no business saving. Given these assumptions, we can say that each dollar spent on production translates directly into a dollar of disposable income. Therefore, gross domestic product, or GDP, equals aggregate income, and also equals disposable income. In the last chapter we focused on real disposable income; in this chapter we focus on real GDP, which, given the simplifying assumptions, is identical to real disposable income. We consider the relation between aggregate spending and real GDP in the economy. By *real GDP* we mean GDP measured in terms of real goods and services produced.

Point to Stress Because this simple model ignores taxes, households are assumed to use income only for consumption and saving. Chapter 11 assumes three uses of income: consumption, saving, and taxes.

The Components of Aggregate Expenditure

Point to Stress Planned aggregate expenditure focuses on the impact on planned spending of changes in income, *other things constant.* One important factor held constant is the price level.

To get us started, suppose the price level in the economy is, say, 130, and we want to see what will be spent by the private sector at various levels of real GDP. Exhibit 1 presents the hypothetical data that will serve as building blocks for constructing the aggregate expenditure function. Much of this exhibit simply puts into tabular form relations that were already introduced as graphs in the previous chapter, namely, the consumption function, saving function, investment function, and net export function. The first column lists the level of real income and output, as measured by real GDP and as denoted by the symbol Y.

Exhibit 1

Hypothetical Schedules for Real GDP, Consumption, Saving, Investment, Net Exports, and Aggregate Expenditure (trillions of dollars)

Real GDP Income = Output (Y) (1)	Consumption (C) (2)	Saving (S) (3)	Planned Investment (I) (4)	Net Exports (NX) (5)	Planned Aggregate Expenditure ($C + I + NX$) (6)	Unintended Inventory Adjustment (7)	Actual Investment (8)
2.8	2.8	0	0.4	–0.1	3.1	–0.3	0.1
3.2	3.1	0.1	0.4	–0.1	3.4	–0.2	0.2
3.6	3.4	0.2	0.4	–0.1	3.7	–0.1	0.3
4.0	3.7	0.3	0.4	–0.1	4.0	0	0.4
4.4	4.0	0.4	0.4	–0.1	4.3	0.1	0.5
4.8	4.3	0.5	0.4	–0.1	4.6	0.2	0.6
5.2	4.6	0.6	0.4	–0.1	4.9	0.3	0.7

The level of real GDP in the first column motivates the actions recorded in the rest of the table. For example, households have only two possible uses for income: consumption and saving. Columns (2) and (3) show that the levels of consumption, *C*, and saving, *S*, increase with income. A second component of spending is investment. Column (4) lists planned investment, *I*, at each level of income. As you can see, planned investment is $0.4 trillion regardless of the level of income; thus, investment is assumed to be autonomous. A third component of spending is net exports, *NX*, listed in column (5), which shows that net exports are –$0.1 trillion at each level of income. Thus, net exports in this case are negative and are assumed to be autonomous. The sum of consumption, *C*, planned investment, *I*, and net exports, *NX*, is listed in column (6) as *planned aggregate expenditure*, which indicates the amount that households, firms, and the rest of the world would like to spend on U.S. output at each level of income. The remaining two columns will be discussed later.

Teaching Tip The vertical intercept for the consumption function in Exhibit 2 is $0.7 trillion. The $C + I$ function has an intercept at $1.1 trillion. The $C + I + NX$ function has an intercept of $1.0 trillion.

Graphical Analysis

Some people find it easier to observe relations in graphs. The consumption, investment, and net export schedules in Exhibit 1 are graphed in Exhibit 2. Real GDP, measured along the horizontal axis, can be interpreted both as the value of aggregate output and as the aggregate income generated by that level of output. Aggregate expenditure is measured on the vertical axis. Because income is measured on the horizontal axis and expenditure on the vertical axis, this graph is often called the **income-expenditure model**.

Income-expenditure model A graph that measures real income on the horizontal axis and aggregate spending on the vertical axis to determine the equilibrium quantity of aggregate output demanded

The consumption function, *C*, the lower line, is drawn to reflect the hypothetical consumption relation presented in Exhibit 1. This is the same consumption function introduced in the last chapter. The top line shows consumption plus investment, $C + I$; this line simply adds the $0.4 trillion in autonomous investment to the consumption function, so the *C* and $C + I$ lines are parallel. Next consider net exports. Because net exports are assumed to be –$0.1 trillion at each level of income, the aggregate expenditure function for the private sector is found by subtracting $0.1 trillion from the $C + I$ line, which yields $C + I + NX$, represented by the middle line and called the aggregate expenditure function. The **aggregate expenditure function** shows, for a given price level, the amount people plan to spend at each level of real GDP. If autonomous net exports were positive, then the aggregate expenditure function would be above the $C + I$ line. If autonomous net exports were equal to zero, then the aggregate expenditure line would be the same as the $C + I$ line.

Aggregate expenditure function A relationship showing, for a given price level, the amount of planned spending for each level of income; the total of $C + I + NX$

Equilibrium Quantity of Real GDP Demanded

We would like to find, for the given price level, the equilibrium quantity of real GDP demanded in the private sector. Refer to panel (a) in Exhibit 3, where the horizontal axis measures real GDP and the vertical axis aggregate expenditure. The aggregate expenditure function just developed in Exhibit 2

EXHIBIT 2

Consumption, Investment, Net Exports, and the Aggregate Expenditure Function

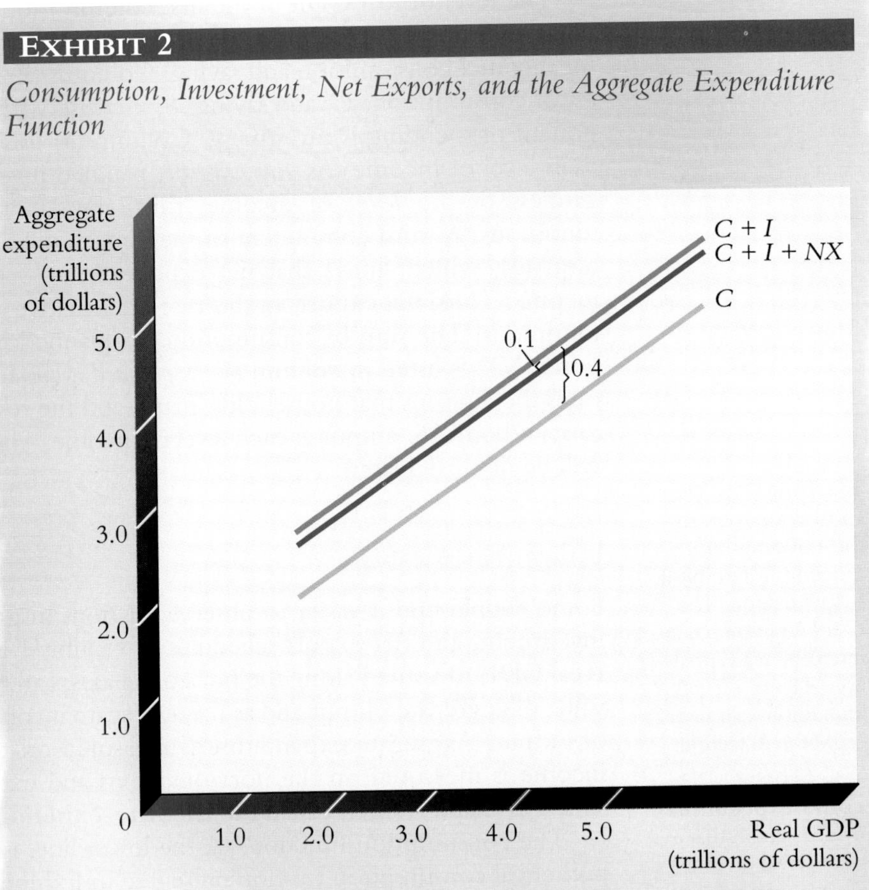

The aggregate expenditure function is the vertical sum of the consumption function, C, the autonomous investment function, I, and the autonomous net export function, NX. Because planned investment and net exports are autonomous, the aggregate expenditure function, $C + I + NX$, is parallel to the consumption function and to the $C + I$ function. And because net exports are assumed to be negative, the aggregate expenditure function is below the $C + I$ line.

Point to Stress The slope of the aggregate expenditure function indicates the impact of changes in income on total planned spending. In this simple model, the slope equals the slope of the consumption function, or the marginal propensity to consume. Since planned investment and net exports are autonomous (that is, do not vary with income), they do not affect the slope. Appendix A presents a model in which net exports affect the slope of the aggregate expenditure function—it becomes the marginal propensity to consume plus the marginal propensity to import.

is presented in Exhibit 3 as $C + I + NX$. *The equilibrium quantity of aggregate output demanded will be achieved where aggregate expenditure, measured along the vertical axis, equals the amount produced, measured along the horizontal axis.*

To gain perspective on the relation between spending and income, we use a handy analytical device: the 45-degree ray from the origin, first discussed in the appendix to Chapter 1. Recall that the special feature of this line is that any point along it is exactly the same distance from each axis. Since the line identifies all points where spending and real GDP are equal, it offers an easy way to find the point along the aggregate expenditure function that is exactly the same distance from each axis. The 45-degree line therefore can be used to find where aggregate expenditure equals real GDP—that is, where planned

EXHIBIT 3

Deriving the Equilibrium Output Demanded for a Given Price Level

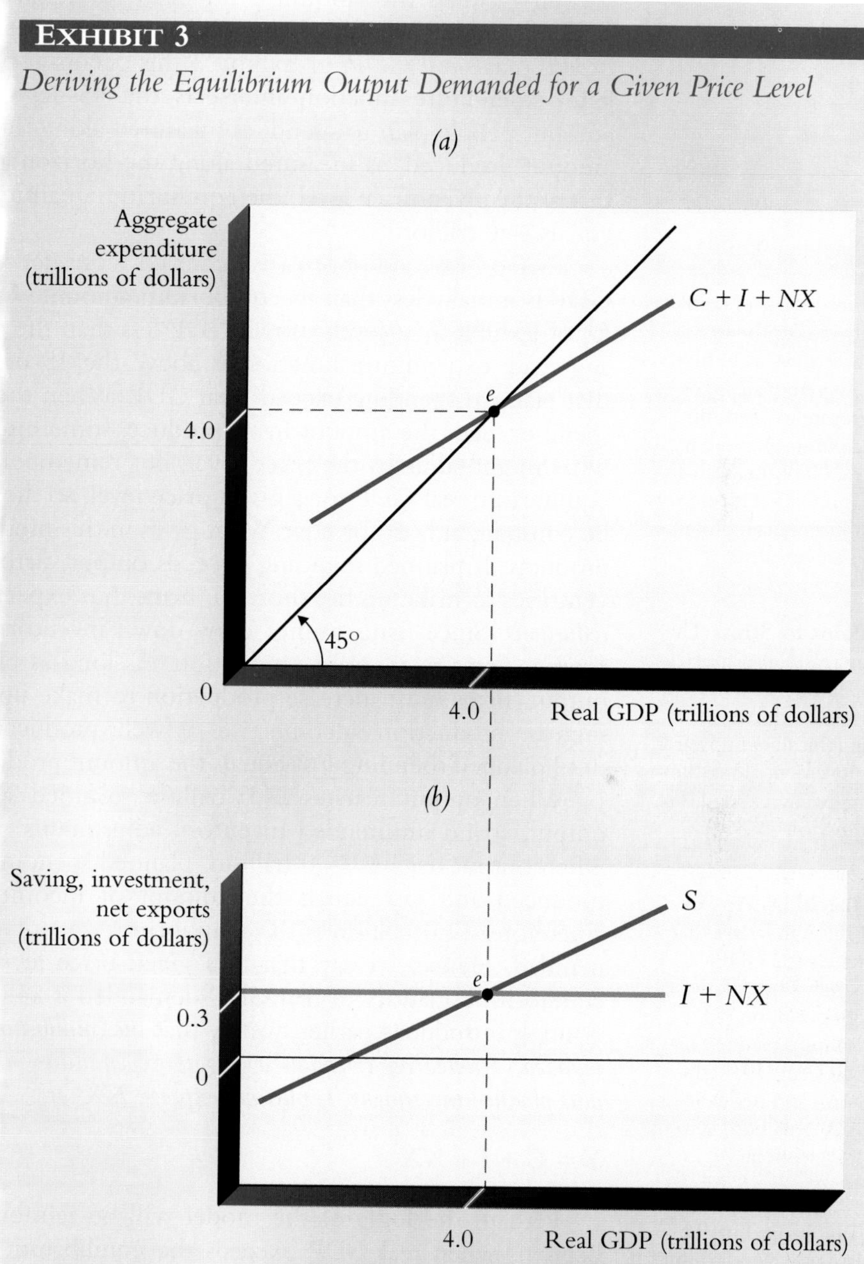

The equilibrium quantity of aggregate output demanded, given the price level, is found where aggregate expenditure equals real GDP—that is, where the amount people and firms want to spend equals the amount produced. In equilibrium, the leakages from the circular flow, in this case saving, *S*, equal the injections, in this case investment plus net exports, *I* + *NX*.

spending equals the amount produced. *The equilibrium quantity of aggregate output demanded occurs where the sum of consumption, planned investment, and net exports equals real GDP*; in Exhibit 3 this occurs at point *e*, where the aggregate expenditure function intersects the 45-degree line. At point *e*, the amount people plan to spend, as measured along the vertical axis, equals the amount produced, as measured along the horizontal axis. We can conclude that at the given price level, the equilibrium quantity of real GDP demanded equals $4.0 trillion.

Teaching Tip Relate points in Exhibit 3 to the left of equilibrium to the first three rows of Exhibit 1, where planned aggregate expenditure (column 6) exceeds real GDP (column 1). Unintended inventory adjustments (column 7) are negative.

To see how equilibrium is achieved, consider what happens when real GDP is initially less than its equilibrium amount. As you can see from panel (a) of Exhibit 3, at levels of real GDP less than the equilibrium amount, the aggregate expenditure function is above the 45-degree line. This indicates that planned spending exceeds real GDP. When the amount people plan to spend exceeds the amount firms produce, something has to give. Ordinarily what might adjust is the price level, but remember that we are seeking the equilibrium real GDP for a given price level, so the price level is assumed to be constant, at least for now. What gives in this model are firms' *inventories* of products. If planned spending exceeds output, firms must dig into their inventories to make up the shortfall; firms thus experience *unintended inventory reductions*. Since firms cannot draw down inventories indefinitely, shortages prompt firms to increase production. As long as planned spending exceeds output, firms must increase production to make up the difference. As firms increase production, income rises as well; production and income will rise until planned spending just equals the amount produced.

Point to Stress The increases in planned spending as income rises are portrayed graphically as upward movement along the aggregate expenditure function.

When output reaches $4.0 trillion, planned spending exactly matches output, so no unintended inventory adjustments occur. More importantly, when output reaches $4.0 trillion, planned spending just equals the amount produced and just equals the amount of income available for spending. Therefore, $4.0 trillion is the equilibrium quantity of aggregate output demanded. Hence, we say that at a given price level (in this case, 130), the equilibrium quantity of real GDP demanded is $4.0 trillion. In terms of the symbols introduced earlier, we say that *the equilibrium quantity of real GDP demanded, denoted as Y, equals aggregate expenditure—the sum of consumption, C, plus planned investment, I, plus net exports, NX, or*

Teaching Tip Exhibit 1 indicates that when real GDP equals $4.0 trillion, consumption ($3.7 trillion), planned investment ($0.4 trillion), and net exports (–$0.1 trillion) sum to $4.0 trillion.

$$\boldsymbol{Y = C + I + NX}$$

Perhaps the logic of the model will be reinforced if we consider what happens when real GDP exceeds the equilibrium level—that is, when the aggregate expenditure function is below the 45-degree line. Note in panel (a) of Exhibit 3 that, along that portion of the aggregate expenditure function to the right of point *e*, planned spending falls short of production. At levels of real GDP higher than the equilibrium level, the amount produced exceeds what people plan to buy, so unsold goods pile up. This swells inventories beyond the level that firms would like to hold. As a result of these *unintended inventory increases*, firms reduce their output. Firms will continue to cut production until the amount they produce just equals aggregate expenditure, which occurs at a level of real GDP of $4.0 trillion.

Teaching Tip Relate points in Exhibit 3 to the right of equilibrium to the last four rows of Exhibit 1, where planned aggregate expenditure (column 6) is below real GDP (column 1). Unintended inventory adjustments (column 7) are positive.

Leakages Equal Planned Injections

Teaching Tip The vertical intercept of the saving function is –\$0.7 trillion.

We can draw on our study of the circular flow model in Chapter 6 to focus on leakages and injections. We will see that, in equilibrium, the leakage of saving must equal the injections of planned investment plus net exports; that is, $S = I + NX$. The same equilibrium derived in panel (a) of Exhibit 3 can be found using the leakages-injections framework, as shown in panel (b). Note that panel (b) has been placed under panel (a) so that levels of real GDP, measured along the horizontal axis, line up in each panel. The upward-sloping saving function, S, introduced in the previous chapter, represents a leakage from the circular flow. The horizontal line, $I + NX$, drawn at \$0.3 trillion, represents autonomous investment plus autonomous net exports, the injections into the circular flow. The two lines intersect where real GDP equals \$4.0 trillion, which is where saving equals planned investment plus net exports, or where the leakages from the circular flow equal the planned injections into the circular flow. This same equality can be computed from the numbers given in Exhibit 1.

Teaching Tip Refer to the first three rows of Exhibit 1, where GDP is less than \$4.0 trillion: saving (column 3) is below the sum of planned investment (column 4) and net exports (column 5). In contrast, in the last four rows, where GDP is above \$4.0 trillion, saving exceeds the sum of planned investment and net exports.

At levels of real GDP that are below the equilibrium value, planned injections exceed leakages. The injections pump up real GDP, so real GDP tends to rise. At levels of real GDP above its equilibrium value, leakages exceed planned injections; the leakages siphon off spending power, which reduces real GDP. To get some feel for how leakages and planned injections help establish equilibrium real GDP, consider the analogy of a bathtub that is partially filled with water. If the rate at which water comes from the faucet exceeds the rate at which water leaks from the tub through the drain, then the water level in the tub will rise. But if the leakage rate exceeds the faucet rate, the water level will fall. Only when the faucet rate equals the leakage rate will the water level remain unchanged, or be in equilibrium.

In summary, the equilibrium value of real GDP demanded can be found using either the income-expenditure approach illustrated in the upper panel of Exhibit 3 or the leakages-injections approach illustrated in the lower panel.

Investment and Unintended Inventory Adjustments

In the income-expenditure model, firms dip into their inventories when planned spending exceeds output and add to their inventories when planned spending falls short of output. Recall that changes in inventories are viewed as changes in investment. The final column of Exhibit 1 lists the actual investment that occurs at each level of income. *Actual investment* equals planned investment plus any unintended change in inventories. If the unintended change in inventories is negative—that is, if firms dip into inventories more than they planned to—actual investment is less than planned investment. For example, when aggregate expenditure exceeds real GDP, firms experience an unintended inventory reduction, so actual investment is less than planned investment. If aggregate expenditure is below real GDP, there is an unintended accumulation of inventories, so actual investment exceeds planned investment.

Only in equilibrium does planned investment equal actual investment. Production of the equilibrium quantity of aggregate output demanded generates just enough income to purchase that output. At any other level of real GDP, planned aggregate expenditure either exceeds or falls short of aggregate output. Consider the equalities that hold in equilibrium. At the equilibrium points *e* in the two panels of Exhibit 3, aggregate expenditure equals the amount produced and also equals the income arising from that production. Also, saving (the leakage from the circular flow) equals planned investment plus net exports (the planned injections into the circular flow). Finally, in equilibrium, planned investment equals actual investment, so there are no unintended inventory changes. All these equalities can be observed in Exhibit 1.

In summary, given the price level, the equilibrium level of aggregate output demanded is achieved only when the amount people plan to spend equals the amount produced, which happens only when leakages from the circular flow equal planned injections into that flow. *Hence, for a given price level, there is only one quantity of output demanded at which planned spending equals income.* We have now established the forces that determine the equilibrium quantity of real GDP demanded for a given price level. In the next section we examine the effect of a shift in the aggregate expenditure function on the equilibrium quantity of aggregate output demanded.

Effect of Shifts in the Aggregate Expenditure Function

In the previous section we employed the aggregate expenditure function to determine the equilibrium level of aggregate output demanded for a particular price level. In this section we will continue to assume that the price level remains unchanged, as we trace the effects of shifts in the aggregate expenditure function on the equilibrium quantity of aggregate output demanded. Like a stone thrown into a still pond, any shift in the aggregate expenditure function creates ripples through the economy, generating changes in aggregate output that may far exceed any initial shift in spending.

Effects of an Increase in Aggregate Expenditure

Point to Stress
Since the initial change in spending is unrelated to income, it causes a parallel shift in the aggregate expenditure function. The initial spending change can be called an *autonomous* change.

We begin in equilibrium at point *e* in Exhibit 4. The equilibrium point shows where planned spending of $4.0 trillion equals real GDP. Now let's consider the effect of an increase in the aggregate expenditure function. Suppose firms become more optimistic about future profit prospects, so they increase their planned investment. Specifically, suppose planned investment increases by $0.1 trillion to $0.5 trillion per year, as reflected in Exhibit 4 by an increase in the aggregate expenditure function, which shifts up by $0.1 trillion, from $C + I + NX$ to $C + I' + NX$. What happens to the equilibrium level of real GDP demanded? An instinctive response is to conclude that equilibrium will increase by $0.1 trillion, but in this case instinct is a poor guide.

EXHIBIT 4

Effect of an Increase in Autonomous Investment

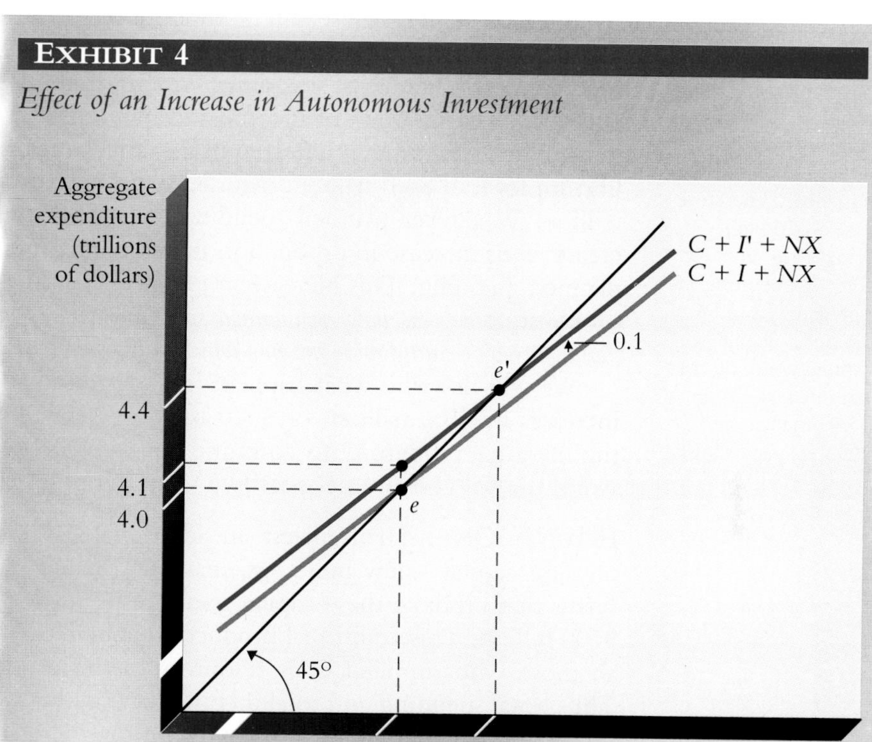

The economy is initially in equilibrium at point *e*, where spending and real GDP both equal \$4.0 trillion. A \$0.1 trillion increase in autonomous investment shifts the aggregate expenditure function vertically by \$0.1 trillion from $C + I + NX$ to $C + I' + NX$. Real GDP rises until it equals spending at point *e'*. As a result of the \$0.1 trillion increase in autonomous investment, real GDP demanded increases by \$0.4 trillion, to \$4.4 trillion.

In Exhibit 4 you can see that at point *e*, the initial amount of real GDP demanded equals \$4.0 trillion. As a result of the \$0.1 trillion increase in the aggregate expenditure function, the equilibrium value shifts up to point *e'*, where the quantity of real GDP demanded equals \$4.4 trillion. The \$0.1 trillion increase in investment has somehow increased the equilibrium quantity of real GDP demanded by \$0.4 trillion. Thus, each dollar of increased investment has been multiplied fourfold. The **multiplier** equals the ratio of a change in equilibrium output to the initial change in expenditure that caused it. In our example the multiplier equals 0.4/0.1, or 4. Later we will provide a specific formula for the multiplier, but first we explore the source of the multiplier magic.

Multiplier The ratio of a change in equilibrium income to the initial change in expenditure that brought it about

The Multiplier and the Circular Flow

The idea of the circular flow is central to an understanding of the process of adjustment from one equilibrium quantity of output demanded to another.

Point to Stress Unlike the initial autonomous change in spending, subsequent spending changes are the result of a change in income. Therefore, these additional changes are shown as a movement along the aggregate expenditure function. Changes in planned spending that result from a change in income can be called *induced* changes.

As noted earlier, real GDP can be thought of as both the value of production and the income arising from that production. Recall that production yields income, which generates spending. We can think of each trip around the circular flow as a "round" of income and spending. A shift up in the aggregate expenditure function, as reflected in Exhibit 4, means that, at the initial equilibrium level of $4.0 trillion, planned spending now exceeds output by $0.1 trillion. Whenever planned spending exceeds output, production must increase. This increase in production increases income, which in turn increases planned spending. This increase in planned spending fuels yet another round of adjustments. *As long as planned spending exceeds output, production will expand, thereby creating more income, which will generate still more spending.*

We will describe what happens in each round when planned investment increases by $0.1 trillion, or $100 billion. We will continue to assume that the marginal propensity to consume equals 3/4, or 0.75, though in the real world the MPC is not necessarily 3/4 or any other constant value.

Round One. Firms invest an additional $100 billion per year in new physical capital—new buildings, machines, trucks, computers, and the like. Firms that produce these capital goods respond by increasing production by $100 billion. This additional production generates $100 billion in income to all those who supplied their resources to the production of capital goods. Thus, total spending and total income increase by $100 billion in what is the first round of new spending arising from the increase in planned investment. The income-generating process does not stop there, however, because those who receive this additional income spend some of it and save some of it, laying the basis for round two of spending and income.

Round Two. Given a marginal propensity to consume of 3/4, or 0.75, those who receive the $100 billion as income will spend a total of $75 billion on toasters, movies, automobiles, and thousands of other goods and services; the other $25 billion of that $100 billion will be saved. Thus, during the second round, the $100 billion in new income supports a $75 billion increase in consumption and a $25 billion increase in saving.

Round Three and Beyond. Focus now on the $75 billion that went toward consumption during round two. Production increases in the second round by $75 billion to satisfy the increase in spending. This production generates an equal amount of income to those who produced the additional goods and services purchased. Again, based on the marginal propensity to consume, we know that three-quarters of the additional income will be consumed and one-quarter will be saved. Thus, $56.25 billion will be spent on still more goods and services, and $18.75 billion will be saved. This spending continues to generate income, three-quarters of which is spent, thereby generating still more income.

Teaching Tip In an expanded income-expenditure model in which imports vary with income, income leaks into imports as well as into saving. Import spending flows out of the country and therefore does not fuel more domestic income.

When does the income-generating machine run out of gas? Saving leaks from the circular flow during every round. *The more income that leaks as saving, the less that remains to fuel still more spending and income.* When the $100 billion initial increase in investment has leaked completely from the circular flow as saving, no new income or spending can be created, so the process stops.

EXHIBIT 5

Tracking the Rounds of Spending Following a \$100 Billion Increase in Autonomous Spending (billions of dollars)

Round (1)	New Spending This Round (2)	Cumulative New Spending (3)	New Saving This Round (4)	Cumulative New Saving (5)
1	100	100	—	—
2	75	175	25	25
3	56.25	231.25	18.75	43.75
4	42.19	273.44	14.06	57.81
⋮	⋮	⋮	⋮	⋮
∞	0	400	0	100

Exhibit 5 summarizes in a more systematic way the multiplier process. The new spending generated in each round is shown in column (2) and the accumulation of new spending is shown in column (3). The new saving from each round is shown in column (4) and the accumulation of new saving in column (5). The first several rounds are listed, and subsequent rounds are summarized. For example, the new spending accumulated as of the third round is \$231.25 billion—the sum of the first three rounds of spending. The new saving accumulated from the first three rounds is \$43.75 billion. When the increase in spending has run its course, the cumulative effect has been to increase spending by \$400 billion and to increase saving by \$100 billion. Saving increases just enough to finance the \$100 billion increase in autonomous investment.

Note that in our example planned investment increased by \$100 billion, or \$0.1 trillion, per year. *If this higher level of planned investment is not sustained in the following year, equilibrium spending will fall.* For example, if planned investment returns to \$0.4 trillion, other things constant, equilibrium spending will return to \$4.0 trillion.

Tracking Rounds with the Income-Expenditure Model

Yet another way to understand the workings of the multiplier is to follow the rounds of spending by reference to the aggregate expenditure function presented in Exhibit 6. We begin as before at point *e*, where planned spending and income each equals \$4.0 trillion. Recall that changes in spending are measured along the vertical axis and changes in income are measured along the horizontal axis. The first round of spending results from the \$100 billion increase in investment, reflected by the shift in the expenditure function from $C + I + NX$ up to $C + I' + NX$. This new spending is satisfied initially by an unplanned reduction in inventories. The initial increase in spending is reflected by the movement from point *e* up to point *a* on the new aggregate expenditure function.

Point to Stress In Exhibit 6, the initial autonomous change in planned spending is represented by the movement from point *e* to point *a*—a shift in the spending function. Subsequent induced spending increases (which result from rising income) are represented by movements along the new spending function from point *a* to point *e′*. In this example, the autonomous spending change is $100 billion, and induced spending changes total $300 billion. Note that induced spending changes equal the marginal propensity to consume times the total change in real GDP. In total, spending increases by $400 billion.

EXHIBIT 6

The Geometry of the Multiplier

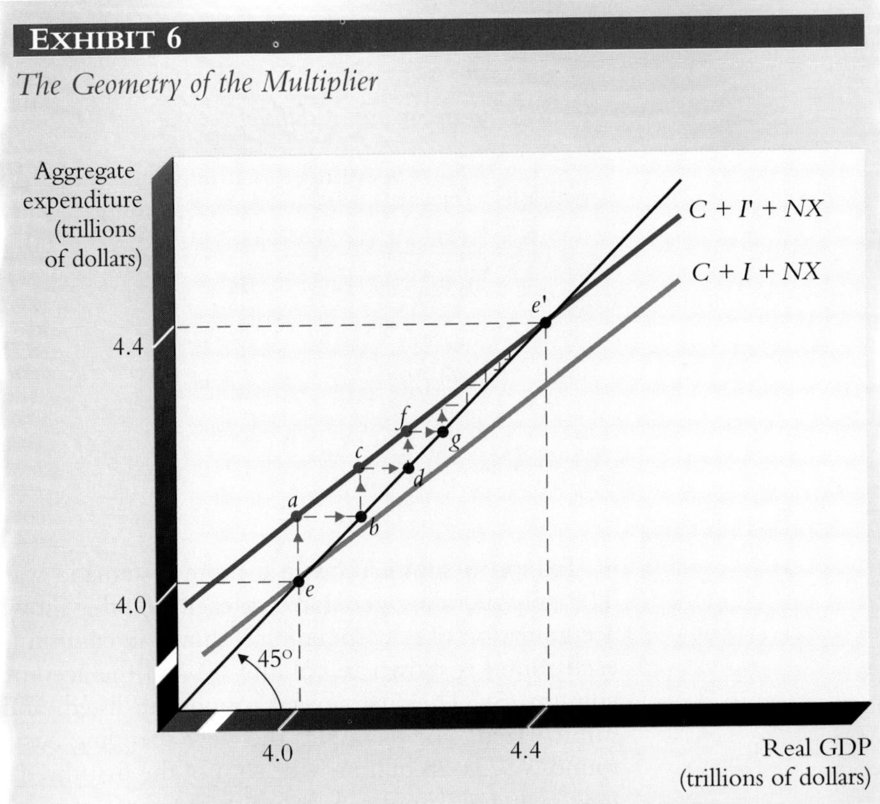

With the economy in equilibrium at point *e*, spending increases by $100 billion. At the initial level of income, this is shown by the movement from point *e* on the old aggregate expenditure function ($C + I + NX$) to point *a* on the new one ($C + I' + NX$). As businesses expand production to satisfy the increased demand, output and income rise by $100 billion, as expressed by the movement from point *a* to point *b*. This is round one.

With income now $100 billion higher, consumption spending rises by $75 billion. This spending causes a reduction in inventories, shown by the movement from point *b* to point *c*. As firms increase output to satisfy the higher level of spending, income also increases by $75 billion, as indicated by the movement from point *c* to point *d*. This process continues until equilibrium is reestablished with aggregate expenditure equal to income at point *e′*.

A reduction in inventories does not translate directly into an increase in income, because these inventories generated income when they were produced in some previous period. But as firms expand output by $100 billion to replenish their inventories, total income also increases by $100 billion, as expressed by the move from point *a* over to point *b*. The two-stage movement from point *e* to point *b* represents the first round in the multiplier process.

After the first round, both spending and income have increased by $100 billion. This increase in income results in an increase in spending in the second round of $75 billion, which is initially met by reductions in inventories, as shown by the movement from point *b* up to point *c*. But as firms expand output to satisfy the new, higher level of spending, income to those who produced that output also increases by $75 billion, as indicated by the movement from point *c* over to point *d*. The process continues in this fashion, with each new round of spending generating an equal amount of income until the new equilibrium quantity of real GDP demanded is reached at point *e′*. Given a constant price level, the equilibrium quantity of real GDP demanded increases from $4.0 trillion to $4.4 trillion. The equilibrium quantity demanded will remain at $4.4 trillion only if planned investment remains at its higher level.

As we will see, the equilibrium quantity of real GDP demanded would have increased by the same amount if consumers had decided to spend $100 billion more at each level of income—that is, if the consumption function rather than the investment function had shifted up by $100 billion. Equilibrium real GDP demanded would likewise have increased if autonomous net exports had increased by $100 billion. *The change in the equilibrium quantity of aggregate output demanded depends on how much the aggregate expenditure function shifts, not which spending component causes the shift.*

Numerical Value of the Multiplier

Tracing the rounds of spending is one way to determine the effects of a particular change in spending, but this process is slow and tedious. What we need is a quick way of translating changes in planned spending into changes in the equilibrium level of real output demanded. Recall that the expansion stemming from an increase in autonomous spending depended on the marginal propensity to consume. There is a relation between the multiplier and the marginal propensity to consume that proves useful in formulating the multiplier. *The larger the fraction of an increase in income that is respent, the greater the multiplier.* The marginal propensity to consume and the multiplier are directly related; the larger the MPC, the larger the multiplier.

Teaching Tip If you plan to use more complicated multiplier formulas in which imports and/or taxes vary with income, students will find it useful if you explain here that the value of the multiplier is equal to 1/1 – slope of aggregate expenditure function.

$$\textbf{The simple multiplier} = \frac{1}{1 - \text{MPC}}$$

Since the MPC is 3/4, the denominator equals 1 – 3/4, or 1/4, and the simple multiplier equals the reciprocal of 1/4, which is 4. If the MPC were 4/5, the denominator would equal 1 – 4/5, or 1/5, and the simple multiplier would equal the reciprocal of 1/5, which is 5.[1]

---

1. A more formal way of deriving the spending multiplier is to total the additions to spending arising from each new round of income and spending. For example, a $1 increase in investment generates $1 in spending in the first round. In the second round, it generates $1 times the MPC. In the third round, the new spending equals the spending that arose in the second round ($1 × MPC) times the MPC. This goes on round after round, with each new round equal to the spending from the previous round times the MPC. Mathematicians have shown that the sum of an infinite series of rounds, each of which is a constant fraction of the previous round, is 1/(1 – MPC) times the initial amount. In our context, 1/(1 – MPC) is the simple multiplier.

Recall from Chapter 8 that the MPC and the MPS add up to 1, so 1 minus the MPC equals the MPS. With this information, we can define the simple multiplier in terms of the MPS as follows:

$$\textbf{The simple multiplier} = \frac{\mathbf{1}}{\mathbf{1 - MPC}} = \frac{\mathbf{1}}{\mathbf{MPS}}$$

When we state the equation this way, we can see that the smaller the MPS, the larger the fraction of each fresh round of income that is spent, so the larger the multiplier. *The simple multiplier is the reciprocal of the MPS.*

The focus of the multiplier thus far has been the national economy. The idea of the multiplier has some relevance for regional and state economies as well, as shown in the following case study.

CASE STUDY

Hard Times in Connecticut

Because of a cutback in federal defense spending and a fall in worldwide orders for commercial aircraft, the United Technologies Corporation (UTC), a major producer of jet engines, announced in January of 1993 that by the end of 1994 it would eliminate 10,000 manufacturing jobs in Connecticut. UTC also planned to reduce its orders from dozens of Connecticut firms that supplied everything from precision parts to janitorial services, thereby causing several thousand more job losses in the state. The direct layoffs as well as expected layoffs by subcontractors reflect an initial payroll loss exceeding $1 billion.

In a state with an expanding economy, job losses in one sector could be made up at least in part by job expansions in other sectors. But such losses will be especially painful in Connecticut, where a long recession has already reduced state jobs by 12 percent over the past four years. Consequently, those who lose high-paying jobs making jet engines face grim alternatives.

This loss in employment and payroll will ripple through the Connecticut economy, reducing the demand for housing, clothing, entertainment, restaurant meals, and other goods and services this pay would have purchased. For example, the unemployed engine makers will eat out less frequently, reducing the income of restaurant owners, workers, and suppliers. (The number of restaurants in Hartford has in fact already declined because of the state's long recession, cutting the number of jobs in this industry and cutting the average tips of remaining waiters, waitresses, and bartenders.) Those who lose restaurant jobs and those restaurant workers who are left will have less to spend, and they in turn will reduce their demand for goods and services.

Thus, job losses will have a multiplier effect in Connecticut. But there will also be job losses beyond the state's borders. For example, the number of new auto purchases has already fallen sharply in Connecticut, and many auto dealers have gone out of business. But reduced auto sales in Connecticut have also cut the jobs and incomes of auto workers living in places such as Detroit and San Diego. Similarly, some restaurants that closed in Connecticut were owned by national chains, so the owners losing income likely resided outside the state. Thus, the number of job losses resulting from UTC's job

cuts will be greater for the nation as a whole than for Connecticut alone. Therefore, the spending multiplier is greater for the nation as a whole than for Connecticut.

Sources: Michael Remez, "State Suppliers to Feel Big Sting from Pratt Cuts," *Hartford Courant*, 28 January 1993; and Patricia Seremet, "As Restaurant Trade Slips, Tips Dwindle," *Hartford Courant*, 29 December 1992.

Effect of Changes in the Price Level

Thus far in this chapter we have used the aggregate expenditure function to derive the equilibrium quantity of real GDP demanded *for a given price level.* But for each price level there is a specific aggregate expenditure function, which yields a unique equilibrium quantity of real GDP demanded.

Changes in the Price Level

Point to Stress In highlighting the impact of changes in the price level, it is assumed that other factors are held constant. The "other factors" include variables such as the nominal level of net wealth, the nominal supply of money, and the level of foreign prices.

What is the effect of a decrease in the price level on the economy's aggregate expenditure function and, in turn, on the equilibrium quantity of real GDP demanded? Recall that consumers hold many assets that are fixed in money terms, and a decrease in the price level increases the real value of these dollar-denominated assets. Consumers therefore feel wealthier as a result of a decrease in the price level, so they are more willing to spend at every level of income. For reasons that will be more fully explained in a later chapter, a lower price level also tends to reduce the market rate of interest, and a lower interest rate increases planned investment. Finally, a lower price level means that foreign goods are now relatively more expensive to U.S. consumers and U.S. goods are relatively cheaper abroad. So exports will rise and imports will fall, increasing net exports. *A decrease in the price level therefore increases consumption, planned investment, and net exports, which all increase aggregate spending.* This increase in the aggregate expenditure function increases the equilibrium quantity of real GDP demanded.

The opposite holds if the price level increases. At a higher price level, the value of assets fixed in dollars decreases. Consumers on average are poorer and so are more inclined to increase saving in order to restore their assets to some desired level. This greater saving means less consumption at each level of real GDP. A higher price level also tends to increase the market rate of interest, which decreases planned investment. Finally, a higher U.S. price level makes U.S. products relatively more expensive abroad and makes foreign products relatively cheaper to Americans, so exports decrease and imports increase. Thus consumption, planned investment, and net exports decrease at each level of real GDP. A lower aggregate expenditure function leads to a lower equilibrium quantity of real GDP demanded.

Each panel of Exhibit 7 represents a different way of expressing the effects of a change in the price level on the quantity of real GDP demanded. Panel (a) presents the income-expenditure framework and panel (b) the aggregate demand framework. Again, the two panels are aligned so that levels of real GDP on the horizontal axes correspond. At the initial price level of 130 in panel (a), the aggregate expenditure function, $C + I + NX$, intersects the 45-degree line at point *e* to yield $4.0 trillion, the equilibrium quantity of real GDP demanded. Panel (b) shows more directly the link between the quantity of real GDP demanded and the price level. As you can see, when the price level is 130, the quantity demanded is $4.0 trillion. This combination of price level and real GDP is identified by point *e* on the aggregate demand curve. Thus, the equilibrium quantity of real output demanded for a particular price level in panel (a) yields one combination of price level and quantity demanded, point *e*, on the aggregate demand curve in panel (b).

Teaching Tip The change in the equilibrium level of real GDP demanded ($0.5 trillion) is equal to the initial shift in planned spending caused by the price level drop times the multiplier.

Consider now the effects of a decrease in the price level. Suppose the price level falls from 130 to, say, 120. As explained earlier, a fall in the price level causes consumption, planned investment, and net exports to increase, as reflected in panel (a) of Exhibit 7 by the shift up in the aggregate expenditure function from $C + I + NX$ to $C' + I' + NX'$. An increase in planned spending at each level of income increases the equilibrium level of real GDP demanded from $4.0 trillion to $4.5 trillion, as indicated by the intersection of the top aggregate expenditure function with the 45-degree line at point e'. This same price increase can be viewed more directly in panel (b). As you can see, when the price level decreases to 120, the quantity of real GDP demanded increases to $4.5 trillion.

Point to Stress Along the aggregate demand curve, the price level varies, but factors such as the nominal level of net wealth, expectations, foreign income levels, and so forth are held constant.

Return now to the initial price level of 130 and consider the effect of an increase in the price level to, say, 140. An increase in the price level reduces consumption, planned investment, and net exports. This reduction in planned spending is reflected in panel (a) of Exhibit 7 by a decrease in the aggregate expenditure function from $C + I + NX$ to $C'' + I'' + NX''$. As a result of this decrease in planned spending, the equilibrium quantity of real GDP demanded declines from $4.0 trillion to $3.5 trillion. Panel (b) shows that an increase in the price level from 130 to 140 decreases the quantity of real GDP demanded from $4.0 trillion to $3.5 trillion.

The aggregate expenditure function and the aggregate demand curve portray real output from different perspectives. The aggregate expenditure function shows, for a given price level, how planned spending relates to the level of real GDP in the economy. The aggregate demand curve shows, for various price levels, the quantity of real GDP demanded.

Point to Stress The horizontal shift in the aggregate demand curve equals the initial autonomous change in consumption times the multiplier. This multiplier process assumes that the price level remains unchanged at 130.

The Multiplier and Shifts in Aggregate Demand

Now that we have some idea how the aggregate expenditure function and the aggregate demand curve relate, we can trace the link between a shift in the aggregate expenditure function caused by some factor other than a change in price and the resulting shift in the aggregate demand curve. Suppose, for example, that an increase in consumer confidence spurs a $0.1 trillion increase in

EXHIBIT 7

The Income-Expenditure Approach and the Aggregate Demand Curve

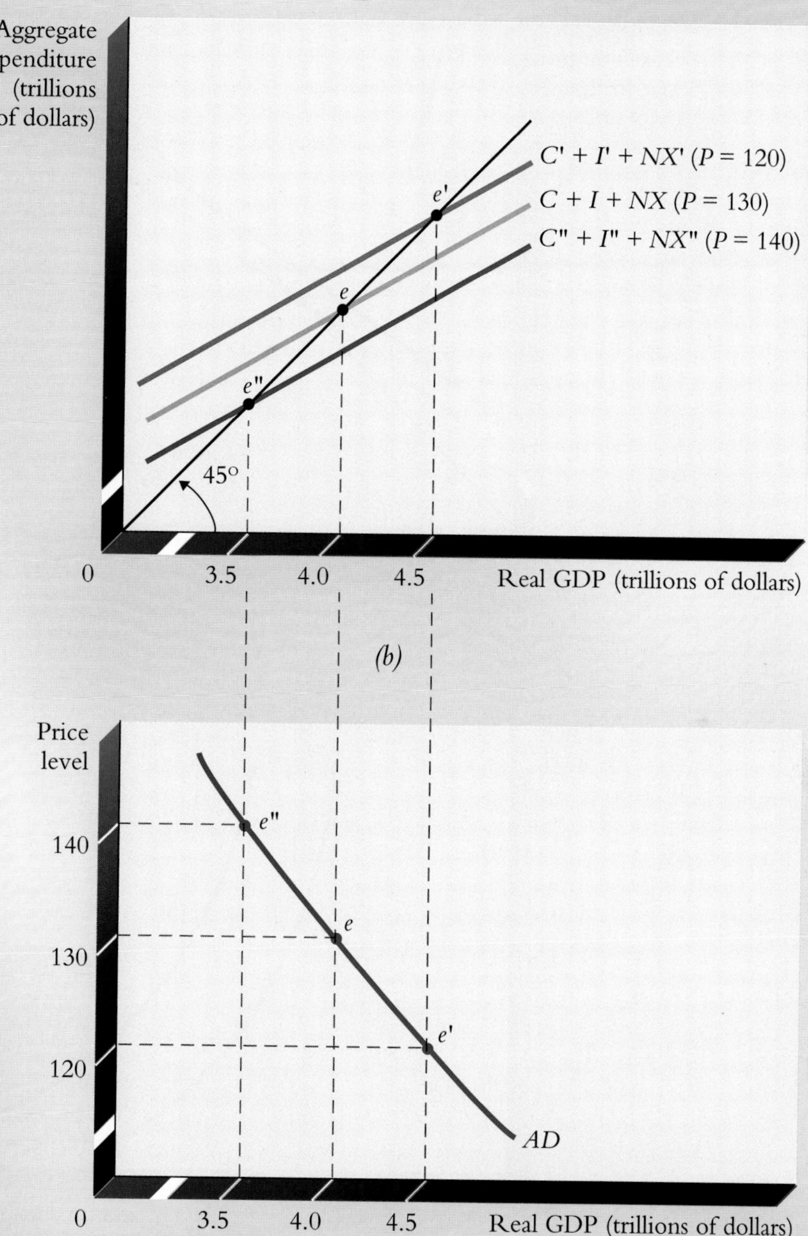

At the initial price level of 130, aggregate expenditure is $C + I + NX$, and equilibrium GDP is \$4.0 trillion. Hence, price level 130 is associated with the level of output of \$4.0 trillion to determine one point (point *e*) on the aggregate demand curve in panel (b).

At the higher price level of 140, consumption is lower (C''), aggregate expenditure is lower ($C'' + I'' + NX''$), and equilibrium GDP is lower. This price-output combination is plotted as point e'' in panel (b). At the lower price level of 120, aggregate expenditure is higher ($C' + I' + NX'$) and so is equilibrium GDP. That price-output combination is plotted as point e' in panel (b).

Connecting points e, e', and e'' gives us the downward-sloping aggregate demand curve that shows how much real GDP will be demanded at each price level.

EXHIBIT 8

A Shift in the Aggregate Expenditure Function and a Shift in the Aggregate Demand Curve

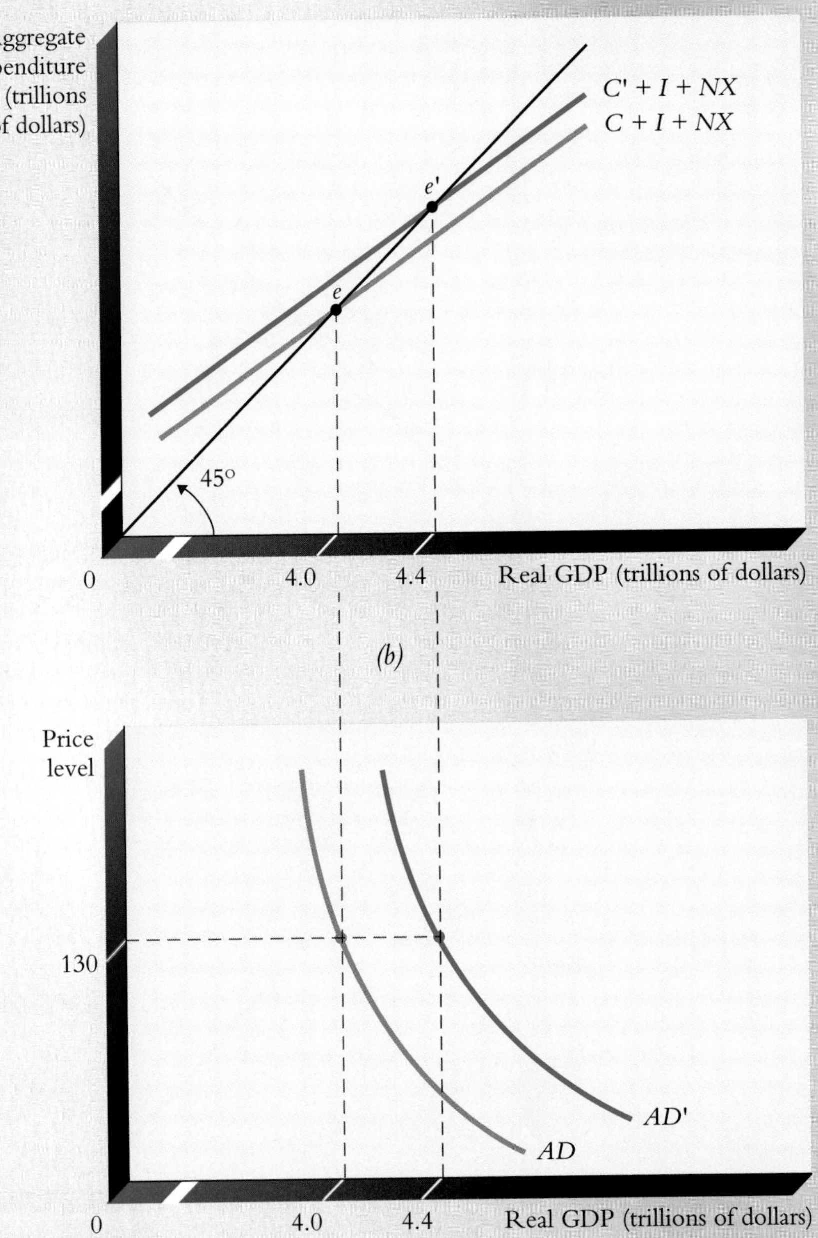

A shift in the aggregate expenditure function that is not due to a change in the price level will cause a shift in the aggregate demand curve. In panel (a), an increase in consumption, with the price level fixed at 130, causes aggregate expenditure to increase from $C + I + NX$ to $C' + I + NX$. As a result, the equilibrium level of real GDP demanded increases from \$4.0 trillion to \$4.4 trillion. In panel (b), the aggregate demand curve has shifted from *AD* to *AD'*. At the prevailing price level, the amount of output demanded has increased by \$0.4 trillion.

consumption at each level of real GDP. The consumption function therefore shifts up by \$0.1 trillion.

Exhibit 8 shows how shifts in the aggregate expenditure function and shifts in the aggregate demand curve are related. In panel (a), a \$0.1 trillion increase in consumption shifts the aggregate expenditure function up by \$0.1 trillion, from $C + I + NX$ to $C' + I + NX$. As we have seen, because of the multiplier effect, such an increase in consumption ultimately raises the equilibrium quantity of real GDP demanded from \$4.0 trillion to \$4.4 trillion. Panel (b) shows the effects of the increase in consumption on the aggregate demand curve. The aggregate demand curve shifts to the right, from AD to AD'. At the prevailing price level of 130, the quantity demanded has increased from \$4.0 trillion to \$4.4 trillion as a result of the \$0.1 trillion increase in consumption.

CONCLUSION

The central ideas of this chapter are the forces that determine the equilibrium quantity of aggregate output demanded and the relation between the spending multiplier and changes in the equilibrium level of aggregate output demanded. As we shall see, the discussion of the multiplier exaggerates the actual effect we might expect from a given shift in consumption, investment, or net exports. For one thing, we assume that the price level remains constant in the face of shifts in the aggregate demand curve. Incorporating aggregate supply into the analysis tends to reduce the size of the multiplier because of resulting price changes. Moreover, as income increases there are other leakages in the circular flow in addition to saving, such as income taxes and increased spending on imports, and these leakages also tend to reduce the size of the multiplier. Finally, although we have presented the process in a timeless framework, the multiplier takes time to work itself out—perhaps as much as two years.

So our simple multiplier overstates the real-world multiplier. Our approach to calculating the simple multiplier is akin to determining the miles a car travels on a gallon of gasoline by testing cars on a treadmill, where they confront no wind resistance, no hills, no potholes, and no bad drivers. Although the tests are obviously unrealistic, the results are still valuable for comparative purposes. We can say, for example, that a Honda Civic has twice the fuel efficiency of a Lincoln Town Car. Similarly, we can examine the effects of various changes in the aggregate expenditure function to see which changes have the greatest impact on the quantity of real output demanded. The simple multiplier provides a first approximation of the effect of a shift in the aggregate expenditure function on the equilibrium quantity of real output demanded, just as mileage tests on a treadmill provide a first, albeit high, estimate of actual fuel efficiency.

This chapter focused on aggregate spending arising from the private sector. A simplifying assumption used throughout was that net exports did not vary with the level of income. Appendix A adds more realism by looking at the effect of imports that increase with income. Since imports represent a leakage from the circular flow, this more realistic approach reduces the size of the multiplier.

Thus far we have determined the equilibrium quantity of aggregate output demanded using several approaches. We told stories, examined tables, and graphed the aggregate expenditure function. With the various approaches we showed that for each price level there is a specific quantity of aggregate output demanded, other things constant. In Appendix B we will use algebra to derive the equilibrium quantity and the multiplier.

SUMMARY

1. By vertically summing the consumption, planned investment, and net export functions, we derive the aggregate expenditure function, which indicates, for a given price level, the amount that households and firms plan to spend at each level of income.

2. At a given price level, the equilibrium quantity of aggregate output demanded is achieved where the amount firms and households plan to spend just equals the amount produced. Planned spending equals aggregate output. And leakages from the circular flow equal the planned injections, which means that, for an economy with no government sector, saving equals planned investment plus net exports.

3. Any change in the aggregate expenditure function will generate a change in income that, in turn, affects spending. The multiplier indicates the multiple by which a shift in planned spending changes the equilibrium level of aggregate output demanded. The simple multiplier examined in this chapter equals $1/(1 - MPC)$. The greater the MPC, the more of each dollar of income that will be spent, and the greater the multiplier.

4. A change in the price level alters the amount consumers purchase at each level of real income. A higher price level results in a downward shift in the aggregate expenditure function, leading to a lower equilibrium quantity of aggregate output demanded. A lower price level results in an upward shift in the aggregate expenditure function, leading to a greater equilibrium quantity of aggregate output demanded. By tracing the equilibrium output demanded at alternative price levels, we can use the income-expenditure framework to derive the aggregate demand curve.

QUESTIONS AND PROBLEMS

1. (Actual Investment Versus Planned Investment) Recently General Motors experienced inventories equal to about one hundred days' production. Usual inventories are about thirty days' production. How does this situation relate to the concept of unplanned investment as discussed in the chapter? How will GM react to such a problem?

2. (Equilibrium) What roles do inventories play in the establishment of equilibrium for aggregate output? To answer this question, suppose that firms are either overproducing or underproducing.

3. (The Multiplier) Suppose that the MPC for the United States is about 0.90 and that a movie studio travels to Montana to make an adventure film. The production of the movie will inject $30 million into the Montana economy initially. One bright economics student claims this $30 million will generate $300 million in additional income for the state. However, some people believe this is an overestimate. What information is needed to decide who is correct?

4. (The Multiplier) What factors would speed up or slow down the multiplier process?

5. (The Multiplier) "A rise in planned investment spending in an economy will lead to a rise in consumer spending." Use the concept of the multiplier to verify this statement.

6. (The Multiplier) Create a table similar to Exhibit 5 in this chapter, given that the marginal propensity to consume is equal to 0.90. Assuming the same $100 billion increase in autonomous spending, list the values for each of the first four rounds and determine the overall effect of the increase.

7. (Paradox of Thrift) When consumer confidence falls, consumers generally attempt to save a little more money to prepare for bad times ahead. Why does such rational action by consumers make society worse off?

8. (Aggregate Expenditure Function) Students often have trouble understanding why aggregate expenditure both depends on income and determines income. Use the economic concept of equilibrium to resolve this seeming paradox.

9. (Multiplier) Suppose that the marginal propensity to consume is 0.80 and autonomous investment is $500 billion. Assume that the world consists of only households and firms.
   a. What is the level of saving at the equilibrium quantity of aggregate output demanded? Explain.
   b. Suppose that consumption equals $100 billion when aggregate output (income) is zero. Graph the saving function and the investment function, showing equilibrium quantity of output demanded.
   c. What is the value of the multiplier?
   d. Explain why the multiplier is related to the slope of the consumption function.

10. (Multiplier and Aggregate Demand) Suppose that at an average price level of 100, equilibrium output demanded is $1,000 billion, and that each point change in the price level causes the aggregate expenditure function to shift by $5 billion. Using a multiplier of 4, do the following:
   a. Construct the aggregate demand curve.
   b. Determine its slope.
   c. Explain how a change in the multiplier would affect the slope of the aggregate demand curve.
   d. State how much an increase in saving of $100 billion would affect the aggregate demand curve. Be specific.

11. (The Multiplier) According to the text, the larger the multiplier, the larger the change in equilibrium real GDP resulting from a change in autonomous aggregate expenditure. Show that this is true using a graph of the aggregate expenditure function with the 45-degree line.

12. (Investment and the Multiplier) The text assumes that all investment is autonomous. What would happen to the size of the multiplier if planned investment increased with the level of real GDP? Explain.

13. (Aggregate Demand) Suppose the changes in real GDP illustrated in Exhibit 7 were based upon a multiplier equal to 5. Construct the *AD* curve for the same shifts in aggregate expenditure assuming that the multiplier is equal to 8, and the starting point is *e* in both panels.

14. (Hard Times in Connecticut) Suppose that instead of cutting back on their spending, consumers in the state of Connecticut shifted their spending from automobiles to real estate. What kinds of impacts, direct and multiplier, would you anticipate as a result?

15. (Hard Times in Connecticut) Why is the size of the spending multiplier time-related?

APPENDIX A
Variable Net Exports

This chapter thus far has assumed that net exports do not vary with the level of income. A more realistic approach allows net exports to vary inversely with the level of income. Such a model of net exports was developed in the appendix to the last chapter. This net export function is presented in panel (a) of Exhibit 9. The higher the income level in the economy, the more that is spent on imports, so the lower the net exports. (If you need a reminder of how this relationship was derived, refer to the appendix in the previous chapter.)

Panel (b) of Exhibit 9 shows what happens when variable net exports are added to consumption and investment. We add the variable net export function to the $C + I$ function to derive the $C + I + (X - M)$ spending function. (Note that we use $X - M$ for variable net exports here to distinguish them from autonomous net exports, which in the body of the chapter were denoted as *NX*.) Perhaps the easiest way to see how the addition of net exports affects aggregate expenditure is to begin where real GDP equals \$2.0 trillion. Since net exports equal zero when real GDP equals \$2.0 trillion, the addition of net exports has no effect on the aggregate expenditure function at that level of income. Therefore, $C + I$ and $C + I + (X - M)$ intersect where real GDP equals \$2.0 trillion. At real GDP levels less than \$2.0 trillion, net exports are positive, so the $C + I + (X - M)$ line is above the $C + I$ line. At income levels greater than \$2.0 trillion, net exports are negative, so $C + I + (X - M)$ is below $C + I$. *Because net exports and real GDP are inversely related, the addition of net exports has the effect of flattening out, or reducing the slope of, the aggregate expenditure function.*

Net Exports and the Spending Multiplier

The inclusion of variable net exports makes the model more realistic but more complicated, and it requires a reformulation of the multiplier. When net exports were autonomous, only the marginal propensity to consume determined how much would be spent and how much would be saved as income increased. The inclusion of variable net exports means that as income increases, U.S. residents spend more on imports. The **marginal propensity to import**, or **MPI**, indicates the fraction of each additional dollar of income that is spent on imported products. Imports are a leakage from the circular flow. Thus, there are now two leakages that grow with income: saving and imports. The introduction of this additional leakage changes the value of the multiplier from 1/MPS to

$$\textbf{Multiplier with net exports} = \frac{1}{\textbf{MPS + MPI}}$$

The larger the marginal propensity to import, the greater the leakage during each round of spending and the smaller the resulting spending multiplier. We assume that the MPI equals about 1/10, or 0.10. If the marginal propensity to save is 0.25 and the marginal propensity to import is 0.10, then only 65 cents of each additional dollar of disposable income is spent on U.S. products. We can compute the new multiplier as follows:

$$\textbf{Multiplier} = \frac{1}{\textbf{MPS + MPI}} = \frac{1}{\textbf{0.25 + 0.10}}$$

$$= \frac{1}{\textbf{0.35}} = \textbf{2.86}$$

Thus the inclusion of net exports reduces the multiplier in our hypothetical example from 4 to less than 3. *Because some of each additional dollar of income is spent on imports, less is spent on U.S. products, so any given shift in the aggregate expenditure function will have less of an impact on equilibrium output.*

EXHIBIT 9

Net Exports and the Aggregate Expenditure Function

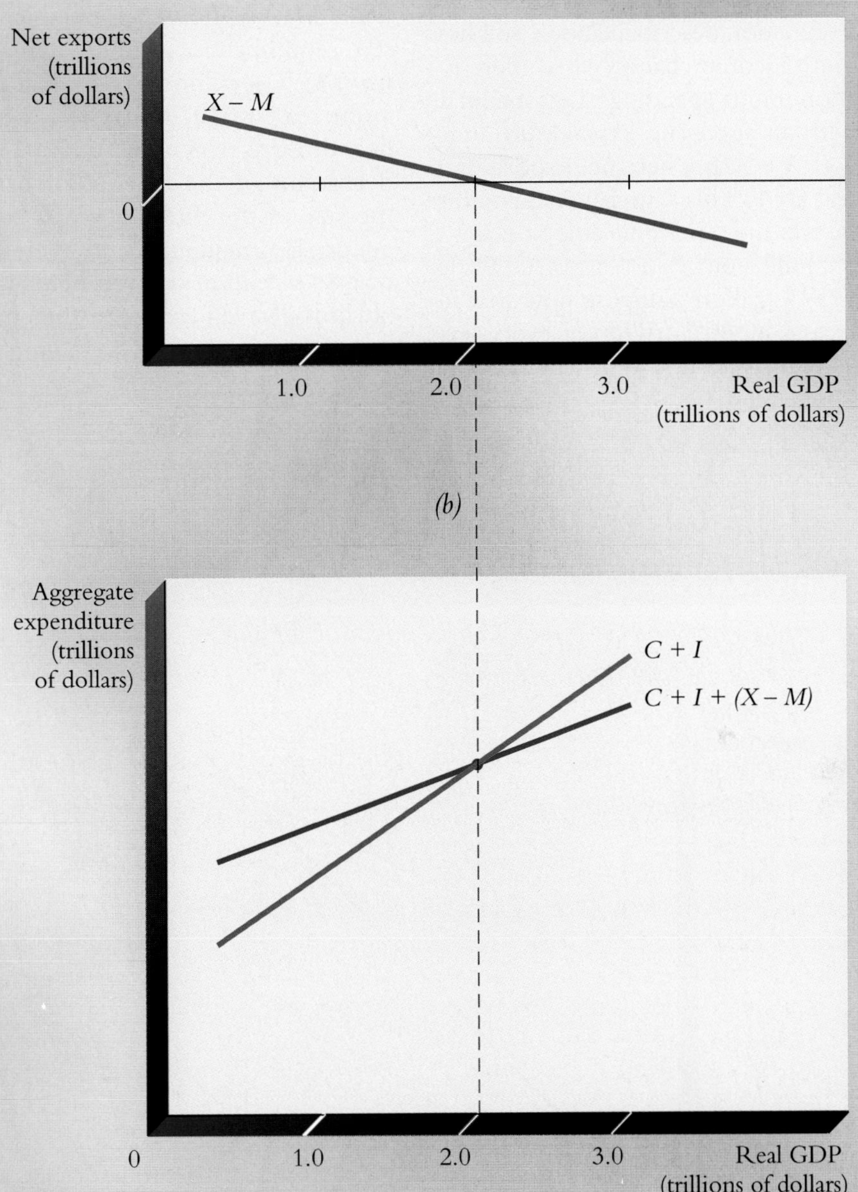

In panel (a), net exports, $X - M$, equal exports minus imports. Net exports are added to consumption plus investment in panel (b) to yield $C + I + (X - M)$. The addition of net exports has the effect of rotating the spending function about the point where net exports are zero, which occurs where real GDP is $2.0 trillion. In the above example, including net exports reduces the equilibrium quantity of real GDP demanded.

A Shift in Autonomous Spending

What is the level of equilibrium real GDP given the net export function described above, and how does equilibrium income change when there is a change in autonomous spending? Let's begin in Exhibit 10 with an aggregate expenditure function of $C + I + (X - M)$, where net exports are a function of real GDP. This aggregate expenditure function intersects the 45-degree line at point *e*, indicating an equilibrium value of real GDP demanded of $3.714 trillion. Suppose now that investment increases by $0.1 trillion at every level of income. This increase in investment will shift the entire aggregate expenditure function up by $0.1 trillion, from $C + I + (X - M)$ to $C + I' + (X - M)$, as shown in Exhibit 10. As you can see, equilibrium output demanded increases from $3.714 trillion to $4.0 trillion, representing an increase of $0.286 trillion, which is $0.1 trillion times the spending multiplier of 2.86. (The derivation of the these equilibrium values and the size of the multiplier will be shown in Appendix B.) Incidentally, it's merely a coincidence that $4.0 trillion derived here is the same equilibrium derived earlier in the chapter when autonomous net exports were employed.

EXHIBIT 10

Effect of a Shift in Autonomous Spending on Equilibrium Income

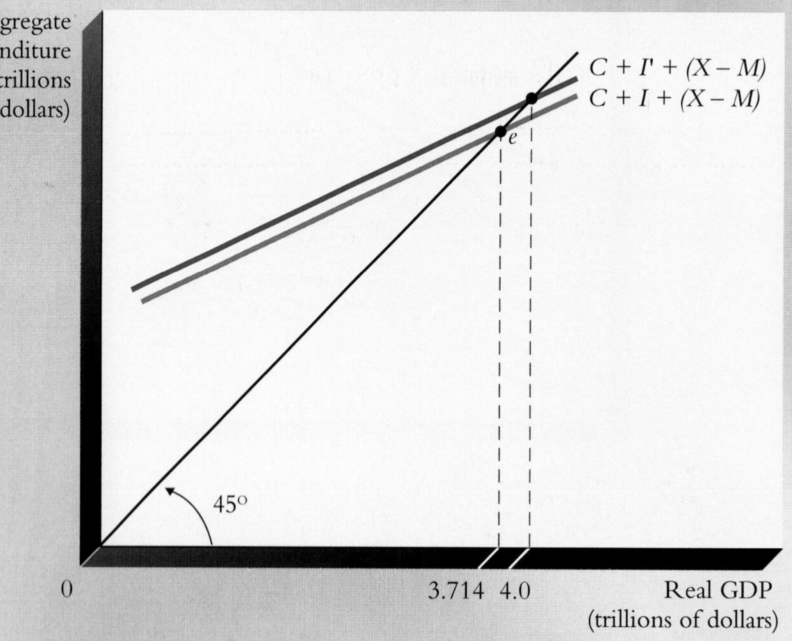

An increase in planned investment, other things constant, shifts the spending function up from $C + I + (X - M)$ to $C + I' + (X - M)$, yielding a larger equilibrium quantity of real GDP demanded.

APPENDIX B
Algebra of Private-Sector Demand

This appendix will explain the algebra behind the material in the chapter, deriving the equilibrium value of aggregate output demanded. You should see some similarity between the presentation here and the description of the circular flow explaining the national income accounts.

The Aggregate Expenditure Function

We begin with the heart of the income-expenditure model: the consumption function. The consumption function used throughout this chapter and the previous chapter was a straight line; the equation for this line can be written as

$$C = 0.7 + 0.75Y$$

where Y equals the level of real GDP, or real income. This line, or consumption function, intercepts the vertical axis at \$0.7 trillion and has a slope of 0.75. Consumption at each level of income therefore equals \$0.7 trillion plus 0.75 times the level of income. Theoretically, \$0.7 trillion will be spent on consumption even if income is zero; \$0.7 trillion is called *autonomous consumption*. In addition, consumption will increase by \$0.75 for each \$1 increase in income. Thus, increases in consumption are said to be *induced* by increases in income. Therefore, consumption has an autonomous portion, \$0.7 trillion, and an induced portion, $0.75Y$.

The second component of spending is investment. The equation for autonomous investment used throughout the chapter can be written simply as $I = \$0.4$ trillion. The third component of spending is net exports, NX, which we assumed to be an autonomous –\$0.1 trillion. Combining these spending elements yields

$$\begin{aligned} C + I + NX &= 0.7 + 0.75Y + 0.4 - 0.1 \\ &= 1.0 + 0.75Y \end{aligned}$$

The right-hand expression describes the aggregate expenditure function used throughout this chapter. This line intercepts the vertical axis at \$1.0 trillion and has a slope of 0.75. Thus, autonomous consumption plus autonomous investment plus autonomous net exports equals \$1.0 trillion. In equilibrium, real GDP, Y, equals aggregate spending:

$$Y = C + I + NX$$

To find the equilibrium level of Y, we find the value of Y in the following equation:

$$Y = \$1.0 \text{ trillion} + 0.75Y$$

By rearranging terms we get

$$0.25Y = \$1.0 \text{ trillion}$$

Dividing both sides of the equation by 0.25 yields an equilibrium value of Y of \$4.0 trillion.

A More General Form of Demand-Side Equilibrium

The advantage of algebra is that it allows us to derive the equilibrium quantity of real GDP demanded in a more general way. Consider a consumption function of the general form

$$C = a + bY$$

where a equals autonomous consumption, the amount of consumption that is independent of the level of income (\$0.7 trillion in our previous example), and b equals the marginal propensity to consume. We can also say that investment equals I and net exports equal NX. At equilibrium, therefore, the quantity of GDP demanded equals the sum of consumption, investment, and net exports, or

Income = Expenditure

$$Y = a + bY + I + NX$$

Again, by rearranging terms and isolating Y on the left-hand side of the equation, we get

$$Y = \frac{1}{1 - b}(a + I + NX)$$

The $(a + I + NX)$ term represents autonomous spending—that is, the amount of spending that occurs even if the level of income equals zero. And $(1 - b)$ equals 1 minus the MPC. In the chapter we showed that 1/(1 – MPC) equals the multiplier. One way of viewing the forces that underlie the determination of equilibrium is to keep in mind that autonomous spending is *multiplied* through the economy until the equilibrium quantity of aggregate output is demanded.

The formula that yields the equilibrium quantity of aggregate output demanded can be used to focus on the origin of the spending multiplier. We can increase autonomous spending by, say, $1, to see what happens to the equilibrium quantity demanded.

$$Y' = \frac{1}{1 - b}(a + I + NX + \$1)$$

The difference between this expression and the initial equilibrium (that is, between Y' and Y) is $\$1/(1 - b)$. Since b equals the MPC, the multiplier equals $1/(1 - b)$. Thus, the change in equilibrium income equals the change in autonomous spending times the multiplier.

Introducing Variable Net Exports

Here we explain the algebra behind variable net exports, first introduced in the appendix to the previous chapter. We begin by stating the equilibrium condition:

$$Y = C + I + (X - M)$$

Exports have been assumed to equal $0.2 trillion at each level of income. Imports increase as income increases and the marginal propensity to import has been assumed to be 0.10. Therefore, net exports are

$$X - M = 0.2 - 0.10Y$$

After incorporating the values for C and I presented earlier, we can express the full equilibrium condition as

$$Y = 0.7 + 0.75Y + 0.4 + 0.2 - 0.10Y$$

which reduces to $0.35Y = \$1.3$ trillion, or $Y = \$3.714$ trillion.

Algebra can be used to generalize these results. If m represents the marginal propensity to import, net exports become $X - mY$. The equilibrium output can be found by solving for Y in the expression

$$Y = a + bY + I + X - mY$$

which yields

$$Y = \frac{1}{1 - b + m}(a + I + X)$$

The expression in parentheses represents autonomous consumption plus autonomous investment plus autonomous exports. In the denominator, $1 - b$ is the marginal propensity to save and m is the marginal propensity to import. We learned in Appendix A that 1/(MPS + MPI) equals the multiplier when net exports are included. Thus, equilibrium output equals the spending multiplier times autonomous spending. And an increase in autonomous spending times the multiplier gives us the resulting increase in the equilibrium quantity of aggregate output demanded.

Appendix Questions

1. (The Spending Multiplier) Suppose that the marginal propensity to consume (MPC) is 0.8 and the marginal propensity to import (MPI) is 0.05.
   a. What is the value of the multiplier?
   b. What would be the change in equilibrium output if investment increased by $100 billion?
   c. Using your answer to part b, calculate the change in the trade balance (net exports) caused by the change in aggregate output.

2. (Equilibrium) Suppose that when aggregate output equals zero, consumption equals $100 billion, autonomous investment equals $200 billion, and net exports equal $100 billion. Suppose also that MPC = 0.9 and MPI = 0.1.
   a. Construct a table showing the level of aggregate spending, net exports, and saving for aggregate output levels of zero, $500 billion, and $1,000 billion.
   b. Use autonomous spending and the multiplier to calculate the equilibrium quantity of aggregate output demanded.
   c. What would the new equilibrium quantity of output demanded be if an *increase* in U.S. interest rates caused net exports to change by $50 billion? Explain.

CHAPTER 10

AGGREGATE SUPPLY

Up to this point we have focused on the quantity of aggregate output demanded for a given price level. We assumed that producers stood ready to supply whatever amount of output was demanded at the given price level, reducing their inventories to cover shortfalls and accumulating inventories to absorb any unsold goods. We were not concerned with what producers would be willing and able to supply, so we have not yet introduced a theory of aggregate supply.

Perhaps no area of macroeconomics is subject to more debate than that of aggregate supply. The debate surrounds the shape of the supply curves and the reasons for that shape. In this chapter, however, we will attempt to develop a single, coherent framework. Although our focus continues to be on economic aggregates, you should not lose sight of the fact that aggregate supply reflects billions of individual production decisions made by millions of individual resource suppliers and firms in the economy. Each firm operates in its own little world, dealing with regular suppliers and customers and keeping a watchful eye on existing and potential competitors. Yet each firm also recognizes that success in large measure is linked to the performance of the economy as a whole. Therefore, the theory of supply we describe here must be consistent with both the microeconomic behavior of individual producers and the macroeconomic behavior of the economy. In the appendix to this chapter we will examine resource markets more closely to strengthen your understanding of the underpinnings of aggregate supply. Topics discussed in this chapter include

- Expected price levels and long-term contracts
- Potential output
- Short-run aggregate supply
- Long-run aggregate supply
- Expansionary and contractionary gaps
- Changes in aggregate supply

AGGREGATE SUPPLY IN THE SHORT RUN

Example "Formal and informal" institutions include property rights, the enforcement of contracts, and so forth. Changes in patent law, for example, would have an impact on aggregate supply.

As you know, *aggregate supply* is the relation between the price level in the economy and the quantity of aggregate output firms are willing and able to supply, other things constant. The other things held constant along a given aggregate supply curve include the supply of resources to producers, the state of technology, and the set of formal and informal institutions that underpin the economic system. The greater the supply of resources, the better the technology, and the greater the production incentives provided by the economic institutions, the greater the aggregate supply. We begin by looking at the supply of the most important resource: labor.

Teaching Tip See the appendix for a more detailed discussion of labor supply.

Labor Supply and Aggregate Supply

Point to Stress The price level refers to output prices, not resource prices. Also stress that the term "wages" refers to total compensation—including employee benefits.

Labor is by far the most important resource, accounting for about three-quarters of cost of production. Labor even has a holiday named after it: Labor Day. The supply of labor in an economy depends on the size and quality of the labor force and household preferences for work versus leisure. Along a given labor supply curve—that is, for a given labor force and given preferences for work versus leisure—the quantity of labor supplied depends on the wage. The higher the wage, other things constant, the greater the quantity of labor supplied.

Nominal wage The wage measured in terms of current dollars; the dollars received in the pay envelope

Real wage The wage measured in terms of dollars of constant purchasing power; hence, the wage measured in terms of the quantity of goods and services it will purchase

So far, so good. Things start getting complicated, however, because the purchasing power of any given dollar wage will depend on the price level in the economy. The higher the price level, the less any given dollar wage will purchase, so the less attractive any given dollar wage is to workers. For example, suppose a worker in 1970 was offered a job paying $20,000 per year. That salary may not impress you today, but the real purchasing power of $20,000 in 1970 equals the real purchasing power of about $75,000 in 1994 dollars. Therefore, we must distinguish between the **nominal wage**, which measures the wage in current dollars (the number of dollars in your pay envelope), and the **real wage**, which measures the wage in constant dollars—that is, dollars of constant purchasing power.

Both workers and employers are concerned about the real wage, not the nominal wage. The problem is that most resource agreements must be negotiated in nominal wages because nobody knows for sure what price level will prevail during the life of the wage agreement. Workers as well as other resource suppliers must reach wage agreements based on the *expected* price level. Some resource prices, such as wages that are set by long-term contracts, must remain in force for extended periods, sometimes for two or three years.

Even where there are no explicit labor contracts, there is often an implicit agreement regarding the nominal wage over some time period. For example, in many firms the standard practice is to revise wages annually. So wage agreements may be either *explicit*, based on a labor contract, or *implicit*, based on the customs or conventions of the market. These explicit and implicit agreements make it difficult to revise the terms of the contract during the life of the agreement even if the price level turns out to be higher or lower than expected. Some contracts may call for cost-of-living adjustments to be made annually during the life of the contract, but research shows that even these adjustments only partially compensate for unexpected increases in the price level.

Potential Output and the Natural Rate of Unemployment

Here's the story. Firms and resource suppliers each begin the production period expecting a certain price level to prevail in the economy. Based on those expectations, they reach agreements on resource prices, such as wages. For example, firms and workers may expect the price level to increase 5 percent next year, so they agree on a nominal wage increase of 5 percent, which will leave the real wage unchanged. If their price-level expectations are realized, the agreed-upon nominal wage yields the expected real wage, so everyone is satisfied with the way things work out. When the actual price level equals the expected price level, we call the resulting level of output the economy's *potential output*. (The concept of potential output is developed more fully in the appendix to this chapter.) *Thus, the potential output is the amount produced when there are no surprises associated with the price level.* So, at the given real wage, workers are supplying just the quantity of labor they want to and firms are hiring just the quantity of labor they want to. Both parties are content with the arrangement.

Teaching Tip Recall the meaning of full employment as discussed in Chapter 7.

We can think of the **potential output** level as the economy's maximum *sustainable* output level, given the supply of resources, the state of technology, and the formal and informal institutions supporting the economy. Potential output is also referred to by other terms, including the *natural rate of output*, the *high-employment level of output*, and the *full-employment level of output*.

Potential output The economy's maximum sustainable output level, given the supply of resources, the state of technology, and the underlying economic institutions; the output level when there are no surprises about the price level

If the economy is producing its potential output, does this mean that all resources in the economy—every worker, every machine, every acre of land—are employed? No. Remember from our discussion of unemployment that even in a vibrant, dynamic economy some workers are unemployed. In a healthy economy there are always both job openings and job seekers. Other resources may be periodically unemployed as well. To remain productive, farmland must at times lie fallow, machines must regularly be shut down for maintenance and repair, trucks must be serviced, even entire plants may be closed for retooling.

The unemployment rate that occurs when the economy is producing its potential GDP is called the **natural rate of unemployment**. The natural rate of unemployment reflects a certain amount of frictional, structural, and seasonal unemployment. When the economy is producing its potential

Natural rate of unemployment The unemployment rate that occurs when the economy is producing its potential level of output

full emplt

output, the number of job openings is equal to the number unemployed for frictional, structural, and seasonal reasons. During the 1960s a widely accepted figure for the natural rate of unemployment was 4 percent of the labor force. Since then the percentage has drifted up for reasons discussed in Chapter 7; today estimates of 5 or 6 percent are most often mentioned.

Example Output per hour of labor in the U.S. business sector in 1990 was 2.5 times output per hour in 1947.

Potential output depends largely on the supply of labor and the productivity of that labor. The supply of labor, in turn, depends on household choices between labor and leisure. At the turn of the century, the average work week was about 54 hours. Because human and physical capital and technology improved during the century, worker productivity per hour increased. The resulting higher real incomes have prompted many households to increase their consumption of leisure, so the average work week is now about 40 hours. Consequently, potential output is lower today than it would be had the labor force not reduced average hours worked.

Example Although the average work week in the United States has dropped to about 40 hours, the average has dropped to about 35 hours in Germany. The average work week in Japan is about 44 hours.

Potential output provides a reference point for the analysis in this chapter. Any increase in the supply of resources in the economy, any technological breakthroughs in the way resources can be combined, or any positive change in the institutional structure of the marketplace will increase the economy's potential output. When the actual price level turns out as anticipated, the expectations of both workers and firms are fulfilled, and the economy produces its potential output. Complications arise, however, when the actual price level that occurs in the economy differs from the expected price level. The *short run* is a period so brief that firms and those who supply resources to firms have insufficient time to adjust to an unexpected price level. In the *long run*, firms and resource suppliers have time to adjust completely to a price level that differs from their expectations.

Actual Price Level Higher Than Expected

As we said, each firm's objective is to maximize profit. Profit equals total revenue minus total cost. In the short run, the pay rates of many resources are fixed by contract. Suppose the price level turns out to be higher than expected. What happens to the quantity of aggregate output supplied? Does it exceed the economy's potential, fall short of that potential, or equal that potential? If firms can increase profits by expanding output when the price level is higher than expected, the quantity supplied will increase. Put another way, if the additional revenue from expanded output exceeds the additional cost, then firms have a profit incentive to increase production. Since the prices of many resources have been fixed for the duration of contracts, firms welcome a price level that is higher than expected. After all, in that situation the prices of their products, on average, are higher than expected, while the costs of at least some of the resources they employ remain constant.

Teaching Tip If your students have not taken microeconomics, an example here would be helpful. If profits are initially $1 million and increasing production by 1,000 units would increase revenues by $500,000 and costs by $250,000, the increased production would raise profits to $1.25 million.

When the price level is higher than expected, if the total revenue the firm receives for the product increases more than the firm's total cost of production, profits rise. Because a price level that is higher than expected results in higher profits in the short run, firms expand aggregate output beyond the economy's potential level. At first it might appear contradictory to talk about producing beyond the economy's potential, but

Example Between 1967 and the present, capacity utilization in U.S. industry has ranged from a low of 74.6 percent in 1975 to a high of 88.4 percent in 1973. During the period 1975 to 1988, capacity utilization peaked at 86.2 percent while unemployment reached a low of 5.8 percent, both in 1979.

remember that potential output implies not zero unemployment but the *natural rate* of unemployment. Even in an economy producing its potential output, there is some unemployed labor and some unused production capacity. The economy has the resilience to push output beyond its potential, and when it does so the unemployment rate falls below the natural rate. If you think of potential GDP as the economy's normal capacity, you get a better understanding of how the economy can temporarily exceed that capacity. For example, during World War II, the United States pulled out all the stops to win the war. Factories operated around the clock. The unemployment rate fell below 2 percent. Overtime was common. People worked longer and harder than they normally would.

Consider your study habits. During most of the term you display your normal capacity for academic work. As the end of the term draws near, however, you probably shift into high gear, finishing term papers, studying late into the night for final exams, and generally running yourself ragged trying to pull things together. During those final frenzied weeks of the term, you study beyond your normal capacity, beyond the schedule you would prefer to follow on a regular or sustained basis. We often observe workers exceeding their normal capacity for short bursts: fireworks displayers around the Fourth of July, accountants during tax preparation time, farmers during harvest time, and elected officials during the last days of a campaign or a legislative session. Similarly, firms and their workers are able, for limited periods, to push output beyond its potential.

Why Costs Rise When Output Exceeds Potential

The economy is flexible enough to expand output beyond potential GDP, just as you can extend yourself during final exams. However, you cannot push yourself for weeks without becoming exhausted—and the economy's resources cannot be stretched indefinitely without putting pressure on production costs. Even though many workers are bound by contracts, wage agreements may require overtime pay for extra hours or weekend work. Firms may have to spend more on recruiting, particularly to hire workers who had been frictionally unemployed. Some firms must resort to hiring workers who are not properly prepared for the available jobs—those who had been structurally unemployed. Retirees may need a bonus to draw them back into the labor force. If few additional workers are available, if available workers are less qualified, or if workers require additional pay for overtime, the nominal pay of labor will increase as output expands in the short run, even though most workers are bound by wage agreements.

Teaching Tip Structural unemployment can also occur because the unemployed do not live where the job openings are. Recruitment and relocation costs would increase the expense of hiring these workers.

Example Lumber is another resource sold in the spot market. Hurricane Andrew resulted in nationwide increases in the cost of plywood in 1992.

The nominal cost of other resources may also increase as output is pushed beyond the economy's potential. As production expands, the demand for resources increases, so the prices of those resources purchased in markets where prices are flexible—such as the spot market for oil—will increase, reflecting their greater scarcity. Also, for the rate of production to expand firms must use their machines and trucks more intensively, so this equipment wears out faster and is more subject to breakdown. Thus, the nominal cost per unit of output rises when production is pushed beyond the economy's potential output. But *because the prices of some resources are fixed in the short run by contracts, the cost of additional production rises less than does the revenue resulting from the higher price level, so profit-maximizing firms increase the quantity supplied.*

In summary, if the price level is greater than expected, firms have a profit incentive to increase the quantity of aggregate output supplied. As firms increase the quantity supplied, however, the per-unit cost of additional output increases. When the price level is higher than expected, firms will maximize profits by expanding output as long as the revenue from additional production exceeds the cost of that production.

The Price Level, Real Wages, and Labor Supply

When the actual price level exceeds the expected price level, the real value of an agreed-upon nominal wage declines. We might ask why workers would be willing to increase the quantity of labor they supply when the price level is higher than expected. One answer is that since labor agreements require workers to offer their labor at the agreed-upon nominal wage, workers are simply complying with their contracts. Another possible explanation is that the contracted wage is higher than it needs to be to attract enough workers. The **efficiency wage theory** argues that by keeping wages above the level required to attract a sufficient number of workers, some firms ensure an abundant worker pool from which to hire. Wages that are higher than necessary also ensure that employees will be less likely to goof off or do anything that might jeopardize what is considered an attractive job. Since wages are higher than they need to be, workers gladly increase the quantity of labor supplied when firms expand output.

Efficiency wage theory The idea that keeping wages above the level required to attract a sufficient pool of workers makes workers compete to keep their jobs and results in greater productivity

Actual Price Level Lower Than Expected

We have discovered that when the price level is greater than expected, firms expand output, but as they do, the per-unit cost of additional production increases. Now let's examine the effects of a price level that is lower than expected. Again, suppose that resource suppliers and firms are expecting a certain price level. If the price level turns out to be lower than expected, production is less attractive to firms. The price firms receive for their output is lower than they expected, but many of their production costs do not fall. In fact, the real cost per unit of resource often goes up if the price level is lower than expected. For example, since the nominal wage has been fixed by labor contracts, a lower price level means that the real wage firms must pay workers actually increases.

Example Between 1974 and 1975, the U.S. capacity utilization rate dropped from 84.2 percent to 74.6 percent. Between July, 1990 and March, 1991, the rate dropped from 83.8 percent to 78.4 percent, while the unemployment rate increased from 5.5 percent to 6.8 percent.

Since production is less profitable when the price level is lower than expected, firms reduce their quantity supplied, and the economy produces less than its potential. The result is that some workers are laid off, those who keep their jobs may work fewer hours, and unemployment rises above its natural rate. Not only is less labor employed, but machines go unused and delivery trucks sit idle—entire plants may even shut down. (You may have read about the auto producers that sometimes halt production for weeks if sales are slower than expected.)

Just as some costs increase in the short run when output is pushed beyond the economy's potential, some costs decline when output falls below the economy's potential. As output falls below potential, some resources become unemployed, so the prices of resources purchased in markets where the price is flexible decline. Moreover, with an abundance of unemployed resources, firms can be more selective about which resources to employ, laying off the least productive first.

The Short-Run Aggregate Supply Curve

Point to Stress An important factor held constant along the *SRAS* curve is the expected price level incorporated in resource price agreements.

To review: If the price level turns out to be higher than expected, the quantity supplied increases beyond the economy's potential output. As output expands, however, the per-unit cost of additional production increases. If the price level turns out to be lower than expected, the quantity supplied shrinks below the economy's potential output. As output declines, the per-unit cost of production falls. All of this is a long way of saying that *in the short run, there is a positive relation between the actual price level and the quantity of aggregate output supplied.*

Short-run aggregate supply (*SRAS*) curve A curve that shows the direct relation between the price level and the quantity of aggregate output supplied, other things constant.

Short run A period during which some resource prices, especially those for labor, are fixed by agreement

What we have been describing is the **short-run aggregate supply (*SRAS*) curve**, which shows the relation between the actual price level and the quantity of aggregate output producers in the economy are willing and able to supply, other things constant. The **short run** in this context is the period during which some resource prices, especially those for labor, are fixed by agreement. For simplicity, we can think of the short run as the duration of labor contracts.

The short-run aggregate supply curve in Exhibit 1, $SRAS_{130}$, is based on the given expected price level, in this case 130. Note that if the price level turns out to be 130, as expected, producers supply the economy's potential level of output, which in Exhibit 1 is $5.0 trillion. This combination of price and quantity supplied is indicated by point *a*. If 130 turns out to be the actual price level, all firms and all resource suppliers will be content to supply that amount, because their supply and demand decisions were based on that expected price level. Nobody is surprised. In Exhibit 1, levels of output that fall short of the economy's potential are shaded in red and levels of output that exceed the economy's potential are shaded in blue.

Teaching Tip Explain that if production costs rise slowly, the prices required by producers to increase output also rise slowly—and the *SRAS* curve is relatively flat. In contrast, if production costs rise rapidly, producers require larger output price increases before they are willing to increase production—and the *SRAS* is therefore relatively steep.

The slope of the aggregate supply curve depends on how quickly the cost of additional production rises as aggregate output expands. If in the short run the increases in production costs per unit are relatively modest, the supply curve will be relatively flat. If these costs increase sharply with increased production, the supply curve will climb sharply. Notice that the short-run aggregate supply curve gets steeper as output increases because resources become more scarce and hence more costly as output increases. At some level of output the supply curve will become vertical, meaning that not one additional unit of aggregate output can be supplied, no matter what the price level. Much of the controversy about the short-run aggregate supply curve involves its shape; extreme shapes range from relatively flat to relatively steep.

EXHIBIT 1

Short-Run Aggregate Supply Curve When the Expected Price Level is 130

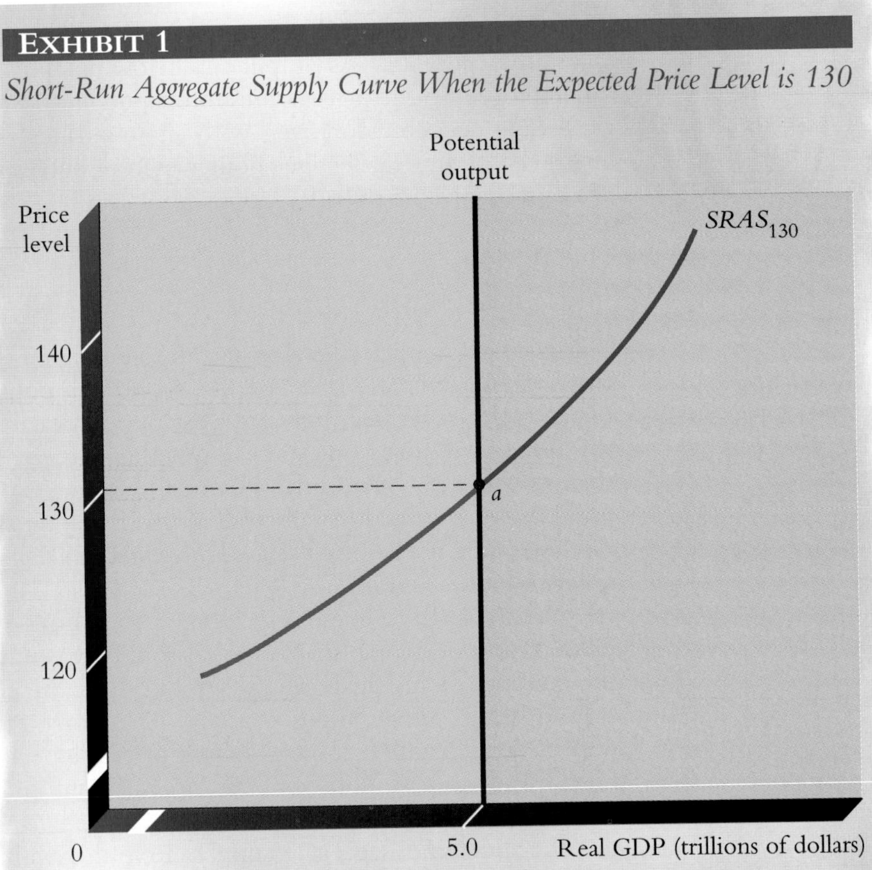

The short-run aggregate supply curve is drawn for a given expected price level of 130. Point *a* shows that if the actual price level equals the expected level, producers supply the potential level of output. If the price level exceeds 130, firms increase the quantity supplied. As they do, the cost of production per unit of output rises. With a price level below 130, firms decrease the quantity supplied. As they do, their cost per unit of output falls. Levels of output that fall short of the economy's potential are shaded red; levels of output that exceed the economy's potential are shaded blue.

AGGREGATE SUPPLY IN THE LONG RUN

A price level that is higher or lower than the expected price level on which the prevailing resource agreements were based will, in the long run, bring about additional adjustments. In the long run, firms and resource suppliers are able to renegotiate all agreements based on knowledge of the actual price level. In this section we examine this long-run adjustment.

Teaching Tip Recall from Chapter 5 that the output and price levels are determined by the interaction of aggregate demand and aggregate supply. Chapter 9 ignored aggregate supply, and Chapter 10 up to now has ignored aggregate demand.

Actual Price Level Higher Than Expected

Let's begin in Exhibit 2 with an expected price level of 130. The short-run aggregate supply curve for that expected price level is $SRAS_{130}$. If the price level turned out as expected, firms would be willing to supply the economy's potential level of output of \$5.0 trillion. Point *a* would reflect the equilibrium combination of price and output levels. Suppose that aggregate demand turns out to be greater than expected, so the actual price level is 135, a price

EXHIBIT 2

Short-Run Equilibrium When the Price Level Exceeds Expectations

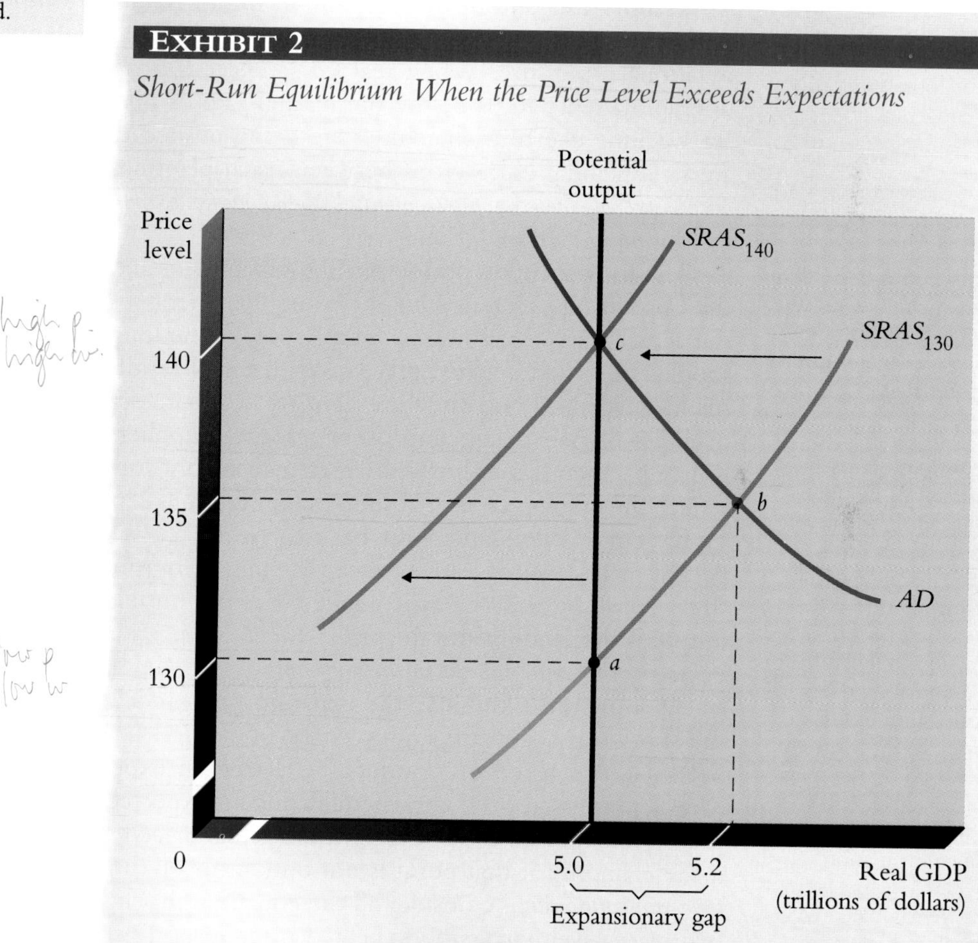

If the expected price level is 130, the short-run aggregate supply curve is $SRAS_{130}$. If the actual price level turns out as expected, the quantity supplied is the potential output, \$5.0 trillion. If the price level is higher than expected, output exceeds potential, as shown by the short-run equilibrium at point *b*. The amount by which output of \$5.2 trillion exceeds the economy's potential output is referred to as the expansionary gap. In the long run, price expectations will be revised upward. As costs rise, the short-run aggregate supply curve shifts upward to $SRAS_{140}$, and the economy moves to long-run equilibrium at point *c*.

Point to Stress As the economy moves to the right along the horizontal axis in Exhibit 2, output and employment both rise. Therefore, the unemployment rate falls.

level higher than expected. When the price level is 135, in the short run firms supply $5.2 trillion, a quantity exceeding the economy's potential of $5.0 trillion. This price and output combination is represented by point *b*, the intersection of the aggregate demand curve, *AD*, with the short-run aggregate supply curve, $SRAS_{130}$. Note again that levels of output exceeding the economy's potential are shaded in blue, and output levels below the economy's potential are shaded in red.

Expansionary gap The amount by which actual output in the short run exceeds the economy's potential output

The amount by which actual output in the short run exceeds the economy's potential is often referred to as the **expansionary gap**; in Exhibit 2 it is the short-run output of $5.2 trillion minus potential output of $5.0 trillion, or $0.2 trillion. As we will see, output exceeding potential GDP creates inflationary pressure. When real GDP exceeds potential output, the actual unemployment rate is below the natural rate of unemployment. Employees are working overtime, machines are being pushed to the limit, and farmers are sandwiching extra crops between usual plantings. *The more the short-run output exceeds the economy's potential, the larger the expansionary gap and the greater the upward pressure on the price level.*

Long run A period during which previous wage contracts and resource price agreements can be renegotiated

The **long run** is a period during which firms and resource suppliers have the opportunity to renegotiate resource payments based on a knowledge of the actual market conditions. Simply put, in the long run firms and resource suppliers know the actual price level that will result from the aggregate demand curve *AD* and they are able to negotiate settlements based on that price level. As workers and other resource suppliers renegotiate higher resource payments, the short-run aggregate supply curve shifts up to the left to reflect the higher cost of resources. In Exhibit 2, the short-run aggregate supply curve eventually shifts back to $SRAS_{140}$, which is based on an expected price level of 140. Notice that the short-run aggregate supply curve shifts up along the aggregate demand curve until the economy's potential output is the equilibrium quantity. *Actual output can exceed the economy's potential in the short run but not in the long run.*

Point to Stress In Exhibit 2, although the actual price level in the short run is 135, price expectations adjust to more than 135 (to 140 in this example). Why? Resource suppliers know that 135 is a price level consistent with existing resource price agreements. However, any increase in compensation when the agreements are renegotiated will result in higher production costs and another round of output price increases.

As shown in Exhibit 2, the expansionary gap is closed by a reduction in the short-run aggregate supply curve from $SRAS_{130}$ to $SRAS_{140}$. Whereas $SRAS_{130}$ was based on contracts reflecting an expected price level of 130, $SRAS_{140}$ is based on contracts reflecting an expected price level of 140. Because the expected price level and the actual price level are identical at point *c*, the economy at that point is not only in short-run equilibrium but also in *long-run equilibrium.* Consider all the equalities that hold at point *c*: (1) the actual price level equals the expected price level; (2) the quantity supplied in the short run equals potential output, which also equals the quantity supplied in the long run; and (3) the quantity supplied equals the quantity demanded. Point *c* will continue to be the equilibrium point unless there is some change in aggregate supply or aggregate demand.

Note that in real terms the situation at *c* is no different from what had been expected at *a*. At both points, firms are willing and able to supply the economy's potential level of output of $5.0 trillion. The same amounts of labor and other resources are employed, and though the price level, the nominal wage rate, and other nominal resource payments are higher at point *c*, real wages and the real return to other resources are the same as they would

Teaching Tip If the real wage was higher at point *c*, the increased compensation would increase the quantity of labor supplied while reducing the quantity demanded. The resulting surplus would drive real wages down.

Point to Stress With an inflation spiral, the economy moves back and forth between an expansionary gap and potential output.

have been at point *a*. For example, suppose that the nominal wage rate was $10 per hour when the expected price was 130. If the expected price level increased from 130 to 140, the nominal wage rate would also increase by the same percentage to $10.77 per hour. With no change in the real wage between points *a* and *c*, firms demand enough labor to produce $5.0 trillion and workers supply enough labor to produce $5.0 trillion.

If suppliers were continually surprised by higher-than-expected price levels, they would continue trying to expand output in the short run beyond the economy's potential level of output. As the economy adjusted in the long run to the higher-than-expected price levels, the short-run aggregate supply curve would shift to the left, creating an inflation spiral. Thus, in the short run, a higher-than-expected price level prompts an increase in the quantity of aggregate output supplied; in the long run, this incorrect price expectation creates inflationary pressure that decreases the short-run aggregate supply curve, resulting in a higher price level and a lower level of output.

If a given increase in the price level, or a given amount of inflation, came to be predicted with accuracy year after year, firms and resource suppliers would build these higher expected price levels into their agreements, raising resource prices enough to keep the real return to resources unchanged. The price level would move up each year by the expected amount, but the economy's output would remain at potential GDP, thereby skipping the round trip beyond the economy's potential and back.

Actual Price Level Lower Than Expected

Point to Stress As the economy moves to the left along the horizontal axis in Exhibit 3, output and employment both drop. Therefore, the unemployment rate rises.

Contractionary gap The amount by which actual output in the short run falls below the economy's potential output

Let's begin again with an expected price level of 130 as presented in Exhibit 3, where blue shading indicates output levels exceeding potential and red shading indicates output levels below potential. If the price level turned out as expected, the resulting equilibrium combination would occur at *a*. Suppose this time that aggregate demand is less than expected, so the price level falls below expectations. The intersection of the aggregate demand curve, *AD*, with $SRAS_{130}$ establishes the short-run equilibrium point, *d*. Production of $4.8 trillion is below the economy's potential. The amount by which actual output falls short of potential GDP is called the **contractionary gap**. In this case the contractionary gap is $0.2 trillion. The unemployment rate is greater than the natural rate.

Example In 1992, General Motors froze salaries and asked its salaried employees to contribute to their health insurance costs. Total compensation therefore dropped.

Because the price level of 125 is lower than the expected level, the nominal wage based on an expected price level of 130 translates into a higher real wage in the short run. But, in the long run, all labor contracts are subject to renegotiation. Since the price level is lower than expected, employers are no longer willing to offer as high a nominal wage. And with the unemployment rate higher than the natural rate, more workers are competing for jobs. At least in theory, the combination of an increase in the pool of unemployed workers and a decline in the price level should make workers more willing to accept a lower nominal wage.

If firms and workers agree on a lower nominal wage, production costs decline, shifting the short-run aggregate supply curve outward. The short-run

EXHIBIT 3

Short-Run Equilibrium When the Price Level is Below Expectations

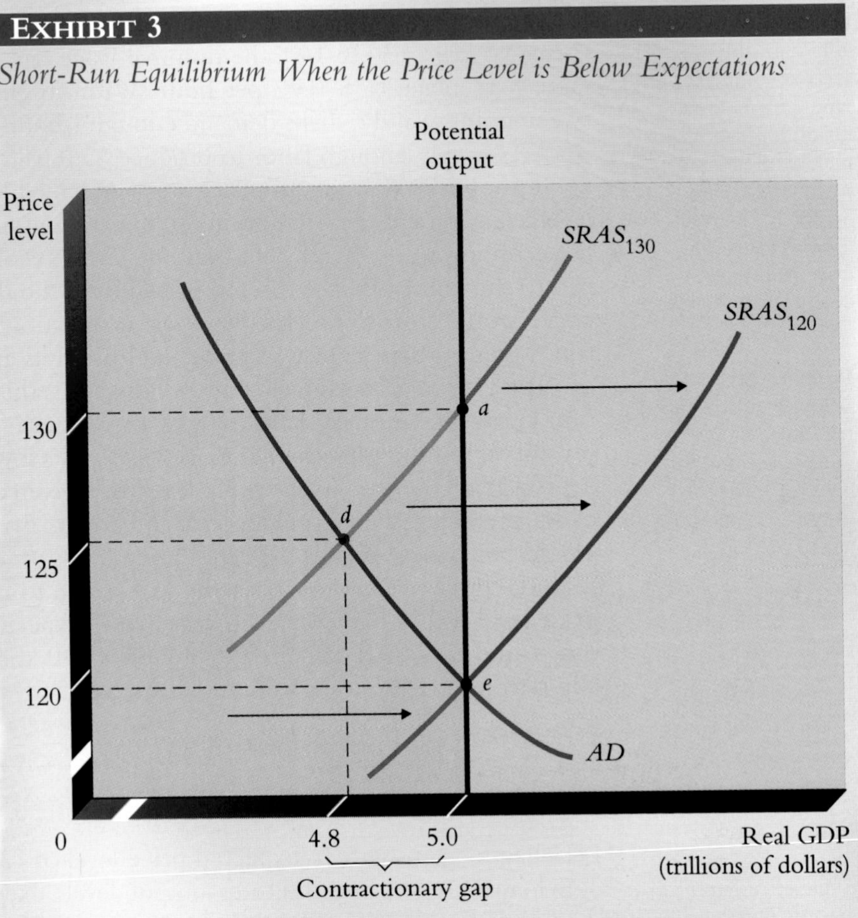

When the price level is below expectations, as indicated by the intersection of the aggregate demand curve *AD* with the short-run aggregate supply curve $SRAS_{130}$, short-run equilibrium occurs at point *d*. Production is below the economy's potential by the amount of the contractionary gap, \$0.2 trillion. In the long run, resource suppliers will lower their price expectations. As resource costs fall, the short-run aggregate supply curve shifts out to $SRAS_{120}$, and the economy moves to long-run equilibrium at point *e*, with output at the potential level, \$5.0 trillion.

Point to Stress In Exhibit 3, although the actual price level in the short run is 125, price expectations adjust to less than 125 (to 120 in this example). Why? Resource suppliers know that 125 is a price level consistent with existing resource price agreements. However, any decrease in compensation when the agreements are renegotiated will result in lower production costs, allowing another round of output price decreases.

supply curve will continue to shift outward until it intersects the aggregate demand curve where the economy produces its potential output. This increase in supply is reflected in Exhibit 3 by a shift to the right in the short-run aggregate supply curve from $SRAS_{130}$ to $SRAS_{120}$. *If the price level and nominal wages are flexible, the short-run aggregate supply curve will move outward until the economy produces its potential output.* The new short-run aggregate supply curve is based on an expected price level of 120. Because the expected price level and the actual price level are the same, the economy is now in long-run equilibrium at point *e*.

Although the nominal wage is lower at point *e* than what was originally agreed upon when the expected price level was 130, the real wage is the same at *e* as it would have been at *a*. Since the real wage is the same, the amount of labor that workers supply is the same and real output is the same. All that has changed between *a* and *e* is the price level, the nominal wage, and other nominal resource payments. It was classical economists who first argued that flexible wages and prices promote an adjustment that can restore the economy to its potential output.

We conclude that when incorrect expectations cause firms and resource suppliers to overestimate the price level, output in the short run falls below the economy's potential. As long as wages and prices remain flexible, however, firms and workers should be able in the long run to adjust their wage agreements when existing contracts expire; a drop in the nominal wage will shift the short-run aggregate supply curve to the right until the economy once again produces its potential level of output. *If wages and prices do not adjust very quickly to a contractionary gap—that is, if they are, in Keynes's word, "sticky"—then shifts in the short-run aggregate supply curve may be very slow to move the economy to its potential output. The economy can therefore appear stuck at an output and employment level below its potential.*

depression

Tracing Potential Output

If wages and prices are flexible enough, the economy in the long run will produce its potential level of output, as indicated in Exhibit 4 by the vertical line drawn at the economy's potential GDP, estimated here to be \$5.0 trillion. The potential level of output depends on the supply of resources in the economy, on the level of technology, and on the production incentives provided by the formal and informal institutions of the economic system. The vertical line drawn at potential GDP is called the economy's **long-run aggregate supply (*LRAS*) curve.**

Long-run aggregate supply (*LRAS*) curve The vertical line drawn at potential output

Note that as long as wages and prices are flexible, the economy's potential GDP is consistent with any level of prices. *In the long run, the actual price level depends only on the location of the aggregate demand curve.* In Exhibit 4 the initial price level of 130 is determined by the intersection of *AD* with the long-run aggregate supply curve. If the aggregate demand curve shifts out to *AD′*, then in the long run the equilibrium price level will increase to 140, but equilibrium output will remain at the economy's potential GDP. Conversely, a fall in aggregate demand will in the long run lead only to a fall in the price level, with no change in output. *We stress that these long-run movements are more like tendencies than smooth adjustments. The time required for resource prices to adjust may be quite long, particularly when the economy faces a contractionary gap.*

Evidence on Aggregate Supply

What evidence is there that when workers and firms have time to adjust to changes in the price level, the long-run aggregate supply curve can be depicted by a vertical line drawn at the economy's potential GDP? Except

EXHIBIT 4

Long-Run Aggregate Supply Curve

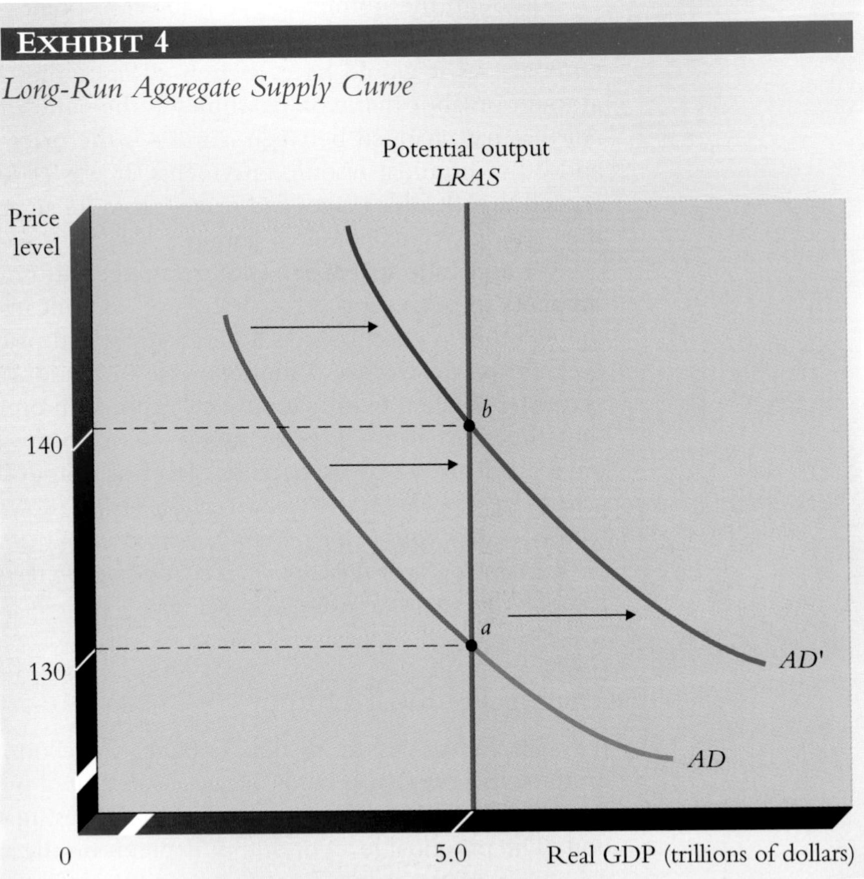

In the long run, when the expected price level equals the actual price level, output will be at the potential level. In the long run, $5.0 trillion will be supplied regardless of the actual price level. The long-run aggregate supply curve, *LRAS*, is a vertical line at potential GDP.

during the Great Depression, unemployment over the last century varied from year to year but typically returned to what would be viewed as the level that was consistent with potential GDP—about 4 or 5 percent. (Exhibit 2 in Chapter 7 graphs the unemployment rate since 1900.)

As the Great Depression taught us, however, the adjustment toward potential output may take years. Herein lies the problem: whereas expansion of output beyond the economy's potential creates labor shortages that in the long run result in a higher nominal wage and a higher price level, reductions in output below the economy's potential GDP do not appear to generate enough downward pressure to lower the nominal wage. Studies have found that the nominal wage is slow to adjust to high unemployment. Nominal wages have declined in particular industries; for example, during the 1980s nominal wages fell in airlines, steel, and trucking. But seldom have we observed actual declines across the economy in nominal wages, especially since World War II.

Example Average hourly nominal earnings in the United States have increased every year since 1947.

When unemployment is extensive, why do employers appear reluctant to cut nominal wages or to replace existing employees with lower-paid workers from the pool of the unemployed? One possible explanation has already been mentioned. Recall that the *efficiency wage theory* argues that by keeping wages above the level required to attract enough workers, firms make workers compete to keep their jobs. This competition in job performance results in greater productivity. During recessions, firms prefer to lay off workers and reduce the hours of employment for remaining workers rather than to cut wages. Wage cuts may save payroll costs, but they can also reduce morale and have negative effects on worker productivity.

Other possible reasons why downward movement of wages might be sticky include workers' psychological resistance to wage cuts, minimum wage laws, long-term wage contracts, labor union resistance to lower wages, and the fact that recessions since World War II have been shorter and less severe than earlier ones. Hence, nominal wages do not adjust downward as quickly or as substantially as they do upward. The downward response that does occur tends to be slow and relatively weak. Consequently, we say that nominal wages tend to be sticky in the downward direction. *Since nominal wages fall slowly, if at all, the natural supply-side adjustments needed to return the economy to potential output may take so long as to seem ineffective.* Therefore, unemployment in excess of the natural rate could linger.

Example Although average hourly earnings have steadily increased in the United States on a nominal basis, figures adjusted for inflation reveal that average hourly earnings peaked in 1973.

Note one final point. Even though the nominal wage seldom falls, a decline in the nominal wage is not necessary to close a contractionary gap. All that is needed is a fall in the real wage. And the real wage will fall as long as the price level increases more than the nominal wage. For example, if the price level increases by 2 percent and the nominal wage remains unchanged, the real wage falls by 2 percent. As long as the real wage falls enough, firms will be willing to demand enough additional labor to produce the economy's potential output. Over the last decade, nominal wage increases have on average trailed increases in the price level, so the real wage has fallen.

CHANGES IN AGGREGATE SUPPLY

So far we have shown that, given the supply of resources in the economy, the state of technology, and the institutional structure of the economic system, the short-run aggregate supply curve depends on the expected price level. Also, when the actual price level differs from the price level on which prevailing contracts are based, market forces are set in motion that, in the long run, shift the short-run aggregate supply curve until the economy produces its potential level of output. In this section we will consider factors other than the expected price level that may affect aggregate supply. We distinguish between long-term trends in aggregate supply and **supply shocks**, which are unexpected events that affect aggregate supply, sometimes only temporarily.

Supply shocks Unexpected events that affect aggregate supply; sometimes the effect is only temporary

Increases in Aggregate Supply

The economy's potential output is based on the willingness and ability of households to supply resources to firms, on the level of technology, and on the institutional underpinnings of the economic system. Any change in the supply of resources, in the way existing resources can be combined, or in the economic system may affect the economy's potential output.[1] For example, labor supply may change because of a change in the size of the labor force or a change in household preferences for labor versus leisure. The U.S. labor force has doubled since 1948 as a result of a growth in population and a rising labor force participation rate, especially among women. At the same time, job training, education, and on-the-job experience have increased the quality of labor. Increases in both the quantity and the quality of the labor force have increased the economy's potential GDP, or long-run aggregate supply.

Example Business investors consider factors such as the reliability of the infrastructure, the stability of government, and the expectations of sufficient rates of return when considering building a plant. African nations have very inexpensive labor costs, but capital operating costs are 50 percent to 100 percent higher than in South Asia where the return on investment is nine times greater than in Africa. Twenty-five years ago the two regions were even.

The quantity and quality of other resources also change over time. The capital stock—the amount of machines, buildings, and trucks—increases whenever the economy's gross investment exceeds the depreciation of capital. Even the quantity and quality of land can be increased—for example, by claiming land from the sea, as is done in the Netherlands, or by revitalizing soil that has lost its fertility. These increases in the quantity and quality of resources expand the economy's potential output. *Changes in the labor force and in the supply of other key resources tend to occur gradually over time.* Institutional changes that define property rights more clearly or make contracts more easily enforced will increase the incentives to undertake productive activity. For example, more firms will be started if the founders have greater control over the use of resources and get to keep most of the profits.

Exhibit 5 shows the effects of a shift in the economy's potential output from \$5.0 trillion to \$5.5 trillion. Notice that since in both cases resource contracts are based on an expected price level of 130, the short-run aggregate supply curve shifts to the right as well, from $SRAS_{130}$ to $SRAS'_{130}$. Thus, improvements in the economy's ability to produce will shift both the economy's potential output and its short-run aggregate supply curve.

Beneficial supply shocks Unexpected events that increase aggregate supply, sometimes only temporarily

In contrast to the gradual, or long-term, changes that often occur in the supply of resources, **beneficial supply shocks** are unexpected events that increase aggregate supply, sometimes only temporarily. For example, in the mid-1980s, the per-barrel price of oil dropped from over \$30 to about \$10. Other beneficial shocks include (1) abundant harvests around the world that increase the supply of food, (2) discoveries of natural resources, such as the oil in Alaska and the North Sea, (3) changes in the economic system that promote more production, such as legislation that reduces the number of groundless lawsuits, and (4) technological breakthroughs that allow firms to combine resources more efficiently, such as the microchip, which revolutionized the way information is gathered, processed, and transmitted.

1. Changes in the economy's potential GDP over time are discussed in greater detail in Chapter 17, which examines U.S. economic growth and productivity.

EXHIBIT 5

Effects of a Gradual Change in the Supply of Resources

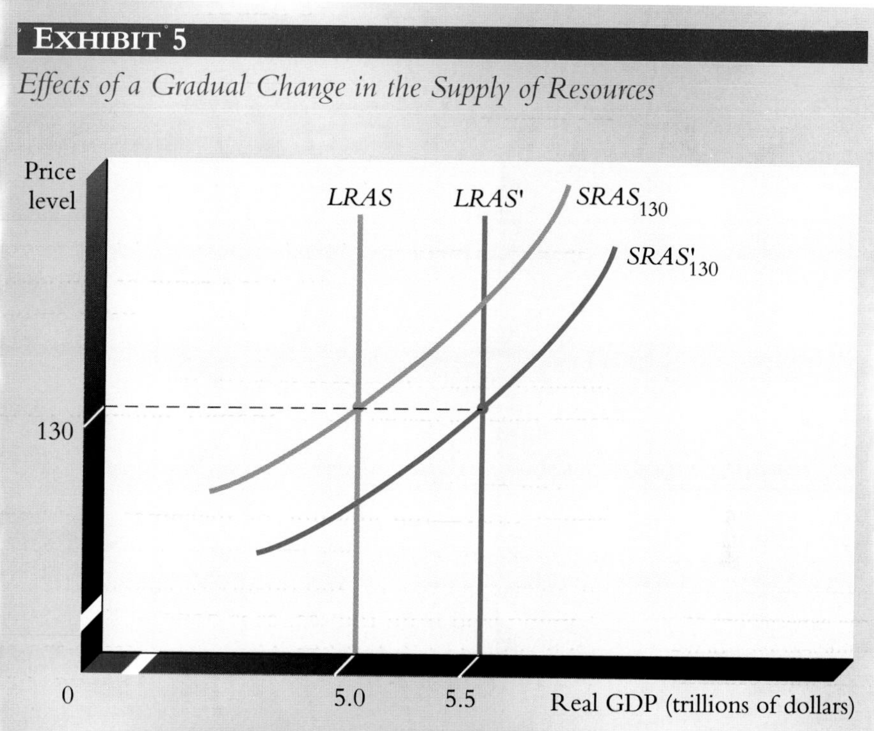

A gradual increase in the supply of available resources increases the potential level of GDP from $5.0 trillion to $5.5 trillion. Both the long- and short-run aggregate supply curves shift to the right.

Exhibit 6 reflects the effect of a beneficial supply shock on short-run and long-run aggregate supply. Note that *for a given aggregate demand curve, the happy outcome of a beneficial supply shock is an increase in output and a decrease in the price level.* For example, the 1986 decline in oil prices helped boost output and lower the inflation rate that year to only 1.9 percent, the lowest rate since the early 1960s. A beneficial supply shock might be only temporary. For example, since 1986 oil prices have increased to $20 per barrel; and one season's favorable growing conditions do not represent a permanent change in the climate.

Example Food production in sub-Saharan Africa has declined by 20 percent since 1970. In part this is due to encroachments by the Sahara desert. In part it is due to government policies that discouraged investment in agriculture by keeping food prices low.

Decreases in Aggregate Supply

Any reduction in the supply of a key resource reduces both potential output and short-run aggregate supply. We noted earlier that the average work week has become shorter, decreasing from about 54 hours at the turn of the century to about 40 hours today. This decline in the supply of labor has reduced potential output below what it would have been had hours not declined. A change in the composition of the work force toward younger, less experienced workers could also reduce aggregate supply. As we said,

EXHIBIT 6

Effects of Supply Shocks on Aggregate Supply

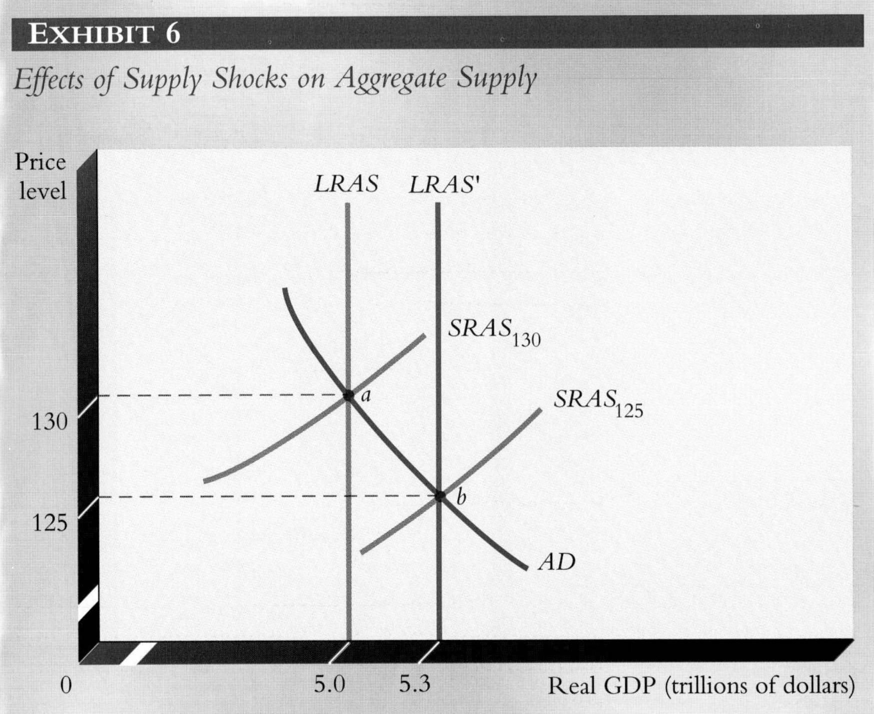

Given the aggregate demand curve, a supply shock shifts both the short-run aggregate supply curve and the long-run aggregate supply curve, or potential output. A beneficial supply shock lowers the price level and increases output, as reflected by the change in equilibrium from point *a* to point *b*. An adverse supply shock can be represented by a move from point *b* to point *a*, where the price level is higher but output is lower.

changes in the supply of labor tend to occur gradually over time. In Exhibit 5, a gradual drop in supply would be represented by a shift to the left in potential output (in this case from $5.5 trillion to $5.0 trillion).

Adverse supply shocks Unexpected events that reduce aggregate supply, sometimes only temporarily

Example Hurricane Andrew damaged about 80 percent of the farms in south Florida.

Adverse supply shocks are unexpected events that reduce aggregate supply, sometimes only temporarily. For example, a national drought could temporarily reduce the supply of a variety of products, including food, building materials, and raw materials such as cotton and flax used in textiles. A lack of rain could also affect water-powered energy sources. Or a government that had been stable could be toppled, creating much uncertainty about property rights and the validity of contracts. Such a change in the institutional underpinnings of the economic system would likely reduce production incentives. An adverse supply shock can be reflected by a shift to the left in the short-run aggregate supply curve and a decrease in the level of potential output. Imagine starting at equilibrium point *b* in Exhibit 6, where the output level is $5.3 trillion and the price level is 125. Given the aggregate demand curve, the effect of an adverse supply shock would be represented by a shift up and to the left in the equilibrium point, from point *b* to point *a*, reducing output to $5.0 trillion and increasing the price level to 130.

The combination of reduced output and a higher price level is often referred to as stagflation. The United States encountered stagflation during the 1970s, when the economy was rocked by a series of adverse supply shocks, such as crop failures around the globe and the fourfold increase in oil prices achieved by OPEC in 1974. If the condition that reduces aggregate supply is only temporary, such as a drought, aggregate supply should increase when the source of the shock disappears. But some economists have begun to question an economy's ability to bounce back from swings in economic activity, as discussed in the following case study.

CASE STUDY

Why Is Unemployment So High in Europe?

Hysteresis The theory that a sustained period of high (or low) unemployment can increase (or decrease) the natural rate of unemployment

Between World War II and the mid-1970s, unemployment rates in Western Europe were relatively low. For example, between 1960 and 1974 the rate in France and Great Britain never reached as high as 4 percent. The world-wide recession of the 1970s, however, caused the unemployment rates to drift up. The problem was that unemployment continued to climb long after these recessions were over. The unemployment rates in France, Great Britain, and Italy remained above 10 percent for most of the 1980s. After a modest decline in the late 1980s, rates again topped 10 percent in the early 1990s.

Some observers argue that this increase in unemployment rates reflected an increase in the underlying natural rate of unemployment. Those economists who have studied the issue have borrowed a term from physics, *hysteresis*, to explain what they believe happened to the natural rate of unemployment. When applied to the unemployment rate, the term **hysteresis** means that the natural rate of unemployment depends in part on the recent history of unemployment. The longer the actual unemployment rate remains above what had been considered the natural rate, the more the natural rate itself will increase.

Here are two possible explanations for this phenomenon. Those out of work can lose valuable job skills, thereby reducing their ability to find a job even after the economy recovers. Or, as weeks of unemployment turn into months, the shock and stigma of being unemployed may diminish, so the work ethic weakens, as does the desire to find a job. What's more, some European countries offer relatively generous and lengthy unemployment benefits, reducing the hardship of unemployment.

Keep in mind that hysteresis remains just a theory to explain high unemployment rates in Western Europe. The theory seems to have less relevance to the United States, where rates dropped throughout most of the 1980s. Still, as noted earlier, some argue that the natural rate of unemployment seems to have drifted up in the United States from about 4 percent in the 1960s to 5 or 6 percent today.

Sources: Olivier Blanchard and Lawrence Summers, "Beyond the Natural Rate Hypothesis," *American Economic Review* 78 (May 1988):182–187; "Economic and Financial Indicators," *The Economist* 22 (August 1992).

Conclusion

Perhaps no subject in macroeconomics remains more debatable than that of aggregate supply. The debate involves the slope of the aggregate supply curve and the reasons for that slope. No two introductory economics books are likely to discuss the topic in exactly the same way. This chapter called attention to the expected price level as a key determinant of the nominal resource prices that shape aggregate supply in the short run. If firms and resource suppliers can, in the long run, fully adjust to unexpected changes in the price level, the economy will produce its potential output.

The appendix to this chapter takes a closer look at the relation between resource markets and potential output. The next chapter will introduce government and show if and how public policy might be instrumental in moving the economy toward its potential GDP.

Summary

1. Short-run aggregate supply is based on resource contracts that reflect the expected price level. If the expected price level actually occurs, the economy produces its potential level of output. If the actual price level exceeds the expected price level, short-run equilibrium outputs exceed the economy's potential, opening up an expansionary gap. If the actual price level is below the expected price level, short-run equilibrium output falls short of the economy's potential, opening up a contractionary gap. The short-run aggregate supply curve slopes upward.

2. Output can exceed the economy's potential in the short run, but in the long run a higher nominal wage will be negotiated at the first opportunity. This higher nominal wage increases the cost of production, shifting the short-run aggregate supply curve back until equilibrium output equals the economy's potential.

3. If output in the short run falls short of the economy's potential, and if wages and prices in the economy are flexible, then a lower real wage will reduce production costs, shifting the short-run aggregate supply curve out until equilibrium output equals the economy's potential.

4. Empirical evidence suggests that when output exceeds the economy's potential, wage and price levels increase. But there is less evidence to support a downward movement of wage and price levels when output is below the economy's potential. Wages appear to be somewhat "sticky" in the downward direction.

5. The long-run aggregate supply curve, or the economy's potential level of output, depends on the amount and quality of resources available in the economy, the state of technology, and formal and informal institutions supporting the economic system. Increases in resource availability, improvements in technology, or institutional changes that provide greater production incentives increase aggregate supply and potential output. Supply shocks are unexpected and sometimes temporary changes in aggregate supply. Beneficial supply shocks lead to increased output and a lower price level. Adverse supply shocks result in stagflation: reduced output and a higher price level.

Questions and Problems

1. (Short Run) In the short run, prices may go up faster than costs do. The chapter discusses why this might happen. Suppose that labor and management agree to adjust wages for changes in the price level. How would such adjustments affect the slope of the aggregate supply curve?

2. (Real Wages) Suppose that nominal wages in the economy are rising at 10 percent per year and the price level is rising at 8 percent per year. What is happening to the real wage rate under these circumstances? Will workers immediately notice what is happening to their real wages?

3. (Potential Output) What factors might affect the potential level of output of the economy? Would a severe epidemic be likely to alter the level of potential output? Would the effect depend on the length of the epidemic?

4. (Natural Rate of Unemployment) How is it possible for the natural rate of unemployment to remain constant (or even to rise) while the level of potential output rises? Is this happening in the United States today?

5. (Expansionary Gap) Why doesn't a reduction in the supply of resources create an expansionary gap? Is it possible for the price level to rise without creating an expansionary gap?

6. (Contractionary Gaps) After reviewing Exhibit 3 in this chapter, explain why contractionary gaps occur only in the short run and only when the actual price level is below what was expected.

7. (Shifts in Aggregate Supply) How have advances in medicine and pharmaceuticals affected aggregate supply in the United States over the last fifty years? When the population is growing and new jobs must be found, how important is technology for maintaining low unemployment?

8. (Long Run) The long-run aggregate supply curve is vertical at the economy's potential output level. Why would the long-run aggregate supply curve have to be centered at this level of output rather than below or above the potential level?

9. (Long-Run Adjustment) In the long run, why do differences between the actual price level and the expected price level lead to changes in the level of nominal wages? Why do these changes cause shifts in the short-run aggregate supply curve?

10. (Wages) In Exhibit 2 in this chapter, how does the real wage rate at point *a* compare with the real wage rate at point *c*? How do nominal wages compare?

11. (Supply) Describe how each of the following influences the slope of the aggregate supply curve in the short run.
    a. The level of the natural rate of unemployment
    b. The efficiency wage theory

12. (Long-Run Adjustment) The ability of the economy to eliminate any imbalances between actual output and potential output is sometimes called "self-correction." Using an aggregate supply and aggregate demand diagram, show why this self-correction process involves only *temporary* periods of inflation or deflation.

13. (Short-Run Aggregate Supply) Suppose you own a business and you observe an increase in the industry price level for the product you produce. If you think that this price increase is strictly for your industry and not for the economy as a whole, what will your likely output response be? Explain.

14. (Natural Rate of Unemployment) Pretend that you are an economist hired by the President to "do something to get the rate of unemployment down." The policy options available to you, however, do not change the natural rate of unemployment. If the economy is currently operating at the natural rate, what is the key to being able to reduce unemployment? What are the consequences of your policies?

15. (Efficiency Wage) According to the efficiency wage theory, employers are reluctant to cut nominal wages when faced with a reduction in output demand and price, preferring instead to lay off workers and thereby create cyclical unemployment. Is there anything in the efficiency wage model that might explain an increase in the natural rate of unemployment?

16. (Price Expectations) Explain why the speed and accuracy of adjustments in price expectations are important in determining output responses to fluctuations in aggregate demand.

17. (Real Wage Adjustment) Can you think of any reasons why labor in specific industries might wish not to have wages indexed perfectly to changes in the aggregate price level?

18. (Unemployment in Europe) According to the Single European Act of 1986 and the Maastricht Agreement of 1992, the member countries of the European Community will comprise an "area without internal frontiers" by the end of 1992. What impact might this have on Europe's natural rate of unemployment?

19. (Unemployment in Europe) Is it possible that hysteresis could actually contribute to the reduction in the natural unemployment rate? Explain.

APPENDIX
The Market for Resources

So far we have not discussed in detail the pricing and output decisions of individual firms and resource suppliers. Resource markets play a key role in shaping aggregate supply. This appendix describes the behavior of resource markets, particularly the market for labor, which accounts for about three-quarters of production costs.

The key actors on the supply side are households and firms. We already know that (1) households supply resources and demand goods and services to maximize utility and (2) firms demand resources and supply goods and services to maximize profit. The willingness and ability of households to supply resources to firms depend on the expected earnings of these resources. The higher the expected earnings, other things constant, the greater the quantity of resources supplied to firms. We initially assume that resource suppliers and demanders, when they formulate their wage agreements, know what the price level will be and are able to adjust their supply and demand based on that price level.

The Market for Labor

Although many resources are required for production, we focus primarily on labor because it accounts for most of the cost. What's more, aggregate employment is a key measure of the economy's performance and is thus of special interest to public policy makers. The interaction between the supply of labor by households and the demand for labor by firms determines the equilibrium wage rate and employment level in the economy. The level of employment, in turn, determines the quantity of aggregate output supplied in the economy. Even without a full-scale discussion of the market for labor, we can get some idea of the forces shaping the supply and demand for labor.

SUPPLY OF LABOR. Individuals can use their time in two ways: for labor or for leisure. For simplicity, let's define *leisure* as all noncompensated uses of time, including watching TV, sleeping, studying, and making a sandwich. The wage rate is the reward per unit of time for supplying labor to the market. The higher the wage rate, other things constant, the greater the reward for working—that is, the more goods and services that can be purchased with the earnings from each hour devoted to market work. One of the factors held constant when we compare alternative wage rates is the expected price level. For a given expected price level, any change in the nominal wage—the wage measured in terms of nominal dollars—also produces a change in the real wage—the wage measured in real dollars—that is, in terms of the quantity of goods and services it will purchase. *For a given expected price level, workers believe they can buy more goods and services as the nominal wage increases.*

The higher the nominal wage, given the expected price level, the more goods and services that can be exchanged for an hour of work. Hence, the higher the nominal wage, the higher the opportunity cost of leisure, so the more labor households will supply. *The supply curve for labor by households therefore slopes upward, indicating that the quantity of labor supplied increases as the nominal wage rate increases, other things constant.*

Exhibit 7 presents such an upward-sloping market supply curve for labor, S_{130}. The nominal wage rate is measured on the vertical axis and the quantity of labor on the horizontal axis. This market supply curve for labor is the horizontal sum of all individual workers' supply-of-labor curves. Because the market supply curve is drawn for a given expected price level, in this case, 130, increases in the nominal wage along the supply curve also represent increases in the real wage.

DEMAND FOR LABOR. What determines how much of a particular resource a firm will employ? A firm values resources because they produce goods and services that can be sold for a profit. A firm will employ additional labor as long as doing so adds more to revenue than to its cost. A firm will stop hiring more labor when additional units of labor add more to cost than to

EXHIBIT 7

Labor Supply

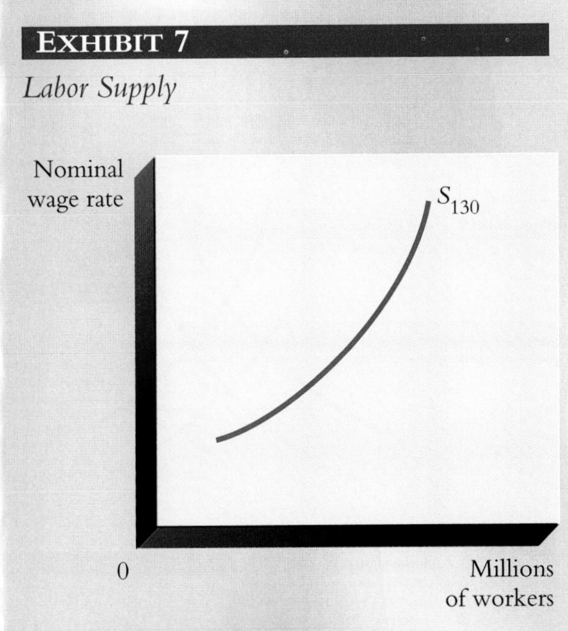

For a given price level of 130, an increase in the nominal wage rate means an increase in the real wage rate. A higher real wage increases the quantity of labor supplied; thus the labor supply curve, S_{130}, slopes upward.

revenue. So each unit of labor (as well as each unit of other resources) must at least pay for itself. The most a firm is willing to pay for an additional unit of labor is that unit's marginal value: the increase in total revenue resulting from each unit of labor's production. The question is, What happens to the marginal value of labor as additional units of labor are employed? Does it go up, go down, or remain the same?

The **law of diminishing marginal returns** says that as additional units of labor are employed while the quantities of other resources are held constant, at some point the quantity of additional output produced begins to decline. This law tells us that the more labor employed, the lower the marginal value added by each additional unit of labor. Remember, the firm will pay no more for each additional unit of labor than the value to the firm of what that unit of labor produces. Since the marginal value of labor declines as more labor is employed, the amount a firm is willing to pay for each additional unit of labor, which is shown by the firm's demand curve for labor, also declines as more labor is employed.

The demand for labor in the economy is reflected by the downward-sloping market demand curve for labor, D_{130}, in Exhibit 8. The market demand curve for labor is the horizontal sum of all firms' demand for labor curves. This downward-sloping demand curve shows that, given the expected price level in the economy of 130, the lower the nominal wage, the greater the quantity of labor firms demand. Because the market demand curve is drawn assuming a given expected price level, decreases in the nominal wage along the demand curve also represent decreases in the expected real wage. The supply and demand curves for labor intersect at the

EXHIBIT 8

The Labor Market

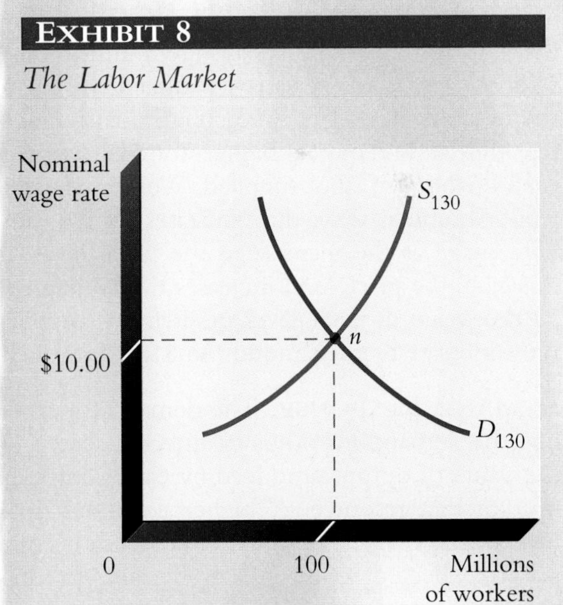

The downward-sloping labor demand curve, D_{130}, indicates that firms increase the quantity of labor demanded as the real wage falls. For a given price level, the intersection of the labor supply and demand curves at point *n* determines the nominal wage rate and the equilibrium level of employment.

equilibrium point, *n*, to yield the equilibrium wage rate of $10.00 and the equilibrium quantity of labor of 100 million workers. In equilibrium, the wage equals labor's marginal value.

Changes in the Expected Price Level

What will happen to the wage and employment level if the price level expected to prevail in the economy is higher than 130? Suppose it is 140.

SUPPLY RESPONSE. With a higher expected price level, workers expect that a given nominal wage will be worth less in real terms because each dollar is expected to purchase less in real goods and services. So under these conditions a higher nominal wage will be required to coax workers to give up the same amount of leisure as they did when the expected price level was lower.

The labor supply curve will therefore shift to the left, from S_{130} to S_{140}, as shown in Exhibit 9, indicating that workers have reduced the quantity of labor they supply at each nominal wage, or that they now require a higher nominal wage for each quantity of labor supplied. Workers must be paid a nominal wage that increases by the same percentage as the increase in the price level. In this case, the price level increases by 7.7 percent, so the wage at each level of quantity supplied must increase by that amount, to $10.77.

EXHIBIT 9

Effect of a Higher Expected Price Level on Nominal Wage and Employment

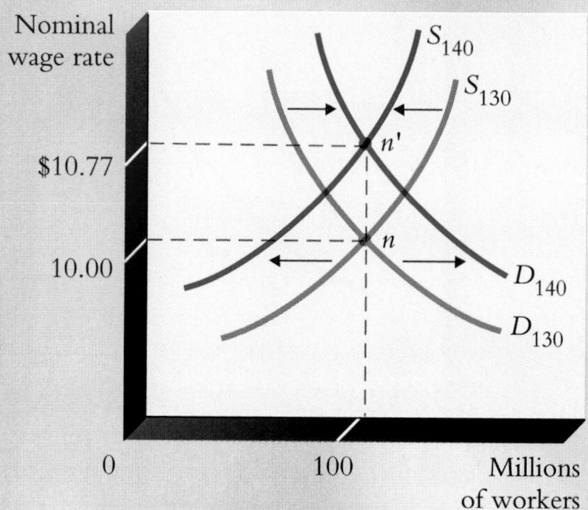

A higher price level reduces the quantity of labor supplied at any given nominal wage rate; the labor supply curve shifts from S_{130} to S_{140} as the price level rises from 130 to 140. At the same time, the higher price level increases the quantity of labor firms demand at any given nominal wage rate; the labor demand curve shifts from D_{130} to D_{140}. These two effects of a higher price level offset each other, so the equilibrium level of employment is unchanged at 100 million workers. The real wage at point *n′* is the same as at point *n*.

DEMAND RESPONSE. The demand for labor, like the demand for other resources, is based on the value of output produced by each additional unit of that resource. A higher expected price level means that the nominal value of labor's output is expected to be greater because product prices are expected to be higher. Since an increase in the expected price level from 130 to 140 increases the revenue generated by each additional unit of labor, firms will be willing to pay a higher nominal wage for each additional unit of labor. This increase in labor demand is reflected in Exhibit 9 by a shift of the labor demand curve to the right, from D_{130} to D_{140}. This increased demand for labor indicates that firms are willing to hire more workers at each nominal wage, or are willing to pay a higher nominal wage for a given quantity of labor. Specifically, if the expected price level increases by 7.7 percent, firms' demand for labor increases by 7.7 percent, indicating that for any given level of employment, firms are willing to pay a nominal wage that is 7.7 percent higher than before.

NEW EQUILIBRIUM. As a result of the higher expected price level, the new supply and demand curves intersect at point *n′*, which corresponds to a nominal wage rate of $10.77. Notice that the increased demand for labor just offsets the decreased supply of labor, leaving the equilibrium quantity of labor unchanged at 100 million workers. The nominal wage has increased, but the increase in the expected price level has left the real wage unchanged. As noted earlier, to derive the expected real wage, we can divide the nominal wage by the expected price level. Specifically, the higher wage rate, $10.77, divided by the higher expected price level, 140, is equal to the original wage rate, $10.00, divided by the original expected price level of 130. In each case the real wage (computed here in terms of 1987 dollars) is $7.69. If both expected prices and nominal wages go up by the same percentage, the expected real wage remains unchanged. Because the expected real wage is the same, the equilibrium quantity of labor remains unchanged.

If we traced the effects of a lower expected price level on the market for resources, we would find that the equilibrium nominal wage falls by the same percent as the expected price level. With nominal wages and expected prices falling by the same percentage, the expected real wage remains unchanged, so equilibrium employment also remains unchanged.

Potential GDP

For a given expected price level, there are supply and demand curves for each type of resource in the economy. The intersection of supply and demand yields for each resource an equilibrium resource price and quantity employed. Imagine all these resource markets as operating simultaneously. How do all these inputs relate to aggregate output? The amount produced depends on the state of technology that exists in the economy and the institutional structure of the economic system. The more advanced the technology or the greater the production incentives provided by the institutional structure, the more output is produced from given amounts of resources. The quantities of the various resources employed, combined with the state of technology and the institutional structure, determine the level of aggregate output for the given expected price level. Point *a* in Exhibit 10 indicates that when the expected price level is 130, the level of real GDP in the economy is $5.0 trillion.

As we have seen, if the expected price level is higher or lower than 130 and if firms and resource suppliers can adjust their supply and demand for resources to reflect the change in expectations, then the same quantities of resources are employed. If the quantities of resources employed remain unchanged, real GDP also remains unchanged. Point *c* in Exhibit 10 shows that when the expected price level is 140, real GDP is $5.0 trillion. Point *b* shows that when the expected price level is lower, say 120, the economy's output is still $5.0 trillion.

The vertical line at a real GDP level of $5.0 trillion in Exhibit 10 traces the long-run relation between alternative expected price levels and the

EXHIBIT 10

Real GDP for Alternative Price Levels

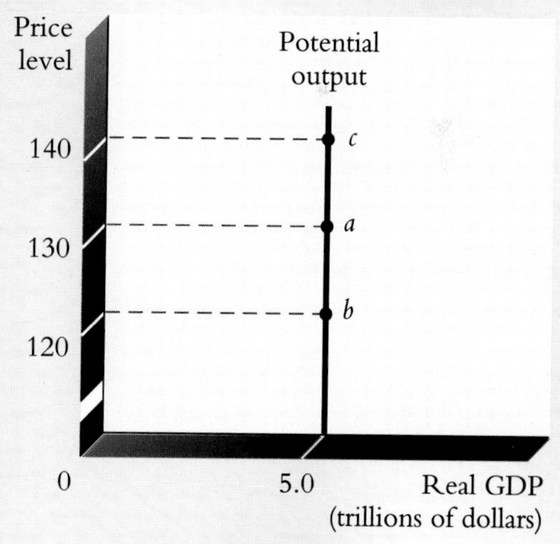

In the long run, changes in the price level will be matched by changes in the nominal wage rate. With the real wage unchanged, the level of employment is unchanged. With employment unchanged, potential output does not vary. So regardless of the price level, the long-run quantity of output supplied is potential output, which in this example equals $5.0 trillion.

quantity of output produced. The economy's potential GDP is \$5.0 trillion, the amount produced when all resource owners and firms have *fully adjusted* to the actual price level in the economy; in other words, the quantity supplied equals the quantity demanded in each resource market, and the expected price level equals the actual price level. For example, the amount of labor that workers are willing and able to supply at the prevailing wage just equals the amount of labor firms are willing and able to demand. Notice that potential GDP is the same regardless of the price level: the amount of output produced in the economy is independent of the expected price level. *Potential output is determined by real factors: the quantity and quality of resources available, the level of technology, and the formal and informal institutions supporting the economic system.*

APPENDIX QUESTIONS

1. (Labor Supply Curve) In Exhibit 7 the supply of labor slopes upward against the nominal wage level. Yet some economists believe that at a high enough nominal wage rate, the supply curve might bend backward. Can you suggest a reason why this might be true?
2. (Equilibrium Level of Employment) Use labor supply and labor demand curves to show the impact on the equilibrium level of employment (and therefore on potential output) of each of the following:
   a. An increase in the price level
   b. A technological improvement
   c. A reduction in the size of the labor force

PART 3
Fiscal and Monetary Policy

CHAPTER 11

FISCAL POLICY, AGGREGATE DEMAND, AND EQUILIBRIUM OUTPUT

During the 1992 presidential campaign, the candidates argued about the best way to revive the economy, which at the time was barely recovering from the 1990–1991 recession. George Bush proposed tax cuts and a relatively smaller role for government. Bill Clinton proposed increases in government spending to be financed by tax increases on top income earners. And Ross Perot wanted to reduce the huge federal budget deficits that had become a part of the fiscal landscape since the early 1980s. So far we have examined aggregate demand only for the private sector, focusing on consumption, investment, and net exports. To examine the possible effects of public policies, we need to get government into the picture.

In this chapter, we first explore the effects of government purchases, transfer payments, and taxes on the equilibrium quantity of real GDP demanded. Next we bring in aggregate supply and consider the impact of government on the equilibrium level of income and employment in the economy. We examine the role of fiscal policy in moving the economy to its potential level of output. Finally, we review fiscal policy as it has been practiced since World War II. Throughout the chapter we will use relatively simple tax and spending programs to convey an intuitive idea of fiscal policy. A more complex treatment, along with the algebraic formulations behind the numbers, particularly for the relevant multipliers, is given in the appendix to the chapter. Topics discussed in this chapter include

- Fiscal policy
- Government purchases
- Net taxes
- Discretionary fiscal policy
- Automatic stabilizers
- Limits of fiscal policy

Theory of Fiscal Policy

As introduced in Chapter 4, *fiscal policy* is the deliberate control of government purchases, transfer payments, and taxes in order to influence macroeconomic variables such as employment, the price level, and the level of GDP. Fiscal policy is carried out primarily at the federal level, though governments at all levels have an impact on the economy.

Example In 1992, the state legislature in Ohio passed a bill authorizing a package of lower income taxes and property taxes on corporations designed to lure new firms to the state and increase employment.

Using the aggregate expenditure framework developed earlier, we will initially focus on the demand side to consider the effect of changes in government purchases, transfer payments, and taxes on the equilibrium level of real GDP demanded. The short story is that at a given price level, an increase in government purchases or in transfer payments increases the level of real GDP demanded and an increase in taxes decreases the level of real GDP demanded, other things constant. In this section we show how and why.

Government Purchases

We begin with the activity that directly and immediately affects aggregate demand: government purchases of goods and services. The federal government purchases thousands of goods and services, ranging from weapon systems to the services of those who maintain the White House grounds. State and local governments also purchase thousands of goods and services, ranging from library books to the services of college professors. In the United States, government purchases of goods and services account for about 20 percent of GDP. Most government purchases are made not by the federal government but by state and local governments.

Example A little less than 40 percent of total U.S. government purchases of goods and services are made by the federal government.

Since decisions about government purchases are largely under the control of public officials, we assume these purchases do not depend directly on the level of income in the economy. We therefore assume that government purchases during a given year are *autonomous*, or independent of the level of income. **Autonomous government purchases** do not vary with the level of real GDP.

Autonomous government purchases Government purchases that do not vary with the level of real GDP

Net Taxes

Tax rev – transf paymts

Government purchases represent only one of the two components of government outlays; the other is transfer payments, such as Social Security and welfare benefits. Transfer payments are outright grants from governments to households. Some taxes are therefore returned to households as transfer payments. Taxes and transfer payments both affect aggregate spending indirectly by changing disposable income and thereby changing consumption. Taxes have a negative effect on consumption and transfer payments have a positive effect.

Example Transfer payments make up about one-third of total spending by federal, state, and local governments. About 75 percent of transfer payments are made by the federal government.

In terms of consumption, what is important is the combined effect on disposable income of taxes and transfer payments. By subtracting taxes from real GDP and then adding transfer payments back in, we transform real GDP into *disposable income*. Disposable income is the take-home pay—the income households can spend or save. To streamline the discussion, we will define **net taxes, NT**, as taxes minus transfer payments. For simplicity we will assume that net taxes are *autonomous*, so they remain constant regardless of the level of real GDP. Hence, **autonomous net taxes** are independent of the level of real GDP.

Net taxes, or NT Taxes minus transfer payments

Autonomous net taxes Taxes minus transfers, independent of the level of real GDP

Components of Aggregate Expenditure

The schedules in Exhibit 1 reflect the same data used in earlier chapters, but we now add the government sector. In particular we assume that autonomous government purchases are equal to $0.8 trillion and that these purchases are paid for by $0.8 trillion in autonomous net taxes. Since government purchases equal net taxes, the government budget is balanced. We want to see how a balanced budget works before we look at the effect of budget deficits or budget surpluses.

The first column in Exhibit 1 lists a range of possible levels of real GDP in the economy. The second column indicates the autonomous net taxes of $0.8 trillion at each level of real GDP. By subtracting net taxes from real GDP, we get disposable income, listed in column (3). Note that at all levels of real GDP, disposable income equals real GDP minus autonomous net taxes of $0.8 trillion. Each time real GDP increases by $0.4 trillion, disposable income also increases by $0.4 trillion. Disposable income determines how much households consume, which is listed in column (4), and how much they save, listed in column (5). Each time real GDP and disposable income increase by $0.4 trillion, consumption increases by $0.3 trillion and saving increases by $0.1 trillion. Thus, the marginal propensity to consume and the marginal propensity to save remain, as before, at 0.75 and 0.25.

Point to Stress *Autonomous* net taxes are assumed only to keep our model simpler. For example, income tax revenues tend to fall and unemployment compensation tends to rise during recessions. The appendix discusses the model in which net taxes vary with the level of national income.

Columns (6) and (7) list autonomous planned investment of $0.4 trillion and autonomous net exports of –$0.1 trillion. Column (8) lists autonomous

EXHIBIT 1

Schedules for Real GDP, with Net Taxes and Government Purchases (trillions of dollars)

Real GDP *(Y)* **(1)**	**Net Taxes** *(NT)* **(2)**	**Disposable Income** *(Y–NT)* **(3) = (1) – (2)**	**Consumption** *(C)* **(4)**	**Saving** *(S)* **(5)**	**Planned Investment** *(I)* **(6)**	**Net Exports** *(NX)* **(7)**	**Government Purchases** *(G)* **(8)**	**Planned Aggregate Expenditure** *(C+I+NX+G)* **(9)**
4.0	0.8	3.2	3.1	0.1	0.4	–0.1	0.8	4.2
4.4	0.8	3.6	3.4	0.2	0.4	–0.1	0.8	4.5
4.8	**0.8**	**4.0**	**3.7**	**0.3**	**0.4**	**–0.1**	**0.8**	**4.8**
5.2	0.8	4.4	4.0	0.4	0.4	–0.1	0.8	5.1
5.6	0.8	4.8	4.3	0.5	0.4	–0.1	0.8	5.4

Point to Stress In using Exhibit 1, a distinction must now be made between real GDP and disposable income. In Chapter 9, net taxes were omitted from the analysis, so real GDP and disposable income were the same.

government purchases of \$0.8 trillion. Column (9) lists the planned aggregate expenditure, which is simply the sum of consumption, planned investment, net exports, and government purchases. Note that in this simple model only consumption depends on the level of income. All the other sources of spending are assumed to be autonomous, or independent of income. So after we introduce autonomous net taxes and autonomous government purchases, the only spending component that varies with the level of real GDP is consumption; an increase in real GDP increases disposable income, which increases the amount spent on consumption.

Recall that for a given price level the equilibrium quantity of aggregate output demanded is achieved when the amount people want to spend equals the amount produced. More precisely, the equilibrium quantity of real GDP demanded is achieved when planned aggregate expenditure equals real GDP.

Equilibrium Aggregate Output Demanded

Teaching Tip Recall the role of unintended inventory changes.

Exhibit 1 shows how the economy converges to the equilibrium level of real GDP demanded. At levels of real GDP less than \$4.8 trillion, planned spending exceeds output, so equilibrium real GDP increases. At levels of real GDP greater than \$4.8 trillion, output exceeds planned spending, so real GDP falls. As you can see, the equilibrium level of real GDP demanded occurs where planned spending and output equal \$4.8 trillion. *In equilibrium not only does planned aggregate expenditure equal real GDP but planned injections equal leakages.* Specifically, the injections of planned investment (\$0.4 trillion) plus net exports (–\$0.1 trillion) plus government purchases (\$0.8 trillion) equal the leakages of saving (\$0.3 trillion) plus net taxes (\$0.8 trillion).

The equilibrium quantity of aggregate output demanded at a given price level can be determined graphically, as illustrated in Exhibit 2. As a reference point, the private sector equilibrium derived in Chapter 9 is found at point *a*, where the aggregate expenditure function for the private sector, $C + I + NX$, crosses the 45-degree line, yielding an equilibrium quantity of real GDP demanded of \$4.0 trillion. To the private sector spending, we add \$0.8 trillion in government purchases and in net taxes, yielding an aggregate expenditure function of $C' + I + NX + G$, where C' reflects the consumption function after net taxes have reduced disposable income at each level of real GDP. Again, the 45-degree reference line provides a ready way of identifying where planned spending equals the amount produced. Equilibrium occurs at point *b*, where planned spending and real GDP both equal \$4.8 trillion.

Teaching Tip See the appendix for the algebraic derivation of equilibrium at real GDP of \$4.8 trillion.

Adding \$0.8 trillion in autonomous government purchases and in autonomous net taxes to private sector spending, other things constant, increases the aggregate quantity demanded at the given price level from \$4.0 trillion to \$4.8 trillion, or by \$0.8 trillion. We will soon see why it is no coincidence that if government purchases and net taxes increase by the same amount, equilibrium real GDP demanded will also increase by that amount. But first let's develop a more general feel for the effects of changes in government purchases and in net taxes.

Teaching Tip In Exhibit 2, the vertical intercept of $C + I + NX$ is \$1.0 trillion (note that autonomous consumption is \$0.7 trillion). The vertical intercept of $C' + I + NX + G$ is \$1.2 trillion. With only consumption varying with income, the slope of both lines equals the marginal propensity to consume, or 0.75.

EXHIBIT 2

Effect of Net Taxes and Government Purchases on Aggregate Expenditure and Real GDP Demanded

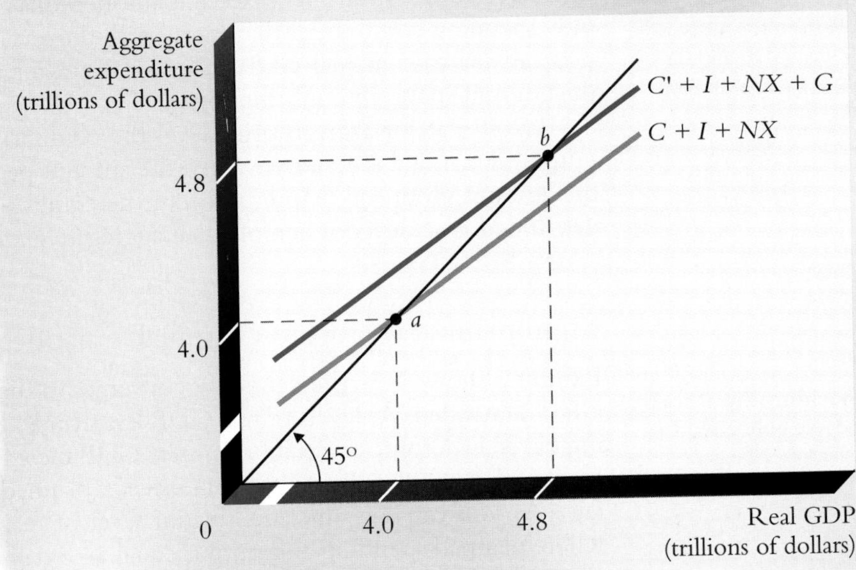

The introduction of net taxes and government purchases increases planned aggregate expenditure. This effect is shown by the shift in the aggregate expenditure line from $C + I + NX$ to $C' + I + NX + G$. As a result of this extra spending, the level of real GDP demanded increases from \$4.0 trillion to \$4.8 trillion.

Teaching Tip The vertical intercept of $C' + I + NX + G'$ equals \$1.6 trillion. You can identify the initial change in aggregate expenditure (as the spending function shifts up) by calling it *autonomous*, whereas subsequent changes in spending (as the economy moves up along the new spending function) are *induced*.

Point to Stress Equilibrium real GDP demanded will remain at the new level only if the increase in government purchases is permanent.

Changes in Government Purchases

Let's begin in Exhibit 3 with the equilibrium level of real GDP demanded of \$4.8 trillion, as reflected at point *b*, where $C' + I + NX + G$ crosses the 45-degree line. Now suppose government purchases increase by \$0.4 trillion, assuming other things, including net taxes, remain constant. This new spending shifts the aggregate expenditure function up by \$0.4 trillion, to $C' + I + NX + G'$. The increase in government purchases multiplies through the economy, increasing real GDP, which increases disposable income, which increases the quantity consumed. Increases in the quantity consumed then take on a life of their own, increasing real GDP, which increases disposable income, which in turn increases quantity consumed. The \$0.4 trillion increase in government purchases directly increases real GDP, and this sets off a series of rounds of increases in quantity consumed.

The initial increase of \$0.4 trillion in government purchases eventually increases the quantity of real GDP demanded at the given price level from \$4.8 trillion to \$6.4 trillion. Since equilibrium output increases by \$1.6 trillion as a result of an increase of \$0.4 trillion in government purchases, the

EXHIBIT 3

Effect of a $0.4 Trillion Increase in Government Purchases on Aggregate Expenditure and Real GDP Demanded

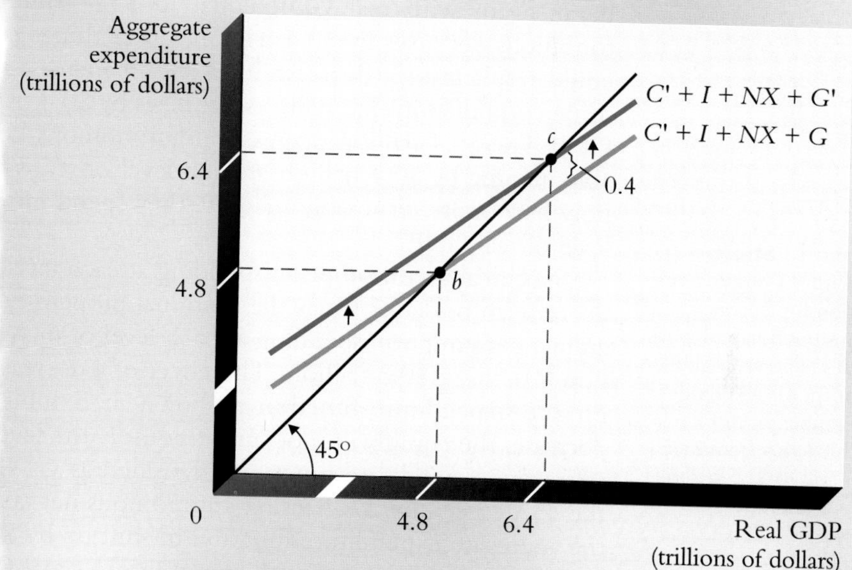

As a result of a $0.4 trillion increase in government purchases, the aggregate expenditure function shifts up by $0.4 trillion, increasing the level of real GDP demanded by $1.6 trillion.

Teaching Tip This and all subsequent multipliers in the chapter are derived in the appendix. Point out to students that the multipliers increase if the marginal propensity to consume increases. For example, if the marginal propensity to consume is 0.8, the multiplier increases from 4 to 5, and equilibrium real GDP demanded would increase by $2.0 trillion.

Point to Stress Increased consumption equals the marginal propensity to consume times the increase in real GDP. Total planned spending (autonomous plus induced) rises by the same amount as the increase in real GDP.

government-purchases multiplier in our example is equal to 4. *As long as consumption is the only source of spending that varies with income, the multiplier for a change in autonomous government purchases, other things constant, equals 1/(1 − MPC),* or 1/(1 − 0.75) in our example. Thus, we can say that for a given price level, and given that only consumption varies with income,

$$\textbf{Change in } Y = \textbf{Change in } G \times \frac{1}{1 - \textbf{MPC}}$$

This same multiplier was discussed in Chapter 9, where we focused on shifts in consumption, autonomous planned investment, and autonomous net exports.

Remember that one thing held constant when government purchases increase is net taxes. Since the budget was in balance prior to an increase in government purchases, an increase in government purchases of $0.4 trillion results in a budget deficit of $0.4 trillion. The $1.6 trillion increase in real GDP increases consumption by $1.2 trillion and saving by $0.4 trillion. Saving increases just enough to finance the $0.4 trillion in government borrowing, so planned injections once again equal leakages.

Changes in Autonomous Net Taxes

A change in autonomous net taxes will also affect the equilibrium quantity of real GDP demanded, but the effect is less direct than with government purchases. A decrease in net taxes, other things constant, increases disposable income at each level of real GDP, so consumption increases. Suppose we begin again with real GDP equal to $4.8 trillion and then reduce autonomous net taxes by $0.4 trillion, other things constant. Such a decrease could result from a decrease in taxes, an increase in transfer payments, or some combination that reduces net taxes by $0.4 trillion at each level of real GDP. The $0.4 trillion decrease in autonomous net taxes increases disposable income by $0.4 trillion at each level of real GDP. Because households now have more disposable income, they spend more and save more at each level of real GDP.

Point to Stress There is a negative relationship between consumption and net taxes. The vertical intercept of the spending function in Exhibit 4 *rises* from $1.2 trillion to $1.5 trillion as autonomous net taxes *fall* by $0.4 trillion.

Specifically, consumption spending at each level of real GDP rises by the decrease in net taxes times the marginal propensity to consume. In our example, consumption spending at each level of income increases by $0.4 trillion × 0.75, or $0.3 trillion. The effect of a decrease in net taxes on the aggregate expenditure function is shown in Exhibit 4. Prior to the net tax decrease, the equilibrium occurs at point *b*, the level of real GDP where the aggregate expenditure function, identified as $C' + I + NX + G$, intersects the 45-degree line. Decreasing autonomous net taxes by $0.4 trillion causes the aggregate expenditure function to shift up by $0.3 trillion at all levels of income. As a result, the equilibrium level of real GDP demanded increases by $1.2 trillion, from $4.8 trillion to $6.0 trillion per year.

Point to Stress Equilibrium real GDP demanded remains at the higher level only if the cut in autonomous net taxes is permanent.

For any given decrease in autonomous net taxes, the consumption function shifts up by the amount of the decrease times the marginal propensity to consume. In our example, we decreased autonomous net taxes by $0.4 trillion, so consumption at each level of real GDP increased by $0.3 trillion, or $0.4 trillion multiplied by 0.75. *The effect of a change in autonomous net taxes on the equilibrium quantity of real GDP demanded equals the resulting shift in the consumption function times the autonomous spending multiplier.* Thus, we can say that the effect of a change in autonomous net taxes is the

Teaching Tip The total change in consumption is $1.2 trillion, a $0.3 trillion autonomous change plus $0.9 trillion in induced changes.

$$\textbf{Change in } Y = (-\,\textbf{MPC} \times \textbf{change in } NT) \times \frac{1}{1 - \textbf{MPC}}$$

This equation can be rewritten as the

$$\textbf{Change in } Y = \textbf{change in } NT \times \frac{-\,\textbf{MPC}}{1 - \textbf{MPC}}$$

The second equation shows that the multiplier for a change in autonomous net taxes equals –MPC/(1 – MPC). For example, with an MPC of 0.75, the multiplier equals –3. In our example, a decrease of $0.4 trillion in autonomous net taxes resulted in an increase in real GDP demanded of $1.2 trillion. As another example, an increase in autonomous net taxes of $0.4 trillion would decrease real GDP demanded by $1.2 trillion.

EXHIBIT 4

Effect of a \$0.4 Trillion Decrease in Autonomous Net Taxes on Aggregate Expenditure and Real GDP Demanded

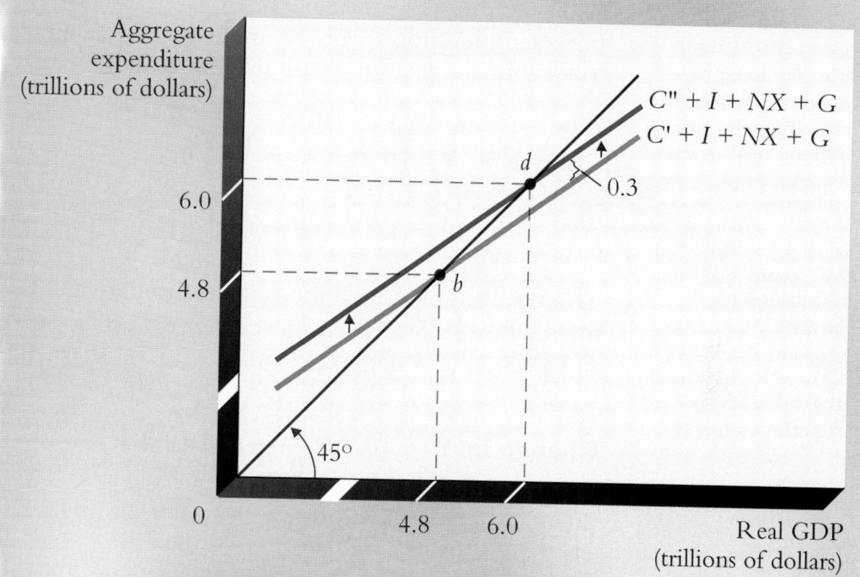

As a result of a decrease in autonomous net taxes of \$0.4 trillion, the consumption function shifts up by \$0.3 trillion, as does the aggregate expenditure function. A \$0.3 trillion increase in aggregate expenditure increases the level of real GDP demanded by \$1.2 trillion.

Changes in Net Taxes and Government Purchases Combined

It may prove useful at this point to compare the autonomous net tax multiplier with the multiplier for autonomous government purchases. First, changes in government purchases and in net taxes have opposite effects on the level of real GDP demanded. Second, the absolute value of the multiplier is greater for a given change in government purchases than for an identical change in autonomous net taxes. This holds because changes in government purchases directly affect aggregate spending; each \$100 increase in government purchases increases spending in the first round by \$100. In contrast, a change in autonomous net taxes changes consumption indirectly by way of a change in disposable income. Thus, a \$100 increase in net taxes reduces disposable income by \$100, which, with an MPC of 0.75, reduces consumption in the first round by \$75.

Example During the 1992 presidential campaign, both Bill Clinton and George Bush called for changes in both taxes and government spending. For example, Clinton proposed an \$80 billion public-works project and higher taxes on households with incomes above \$200,000.

We are now in a position to consider the combined effects of changes in autonomous government purchases and in autonomous net taxes. The effect of a change in *G* on *Y* equals the change in *G* times 1/(1 – MPC). The effect of a change in *NT* on *Y* equals the change in *NT* times –MPC/(1 – MPC).

Example Combining the changes in Exhibit 3 and Exhibit 4 would generate an aggregate expenditure function with a vertical intercept of $1.9 trillion ($0.7 trillion above the spending function in Exhibit 2). Equilibrium real GDP demanded would be $7.6 trillion, an increase of $2.8 trillion over the $4.8 trillion equilibrium in Exhibit 2. The $2.8 trillion increase equals

(0.4 × 1/0.25) + (-0.4 × -0.75/0.25).

The overall effect of changing autonomous government purchases and autonomous taxes can be determined by combining their individual effects:

$$\textbf{Change in } Y = \left(\textbf{change in } G \times \frac{1}{1 - \text{MPC}}\right) + \left(\textbf{change in } NT \times \frac{-\text{MPC}}{1 - \text{MPC}}\right)$$

For example, suppose government purchases increase by $0.2 trillion and autonomous net taxes increase by $0.1 trillion:

$$\textbf{Change in } Y = \left(0.2 \times \frac{1}{0.25}\right) + \left(0.1 \times \frac{-0.75}{0.25}\right)$$

$$= 0.8 - 0.3 = 0.5$$

The resulting budget deficit has a stimulative effect, increasing real GDP demanded by $0.5 trillion. As another example, suppose government purchases and autonomous net taxes each increase by $0.2 trillion:

$$\textbf{Change in } Y = \left(0.2 \times \frac{1}{0.25}\right) + \left(0.2 \times \frac{-0.75}{0.25}\right)$$

$$= 0.8 - 0.6 = 0.2$$

Balanced budget multiplier A factor that shows that identical changes in government purchases and net taxes change equilibrium real GDP demanded by that same amount

The result is a $0.2 trillion increase in real GDP demanded. Recall that throughout these examples the multiplier for autonomous government purchases has been 4, but the autonomous net tax multiplier has been –3. Adding these two multipliers together yields a net multiplier of 1—what we call the **balanced budget multiplier**, which shows that if government purchases and net taxes change by the same amount, other things constant, the equilibrium quantity of aggregate output demanded also changes by that amount. The appendix offers a more general derivation of this balanced budget multiplier.

Point to Stress You can only add the multipliers when the change in government purchases and the change in net taxes are equal. Otherwise, their combined effect must be determined as in the formula given above.

To summarize, the overall impact of government on aggregate demand will depend on the combined effect of government purchases and net taxes. Generally, *an increase in government purchases or a reduction in net taxes, other things constant, will increase the equilibrium real GDP demanded.* If government purchases exceed net taxes, there will be a budget deficit; government deficits are discussed in greater detail in Chapter 16.

Thus far in this chapter we have ignored the supply side, focusing on the quantity of aggregate output demanded at the given price level. We are now in a position to consider the effects of aggregate supply.

COMBINING AGGREGATE DEMAND WITH AGGREGATE SUPPLY

In the previous chapter we introduced the possibility that natural market forces may take a long time to close a contractionary gap. Let's consider the effect of fiscal policy in such a situation.

Teaching Tip The multipliers developed in the chapter assume that neither net taxes nor imports vary with the level of national income. Allowing either to vary with income will reduce the slope of the aggregate expenditure function and the size of the multipliers. See the appendix for development of this expanded model.

Fiscal Policy with a Contractionary Gap

With long-term labor contracts reflecting the expected price level of, say, 130, firms plan to produce the economy's potential level of output of $5.0 trillion, as shown in Exhibit 5. Suppose aggregate demand, which now includes the government sector, is not sufficient to clear the market at the expected price level. The short-run aggregate supply curve, $SRAS_{130}$, and the aggregate demand curve, *AD*, intersect at point *e* to yield the short-run equilibrium output of $4.8 trillion and price level of 125. Since output falls short of the economy's potential, there is a contractionary gap equal to $0.2 trillion, as Exhibit 5 shows.

EXHIBIT 5

Fiscal Policy and a Contractionary Gap

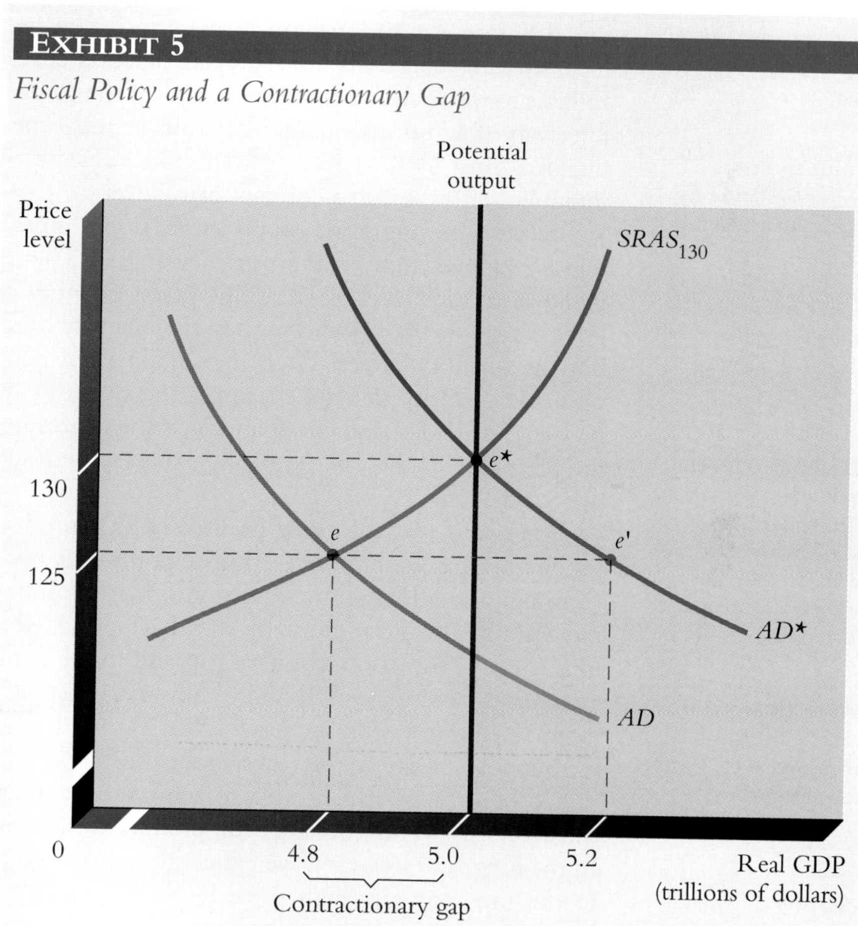

The aggregate demand curve, *AD*, and the short-run aggregate supply curve, $SRAS_{130}$, intersect at point *e*. Because the price level of 125 is below the expected price level of 130, the level of output falls short of the economy's potential. The resulting contractionary gap is $0.2 trillion. This gap can be closed by an expansionary fiscal policy. An increase in government purchases, a decrease in net taxes, or some combination of the two could shift aggregate demand to AD^*, moving the economy to its potential level of output at e^*.

Point to Stress The economy would also return to potential output if resource prices rose more slowly than output prices rose.

Example In 1992, the Japanese government announced an $87 billion increase in government spending to stimulate the economy.

Point to Stress The *horizontal* shift in the aggregate demand curve (from *e* to *e′* in Exhibit 5) equals the simple multiplier times the autonomous change in planned spending.

Teaching Tip The output price level must rise because some resource prices will rise as output and employment are increased.

Point to Stress Resource prices will be increased as contracts are renegotiated.

If markets adjusted to the resulting increase in unemployed resources, the money price of all resources would in the long run drop enough that the short-run aggregate supply curve would shift out and return the economy to its potential output. However, history suggests that wages and other resource prices may be slow to adjust to a contractionary gap. Suppose policy makers believe that the return to potential output will take too long. If the policy makers' timing is right and if just the right fiscal policy is introduced, it may stimulate aggregate demand enough to return the economy to its potential level of output.

When the economy is at a level of output that is below its potential, what is the effect of an expansionary fiscal policy, such as increasing government purchases, increasing transfer payments, decreasing taxes, or some combination of these? Suppose a $0.1 trillion increase in government purchases provides the fiscal stimulus that shifts the aggregate demand curve to the right, as shown in Exhibit 5 by the shift from *AD* to *AD**. If the price level remained at 125, this injection of additional spending would increase the equilibrium quantity demanded from $4.8 to $5.2 trillion. This increase of $0.4 trillion reflects the multiplier effect, given a constant price level.

Because the aggregate supply curve slopes upward, however, more output will be supplied only if the price level rises. There is an excess quantity demanded at price level of 125. This excess quantity demanded causes the price level to rise. As the price level rises, the quantity of real GDP supplied increases but the quantity of real GDP demanded decreases. The price level will rise until the quantity demanded equals the quantity supplied. In Exhibit 5, the new aggregate demand curve intersects the aggregate supply curve at *e**, where the price level is the one originally expected and output equals potential GDP of $5.0 trillion.

Since 130 was the price level on which producers originally based their production plans, the intersection at point *e** is not only a short-run equilibrium but also a long-run equilibrium. If fiscal policy makers have been accurate enough (or lucky enough), they have provided the appropriate fiscal stimulus to close the contractionary gap and foster a long-run equilibrium at the economy's potential GDP. Note, however, that the increase in output is accompanied by a rise in the price level.

Suppose policy makers overshoot the mark, and aggregate demand turns out to be greater than needed to achieve potential GDP. As we have shown, the economy will in the short run produce beyond its potential level of output. In the long run, however, we expect that firms and resource owners will adjust to the unexpectedly high price level. The short-run supply curve will shift back until it intersects the aggregate demand curve at potential output, increasing the price level but reducing the level of output.

Fiscal Policy with an Expansionary Gap

Suppose the short-run equilibrium price level exceeds the level on which long-term contracts are based, so output exceeds potential GDP. In Exhibit 6, the short-run aggregate supply curve is again based on an expected price level of 130, but the aggregate demand curve, *AD″*, is such that the actual price

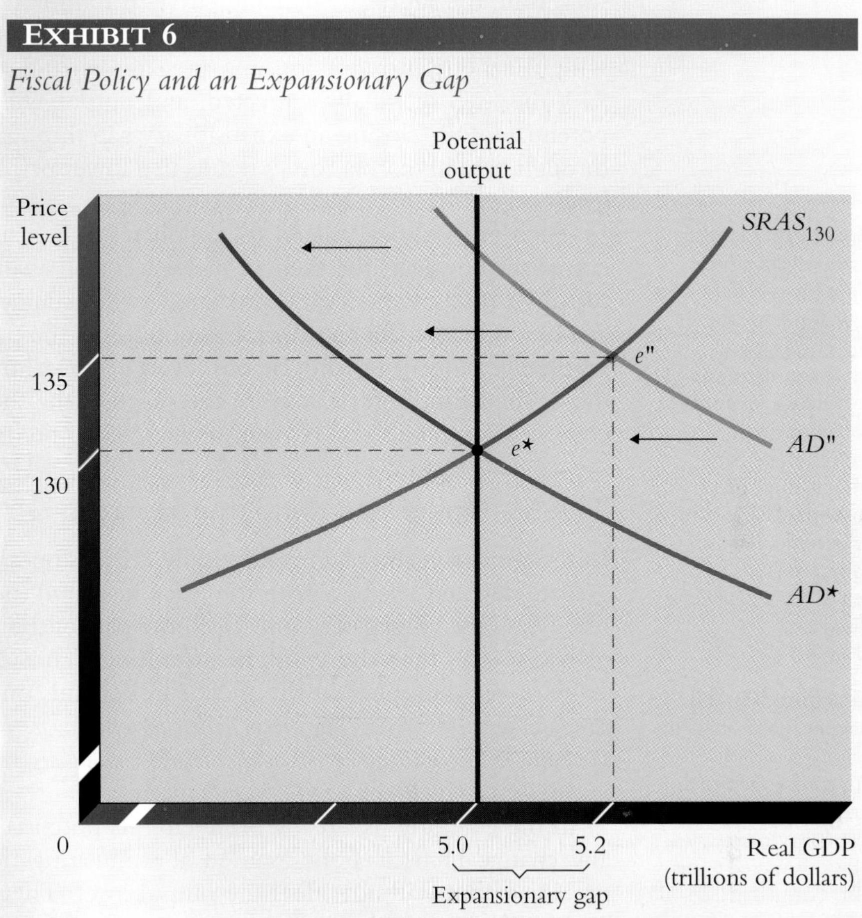

EXHIBIT 6

Fiscal Policy and an Expansionary Gap

With the price level of 135, above the expected level of 130, there is an expansionary gap equal to \$0.2 trillion. The gap can be eliminated by a contractionary fiscal policy. An increase in net taxes, a decrease in government purchases, or some combination of the two could shift the aggregate demand curve back to AD^* and return the economy to potential output at point e^*.

level exceeds the expected price level. So the short-run level of equilibrium output is initially \$5.2 trillion, an amount exceeding the economy's potential output. The economy therefore faces an expansionary gap of \$0.2 trillion. Ordinarily, this gap would be closed by an upward shift in the short-run aggregate supply curve, which would return the economy to the potential level of output but in the process increase the price level.

Example In 1992, the Italian government announced a \$72 billion austerity package of government spending cuts and new taxes.

The use of fiscal policy, however, opens the door to another possibility. By increasing net taxes, reducing government purchases, or using some combination of these approaches, the government can employ fiscal policy to reduce aggregate demand, thereby returning the economy to its potential level of output while avoiding an increase in the price level. If this fiscal policy is successful, the aggregate demand curve in Exhibit 6 will shift to the left from AD'' to AD^*, and equilibrium will move from point e'' to point e^*. Again, with just the right reduction in aggregate demand, the price level will fall to 130, the level originally expected, and output will fall to $5.0 trillion, the potential GDP. Closing an expansionary gap through fiscal policy rather than through natural market forces results in a lower price level, not a higher price level.

Teaching Tip Estimates of spending multipliers will be too low, for example, if the government underestimates the marginal propensity to consume or overestimates the marginal propensity to import. The role of expectations is also important; see Chapter 15 for a detailed discussion.

Such precisely calculated fiscal policies as described here are hard to accomplish, however, for their proper execution assumes that (1) the relevant spending multipliers can be predicted with accuracy, (2) aggregate demand can be shifted by the appropriate amount, (3) the potential level of output is accurately gauged, (4) the various levels of government can somehow coordinate their fiscal efforts, and (5) the shape of the short-run aggregate supply curve is known and will remain unchanged by the fiscal policy itself.

The Multiplier and the Time Horizon

In the short run, the aggregate supply curve slopes upward, so a shift in aggregate demand changes both the price level and the level of output. Therefore when the aggregate supply becomes part of the picture, the actual multiplier is smaller than the multiplier assuming a constant price level. The exact value of the multiplier in the short run depends on the steepness of the aggregate supply curve. *The steeper the short-run aggregate supply curve, the smaller the value of the multiplier—that is, the less impact a given shift in the aggregate demand curve will have on equilibrium output.*

Teaching Tip The steeper the short-run aggregate supply curve, the greater the price increases required to induce suppliers to increase output. Greater price increases have a larger dampening effect on total spending.

If the economy is already producing its potential output, in the long run any change in fiscal policy aimed at stimulating demand will increase the price level but will not affect the output level. Therefore, *if the economy is already at the potential level of output, the spending multiplier in the long run is zero.* We now have some idea of how fiscal policy can work in theory. Let's look at how fiscal policy has been applied over the years.

Fiscal Policy in Practice

It is said that geologists learn much more about the nature of the earth's crust from one major upheaval, such as an earthquake or a volcanic eruption, than from a dozen more common events. Likewise, economists learned more about the economy from the Great Depression than from many more modest economic fluctuations. Even though it began over six decades ago, economists continue to sift and refine the data from that economic calamity, looking for hints about how the economy really works.

The Great Depression and World War II

Until the 1930s fiscal policy was not used as a tool to influence the performance of the macroeconomy. Since the classical approach assumed that the economy would tend toward its potential GDP, there appeared to be no need for government intervention in the economy. At the time most economists believed that any attempted cure could do more harm than the disease.

Three developments in the years following the onset of the Great Depression bolstered the use of fiscal policy in the United States. The first was the influence of Keynes's *General Theory*, which argued that the natural forces would not necessarily move the economy toward potential output. Keynes thought the economy could become stuck at a level of output that was well below its potential, in which case it would be necessary for government to increase aggregate demand so as to stimulate output and employment. The second development was the impact of World War II on output and employment. The demands of war greatly increased expenditures and in the process virtually eliminated unemployment, pulling the U.S. economy out of the Depression. The third development, largely a consequence of the first two, was the passage of the Employment Act of 1946, which gave the federal government the responsibility for promoting full employment and price stability.

Example After adjustment for inflation, U.S. federal government purchases in 1944 were more than eleven times greater than in 1940. The civilian unemployment rate fell from 14.6 percent in 1940 to 1.2 percent in 1944.

Prior to the Great Depression, the most important fiscal policy was trying to match revenues and expenditures to balance the budget. Indeed, to head off a modest federal deficit in 1932, a tax increase was approved, an increase that deepened the depression. In the wake of Keynes and World War II, however, economists and policy makers grew more receptive to the view that fiscal policy could be used to influence aggregate demand and thereby improve economic stability. No longer was the objective of fiscal policy to balance the budget but to promote full employment with price stability.

Point to Stress The chapter's earlier simplifying assumption of *autonomous* net taxes ignores the role of automatic stabilizers, which alter the slopes of the aggregate expenditure and aggregate demand functions.

Automatic Stabilizers

The tools of fiscal policy can be divided into two major categories: automatic stabilizers and discretionary fiscal policy. **Automatic stabilizers**, such as the federal income tax and unemployment insurance, are stabilization policies that, once adopted, require no congressional action to operate year after year. **Discretionary fiscal policy** requires ongoing decisions about government spending and taxation to promote full employment and price stability. So far this chapter has focused mostly on discretionary fiscal policy: conscious decisions to change government purchases or net taxation. Now let's get a clearer picture of automatic stabilizers.

Automatic stabilizers Structural features of government spending and taxation that smooth fluctuations in disposable income over the business cycle

Discretionary fiscal policy The deliberate manipulation of government spending or taxation in order to promote full employment and price stability

Automatic stabilizers smooth fluctuations in disposable income over the business cycle, so that consumption varies by less than does real GDP. Automatic stabilizers stimulate aggregate demand during periods of recession and dampen aggregate demand during periods of expansion. Let's consider the federal income tax. As the economy expands and employment increases, more and more people get jobs and pay taxes. Because the personal income tax is progressive, the fraction paid in taxes increases with income, so taxes grow faster than income. With a growing share of income going to taxes during expansions, there is proportionately less available for consumption. So the progressive income tax relieves some of the inflationary pressure that might arise from an increase in aggregate demand due to rising employment. Conversely, when the economy is in recession, unemployment increases and tax revenues fall more than real GDP, so disposable income does not fall as much as does real GDP. Thus, an income tax, particularly a progressive income tax, cushions declines in disposable income, in consumption, and in aggregate demand.

Example During 1992, passage of legislation to extend the time period during which an individual can receive unemployment compensation represented a *discretionary* change.

Another automatic stabilizer is unemployment insurance. During an economic expansion, the unemployment insurance system automatically increases the flow of unemployment insurance premiums from the income stream into the unemployment insurance fund, thereby moderating aggregate demand. During a recession, unemployment increases and the system reverses itself: unemployment compensation automatically flows from the insurance fund to those who are unemployed, thereby increasing their disposable income and propping up consumption and aggregate demand. Likewise, welfare benefits automatically increase as more people become eligible during hard times. *As a result of these automatic stabilizers, disposable income varies less during economic fluctuations than does GDP.*

Most automatic stabilizers, such as unemployment insurance, welfare benefits, and the progressive income tax, were designed not so much as automatic stabilizers but as income redistribution programs. Their beneficial roles as automatic stabilizers are secondary effects of the legislation. Automatic stabilizers do not eliminate the fluctuations in the economy that are caused by the business cycle, but they do reduce the magnitude of the fluctuations. The stronger and more effective the automatic stabilizers are, the less need there is for discretionary fiscal policy.

The Golden Age of Fiscal Policy

The decade of the 1960s was the Golden Age of fiscal policy. John F. Kennedy was the first U.S. president to argue that a federal budget deficit would stimulate an economy experiencing a contractionary gap. He expanded the scope of fiscal policy from simply moderating business fluctuations to promoting long-term economic growth, and he set numerical targets of no more than 4 percent unemployment and no less than a 4.5 percent annual growth rate of output. Fiscal policy was also used on occasion to provide an extra kick to a recovery, as in 1964, when income tax rates were cut to keep a recovery alive. *This tax cut, introduced to stimulate business investment, consumption, and employment, was perhaps the shining example of the successful use of fiscal policy during the 1960s.* The tax cut seemed to work wonders, increasing disposable income and consumption. The unemployment rate dropped below 5 percent for the first time in seven years, the inflation rate was under 2 percent, and the federal budget deficit in 1964 was only about 1 percent of GDP (compared to an average of more than 4 percent since 1982).

Teaching Tip The 106-month U.S. economic expansion from February, 1961 through December, 1969 was the longest in records back to 1857. In part this expansion was fueled by wartime spending.

Example Between 1973 and 1975, inflation rose from 6.2 percent to 9.1 percent and the civilian unemployment rate rose from 4.9 percent to 8.5 percent.

Fiscal policy is a type of demand-management policy because the idea is to increase or decrease aggregate demand to smooth business fluctuations. But the problem during much of the 1970s was stagflation—the double trouble of higher inflation and higher unemployment resulting from a decrease in aggregate supply. Demand-management policies were ill-suited to solving the problem of stagflation because an increase in aggregate demand would agravate inflation, whereas a decrease in aggregate demand would aggravate unemployment.

Other concerns also caused economists and policy makers to question the effectiveness of discretionary fiscal policy: the difficulty of estimating the natural rate of unemployment, the time lags involved in implementing fiscal policy, the distinction between current and permanent income, and possible feedback effects of fiscal policy on aggregate supply. We will consider each of these concerns in turn.

Fiscal Policy and the Natural Rate of Unemployment

Example Some economists claim that discretionary government policies introduced during the Carter administration reduced the unemployment rate below the natural rate in 1979, contributing to record inflation rates in 1979 and 1980.

As we have said, the unemployment rate that occurs when the economy is producing its potential GDP is called the natural rate of unemployment. For discretionary policy purposes it is important that public officials correctly estimate this natural rate. Suppose the economy is producing at its potential output, and the natural rate of unemployment is 6 percent. What if government officials believe the natural rate is 5 percent and attempt to increase output and reduce unemployment through fiscal policy? Fiscal policy will appear to succeed in the short run because output and employment will expand. But stimulating aggregate demand will in the long run result only in a higher price level, while the level of output falls back to the economy's potential. Thus, temporary increases in output may persuade policy makers that their plan was a good one, even though attempts to increase production beyond potential GDP in the long run lead only to inflation.

Lags in Fiscal Policy

Point to Stress If discretionary fiscal policy takes effect only after the economy turns itself around, the policy may serve to decrease stability in the economy.

The time required to approve and implement fiscal legislation may hamper its effectiveness and weaken fiscal policy as a tool of economic stabilization. Even if the fiscal prescription is appropriate for the economy at the time it is proposed, the months and sometimes years required to approve legislation and to implement the change may make the medicine too little too late, taking effect only after the economy has already turned itself around. Since a recession does not become official until six months after it begins and since the average recession lasts on average little more than a year, this leaves a narrow window of time to execute discretionary fiscal policy. (More will be said about timing problems in Chapter 15.)

Discretionary Policy and Permanent Income

It was once thought that discretionary fiscal policy could be turned on and off like a water faucet, stimulating the economy by just the right amount. Given the marginal propensity to consume, a relationship that Keynes believed was among the most stable in macroeconomics, tax changes could increase or decrease disposable income to bring about the desired change in consumption. A more recent view is that people base their consumption decisions not merely on their current, or transitory, income, but on their permanent income.

Permanent income Income that individuals expect to receive on average over the long term

Permanent income is the income a person expects to receive on average over the long term. If people base consumption decisions more on their permanent incomes, consumption will be less responsive to *temporary* changes in income than to permanent ones. The short-term manipulation of the tax rates to foster potential output will not yield the desired effects as long as people view the tax changes as only temporary. For example, in 1967, at a time when the U.S. economy was producing its potential level of output, the escalating war in Vietnam increased military spending, pushing the economy beyond its potential. The combination of a booming domestic economy and a widening war produced an expansionary gap by 1968. That year Congress approved a temporary tax surcharge, which raised income tax rates for eighteen months. The idea was to reduce disposable income, thereby reducing consumption and aggregate demand as a way of relieving inflationary pressure in the economy. But the reduction in aggregate demand turned out to be disappointingly small, and inflation was little affected. Although several factors may have contributed to the failure of higher taxes to reduce consumption, most economists agree that the *temporary* nature of the tax increase meant that consumers faced only a small downward revision in their permanent income. Since permanent income changed little, consumption changed little. Consumers simply saved less. *To the extent that consumers make decisions based on their permanent income, attempts to fine tune the economy over the business cycle with temporary tax-rate adjustments will be less effective.*

Example U.S. inflation was less than 2 percent every year from 1959 through 1965 and was still only 3.1 percent in 1967. Inflation rose to 4.2 percent in 1968 and 5.5 percent in 1969.

Example Saving by individuals totalled $79.5 billion in 1968 and $73.9 billion in 1969, although the economy was in an expansion in 1969. This was the first drop in saving since the recession year of 1961.

Feedback Effects of Fiscal Policy on Aggregate Supply

So far we have limited our discussion of fiscal policy to its effect on aggregate demand. Fiscal policy may also affect aggregate supply, though often the effect is unintentional. For example, suppose the government increases transfer payments to the jobless and finances the transfers by an increase in income taxes on those who have jobs. Since the increase in transfers is offset by an increase in taxes, net taxes remain unchanged, as does disposable income. If the marginal propensity to consume is the same for both groups, the reduction in spending by those whose taxes increase should be just offset by the increase in spending by transfer recipients. Thus, according to a theory of fiscal policy focusing on aggregate demand, there should be no change in aggregate demand and hence no change in equilibrium real GDP.

Teaching Tip Recall the discussion in Chaper 1 of the pitfall of ignoring secondary effects.

Example Consider the possible effect of the increased duration of unemployment compensation passed by Congress in 1992.

But consider the possible effects of these changes on the supply of labor. The unemployed who benefit from increased transfers may stop looking for work or may look for work at a more leisurely pace. Conversely, workers who find their after-tax wage reduced by the higher tax may be less willing to work extra hours or to work a second job. In short, the supply of labor could fall as a result of an increase in transfers to the unemployed. A decrease in the supply of labor would decrease aggregate supply, reducing the economy's potential GDP.

Both automatic stabilizers and discretionary fiscal policy may affect individual incentives to work, to spend, to save, and to invest, though these effects are usually unintended. We should keep these secondary effects in mind when we evaluate fiscal policies. It was concern about the effects of taxes on the supply of labor that served as a basis for tax cuts introduced in 1981, as we will see next.

Giant U.S. Budget Deficits of the 1980s and 1990s

In 1981 President Reagan and Congress agreed on a 23 percent tax reduction over three years and a major buildup in defense spending, with no substantial offsetting reductions in domestic programs. This tax cut reflected a supply-side philosophy that reductions in tax rates would make people willing to work harder because they could keep more of what they earned. Lower taxes would increase the supply of labor and the supply of other resources in the economy and thereby increase aggregate supply and the economy's potential GDP. In its strongest form, the supply-side theory held that enough additional real GDP would be generated by the tax cuts that total tax revenues would actually increase.

Productivity did increase during the 1980s: output per worker increased at an annual rate of 1.6 percent, compared to only 0.8 percent from 1973 to 1979. Research and development, the fountainhead of technological breakthroughs, also increased. Despite the growth in labor productivity, however, real GDP did not grow enough to generate the revenue required to fund growing government spending; the resulting budget deficits were huge. Until 1981 deficits had been relatively small, typically less than 1 percent of the economy's potential GDP. But deficits had grown to about $200 billion a year by the middle of the decade—5 percent of GDP. These deficits were the greatest ever experienced during peacetime. The recession of the early 1990s and the federal cost of bank failures pushed the federal deficit up to 6 percent of GDP in 1992.

Example According to records back to 1857, the 92-month U.S. expansion from November, 1982 through July, 1990 is second only to the wartime expansion of the 1960s.

The combination of tax cuts with increases in spending led to the higher deficits. Although they did not make a conscious decision to do so, policy makers in effect implemented an expansionary fiscal policy during the 1980s. *The stimulus of huge federal deficits helped sustain a continued expansion during the 1980s—the longest peacetime expansion in this century.* In Chapter 16 we will look at the effects of these deficits in detail. The results of the entire supply-side experiment are examined more closely in Chapter 17.

We close the chapter with a look at how political considerations may shape discretionary policies.

CASE STUDY

Discretionary Policy and Presidential Elections

After the recession of 1990–1991, the economy was slow to recover. At the time of the presidential election in 1992, the unemployment rate still languished at 7.5 percent, up two percentage points from where it stood in 1988, when President Bush was first elected. The higher unemployment rate was too much of a hurdle to overcome and Bush was not reelected.

The link between economic performance and reelection success goes back a long way. Ray Fair of Yale University examined presidential elections between 1916 and 1976 and found that the state of the economy had a clear impact on the elections' outcomes. Specifically, he found that a declining unemployment rate and strong growth of real GDP per person during the election year increased the chances of election for the candidate of the incumbent party.

Political business cycles Business cycles that result when discretionary policy is manipulated for political gain

Another Yale economist, William Nordhaus, developed a theory of **political business cycles** to argue that incumbent presidents use expansionary discretionary policies to stimulate the economy, often only temporarily, during an election year. Their objective is to increase the chances of being reelected by causing a fall in the unemployment rate and an increase in output. For example, observers claim that President Nixon used expansionary policies to increase his chances for reelection in 1972.

The evidence to support the theory of political business cycles is not persuasive. One problem is that the theory limits presidential motivation to reelection, when in fact presidents may have other policy objectives. For example, in the spring of 1992 President Bush passed up an opportunity to stimulate the economy with a middle-class tax cut because the measure also called for tax increases on a much smaller group—upper-income taxpayers.

An alternative theory is that Democrats care relatively more about unemployment and relatively less about inflation than do Republicans. This theory is supported by evidence indicating that during a Democratic administration unemployment is more likely to fall and inflation is more likely to rise than during a Republican administration. Republican presidents tend to pursue contractionary policies soon after coming into office and are more willing to endure a recession in order to reduce inflation. (The country suffered a recession during the second year of the term of each of the last four Republican presidents.) Democratic presidents tend to pursue expansionary policies to reduce unemployment and are willing to put up with higher inflation to do so.

Sources: *Economic Report of the President*, January 1993; Ray Fair, "The Effects of Economic Events on Votes for President," *Review of Economics and Statistics* (May 1978): 159–172; William Nordhaus, "Alternative Approaches to the Political Business Cycle," *Brookings Papers on Economic Activity* 2 (1989): 1–49.

CONCLUSION

Because of huge federal deficits, the explicit use of discretionary fiscal policy as a tool for economic stabilization has been in decline. It is hard to fight recessions with deficit spending when federal budget deficits have already become huge during economic expansions. President Clinton proposed a modest stimulus package in early 1993 to boost the recovery that was underway, but his opponents said the proposal would increase the deficit. Another important tool for economic stabilization is monetary policy, which is the regulation of the money supply by the Federal Reserve System. In the next three chapters we will introduce money and financial institutions, examine monetary policy, and discuss the impact of monetary and fiscal policy on economic stability and growth.

SUMMARY

1. The effect of a change in autonomous government purchases on the equilibrium quantity of aggregate output demanded is the same as that of a change in any other type of autonomous spending. The simple multiplier equals 1/(1 – MPC).

2. A change in net taxes (taxes minus transfer payments) affects consumption by changing disposable income; thus, a given change in net taxes does not affect spending as much as an identical change in government purchases would. The multiplier for a change in autonomous net taxes equals –MPC/(1 – MPC).

3. If both taxes and government purchases change by the same amount, the equilibrium quantity of aggregate output demanded will also change by that amount, so the balanced-budget multiplier equals 1.

4. In order to close a contractionary gap, government purchases or transfer payments can be increased or taxes can be reduced to increase aggregate demand. Because the short-run aggregate supply curve slopes upward, the increase in aggregate demand will raise both output and the price level in the short run. Fiscal policy aimed at reducing aggregate demand in order to close an expansionary gap will result in a reduction in both output and the price level.

5. Fiscal policy focuses primarily on the demand side, not the supply side. The problems of the 1970s, however, resulted more from a decline in aggregate supply than from a decline in aggregate demand. Since then, a variety of concerns have discouraged the explicit use of fiscal policy to influence aggregate demand. The tax cuts of the early 1980s were introduced as a way of increasing aggregate supply. Because these tax cuts were accompanied by a growth in federal spending, the result was huge deficits that stimulated aggregate demand.

QUESTIONS AND PROBLEMS

1. (Autonomous Net Taxes) Would people who expected their incomes to rise in the future favor an autonomous tax or a proportional income tax? Would an autonomous tax be easy to institute in the United States? What groups would favor an autonomous tax, and what groups would oppose it?

2. (Balanced Budget Multiplier) "Taxes are just the opposite of government spending. Therefore, a rise in taxes must completely offset an equal rise in government spending." Although this argument sounds true, it is not. Use the concept of the balanced budget multiplier to explain the error in logic.

3. (Tax Multiplier) Explain why the tax multiplier for autonomous net taxes is equal to the government spending multiplier times the marginal propensity to consume. If the MPC falls, what happens to the tax multiplier?

4. (Automatic Stabilizers) Often during recessions there is a large increase in the number of young people who volunteer for military service. Would this rise be considered a type of automatic stabilizer? Why or why not?

5. (Automatic Stabilizers) Recent federal legislation requires welfare recipients to work at certain public jobs in order to receive their benefits. Without debating the merits of the program, explain whether you think this plan would strengthen or weaken the automatic stabilizer effect of the welfare system. Why?

6. (Permanent Income) "If the federal government wants to stimulate consumption by means of a tax cut, it should set up tax cuts that last a long time. If the government wants to stimulate savings in the

short run, it should create a one-year tax cut." Evaluate these statements.

7. (Fiscal Policy) Will a 10-percent cut in a proportional income tax rate reduce government revenues by 10 percent? Why or why not? What would happen if there were a 10 percent cut in autonomous net taxes?

8. (Fiscal Policy) The chapter shows that increased government spending, with taxes held constant, can eliminate a deflationary gap. How might a tax cut achieve the same results? Must the tax cut be larger than the earlier increase in government spending? Why or why not?

9. (Fiscal Policy) Proponents of the federal highway bill, which passed in 1987 over presidential veto, claimed that such spending would be good for the economy. How would you justify their claims? How would you justify the administration's opposing position?

10. (Effects of Fiscal Policy) Recently some legislators have called for tax increases to reduce the federal budget deficit. Conservatives have countered that such tax increases could plunge the economy into a recession. Using aggregate supply and aggregate demand, explain how increases in taxes would lead to a loss of output and a dampening of prices. Are there arguments on both sides?

11. (Fiscal Policy) Suppose that the economy is experiencing a contractionary gap of $500 billion. Answer the following questions, assuming that autonomous spending equals $400 billion, all taxes are autonomous taxes, the MPC equals 0.9, and the price level remains constant.
   a. What is the level of potential output?
   b. What change in government spending would eliminate this contractionary gap?
   c. What change in the lump-sum tax would eliminate this gap?
   d. What "balanced budget" change in government spending would eliminate this gap?
   e. How would your answers change if the price level changed?
   f. How would your answers to part (b) change if taxes were proportional to income?

12. (Fiscal Policy) Explain why effective discretionary fiscal policy requires information about each of the following:
   a. The slope of the short-run aggregate supply curve
   b. The slope of the aggregate demand curve
   c. The natural rate of unemployment
   d. The size of the multiplier
   e. The speed with which self-correcting forces operate

13. (Consumption) Answer the questions below, using the following data.

Disposable Income	*Consumption*
$ 0	$ 500
500	900
1,000	1,300
1,500	1,700

   a. Assuming that net taxes are equal to $200 regardless of the level of income, graph consumption against income (as opposed to disposable income).
   b. How would an increase in net taxes to $300 affect your consumption function?
   c. If the level of taxes were related to the level of income (i. e., income taxes were proportional), how would this affect your consumption function?

14. (Fiscal Multipliers) Explain how each of the following might be expected to influence the effective size of the fiscal multipliers (i. e., the change in real GDP resulting from a fiscal stimulus).
   a. Short run versus long run
   b. The ratio of actual to potential GDP

15. (Budget Deficits) The large deficits of the 1980s and 1990s have led some to call for a constitutional amendment requiring the federal budget to be balanced annually. What would such a solution do to the automatic stabilizers that are currently a part of the fiscal package?

16. (Aggregate Supply and Fiscal Policy) In the previous chapter, the short-run aggregate supply curve was based on differences between actual and expected aggregate price levels. How would the speed at which expectations adjusted to such differences affect the case for discretionary fiscal policy?

17. (Fiscal Multipliers) Suppose that investment, in addition to having an autonomous component, also had a component that varied directly with the level of real GDP. How would this affect the size of the fiscal multiplier?

18. (Discretionary Policy) Suppose that fiscal policy creates changes in output faster than changes in prices. How might such timing play a role in the theory of political business cycles?

19. (Discretionary Policy) Some people have argued that fiscal policy is likely to be less successful in pulling an economy out of a contractionary gap than it used to be because of the large budget deficits over the past few years. Why do you suppose that they make such an argument and what implications does it carry for the political business cycle?

APPENDIX
The Algebra of Demand-Side Fiscal Policy

In this appendix we will continue to focus on aggregate demand, using algebra. We will first solve for the equilibrium real GDP demanded as found in this chapter and then derive the relevant multipliers. Initially we assume net exports and net taxes are autonomous. Then we incorporate variable net exports and proportional income taxes into the framework. Simple multiplier effects assume a given price level, so we will be limiting the analysis to shifts in the aggregate demand curve.

The equilibrium quantity of aggregate output demanded occurs where aggregate expenditure equals real GDP. Aggregate expenditure is equal to the sum of consumption (C), investment (I), net exports (NX), and government purchases (G). Algebraically, we can write the equilibrium condition as

$$Y = C + I + NX + G$$

To flesh out the equilibrium aggregate expenditure, we begin with the first spending component: consumption. The consumption function is

$$C = 0.7 + 0.75(Y - 0.8)$$

where 0.7 is autonomous consumption measured in trillions of dollars, 0.75 is the marginal propensity to consume, Y is income, or real GDP, and 0.8 is autonomous net taxes in trillions of dollars. Thus, $(Y - 0.8)$ is real GDP minus net taxes, which equals disposable income.

The other components of aggregate expenditure are assumed to be independent of income, or autonomous. We assumed investment spending to be \$0.4 trillion, net exports to be −\$0.1 trillion, and government purchases to be \$0.8 trillion. Again, we can write the equilibrium condition as

$$Y = C + I + NX + G$$

Substituting the numerical values for each spending component, we get

$$Y = 0.7 + 0.75(Y - 0.8) + 0.4 - 0.1 + 0.8$$

Notice that there is only one variable in this expression: Y. If we rewrite the expression as

$$Y - 0.75Y = 0.7 - 0.6 + 0.4 - 0.1 + 0.8$$
$$0.25Y = 1.2$$

we can solve for the equilibrium level of real GDP demanded:

$$Y = \frac{1.2}{0.25}$$
$$Y = \$4.8 \text{ trillion}$$

Government Purchases Multiplier

The benefit of algebra is that we can derive in a more general way the equilibrium real GDP demanded. With autonomous net taxes equal to NT, the general form of the consumption function is

$$C = a + b(Y - NT)$$

where a equals autonomous consumption and b equals the marginal propensity to consume. To consumption we add the other spending components, NX, I, and G, to yield

$$Y = a + b(Y - NT) + I + NX + G$$

By rearranging terms and isolating Y on the left-hand side of the equation, we get

$$Y = \frac{a - bNT + I + NX + G}{1 - b}$$

which is the equilibrium quantity of GDP demanded, given the prevailing price level. Notice that when b, the marginal propensity to consume, is equal to 0.75, the equilibrium GDP is

$$Y = \frac{1}{0.25} \times (a - 0.75NT + I + NX + G)$$
$$= \text{multiplier} \times \text{autonomous spending}$$

To derive the government purchases multiplier, let's consider the effect of a \$1 increase in government purchases, other things constant:

$$Y' = \frac{a - bNT + I + NX + G + \$1}{1 - b}$$

The difference between Y' and Y—that is, the difference in the equilibrium quantity demanded after addition of \$1 in government purchases—is

$$Y' - Y = \frac{\$1}{1 - b}$$

Thus, the effect of adding \$1 to government purchases is to increase the equilibrium quantity of real GDP demanded by \$1 divided by $(1 - b)$, or \$1 divided by (1 – MPC). Dividing a number by (1 – MPC) is the same as multiplying it by 1/(1 – MPC). So the multiplier for a change in autonomous spending is the same as the one derived previously in connection with changes in autonomous consumption, investment, and net exports. The higher the marginal propensity to consume, the smaller the denominator, so the larger the spending multiplier.

Autonomous Net-Tax Multiplier

Instead of focusing on a \$1 increase in government purchases, consider the effects on the equilibrium quantity of GDP demanded of a \$1 increase in autonomous net taxes. We begin with Y, the equilibrium derived earlier, then increase net taxes by \$1 to see what happens to the equilibrium level of real GDP. Increasing net taxes by \$1 yields

$$Y'' = \frac{a - b(NT + \$1) + I + NX + G}{1 - b}$$

The difference between this equilibrium and the original equilibrium is

$$Y'' - Y = \frac{\$1(-b)}{1 - b}$$

Since b is the marginal propensity to consume, this difference in equilibrium values can be expressed as \$1 times –MPC/(1 – MPC), the autonomous net-tax multiplier discussed in this chapter. With the MPC equal to 0.75, the autonomous net-tax multiplier equals –0.75/0.25, or –3, so the effect of increasing the net taxes by \$1 is to reduce equilibrium income by \$3. With an MPC equal to 0.80 the autonomous net tax multiplier equals –0.80/0.20, or –4.

The Multiplier When Both G and *NT* Change

In this chapter we discussed the combined effects of government purchases and net taxes. Suppose that both increase by \$1. We can bring together the two changes in the following equation:

$$Y^* = \frac{a - b(NT + \$1) + I + NX + G + \$1}{1 - b}$$

The difference between this equilibrium and Y, the income level before introduction of any changes in G or NT, is

$$Y^* - Y = \frac{\$1(-b) + \$1}{1 - b}$$

which can be simplified to

$$Y^* - Y = \frac{\$1(1 - b)}{1 - b} = \$1$$

Equilibrium income increases by \$1 as a result of \$1 increases in both government purchases and net taxes. The *balanced budget multiplier* is equal to 1. More generally, we can say that if ΔNT represents the change in autonomous net taxes and

ΔG represents the change in government purchases, the resulting change in equilibrium income, ΔY, can be expressed as

$$\Delta Y = \frac{\Delta G - b\Delta NT}{1 - b}$$

The Multiplier with a Proportional Income Tax

An autonomous net tax is relatively easy to manipulate, but it is not very realistic. Instead of an autonomous net tax, suppose we introduce a **proportional income tax** equal to t, where t lies between zero and 1. Tax collections equal real GDP, Y, times the tax rate, t. With tax collections of Yt, disposable income equals

$$Y - Yt = Y(1 - t)$$

We plug this value for disposable income into the consumption function to yield

$$C = a + bY(1 - t)$$

To consumption we add the other components of aggregate expenditure, I, NX, and G, to get

$$Y = a + bY(1 - t) + I + NX + G$$

Moving all the Y terms to the left-hand side of the equation yields

$$Y - bY(1 - t) = a + I + NX + G$$

or

$$Y[1 - b(1 - t)] = a + I + NX + G$$

By isolating Y on the left-hand side of the equation, we get

$$Y = \frac{a + I + NX + G}{1 - b(1 - t)}$$

The numerator on the right-hand side consists of the autonomous spending components. A \$1 change in any of these components would change equilibrium income by

$$\Delta Y = \frac{\$1}{1 - b(1 - t)}$$

Thus, the autonomous spending multiplier when there is a proportional income tax equals $1/[1 - b(1 - t)]$. Note that as the tax rate increases, the denominator increases, so the multiplier gets smaller. *The higher the proportional tax rate, other things constant, the smaller the multiplier. Because a higher tax rate reduces disposable income, a higher tax rate reduces spending during each round of the expansion process.*

The Inclusion of Variable Net Exports

If you have been reading the appendixes along with the chapters, you are already acquainted with how variable net exports fit into the picture. *The addition of variable net exports causes the aggregate expenditure function to flatten out, because net exports decrease as real income increases.* The fraction of each additional dollar of income that is spent on imports is specified by the *marginal propensity to import*. Dollars spent on imports are paid to foreign producers, not domestic producers. With less of each dollar of income spent on domestic goods, the multiplier loses some punch.

With variable net exports equal to $X - M$, equilibrium real GDP demanded can be derived from the following equation:

$$Y = C + I + X - M + G$$

Variable imports, M, were expressed in an earlier appendix as mY, where m is the marginal propensity to import. When autonomous net taxes are employed, we can express consumption and imports more fully in the equilibrium equation as

$$Y = a + b(Y - NT) + I + X - m(Y - NT) + G$$

which reduces to

$$Y = \frac{a - bNT + I + X + mNT + G}{1 - b + m}$$

The numerator equals autonomous spending, and 1 over the denominator equals the spending multiplier for a model with autonomous government purchases, autonomous net taxes, and imports that vary with income. The higher the marginal propensity to consume, b, the smaller the denominator and the greater the value of the spending multiplier. The higher the marginal propensity to import, m, the larger the denominator, so the smaller the spending multiplier. Simply put, the higher the marginal propensity to consume and the smaller the marginal propensity to import, the larger the multiplier.

When a proportional income tax is employed, equilibrium income can be derived algebraically as

$$Y = a + bY(1 - t) + I + X - mY(1 - t) + G$$

This equation reduces to

$$Y = \frac{a + I + X + G}{1 - b + m + t(b - m)}$$

The higher the proportional tax rate, t, or the higher the marginal propensity to import, m, the larger the denominator, so the smaller the multiplier resulting from a change in autonomous spending.

Since we first introduced the simple spending multiplier, we have examined some considerations that reduce that simple multiplier—namely, a smaller marginal propensity to consume, a higher proportional income tax, a higher marginal propensity to import, and an upward-sloping aggregate supply curve. Once we introduce money in the next two chapters, we will consider other constraints on the spending multiplier.

Appendix Questions

1. (Equilibrium) Suppose that the autonomous levels of consumption, investment, and net exports are \$500 billion, \$300 billion, and \$100 billion, respectively. Suppose further that the MPC is 0.85, the marginal propensity to import (MPI) is 0.05, and income is taxed at a proportional rate of 0.25. If aggregate equilibrium output is \$2,500 billion,
   a. What is the level of autonomous government spending?
   b. What is the size of the government deficit (or surplus) at this equilibrium output?
   c. What is the size of the trade balance at this output?
   d. What is the level of savings at this output?
   e. What change in autonomous spending is required to change equilibrium output by \$500 billion?
2. (The Multiplier) Using a 45-degree line diagram, show the following:
   a. The size of the multiplier when the slope of the aggregate expenditure function is 1
   b. The size of the multiplier when the slope of the aggregate expenditure function is zero
   c. How increases in MPS, the marginal propensity to import, and the proportional income tax rate affect the slope of the aggregate expenditure function and therefore the size of the multiplier

CHAPTER 12

MONEY AND THE FINANCIAL SYSTEM

Money has been a source of fascination since earliest times. It has come to symbolize all personal and business finance. There is *Money* magazine, the "Money" section of *USA Today*, and cable TV shows such as "Moneyline," "Moneyweek," and "Your Money." Money in today's economy represents a sophisticated system of IOUs. With money, you can articulate your preferences clearly—after all, money talks.

Money is the oil that lubricates the wheels of commerce. Just as oil makes for an easier fit among interacting gears, money reduces the friction of voluntary exchange. Too little oil can leave some parts creaking; too much oil can gum up the works. Similarly, too little or too much money in circulation makes exchange more difficult and creates economic problems.

In this chapter we will first discuss the evolution of money, moving from the most primitive economy to our own. Then we will review monetary developments in the United States, focusing primarily on the twentieth century. Topics discussed in this chapter include

- Barter and the double coincidence of wants
- Functions of money
- Commodity and fiat moneys
- Federal Reserve System
- Depository institutions
- Banking problems of the 1990s

THE EVOLUTION OF MONEY

In the beginning there was no money. The earliest families were largely self-sufficient. Each family produced all it consumed and consumed all it

Point to Stress Money continues to evolve to meet the ever-changing requirements of a dynamic society.

produced, so there was little need for exchange. Without exchange, there was no need for money. When specialization first emerged, as some people went hunting and others took up farming, hunters and farmers had to trade. Thus, the specialization of labor resulted in exchange, but the kinds of goods traded were limited enough that people could easily exchange their products directly for other products—a system called *barter.*

Barter and the Double Coincidence of Wants

Double coincidence of wants A situation in which two traders are willing to exchange their products directly

Barter depends on a **double coincidence of wants**, which occurs only when traders are willing to exchange their products for what others are selling. The hunter must be willing to exchange hides for the corn offered by the farmer, *and* the farmer must be willing to exchange corn for the hides offered by the hunter. As long as specialization was limited, mutually beneficial trades were relatively easy to discover. As the economy developed, however, greater specialization in the division of labor increased the difficulty of finding goods that each trader wanted to exchange. Rather than just two possible types of producers, there were, say, a hundred types of producers.

Example If an economy trades 1,000 different goods, a barter economy would require 499,500 prices whereas a money economy would require only 1,000 prices.

In a barter system, traders must not only discover a double coincidence of wants; they must also agree on a rate of exchange after they connect—that is, how many hides should be exchanged for a bushel of corn. When only two goods are produced, only one exchange rate must be determined, but as the number of goods produced in the economy increases, the number of exchange rates grows sharply. For example, if there are one hundred different goods, then 4,950 exchange rates must be determined. Increased specialization made the barter system of exchange more time-consuming and more cumbersome.

Teaching Tip The general formula for determining the number of different exchange ratios required for n number of commodities is

$$\frac{n(n-1)}{2}$$

Negotiating the exchange rates among commodities is complicated in a barter economy because there is no common measure of value. Sometimes differences between the relative values of products make barter difficult. For example, suppose the hunter wants to buy a home, which exchanges for 2,000 hides. The hunter will be hard-pressed to find a home seller in need of that many hides. These difficulties with barter have led people in even very simple economies to use money.

Earliest Money and Its Functions

Nobody actually recorded the emergence of money. Thus, we can only speculate about how money first came into use. Through the experience accumulated from repeated exchanges, traders may have found that there were certain goods for which there was always a ready market. If a trader could not find a good he or she desired personally, some good with a ready market could be accepted instead. So traders began to accept certain goods not for immediate consumption but because these goods would be accepted by others and therefore could be retraded later. For example, corn might become accepted because traders knew corn was always in demand. As one good became generally accepted in return for all other goods, that good began to

Money Anything that is generally acceptable in exchange for goods and services

Point to Stress The use of money reduces the time needed to make optimal economic decisions and thus increases efficiency in the economy.

function as **money**. *Any commodity that acquires a high degree of acceptability throughout an economy thereby becomes money.* Money fulfills three important functions: most importantly, it serves as a medium of exchange; money also serves as a standard of value and a store of wealth. Money's function as a medium of exchange is what distinguishes it from other assets such as stocks, bonds, or real estate.

Medium of exchange Anything that facilitates trade by being generally accepted by all parties in payment for goods or services

MEDIUM OF EXCHANGE. Separating the sale of one good from the purchase of another requires something acceptable to all parties involved in the transaction. If a community, by luck or by design, can find one commodity that everyone will accept in exchange for whatever is sold, traders can save much time, disappointment, and sheer aggravation. Suppose corn plays this role, a role that clearly goes beyond its usual function as food. We then call corn a medium of exchange because it is accepted in exchange by all buyers and sellers, whether or not they want corn to eat. A **medium of exchange** is anything that is generally accepted in payment for goods and services sold. The person who accepts corn in exchange for some product may already have more corn than the entire family could eat in a year, but the corn is not accepted with a view toward consumption. It is accepted because it can be exchanged later for whatever is desired whenever it is desired.

Commodity money Anything that serves both as money and as a commodity

Example During the Roman Empire, Caesar's soldiers were paid in part with salt. The salt portion of pay was called the *salarium*, origin of the modern word salary.

Because in this example corn both is a commodity and serves as money, we call it a **commodity money**. The earliest money was commodity money. Consider some commodities used as money over the centuries. Cattle served as money, first for the Greeks and then for the Romans. In fact, the word "pecuniary" ("of or relating to money") comes from the Latin word *pecus*, meaning "cattle." The so-called precious metals—gold and silver—were long popular as commodity moneys. Other commodity moneys used at various times include tobacco and wampum (polished strings of shells) in colonial America, tea pressed into small cakes in Russia, and dates in North Africa. Whatever serves as a medium of exchange is called money, no matter what it is, no matter how it first comes to serve as a medium of exchange, and no matter why it continues to serve this function.

Standard of value A common unit for measuring the value of every good or service

STANDARD OF VALUE. As one commodity, such as corn, becomes widely accepted, the prices of all other goods come to be quoted in terms of that good. The chosen commodity becomes a common **standard of value**. The price of shoes or pots is expressed in terms of bushels of corn. Thus, not only does corn serve as a medium of exchange; it also becomes a yardstick for measuring the value of all goods and services. Rather than having to quote the rate of exchange for each good in terms of every other good, as was the case in the barter economy, people can measure the price of everything in terms of corn. For example, if a pair of shoes sells for two bushels of corn and a five-gallon pot sells for one bushel of corn, then one pair of shoes has the same value in exchange as two five-gallon pots.

Store of wealth Anything that retains its purchasing power over time

STORE OF WEALTH. Because people often do not want to make purchases at the time they sell an item, the purchasing power acquired through sales must somehow be preserved. Money serves as a **store of wealth** when it retains purchasing power over time. The cobbler accepts corn in exchange for shoes, believing that other producers will later accept corn in exchange for whatever the cobbler demands. Corn represents a way of conserving purchasing power so that purchases can be deferred until later. The better money is at preserving purchasing power, the better it serves as a store of wealth.

Problems with Commodity Money

There are problems with most commodity moneys, including corn. First, corn must be properly stored or its quality deteriorates; even then, it will not maintain its quality for long. Second, corn is bulky, so exchanges for major purchases become unwieldy. For example, if a new home cost 50,000 bushels of corn, many truckloads of corn would be involved in its purchase. Third, money may not be easily divisible into smaller units. For example, when cattle served as money, a price that amounted to a fraction of a cow posed an exchange problem. Fourth, if all corn is valued equally in exchange, people will tend to keep the best corn and trade away the lowest-quality corn. The quality of corn in circulation will therefore decline, reducing its acceptability. Sir Thomas Gresham, founder of the Royal Exchange of London, noted back in the sixteenth century that "bad money drives out good money," and this has come to be known as **Gresham's Law**. People tend to trade away inferior money and hoard the best.

Gresham's Law People tend to trade away inferior money and hoard the best

A final problem with corn, as with other commodity money, is that the value of corn depends on its supply and demand, which may vary unpredictably. If a bumper crop increased the supply of corn, corn would likely become less valuable, so more corn would be exchanged for all other goods. Any change in the demand for corn as food would alter the amount available as a medium of exchange, and this, too, would influence the value of corn. Erratic fluctuations in the market for corn limit its usefulness as money, particularly as a store of wealth. If people cannot rely on the value of corn over time, they will be reluctant to hold it as a store of wealth. More generally, *since the value of money depends on its limited supply, anything that can be easily gathered or produced by anyone does not serve well as a commodity money.* For example, leaves would not serve well as a commodity money. In short, the best commodity money is durable, divisible, of uniform quality, and in limited supply.

Teaching Tip Portability was also a consideration with commodity money. For example, gold was much more convenient to transport than a copper coin once used in Sweden that weighed 31 pounds.

Metallic Money and Coins

Throughout history several metals, including iron and copper, have been used as commodity moneys. But silver and gold have always been held in highest regard. The division of commodity money into units was often quite natural, as in a bushel of corn or a head of cattle. When rock salt was used as money, it was cut into uniform bricks. Since salt was usually of consistent quality, a trader had only to count the bricks to determine the amount of money. With precious metals, however, both the quantity and the quality became open to question. Because precious metals could be debased with cheaper metals, the quantity and the quality of the metal had to be ascertained with each exchange.

Example Because gold was so scarce, silver was the dominant basis of currency until the nineteenth-century gold discoveries in Australia and California.

Example There is evidence that coins replaced barley as money in Sumaria sometime between 3000 and 2500 B.C.

Example Wooden nickels were issued in some parts of the United States during the Great Depression. The unemployed could exchange the nickels for food.

This quality-control problem was addressed by coining the metal. *Coinage determined both the amount of metal and the quality of the metal.* The use of coins allowed payment by count rather than by weight. A table on which this money was counted came to be called the counter—a term still used today. Initially, coins were stamped on only one side, but undetectable amounts of the metal could be shaved from the smooth side of the coin. To prevent such shaving, coins were stamped on both sides. But another problem arose: because the borders of coins remained smooth, small amounts of the metal could be clipped from the edges. To prevent clipping, coins were bordered with a well-defined rim and were milled around the edges. If you have a dime or a quarter, notice the tiny serrations on the edge and the words along the border. These features, throwbacks from the time when these coins were silver rather than cheaper metals, prevented the recipient from "getting clipped" or getting stuck with "light money."

Seigniorage The difference between the face value of money and the cost of supplying it; the "profit" from issuing money

Token money The name given to money whose face value exceeds the value of the material from which it is made

The power to coin money was viewed to be vested in the seignior, or feudal lord. When the face value of the coin exceeds the cost of coinage, the minting of coins becomes a source of revenue to the seignior. **Seigniorage** refers to the revenue earned from coinage by the seignior. For example, a coin with a face value of, say, \$10, could be made for, say, \$1, resulting in seigniorage of \$9. **Token money** is the name given to money whose face value exceeds the value of the material from which it is made. Coins (and paper money) now in circulation in the United States are token money. For example, the twenty-five-cent coin costs the U.S. Mint only about three cents to make.

Money and Banking

Banking, as the term is understood today, dates back to London goldsmiths of the seventeenth century. Because goldsmiths had safes in which to store gold, others in the community came to rely on goldsmiths to hold their money and other valuables for safekeeping. The goldsmith had to give depositors their money back on request, but since withdrawals by one depositor tended to be offset by deposits by others, the amount of idle cash, or gold, in the vault tended to remain relatively constant over time. Goldsmiths found that they could earn interest by making loans from this pool of idle cash.

Example Although the goldsmiths are the origin of the modern banking system, banks during the Roman Empire were known to issue letters of credit to save clients the expense of transporting heavy metal currency to distant parts of the empire. Banking declined after the fall of the empire.

Keeping one's money on deposit with a goldsmith was safer than leaving the money where it could be easily stolen, but it was a nuisance to have to visit the goldsmith each time money was needed. For example, the farmer would visit the goldsmith to withdraw enough money to buy a horse. The farmer would then pay the horse trader, who would promptly deposit the receipts with the goldsmith. Thus, money took a round trip from goldsmith to farmer to horse trader and back to goldsmith. Because depositors grew tired of going to the goldsmith every time they needed to make a purchase, they instituted a practice whereby a purchaser, such as the farmer, could write the goldsmith instructions to pay someone else, such as the horse trader, a given amount from the purchaser's account. The payment amounted to having the goldsmith move gold from one stack (the farmer's) to another (the horse trader's). *These written instructions to the goldsmith were the first checks.* Checks have since become official-looking instruction forms, but they need not be, as evidenced by the actions of a Montana man who recently paid a speeding fine with a check written on a clean but frayed pair of underpants. The Western Federal Savings and Loan of Missoula honored the check.[1]

Example The receipts issued by the goldsmiths for each item deposited were the forerunners of bank notes. The first European bank to issue bank notes was the Bank of Sweden in 1656.

By combining the idea of cash loans with checking, the goldsmith soon discovered how to make loans by check. The check was a claim against the goldsmith, but the borrower's promise to repay the loan became the goldsmith's asset. *The goldsmith could extend a loan by creating an account against which the borrower could write checks. In this way goldsmiths, or banks, were able to "create money"—that is, to create claims against themselves that were generally accepted as a means of payment—as a medium of exchange.* This money, though based only on an entry in the goldsmith's ledger, was accepted because of the public's confidence that these claims would be honored.

Fractional reserve banking system A banking system in which only a portion of deposits in the depository institutions is backed up by reserves

The total claims against the goldsmith consisted of customer deposits plus deposits created through loans. Because these claims exceeded the value of gold on reserve, this was the beginning of a **fractional reserve banking system**, a system whereby bank reserves amount to only a fraction of deposits. The *reserve ratio* measures reserves as a proportion of total claims against the goldsmith, or total deposits. For example, if the goldsmith had gold valued at $5,000 but claims, or deposits, totalling $10,000, the reserve ratio was 50 percent.

Paper Money

Bank notes Papers promising a specific amount of money in gold to bearers who presented them to issuing banks for redemption; an early type of money

Another way a bank could create claims against itself was to issue bank notes. In London, goldsmith bankers introduced bank notes about the same time they introduced checks. **Bank notes** were pieces of paper promising that the bearer would receive something of value upon presenting the notes to the issuing bank for redemption. *Whereas checks could be redeemed only by the individual to whom the deposit was directed, notes could be redeemed by anyone who held them.* Paper money was often "as good as gold," since the bearer could usually, upon request, redeem the note for gold. In terms of convenience, paper money was often better than gold because it took up less space and was easier to carry.

Teaching Tip Without the invention of paper money, there would not have been enough precious metal to finance the huge expansion of world output and trade since the eighteenth century.

The amount of paper money issued depended on the bank's estimate of the proportion of notes that would be redeemed. The greater the redemption rate, the fewer notes that could be issued based on a given amount of reserves. Initially, these promises to pay were issued by private individuals or banks, but over time governments took a larger role in printing and circulating notes.

Fiat money Money not redeemable for any commodity; its status as money is conferred by the government

Once paper money became widely accepted, it was perhaps inevitable that governments would begin issuing **fiat money**, which consists of paper money that derives its status as money from the power of the state, or by *fiat.* Fiat money is money because the government says it is money. Fiat money is not redeemable for anything other than more fiat money; it is not backed by a promise to pay something of intrinsic value. You can think of fiat money as mere paper money. It is acceptable not because it is intrinsically useful or valuable—as was corn or gold or silver—but because the government

1. As reported in "Legal Briefs," *Newsweek*, Feb. 3, 1992, p. 7.

Legal tender Anything that creditors are required to accept as payment for debts

requires that it be accepted as payment. Fiat money is declared **legal tender** by the government, meaning that creditors must accept it as payment for debts. *Gradually, people came to accept fiat money because they believed that others would accept it as well.* The money issued in the United States today, and indeed paper money throughout most of the world, is largely fiat money. In a way, a well-regulated system of fiat money is more efficient for an economy than commodity money, since fiat money uses only the resources required to produce and police the money supply, whereas commodity money requires that valued commodities be used directly or held in reserve to support the system.

Point to Stress An item need not be legal tender to be money. For example, checkable deposits are not legal tender.

The Value of Money

Why does money have value? As we have seen, various commodities served as the earliest moneys. Commodities such as tobacco and gold had value in use even if for some reason they became less acceptable in exchange. The commodity feature of early money bolstered confidence in its acceptability. When paper money came into use, its acceptability was initially fostered by the promise to redeem it for gold, silver, or other items of value. But since most paper money throughout the world is now fiat money, there is no promise of redemption.

Point to Stress As long as one can find others who will give up goods and services to receive a given item, it makes little difference what item is used for money.

So why can a piece of paper bearing the image of Alexander Hamilton and the number 10 in each corner be exchanged for a large pepperoni pizza or anything else selling for $10? People accept these pieces of paper because they believe others will do so. *Fiat money has no value other than its ability to be exchanged for goods and services now and in the future. Its value lies in people's belief in its value.*

Point to Stress Stability in the value of money is essential, but stability does not mean constancy. Slow and steady changes in value can be consistent with monetary efficiency.

The value of money is reflected in its *purchasing power*: the rate at which money is exchanged for goods and services. The higher the price level, the fewer goods and services that can be purchased with each dollar, so the less each dollar is worth. Changes in the purchasing power of each dollar over time vary inversely with changes in the price level. As the price level increases, the purchasing power of money falls. To measure the purchasing power of the dollar in a particular year, first compute the price index for that year, then divide 100 by that price index. For example, relative to the base period 1982–1984, the consumer price index for March 1993 was 143.6. The value of a dollar in March 1993 was therefore 100/143.6, or about $0.70, measured in 1982–1984 dollars. Exhibit 1 chronicles the steady decline since 1960 in the value of the dollar measured in terms of its average value in 1982–1984.

When Money Performs Poorly

Example During the height of Hungarian hyperinflation in 1945 and 1946, prices doubled every two to three days.

One way to understand the functions of money is to look at situations in which money did not perform these functions well. In Chapter 7 we examined the hyperinflation of Bolivia. With prices growing by the hour, money no longer represented a stable store of wealth, so people were unwilling to hold money. With the price level rising rapidly, some merchants were quicker to raise their prices than others, so relative prices became distorted. Thus, money became less useful as a standard of value—that is, as a way of

EXHIBIT 1

Purchasing Power of a Dollar Measured in 1982–1984 Constant Dollars

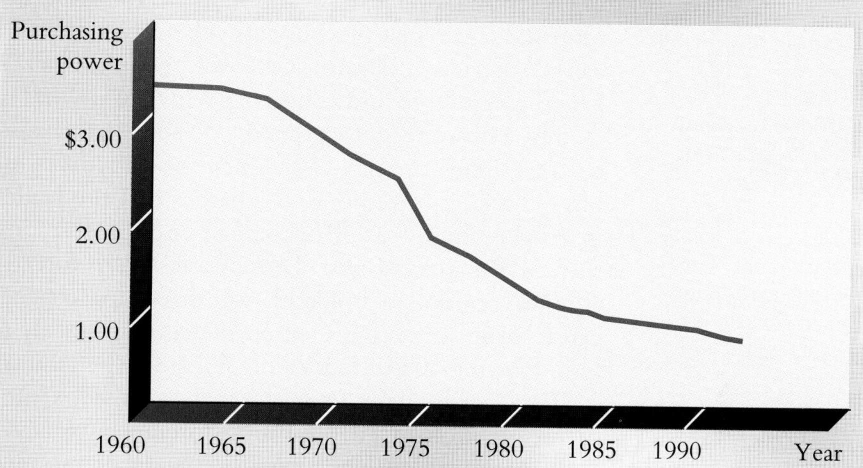

An increase in the price level reduces the amount of goods and services that can be purchased with a dollar. Since 1960 the price level has risen every year, so the purchasing power of the dollar has fallen continually.

Source: *Economic Report of the President,* January 1993.

> **Teaching Tip** If people lose confidence in money, they try to dispose of it as quickly as possible. The increase in the turnover rate of money aggravates inflation, further reducing the value of money.

comparing the price of one good to that of another. Money still served as a medium of exchange, but the store of wealth and standard of value roles were undermined by hyperinflation.

At some point, a currency may become so inflated that people will no longer accept it in payment and will resort to barter. Barter is inefficient compared to a smoothly functioning monetary system, but it may be more efficient than trying to use money during hyperinflation. Likewise, if the supply of money dries up or if the price system is not allowed to function properly, barter may be the only remaining alternative. The following case study discusses instances when money performed poorly.

CASE STUDY

When the Monetary System Breaks Down

After Germany lost World War II, money in that country became largely useless because, despite tremendous inflationary pressure in the economy, the occupation forces imposed strict price controls. Since prices were set well below what people thought they should be, sellers stopped accepting money, forcing people to use barter. Experts estimate that because of the lack of a viable medium of exchange, the German economy produced only half the output that it would have produced with a smoothly functioning monetary system. The "economic miracle" that occurred in Germany immediately after 1948 can be credited in large part to that country's adoption of a reliable monetary system.

Example Because of a shortage of French money, in 1865 Canadian residents began using playing cards marked for certain values and signed by the French colonial governor. These playing cards continued in circulation for seventy years.

Money became extremely scarce during the nineteenth century in Brazil because of a copper shortage. Money-financed transactions were temporarily impossible because copper coins could no longer be minted. In response to this crisis, some merchants and tavern keepers printed vouchers redeemable in goods and services. These vouchers circulated as money until copper coins returned to circulation. Similarly, there was often a shortage of money in the early American colonies. One way people dealt with the problem was by keeping careful records, showing who owed what to whom.

For a more recent example, consider Panama, a Central American country that relies on the U.S. dollar as a medium of exchange. In 1988 the United States, in response to charges that the leader of Panama was involved in drug dealing, froze Panamanian assets in the United States, precipitating a run on Panama's banks. Those banks were forced to close for nine weeks. The flow of dollars in circulation dried up, so people resorted to barter. Because barter is much less efficient than a smoothly functioning monetary system, Panama's GDP reportedly fell by 30 percent in 1988.

For decades workers in the former Soviet Union were barred, at the risk of prison, from even possessing foreign currency. It became the forbidden fruit. As Russia gropes toward a market economy, the monetary system has been under heavy strain. In 1992 Russia's Parliament legalized the widespread practice of paying workers in dollars, as the country's crumbling economy and high inflation made the ruble a hot potato.

Teaching Tip Financial intermediation, or "indirect finance," is an alternative to the purchases of stocks and bonds by savers.

Thus, when the supply of money shrinks or when the official money fails to serve as a medium of exchange, some other mechanism may arise to facilitate exchange. But this second-best alternative is seldom as efficient as a smoothly functioning monetary system because more resources must be diverted from the production of goods and services to carrying out exchange. A poorly functioning monetary system results in higher transaction costs. It has been said that no machine increases the economy's productivity as much as properly functioning money. Indeed, it seems hard to overstate the value of a reliable monetary system.

Financial Institutions in the United States

Financial intermediaries Institutions that serve as go-betweens, accepting funds from savers and lending those funds to borrowers

You already learned about the origin of modern banks: goldsmiths lent money from deposits held for safekeeping. So you now have some idea of the way banks operate. Recall from the circular flow model discussed earlier that household saving flows into financial markets and is lent to investors. Financial institutions attract the funds of savers and lend these funds to borrowers, serving as intermediaries that link savers to borrowers. Financial institutions, or **financial intermediaries**, earn a profit by "buying low and selling high"—that is, by paying a lower interest rate to savers than they charge borrowers.

Commercial Banks and Thrifts

Depository institutions Commercial banks and other financial institutions that accept deposits from the public

Commercial banks Depository institutions that make short-term loans primarily to businesses

Demand deposits Accounts at financial institutions that pay no interest and on which depositors can write checks to obtain their deposits at any time

Thrift institutions, or **thrifts** Depository institutions that make long-term loans primarily to households

Example In recent years, financial institutions have been particularly successful in establishing a wide gap between the cost of their funds and the interest rates charged on credit cards.

A wide variety of financial intermediaries respond to the economy's demand for financial services. **Depository institutions**, such as commercial banks, savings and loan associations, mutual savings banks, and credit unions, obtain funds primarily by accepting *deposits* from the public—hence their name. Other financial intermediaries, such as finance companies, insurance companies, and pension funds, acquire funds not through customer deposits but by collecting premiums or by borrowing. Our emphasis will be on depository institutions because they play a key role in providing the nation's money supply. Depository institutions can be classified broadly into two types: commercial banks and thrift institutions.

Commercial banks are the oldest, largest, and most diversified of depository institutions. They are called **commercial banks** because historically they made loans primarily to commercial ventures, or businesses, rather than to households. Commercial banks hold two-thirds of all deposits of depository institutions. Until recently, commercial banks were the only depository institutions that offered demand deposits, or checking accounts. **Demand deposits** are so named because a depositor with such an account can write a check to *demand* those deposits at any time. **Thrift institutions**, or **thrifts**, include savings and loan associations, mutual savings banks, and credit unions. Historically, savings and loan associations and mutual savings banks specialized in making mortgage loans, which are loans to finance real estate purchases. Credit unions extended loans only to their "members" to finance homes or other major consumer goods such as cars.

Development of the Dual Banking System

Teaching Tip The United States has approximately 12,000 commercial banks, 4,000 savings and loans, 800 mutual savings banks (mostly in New York and New England), and 20,000 credit unions. Commercial banks hold the most assets; credit unions hold the fewest assets.

Before 1863 each commercial bank in the United States was chartered by the state in which it operated. These banks, like the English goldsmiths, issued bank notes. More than 10,000 different kinds of notes circulated and nearly all were, at least in theory, redeemable for gold. To redeem a note, the bearer had to present it to the issuing bank. Since a bank's notes in circulation were a source of profit, many banks tried to discourage redemption by locating out in the sticks—out where the wildcats lived. Thus, this period of banking became known as the "wildcat era." Because state regulations were lax, bank failures were common and many people were stuck with worthless notes. Most well-known notes were counterfeited. In fact, by 1860 one-third of the notes in circulation were counterfeits.

There was growing dissatisfaction with what some people viewed as disarray in note issues by *state banks*—that is, banks with state charters. The National Banking Act of 1863 and its later amendments created a new system of federally chartered banks called *national banks.* National banks were authorized to issue notes and were regulated by the Office of the Comptroller of the Currency, part of the U.S. Treasury. At this time a tax was introduced on the notes issued by state-chartered banks, the idea being to tax state bank notes out of existence. But state banks survived by substituting checks for notes.

Example Of forty banks established in Michigan in 1837, thirty-six failed within two years.

Borrowers were issued checking accounts rather than bank notes. State banks thereby held on, and to this day the United States has a *dual banking system* consisting of both state banks and national banks.

Example The first national bank was opened in Philadelphia on June 20, 1863.

Birth of the Federal Reserve System

During the nineteenth century, the economy experienced a number of panic "runs" on banks by depositors. A panic was usually set off by the failure of some prominent financial institution. Following such a failure, banks were besieged by fearful customers. Borrowers wanted additional loans and extensions of credit, and depositors wanted their money back. The failure of the Knickerbocker Trust Company in New York set off the Panic of 1907. This financial calamity underscored the lack of banking stability and so aroused the public that in 1908 Congress established the National Monetary Commission to study the banking system and make recommendations. That group's deliberations led to the Federal Reserve Act, passed in 1913 and implemented in 1914, which established the **Federal Reserve System** as the central bank and monetary authority of the United States. *Throughout most of its history, the United States had what is called a decentralized banking system. The Federal Reserve Act moved the country toward a system that was partly centralized and partly decentralized.*

Federal Reserve System The central bank and monetary authority of the United States, known as "the Fed"

Nearly all industrialized countries had formed central banks by 1900—the Bundesbank in Germany, the Bank of Japan, the Bank of England. But the American public's suspicion of such monopoly power led to the establishment of not one central bank but separate semiautonomous central banks in twelve Federal Reserve districts around the country. The new banks were named after the cities in which they were located—the Federal Reserve Bank of Boston, New York, Chicago, San Francisco, and so on. All national banks were required to become members of the Federal Reserve System and became subject to new regulations issued by *the Fed*, as it came to be known. For state banks, membership was voluntary; most state banks did not join because they did not want to comply with the new regulations.

Example The Bank of England was founded in 1694 by a group of merchants. Although it became accepted by other banks as a de facto central bank, held the country's gold reserves, and provided ultimate support for the country's financial structure, it was not nationalized until 1947.

Powers of the Federal Reserve System

According to the 1913 act, the Federal Reserve System was to be directed by the Federal Reserve Board. This board was authorized "to exercise general supervision" over the twelve Reserve banks. The Federal Reserve's task was to ensure the availability of enough money and credit in the banking system to support a growing economy. The power to issue bank notes was taken away from national banks and turned over to the Federal Reserve banks. (Take out a dollar and notice what it says across the top: FEDERAL RESERVE NOTE. The seal to the left of George Washington's picture identifies which Reserve bank issued the note.) The Federal Reserve was also given other powers: *the abilities to buy and sell government securities, to extend loans to member banks, to clear checks, and to require that member banks hold reserves equal at least to some fraction of their deposits.*

Teaching Tip A major weakness of the national banking system established in 1863 was that the volume of bank notes tended to fall during economic expansions and rise during contractions.

Federal Reserve banks typically do not deal with the public directly. Each may be thought of as a bankers' bank. Reserve banks hold deposits of member banks, just as depository institutions hold deposits of the public. Reserve banks extend loans to member banks just as depository institutions extend loans to the public. In addition to serving as bankers' banks, Reserve banks serve as bankers to the federal government, holding government deposits and lending money to the government by purchasing federal securities.

Federal Reserve banks get their name from the fact that they hold member bank *reserves* on deposit, both to promote banking safety and to facilitate interbank transfers of funds. **Reserves** are funds that banks use to satisfy the cash demands of their customers. These reserves allow Reserve banks to clear checks written by a depositor in one commercial bank and deposited in another commercial bank. This check clearance is, on a larger scale, much like the goldsmith's moving of gold reserves from the farmer's account to the horse trader's account. As noted earlier, Reserve banks also make loans to member banks. The interest rate charged banks for these so-called *discount loans* is called the **discount rate**. By making discount loans to banks, the Fed can increase reserves in the banking system.

Reserves Funds that banks use to satisfy the cash demands of their customers; reserves consist of deposits at the Fed plus currency that is physically held by banks

Discount rate The interest rate the Federal Reserve charges banks for discount loans

Member banks are required to own stock in the Federal Reserve bank in their district, and this stock ownership entitles them to vote for the Board of Directors of their district Federal Reserve bank. Member banks earn a guaranteed dividend of 6 percent on their ownership of the Reserve banks. Any additional profit earned by the Reserve banks is turned over to the U.S. Treasury. Twelve commercial bankers, one representing each Federal Reserve district, also make up the *Federal Advisory Council*, which advises the Fed.

Teaching Tip When the Fed was established, it was thought that the discount rate would be the major monetary tool. Therefore, in keeping with the suspicion of monopoly power, the power to propose discount rates for each district was given to the individual Reserve banks.

Teaching Tip Each Reserve bank is controlled by nine directors. Six are elected by member banks; three are appointed by the Board of Governors.

Banking During the Great Depression

From 1913 to 1929, both the Federal Reserve System and the national economy performed relatively well. But the stock market crash of 1929 was followed by the Great Depression, bringing a new set of problems for the Federal Reserve System. Frightened depositors wanted their money back, precipitating bank runs. But the Fed failed to respond to the crisis; it failed to act as a lender of last resort—that is, it did not lend banks the money they needed to satisfy deposit withdrawals in cases of runs on otherwise sound banks. Between 1930 and 1933, about 9,000 banks failed—roughly half of the banks in existence.

The Federal Reserve System was established precisely to prevent such panics and to add stability to the banking system. What went wrong? In a word, everything. Between 1930 and 1933, the support offered by the Federal Reserve System seemed to crumble in stages. As businesses failed, they were unable to repay their loans. These defaults on loans led to the initial bank failures. As the crisis deepened, the public grew more concerned about the safety of deposits, so cash withdrawals increased. To satisfy the increased demand for currency, banks were forced to sell their holdings of stocks and bonds. But with many banks looking to sell and with few buyers, securities markets collapsed, sharply reducing the market value of these bank assets. Many banks did not have the resources to survive.

The Fed should have extended loans on a large scale to banks experiencing a short-run shortage of cash, much as it did a half century later during the stock market crash of 1987. The Fed failed to act because it did not understand either the gravity of the situation or its own power to assist troubled banks. The Fed viewed bank failure as a regrettable but inevitable consequence of poor bank management or prior speculative excesses, or simply as the effect of a collapsing economy. The Fed did not seem to understand that the banking system's instability was contributing to the deterioration of the economy. For example, the stock market collapsed in part because many banks were trying to sell their securities at the same time. And the collapse came just when banks were badly in need of cash. Fed officials appeared concerned primarily with the solvency of the Federal Reserve banks. They did not seem to realize that because Federal Reserve banks had unlimited money-creating power, they could not fail.

Roosevelt's Reforms

In his first inaugural address, President Franklin D. Roosevelt said, "The only thing we have to fear is fear itself," a view that was especially applicable to a fractional reserve banking system. Most banks were sound as long as people had confidence in the safety of their deposits. *But if many people became frightened and tried to withdraw their money, they could not do so because each bank held reserves amounting to only a fraction of its deposits.*

Upon taking office in March of 1933, President Roosevelt attempted to soothe prevailing fears by declaring a "banking holiday," which closed all banks for a week. A national suspension of banking business for a week was unprecedented, yet it was welcomed as a sign that something would be done. Roosevelt also proposed the Banking Acts of 1933 and 1935 and other measures to introduce a variety of reforms aimed at shoring up the banking system and centralizing the power of the Federal Reserve in Washington. Let's consider the most important features of this legislation.

Teaching Tip To make the board representative of the country as a whole, no more than one member can come from each reserve district. Members may not be reappointed after their fourteen-year terms.

BOARD OF GOVERNORS. The Federal Reserve Board was renamed the Board of Governors, and it became responsible for setting and implementing the nation's monetary policy. Recall that *monetary policy* is the regulation of the economy's money supply to promote macroeconomic objectives. All twelve Reserve banks came under the authority of the Board of Governors, which consists of seven members appointed by the president and confirmed by the Senate. Each governor serves a fourteen-year term, and the terms are staggered so that one governor is appointed every two years. The president also appoints one of the governors to chair the board for a four-year term. A president bent on changing the direction of monetary policy could be sure of changing only two members in a single presidential term and four members in two terms. Thus, board membership is relatively stable, and in one four-year term a president has only limited control over the board's monetary policy. *The idea was to insulate monetary authorities from short-term political pressures.*

Teaching Tip The presidents of districts other than New York rotate through one-year terms on the FOMC. Every reserve president normally attends and participates in FOMC meetings, although only members can vote.

Open-market operations Purchases and sales of government securities by the Federal Reserve in an effort to change the money supply

Teaching Tip The Federal Advisory Committee in Exhibit 2 consists of representatives selected by the board of directors of each Reserve bank. They keep the Board of Governors informed of problems in each district.

FEDERAL OPEN MARKET COMMITTEE. Originally, the power of the Federal Reserve was vested in each of the twelve Reserve banks. The Banking Acts established the *Federal Open Market Committee (FOMC)* to consolidate decisions about the most important tool of monetary policy—**open-market operations**, which are purchases and sales of U.S. government securities by the Fed. (Open-market operations will be examined in the next chapter.) The FOMC consists of the seven board governors plus five presidents from the Reserve banks. Open-market operations are carried out in New York, and the president of the New York Fed is always on the FOMC. The organizational structure of the Federal Reserve System as it now stands is presented in Exhibit 2.

RESERVE REQUIREMENTS. As noted earlier, because reserves amount to only a fraction of deposits, we have a *fractional reserve* banking system. Specific reserve requirements had been established by the Federal Reserve Act of 1914. Member banks were required to hold in reserves no less than a certain percentage of their deposits. The Banking Acts of 1933 and 1935 authorized the Board of Governors to vary reserve requirements within a range, thereby giving the Fed an additional tool of monetary policy.

EXHIBIT 3

Organization Chart for the Federal Reserve System

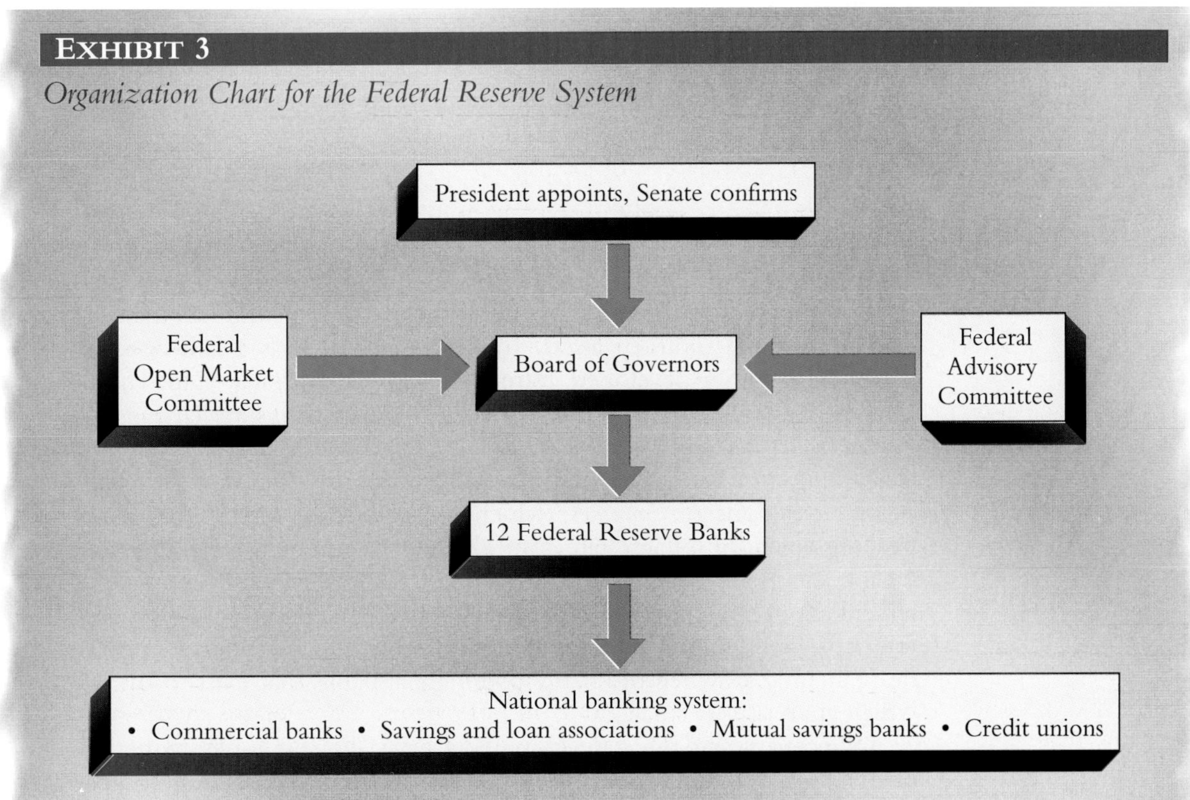

Thus, as of 1935, the Federal Reserve System had a variety of tools to regulate the money supply, including *(1) conducting open-market operations—buying and selling U.S. government securities; (2) setting the legal reserve requirement for member banks; and (3) setting the discount rate—the interest rate charged by the Reserve banks for loans to member banks.* We will explore these tools in greater detail in the next chapter.

Teaching Tip
Ninety-nine percent of all deposit accounts are protected, but due to the large size of some deposits, only two-thirds of total deposits are covered.

FDIC. One cause of bank failures during the depression was the lack of confidence depositors had in the safety of their bank deposits. The Federal Deposit Insurance Corporation (FDIC) was established in 1933 to insure each deposit account held in member banks for up to $2,500. Today the ceiling is $100,000 per account. Members of the Federal Reserve System are required to purchase FDIC insurance; the program is voluntary for others. Today about 97 percent of commercial banks and about 90 percent of savings and loan associations are insured by the FDIC. The rest are insured by private companies or state reserve funds. *Deposit insurance worked wonders to reduce bank runs by calming fears about bank safety.*

RESTRICTING BANK INVESTMENT PRACTICES. As part of the Banking Act of 1933, commercial banks were forbidden to buy and sell corporate stocks and bonds. The belief was that when commercial banks hold assets that fluctuate widely in value, the stability of the banking system is endangered. *The act limited bank assets primarily to loans and government securities.* Also, bank failures were thought to have resulted in part from interest-rate competition among banks for customer deposits. To reduce such competition, the Fed was empowered to set the maximum interest rates that could be paid on commercial bank deposits. ceiling.

Branch Banking Restrictions

The United States has about 12,000 commercial banks—more than any other country. And the ten largest commercial banks hold less than 40 percent of banking industry assets. In contrast, as few as a half-dozen banks dominate in other developed countries, such as Australia, Canada, and the United Kingdom. Nine of the world's ten largest banks are Japanese. *So the United States has more banks than other countries and bank assets are distributed more evenly across banks.* The number of banks in this country reflects government restrictions on *branches*, which are additional offices that carry out banking operations. Each state controls the type and number of branches that a bank can open. States on the East Coast and West Coast tend to be more lenient about branches than do states in between. Federal legislation prohibits interstate branching. The combination of intrastate and interstate restrictions on branching spawned the many commercial banks that exist today, most of which are relatively small.

Bank holding company A corporation that owns banks

In recent years, three developments have allowed banks to get around branching restrictions. The first is the rise of the bank holding company. A **bank holding company** is a corporation that may own several different banks. Many states now permit holding companies to cross state lines, thereby skirting federal prohibitions against interstate banking. Moreover, a holding company can provide other services that banks are not authorized to offer, such as financial advising, leasing, and credit card services. And a holding company has the ability to attract funds from sources that are not available to banks. Holding companies have blossomed in recent years, and today more than three-quarters of the nation's demand deposits are in banks owned by holding companies. The nation's major banks are all owned by holding companies.

Teaching Tip A major cause of the growth in holding companies was the relaxation of legal restrictions since the mid-1970s.

Another important development that has allowed banks to extend their presence is the automatic teller machine. In some states banks have bypassed branching restrictions by having several banks share the same machine. Thus, *holding companies and automatic teller machines have allowed banks to avoid branching restrictions and thereby cover more territory.*

Example In 1990, 75,000 automatic teller machines in the United States accounted for five billion transactions.

As we shall see, recent financial weakness of some banks has forced them to merge with stronger banks, and these mergers have spread the presence of the merged bank within states and across the country. For example, recent mergers between Chemical Bank and Manufacturers Hanover and between BankAmerica and Security Pacific have resulted in banks with a broader geographical presence.

The Quiet Life of Depository Institutions

Restrictions imposed on depository institutions during the 1930s made banking a heavily regulated industry, something like a public utility. The federal government insured most deposits. Depository institutions, in turn, surrendered much of their freedom to wheel and deal. The assets they could acquire were carefully limited, as were the interest rates they could offer depositors. Households typically left their money in savings accounts earning 5 percent or less; checking deposits earned no interest. Banks and thrifts quietly accepted these deposits and made loans, earning their profit on the interest differential. The banking business became comfortable and was largely insulated from the rigors of competition. As the expression "banker's hours" suggests, banks closed at 2:00 or 3:00 in the afternoon and remained closed on weekends. Banking was considered stuffy, even boring. In this staid business climate, offering a free toaster as a deposit bonus was considered state-of-the-art marketing.

Savings and loan associations and mutual savings banks were even more sheltered than commercial banks. They might pay 4 percent interest on deposits that were loaned out at 7 percent interest for thirty-year home mortgages. If the loan went into default and the mortgage had to be foreclosed, rising postwar housing values made the house worth more than the unpaid loan. Under the circumstances, it was difficult to make a bad mortgage loan. But the quiet world of banking was shaken by developments in the 1970s that ultimately led to the elimination of many restrictions introduced during the 1930s. Let's look at what happened.

Recent Problems with Depository Institutions

Money market mutual fund A collection of short-term interest-earning assets purchased with funds collected from many shareholders

The surge of inflation during the 1970s increased interest rates in the economy, and the sleepy world of the banker has not been the same since. In October 1972, Merrill Lynch, a major brokerage house, introduced an account combining a **money market mutual fund** with check-writing privileges. Money market mutual fund shares represent a claim on a portfolio, or collection, of short-term interest-earning assets. By pooling the funds of many shareholders, the managers of a money market mutual fund can acquire a diversified portfolio of assets offering shareholders higher rates of interest than those offered by most depository institutions. Money market mutual funds proved to be stiff competitors for bank deposits.

Depository Institutions Were Losing Deposits

Example Between 1978 and 1981, the average yield on three-month Treasury bills rose from 7.2 percent to 14.0 percent. Money market mutual fund assets grew from $6.4 billion to $150.6 billion.

Federal Reserve regulations establishing ceilings on the interest rates that depository institutions could offer their depositors reduced interest-rate competition for deposits *among* depository institutions. Depository institutions still competed for deposits in other ways, such as by offering free toasters or providing drive-through windows. As long as the interest-rate ceilings were at or above prevailing market rates of interest, the banking system as a whole did not have to worry about outside competition for customer deposits. When market interest rates rose above the ceiling that banks and thrifts could offer, however, many savers withdrew their deposits from banks and thrifts and put them into higher-yielding alternatives, such as money market mutual funds. The banks had used savers' deposits to make loans; when savers withdrew their deposits, banks and thrifts had to replace the funds needed to support their loans by borrowing at prevailing interest rates, which were typically higher than banks and thrifts earned on their loans.

Because their loans were typically for short periods, commercial banks encountered less of a problem when interest rates rose. Their problem could be resolved in the short run as outstanding loans were repaid. But thrifts had made loans for long-term mortgages, loans that had to be carried for years. *Because thrifts had to pay more interest to borrow funds than they were earning on these mortgages, they were in big trouble and many failed.*

Bank Deregulation

Example The major deregulation bills were the Depository Institutions Deregulation and Monetary Control Act of 1980 and the Depository Institutions (or Garn-St. Germain) Act of 1982.

In response to the loss of deposits and other problems of depository institutions, Congress tried to ease the regulations, giving banks and thrifts greater discretion in their operations. For example, the interest-rate ceilings for deposits were eliminated and all depository institutions were authorized to offer checking accounts. Thrifts were given wider latitude in making loans and in the kinds of assets they could acquire. Additionally, all depository institutions were allowed to offer money market deposit accounts in order to compete more effectively with those money market funds already offered by other financial institutions.

Some states, such as California and Texas, largely deregulated state-chartered savings and loan associations. The combination of deposit insurance, unregulated interest rates, and a wider latitude in the kinds of assets that could be purchased gave savings and loan associations a green light to compete for large sums of money in national markets and to acquire assets as they pleased. Once-staid financial institutions moved into the fast lane.

Thus, with deregulation, thrifts could wheel and deal, but with the benefit of deposit insurance. Many troubled thrifts could attract funds only by offering high interest rates. The high rates they had to pay to attract deposits required thrifts to gamble to earn still higher returns on the assets acquired. Deposit insurance encouraged some thrifts to take big risks because they knew their depositors would be protected by deposit insurance. For the thrift owner, the gamble became "heads I win, tails the deposit insurer loses." Thrift owners were therefore willing and able to "bet the bank" trying to get out of their financial bind.

Meanwhile, most depositors paid little attention to their bank's health since deposits were insured. *Thus deposit insurance, originally introduced during the Great Depression to prevent bank panics, caused depositors to become complacent about the safety of their deposits and caused those who ran the banks and thrifts to take unwarranted risks because they were gambling with other people's money.*

Teaching Tip More than 80 percent of all U.S. thrift insolvencies since 1934 have occurred since 1980. The FSLIC had assets of $5 billion in 1985. By 1988, it faced a deficit of $12 billion.

The result was a disaster, and depository institutions, particularly thrifts, failed at record rates. The number of thrifts in existence dropped by half between 1980 and 1991. And half of those remaining in 1991 were expected to disappear by the year 2000 through mergers or failures. Investigations of failed depository institutions turned up not only poor management but in some cases outright criminal behavior.

Bailing Out the Thrifts

Teaching Tip The bailout bill is the Financial Institutions Reform, Recovery, and Enforcement Act of 1989.

The insolvency and collapse of a growing number of thrifts finally prompted Congress in August of 1989 to approve the largest financial bailout of any industry in history—a measure estimated to cost up to $300 billion and a measure contributing to current federal deficits. Taxpayers are expected to pay nearly two-thirds of the total cost, with the thrift industry paying the remaining third through higher deposit insurance premiums. The money is to be spent over a period of years to shut down failing thrifts and pay off insured depositors.

The bailout measure imposed new regulations on the composition of thrift portfolios. Thrifts are no longer allowed to buy high-risk bonds, or "junk" bonds, and had to sell their holdings of such bonds by 1994. Thrifts must hold at least 70 percent of their assets in mortgages. When the dust settles, failures and mergers could reduce the number of thrifts to as few as 1,000, only about 25 percent of their number in the early 1980s. Despite the billions that will be spent on the rescue, more funds may yet be needed. Additional legislation was passed in 1991, but efforts to reduce the limits on deposit insurance failed.

Part of the cleanup involves selling the office buildings, shopping malls, apartment buildings, land, and other assets formerly taken over by insolvent thrifts. A glut of such properties dragged down market values and reduced the federal government's ability to recoup its losses from deposit insurance. The problem is discussed in the following case study.

CASE STUDY

Easy Money, Empty Buildings

During the 1980s, office buildings shot up like weeds. A ready supply of financing from banks and thrifts coupled with generous 1981 tax law provisions for developers made new buildings look like sure-fire investments. The one-two punch of easy financing and tax incentives turned office-building construction into a growth industry. But the growth in office-building construction occurred just as the financial service sector, the sector that was expected to fill those buildings with office workers, was starting to contract.

The increased supply of office buildings and decreased demand left many new buildings only partially filled or even empty. Vacancy rates in cities such as Boston and New York doubled to 20 percent. The excess quantity supplied depressed rents, which in real terms by 1992 were only half what they were in 1987. Building developers were not earning enough in rent to pay off their loans, so they defaulted. The banks and thrifts that financed construction became reluctant owners of these failed properties. They tried to sell the properties, but with many buildings for sale and few buyers, market values fell sharply. Many banks could not hang on and were dragged under by these loans.

Commercial property values in the United States are in a depression that will take years to work through. A lot of investors lost money, especially developers and those who bankrolled the construction. The sad part for the economy as a whole is that money that could have gone to advancing technology, to more efficent machines, to better education, or to improved highways instead went to finance unused or underemployed buildings. U.S. workers in the 1990s will be less productive because much investment during the 1980s went not into productive capital but into what turned out to be gleaming office buildings that were not needed.

Source: "Still Flat on Its Back," *The Economist*, 16 May 1992.

Commercial Banks Were Also Failing

Teaching Tip The United States is not alone in experiencing upheaval in its banking system. Rapidly rising real estate prices in Japan in the 1980s led to massive bank loans that soured when real estate prices collapsed. Most finance companies financed by Japanese banks are now broke.

The U.S. banking system experienced more change and upheaval during the 1980s and early 1990s than at any other time since the Great Depression. As they had in the case of thrifts, risky decisions based on deposit insurance and the slump in property values hastened the demise of many commercial banks. Hundreds of troubled commercial banks such as Continental Illinois, First Republic Bank of Dallas, and the Bank of New England were taken over by the FDIC or forced to merge with healthier banks. Other major banks were in trouble, many with questionable loans still on the books. Banks in Texas and Oklahoma failed because loans to oil drillers and farmers went sour. Banks in the Northeast failed because falling real estate values caused borrowers to default. Exhibit 3 shows the number of bank failures per year since 1935. The rising tide of failures during the 1980s is clear.

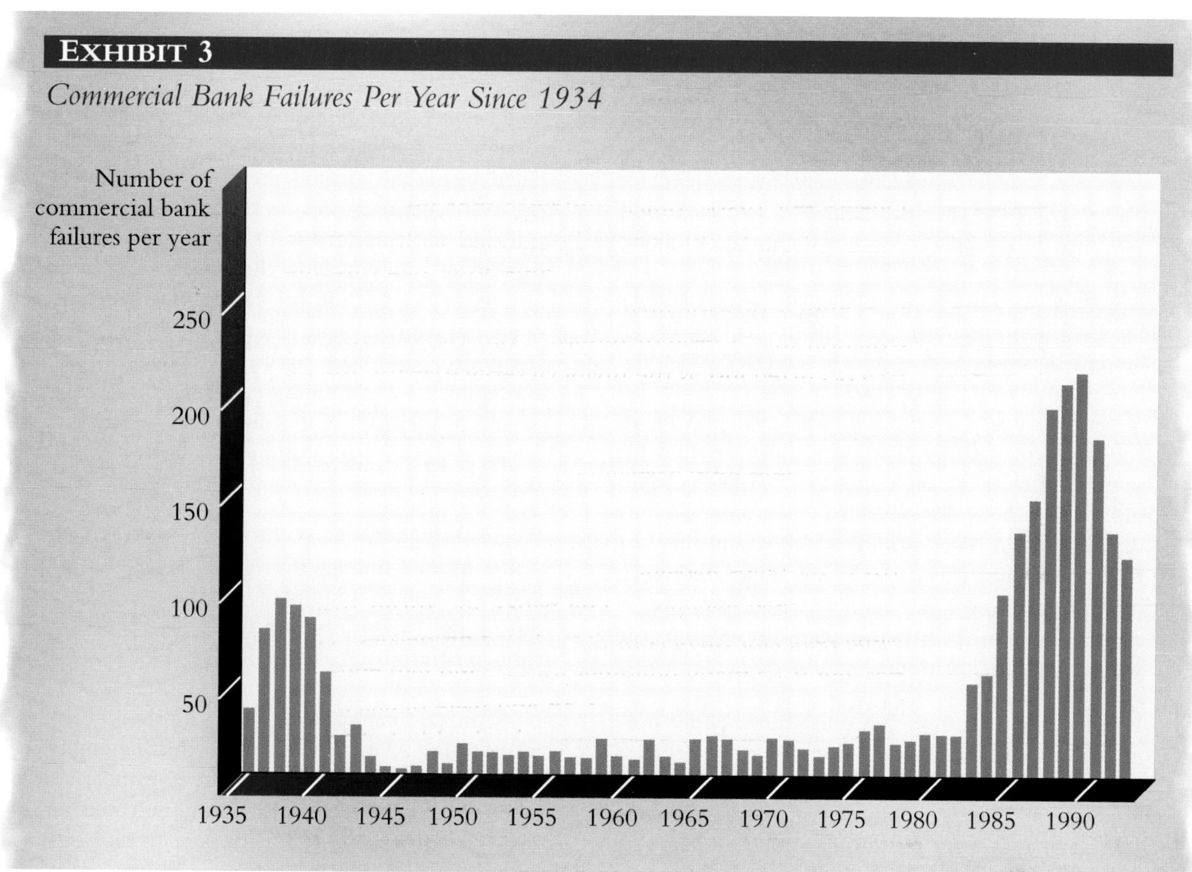

Source: Federal Deposit Insurance Corporation.

CONCLUSION

Example In 1933, almost 4,000 U.S. banks failed. Between 1971 and 1980, only 83 banks failed. In 1989, the worst year since 1933, 206 failures occurred. However, unlike in 1933, less than one-half of failed banks ceased operation, as many merged with stronger banks.

Banking has evolved from one of the most staid industries to one of the most competitive. Deregulation and branching innovations have made it easier to enter the industry and have increased the kinds of activities that banks can undertake. Reforms have given the Fed more uniform control over all depository institutions and have given the institutions greater access to the services provided by the Fed. Thus, all depository institutions can compete on more equal footing.

Deregulation provides greater freedom not only to prosper but also to fail. Problems of the thrifts began when they had to pay more interest on their deposits than they were earning on their loans. Losses mounted because deposit insurance encouraged thrifts to gamble big to get even. In the Darwinian world of deregulated banking, only the fittest will survive. Failures of depository institutions create a special problem, however, because these institutions provide the financial underpinning of the nation's money supply, as we will see in the next chapter. There we will examine more closely how banks operate and how banks help supply the nation's money.

Summary

1. Barter was the first form of exchange. As the degree of specialization grew, it became more difficult to discover the double coincidence of wants required for barter. The time and inconvenience associated with barter led even simple economies to introduce money.

2. Anything that acquires a high degree of acceptability throughout an economy as a medium of exchange thereby becomes money. The first money was commodity money: a good such as salt or gold also served as money. Eventually, what changed hands was a piece of paper that could be redeemed for something of value, such as silver or gold. As paper money became widely accepted, governments eventually introduced fiat money, which is paper money that cannot be redeemed for anything other than more paper money. Fiat money is given its status as money by law. Most currencies throughout the world today are fiat money.

3. People accept fiat money because they believe others will do so as well. The value of money depends on how much it will buy. If money fails to serve as a medium of exchange, traders will resort to some second-best means of exchange, such as barter, a careful system of record keeping, or some informal commodity money. When the monetary system breaks down, more time must be devoted to exchange and less to production, so the economy's efficiency suffers.

4. The Federal Reserve System was established in 1914 to stabilize the banking system. After many banks failed during the Great Depression, the powers of the Fed were increased and centralized. The Fed's control over all depository institutions was extended by legislation passed during the 1980s. The primary powers of the Fed are to (1) conduct open-market operations (buying and selling U.S. government securities to control the money supply), (2) establish and enforce reserve requirements for depository institutions, and (3) set the discount rate (the rate at which depository institutions can borrow from the Fed).

5. Regulations introduced during the Great Depression turned banking into a closely regulated and largely predictable industry. But high interest rates during the 1970s disturbed the quiet life of depository institutions. Reforms in the 1980s were designed to give depository institutions greater flexibility in competing with other kinds of financial institutions. Many thrifts used this flexibility to gamble on investments, but these gambles often failed, causing hundreds of thrifts to go bankrupt. In 1989 Congress approved a measure to close failing thrifts, pay off insured deposits, and regulate more closely the operations of remaining thrifts. Commercial banks also experienced record failures during the 1980s, but their problems were not as serious as those affecting the thrifts.

Questions and Problems

1. (Barter) Most of us have heard stories of the old general store, where many different goods could be exchanged. Why would such a store help reduce transactions costs in economies where there was a considerable amount of barter? Would flea markets that met twice a month have the same effect?

2. (Commodity Money) In medieval Japan rice was used for money. Why do you think this commodity was chosen to serve as money? What would happen to prices in general if there was a particularly good harvest one year?

3. (Store of Wealth) "If an economy had only two goods (both nondurable), there would be no need for money because exchange would always be between those two goods." Does this statement disregard some important function of money?

4. (Gresham's Law) Early in the history of the United States, tobacco was used as money. If you were a tobacco farmer and you had two loads of tobacco that were of different qualities, which would eventually be used for money and which for smoking? Under what conditions would both types of tobacco be used for money?

5. (Fractional Reserve Banking System) What factors or conditions in the economy would lead a bank to increase the fraction of its deposits held as reserves? Would a bank hold greater reserves during certain seasons? Why?

6. (Fiat Money) Most economists believe that fiat money has value only to the extent that people believe it will retain its value. What does this seemingly circular statement mean? How could people lose faith in that money?

7. (Savings and Loans) In the early 1980s, the number of savings and loan institutions in the United States decreased drastically. Why? How did the government deal with the situation?

8. (Federal Reserve System) Why are most Federal Reserve banks located in the East?

9. (Bank Failures) Why has the steep reduction in the prices of oil and farmland led to the largest number of bank failures in the United States since the Great Depression? Would the United States be better off with higher oil prices and higher food prices? Why or why not?

10. (Bank Restrictions) Eurodollars are dollar denominated deposits held in banks outside the United States. Such deposits earn high rates of interest. Did ceilings on the interest rates that banks could offer depositors help foster the development of the Eurodollar market?

11. (Money Versus Barter) "Without money, everything would be more expensive." This statement is both true and false. Explain.

12. (Money) Show that a barter system with n goods has $n(n - 1)/2$ exchange rates but this same system with money added has only n exchange rates.

13. (Money) When monetary systems were based on monetary units whose values were determined by their gold content, new discoveries of gold were frequently followed by periods of inflation. Explain.

14. (Banks and Interest Rates) Banks and other financial intermediaries typically borrow short (e.g., accept short-maturity deposits) and lend long (e.g., offer thirty-year mortgages). Because long-term interest rates generally are higher than short-term rates, banks can "live off the spread." Why do you think that rising rates can create profit problems for banks?

15. (Deregulation) Some economists argue that deregulated deposit rates combined with deposit insurance have led to financial "black holes." Why do you think they make such an argument?

16. (Money Versus Barter) Suppose that you wanted to purchase a house, making payments over the next twenty years. Explain the advantage of money over a pure barter system for handling such a transaction.

17. (Federal Reserve) When the Federal Reserve System was initially established, its power was largely decentralized in the individual Federal Reserve banks rather than in Washington. Can you suggest a reason for this power structure?

18. (Branching Restriction) As noted in the text, the United States is one of the few industrialized countries with restrictions on bank branching. These restrictions are applied both within states and across state lines. What reasons can you suggest for such restrictions?

19. (Money) Why is universal acceptability such an important characteristic of money? What other characteristics can you think of that might be important?

20. (FDIC) The insurance premiums paid by banks for deposit insurance have historically been a flat percentage of bank deposits. Is this an unusual premium structure? How might this have contributed to the recent banking crisis?

21. (When the Monetary System Breaks Down) As the first case study suggests, if the supply of money is not appropriate (i.e., either too small or too big), problems for the economy inevitably result. In this country we have several different measures of the money supply. Why do you think that the money supply is so hard to measure?

22. (When the Monetary System Breaks Down) When the government issues fiat money, it must declare it to be legal tender, which means that it *must* be accepted for payment. Yet in contrast to other forms of money, the acceptability of legal tender depends upon the quantity of it that is issued. Explain.

23. (Easy Money, Empty Buildings) The collapse of the commercial property market has had a decidedly regional flavor. The result has been a banking industry also characterized by regional failure. Do you think that branching restrictions could have contributed to the problem?

24. (Easy Money, Empty Buildings) A relatively recent development in the banking industry is a secondary (or resale) market for real estate loans and other kinds of loans by banks. What impact might this secondary market have on the banking industry problems addressed in this case study?

CHAPTER 13

BANKING AND THE MONEY SUPPLY

Why are we so interested in banks? After all, isn't banking a business like any other—dry cleaning, lawn mowing, or house painting? Why not devote the chapter to house painting? Banks are of special interest in macroeconomics because, like the London goldsmith, banks can change a borrower's IOU into money. *Banks have the ability to create money, and money is a key ingredient in a healthy economy.*

As noted in the last chapter, regulatory reforms have eliminated many of the distinctions between commercial banks and thrift institutions. Thrifts represent a dwindling share of depository institutions—less than 20 percent. So from now on depository institutions will usually be referred to more simply as banks. We will first consider the role of banks in the economy and the types of deposits they hold. Then we will examine how banks work and show how the money supply expands through the creation of deposits. We will also consider the operation of the Federal Reserve System in more detail. As we will see, the Federal Reserve attempts to control the growth of the money supply by controlling bank reserves. Topics discussed in this chapter include

- Checkable deposits
- Near moneys
- Monetary aggregates
- Balance sheets
- Money creation process
- Money multiplier

BANKS, THEIR DEPOSITS, AND THE MONEY SUPPLY

Banks attract their funds from savers and lend these funds to borrowers. Savers need a safe place for their money and borrowers need credit, so banks try to earn a profit by serving both groups. Banks attempt to identify borrowers who are willing to pay interest but who also are able to repay the loans. At the same time, banks must attract and retain deposits from savers who believe their money will be looked after carefully. Hence, banks try to present an image of sober dignity—an image meant to foster assurance. Even their names are selected to inspire depositor confidence. Banks are more apt to be called First Trust, Security National, or Federal Savings than Benny's Bank, Easy Money Bank and Trust, or Last Chance Savings and Loan. In contrast, *finance companies* are financial intermediaries that do not get their funds from depositors, so they can choose names aimed more at borrowers—names such as Household Finance and The Money Store.

Example General Motors Acceptance Corporation (GMAC) obtains funds through the issue of commercial paper, stocks, and bonds.

Banks Are Financial Intermediaries

Banks extend, structure, and monitor loans, and diversify risk. *By bringing together the two sides of the market, banks serve as financial intermediaries.* They gather various amounts from savers and package these funds into the amounts demanded by borrowers. The amount and duration of saving differ among savers. Some savers need their money back next week, some next year, some only after retirement. Likewise, the amount and duration of loans vary among borrowers.

Teaching Tip The large size of financial institutions allows them to hire financial experts specializing in evaluating creditworthiness.

COPING WITH ASYMMETRIC INFORMATION. Banks have an abiding interest in knowing how likely a borrower will be to repay the loan. But borrowers have more reliable information about their credit history and financial plans than do lenders. Thus, we say that in the market for loans there is **asymmetric information**: an inequality in the information known by each party to the transaction. This asymmetry would not create a problem if borrowers could be relied upon to communicate information accurately to lenders. Some borrowers, however, have an incentive to suppress vital information, such as other debts incurred, a troubled financial history, or plans to invest the borrowed funds in a risky enterprise. Because banks have experience and expertise in evaluating the creditworthiness of loan applicants, banks have a greater ability than do individual savers to cope with the asymmetric information problem that arises in this market. Moreover, because banks have abundant experience in drawing up and enforcing contracts with borrowers, they can do so more cheaply than could individual savers. The economy is more efficient because banks develop expertise in evaluating borrowers, structuring loans, and enforcing loan contracts.

Asymmetric information An inequality in the information known by each party to a transactiion

Point to Stress Operating with a large pool of funds and expert financial management, financial institutions can acquire a range of securities selected to offset risk.

MINIMIZING RISK THROUGH DIVERSIFICATION. By creating a diversified portfolio of assets rather than lending funds to a single borrower, banks reduce the risk to each individual saver. All the eggs are not in one basket. A bank lends a tiny fraction of each saver's deposits to each of the many borrowers it finances. If one of these borrowers fails to repay the loan, this failure will hardly make a ripple in the balance sheet of a large, diversified bank. Certainly, such a default does not represent the personal disaster it would if one saver's entire nest egg had been loaned directly to that defaulting borrower.

Point to Stress Checkable deposits are the primary medium of exchange in the United States.

Money and Liquidity

When a bank accepts a deposit, it promises to repay the depositor that amount. The deposit therefore becomes an amount the bank owes—it becomes a **liability**. When the bank lends these funds to a borrower, the borrower's promise to repay the loan becomes an amount owed to the bank—it becomes an **asset**. Although the principle is the same, different kinds of banks have different kinds of liabilities and assets.

Liability Anything that is owed to another individual or institution

Asset Anything of value that is owned

Suppose you have some cash in your pocket. If you deposit this cash in a checking account, you can then write checks directing your bank to pay someone from your account. When you think of money, what most likely comes to mind is currency—dollar bills and coins. In reality, however, money consists primarily of a particular class of bank liabilities—**checkable deposits**, or deposits against which checks can be written. The checks themselves are not money; it is the checkable deposits that are money. Banks hold a variety of checkable deposits. The most important checkable deposits over the years have been demand deposits, which are held by commercial banks and do not earn interest. In recent years financial institutions have developed other kinds of accounts that carry check-writing privileges while also earning interest, such as negotiable order of withdrawal (NOW) accounts.

Checkable deposits Deposits in financial institutions against which checks can be written

Monetary aggregates are various measures of the money supply used by the Federal Reserve. The money supply is most narrowly defined as **M1**, which consists of currency (including coins) held by the nonbanking public, checkable deposits, and travelers checks. (Note that currency held by banks is not counted as part of the money supply.) Currency has been declared legal tender by the federal government; you'll recall that this means that if currency is offered as payment, it must be accepted. Checkable deposits are the liabilities of the issuing banks, which stand ready to convert these deposits into currency. Checks are not legal tender, so sellers need not accept checks, as signs that say "No Checks!" attest. Yet checks are so widely accepted as a medium of exchange that checkable deposits are counted as part of the money supply.

Monetary aggregates Measures of the economy's money supply

M1 A measure of the money supply consisting of currency and coin held by the nonbank public, checkable deposits, and travelers checks

The primary currency circulating in the United States consists of Federal Reserve notes, which are issued by and are the liability of the Federal Reserve banks. Federal Reserve notes are IOUs from the Fed to the bearer. But unlike other IOUs, they can be redeemed only for more IOUs. If you present a $20 note to the Fed for redemption, you will receive your choice of two $10s, four $5s, twenty $1s, or some other combination of currency and coins totaling $20. Since Federal Reserve notes are redeemable for nothing other than more Federal Reserve notes, U.S. currency is *fiat money*, as noted already. The other component of currency is coins, manufactured and distributed by the U.S. Bureau of the Mint. Our coins are token coins because their metal value is less—much less—than their face value.

Liquidity describes the ease with which an asset can be converted into the medium of exchange without a significant loss of value. The most liquid asset is money itself—currency held by the nonbanking public and checkable deposits, with currency being the more liquid of the two. In contrast, assets such as automobiles, real estate, and rare stamps rank low in liquidity. True, you could sell your automobile in minutes if you were willing to exchange it for a pittance, but selling your car for its market value would take time and would involve some transaction costs.

Liquidity A measure of the ease with which an asset can be converted into money without significant loss in its value

Example The U.S. Treasury issued gold certificates from 1866 to 1933; silver certificates were issued from 1878 to 1963. Fed assets continue to include some gold certificates.

Other Deposits: Near Moneys

We regard currency and checkable deposits as money because each serves as a medium of exchange; they are also a standard of value and a store of wealth. Some other kinds of assets appear to perform the standard-of-value and store-of-wealth functions and are also readily convertible to currency or to checkable deposits. Because these financial assets are so close to money, we call them **near moneys**. Near moneys are like money in all ways except that they do not serve as a medium of exchange, so near moneys are less liquid than money. Important forms of near money include time deposits, savings deposits, and money market mutual fund accounts.

Example Federal Reserve statistics show that U.S. households use currency for about 34 percent of transactions and checkable deposits for about 48 percent.

Near moneys Financial assets that are like money but that do not serve as mediums of exchange

Time deposits earn a fixed rate of interest if they are held for the specified period, which can range anywhere from thirty days to several years. Premature withdrawals may be penalized. **Savings deposits** earn interest but have no specific maturity date. Neither time nor savings deposits serve directly as a medium of exchange, so they are not included in M1, the narrowest definition of money. But many banks now allow depositors to transfer time and savings deposits to checking accounts with just a phone call or by pressing a few buttons on an automatic teller machine, so distinctions between the narrowest definition of money and near moneys have become blurred.

Time deposits Deposits that earn a fixed rate of interest if they are held for the specified period, which can range anywhere from thirty days to several years

Savings deposits Deposits that earn interest but have no specific maturity date

Money market mutual fund accounts, discussed in the previous chapter, represent another near money. Because of restrictions on the minimum balance, on the number of checks that can be written per month, and on the minimum amount of each check, these popular accounts are not viewed as money based on the narrowest definition.

Because of the similarity between money and near moneys, the definition of money often broadens to include near moneys. Recall that M1 consists of currency (including coins) held by the nonbanking public, checkable deposits, and travelers checks. **M2** is a monetary aggregate that includes M1 plus savings deposits, small time deposits, and money market mutual fund accounts. **M3** includes M2 plus *negotiable certificates of deposit*, which are issued by commercial banks to large savers in minimum denominations of $100,000. Negotiable certificates of deposit can be sold to a third party

M2 A monetary aggregate consisting of M1 plus savings deposits, small time deposits, and money market mutual funds

M3 A monetary aggregate consisting of M2 plus negotiable certificates of deposit

Teaching Tip Time deposits represent about one-third of commercial bank assets; savings deposits are about 17 percent.

Teaching Tip The M2 and M3 definitions are simplified. M2 also includes overnight Eurodollar deposits and repurchase agreements; M3 includes term Eurodollar deposits and repurchase agreements. IRA and Keogh deposits are not counted as part of the money supply.

Example Federal Reserve statistics indicate that households use credit cards for about 8 percent of transactions.

Teaching Tip The checkable deposits in M1 include demand deposits at commercial banks and *other checkable deposits* (OCD) that include NOW accounts, ATS accounts at depository institutions, demand deposits at thrift institutions, and credit union share draft accounts. Prior to 1980, only commercial banks could offer checkable deposits. OCDs grew from 4 percent of M1 in 1979 to 36 percent in 1990.

before maturity. In subsequent discussions, when we refer to the "money supply," we will usually be talking about M1, the narrow definition of money.

The size and relative importance of each monetary aggregate are presented in Exhibit 1. As you can see, M2 is more than three times larger than M1, and M3 is about four times larger. Thus, *the narrow definition of money describes only a fraction of broader aggregates.* And distinctions between M1 and M2 grow less meaningful as banks allow depositors to transfer funds from one account to another.

You may have noticed that our discussion of money did not include credit cards, such as VISA and MasterCard. Shouldn't credit cards be included in any definition of money? After all, most sellers accept credit cards as readily as they do cash or checks (some even prefer credit cards to checks). Credit cards themselves are not money, however—they are simply a means of obtaining a short-term loan from the card issuer. If you purchase plane tickets from a travel agent using a credit card, the transaction is not complete until the card issuer pays for the tickets. The credit card has not eliminated the use of money; it has merely postponed the travel agent's receipt of money. Credit cards also reduce the amount of money people must carry with them.

EXHIBIT 1

Alternative Measures of the Money Supply (October 1992)

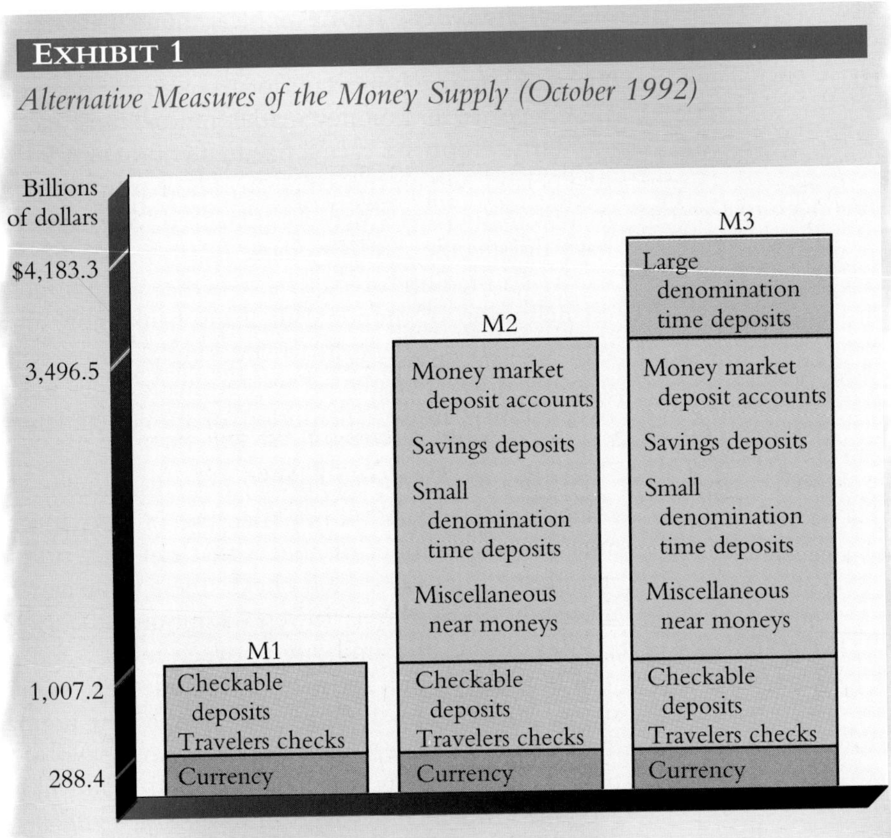

Source: *Federal Reserve Bulletin,* January 1993.

How Banks Operate

Banks are profit-making institutions in the business of taking people's money on deposit and lending out a large portion of that money, earning a profit on the difference between the interest paid on deposits and the interest received from loans. We could consider the operation of any type of bank (commercial bank, savings and loan, mutual savings bank, or credit union), but we will focus on commercial banks because they are the most important depository institutions in terms of total assets. Moreover, the operating principles that apply to credit expansion in commercial banks generally apply to other depository institutions as well.

Starting a Bank

Let's begin with the formation of a bank. Suppose some business leaders in your hometown decide to form a commercial bank called Home Bank. To obtain a *charter*, or the right to operate, they must apply to the U.S. Comptroller of the Currency in the case of a national bank or to the state banking authority in the case of a state bank. When the chartering agency reviews the application, it considers the quality of the bank's management, the amount of money the owners plan to invest, the need for an additional bank in the region, and the probable earnings of the bank.

Teaching Tip U.S. banks traditionally have been financed by issuing common stock. Since 1962, they have also been permitted to sell debentures.

Suppose the founders plan to invest $100,000 in the bank, and they so indicate on their application for a national charter. When their application is approved, they issue themselves shares of stock—paper certificates indicating ownership. Thus, they exchange $100,000 in cash for shares of stock in the bank. These shares, which provide evidence of ownership, are called the *owners' equity*, or the **net worth**, of the bank. Part of the $100,000, say $20,000, is used to buy shares in their district Federal Reserve bank, thereby establishing Home Bank as a member of the Federal Reserve System. (Recall that all national banks must belong to the Fed.) With the remaining $80,000, the owners acquire and furnish the bank building.

Net worth The difference between the values of an institution's assets and liabilities

Balance sheet A financial statement that shows assets, liabilities, and net worth at a given point in time

To focus our discussion, we will examine the bank's **balance sheet**, presented in Exhibit 2. As the name implies, a balance sheet shows a balance between the two sides of the bank's accounts. The left-hand side lists the bank's

Exhibit 2

Home Bank's Balance Sheet

Assets		Liabilities and Net Worth	
Building and furniture	$ 80,000	Net worth	$100,000
Stock in district Fed	20,000		
Total	$100,000	Total	$100,000

Teaching Tip Net worth also includes any retained earnings accumulated through the bank's operations.

assets. An asset is any physical property or financial claim owned by the bank. At this early stage, assets include the building and equipment owned by Home Bank plus its stock in the district Federal Reserve bank. The right-hand side lists the bank's liabilities and net worth. So far the right-hand side includes only the net worth of $100,000, an amount that also equals the bank's assets to this point. The two sides of the ledger must always be equal, or in *balance*—hence the name balance sheet. Since the two sides must be in balance, assets must equal liabilities plus net worth:

Assets = liabilities + net worth

Point to Stress This transaction does not represent a change in the size of M1, only a change in the composition of M1.

The bank is now ready to open. Opening day is the bank's lucky day, because its first customer comes in with a briefcase full of $100 bills and puts $1,000,000 into a checkable deposit account. As a result of this deposit, the bank's assets increase by $1,000,000 in cash, and its liabilities increase by $1,000,000 in checkable deposits. Exhibit 3 shows the effects of this transaction on Home Bank's balance sheet. The customer has deposited $1,000,000 in the bank, so the bank owes the customer the amount deposited. On the right-hand side there are now two kinds of claims on the bank's assets: claims by the owners, called net worth, and claims by nonowners, called liabilities, which at this point consist of checkable deposits.

Point to Stress Legal reserve requirements are a tool of U.S. monetary policy; they are not necessary to ensure bank safety. Great Britain and Canada do not impose legal reserve requirements.

Reserve Accounts

Required reserve ratio The proportion of deposits a depository institution is legally required to hold in the form of reserves

Required reserves The dollar amount of reserves a depository institution is legally required to hold

Where do we go from here? As mentioned in the previous chapter, banks are required by the Federal Reserve System to set aside, or to hold in reserve, a certain percentage of their deposits. The **required reserve ratio** dictates the minimum *proportion* of deposits that must be held in reserve. Suppose the required reserve ratio on checkable deposits is 10 percent. Home Bank must therefore hold in reserve 10 percent of checkable deposits. The dollar amount that must be held in reserve is called **required reserves**—deposits multiplied by the required reserve ratio. Home Bank must therefore hold $100,000 as required reserves, which equal checkable deposits of $1,000,000 multiplied by 0.10. A bank can hold reserves either

EXHIBIT 3

Home Bank's Balance Sheet After $1,000,000 Deposit

Assets		Liabilities and Net Worth	
Cash	$1,000,000	Checkable deposits	$1,000,000
Building and furniture	80,000	Net worth	100,000
Stock in district Fed	20,000		
Total	$1,100,000	Total	$1,100,000

Point to Stress Bank reserves do not earn income.

as cash in its vault or as reserves deposited at the Fed, but neither earns the bank any interest income. All depository institutions are subject to the reserve requirements established by the Fed.

Suppose Home Bank opens a reserve account with the district Federal Reserve bank and deposits $100,000 in cash. Home Bank's balance sheet now looks like Exhibit 4, where reserves are divided between cash in the vault and deposits with the Fed. Home Bank's reserves exceed the required reserves by $900,000. Reserves in excess of required reserves are called **excess reserves**. A bank's actual reserves therefore consist of required reserves plus excess reserves. So far Home Bank has not earned a penny. Excess reserves, however, can be used to make loans or to purchase other interest-bearing assets, such as government securities.

Excess reserves Reserves held by depository institutions in excess of required reserves

Competing Objectives: Liquidity Versus Profitability

Like the early goldsmiths, modern-day banks must be prepared to satisfy depositors' requests for funds. A bank loses reserves whenever a depositor demands cash or whenever a depositor writes a check that gets deposited in another bank. The bank wants to be in a position to satisfy all demands for its reserves, even if many depositors ask for their money at the same time or even if many checks are written against its checkable deposits. Banks could fail if they lacked sufficient reserves to meet all depositor requests for funds. Required reserves are not meant to be used to meet depositor requests for funds, so banks often hold excess reserves or hold some assets that can be easily liquidated to satisfy any unexpected demand for funds. Banks may also want to have excess reserves on hand in case a valued customer needs an immediate loan.

The bank manager must therefore structure the portfolio of assets with an eye toward liquidity, or safety, but must not forget that the bank's survival also depends on profitability. *The two objectives of liquidity and profitability are at odds.* For example, the bank will generally find that the assets offering the highest interest rate tend to be less liquid than other assets of comparable risk. The most liquid asset is bank reserves, either in the bank's vault as cash or on account with the Fed, but reserves yield no interest. At one extreme, consider a

Teaching Tip U.S. bank liquidity has been generally declining since World War II as a result of more efficient use of bank funds.

EXHIBIT 4

Home Bank's Balance Sheet After $100,000 Deposit with the Fed

Assets		**Liabilities and Net Worth**	
Deposits with Fed	$ 100,000	Checkable deposits	$1,000,000
Cash	900,000	Net worth	100,000
Building and furniture	80,000		
Stock in district Fed	20,000		
Total	$1,100,000	Total	$1,100,000

bank that is completely liquid, holding all its assets as cash reserves. Such a bank would clearly have no difficulty meeting depositors' demands for funds. The bank is playing it safe—too safe. Since it holds no interest-earning assets, the bank will earn no income and will fail. At the other extreme, imagine a bank that uses all its excess reserves to acquire high-yielding but highly illiquid assets, such as long-term loans. Such a bank would run into liquidity problems any time withdrawals exceeded deposits.

The bank portfolio manager's task is to strike just the right balance between liquidity, or safety, and profitability. The manager's choice of assets is limited by legal restrictions on the kinds of assets a bank can own. The kinds of assets banks can acquire are limited primarily to loans and government securities.

Suppose Home Bank extends a $400,000 building loan to a local business. The bank also lends $100,000 for a home purchase. In addition to making loans, Home Bank also purchases $250,000 worth of U.S. government securities and $100,000 worth of other securities, primarily those issued by state and local governments. Finally, to ensure sufficient liquidity, the bank keeps $50,000 in cash as excess reserves. Exhibit 5 reflects Home Bank's revised balance sheet. The bank has exchanged $850,000 of its $900,000 in excess reserves for interest-earning assets. It still has $150,000 in reserves: $100,000 in required reserves on deposit with the Fed and $50,000 in excess reserves as cash in the vault.

Teaching Tip The federal funds market gets its name from the fact that the funds generally do not leave the Fed—they are just transferred between accounts. Most loans are overnight, although they may be for as long as three days.

Since reserves earn no interest, banks usually try to keep their excess reserves at a minimum. Banks continuously "sweep" their accounts to find excess reserves that can be put to some interest-bearing use. They do not let excess reserves remain idle even overnight. The **federal funds market** provides for day-to-day lending and borrowing among banks of excess reserves on account at the Fed. For example, suppose that at the end of the business day Home Bank has excess reserves of $50,000 on account at the Fed and is willing to loan that amount to another bank that finished the day with a reserve deficiency of $50,000. These two banks are brought together by a broker who

Federal funds market A market for day-to-day lending and borrowing of reserves among financial institutions

EXHIBIT 5

Home Bank's Balance Sheet After Purchase of Assets with Excess Reserves

Assets		Liabilities and Net Worth	
Deposits with Fed	$ 100,000	Checkable deposits	$1,000,000
Cash	50,000	Net worth	100,000
Business loans	400,000		
Mortgage loans	100,000		
U.S. government securities	250,000		
Other securities	100,000		
Building and furniture	80,000		
Stock in district Fed	20,000		
Total	$1,100,000	Total	$1,100,000

EXHIBIT 6

Consolidated Balance Sheet of U.S. Commercial Banks as of October 28, 1992 (billions of dollars)

Assets		Liabilities and Net Worth	
Deposits with Fed	$ 24.5	Checkable deposits	$ 718.2
Cash	179.2	Savings deposits	738.8
Loans	2,260.8	Time deposits	1,021.7
U.S. government securities	643.0	Borrowings	491.8
Other securities	166.7	Other liabilities	340.0
Other assets	299.8	Net worth	263.5
Total	$3,574.0	Total	$3,574.0

Source: *Federal Reserve Bulletin,* January 1993.

Federal funds rate The interest rate prevailing in the federal funds market

Teaching Tip Commercial banks got their name because, historically, the largest category of bank loans was commercial and industrial. Today, real estate loans have surpassed commercial loans; individual consumer loans are the third largest category.

specializes in the market for federal funds—that is, the market for excess reserves at the Fed. The interest rate paid on this loan is called the **federal funds rate**, which is determined by the supply and demand for federal funds. Borrowers in the federal funds market tend to be large commercial banks in New York and Chicago that need reserves because of large, unexpected outflows of deposits.

To get some feel for banks in the United States, consider the consolidated balance sheet for all commercial banks shown in Exhibit 6. The consolidated picture bears some resemblance to that of our hypothetical bank, particularly on the assets side. On the liabilities side, bank deposits are sorted into three types: checkable deposits, savings deposits, and time deposits. Only checkable deposits have reserve requirements.

Before we discuss how Home Bank can create money, we must bring into the picture another important institution: the Federal Reserve. We will take a closer look at how the Fed operates, beginning with a simplified version of the Fed's balance sheet.

The Fed's Balance Sheet

Point to Stress The Fed holds most of its U.S. government securities as tools for monetary policy, not in order to lend money to the U.S. Treasury.

In its capacity as a bankers' bank, the Fed clears checks for, extends loans to, and holds deposits of depository institutions. In its capacity as banker to the federal government, the Fed holds deposits of the U.S. Treasury and also lends money to the federal government by purchasing U.S. government securities. The operation of Federal Reserve banks, like that of depository institutions, can be best studied by reviewing their balance sheet. Exhibit 7 presents a consolidated balance sheet for all Federal Reserve banks. *Over three-fourths of the Federal Reserve's assets are U.S. government securities.* These securities are assets of the Fed because they are IOUs from the federal government. Another asset is discount loans made by the Fed to banks. These loans are assets of the Fed because they are IOUs from the borrowing institutions.

EXHIBIT 7

Consolidated Balance Sheet of Federal Reserve Banks as of October 31, 1992 (billions of dollars)

Assets		Liabilities and Net Worth	
U.S. government securities	$282.9	Federal Reserve notes in circulation	$300.0
Discount loans to banks	0.1	Deposits of depository institutions	29.3
Coins	0.5	U.S. Treasury deposits	4.4
Other assets	62.8	Other liabilities	7.2
		Net worth	5.4
Total	$346.3	Total	$346.3

Source: *Federal Reserve Bulletin,* January 1993.

Turning now to the other side of the balance sheet, we can see that *Federal Reserve notes in circulation account for over three-fourths of the Fed's liabilities.* Just as the goldsmiths issued notes, the Fed issues financial claims on itself. These notes represent *accounting* liabilities to the Fed because note holders can redeem them with the Fed. As we have said, however, since we have a fiat money system, those who redeem notes are simply given other notes, so *these notes are not true economic liabilities.*

Since banks can ask to have their reserves on deposit with the Fed returned to them at any time, these deposits are another liability of the Fed. These deposits are an important part of bank reserves and facilitate the check-clearing process, which will be examined shortly. The deposits of the U.S. Treasury are also a liability of the Fed.

Example About 95 percent of Fed earnings have been turned over to the Treasury since the Fed's establishment.

The two primary assets held by the Federal Reserve banks—U.S. securities and discount loans—earn interest for Reserve banks, whereas their two primary liabilities—Federal Reserve notes and reserves deposited by banks—require no interest payments by Reserve banks. *The Fed is therefore both literally and figuratively a money machine. It is literally a money machine because it provides the economy with Federal Reserve notes, and it is figuratively a money machine because its assets earn interest but its liabilities pay no interest.* The Fed finances its normal business expenses with this interest income and turns over any additional income to the U.S. Treasury.

Teaching Tip The Fed also holds deposits for foreign governments, foreign banks, the International Monetary Fund, and the World Bank.

What the balance sheet does not reflect is the Fed's responsibility for the stability of financial markets. The Fed, through its regulation of financial markets, tries to prevent major disruptions and widespread panics. For example, during the stock market crash of 1987, Fed Chairman Alan Greenspan worked behind the scenes to ensure that banks had enough liquidity to provide the essential borrowing needed to calm the panic. In 1989, when a similar crash threatened, the Fed again stepped in to ensure the necessary liquidity.

The Fed is also an active trader in foreign exchange markets. Foreign currency operations are carried out by the New York Fed's foreign trading desk in cooperation with the U.S. Treasury. Some of the "other" Fed assets listed in Exhibit 7 are securities issued by foreign governments. For example, in order to influence foreign exchange rates, the Fed can sell German securities and receive marks in exchange. The marks can then be used to buy dollars from a U.S. bank. These transactions increase both the supply of marks and the demand for dollars, thereby affecting the exchange rate between the two currencies.

Independence of the Fed

Federal law requires the Fed "to promote effectively the goals of maximum employment, stable prices, and moderate long-term interest rates." The law leaves it up to the Fed how best to pursue these goals. The Fed does not rely on congressional appropriations, so Congress cannot attempt to influence the Fed by withholding funds. In fact, the Fed makes a "profit" of about $20 billion a year, which it turns over to the U.S. Treasury. Thus, although the U.S. president appoints members of the Board of Governors and these appointments must be approved by the Senate, the Fed operates with some independence from the president and the Congress.

Point to Stress Although the Fed must report to Congress, it need not seek Congressional or presidential advice or consent for its actions.

But the president and the Congress at times may try to influence the Fed. By law the Fed must report its monetary policy plans to Congress twice a year and discuss the relation between those plans and the president's objectives. Since Congressional legislation established and authorized the Fed, Congress could rewrite those laws if the Fed seems unresponsive to Congressional concerns. Often Congress tries to pressure the Fed to stimulate the economy by increasing the supply of money. Consider central bank independence around the world in the following case study.

CASE STUDY

Central Bank Independence and Price Stability

Some economists argue that the Fed would do better in the long run if it was committed to the single goal of price stability. Consider the experience in Germany. By law, the Bundesbank, the German central bank, is not subject to instructions from the government or from any other authority. And by law the goal of price stability is given the highest priority. Since 1960, the German inflation rate has been only half the U.S. rate. The story is similar in Japan. Since 1975 there has been a strong commitment by the Japanese central bank to low inflation, and inflation in Japan since 1975 has averaged only half the U.S. rate.

When central banks for seventeen advanced industrial countries are ranked from least independent to most independent, inflation is the lowest in countries with the most independent central banks and highest in countries with the least independent central banks. For example, the most independent central banks are in Germany and Switzerland, and their average inflation rate from 1973 to 1988 was about 3 percent per year. The least independent banks during that period were in Spain, New Zealand, Australia, and Italy, where the rate of inflation averaged 11.5 percent per year. The U.S. central bank is considered relatively independent; our inflation rate, averaging about 6.5 percent between 1973 and 1988, was between the average rates for the most independent and least independent groups.

Australia and New Zealand have recently amended the laws governing their central banks to make price stability the primary goal. Chile and Argentina, developing countries that recently experienced hyperinflation, have tried to establish central bank credibility by legislating more central bank independence. What's more, the Maastricht agreement, which defines the framework for establishing a central bank for the European Community, makes price stability the main objective. Thus, many countries around the world, in pursuit of more price stability, are moving toward a more independent central bank.

Sources: Alberto Alesina and Lawrence Summers, "Central Bank Independence and Macroeconomic Performance: Some Comparative Evidence," Harvard University (mimeo), 1990; and *1991 Annual Report*, Federal Reserve bank of Cleveland.

How Banks Create Money

We are now in a position to examine how an individual bank and the banking system as a whole can affect the supply of money. Since you already have some acquaintance with balance sheets, we will consider only those entries that change. In the process we will also see how the Federal Reserve System can influence the money supply. Our discussion will focus on the behavior of commercial banks because these are the largest and most important of depository institutions, though thrifts can carry out similar activities.

Creating Money Through Excess Reserves

The key variable in determining the nation's money supply is the amount of reserves in the banking system. As we shall see, excess reserves are the raw material the banking system employs to create money. The Fed can influence the amount of excess reserves by buying or selling U.S. government securities, by lending reserves to banks through the discount window, and by changing the required reserve ratio. The most important of these is buying or selling U.S. government securities, an activity called *open-market operations* because the Fed buys or sells these securities in the open market.

Point to Stress
Open-market operations involve buying and selling securities issued *previously* by the Treasury. They are not designed to finance government operations.

Assume there are no excess reserves in the banking system initially and that the reserve requirement on checkable deposits is 10 percent. To start the process rolling, suppose the Federal Reserve purchases a $1,000 U.S. security from Home Bank, increasing Home Bank's reserve account at the district Federal Reserve bank by $1,000. Where does the Fed get these reserves? The Fed creates reserves out of thin air!

Exhibit 8 shows how the balance sheets for the Fed and for Home Bank *change* as a result of the transaction. U.S. securities are up by $1,000 at the Fed and down that same amount at Home Bank; both changes are on the asset

EXHIBIT 8

Changes in the Fed's and Home Bank's Balance Sheets After the Fed Buys $1,000 in Securities from Home Bank

Fed's Balance Sheet

Assets		Liabilities and Net Worth	
U.S. securities	+ 1,000	Home Bank deposits	+ 1,000

Home Bank's Balance Sheet

Assets		Liabilities and Net Worth	
Deposits with Fed	+ 1,000		
U.S. securities	– 1,000		

Point to Stress Although legal reserves have increased by $1,000, required reserves are unchanged.

side of the ledger. Home Bank's deposits with the Fed are also up by $1,000, which shows up as an asset for Home Bank but a liability for the Fed. Home Bank's balance sheet indicates that it has simply exchanged one asset, U.S. securities, for another asset, reserves on deposit with the Fed. So far the money supply has not changed because neither U.S. securities nor Home Bank's reserves at the Fed are part of the money supply. Nor have Home Bank's total assets changed. But the increase in Home Bank's reserves can fuel an increase in the money supply, as we will observe in the following series of rounds.

ROUND ONE. After selling the security, Home Bank has $1,000 in excess reserves. The opportunity cost of holding excess reserves is the forgone interest that could be earned by putting them to some interest-earning use. So Home Bank will put excess reserves to work. Suppose Home Bank is your regular bank and you apply for a $1,000 student loan to help pay tuition. Home Bank approves your loan and consequently increases your checking account by $1,000. *Home Bank has converted your promise to repay the loan, your IOU, into a $1,000 checkable deposit, thereby increasing the money supply by $1,000.* Home Bank has created money from your promise—it has created money out of thin air. Exhibit 9 shows how Home Bank's balance sheet changes as a result of the loan. On the asset side, loans increase by $1,000 because your IOU becomes an asset to the bank. On the liability side, checkable deposits increase by $1,000 because Home Bank has increased your account by that amount. Exhibit 9 also illustrates how your balance sheet changes. On the asset side, your checkable deposits are now up by $1,000. On the other side, you now owe Home Bank the loan, increasing your liabilities by $1,000.

Point to Stress Any net change in assets must be balanced by an equal net change in liabilities and net worth.

ROUND TWO. When you write a $1,000 check to your college, your college promptly deposits this check in its checking account at College Bank. College Bank then increases the college's account by $1,000 and presents the

Exhibit 9

Changes in Home Bank's Balance Sheet and Your Balance Sheet After Home Bank Lends You $1,000

Home Bank's Balance Sheet

Assets		Liabilities and Net Worth	
Loans	+ 1,000	Checkable deposits	+ 1,000

Your Balance Sheet

Assets		Liabilities and Net Worth	
Checkable deposits	+ 1,000	Loan from Home Bank	+ 1,000

check to the Fed. The Fed reduces Home Bank's reserve deposits by $1,000 and increases College Bank's reserve deposits by the same amount. The Fed then sends the check to Home Bank, which reduces your checkable deposits by $1,000. The Fed has cleared your check by settling the claim that College Bank had on Home Bank. Consider the balance sheets in Exhibit 10, which reflect the changes after your check clears. Home Bank's deposits at the Fed and checkable deposits are both down by $1,000. And College Bank's deposits at the Fed and checkable deposits are both up by $1,000. Checkable deposits have simply shifted from Home Bank to College Bank.

Let's review what has happened to Home Bank's balance sheet. Home Bank initially exchanged U.S. securities for excess reserves (Exhibit 8), then extended a loan to you by increasing your checking account by $1,000 (Exhibit 9). When the check you wrote for tuition cleared, Home Bank lost its

Exhibit 10

Changes in Home Bank's and College Bank's Balance Sheets After Your Tuition Check to College Bank Clears

Home Bank's Balance Sheet

Assets		Liabilities and Net Worth	
Deposits with Fed	– 1,000	Checkable deposits	– 1,000

College Bank's Balance Sheet

Assets		Liabilities and Net Worth	
Deposits with Fed	+ 1,000	Checkable deposits	+ 1,000

Teaching Tip In Exhibit 8, Home Bank has no change in checkable deposits. Therefore, any change in deposits with the Fed represents excess reserves. In Exhibit 10, College Bank's checkable deposits rise. Therefore, the change in excess reserves is less than the change in deposits with the Fed.

Point to Stress To this point, Home Bank has created $1,000 worth of new money and College Bank has created $900 worth of money.

excess reserves to College Bank and reduced your checking account by $1,000 (Exhibit 10). Home Bank, by selling U.S. securities to the Fed and lending out the excess reserves, has exchanged one asset, U.S. securities, for another asset, your IOU. But in the process the reserves in the banking system and the money supply have increased, for College Bank's reserves and checkable deposits are now up by $1,000, and checkable deposits are money.

So College Bank has $1,000 more in reserves on deposit with the Fed. After setting aside $100, or 10 percent of your college's increase in deposits, as required reserves, College Bank has $900 in excess reserves, which can be loaned, used to purchase some other interest-bearing asset, or simply left idle. Suppose these excess reserves are loaned to an enterprising business student who plans to open an all-night bait-and-doughnut shop to lure early morning anglers on their way to a nearby lake. College Bank extends the loan by providing the entrepreneur with a checking account balance of $900. As shown in Exhibit 11, College Bank's assets are up by the $900 loan, and its liabilities are up by the $900 increase in checkable deposits extended as a loan to the business student. *College Bank has converted the student's promise to repay the loan into money.*

Suppose the student spends the $900 on equipment at Wholesale Hardware, which deposits the check in its bank, Merchants Trust. Merchants Trust increases the hardware store's checkable deposits by $900 and sends the check to the Fed for clearance. The Fed increases Merchants Trust's reserve deposits by $900 and decreases College Bank's reserve deposits by the same amount. The Fed then sends the check to College Bank, which reduces the borrower's checkable deposit account by $900.

Exhibit 12 shows the effects of these transactions on the balance sheets of the two banks. As you can see, deposits at the Fed and checkable deposits are down by $900 at College Bank and up by that amount at Merchants Trust. Checkable deposits in the banking system at this point are $1,900 over what they were before we started: your college has $1,000 more in checkable deposits at College Bank because you paid tuition, and the hardware store has $900 more in its account at Merchants Trust because of the enterprising student's equipment purchase.

ROUND THREE AND BEYOND. Merchants Trust holds $90 of the $900 deposited as required reserves, which leaves $810 in excess reserves. Suppose this $810 is loaned to an unscrupulous English major who is starting a new

EXHIBIT 11

Changes in College Bank's Balance Sheet After the Bank Makes a $900 Loan

Assets		Liabilities and Net Worth	
Loans	+ 900	Checkable deposits	+ 900

EXHIBIT 12

Changes in College Bank's and Merchants Trust's Balance Sheets After the Borrower's Check for $900 to Hardware Store Clears

College Bank's Balance Sheet

Assets		Liabilities and Net Worth	
Deposits with Fed	– 900	Checkable deposits	– 900

Merchants Trust's Balance Sheet

Assets		Liabilities and Net Worth	
Deposits with Fed	+ 900	Checkable deposits	+ 900

Point to Stress Total money created to this point is $1,000 by Home Bank, $900 by College, and $810 by Merchants Trust.

venture called "Term Papers 'R' Us." The English major hopes to sell research to students with more money than brains. Exhibit 13 shows that Merchants Trust's assets are up by $810 in loans, and its liabilities are up by the same amount in checkable deposits.

The loan of $810 is spent at the college bookstore for a complete set of *Cliffs Notes.* The bookstore then deposits the check in its account at Fidelity Bank. Fidelity Bank credits the bookstore's checkable deposits with $810 and sends the check to the Fed for clearance. The Fed reduces Merchants Trust's reserves by $810 and increases Fidelity Bank's by the same amount. The Fed then sends the check to Merchants Trust, which reduces the English major's checkable deposits by $810. Exhibit 14 presents the changes in the balance sheets of Merchants Trust and Fidelity Bank after the check clears. Deposits at the Fed and checkable deposits are down by $810 at Merchants Trust and up by the same amount at Fidelity Bank.

Point to Stress The $729 loan represents the creation of more money. Total money created to this point is $3,439.

At this point checkable deposits in the banking system, and the money supply in the economy, are up by $2,710: your college's $1,000 checkable deposit at College Bank, plus the hardware store's $900 checkable deposit at Merchants Trust, plus the bookstore's $810 checkable deposit at Fidelity Bank. We could continue the credit expansion process with Fidelity Bank, which sets aside $81 in required reserves and uses the $729 in excess reserves as a basis for additional loans, but by now you get the idea.

EXHIBIT 13

Changes in Merchants Trust's Balance Sheet After an $810 Loan to English Major

Assets		Liabilities and Net Worth	
Loans	+ 810	Checkable deposits	+ 810

EXHIBIT 14

Changes in Merchants Trust's and Fidelity Bank's Balance Sheets After English Major's Check to Bookstore Clears

Merchants Trust's Balance Sheet

Assets		Liabilities and Net Worth	
Deposits with Fed	− 810	Checkable deposits	− 810

Fidelity Bank's Balance Sheet

Assets		Liabilities and Net Worth	
Deposits with Fed	+ 810	Checkable deposits	+ 810

Notice the pattern of deposits and loans emerging from the analysis. Each time a bank receives new deposits, 10 percent is set aside to satisfy the reserve requirement. The rest becomes excess reserves, which can be lent, used to purchase government securities, or left idle. In our example excess reserves were lent and then spent by the borrower. This spending became another bank's checkable deposits, thereby generating excess reserves to fund still more loans. Thus, the excess reserves created initially by the Federal Reserve's purchase of U.S. securities were passed from one bank to the next in the chain. Each bank set aside 10 percent of new deposits as required reserves and loaned out the remaining 90 percent.

Point to Stress
Throughout the example, the total new reserves in the system always equals the initial $1,000 created by the Fed. For example, by the end of round 3, Home Bank retains none of the new reserves, College Bank retains $100, Merchants Trust retains $90, and Fidelity Bank holds $810.

An individual bank in a banking system can lend no more than its excess reserves because borrowers usually spend the amount borrowed. When a check clears, it reduces the reserves at one bank but does not reduce reserves for the banking system as a whole. A check drawn against one account will typically be deposited in another account—if not in the same bank, then in another. Thus, when a bank makes a loan and creates checkable deposits, the excess reserves on which that loan was based usually find their way back into the banking system. The recipient bank uses the new deposit to extend more loans and create more checkable deposits. The potential expansion of checkable deposits in the banking system therefore equals some multiple of the initial increase in excess reserves. Our example assumes that banks do not allow excess reserves to remain idle and that the public does not choose to hold some of the newly created money as cash.

Teaching Tip
Changing the required reserve ratio changes excess reserves without affecting total reserves. Open-market operations and changes in the discount rate alter excess reserves by altering total reserves.

Summary of Rounds

To review: *The initial and most important step in the process described in the preceding section is the Fed's injection of $1,000 in new reserves into the banking system.* In our example this resulted from the Fed's $1,000 purchase of U.S. securities, but Home Bank's excess reserves would also increase if Home

Teaching Tip Advanced students may be interested to know that if a bank knows that a certain percentage of loan-created deposits will be retained, it can lend an amount greater than its excess reserves. For example, if Home Bank generally retains 25 percent of loan-created deposits, it can lend $1,290 after it sells its $1,000 security. Seventy-five percent, or about $968, will be withdrawn, leaving about $322 ($1,290 – $968) in checkable deposits. The remaining deposits with the Fed of $32 ($1,000 – $968) will cover required reserves.

Point to Stress In Exhibit 15, the change in M1 equals the $10,000 change in checkable deposits supported by the $1,000 in new reserves. Note that $1,000 equals the reserve requirement times new checkable deposits. If the initial $1,000 loan by Home Bank is added to the numbers, the change in checkable deposits matches the amount of new loans.

Bank borrowed $1,000 in discount loans from the Fed, or if the Fed freed up $1,000 in excess reserves by lowering the reserve requirement.

Home Bank uses this $1,000 in excess reserves to offer you a college loan. You pay your tuition bill, and your college deposits the check in its bank. This deposit precipitates a series of rounds that expand the money supply. These rounds are summarized in Exhibit 15, where the banks are listed along the left-hand margin. Column (1) lists the increase in checkable deposits (and reserves) at each bank, column (2) lists the increase in required reserves resulting from the increase in checkable deposits, and column (3) lists the increase in loans each bank extends as a result of the increase in excess reserves. As you can see, the change in loans equals the change in checkable deposits minus the change in required reserves. Each bank loans out an amount equal to its excess reserves.

The increase in College Bank's checkable deposits is the change in the money supply arising from the first round. This $1,000 deposit translates into $100 in required reserves leaving $900 in new loans. The $900 lent by College Bank ends up as checkable deposits in Merchants Trust, which sets aside $90 in required reserves and lends the balance of $810. The loan is spent and is deposited in an account at Fidelity Bank, which sets aside $81 as reserves and lends the balance. Theoretically, the process will continue until there are no more excess reserves in the system to serve as a basis for additional loans.

The banking system increases the money supply by a multiple of new reserves and thereby appears to perform magic. Can banks simply create credit balances out of thin air? As we have seen, the answer is yes. However, since people borrow money not to hold idle checkable deposits but to spend the borrowed funds, banks must have enough excess reserves to back up their loans. Credit expansion stops when the new reserves introduced into the banking system have been converted into required reserves. In our example, $1,000 in new reserves was introduced when the Fed purchased U.S. securities from Home Bank. The credit expansion process stops when the increase in required reserves resulting from credit expansion equals $1,000. Because

EXHIBIT 15

Summary of the Credit Expansion Process Resulting from the Fed's Purchase of $1,000 in U.S. Securities from Home Bank

Bank	Increase in Checkable Deposits (1)	Increase in Required Reserves (2)	Increase in Loans (3) = (1) – (2)
1. College Bank	$ 1,000	$ 100	$ 900
2. Merchants Trust	900	90	810
3. Fidelity Bank	810	81	729
All remaining rounds	7,290	729	6,561
Totals	$10,000	$ 1,000	$ 9,000

the entire process begins with the Fed creating $1,000 in reserves out of thin air, the Fed can rightfully claim that "The buck starts here," which is a slogan on New York Fed T-shirts.

Some Other Possibilities

Suppose that instead of buying the $1,000 worth of U.S. securities from Home Bank, the Fed buys them from a securities dealer and pays by issuing $1,000 in Federal Reserve notes. Exhibit 16 shows the resulting change in the Fed's and the dealer's balance sheets. The Fed acquires assets of $1,000 in securities; the Fed's liabilities increase by $1,000 in the form of new Federal Reserve notes in circulation. The securities dealer's balance sheet simply reflects a change in the mix of financial assets, with securities down by $1,000 and currency up by the same amount. The Fed has increased the money supply by $1,000 by exchanging Federal Reserve notes, which become part of the money supply when in the hands of the public, for U.S. securities, which are not part of the money supply. Once the securities dealer puts this cash into a checkable deposit—or spends the cash, so the money ends up in someone else's checkable deposit—the banking system's credit expansion process will be off and running.

Teaching Tip When the Fed buys the $1,000 security from the nonbanking public, the direct increase in M1 is $1,000. Subsequent deposit of these funds creates excess reserves of $900, which supports an additional $9,000 increase in M1.

Recall that when the Fed buys U.S. securities from banks, bank reserves are increased; *the excess reserves serve as fuel for the money expansion process.* When the Fed buys U.S. securities from the nonbanking public, such as securities dealers, the money supply is increased directly. When deposited in banks, these new deposits generate excess reserves to fuel the money expansion process. Thus, whether the Fed buys securities from banks or from the public, the purchase sooner or later increases bank reserves, thereby promoting the expansion of credit.

EXHIBIT 16

Changes in the Fed's and Securities Dealer's Balance Sheets After the Fed Purchases $1,000 in Securities from the Dealer and Pays with $1,000 in Federal Reserve Notes

Fed's Balance Sheet

Assets		Liabilities and Net Worth	
U.S. securities	+ 1,000	Federal Reserve notes in circulation	+ 1,000

Securities Dealer's Balance Sheet

Assets		Liabilities and Net Worth	
U.S. securities	– 1,000		
Cash	+ 1,000		

Point to Stress
When the Fed sells securities, reserves drop as the Fed reduces banks' deposits with the Fed. Reserves drop immediately if the sale is to a bank. If the sale is to the nonbanking public, reserves drop when the buyer's check clears through the Fed.

The Fed expands the money supply when it purchases U.S. securities, but it also expands the money supply whenever it pays for anything else, from the salaries of the Board of Governors to the phone bill for the securities trading desk. Conversely, the Fed reduces the money supply when it sells U.S. securities, but it also reduces the money supply whenever it sells anything else, from Fed publications to used furniture. In this chapter we limited discussion of the Fed's buying and selling to U.S. securities because open-market operations represent the overwhelming share of the Fed's total buying and selling. Since the Fed is the only bank with the authority to print money, it is the only bank not constrained by reserve requirements. Indeed, the expressions "required reserves" and "excess reserves" do not apply to the Fed. The Fed can issue whatever money the economy needs.

Excess Reserves, Reserve Requirements, and Credit Expansion

One way the banking system as a whole eliminates excess reserves is by expanding credit. With a 10 percent reserve requirement, an initial injection of $1,000 in new reserves by the Fed could support a maximum of $10,000 in new checkable deposits in the banking system as a whole, *assuming no bank holds excess reserves and nobody withdraws cash.* We can think of the $1,000 injection as the source of the $1,000 in reserves required to support the expansion of $10,000 in new checkable deposits.

Money multiplier The multiple by which the money supply increases as a result of an increase in excess reserves in the banking system

Simple money multiplier The reciprocal of the required reserve ratio, or $1/r$

The multiple by which the money supply increases as a result of an increase in the banking system's excess reserves is called the **money multiplier**. The **simple money multiplier** equals the reciprocal of the required reserve ratio. The simple money multiplier is therefore $1/r$, where r is the reserve requirement. In our example the reserve requirement was 10 percent, or 0.10, so the reciprocal is 1/0.10, which equals 10. The formula for the multiple expansion of checkable deposits can be written as

Change in checkable deposits = change in excess reserves × 1/*r*

If banks hold no excess reserves and nobody withdraws cash, then total reserves must equal checkable deposits times the reserve requirement. Or, total reserves divided by the reserve requirement must equal checkable deposits. Since we assume that banks are "all loaned up," any increase by the Fed in bank reserves is an increase in excess reserves. Thus, if the Fed increases bank reserves, the potential increase in checkable deposits equals the increase in excess reserves divided by the reserve requirement, which is the multiple expansion formula just presented. The simple multiplier assumes that banks hold no excess reserves and the public withdraws no cash.

Point to Stress The simple money multiplier calculates the maximum possible increase in the money supply.

The higher the reserve requirement, the more of each deposit that must be held as reserves, so the less that is available in excess reserves, and the smaller the money multiplier. If the reserve requirement were 20 percent instead of 10 percent, each bank would have to set aside twice as much for required reserves. The simple money multiplier in this case would be 1/0.20 = 5, and the potential increase in checkable deposits resulting from an initial $1,000 increase in excess reserves would therefore be $1,000 × 5 = $5,000. Deposits in the banking system could be expanded by only half as much as when the reserve requirement was 10 percent. *Excess reserves fuel the deposit expansion process, and a higher reserve requirement drains this fuel from the banking system, thereby reducing the money multiplier.*

On the other hand, with a reserve requirement of only 5 percent, banks would set aside less for required reserves and would consequently be able to make more loans because they would have greater excess reserves. The simple money multiplier in that case would be 1/0.05 = 20. With $1,000 in new reserves and a 5 percent reserve requirement, the banking system could increase the money supply by $1,000 × 20 = $20,000.

In summary, it all begins with an injection of new reserves into the banking system by the Fed. An individual bank loans only an amount no greater than its excess reserves. The proceeds of this loan are redeposited in the banking system and serve as the basis for additional excess reserves. An increase in bank reserves gives rise to a multiple expansion of checkable deposits, and checkable deposits are money. *The fractional reserve requirement is the key to the multiple expansion of checkable deposits in the banking system.* If each deposit had to be backed by 100 percent reserves, each $1 injected into reserves could create at most a $1 expansion of the money supply; the Fed, by purchasing securities, reducing the discount rate, or lowering the required reserve ratio, could still help create excess reserves that would result in an expanded money supply, but that expansion would amount to at most no more than excess reserves, rather than a multiple of excess reserves.

Teaching Tip If the nonbanking public converts currency in circulation into checkable deposits, this also creates excess reserves and fuels an expansion of the money supply. However, the expansion is smaller than if the Fed injects reserves, since the initial change in excess reserves is smaller.

Now that we have been through the entire money expansion process, we can return to the beginning and consider what would happen if Home Bank, instead of extending loans, used its excess reserves to purchase U.S. securities. If Home Bank purchased U.S. securities from the public, Home Bank's payment would eventually get deposited in a bank, and these new deposits will fuel the money creation process. For the money multiplier to operate, the bank need not use excess reserves in a specific way; the bank could use them to pay all its employees a Christmas bonus, for that matter. *As long as the bank does not allow excess reserves to sit idle or use them to simply buy government securities from the Fed, these excess reserves can fund an expansion of the money supply.*

Teaching Tip Cash holdings as a percent of deposits vary seasonally. For example, currency holdings tend to increase during the Christmas shopping season. Leakages from the M1 money-creation process also occur as the nonbanking public decides to hold more of its funds in time or savings deposits—which are excluded from M1.

Limitations of Money Expansion

Various leakages from the multiple expansion process tend to reduce the size of the money multiplier, which is why we refer to $1/r$ as the *simple* money multiplier. Here we will consider leakages into cash and into excess reserves. Our example assumed that people do not choose to hold a portion of the new deposits in cash. *To the extent that people prefer to hold cash, the actual money multiplier is less than the simple money multiplier because cash withdrawals reduce reserves in the banking system.* With a reduction in reserves, banks have less ability to extend loans or buy securities. Likewise, if banks chose to allow their

Teaching Tip
Banks' willingness to hold excess reserves varies as changes in interest rates alter the opportunity cost of retaining reserves. Because bank and nonbank behaviors vary, the money multiplier is not a constant.

excess reserves to sit idle, these idle reserves would not fuel expansion of the money supply. However, since banks earn no interest on idle reserves but do earn interest on loans and investments, banks carefully monitor their excess reserves, keeping them as low as possible.

Multiple Contraction of Money and Credit

We have already outlined the mechanics of the banking system, so the story of how the Federal Reserve System can reduce bank reserves, thereby reducing banks' ability to increase loans, can be a brief one. Again, we begin with no excess reserves and a reserve requirement of 10 percent. Suppose that rather than buying U.S. securities, the Fed *sells* Home Bank $1,000 worth of U.S. securities. Home Bank pays with a check written against its reserve account at the district Federal Reserve bank. The Fed therefore reduces Home Bank's reserve account by $1,000. As Exhibit 17 indicates, the Fed's assets decline by $1,000 in U.S. securities. The Fed's liabilities decline by $1,000 in Home Bank's reserve deposits. Home Bank's balance sheet indicates the change in the composition of assets: its deposits with the Fed are down by $1,000, and its securities are up by that amount.

Since Home Bank had no excess reserves at the outset, something has to give. To replenish reserves, Home Bank can recall loans, sell some other asset, or borrow additional reserves. Suppose Home Bank calls in loans amounting to $1,000, and those who repay the loans do so with checks written against College Bank. When the checks clear, Home Bank's reserves are up by $1,000, just enough to satisfy its reserve requirement, but College Bank's reserves are down by $1,000. Since we assumed that there were no excess reserves at the outset, the loss of $1,000 in reserves leaves College Bank short of its required reserves. Specifically, in keeping with the legal reserve requirement, College Bank had $100 in required reserves supporting the $1,000

EXHIBIT 17

Changes in Balance Sheets After the Fed Sells $1,000 in Securities to Home Bank

Fed's Balance Sheet

Assets		Liabilities and Net Worth	
U.S. securities	– 1,000	Home Bank deposits	– 1,000

Home Bank's Balance Sheet

Assets		Liabilities and Net Worth	
U.S. securities	+ 1,000		
Deposits with Fed	– 1,000		

checkable deposits, so its reserves are now $900 below the required level. College Bank must therefore recall $900 in loans or otherwise try to replenish the $900 in required reserves.

Point to Stress A contraction of the money supply can also be fueled by an increase in the required reserve ratio.

And so it goes down the line. The Federal Reserve's sale of U.S. securities reduces bank reserves, forcing banks to recall loans or to replenish reserves somehow. *The maximum possible effect is to reduce the money supply by the amount of the original reduction in bank reserves times the simple money multiplier, which again equals 1 divided by the reserve requirement, or 1/r.* In our example the Fed's sale of $1,000 in U.S. securities to Home Bank could utimately reduce the money supply by up to $10,000.

Change in the Discount Rate

The focus thus far has been on open-market operations because this activity represents the primary tool of monetary policy. But there are other tools. The discount rate is the interest rate the Fed charges on loans to banks. The Fed can decrease or increase the discount rate as a way to encourage or discourage borrowing from the Fed. When the Fed decreases the discount rate, other things constant, borrowing from the Fed becomes cheaper, so the quantity of discount loans demanded increases. As borrowing increases, excess reserves in the banking system increase. These excess reserves serve as fuel for an expansion of the money supply. Thus, *a lower discount rate tends to expand the money supply.*

Teaching Tip Lowering the discount rate may not expand the money supply if the banks do not perceive profitable investment opportunities on which to use such borrowed funds.

On the other hand, an increase in the discount rate makes borrowing from the Fed less attractive, so the quantity of discount loans demanded decreases. As loans decrease, reserves in the banking system decrease. As reserves decrease so do excess reserves, reducing the banking system's ability to expand the money supply. Thus, *a higher discount rate tends to decrease the money supply.*

CONCLUSION

Banks play a unique role in the economy because they can transform someone's IOU into a checkable deposit, and a checkable deposit is money. The banking system's ability to expand the money supply depends on the amount of excess reserves in the system. Note the control that the Fed has over the money creation process. Through open-market operations, the Fed can vary the supply of new reserves by buying or selling U.S. securities. In our example it was the purchase of $1,000 worth of U.S. securities that started the ball rolling. The Fed can also increase reserves by lowering the discount rate enough to stimulate bank borrowing from the Fed. And by reducing the required reserve ratio, the Fed can not only create excess reserves in the banking system but increase the money multiplier. In practice, the Fed rarely changes the reserve requirement because of the disruptive effect of such a change on the banking system. And the Fed uses changes in the discount rate more as a signal of its policy goals than as a means of altering the money supply. *The Fed relies primarily on open-market operations to control the money supply.* In the next chapter we will consider the effects of the money supply on the economy.

SUMMARY

1. Banks are unlike other businesses in that they can turn a borrower's IOU into money—they can create money. Banks match the varying desires of savers in terms of amount and duration with the varying desires of borrowers. Banks evaluate loan applications and diversify portfolios of assets to minimize the risk to any one saver.
2. The money supply is most narrowly defined as M1, which consists of currency held by the nonbanking public plus checkable deposits and travelers checks. Broader monetary aggregates include other kinds of deposits. M2 includes M1 plus savings deposits, small time deposits, and money market mutual funds. M3 includes M2 plus large time deposits, or what are called negotiable certificates of deposit.
3. In acquiring portfolios of assets, banks attempt to maximize profits while simultaneously maintaining liquidity sufficient to satisfy depositors' demands for funds. There is a tradeoff between profitability and liquidity.
4. Any single bank can expand the money supply by the amount of its excess reserves. For the banking system as a whole, the maximum expansion of the money supply equals excess reserves in the banking system times the money multiplier. The simple money multiplier equals the reciprocal of the reserve ratio. The money multiplier is reduced to the extent that banks choose to hold some excess reserves as idle cash balances or the public wishes to withdraw cash from the banking system.
5. The key to changes in the money supply is the effect of the Fed's actions on excess reserves in the banking system. To pursue an expansionary monetary policy, the Fed can buy U.S. securities, reduce the discount rate, or lower the reserve requirement. To pursue a tight monetary policy, the Fed can sell U.S. securities, increase the discount rate, or increase the reserve requirement. The most important monetary tool for the Fed is open-market operations—buying or selling U.S. securities.

QUESTIONS AND PROBLEMS

1. (Demand Deposits) Checks are not used in some countries, such as Japan and Taiwan. What costs are associated with relying only on currency? What benefits might there be? Why do you think such countries elect to avoid demand deposits?
2. (Near Moneys) Coca-Cola is a good substitute for Pepsi. Coffee is probably a poor substitute. How can the same principle be applied to the various types of money? Are a hundred pennies a perfect substitute for a dollar bill?
3. (Bank Balance Sheets) Show how each of the following initially affects bank assets and liabilities. Assume a required reserve ratio of 0.05.
   a. The Fed purchases $10 million worth of securities from banks.
   b. The Fed loans the banking system $5 million.
   c. The required reserve ratio is raised to 0.10.
4. (Reserves) Technically bank reserves are defined as vault cash plus bank deposits held at the Federal Reserve. These can be divided between required reserves and excess reserves. Usually banks hold some positive amount of excess reserves. During the Great Depression, excess reserves rose dramatically. What reasons can you suggest for this increase?
5. (Reserve Requirements) Explain why a reduction in the required reserve ratio cannot increase reserves in the banking system. Is the same true of discount loans from the Fed? What would happen if the Fed bought securities from or sold securities to the banking system?

6. (Money Supply) Why are there different measures of money (for example, M1 and M2)? Could one measure of money rise while another measure fell? How?
7. (Money Supply) Suppose that $1,000 is moved from a savings account at a commercial bank to a checking account at the same bank. Which of the following statements will be true and which will be false?
   a. The level of currency will initially fall.
   b. The level of M1 will initially rise.
   c. The level of M2 will initially rise.
   d. The level of bank reserves will increase.
8. (Money Supply) Often it is claimed that banks create money by making loans. How can private banks create money? Isn't the government the only institution that can legally create money?
9. (Credit Cards) Many people have complained recently about the high interest rates consumers are being charged for the use of credit cards. What are the arguments for and against the high rates?
10. (Money Multiplier) Suppose that the Federal Reserve lowers the required reserve ratio from 0.10 to 0.05. How will this affect the money multiplier, assuming that excess reserves are held to zero and there are no currency leakages?
11. (Bank Balance Sheet) Show how each of the following would affect a bank's balance sheet.
    a. Someone makes a $10,000 deposit.
    b. The bank makes a $3,000 cash loan.
    c. The bank makes a line-of-credit loan of $1,000 by establishing a checking account for $1,000.
    d. The line-of-credit loan gets spent.
    e. The bank has to write off a loan because the borrower defaults.
12. (Bank Management) Explain why a bank's manager must strike a balance between liquidity and profitability on the bank's balance sheet.
13. (Money Creation) Suppose Bank A, which faces a reserve requirement of 10 percent, receives a $1,000 deposit.
    a. Assuming it wishes to hold no excess reserves, determine how much the bank should lend. Show your answer on Bank A's balance sheet.
    b. Assuming that the loan shown in Bank A's balance sheet is redeposited in Bank B, show the changes in Bank B's balance sheet as it lends out the maximum possible.
    c. Repeat this process for Banks C, D, and E.
    d. Using the simple money multiplier, calculate the total change in the money supply resulting from the $1,000 initial deposit.
    e. Calculate the changes in the balance sheets for Banks A, B, C, D, and E if each wished to hold 5 percent excess reserves. How would holding this level of excess reserves affect the total change in the money supply?
14. (Reserve Requirements) As part of the Monetary Control Act of 1980, the Fed was given the power to set reserve requirements for *all* depository institutions. Because the effect was to increase the reserve ratio for many institutions, the changes were phased in over a seven-year period. Why do you think such a long phase-in period was selected?
15. (Bank Management) In essence, banks "borrow" from their depositors and loan out the money. Although the loans that banks make are often long-term loans, banks promise depositors immediate access to their accounts. How can they do this? What feature of depositor behavior are they relying on?
16. (Bank Management) Look at the consolidated balance sheet of the banking industry in Exhibit 6. What kinds of changes in the mix of assets and liabilities would you expect to occur if banks expect interest rates to increase in the future? Explain.
17. (Fed Balance Sheet) Exhibit 7 shows the Fed's balance sheet. According to the balance sheet, what are the Fed's sources of income? Which source is most important?
18. (Money Creation) The Monetary Control Act of 1980 gave the Fed the right to set reserve requirements for all depository institutions offering checkable deposits. How do you think this changed the Fed's ability to control the money supply?
19. (Money Multiplier) The text suggests that if excess reserves are held by banks instead of being loaned out, and cash is held by the public, the size of the money multiplier will be reduced. These factors are not constant. Suggest some reasons for why they vary.
20. (Central Bank Independence) One source of independence for the Fed, as suggested in Chapter 12, is the length of term for members of the Board of Governors. Given that the Fed's operating expenses are less than $1.5 billion, is there anything in Exhibit 7 that suggests another reason why the Fed can remain independent of Congress?
21. (Central Bank Independence) How would a return to some form of commodity-based money, as advocated by some, affect the independence of the Fed?

CHAPTER 14

MONETARY THEORY AND POLICY

Point to Stress Monetary policy refers to changes in the supply of money made in order to influence aggregate economic activity.

Monetary policy Regulation of the money supply by the Fed in order to influence aggregate economic activity; the Fed's role in supplying money to the economy

Monetary theory The study of the effect of money on the economy

Thus far we have focused on how money is created in the banking system. We have established that the Federal Reserve can influence the supply of money mainly through its control over excess reserves. How does the supply of money in the economy affect your chances of finding a job, your ability to finance a new car, the interest rate you pay on credit cards, or the ease of securing a student loan and the interest on that loan? The supply of money in the economy affects you in a variety of ways, but to understand those effects we must dig a little deeper.

The Fed's role in supplying money to the economy is called **monetary policy**. The problem is *how* the Fed should use this power. More fundamentally, what is the relation between the supply of money and the economic health of the economy? The study of the effect of money on the economy is called **monetary theory**. A central concern of monetary theory is the effect of the quantity of money on the economy's price level and on the level of output. What have economic theory and the historical record taught us about the relation between the quantity of money in the economy and other macroeconomic variables?

Until now we have not emphasized differences among competing theories of how the economy works. The role of money in the economy, however, remains subject to debate. In this chapter we will consider two approaches to the way money affects the economy: the Keynesian view and the monetarist view. The Keynesian view will be discussed first because we have already used it to develop the concept of aggregate demand. Then we will consider the monetarist view and show how the two views are related. Our discussion will present a simplified version of each theory, ignoring variations among interpretations. Note that although these two theories are different, they are not mutually exclusive. Each traces a different path between changes in the money supply and changes in aggregate demand. Most economists now accept elements of both theories. Topics discussed in this chapter include

- Demand for money
- Supply of money
- Keynesian view of monetary policy
- Monetarist view of monetary policy
- Equation of exchange
- Velocity of money
- Monetary targets

THE DEMAND AND SUPPLY OF MONEY

We begin with an important distinction: the distinction between *money* and *income*. Earlier we explained the difference between stocks and flows. You will recall that a stock is an amount measured at a particular point in time, such as the amount of food in your refrigerator or the amount of gasoline in your car's tank. In contrast, a flow is an amount per unit of time, such as the calories you consume per day or the miles you drive per week.

Teaching Tip The monetary aggregates (M1, M2, M3) introduced in Chapter 13 are also known as the "money stock measures."

Teaching Tip GDP is a flow measure, as are all the national income accounts introduced in Chapter 6.

How much money do you have with you right now? That amount is a stock. Likewise, the *stock* of money in the economy is measured at a particular point in time; it equals the amount people have with them (both currency and travelers checks) and the amount deposited in their checking accounts, plus any money squirreled away in mattresses, piggy banks, or wherever. Income, in contrast, is a *flow*, indicating how many dollars you receive per period of time. Income has little meaning unless the time period is specified. You would not know whether to be impressed that a friend earned $100 unless you knew whether this was earnings per week, per day, or per hour.

The demand for money is a desire to hold a particular amount of money. It may seem odd at first to be talking about the demand for money. You might think that people would demand all the money they could get their hands on. But remember that money, the stock, is not the same as income, the flow. People express their demand for income by selling their labor and other resources. People express their demand for money by holding some of their wealth as money even though there is an opportunity cost of doing so. But we are getting ahead of ourselves. The question we want to ask initially is why people demand money. Why do people have money in their purses or wallets and maintain cash balances in their checking accounts? The most obvious reason people demand money is because it is a convenient medium of exchange. *People demand money to carry out transactions.*

Point to Stress The discussion of the demand for money relies mainly on the M1 definition of money.

The Demand for Money

Because barter represents an insignificant portion of exchange in the modern industrial economy, households, firms, governments, and foreigners need money to conduct their daily transactions. Consumers need money to buy products, and firms need money to pay for resources. When credit cards are involved, the payment of money is delayed briefly, but all accounts must eventually be settled with money. Thus, *money allows people to carry out their economic transactions more easily*.

Transactions demand for money The demand for money to support the exchange of goods and services

The demand for money to support exchange is called the **transactions demand for money**. The greater the number of transactions to be financed in a given period, the greater the quantity of money demanded for transactions. So the more active the economy is—that is, the greater the volume of exchange as reflected by real GDP—the greater the transactions demand for money. Also, the higher the price level, the greater the transactions demand for money. The more things cost on average, the more dollars required to purchase them.

Point to Stress The demand for money refers to demand for both currency and checkable deposits. "Normal" expenditures includes items such as rent and mortgage payments, utility expenses, and car loan payments.

Your transactions demand for money supports both expenditures you expect in the course of your normal economic affairs and certain unexpected expenditures. If you plan to buy lunch tomorrow, you will carry enough money to pay for it. But you also want to be able to pay for other possible contingencies. For example, you could have car trouble or you could come across an unexpected sale on a favorite item. You may have a little extra money with you right now for who knows what. Even *you* don't know.

The transactions demand for money is rooted in money's role as a medium of exchange. As we have seen, however, money is more than a medium of exchange; it is also a store of wealth. Because a household's income and expenditures are not perfectly matched each period, purchasing power is often saved to finance future expenditures. People save for a new home, for college, for retirement. The Keynesian view of money focuses on two ways in which people can store their purchasing power: (1) in the form of money and (2) in the form of other financial assets, such as private and government securities. When people purchase securities and other financial assets, they are lending their money and are paid interest for doing so.

Teaching Tip Generally, the more liquid an asset, the lower its rate of return. However, liquidating assets is not free: converting to cash involves transactions costs such as brokerage fees. Any legal, institutional, or technological change that reduces transactions reduces the demand for money.

The demand for any asset depends on the flow of services it provides. The big advantage of money as a store of wealth is its liquidity: money can be immediately exchanged for whatever is for sale. In contrast, other financial assets, such as private and government securities, must first be *liquidated*, or exchanged for money, which can then be used to buy goods and services. Money, however, has one major disadvantage when compared to other types of financial assets. Money in the form of currency and traveler's checks earns no interest, and the interest rate earned on other types of money, such as checkable deposits, is typically below that earned on other financial assets. So those who hold their wealth in the form of money forgo some interest that could be earned on some other financial asset. For example, suppose a corporation could earn 5 percent more by holding financial assets other than money. The opportunity cost of holding $10 million as money rather than as some other financial asset would amount to over $40,000 per month. *The interest forgone represents the opportunity cost of holding money*. When interest rates are high, as they were during the early 1980s, people move their money out of cash and checkable deposits and into higher-yielding assets, such as private or government securities.

Example Corporations hold checkable deposits in the form of demand deposits, which earn no interest. Demand deposits continue to constitute about one-third of the M1 monetary aggregate.

Money Demand and Interest Rates

When the market rate of interest is low, other things constant, the cost of holding money—the cost of liquidity—is low, so people hold a larger fraction of their wealth in the form of money. When the market rate of interest is high, the cost of holding money is high, so people hold less of their wealth in money and more of their wealth in other financial assets that pay more interest. Thus, other things constant, the quantity of money demanded varies inversely with the market rate of interest.

Teaching Tip Interest rates on assets in M1 tend to be more stable than other interest rates. Thus, the gap between M1 assets and other assets varies directly with increases and decreases in market interest rates.

The money demand curve, D_m, in Exhibit 1 shows the quantity of money people in the economy demand at alternative interest rates, other things constant. *The money demand curve slopes downward because the lower the interest rate, the lower the opportunity cost of holding assets as money.* Movements along the curve reflect the effects of changes in the interest rate on the quantity of money demanded. *Held constant along the curve are the price level and the real GDP. If either increases, the transactions demand for money increases, which shifts the money demand curve to the right.*

Supply of Money and the Equilibrium Interest Rate

The supply of money—the stock of money available in the economy at a particular time—is determined primarily by the Fed through its control over

EXHIBIT 1

Demand for Money

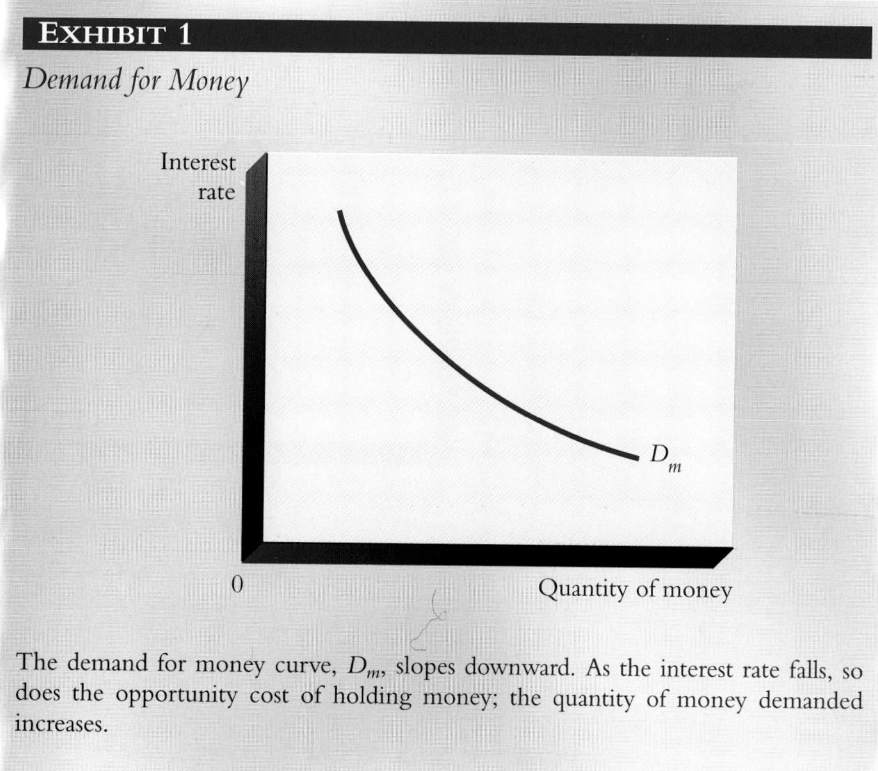

The demand for money curve, D_m, slopes downward. As the interest rate falls, so does the opportunity cost of holding money; the quantity of money demanded increases.

Teaching Tip The money multiplier discussed in Chapter 13 rises as interest rates rise. Therefore, the Fed tries to estimate currency leakages and banks' excess reserve retention rates in determining appropriate actions to meet money supply goals.

excess reserves in the banking system. We can express the supply of money, S_m, as a vertical line, as in Exhibit 2. *By drawing the supply curve as vertical, we are making the simplifying assumption that the quantity of money supplied is independent of the interest rate.* (In reality, as the interest rate increases, banks offer higher interest rates to depositors. Banks are also less inclined to allow excess reserves to sit idle as the interest rate rises. Thus, in reality, the money supply is directly related to the interest rate—that is, the money supply curve tends to slope upward.)

The intersection of the supply of money, S_m, and the demand for money, D_m, determines the equilibrium rate of interest, *i*: the interest rate that equates the quantity of money supplied in the economy with the quantity of money demanded. At interest rates above the equilibrium level, the opportunity cost of holding money is higher, so the quantity of money people want to hold is less than the quantity supplied. At interest rates below the equilibrium level, the op-

EXHIBIT 2

Effect of an Increase in the Money Supply

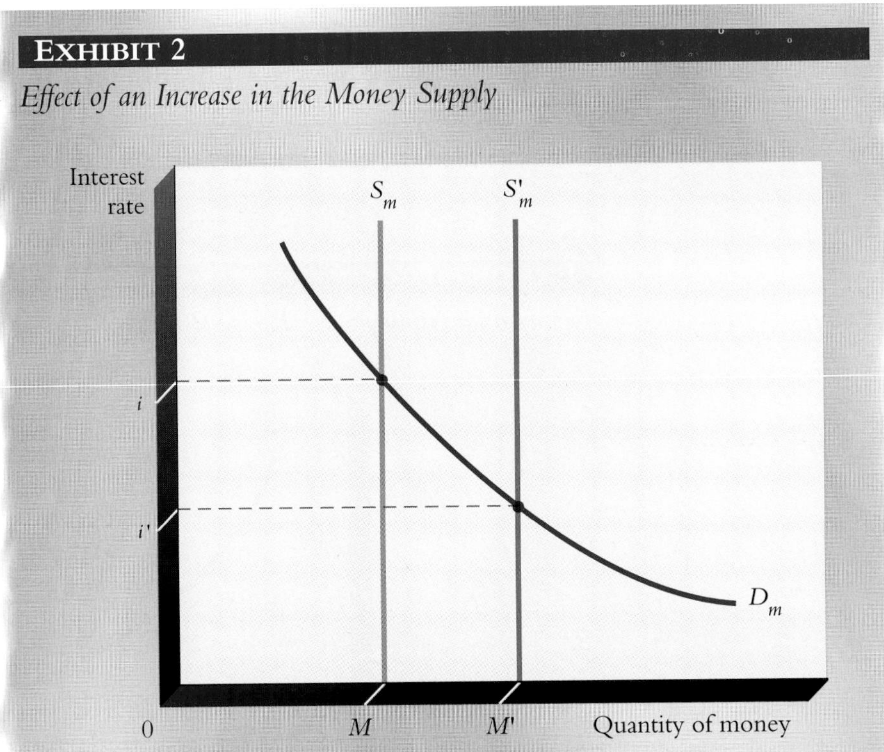

Since the supply of money is determined by the Federal Reserve, it can be represented by a vertical line. The intersection of the supply of money, S_m, and the demand for money, D_m, determines the equilibrium interest rate, *i*. Following an increase in the money supply to S'_m, the quantity of money supplied exceeds the quantity demanded at the original interest rate, *i*. People who are holding more money than they would like attempt to exchange money for bonds or other financial assets. In doing so, they drive the interest rate down to *i′*, where quantity demanded equals the new quantity supplied.

Point to Stress The Fed can buy government securities in the open market, lower the discount rate, or reduce required reserve ratios. Open-market operations are the most frequently used method (usually daily), changing required reserve ratios the least frequently used. (The last change was in December, 1990, on nonpersonal time deposits.)

portunity cost of holding money is lower, so the quantity of money people want to hold is greater than the quantity supplied.

If the Fed increases the money supply, the money supply curve shifts to the right, as shown by the movement from S_m to S'_m in Exhibit 2. The quantity supplied now exceeds the quantity demanded at the original interest rate, *i*. Because of the increased supply of money, there is now more money in the hands of the public, so people are *able* to hold a greater quantity of money. But at interest rate *i* they are *unwilling* to hold that much. Since people are now holding more of their wealth as money than they would like, they attempt to exchange money for financial assets that earn a higher interest. Simply put, people increase the amount of money they are willing to lend. This greater supply of lending reduces the market rate of interest. Because people are more willing to exchange money for other financial assets, the market rate of interest declines. (You may recall from the market for loans introduced back in Chapter 7 that an increase in the supply of loanable funds reduces the market rate of interest.)

Teaching Tip With open-market operations, the Fed also has some direct influence on the interest rate. As the Fed buys securities, security prices rise and their yields drop. There is an inverse relationship between security prices and security yields.

As the interest rate falls, the quantity of money that people are willing to hold increases. The interest rate falls until the quantity demanded just equals the quantity supplied. With the decline in the rate of interest to *i*′ in Exhibit 2, the opportunity cost of holding money falls just enough that the public is willing to demand, or to hold, the increased supply of money. *For a given demand for money, increases in the supply of money lower the rate of interest, and decreases in the supply of money raise the rate of interest.*

Now that you have some idea how money demand and supply determine the market rate of interest, you are ready to see how money fits into the model of the macroeconomy we have developed thus far. Specifically, we will observe how changes in the supply of money affect aggregate demand and equilibrium output.

MONEY AND AGGREGATE DEMAND

Point to Stress Levels of income and employment are determined by the interaction of aggregate supply and aggregate demand. Fiscal policy is designed to affect aggregate demand.

Aggregate demand, as you will recall, is the sum of consumption, planned investment, government purchases, and net exports at various price levels. We saw that through fiscal policy, the federal government tries to influence aggregate demand and the level of income and employment in the economy. Fiscal policy affects aggregate demand directly through changes in government purchases and indirectly through the effects of taxes on consumption, investment, and net exports. In contrast to the more or less direct effect fiscal policy has on aggregate demand, monetary policy is less direct.

Interest Rates and Planned Investment

Monetary policy influences the market rate of interest, which, in turn, affects the level of planned investment, a component of aggregate demand. Let's work through the sequence of causality in a specific economic setting. Suppose the Federal Reserve believes that the economy is operating well below its potential level of output and decides to increase the money supply to stimulate output and employment. Recall that the Fed can expand the money supply by (1) purchasing U.S. government securities, (2) lowering the interest rate at which banks can borrow from the Fed, or (3) lowering reserve requirements.

The four panels of Exhibit 3 trace the links between changes in the money supply and changes in aggregate demand. We begin with the equilibrium rate of interest *i*, which is located in panel (a) at the intersection of the demand for money, D_m, with the supply of money, S_m. Suppose the Fed purchases U.S. securities and thereby increases the money supply, as shown in panel (a) by the shift to the right in the money supply curve from S_m to S'_m. With the increase in the supply of money, people are holding more of their wealth in money than they would prefer at initial interest rate *i*, so they try to exchange one form of wealth, money, for other financial assets. This greater willingness to lend has no direct effect on aggregate demand, but it does reduce the market rate of interest.

Point to Stress
When the interest rate declines, businesses become willing to undertake investment projects with expected rates of return that were too low under the old, higher interest rate.

A decline in the interest rate, other things constant, reduces the opportunity cost of financing new plant and equipment, thereby making new business investment more profitable. Likewise, a lower interest rate reduces the cost of a mortgage on new housing, so housing investment increases. Thus, the decline in the rate of interest increases the quantity of investment demanded. Panel (b) shows the demand for investment, D_i, first introduced in Chapter 8. When the interest rate falls from *i* to *i'*, the quantity of investment demanded increases from *I* to *I'*.

The aggregate expenditure function in panel (c) shifts up by the increase in planned investment, from $C + I + NX + G$ to $C + I' + NX + G$. The spending multiplier magnifies this increase in investment, leading to a greater increase in the equilibrium quantity of real GDP demanded at the prevailing price level. The quantity demanded increases from *Y* to *Y'*, as reflected in panel (c) by the intersection of the new aggregate expenditure function with the 45-degree line. This same increase is also reflected in panel (d), given price level *P*, by the shift in the aggregate demand curve from *AD* to *AD'*.

The sequence of events can be summarized by the following flowchart:

$$\boldsymbol{M \uparrow \rightarrow i \downarrow \rightarrow I \uparrow \rightarrow (C + I + NX + G) \uparrow \rightarrow AD \uparrow \rightarrow Y \uparrow}$$

An increase in the money supply, *M*, reduces the interest rate, *i*. The lower interest rate stimulates investment spending, *I*, which shifts up the aggregate expenditure function, increasing the quantity of aggregate output demanded from *Y* to *Y'*. This increase in the quantity of real GDP demanded at a particular price level is reflected by a shift to the right in the aggregate demand curve, from *AD* to *AD'*.[1]

1. The graphs are actually more complicated than those we have presented. Since the demand for money depends on the level of real GDP, an increase in the quantity of real GDP demanded would shift the money demand curve to the right in panel (a). For simplicity, we have not shown a shift in the money demand curve. If we had shifted the money demand curve, the equilibrium interest rate would still have fallen, but not by as much, so investment and aggregate demand would not have increased by as much.

EXHIBIT 3

Effects of an Increase in the Money Supply on Interest Rates, Investment, Aggregate Expenditure, and Aggregate Demand

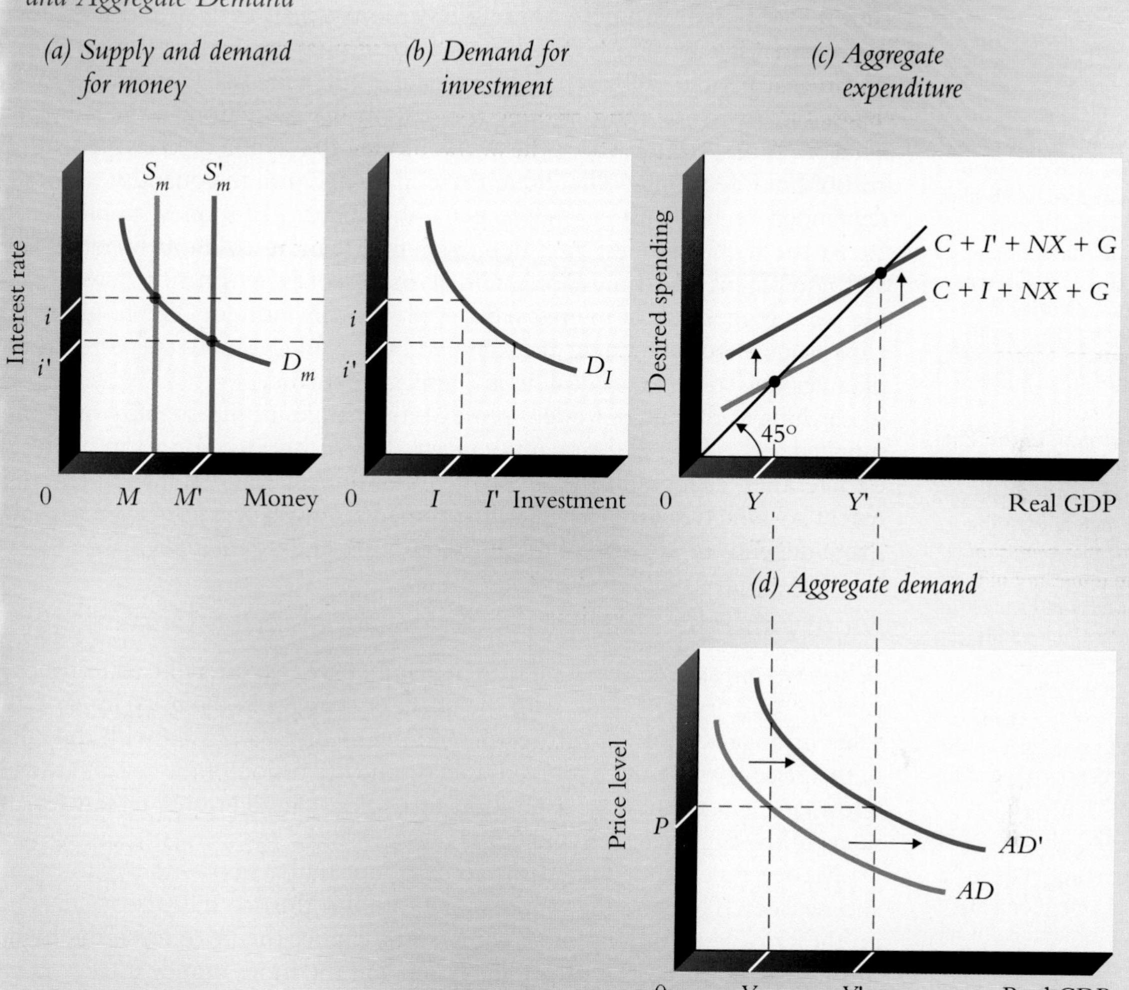

In panel (a), an increase in the money supply drives the interest rate down to i'. With the cost of borrowing now lower, the level of investment spending increases from I to I', as shown in panel (b). More investment spending drives aggregate expenditure up from $C + I + G + NX$ to $C + I' + G + NX$, as shown in panel (c). The increase expenditure sets off the multiplier process, so the quantity of aggregate output demanded increases from Y to Y'. The increase is shown by the shift to the right in the aggregate demand curve in panel (d).

Point to Stress The Fed can sell government securities in the open market, raise the discount rate, or increase required reserve ratios.

Teaching Tip With open-market operations, the Fed also has some direct influence on the interest rate. As the Fed sells securities, security prices fall and their yields rise.

Point to Stress The size of the impact on aggregate demand of a change in the money supply depends on (1) the sensitivity of interest rates to changes in the money supply, (2) the sensitivity of planned investment to interest rate changes, and (3) the size of the fixed-priced spending multiplier.

Teaching Tip See Chapter 5 for a discussion of the impact of price changes on real wealth and thus consumption and of domestic price changes on net exports, other things held constant.

We will now trace the same sequence in reverse, but we will dispense with the graphs. (You may wish to provide them.) Suppose the Federal Reserve decides to reduce the money supply to cool down an overheated economy. Given the money demand curve, a reduction in the supply of money means that people are now holding less money than they would like at the initial interest rate. The excess demand for money at the initial interest rate means that people will attempt to exchange other financial assets for money. These efforts to get more money translate into a reduction in the supply of loanable funds, which raises the market rate of interest, or the opportunity cost of holding money. The interest rate increases until the quantity of money demanded declines just enough to equal the quantity of money supplied.

At the higher interest rate, businesses find it more costly to finance plants and equipment and households find it more costly to finance new homes. Hence, a higher rate of interest reduces planned investment. The resulting decline in planned investment is magnified by the autonomous spending multiplier, leading to a greater decline in aggregate demand.

As long as the interest rate is sensitive to changes in the quantity of money supplied and as long as the quantity invested is sensitive to changes in the interest rate, then changes in the supply of money affect planned investment. The extent to which a given change in planned investment affects aggregate demand depends on the size of the autonomous spending multiplier.

Money and the Shape of the Aggregate Demand Curve

When we introduced the aggregate demand curve, we offered two reasons for its shape: the first had to do with the effect of changes in the price level on the value of dollar-denominated wealth, and the second had to do with the effect of the price level on net exports. Based on the discussion of money and the interest rate, we are now in a position to explore an additional reason for the shape of the aggregate demand curve.

Money is demanded primarily to carry out transactions—to pay for goods and services. The amount of money required to finance transactions depends on the price level, among other things. The higher the price level, the higher the average dollar cost of each transaction, and the more money it takes to pay for a given level of real GDP. So the demand for money increases as the price level increases, other things constant. For a given supply of money, an increase in the demand for money leads to a higher interest rate. An increase in the interest rate reduces the quantity of planned investment. This decline in investment reduces the quantity of real GDP demanded.

The two panels of Exhibit 4 represent this relationship graphically. Panel (a) shows the economy's supply and demand for money, and panel (b) shows the aggregate demand curve. We begin with an interest rate of i in panel (a) and a price level of P in panel (b). The equilibrium interest rate is determined by the intersection of the money supply curve, S_m, and the money demand curve, D_m; this intersection occurs at point *a* in panel (a). Note that D_m is the demand for money when the price level is P. Point *a* in panel (b) indicates that when the price level is P, the quantity of real GDP demanded is Y.

If the price level increases to P', the amount of money needed to support a given level of transactions increases, so the demand for money shifts to the

EXHIBIT 4

Effect of a Change in the Price Level on Quantity Demanded

(a) Supply and demand for money

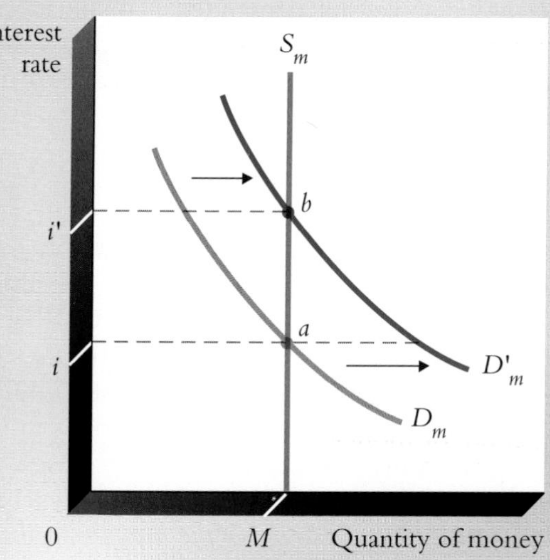

(b) Aggregate demand

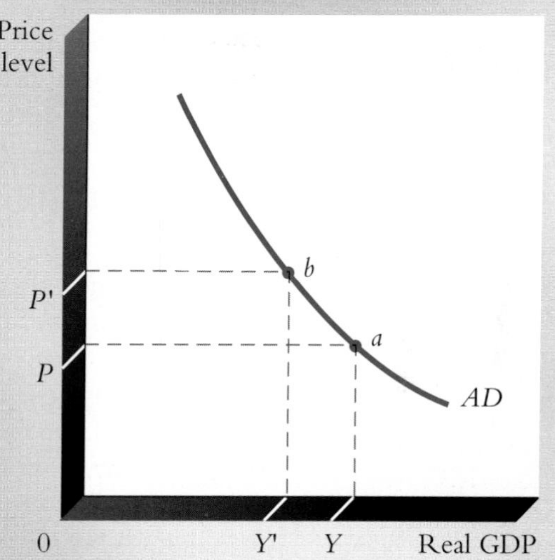

An increase in the price level from P to P' increases the transactions demand for money from D_m to D'_m and drives the interest rate up from i to i'. The rise in the interest rate reduces investment spending and aggregate expenditure. Through the multiplier process, the quantity of aggregate output demanded falls from Y to Y'. Panel (b) shows that higher price levels are associated with lower quantities of real output demanded. Changes in the price level lead to movements along the aggregate demand curve.

Point to Stress In Exhibit 4, the change in the interest rates results from a price-level change. Therefore, there is a movement along a given aggregate demand curve. In Exhibit 3, the interest-rate change did not result from a price-level change, but rather from a money-supply change. Therefore, the entire aggregate demand curve shifted.

right, from D_m to D'_m in panel (a). People demand more money at every interest rate. People try to get more money to support transactions at the higher price level by exchanging some of their other financial assets for money. But S_m is the existing money stock; there is no more. *As people try to get more money, they reduce their supply of loanable funds, which drives up the interest rate.* The interest rate rises until the quantity of money demanded just equals the given supply of money, as shown by equilibrium point *b* in panel (a).

An increase in the interest rate has a now-familiar effect on the quantity of aggregate output demanded. When the interest rate increases, investment becomes more costly, so investment spending declines. Thus, as the price level increases from P to P' in panel (b), the higher demand for money drives up the interest rate and reduces the quantity of planned investment. This decline in investment results in a reduction in the quantity of aggregate output demanded from Y to Y', reflected by the movement along the aggregate demand curve in panel (b) from point *a* to point *b*.

In summary, the aggregate demand curve is drawn assuming a given supply of money in the economy. Changes in the price level alter the amount of money needed to carry out transactions, thereby shifting the money demand curve. A higher price level leads to a higher interest rate, which results in less investment and a decrease in the quantity of aggregate output demanded. A lower price level leads to a lower interest rate, resulting in more investment and an increase in the quantity of aggregate output demanded. This relation between the price level and the interest rate provides another reason why the aggregate demand curve slopes down to the right.

Adding Aggregate Supply

Even after we determine the effect of a change in the money supply on aggregate demand, we still have only half the story. To determine the ultimate effects of monetary policy on the equilibrium level of real GDP in the economy, we must introduce the supply side. We need an aggregate supply curve to tell us how a given shift in aggregate demand affects real GDP and the price level. In the short run, the aggregate supply curve slopes upward, so the quantity supplied will expand only if the price level increases. *For a given shift in the aggregate demand curve, the steeper the short-run aggregate supply curve, the smaller the increase in real GDP and the larger the increase in the price level.*

Assume the economy is producing at point *a* in Exhibit 5, where the aggregate demand curve, *AD*, intersects the short-run aggregate supply curve, $SRAS_{130}$, yielding a short-run equilibrium output of $4.8 trillion and a price level of 125. As you can see, the actual price level of 125 is below the expected price level of 130, so the short-run equilibrium output of $4.8 trillion is below the economy's potential of $5.0 trillion. The contractionary gap equals the difference, or $0.2 trillion. (Output levels below the economy's potential are shaded in red, and those above that potential are shaded in blue.)

Example After the contraction in the U.S. economy began in August, 1990, the discount rate at the New York reserve bank fell from 7.0 percent to 3.0 percent in late 1992. In addition, the federal funds rate fell from 8.13 percent to 3.0 percent as the Fed pumped reserves into the banking system.

The Fed can wait to see whether natural market forces close the gap by shifting the short-run aggregate supply curve to the right, or the Fed can intervene and attempt to close the gap with an expansionary monetary policy. Suppose the Fed decides to increase the money supply in order to lower interest rates and stimulate investment spending. The increased investment shifts aggregate demand from *AD* out to *AD'*. If the Fed increases the money supply by exactly the appropriate amount, the new equilibrium is achieved at point *b*, where the economy is producing its potential output. Given all the connections in the chain of causality between changes in the money supply and changes in equilibrium output, it would actually be quite difficult for the Fed to execute such a precise monetary policy (but more on that later).

To review: An initial increase in the money supply reduces the market rate of interest, resulting in an increase in investment and a consequent increase in aggregate demand. As aggregate demand increases along a given short-run aggregate supply curve, both the equilibrium price and output increase. *As long as the short-run aggregate supply curve slopes upward, the short-run effect of an increase in the money supply is an increase in both output and the price level.*

EXHIBIT 5

Expansionary Monetary Policy to Correct a Contractionary Gap

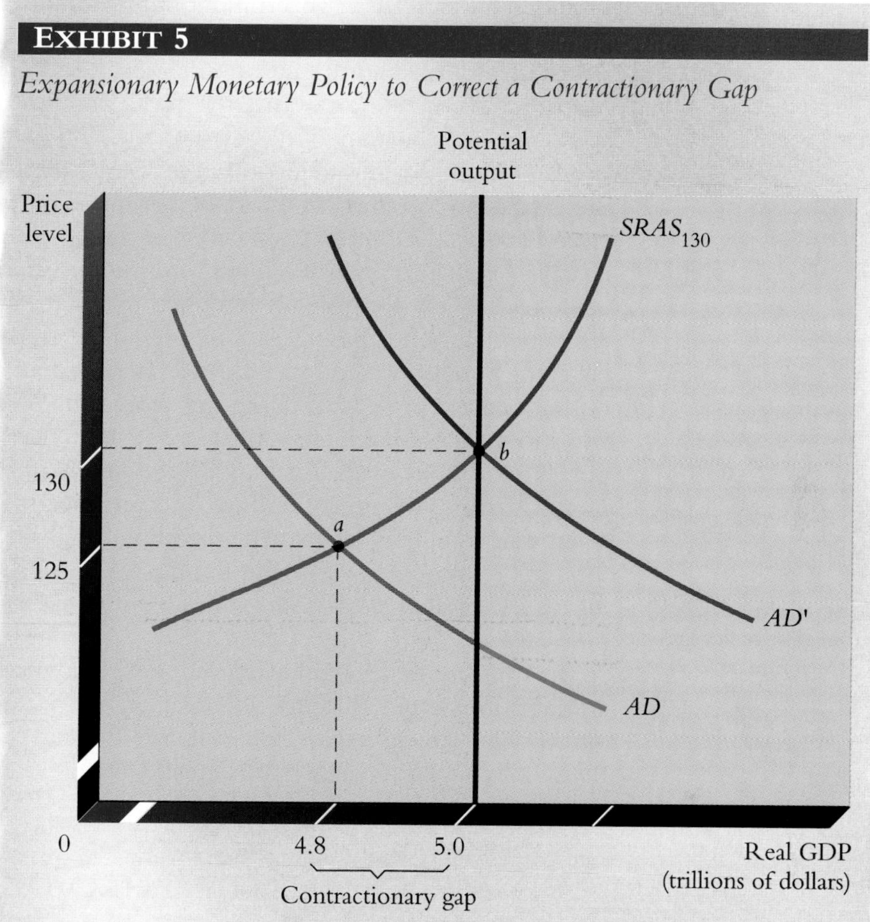

At point *e*, the economy is producing below potential. There is a contractionary gap equal to $Y\star - Y$. If the Federal Reserve increases the money supply, the aggregate demand curve shifts to $AD\star$. At the old price level, *P*, the quantity of output demanded is Y' but the quantity supplied is *Y*. The excess demand causes the price level to rise. Equilibrium will be reestablished at point $e\star$, with price level $P\star$ and output at the potential level, $Y\star$.

Fiscal Policy and Money

Now that we have introduced the effects that money has on aggregate demand and equilibrium output, we can take another look at the effects of fiscal policy, this time incorporating monetary effects. Suppose there is an increase in government purchases, other things constant. In Chapter 11 we found that an increase in government purchases increases aggregate demand and, in the short run, leads to both a greater output and a higher price level. Once money enters the picture, however, we must recognize that an increase in either real output or the price level increases the demand for money.

Teaching Tip The greater the impact of increased government purchases on the interest rate and the greater the sensitivity of planned investment to the interest rate, the greater the crowding-out effect.

Thus, an increase in government purchases increases money demand. For a given supply of money, an increase in money demand leads to a higher interest rate. But a higher interest rate *reduces* the quantity of investment demanded. We therefore say that the fiscal stimulus of government purchases *crowds out* some investment. (Crowding out will be considered more carefully in a later chapter.) This reduction in investment will, to some extent, dampen the expansionary effects of fiscal policy on real output. Hence, *the inclusion of money in the fiscal framework introduces yet another reason why the simple spending multiplier overstates the increase in real output arising from any given fiscal stimulus.*

Point to Stress The discussion of crowding out assumes a given money supply. The Fed can counteract the crowding out by altering the money supply.

Likewise, any fiscal policy designed to reduce aggregate demand will be tempered by monetary effects. Suppose, in an attempt to cool inflation, government purchases are reduced. As aggregate demand declines, equilibrium output and the price level fall in the short run. With a lower level of output and a lower price level, less money is needed to carry out transactions, so the demand for money falls. Again, with the supply of money unchanged, a drop in the demand for money leads to a lower interest rate. This drop in the interest rate stimulates investment spending, to some extent offsetting the effects of the drop in government purchases. Thus, *given the supply of money, the impact of changes in the demand for money on interest rates reduces the effectiveness of fiscal policy.*

Monetarism A school of thought that attaches great significance to variations in the money supply as a primary determinant of aggregate demand

In the Keynesian framework, money influences aggregate demand and equilibrium output through its effect on the interest rate. Another framework, called **monetarism**, focuses more directly on the effects of changes in the money supply on aggregate demand. We next examine this approach.

MONETARISM AND THE QUANTITY THEORY

Example According to the Fed-sponsored Survey of Consumer Finances (1989), family ownership of assets is divided, with 28 percent in financial assets and 72 percent in nonfinancial assets. The largest single asset of most families is their principle residence (32 percent). Other significant assets are investment real estate (15 percent) and business investment (18 percent).

The Keynesian approach assumes that the only alternative to holding money as a store of wealth is holding other *financial* assets. In this view, an increased supply of money makes people want to exchange money for other financial assets, which lowers the rate of interest and stimulates investment. Thus, changes in the money supply affect aggregate demand through changes in the interest rate. Another group of economists, called *monetarists*, concurs that money works through interest rates, but they also see a more direct role for money in aggregate spending.

Monetarism

The father of modern monetarism is Nobel Prize winner Milton Friedman, who spent most of his career at the University of Chicago. Friedman argues that people hold their wealth in several forms. Money is just one asset among many that can serve as a store of wealth. In addition to other financial assets, people hold *real* assets, such as real estate and automobiles. An increase in the money supply means that at the initial interest rate the quantity of money supplied exceeds the quantity demanded. People are therefore holding more of their wealth in the form of money than they would like. As they attempt to reduce their money holdings, people increase their demand for all kinds of assets, including homes and other durable goods. So in the monetarist view, an increase in the supply of money increases the demand for both other financial assets and real assets. This increased desire to buy real assets increases aggregate demand directly. Monetarists rely on a framework called the equation of exchange, which we will examine next.

Teaching Tip The equation of exchange was developed by the classical economist Irving Fisher (1867–1947).

The Equation of Exchange

Equation of exchange The quantity of money, *M*, multiplied by its velocity, *V*, equals nominal income, which is the product of the price level, *P*, and real GDP, *Y*.

Every transaction in the economy involves a two-way swap: the seller surrenders goods and services for money, and the buyer surrenders money equal in value to the asking price. One way of expressing this relation among key variables in the economy is the **equation of exchange**, first developed by the classical economists. Although this equation can be arranged in different ways depending on the variables to be emphasized, the basic version is

$$M \times V = P \times Y$$

Velocity of money The average number of times per year a dollar is used to purchase final goods and services

where M is the quantity of money in the economy; V is the **velocity of money**, or the average number of times per year each dollar is used to purchase final goods and services; P is the price level; and Y is real national output, or real GDP. The equation of exchange says that the quantity of money in circulation, M, multiplied by the number of times that money turns over (changes hands), V, equals the average price level of products sold, P, times real output, Y. The price level, P, times real output, Y, equals the economy's nominal income and output.

Example In 1992, nominal GDP was approximately $5.95 trillion, while the M1 money supply was only $1,026.6 billion. On average, each dollar in M1 would have turned over 5.8 times in order to pay for the year's production of final goods and services.

Consider a simple economy in which total sales during the year consist of 1,000 bags of popcorn at $1 each and 1,000 six-packs of Pepsi at $3 each. The total output, Y, equals 2,000 units, and the average price level, P, is $2 per unit. The nominal value of output, $P \times Y$, equals $2 × 2,000, or $4,000, which also equals the income received by resource suppliers. Suppose the total money supply in this economy is $500. How often is each dollar used on average to pay for final goods and services during the year? In other words, what is the velocity of money? We can derive the velocity by rearranging the equation of exchange to yield

$$V = \frac{P \times Y}{M} = \frac{\$4{,}000}{\$500} = 8$$

Given the value of total output and the money supply, each dollar on average must have turned over eight times to finance final goods and services. There is no other way these market transactions could occur. Velocity is implied by the values of the other variables. Incidentally, velocity does not

Teaching Tip The velocity of money discussed to this point is termed the *income* velocity of money. It is stressed because GDP is the focus of macroeconomic policy decisions. An alternative velocity measure, which considers spending on all goods and services, is known as the *transactions* velocity of money.

reflect spending on intermediate goods, second-hand goods, or financial assets, even though such spending also takes place in the economy. Thus, each dollar, in fact, works harder than is implied by velocity, which reflects spending on only final goods and services.

Classical economists developed the equation of exchange as a way of explaining how much money was needed to finance a given amount of spending. The equation says that total spending ($M \times V$) is always equal to total receipts ($P \times Y$), as was the case in our circular flow analysis. As described thus far, however, the equation of exchange is simply an *identity*—a relation expressed in such a way that it is true by definition. Another example of an identity would be a relation equating miles per gallon to the distance driven divided by the gasoline required.

The Quantity Theory of Money

Quantity theory of money The theory that the velocity of money is predictable, so changes in the money supply have predictable effects on nominal income

How do monetarists use the equation of exchange? They claim that velocity varies over time in a predictable manner unrelated to changes in the money supply. By arguing that velocity is predictable, monetarists transformed the equation of exchange from an identity into a theory: the quantity theory of money. The **quantity theory of money** states that if the velocity of money is stable or at least predictable, then the equation of exchange can be used to predict the effects of changes in the money supply on nominal income, $P \times Y$. For example, if M is increased by 10 percent and if V remains constant, then $P \times Y$, which measures nominal income, must also increase by 10 percent.

Teaching Tip Monetarists assume that velocity is influenced by a different set of variables than those affecting the money supply. Thus, changes in the money supply do not alter velocity.

Thus, increases in the money supply increase aggregate demand, and the increase in aggregate demand results in a higher nominal income. How is this increase in nominal income ($P \times Y$) divided between changes in the price level and changes in real GDP? The answer does not lie in the quantity theory, for that theory is stated only in terms of nominal income. The answer lies in the shape of the aggregate supply curve. In the short run, the aggregate supply curve slopes upward, so a shift to the right in the aggregate demand curve will increase both real output and the price level. If there is much unemployment and much idle capacity, short-run changes in the price level may be relatively small. If the economy is already producing its potential output, short-run changes in the price level will be relatively large.

Teaching Tip The equation of exchange can be rewritten as $P = (M \times V)/Y$. The percentage change in P is approximately equal to the percentage change in M plus the percentage change in V minus the percentage change in Y.

So, *in the short run, changes in nominal output are divided between changes in real GDP and changes in the price level.* In the long run, the aggregate supply curve is vertical at the economy's potential level of output. If the economy is already operating at its potential output, then a shift to the right in the aggregate demand curve will in the long run increase only the price level, leaving output unchanged at potential GDP. Thus, *in the long run, increases in the money supply result only in higher prices*. Note that the economy's potential level of output is not affected by changes in the money supply.

Although monetarists believe that there is a relation between changes in the money supply and changes in nominal income, they caution that there may be long and unpredictable time lags before changes in actions by the Fed affect aggregate demand. Consequently, monetarists consider monetary policy a poor instrument for changing nominal income. In the next chapter we will examine the problem of lags and consider the policy implications of these lags.

To review: *What turns the equation of exchange from an identity into a theory is the monetarist assertion that changes in velocity are predictable, at least in the long run.* If velocity *is* predictable, changes in the money supply affect nominal income in a predictable way. Velocity is therefore a key component of the quantity theory of money. Let's consider some factors that influence velocity.

What Determines the Velocity of Money?

Teaching Tip Households are not concerned with the velocity of money per se. But the velocity of money varies inversely with the amount of money people want to hold. Besides the factors discussed in this section, people's desire to hold money can also be affected by expectations of future economic and political stability.

Velocity depends on the customs and conventions of commerce. In colonial times money might be tied up in transit for days as a courier on horseback carried a payment from a merchant in Boston to one in Baltimore. Today the electronic transmission of funds takes only seconds, so the same stock of money can move around much more quickly to finance many more transactions. *The velocity of money has also been increased by a variety of commercial innovations that have facilitated exchange.* For example, a wider use of charge accounts and credit cards has reduced the need for shoppers to carry cash to support transactions. Likewise, automatic teller machines have made cash more accessible any time, so people have reduced their "walking around" money. Monetarists argue that although such changes can affect velocity, financial innovations do not occur suddenly or frequently. Moreover, their effects are predictable, so the quantity theory remains a useful model.

Another institutional factor that determines velocity is the frequency with which people get paid. If workers are paid $1,000 every two weeks and gradually spend the entire paycheck during that period, each worker's average money balance during the pay period is $500. If workers are paid $500 once a week, however, their average money balance falls to $250. Thus, the more often workers are paid, other things constant, the lower their average money balances, so the more active the money supply and the greater its velocity. Again, payment practices change slowly over time, and the effects of these changes on velocity are predictable.

Teaching Tip Monetarists emphasize the influences on velocity of permanent income and expected inflation.

The better money serves as a store of wealth, the more of it people want to hold, so the lower its velocity. For example, the introduction of interest-bearing checking accounts made money a better store of wealth. On the other hand, when inflation is high, money is not as good a store of wealth; people become more reluctant to hold money and try to exchange it for some asset that during inflation retains its value better. This reduction in people's willingness to hold money during periods of high inflation increases the velocity of money. Thus, *velocity increases with a rise in inflation, other things constant.*

The Keynesian Approach and the Equation of Exchange

How does the Keynesian approach look from the viewpoint of the equation of exchange? Recall that since the equation of exchange is an identity, not a theory, we should be able to explain how the Keynesian theory fits in with this identity. Suppose an increase in the aggregate expenditure function increases aggregate demand. An increase in aggregate demand increases the price level, the level of real output, or both, thereby increasing the transactions demand for money. For a given supply of money in the economy, an increase in the money demand curve raises the interest rate. The higher opportunity cost of holding money reduces the quantity of money people want to hold as an asset, so idle cash balances decline and the velocity of money increases. Because of this increase in velocity, a given supply of money is able to support the increase in aggregate demand.

Teaching Tip The *total* amount of money people hold does not change: they hold more for transactions purposes, less for asset purposes.

Thus, in the Keynesian framework, an increase in aggregate demand increases the velocity of money enough that the existing money supply is sufficient to support the higher level of nominal spending. Dollars that had been relaxing comfortably in checking accounts or coffee cans are put to work. The equation of exchange remains in balance, $M \times V = P \times Y$, even though M has not changed. The increase in V allows the existing supply of money to support a higher level of nominal income. According to the Keynesian view, *money works harder when the interest rate rises.*

Conversely, suppose a reduction in the aggregate expenditure function reduces aggregate demand, thereby reducing the transactions demand for money. For a given supply of money in the economy, a drop in the demand for money results in a lower interest rate, which lowers the opportunity cost of holding money. With the opportunity cost lower, people increase the amount of money they are willing to hold as an asset, so idle cash balances increase and the velocity of money falls. The existing money supply supports a lower level of nominal output.

Point to Stress Monetarists deemphasize the influence on velocity of changes in the interest rate. Therefore, a change in the money supply does not affect velocity.

In the Keynesian approach, the velocity of money varies directly with the interest rate. This link between the interest rate and velocity weakens the force of the quantity theory of money. Here is why. The quantity theory states that because velocity is relatively stable, an increase in the supply of money leads to an increase in nominal income. But since an increase in the supply of money reduces the interest rate, people may be content to hold some of the increased supply of money as idle cash balances. If a decline in the interest rate reduces velocity, then an increase in the money supply is to some extent offset by a reduction in velocity.

The usefulness of the modern quantity theory hinges on how stable and predictable the velocity of money is. Even a small unexpected change in velocity could undermine the ability of the equation of exchange to predict nominal income. For example, if velocity turned out to be 5 percent less than expected, then nominal GDP would also be 5 percent less than expected. Let's examine the stability of velocity over the years.

How Stable Is Velocity?

Exhibit 6 graphs velocity since 1915, measured as nominal GDP divided by M1. Based on this exhibit, is it reasonable to conclude that velocity is relatively stable? That depends on the time period considered and what is meant by "relatively stable." As you can see, from 1915 to 1947 velocity fluctuated a

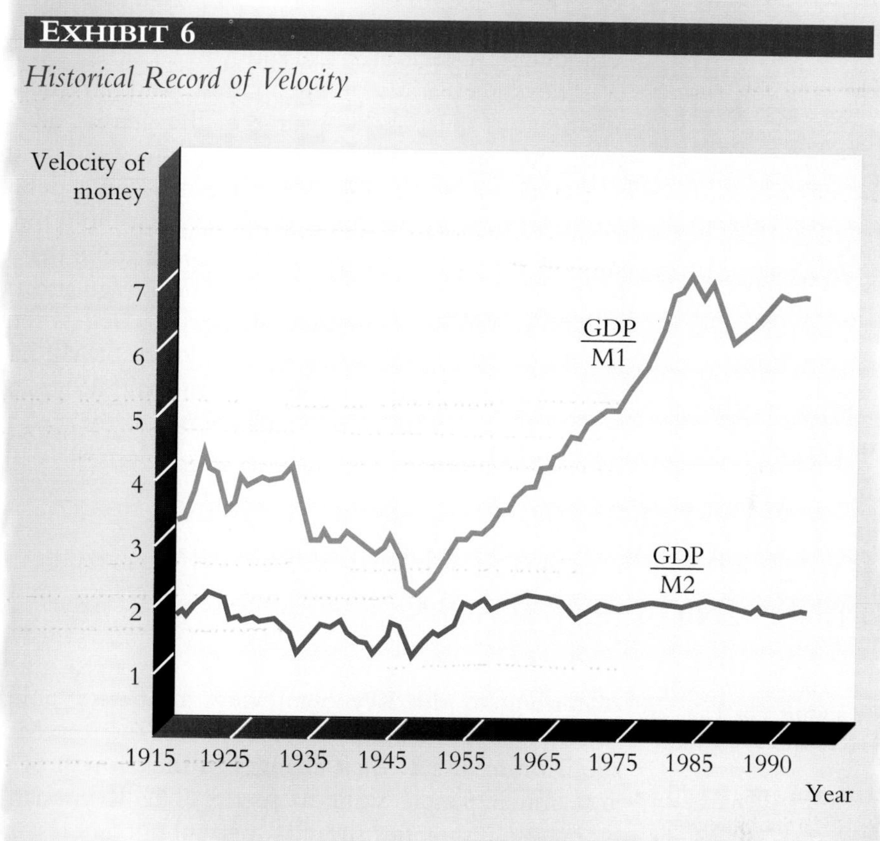

Sources: *Long-Term Economic Growth,* 1860–1970 (Washington, D.C.: U.S. Government Printing Office, 1973) and *Economic Report of the President,* January, 1993.

Teaching Tip Many analysts connect the upward trend in velocity from 1947 to 1979 with generally rising inflation and interest rates during this period and the regulatory constraints (such as interest-rate ceilings on bank deposits).

fair amount, but the trend was downward. From 1947 to 1979 there was an overall upward trend in velocity, with less variability than before. In fact, between 1973 and 1979 velocity grew each year at a rate of between 3.0 and 4.3 percent. *Velocity appeared so relatively stable during this six-year stretch that some economists began to talk about an economic law relating the money supply to nominal GDP.* More attention was thus accorded monetarism during the latter part of the 1970s. Whereas the decade of the 1960s was the high point of Keynesianism, the period of the late 1970s was perhaps the high point of monetarism.

Teaching Tip M1 velocity now varies substantially with changes in interest rates. The opportunity costs of M1 assets are highly variable, as rates on other checkable deposits in M1 are slow to react to changes in market interest rates.

After 1979, however, the velocity of M1 became more erratic. After jumping by 4.9 percent in 1981, it dropped by 4.6 percent during the recession year of 1982, the largest decline since 1947. This swing meant that nominal GDP was 9.5 percent lower in 1982 than it would have been had velocity continued to grow in 1982 as it had in 1981. Velocity has fluctuated since 1982. In general, between 1979 and 1992 the velocity of M1, on average, declined sharply, but year-to-year changes in velocity increased. Thus velocity was falling but becoming more erratic. The equation of exchange consequently became less reliable as a short-run predictor of the effects of a change in M1 on nominal GDP. There is less talk now about economic laws

Example From 1961 to 1981, M2 velocity grew on average at a slow 0.2 percent per year. The long-run trendless nature of M2 velocity seemed unaffected by events in the 1980s. In 1987, in reaction to interest-rate volatility, the Fed changed M1 from a "targeted" to a "monitored" variable and stopped reporting M1 growth targets.

relating money supply to nominal GDP. Some economists believe that the link between the money supply and nominal GDP has been disturbed only temporarily. Others aren't so sure.

The deregulation of the interest paid on checkable deposits has been identified as the possible source of the demise of a predictable relation between M1 and nominal income. Prior to 1980, with minor exceptions, interest was not paid on checkable deposits. Since people can now earn interest on their checking accounts, they choose to hold more money, thus reducing the velocity of money. Some economists argue that the definition of money has really changed due to changes in bank regulations. Therefore, a better definition of money—one that will perhaps be less sensitive to interest rates—should be developed. In fact, the velocity of M2 has been more stable than the velocity of M1, especially since the mid-1950s, as you can see in Exhibit 6. In setting targets for monetary growth, the Fed now relies more on M2 than on M1.

Monetary Targets: Money Supply Versus Interest Rates

Teaching Tip The Fed cannot directly achieve its *ultimate* goals of GDP growth, inflation, and unemployment. Nor are its *intermediate* targets of the money supply and overall interest rates directly and completely under its control. Therefore, Fed operations emphasize *operating* targets such as the federal funds rates, the level of nonborrowed bank reserves, or the level of borrowed bank reserves.

According to the Keynesian view, monetary policy affects the economy largely by influencing the market rate of interest. Monetarists think the linkage is more direct—that changes in the growth of the money supply affect how much people want to spend. The Keynesian approach suggests that monetary authorities should worry about interest rates; the monetarist approach suggests that the money supply is of more direct importance. There is much debate over whether monetary authorities should focus on keeping the money stock stable or on keeping the interest rate stable. As we will see, the Fed does not have enough tools to do both.

Contrasting Policies

To demonstrate the effects of different policies, we will begin with the money market in equilibrium at point *e* in Exhibit 7. The interest rate is *i* and the money stock is *M*, values the monetary authorities find quite appropriate. Suppose there is an increase in the demand for money in the economy, perhaps because of an increase in aggregate demand. The money demand curve shifts to the right from D_m to D'_m.

Example The federal funds rate has been much more flexible since 1979 when the Fed dropped the rate as its primary operating target.

When confronted with an increase in the demand for money, monetary authorities can do one of the following two things: they can do nothing, allowing the interest rate to rise, or they can increase the supply of money in an attempt to keep the interest rate constant. If monetary authorities do nothing, the quantity of money in the economy will remain the same, but the interest rate will rise because the greater demand for money will shift the equilibrium up from point *e* to point *e′*. Alternatively, monetary authorities can try to keep the interest rate at its initial level by

EXHIBIT 7

Targeting Interest Rates Versus the Supply of Money

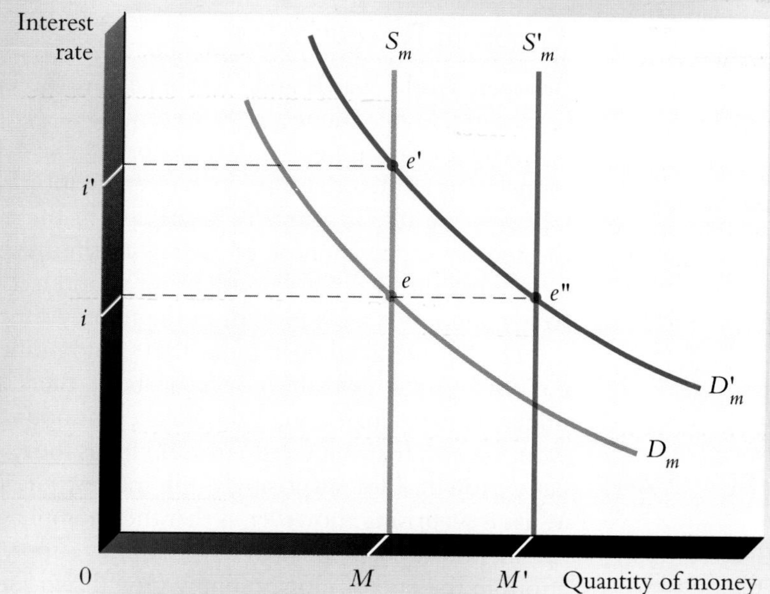

An increase in the price level or in real GDP increases the demand for money from D_m to D'_m. If the Federal Reserve holds the money supply at S_m, interest rates will rise from i (at point e) to i' (at point e'). Alternatively, the Fed could hold the interest rate constant by increasing the supply of money to S'_m. The Fed may choose any point along the money demand curve, D'_m.

increasing the supply of money from S_m to S'_m. In terms of possible combinations of the money stock and the interest rate, monetary authorities must choose from points lying along the new money demand curve.

Teaching Tip Monetary rules governing Fed operations are discussed in Chapter 15.

A growing economy usually needs a growing money supply. If monetary authorities maintain a constant growth in the money supply, the interest rate will probably fluctuate unless the growth in the supply of money each period just happens to match the growth in the demand for money. Alternatively, monetary authorities could try to adjust the money supply in each period by the amount needed to keep the interest rate stable. With this approach, changes in the money supply would have to offset any changes in the demand for money.

Interest-rate fluctuations could be considered undesirable if they created fluctuations in investment. For interest rates to remain stable during economic expansions, the money supply should grow at the same rate as the demand for money. Likewise, for interest rates to remain stable during economic contractions, the money supply should decline by the same rate as the demand for money. Hence, if monetary authorities attempted to maintain the interest rate

Example Milton Friedman blames much of the Great Depression on Fed policies that allowed the money supply to drop by one-third.

Teaching Tip The Fed began announcing target ranges for the monetary aggregates in 1975. From 1975 to 1979, the Fed set tolerance ranges for the federal funds rates (an operating target) designed to foster the target growth rates for the monetary aggregates (intermediate targets).

Example In December 1980, the federal funds rate reached 20 percent.

Example Between 1975 and 1979, annual growth of M1 ranged from 5.8 percent to 7.9 percent. From 1979 to 1982, M1 growth ranged from 2.4 percent to 9.0 percent.

Example CPI inflation was 11.3 percent in 1979, 13.5 percent in 1980, 10.3 percent in 1981, 6.2 percent in 1982, and 3.2 percent in 1983.

at some predetermined level, the money supply would have to increase during periods of economic expansion and decrease during periods of economic contraction. Unfortunately, *such changes in the money supply would tend to reinforce fluctuations in economic activity, thereby adding more instability to the economy.*

Targets in Recent Years

Between World War II and October 1979, the Fed attempted to stabilize interest rates. Stable interest rates were viewed as a prerequisite for an attractive investment environment and, thus, for a stable economy. Friedman and other monetarists argued that this exclusive attention to interest rates made monetary policy a major source of instability in the economy because changes in the money supply reinforced swings in the business cycle. Monetarists proposed that the Fed pay less attention to interest rates and instead focus on a steady and predictable growth in the money supply.

The debate raged during the 1970s, and monetarists made some important converts. Amid growing concern about the rising inflation rate, the Fed, under its new chairman, Paul Volcker, announced in October 1979 that it would deemphasize interest rates and focus more on specified targets for monetary growth. Not surprisingly, the interest rate became much more volatile. What *is* surprising, however, is that the deemphasis on interest rates did *not* result in a more stable growth in the money supply. After October 1979 fluctuations in the rate of money supply growth *increased* rather than decreased.

Many observers believe that a sharp reduction in money growth in the latter half of 1981 caused the recession of 1982, the most severe since the Great Depression. Inflation declined rapidly, but the unemployment rate jumped to over 10 percent. People got worried. As you might expect, the Fed was widely criticized for its monetary policy. Volcker was denounced by farmers, politicians, and businesspeople. Feelings ran high. Volcker was reportedly even given Secret Service protection. In October 1982, three years after the focus on interest rates was dropped, Volcker announced that the Fed would pay attention to both interest rates *and* money growth.

Monetarists do not acknowledge that the attempt to focus on the money supply was a failure. Rather, they argue that the Fed never really implemented a policy of steady, predictable growth in the money supply, so the three-year period should not be viewed as a test of the effectiveness of monetarism. Some monetarists even believe that the Fed espoused monetarism simply as a smokescreen for putting the brakes on inflation rates that exceeded 12 percent in 1979 and 1980. According to this argument, Congress would have objected if the Fed had announced an explicit policy to raise interest rates to cool inflation.

Interest Rates and International Finance

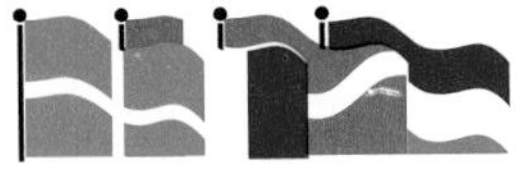

Thus far we have confined the discussion of monetary policy to domestic issues. But international transactions complicate the picture, as savers throughout the world have a strong financial incentive to seek out the highest interest rate. For a Japanese saver, for example, the alternatives might be to buy

Japanese corporate bonds paying, say, 4 percent or to buy U.S. corporate bonds paying 7 percent. To purchase U.S. corporate bonds, that Japanese saver would first have to purchase U.S. dollars with Japanese yen. Therefore, relatively high interest rates in the United States cause foreigners to exchange their own currencies for dollars. This increase in the demand for dollars causes the dollar to appreciate relative to other currencies.

For example, during the first half of the 1980s, real interest rates in the United States were higher than foreign interest rates, and the U.S. dollar appreciated by about 55 percent. Interest rates, therefore, affect not only domestic investment but the value of the dollar on world currency markets. An appreciated dollar means that U.S. residents find foreign goods cheaper and foreigners find U.S. goods more expensive, so imports increase and exports decrease. The result is a reduction in aggregate demand.

Real interest rates in the United States began a sharp decline in early 1985, a decline that continued until 1987. During that same period, the U.S. dollar fell nearly to its 1980 level. When U.S. interest rates fall relative to foreign interest rates, the foreign demand for U.S. dollars also falls and the dollar tends to depreciate. A depreciated dollar means that U.S. residents find foreign goods more expensive and foreigners find U.S. goods cheaper, so imports decrease and exports increase. The result is an increase in aggregate demand.

Fed Policy Since 1982

Between 1982 and 1987 the monetary policy was to accommodate the increased demand for money in a growing economy. In 1987, as the economy approached its potential output, the Fed, under Chairman Alan Greenspan, began to tighten the money supply because of fears of inflation. For example, between 1988 and 1989 the money supply grew by only 1 percent, and the tighter monetary policy caused interest rates to rise. The federal funds rate, the rate charged for overnight borrowing of reserves between banks, climbed from 6.5 percent in 1988 to nearly 10 percent in 1989. Higher U.S. interest rates also caused the dollar to appreciate against foreign currencies.

Example In 1992, the German central bank increased interest rates to a level approximately 6.5 percent above the equivalent U.S. rate. The dollar reached its lowest value against the German mark since World War II, and the U.S. trade deficit began to rise. The rising trade deficit contributed to slow U.S. growth in 1992.

Some observers thought the Fed had become too earnest in its efforts to prevent higher inflation and would instead cause a recession. In June of 1989, fears of a recession caused the Fed to pursue a more expansionary monetary policy, a policy aimed at lowering interest rates. In the process, the Fed also wanted to halt the appreciation of the dollar. Interest rates did fall and the dollar did depreciate, but none of this headed off a recession, which began in July of 1990. For the next two years, the Fed tried to lower interest rates as a way of stimulating the economy. By 1992 the M1 was growing at 10 percent a year and the funds rate had fallen under 4 percent—a level not seen in three decades. But the unemployment rate had climbed from 5.2 percent in 1989 to 7.6 percent in 1992.

Though short-term rates fell, long-term rates remained relatively high (about 5 percentage points above the federal funds rate.) Long-term lenders believed that the easier monetary policy since 1989 would ultimately translate into more inflation down the road, so long-term lenders required higher rates as a hedge against inflation. Moreover, few believed the federal government was going to do much about the ballooning federal deficit, a deficit that could eventually worsen inflation.

The Fed is always feeling its way, looking for signs about the direction of the economy and clues to what its monetary policy should be. Chairman Greenspan has said that the Fed would not focus exclusively on the money supply. He said that "intermediate-term movements" in the money supply "are not linked closely enough with those of nominal income to justify a single-minded focus on the money supply."[2] In its quest for economic stability, the Fed has recently developed a new monetary indicator. We close this chapter with a case study discussing this indicator.

CASE STUDY

The Fed's New Monetary Indicator: The Long-Run Price Level

Point to Stress Since the $P^{\star}$ analysis assumes a constant $V^{\star}$ and stable growth of $Y^{\star}$ (approximately 2.5 percent), the long-run inflation rate becomes a function of the money supply.

In their pursuit of price stability, Fed officials have begun considering a new indicator of inflationary pressure in the economy: the *long-run equilibrium price level*, which is the level that prices are expected to reach when the economy produces its potential output. By comparing the long-run price level to the current price level in the economy, Fed officials hope to develop insights into the likely course of inflation.

The long-run price level, as estimated by the Fed, is derived from the equation of exchange, $M \times V^{\star} = P^{\star} \times Y^{\star}$, where M is the money supply (measured as M2), $V^{\star}$ is the average velocity of M2 over the long run, $P^{\star}$ is the long-run equilibrium price level, and $Y^{\star}$ is real potential output. The equation of exchange can be rearranged to yield the long-run equilibrium price level: $P^{\star} = (M \times V^{\star})/Y^{\star}$. You can think of $P^{\star}$ as the price level that will eventually occur when the economy achieves its potential output, given the current money supply and the average velocity of money.

In deriving $P^{\star}$, the Fed knows the value of M2, but it must estimate both potential output and the average velocity. Estimates of potential output are based on an analysis of the U.S. economy's long-run trend in real output. The velocity of M2 varies in the short run, but research shows that over sufficiently long periods, velocity returns to an average value; that is, the velocity of M2 seems constant over the long run. As an estimate of long-run velocity, the Fed uses the average value of velocity since 1955.

Once they estimate $P^{\star}$, Fed analysts compare it to the economy's current price level. The difference between the two price levels provides policy makers with an indication of the likely direction of inflation. Empirical evidence suggests that when the long-run equilibrium price level is below the current price level, inflation tends to decrease. When the long-run equilibrium price level exceeds the current price level, inflation tends to increase. And when the long-run equilibrium price level equals the current price level, inflation remains the same. Therefore, the difference between the current price level and the long-run equilibrium price level provides the Fed

2. "Greenspan Asks That Fed Be Allowed to Pay Interest," *Wall Street Journal*, 11 March 1992.

with additional information on how to pursue price stability. For example, if the current price level is below the long-run equilibrium price level, it is likely that there is inflationary pressure in the economy, so the Fed may want to pursue a less inflationary monetary policy. That is, by reducing M2, monetary authorities can reduce the long-run equilibrium price level.

Using the tools of aggregate supply and aggregate demand developed earlier, we can offer a crude explanation for the empirical relation observed between the current price level and the long-run equilibrium price level. Exhibit 8 presents the economy's long-run aggregate supply curve as a vertical line drawn at the economy's potential output, $Y^\star$. The long-run equilibrium price level, $P^\star$, is determined by the intersection of the aggregate demand curve and the long-run aggregate supply curve. Suppose, however, that the short-run equilibrium occurs at point *e*, where current output is below the economy's potential. At point *e*, the current price level, *P*, exceeds the long-run equilibrium price level, $P^\star$, indicating that the price

EXHIBIT 8

Long-Run Price Level as an Indicator of the Likely Course of Inflation

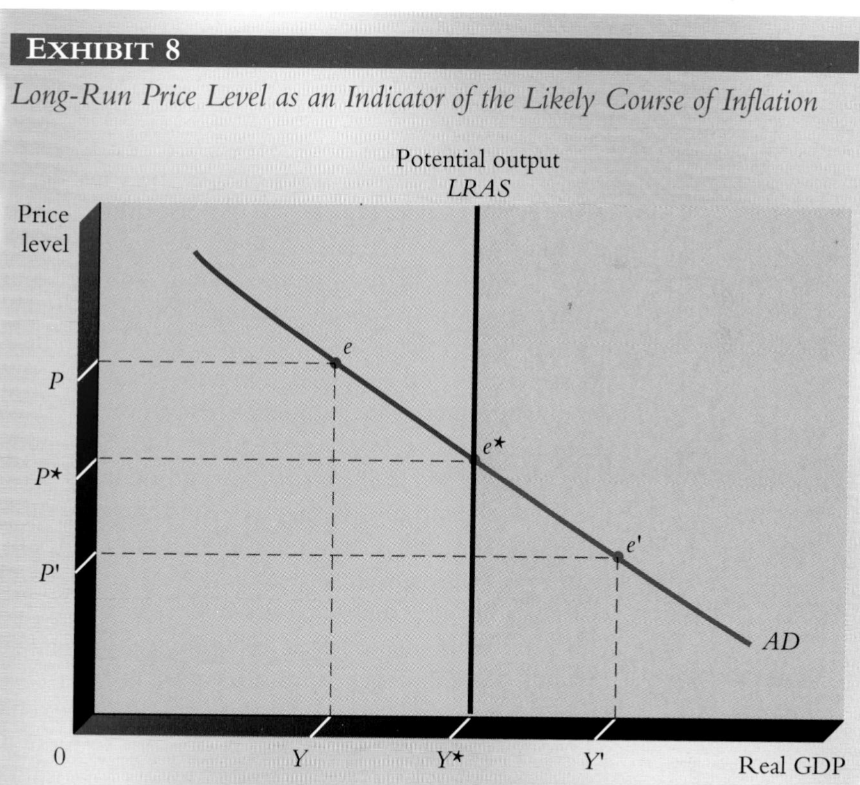

The difference between the current price level and the long-run equilibrium price level provides Fed officials with an indication of the likely course of inflation. If the current price level, *P*, exceeds the long-run price level, $P^\star$, inflation will tend to fall over the long run. If the current price level, P', is below $P^\star$, inflation will tend to increase. And if the current price level equals $P^\star$, inflation will remain unchanged.

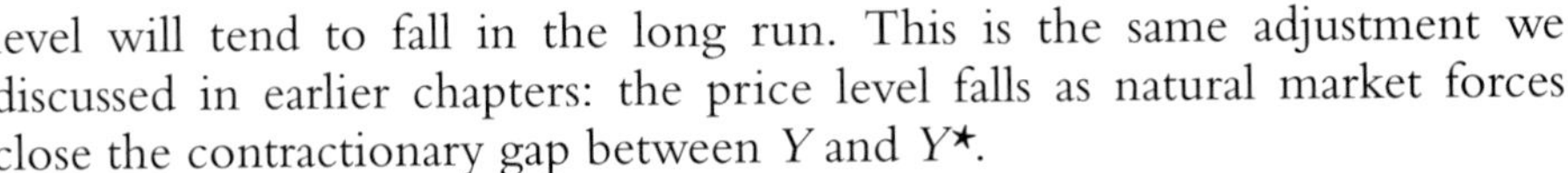

level will tend to fall in the long run. This is the same adjustment we discussed in earlier chapters: the price level falls as natural market forces close the contractionary gap between Y and $Y^\star$.

Conversely, if the short-run equilibrium occurs at point e', current output, Y', exceeds the economy's potential output and the current price level, P', is below the long-run equilibrium price level. The Fed's model predicts that when the current price level is below the long-run equilibrium price level, the price level will tend to rise. Again, this is the natural market adjustment to an expansionary gap. If the short-run equilibrium occurs at point $e^\star$, the current price level equals the long-run price level, so the price level (or inflation) is expected to remain stable.

Sources: John B. Carlson, "The Indicator P-Star: Just What Does It Indicate?" *Economic Commentary*, Federal Reserve Bank of Cleveland, September 15, 1989; and Thomas M. Humphrey, "Precursors of the P-Star Model," *Economic Review*, Federal Reserve Bank of Richmond, July/August 1989.

Conclusion

We have described two ways of viewing the effects of money on the economy's performance, but we should not overstate the differences. In the Keynesian model, an increase in the money supply means that people are holding more money than they would like at prevailing interest rates, so they exchange one form of wealth, money, for other financial assets, such as private or government securities. This increased demand for other financial assets has no direct effect on aggregate demand, but it does reduce the interest rate, and this lower interest rate stimulates investment. The increase in planned investment is magnified by the spending multiplier, increasing aggregate demand. The ultimate effect of this increase in demand on real output and the price level will depend on the shape of the aggregate supply curve.

In the monetarist framework, changes in the money supply act more directly on both output and prices. If velocity is relatively stable or at least fairly predictable, then changes in the money supply will have a predictable effect on nominal income and output in the economy. The mechanism through which changes in money translate into changes in nominal income is no more complicated than the equation of exchange. Increase the supply of money in the economy, and people try to reduce their money balances to the desired level by exchanging money for other assets, including houses and cars. This greater spending leads to an increase in aggregate demand and to a greater nominal output.

Each model employs a different perspective to examine the way the economy works. The Keynesian approach uses the 45-degree income-expenditure model, with the components of aggregate spending as basic building blocks. The monetarist approach uses the equation of exchange, with the elements of that equation as basic building blocks. To understand why these are alternative ways of viewing the same thing, consider the following analogy.

Suppose city officials, concerned about traffic congestion, ask their engineers and planners to estimate the total number of trips made from the suburbs to the city each month. The city engineers check with the state department of motor vehicles and find that 100,000 cars are registered to suburban residents. The engineers then estimate that each car makes an average of fifteen trips to the city per month, for a total of 1.5 million trips. In contrast, the city planners consider the number of trips to the city by suburban residents. They estimate that those suburbanites who commute to work make 700,000 trips per month, shoppers make 500,000 trips per month, and joyriders make 300,000 trips per month, for a total of 1.5 million trips.

The engineers focus on the number of cars and the average number of trips taken by each. Likewise, monetarists, to arrive at total spending, focus on the money supply and the average number of "trips" each dollar takes—that is, the average number of times each dollar is spent. Note that the engineers count all registered vehicles, even though some may sit in garages. Similarly, monetarists count all dollars, even though some remain idle in checking accounts or piggy banks. In contrast, the city planners focus not on the number of cars but on the different sources of trips to the city by suburban residents. Likewise, Keynesians focus not on the money stock but on the spending by various sectors in the economy.

Summary

1. The demand for money represents the sum of the transactions demand for money and the demand for money as a store of wealth. The opportunity cost of holding money is the higher interest that could be earned by holding other financial assets. The quantity of money demanded is inversely related to the interest rate. The demand for money increases with an increase in the price level or in real GDP.

2. The supply of money is determined by the Fed. The intersection of the supply and demand for money determines the equilibrium interest rate. According to the Keynesian view, an increase in the supply of money reduces the rate of interest, which increases investment spending. This increase in investment increases aggregate demand and the equilibrium level of income and output in the economy.

3. Monetarists focus on the role of money through the equation of exchange, which states that the money stock, M, multiplied by the average number of times, V, each dollar is used to pay for final output, equals the price level, P, multiplied by real GDP, Y.

4. Monetarists and Keynesians agree that an increase in the supply of money results in a lower interest rate and greater investment. But monetarists also claim that when the supply of money increases, people exchange money for real assets, such as homes and cars. Monetarists argue that velocity is stable enough that the effect of changes in the money supply on nominal output can be predicted, at least in the long run. During most of the 1970s, velocity appeared relatively stable, but since 1979 the velocity of M1 has been so variable that economists began to question the usefulness of the quantity theory, at least in the short run. Velocity has been more stable for M2 than for M1.

5. The Fed's model, based on the long-run equilibrium price level, predicts that inflation (1) will fall when the current price level is above the long-run equilibrium price level, (2) will rise when the current price level is below the long-run equilibrium price level, and (3) will remain unchanged when the current price level equals the long-run equilibrium price level.

QUESTIONS AND PROBLEMS

1. (Transactions Demand for Money) It is sometimes said that not only consumers but also businesses have a transactions demand for money. Explain why businesses would hold both demand deposits and currency. Are the factors that affect the demand for money by consumers the same as those that affect the demand by businesses?

2. (Opportunity Costs) How has lifting the prohibition against paying interest on checkable deposits affected the opportunity cost of holding currency? What has the effect been on the opportunity cost of holding checkable deposits? Will currency leakages and thus the money multiplier also be affected?

3. (Chain of Causation) There are two important links in the chain of causality for monetary policy: the link between an increase in the money supply and a drop in interest rates and the link between a drop in interest rates and a rise in investment spending. What would cause these two links to fail? Might both links fail at the same time?

4. (Demand for Money) If money is so versatile and can buy anything, why don't people demand an *infinite* amount of money? Does it really make sense to talk about a demand for money?

5. (Demand for Money) Would the quantity of money demanded be less sensitive to changes in interest rates if we defined money as M2 instead of M1? Would the same hold true if there was a ceiling on interest paid on savings accounts?

6. (Fiscal Policy and Monetary Policy) Explain why incorporating money into our macroeconomic framework moderates the effects of fiscal policy. That is, how does the existence of the supply and demand for money diminish the effects of increased government spending?

7. (Monetarism) Monetarists claim that a steady, constant growth in the money supply that is compatible with the long-run economic growth of the economy is the best type of monetary policy. What are the strengths and weaknesses of this approach?

8. (Velocity) The existence of automatic tellers for twenty-four-hour withdrawal of cash may have led to a reduction in the average amount of currency held by individuals. What effect would such a reduction have on the velocity of money? Have any other financial innovations affected velocity?

9. (Velocity) Why do some economists believe that higher expected inflation will generally lead to a rise in velocity?

10. (Monetary Targets) One problem with targeting the money supply is that it is not measured continuously as interest rates are. However, there are also some problems associated with using an interest-rate target for monetary policy. What are these problems?

11. (Monetary Policy) Using money supply-demand and aggregate expenditure diagrams, show how the sensitivity of money demand and aggregate expenditure to interest-rate changes influences the effectiveness of monetary policy in shifting the aggregate demand curve.

12. (Money Demand) Suppose the amount of money you hold for transactions purposes equals your average checking account balance (i.e., you never carry cash). Assume that your paycheck of $1,000 per month is deposited directly into your account and you spend your money at a uniform (constant) rate such that at the end of each month your checking balance is zero.
    a. What is your transactions demand for money?
    b. How would each of the following affect your money demand level?
        i. You are paid $500 twice a month instead of $1,000 once a month.
        ii. You are uncertain about your total spending each month.
        iii. You spend a lot in the beginning of each month (e.g., for rent) and little at the end of each month.
        iv. Your monthly income increases.

13. (Interest Rates) In Chapter 7 we noted that interest rates are determined in the loanable funds market. How is this fact consistent with the idea that interest rates are based on money demand and money supply?

14. (Velocity of Money) Using the equation of exchange, show why fiscal policy alone cannot increase nominal GDP if the velocity of money is constant.

15. (Velocity and Money Demand) How would the sensitivity of money demand to interest-rate levels be likely to influence the stability of the velocity of money?

16. (Money Demand) Suppose you are holding money balances and are considering using them to purchase an interest-earning asset. If you believe interest rates to be currently unusually low, how would this affect your current demand for money balances?

17. (Monetary Equilibrium) Exhibit 2 shows the impact on interest rates of an increase in the supply of money. Considering the transactions demand for money and the impact of money on aggregate demand as illustrated in Exhibit 3, why is the new interest rate shown in Exhibit 2 likely to be too low to be a new equilibrium rate?

18. (Quantity Theory) The quantity theory, in explaining the short-run impact of a change in the money supply on the economy, states that the impact on nominal GDP can be determined without any information on the *AD* curve, so long as the velocity of money is predictable. Discuss this assertion.

19. (Money and Interest Rates) The opportunity cost of holding money is the rate of interest. Which interest rate should be used, nominal or real? Explain.

20. (Money Versus Interest Rates) Explain why it is important to know the source of variation in money demand in order to know whether the Fed should target the money supply or interest rates.

21. (The Long-Run Price Level) Suppose that the money supply and the velocity of money are known. Using the equation of exchange, show that if actual P is below $P^\star$, then actual output must be above potential output (and hence an inflationary situation exists).

22. (The Long-Run Price Level) Suppose the Fed has determined that $P^\star$ lies below the actual price level. What will happen to $P^\star$ if the Fed takes action to correct output to potential GDP?

CHAPTER 15

THE POLICY DEBATE: ACTIVISM VERSUS NONACTIVISM

Activists Those who consider the private sector to be relatively unstable and able to absorb economic shocks only with the aid of discretionary government policy

Nonactivists Those who consider the private sector to be relatively stable and able to absorb economic shocks without discretionary government policy

Although we distinguished between Keynesians and monetarists in the last chapter, in matters of public policy a more general way of sorting out macroeconomists is into activists and nonactivists. **Activists** consider the private sector to be relatively unstable and unable to absorb shocks when they occur; **nonactivists** consider the private sector to be relatively stable and able to absorb shocks when they occur. According to activists, economic fluctuations arise primarily from the private sector, particularly investment. Essentially, activists would say "The economy has fallen and it can't get up." Nonactivists believe, however, that when the economy gets off track, natural market forces get it back on track; discretionary government policy often does more harm than good.

In this chapter we will compare the merits of active government intervention in the economy with those of passive reliance on natural market forces. We will also consider the crucial role that expectations play in determining the effectiveness of stabilization policy. We will show why unanticipated stabilization policies have more impact on employment and output than do anticipated policies. The chapter closes with a consideration of the tradeoff between unemployment and inflation. As you read, keep in mind that issues of macroeconomic policy remain the most widely debated of economic questions. Topics discussed in this chapter include

- Activist versus nonactivist policy
- Self-correcting mechanisms
- Rational expectations
- Policy rules and policy credibility
- The time inconsistency problem
- The short-run and long-run Phillips curves
- Natural rate hypothesis

Activism Versus Nonactivism

Teaching Tip The issue of activism versus nonactivism was an important topic during the 1992 presidential campaign.

According to activists, discretionary government policy can reduce the costs imposed by an unstable private sector. According to nonactivists, discretionary policy is part of the problem, not part of the solution. The two groups differ in their beliefs about how quickly wages and prices adjust to an excess supply or excess demand for labor—that is, how quickly natural market forces operate.

Closing a Contractionary Gap

Perhaps the best way to describe the views of each group is by examining a particular macroeconomic problem. Suppose the economy is in short-run equilibrium at point *a* in panel (a) of Exhibit 1, with a real GDP of $4.8 trillion, which is below the economy's potential of $5.0 trillion. The contractionary gap of $0.2 trillion results in unemployment that exceeds its natural rate (the rate of unemployment when the economy is producing its potential output). What should public officials do when confronted with this situation?

Point to Stress The point of contention between activists and nonactivists is not whether the economy can adjust back to potential GDP without government intervention, but whether such an adjustment will occur during a *reasonable* period. Also, note that in panel (a) of Exhibit 1, new wage agreements reflect an expected price level of 120.

Nonactivists, like their classical predecessors, have more faith in the self-correcting mechanisms of the economy than do activists. In what sense is the economy self-correcting? According to nonactivists, wages and prices are flexible enough to adjust within a reasonable period to labor shortages or surpluses. The high unemployment in panel (a) will cause wages to fall, which will reduce production costs, which will increase the short-run aggregate supply curve. (Money wages need not actually fall; money wage increases may simply lag behind increases in the price level, so that real wages fall.) According to the nonactivists, the short-run aggregate supply curve will, within a reasonable period, shift out from $SRAS_{130}$ to $SRAS_{120}$, moving the economy to its potential level of output at point *b*. *Nonactivists view the economy as inherently stable, gravitating in a reasonable amount of time toward potential GDP. Consequently they see little reason for active government intervention.* The *nonactivist* approach to a contractionary gap is to allow natural market forces to close the gap.

Activists, on the other hand, believe that prices and wages are not very flexible, particularly in the downward direction. When supply shocks or sagging demand result in unemployment that exceeds the natural rate, the economy does not quickly adjust to eliminate this unemployment. Activists argue that even when there is much unemployment in the economy, the renegotiation of long-term wage contracts in line with a lower expected price level may take a long time. Thus, the wage reductions required to shift the short-run aggregate supply curve out may also take a long time, even years. The longer natural market forces take to lower unemployment to the natural rate, the greater the forgone output during the adjustment period and the greater the economic and psychic costs to those who are unemployed during that period. Because activists associate a high cost with the nonactivist approach, they believe that the economy needs an *active* fiscal and/or monetary policy to alter aggregate demand to achieve the natural rate of output and price stability.

Point to Stress The greater the length of time needed for an automatic adjustment, the greater the cost of the contractionary gap and the greater the justification for discretionary policy changes.

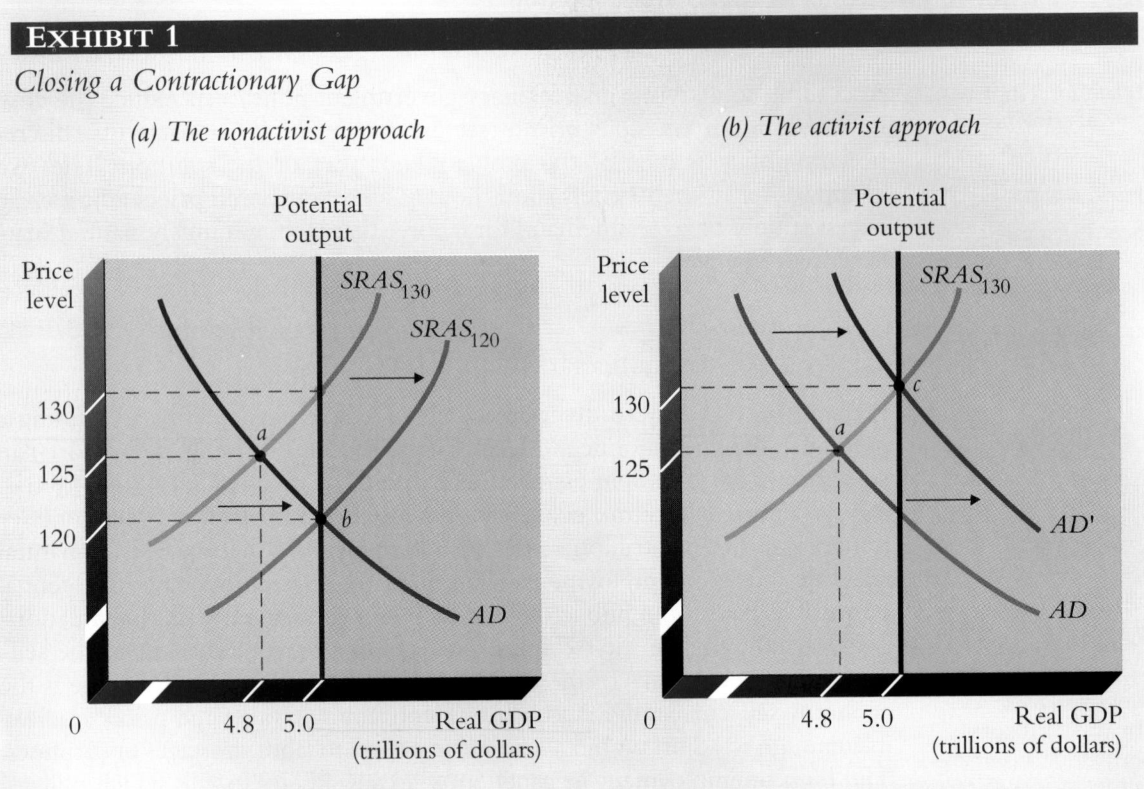

At point *a*, the economy is in short-run equilibrium. Unemployment is above the natural rate. According to nonactivists, that high unemployment will eventually cause wages to fall, reducing firms' cost of doing business. The decline in costs will cause the short-run aggregate supply curve to shift out to $SRAS_{120}$, moving the economy to its potential level of output at point *b*.

At point *a*, the economy is in short-run equilibrium. Unemployment is above the natural rate. To reduce unemployment, the government employs an activist policy to shift the aggregate demand curve from *AD* to *AD′*. If the policy works, the economy moves to its potential level of output at point *c*.

Example In October 1992, the German central bank announced interest-rate drops to counteract the slowing German economy.

A decision by the government to intervene in the economy to speed the return to potential output—that is, a decision to use discretionary policy—reflects an *activist* approach. In panel (b) of Exhibit 1 we begin at the same point *a* as in panel (a). At point *a* the short-run equilibrium output is below the potential output, so the economy is experiencing a contractionary gap. Through monetary policy, fiscal policy, or some mix of the two, activist policy makers attempt to increase aggregate demand from *AD* to *AD′*, moving equilibrium from point *a* to point *c* and closing the contractionary gap. One cost of such a policy is an increase in the price level. To the extent that the stimulus to aggregate demand arises from a budget deficit, another cost of the policy is an increase in the national debt, a cost that will be examined more closely in the next chapter.

Closing an Expansionary Gap

Let's consider the situation in which the short-run equilibrium output exceeds the economy's potential. Suppose that the actual price level of 135 exceeds the expected price level of 130, causing an expansionary gap of $0.2 trillion, as shown in Exhibit 2. In the absence of any discretionary government policy, natural market forces will, according to nonactivists, prompt firms and workers to negotiate higher wage agreements. These higher nominal wages will increase production costs, shifting the short-run supply curve up and to the left, from $SRAS_{130}$ to $SRAS_{140}$, leading to a higher price level and reducing output to the economy's potential. So the natural adjustment process will result in a higher price level, or inflation.

Point to Stress The higher wage agreements reflect a new expected price level of 140.

EXHIBIT 2

Policy Responses to an Expansionary Gap

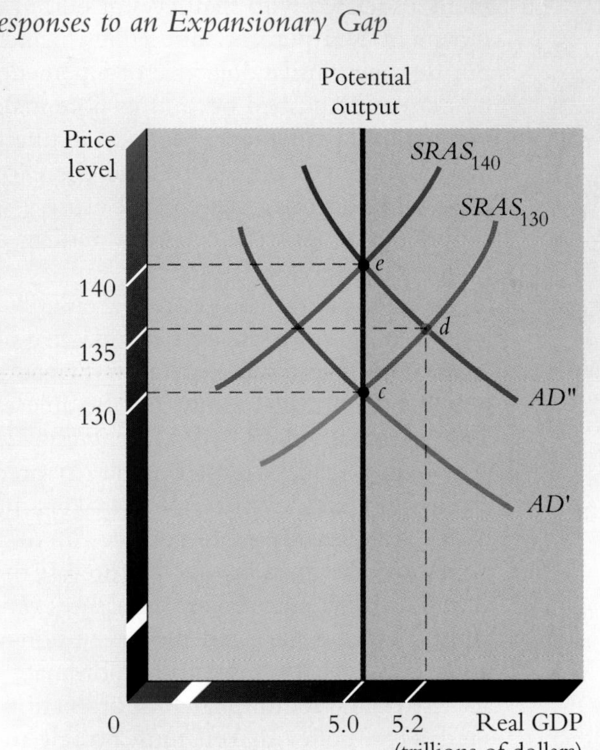

At point *d*, the economy is in short-run equilibrium, producing $5.2 trillion. Unemployment is below the natural rate. If the government makes no change in policy, natural market forces will eventually bring about a higher negotiated wage, shifting the short-run supply curve up to $SRAS_{140}$. The new equilibrium at point *e* will result in a higher price level and a lower level of output and employment. An activist policy might be able to reduce aggregate demand, shifting the equilibrium from point *d* to point *c*, thus closing the expansionary gap without increasing the price level.

Activists see discretionary policy as a way of returning the economy to its potential output without fostering an increase in the price level, or inflation. Activists believe that if aggregate demand can be reduced from AD'' to AD', then the equilibrium point will move down along the initial supply curve from *d* to *c*. *Whereas natural market forces close an expansionary gap by raising the price level, just the right discretionary policy closes the gap by lowering the price level.* Thus, the correct discretionary policy can relieve the inflationary pressure associated with an expansionary gap.

Problems with Activist Policy

Example In the P^* analysis, if the Fed overestimates Y^*, then it underestimates P^*. Thinking P exceeds P^*, the Fed may ease monetary policy during a period when inflationary pressures are growing (i.e., when P^* exceeds P).

Teaching Tip With the short-run aggregate supply curve shifting up, the government can maintain actual unemployment below the natural rate only by constantly increasing aggregate demand.

Example Despite Fed policies during 1991–1992 that left short-term interest rates at their lowest levels since the 1960s, economic growth remained very low relative to normal post-recession growth levels. Total bank lending dropped steadily while banks' holdings of Treasury notes and bills increased dramatically.

The timely adoption and implementation of an appropriate activist policy is not easy. One problem confronting policy makers is the difficulty of identifying the economy's potential level of output and the amount of unemployment associated with that level of output. Suppose the natural rate of unemployment is 6 percent, but policy makers believe it is 5 percent. As they pursue their elusive objective of 5 percent unemployment, the economy will be constantly pushed beyond its potential, creating higher prices in the long run with no permanent reduction in unemployment. Recall that in the short run, if output is pushed beyond the economy's potential, an expansionary gap will be created, which will cause a shift up in the short-run aggregate supply curve until the economy returns to its potential level of output at a higher price level.

Even if policy makers can accurately estimate the economy's potential level of output, formulating an effective policy requires abundant knowledge of the current and future states of the economy. To pursue an effective activist policy, policy makers must *first* be able to forecast what aggregate demand and aggregate supply would be without government intervention. Simply put, policy makers must be able to predict what would happen with no change in policy. *Second*, policy makers must have in their discretionary arsenal the tools necessary to achieve the desired result relatively quickly. *Third*, policy makers must be able to forecast the effects of any new policy on the economy's key performance measures. *Fourth*, policy makers must work together. Fiscal policy and monetary policy are pursued by separate government bodies that often fail to coordinate their efforts. To the extent that an activist policy requires such coordination, the policy may not work as desired. *Fifth*, policy makers must be able to implement the appropriate policy, even if that policy involves short-term political costs. For example, during inflationary times the optimal policy may call for a tax increase or slower money growth, policies that may not be popular because of their negative effects on employment. *Finally*, policy makers must be able to deal with a variety of lags. As we will see next, these lags compound the problems of pursuing an activist policy.

The Problem of Lags

So far we have ignored the time required to implement policy. That is, we have assumed that the desired policy was selected and implemented in no time. We have also assumed that, once implemented, the policy worked as advertised—again, in no time. Actually, there may be long, sometimes unpredictable, delays at several stages in the process. These lags reduce the effectiveness of discretionary policies.

Recognition lag The time needed to identify a macroeconomic problem and assess its seriousness

First, there is a **recognition lag**, which is the time it takes to identify a problem and determine how serious it is. Time is required to accumulate data indicating that the economy is indeed performing below its potential. Even if initial data provide early warning signals, these data are often subsequently revised. Therefore, policy makers often await additional evidence of trouble rather than risk responding to what may turn out to be a false alarm. In fact, a recession does not become official until more than six months after it begins. And since the average recession lasts about a year, the recession is nearly half over before it is officially recognized as such.

Decision-making lag The time needed to decide what changes to make in government policy after a macroeconomic problem is identified

When enough evidence has accumulated, policy makers usually take time deciding what to do, so there is a **decision-making lag**. In the case of fiscal policy, Congress and the president must develop and agree upon an appropriate course of action. Fiscal legislation usually takes months to pass; it can take more than a year. On the other hand, Federal Reserve authorities can decide on the appropriate monetary policy much more quickly than can those in charge of fiscal policy, so the decision-making lag is shorter for monetary policy.

Implementation lag The time needed to introduce a change in monetary or fiscal policy

Teaching Tip The main policy-making arm of the Fed is the Federal Open Market Committee, which has only twelve members. See Chapter 16 for a discussion of the far more complicated budget process involved in fiscal policy.

Once a decision has been made, the new policy must be introduced, which often involves an **implementation lag**. Again, monetary policy has the advantage: after a policy has been adopted, the Fed can buy or sell U.S. securities, change the discount rate, or alter reserve requirements relatively quickly. The implementation lag is longer for fiscal policy. For example, if tax rates change, new tax forms must be printed and distributed. If government spending changes, the appropriate government agencies must get involved. The implementation of fiscal policy can take more than a year. For example, in February 1983 the nation's unemployment rate reached 10.3 percent, with 11.5 million unemployed. The following month the Emergency Jobs Appropriation Act was passed, providing $9 billion to create what supporters of the measure claimed would be hundreds of thousands of new jobs. Fifteen months later, only $3.1 billion had been spent and only 35,000 new jobs had been created, according to a Government Accounting Office study. By that time, the economy had recovered on its own, reducing the unemployment rate to 7.1 percent and increasing the number employed by 6.2 million. Thus, this public spending program was implemented only after the recession had bottomed out.

Effectiveness lag The time necessary for changes in monetary or fiscal policy to have an effect on the economy

Teaching Tip A change in open-market operations simply requires the issuing of a directive to the Trading Desk at the New York Reserve bank.

Once a policy has been implemented, there is an **effectiveness lag** before the full impact of the policy registers on the economy. One problem with monetary policy is that the lag between a change in the money supply and its effect on aggregate demand and output is long and variable, ranging from several months up to three years. Once enacted, fiscal policy usually requires three to six months to take effect and between nine and eighteen months to register its full effect.

These various lags make an activist policy difficult to pursue. If natural market forces fail to reduce unemployment, then longer lags increase the total output forgone by the economy and the psychic costs imposed on unemployed

Teaching Tip In terms of aggregate demand and aggregate supply analysis, nonactivists argue that the short-run aggregate supply curve shifts the economy back to potential GDP before government actions can shift the aggregate demand. Therefore, the new equilibrium occurs at the intersection of a new short-run aggregate supply curve and a new aggregate demand—to the right of potential GDP.

workers. The more variable the lags are, the harder it is to predict when a particular policy will take effect and what the state of the economy will be at that time. To nonactivists, these lags are reason enough to avoid discretionary policy, particularly because the average contraction, or recession, since World War II has lasted only about a year. *Nonactivists argue that an active stabilization policy imposes troubling fluctuations in the price level and in the level of output because it often takes hold only after market forces have already returned the economy to its potential level of output.*

Talk in the media about "jump-starting" the economy reflects the activist approach, which views the economy as a sputtering machine that can be fixed by an expert mechanic. Nonactivists would argue that the economy is more like a supertanker on automatic pilot. The policy question then becomes whether to trust that automatic pilot (i.e., the self-correcting tendencies of the economy) or to try to override the mechanism with activist discretionary policies.[1]

Example Estimates of the percentage of "distressed workers" in the labor force in 1992 were as high as 40 percent. As well as unemployed workers, this category included those working below their skill levels, those working only part time, those working at or below poverty-level wages, and discouraged workers.

Review of Policy Perspectives

Activists and nonactivists have different views about the natural stability of the economy and the ability of the government to implement appropriate discretionary policies. Hence they disagree about the role of government in the economy. As we have seen, activists think that the natural adjustments of wages and prices can be excruciatingly slow, particularly when unemployment is high, as during the Great Depression. Prolonged high unemployment means that much output must be sacrificed, and the unemployed must suffer personal hardship during the slow adjustment period. If high unemployment lasts a long time, labor skills may grow rusty, some long-term unemployed workers may drop out of the labor force, and firms may neglect their capital stock, causing it to depreciate faster. Therefore, prolonged unemployment may cause the economy's potential GDP to fall, as the case study of hysteresis in Chapter 10 suggested.

Thus, activists associate a high cost with the failure to pursue a discretionary policy. And despite the lags involved, activists prefer action—whether through fiscal policy, monetary policy, or some combination of the two—to inaction. Nonactivists, on the other hand, believe that uncertain lags and ignorance about how the economy works prevent the government from accurately determining or effectively implementing the appropriate activist policy. Therefore, nonactivists would rather rely on the economy's natural ability to correct itself and on the government's automatic stabilizers than pursue a misguided activist policy.

In a small way, differences between activists and nonactivists came out in 1992, when a slow recovery from a recession collided with a presidential election, as discussed in the following case study.

1. This analogy was contributed by J. W. Mixon, Jr. to *The Teaching Economist* 4 (Spring 1992): 3, edited by W. A. McEachern.

CASE STUDY

The '92 Presidential Campaign

Teaching Tip In December 1991, Michael Boskin, head of President Bush's Council of Economic Advisers, recommended a $50 to $75 billion package of tax cuts and spending increases to speed the recovery. He argued that in fact the effect of the federal budget was neutral and that state budgets were somewhat contractionary. However, Boskin's advice was ignored.

In the third quarter of 1990 the U.S. economy slipped into a recession. Because of huge federal deficits, policy makers were reluctant to turn to discretionary fiscal policy to stimulate the economy. That task was left to monetary policy. The Fed supplied additional reserves to the banking system and cut the discount rate several times, moves aimed at expanding the money supply and reducing interest rates to stimulate spending. The recession lasted only three quarters, but the recovery was sluggish, with a growth rate slower than usual.

That was the economic setting for the presidential election of 1992 between Democratic challenger Bill Clinton and Republican President George Bush. Since monetary policy did not seem to be providing a sufficient kick, was additional fiscal stimulus a viable option? Since the federal budget in 1992 was already over $300 billion, a record level, would a higher deficit do more harm than good?

Bush's biggest liability during the campaign was the sluggish recovery and mounting federal debt; these were Clinton's biggest assets. Clinton's economic positions were that (1) Bush had not done enough to revive the economy; (2) Bush and his predecessor, President Reagan, were responsible for the rise in federal deficits and the resulting federal debt; and (3) Bush could not be trusted because he broke his pledge of no new taxes by signing a tax increase in 1990. Clinton called for raising the marginal tax rate on the top 2 percent of taxpayers and cutting taxes for the middle class. He also promised to create jobs through government spending that would "invest in America."

Bush tried to point out that technically the recession was over and the economy was on the right track. He blamed a Democratic Congress for blocking his recovery proposals, and he renewed his pledge of no new taxes (saying he really meant it this time). Bush promised to cut taxes by 1 percent as a way of shifting spending from government bureaucrats back to households.

Though both candidates were short on specifics, Clinton saw a stronger role for government, and Bush saw a stronger role for the private sector. Clinton was more the *activist*, and Bush was more the *nonactivist*. Neither candidate proposed aggressive deficit-reducing measures. Both apparently recognized that there were few votes to be gained by raising taxes or cutting government programs. Only third-party candidate Ross Perot made an issue of the deficit. In the end, the negative economic reports that dominated the news made people willing to gamble on Clinton. Evidently, during hard times an activist policy has more voter appeal than a nonactivist policy.

Sources: David Wessel, "Wanted: Fiscal Stimulus Without Higher Taxes," *Wall Street Journal*, 5 October 1992; and Herbert Stein, "The Inane Campaign Gives Me a Pain," *Wall Street Journal*, 7 October 1992.

MACROECONOMIC POLICY AND EXPECTATIONS

The effectiveness of a particular government policy depends on what people expect. As we observed in Chapter 10, the short-run aggregate supply curve is drawn for a given expected price level reflected in long-term wage contracts. If workers and firms expect more inflation, their labor agreements will reflect these inflationary expectations. An influential approach in macroeconomics, called the **rational expectations** school, argues that people form expectations on the basis of all available information, including information about the probable future action of policy makers. Thus, aggregate supply depends on what sort of macroeconomic course policy makers are expected to pursue. For example, if people observe that the government tries to stimulate aggregate demand every time real output falls below the economy's potential, they will come to anticipate the effects of this policy on the levels of price and output.

Rational expectations A school of thought that claims people form expectations based on all available information, including the probable future actions of government policy makers

Monetary authorities must testify before Congress regularly, indicating the monetary policy they plan to pursue. We will consider the role of expectations in the context of monetary policy by examining the relation between policy pronouncements and equilibrium output. We could employ a similar approach with fiscal policy, but active discretionary fiscal policy over the last decade has been overshadowed by the huge federal deficits. To be sure, there is still talk about tax cuts and spending programs to "jump start" the economy (such as President Clinton's $16 billion stimulus proposal in the spring of 1993), and automatic fiscal stabilizers (e.g., unemployment insurance, progressive income taxes, means-tested programs, etc.) continue in force, but monetary policy has been center stage.

Teaching Tip The rational expectations school was developed during the 1970s. Its major proponents were Robert Lucas and Thomas Sargent.

Example The Fed reduced short-term interest rates twenty-four times in 1991 and 1992. Some analysts began to question whether interest rates were now so low that monetary policy had become ineffective.

Monetary Policy and Expectations

Suppose the economy is producing at its potential rate of output. At the beginning of the year, firms and employees must negotiate wage agreements. While negotiations are under way, the Fed announces that throughout the year its policy will limit the growth in the money supply to that sufficient to serve the money needs of an economy producing at the potential level. Thus the Fed plans to hold the price level constant. This seems to be the appropriate policy since the level of unemployment is already at the natural rate. Until the year is under way and monetary policy is actually implemented, however, the public cannot be sure what the Fed will do. Firms and workers understand that the Fed's plans appear optimal under the circumstances, since a sharp increase in the money supply would, in the long run, simply lead to a higher price level.

Teaching Tip If potential GDP increases each year, the money supply needs to grow just to keep the price level from falling.

Teaching Tip The constant price level goal requires that the Fed be *able* to predict the money needs of the economy accurately.

If workers limited their wage increase demands to any growth in labor productivity, this would be consistent with the Fed's announced policy of a constant price level. Alternatively, workers can try for higher wages, but that option will ultimately lead to inflation. Suppose workers and firms believe the Fed's pronouncements and agree on wage settlements based on expectations of a constant price level. If the Fed follows through, as promised, then the price level will be constant, output will remain at the economy's potential, and unemployment will remain at the natural rate. A constant price level is the optimal outcome in the long run. The situation is depicted in Exhibit 3, where the short-run aggregate supply curve, $SRAS_{130}$, is based on wage contracts reflecting an expected price level of 130. If the Fed follows the announced course, aggregate demand will be *AD* and equilibrium will be at point *a*, where the price level is as expected and the economy is producing $5.0 trillion, the potential level of output.

Suppose, however, that after workers and firms have signed labor pacts—that is, after the short-run aggregate supply curve has been determined—public officials become dissatisfied with the prevailing level of unemployment. Perhaps election-year concern about unemployment, an underestimation of

EXHIBIT 3

Short-Run Effects of an Unexpected Increase in the Money Supply

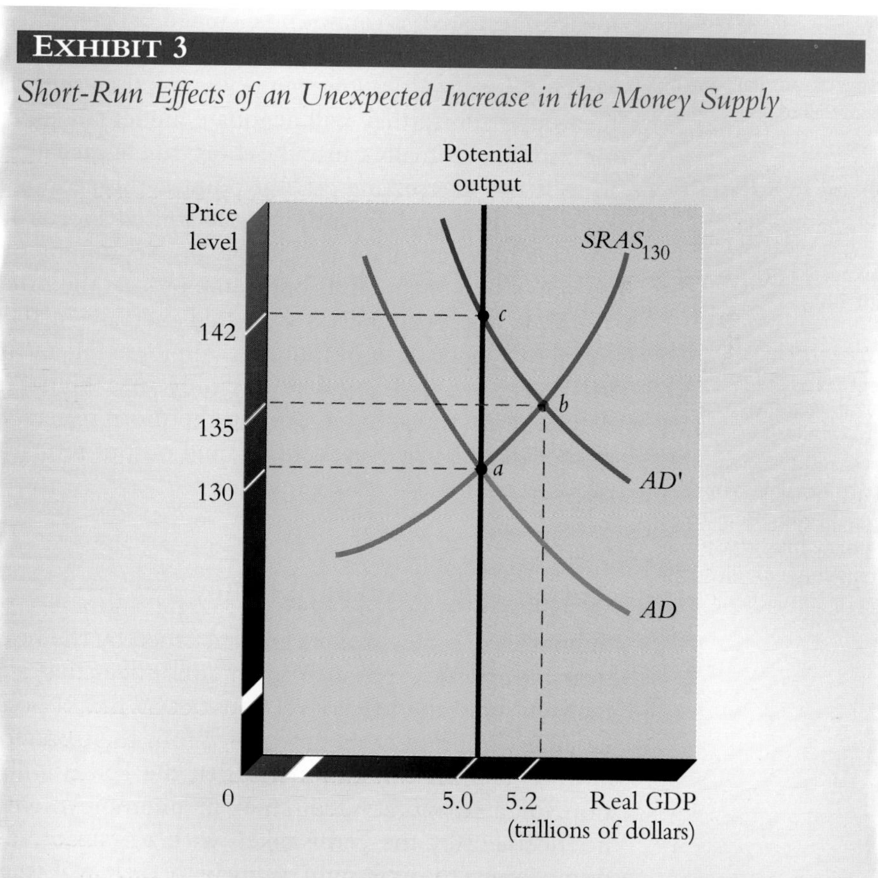

At point *a*, firms and workers expect the price level to be 130; supply curve $SRAS_{130}$ reflects those expectations. If the Federal Reserve unexpectedly increases the money supply, the aggregate demand curve will be *AD′* rather than *AD*. Output will temporarily rise above the potential rate (at point *b*), but in the long run it will fall back to the potential rate at point *c*. The short-run effect of monetary policy is a higher level of output, but the long-run effect is just an increase in the price level.

Teaching Tip Recall the discussion of the political business cycle in Chapter 11.

the natural rate of unemployment, or a false alarm about the onset of a recession prompts officials to pressure the Fed into stimulating aggregate demand and lowering unemployment in the short run by increasing the money supply more than was expected.

The unexpected increase in the money supply increases aggregate demand beyond *AD*, the level anticipated by firms and employees, to *AD′*. The expansionary monetary policy stimulates output and employment in the short run to equilibrium point *b*. Output increases to $5.2 trillion, and the price level increases to 135. This temporary boost in output and reduction in unemployment lasts perhaps long enough to help public officials get reelected. The **time inconsistency problem** arises when policy makers have an incentive to announce one policy to influence expectations but then pursue a different policy once those expectations have been formed and acted upon. As we shall see in the next section, one solution to the time inconsistency problem is to take discretion away from the policy makers so that once a policy is announced, it cannot be changed.

Time inconsistency problem The problem that arises when policy makers have an incentive to announce one policy to influence expectations but then to pursue a different policy once those expectations have been formed and acted upon

In the short run, workers are locked into wage levels that, because of the higher price level, are lower in real terms than they had bargained for. At their next opportunity, they will negotiate higher wages. These higher wage agreements will eventually cause the short-run aggregate supply curve in Exhibit 3 to shift up, intersecting *AD′* at point *c*, the economy's potential output. (To keep the diagram less cluttered, the shifted short-run aggregate supply curve has not been included in Exhibit 3.) So output once again returns to the economy's potential GDP, but in the process the price level rises to 142.

Point to Stress The higher negotiated wages reflect a new expected price level of 142.

Thus, the greater-than-expected increase in the money supply causes a short-run increase in output and employment; in the long run, the increase in the aggregate demand results only in a higher price level, or inflation. After a short-run surge in output, the short-run aggregate supply curve shifts to the left, the price level climbs, and output returns once again to the economy's potential.

Teaching Tip Nominal wages have risen, but the real wage simply returns to the level that existed before the change in monetary policy (in the static environment illustrated in Exhibit 3).

Anticipating Monetary Policy

Suppose Fed policy makers grow alarmed by the resulting inflation. The next time around the Fed once again announces that it plans a monetary policy that will hold the price level constant at 142, a policy aimed at keeping the economy's output at its potential. From their previous experience, however, workers and firms have learned that the Fed is willing to trade higher inflation for a temporary reduction in unemployment. Consequently, the announcement by the Fed is taken with a grain of salt. Workers, in particular, do not want to get caught again with their real wages down should the Fed implement a stimulative monetary policy, so a high-wage-increase settlement is reached.

In effect, workers and firms are betting that when the chips are down, monetary authorities will pursue an expansionary monetary policy regardless of their pronouncement to the contrary. The short-run aggregate supply curve reflecting these high-wage-increase agreements is depicted by $SRAS_{152}$ in

Exhibit 4, where 152 is the expected price level. Note that AD' is the aggregate demand that would result if the announced constant-price-level policy were pursued; that demand curve intersects the potential output line at point *c*, where the price level is 142. But AD'' is the aggregate demand that firms and workers expect based on a high-money-growth policy. Firms and workers have agreed to wage settlements that will produce the economy's potential level of output if the Fed behaves as *expected*, not as *announced*.

EXHIBIT 4

Short-Run Effects of an Unexpected Decrease in the Money Supply

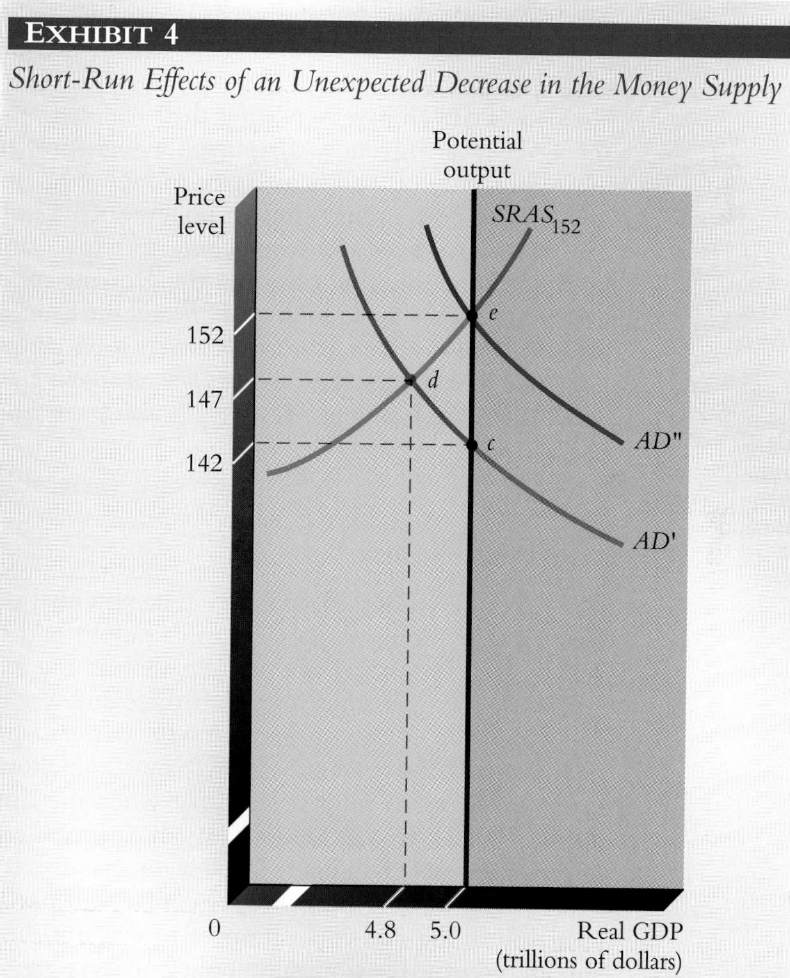

The Fed announces a monetary policy that will keep the price level at 142. Firms and workers, however, do not believe the announcement; they think the monetary policy will be expansionary. The short-run aggregate supply curve, $SRAS_{152}$, reflects their forecasts of the price level. The Fed must then decide what to do. If it follows the noninflation policy, aggregate demand will be AD', and output will fall below potential to point *d*. To keep the economy performing at its potential, the Fed must increase the money supply by as much as workers and firms expected.

Monetary authorities must now decide whether to stick with their announcement of holding the price level constant or follow a more expansionary monetary policy. If they pursue the constant-price-level policy, aggregate demand will turn out to be AD' and short-run equilibrium will occur at point *d*. Short-run output will fall below the economy's potential, resulting in unemployment above the natural rate. If the monetary authorities want to keep the economy performing at its potential, they have only one alternative: to meet workers' and firms' expectations. Monetary authorities *must* increase the money supply by more than they had announced. Such a policy will result in an aggregate demand of AD'', leading to an equilibrium at point *e*, where the economy produces its potential output, but the price level has climbed to 152.

Teaching Tip The process of increasing the money supply in reaction to the workers' negotiating higher wages is called *monetary validation.*

Thus, firms and workers enter their negotiations with the realization that the Fed has an incentive to pursue a high-growth-rate monetary course. Therefore, workers and firms agree to high wage increases, and the Fed follows with a high-money-growth policy. Such a policy results in more inflation. Once workers and firms come to expect an expansionary monetary policy and the resulting inflation, the growing money supply does not spur even a temporary boost in output beyond the economy's potential. *Economists of the rational expectations school believe that an expansionary monetary policy, if fully and correctly anticipated, has no effect on output or employment. Only unanticipated or incorrectly anticipated changes in policy can have an impact on output and employment.*

Teaching Tip The rational expectations school assumes that wages and prices are able to adjust quickly to changes in government policies. Critics argue that the U.S. system of three-year decentralized wage bargaining with staggered contract expiration dates casts serious doubt on the validity of this assumption.

Policy Credibility

If the economy is already producing its potential output, an unexpected increase in the money supply increases output and employment temporarily. The costs, however, are not only inflation in the long term but also a loss of credibility the next time around. Is there any way out of this cycle? For the Fed to get on a slow-money-growth, constant-price-level course, its announcements of slow money growth must somehow be *credible*, or believable. Firms and workers must believe that when the time comes to make a hard decision, the Fed will follow through as promised. Perhaps the Fed could offer some sort of insurance policy to make everyone believe that policy makers who deviate from the set course will pay dearly—for example, the chairman of the Fed could promise to resign if the Fed does not pursue the announced course. Ironically, policy makers are often more credible and therefore more effective if they have their discretion taken away. In this case a hard-and-fast rule could be substituted for a policy maker's discretion. Policy rules will be considered in the next section.

Consider the problems facing central banks in countries that have experienced hyperinflation. For an anti-inflation policy to succeed at the least possible cost in forgone output, the public must believe the announcements of central bankers. How do they establish credibility? Some economists believe that the most efficient anti-inflation policy is **cold turkey**, which is to announce and execute tough measures to stop inflation, such as halting the

Cold turkey The announcement and execution of tough measures to reduce high inflation

Teaching Tip The longer the period needed to adjust price expectations downward, the longer the contractionary gap resulting from an anti-inflationary policy lasts.

Example In December 1982 the U.S. civilian unemployment rate hit its highest point since before World War II: 10.8 percent.

Teaching Tip The Fed often comes under pressure from the president to take a short-term view of its targets.

growth in the money supply. For example, in 1985 the annual rate of inflation in Bolivia was running at 20,000 percent when the new government announced a stern "New Economic Policy." The tough new measures worked and inflation was stopped within a month, with only a 5-percent loss on output. Around the world credible anti-inflation policies have been successful.[2] Drastic measures may involve costs. For example, Fed Chairman Volcker's sharp measures to curb high U.S. inflation during the early 1980s were said to have precipitated the worst recession since the Great Depression.

If policy makers thought of their reputations as valuable resources to be handled with care, they might be more reluctant to seek short-term reductions in unemployment. For example, suppose that by sticking to a zero-inflation or low-inflation policy for several years, the Fed persuaded the public that such a policy would continue in future years. As firms and workers came to realize that the Fed is credible, they would be more willing to sign wage contracts that assume a tight monetary policy.

Much depends on the Fed's time horizon. If policy makers take the long view of their duties, they will be reluctant to risk their long-run policy effectiveness for a temporary reduction in unemployment. If Fed officials realize that their credibility is hard to develop but easy to undermine, they will carefully weigh the effects of their actions on their reputations and follow what nonactivists believe is the optimal policy: slow, steady growth in the money supply. We next consider policy rules.

Policy Rules Versus Discretion

Teaching Tip See Chapter 16 for another predetermined rule that has been suggested for fiscal policy: the balanced budget amendment.

Point to Stress The validity of monetarist recommendations rests, in part, on the assumption of a stable and predictable velocity of money.

As we have noted, activists believe that the economy is inherently unstable and that discretionary policy is needed to eliminate excessive unemployment when it arises. Nonactivists believe that the economy is inherently stable, so discretionary policy is not only unnecessary but causes destabilizing swings in aggregate demand that ultimately lead to more inflation. In place of discretionary policy, nonactivists advocate predetermined rules to guide the actions of policy makers. In the context of fiscal policy, these predetermined rules take the form of automatic stabilizers, such as unemployment insurance, a progressive income tax, and antipoverty programs. In this section we examine the arguments for rules versus discretion in the context of monetary policy.

Rationale for Monetary Rules

As noted in the previous chapter, monetarists believe that changes in the quantity of money have a major influence on changes in nominal income.

2. For a discussion about how four hyperinflations in the 1920s ended, see Thomas Sargent, "The Ends of Four Big Inflations," in Robert Hall, ed., *Inflation: Causes and Consequences* (Chicago: University of Chicago Press, 1982): 41–98.

They also believe that moderate, predictable growth in the money supply is better for the economy in the long run than any discretionary monetary policy. In fact, monetarists attribute most past instability in nominal income to unstable money growth. Perhaps the strongest advocate of a monetary rule is Milton Friedman, who said:

My own prescription is still that the monetary authority go all the way in avoiding such swings by adopting publicly the policy of achieving a specified rate of growth in a specified monetary total. The precise rate of growth, like the precise monetary total, is less important than the adoption of some stated and known rate.[3]

Teaching Tip In an interview in the October 3, 1977 issue of *Newsweek*, Friedman stated that the "one and only basic cause of inflation (is) too high a rate of growth in the quantity of money. . . ."

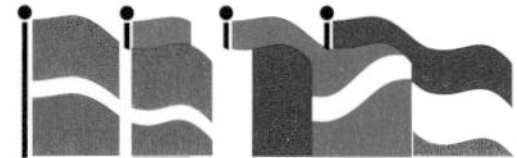

In addition, Friedman contends that in the long run *excessive* increases in the money supply result in inflation. Panel (b) in Exhibit 5 illustrates the relation between the average annual growth rate in the money supply (broadly defined) from 1980 to 1990 and the average annual rate of inflation from 1980 to 1990 for the eighty-five countries for which complete data are available. As you can see, the points fall rather neatly along the trend line, showing a positive relation between money growth and inflation. Argentina, Bolivia, and Israel—the three countries that experienced annual inflation exceeding 100 percent—also had an annual growth in the money supply exceeding 100 percent. For example, Argentina, which had the highest average annual inflation rate over the ten-year period in the sample, at 395 percent, also had the highest average annual rate of growth in the money supply, at 369 percent.

Since most countries are bunched below an inflation rate of 20 percent, these points have been broken out in finer detail in panel (a). Countries with low rates of money growth also experienced low rates of inflation. More generally, over the past two decades, nominal GDP in the United States has grown at an annual rate of 8.6 percent, and the stock of M2 has grown by 8.2 percent. Such evidence has led Friedman and others to advocate a steady *and moderate* increase in the money supply year after year.

Kinds of Rules

Teaching Tip A constant-growth-rate rule for monetary policy might, for example, set the money growth rate equal to the long-term growth trend of potential GDP.

A *monetary rule* specifies the relation that ties policy instruments, such as the growth in the money supply, to policy objectives, such as keeping inflation below a certain rate. A rule can specify that there is no policy relation. For example, it might state that the rate of growth in the money supply will be constant regardless of how the economy actually performs. Such a rule represents the most passive form of monetary policy.

A more active approach might be to link money supply growth to some measure of economic performance. For example, a rule might state that the money supply will grow as fast as real GDP, that the money supply will be adjusted to offset the growth in inflation (as inflation heats up, the growth in the money supply will be slowed), that the money supply will be adjusted to maintain a constant interest rate, or that the money supply will be adjusted to maintain a constant rate of inflation. These monetary policies are active in

3. Milton Friedman, "The Role of Monetary Policy," *American Economic Review* 58 (March 1968): 16.

EXHIBIT 5

Annual Inflation and Money Growth in Eighty-Five Countries: 1980–1990

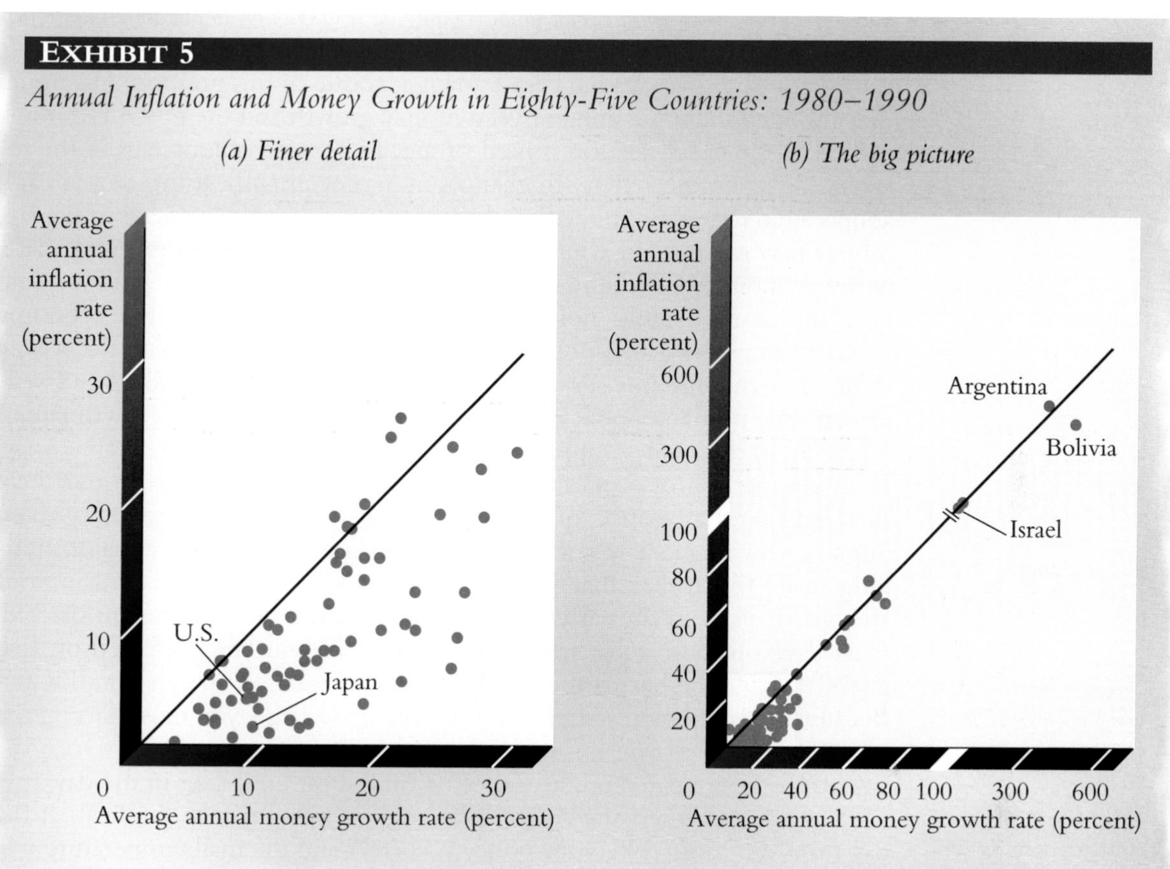

Source: The World Bank, *World Development Report 1992* (New York: Oxford University Press, 1992), Table 13.

the sense that they respond to events. But because the response has been predetermined—that is, because it has been established by a previously adopted policy—little discretion is required of policy makers. Such a policy, however, does not completely eliminate discretion on the part of policy makers, because they must still determine what growth rate in the money supply will achieve the desired results. Policy makers must decide, for example, how much money should grow next year to match the growth in real GDP or to keep interest rates constant.

If monetary authorities are not penalized for departing from a predetermined rule, then it is not much of a rule. During the 1980s the Fed set targets for the growth in M1. When actual money growth exceeded planned growth, the Fed simply increased its targets during the year. Although actual money growth still exceeded the revised target, Fed officials were not penalized for overshooting their targets.

Point to Stress The two groups of economists mentioned represent the nonactivists discussed in the beginning of the chapter.

Why Rules?

The rationale for rules arises from two different models of how the economy works. One group of economists contends that *the economy is so complex and economic aggregates interact in such inscrutable ways and with such varied lags that policy makers cannot comprehend what is going on well enough to pursue an appropriate monetary or fiscal discretionary policy.* With regard to monetary policy, Milton Friedman is perhaps the best-known advocate of this position. He argues that although there is a link between money growth and the growth in nominal GDP, the exact relation is hard to specify because of long lags in the response of economic activity to changes in money growth. If the central bank adopts a discretionary policy that is based on an incorrect estimate of the lag, money may expand just when a tighter monetary policy is more appropriate. Many economists believe that even if an appropriate monetary policy would have the desired result, nobody knows enough about how the economy works to implement that policy at the right time. To avoid doing the wrong thing at the wrong time, Friedman recommends that the Fed follow a fixed-growth-rate monetary policy year after year, such as an annual growth rate of 3 percent in the money supply.

A comparison of economic forecasters and weather forecasters may help shed light on the position of those who advocate the use of monetary rules. Suppose you are in charge of the heating and cooling system at a major shopping mall. You realize that weather forecasters have a poor record in your area, particularly in the early spring, when days can be either warm or cold. Each day you must guess what the temperature will be and, based on that guess, decide whether to fire up the heater or turn on the air conditioner. Because the ventilation system and the mall are so large, you must start up the system long before you know for sure what the weather will be. Once the system has been turned on, it cannot be turned off until later in the day.

Teaching Tip The heating/cooling problem can be related to the recognition lag (predicting the weather), the implementation lag (the time required for the system to come on), and the effectiveness lag (the time it takes for the system to actually affect the temperature in the mall).

Suppose you guess the day will be cold, so you turn on the heat. If the day turns out to be cold, your policy is correct and the mall temperature will be just right. But if the day turns out to be warm, the heater will make the mall unbearable. You would have been better off with no heat. In contrast, if you turn on the air conditioner expecting a warm day but the day turns out to be cold, the mall will be very cold. The lesson is that if you have little ability to predict the weather, you should use neither heat nor air conditioning. Similarly, if monetary officials cannot predict the course of the economy, they should not try to fine-tune monetary policy. Complicating the prediction problem is the fact that monetary officials are not sure about the lags involved with monetary policy. The situation is comparable to your not knowing for sure when you turn the switch to "on" how long the system will actually take to come on.

The above analogy applies only if the cost of doing nothing—using neither heat nor air conditioning—is relatively low. In the early spring, you can assume that there is little risk of the temperatures being so cold that water pipes will freeze or so hot that the walls will sweat. This assumption is like the nonactivists' assumption that the economy is inherently stable and periods of prolonged unemployment are unlikely. In such an economy, the costs of *not* intervening are relatively low. In contrast, activists believe that there can be wide and prolonged swings in the economy (analogous to wide and prolonged swings in temperature), so activists believe that doing nothing involves significant risks.

Rules and Rational Expectations

Another group of economists also advocates economic rules, but not because they believe we know too little about how the economy works. Proponents of the *rational expectations* approach claim that people on average have a good idea about how the economy works and what to expect from policy makers. Individuals and firms know enough about the monetary and fiscal policies pursued in the past to anticipate, with reasonable accuracy, future policies and the effects of these policies on the economy. Some individuals will forecast too high and some too low, but on average forecasts will turn out to be correct. Earlier we argued that only when the public was surprised by the Fed did monetary policy have an effect on output. *To the extent that monetary policy is fully anticipated by workers and firms, it has no effect on the level of output; it affects only the level of prices.* Thus, only unexpected changes in policy can bring about short-run changes in output.

Point to Stress The Fed has been announcing its target growth rates for the monetary aggregates since 1975, but there is no guarantee that it will stay within the announced ranges.

Since in the long run changes in the money supply affect only the rate of inflation, not real output, followers of the rational expectations theory believe that the Fed should not try to pursue a discretionary monetary policy. Instead, the Fed should follow a predictable monetary rule. A monetary rule would reduce monetary surprises and would therefore reduce departures from the natural rate of output. *Whereas Friedman advocates a rule because of the Fed's ignorance about the lag structure of the economy, those who subscribe to the rational expectations theory advocate a predictable rule to avoid monetary surprises, which result in departures from the natural rate of output.*

Despite support by some economists for rules rather than discretion, central bankers appear reluctant to follow hard-and-fast rules about the course of future policy. Discretion appears to rule the day. As Paul Volcker, the former Fed chairman, argued:

> *The appeal of a simple rule is obvious. It would simplify our job at the Federal Reserve, make monetary policy easy to understand, and facilitate monitoring of our performance. And if the rule worked, it would reduce uncertainty. . . . But unfortunately, I know of no rule that can be relied on with sufficient consistency in our complex and constantly evolving economy.*[4]

Aggregate demand and aggregate supply provide a way of picturing how output and the price level adjust to a new equilibrium, but this picture says little about how fast this adjustment occurs. The speed of adjustment is really an empirical question, and an empirical tool, the Phillips curve, has been developed to focus on the issue of timing. We next examine the Phillips curve.

---

4. Statement of Paul Volcker, Chairman of the Board of Governors of the Federal Reserve System, before the Subcommittee on Domestic Monetary Policy of the Committee on Banking, Finance, and Urban Affairs, U.S. House of Representatives, August 1983.

THE PHILLIPS CURVE

Teaching Tip Using changes in money wages as a measure of inflation is based on the idea that the inflation rate equals the difference between the rate of nominal wage growth and the rate of labor productivity growth.

At one time, policy makers thought they faced a fairly stable long-run tradeoff between inflation and unemployment. This view was suggested by the research of New Zealand economist A. W. Phillips, who in 1958 published an article that examined the historical relation between inflation and unemployment, using data from the United Kingdom.[5] Based on about one hundred years of evidence, his data suggested an inverse relation between the unemployment rate and changes in money wages (serving as a measure of inflation). This relation implied that the opportunity cost of reducing unemployment was higher inflation, and the opportunity cost of reducing inflation was higher unemployment.

Phillips curve A curve showing possible combinations of the inflation rate and the unemployment rate, given the expected price level

The possible options with respect to unemployment and inflation are illustrated by the **Phillips curve** in Exhibit 6. The unemployment rate is measured along the horizontal axis and the inflation rate along the vertical axis. Let's begin at point *a*, which depicts one possible combination of unemployment and inflation. Fiscal or monetary policy could be used to stimulate output and thereby reduce unemployment, moving the economy from point *a* to point *b*. Notice, however, that the reduction in unemployment comes at the cost of higher inflation. A reduction in unemployment with no offsetting change in inflation would be represented by point *c*. But as you can see, that alternative is not an option available on the curve. Thus, policy makers were thought to face a difficult tradeoff: they could choose either lower inflation and higher unemployment or lower unemployment and higher inflation.

Teaching Tip In the original Phillips curve scenario, inflation is a function of the difference between the actual unemployment rate and the natural rate of unemployment.

The Phillips curve is not so much a theory as a statistical observation. Although not everyone accepted the policy implications of the Phillips curve, during the 1960s policy makers increasingly came to believe that they faced a stable, long-run tradeoff between unemployment and inflation. The Phillips curve was developed during a period when inflation was low and the primary disturbances in the economy were to aggregate demand. Changes in aggregate demand can be viewed as movements along a given short-run aggregate supply curve. If aggregate demand increased, the price level increased, but unemployment decreased. If aggregate demand decreased, the price level decreased, but unemployment increased. Many economists therefore assumed that there was a tradeoff between inflation and unemployment; hence, with appropriate demand-management policies, government policy makers could choose any point along the Phillips curve.

Teaching Tip In the labor market, an increase in output prices (as aggregate demand rises) causes an increase in the demand for labor. Employment then rises as long as wage increases lag behind the output price increase. See the appendix to Chapter 10.

The experience in the 1970s proved this view wrong for two reasons. First, some of the biggest disturbances were supply shocks, such as the shocks created by the oil embargoes and worldwide crop failures; these shocks resulted in leftward shifts in the aggregate supply curve. A reduction in aggregate supply led to both higher inflation and higher unemployment. This stagflation was at

Point to Stress Inflation-unemployment combinations in the 1970s were *above* the Phillips curve developed in the 1960s.

5. A. W. Phillips, "Relation Between Unemployment and the Rate of Change in Money Wage Rates in the United Kingdom, 1861–1957," *Economica* 25 (November 1958): 283–299.

EXHIBIT 6

Hypothetical Phillips Curve

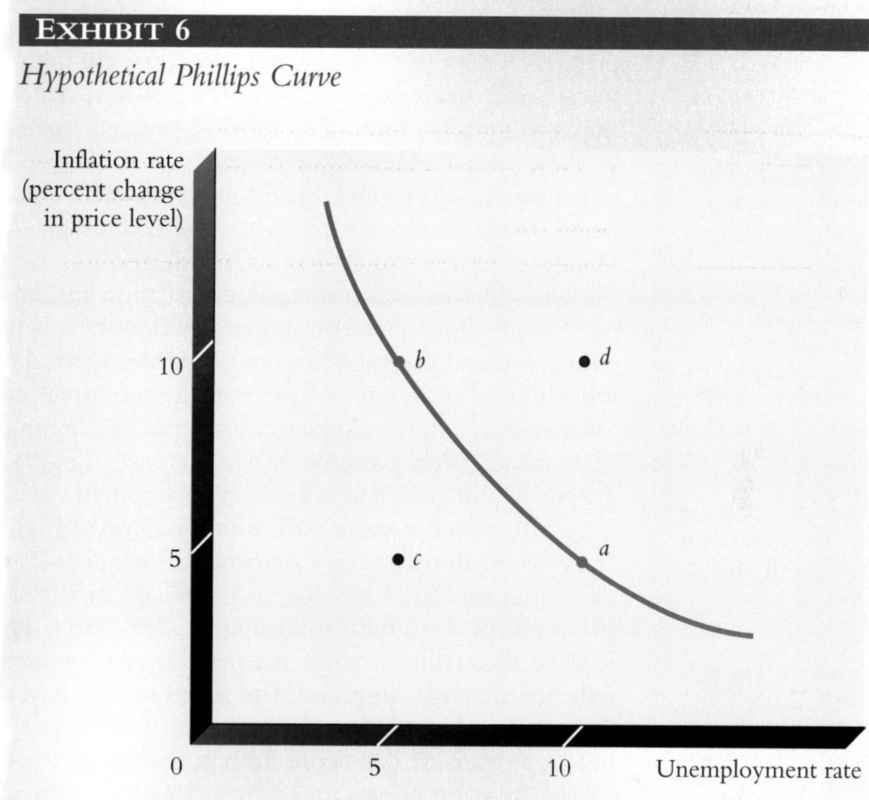

Points *a* and *b* lie on the Phillips curve and represent alternative combinations of the inflation rate and the unemployment rate that are attainable as long as the curve itself does not shift. Points *c* and *d* are off the curve; they are not attainable combinations.

odds with the Phillips curve. Second, economists learned that when the short-run equilibrium output exceeds potential output, the economy opens an expansionary gap. As this gap is closed by the upward movement of the short-run aggregate supply curve, the results are greater inflation and higher unemployment—again, results inconsistent with a given Phillips curve.

The combination of high inflation and high unemployment resulting from stagflation and expansionary gaps is represented by an outcome such as point *d* in Exhibit 6. By the end of the 1970s, increases in inflation and unemployment suggested either that the Phillips curve had shifted out or that it no longer existed. The situation called for a reexamination of the Phillips curve, a reexamination that led economists to distinguish between the short-run Phillips curve and the long-run Phillips curve.

Short-Run Phillips Curve

To discuss the underpinnings of the Phillips curve, we must return to the short-run aggregate supply curve. We begin by assuming that the price level

simplify.

Point to Stress The tradeoff along the short-run Phillips curve corresponds to movements of the aggregate demand curve along a fixed short-run aggregate supply curve. Both the Phillips curve and the aggregate supply curve assume wage contracts will be based on a given expected price level. At point *a* in both panels of Exhibit 7, this expected price level equals the actual price level—or, expected inflation equals actual inflation.

Teaching Tip In Exhibit 7, the real wage falls as the economy moves to point *b*; the real wage rises as the economy moves to point *c*.

this year is reflected by a price index of, say, 100. Suppose that people expect prices to be about 4 percent higher next year than this year, so the expected price level next year will be 104. Workers will therefore negotiate labor contracts based on an expected price level of 104, which is 4 percent higher than the current price level. As the short-run aggregate supply curve in Exhibit 7(a) indicates, if *AD* is the aggregate demand curve and the price level is 104, as expected, output will equal the economy's potential GDP, shown here to be $5.0 trillion. Recall that when the economy produces its potential GDP, unemployment is equal to the natural rate.

The short-run relation between inflation and unemployment is presented in Exhibit 7(b), where the unemployment rate is measured along the horizontal axis and the inflation rate along the vertical axis. Panel (a) shows that when the inflation rate is 4 percent, the economy produces its potential GDP. When the economy produces its potential GDP, unemployment is at the natural rate, which we assume to be 6 percent in panel (b). The combination of 4 percent inflation and 6 percent unemployment is reflected by point *a* in panel (b), which corresponds to point *a* in panel (a).

What if the aggregate demand curve turns out to be greater than expected, as indicated by *AD′* in panel (a)? In the short run, the greater demand results in equilibrium point *b*, with a price level of 106 and an output level of $5.1 trillion. Since the price level is greater than the expected level reflected in wage contracts, the inflation rate is also greater than expected. Specifically, the inflation rate turns out to be 6 percent, not 4 percent. Output now exceeds the economy's potential, so the unemployment rate falls below the natural rate, to 5 percent. This combination of a higher inflation rate and a lower level of unemployment is depicted by point *b* in panel (b), which corresponds to point *b* in panel (a).

What if aggregate demand turns out to be less than expected, as indicated by *AD″* in panel (a)? In the short run, the lower demand results in equilibrium point *c*, where the price level of 102 is lower than the expected level reflected in labor contracts, and output of $4.9 trillion is below potential GDP. With a lower-than-expected price level, the inflation rate is 2 percent rather than the expected 4 percent. With output below the economy's potential, the unemployment rate is 7 percent, which exceeds the natural rate. This combination of lower-than-expected inflation and higher-than-expected unemployment is reflected by point *c* on the curve in panel (b).

As you can see, the short-run aggregate supply curve in panel (a) can be used to establish the inverse relation between the inflation rate and the level of unemployment illustrated in panel (b). This latter curve is called a **short-run Phillips curve**, and it is generated by the intersection of alternative aggregate demand curves with a given short-run aggregate supply curve. *The short-run Phillips curve is therefore based on labor contracts reflecting a given expected price level, which implies a given expected rate of inflation.* The short-run Phillips curve in panel (b) is based on an expected inflation rate of 4 percent. If inflation turns out as expected, unemployment will equal the natural rate. If inflation is higher than expected, unemployment in the short run will fall below the natural rate. If inflation is lower than expected, unemployment in the short run will exceed the natural rate.

Short-run Phillips curve A curve that, based on an expected price level, reflects an inverse relation between the inflation rate and the level of unemployment

EXHIBIT 7

Relation Between the Short-Run Aggregate Supply Curve and the Short-Run Phillips Curve

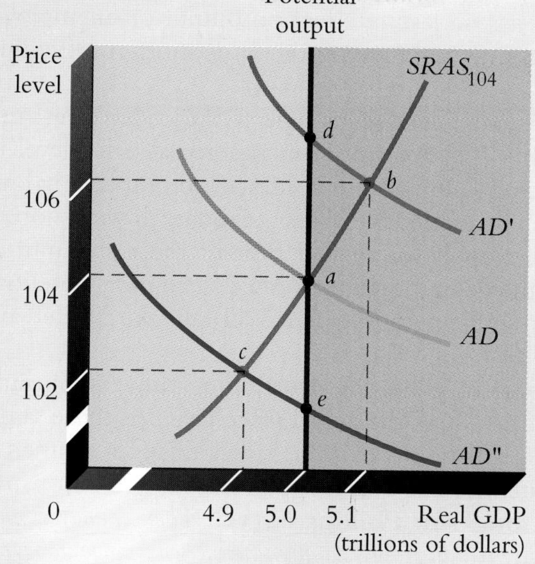

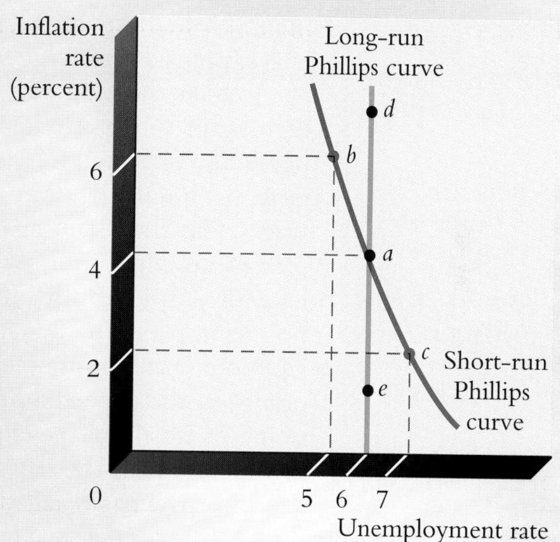

If people expect a price level of 104, which is 4 percent higher than the current level, and if *AD* is the aggregate demand curve, then the price level will actually be 104 and output will be at the potential rate. Point *a* in both panels represents this situation. Unemployment will be at the natural rate, 6 percent.

If aggregate demand is higher than expected (*AD′* instead of *AD*), the economy will be at point *b* in both panels. If aggregate demand is less than expected (*AD″* rather than *AD*), short-run equilibrium will be at point *c*; the price level, 102, will be lower than expected, and output will be below the potential rate. The lower inflation rate and higher unemployment rate are shown as point *c* in panel (b). In panel (b), points *a*, *b*, and *c* trace the short-run Phillips curve.

In the long run, the actual price level equals the expected price level and output is at the potential level, $5.0 trillion, in panel (a), and unemployment is at the natural rate, 6 percent, in panel (b). Points *a*, *d*, and *e* represent that situation; they lie on the vertical long-run Phillips curve.

Long-Run Phillips Curve

If inflation is higher than was expected when long-term labor contracts were negotiated, output can exceed the economy's potential in the short run, but not in the long run. Labor shortages and worker dissatisfaction with shrinking real wages will lead to higher wage agreements during the next round of negotiations. The short-run aggregate supply curve will shift up to the left until it passes through point *d* in Exhibit 7(a), returning the economy to its

Teaching Tip At point *d* in panel (b) of Exhibit 7, a higher expected inflation reflected in long-term contracts equals higher actual inflation. The upward adjustment in expected inflation shifts the short-run Phillips curve upward so it goes through point *d*.

Teaching Tip At point *e* in panel (b) of Exhibit 7, a lower expected inflation reflected in long-term contracts equals lower actual inflation. The downward adjustment in expected inflation shifts the short-run Phillips curve downward so it goes through point *e*.

Long-run Phillips curve A vertical line drawn at the economy's natural rate of unemployment that traces equilibrium points that can occur when employers and workers have the time and the ability to adjust fully to any unexpected change in aggregate demand

Natural rate hypothesis The natural rate of unemployment is largely independent of the stimulus provided by monetary or fiscal policy

Weak version of the natural rate hypothesis Policy makers can influence the tradeoff between unemployment and inflation in the short run but not in the long run

potential level of output. Point *d* represents a higher price level, but notice that the higher price level is no longer associated with reduced unemployment. The economy, in closing the expansionary gap, thus experiences both higher unemployment and a higher price level. At point *d* in panel (a), the economy is producing its potential GDP, which means that unemployment equals the natural rate. This combination of the natural rate of unemployment and higher inflation is depicted by point *d* in panel (b). The unexpectedly higher aggregate demand has no lasting effect on output or unemployment. Note that whereas points *a, b,* and *c* are on the same short-run Phillips curve, point *d* is not.

To trace the long-run effects of a lower-than-expected price level, let's return again to point *c* in Exhibit 7(a). At this point the actual price level is below the expected level reflected in long-term contracts, so output is below potential GDP. If, over time, firms and workers negotiate lower money wages, the short-run aggregate supply curve will shift to the right until it passes through point *e*, where the economy returns once again to its potential level of output. Both inflation and unemployment will fall, as reflected by point *e* in panel (b).

Note that points *a, d,* and *e* in panel (a) depict long-run equilibrium points, so the expected price level equals the actual price level. At those same points in panel (b), the expected inflation equals the actual inflation, so unemployment equals the natural rate. We can connect points *a, d,* and *e* in panel (b) to form what is called the **long-run Phillips curve**. *When employers and workers have the time and the ability to adjust fully to any unexpected change in aggregate demand, the long-run Phillips curve is a vertical line drawn at the economy's natural rate of unemployment*, as shown in panel (b). As long as prices and wages are flexible, the rate of unemployment is, in the long run, independent of the rate of inflation. *Thus, in the long run, policy makers cannot choose between unemployment and inflation. They can choose only among alternative levels of inflation.*

Natural Rate Hypothesis

As mentioned in Chapter 10, the natural rate of unemployment is the rate that is consistent with the economy's potential level of output, which we have discussed extensively already. An important idea to emerge from this reexamination of the Phillips curve is the **natural rate hypothesis**, which holds that in the long run the economy tends toward the natural rate of unemployment. This natural rate is largely independent of the level of the *aggregate demand* stimulus provided by monetary or fiscal policy. Policy makers may be able to push the economy beyond its natural, or potential, rate of production temporarily, but only if the public does not anticipate the resulting level of aggregate demand and the resulting price level.

WEAK VERSION. The **weak version of the natural rate hypothesis** is that policy makers can influence the tradeoff between unemployment and inflation in the short run but not in the long run. Unemployment could be maintained below the natural rate, but only at the cost of ever-increasing

Teaching Tip Expected inflation reflected in long-term contracts is fixed along a short-run Phillips curve but varies along the long-run curve.

inflation. For example, if the Fed increased the money supply at a faster and faster rate, actual inflation would rise faster and faster, continually exceeding expected inflation. But such a policy is clearly self-limiting. In the long run, monetary or fiscal policy affects only the rate of inflation, not the rate of unemployment; in the long run, there is no tradeoff between inflation and unemployment.

Strong version of the natural rate hypothesis The short-run gains in employment resulting from monetary or fiscal surprises diminish as the public comes to expect as much

Strong Version. In the **strong version of the natural rate hypothesis**, even this short-run kick becomes smaller and smaller over time. According to the rational expectations theory, market participants gain experience as time goes by, so they adjust more and more rapidly to policy decisions expected to affect the price level. As market participants learn more about the behavior of policy makers, the cycles generated by short-run fluctuations in inflation and unemployment that result from discretionary policy get smaller and smaller. People become more adept not only at predicting the effects of a policy on the economy but also at predicting the policy itself. It becomes more and more difficult for policy makers to surprise the public. Therefore, the short-run gains in employment resulting from monetary or fiscal surprises diminish as the public comes to expect as much. An implication of the natural rate hypothesis is that *regardless of policy makers' concerns about unemployment, the policy that results in low inflation is generally going to be the optimal policy in the long run.*

Teaching Tip Recall from the Phillips curve analysis that the actual unemployment rate can be below the natural rate only if actual inflation exceeds the expected inflation reflected in long-term contracts. Since expected inflation will adjust upward over time to match higher actual inflation, actual inflation must rise continually to remain above expected inflation.

Inflation and Unemployment Evidence

What has been the actual relation between unemployment and inflation in the United States? In Exhibit 8, the relation for each year since 1960 is represented by a point, with the unemployment rate measured along the horizontal axis and the inflation rate measured along the vertical axis. Superimposed on these points is a series of short-run Phillips curves showing patterns of unemployment and inflation during four distinct periods since 1960. Remember, each short-run Phillips curve is drawn for a given expected rate of inflation. A change in inflationary expectations results in a shift in the short-run Phillips curve.

Point to Stress Since fiscal and monetary policies affect aggregate demand, they typically affect neither the natural rate of unemployment nor the position of the long-run Phillips curve.

Notice that the clearest tradeoff between unemployment and inflation seems to have occurred between 1960 and 1969; the points for those years fit neatly along the curve. In the early part of the decade, inflation was low but unemployment was high; as the 1960s progressed, unemployment declined but inflation increased. The average inflation rate during the decade was only 2.5 percent, and the average unemployment rate was 4.8 percent.

The short-run Phillips curve appears to have shifted up to the right for the period 1970 to 1973, when inflation and unemployment both climbed to an average of 5.2 percent. In 1974 sharp increases in oil prices and crop failures around the world sparked another shift in the curve. Though points for the decade between 1974 and 1983 do not lie as neatly along the curve as points for earlier periods do, a tradeoff between inflation and unemployment is still evident. During the 1974–1983 period, inflation rose on average to 8.2 percent and unemployment climbed on average to 7.5 percent.

EXHIBIT 8

Short-Run Phillips Curves Since 1960

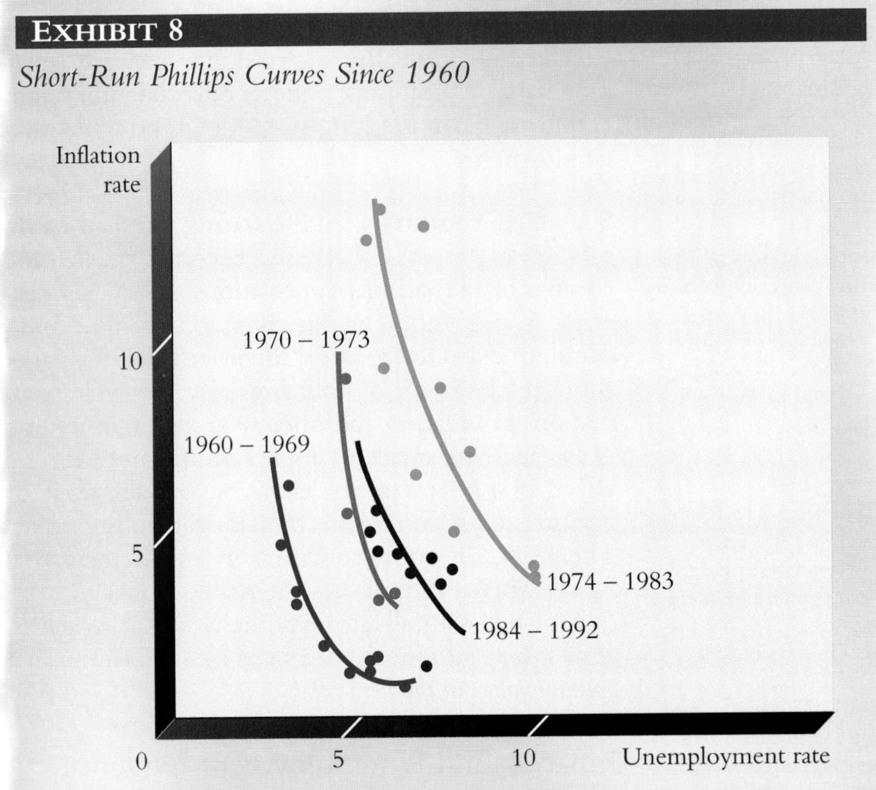

The figure shows unemployment–inflation rate combinations since 1960. Note that the short-run Phillips curve has shifted as inflation expectations have changed.

Teaching Tip Proponents of zero inflation also argue that inflation reduces growth by (1) increasing uncertainty and therefore reducing planned investment, (2) interacting with the U.S. tax code to reduce capital gains and further reduce investment, and (3) causing the allocation of scarce resources to inflation-hedging schemes rather than productive investments.

Teaching Tip See Chapter 7.

Finally, after recessions in the early 1980s, the short-run Phillips curve seems to have shifted down since 1983; average inflation for 1984–1992 fell to 3.9 percent and average unemployment fell to 6.4 percent. Changes in the average unemployment rate across periods since 1960 suggest that the underlying natural rate of unemployment may have shifted as well. (You'll recall that earlier we discussed the possibility that the natural rate has drifted higher since the 1960s.)

As noted earlier, a conclusion of the natural rate hypothesis is that the policy that results in zero or low inflation is generally going to be the optimal policy in the long run. We next consider efforts to reach zero inflation.

In Pursuit of Zero Inflation

Any amount of inflation interferes with the primary function of market prices, which is providing information about relative scarcities. With zero inflation, any increase in the price of an item is a signal that its relative price has increased. But with inflation greater than zero, an increase in the price of a given item sends a signal that mixes information about the relative scarcity of this item with information about the general rise in prices.

In 1989 a resolution was proposed in Congress directing the Fed "to adopt and pursue monetary policies leading to, and then maintaining, zero inflation." According to the resolution, inflation would be considered eliminated "when the expected rate of change in the general level of prices ceases to be a factor in individual decisionmaking."[6] Federal Reserve Chairman Alan Greenspan testified in support of the congressional resolution, stating that he thought the goal was attainable within the five years specified in the resolution. He said that although the zero-inflation goal could involve some reduced output in the short run, it need not create a recession. Short-run output losses could be more than offset by the long-run gain that would result from a more stable investment and employment climate.[7] The resolution was not approved by Congress.

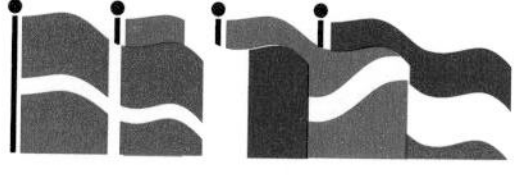

As mentioned in the earlier case study in Chapter 13, more governments around the world are committing themselves to a more independent central bank that has price stability as a goal. And those countries with a more independent central bank, such as Germany, Switzerland, and Japan, also have experienced lower inflation over the last two decades than countries where the central bank is less independent. If price stability does take root in major industrial countries, money will serve as a more reliable store of wealth, so tangible assets, such as real estate, gold, and works of art, will become less attractive as a store of wealth.

Conclusion

Example According to German law, the goal of price stability must be given highest priority whenever another goal might conflict with maintaining price stability. However, in October 1992, the German central bank announced a policy of monetary easing, despite the fact that inflation was above its medium-term target and rising. The policy change was in response to fiscal strains on the government, the slow reconstruction of former East Germany, and shrinking exports as other western European economies slowed.

This chapter examined the policy implications of activism versus nonactivism. The important question is whether the economy is (1) essentially stable and self-correcting when it gets off track or (2) essentially unstable and in need of activist policies. Activists believe that the federal government should reduce swings in the business cycle by stimulating a sluggish economy when output falls below its potential level and by dampening an overheated economy when output exceeds its potential level. Activists argue that government attempts to insulate the economy from the ups and downs of the business cycle may be far from perfect, but they are better than nothing. Nonactivists, on the other hand, believe that discretionary policy may contribute to the cyclical swings in the economy, leading to higher inflation in the long run with no permanent effect on either output or employment. Nonactivists rely more on passive policies such as a rules for monetary policy and automatic stabilizers for fiscal policy.

The activist-nonactivist debate in this chapter has focused on monetary policy primarily because discretionary fiscal policy in recent years has been hampered by chronic federal deficits that have ballooned the national debt. In the next chapter we will take a closer look at these deficits and the debt that has resulted.

6. House Joint Resolution 409, 101st Congress, 1st session, September 25, 1989.
7. Greenspan's testimony was reported by Lindley H. Clark in "Do We Want or Need Zero Inflation," *Wall Street Journal*, November 6, 1989.

SUMMARY

1. Activists view the private sector—particularly fluctuations in investment—as the main source of economic instability in the economy. Because the return to potential output can be slow and painful, activists recommend that the government intervene with monetary or fiscal policy to stimulate aggregate demand when actual output is below potential output.

2. Nonactivists argue that the economy has a natural resiliency which will cause output to return to its potential level within a reasonable amount of time even if upset by some shock. Nonactivists also point to the variable and uncertain lags associated with discretionary policy as reason enough to steer clear of active intervention.

3. Nonactivists suggest that the government should follow steady and predictable policies and avoid trying to stimulate or dampen aggregate demand over the business cycle. Nonactivists prefer passive policies as reflected by monetary rules and automatic fiscal stabilizers.

4. At one time public officials were thought to face a stable tradeoff between higher unemployment and higher inflation. Recent evidence suggests that if there is a tradeoff, it is only in the short run, not in the long run. Expansionary fiscal or monetary policies, if unexpected, can stimulate output and employment in the short run. But if the economy is already at or near its potential output, these expansionary policies will in the long run result only in higher inflation.

QUESTIONS AND PROBLEMS

1. (Activists Versus Nonactivists) One issue that activists and nonactivists argue about is whether interest rates can be kept low by the actions of the Federal Reserve. Does it seem reasonable that the Fed can keep nominal interest rates permanently low by injecting more and more money into the economy? Why or why not?

2. (Aggregate Supply) What is the variable that naturally adjusts in the labor market, shifting the aggregate supply curve to guarantee full employment at the natural rate? Is it reasonable to assume that the aggregate supply curve shifts up more easily and quickly than it shifts down? Why or why not?

3. (Rational Expectations) Can the government fool the public with erratic monetary and fiscal policy if the public has rational expectations? Suppose that the government uses a monetarist rule. How will rational expectations affect the impact of the rule?

4. (Rational Expectations) Some economists in the late 1970s believed that it might be possible to reduce the very high inflation rate then prevailing without causing higher unemployment. However, they emphasized that the Fed would have to make clear its intention and stick to its policy. In the end, inflation fell dramatically, but not without producing very high unemployment. Is this evidence against the rational expectations hypothesis? Why or why not?

5. (Macroeconomic Policy) Some economists argue that only unanticipated increases in the money supply cause increases in GDP. Explain why this may be the case.

6. (Macroeconomic Policy) An activist economist in the government argues that the current rate of unemployment could be greatly reduced through fiscal and monetary policies. The nonactivist claims that such policies would create price instability. What information must the government have to decide whose advice is better?

7. (Rules) There has been a great deal of talk about a balanced-budget amendment to the Constitution. This would be a rule for fiscal policy. How would you evaluate this rule based on the macroeconomic model discussed in the text?

8. (Phillips Curve) Why does a movement up the short-run Phillips curve imply a declining real wage

for workers? Would workers allow this decline to continue unabated? How would the short-run Phillips curve adjust to changes in workers' perceptions about their real wage?

9. (Natural Rate of Unemployment) The natural rate of unemployment was once characterized as "inevitable unemployment" in the *Economic Report of the President.* Why would such words be chosen? What determines the natural rate of employment?

10. (Potential GNP) Why is it hard for policy makers to decide if the economy is operating at its potential output level? Why don't they just look to see if there is full employment?

11. (Activists Versus Nonactivists) Discuss the role each of the following should play in the debate between activists and nonactivists.
    a. The speed of adjustments in nominal wages
    b. The speed of adjustments in expectations about inflation
    c. The existence of lags in policy creation and implementation
    d. Variability in the natural rate of unemployment over time

12. (Phillips Curve) Describe the different Phillips curve tradeoffs implied by the activist viewpoint, the weak version of rational expectations, and the strong version of rational expectations.

13. (Phillips Curve) The original Phillips curve research compared the unemployment rate with the rate of nominal wage adjustment (i. e., it was a wage Phillips curve). Show how you would construct a price Phillips curve, like those shown in the text, based on a wage Phillips curve.

14. (Phillips Curve) According to the Phillips curve discussion, changes in expected inflation rates will shift the short-run Phillips curve. What will shift the long-run Phillips curve?

15. (Phillips Curve) Suppose the economy is at point *d* on the long-run Phillips curve shown in Exhibit 7. If that inflation rate is unacceptably high, how can policy makers get the inflation rate down? Would rational expectations help or hurt their efforts?

16. (Rational Expectations) Suppose the economy is operating at the natural rate of unemployment and the Fed announces an expansionary monetary policy designed to lower the unemployment rate. According to Chapter 14, this policy should reduce nominal interest rates. According to the rational expectations model, however, nominal interest rates will *increase*. Explain.

17. (Automatic Stabilizers and the Phillips Curve) In Chapter 11 you learned about automatic stabilizers. How do you see such stabilizers influencing the movement along the short-run Phillips curve and consequently the variability in the rate of inflation? Are automatic stabilizers an example of a fiscal policy rule?

18. (Expectations and Policy) Suppose that people in an election year believe that public policy makers are going to pursue expansionary policies to enhance their reelection chances. Why might such expectations put pressure on officials to pursue such policies even if they weren't planning to?

19. (The '92 Presidential Campaign) During 1991–1992 the Fed aggressively attempted to reduce interest rates in an effort to revive a sluggish economy. Short-term rates fell, but long-term rates were much slower to fall. Why do you suppose this happened?

20. (The '92 Presidential Campaign) Ross Perot made quickly bringing down the deficit his main campaign theme. At the same time, some economists warned that the policies necessary to achieve such deficit reduction would be too damaging to the economy in the short run. Discuss the consequences of such a policy in the context of Exhibit 7.

CHAPTER 16

BUDGETS, DEFICITS, AND PUBLIC POLICY

The word *budget* is derived from the Old French word *bougette*, which means "little bag." The annual federal budget is now over $1,500,000,000,000—over one and a half trillion dollars. Big money! If this "little bag" contained $100 bills, it would weigh over 15,000 *tons*! These $100 bills would fill to the legal limit six hundred trailer trucks. These $100 bills could paper over a ten-lane highway stretching from Portland, Maine to Los Angeles, California. This budget could buy every U.S. household a new Mercedes every three years. If President Clinton's sole function were to pay the bills by writing million-dollar checks, he would have to write three checks a minute, 24 hours a day, 365 days a year to keep up with federal spending.

Teaching Tip Only the federal budget plays a major role as a stabilization tool. Most states are legally required to have balanced budgets.

In this chapter we first examine the federal budget process, then turn to what appears to be the major budget concern today: the giant budget deficits of the 1980s and 1990s and the resulting national debt. We look at the source of deficits over the years and the immediate effects of deficits on the economy. We then examine the short-run and long-run effects of the national debt. Topics discussed in this chapter include

- The budget process
- Rationale for deficits
- Impact of deficits
- The burden of the debt
- Measures to reduce deficits

THE FEDERAL BUDGET PROCESS

Government budget A plan for government expenditures and revenues for a specified period, usually a year

The **government budget** is a plan for government expenditures and revenues for a specified period, usually a year. The period covered by the federal budget is called the *fiscal year,* and it runs from October 1 of one year to September 30 of the following year. Most of the federal budget benefits individuals through cash transfer programs such as Social Security and Aid to Families with Dependent Children and in-kind transfer programs such as Medicare, Medicaid, and food stamps. One-fifth of the budget goes to national defense and one-seventh goes to pay interest on the national debt. Exhibit 1 provides a percentage breakdown of federal spending by major category. (For a percentage breakdown during the past fifty years, see Exhibit 4 in Chapter 4.)

Example Medicare and Medicaid combined are expected to take the largest share of the budget by the year 2000. Medicare has been growing since 1967 at an annual rate of 10 percent after inflation; real growth for Medicaid has been 15.9 percent.

The Presidential Role in the Budget Process

Before 1921 the federal budget played a minor role in the economy, with federal spending, except during wartime, accounting for less than 3 percent of GDP (versus more than 22 percent today). Federal agencies made budget requests directly to Congress, bypassing the president entirely. Legislation in

EXHIBIT 1

Composition of Federal Expenditures: Fiscal Year 1993

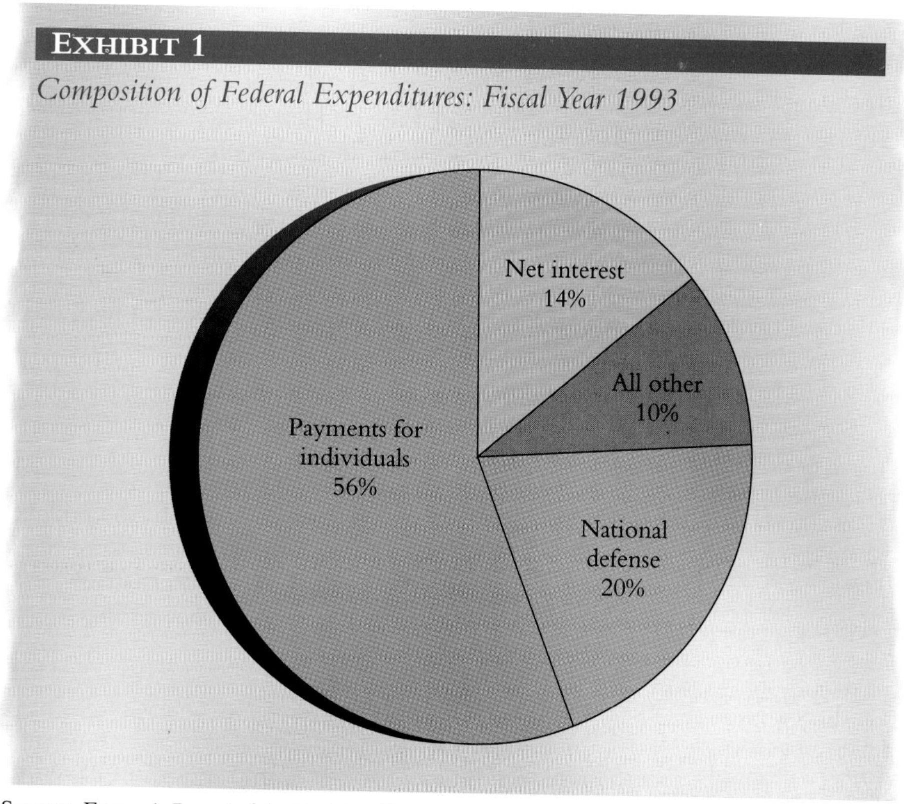

Source: *Economic Report of the President,* January 1993.

1921 created the Office of Management and Budget (OMB) to examine agency budget requests and to help the president develop a budget proposal. Later, the Employment Act of 1946 created the Council of Economic Advisers to forecast economic activity and assist the president in formulating an appropriate fiscal policy. During the 1960s and 1970s, various measures were introduced by the executive branch to improve the evaluation of government programs. By the mid-1970s the president had in place the staff and the procedures to translate policy into a budget proposal to be presented to the Congress.

Teaching Tip The budget timetable was set by the Full Employment and Balanced Growth Act of 1978.

Development of the president's budget begins a year before it is submitted to Congress, with each agency preparing a budget request. The formal budget process begins in January, with the president's submission to Congress of a fat book called *The Budget of the United States Government*. This document details the president's proposals about what should be spent in the upcoming year and how this spending should be financed. At this stage, however, the president's budget is little more than detailed suggestions for congressional consideration. Soon after a budget is proposed, the *Economic Report of the President* is also transmitted to Congress. This report, required under the Employment Act of 1946 and written by the Council of Economic Advisers, reflects the administration's views about the state of the economy and includes fiscal policy recommendations for fostering "maximum employment, production, and purchasing power."

Point to Stress Recall the decision-making and implementation policy lags discussed in Chapter 15.

The Congressional Role in the Budget Process

Teaching Tip Neither expenditures nor revenues are known with certainty. Actual budgets depend on the state of the economy, and estimates can vary substantially. Fiscal year 1992's budget deficit was initially forecast at $368 billion by the Congressional Budget Office (CBO) and $399 billion by the White House. In the summer of 1992, these forecasts were revised to $314 billion and $334 billion, respectively. The actual deficit was about $290 billion. The concept of the structural deficit is discussed later in the chapter.

The Congressional budget cycle begins in January, when the president's budget is delivered to Congress. Budget committees in the House and the Senate agree on the size of the budget, spending by major category, and expected revenues. Once an overall budget approach has been approved by Congress as a *budget resolution*, this resolution is supposed to discipline the many committees and subcommittees that authorize spending by establishing the framework that guides spending and revenue decisions. The budget cycle ends on October 1, when the new fiscal year begins. Thus, the federal budget has a congressional gestation period of about nine months, though, as we have noted, the president's budget begins taking shape a year before the January submission.

The spending side of the budget is usually outlined in more detail than the revenue side. Most taxes are collected on the basis of certain rules and schedules that change infrequently. Of special interest is the bottom line, the relation between *budgeted* expenditures and *projected* revenues. The difference between expenditures and revenues is one measure of the budget's fiscal impact. *When expenditures exceed revenues, the budget is projected to be in deficit; a rising deficit is expected to stimulate aggregate demand*. Alternatively, *when revenues exceed expenditures, the budget is projected to be in surplus; a rising surplus is expected to dampen aggregate demand.*

Problems with the Budget Process

The federal budget process sounds good on paper, but it does not work well in practice. There are several problems.

Continuing resolutions Budget agreements that allow agencies, in the absence of an approved budget, to spend at the rate of the previous year's budget

CONTINUING RESOLUTIONS INSTEAD OF BUDGET DECISIONS. The budget timetable discussed above is often ignored by Congress. Because deadlines are often missed, budgets typically run from year to year based on **continuing resolutions**, which are agreements to allow agencies, in the absence of an approved budget, to spend at the rate of the previous year's budget. Poorly conceived programs continue through sheer inertia; successful programs cannot be expanded. On occasion the president has to shut down the entire government temporarily because not even the continuing resolution can be approved in time.

Teaching Tip The Senate considers the budget after the House of Representatives passes its version. The budget is sent to the president after Congress passes a joint version.

OVERLAPPING COMMITTEE AUTHORITY. An overlap in budget authority across the many committees and subcommittees requires the executive branch of government to defend the same section of the president's budget before several committees in both the House and the Senate. Those responsible for running the federal government end up spending much of their time testifying before assorted congressional committees. Because several committees have jurisdiction over the same area, no committee really has final authority, so matters often remain unresolved even after extensive committee deliberations.

LENGTHY BUDGET PROCESS. You can imagine the difficulty of using the budget as a tool of fiscal policy when the budget process takes so long. Given that the average recession lasts only about a year and that budget preparations begin more than a year and a half before the budget goes into effect, planning discretionary fiscal measures to address recessions through the budget process is difficult. That's one reason why congressional attempts to stimulate an ailing economy often seem so half-hearted; by the time Congress agrees on a fiscal remedy, the economy has often taken a turn for the better on its own. For example, by the spring of 1993 the recession had been over for two years, yet President Clinton proposed a stimulus package of spending projects.

Teaching Tip Uncontrollable expenditures include interest on the national debt, food stamps, benefits for Social Security, railroad retirement, federal employee retirement, Medicare, Medicaid, and unemployment compensation. Most benefits in the entitlement programs rise automatically each year since they are indexed to inflation.

UNCONTROLLABLE BUDGET ITEMS. Congress has only limited control over much of the budget. Some budget items, such as interest on the national debt, cannot be changed in the near term. *About three-quarters of the budget falls into expenditure categories that are determined by existing laws*. For example, once Congress establishes eligibility criteria, *entitlement programs* such as Social Security take on a life of their own, with each annual appropriation simply reflecting the amount required to support the expected number of entitled beneficiaries. Congress has no say in such appropriations unless it chooses to change the eligibility criteria or the level of benefits.

OVERLY DETAILED BUDGET. The federal budget is divided into thousands of accounts and subaccounts. Congress tends to budget in such minute detail that the big picture often gets lost. To the extent that the budget is a way of making political payoffs, such micromanagement allows Congress to reward friends and punish enemies with great precision. For example, though a huge deficit was projected, Congress still found room in 1992 for $2.7 million to build a freshwater catfish farm in Arkansas, $2.5 million to remove asbestos from a meatpacking plant in Iowa, and $10 million to build a ramp to the Milwaukee Brewers stadium parking lot. Moreover, the president has little control over the specifics of the budget and must either accept or veto the entire budget as is. Since the president usually receives the budget at the eleventh hour, a veto would shut down the government, so budget vetoes are rare. This *detailed budgeting not only is time-consuming but also reduces the flexibility of fiscal policy*. When economic conditions change or when there is a shift in the demand for certain kinds of publicly provided goods, the federal government cannot easily reallocate funds from one account to another.

Suggested Budget Reforms

Several reforms have been suggested to improve the budget process. First, the annual budget could be converted into a two-year budget, or *biennial budget*. As it is, Congress spends nearly all of the year working on the budget. The executive branch is always dealing with three budgets: administering an approved budget, defending a proposed budget before congressional committees, and preparing yet another budget for submission to Congress. If decisions were made for two years at a time, Congress would not be continually involved with budget deliberations, and executive branch heads could run their agencies rather than marching from committee hearing to committee hearing. Two-year budgets, however, would require longer-term economic forecasts of the economy and would be even less useful than the one-year budget as a tool of discretionary fiscal policy.

Point to Stress Forecasts are needed to estimate budget items such as interest on the debt, benefits in entitlement programs, and tax revenues.

Another possible reform would be for Congress to simplify the budget document by concentrating on major groupings and eliminating line items. Each agency head could then be given an overall budget, along with the discretion to allocate funds in a manner consistent with the perceived demands for agency services. We will consider other reforms later in the chapter after we discuss the federal deficit.

FEDERAL BUDGET DEFICITS

Budget deficit Amount by which government spending during the year exceeds government revenues

The big budget story in recent years has been the giant federal deficits. When government spending—that is, government purchases plus transfer payments—exceeds government revenues, the result is a **budget deficit**. Since 1960 the federal government has experienced a budget deficit every year but one. To place deficits in perspective, we will first examine the economic rationale for deficit financing.

Rationale for Deficits

Deficit financing has been justified for outlays that increase the economy's productivity—outlays for investments such as highways, waterways, and dams.

Example Even deficits during the Great Depression were small relative to wartime deficits. The deficit in 1933 was $33 billion (in 1992 dollars). Deficits in 1943 through 1945 approached or exceeded $450 billion (in 1992 dollars) each year. However, by 1947 the government was running a $26 billion surplus (in 1992 dollars).

Example Social Security, Aid to Families with Dependent Children, and unemployment compensation were all instituted during the 1930s. However, social spending exploded after the mid-1960s when programs such as Medicaid and food stamps were established.

The cost of these capital goods should be borne in part by future taxpayers, who will also benefit from these investments. This rationale is used to fund capital projects at the state and local level, but a capital budget as such has not been part of the federal budget process.

Until the Great Depression, federal deficits occurred only during wartime. Because wars involved much hardship, public officials were understandably reluctant to increase taxes to finance war-related expenditures. Deficits arising during wars were largely self-correcting, however, because after each war government expenditures dropped faster than did government revenues.

The depression led John Maynard Keynes to develop an expanded role for the federal budget. As you know, the Keynesian prescription for fighting an economic slump was for the federal government to stimulate aggregate demand through deficit spending. As a result of the depression, automatic stabilizers were also introduced; these increase government spending during recessions and decrease it during expansions. The federal deficit increases during recessions because, as economic activity slows down, unemployment rises, increasing government outlays for unemployment benefits and other transfer payments. Furthermore, tax revenues decline during recessions. For example, as a result of the 1990–1991 recession, tax revenues from corporations fell by $14 billion between 1989 and 1992, while payments for "income security" jumped by $60 billion. An economic recovery is the other side of the coin. As business activity expands, so do jobs, personal income, and corporate profits, causing federal revenues to swell. With reduced joblessness, transfer payments decline. Thus, the federal deficit falls.

Budget Philosophies and Deficits

Annually balanced budget Budget philosophy prior to the Great Depression; aimed at equating revenues with expenditures, except during times of war

Cyclically balanced budget Budget philosophy calling for budget deficits during recessions to be financed by budget surpluses during expansions

Functional finance Budget philosophy aiming fiscal policy at achieving potential GDP rather than balancing budgets either annually or over the business cycle

Several budget philosophies have emerged over the years. Fiscal policy prior to the Great Depression aimed at maintaining an **annually balanced budget**, except during times of war. Since tax revenues tend to rise during expansions and fall during recessions, the annually balanced budget calls for the federal government to increase spending during expansions and reduce spending during recessions. But such spending will worsen fluctuations in the business cycle, overheating the economy during expansions and increasing unemployment during recessions.

A second budget philosophy is to have a **cyclically balanced budget**, which calls for budget deficits during recessions and budget surpluses during expansions. Fiscal policy is thereby able to dampen swings in the business cycle yet not increase budget debt over that cycle. (Budget debt, recall, is the net accumulation of deficits.) Many state governments have established "rainy day" funds to build up budget surpluses during the good times for use during hard times.

A third budget philosophy is **functional finance**, which says that policy makers should be less concerned with balancing the budget annually or even over the business cycle than with seeing that the economy produces its potential output. The functional finance philosophy argues that one of the

Teaching Tip The procyclical nature of annually balanced budgets developed after 1913. The federal income tax was not established until the passage of a constitutional amendment in that year.

federal government's primary responsibilities is to promote economic stability at the potential level of output. If the budget needed to keep the economy operating at its potential involves chronic deficits, so be it.

Since the Great Depression, budgets in this country have been neither annually nor cyclically balanced. *Although budget deficits have been greater during recessions than during expansions, the federal budget has been in deficit in all but eight years since 1931.* In fact, the budget has been in deficit in all but one year since 1960. Exhibit 2 shows the deficit since 1979, with periods of recession shaded. As you can see, deficits worsened during the recessions of the early 1980s and early 1990s. But the deficit continued to grow for four years after the 1982 recession was over.

Structural deficit A measure of what the federal budget deficit would be if the economy were producing its potential level of output

Because GDP fluctuates as the economy moves through the business cycle, actual budgets are not a good measure of fiscal policy. For example, the government could be pursuing a tight fiscal policy, reducing spending and increasing taxes, yet a recession could still create a substantial deficit. The **structural deficit** is an estimate of what the deficit or surplus would be if the economy were producing at its potential. That part of the deficit or surplus arising from the business cycle is filtered out. *The larger the structural deficit, the more stimulative the fiscal policy*. The structural deficit since 1979 is also presented in Exhibit 2. Notice that since 1979 the structural deficit has been stimulative.

EXHIBIT 2

Federal Deficits and Business Cycles Since 1979

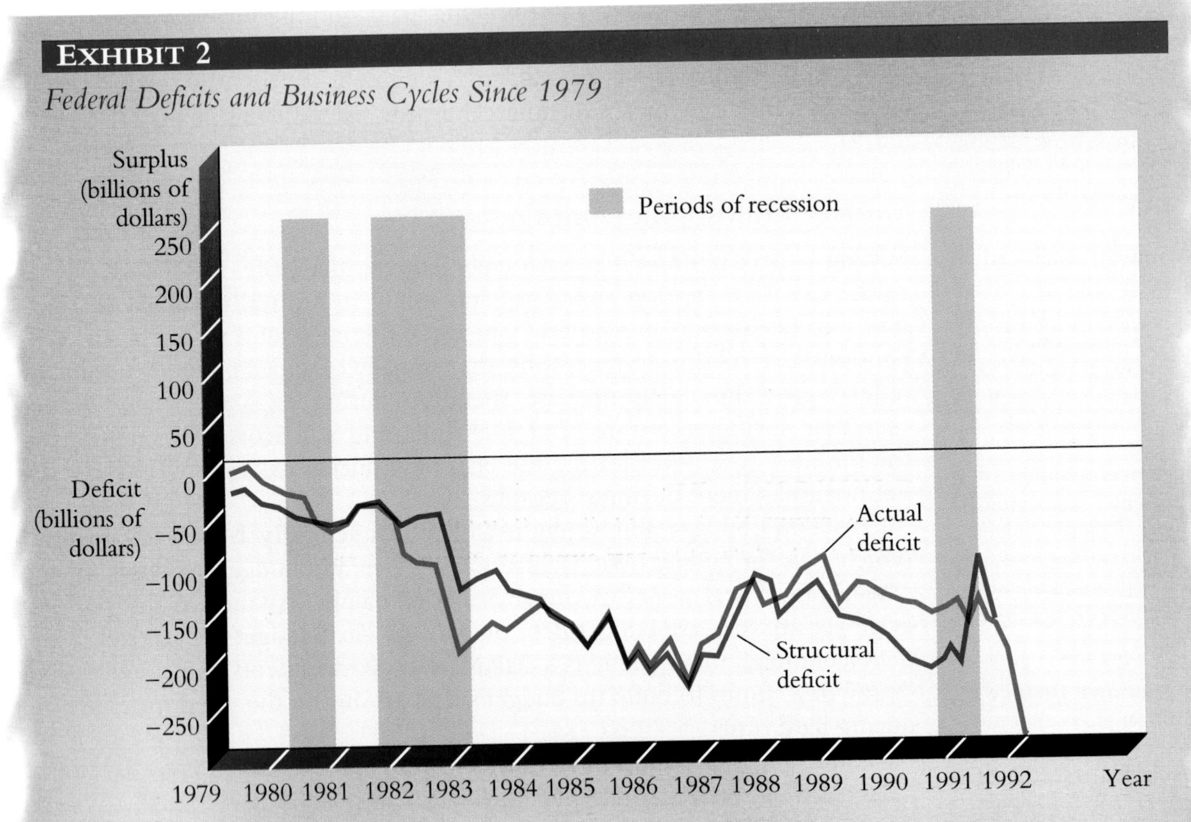

Source: Federal Reserve Bank of St. Louis, *Monetary Trends*, various issues.

Deficits in the 1980s

In 1981 President Reagan, charged up by his stunning election victory, secured a three-year budget resolution that included a historic tax cut along with increases in defense spending. Some so-called *supply-side* proponents argued that tax cuts would stimulate enough economic activity to keep tax revenues from falling. The congressional budget resolution adopted in 1981 was based on an assumption that unspecified spending cuts would bring the two sides of the budget into balance, but the promised cuts in spending were never made. Moreover, overly optimistic revenue projections were built into the budget.

Example Fiscal year 1992 had a record deficit of $290 billion, after six consecutive quarters of slow but positive growth. Fiscal year 1993 was projected to have a deficit of $327 billion, but President Clinton introduced tax increases and spending cuts to reduce the deficit.

Teaching Tip Note, however, the size of the structural deficits in Exhibit 2 during the Reagan administration.

The budget projected that real GDP would grow by 5.2 percent in 1982, but the economy actually fell into a recession and instead output dropped by 2.1 percent. The recession caused the automatic stabilizers in the budget to take over, thereby reducing revenues and increasing spending still more. Since spending was underestimated and revenue was overestimated, the deficit in 1982 was about 4 percent of GDP, one of the largest peacetime deficits in history. The deficit served as a backdrop for budget debates in the early 1980s. President Reagan's budget strategy called for increases in defense spending, but he promised to veto any new taxes or any cuts in Social Security. The deficit climbed above 6 percent of GDP in 1983. During the presidential campaign of 1984, candidate Walter Mondale warned that taxes would have to be increased to reduce the deficits. President Reagan, however, blamed the deficits on the recession and predicted that as the economy improved the deficit would disappear even without tax increases; he claimed the country would "grow out of" the deficits.

Reagan won the 1984 election but he lost the argument about the deficit. The federal government had cut tax rates but did not cut expenditures. *Although revenues as a percentage of GDP declined, federal spending rose from 22.5 percent of GDP in 1980 to 24.4 percent in 1986.* Exhibit 3 presents the federal budget deficit as a percentage of GDP since 1980. As you can see, the deficit climbed in the early 1980s, declined somewhat as the economy improved after the recession of 1982, but increased in 1990 with the onset of another recession.

Deficit Reduction Laws

The Gramm-Rudman-Holling (GRH) measure, enacted in 1985, introduced a schedule of targets aimed at eliminating the deficit by 1991. The law required automatic across-the-board budget reductions if the targets for deficit reductions were not met. But two-thirds of the budget was exempt from such cuts. What's more, the Supreme Court ruled parts of the law unconstitutional. Nonetheless, Congress vowed to maintain the spirit of the law. Overall the GRH measure helped Congress focus on the budget problem, but actual reductions in the deficit were modest.

During the 1988 presidential campaign, both major candidates largely ignored the issue of the deficit, since to make much of it would only raise the question of what was to be done, and neither candidate wanted to talk

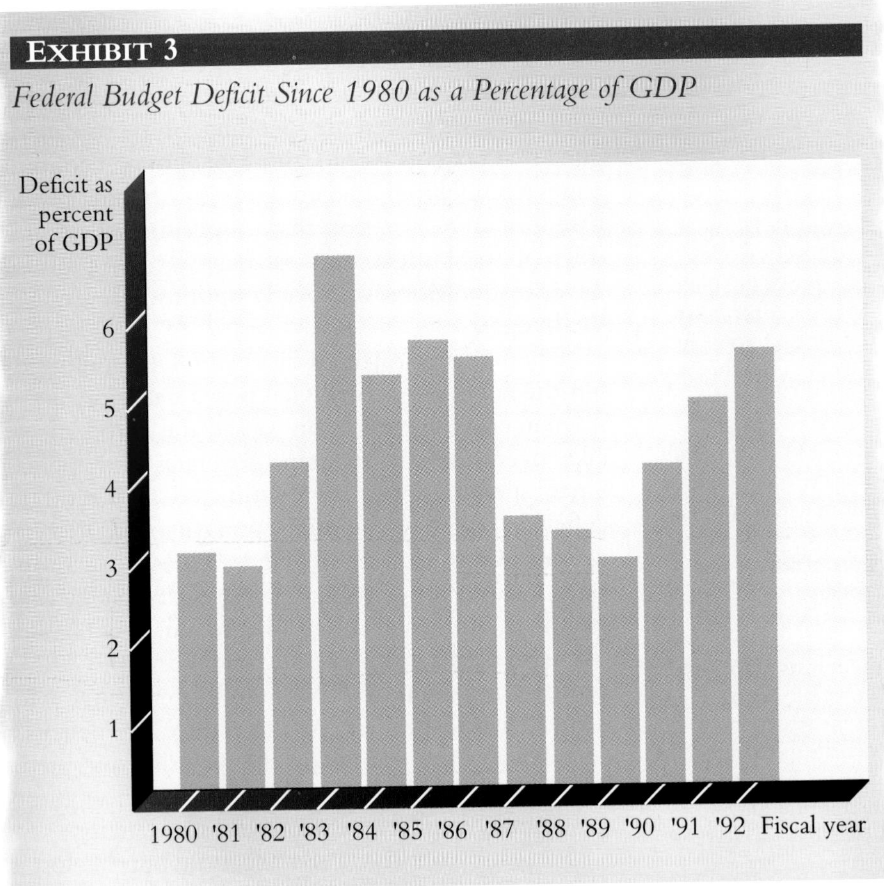

Source: U.S. Commerce Department; *Economic Report of the President,* January 1993.

about taxes. Congress dealt with GRH deficit limits mostly by raising them. For example, the original GRH deficit target for 1990 was $36 billion; that target was eventually raised to $100 billion. The actual deficit that year was $221 billion, due in part to a recession that began toward the end of the fiscal year.

With concern about the deficit growing, Congress and President Bush agreed to the 1990 Budget Enforcement Act (BEA), a package of spending cuts and tax increases aimed at trimming the projected deficit. Rather than relying exclusively on a deficit cap, as did the GRH law, the new law applied spending caps to three broad areas of discretionary spending (defense, international programs, and domestic programs). If the caps are exceeded, automatic across-the-board cuts are to be applied to that area of spending. The BEA also has a pay-as-you-go feature requiring that any proposals to increase spending or decrease revenues must be offset by new revenue increases or spending cuts. Some cynics viewed the new law simply as a way putting off hard decisions about the federal deficit until after the 1992 presidential election.

Recent projections by the Congressional Budget Office predict that the actual deficit during the first half of the 1990s will exceed legislated deficit targets by a substantial amount. Worse still, the deficit is expected to start climbing once again after 1996. Thus, the budget agreement of 1990, even though it raised taxes and cut spending, is not expected to resolve the problem of the deficit. The subject of the deficit was largely avoided during the 1992 campaign. Since his election, however, President Clinton has proposed tax increases and spending cuts to reduce the deficit. Despite these efforts, the deficit is projected to grow again by 1997.

Why Deficits? Why Now?

Why have federal budget deficits become the status quo? The most obvious answer is that Congress is not required to balance the budget. In contrast, forty-nine states now require a balanced budget. As mentioned already, current deficits have been caused by a combination of tax cuts and spending increases. But why has the budget been in deficit for all but eight years since 1931? As an explanation, let's consider one widely accepted model of how the government works. Elected officials attempt to maximize political support, including votes and campaign contributions. Voters like public spending programs but dislike taxes, so spending programs win support and taxes lose support. Because of this asymmetry in the relative payoffs, candidates attempt to maximize their chances of being elected by offering a budget that is long on benefits but short on taxes. Moreover, the many fragmented congressional committees push their favorite programs with little concern about the overall budget. For example, the 1990 defense bill included eighteen F-14D fighter jets and thirty-six V-22 Osprey aircraft because the planes were produced by firms located in key congressional districts, even though the Pentagon did not want the planes.

Teaching Tip See Chapter 4 for a discussion of elected officials as vote maximizers. Chapter 30 provides further information about behavior in a representative democracy.

Teaching Tip Prior to the 1960s, surpluses still tended to occur during peacetime expansion years: 1947, 1948, 1951, 1956, and 1957.

This asymmetry in favor of spending may explain why we have deficits, but it does not explain why deficits were not typical before the Great Depression. If voters and politicians have always favored spending programs over taxes, why has it been only since the depression that deficits have predominated? Nobel laureate James Buchanan argues that the rational self-interest of elected officials has always given them a preference for nontax sources of revenue. Prior to Keynes, however, they were constrained from resorting to deficit financing by the view that such a fiscal policy was *immoral*. According to Buchanan, Victorian fiscal morality dictated adherence to a balanced budget. Keynes revolted against those precepts, replacing the notion of the moral superiority of a balanced budget with an economic argument about why deficits could be good for the country. *After Keynes, it was no longer considered immoral for people, through their government, to spend more than they were willing to tax themselves.*

The Relation Between Deficits and Other Aggregate Variables

There is much talk in the news media about the relations among deficits, interest rates, and inflation. To develop a clearer understanding of these relations, let's consider the following simplification. We begin with the federal budget in balance and the economy producing its potential GDP (point *a* in Exhibit 4). Thus, the *structural deficit*—the deficit when the economy produces

EXHIBIT 4

Deficits and Other Measures of the Economy's Performance

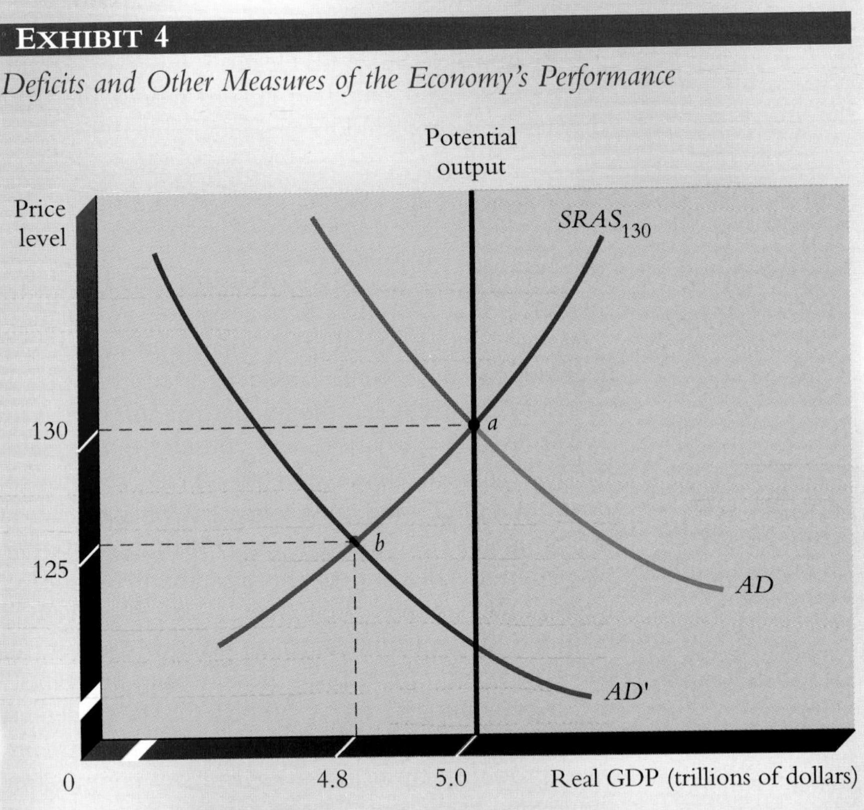

At point *a*, the federal budget is in balance and output is at potential. A decline in aggregate demand to *AD′* triggers automatic stabilizers. Tax revenues fall, transfer payments increase, and the budget moves to a deficit position. In this case the deficit is associated with falling output and a falling price level.

With the economy now at point *b*, suppose policy makers stimulate aggregate demand through expansionary fiscal policy. Tax revenues fall, government expenditures increase, and the deficit grows larger. Here the deficit is associated with rising output and a rising price level.

its potential output—is equal to zero in this example. The short-run aggregate supply curve is based on long-term labor contracts reflecting an expected price level of 130.

Suppose an unexpected decline in private-sector spending reduces aggregate demand. As output and employment decline, the automatic stabilizers kick in, reducing tax revenues and increasing transfer payments. These stabilizers keep aggregate demand from falling as much as it would without them. Still, the aggregate demand curve drops from *AD* to *AD′*, resulting in a short-run equilibrium at output level of $4.8 trillion. This combination of reduced tax revenues and increased government outlays results in a budget deficit. According to research, every 1 percent increase in the unemployment rate increases the federal deficit by over $30 billion.

Point to Stress The deficit does not *cause* the falling real output and prices.

Teaching Tip The impact of a deficit on interest rates also depends on Fed policy. Fed purchases of securities can offset the tendency of Treasury sales of securities to raise interest rates.

Point to Stress Unlike the deficit resulting from automatic stabilizers, the deficit resulting from discretionary policy *causes* the changes in real output and prices. Again, any effect on interest rates can be counteracted through monetary policy. Note the high German interest rates in 1992 relative to U.S. rates although Germany and the United States had similar budget deficits as a percentage of GDP (see Exhibit 5). Monetary policy was much easier to implement in the United States.

Example Between 1965 and 1966, real government spending rose 12.9 percent with no increase in taxes. Interest rates increased 30 percent. Residential investment dropped 23 percent in 1966, and nonresidential investment dropped 13 percent in 1967. In 1990, borrowing to finance the deficit absorbed 58 percent of national saving.

Now let's consider the association between this deficit and what happens to real output, the price level, and interest rates. The first two are easy to predict: the deficit resulting from the automatic stabilizers is associated with falling real output and a falling price level. But the interaction of two opposing forces determines the interest rate. First, when output and the price level decline, the transactions demand for money declines as well, so the interest rate tends to fall. Second, to finance the government deficit, the U.S. Treasury must sell securities, and this additional supply of securities in the market will put upward pressure on interest rates. The net effect on interest rates will depend on which force is stronger, the falling demand for money or the rising supply of government securities. Thus, *a deficit resulting from automatic stabilizers will be associated with a lower level of price and output, but the effect on the interest rate depends on opposing market pressures.*

At point *b*, the economy is in recession, with a short-run equilibrium output that is below the economy's potential. Policy makers can either do nothing and wait for natural market forces to correct the problem of unemployment or intervene in some way. Recall that activists believe that if no government action is taken, the adjustment to potential output could be long and painful, with much unemployment and much forgone output. Nonactivists believe that government intervention involves unpredictable lags and may affect aggregate demand only after the economy has naturally returned to its potential.

Suppose the government increases its spending without changing taxes. To finance this increase in the deficit, the Treasury must sell more securities to the public, a move that tends to put upward pressure on interest rates. According to the activist view, the appropriate increase in government spending could stimulate aggregate demand just enough to return the economy to its potential GDP. The effects of this policy would be represented in Exhibit 4 by a movement from point *b* back to point *a*. In essence, increased government demand offsets the decline in private sector demand. You might say that this is fiscal policy at its best; the deficit is used to nudge the economy back to its potential output.

What is the relation between the deficit that results from this discretionary fiscal policy and the other macroeconomic aggregates of concern? This deficit is associated with a greater output and a higher price level. The interest rate rises not only because the Treasury sells bonds to finance the deficit but also because the higher price and output levels increase the demand for money. Thus, *the deficit that arises from discretionary fiscal policy is associated with a higher real output, a higher price level, and a higher interest rate.*

Consequently, there is no necessary relation between deficits and various measures of economic performance. In the first instance the deficit results from the operation of automatic stabilizers that cushion the fall in private-sector spending; in the second instance the deficit results from a discretionary fiscal policy aimed at increasing aggregate demand.

Crowding Out and Crowding In

Suppose the federal government decides to expand the interstate highway system with a program that will cost $10 billion this year. But taxes are not increased to finance it. To pay for the new system, the U.S. Treasury sells securities, or IOUs. The government's increased demand for credit raises interest rates in the market for loans. Higher interest rates in turn discourage, or crowd out, some private investment, reducing the expansionary effect of the deficit. The extent of **crowding out** is a matter of debate. Some argue that although borrowing from the public may displace some private-sector borrowing, discretionary fiscal policy will result in a net increase in aggregate demand, leading to greater output and employment. Others believe the crowding out is more extensive, so borrowing from the public in this way could result in little or no increase in aggregate demand and output. The fact is that during the 1980s real long-term interest rates (the interest rate on government bonds minus the inflation rate) averaged 5.7 percent compared to only 0.4 percent during the 1970s. Real long-term interest rates in the United States continued to be high into the 1990s.

Crowding out The displacement of interest-sensitive private investment that occurs when increased government spending drives up interest rates

Although crowding out is likely to occur to some degree, there is another possibility. If the economy is operating well below its potential, the additional fiscal stimulus provided by deficit spending could encourage firms to invest more and could thus result in a higher level of investment. Recall that an important determinant of investment is business expectations. A government deficit could stimulate a weak economy, increasing aggregate demand and putting a sunny face on business expectations. As business expectations grow more favorable, firms could become more willing to invest. This ability of government deficits to stimulate private investment is sometimes called **crowding in**, to distinguish it from crowding out.

Teaching Tip Complete or extensive crowding out represents another argument for nonactivist fiscal policy. Crowding in would be an argument for activist policy.

Crowding in The potential for government spending to stimulate private investment in an otherwise sluggish economy

Were you ever unwilling to enter a restaurant because it was too crowded? You simply did not want to put up with the hassle and long wait and were thus "crowded out." Similarly, large government deficits may "crowd out" some investors by driving up interest rates. Alternatively, did you ever pass up a restaurant because the place seemed dead—it had few customers? Perhaps you wondered why few people chose to eat there. With just a few more customers, you might have stopped in—you might have been willing to "crowd in." Similarly, businesses may be reluctant to invest in a seemingly dead economy. The economic stimulus resulting from deficit spending could encourage come investors to "crowd in."

The Twin Deficits

We have already discussed the huge federal deficits that began in the early 1980s. To finance the deficits, the U.S. Treasury had to sell securities, driving up the market rate of interest. With U.S. interest rates relatively high, foreigners were more willing to save by investing in dollar-denominated assets. To buy such assets, foreigners had to exchange their currencies for dollars. This greater demand for dollars caused the dollar to appreciate relative to foreign currencies. The rising value of the dollar made foreign goods cheaper in the United States and U.S. goods more expensive abroad. Thus, U.S. imports increased and U.S. exports decreased, so the foreign trade deficit increased.

Teaching Tip The drop in net exports represented another form of crowding out. The more net exports are crowded out, the larger the flow of funds from abroad, and the less private investment is crowded out.

The higher trade deficits meant that foreigners were accumulating dollars. Foreigners invested these dollars in U.S. assets, including U.S. government securities, and thereby helped fund the giant federal deficits. The increase in funds from abroad in the 1980s was both good news and bad news for the U.S. economy. The good news was that the supply of foreign funds increased investment in the United States over what it would have been in the absence of these funds. Higher investment led to greater worker productivity and more economic growth. Ask residents what they think of foreign investment in their town; they will likely say it's great.

But the foreign supply of funds reflected the fact that the saving rate in the United States is now about the lowest it has been since the Great Depression, and the United States is now the largest borrower in the world. Such a pattern could pose problems in the long run. The United States has surrendered a certain amount of control over its economy to foreign investors. The return on foreign investments in the United States will flow abroad.

By the early 1990s, the Federal Reserve reduced U.S. interest rates, which has made the U.S. assets less attractive to foreigners. As a result, the value of the dollar has fallen on foreign exchange markets. The recession of 1990–1991 and the sluggish recovery also reduced imports, thus reducing the trade deficit. In short, by the early 1990s the inflow of savings from abroad had slowed.

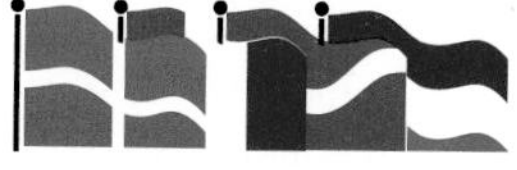

Deficits in Other Countries

Example Japan's surplus allowed it to announce spending increases in 1992 in response to a 7.6 percent drop in industrial production. After months of allowing Germany's deficit to drive up interest rates, the Bundesbank reversed its traditional anti-inflationary stance by announcing interest rate cuts in late 1992 in response to a downturn in its economy. Italy proclaimed a $72 billion austerity package of lower spending and higher taxes to cut its deficit.

In sheer size, the United States has had the largest government deficit throughout the world, but when measured as a percentage of GDP, we are in the middle of the pack. Exhibit 5 shows how the government deficit in the United States for 1992 compared to deficits in other industrial countries. Due in part to a worldwide recession in the early 1990s, government deficits in industrial countries were higher in 1992 than at the end of the 1980s.

Of the eighteen countries in the exhibit, only Japan had a budget surplus in 1992; this compares to seven surpluses among these eighteen countries in 1989. The integration of what had been Eastern Germany into Germany proved costly; the German national deficit was 4 percent of GDP in 1992, which was down slightly from 5 percent in 1991. As a consequence, Germany needed all of its domestic sources of investment and may even have to import savings from abroad. The German Bundesbank increased German interest rates to attract the necessary funds.

The biggest deficits were in Greece and Italy. The deficit in Greece of 15 percent in 1992 was actually an improvement from the 18 percent deficit in 1989. Italy's deficit of 10 percent of GDP in 1992 was only the most recent of a long series of deficits resulting from what is considered to be the most inefficient and wasteful government in Europe. But chronic deficits are catching up with Italy; as we will see shortly, public-sector debt now exceeds Italy's gross domestic product, and the Italian government is in turmoil.

EXHIBIT 5

National Government Surpluses or Deficits in 1992 as a Percentage of GDP

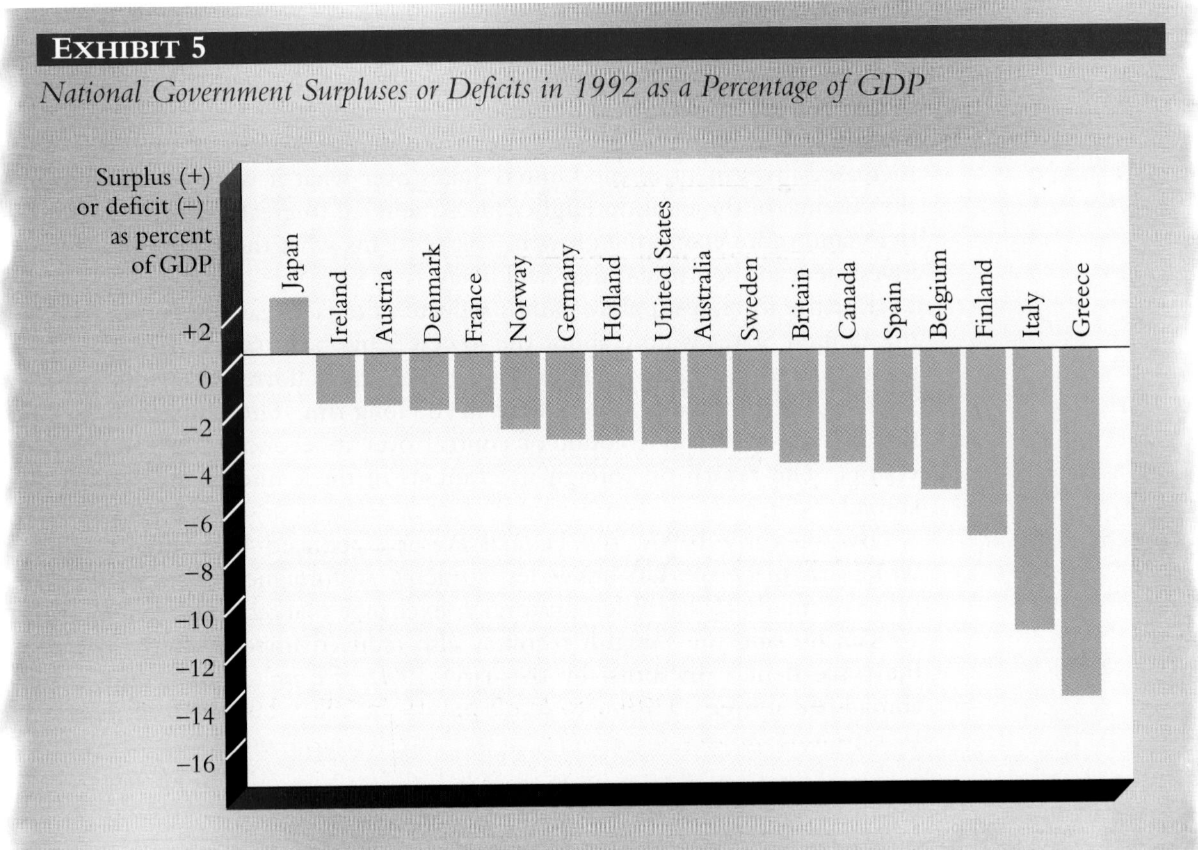

Sources: Organization for Economic Cooperation and Development, as reported in *The Economist,* 15 August 1992: 90.

THE BALLOONING NATIONAL DEBT

National debt The net accumulation of federal budget deficits

Whereas the federal deficit is a flow variable measuring the amount by which expenditures exceed revenues in a particular year, the federal debt, or the **national debt**, is a stock variable measuring the net accumulation of past deficits. Federal deficits add up. It took thirty-nine presidents, six wars, the Great Depression, and more than two hundred years for the federal debt to reach $1 trillion, as it did in 1981. It took only two presidents and another eleven years for that debt to top $4 trillion, as it did in 1992. Ironically, this quadrupling of the national debt occurred primarily under President Reagan, who was initially elected on a promise to balance the budget.

In talking about the national debt, we distinguish between the gross debt and debt held by the public. The *gross debt* includes U.S. Treasury securities purchased by various federal agencies, such as the Social Security trust fund. Since this is debt the federal government owes to itself, we often ignore such

Teaching Tip Publicly held debt also includes that held by state and local governments. The bulk of Fed assets are government securities (mainly for controlling the money supply). Government securities also represent the second largest asset group of U.S. commercial banks, and their holdings of Treasury bills and notes increased 23 percent between the fall of 1991 and the fall of 1992.

debt to focus on *debt held by the public*, which includes debt held by banks (including Federal Reserve banks), firms, households, and foreign entities. As of 1993, the gross national debt stood at about $4.4 trillion and the debt held by the public stood at $3.3 trillion. Even if Clinton's proposals for deficit reduction are approved by Congress, another $1 trillion will be added to the debt during Clinton's first term.

The National Debt Since World War II

The top line in Exhibit 6(a) represents the debt held by the public since World War II, as measured in current dollars. At the end of World War II, the federal debt held by the public was $242 billion, about $200 billion of which resulted from financing the war. Between 1946 and the mid-1970s, the national debt grew slowly. By 1974 the national debt had increased to only $344 billion; by 1993, however, the debt held by the public had jumped to over $3.3 trillion.

Because of inflation, the 1993 dollar purchases far less than did the 1946 dollar. Thus, a dollar's worth of debt in 1993 does not represent as great a liability as a dollar's worth of debt in 1946. To adjust for inflation, we can measure the debt in constant dollars. As the lower line in Exhibit 6(a) shows, in 1946 constant dollars, the national debt actually declined from $242 billion in 1946 to $165 billion in 1980, but then climbed to $437 billion in 1993. Hence, when figures are adjusted for inflation, the growth of the national debt is not nearly as dramatic. Measured in *constant dollars*, the federal debt declined between 1946 and 1980 but grew at an average annual rate of 7.8 percent between 1974 and 1993.

Debt Relative to GDP

Another way to measure debt over time is to relate it to the economy's production and income, or GDP (just as a bank might compare the size of a mortgage to a borrower's income). Exhibit 6(b) shows debt held by the public as a percentage of GDP. In 1946 the national debt was 114 percent of GDP. Between 1946 and 1980, debt as a percentage of GDP declined to only 27 percent, but then climbed to 54 percent by 1993.

Let's consider briefly why debt has changed relative to GDP. For debt as a percentage of GDP to decline, GDP must grow faster than debt. Nominal national debt grew by only 3.2 percent per year between 1946 and 1980, a period during which nominal GDP grew by 7.7 percent per year. National debt as a percentage of GDP therefore fell between 1946 and 1974, as reflected in Exhibit 6(b). Between 1980 and 1993, however, nominal debt grew by a whopping 12.6 percent per year, whereas nominal GDP grew by only 6.6 percent per year, so debt as a percentage of GDP increased.

Example The trend was expected to continue for 1993 with economic growth projected at only 2.6 percent and deficit growth projected at 18 percent.

Thus far we have examined the national debt using the federal government's accounting system, which is unlike the system used by The Gap or Motown Records. The case study that begins on page 403 considers what would happen to the deficit if we used conventional accounting practices.

EXHIBIT 6

Postwar Measures of Federal Debt Held by the Public

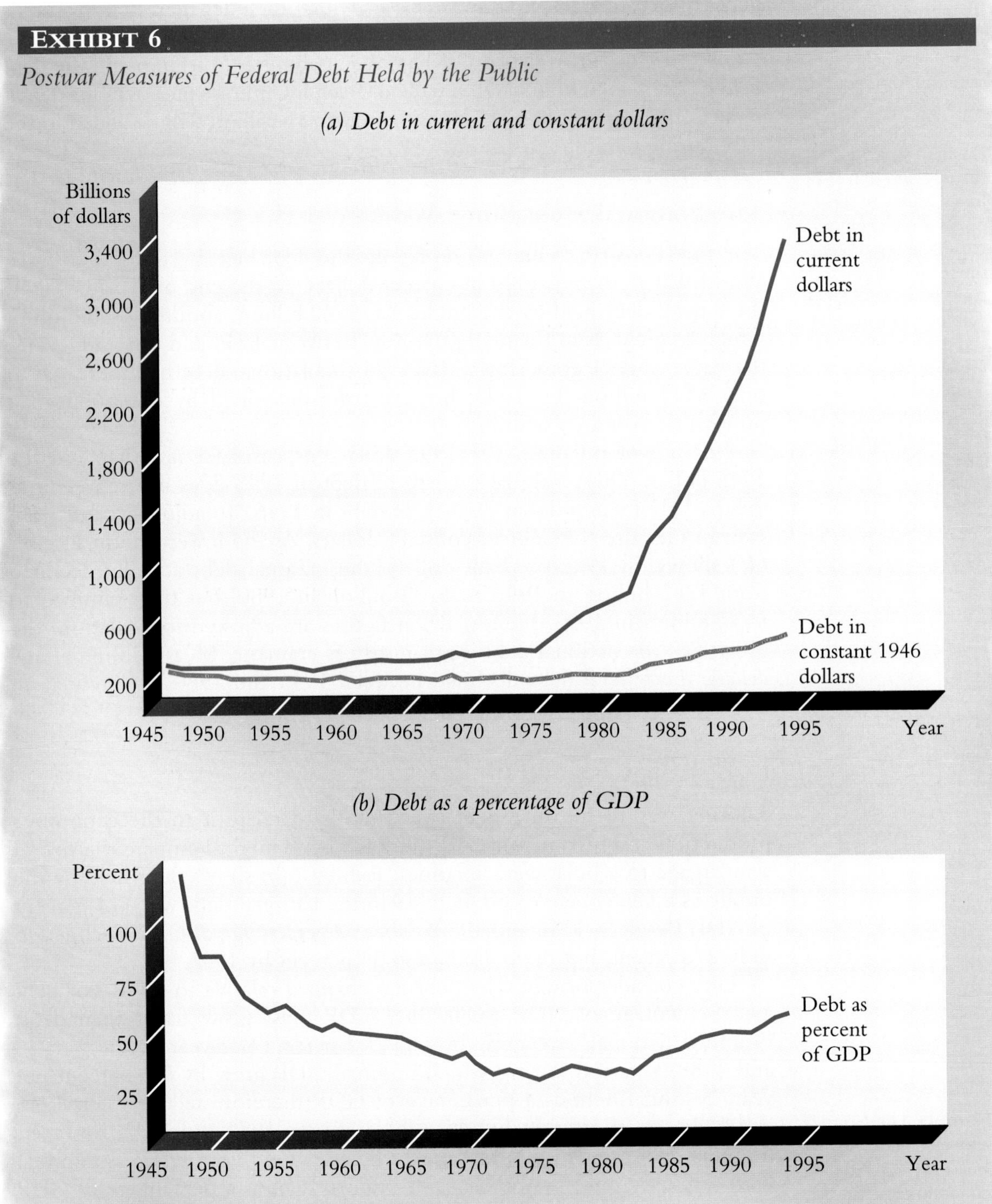

Source: Computed using data from *Economic Report of the President,* January 1993.

CASE STUDY

Another View of Federal Debt

Firms in the private sector budget by (1) capital accounts, which reflect spending for such capital resources as plant and equipment, and (2) current accounts, which include expenditures for all other resources, such as wages, energy, and raw materials. The federal budget mixes current and capital expenditures together. Robert Eisner of Northwestern University argues that the federal accounting system, by ignoring a capital budget, yields a distorted measure of national debt.

Eisner develops a capital budget to derive what he believes is a more realistic federal budget picture. Although we will use his figures for 1984 as an example of how to carry out the calculations, his methodology could be used for any year. He first computes the federal government's "net debt," which is its financial liabilities minus its financial assets. The primary financial liability is government securities. To derive the 1984 market value of government securities, Eisner had to find the market value that year of all U.S. government security issues outstanding. Securities that were initially sold at an interest rate below the 1984 rate would be less attractive on the market than 1984 issues; they would sell at a *discount*, meaning that their market value was lower than their face value. Conversely, securities that were initially sold when interest rates were higher than those prevailing in 1984 would be more attractive than 1984 issues and would sell at a *premium*, with a market value exceeding their face value. According to Eisner's computations, the market value of the federal debt totaled $2,063 billion in 1984.

Next, Eisner adds up federal financial assets: cash on hand, taxes still to be received, and loans made by the federal government to students, businesses, farmers, home buyers, and other countries. He adjusts the value of these loans as he does the value of liabilities. In 1984 these financial assets had a market value of $887 billion. By subtracting the market value of these assets from the market value of debt, Eisner derived a "net debt" of $1,176 billion, only two-thirds the reported national debt in 1984 of $1,817 billion.

But Eisner is not finished. He further argues that the federal government, like businesses, owns tangible assets, such as buildings, power plants, military installations, highways, hospitals, public housing, and millions of acres of federal land. He calculated that the value of these tangible assets in 1984 was $1,118 billion. These assets minus the government "net debt" of $1,176 billion yields a government "net worth" of –$58 billion. Thus, in Eisner's view, instead of being "in the red" by over $2 trillion in 1984, the federal government was "in the red" by only $58 billion. He performed these calculations for several years between 1945 and 1984, and his findings indicate that the net worth of the U.S. government peaked in 1980 at $382 billion.

Eisner's broader view of the budget points to the false economy associated with attempting to balance the budget by selling federal assets, such as national park land, or by slashing spending on the public infrastructure. Selling tangible assets to finance current expenditures reduces the current deficit but also reduces the federal government's net worth. Since 1984 the national debt has doubled, so the federal government's net worth today would be more in the red than in 1984 if calculated using Eisner's method. In 1992 New Zealand was the first country in the world to report a government balance sheet that keeps track of the value of government assets such as highways and liabilities such as pension programs.

Source: Robert Eisner, *How Real Is the Federal Deficit?* (New York: Free Press, 1986); "Budget Deficits: Rhetoric and Reality," *Journal of Economic Perspectives*, 3 (Spring 1989): 73–94; and "Lessons from the Kiwis," *The Economist*, 3 October 1992.

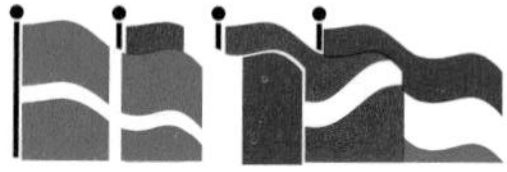

An International Perspective on National Debt

How does public-sector debt in the United States compare to debt levels in other countries? Exhibit 7 compares the U.S. public-sector debt levels as a percentage of GDP with thirteen other industrial countries. Two measures of debt are used: total debt and net debt. The total debt includes all outstanding liabilities of federal, state, and local governments. Net debt is calculated by subtracting the governments' financial assets, such as loans to students and farmers, stock shares, cash on hand and foreign exchange on reserve. Note

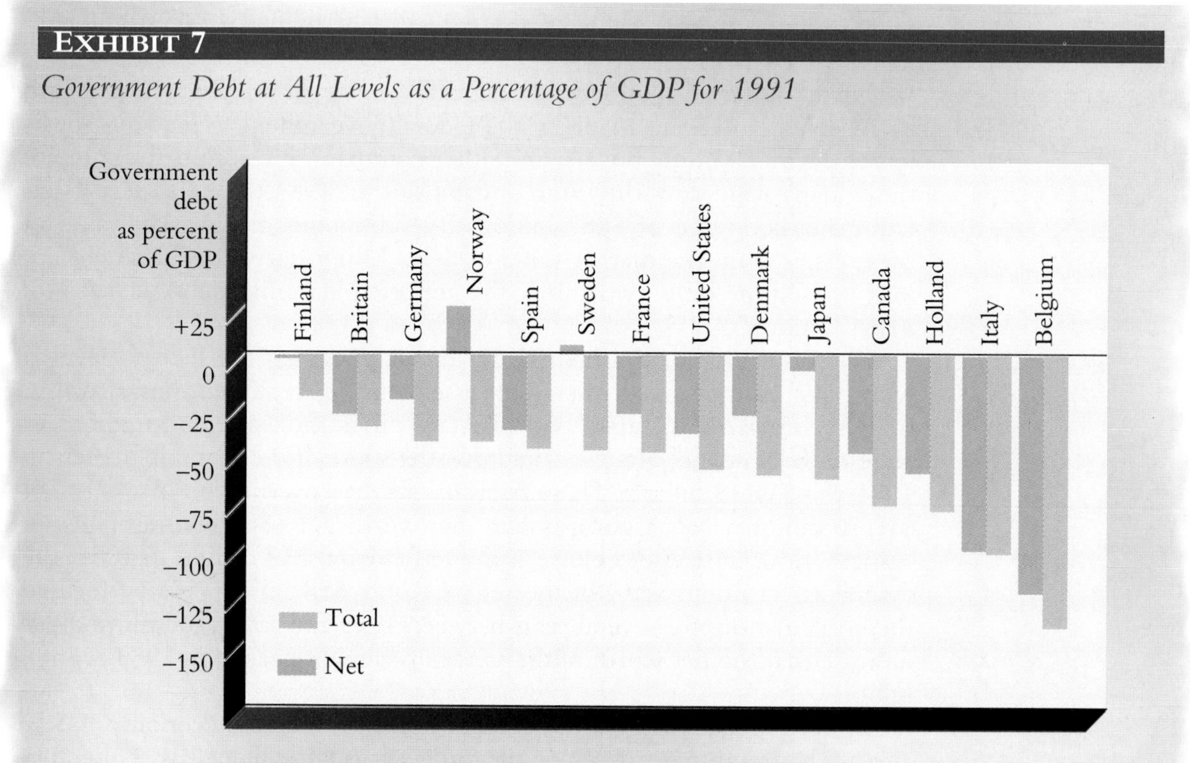

EXHIBIT 7

Government Debt at All Levels as a Percentage of GDP for 1991

Source: Organization for Economic Cooperation and Development, as reported in *The Economist,* 26 September 1992: 120.

that the value of tangible assets owned by the public sector, such as buildings and national parks, is ignored in this exhibit.

As you can see in Exhibit 7, despite the huge increase in federal debt since 1980, the United States is again in the middle of the pack of industrial countries, with total debt for all levels of government combined a little more than 50 percent of GDP and net debt about 35 percent. When net debt is considered, Norway and Sweden had a net public-sector surplus, and Japan's public-sector debt nearly disappears.

Interest Payments on the Debt

Teaching Tip The government sells thirteen- and twenty-six-week Treasury bills (auctioned every Monday), nine-month and twelve-month bills (sold monthly), Treasury notes with original maturities of from one to seven years, and Treasury bonds with original maturities greater than seven years.

Example The 1993 debt was projected to amount to $17,300 per person by the end of the fiscal year.

Purchasers of government securities range from individuals who buy a $25 savings bond to institutions that buy $1 million Treasury notes. When these securities mature, the government issues more securities to pay them off. Because most government securities are short term, the national debt "turns over" rapidly—about 45 percent of the debt is refinanced every twelve months. With over $150 billion coming due each month, debt service payments are quite sensitive to movements in interest rates. A one-percent increase in the nominal interest rate paid by the government increases its annual interest costs by over $10 billion during the first year and by $30 billion during the second year.

Since 1960, interest payments on the national debt have grown every year. As a percentage of the federal budget, interest payments grew from 6 percent in 1960 to 14 percent in 1993. Interest payments as a percentage of federal personal income tax collections have doubled from about 20 percent in 1980 to about 40 percent in 1993. Interest payments will soon eat up half of personal income taxes. Part of the problem of the debt is that it is an abstraction. To put interest payments in context: In 1993 interest payments on the national debt amounted to about $250 per month for each of the 68 million U.S. families; that's equivalent to a second car payment.

Interest Payments and Seigniorage

One factor that influences interest payments is *seigniorage*. You'll recall that this term was originally used to refer to the profit the "lord of the manor" derived from issuing coins whose metallic value was less than their face, or exchange, value. In the modern setting, seigniorage refers to the revenue that the U.S. Treasury receives because the Federal Reserve System can create money. As you know, the Fed adds money to the economy by purchasing Treasury securities from the public. Although the Fed earns interest on these securities, it pays no interest on the money it creates.

Point to Stress Seigniorage has seldom amounted to more than 10 to 13 percent of total interest on the debt.

Some of the interest received by the Fed is used to cover its operating expenses, including paying dividends to member banks, which are stockholders of the Federal Reserve banks. Most of the interest, however, is returned to the U.S. Treasury. Since 1913 the Fed has returned an average of 87 percent of its earnings to the Treasury. For example, in 1992 the Federal Reserve System returned about $21 billion to the Treasury. *Seigniorage, a by-product of monetary policy, reduces the net interest payment in any given year and thereby reduces the deficit.*

Who Bears the Burden of the Debt?

Deficit spending is a way to increase current expenditures. The national debt raises moral questions about the right of one generation of taxpayers to bequeath to the next generation the burden of its own borrowing. The director of the Congressional Budget Office has argued before Congress that "by running up large federal deficits, the current generation is lowering the living standard for its children and grandchildren." Similarly, Nobel laureate Franco Modigliani believes that deficit spending amounts to "enjoying it now and paying it later" by pushing the bill on to future generations in the form of the higher taxes that will be required to cover interest and principal. And Benjamin Friedman of Harvard University says "America has thrown a party and billed the tab to the future. The costs, which are only beginning to come due, will include a lower standard of living for individual Americans and reduced American influence and importance in world affairs."[1] To what extent do budget deficits shift the burden to future generations? Let's consider arguments about the burden of the debt.

Teaching Tip Lower future living standards are less likely to occur to the extent that government debt finances capital expenditures that yield returns sufficient to justify the debt cost. Lower living standards are more likely to occur to the extent that debt is used to finance operating expenses—especially for services that the private sector could provide more efficiently.

FOREIGN OWNERSHIP OF DEBT. It is often argued that the debt is not a burden to future generations because, although future generations must service the debt, those same generations will receive the debt service payments. It's true that if U.S. citizens forgo present consumption to buy bonds, they or their heirs will receive the interest payments, so debt service payments will stay in the country. But foreigners who purchase U.S. government securities forgo the present consumption and receive the future benefits. An influx of foreign capital reduces the amount of current consumption that Americans must sacrifice to finance the national debt. *A reliance on foreigners, however, increases the burden of the debt on future generations because future debt service payments no longer remain in the country.* Foreign holdings of debt have ranged between 10 and 15 percent of the total.

CROWDING OUT AND CAPITAL FORMATION. As we have said, government borrowing drives up interest rates, crowding out some private investment by making it more costly. The higher interest rates resulting from government borrowing increase foreign demand for dollars, as foreigners try to invest in dollar-denominated assets. This increased demand for dollars causes the dollar to appreciate on foreign exchange markets, leading to more imports and fewer exports, so higher interest rates could reduce net exports as well as crowd out some domestic investment.

Therefore, deficit spending does not expand aggregate demand as much as the autonomous spending multiplier would suggest. The long-run opportunity cost of crowding out will depend on how the government spends the borrowed dollars. If additional federal outlays are oriented toward investments such as improving interstate highways or educating the work force, the public investment may be as productive as any private investment forgone.

1. Benjamin Friedman, *Day of Reckoning* (New York: Random House, 1988).

Example On average, Japan's annual real growth rate has exceeded the U.S. rate since 1961.

Hence, there should be no harmful effects on the economy's long-run productive capability. If, however, the additional borrowed dollars go toward current consumption, such as farm subsidies or retirement benefits, the economy's capital formation will be less than it would otherwise be. With less investment today, there is less of an endowment of capital equipment and technology for future generations.

U.S. investment as a percentage of GDP is much lower than in Japan. Over time, a decline in the rate of investment reduces the amount and quality of capital available in the economy, which reduces both productivity and the economy's ability to grow. Thus, government deficits of one generation can reduce the standard of living for the next. In this sense the deficit of one generation imposes a burden on future generations.

Reducing the Deficit

Example During the 1992 presidential campaign, Ross Perot called for higher taxes on income, gas, cigarettes, and Social Security benefits, as well as an increase in Medicare premiums and limited deductions for home mortgages.

Teaching Tip A 1992 study by a bipartisan commission concluded that the line-item veto would be unlikely to trim more than 2 percent, or about $30 billion, from government spending. The line-item veto would not apply to the fastest-growing portion of the budget: entitlement programs.

Line-item veto A provision to allow the president to reject particular portions of the budget rather than simply accept or reject the entire budget

Among economists, there is some disagreement over whether the current deficits pose a major problem for the country. Most agree that chronic deficits are undesirable, but current prospects for substantial reductions in the deficit are not good. As we have seen, recent legislation, including the so-called Gramm-Rudman-Hollings Act of 1985 and the Budget Enforcement Act of 1990, have not done the job. One way of eliminating the deficit is to raise taxes enough to cover it, but some economists believe that higher taxes could substantially slow the economy. Some also believe that the giant deficits, while undesirable in themselves, have at least slowed the growth in federal spending (federal spending as a percentage of GDP fell slightly between 1986 and 1989, but it has since increased). According to this view, a tax hike would simply support higher government spending and do little for the deficit.

As mentioned earlier, elected officials pay a political price for raising taxes and thus are understandably reluctant to do so. A promise to raise taxes could prove hazardous to a politician's career, as Walter Mondale, the Democratic candidate for president in 1984, can attest. Instead, members of Congress pursue reelection by supporting innumerable programs for special-interest constituencies. Individual members of Congress tend to spend for narrow purposes and in so doing tend to overspend in total.

Line-Item Veto

One proposal designed to reduce the impact of special interests on the budget and at the same time provide the executive branch with more flexibility is to give the president a line-item veto. The **line-item veto** would allow the president to reject particular portions of the budget rather than simply accept or reject the entire budget, as is now the case. An argument for the line-item veto is that the president is the only elected representative with a broad enough constituency to reject the special-interest programs often embedded in the budget. To approve a vetoed item, Congress would have to demonstrate a strong preference for the project by coming up with a two-thirds majority. The governors of forty-three states have the line-item veto for their state budgets.

Balanced Budget Amendment

Balanced budget amendment Proposed amendment to the U.S. Constitution requiring a balanced federal budget

Another attempt to force the government to control spending is a proposed amendment to the U.S. Constitution requiring a balanced federal budget. Professor James Buchanan argues that a **balanced budget amendment** could replace the moral force that required balanced budgets before Keynes freed lawmakers of this constraint.

There have been two kinds of criticisms of the balanced budget amendment. The first stems from the belief that the amendment would work too well. Both autonomous and discretionary fiscal policies use deficits and surpluses as policy tools to stimulate the economy during recessions and to dampen the economy during expansions. A balanced budget requirement would reduce the government's ability to employ fiscal policy to cope with business fluctuations, particularly recessions. Another problem with requiring a balanced budget is that tax rates would have to be raised during recessions. The higher rates would not only reduce disposable income but might reduce incentives to work and to invest. To allow some room for fiscal policy, proposed balanced budget amendments typically allow Congress the ability to override this restriction with a greater-than-majority vote, such as two-thirds or three-fifths. Despite this escape clause, some policy makers remain concerned that fiscal policy would be undermined by a balanced budget amendment. But discretionary fiscal policy has been largely undermined anyway by large chronic deficits (though automatic stabilizers still operate).

Example A bipartisan study sponsored in 1992 by the Center for Strategic and International Studies concluded that an amendment requiring a balanced budget within five years would force spending cuts or tax increases totaling $630 billion.

A second kind of criticism of a balanced budget amendment is that any budget restriction would probably be difficult to specify and easy to bypass. Even if such a measure held down spending by the federal government, authority for certain types of spending could simply be pushed down to lower levels of government. Another fear is that the federal government would use greater regulation of the economy to achieve what it could not fund directly through the budget. For example, rather than subsidizing an employment training program for unskilled workers, the government might simply require employers to hire and train such workers. Some people think that such government intervention in the market might ultimately prove to be less efficient than using the budget to achieve the desired outcome. Congress narrowly defeated a balanced-budget amendment in 1992.

Conclusion

Keynes introduced the idea that federal deficit spending is an appropriate fiscal policy when private aggregate demand is lacking. The federal budget has not been the same since. The federal budget has been in deficit every year but one since 1960. Since the early 1980s giant federal deficits have dominated the fiscal policy debate. One reason budget deficits are hard to reduce is that the pain of such reduction comes in the near term but the benefits are off in the future. As people get used to huge deficits, the numbers seem less scary, and politicians grow more reluctant to incur the political cost of fixing the problem. Italy experienced huge federal deficits for years and they became standard practice. But these huge deficits eventually bore the bitter fruit of political and economic crisis in that country.

The macroeconomic focus thus far has been on the effects of fiscal and monetary policy in promoting potential output and price stability. In the next chapter we will consider another macroeconomic policy objective: economic growth.

SUMMARY

1. The federal budget process suffers from a variety of problems, including overlapping committee jurisdictions, lengthy budget deliberations, extensive use of continuing resolutions, budgeting in too much detail, and a lack of year-to-year control over most of the budget. Suggested improvements include instituting a biennial budget and budgeting in less detail.

2. Deficits usually rise during wars and severe recessions, but huge deficits occurred during the economic expansion of the 1980s. The deficits arose from a combination of tax cuts during the early 1980s and growth in federal spending. As a percentage of GDP, the national debt has more than doubled since 1980.

3. There is no clear, consistent relation between deficits and other measures of macroeconomic performance, such as output, the price level, and interest rates. If a fall in aggregate demand results in a recession, deficits increase because of automatic stabilizers, but output, the price level, and, at times, the interest rate all tend to decline. If discretionary fiscal policy is used to rekindle aggregate demand, deficits increase, and so do output, the price level, and the interest rate.

4. To the extent that deficits crowd out private capital formation, this decline in investment reduces the economy's ability to grow. To the extent that deficits drive up interest rates, the greater demand for dollars on foreign exchange markets drives up the value of the dollar and reduces net exports. Foreign holdings of debt also impose a burden on future generations because future payments to service this debt are paid to foreigners and are consequently not available to U.S. citizens. Thus, the deficits of one generation can reduce the standard of living of the next.

5. Several proposals have been put forth to reduce the giant federal deficits. The Gramm-Rudman-Hollings Act of 1985 and the Budget Enforcement Act of 1990 each put a small dent in the deficit. Other possible remedies include tax increases, expenditure reductions, the line-item veto, and a balanced budget amendment.

QUESTIONS AND PROBLEMS

1. (Federal Budget Process) Why wouldn't a general freeze on federal government spending stop some government spending from increasing? Why can't the government control expenditures on interest payments on the national debt in the short run?

2. (Government Budget Deficits) Recessions have often led to large budget deficits. However, the years 1983–1987 were years of recovery for the economy. How, then, were the largest deficits in history produced during these years?

3. (Government Budget Deficits) During the 1984 presidential campaign, President Reagan claimed that the country would grow out of the deficit it was experiencing. What was the reasoning behind his statement? Did the economy in fact grow out of the deficit?

4. (Crowding Out) Is it possible for U.S. federal budget deficits to crowd out investment spending in other countries? How could German or British investment be hurt by large U.S. budget deficits?

5. (Government Debt) Consider a capital budget for the government, as described in the chapter. Suppose that interest rates in the United States rose. How would this affect the net worth of the government, as computed by Eisner? If the government attempted to sell off assets to reduce the deficit, what effect would this sale of assets have on the government's net worth?

6. (Seigniorage) Earlier in the text we noted that the Fed pays no interest to commercial banks that hold reserves with the Fed. If the Fed were forced to pay interest, how would this affect the level of seigniorage returned to the U.S. Treasury? How might this complicate attempts to reduce federal budget deficits?

7. (Government Sale of Assets) Some commentators have satirically suggested that the government sell Yellowstone National Park to reduce the deficit. Assuming more appropriate candidates could be found, there are still problems with the sale of assets. Why do such sales reduce the deficit only in the year of sale? Are there other reasons to conduct such sales? How would you decide which assets should be sold and which should not be sold?

8. (Budget Deficits) One alternative to balancing the budget annually or cyclically is to produce a government budget that would be balanced if the economy were at full-employment output. Given the cyclical nature of government tax revenues and spending, how would the budget deficit or surplus vary over the business cycle?

9. (Crowding Out) One kind of crowding out caused by government budget deficits is called *international* crowding out. Explain why a reduction in net exports is likely to occur.

10. (Budget Deficits) If individuals continually spend more than they take in, eventually they must declare bankruptcy. Why is this not the case with the federal government?

11. (Debt Burden) Suppose that government budget deficits are financed to a considerable extent by foreign sources. How does this create a potential burden for the domestic economy in the future?

12. (Balancing the Budget) Explain how a rule *requiring* the federal government to annually balance its budget could be *de*stabilizing to the economy as far as fiscal activity is concerned.

13. (Federal Debt) During the 1992 presidential campaign, Ross Perot expressed concern about the amount of the federal debt held in short-run securities. What do you see as the benefits and costs of such a strategy of federal debt offerings?

14. (Debt Service) According to the text, the percentage of federal income tax revenues necessary to service the debt has doubled since 1980. What problems does this create for public officials and spending programs? Do you need to run a budget surplus to "solve" the problem?

15. (Structural Deficits) Exhibit 2 presents deficit data for the years 1979–1992. In which years did the economy experience a contractionary gap? An expansionary gap? Explain your answers.

16. (Time Deficits) Since 1979, countries in the European Monetary System have attempted to maintain relatively rigid exchange rates by pricing their currencies to the European Currency Unit, or ECU. In 1992, however, several countries were under tremendous pressure to float or devalue their currencies because of high interest rates in Germany. Discuss.

17. (Functional Finance) The functional finance approach to budget deficits would have the federal budget set so as to promote an economy operating at potential output levels. What operational problems might you expect if the country were to use this kind of budgetary philosophy?

18. (Another View of Federal Debt) Virtually all of the financial assets and liabilities of the federal government have fixed interest-rate payments. What would happen to the government's "net debt" position if interest rates increased? Are both assets and liabilities equally risky?

19. (Another View of Federal Debt) Many of the federal government's tangible assets may have limited private-sector value beyond the land (e.g., a military base). Should the government count the value (i.e., cost) of structures, etc., in valuing tangible assets for determining net worth estimates?

CHAPTER 17

PRODUCTIVITY AND GROWTH

Two centuries ago, most Americans were employed in agriculture, in jobs whose hours were long and rewards unpredictable. Nonagricultural workers had it no better; they worked from sunrise to sunset for a wage that exchanged for the bare necessities. There was little intellectual stimulus and little contact with the outside world. A typical worker's home in the year 1790 was described as follows: "Sand sprinkled on the floor did duty as a carpet. . . . What a stove was he did not know. Coal he had never seen. Matches he had never heard of. . . . He rarely tasted fresh meat. . . . If the food of an artisan would now be thought coarse, his clothes would be thought abominable."[1]

The single most important factor determining a nation's standard of living in the long run is the productivity of its resources. A nation prospers by making more efficient use of its resources. Even relatively small increases in the growth rate in productivity can, if maintained over time, have large effects on living standards. Growing productivity is therefore key to a higher standard of living. In the last two centuries, there has been a tremendous increase in U.S. productivity and in the variety of products available. This growth in productivity has put the U.S. standard of living ahead of nearly every other nation on earth.

For the last two decades, however, U.S. productivity growth appears to have slowed down. This slowdown could threaten continued prosperity and will affect the standard of living you experience during your lifetime.

1. E. L. Bogart, *The Economic History of the United States* (New York: Longmans, Green, and Co., 1912), 157–158.

Example A 1992 study by the McKinsey Global Institute indicated that the productivity of U.S. workers is 11 percent higher than that of West German workers and 23 percent higher than that of Japanese workers.

In this chapter we consider the sources of economic growth and examine the recent slowdown in productivity growth. We also analyze the government's role in fostering economic growth and productivity, an issue that gained increased attention in the Clinton administration. A detailed picture of growth and productivity is provided in "A Closer Look," which appears at the end of this chapter. We should note at the outset that, though the *growth* in U.S. productivity has recently lagged behind the historical trend and behind the growth in most other industrial countries, the *level* of productivity still ranks U.S. workers first in the world. So this chapter is more about the growth in productivity than about the level of productivity, and it is more about the future economic leadership of the United States than about our current ranking. Topics discussed in this chapter include

- Labor productivity
- Slowdown in productivity growth
- Technological change
- Research and development
- Policies to change potential GDP
- Supply-side tax cuts

PRODUCTIVITY AND GROWTH

Economic growth is a complicated process and one we do not yet fully understand. Since before Adam Smith inquired into the *Wealth of Nations,* economists have been trying to discover what makes some economies prosper while others founder. Because the capitalist economy is not the product of conscious design, however, it does not divulge its secrets readily, nor can it be easily manipulated in pursuit of growth objectives. We cannot simply push here and pull there to achieve the desired result. Changing the economy is not like remodeling a home by moving a wall out to expand the kitchen. Since we have no clear copy of the economy's blueprint, we cannot make changes to specifications.

Example According to the McKinsey Global Institute, an average full-time worker in the United States produced $49,600 worth of goods and services in 1992, compared to $47,000 in France, $44,200 in Germany, and $38,200 in Japan.

Productivity

Productivity The ratio of a specific measure of output to a specific measure of input

Productivity measures how efficiently resources are employed. In simplest terms, the greater the productivity, the more goods and services can be produced from a given amount of resources. **Productivity** is defined as the ratio of a specific measure of output to a specific measure of input. It usually reflects an average, expressing total output divided by the total input of a specific kind of resource. For example, *labor productivity* is the output per unit of labor and is measured as total output divided by the number of units of labor employed to produce that output.

We can talk about the productivity of any resource, such as land, labor, or capital. When agricultural products made up the bulk of total output, land productivity, or bushels of grain per acre, was the key measure of economic welfare. Where soil was rocky and barren, people were less prosperous than

Example Japan's land mass is only 143,750 square miles; Germany's is only 137,744 square miles; the United States has 3,618,769 square miles.

where soil was fertile and fruitful. Even today, in many developing countries throughout the world, the productivity of the soil determines the standard of living in the region. Industrialization and trade, however, have liberated many economies from dependence on soil quality. Today some of the world's richest economies have little land or have land of poor fertility.

Labor Productivity

Labor is the resource most commonly used in measuring productivity. Why labor? First, labor accounts for a relatively large share—about three-fourths—of the cost of production. Second, labor is more easily measured than other inputs, whether we speak of hours per week or full-time workers per year. Statistics about employment and hours worked are more readily available and more reliable than those about other resource use.

The resource most responsible for increasing labor productivity is capital. For example, consider the difference between digging a ditch with a teaspoon and digging it with a shovel. Now compare that shovel to a backhoe. You can see that the addition of capital makes the digger more productive. As mentioned in Chapter 1, there are two broad categories of capital: human capital and physical capital. Human capital is the accumulated knowledge, skill, and experience of the labor force. As individual workers acquire more human capital, their productivity, and hence their incomes, grow. For example, a worker may learn how to operate a backhoe. You are reading this book right now to enhance your human capital. Physical capital includes the machines, buildings, roads, airports, communication networks, and other manufactured creations used to produce goods and services. As a nation accumulates more capital per worker, labor productivity tends to increase and the nation gets richer.

Example According to Edward Denison (see footnote 2), 20 percent of U.S. growth from 1929 to 1982 in national income per person employed was due to increases in capital; 27 percent was due to improvements in education.

The Per-Worker Production Function

Per-worker production function The relation between the amount of capital per worker in the economy and the output per worker

We can express the relation between the amount of capital per worker and the output per worker as an economy's **per-worker production function**. Exhibit 1 shows the relation between the amount of capital per worker, measured along the horizontal axis, and output per worker, measured along the vertical axis. The production function, *PF*, slopes upward from left to right because an increase in the amount of capital per worker helps each worker produce more output. For example, a bigger truck makes the truck driver more productive. Any point on the curve shows the relation in the economy between the amount of capital per worker and the output per worker. For example, when there are *k* units of capital per worker, the output per worker in the economy is *y*.

Point to Stress The law of diminishing returns applies while one resource is varied and other resources and the level of technology are held constant.

As the quantity of capital per worker increases, the output per worker increases as well but at a diminishing rate, as reflected by movement along the per-worker production function. The bowed-out shape of this curve reflects the *law of diminishing marginal returns*, which when applied to capital says that the larger the capital stock already is, the less additional output can be gained

EXHIBIT 1

Per-Worker Production Function

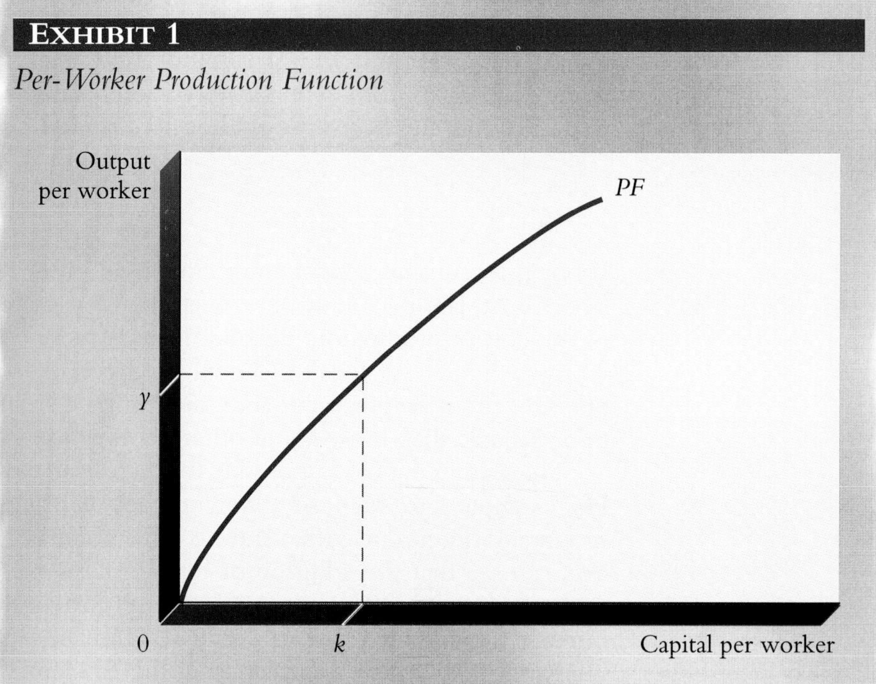

As the capital stock in a nation increases, each worker can produce more, so output per worker increases. The per-worker production function, *PF*, shows the direct relation between the amount of capital per worker, *k*, and the output per worker, *y*. The bowed shape of *PF* reflects the law of diminishing marginal returns as more capital is added.

by increasing the capital stock still more. For example, beyond some size, bigger trucks add less and less to productivity because they are too unwieldy to do the job. Thus, given the technology and the supply of other resources, the additional gains from more capital accumulation eventually diminish. Beyond some point, the additional output from more capital is not worth the cost of that capital.

Example Denison's study indicated that 55 percent of U.S. productivity growth from 1929 to 1982 resulted from "advances in knowledge," which includes managerial, organizational, and technological improvements.

Held constant along a per-worker production function is the level of technology prevailing in the economy. Technological change represents a major source of increasing productivity. Technological change usually improves the quality of capital. For example, the automobile is more efficient than the horse and buggy, the word processor more efficient than the typewriter, a Lotus spreadsheet more efficient than a pencil and paper, and the fiber-optics telephone line more efficient than copper wire. Improving technology is reflected in Exhibit 2 by an upward rotation in the per-worker production function from *PF* to *PF′*. As a result of the technological breakthrough, more output is produced at each level of capital per worker. For example, when there are *k* units of capital per worker, the improvement in technology increases the output per worker in the economy from *y* to *y′*.

EXHIBIT 2

Impact of a Technological Breakthrough on the Per-Worker Production Function

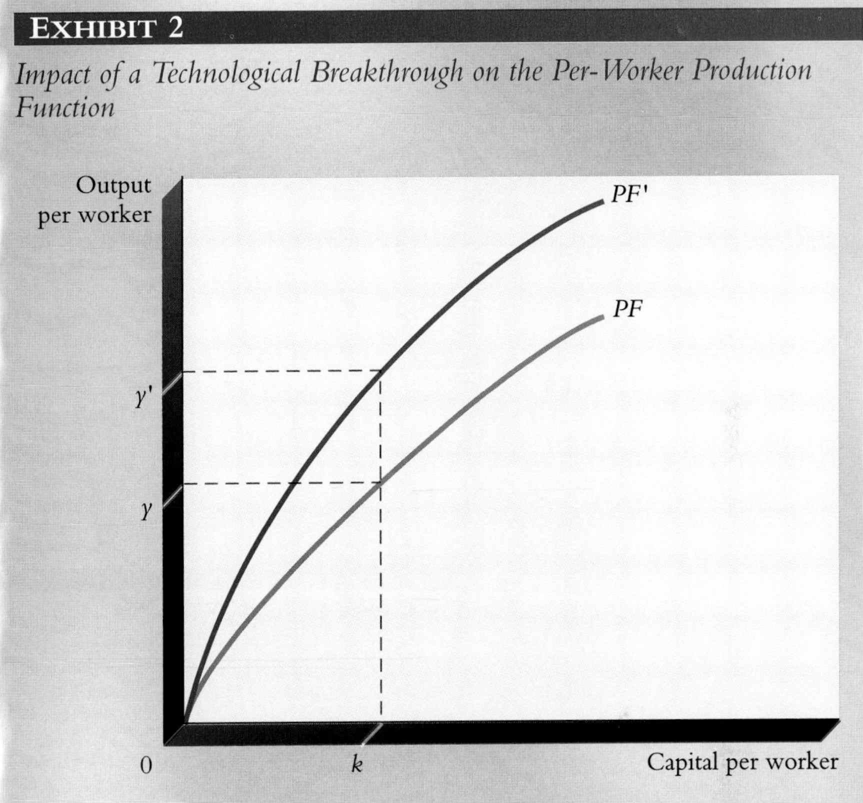

A technological breakthrough increases the output per worker at each level of capital per worker. Better technology makes workers more productive.

Thus, two changes in capital improve worker productivity: (1) an increase in the *quantity* of capital, as reflected by a movement along the curve, and (2) an improvement in the *quality* of capital, as reflected by technological change that rotates the curve upward. Over time, improvements in the standard of living result from both more capital per worker and better capital per worker.

Teaching Tip
Labor productivity also exhibits cyclical behavior—rising during the first half of expansions, falling during the later months of expansions and early months of recessions, rising again late in recessions. Therefore, it is important not to place too much emphasis on quarterly announcements of productivity changes.

Long-Term Productivity Growth

Exhibit 3 offers a long-run perspective on growth in the United States, showing annual productivity growth over the last 120 years as measured by real output per work hour. Productivity growth is averaged by decade, beginning with the decade that ended in 1880 and ending with the decade that ended in 1990. The huge dip in productivity growth during the 1930s due to the Great Depression and the big jump during the 1940s due to World War II are unmistakable. During the entire 120-year period, labor productivity grew by an average of 2.2 percent per year. This may not seem like much, but because of the power of compounding, output per work hour grew

EXHIBIT 3

Long-Term Trend in Labor Productivity

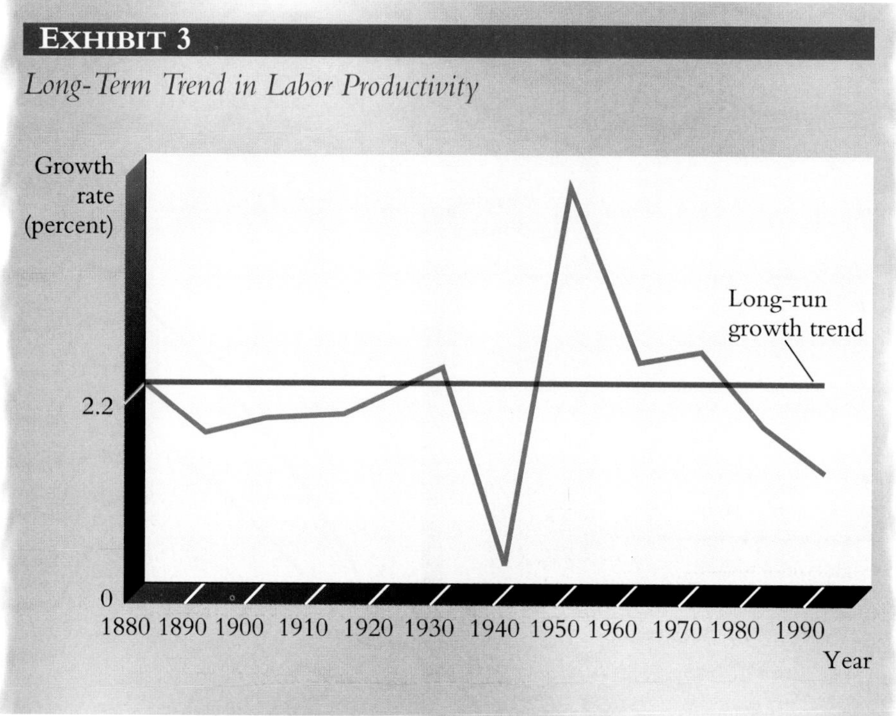

Source: Angus Maddison, *Phases of Capitalist Development* (New York: Oxford University Press, 1982), 212. Updated for 1990 by author.

about 1,260 percent during the 120-year span. To put this in perspective, suppose that in 1870 a worker on average mined a ton of coal per hour. If coal miners experienced a 1,260 percent increase in their labor productivity, the 1990 version of that worker could mine 12.6 more tons of coal per hour.

Over long periods, tiny differences in productivity growth rates have significant impacts on the economy's ability to produce. For example, if productivity had grown by 2.0 percent per year instead of 2.2 percent during the period, output per work hour since 1870 would have increased by only 975 percent, not 1,260 percent. On the other hand, if productivity had increased an average of 2.4 percent per year, output per work hour since 1870 would have increased by 1,620 percent! The wheels of progress grind slowly but they grind very fine, and the cumulative effect is powerful.

The Recent Slowdown in Productivity Growth

By breaking productivity data down into time periods other than decades, we can examine in greater detail productivity since World War II. The growth in output per labor hour declined from 2.8 percent per year between 1948 and 1973 to 0.7 percent per year between 1973 and 1981. Productivity growth then rebounded slightly to 1.0 percent between 1981 and 1992. *Thus, the rate of growth in labor productivity during the last two decades has been less than half what it was during the quarter century following World War II and less than it was during the previous century.*

Example Per-capita GDP in the United Kingdom was surpassed by the United States in 1890, Sweden in the 1940s, France and Germany in 1960, and Japan in 1970.

Such a drop in labor productivity growth usually means the standard of living also grows more slowly. For example, between 1948 and 1973, median family income adjusted for inflation more than doubled. But between 1973 and 1992 real income for the median family grew by a total of only 5 percent. The long-run implications of the recent slowdown are serious. The United Kingdom was once the richest economy on earth, but half a century of productivity growth less than 1 percentage point below the U.S. rate has left the United Kingdom with a GDP per capita that is 30 percent below that of the United States.

Why the Slowdown in Labor Productivity Growth?

Teaching Tip Since productivity growth slowed throughout the industrial world, some analysts also blame the slowdown on increased inflation worldwide, which increased uncertainty, decreased the efficiency of resource allocation, and shortened investment horizons.

A thorough explanation of the recent slowdown in productivity growth should not only account for the overall trend from period to period but also explain differences in productivity growth across economic sectors. Nobody has yet developed such an explanation. All we have are possible reasons for the slowdown. As you will see, economists are unable to say for sure which factors really contributed to the slowdown. Nonetheless, possible contributors to the slowdown are worth discussing because they give us a better understanding of factors that could affect productivity.

Factors that economists believe may have contributed to the slowdown in productivity growth include (1) reduced capital formation, (2) changes in human resources, (3) higher energy prices, (4) the changing composition of output, (5) greater government regulation, (6) higher federal deficits, and (7) reduced spending on research and development. This last possibility is potentially so important that it warrants extensive discussion. But let's begin by examining the first six factors.

Rate of Capital Formation

Example Not all analysts agree on the main causes of the productivity slowdown. John Kendrick blamed 35 percent of the U.S. productivity slowdown on slower growth in capital per worker.

As we have said, the productivity of labor depends in part on the amount of capital supporting each worker. *A slowdown in the growth of the capital per worker has been suggested as a reason for the slower productivity growth, but the relative importance of this is unclear.* Edward Denison, who is perhaps the leading authority on U.S. productivity, concludes that the small decline in the growth of capital per worker contributed only modestly to the decrease in productivity growth.[2]

Changing Human Resources

An important component in the production function is the quality of labor—the skill level and level of education of workers. Some economists

2. Edward F. Denison, *Trends in American Economic Growth, 1929–1982* (Washington, D.C.: Brookings Institution, 1985).

Example Denison estimated that both a reduction in average hours worked and changes in the composition of the labor force reduced the growth of per-capita GDP between 1929 and 1982. However, when he included improvements in education in the labor component, he concluded that 15 percent of growth was due to changes in labor.

Example Average verbal scores on the Scholastic Aptitude Test in 1992 were 40 points below the 1969 average; 1992 math scores were 17 points below the 1969 average.

Example In a 1982 paper for the NBER, Michael Bruno of the Hebrew University of Jerusalem attributed more than one-half of the worldwide slowdown in manufacturing productivity to higher relative prices of energy and raw materials.

argue that changes in the composition of the labor force have contributed to the decline in productivity growth. Individuals who are just entering the labor force are typically less productive because they have fewer skills and less work experience than those who are already in the labor force. As long as the proportion of new workers remains constant over time, their presence should not affect productivity measures. However, if the share of employment accounted for by new workers increases, as it has since 1966, then productivity growth may suffer. Moreover, the skill level of immigrants coming to this country since 1970 has on average been lower than it was prior to 1970. Offsetting to some extent the increase in the number of less experienced workers has been the increase in the education and training of the work force as a whole. *Most researchers agree that the net effect of the change in composition of the work force on the decline in the growth of labor productivity has been small.* Furthermore, as the labor force matures and workers develop more experience, labor productivity should grow more quickly.

Improvements in the amount and quality of schooling have contributed substantially to productivity growth for much of this century. Beginning in 1967, however, standardized test scores declined nationwide.[3] Though these scores are far from a perfect measure of ability, the fall in test scores, which continued until 1980, suggested that the quality of young entrants into the work force had decreased. Such a decrease has been identified as another source of the decline in productivity growth.

Higher Energy Prices in the 1970s

The sharp rise in energy prices during the 1970s has been put forth as a cause of the decline in productivity growth during the period. The price of a barrel of crude oil increased from $6.81 in 1973 to $21.67 in 1975 (measured in 1987 constant dollars). With higher energy prices, some existing capital stock became uneconomical, since it was designed during an era of relatively cheap fuel. *Higher energy prices encouraged firms to substitute labor for energy in the production process, which increased labor usage per unit of output.* During the conversion to a more energy-efficient economy—so the argument goes—the growth rate was held down. Real GDP declined by 1 percent between 1973 and 1975. Several economists conclude that the increase in energy prices that began in 1973 was an important contributor to the decline in U.S. productivity growth.[4] Productivity in fact declined by 2 percent in 1974, the largest drop yet recorded.

Not everyone agrees. *Some economists argue that energy costs represent such a small proportion of total costs that higher energy costs should not greatly affect productivity growth.* Denison says that higher energy costs during the 1970s

3. See John H. Bishop, "Is the Test Score Decline Responsible for the Productivity Growth Decline?" *American Economic Review* 79 (March 1989): 178–197.

4. See, for example, Dale W. Jorgenson, "Productivity and Postwar U.S. Economic Growth," *Journal of Economic Perspectives* 2 (Fall 1988): 23–41.

contributed only 0.1 percent to the decline in productivity growth. During the 1980s the reduction in energy prices caused yet another major conversion in resource usage, a shift that should eventually enhance labor productivity.

Changing Composition of Output

Average productivity will decline if workers shift from sectors where substantial capital formation and technological change increase labor productivity to sectors where capital formation and technological change are less important. Labor productivity can be increased more easily in the goods-producing sector (manufacturing and farming), where machines can be readily introduced, than in the service sector (government, education, transportation, finance, health care, retailing, and entertainment), where machines are less important. For example, there are more opportunities for technological change when producing cars than when producing haircuts.

Since 1948 productivity has grown by an average of 2.1 percent in the goods-producing sector but only by 1.4 percent in the service sector. But the goods-producing sector's share of total employment has declined from about 40 percent in 1948 to about 20 percent today. *The service sector's growing share of the labor force has lowered the growth rate of productivity in the economy as a whole.* Most economists who have explored the issue agree that the shift from high-productivity to low-productivity sectors accounts for some of the slowdown. Some claim the shift is responsible for more than half the decline.

Increased Government Regulation

Another factor cited as a source of slower productivity growth is the more pervasive role of government in the economy, both in its regulatory function and more generally in its impact on the direction of economic activity. Government regulation grew sharply between the mid-1960s and the late 1970s. In one three-year period, five major regulatory bodies were established by the federal government, including the Environmental Protection Agency and the Occupational Safety and Health Administration. Some regulation may have a positive effect on worker productivity. For example, better worker health and a safer work environment can reduce the cost of health insurance and reduce worker turnover. But some regulations may divert resources from direct production and thereby reduce productivity. For example, requirements for greater safety in coal mines have been cited as a source of lackluster productivity in that industry. The control of toxic emissions, the improvement of safety in the workplace, and the like may ultimately increase the quality of life in the nation, but they add little to output as measured by GDP per worker.

Example Kendrick attributed 15 percent of the U.S. productivity slowdown, 27 percent of the West German slowdown, and 13 percent of the Japanese slowdown to increased government regulations. One factor often cited is the cost of the paperwork associated with meeting regulations.

One way to view government's role in the economy in a wider context is to look at the relation between economic growth and the share of GDP that goes to the federal government. In the thirty-seven years between 1892 and 1929, federal expenditures averaged about 4.5 percent of GDP and federal revenues about 3.5 percent, with most of the difference due to deficits created during World War I.[5] In the thirty-seven years between 1948 and 1985, federal expenditures averaged about 20 percent and revenues about 18.5 percent of GDP. During the earlier period, real GDP rose at an annual rate of 3.4 percent. In the more recent period, the era of big government, real GDP also rose by 3.4 percent annually. In terms of productivity, output per worker-hour rose by 1.5 percent per year during the small-government period and by 2.4 percent per year during the big-government period. These statistics suggest that *it is too simplistic to conclude that government regulations are major obstacles to economic growth and productivity.*

Huge Government Deficits

In his first State of the Union address, President Clinton argued that large federal deficits were responsible for the declining growth in labor productivity. He said that to finance the deficits the federal government must borrow huge amounts, thereby "crowding out" other borrowers who could invest in physical capital, in human capital, and in research and development. By raising tax rates and reducing the growth rate in government spending, Clinton proposed reducing the federal deficit as a way of increasing productivity and growth.

Despite President Clinton's assertion, the link between federal deficits and labor productivity growth remains unclear. For example, between 1973 and 1981, federal deficits averaged less than $50 billion per year; during that same period, as noted earlier, labor productivity grew by an average of only 0.7 percent per year. Between 1982 and 1992 federal deficits averaged $200 billion per year, but labor productivity averaged 1.0 percent per year. Thus, labor productivity on average grew somewhat faster during the period of higher average deficits. Nobody would argue that huge deficits boost labor productivity, especially over the long term, but we cannot simply attribute the decline in productivity growth to higher federal deficits.

Example Both Denison and Kendrick cite slower advances in knowledge as a major cause of the productivity slowdown.

Perhaps the single most important contributor to productivity growth is technological change. In the next section we will examine research and development, the fuel for technological change.

Research and Development

Simon Kuznets, who won the Nobel Prize in part for his analysis of the sources of economic growth, claimed that technological change and the ability to apply this change to all aspects of production were the driving force behind modern economic growth in developed market economies. Kuznets argued that changes in the *quantities* of labor and capital accounted for only

5. See Herbert Stein, "Should Growth Be a Priority of National Policy?" *Challenge* (March–April 1986): 11–17.

one-tenth of the increase in economic growth. Nine-tenths of the increase was a result of improvements in the *quality* of inputs.

Basic and Applied Research

A major contributor to productivity has been an improvement in the quality of human and physical capital. In terms of human capital, this quality improvement results from more education and more job training. In terms of physical capital, quality improvement results from better technology embodied in this capital. Improvements in technology arise from scientific discovery, which is the result of research.

Basic research The search for knowledge without regard to how that knowledge will be used; a first step toward technological advancement

Applied research Research that seeks to answer particular questions or to apply scientific discoveries to the development of specific products

We distinguish between basic research and applied research. **Basic research**, the search for knowledge without regard to how that knowledge will be used, is a first step toward technological advancement. In terms of economic growth, however, scientific discoveries are meaningless until they are implemented—which requires applied research. **Applied research** typically seeks to answer particular questions or to apply scientific discoveries to the development of specific products. Since technological breakthroughs may or may not have commercial possibilities, basic research has less of an immediate payoff than applied research. But basic research is likely to yield a higher rate of return to society as a whole than applied research.

If a technological breakthrough is thought to have economic value in the marketplace, it becomes *embodied* in new capital. Such technological innovation increases the productivity of other resources by permitting them to be combined in more efficient ways, so total output is increased. *From the wheel to assembly-line robots, capital embodies the fruits of scientific inquiry and serves as the primary engine for economic growth.*

Example The Sony Corporation purchased the transistor from Bell Laboratories for $25,000 and then developed the transistor radio.

Example Kendrick concluded that 35 percent of the U.S. productivity growth slowdown was due to a decline in the relative importance of research and development and technical innovation.

Expenditures for Research and Development

Since technological advances spring from the process of research and development (R&D), expenditures on R&D represent one measure of the economy's efforts to improve productivity through technological discovery. With the exceptions of the late 1960s and mid-1970s, company-financed R&D has grown steadily for the last three decades, but federally supported R&D fell sharply during the 1970s. Some economists believe that the slowdown during the 1970s in the growth of R&D proved costly to the economy in terms of forgone growth opportunities. As we have seen, the decline in federal R&D was part of the problem. But research suggests that a dollar of federally supported R&D contributes less to economic growth than does a dollar of company-supported R&D,[6] perhaps because much federally supported R&D has military objectives. Thus, although the decline in federal R&D may have contributed to the slowdown in productivity during the 1970s, the impact

6. See, for example, Zvi Griliches, "Productivity, R&D, and Basic Research at the Firm Level in the 1970s," *American Economic Review* 76 (March 1986): 141–154.

would have been greater if the decline in R&D had occurred primarily in the private sector. Still, there was a modest decline in the late 1960s and mid-1970s in company-financed R&D.

Teaching Tip As technology becomes more difficult and expensive to develop, technical alliances may grow. For example, IBM, Siemens AG (of Germany), and Toshiba Corporation are working together on the development of advanced computer memory chips. EO, Inc., a California company that developed a personal communicator—combining the capabilities of pager, phone, fax, computer, and electronic organizer—is backed by AT&T, Matsushita Electric Industrial Corp., and Marubeni Corp.

The fruit of R&D is inventions and technological breakthroughs. Did the slowdown in R&D expenditures during the 1970s influence inventive activity? One measure of inventive activity is the number of patents granted by the U.S. Patent Office, the agency established by Congress in 1790 to grant inventors the exclusive rights to their discoveries. In fact, there is a strong relation both within firms and across firms between R&D expenditures and the number of patents granted. Patents granted per year fell during the 1970s, dropping from about 75,000 in 1971 to about 50,000 by 1979. More troubling still is that nearly all the decline came in patents granted to U.S. corporations and individuals (as opposed to foreign corporations and individuals). There has since been an increase in the total number of patents, but most of the increase has been in patents granted to foreign corporations. For example, there has been sharp growth in U.S. patents granted to the major Japanese electronics and motor vehicle firms. Overall, patents granted to foreigners climbed from one-fifth of the total in the 1960s to nearly one-half today.

The federal government has tried to stimulate private R&D by providing special investment tax incentives for this activity. A review of the effects of this program, however, indicates that federal tax incentives introduced in 1981 to stimulate new R&D expenditures were not cost-effective.[7] Because of the special tax benefits accorded R&D outlays, firms became much more liberal in their definitions of R&D. The program cost about $1.5 billion per year in forgone tax revenue, yet it increased R&D by only $0.5 billion.

Teaching Tip In Japan, the government may request banks to extend long-term, low-interest loans to certain firms. The Ministry of International Trade and Industry may recommend direct government aid.

Industrial Policy

In recent years policy makers have debated whether or not the federal government should become more involved in shaping the nation's technological future. One concern is that technologies of the future often require huge sums to develop and implement, sums that individual firms cannot always raise. Another concern is that some technological breakthroughs benefit other industries, but the firm that develops the breakthrough may not be in a position to benefit from these spillover effects, so individual firms may underinvest in such developments. The proposed solution is to have the government more involved.

Industrial policy The view that government, using taxes, subsidies, and regulations, should nurture the industries and technologies of the future to give domestic industries an advantage over foreign competition

Industrial policy is the idea that government, using taxes, subsidies, and regulations, should nurture the industries and technologies of the future to give domestic industries an advantage over foreign competition. The objective is to secure a leading role for domestic industry in the future. One example of European industrial policy is Airbus Industrie, a four-nation aircraft consortium. With an estimated $20 billion in aid from European governments, the aircraft producer has taken business away from McDonnell-

7. Edwin Mansfield, "The R&D Tax Credit and Other Technology Policy Issues," *American Economic Review* 76 (May 1986): 190–194.

Douglas and has become Boeing's main challenger. When Airbus seeks business orders around the world, it can draw on its government backing to promise special terms, such as landing rights at key European airports and an easing of regulatory constraints. U.S. producers have no such ties to government and therefore no such goodies to offer. Industrial policy is discussed in the following case study.

CASE STUDY

Picking The Technological Winners

Example The Honda Corporation was unable to receive government aid because Japanese policy makers believed that their auto industry should have only two manufacturers, Toyota and Nissan.

U.S. industrial policy over the years, though not called such, has been aimed at creating the world's most advanced military industry. For example, the Defense Advanced Research Projects Agency tries to help develop new technologies, such as computer graphics, semiconductors, and computer-controlled machine tools. With the demise of the Soviet Union, defense technologies have become less important. Some argue U.S. industrial policy should shift from a military to a civilian focus. President Bill Clinton promised during his campaign that he would establish a powerful agency to help finance and coordinate R&D for what he called "cutting-edge products and technologies." He has also proposed bringing together businesses, universities, and laboratories to carry out R&D in civilian technologies.

Skeptics wonder whether the same government that has brought us huge deficits should be trusted to identify emerging technologies and to pick the firms that will lead the way. Critics of industrial policy believe the market is a better allocator of scarce resources than the government. For example, the costly attempt of European governments to develop the supersonic transport (SST) did not work out. As another example, in the early 1980s the U.S. government spent $1 billion to help military contractors try to develop a high-speed computer circuit. But Intel, a company receiving no federal support from the program, was the first to successfully develop the circuit.

There is also concern that the industrial policy would evolve into another government give-away program. Rather than going to the most promising technologies, the money and the competitive advantages would be awarded based on political influence. Critics also wonder how wise it is to sponsor corporate research when beneficiaries may share their expertise with foreign companies and may even build factories abroad. Sematech, for example, is a U.S. government–backed alliance of companies in the semiconductor industry. One of its members, Advanced Micro Devices, recently teamed up with a Japanese company to make semiconductors in Japan.

Professor Gene Grossman of Princeton University, after surveying the available evidence on industrial policy, concludes that government's track record at backing winners is poor. He says there are better alternatives to industrial policy, such as tax incentives for all R&D, that do not require the targeting of specific industries. Many economists would prefer to let IBM, Hewlett-Packard, or some upstart gamble on the important technologies for the future.

Sources: Steven Greenhouse, "The Calls for Industrial Policy Grow Louder," *New York Times* 19 July 1992, p. 5; and Gene Grossman, "Promoting Industrial Activities: A Survey of Recent Arguments and Evidence," *OECD Economic Studies* (Spring 1990): 87–125.

Does Technological Change Lead to Unemployment?

Technological change can sometimes free resources for new uses. For example, now that fiber-optics technology has become the best means of communicating, the copper from existing telephone lines is becoming available for other uses. In fact, AT&T controls most of the world's known copper deposits in the form of existing wires and cables that will gradually be replaced by fiber optics.

Example Some analysts claim that the computer chip has caused more industrial dislocation than any other advance in the history of capitalism.

Technological change often reduces the number of workers needed to produce a given amount of output. Consequently, some observers fear that new technology will throw workers out of their jobs and lead to higher unemployment. True, technological change can lead to structural unemployment in some industries, but it can also increase production and employment by making products more affordable. For example, the introduction of the assembly line made automobiles more affordable to the average household, stimulating production and employment in that industry. Even in industries where some workers are displaced by machines, those who keep their jobs are more productive and those who are displaced typically go on to find other jobs producing the goods and services demanded in a growing economy. As long as wants are unlimited, displaced workers will usually find other employment.

Although data for the nineteenth century are sketchy, there is no evidence that the unemployment rate is any higher today than it was 125 years ago. Since then real income per capita has increased more than twelvefold and the length of the average work week has decreased more than one-third. Though technological change may displace some workers in the short run, the long run benefits include higher real incomes and more leisure—in short, a higher standard of living.

If technological change caused more unemployment, then the slowdown in productivity growth that occurred over the last two decades should have resulted in lower unemployment. But, in fact, the unemployment rate has drifted up during the last two decades when compared to the high productivity growth decades of the 1950s and 1960s. And if technological change caused more unemployment, then unemployment rates should be lower where modern technology has not yet been introduced, such as in developing countries. But, in fact, the unemployment rate is typically higher in such countries, and those who are employed there earn relatively little because they are not very productive.

International Comparisons

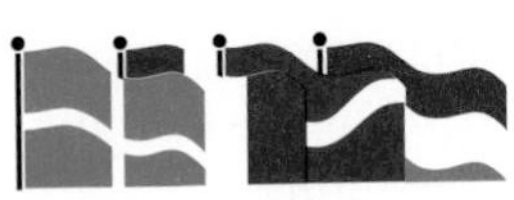

So far we have focused on growth as measured by rising labor productivity—that is, growth achieved by getting more output from each hour worked. The economy may also grow by employing more workers. *Output per capita* captures the combined effects of growing productivity and a growing work force. If the work force grows faster than the population as a whole, output per capita can increase faster than productivity per worker.

EXHIBIT 4

Average Growth Rate Per Year in Real GDP Per Capita, 1948–1992

Country	1948–1973	1973–1981	1981–1992
United States	2.2%	1.1%	1.3%
Japan	7.8	2.7	2.6
West Germany	5.7	2.0	1.9
United Kingdom	2.6	0.7	1.7
Italy	5.0	2.2	1.7
France	4.3	2.1	1.3
Canada	2.8	2.5	1.3

Sources: *Economic Report of the President,* January 1989, Table 1–1; *Economic Report of the President,* January 1993; and *Statistical Abstract of the United States 1992,* U.S. Department of Commerce, Table 1370.

Teaching Tip Some economists claim that the period from the end of World War II to the mid-1960s was one of unusually high productivity growth by historical standards. Therefore, to compare current performance to this earlier period is inappropriate. Michael Darby concludes that there has been no major change in U.S. productivity growth ("The U.S. Productivity Slowdown: A Case of Statistical Myopia," *American Economic Review,* June 1984).

Exhibit 4 presents the *real GDP growth rate per capita* for three periods between 1948 and 1992 for the United States and six other leading industrial countries. The 2.2 percent U.S. annual growth rate during 1948–1973 was less than half the 4.7 percent average for the six other developed countries listed. The United States had the lowest growth rate during that time largely because, with the exception of Canada, the other countries were starting from such a low level of productivity after being ravaged by World War II. Likewise, during 1973–1981 the U.S. annual growth rate of 1.1 percent was little more than half the 2.0 percent average growth rate for the six other countries.

Since 1981, however, the U.S. annual growth rate of 1.3 was closer to the 1.7 percent average for the six other countries. In fact, between the periods 1948–1973 and 1981–1992, the U.S. annual growth rate declined from 2.2 percent to 1.3, but growth rates for the other six countries declined on average from 4.7 to 1.7. Japan's growth rate fell by two-thirds, from 7.8 percent to 2.6 percent, between those two periods.

Note that between 1981 and 1992 the growth rate in GDP per capita was about 1.3 percent per year, while the growth rate in output per labor hour was only 1.0 percent per year. What explains the difference? *During that period the growth in employment exceeded the growth in population so output per capita grew faster than output labor hour.* Both the shift of baby-boom workers to the labor force and the increase in the labor force participation rate of married females increased the labor force participation rate.

Convergence A theory that economies around the world will grow more alike over time, with poorer countries catching up with richer countries

Do Economies Converge?

The **convergence** theory argues that economies around the world will grow more alike, with poorer countries catching up with richer countries. It is easier to copy new technology once it is developed than to develop that technology in the first place. Countries that start out far behind have the advantage of being able to increase their productivity by copying existing technology. But economies that are already using the latest technology can boost productivity only with a steady stream of technological breakthroughs.

The convergence theory says that less developed countries will grow faster than more developed countries. The empirical evidence for this theory is mixed. For example, since 1950 there has been little tendency for the poorest countries of the world to close the gap with more developed countries. One reason why convergence may not occur is the vast differences in the quality of *human capital* across countries. Whereas technology is indeed portable, the knowledge, skill, and training often required to appreciate and take advantage of that technology are not. And countries with a high level of human capital can make up for other shortcomings. For example, the physical capital stock in Japan and Germany was mostly destroyed during World War II. But the two countries retained enough of their well-educated and highly skilled labor force to become industrial leaders again in little more than a generation.[8]

Teaching Tip With some exceptions, less developed countries tend to have lower average education levels and higher illiteracy rates than the major industrialized countries.

Government Policies and Potential GDP

Economic growth is reflected as an increase in the economy's potential output—that is, the rate of output the economy can produce on a sustained basis. What will cause potential output to increase? The economy's potential output can be increased either by increasing output per labor hour or by increasing the number employed. One way to increase employment is to reduce the number unemployed. Unemployed workers cannot be immediately matched with job vacancies because of imperfections in the labor market. Reducing these imperfections can increase the economy's potential GDP. By spelling out these imperfections and exploring policy options for reducing them, we can better understand how the economy works. In this section we consider government policies and employment practices that affect the unemployment rate.

Point to Stress Potential GDP can increase as a result of a decrease in the number unemployed—that is, by a reduction in the number frictionally and structurally unemployed—when the economy is at the natural rate of unemployment.

Policies to Reduce Skills Mismatch

As we have mentioned, the classified ads are filled with job openings at the same time that millions of people are unemployed. Many unemployed workers simply do not have the skills required to fill the available jobs. For example, new entrants into the work force, particularly recent high school dropouts, have never held a job and have never had an opportunity to develop marketable skills. For most new entrants, the problem is landing that

8. Further issues of economic development are discussed in Chapter 35, which is entitled "Problems of Economic Development."

Teaching Tip Public training programs, such as the Manpower Development and Training Act (1962) and the Comprehensive Employment and Training Act (1973), have been tried frequently. Both Bill Clinton and George Bush called for retraining programs during the 1992 presidential campaign, and President Clinton has promoted such programs.

first job. Government policies that promote education and training of those who are most vulnerable to structural unemployment will reduce this source of unemployment and increase the economy's potential GDP. Primary and secondary schools impart the basic knowledge that is usually demanded by employers, but many students fail to finish high school and jobs often demand vocational training or higher education or both. *Wage subsidy programs* from the government to employers encourage employers to hire and train those who otherwise lack the necessary skills to get jobs. For years employers have had training programs to teach specific job skills. But some employers have been forced to teach potential employees more basic skills, such as how to apply for a job, how to dress, and how to get along with other employees.

Policies to Reduce Location Mismatch

Teaching Tip Wage subsidies are designed to reduce the cost of labor to employers to the point where it is worthwhile to hire those workers whose initial productivity is low.

This is a big country, and the national unemployment rate often masks wide differences among regions, as noted in Chapter 7. At any given time, the unemployment rate in some states may be only half the national average, while other states experience rates far exceeding the national average. Some unemployment arises from a locational mismatch: those seeking employment in one region are qualified only for job openings in another region. Employment opportunities may differ even within a metropolitan area. Those unemployed in the central city may qualify for job openings in the suburbs but may be unaware of these opportunities or may be unable to commute to them.

Example In 1987, civilian unemployment ranged from a low of 2.5 percent in New Hampshire to a high of 12 percent in Louisiana.

Programs that help job searchers to identify and secure positions will reduce unemployment that arises from locational mismatches. By establishing government employment agencies and making moving expenses and job-search costs tax deductible (for taxpayers who itemize on their tax returns), the government has tried to encourage mobility to find work. As an example of what can be done to reduce structural unemployment, consider one company's efforts. During the late 1980s, the hotels and casinos in Atlantic City, New Jersey had hundreds of job openings that could not be filled from the local labor pool. Representatives from one hotel went to a region of Ohio where there was high unemployment to interview job applicants. With the help of local officials in Ohio, the hotel hired and relocated over one hundred people.

Because local employment opportunities reflect the ups and downs of local economies, interregional differences in unemployment are difficult to eliminate altogether. The demand for labor is derived from the market value of labor's product. When the demand for goods produced in a particular region changes, this alters employment opportunities. For example, when oil prices were climbing, the Texas economy blossomed and jobs were abundant. Migrants from the Northeast poured into Houston and Dallas looking for work. But when oil prices tumbled, the Texas economy withered and the resulting unemployment left many recent arrivals stranded with no jobs and with no family ties in the area.

Legal and Social Practices

Economic and social policies serve a variety of objectives, but sometimes they cause unemployment by interfering with the labor market.

Point to Stress Recall from Chapter 3 that when a price floor is set above equilibrium, a surplus results.

THE MINIMUM WAGE LAW. The minimum wage law makes it more difficult for some individuals who have few or no skills to find work. Some people, particularly those just entering the labor market, are handicapped by the minimum wage law because they have so few skills and so little work experience that their labor productivity may fall below the minimum wage. Imagine trying to climb a ladder when the bottom rung has been removed. Workers who are unable to reach the next highest rung—that is, those who lack the skills to warrant even a minimum wage—may be shut out of the job market entirely. If labor markets were allowed to move to a market-clearing wage, unemployment would be reduced. Moreover, to the extent that the minimum wage law places a floor under wages, wages become less flexible downward and are therefore less likely to fall when unemployment is high. In 1991 the minimum wage increased to $4.25 an hour; a lower minimum of $3.61 an hour was established for workers considered to be in training.

Teaching Tip The minimum wage was established by the Fair Labor Standards Act of 1938, with an initial hourly rate of $0.25.

RESTRICTED ENTRY AND DISCRIMINATION. Any practice that prohibits qualified workers from entering certain trades or professions reduces employment opportunities and lowers the economy's potential GDP. Labor unions and professional associations often control entry into certain jobs and prevent some people from pursuing those trades. Restrictions based on any criteria other than ability, such as race or gender, increase the unemployment rate within the groups that are discriminated against. This problem can be resolved by ensuring that all qualified applicants are allowed to compete for any job. In an effort to ensure equal access to jobs and promotions, the Equal Employment Opportunity Commission was established by the Civil Rights Act of 1964.

Teaching Tip See Chapter 29 for a discussion of why producer groups may lobby for restricted entry.

INCENTIVE PROBLEMS. Finally, some are concerned that the existing social service support system, by providing unemployment benefits that replace most of the after-tax income that could be earned by working, may decrease employment incentives. Public officials are torn between providing adequate support for a family in need and providing incentives to promote self-sufficiency. To address this issue, federal and state governments have introduced welfare reforms aimed at providing recipients with the incentive and the training to enter the work force.

Example Phillip Cagan concluded that 0.34 percent of the 1.23 percent increase from 1955 to 1975 in the natural rate of unemployment was due to unemployment compensation (*Persistent Inflation*, Columbia University Press, 1979).

THE SUPPLY-SIDE EXPERIMENT

In 1981 President Reagan said that his proposed tax cut would revive lagging productivity, restore U.S. competitiveness in world markets, and spur the steady growth of jobs, production, and real income. The tax cut was heralded

Teaching Tip Supply-siders argued that tax cuts would increase the supply of both labor and capital, thus increasing aggregate supply. Studies of how individual workers actually react to tax cuts yield ambiguous results.

as more than just tax relief for individual taxpayers. It was a way of achieving economic growth—a means of unleashing the animal spirits of enterprise to foster productive activity. According to proponents of the supply-side philosophy that motivated the tax cut, the ensuing economic growth would yield enough new revenue to offset the direct loss of revenue from the lower tax rates. The higher level of economic activity would also generate the additional saving required to finance an increase in investment. The supply-side tax cut approved in 1981 therefore hinged on generating enough growth to balance the budget. The economy's potential GDP was supposed to increase dramatically. Otherwise, federal revenues would fall short of federal expenditures, and the resulting budget deficit would soak up the private saving needed to finance investment.

The largest income tax cut in history, the 1981 tax cut, emphasized reductions in the marginal tax rates. The measure also accelerated the rate at which businesses could deduct capital costs in computing their corporate income taxes. Thus, there were tax cuts for both individuals and businesses. What has transpired since the tax cut? From 1981 to 1991 federal spending grew at a rate of 7.6 percent per year and federal receipts grew at a rate of 6.2 percent per year. The result has been a large and growing federal deficit. Let's look more closely at events during the 1980s.

Results of the Supply-Side Experiment

Teaching Tip See Chapters 11 and 16.

Earlier chapters discussed the results of the supply-side experiment. Taking the 1981–1988 period as the time frame for the examination, we can make some tentative observations. Although it is difficult to untangle the growth generated by the tax cuts from the cyclical upswing following the recession of 1981–1982, we can say that between 1981 and 1988 employment climbed by fifteen million and unemployment fell by two million workers. This combination of rising employment and falling unemployment spurred the growth in output per capita. The growth rate in output per capita increased by 2.0 percent per year between 1981 and 1988. This rate was higher than the 1.1 percent average during 1973–1981 but lower than the 2.2 percent rate during 1948–1973. *Despite the growth in employment, government revenues did not expand enough to offset the combination of tax cuts and increased government spending. The resulting federal deficits have been huge, as has been well documented already. The federal debt has quadrupled since 1981.*

Does the growth in employment and in real GDP per capita mark the supply-side experiment as a success? Part of the growth in employment and output could be explained by the economic stimulus provided by the huge federal deficits during the period. One surprising result of the experiment was that despite the federal deficit, which would tend to crowd out private investment, the proportion of national income that went to business investment during the years following the recession of 1982 was the same as the average during the five expansionary periods between 1954

Point to Stress Net exports were crowded out rather than investment.

and 1980. Investment failed to decline because there was an unusually large inflow of saving from abroad. High real U.S. interest rates, a strong dollar during the first half of the decade, and a stable political climate combined to make the United States an attractive place for foreigners to put their savings during the 1980s.

In 1984 U.S. private saving was 7.4 percent of GDP. Because of the large federal deficit, dissaving by the government sector (including federal, state, and local governments) amounted to 3.4 percent of GDP. Without foreign capital, private saving could only have supported investment amounting to 4.0 percent (7.4 percent minus 3.4 percent) of GDP. But actual domestic investment amounted to 6.4 percent of GDP, with the difference of 2.4 percent coming from the foreign inflow of saving. The flow of saving from abroad made a positive contribution to U.S. productivity, but enthusiasm for foreign saving should be tempered by the realization that foreigners are accumulating U.S. assets. The return on these investments will flow to foreigners, not to Americans.

Teaching Tip The flow of saving from abroad lessened in the early 1990s as the German and Japanese economies slowed.

During years of large federal deficits, U.S. consumption, investment, and government purchases exceed U.S. income and output. How can this occur? Domestic spending can exceed domestic output because U.S. households, firms, and governments borrow from abroad to help buy foreign production. Thus, during the last decade, U.S. imports exceeded exports, and the resulting trade deficit was financed in part by borrowing from abroad.

Tax Levels and Economic Growth Around the World

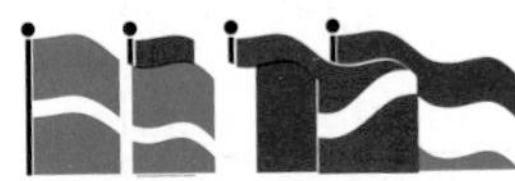

What has been the relation between tax rates and economic growth around the world? From a supply-side perspective, the taxes expected to have the most negative effect on the incentives to work and to invest are taxes on personal income and on business profits. The link between these taxes and economic growth is examined in Exhibit 5. Taxes on income and profit as a percentage of GDP are measured along the horizontal axis and the average growth in real GDP per capita between 1960 and 1989 is measured on the vertical axis. Data for twenty-three leading industrial countries are plotted in the exhibit, with some key countries identified.

Teaching Tip A 1992 bipartisan commission recommended replacing the federal income tax with a consumption-based tax. Taxes would be levied on the portion of an individual's personal income or a corporation's cash flow that was not saved, used to purchase financial assets, or used for capital formation.

Although the data points do not fall into a perfect line, you can see that the countries with the lower taxes tended to grow more than those with the higher taxes. The United States, for example, shows a higher-than-average tax rate and a lower-than-average growth rate. You need little imagination to draw a line sloping down to the right to reflect an inverse relation between taxes as a percentage of GDP and the growth rate in real GDP per capita. Growth rates on average were about one-third higher for countries with tax levels below the median than for those with tax levels at or above the median. Note that the exhibit graphs only taxes on income and profits. Taxes directed toward consumption, such as the sales tax or the tax on value added, may discourage consumption but not production.

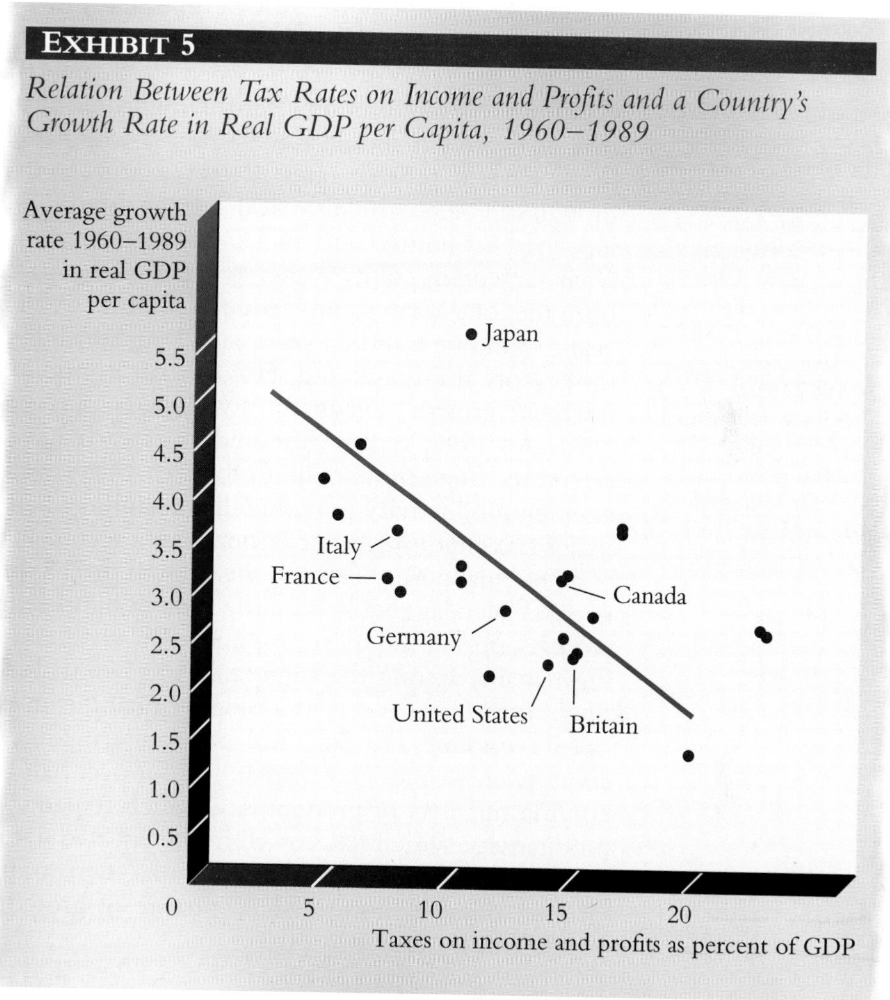

Source: "America Meets Europe in Wyoming," *The Economist,* 12 September 1992: 75. ©1992 The Economist Newspaper Group, Inc. Reprinted with permission. Further reproduction prohibited.

CONCLUSION

The productivity of an economy depends on the availability and quality of various resources, the level of technology, methods for organizing production, the energy and enterprise of entrepreneurs and workers, and a variety of institutional and social factors that affect the incentives and behavior of various resource suppliers. These factors interact to determine the level and growth of productivity. The factors that contribute to productivity are strongly correlated with one another. A country with low productivity will probably be deficient in the quality of its work force, in the quantity or quality of its physical capital, and in the level of its technology. Similarly, a country with high productivity is likely to excel in all measures.

Example In 1992, Ford and Chrysler became the world's lowest-cost producers of cars and trucks as the average number of assembly workers per vehicle fell from 4.71 to 3.01 at Ford and from 5.63 to 3.76 at Chrysler. High manufacturing costs in Germany led BMW to break ground in 1992 on an assembly plant in South Carolina. Mercedes-Benz also plans to make cars in the United States.

Recent productivity growth appears slow compared to the high growth rates immediately following World War II. Many economists believe that the rapid growth between 1948 and 1973 occurred because the economy was catching up after the doldrums of the Great Depression and that such growth should not be used as the benchmark against which to judge current growth rates. Between 1981 and 1992 U.S. productivity, though still below the historical average, was close to growth rates in other industrial economies.

If U.S. productivity grows at a rate of 2.2 percent per year, which has been the long-term trend, output per worker will double every thirty-two years, so in one hundred years each hour of labor will produce about eight times more real goods and services than it produces today. But if our productivity growth remains at 1.0 percent per year, the average between 1981 and 1992, in one hundred years each hour of labor will yield less than three times more than it produces today. In the long run, small differences in productivity growth will determine whether the United States remains an economic leader or becomes a second-rate economy.

One final point: Though the growth in U.S. productivity has in recent decades been lagging behind the growth in other industrial countries, U.S. workers are still the most productive on earth and the U.S. standard of living remains among the highest in the world. Real per-capita income in the United States is one-third higher than it is in Japan and in other developed economies. In fact, real per-capita income in the United States is about twenty times greater than it is for over half the human race. So don't confuse our *level* of productivity, which remains tops, with our *growth* in productivity, which has slowed in the last two decades. As a way of underscoring these points, "A Closer Look," which appears at the end of this chapter, offers a more detailed picture of growth and productivity since World War II.

SUMMARY

1. Because the population is continually increasing, an economy must produce more goods and services simply to maintain its standard of living. If output grows faster than the population, the standard of living will usually rise.

2. Over the last 120 years, labor productivity has increased an average of 2.2 percent per year. The wheels of progress appear to turn very slowly, but the cumulative effect is powerful: the output per hour of work was 1,260 percent greater in 1990 than in 1870. Research suggests that the quality of labor and capital is much more important than the quantity of these resources. Productivity growth has slowed somewhat in the last two decades, especially in comparison to the robust growth during and immediately following World War II.

3. A variety of factors could explain the recent decline in productivity growth, including (1) a slower rate of growth in physical capital formation, (2) a slower rate of growth in human capital formation, (3) higher energy prices during the 1970s, (4) the changing composition of output, (5) growth in government regulations, (6) higher federal deficits, and (7) a decline in research and development expenditures.

4. Various government policies are aimed at reducing imperfections in the labor market in order to lower the natural rate of unemployment and expand the economy's potential output. Some programs are aimed at reducing the skills mismatch and the location mismatch. Potential output is diminished when any restriction prevents workers from selling their labor where it is valued the most.

5. Supply-side economic policies of the 1980s included tax cuts to provide incentives to increase aggregate supply. But government spending increased more quickly than revenue, and the national debt exploded.

Questions and Problems

1. (Education and Growth) Many developing countries pay for students to come to the United States to study. How might those countries benefit from such expenditures? Does the United States also benefit? What groups might be hurt?

2. (Agricultural Productivity) As population grows, land of lower quality is brought under cultivation to produce more food. This suggests that in predominantly agricultural economies with growing populations, agricultural productivity must fall. Is this a valid conclusion?

3. (Japanese Productivity) Japanese universities graduate more engineers each year than U.S. universities do. However, the United States graduates vastly more attorneys. How would you relate these facts to the slow growth in U.S. productivity compared to that of Japanese productivity? Is the United States burdened by too much regulation and litigation? Can productivity conflict with fairness and justice?

4. (Japanese–U.S. Productivity) The Japanese secondary school year is considerably longer than the U.S. year. However, a smaller percentage of secondary school graduates go to college in Japan. Do differences in educational systems explain the differences in productivity growth between the two countries? Why or why not?

5. (Capital Formation and Productivity) There has been much debate in the United States over the long-run effects of the Social Security system on growth and productivity. The current program transfers taxes directly to older individuals, who spend the transfers. The young see their contributions as savings, but are these contributions really savings? How could such a system reduce the overall rate of saving and capital formation in the economy?

6. (Quality and Productivity) Some economists have argued that it is not simply the quantity of investment in the economy that determines productivity growth but also the quality of investment expenditures. What is meant by the "quality of investment," and how might such quality be improved?

7. (Expanding Potential Output) Explain how the community college system, which offers a wide range of practical courses, affects the nation's potential output level. What impact does it have on structural unemployment?

8. (Job Location Mismatch) What factors might contribute to a worker's decision to remain unemployed rather than move to another region where work is available? Consider such issues as marriage, children, and home ownership.

9. (Supply-Side Economics) During the early years of the Reagan administration, there was considerable optimism about supply-side economics. How were tax cuts expected to affect aggregate supply? What other incentives for growth and productivity were advocated? Were such measures successful? Why or why not?

10. (Technology and Productivity) What measures can government take to promote the development of practical technologies? Is the strict enforcement of patent laws important to research and development? Why or why not?

11. (Productivity and Living Standards) A considerable amount of regulatory legislation involves so-called environmental impact considerations. The result has been a reduction in output per unit of labor, which some say has lowered our standard of living. Defend or refute this position.

12. (Investment Policies) Using a supply-demand diagram for loanable funds (see Chapter 7 for review), show the consequences for capital formation, and therefore productivity growth, of each of the following:
    a. Repeal of the deductibility of consumer interest payments
    b. A reduction in the tax rate on corporate income
    c. Elimination of the deductibility of mortgage interest payments

13. (Trade and Productivity) International trade is supposed to enhance efficiency by allowing greater specialization of resources. Yet it may well result in an increase in structural unemployment. Explain.

14. (Supply-Side Economics) Supply-side policies are supposed to increase potential GDP by stimulating resources and productivity. Yet cuts in personal tax rates create higher federal budget deficits and crowding out. Doesn't this contradict the supply-side story?

15. (Productivity Measurement) Chapter 6 discussed some limitations of national income accounting. How might some of the ideas discussed there contribute to the productivity slowdown?

16. (Labor Productivity) Exhibit 1 shows a per-worker production function illustrating the fact that increasing capital per worker yields decreasing increments to total output and therefore slowed productivity growth. Yet the change in the composition of output toward service (and thus a more labor-intensive focus of production) means a lower capital-per-worker ratio, which also is said to lower labor productivity. Do these two views contradict each other?

17. (Productivity and the Standard of Living) Productivity changes are certainly important in determining long-term changes in living standards, yet other factors also play a role. Do you think the increasing importance of international trade in the U.S. national accounts can be changing the way productivity growth is linked to improved living standards?

18. (Productivity and Employment) Explain why government policies to reduce unemployment could both increase output per capita and decrease labor productivity. Which outcome is a better gauge of the impact of the policies on aggregate well-being?

19. (Picking the Technological Winners) Can you make a case for public-sector ownership of technology?

20. (Picking the Technological Winners) In what sense could reducing the size of the federal budget deficit be considered "industrial policy"?

A CLOSER LOOK

LABOR PRODUCTIVITY SINCE WORLD WAR II

Throughout the chapter we have considered the factors that shape production and growth. The key to economic growth is worker productivity. Here we take "A Closer Look" at the relation between worker productivity and economic prosperity since 1947. We begin with the level of employment and gradually build to real GDP per capita—the goods and services produced per person. In each case we convert the raw values to index numbers, using 1947 as the base year. This approach is developed in the series of overlays presented as part of Exhibit 6. When you turn the page, you will find Exhibit 6 on the right-hand page and an explanation on the left-hand page. Please turn the page.

U.S. EMPLOYMENT We begin with the key economomic resource: labor. The Base Page of Exhibit 6 shows an index of U.S. employment between 1947 and 1992. (To see the Base Page clearly, lift the transparencies and keep them in your hand.) Employment is indexed to the base year of 1947. As you can see, employment tended to grow from year to year except during recessions, which are shaded in red. Over the entire period, the index grew from 1.00 in 1947 to 2.06 in 1992. (Actual employment increased from 57.0 million in 1947 to 117.6 million in 1992. Though not shown in the exhibit, employment as a percent of the U.S. population climbed from 39.5 percent in 1947 to 46.0 percent in 1992.)

WORKER PRODUCTIVITY Employment is important to economic prosperity, but more important is the productivity per worker. After all, many developing countries have abundant labor but still produce relatively little. Labor productivity can be measured as the real output per hour of labor. An index of output per hour of labor between 1947 and 1992 is presented as the First Overlay of Exhibit 6. (Place the First Overlay over the Base Page.) The index uses productivity in 1947 as the base year. Overall, the index rose from 1.00 in 1947 to 2.60 in 1992, so labor productivity during the period rose by 160 percent.

REAL GDP As we have seen, between 1947 and 1992 employment more than doubled, as did the output per labor hour. Real GDP reflects both total employment and the productivity of each worker; an increase in both measures bodes well for total production. Real GDP, again indexed to 1947, is presented as the Second Overlay. (Add the Second Overlay to the exhibit.) You can see that recessions temporarily halted the growth of real GDP, but the growth over the long term is clearly upward. Between 1947 and 1992 real GDP nearly quadrupled.

REAL GDP PER CAPITA The bottom line in terms of the nation's standard of living is not total production but production per capita. We already know enough to suspect that production per capita increased during the period. First, labor productivity increased, and, second, employment as a percentage of the population increased. To observe real GDP per capita during the period, add the Third Overlay to the exhibit. Note that the index of real GDP per capita grew more slowly than the index of real GDP because population was growing, so over time real GDP was divided by a larger and larger number. Still, the index of real GDP per capita increased by 121 percent in the United States, indicating that more than twice as much was produced per capita in 1992 than in 1947.

EXHIBIT 6

Employment, Labor Productivity, and Economic Growth Since 1947 (all indexed to 1947)

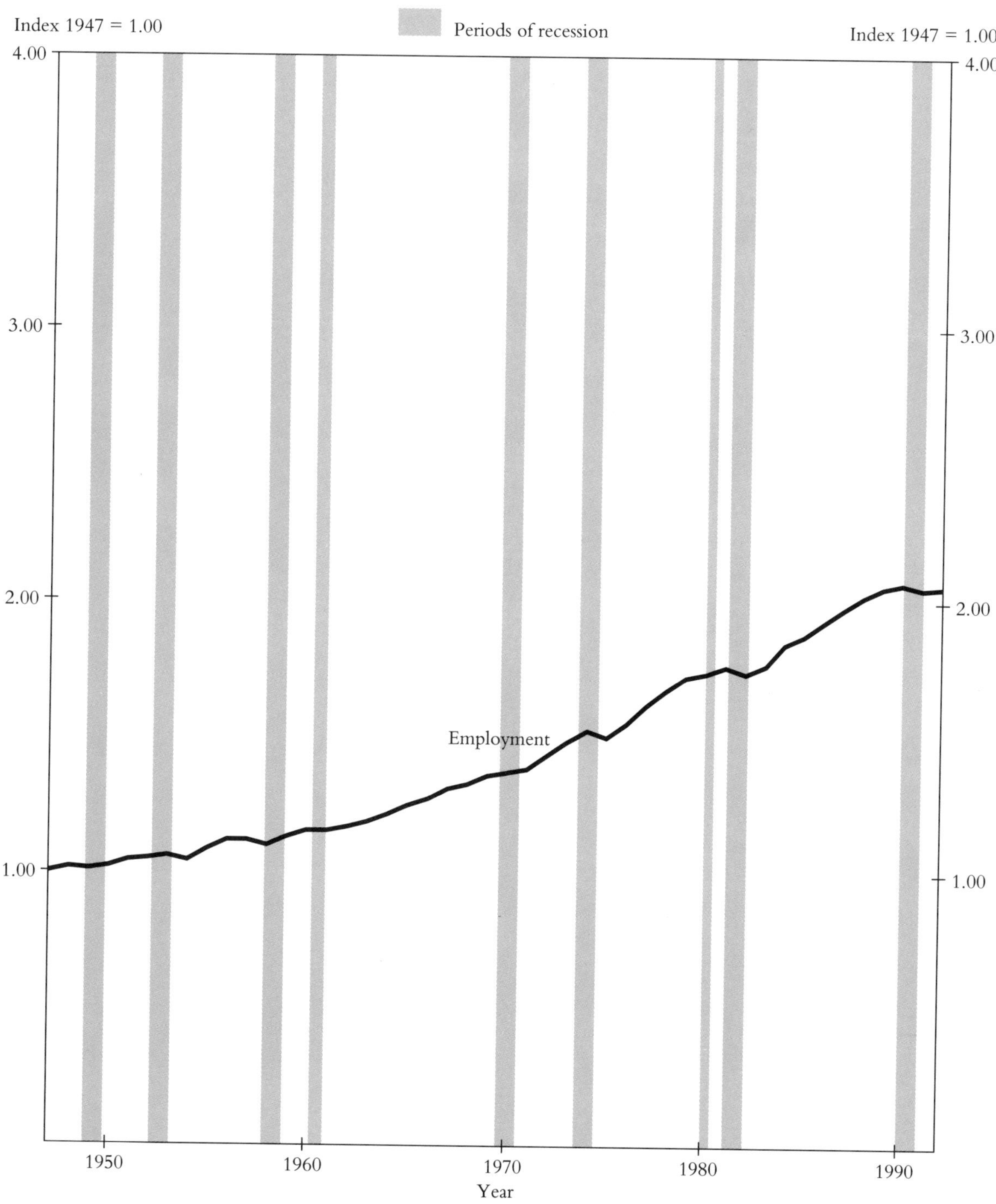

Sources: Computed based on data found in the *Economic Report of the President,* February 1983 and January 1993.

PART 4

Introduction to the Market System

CHAPTER 18

ELASTICITY OF DEMAND AND SUPPLY

As noted in Chapter 1, macroeconomics focuses on aggregate markets—on the big picture. But the big picture is a mosaic pieced together from individual decisions made by domestic households, firms, governments, and the rest of the world. To understand how the economy works, we must take a closer look at these individual decisions. In market economies, the price system guides production and consumption. Prices inform consumers and producers about the relative scarcity of goods and resources. In this chapter we consider how responsive producers and consumers are to price changes.

Teaching Tip
Knowledge of elasticities also will help a firm predict the impact on its revenues of movements through the business cycle, of competitors' price changes, and so forth.

A downward-sloping demand curve and an upward-sloping supply curve combine to form a powerful analytical tool. To add greater precision to our analytical ability, we must examine the shape and position of the demand and supply curves. Firms are willing to pay dearly for predictions about the impact of a change in price on quantity demanded. For example, between 1990 and 1992 the price of the Sears LXI Camcorder dropped from $999 to $699. Sears would like to be able to predict the effect of such a price drop on the quantity demanded. Governments would also like to know the effect of sales taxes on quantity supplied and quantity demanded. For example, state governments would like to know the effect of an increase in the gasoline tax on tax revenues. To answer such questions, we need to know how sensitive quantity demanded or quantity supplied is to a change in price. Price *elasticity* is the tool used to measure sensitivity. Topics discussed in this chapter include

- Price elasticity of demand
- Determinants of price elasticity
- Price elasticity of supply
- Income elasticity of demand
- Cross-price elasticity

PRICE ELASTICITY OF DEMAND

Point to Stress The law of demand refers to the *direction* of the relationship between quantity demanded and price; price elasticity of demand refers to the *relative size* of the relationship.

As we said, producers would like to know the impact of a price change on quantity demanded. For example, if consumers sharply reduce their taco purchases when the price of tacos goes up, taco producers may find that total revenue falls as the price rises. Consider the two demand curves in Exhibit 1. In each case the price per unit has increased by 25 percent, from \$1 to \$1.25, but the effect on the quantity demanded differs in the two panels. In panel (a), the quantity demanded drops from 100 to 90, a 10-percent decline; in panel (b), it drops from 100 to 70, a 30-percent decline. Consumers are more responsive to the price increase in panel (b) than in panel (a). The responsiveness of quantity demanded to a change in price is measured by the price elasticity of demand. *Elasticity* is simply another word for *responsiveness.*

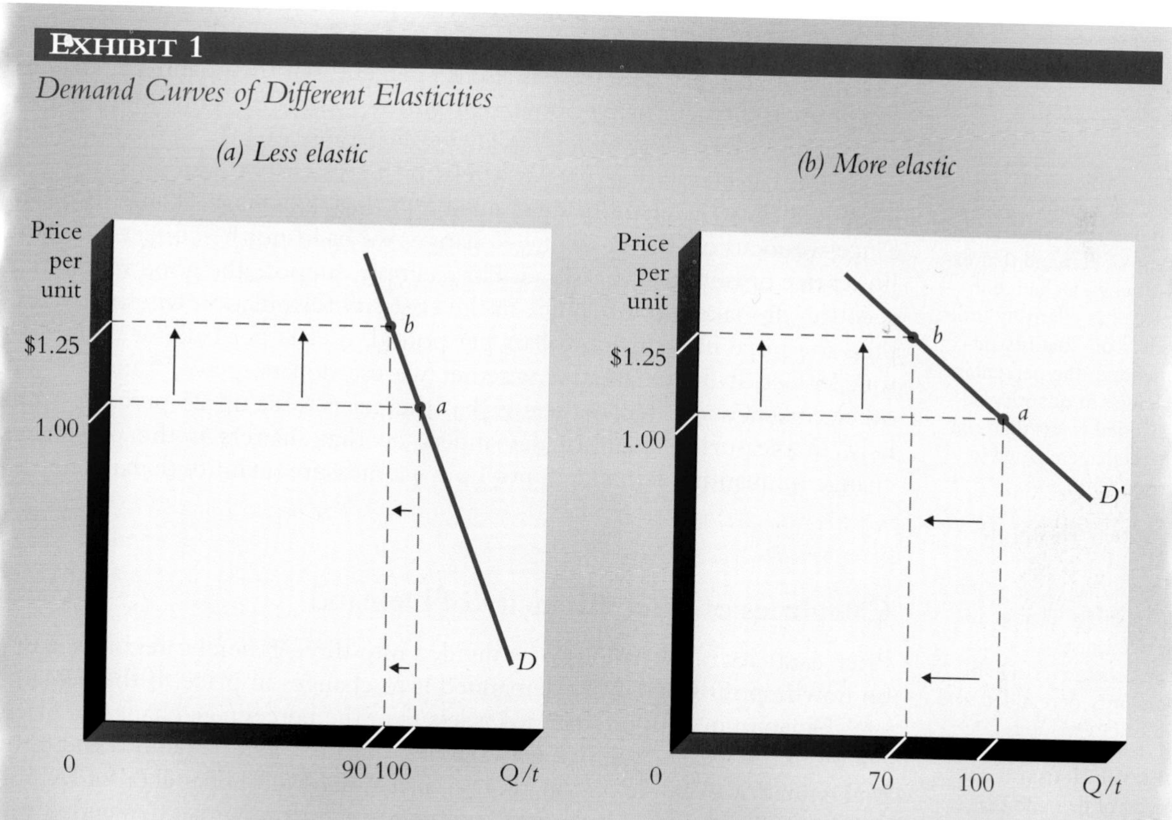

For a given change in price, the less elastic the demand, the smaller the change in quantity demanded. In panel (a), a 25-percent increase in price leads to a 10-percent decrease in quantity demanded. In panel (b), with more elastic demand *D′*, the same 25-percent price increase leads to a 30-percent decrease in quantity demanded.

Calculating Price Elasticity of Demand

Price elasticity of demand A measure of the responsiveness of quantity demanded to a price change; the percentage change in quantity demanded divided by the percentage change in price

Point to Stress Like the law of demand, price elasticity of demand considers the relationship between the quantity demanded of a good and its price, *other things constant.*

In simplest terms, the **price elasticity of demand** is equal to the percentage change in the quantity demanded divided by the percentage change in price. This relation can be represented by the equation

$$\textbf{Price elasticity of demand} = \frac{\textbf{percentage change in quantity demanded}}{\textbf{percentage change in price}}$$

Recall that the law of demand states that price and quantity demanded are inversely related: the change in price and the change in quantity demanded will always be in opposite directions. Hence, in the preceding elasticity formula the numerator and the denominator will have opposite signs, so the price elasticity of demand will always have a negative value. For simplicity, we will use the *absolute value* of the elasticity, which means that we drop the minus sign.

In panel (a) of Exhibit 1, when the price increases from \$1.00 to \$1.25, an increase of 25 percent [(1.25 – 1.00)/1.00], the quantity demanded decreases from 100 to 90, a drop of only 10 percent [(90 – 100)/100]. In this case the resulting elasticity is –10%/25%, which has an absolute value of 0.4. In panel (b), the price increase is also 25 percent, but the quantity demanded falls from 100 to 70, or by 30 percent [(70 – 100)/100]. Thus, the resulting elasticity is –30%/25%, which has an absolute value of 1.2.

Note that elasticity expresses a relation between two amounts: the percentage change in quantity demanded and the percentage change in price. Since we focus on the percentage change, we need not be concerned about how price or output is measured. For example, suppose the good in question is cotton. It makes no difference in the elasticity formulation whether we express the price in terms of dollars per pound, dollars per bale, or dollars per ton. In fact, it doesn't matter whether we use dollars, pesos, francs, or any other currency. All that matters is that the price went up 25 percent. Similarly, in measuring quantity demanded, all that matters is the percentage change in quantity demanded, not how we measure quantity demanded.

Inelastic demand The type of demand that exists when a change in price has relatively little effect on quantity demanded; the percentage change in quantity demanded is less than the percentage change in price

Unitary elastic demand The type of demand that exists when a percentage change in price causes an equal percentage change in quantity demanded; the elasticity value is one

Elastic demand The type of demand that exists when a change in price has a relatively large effect on quantity demanded; the percentage change in quantity demanded exceeds the percentage change in price

Categories of Price Elasticity of Demand

Price elasticity of demand can be divided into three general categories, based on how responsive quantity demanded is to changes in price. If the percentage change in quantity demanded is less than the percentage change in price, the resulting price elasticity has a value less than 1.0, and demand is said to be **inelastic**. For example, in the range of prices depicted in panel (a) of Exhibit 1, demand is inelastic. If the percentage change in quantity demanded just equals the percentage change in price, the resulting price elasticity has a value equal to 1.0, and demand is said to be of **unitary elasticity**. Finally, if the quantity demanded changes by a greater percentage than does the price, the resulting price elasticity has a value greater than 1.0, and demand is said to be **elastic**. For example, in the price range depicted in panel (b) of Exhibit 1,

Point to Stress The elasticity coefficient indicates the percentage change in the quantity demanded resulting from a 1-percent change in the price. Thus, a value of 0.4 indicates that a 10-percent price increase generates a 4-percent reduction in the quantity demanded; with an elasticity value of 1.2, the quantity demanded falls by 12 percent.

demand is elastic. In summary, *demand is inelastic if price elasticity is less than 1.0, of unitary elasticity if price elasticity is equal to 1.0, and elastic if price elasticity is greater than 1.0.*

Refining the Calculations: The Midpoint Formula

The discussion to this point has glossed over a tricky little problem in calculating elasticity. Using our simple formula, we get a different elasticity value depending on whether we move from point *a* to point *b* or from point *b* to point *a*. Consider the case in panel (a) of Exhibit 1, where the price increases from $1.00 to $1.25, an increase of 25 percent, and the quantity decreases from 100 to 90 units, a decrease of 10 percent. The elasticity was calculated as –10%/25%, which has an absolute value of 0.4. If, however, we begin with a price of $1.25 and lower it to $1.00, this change represents a price drop of 20 percent [(1.25 – 1.00)/1.25]; quantity demanded then increases from 90 to 100, an increase of 11 percent [(100 – 90)/90]. The resulting elasticity is –11%/20%, which has an absolute value of 0.55, which is obviously different from 0.4.

Teaching Tip Indicate the different categories of price elasticity along a number line ranging from zero to infinity.

The problem is that although the *amounts* of changes in price and in quantity are the same whether we go from the higher to the lower price or the other way around (that is, the price changes by $0.25, and the quantity demanded changes by 10 units), the *base* for calculating the percentage change depends on the initial price and the initial quantity. Consequently, when we begin with $1.00 and raise the price by $0.25, the base is different from what it is when we begin with $1.25 and lower the price by $0.25. Economists have solved the problem by using the *midpoint* between the initial value and the new value as the base. The midpoint is simply the average of the initial value and the new value. Thus, when the price increases from $1.00 to $1.25, the base used in calculating the percentage change is not $1.00 but $1.125 [($1.25 + $1.00)/2]. The percentage change in price is therefore 0.25/1.125, or 22 percent. And the base will be the same whether we consider a change from $1.00 to $1.25 or from $1.25 to $1.00.

Point to Stress The midpoint value of 0.48 lies between the values of 0.4 (from point *a* to point *b*) and 0.55 (from point *b* to point *a*) calculated with the simple elasticity formula.

The same holds for changes in quantity demanded. When the quantity demanded falls from 100 to 90, the base is not 100 but 95 [(90 + 100)/2]. Thus, the percentage change in quantity demanded calculated by the midpoint method is 10/95, which equals 10.5 percent. The resulting elasticity of demand is the percentage change in quantity, 10.5 percent, divided by the percentage change in price, 22 percent, which is equal to 0.48. Because the midpoint formula uses the same base, the value for the elasticity will be the same for a price drop from $1.25 to $1.00 as for a price increase from $1.00 to $1.25.

Midpoint elasticity formula Computes the percentage change by using the average quantity and the average price as bases rather than the initial price and the initial quantity

Let's develop the midpoint formula for the changes in price and quantity shown in Exhibit 2. As you can see, if the price increases from p to p', the quantity demanded decreases from q_D to q'_D. The **midpoint elasticity formula** for calculating the price elasticity of demand, E_D, between the two points is

EXHIBIT 2

Price Elasticity of Demand Using the Midpoint Formula

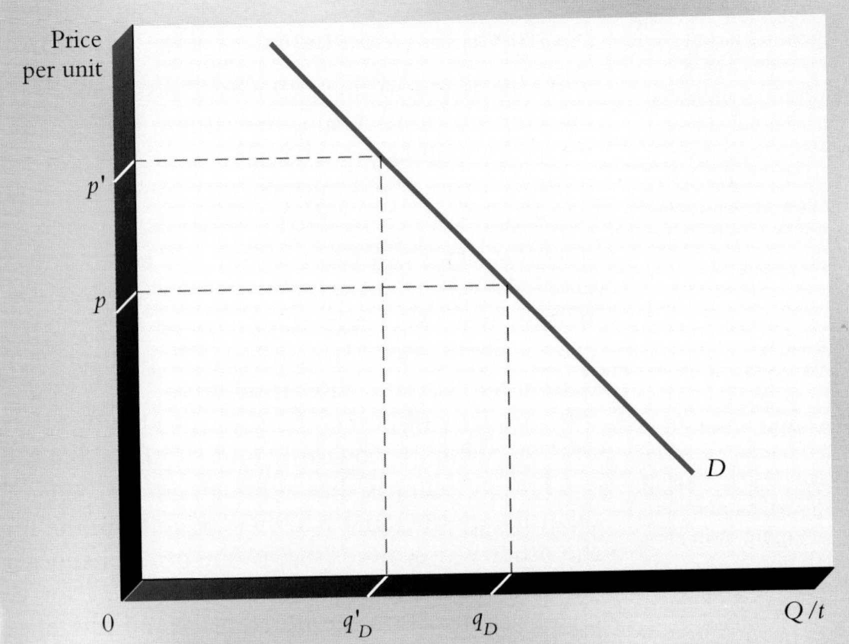

If the price increases from p to p', the quantity demanded decreases from q_D to q'_D. The midpoint elasticity formula for calculating the price elasticity of demand is found by using the average price $[(p + p')/2]$ and the average quantity $[(q_D + q'_D)/2]$ as denominators in computing the percentage change in price and percentage change in quantity demanded.

$$E_D = \frac{q'_D - q_D}{(q'_D + q_D)/2} \div \frac{p' - p}{(p' + p)/2}$$

The 2s cancel out to yield

$$E_D = \frac{q'_D - q_D}{q'_D + q_D} \div \frac{p' - p}{p' + p}$$

Teaching Tip In panel (b) of Exhibit 1, the elasticity value using the midpoint formula is 1.59 (versus 1.2 from point *a* to point *b* and 2.15 from point *b* to point *a*, values produced by using the simple formula).

With the midpoint formula, it makes no difference in the computed elasticity whether the change is from a lower to a higher price or from a higher to a lower price.

Elasticity and Total Revenue

One reason producers want to know the price elasticity of demand is that it tells them what will happen to their total revenue if the price is changed.

Total revenue Price multiplied by the quantity sold at that price

Teaching Tip Moving from point *b* to point *a* in panel (a) of Exhibit 1, demand is inelastic and total revenue falls from $112.50 to $100.00; in panel (b), demand is elastic and total revenue rises from $87.50 to $100.00.

Example In 1980, the former Soviet Union restricted shipments of titanium to the world market. The price of titanium rose from $4 per pound to $20 per pound, and Soviet total revenue from titanium sales rose. Demand was inelastic.

Total revenue is the price of the product multiplied by the quantity sold at that price, or $TR = p \times q$. What happens to total revenue when the price decreases? According to the law of demand, if the price falls, the quantity demanded increases. The lower price means producers get less per unit, which tends to decrease total revenue, but increased quantity demanded resulting from a lower price tends to increase total revenue. The overall change in total revenue resulting from a lower price is the net result of these opposite effects. If the positive effect of a greater quantity demanded exceeds the negative effect of a lower price, total revenue will rise. More specifically, when demand is *elastic*, the percentage increase in quantity demanded exceeds the percentage decrease in price, so total revenue increases. When demand is of *unitary elasticity*, the percentage increase in quantity demanded is just equal to the percentage decrease in price, so total revenue remains unchanged. Finally, when demand is *inelastic*, the percentage increase in quantity demanded is less than the percentage decrease in price, so total revenue decreases.

Price Elasticity and the Linear Demand Curve

Linear demand curve A straight-line demand curve

The price elasticity of demand usually varies along a demand curve. An examination of the elasticity of a particular type of demand curve, the linear demand curve, will tie together the concepts examined thus far. A **linear demand curve** is simply a straight-line demand curve. Panel (a) of Exhibit 3 presents a linear demand curve, and panel (b) presents the total revenue generated at each price-quantity combination along the demand curve. Recall that total revenue equals price times quantity.

Since the demand curve in panel (a) is linear, the slope is constant, so a given decrease in price always causes the same unit increase in quantity demanded. For example, a $10 price drop in price always increases quantity demanded by 100 units. But *the price elasticity of demand is greater on the higher-price end of the demand curve than on the lower-price end*. Here is why. Because the quantity demanded is smaller at the upper end of the demand curve than at the lower end, a 100-unit increase in quantity demanded represents a greater percentage change at the upper end than at the lower end. But because the price *level* is higher at the upper end than at the lower end of the curve, a $10 decrease in price represents a smaller percentage change in price at the upper end than at the lower end. Thus, at the upper end of the demand curve, the percentage increase in quantity demanded is relatively large and the percentage decrease in price is relatively small, so the price elasticity of demand is relatively large. At the lower end of the demand curve, the percentage increase in quantity demanded is relatively small and the percentage decrease in price is relatively large, so the price elasticity of demand is relatively small.

Teaching Tip Demand curves with the same slopes need not have the same price elasticities of demand. Along two parallel, linear, downward-sloping demand curves, the curve farther from the origin is less elastic at each price. The base quantities are larger; therefore, the percentage change in quantity demanded is smaller for each price change.

Consider a movement from point *a* to point *b* on the upper end of the demand curve. Using the midpoint formula, we find that a $10 price drop amounts to a percentage change of 10/85, or about 12 percent. The 100-unit increase in quantity demanded is a percentage change of 100/150, or 66 percent. Therefore, the price elasticity of demand between points *a* and *b* is

EXHIBIT 3

Demand, Price Elasticity, and Total Revenue

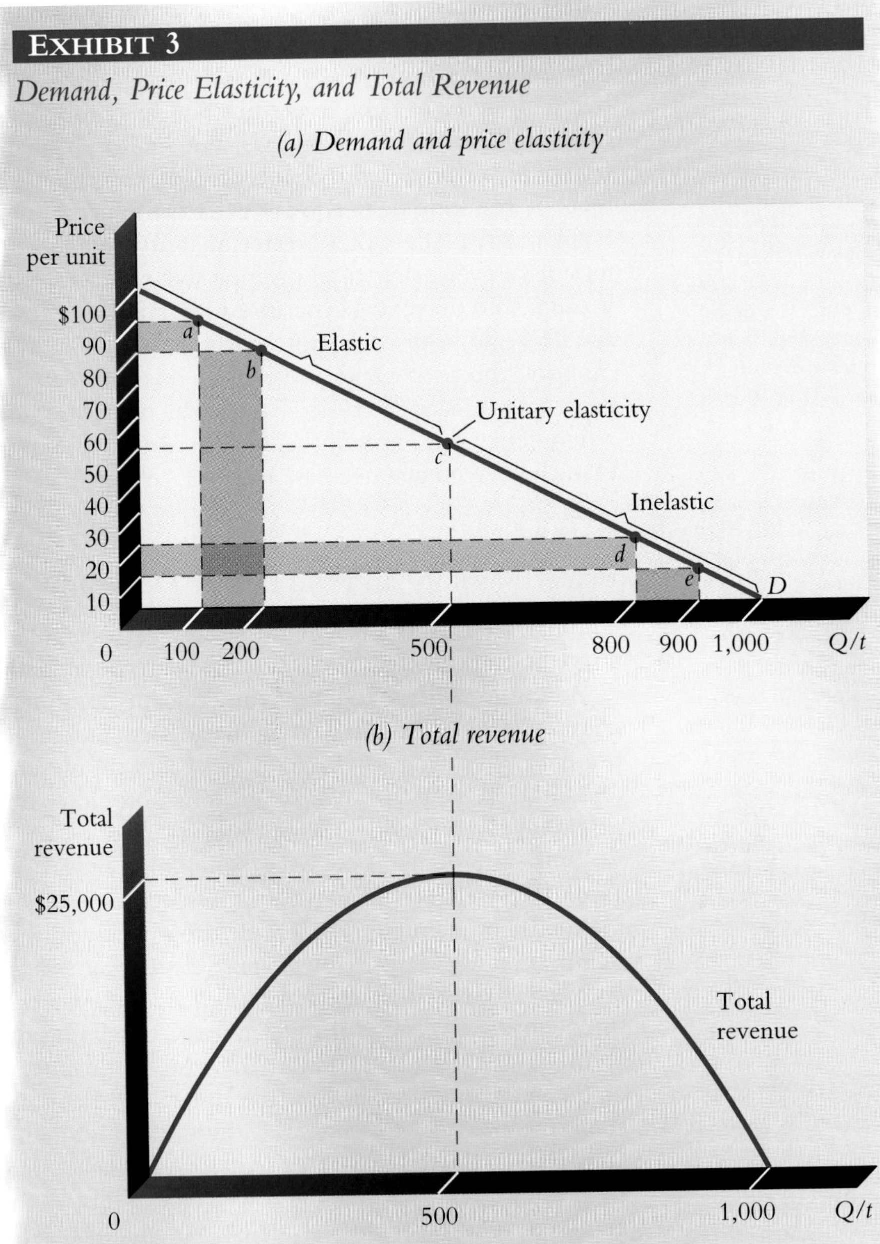

Where demand is elastic in panel (a), total revenue in panel (b) increases following a price decrease. Total revenue attains its maximum value at the level of output where demand is of unitary elasticity. Where demand is inelastic, further decreases in price cause total revenue to fall.

Teaching Tip The coefficient of price elasticity of demand varies from infinity, where the curve intersects the price axis, to zero, where it intersects the quantity axis.

66%/12%, which equals 5.5. Between points *d* and *e* on the lower end, however, the $10 price decrease is a percentage change of 10/15, or 66 percent, and the 100-unit quantity increase is a percentage change of 100/850, or only 12 percent. The price elasticity of demand thus falls to 12%/66%, or 0.18. In other words, *if the demand curve is linear, consumers are more responsive to a given price change when the price range for a product is relatively high than when the price range is relatively low.*

The price elasticity of demand falls steadily as we move down the curve. At a point halfway down the linear demand curve in Exhibit 3, the elasticity is equal to 1.0. *This halfway point divides the demand curve into an elastic upper half and an inelastic lower half.* You can observe the clear relation between the elasticity of the demand curve in the upper diagram and total revenue in the lower diagram. Note that where the demand curve is elastic, a decrease in price increases total revenue because the gain in revenue from selling more units (represented by the large blue rectangle in the top panel) exceeds the loss in revenue from selling at the lower price (the small red rectangle). Where the demand curve is inelastic, a price decrease reduces total revenue because the gain in revenue from selling more units (the small blue rectangle) is less than the loss in revenue from selling at the lower price (the large red rectangle). Where the demand curve is of unitary elasticity, the gain and loss of revenue exactly cancel each other out, so total revenue at that point remains constant (hence total revenue "peaks out" in the lower portion of the exhibit).

Point to Stress In the elastic range of a demand curve, price and total revenue move in opposite directions. In the inelastic range, price and total revenue move in the same direction.

In summary, total revenue increases as the price declines until the midpoint of the demand curve is reached, where total revenue peaks. In Exhibit 3, total revenue peaks at $25,000 when quantity demanded equals 500 units. Below the midpoint of the demand curve, total revenue declines as the price falls. More generally, regardless of whether the demand curve is a straight line or a curve, there is a relation between the price elasticity of demand and total revenue: a price decrease *increases* total revenue if demand is elastic, *decreases* total revenue if demand is inelastic, and *has no effect* on total revenue if demand is of unitary elasticity. Finally, note that a downward-sloping linear demand curve has a constant slope but a varying elasticity, so the slope of a demand curve is not the same as the price elasticity of that demand curve.

Point to Stress A perfectly elastic demand curve has a slope of zero but an elasticity value of infinity. If the price rises, total revenue falls to zero.

Constant-Elasticity Demand Curves

Price elasticity varies along a linear demand curve unless the demand curve is horizontal or vertical, as in panels (a) and (b) of Exhibit 4. These two demand curves, along with the demand curve in panel (c), are called *constant-elasticity demand curves* because the elasticity does not change along the curves.

Perfectly elastic demand curve A horizontal line reflecting the fact that any price increase reduces quantity demanded to zero; the elasticity value is infinity

PERFECTLY ELASTIC DEMAND. The horizontal demand curve in panel (a) indicates that consumers will demand all that is offered for sale at the given price *p*. If the price rises above *p*, however, the quantity demanded drops to zero. This demand curve is said to be **perfectly elastic**, and its numerical elasticity value is infinity, the highest possible value. You may think this is an odd sort of demand curve: consumers, as a result of a small increase

EXHIBIT 4

Three Constant-Elasticity Demand Curves

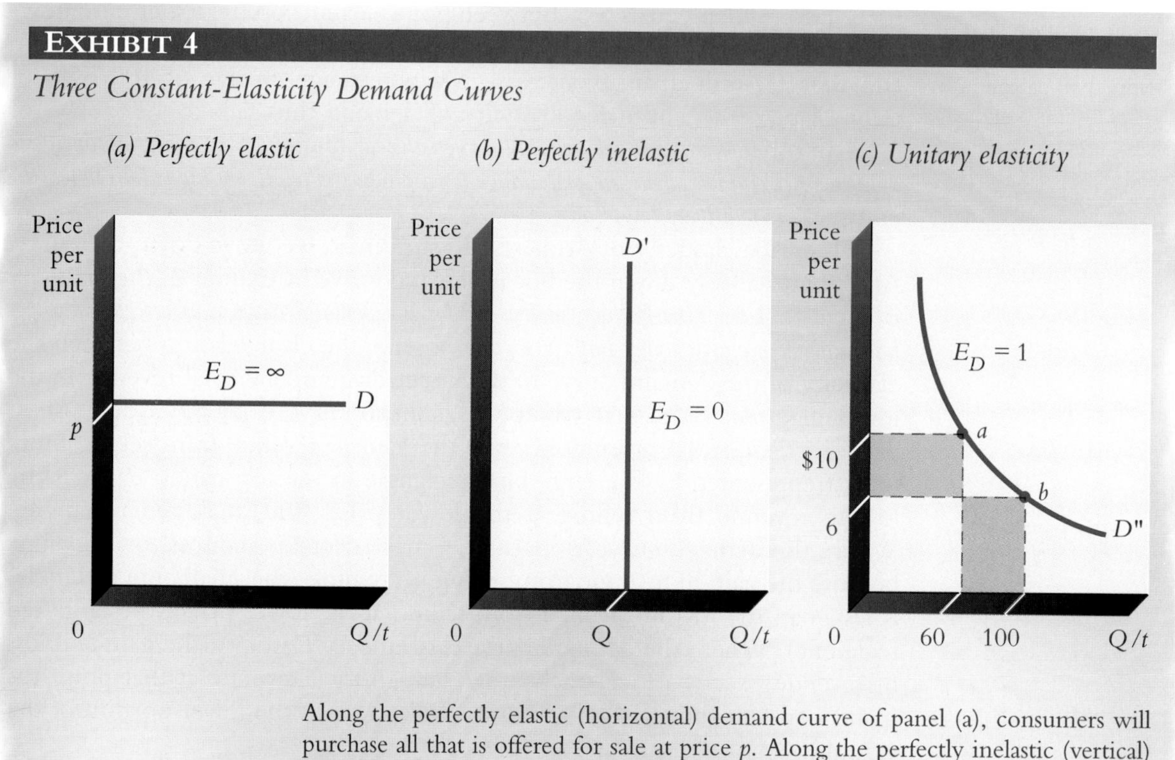

Along the perfectly elastic (horizontal) demand curve of panel (a), consumers will purchase all that is offered for sale at price *p*. Along the perfectly inelastic (vertical) demand curve of panel (b), consumers will purchase quantity Q regardless of price. Along the unitary elastic demand curve of panel (c), total revenue is the same for every price-quantity combination.

in price, go from demanding as much as is available to demanding nothing. As you will see later, this curve describes the demand for the output of any individual producer when many producers are selling identical products.

PERFECTLY INELASTIC DEMAND. The vertical demand curve in panel (b) of Exhibit 4 represents the situation in which quantity demanded does not vary at all when the price changes. This demand curve expresses consumers' sentiment that "price is no object." For example, if you were very rich and needed insulin injections to stay alive, price would be no object. No matter how high the price of the insulin, you would continue to demand the amount necessary to stay alive. Likewise, price might not be an object if an oil tycoon came across a diamond necklace that she simply had to have. Vertical demand curves are called **perfectly inelastic** because price changes do not affect quantity demanded, at least not over the range of prices shown by the demand curve. Since the percentage change in quantity is zero for any given percentage change in price, the numerical value of the elasticity is zero.

Perfectly inelastic demand curve A vertical line reflecting the fact that a price change has no effect on the quantity demanded; the elasticity value is zero

UNITARY ELASTICITY. Panel (c) in Exhibit 4 presents a demand curve that is of unitary elasticity everywhere along the curve. This means that a percentage change in price will always result in an identical percentage change

EXHIBIT 5

Summary of Price Elasticity of Demand

Absolute Price Elasticity Value	Type of Demand	Effects of a 10-Percent Increase in Price: What Happens to Quantity Demanded	Effects of a 10-Percent Increase in Price: What Happens to Total Revenue
$\|E_D\| = 0$	Perfectly inelastic	No change	Increases by 10 percent
$0 < \|E_D\| < 1$	Inelastic	Drops by less than 10 percent	Increases by less than 10 percent
$\|E_D\| = 1$	Unitary elasticity	Drops by 10 percent	No change
$1 < \|E_D\| < \infty$	Elastic	Drops by more than 10 percent	Decreases
$\|E_D\| = \infty$	Perfectly elastic	Drops to 0	Drops to 0

in quantity demanded. Because percentage changes in price and in quantity will be equal and offsetting, total revenue will be the same for every price-quantity combination along the curve. For example, when the price falls from $10 to $6, the quantity demanded increases from 60 to 100 units. The red shaded rectangle represents the loss in total revenue because all units are sold at the lower price; the blue shaded rectangle represents the gain in total revenue because more units are sold when the price drops. Because the demand curve is of unitary elasticity, the revenue gained by selling more units just equals the revenue lost by lowering the price on all units, so total revenue is unchanged at $600. A demand curve of unitary elasticity all along the curve would actually be quite rare.

Point to Stress A perfectly inelastic demand curve has a slope of infinity but an elasticity value of zero. If the price rises, there is a proportional increase in total revenue.

Constant elasticity of demand The type of demand that exists when price elasticity is the same everywhere along the curve; the elasticity value is constant

Each of the demand curves in Exhibit 4 is called a **constant-elasticity** demand curve because the elasticity is the same all along the curve. In contrast, the downward-sloping linear demand curve examined earlier had a different elasticity value at each point along the curve. Exhibit 5 lists the absolute values of the five categories of price elasticity we have discussed, summarizing the varying effects of a 10-percent increase in the price on quantity demanded and on total revenue. Give this exhibit some thought, and see if you can draw a demand curve to reflect each type of elasticity.

DETERMINANTS OF THE PRICE ELASTICITY OF DEMAND

Thus far we have explored the technical properties of demand elasticity. We have not yet considered why the price elasticities of demand vary for different goods. Several characteristics influence the price elasticity of demand for a good. We will examine each of these in detail.

Availability of Substitutes

Example In late 1992, IBM introduced a new line of low-priced personal computers, PS/ValuePoint, in recognition of the growing number of customers who regard different personal computer brands as very close substitutes and shop for the lowest price.

As noted in Chapter 3, your particular wants can be satisfied in a variety of different ways. If the price of pizza increases, other foods become relatively cheaper. If close substitutes are available, an increase in the price of pizza will encourage consumers to shift to these substitutes and to lower the quantity of pizza demanded. But if nothing else comes close to satisfying the desire for pizza, the quantity of pizza demanded will not decline as much. *The greater the availability of substitutes for a good and the closer these substitutes, the greater the price elasticity of demand.* It's been reported that the price of an umbrella on a New York City street corner is $3 is fair weather and $5 in the rain. The price is higher during rainy weather because there are fewer close substitutes.

Example In Exhibit 7, note the high long-run elasticity for Chevrolets relative to the elasticity for automobiles.

The number and similarity of substitutes depend on how we define the good. *The more broadly we define a good, the fewer substitutes there will be and the less elastic the demand will be.* For example, the demand for shoes will be less elastic than the demand for running shoes because there are few substitutes for shoes but several substitutes for running shoes, such as sneakers, tennis shoes, cross-trainers, and the like. The demand for running shoes, however, will be less elastic than the demand for Nike running shoes because the consumer has more substitutes for Nikes, including Reeboks, New Balance, and so on. Finally, the demand for Nike running shoes will be less elastic than the demand for a specific model of Nikes, such as Nike Airs.

Example Titanium (mentioned in an earlier example) has no close substitutes when used in airplane manufacture—thus, demand for titanium is inelastic.

For some goods, such as insulin, there are simply no close substitutes. The demand for such goods tends to be less elastic than for goods with close substitutes. Because a producer would like to be able to increase price without having consumers switch to substitutes, the producer would like consumers to think there are no substitutes for the particular product. Much advertising is aimed at establishing in the consumer's mind the uniqueness of a particular product. For example, Reebok has spent millions touting the Reebok Pump, in an attempt to both increase demand and make the demand for the Pump more inelastic.

Proportion of the Consumer's Budget Spent on a Good

Recall that a higher price reduces quantity demanded in part because a higher price causes the real spending power of consumer income to decline. A demand curve reflects both the willingness and the ability to purchase a good at alternative prices. Because spending on certain goods represents a large share of the consumer's budget, a change in the price of such a good has a substantial impact on the quantity that consumers are *able* to purchase. An increase in the price of housing, for example, reduces the ability to purchase housing. The income effect of a higher housing price is to reduce the quantity demanded. In contrast, the income effect of an increase in the price of paper towels is trivial because paper towels represent such a small proportion of any budget. *The more important the item is as a proportion of the consumer's budget, other things constant, the greater will be the income effect of a change in price.* The smaller the spending on the item as a proportion of the budget, the smaller will be the income effect of a change in price.

Example In Exhibit 7, note the long-run elasticity of demand for residential natural gas versus the elasticity of demand for newspapers and magazines.

Hence, a change in the price of housing, automobiles, or college creates more of an income effect than a change in the price of paper towels, pencils, or flash-light batteries.

A Matter of Time

Consumers can substitute lower-priced goods for higher-priced goods, but this substitution usually takes time. Suppose your college announces a substantial increase in room and board fees effective immediately. Some students will move off campus as soon as they can. Others will wait until the end of the school year. And, over time, fewer students may apply for admission, and more incoming students will choose off-campus housing. Thus, *the longer the adjustment period considered, the greater the ability to substitute away from relatively higher-priced products toward lower-priced substitutes, and the more responsive the change in quantity demanded to a given change in price.*

Exhibit 6 demonstrates how demand becomes more elastic over time. As-

EXHIBIT 6

Demand Becomes More Elastic Over Time

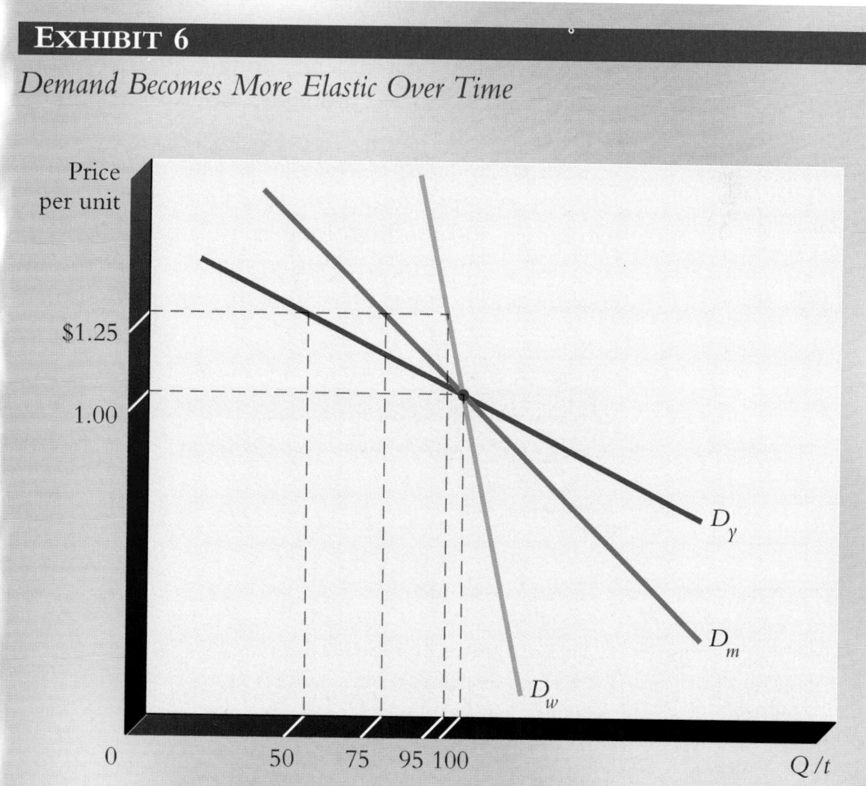

D_w is the demand curve one week after a price increase from $1.00 to $1.25. Along this curve, quantity demanded falls from 100 to 95. One month after the price increase, quantity demanded has fallen to 75 along D_m. One year after the price increase, quantity demanded has fallen to 50 along D_y. D_y is more elastic than D_m, which is more elastic than D_w.

Point to Stress Although elasticity varies along downward-sloping linear demand curves, the elasticities of intersecting curves *at the intersection point* can be compared by comparing slopes.

suming that the initial price is $1.00, let D_w be the demand curve one week after a price change; D_m, one month after; and D_y, one year after. If the price increases from $1.00 to $1.25, the reduction in quantity demanded will be greater as consumers have longer to identify and adopt substitutes. For example, the demand curve D_w shows that one week after the price increase the quantity demanded has not declined much—in this case from 100 to 95. The demand curve D_m indicates a greater reduction in quantity demanded after one month, and demand curve D_y shows the greatest reduction in quantity demanded after one year. Notice that *among these demand curves and over the range starting from the point of intersection, the flatter the demand curve, the more price elastic the demand.*

Elasticity Estimates

Let's consider some estimates of the price elasticity of demand for particular goods and services. As we have said, the substitution of relatively lower-priced goods for newly higher-priced goods often takes time. Thus, when estimating price elasticity, we often distinguish between a period during which consumers have little time to adjust—let's call it the short run—and a period during which consumers can fully adjust to a price change—let's call it the long run. Exhibit 7 provides some short-run and long-run price elasticity estimates for selected products. (For some products, only short-run or long-run estimates are available.)

The price elasticity is greater in the long run because consumers have more time to adjust. For example, notice the low short-run elasticity of demand for residential natural gas and the high long-run elasticity. If the relative price of natural gas rose today, consumers might cut back a small amount in the short run in their cooking and heating. Over time, however, consumers would switch to now rel-

EXHIBIT 7

Selected Price Elasticities of Demand

Product	Short Run	Long Run
Air travel	0.1	2.4
Electricity (residential)	0.1	1.9
Gasoline	0.2	0.5
Medical care and hospitalization	0.3	0.9
Newspapers, magazines	0.1	0.5
Natural gas (residential)	0.1	10.7
Alcohol	0.9	3.6
Movies	0.9	3.7
Milk	0.4	—
Automobiles	—	1.5
Chevrolets	—	4.0

Source: H. S. Houthakker and L. D. Taylor, *Consumer Demand in the United States: Analyses and Projections,* 2d ed. (Cambridge, MA: Harvard University Press, 1970).

Point to Stress The elasticity coefficient indicates the percentage change in the quantity supplied resulting from a 1-percent change in the price. Thus, a value of 0.5 indicates that a 10-percent price increase generates a 5-percent increase in the quantity supplied.

atively cheaper energy sources such as oil or electricity or they might purchase a more energy-efficient gas burner. So the price elasticity of demand is more elastic in the long run than in the short run. Notice also in Exhibit 7 that the long-run price elasticity of demand for Chevrolets exceeds the price elasticity for automobiles in general. There are many more substitutes for Chevrolets than for automobiles. A luxury tax introduced in 1991 raised the price of expensive automobiles; as a result the quantity demanded fell sharply for such luxury models as Rolls-Royce, Mercedes, and Porsche.

PRICE ELASTICITY OF SUPPLY

Price elasticity of supply A measure of the responsiveness of quantity supplied to a price change; the percentage change in quantity supplied divided by the percentage change in price

Prices signal both sides of the market about the relative scarcity of products; high prices discourage consumption but encourage production. The price elasticity of demand is a measure of how consumers respond to a price change. Similarly, the **price elasticity of supply** measures how responsive producers are to a price change. This elasticity is calculated in the same way as demand elasticity, but using the percentage change in quantity supplied instead of the percentage change in quantity demanded. In simplest terms the price elasticity of supply equals the percentage change in quantity supplied divided by the percentage change in price.

Let's develop the midpoint formula for the changes in price and quantity supplied shown in Exhibit 8. As you can see, if the price increases from p to p', the quantity supplied increases from q_S to q'_S. The *midpoint elasticity formula* for calculating the price elasticity of supply, E_S, between the two points is

$$E_S = \frac{q'_S - q_S}{q'_S + q_S/2} \div \frac{p' - p}{p' + p/2}$$

Again, the 2s cancel out so the formula reduces to

$$E_S = \frac{q'_S - q_S}{(q'_S + q_S)} \div \frac{p' - p}{(p' + p)}$$

Teaching Tip As with the demand curve, the concepts of slope and elasticity are not equivalent along the supply curve. A perfectly elastic supply curve has a slope of zero but an elasticity value of infinity. A perfectly inelastic supply curve has a slope of infinity and an elasticity value of zero.

Since price and quantity supplied are usually directly related, the percentage change in price and the percentage change in quantity supplied usually move in the same direction, so the price elasticity of supply is usually positive.

Categories of Supply Elasticity

The terminology for supply elasticity is the same as for demand elasticity: if the value is less than 1.0, supply is *inelastic*; if supply elasticity has a value greater than 1.0, supply is *elastic*; and if the value is equal to 1.0, supply is of *unitary elasticity*. There are also some special values of supply elasticity to be considered.

EXHIBIT 8

Price Elasticity of Supply Using the Midpoint Formula

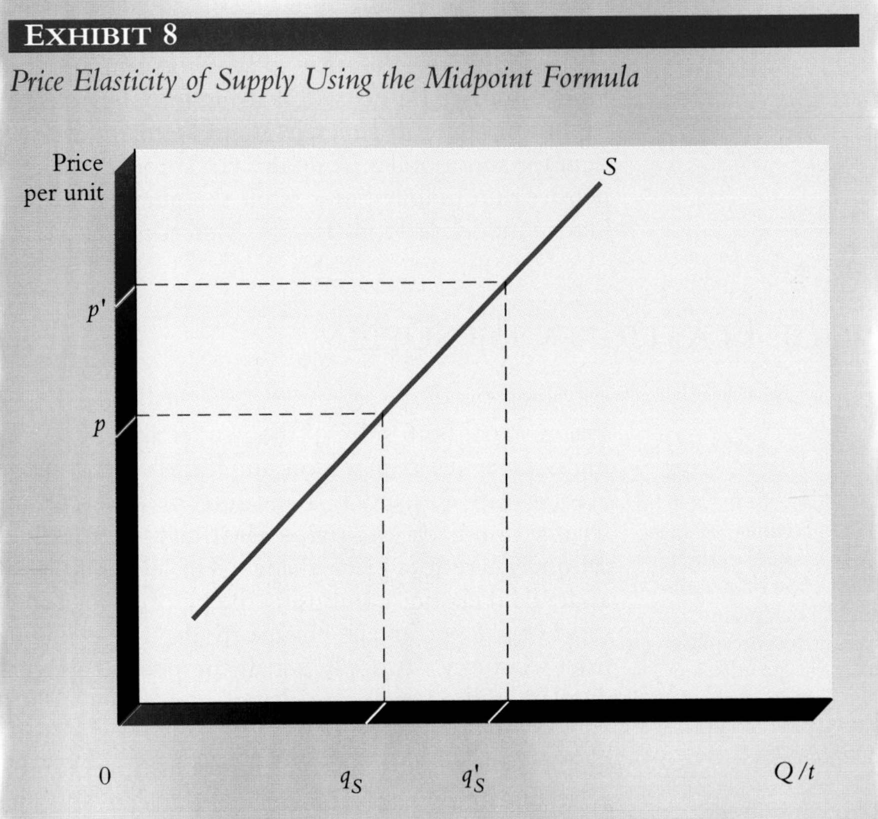

If the price increases from p to p', the quantity supplied increases from q_S to q'_S. The midpoint formula for calculating the price elasticity of supply is found by using the average price $[(p' + p)/2]$ and the average quantity $[(q'_S + q_S)/2]$ as denominators in computing the percentage change in price and the percentage change in quantity supplied.

Teaching Tip Individual consumers face perfectly elastic supply curves when each consumer represents a small fraction of the entire market—too small a fraction for the consumer's buying behavior to affect the price.

Perfectly elastic supply curve A horizontal line reflecting the fact that any price decrease reduces the quantity supplied to zero; the elasticity value is infinity

PERFECTLY ELASTIC SUPPLY. At one extreme is the horizontal supply curve, such as supply curve *S* in panel (a) of Exhibit 9. In this case producers will supply none of the good at a price below *p* but will supply any amount at a price of *p*. The quantity actually supplied at price *p* will depend on the quantity demanded at that price. Because a tiny increase from a price just below *p* to a price of *p* will result in an unlimited supply, this curve is said to reflect **perfectly elastic supply**, with a mathematical elasticity value of infinity. As individual consumers, we typically face perfectly elastic supply curves. When we go to the supermarket, we usually can buy as much as we want at the prevailing price. This is not to say that all consumers together could buy an unlimited amount at the prevailing price. (Recall the fallacy of composition: what is true for any individual consumer is not necessarily true for all consumers as a group.)

EXHIBIT 9

Three Constant-Elasticity Supply Curves

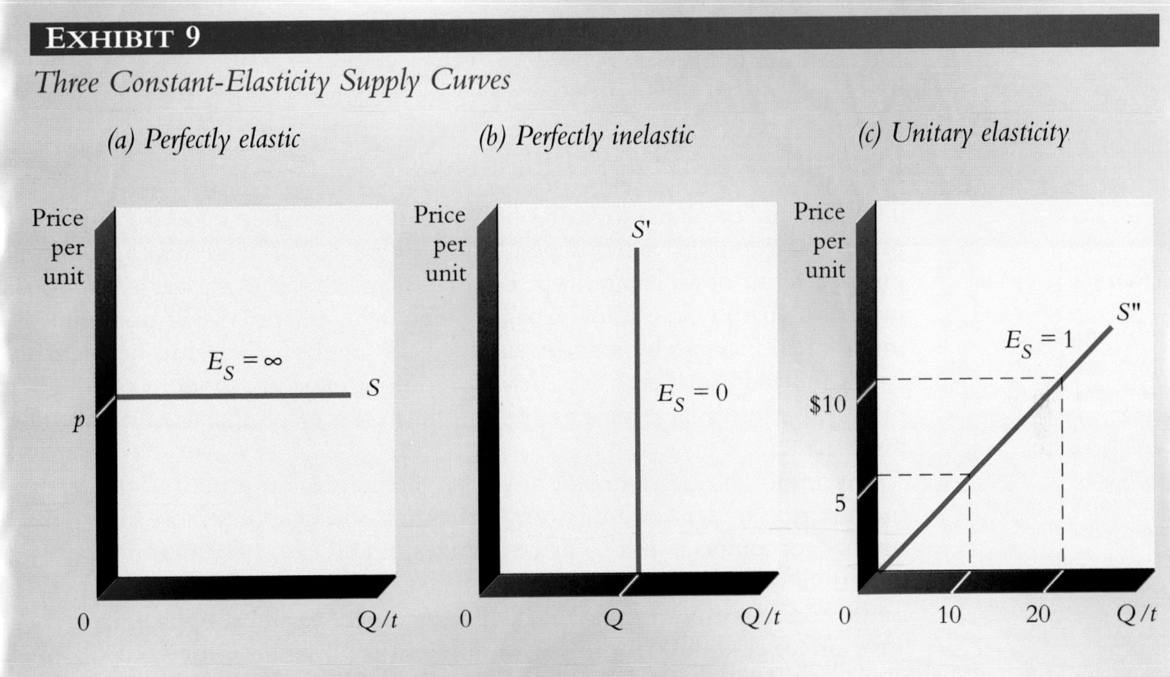

Supply curve S in panel (a) is perfectly elastic (horizontal). Along S, firms will supply any amount of output demanded at price p. Supply curve S' is perfectly inelastic (vertical). S' shows that the quantity supplied is independent of the price. In panel (c), S'' is a ray, which has a price elasticity of supply that is unitary. Any percentage change in price will result in the same percentage change in quantity supplied.

Perfectly inelastic supply curve A vertical line reflecting the fact that a price change has no effect on the quantity supplied; the elasticity value is zero

Unitary elastic supply A percentage change in price causes an equal percentage change in quantity supplied; depicted by a supply curve that is a ray from the origin; the elasticity value is one

PERFECTLY INELASTIC SUPPLY. The most unresponsive relation between price and quantity supplied is the one in which there is no change in the quantity supplied when the price changes. Such a case is represented by the vertical supply curve S' in panel (b) of Exhibit 9. Because the percentage change in quantity supplied is zero, regardless of the change in price, the value of the supply elasticity equals zero. This curve reflects **perfectly inelastic supply**. Any good that is in fixed supply, such as Picasso paintings or 1978 Dom Perignon champagne, will have a perfectly inelastic supply curve. Not surprisingly, the price of Picasso's paintings jumped upon news of his death because his death meant an end to additional output and hence a reduction in the expected total supply of his work. Similarly, the death of pop artist Andy Warhol meant a decrease in the expected supply of his work; art dealers immediately raised prices to as much as three times what they had been only minutes earlier.

UNITARY ELASTIC SUPPLY. Any supply curve that can be represented as a ray from the origin—that is, a straight line from the origin, such as S'' in Exhibit 9(c)—is of **unitary elasticity**. This means that a percentage change in price will always result in an identical percentage change in quantity supplied. For example, along S'' a doubling of the price results in a doubling of the quantity supplied.

Determinants of Supply Elasticity

The elasticity of supply indicates how responsive producers are to a change in price. Their responsiveness depends on how easy or difficult it is to alter output as a result of a change in price. If the cost of supplying each additional unit rises sharply as output expands, then a higher price will not result in much of an increase in quantity supplied, so supply will tend to be inelastic. But if the additional cost rises slowly as output expands, the lure of a higher price will cause a large increase in output. In this case supply will tend to be more elastic.

Example Crop production would tend to rise more for a given price increase in countries where additional arable land is readily available than in countries where additional planting requires draining swampy land or irrigating dry land.

An important determinant of supply elasticity is the length of the adjustment period under consideration. Just as demand becomes more elastic over time as consumers adjust to price changes, supply also becomes more elastic over time as producers adjust to price changes. The longer the time period under consideration, the more able producers are to adjust to changes in relative prices. Exhibit 10 presents a different supply curve for each of three time periods. S_w is the supply curve when the period of adjustment is a week. As you can see, a higher price will not elicit much of a response in quantity supplied because firms have little time to adjust. Thus, such a supply curve will tend to slope steeply, reflecting inelastic supply.

S_m is the supply curve when the adjustment period under consideration is a month. In that time firms can more easily adjust the rate at which they employ some resources. As a result, firms have a greater ability to vary output. Thus, the supply curve is more elastic when the adjustment period is a month than when it is a week. The supply curve is still more elastic when the adjustment period is a year, as shown by S_y. In a year firms can vary most, if not all, inputs; if all inputs can be varied, then a higher price may draw new firms into the market. So a given price increase will elicit a greater response in quantity supplied. For example, if the price of oil increases, oil producers in the short run can try to pump more from existing wells, but in the long run they can try to discover more oil in the remote jungles of the Amazon or the stormy waters of the North Sea. Empirical estimates have confirmed the positive link between the price elasticity of supply and the length of the adjustment period. *The elasticity of supply is therefore greater the longer the period of adjustment.* Firms' ability to alter supply in response to price changes differs across industries. The response time will be slower for producers of electricity, oil, and timber than for real estate sales, video rentals, and lawn mowing.

Example In recent years, demand for digital pianos has been rising relative to demand for acoustic pianos. Yamaha Corp. has responded the most quickly and now dominates the U.S. market. Baldwin Piano and Organ Co. produces mostly acoustic pianos but is already planning significant increases in its digital piano production. Steinway and Sons is just looking into digital technology, and Kimball Pianos plans to stick solely to acoustic pianos. The supply of digital pianos will be more elastic in the long run as Baldwin and later Steinway develop capacity.

Now that you have been introduced to the elasticities of demand and supply, your understanding of elasticity will be reinforced by working through an example involving both demand and supply. In the next section we show the effects of a sales tax on equilibrium price and quantity, and we link these effects to elasticities.

EXHIBIT 10

Market Supply Becomes More Elastic Over Time

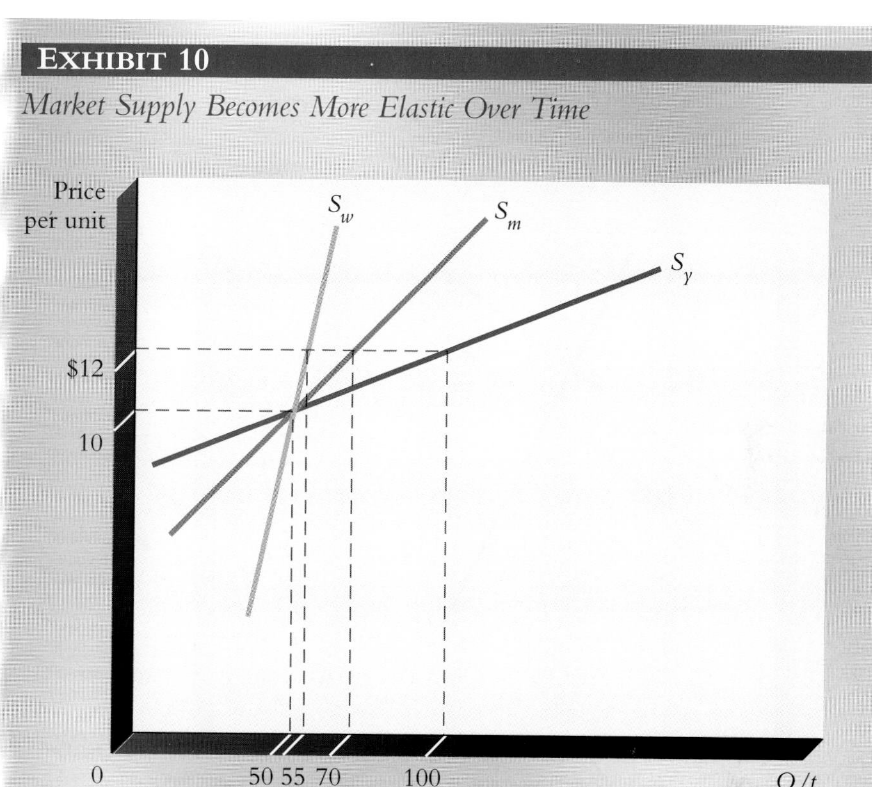

The supply curve one week after a price increase, S_w, is less elastic than the curve one month later, S_m, which is less elastic than the curve one year later, S_y. Given a price increase from $10 to $12, quantity supplied increases to 55 units after one week, to 70 units after one month, and to 100 units after one year.

ELASTICITY AND TAX INCIDENCE: AN APPLICATION

Suppose a tax of $0.20 is imposed on each pack of cigarettes sold. There is much confusion about who exactly pays the tax. Is it paid by producers or by consumers? As you will see, the *tax incidence*—that is, who ultimately pays the tax—depends on the elasticities of supply and demand.

Demand Elasticity and Tax Incidence

Panel (a) in Exhibit 11 depicts the supply, *S*, and demand, *D*, for cigarettes. Before the tax is imposed, the intersection of supply and demand yields an equilibrium price of $1 per pack and an equilibrium quantity of 10 million packs per day. Now suppose a tax of $0.20 is imposed on each pack of cigarettes sold. Recall that the supply curve represents the amount that producers

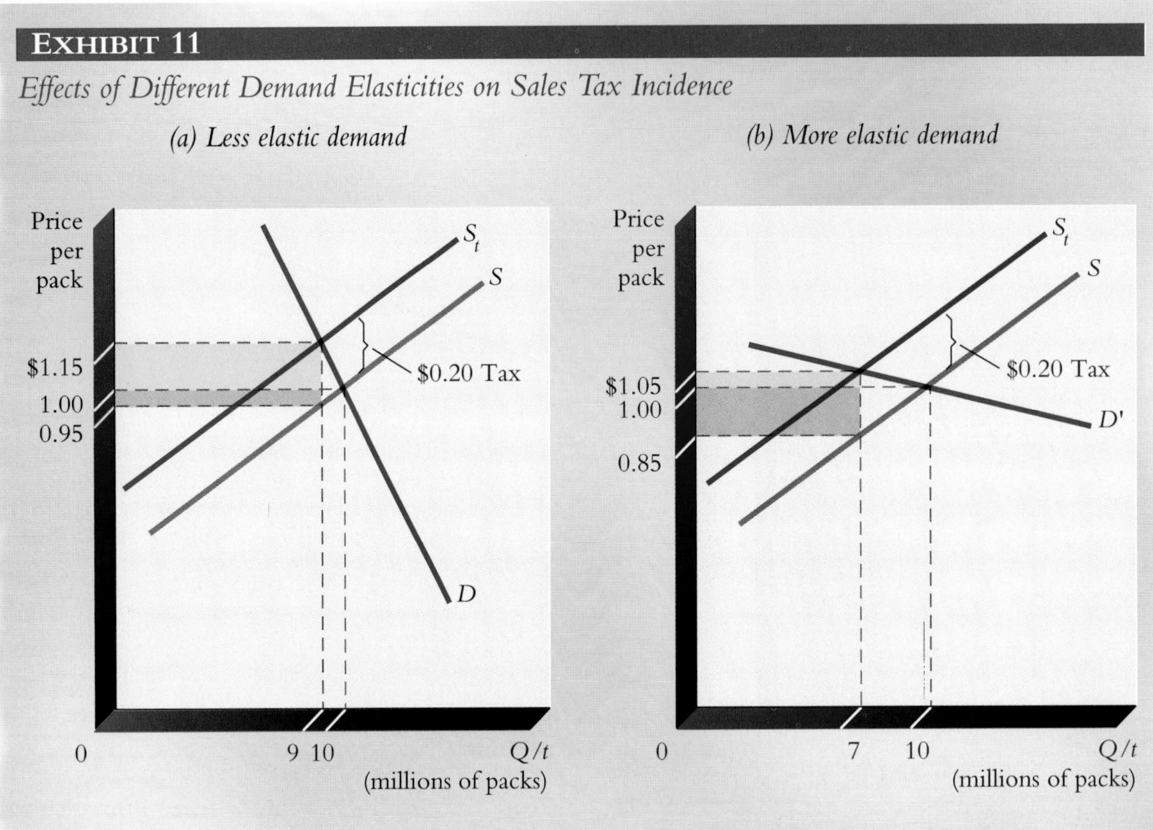

EXHIBIT 11

Effects of Different Demand Elasticities on Sales Tax Incidence

The imposition of a $0.20 per pack tax shifts the supply curve vertically from S to S_t. In panel (a), with less elastic demand, the market price rises from $1.00 to $1.15 per pack and the quantity demanded and supplied falls from 10 million packs to 9 million. In panel (b), with more elastic demand, the same tax leads to an increase in price from $1.00 to $1.05 per pack; the quantity demanded and supplied falls from 10 million packs to 7 million. The more elastic the demand, the more the tax is paid by producers in the form of a lower price net of taxes.

are willing and able to supply at each price. Since producers are now required to pay the government $0.20 for each pack of cigarettes they sell, the tax adds $0.20 to the supply price at each level of output, so the tax causes a $0.20 vertical shift in the supply curve, from S up to S_t. *The effect of the tax is to shift up the supply of cigarettes by the vertical amount of $0.20—the amount of the tax.* The demand curve remains the same since nothing has happened to the demand curve; only the quantity demanded will change.

Since suppliers are the ones who collect the tax for the government, they at first appear to be the ones who pay the tax. But let's take a closer look. The result of the tax in panel (a) is to raise the equilibrium price from $1.00 to $1.15 and to decrease the equilibrium quantity from 10 million to 9 million packs. As a result of the tax, consumers pay $1.15, or $0.15 more per pack, and the net-of-tax amount that producers receive is $0.95, or $0.05 less per

Teaching Tip Producers still require \$1.00 per pack to produce 10 million packs. Therefore, after the \$0.20 tax is imposed, the price *at 10 million* packs must rise to \$1.20 so producers retain \$1.00 after passing the tax on to the government. However, given the shapes of the demand and supply curves in Exhibit 11, a surplus occurs if the price rises all the way to \$1.20.

Point to Stress Although elasticity varies along a downward-sloping linear demand curve, the flatter slope of D' indicates greater elasticity when comparing the curves at the common starting point of \$1.00 and 10 million packs.

pack. Thus, \$0.15 of the \$0.20 tax is paid by consumers in the form of a higher price, and \$0.05 is paid by suppliers in the form of a reduction in the amount they receive per pack.

The shaded area represents the total taxes collected, which equal the tax per pack of \$0.20 times the 9 million packs sold, for a total of \$1.8 million. You can see that the original price line of \$1 divides the shaded area into two segments, representing the portion of the tax paid by consumers through a higher price (the lighter shading) and the portion paid by producers through a lower net price (the darker shading).

The same situation is depicted in panel (b) of Exhibit 11, with the single difference being that the demand curve, D', is more elastic than the demand curve in panel (a). In panel (b) consumers cut quantity demanded more sharply in response to a change in price, so the suppliers cannot as easily pass the tax along as a higher price. Hence, the price increases by only \$0.05, to \$1.05, and the net-of-tax receipts of producers decline by \$0.15 per pack, to \$0.85. Total tax revenues equal \$0.20 per pack times 7 million packs sold, or \$1.4 million. Again, the light blue rectangle depicts the portion of the total taxes paid by consumers through a higher price, and the dark blue rectangle depicts the portion of the total taxes paid by producers through a lower price net of taxes. Note that the amount by which the price increases and the amount by which the producers' net price declines must always sum to \$0.20, the amount of the tax per unit.

Thus, the tax is the difference between the price consumers pay and the price producers receive. More generally, as long as the supply curve slopes upward, *the more elastic the demand, the less the tax is passed on to consumers as a higher price and the more the tax is levied on producers, who receive a lower after-tax price for their product.* Also note that the amount sold falls more in panel (b) than in panel (a): other things constant, the total tax revenue is lower when demand is more elastic. Because tax revenue falls as demand elasticity increases, governments tend to tax those products, such as cigarettes and gasoline, for which demand is relatively inelastic.

Teaching Tip If demand is perfectly elastic or supply perfectly inelastic, the price does not rise, and the producers pay the entire tax. If demand is perfectly inelastic or supply perfectly elastic, the price rises by the full amount of the tax, so consumers pay the entire tax.

Supply Elasticity and Tax Incidence

The effect of the elasticity of supply on the tax incidence is shown in Exhibit 12. The supply curve in panel (a) is more elastic than the one in panel (b). In both panels the demand curve is the same and the supply curve shifts vertically by \$0.20 to reflect the \$0.20 tax per pack. Notice that in panel (a) the equilibrium price rises to \$1.15—a \$0.15 increase over the pretax price. But in panel (b) the price increases by only \$0.05. Thus, more of the tax is passed on to consumers in panel (a), where supply is more elastic, than in panel (b), where supply is less elastic. More generally, as long as the demand curve slopes downward, *the more elastic the supply, the more the tax is passed on to consumers and the less it is levied on producers.* We conclude that *the less elastic the demand and the more elastic the supply, the higher the proportion of the tax paid by consumers.*

EXHIBIT 12

Effects of Different Supply Elasticities on Sales Tax Incidence

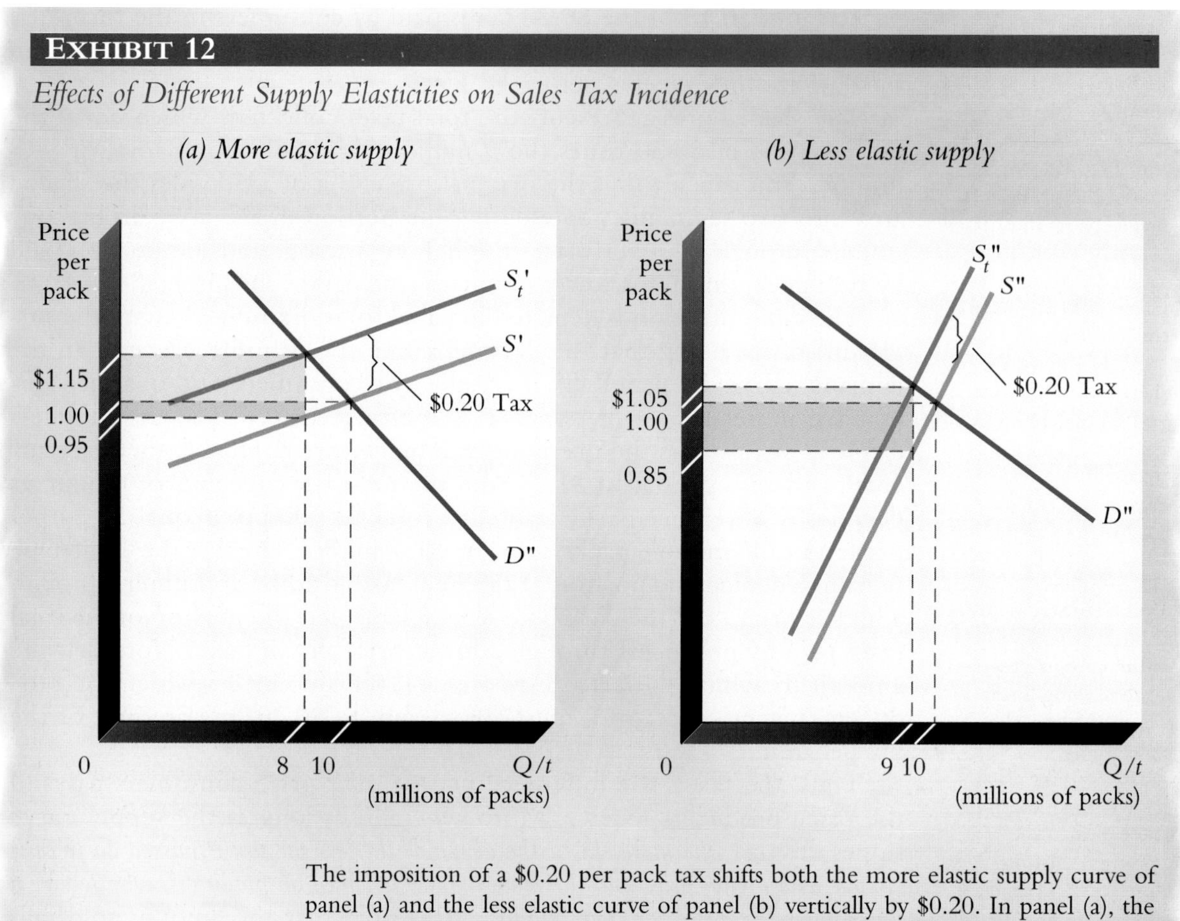

The imposition of a $0.20 per pack tax shifts both the more elastic supply curve of panel (a) and the less elastic curve of panel (b) vertically by $0.20. In panel (a), the market price rises from $1.00 per pack to $1.15; in panel (b), the price rises to $1.05 per pack. Thus, the more elastic the supply, the more the tax is paid by consumers.

OTHER ELASTICITY MEASURES

The price elasticities of demand and supply are frequently used in economic analysis, but other elasticities also provide useful information. The price elasticity of demand measures the responsiveness of the quantity of a particular product demanded to changes in its price, but we are also interested in how demand responds to other events, such as a change in consumer income or a change in the price of a related good.

Teaching Tip Indicate the different categories of income and cross-price elasticities along number lines ranging from negative to positive infinity.

Income Elasticity of Demand

What happens to the demand for new cars, garden supplies, or sweaters if consumer income increases by, say, 10 percent? The answer to this question is

Income elasticity of demand The percentage change in quantity demanded (holding the price constant) divided by the percentage change in income

Teaching Tip The value of income elasticity is determined using the midpoint formula

$$\frac{\frac{q'_D - q_D}{q'_D + q_D}}{\frac{I' - I}{I' + I}}$$

where I equals income. A value of −2 means that a 10-percent increase in income reduces the quantity demanded by 20 percent.

Example Normally, peanut butter sales rise during recessions as people replace higher-priced sandwich meats. However, a 1990–1991 drought doubled peanut prices in late 1990, so peanut butter prices rose substantially. As a result, peanut butter sales dropped during the 1991 recession year.

of great interest to producers of these and other goods because it allows them to predict the effect of rising incomes on unit sales and on total revenues. The **income elasticity of demand** measures how demand changes in response to a change in income, with prices held constant. Whereas the price elasticity of demand measures the sensitivity of a change in quantity demanded to a change in price along a given demand curve, *the income elasticity of demand measures the sensitivity of a change in demand to a change in income.* More specifically, the income elasticity of demand measures, at a given price, the percentage change in quantity demanded divided by the percentage change in income that caused it.

As noted in Chapter 3, the demand for some products, such as bus rides and laundromat services, actually declines as income increases. Thus, the value of the income elasticity of demand for such products will be negative. Goods with a value of income elasticity less than zero are called *inferior goods*. The demand for most goods increases as income increases. These goods are called *normal goods*, and they have an income elasticity greater than zero.

Let's take a closer look at normal goods. Sometimes demand increases with rising income but by a smaller percentage than that by which income increases. In such cases the value of income elasticity is greater than zero but less than 1. For example, people spend more on food as their incomes rise, but the percentage increase in spending is less than the percentage increase in income. Normal goods with a value of income elasticity less than 1 are said to be *income inelastic* and are sometimes called *necessities*. Goods with a value of income elasticity greater than 1 are said to be *income elastic* and are sometimes called *luxuries*, such as fine cars, meals at fancy restaurants, and ski vacations to the Swiss Alps. During 1990 and 1991 the U.S. economy experienced a recession, meaning that national income declined; as a result, the demand for meals at fancy restaurants declined, and some restaurants went out of business. During the same period, the demand for basic foods such as bread, sugar, and cheese changed very little. The terms *necessities* and *luxuries* are not meant to imply some value judgment about the merit of particular goods; they are simply convenient definitions economists use to classify economic behavior.

Exhibit 13 presents income elasticity estimates for various goods and services. The demands for major items such as private education, owner-occupied housing, automobiles, furniture, and dental care are income elastic, so these goods are considered luxuries. Products with a value of income elasticity less than 1 are necessities, such as food, physicians' services, gasoline, and rental housing. Thus, whereas restaurant meals are income elastic, more direct food purchases are inelastic. As income increases, spending at grocery stores increases less than spending at restaurants. Similarly, owner-occupied housing is income elastic but rental housing is inelastic, suggesting that as income rises the demand for rental housing rises less than the demand for owner-occupied housing. Flour is considered an inferior good because it has negative income elasticity. As income increases, consumers switch from home baking to purchasing baked goods. Exhibit 13 indicates that the demand for food is income inelastic. The demand for food also tends to be price inelastic. This combination of price and income inelasticities creates special problems in agricultural markets, as described in the following case study.

Teaching Tip Income elasticity of demand is important in determining how a firm's sales react to movements of the economy through the business cycle. Demand for automobiles and airline travel have high income elasticities. As a result, profits vary widely with income, and stock market prices of firms in those industries are cyclical, their values fall during recessions and rise during expansions.

EXHIBIT 13

Selected Income Elasticities of Demand

Product	Income Elasticity
Private education	2.46
Automobiles	2.45
Owner-occupied housing	1.49
Furniture	1.48
Dental services	1.42
Restaurant meals	1.40
Shoes	1.10
Clothing	1.02
Beer	0.93
Physicians' services	0.75
Food	0.51
Cigarettes	0.50
Gasoline and oil	0.48
Rental housing	0.43
Coffee	0.29
Flour	−0.36

Sources: T. F. Hogerty and K. G. Elzinga, "The Demand for Beer," *Review of Economics and Statistics* (May 1972); H. S. Houthakker and L. D. Taylor, *Consumer Demand in the United States: Analyses and Projections,* 2d ed. (Cambridge, MA: Harvard University Press, 1970); J. J. Hughes, "Note on the U.S. Demand for Coffee," *American Journal of Agricultural Economics* (November 1969); S. M. Sackrin, "Factors Affecting the Demand for Cigarettes," *Agricultural Economics Research* (July 1962); H. Wold and C. E. Leser, "Commodity Group Expenditure Functions for the United Kingdom, 1948–57," *Econometrica* (January 1961).

CASE STUDY

The Demand for Food and "The Farm Problem"

Teaching Tip The more price inelastic the demand for a good, the greater the price swings associated with a given change in supply.

Despite decades of federal support through various farm assistance programs, the number of farmers continues to drop. By the early 1990s, the United States had only 4.5 million farms, down from 23 million in 1950. The demise of the family farm can be traced to the price and income elasticities of demand for farm products and to technological breakthroughs that made larger farms more efficient.

Many of the forces that determine farm production are beyond the farmer's control. Temperature, rain, insects, and other external forces affect crop size and quality. For example, the summer of 1988 was hot and dry, cutting farm production sharply. These swings in production create special problems for farmers because the demand for most farm crops, such as milk, eggs, corn, potatoes, oats, sugar, and beef, is price inelastic.

The effect of an inelastic demand curve on farm revenue is illustrated in Exhibit 14. Farmers in a normal year supply 10 billion bushels of grain at a market price of $5 per bushel. Total revenue, which is price times quantity, comes to $50 billion in our hypothetical example. Suppose that more favorable growing conditions increase crop production to 11 billion bushels, an

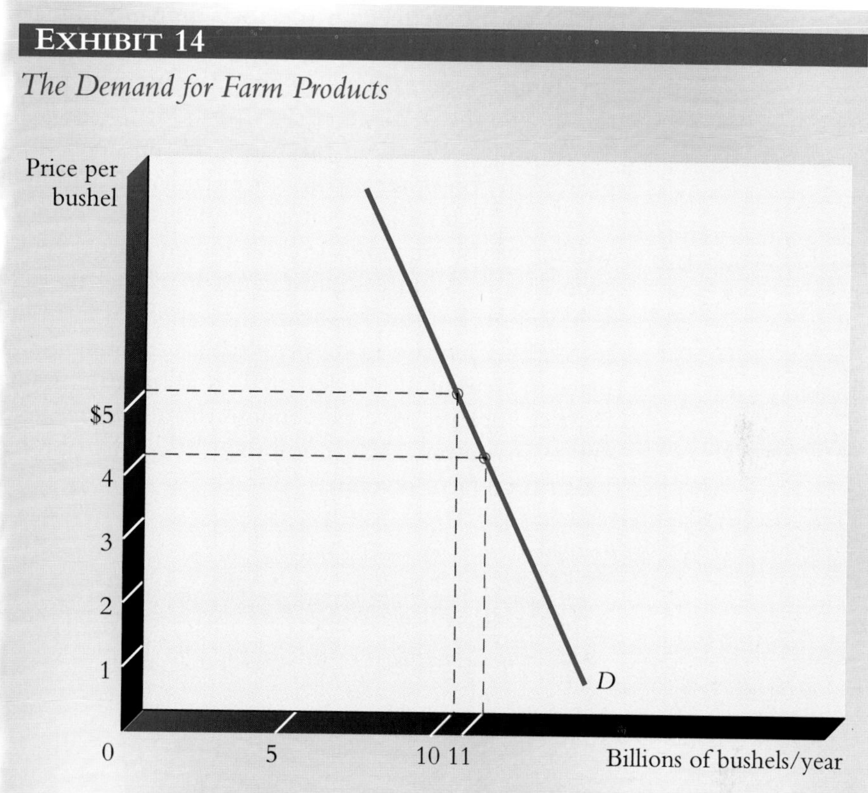

The demand for farm products tends to be price inelastic. As the market price falls, total revenue also falls.

increase of 10 percent. Because demand is price inelastic, the average price in our example must fall by more than 10 percent, say, to $4 per bushel, in order to clear the market of the additional billion bushels. Thus, the 10-percent increase in farm production can be sold only if the price drops by 20 percent.

Example In 1992, U.S. farmers experienced large increases in the corn, soybean, and wheat crops over 1991 levels. As a result, net farm income fell for the second straight year.

Because, in percentage terms, the drop in price exceeds the increase in output, total revenue declines—from $50 billion to $44 billion. So, farm revenue drops by over 10 percent, despite the 10-percent increase in production. *A demand curve that is price inelastic reverses the effect of changes in output on farm income, so that an increase in output reduces income.* Of course, the up side of an inelastic demand curve is that a lower-than-normal crop results in a proportionately higher price and a higher total revenue.

Weather-generated changes in farm production create substantial year-to-year swings in farm revenue. This problem is compounded in the long run by the fact that the demand for food tends to be *income inelastic.* People can eat only so much, and they do not eat much more in response to an increase in income. As their incomes increase, households may spend more to eat because they cook less and buy more prepared foods and more restaurant meals. But the switch from home cooking to packaged foods and restaurant meals has little effect on the total demand for farm products. Thus, as the economy grows over time and real incomes rise, the demand for farm products tends to increase by less than the increase in real income, as reflected by the shift in the demand curve from *D* to *D′* in Exhibit 15.

Although the demand for farm products has not kept up with the growth in consumer income over time, the supply has increased sharply because of technological improvements in production. Farm output per worker was seven times greater in the early 1990s than in 1950 because of such factors as more sophisticated machines, better fertilizers, and healthier seed strains. Exhibit 15 shows the supply of farm products increasing from *S* to *S′*. The increase in supply exceeds the increase in demand, so the relative price of farm products declined. And because the demand for farm products is price inelastic, the percentage drop in price exceeds the percentage increase in output. The combined effect in our hypothetical example is a lower total farm revenue.

EXHIBIT 15

The Effect of Increases in Supply and Demand on Farm Revenue

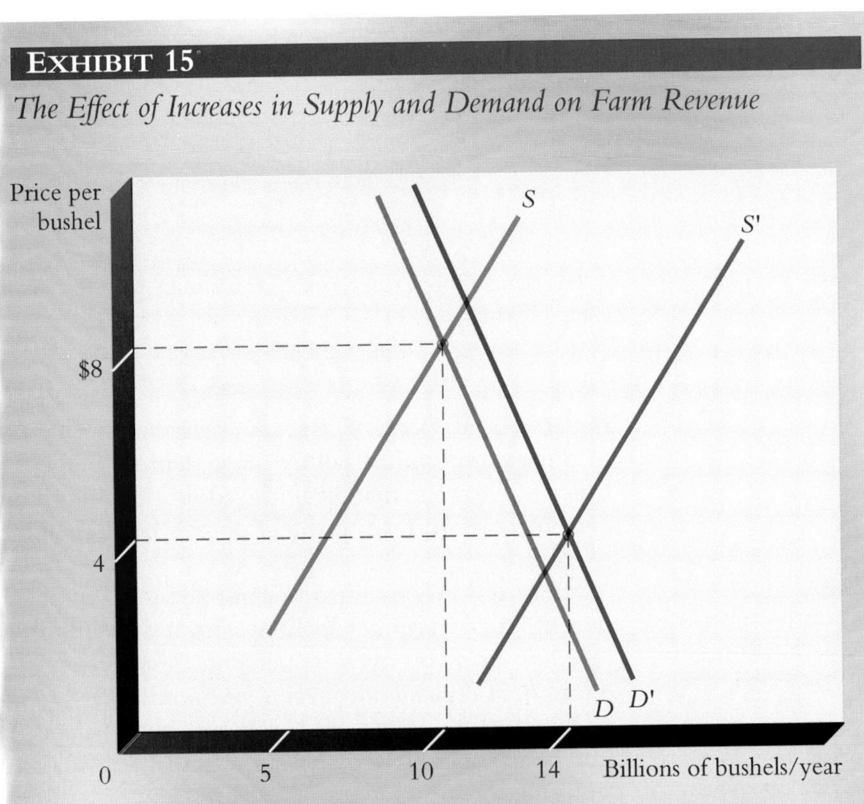

Over time, technological advances in farming have increased the supply of farm products sharply. In addition, increases in household income over time have increased the demand for farm products. But because increases in the supply of farm products have exceeded increases in demand, the combined effect has been a drop in the market prices and a fall in total farm revenue.

In fact, total farm income in the early 1990s in the United States, adjusted for inflation, was little more than half what it had been in the early 1950s. Although total farm income declined, the number of farmers declined even more, so income per farmer increased. Because the poorest farmers left the industry, the average income of remaining farm households now exceeds the average income of nonfarm households.

Example Wheat and corn sales to the former Soviet Union fell 33 percent in 1992.

Another wild card in the farm revenue equation is unstable foreign demand. Foreign demand for U.S. crops depends on foreign production and prices, on the exchange rate between the dollar and foreign currencies, and on public policy with regard to foreign trade. Farm exports have at times been caught up in foreign policy, as when President Carter placed an embargo on U.S. grain sales to what had been the Soviet Union. U.S. representatives are currently trying to resolve issues regarding agricultural trade with Europe. Thus, many of the forces shaping the market for farm products are beyond the farmer's control. And demand that is both price inelastic and income inelastic magnifies the effects of changes in farm output on total revenue.

Sources: Bruce L. Gardner, "Changing Economic Perspective on the Farm Problem," *Journal of Economic Literature*, Vol. 30 (March 1992): 62–105; and *Economic Report of the President*, 1992, Tables B-93 to B-98.

Cross-price elasticity of demand The percentage change in the quantity demanded of one good (holding the price constant) divided by the percentage change in the price of another good

Cross-Price Elasticity of Demand

The responsiveness of demand for one good to changes in the price of another good is called the **cross-price elasticity of demand**. It is defined as the percentage change in the quantity demanded of one good (holding the price constant) divided by the percentage change in price of another good. Its numerical value can be positive, negative, or zero, depending on whether the two goods in question are substitutes, complements, or unrelated.

Teaching Tip Knowledge of cross-price elasticities helps a firm predict the impact on its sales of the pricing behavior of competing firms. On the eve of unveiling its new line of low-cost personal computers in October 1992, IBM slashed its prices to counter an unexpected price cut by rival Compaq Computer Corp on its low-cost line.

SUBSTITUTES. If an increase in the price of one good leads to an increase in the demand for another good, the value of their cross-price elasticity is positive, and the goods are considered *substitutes*. For example, an increase in the price of Coke, other things constant, will increase the demand for Pepsi, reflecting the fact that the two are substitutes.

COMPLEMENTS. If an increase in the price of one good leads to a decrease in the demand for another good, the value of their cross-price elasticity is negative, and the goods are considered *complements*. For example, an increase in the price of gasoline, other things constant, will reduce the demand for tires because people will drive less and so will replace their tires less frequently. Gasoline and tires have a negative cross-price elasticity and are complements.

In summary, when the change in demand for one good has the same sign as the change in price of another good, the two goods are substitutes; when the change in demand for one good has the opposite sign from the change in price of another good, the goods are complements. Most pairs of goods selected at random are *unrelated*, so the value of their cross-price elasticity is zero.

CONCLUSION

Because this chapter has tended to be more quantitative than earlier chapters, you may have been preoccupied with the mechanics of the calculations and thus may have overlooked the intuitive appeal and the neat simplicity of the notion of elasticity. *An elasticity measure represents the willingness and ability of buyers and sellers to alter their behavior in response to a change in their economic circumstances.* For example, if the price of a good falls, consumers may be able but not willing to increase their consumption of the good. In this case the demand would be inelastic.

Firms try to estimate the price elasticity of demand for their products. Since a corporation often produces an entire line of products, it also has a special interest in certain cross-price elasticities. For example, the Coca-Cola Corporation needs to know how changing the price of Cherry Coke will affect sales of Classic Coke. Similarly, Procter and Gamble wants to know how changing the price of Safeguard soap will affect sales of Ivory soap. Governments, too, have an ongoing interest in various elasticities. For example, state governments want to know the effect of a 1-percent increase in the sales tax on total tax receipts, and local governments want to know how an increase in income will affect the demand for real estate and hence the revenue generated by a property tax. And international groups are interested in elasticities; for example, the Organization of Petroleum Exporting Countries (OPEC) is concerned about the price elasticity of demand for oil. Many questions can be answered by referring to particular elasticities; some corporate economists estimate elasticities for a living.

SUMMARY

1. The price elasticities of demand and supply indicate how sensitive buyers and sellers are to changes in the price. The greater the response, the greater the elasticity; the less the response, the smaller the elasticity. The price elasticity of demand equals the absolute value of the percentage change in quantity demanded divided by the percentage change in price. If the elasticity has a value of less than 1.0, demand is inelastic; if the value is greater than 1.0, demand is elastic; and if the value is equal to 1.0, demand is of unitary elasticity.

2. If demand is elastic, a price increase will reduce total revenue and a price decrease will increase total revenue. If demand is inelastic, a price increase will increase total revenue and a price decrease will reduce total revenue. And if demand is of unitary elasticity, a price change will leave total revenue unchanged.

3. The midpoint formula uses the average price and average quantity as the base values for computing percentage changes in price and quantity. Computing elasticities based on the midpoint formula ensures that the elasticity calculated between two points on a demand curve or a supply curve will be the same whether the price goes up or down.

4. Along a linear, or straight-line, demand curve, the elasticity of demand falls steadily as the price falls. Constant-elasticity demand curves have the same elasticity everywhere along the curve.

5. Several factors affect the price elasticity of demand. Demand will be more elastic (1) the greater the availability of substitutes and the more they resemble the good demanded, (2) the more narrowly the good is defined, (3) the larger the proportion of the

consumer's budget spent on the product, and (4) the longer the time available to adjust to a change in price.

6. We use the same kind of calculations and the same terminology for the price elasticity of supply as for the price elasticity of demand. If costs rise sharply as output expands, supply will be less elastic. Also, the longer the time period under consideration, the more elastic the supply.

7. The income elasticity of demand measures the responsiveness of demand to changes in consumer income. The income elasticity of demand is positive for normal goods and negative for inferior goods.

8. The cross-price elasticity of demand measures the responsiveness of demand to changes in the price of another product. Two goods are defined as substitutes, complements, or unrelated, depending on whether the value of their cross-price elasticity of demand is positive, negative, or equal to zero.

Questions and Problems

1. (Demand Elasticity) How is it possible for many elasticities to be associated with a single demand curve?

2. (Demand Elasticity) Suppose that a company is concerned only with maximizing its gross revenues. What pricing policy should it follow?

3. (Midpoint Elasticity) Suppose the initial price and quantity demanded of a good are $1 per unit and 50 units, respectively. A reduction in price to $0.20 results in an increase in quantity demanded to 70 units. Show that these data yield a midpoint elasticity of 0.25. A 10-percent rise in the price can be expected to reduce the quantity demanded by what percentage?

4. (Linear Demand and Elasticity) Must the elastic and inelastic sections of a linear demand curve always be of equal length? Why or why not?

5. (Perfectly Inelastic Demand) Why is it impossible for a demand curve to be perfectly inelastic for *all* prices? Consider very high and very low prices.

6. (Demand Elasticity Determinants) What happens to the elasticity of demand for automobile towing services during a large snowstorm? How might this change be different for low-income people and high-income people?

7. (Perfectly Inelastic Supply) Although Picasso paintings are technically in fixed supply, how might their availability be increased?

8. (Tax Incidence) Often it is claimed that a tax on the sale of a specific good will simply be passed on to consumers. What is necessary for this to happen? In what cases might very little of the tax be passed on to consumers?

9. (Cross-Price Elasticity) Rank the following in order of increasing cross-price elasticity (from negative to positive) with coffee:
   a. Mustard
   b. Tea
   c. Cream
   d. Cola

10. (Price Elasticity) Explain why the price elasticity of demand for Coke is greater than that for soft drinks generally. How would one define the price of soft drinks generally in this case?

11. (Elasticity) Fill in values for each point listed in the following table.

P	Q	*Price Elasticity*	*Total Spending*
$10	0	____	____
9	1	____	____
8	2	____	____
7	3	____	____
6	4	____	____
5	5	____	____
4	6	____	____
3	7	____	____
2	8	____	____
1	9	____	____
0	10	____	____

12. (Demand and Elasticity) Suppose that crime and spending on drugs are directly related (i.e., the level of crime increases as drug spending increases) and that the demand for drugs is inelastic. What would happen to the level of crime under each of the following anti-drug policies?
    a. Prosecute pushers only
    b. Prosecute users only
    c. Prosecute both

13. (Tax Incidence) Using supply and demand curves, show why the economic incidence of a sales tax is independent of the statutory incidence (i.e., who legally pays the tax).

14. (Taxes and Elasticity) Suppose a tax is imposed on a good that has a completely inelastic supply curve.
    a. Who pays the tax?
    b. Using supply and demand curves, show how much tax revenue is collected.
    c. How would this tax revenue change if the supply curve became more elastic?

15. (Income Elasticity) Calculate the income elasticity of demand for each of the following goods.

	Income = $10,000	*Income = $20,000*
Good 1	10	20
Good 2	4	5
Good 3	3	3

16. (Substitutes and Complements) Using supply and demand curves, predict the impact on the price and quantity of Good 1 (above) of an increase in the price of Good 2 if
    a. they are substitutes.
    b. they are complements.
    c. Good 2 is price inelastic.

17. (Tax Incidence) In Chapter 4 we defined a regressive tax as one structured so that the tax paid as a percentage of income decreases as income increases. If excise taxes were imposed on each of the goods listed in Exhibit 13, which of these would be regressive? Explain your answer.

18. (Price Elasticity) Suppose that you want to calculate the price elasticity of a linear demand curve at a point instead of over a discrete section of demand (for which the midpoint formula could be used). How would you do it?

19. (Tax Incidence) According to the text, the incidence of an excise tax (for buyers versus sellers) depends upon the relative sizes of the supply and demand elasticities. Can you think of any other people who might be hurt and therefore bear some of the tax burden, if such a tax were imposed? Explain.

20. (Price Elasticity) Suppose that you are hired by the city to set the price for a ticket on the city subway system. This system is characterized by a set of costs that are largely fixed and therefore independent of ridership. How would you determine the price of a subway ticket in order to maximize net revenues to the city?

21. (Cross-Price Elasticities) Suppose that the cross-price elasticity of compact disks to cassettes is 0.8. What would happen to the revenues to cassette producers if compact disk prices were increased by 10 percent, assuming that cassette prices did not change? Be specific in your answer.

Use the following diagram to answer the questions below.

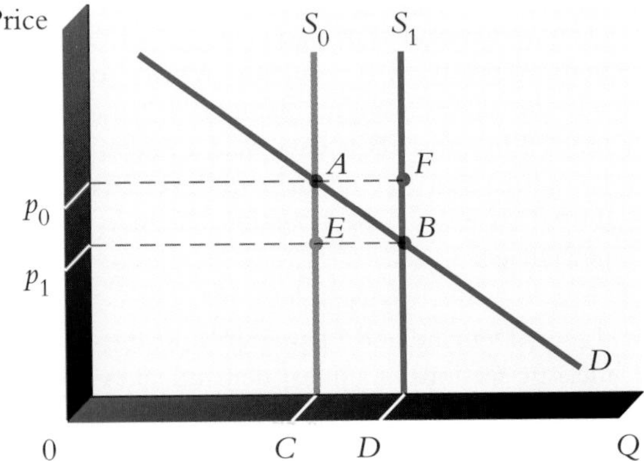

22. (The Farm Problem) Suppose that this diagram represents the supply and demand curves for the farm industry. Show on the diagram how you would determine the change in farm revenues that would occur when the supply increased from S_0 to S_1. If demand is inelastic, what must be true of the relative size of the geometric areas illustrating this change?

23. (The Farm Problem) Suppose that to aid farmers, government decided to stabilize prices at P_0 by buying up the surplus farm products. Show on the diagram how much this would cost the government. How much would farm income change from what it would have been without the government intervention?

CHAPTER 19

CONSUMER CHOICE AND DEMAND

Demand is a key building block in economics. You already learned two reasons why demand curves slope downward. The first is the substitution effect of a price change. When the price of a good falls, consumers substitute the now cheaper good for other goods that provide alternative ways of satisfying the same want. The second reason demand curves slope downward is the income effect of a price change. When the price of a good falls, the real incomes of consumers increase, so more of the good will be purchased as long as the good is normal.

Demand is so important that we need to know more about it. In this chapter we present another way to derive the law of demand, a way that focuses on the logic of consumer choice in a world of scarcity. First we will develop *utility analysis,* which we use to predict which goods and services will be consumed and in what quantities. The objective of this chapter is not to tell you how to maximize your utility but to help you understand more fully the economic implications of your behavior. You do not need a theory to tell you how to behave in a world of scarcity, but you do need a theory to understand your behavior in a world of scarcity. Topics discussed in this chapter include

Point to Stress The purpose of the mathematics in this chapter is not to teach a way to maximize utility but to build a model of a process that consumers already go through. The model can then be used to study the impact of price and income changes on consumer behavior.

- Total and marginal utility
- The law of diminishing marginal utility
- Measuring utility
- Utility-maximizing conditions
- Consumer surplus
- The role of time in demand

UTILITY ANALYSIS

Teaching Tip Utility analysis assumes that *all* goods are comparable and that consumers are capable of ranking preferences in a consistent fashion.

Teaching Tip You can distinguish between *goods,* of which more is preferred to less, and *bads,* of which less is preferred to more. In Exhibit 1, water becomes a bad after four glasses.

Tastes A consumer's attitudes toward and preferences for different goods and services

Suppose you and a friend dine together. If, after dinner, your friend asks how you enjoyed your meal, you might say, "It was delicious" or "I liked it better than my last meal here." You would not say, "It deserves a rating of 86 on the standard satisfaction index." Nor would you say, "I liked mine twice as much as you liked yours." The utility, or satisfaction, you derived from that meal cannot be measured objectively. You cannot give your meal an 86 satisfaction rating and your friend's meal a 43. Each of us can tell whether one personal experience is more satisfying than another, but we cannot make comparisons across individuals. What we *can* do is to infer from behavior that a person likes apples more than oranges if, when the two are priced the same, that person always buys apples.

Tastes and Preferences

As mentioned in Chapter 4, *utility* is the sense of pleasure or satisfaction that comes from consumption. Utility is subjective. The utility you derive from consuming a particular good depends on your **tastes**, which are your attitudes toward and preferences for different goods and services—your likes and dislikes in consumption. Some goods are extremely appealing to you, and others are not. You may not understand, for example, why someone would pay good money for raw oysters, chicken livers, or country music. Economists have little to say about the origin of tastes—why, for example, some people like raw oysters and some do not. *Economists assume simply that tastes are given and are relatively stable—that is, tastes are not changing all the time.* Tastes are considered in the following case study.

CASE STUDY

Study Some Reflections of Tastes

Although we know little about the origin of tastes and preferences, some people are obviously influenced by the consumption behavior of others. The typical consumer may look to supposedly more knowledgeable consumers for advice. Young athletes may want to wear the same brand of athletic shoes as Michael Jordan or use the same tennis racket as Steffi Graf. Manufacturers understand this and are willing to pay large sums for product endorsements. Rolex, for example, offers its $5,000 watch free to trendsetters just so that others will notice that famous people wear that brand.

The other side of the coin is that some people apparently derive utility from advertising their own consumption choices, even to the point of wearing the label on the outside. Thorstein Veblen (1857–1929) argued that those who accumulate wealth want to display their acquisitions as a form of *conspicuous consumption.* The public display of designer jeans, Gucci handbags, $150 Reeboks, and the ultimate driving machine suggests that the utility of some products is linked to public recognition of one's supposedly superior consumer choices.

Tastes are relatively stable, but some tastes seem to evolve over time, often from generation to generation. The clothing styles of one generation sometimes seem comical to the next. After skipping a generation, however, some styles return to popularity. The rock stars of one generation are often has-beens to the next. Tastes evolve in a variety of consumer sectors, including restaurants, movies, TV shows, automobiles, and architecture—to name a few areas. Although tastes appear to evolve over time, we can still consider tastes as given and relatively stable for the period of analysis under consideration.

The Law of Diminishing Marginal Utility

Imagine that it is a hot day. You have just mowed the lawn and are extremely thirsty. You pour yourself a glass of cold water. That first glass is wonderful, and it puts a serious dent in your thirst; the next one is not quite as wonderful, but it is still pretty good; the third is just fair; and the fourth glass you barely finish. Let's talk about the *utility,* or satisfaction, you get from consuming water.

Total utility The total satisfaction a consumer derives from consumption

Marginal utility The change in total utility derived from a one-unit change in consumption of a good

Law of diminishing marginal utility The more of a good consumed per period, the smaller the increase in total utility from consuming one more unit, other things constant

Point to Stress Total utility is a function of the total quantities of all n goods consumed: $TU = f(q_1, q_2, \ldots, q_n)$. Marginal utility is the change in total utility that results from varying consumption of *one* good i by small amounts while holding other consumption constant: $MU = \Delta TU / \Delta q_i$.

We distinguish between total utility and marginal utility. **Total utility** is total satisfaction a consumer derives from consuming the good. For example, when you drink four glasses of water, total utility is the total satisfaction you derive from your consumption of that water. **Marginal utility** is the change in total utility resulting from a one-unit change in consumption of a good. For example, the marginal utility of the third glass of water is the change in total utility resulting from consuming that third glass of water; put another way, the marginal utility is the total utility from consuming three glasses of water minus the total utility of consuming two glasses of water.

Your experience with the water reflects a basic principle of utility analysis: the **law of diminishing marginal utility**. This law states that the more of a good an individual consumes per time period, other things constant, the smaller the increase in total utility—that is, the smaller the marginal utility of each additional unit consumed. The marginal utility you derive from each glass of water declines as your rate of consumption increases. You enjoy the first glass a lot, but each additional glass provides less and less marginal utility. If someone forced you to drink a fifth glass, you probably would not enjoy it; your marginal utility from a fifth glass would likely be negative.

Diminishing marginal utility is a feature of all consumption. A second Big Mac may provide some marginal utility, but the marginal utility of a third one during the same meal would be slight or even negative. You may still enjoy a second video movie on Friday night, but a third and fourth video get a bit numbing. That first Vat O' Slurpee may be just what you needed on a hot day, but a second one is too much. Marginal utility does not always decline right away or very quickly. For example, you may eat many potato chips before the marginal utility of additional chips begins to fall. After a long winter, that first warm day of spring is something special and is the cause of "spring fever." The fever is cured, however, by many warm days like the first. By the time August arrives, people attach much less marginal utility to yet another warm day. For some goods the drop in marginal utility with additional consumption is more dramatic. A second copy of the same daily newspaper would likely provide you with no marginal utility (in fact, the design of newspaper vending machines relies on the fact that you will not want to take more than one paper). Likewise, a second viewing of the same movie at one sitting often yields no additional utility.

MEASURING UTILITY

Example A 1992 survey asked people if they would be willing to give up watching television entirely for $1,000,000. Such a choice would be based on the total utility of television viewing. However, real choices are usually based on marginal utilities—for example, watching a little less or a little more television.

So far our descriptions of utility have used such words as "wonderful," "good," and "fair." We cannot push the analysis of utility very far if we are limited to such subjective language. If we want to predict behavior based on changes in the economic environment, we must develop a consistent way of viewing utility.

Units of Utility

Let's go back to the water example. Although there really is no objective way of measuring utility, if pressed you might be able to be more specific about how much you enjoyed each glass of water. For example, you might say the first glass was twice as good as the second, the second was twice as good as the third, the third was twice as good as the fourth, but a fifth glass would have been a pain to finish. Let's assign arbitrary numbers to the amount of utility from each quantity consumed, such that the pattern of numbers matches the pattern of your satisfaction.

To be more specific, suppose we talk in terms of units of utility. Let's say the first glass of water provides you with 40 units of utility, the second glass yields 20, the third yields 10, and the fourth yields 5. A fifth glass would yield negative utility, in this case measured specifically as −2 units of utility. *Developing numerical values for utility allows us to be more specific in attaching relative weights to the utility derived from consumption.* More generally, units of utility measure pleasure, or satisfaction.

You could think of units of utility more playfully as kicks, thrills, yayas, or jollies—as in, getting your jollies from consumption. By attaching a numerical measure to utility, we can compare the total utility a particular consumer receives from different goods as well as the marginal utility the consumer derives from additional consumption of the same good. Thus, we can employ units of utility to evaluate a consumer's preferences for various goods. Note, however, that we cannot compare units of utility across consumers. *Each individual has a uniquely subjective utility scale.*

Point to Stress As long as total utility is rising, marginal utility is positive (although it may be declining if diminishing marginal utility has set in). Marginal utility becomes negative when total utility is falling.

The first column of Exhibit 1 lists possible quantities of water you might consume after mowing the lawn; the second column presents the total utility derived from that consumption; and the third column shows the marginal utility of each additional glass of water consumed. Marginal utility, recall, is

EXHIBIT 1

Utility You Derive from Water After Mowing the Lawn

Units of Water Consumed (8-ounce glass) (q)	Total Utility (TU)	Marginal Utility $\left(MU = \frac{\Delta TU}{\Delta q}\right)$
0	0	—
1	40	40
2	60	20
3	70	10
4	75	5
5	73	−2

the change in total utility that results from consuming an additional unit of the good. You can see from the second column that total utility increases with each of the first four glasses, but by smaller and smaller amounts. The third column shows that the first glass of water yields you 40 units of utility, the second glass yields 20 units, and so on. Marginal utility declines after the first glass of water, becoming negative with the fifth glass. Total utility is the sum of the marginal utilities; it is graphed in panel (a) of Exhibit 2. Again, because of diminishing marginal utility, each glass adds less and less to total utility, so total utility increases but at a decreasing rate. Marginal utility is presented in panel (b).

Point to Stress Consumers maximize total utility subject to cost—that is, they must consider prices and income as well as tastes.

Utility Maximization in a World Without Scarcity

Economists assume that your objective in the consumption of water, as in all consumption, is to *maximize total utility.* So how much water do you consume? If the price of water is zero, you drink water as long as each additional glass increases total utility, which means you consume four glasses of water. *So when a good is free, you increase consumption as long as additional units provide positive marginal utility.*

Example Prior to 1961, Boulder, Colorado charged a flat monthly rate for residential water use. The price of water was thus zero at the margin. A study of "ideal" water use versus actual water use for lawn sprinkling revealed that actual water use ranged from 128 percent to 177 percent of ideal use over the routes monitored. (Steve Hanke, "Demand for Water Under Dynamic Conditions," *Water Resources Research,* October, 1970.)

Let's extend the analysis of utility to a world where you have only two goods from which to choose: food and clothing. We will continue to translate the relative satisfaction you receive from consumption into units of utility. Suppose the total utility and the marginal utility for alternative rates of consumption of these goods, given your tastes and preferences, are as presented in Exhibit 3. You can see from columns (3) and (7) that both goods exhibit diminishing marginal utility. Given this set of preferences, how much of each good will you consume? That depends on the prices of the goods and your income. Without scarcity, the price of each good would be zero and you would increase consumption as long as you derived positive marginal utility from additional units of each good. Thus, in a world without scarcity you would consume at least the first six units of each good because both

EXHIBIT 2

Total Utility and Marginal Utility You Derive from Water After Mowing the Lawn

(a) Total utility

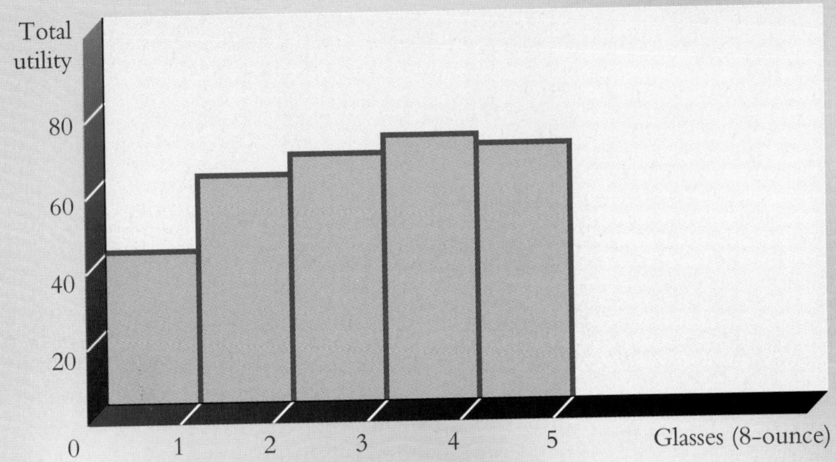

(b) Marginal utility

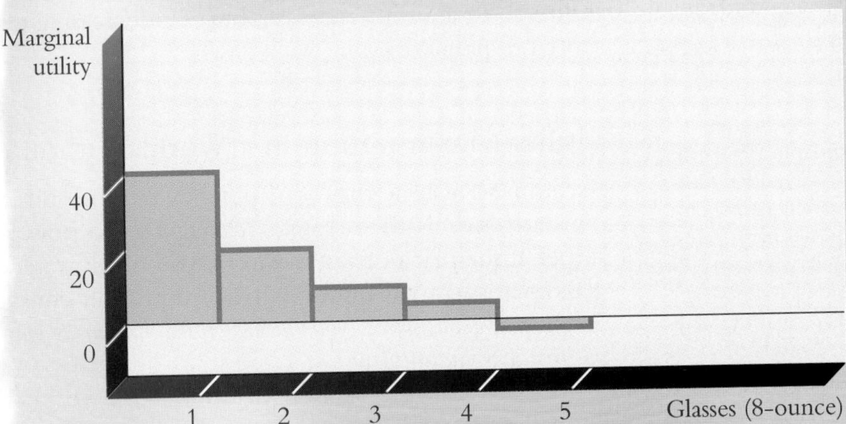

Total utility increases with each of the first four glasses of water consumed (panel a), but by smaller and smaller amounts (panel b). The fifth glass causes total utility to fall, implying that marginal utility is negative in panel (b).

EXHIBIT 3

Total and Marginal Utility from Food and Clothing

Units of Food Consumed per Period (1)	Total Utility of Food (2)	Marginal Utility of Food (3)	Marginal Utility of Food per Dollar Expended (price = $4) (4)	Units of Clothing per Period (5)	Total Utility of Clothing (6)	Marginal Utility of Clothing (7)	Marginal Utility of Clothing per Dollar Expended (price = $2) (8)
0	0	—	—	0	0	—	—
1	25	25	6.25	1	20	20	10.00
2	41	16	4.00	2	34	14	7.00
3	53	12	3.00	3	44	10	5.00
4	62	9	2.25	4	50	6	3.00
5	68	6	1.50	5	54	4	2.00
6	72	4	1.00	6	57	3	1.50

Teaching Tip Exhibit 3 can also be used to determine the impact of a change in income. If the consumer's budget increases to $32 with no change in prices, for example, the new consumer equilibrium shifts to 5 units of food and 6 units of clothing. Both demand curves shift to the right.

goods generate positive marginal utility at that level of consumption. Did you ever go to a party where the food and drinks were free? How much did you eat and drink? You probably ate and drank until you didn't want any more—that is, until the marginal utility of each good consumed declined to zero.

Utility Maximization in a World of Scarcity

Alas, scarcity is our lot, so we should focus on how a consumer chooses in a world shaped by scarcity. To make our example more realistic, suppose the price of food is $4 per unit, the price of clothing is $2 per unit, and your income is $20 per period. Under these conditions, the utility you receive from different goods relative to their prices determines how you allocate your income.

How do you allocate income between the two goods so as to maximize utility? Suppose you start off with some bundle of food and clothing. If you can increase your utility by reallocating expenditures, you will do so, and you will continue to make adjustments as long as you can increase your utility. There may be some trial and error involved in your consumption decision at first, but as you learn from your mistakes you move toward the utility-maximizing position. When no further utility-increasing moves are possible, you have settled on the bundle that maximizes your utility given the prices and your budget; you have arrived at the equilibrium combination. Once you reach this equilibrium, you will maintain this consumption pattern. You have no reason to choose differently unless there is a change in one of the factors that influence your demand, such as your income, relative prices, or your tastes.

Teaching Tip The text's simplified model assumes that consumption of food does not affect the marginal utility from consuming clothing and vice versa. That is, the total utility function is additive:

$$TU = f(q_F + q_C).$$

Teaching Tip When the price at the margin exceeds zero, equilibrium is reached before marginal utility falls to zero.

Example As reported in the Boulder study, the city switched to metered rates for water in 1961. The ratio of actual to ideal lawn sprinkling dropped to a range of 63 percent to 105 percent along the monitored routes, and lawns became browner.

Teaching Tip With a different starting point of 6 units of clothing and 2 units of food, total spending equals the $20 budget and total utility equals 98 units. When clothing consumption drops to 4 units, food consumption can rise to 3 units, and total utility rises to 103 units.

Consumer equilibrium The condition in which an individual consumer's budget is completely exhausted and the last dollar spent on each good yields the same marginal utility

To get the allocation process rolling, suppose you start off spending your entire budget of $20 on food, purchasing 5 units, which yield a total utility of 68 per period. You soon realize that if you reduce food consumption by 1 unit, you can buy the first 2 units of clothing. You thus give up 6 units of utility, the marginal utility of the fifth unit of food, but you gain a total of 34 units of utility from the first 2 units of clothing. Total utility thereby increases from 68 to 96 units of utility per period. Then you notice that if you reduce your food consumption to 3 units, you give up 9 units of utility from the fourth unit of food but gain 16 units of utility from the third and fourth units of clothing. This is another utility-increasing move. Further reductions in food, however, would reduce your total utility because you would give up 12 units of utility from the third unit of food but gain only 7 units of utility from the fifth and sixth units of clothing. Thus, by trial and error, you find that the utility-maximizing equilibrium is to consume 3 units of food and 4 units of clothing, for a total utility of 103. This involves an outlay of $12 on food and $8 on clothing. *You are in equilibrium when consuming this bundle because any change would only lower your total utility.*

THE UTILITY-MAXIMIZING CONDITIONS. When a consumer is in equilibrium, there is no way to increase utility by reallocating the budget. In fact, as you can see from the previous example, once equilibrium has been achieved, any shift in spending from one good to another will decrease utility. We will now examine a special property of the utility-maximizing combination: in equilibrium the last dollar spent on each good yields the same utility. More specifically, *utility is maximized when the marginal utility of a good divided by its price is identical for the last unit of each good purchased.* If this were not so, you could always reallocate your budget to increase your total utility. Let's see how this works.

Columns (4) and (8) in Exhibit 3 indicate the marginal utility of each dollar's worth of food and clothing. Column (4) is derived by dividing the marginal utility of food by the price of food, which is $4. Column (8) is derived the same way, using the marginal utility of clothing and its price of $2. You can see that the equilibrium choice of 3 units of food and 4 units of clothing yields 3 units of utility for the last dollar spent on either good. **Consumer equilibrium** is achieved when the budget is exhausted and the last dollar spent on each good yields the same utility, or

$$\frac{\mathbf{MU_F}}{p_F} = \frac{\mathbf{MU_C}}{p_C}$$

where MU_F is the marginal utility of the last unit of food consumed, p_F is the price of food, MU_C is the marginal utility of the last unit of clothing consumed, and p_C is the price of clothing. If food yields a lower marginal utility per dollar than does clothing, total utility can be increased by reducing food purchases and increasing clothing purchases. For example, if you allocated your budget to 4 units of food and 2 units of clothing, then the last dollar spent on food would yield 2.25 units of utility whereas the last dollar spent

Point to Stress Consumer equilibrium is reached when the per-dollar marginal utilities are equal at a point *where the budget is exhausted.* In Exhibit 3, for example, the per-dollar marginal utilities match for 5 units of food and 6 units of clothing. However, that consumption bundle would cost $32, exceeding the $20 budget. If the per-dollar marginal utilities could be equal at a consumption bundle costing less than $20, the consumer could still increase total utility by increasing consumption.

Teaching Tip Saving can be included as a good by attaching marginal utilities to each dollar saved.

Teaching Tip The need for higher-priced goods to yield higher marginal utilities can be emphasized by rearranging the equilibrium equation as

$$\frac{MU_F}{MU_C} = \frac{p_F}{p_C}$$

Teaching Tip The $3 left over in the budget if the initial consumption bundle is maintained represents the income effect of a price change introduced in Chapter 3.

on clothing would yield 7 units of utility. By reducing your food consumption by 1 unit and increasing your clothing consumption by 2 units, your total utility increases from 96 to 103 and the last dollar spent on food yields 3 units of utility as does the last dollar spent on clothing.

Although we have considered only two goods, the logic of utility maximization applies to any number of goods. The consumer reallocates spending until the last dollar spent on each product yields the same utility. The consumer maximizes utility by equating the ratios of marginal utility of each good consumed to the price of each good. *In equilibrium, higher-priced goods must yield more utility than lower-priced goods—enough additional utility to compensate for their higher price.* In our example, since food costs twice as much as clothing, the marginal utility of the final unit of food consumed must, in equilibrium, be twice that of the final unit of clothing consumed; in fact, 12 units of utility, the marginal utility of the third unit of food, is twice as much as 6 units of utility, the marginal utility of the fourth unit of clothing. Economists do not claim that you consciously equate the ratios of marginal utility to price, but economists do claim that you act as if you made such calculations. *Thus, you decide how much of each good to purchase by considering your relative preferences for the alternative goods, the prices of the alternative goods, and your income.*

Deriving the Law of Demand from Marginal Utility

The purpose of utility analysis is to provide information about the demand curve. How does the previous analysis relate to your demand for food? It yields a single point on your demand curve for food: at a price of $4 per unit, you will demand 3 units per period. This point on the demand curve for food is based on a given income of $20 per period, a given price for clothing of $2 per unit, and the tastes reflected in your utility schedules.

This single point, however, gives us no idea about the shape of your demand curve. To generate another point, let's change the price of food, keep other things constant, and see what happens to the quantity demanded. Suppose the price of food drops from $4 to $3 per unit. What will happen to your consumption decision, given the preferences already outlined in the discussion of Exhibit 3? Exhibit 4 is the same as Exhibit 3 except the price of food has been changed from $4 to $3 per unit. Your original consumption choice was 3 units of food and 4 units of clothing. At that combination, the marginal utility per dollar expended on the third unit of food is 4 but the marginal utility per dollar spent on the fourth unit of clothing is 3. The marginal utility of the last dollar spent on each good is no longer equal across goods. What's more, if you maintained the original combination of food and clothing, you would have $3 left over in your budget because you would be spending only $9 on food. You can increase your utility by consuming a different bundle.

In light of your utility schedules in Exhibit 4, you would increase your consumption of food to 4 units per period. This increase exhausts your budget and equates the marginal utility of the last dollar expended on each good. Your consumption of clothing in this example remains the same (though it could have changed due to the income effect of a price change).

EXHIBIT 4

Total and Marginal Utility from Food and Clothing After Price of Food Decreases from $4 to $3

Units of Food Consumed per Period (1)	Total Utility of Food (2)	Marginal Utility of Food (3)	Marginal Utility of Food per Dollar Expended (price = $3) (4)	Units of Clothing per Period (5)	Total Utility of Clothing (6)	Marginal Utility of Clothing (7)	Marginal Utility of Clothing per Dollar Expended (price = $2) (8)
0	0	—	—	0	0	—	—
1	25	25	8.33	1	20	20	10.00
2	41	16	5.33	2	34	14	7.00
3	53	12	4.00	3	44	10	5.00
4	62	9	3.00	4	50	6	3.00
5	68	6	2.00	5	54	4	2.00
6	72	4	1.33	6	57	3	1.50

But as your consumption of food increases to 4 units, the marginal utility of the fourth unit, 9, divided by the price of $3 yields 3 units of utility per dollar of expenditure, which is the same as for the fourth unit of clothing. You are in equilibrium once again. Your total utility increases by the 9 units of utility you receive from the fourth unit of food; hence, you are clearly better off as a result of the price decrease.

Teaching Tip Lower prices are required to justify buying goods with lower marginal utilities. The behavior of marginal utility determines the price elasticity of demand. The more rapidly marginal utility changes as consumption varies, the smaller the changes in quantity that are needed to return to equilibrium after a given price change—that is, the smaller the coefficient of elasticity.

We now have a second point on your demand curve for food; the two points are presented as *a* and *b* in Exhibit 5. We could continue to change the price of food and thereby generate additional points on the demand curve, but we get some idea of the demand curve's slope from these two points. The shape of the demand curve for food conforms to our expectations based on the law of demand: price and quantity demanded are inversely related. (Try to determine the price elasticity of demand between points *a* and *b*.)

Even animals behave in a way that is consistent with the law of demand. Experiments have been carried out with a variety of animals who must perform specific tasks in exchange for a portion of food or drink. The prices are determined by the tasks performed. Relative prices are then changed by varying the amount of "work" required per portion. Experiments show that animals consume relatively more of a good when its relative price falls. For example, in one experiment the "price" of cherry cola relative to the "price" of root beer was determined by the number of times a white rat had to press a lever. When the "price" of cherry cola became relatively cheaper, the quantity of cherry cola demanded increased.[1]

1. See J. Kagel, R. Battalio, L. Green, and H. Rachlin, "Consumer Demand Theory Applies to Choice Behavior of Rats," in *Limits to Action: The Allocation of Individual Behavior,* J. E. R. Staddon, ed. (New York: Academic Press, 1980), Chapter 8.

EXHIBIT 5

Demand for Food Generated from Marginal Utility

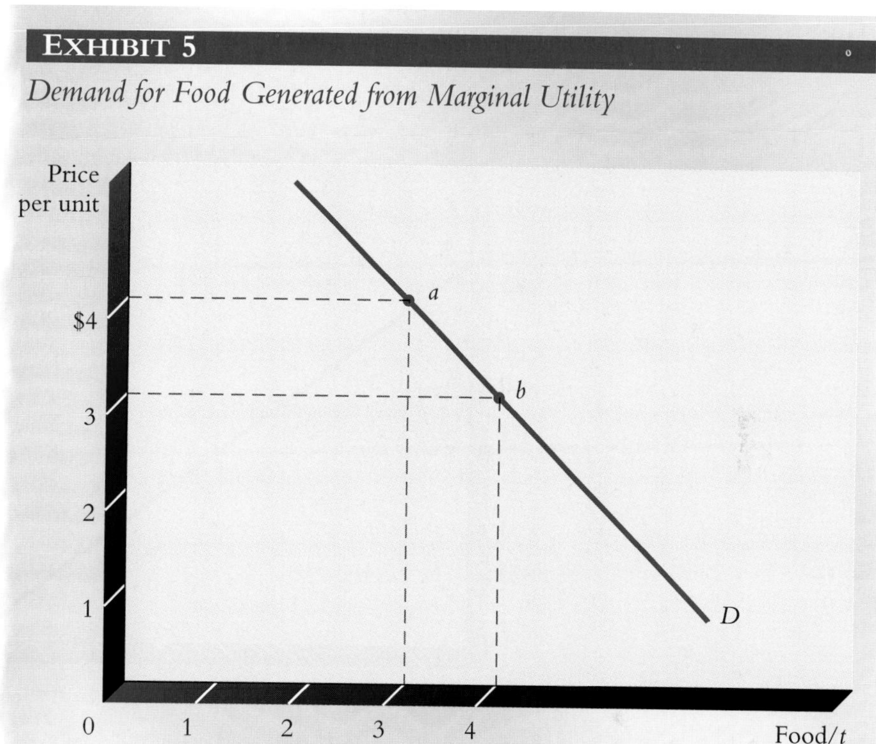

At a price of $4 per unit of food, the consumer is in equilibrium when consuming 3 units of food (point *a*). Marginal utility per dollar is the same for all goods consumed. If the price falls to $3, the consumer will increase consumption to 4 units of food (point *b*). Points *a* and *b* are two points on this consumer's demand curve for food.

We have gone to some length to explain how you (or any consumer) maximize utility. Using a subjective measure of utility, we determined the marginal utility you derived from additional units of the good. This allowed us to construct the tables in Exhibit 3 and Exhibit 4 in order to analyze your consumption choices. In reality, you do not need to perform such calculations, at least not explicitly. Your tastes and preferences will naturally guide you to the most preferred bundle, given your income and the relative prices of goods and services. You are probably not even conscious of your behavior. The urge to maximize utility is like the force of gravity: both work whether or not you understand them. Now that you have some idea of utility, let's consider an application of utility analysis.

Point to Stress The consumer can and does make mistakes. The movement to equilibrium is not instantaneous.

Consumer Surplus

In our example, total utility increased when the price fell from $4 to $3. In this section we take a closer look at how consumers benefit from a lower price. Suppose your demand for pizza is as shown in Exhibit 6, which measures on

EXHIBIT 6

Consumer Surplus

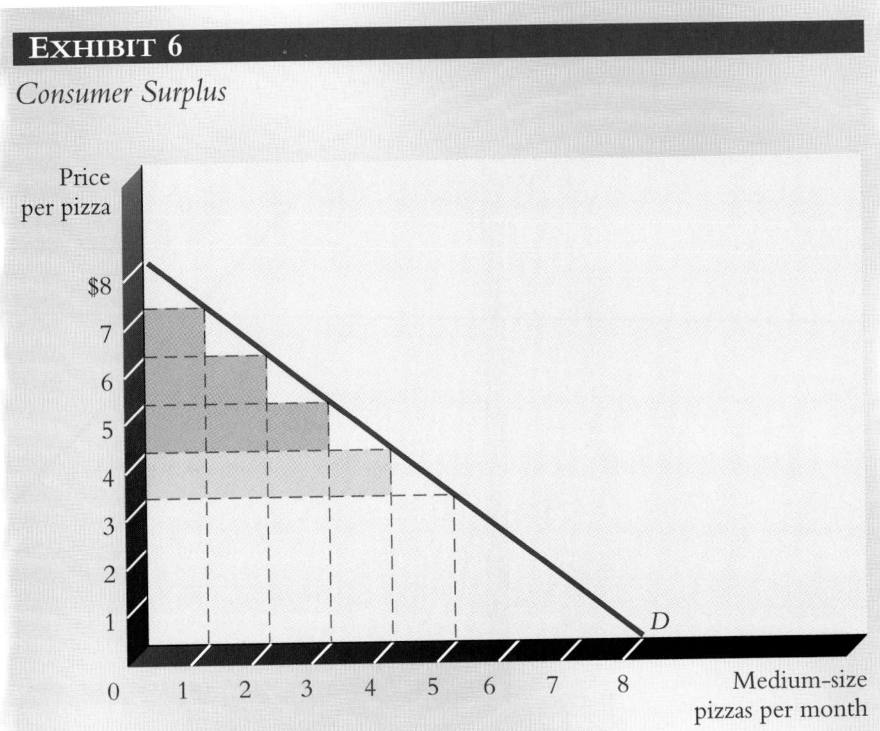

At a given quantity of pizza, the height of the demand curve shows the value of the last unit purchased. The area under the demand curve up to a specific quantity shows the total value the consumer places on that quantity. At a price of $4, the consumer purchases four pizzas. The first pizza is valued at $7, the second at $6, the third at $5, and the fourth at $4; the consumer values four pizzas at $22. Since the consumer pays $4 per pizza, all four can be obtained for $16. The difference between what the consumer would have been willing to pay ($22) and what the consumer actually pays ($16) is called consumer surplus. When the price is $4, the consumer surplus is represented by the dark shaded area under the demand curve above $4. When the price of pizza falls to $3, consumer surplus increases by $4, as reflected by the lighter shaded area.

the horizontal axis the number of medium-size pizzas demanded per month. Recall that in constructing a demand curve, we hold tastes, income, and the prices of related goods constant; only the price of pizza varies.

Teaching Tip Every point on the demand curve satisfies the conditions for consumer equilibrium. Marginal utility falls as the consumer moves to points lower on the curve.

At a price of $8 or above, you find that the marginal utility of other goods that you could buy for $8 is higher than the marginal utility of a pizza. Consequently, you buy no pizza. At a price of $7, you buy one pizza per month, so the marginal utility of the first pizza exceeds what you could have received by spending that money on your best alternative—say, a movie, popcorn, and a Coke. A price of $6 prompts you to buy two pizzas a month. Your marginal valuation of the second pizza is $6. At a price of $5, you buy three pizzas a month, and at $4, you buy four pizzas a month. *In each case the value to you of*

Marginal valuation The dollar value of the marginal utility derived from consuming each additional unit of a good

Point to Stress Although the consumer pays the same price for each unit, the price only reflects what the *last unit* purchased is worth.

Consumer surplus The difference between the maximum amount that a consumer is willing to pay for a given quantity of a good and what the consumer actually pays

Teaching Tip Although total spending fell in this example, a drop in spending is not required for consumer surplus to rise. For example, if the demand curve in Exhibit 6 showed that 5 pizzas would be purchased at a price of $3.50, total spending would rise from $16 for 4 pizzas to $17.50 for 5 pizzas. Consumer surplus would still rise, from $6 to $7.50.

Teaching Tip Consumer C attaches lower marginal utilities and thus lower marginal values to pizzas than do consumers A and B. Lower prices are needed to entice consumer C to enter the market.

the last unit purchased must at least equal the price; otherwise, you would not have purchased that unit. Along the demand curve, therefore, the price reflects your **marginal valuation** of the good, or the dollar value of the marginal utility derived from consuming each additional unit.

Notice that when the price is $4, you purchase each of the four pizzas for that price even though you would have been willing to pay more than $4 apiece for the first three pizzas. The first pizza provides marginal utility you value at $7; the second, marginal utility valued at $6; and the third, marginal utility valued at $5. In fact, you would have been willing to pay $7 for the first, $6 for the second, and $5 for the third. The value of the total utility of the first four pizzas is $7 + $6 + $5 + $4 = $22. Note, however, that when the price is $4, you get all four pizzas for $16. Thus, a price of $4 confers a **consumer surplus**, or bonus, equal to the difference between the maximum amount you would have been willing to pay ($22) and what you actually paid ($16). When the price is $4 per pizza, your consumer surplus is $6, as shown by the six darker shaded blocks in Exhibit 6. The consumer surplus is equal to the value of the total utility you receive from consuming the pizza minus your total spending on pizza.

If the price falls to $3, you purchase five pizzas a month. Evidently you feel that the marginal benefit you receive from the fifth one is worth at least $3. The lower price means that you get to buy all the pizzas for $3 even though most are worth more than $3 to you. Your consumer surplus when the price is $3 is the value of the total utility conferred by the first five pizzas, which is $7 + $6 + $5 + $4 + $3 = $25, minus the cost, which is $3 × 5 = $15. Thus, the consumer surplus is $25 − $15 = $10, as indicated by both the dark and the light shaded blocks in Exhibit 6. When the price declines to $3, you are able to purchase all units for less, so your consumer surplus increases by $4, as indicated by the four lighter shaded blocks in Exhibit 6. You can see why consumers benefit from lower prices.

Market Demand and Consumer Surplus

Let's talk more generally now about the market demand for a good, assuming the market consists of you and two other consumers. *The market demand curve is simply the horizontal sum of the individual demand curves for all consumers in the market.* Exhibit 7 shows how the demand curves for three consumers in the market for pizza are summed horizontally to yield the market demand curve (you are consumer A in this example). At a price of $4 per pizza, for example, consumer A demands 4 units, consumer B demands 2 units, and consumer C demands nothing. The market quantity demanded at a price of $4 is therefore 6 pizzas. At a price of $2 per pizza, A's quantity demanded is 6 units, B's is 4 units, and C's is 2 units, for a total quantity demanded of twelve pizzas. The market demand curve shows the total quantity demanded by all consumers at various prices.

With certain qualifications that we need not go into here, the idea of consumer surplus can be used to examine market demand as well as individual demand. We can sum each consumer's surplus to arrive at the market consumer surplus. *As with individual demand curves, consumer surplus for the market demand*

EXHIBIT 7

Summing Individual Demands to Derive the Market Demand for Pizza

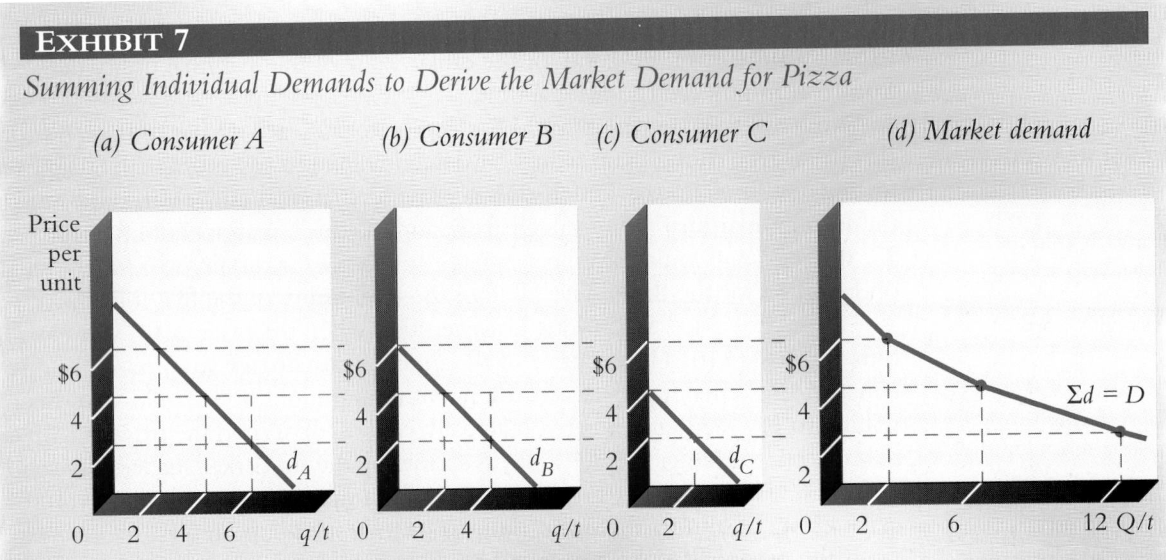

At a price of \$4 per pizza, consumer A demands 4 units, consumer B demands 2 units, and consumer C demands no units. Total market demand at a price of \$4 is $4 + 2 + 0 = 6$ units. At a lower price of \$2 per pizza, consumer A demands 6 units, B demands 4 units, and C demands 2 units. Market demand at a price of \$2 is 12 units. The market demand curve D is the horizontal sum of individual demand curves d_A,d_B, and d_C.

curve is measured by the difference between the value of the total utility received from consumption and the total amount paid for that consumption. Instead of considering just three consumers, we could consider the market demand when there are many consumers in the market. In Exhibit 8 we present the market demand for pizza when there are thousands of consumers in the market. If the price per pizza in Exhibit 8 is \$2, each person increases quantity demanded until the marginal valuation of the last unit each purchases equals \$2. But each consumer gets to buy all the other units for \$2 as well. In Exhibit 8, the dark shading, bounded below by the price of \$2 and above by the demand curve, depicts the market consumer surplus when the price is \$2. The light shading represents the increase in consumer surplus if the price drops to \$1 per unit.

Point to Stress
Consumer surplus is represented by the area below the demand curve down to the prevailing market price.

THE ROLE OF TIME IN DEMAND

Demand measures the desired rate of consumption at alternative prices during a given time period. An important consideration in constructing a demand curve is the time period involved, for it influences the rate of consumption. The longer the time period, the greater the demand, other things constant. The demand for pizza per month is greater than the demand per week or per day.

EXHIBIT 8

Market Demand and Consumer Surplus

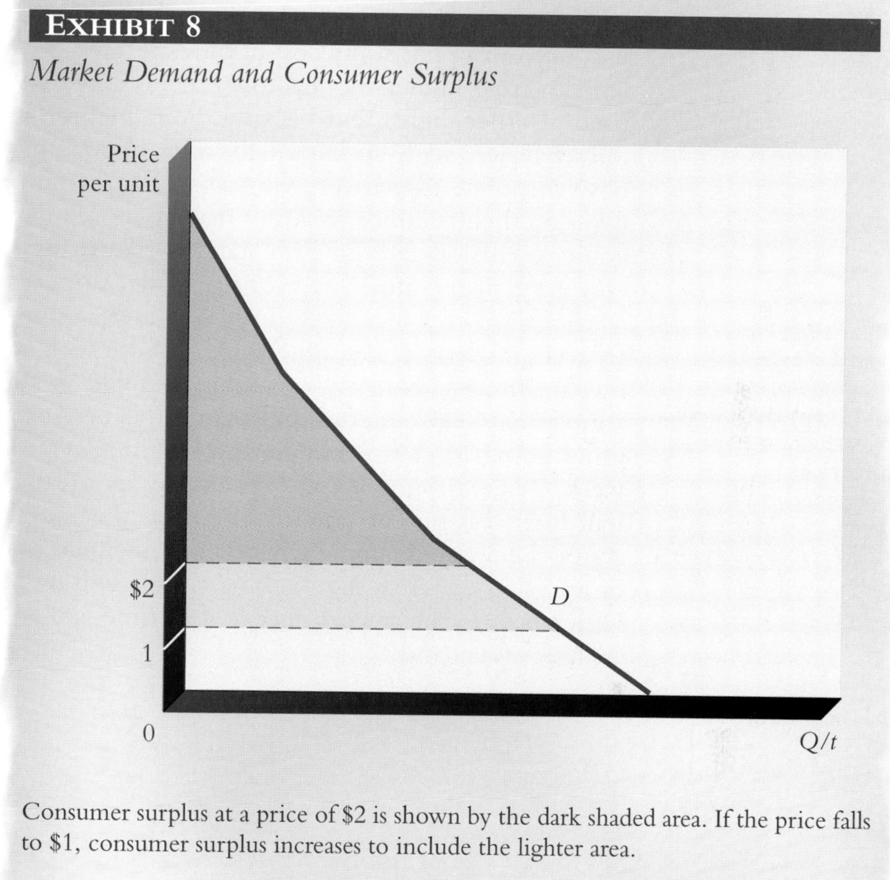

Consumer surplus at a price of $2 is shown by the dark shaded area. If the price falls to $1, consumer surplus increases to include the lighter area.

Teaching Tip Some goods may only have a time price. Consider, for example, the chapter's earlier example of free food and drink at a party. Free municipal health clinics provide another example. A 1973 study in New York City indicated a negative relationship between the time price of free clinics and the quantity demanded—so the law of demand still holds. (Jan P. Acton, "Demand for Health Care Among the Urban Poor, with Special Emphasis on the Role of Time," New York City: Rand Institute, April 1973.)

Teaching Tip The effective price for good X can be written as $p_X + wt_X$, where t_X is the time needed to consume and w is the hourly money wage that the consumer could otherwise be receiving. Therefore, wt_X represents the income value of the required time input to consume good X. As w rises, the effective price rises.

Because consumption does not occur instantaneously, time also plays another important role in demand analysis. Consumption takes time and, as Benjamin Franklin said, time is money—time has a positive value for most people. Consequently, the cost of consumption has two components: the *money price* of the good and the *time price* of the good. Goods are demanded because of the services they offer. Your demand for a lawn mower is based on its ability to cut grass; your interest is not in the mower itself but in the service it provides. Thus, you may be willing to pay more for a mower that does the job faster. Similarly, it is not the toaster, automatic dishwasher, or airline trip that you demand, but the services they provide. Other things held constant, the good that provides the same service in less time is preferred.

The money price of a good is usually the same for all consumers, but the time price of consuming that good differs among individuals, since their opportunity costs of time differ. Your willingness to pay a premium for timesaving goods and services depends on the opportunity cost of your time. Differences in the value of time to different consumers explains many of the consumption patterns observed in the economy.

Consider the alternative ways to get to Europe. You could, for example, take the Concorde or a regular airline. Your mode of travel will depend in part on your opportunity cost of time, because goods with lower time costs tend to have higher money costs. The Concorde takes less than half the time of other flights, but because the Concorde is much more expensive, only travelers with an extremely high opportunity cost of time, such as busy corporate executives, will pay such a premium for faster service. Students on their summer vacations may be more inclined to opt for some discount excursion fare or even standby status; for them, the lower money cost more than compensates for the higher time cost.

Teaching Tip The income and substitution approach does not contradict the approach given earlier in the chapter. See the appendix for graphical utility analysis that incorporates income and substitution effects.

A retired couple is likely to have a lower opportunity cost of time and so will purchase fewer timesaving goods, such as microwave ovens and frozen dinners, than, say, a working couple in the fast lane. The retired couple may clip coupons and search the newspapers for bargains, sometimes going from store to store for particular grocery items on sale that week. The working couple will usually ignore the coupons and sales and will often eat out or purchase items at the more expensive convenience stores. The retired couple will be more inclined to drive across the country on vacation, whereas the working couple will fly to a vacation destination. Differences in the opportunity cost of time add an extra dimension to our analysis of demand.

CONCLUSION

This chapter presented another way to derive demand curves. Rather than relying on the substitution and income effects of a price change, we developed a utility-based analysis of consumer choice. The focus was on the utility, or enjoyment, that consumers receive from consumption. In observing consumer behavior, we assume that for a particular individual, utility can be measured in some systematic way even though different consumers' utility levels cannot be compared. Our ultimate objective is to predict how consumer choice is affected by such variables as a change in price. We judge a theory not by the realism of its assumptions but by the accuracy of its predictions. Based on this criterion, the theory of consumer choice presented in this chapter has proven to be quite useful.

Again, we stress that consumers do not have to understand the material presented in this chapter in order to maximize utility. Economists assume that rational consumers attempt to maximize utility naturally and instinctively. In this chapter we simply tried to analyze that process using a model of consumer choice based on utility analysis. A more general approach to consumer choice, an approach that does not require a specific measure of utility, is developed in the appendix to this chapter.

SUMMARY

1. Utility is the sense of pleasure or satisfaction that comes from consumption; it is the want-satisfying power of goods and services. The utility you receive from consuming a particular good depends on your tastes. We distinguish between the total utility derived from consuming a good and the marginal utility derived from consuming one more unit of the good. The law of diminishing marginal utility says that the greater the amount of a particular good consumed per time period, other things constant, the smaller the increase in total utility received from each additional unit consumed.

2. An assessment of the want-satisfying power of consumption must be made by each individual consumer, so utility is a subjective notion. By translating an individual's subjective measure of satisfaction into units of utility, we can predict a consumer's consumption choice as well as the effect of a change in price on quantity demanded.

3. The consumer's objective is to maximize utility within the limits imposed by income and prices. In a world without scarcity, utility would be maximized by consuming goods until the marginal utility of the last unit of each good consumed was zero. In the real world, a world shaped by scarcity, utility is maximized when the final unit of each good consumed yields the same utility per dollar spent. Put another way, utility is maximized when the marginal utility divided by the price is identical for each good consumed.

4. Utility analysis can be used to construct an individual consumer's demand curve. By changing the price and observing the utility-maximizing levels of consumption, we can generate points along the demand curve.

5. When the price of a good drops, other things constant, the consumer is able to buy all units of the good at the lower price. Thus, we say that consumers typically receive a surplus, or bonus, from consumption, and this surplus increases as the price falls.

6. The market demand curve is simply the horizontal sum of the individual demand curves for all consumers in the market. With some qualifications, consumer surplus for the market demand curve can be measured as the difference between the value of the total utility received from consumption and the total amount paid for that consumption.

7. There are two components to the cost of consumption: the money price of the good and the time price of the good. People with a higher opportunity cost of time are willing to pay a higher money price for goods and services that involve a lower time price.

QUESTIONS AND PROBLEMS

1. (Diminishing Marginal Utility) Some restaurants offer "all you can eat" meals. How is this practice related to diminishing marginal utility? What restrictions must the restaurant impose on the customer in order to make a profit?

2. (Marginal Utility) Consider Exhibit 3 of this chapter; suppose that each number in columns (1) and (5) were multiplied by 2. How would this affect the marginal utility in columns (3) and (7)? Would columns (4) and (8) also be affected?

3. (Marginal Utility) Is it possible for marginal utility to be negative and yet total utility to be positive? Why or why not?

4. (Consumer Equilibrium) Suppose that a consumer has a choice between two goods, X and Y. If the price of X is \$2 per unit and the price of Y is \$3 per unit, how much of X and Y will the consumer purchase, given an income of \$17? Use the following information on marginal utility:

Units	MU_X	MU_Y
1	10	5
2	8	4
3	2	3
4	2	2
5	1	2

5. (Consumer Allocation) Consider two goods, X and Y. Suppose that $MU_X = MU_Y$ and the price of X is less than the price of Y. The rational consumer will increase purchases of X and reduce purchases of Y. Why?

6. (Consumer Allocation) Suppose that $MU_X = 100$ and that the price of X is \$10 and the price of Y is \$5. Assuming that the consumer is in equilibrium, what must the marginal utility of Y be?

7. (Time Price and Money Price) In many amusement parks, you pay an admission fee to the park and then you need not pay for each ride. How are rides allocated in such parks? Is there an incentive for some people to sell their places in line? Why or why not?

8. (Utility Maximization) Suppose that the price of X is twice as high as the price of Y. You are a utility maximizer who consumes some of each good.
   a. What must be true about the relationship between the marginal utility levels of the last unit consumed of each good?
   b. What must be true about the relationship between the marginal utility levels of the last dollar spent on each good?

9. (Marginal Utility and Demand) Suppose that you buy five shirts a year when the price of shirts is \$30 and ten shirts a year when the price of shirts is \$25.
   a. What can you say about the value you place on the third shirt, the seventh shirt, and the twelfth shirt you buy per year?
   b. With diminishing marginal utility, are you deriving any consumer surplus? Explain.

10. (Relative Utility Values) Although utility is purely subjective, you and I consume goods in combinations such that the ratios of the marginal utilities of the last unit consumed of each good are the same for both of us. Why is this true?

11. (Consumer Surplus) In Chapter 18, we noted that the demand curve for any particular good is likely to become more elastic the longer the adjustment period. Given the definition of consumer surplus, does this mean that the consumers of this good are worse off as time goes on? Explain.

12. (Marginal Valuation) The height of the demand curve reflects the marginal valuation of a given unit of the good demanded. An increase in income will, if the good is normal, shift the demand curve to the right and therefore increase the height of the demand curve. Does this mean that consumers get greater marginal utility from each unit of this good than they did before? Explain.

13. (Utility Maximization) Suppose that your best friend moves far away and all the joy goes out of your life. You find that nothing is fun any more and everything you buy gives you only half as much satisfaction as before. How would this state of mind determine the set of goods that you buy?

14. (Consumer Surplus) Suppose that a good is in perfectly elastic supply at a price of \$5. The demand for this good is linear, with the quantity demanded falling to zero when the price rises to \$25. If the slope of this linear demand curve is –0.25, calculate the consumer surplus that occurs when the market is in equilibrium.

15. (Diminishing Marginal Utility) For some goods marginal utility may not decline, and perhaps may even increase, with increased consumption levels, up to some point. However, utility maximization requires that all goods, if consumed at all, must be consumed to the point where marginal utility is diminishing. Discuss.

16. (Some Reflections of Tastes) Advertising to affect tastes may be thought of as an attempt to convert wants to needs. What impact might successful advertising have on the price elasticity of demand? On the income elasticity of demand?

17. (Some Reflections of Tastes) If manufacturers of competing products each advertise to alter tastes toward their products, and the effect is that everything "cancels out," does this mean that all advertising is a waste of resources?

APPENDIX
Indifference Curves

The approach used in the main part of the chapter, marginal utility analysis, requires some numerical measure of utility in order to determine the optimal bundle of goods and services. Economists have developed another, more general, approach to utility and consumer behavior, one that does not require that numbers be attached to specific levels of utility. All the new approach requires is that consumers be able to rank their preferences for various combinations of goods. This new approach is more general and more flexible. We begin with an examination of consumer preferences.

EXHIBIT 9

An Indifference Curve

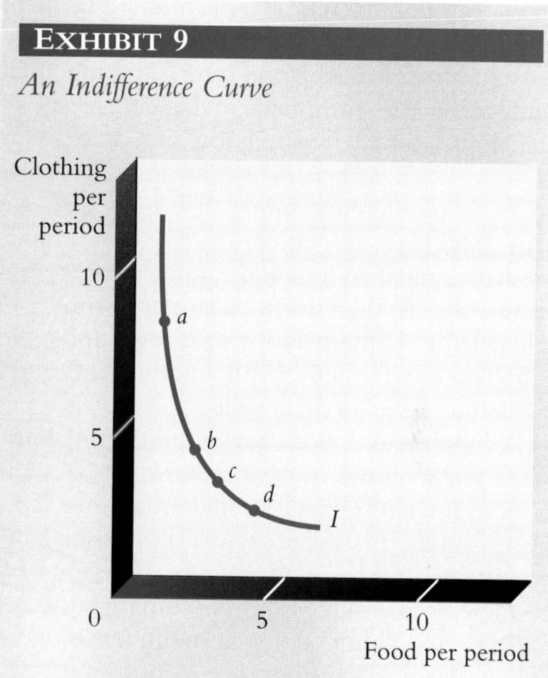

An indifference curve shows all combinations of two goods that provide a consumer with the same total utility. Points *a* through *d* depict four such combinations. Indifference curves have negative slopes and are convex to the origin.

Consumer Preferences

Indifference curve analysis is an approach to the study of consumer behavior that requires no specific measure of utility. An **indifference curve** shows all combinations of goods that provide the consumer with the same total satisfaction, or total utility. Since each of the alternative bundles of goods yields the same utility, the consumer is *indifferent* about which combination is actually consumed. We can best explain the use of indifference curves through the following example.

In the real world consumers choose from among thousands of goods and services, but to keep the analysis manageable, suppose there are only two goods available to consumers: food and clothing. In Exhibit 9, the horizontal axis measures the quantity of food an individual consumes per period. The vertical axis measures the quantity of clothing the individual consumes per period. At point *a,* the individual consumes 8 units of clothing and 1 unit of food. The question is: Holding the consumer's total utility constant, how much clothing would the consumer be willing to give up to get a second unit of food? As you can see, in moving from point *a* to point *b,* the consumer is willing to give up 4 units of clothing to get 1 more unit of food. Total utility is the same at points *a* and *b.* The marginal utility of that additional unit of food is just sufficient to compensate the consumer for decreasing clothing consumption by 4 units. Thus, at point *b,* the person is consuming 4 units of clothing and 2 units of food and is indifferent between this combination and the combination reflected by point *a,* since total utility is the same at both points.

In moving from point *b* to point *c,* again the total utility is constant; the consumer is now willing to give up only 1 unit of clothing to get another unit of food. At point *c,* the consumption bundle consists of 3 units of clothing and 3 units of food. Once at point *c,* the individual is willing to give up only one-half unit of clothing to get another unit of food. Combination *d* therefore consists of 2.5 units of clothing and 4 units of food.

We can connect points *a, b, c,* and *d* to form an indifference curve, *I,* which represents possible combinations of food and clothing that would keep the consumer at the same level of total utility. Since all points on the curve offer the same total utility, or satisfaction, the consumer is indifferent among them—hence the name *indifference curve.* Note that we don't know, nor do we need to know, the value of that total utility—that is, there is no particular number attached to it. Combinations of goods along the indifference curve reflect some constant, though unspecified, level of total utility.

Because both goods yield utility, the consumer prefers more of each rather than less. For the consumer to remain indifferent among bundles of goods, the decrease in utility from consuming less of one good must be just offset by the increase in utility from consuming more of another good. Thus, along an indifference curve there is an inverse relation between the quantity of one good consumed and the quantity of another consumed. Because of this inverse relation, *indifference curves slope downward.*

Indifference curves are also *convex to the origin,* which means that they are bowed inward toward the origin: the slope gets flatter as we move down the curve. Here is why. A consumer's willingness to substitute food for clothing depends on how much of each the individual is currently consuming. At combination *a,* for example, the individual is consuming 8 units of clothing and only 1 unit of food, so there is much clothing relative to food. Because food is relatively scarce in the consumption bundle, another unit of food has a high marginal value and the consumer would be willing to give up 4 units of clothing to get it. Once the consumer reaches point *b,* the amount of food consumed has doubled, so the consumer is not quite so willing to surrender clothing to get another unit of food. In fact, the consumer will forgo only 1 unit of clothing to get 1 more unit of food. This moves the consumer from point *b* to point *c.* At point *c,* the consumer is even less anxious to get still more food, so is willing to give up only one-half unit of clothing to get a fourth unit of food.

The **marginal rate of substitution**, or **MRS**, between food and clothing indicates the maximum amount of food that the consumer is willing to give up to get one more unit of clothing, neither gaining nor losing utility in the process. Because the MRS measures the willingness to trade clothing for food, it depends on the amount of each good the consumer has at the time. Mathematically, the MRS is equal to the absolute value of the slope of the indifference curve. Recall that the slope of any line is the vertical change between two points on the line divided by the corresponding horizontal change. For example, in moving from combination *a* to *b* in Exhibit 9, the consumer is willing to give up 4 units of clothing to get 1 more unit of food; the slope between those two points equals −4, so the MRS is 4. In the move from combination *b* to *c,* the slope is −1, so the MRS is 1. And from *c* to *d,* the slope is −0.5, so the MRS is 0.5.

The **law of diminishing marginal rate of substitution** says that as the consumption of food increases, the amount of clothing that the consumer is willing to give up to get another unit of food declines. With minor exceptions, this law applies more generally to all pairs of goods. Because the marginal rate of substitution of clothing for food declines with an increase in food consumption, the indifference curve has a diminishing slope, meaning that it is convex when viewed from the origin. Suppose that "food per period" measures meals per day. The consumer is willing to give up 4 units of clothing to get a second meal per day and 1 unit of clothing to get a third meal per day but only one-half unit of clothing to get a fourth meal per day. As we move down the indifference curve, the amount of food consumed increases so the marginal utility of additional units of food decreases. Conversely, the amount of clothing consumed decreases and its marginal utility increases. Thus, in moving down the indifference curve, the consumer is willing to give up smaller and smaller amounts of clothing to get additional units of food.

We have focused on a single indifference curve that indicates some constant but unspecified level of utility. We can use the same approach to generate a series of indifference curves, called an **indifference map**, for a particular consumer's consumption of the two goods in question. Each curve in the indifference map reflects a different level of utility. Such a map is shown in Exhibit 10, where indifference curves for a particular consumer are labeled I_1, I_2, I_3, and I_4. Each consumer will have a unique indifference map based on that consumer's preferences.

Curves farther from the origin represent greater consumption levels and therefore higher levels of total utility. The total utility level along I_2 is greater than that along I_1, I_3 is greater than I_2, and so on. We can see this best if we draw a ray from the origin and follow it to higher indifference curves. Such a ray has been included in Exhibit 10. By following that ray to higher and higher indifference curves, we see that the combination on each successive indifference curve reflects greater amounts of *both* goods. Since the consumer values both goods, the greater amounts of each good reflected on higher indifference curves represent higher levels of utility.

Note that indifference curves are not necessarily parallel as Exhibit 10 may suggest. Although they are not necessarily parallel, indifference curves in a consumer's indifference map do not intersect. Exhibit 11 shows why. If indifference curves I and I' intersect at point *i*, then that combination of goods lies on both indifference

EXHIBIT 10

An Indifference Map

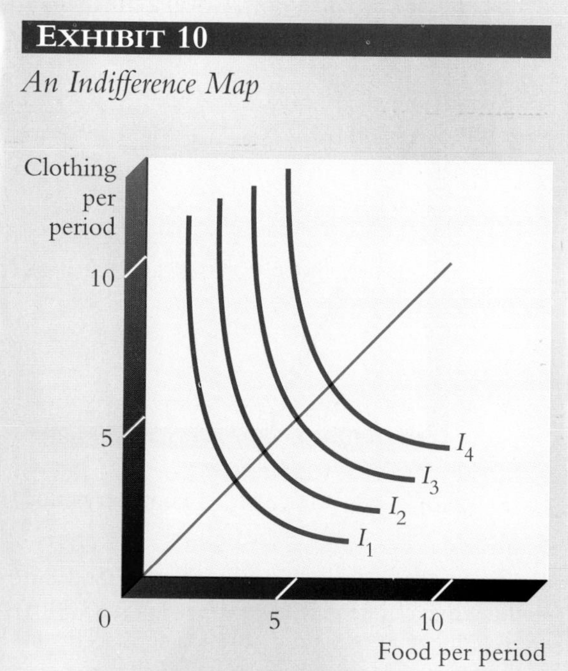

Indifference curves I_1 through I_4 are four examples from a consumer's indifference map. Indifference curves farther from the origin depict higher levels of utility. A ray reflects more of both goods on each higher indifference curve.

EXHIBIT 11

Indifference Curves Do Not Intersect

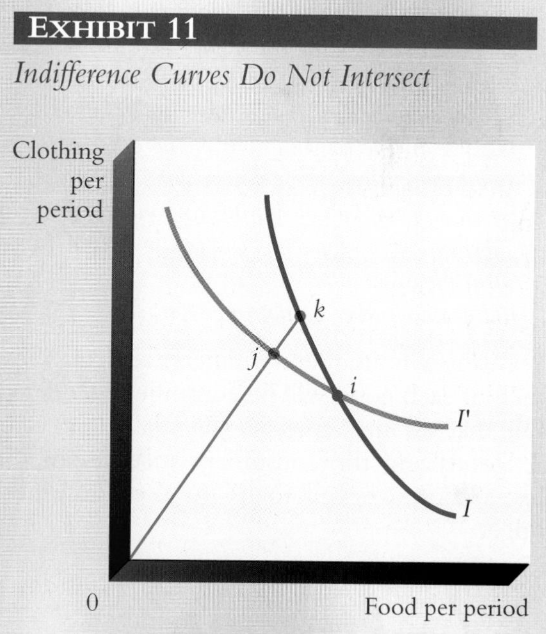

If indifference curves crossed, as at point *i*, then every point on indifference curve I and every point on curve I' would have to reflect the same level of utility as at point *i*. But point *k* is a combination with more food and more clothing than point *j* and so must represent a higher level of utility. This contradiction means that indifference curves cannot intersect.

curves. Since the consumption of the bundle at point i reflects some specific level of utility and since point i lies on both curves, both curves must have this same level of utility. A ray from the origin intersects the curves at points j and k. Combination k has more of both goods than does combination j. Since more is preferred to less, k must provide greater utility than j. Since the utility at point k exceeds the utility at point j, the utility along I must exceed the utility along I'. But we already said that if the two indifference curves intersect at i, they must have equal utility. *Because the curves cannot reflect both an identical utility level and different utility levels, we conclude that the curves cannot intersect.*

Let's summarize the properties of indifference curves.

1. *An indifference curve reflects a constant level of utility, so the consumer is indifferent among consumption combinations along a given curve.*
2. *If total utility is to remain constant, an increase in the consumption of one good must be offset by a decrease in the consumption of the other good, so indifference curves slope downward.*
3. *Because of the law of diminishing marginal rate of substitution, indifference curves are bowed in toward the origin.*
4. *Indifference curves do not intersect.*

Given a consumer's indifference map, how much of each good will be consumed? To determine that we must consider the relative prices of the goods and the consumer's income. In the next section we will focus on the consumer's budget.

The Budget Line

Suppose the price of food is \$4 per unit, the price of clothing is \$2 per unit, and the consumer's budget is \$20 per period. If the entire \$20 is spent on clothing, the consumer can afford to buy 10 units. Alternatively, if the entire \$20 is spent on food, the consumer can afford 5 units. The **budget line** reflects all possible combinations of clothing and food that could be purchased given the consumer's budget and the prices of the goods. In Exhibit 12, the consumer's budget line meets the vertical axis at 10 units of clothing and meets the horizontal axis at 5 units of food. You might think of the budget line as the individual's *consumption possibilities frontier.*

Let's find the slope of the budget line. At the point where the budget line meets the vertical axis, the quantity of clothing that can be purchased equals the consumer's income divided by the price of clothing, or I/p_C, where I is income and p_C is the price of clothing. At the point where the budget line meets the horizontal axis, the quantity of food that can be purchased equals the consumer's income divided by the price of

EXHIBIT 12

The Budget Line

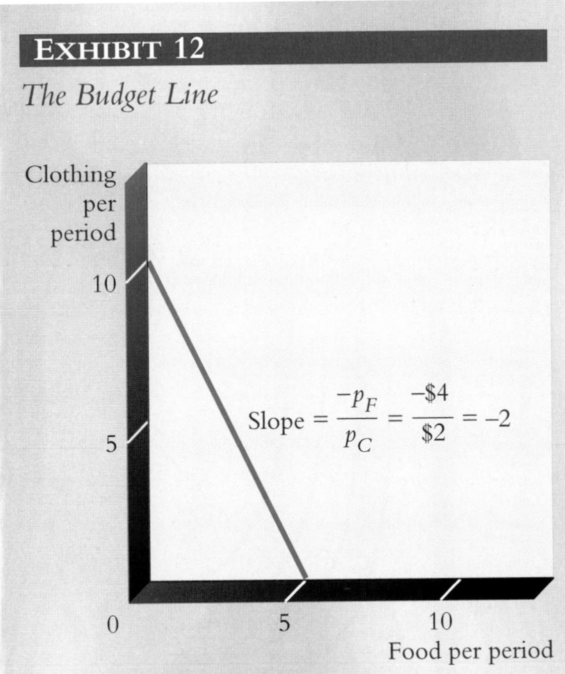

The budget line shows all combinations of food and clothing that can be purchased at fixed prices with a given amount of income. If all income is spent on clothing, 10 units can be purchased. If all income is spent on food, 5 units can be purchased. Points between the vertical intercept and the horizontal intercept represent combinations of some food and some clothing. The slope of the budget line is –2, illustrating that the cost of 1 unit of food is 2 units of clothing.

food, or I/p_F, where p_F is the price of food. The slope of the budget line in Exhibit 12 can be calculated by considering a movement from the vertical intercept to the horizontal intercept. That is, we divide the vertical change ($-I/p_C$) by the horizontal change (I/p_F) as follows:

$$\textbf{Slope of budget line} = -\frac{I/p_C}{I/p_F} = -\frac{p_F}{p_C}$$

Along the budget line, the vertical value falls as the horizontal value increases, so the slope is negative. The slope of the budget line equals minus the food price divided by the clothing price; in our example it is – \$4/\$2, which equals –2. The slope of the budget line indicates what it costs the consumer in terms of forgone clothing to get another unit of food. The consumer must give up 2 units of clothing for each additional unit of food. *Note that the income term cancels out, so the slope of a line depends only on relative prices, not on the level of income.*

As you know, the demand curve shows the quantity that the consumer is willing and able to buy at alternative prices. The indifference curve indicates what the consumer is *willing* to buy. The budget line shows what the consumer is *able* to buy. We must therefore bring together the indifference curve and the budget line to find out what quantity the consumer is both willing and able to buy.

EXHIBIT 13

Utility Maximization

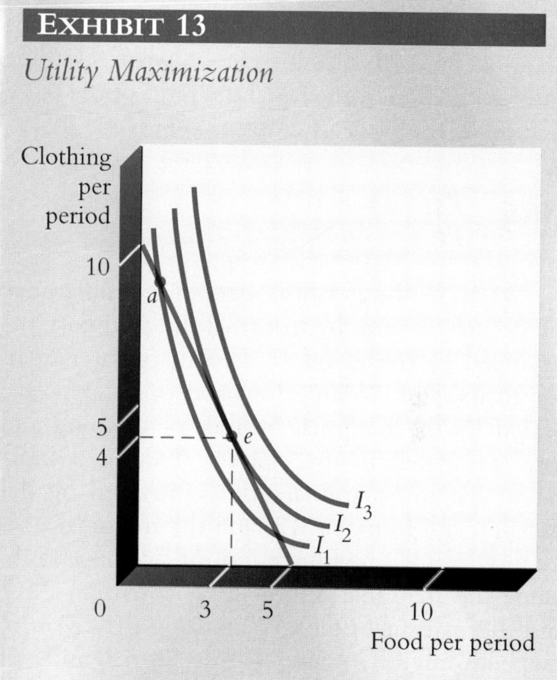

The consumer's utility is maximized at point *e*, where indifference curve I_2 is just tangent to the budget line.

Consumer Equilibrium at the Tangency

As always, the consumer's objective is to maximize utility. We know that indifference curves farther from the origin represent higher levels of utility. The utility-maximizing consumer therefore will select that combination along the budget line in Exhibit 13 that lies on the highest attainable indifference curve. Combination *a* consists of 8 units of clothing costing a total of \$16 and 1 unit of food for \$4, for a total outlay of \$20. Point *a* is on the budget line and thus is a combination the consumer is *able* to consume, but *a* is not on the highest attainable indifference curve. Given prices and income, the consumer maximizes utility at the combination of food and clothing depicted by point *e* in Exhibit 13, where indifference curve I_2 just touches, or *is tangent to,* the budget line. This utility-maximizing consumption bundle consists of 4 units of clothing totaling \$8 and 3 units of food totaling \$12; this combination exhausts the \$20 budget. Other, "better" indifference curves, such as I_3, lie completely above the budget line and are thus unattainable.

Since the consumer is maximizing utility at point *e*, this is an equilibrium outcome. Note that the indifference curve is tangent to the budget line at the equilibrium point, and recall that the slope of a curve equals the slope of a line drawn tangent to that curve. At point *e*, therefore, the slope of the indifference curve equals the slope of the budget line. Recall that the absolute value of the slope of the indifference curve is the consumer's marginal rate of substitution, and the absolute value of the slope of the budget line equals the price ratio. In equilibrium, therefore, the marginal rate of substitution between clothing and food, MRS, must equal the ratio of the price of food to the price of clothing, or

$$\text{MRS} = \frac{p_F}{p_C}$$

What is the relation between indifference curve analysis and the marginal utility theory introduced in the chapter? The marginal rate of substitution of clothing for food can also be revealed by the marginal utilities of clothing and food presented in the chapter. Exhibit 3 indicated that the marginal utility provided by the third unit of food was 12, and the marginal utility provided by the fourth unit of clothing was 6. Since the marginal utility of food (MU_F) is 12 and the marginal utility of clothing (MU_C) is 6, the consumer is willing to give up 2 units of clothing to get 1 more unit of food. Thus, the marginal rate of substitution of clothing for food equals the ratio of food's marginal utility (MU_F) to clothing's marginal utility (MU_C), or

$$\text{MRS} = \frac{MU_F}{MU_C}$$

In fact, the slope of the indifference curve equals $-MU_F/MU_C$. Therefore, in equilibrium, the slope of the indifference curve equals the slope of the budget line. Since the slope of the budget line equals $-p_F/p_C$, the equilibrium condition for the indifference curve approach can be written as

$$-\frac{MU_F}{MU_C} = -\frac{p_F}{p_C}$$

which can be easily rearranged to show that

$$\frac{MU_F}{p_F} = \frac{MU_C}{p_C}$$

This equation is the same equilibrium condition for utility maximization presented in the chapter using marginal utility analysis. The equality says that in equilibrium—that is, when the consumer maximizes total utility—the last dollar spent on each good yields the same marginal utility. If this equality does not hold, the consumer can increase total utility by adjusting consumption until the equality does hold.

Effects of a Change in Income

We have established the equilibrium consumption bundle for a particular consumer, given the consumer's income and product prices. What happens if the consumer's income changes? Suppose, for example, that the consumer's income is cut in half, from \$20 to \$10 per period, yet prices remain as before. Exhibit 14 shows the effects of this reduction in income on the equilibrium bundle consumed. Since income falls but prices remain the same, the new budget line is parallel to, but below, the old budget line. Be-

EXHIBIT 14

Effect of a Reduction in Consumer Income

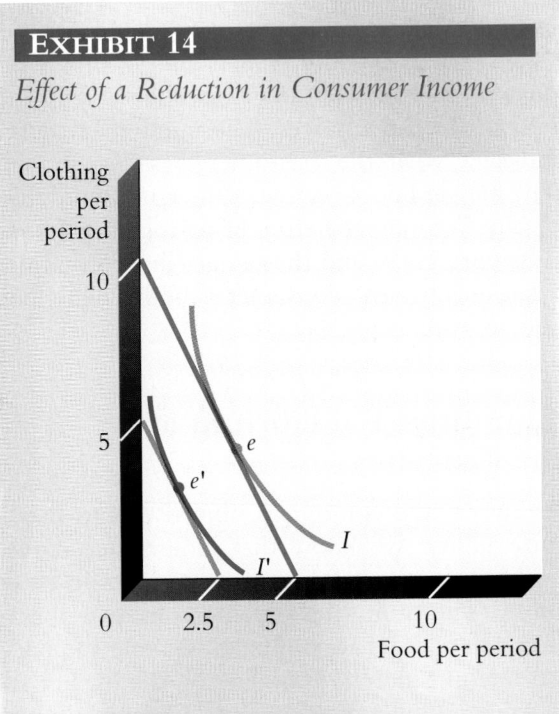

A reduction in income causes a parallel inward shift of the budget line. The consumer is back in equilibrium at point e', where indifference curve I' is tangent to the new, lower budget line.

cause of the decrease in income, the budget now buys less of each good. If the entire budget is devoted to clothing, only 5 units can be purchased; if it is devoted to food, only 2.5 units can be purchased. The consumer once again maximizes utility by consuming that combination of goods that is on the highest attainable indifference curve—in this case point e' on indifference curve I'. The drop in income reduces the consumer's purchasing power, resulting in a lower level of utility. (Note that food and clothing are both normal goods, since a drop in income results in reduced consumption of both.)

Effects of a Change in Price

What happens to equilibrium consumption if there is a change in price? The answer can be found by deriving the demand curve. We begin at point *e,* our initial equilibrium, in panel (a) of Exhibit 15. At point *e,* the person consumes 4 units of clothing and 3 units of food. Suppose that the price of food falls from $4 per unit to $3 per unit, other things constant. A drop in the price of food from $4 to $3 means that, if the entire budget were devoted to food, the consumer could purchase 6.67 units of food (20/3). Since the price of clothing has not changed, however, 10 units of clothing remain the maximum amount that can be purchased. Thus, the budget line's vertical intercept remains fixed at 10 units, but the lower end of the budget line rotates out.

After the price change, the new equilibrium position occurs at e'', where the quantity of food increases from 3 units to 4 units, and, as it happens, the quantity of clothing consumed remains at 4 units. Thus, price and quantity demanded are inversely related, other things constant, and we have again derived the law of demand. The demand curve in panel (b) of Exhibit 15 reflects how price and quantity demanded are related. Specifically, when the price of food falls from $4 per unit to $3 per unit, other things constant, the quantity of food demanded increases from 3 units to 4 units.

EXHIBIT 15

Effect of a Drop in the Price of Food

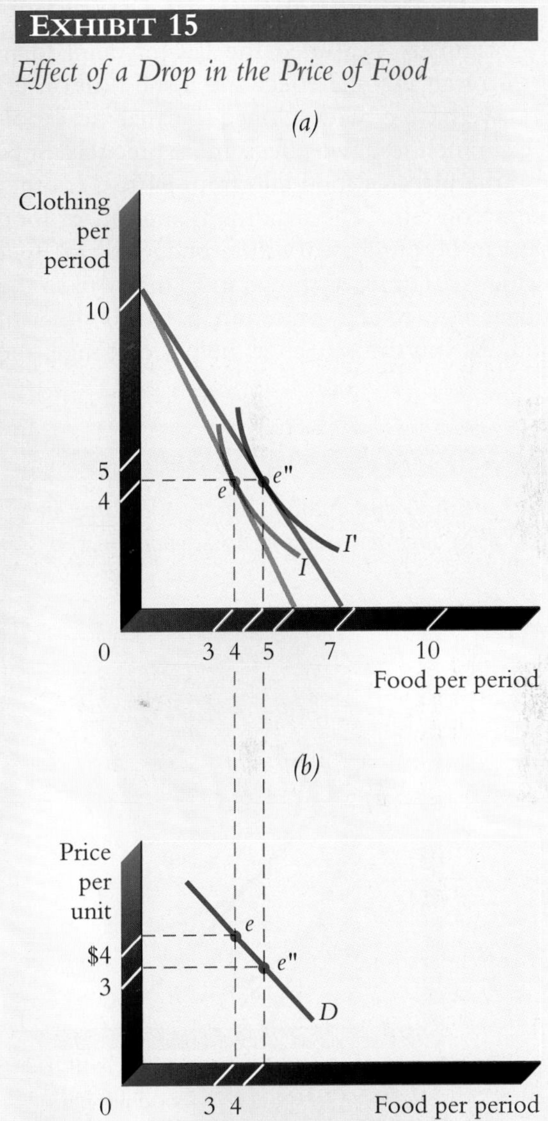

A reduction in the price of food rotates the budget line outward in panel (a). The consumer is back in equilibrium at point e'' along the new budget line. Panel (b) shows that a drop in the price of food from $4 per unit to $3 leads to an increase in quantity demanded from 3 units to 4. Price and quantity demanded are inversely related.

Since the consumer is on a higher indifference curve at e'', the consumer is clearly better off after the price reduction.

Income and Substitution Effects

We originally explained the law of demand in terms of an income effect and a substitution effect. We have now developed the analytical tools to examine these two effects more precisely. Suppose the price of food falls from $4 to $2, other things constant. The maximum amount of food that can be purchased with a budget of $20 per period is 10 units, as shown in Exhibit 16, so the budget line rotates out from 5 to 10 units of food. As you can see, after the price change, the quantity of food demanded increases from 3 units to 5 units. The increase in utility shows that the consumer benefits from the price drop.

The increase in the quantity of food demanded can be broken down into the substitution effect and the income effect of a price change. When the price of food falls, the change in the ratio of the price of food to the price of clothing is reflected by the change in the slope of the budget line. In order to derive the substitution effect, let's assume the consumer must maintain the same level of utility after the price change as before. Given the new set of relative prices, the consumer would increase the quantity of food demanded to the point on indifference curve *I* where the indifference curve is just tangent to *CF,* the dashed budget line. That tangency keeps utility at the initial level but reflects the new set of relative prices. Thus, we adjust the consumer's budget line to correspond to the new relative prices but at an income level that keeps the consumer on the same indifference curve.

The consumer moves down along indifference curve *I* to point *e′*, purchasing less clothing and more food. This change in quantity demanded reflects the *substitution effect* of the lower price of food. The substitution effect always increases the quantity demanded of the good whose price has dropped. Since consumption bundle *e′* represents the same level of utility as consumption bundle *e,* the consumer is neither better off nor worse off at point *e′*.

But at point *e′* the consumer is not spending all the income available. The drop in the price of food has increased the amount of food that can be purchased, as shown by the expanded budget line that runs from 10 units of clothing to 10 units of food. The consumer's *real income* has increased because of the lower price of food. As a result, the consumer is able to attain point *e*★ on indifference curve *I*★. At this point, the person consumes 5 units each of food and clothing. Because prices are held constant during the move from *e′* to *e*★, the change in consumption is due solely to a change in real income. Thus, the change in the quantity of food demanded reflects the *income effect* of the lower food price.

EXHIBIT 16

Substitution and Income Effects of a Drop in the Price of Food from $4 to $2 per Unit

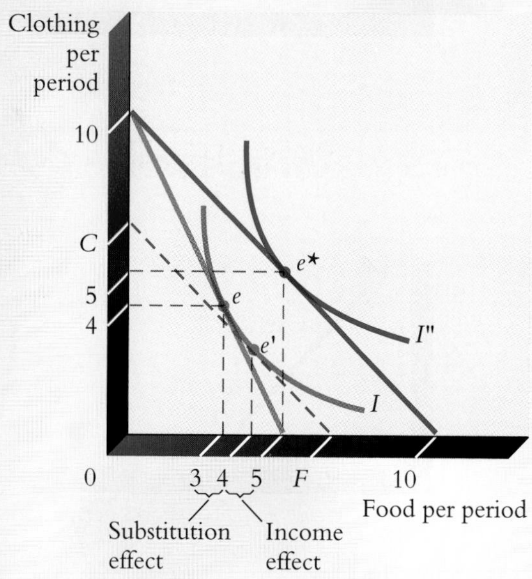

A reduction in the price of food moves the consumer from point *e* to point *e*★. This movement can be decomposed into a substitution effect and an income effect. The substitution effect (from *e* to *e′*) reflects a reaction to a change in relative prices along the original indifference curve. The income effect (from *e′* to *e*★) moves the consumer to a higher indifference curve at the new relative price ratio.

We can now distinguish between the substitution effect and the income effect of a drop in the price of food. The substitution effect is shown by the move from point e to point e' in response to a change in the relative price of food, with the consumer's utility held constant along I. The income effect is shown by the move from e' to $e^{\star}$ in response to an increase in real income, with relative prices held constant.

The overall effect of a change in the price of food is the sum of the substitution effect and the income effect. In our example the substitution effect accounts for a one-unit increase in the quantity of food demanded, as does the income effect. Thus, the income and substitution effects combine to increase the quantity of food demanded by 2 units when the price falls from $4 to $2. The income effect is not always positive. For inferior goods, the income effect is negative, so as the price falls, the income effect can cause consumption to fall, offsetting part or even all of the substitution effect. Incidentally, notice that as a result of the increase in real income, clothing consumption increases as well—from 4 units to 5 units in our example.

Conclusion

Indifference curve analysis does not require us to attach numerical values to particular levels of utility, as marginal utility theory does. The results of indifference curve analysis confirm the conclusions drawn from our simpler models. Indifference curves provide a logical way of viewing consumer choice, but consumers need not be aware of this approach to make rational choices. The purpose of the analysis in this chapter is to predict consumer behavior—not to advise consumers how to maximize utility.

Appendix Questions

1. (Slope of Indifference Curve) The slope of an indifference curve equals the marginal rate of substitution. If two goods were *perfectly* substitutable, what would the indifference curves look like? Explain.
2. (Effects of Change in Income) Suppose that a good is income elastic. What would happen to the tangency solutions on a consumer's indifference map as you varied the consumer's level of income?

CHAPTER 20

COST AND PRODUCTION IN THE FIRM

Each year throughout the world, millions of new firms enter the marketplace, and nearly as many leave. The firm's decision makers must choose what goods and services to produce and what resources to employ; they must also make plans while confronting uncertainty about consumer demand, resource availability, and the intentions of other firms. The lure of profit is so strong, however, that eager entrepreneurs are always ready to pursue their dreams.

The previous chapter explored the consumer behavior underlying the demand curve. This chapter examines the producer behavior underlying the supply curve. More specifically, we examine a firm's production and cost of operation as a prelude to the analysis of supply that will come in the next chapter. In the previous chapter you were asked to think like a consumer. In this chapter you must think like a producer. You may feel more natural as a consumer (after all, you make purchases every day), but you know more about firms than you may realize because you have been around them all your life—bookstores, record stores, video stores, department stores, grocery stores, convenience stores, dry cleaners, gas stations, automobile dealers, restaurants, and more. Although you probably have not yet managed a firm, you already have some idea how firms operate. Topics discussed in this chapter include

- Explicit and implicit costs
- Economic and normal profit
- Increasing and diminishing returns
- Short-run costs
- Long-run costs
- Economies and diseconomies of scale

COST AND PROFIT

Teaching Tip See Chapter 25 for a discussion of entrepreneurial ability and sources of profit. Chapter 27 provides a discussion of alternative theories of firm goals when ownership is separated from control.

When we examined the theory of consumer demand, we assumed that the consumer tried to maximize utility; this objective then provided the motivation for consumer behavior. When we turn to the production side, we assume that the producer tries to *maximize profit*—that is, the difference between the total revenue received from the sale of output and what must be paid to attract resources from their best alternative use. Over time the firms that survive and grow are those that turn out to be the most profitable. Firms that are unprofitable year after year will have more difficulty securing the financing needed to survive. Thus, profit maximization appears to be a reasonable operating assumption for firms.

Teaching Tip For labor resources, wages include the employer's contributions to social security, pension funds, unemployment insurance, health insurance, and so forth. For example, General Motors spent $3.4 billion for health insurance in 1991—adding explicit costs of $900 per vehicle.

Explicit and Implicit Costs

To hire resources, the firm must pay resource owners at least their *opportunity cost*—what the resources could earn in their best alternative use. For resources purchased in resource markets, the corresponding cash payments are good approximations of the opportunity cost. For example, the $3 per pound that Domino's Pizza pays for cheese reflects a price the cheese supplier could get elsewhere. Some resources, however, are owned by the firm (or, more precisely, are owned by the firm's owners), so there are no direct cash payments for their use. For example, the firm does not pay rent to operate in a company-owned building. Similarly, Mom and Pop, the owners and operators of the corner grocery, usually do not pay themselves an hourly wage. But these resources are not free. *Whether resources are owned by the firm or hired in resource markets, resources have an opportunity cost.*

Explicit cost Opportunity cost of a firm's resources that takes the form of actual cash payments

Implicit cost A firm's opportunity cost of using its own resources or those provided by its owners without a corresponding cash payment

A firm's **explicit costs** are the actual cash payments for resources purchased in resource markets: wages, rent, interest, insurance, taxes, and the like. In addition to these direct cash outlays, or explicit costs, the firm also faces **implicit costs**, which are the opportunity costs of using resources owned by the firm or provided by the firm's owners. Examples include the use of a company-owned building, use of company finances, or the time of the firm's owners. Like explicit costs, implicit costs involve an opportunity cost to the firm. But unlike explicit costs, implicit costs usually require no cash payment and no entry in the firm's *accounting statement*, which records the firm's revenues, explicit costs, and accounting profit.

Example Other types of implicit costs are a valuable patent owned by the firm, a popular brand name that could be licensed, capital depreciation in market value beyond that allowed for tax purposes, and so forth.

Alternative Measures of Profit

A particular example will help clarify the distinction between implicit and explicit costs. Meet Wanda Wheeler, an aeronautical engineer who earns $30,000 a year working for the Skyhigh Aircraft Company. On her way home from work one day, she gets an idea for a rounder, more friction-resistant airplane wheel. She decides to quit her job and start a business she calls The Wheeler Dealer. To buy the necessary machines and equipment, she withdraws her savings of $20,000 from a bank account, where it had been earning interest of $1,000 per year. She hires an assistant and starts producing the wheel in her garage, which she had been renting to a neighbor for $100 per month.

Sales are slow at first—people keep telling her she is just trying to reinvent the wheel—but her wheel eventually gets rolling. When Wanda and her accountant examine the firm's performance for the year, they are quite pleased. As you can see in the top part of Exhibit 1, total revenue in 1993 was $75,000. After paying the assistant's salary and covering the cost of raw materials, the firm shows an accounting profit of $40,000. **Accounting profit** equals total revenue minus explicit costs—those cash outlays that take the form of payments to nonowners of the firm. This is the profit used by accountants to determine a firm's taxable income.

Accounting profit A firm's total revenue minus its explicit cost

But accounting profit ignores the opportunity cost of Wanda's own resources used in the firm. First is the opportunity cost of her time. Remember that she quit a $30,000-a-year job to work full-time on her business, thereby forgoing that salary. Second is the $1,000 in interest she forgoes by using her savings. And, third, by using her garage for the business, she forgoes $1,200 per year in rental income. The forgone salary, interest, and rental income are implicit costs because, although Wanda makes no explicit payment for the resources, she gives up income generated from their best alternative uses. **Economic profit** equals total revenue minus all costs, both implicit and explicit; *economic profit takes into account the opportunity cost of resources.* In Exhibit 1, accounting profit of $40,000 less implicit costs of $32,200 equals economic profit of $7,800.

Economic profit A firm's total revenue minus its explicit and implicit costs

What would happen to the accounting statement if Wanda decided to pay herself a salary of, say, $30,000 per year? Explicit costs would increase by $30,000, implicit costs would decrease by $30,000, and accounting profits would decrease by $30,000. Economic profit, however, would not change because it already takes into account both implicit and explicit costs.

EXHIBIT 1

Accounts of Wheeler Dealer, 1993

Total revenue	$75,000
Less explicit costs:	
Assistant's salary	15,000
Material and equipment	20,000
Equals accounting profit	$40,000
Less implicit costs:	
Wanda's forgone salary	$30,000
Forgone interest on savings	1,000
Forgone garage rental	1,200
Equals economic profit	$ 7,800

Normal profit The accounting profit required to induce a firm's owners to employ their resources in the firm; the accounting profit earned when all resources used by the firm are earning their opportunity cost

There is one other important profit level to consider: the accounting profit required to induce the firm's owners to employ their resources in the firm. The level of accounting profit just sufficient to ensure that all resources used by the firm earn their opportunity cost is called a **normal profit**. Wanda's firm is earning a normal profit when the accounting profit equals the sum of the salary she gave up at her regular job ($30,000), the interest she gave up by using her own savings ($1,000), and the rent she gave up on her garage ($1,200). Thus, if the accounting profit is $32,200 per year—the opportunity cost of resources Wanda supplies to the firm—the company earns a normal profit. *Any accounting profit in excess of a normal profit is economic profit.*

Point to Stress Because total cost includes a normal profit, the firm is earning its normal profit whenever economic profit is zero ($TR = TC$). Normal profit varies from firm to firm depending on the owners' alternatives and levels of risk.

If accounting profit is large enough, it can be divided into normal profit and economic profit. The $40,000 in accounting profit earned by Wanda's firm consists of (1) a normal profit of $32,200, which just covers the opportunity cost of Wanda's resources supplied to the firm, and (2) an economic profit of $7,800, which is over and above what these resources could earn in their best alternative use. As long as economic profit is positive, Wanda is better off running her own firm than working for the Skyhigh Aircraft Company. If total revenue had been only $50,000, accounting profit of only $15,000 would cover only half of Wanda's salary, to say nothing of the forgone rent and interest. Since Wanda would not be earning even a normal profit, she would be better off working as an engineer for Skyhigh Aircraft Company.

PRODUCTION IN THE SHORT RUN

We shift now from a look at profit to a look at how firms operate. Suppose a new McDonald's has just opened in your neighborhood, and its business is booming far beyond expectations. The manager responds to the unexpected demand by quickly hiring more workers. But suppose that cars are still backed up into the street waiting for a parking space. The solution is to add a drive-through window, but such an expansion takes time.

Variable resource Any resource that can be quickly varied in the short run to increase or decrease the level of output

Fixed resource Any resource that cannot be varied in the short run

Short run A period during which at least one of a firm's resources cannot be varied

Long run A period during which all the firm's resources are variable

Fixed and Variable Resources

Some resources, such as labor, are called **variable resources** because they can be quickly varied to increase or decrease the output level. Adjustments in other resources, however, take more time; the size of the building, for example, cannot be easily altered. Such resources are therefore called **fixed resources**. When considering the time required to alter the quantity of resources employed, economists distinguish between the short run and the long run. The **short run** is a period during which at least one resource is fixed. Output can be changed by adjusting the variable resources, but the size, or scale, of the firm is fixed in the short run. In the **long run**, however, all resources can be varied. The length of the long run differs from industry to industry because the nature of the production process differs. For example,

Example In 1992, the Saturn factory in Tennessee was unable to keep up with demand for its cars. Among the short-run strategies considered was adding a third shift (by mid-1993) to boost production from 240,000 to 300,000 cars. In the long run, the company could build a second assembly plant at a cost between $500 million and $1 billion.

the size of a McDonald's restaurant can be increased more quickly than can the size of an electric power plant. Thus, the long run for McDonald's is shorter than the long run for an electric company.

The Law of Diminishing Marginal Returns

Let's focus on the short-run link between resource use and the rate of production by considering a hypothetical firm called the Smoother Mover moving company. Suppose the company's fixed resources are already in place and consist of a warehouse, a large moving van, a pickup truck, and moving equipment. In this example, labor will be the only variable resource of significance.

Exhibit 2 presents a schedule relating the amount of labor employed to output; we can call this relation the *production function*. Labor is measured in workers per day, and output is measured in tons of furniture moved per day. The left column shows the units of labor employed, which range from 0 to 8. The tons of furniture moved, or the **total physical product**, at each level of employment is in the center column. The right column shows the **marginal physical product** of each worker—that is, the amount by which the total physical product, or total output, changes with each additional unit of labor, assuming all other resources remain unchanged.

Total physical product The total output produced by a firm

Marginal physical product The change in total physical product that occurs when the usage of a particular resource increases by one unit, all other resources constant

Increasing Marginal Returns. In the moving business, nothing gets produced without labor, so when the quantity of labor is 0, no furniture gets moved and the total physical product is 0. Consider now what happens as we add labor to the fixed amount of capital. If only one worker is employed, that worker alone must do all the driving, packing, crating, and

Example The type of fixed resources can also vary from industry to industry. For example, Snider Mold Co. in Wisconsin has more orders than its workers can fill but cannot find additional skilled workers. In 1992 the National Tooling and Machining Association estimated that the country is experiencing a shortage of 10,000 toolmakers of the type needed by Snider.

Exhibit 2

The Short-Run Relation Between Units of Labor and Tons of Furniture Moved

Units of the Variable Resource (labor/day)	Total Physical Product (tons moved/day)	Marginal Physical Product (tons moved/day)
0	0	—
1	2	2
2	5	3
3	9	4
4	12	3
5	14	2
6	15	1
7	15	0
8	14	−1

Teaching Tip Total physical product indicates the *maximum* output possible given fixed available technology. Marginal physical product equals $\Delta TPP / \Delta q_{resource}$.

Increasing marginal returns Marginal physical product increases experienced by a firm when another unit of a particular resource is employed, other resources constant

Law of diminishing marginal returns When more and more of a variable resource is added to a given amount of a fixed resource, the resulting changes in output will eventually diminish

Teaching Tip Machinery has a most efficient rate of usage. As the rate of usage initially increases toward that point, then, efficiency rises. Consider the impact of rising miles per gallon (or less gas required to travel one mile) as a car accelerates toward the most efficient speed for the engine.

Teaching Tip Again consider the automobile. As a driver accelerates beyond the most efficient speed, miles per gallon drop and the amount of gas required to travel each mile rises.

moving. Some of the larger pieces of furniture, such as couches and beds, cannot easily be moved by one person. Still, in our example one worker manages to move 2 tons of furniture per day.

When a second worker is employed, some division of labor in packing is possible and two workers can handle the larger household items much more easily than one, so total production more than doubles, reaching 5 tons per day. The marginal physical product resulting from adding a second worker is 3 tons per day. Adding a third worker allows for greater specialization, which contributes to increased output; for example, one worker can specialize in packing fragile objects while the other two do the heavy lifting. The total physical product of three workers is 9 tons per day, which is 4 tons more than is produced by two workers. Because the marginal physical product increases, the firm experiences **increasing marginal returns** as each of the first three workers is added. Marginal returns increase because additional workers can specialize and can therefore make more efficient use of the fixed resources.

DIMINISHING MARGINAL RETURNS. The addition of a fourth worker adds to the total product, but not as much as was added by the third worker. Adding still more workers increases total product by successively smaller amounts, so the marginal physical product in Exhibit 2 declines. With each additional worker beyond the third, the advantages of greater specialization decrease. Indeed, with eight workers, the working area becomes so crowded that workers get in each other's way. Transporting workers to and from moving sites cuts into production because workers take up valuable space on the moving van. As a result, the total product actually declines when an eighth worker is added, so the marginal physical product is negative.

Beginning with the fourth worker, the **law of diminishing marginal returns** takes hold. This law states that as additional quantities of the variable resource are combined with a given amount of fixed resources, a point is eventually reached where each additional unit of the variable resource yields a smaller and smaller marginal physical product. *The law of diminishing marginal returns is the most important feature of firm production in the short run.* Evidence of diminishing returns is abundant. As another example, McDonald's can add only so many workers before growing congestion in the work area causes marginal physical product to decline.

The Total and Marginal Physical Product Curves

Panels (a) and (b) of Exhibit 3 illustrate the relation between the total physical product and the marginal physical product, using the data from Exhibit 2. Note that as long as the marginal physical product curve is rising—that is, as long as marginal returns are increasing—the total physical product curve increases by increasing amounts. But as the marginal product begins to decline—that is, when marginal returns start to diminish—total product still increases but at a decreasing rate. At the output level where marginal product becomes negative, the total product curve begins to turn down. So as long as marginal product is positive, total product is increasing.

Example A study by Southern California Edison on reducing fly ash emissions from its power plants indicated that one filter per stack reduced emissions by 50 percent. However, five filters were needed to reduce emissions by 97 percent, and fifteen filters to reduce emissions by 99 percent.

Teaching Tip Marginal physical product is the slope of the total physical product curve. Total physical product reaches its maximum when marginal physical product is zero.

EXHIBIT 3

The Total and Marginal Physical Product of Labor

(a) Total physical product

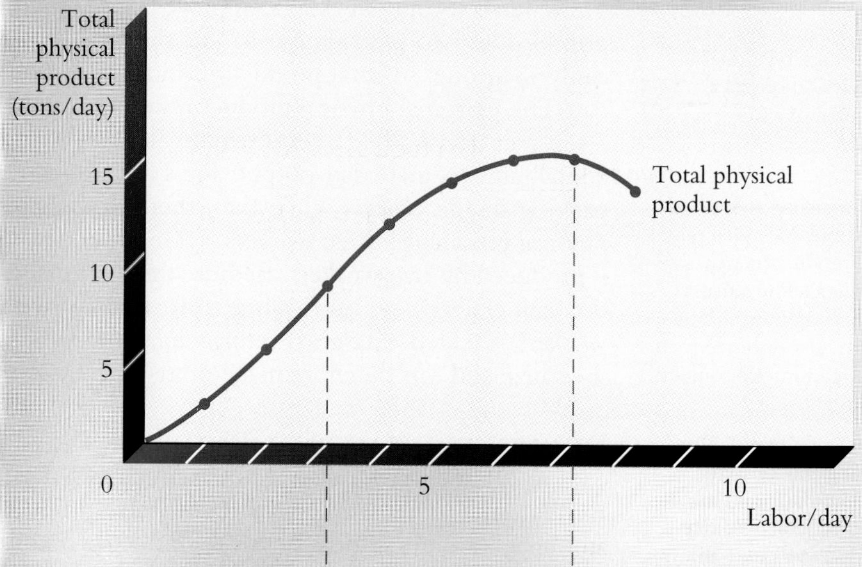

(b) Marginal physical product

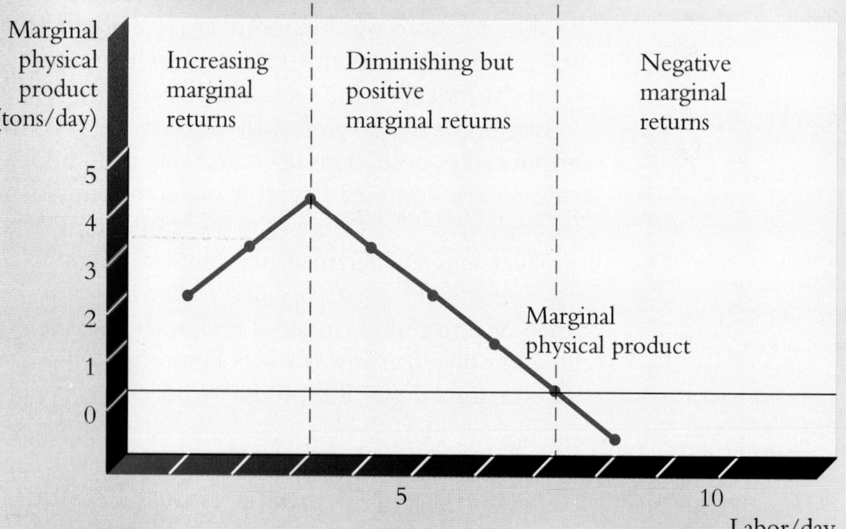

When marginal physical product is rising, total physical product is increasing by increasing amounts. When marginal physical product is decreasing but is still positive, total product is increasing by decreasing amounts. When marginal product equals 0, total product is at a maximum. Finally, when marginal product is negative, total physical product is falling.

COSTS IN THE SHORT RUN

Point to Stress The cost curve assumes fixed resource prices and fixed available technology.

Fixed cost Any production cost that is independent of the firm's rate of output

Variable cost Any production cost that increases as output increases

Point to Stress Column 1 in Exhibit 4 matches column 2 in Exhibit 2, and column 3 in Exhibit 4 matches column 1 in Exhibit 2. Using the same numbers allows the relationship between the production functions and the cost functions to be stressed.

Now that we have examined the relation between the amount of resources used and the level of output, we can consider how the firm's cost of production varies with changes in the level of output. Short-run cost is divided into two categories: fixed cost and variable cost. Simply put, fixed cost is paid to fixed resources and variable cost is paid to variable resources. A firm must pay a **fixed cost** even if no output is produced. Even if the Smoother Mover hires no labor and moves no furniture, this firm must pay for property taxes, insurance premiums, vehicle registration, maintenance, plus principal and interest on any loans for its warehouse, trucks, and equipment. By definition, fixed cost is just that: fixed; it does not vary in the short run because fixed resources do not vary even when the rate of output increases. Let's assume that the firm's *total fixed cost* comes to $200 per day.

As we said, the fixed cost is paid to fixed resources, and the **variable cost**, as the name implies, is paid to variable resources. When output is 0, variable cost is $0 because no variable resources are employed. When output increases, more variable resources are employed so variable cost increases. The amount by which variable cost increases depends on the amount of variable resources employed and the prices of those resources. In our example, variable cost consists of labor costs. Suppose labor costs the firm $100 per worker per day. The *total variable cost* in this example can be found by multiplying $100 times the amount of labor employed.

Total Cost and Marginal Cost in the Short Run

Exhibit 4 presents daily cost data for the Smoother Mover. The table lists the cost of production associated with alternative levels of output. Column

EXHIBIT 4

Short-Run Cost Data for the Smoother Mover

Tons Moved per Day (q) (1)	Total Fixed Cost (TFC) (2)	Workers per Day (3)	Total Variable Cost (TVC) (4)	Total Cost ($TC = TFC + TVC$) (5)	Marginal Cost $\left(MC = \frac{\Delta TC}{\Delta q}\right)$ (6)
0	$200	0	$ 0	$200	—
2	200	1	100	300	$ 50.00
5	200	2	200	400	33.33
9	200	3	300	500	25.00
12	200	4	400	600	33.33
14	200	5	500	700	50.00
15	200	6	600	800	100.00

(1) shows possible levels of output in the short run, measured in tons of furniture per day.

Point to Stress Total cost incorporates both explicit and implicit costs (including a normal profit).

Total Cost. Column (2) indicates the total fixed cost (*TFC*) for each level of output. Note that total fixed cost remains constant at $200 per day regardless of the level of output. Column (3) shows the amount of labor required to produce each level of output and is based on the productivity reported in the previous two exhibits. (Only the first six units of labor are listed because units seven and beyond added nothing to total product.) For example, moving 2 tons requires one worker, 5 tons requires two workers, and so on. Column (4) lists the total variable cost (*TVC*) per day, which equals the cost of $100 per unit of labor times the quantity of labor employed per day. For example, the total variable cost of moving 9 tons of furniture per day is $300 since three workers must be employed. Column (5) lists the **total cost** (*TC*) of each level of output, which is the sum of the total fixed cost and total variable cost: $TC = TFC + TVC$. Note that at 0 units of output, total variable cost is $0, so total cost equals total fixed cost.

Total cost The sum of fixed cost and variable cost

Marginal cost The change in total cost divided by the change in output; the change in total cost resulting from a one-unit change in output

Marginal Cost. Of major interest to the firm is how total cost changes as output changes. More specifically, what is the marginal cost of producing another unit? The **marginal cost** of production listed in column (6) is simply the change in total cost divided by the change in output, or $MC = \Delta TC/\Delta q$. For example, increasing output from 0 to 2 tons increases total cost by $100 ($300 – $200). The marginal cost of each of the first 2 tons is the change in total cost, $100, divided by the change in output, 2, or $100/2, which equals $50. The marginal cost of each of the next three tons equals $100/3, or $33.33.

Teaching Tip Since fixed cost does not change with output, marginal cost must equal marginal *variable* cost. Thus, marginal cost can also be calculated as $MC = \Delta TVC/\Delta q$.

Notice in column (6) that marginal cost first decreases, then increases. *Changes in marginal cost reflect changes in the marginal productivity of the variable resources employed.* Recall from Exhibit 2 that the first three workers contributed to increasing marginal returns, with each worker producing more output than the last. This greater productivity of labor results in a falling marginal cost for the output produced by the first three workers. As more labor is added beyond three workers, however, the firm experiences diminishing marginal returns to labor, so the marginal cost of output increases. *When the firm experiences increasing marginal returns, the marginal cost of output decreases; when the firm experiences diminishing marginal returns, the marginal cost of output increases.*

Teaching Tip When the variable resource is labor, as in Exhibit 4, ΔTC equals the wage rate (w) as labor varies by one unit and Δq equals marginal physical product. Thus, $MC = w/MPP$. Since w remains unchanged, marginal cost falls as marginal physical product rises; marginal cost rises as marginal physical product falls.

Thus, the marginal cost in Exhibit 4 first falls and then rises, because of first increasing and then diminishing marginal returns. Specifically, the labor employed by the Smoother Mover shows increasing marginal returns for the first 9 tons of furniture moved and decreasing marginal returns thereafter. Recall that marginal cost equals the increase in total cost divided by the change in output.

Total and Marginal Cost Curves. Exhibit 5 shows the total cost curves and the marginal cost curve for the data in Exhibit 4. Since total fixed cost does not vary with output, the total fixed cost curve is a horizontal line at the $200 level in panel (a). Total variable cost is $0 when output is 0, so the total variable cost curve starts from the origin. Initially, total variable cost

EXHIBIT 5

Total and Marginal Cost Curves

(a) Total cost curves

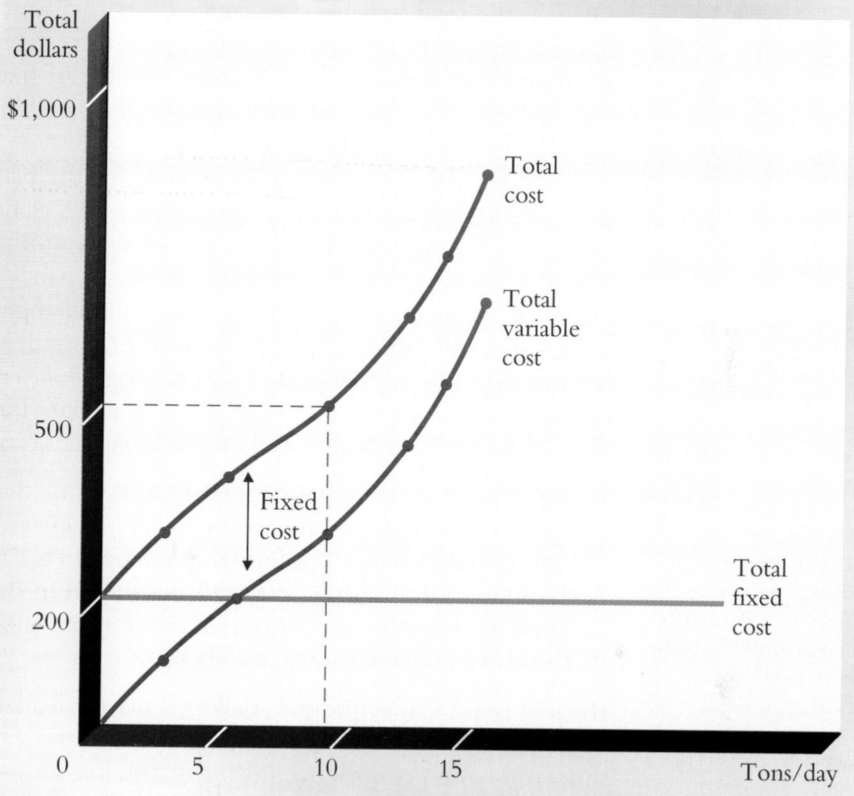

(b) Marginal cost

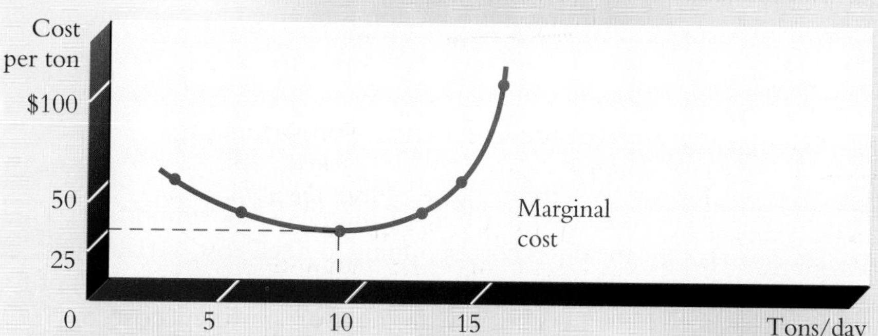

In panel (a), total fixed cost is constant at all levels of output. Total variable cost starts from the origin and increases slowly at first as output increases. When the variable resources generate diminishing marginal returns, total variable cost begins to increase more rapidly. Total cost is the vertical sum of total fixed cost and total variable cost. In panel (b), marginal cost first declines, reflecting increasing marginal returns, and then increases, reflecting diminishing marginal returns.

Point to Stress The product curves are graphed with output measured along the vertical axis, whereas the cost curve graphs have output along the horizontal axis. For the product curves, output is the dependent variable; for the cost curves, it is the independent variable.

Teaching Tip Both the total cost and total variable cost curves become steeper after 9 units of output in Exhibit 5. This is also the output at which the marginal cost curve reaches its minimum and the marginal physical product curve reaches its maximum [see panel (b) of Exhibit 3].

increases slowly as output increases because of increasing marginal returns to labor. As soon as labor reaches the point of diminishing marginal returns, however, total variable cost begins to climb more rapidly as output expands. Overall, the total variable cost curve has a backward S shape. The total cost curve is derived by *vertically* summing the total variable cost curve and the total fixed cost curve. Because a constant amount of fixed cost is added to total variable cost, the total cost curve is the total variable cost curve shifted vertically by the amount of fixed cost.

We have already discussed the reasons for the pattern of marginal cost. In panel (b) of Exhibit 5, the marginal cost curve at first declines and then increases, reflecting labor's increasing and then diminishing marginal returns. There is a clear geometric relation between panels (a) and (b) because the change in total cost resulting from a one-unit change in production equals the marginal cost. With each successive unit of output, the total cost increases by the marginal cost of that unit. Thus, *the slope of the total cost curve at each level of output equals the marginal cost at that level of output*. The total cost curve can be divided into two sections based on what happens to marginal cost:

1. Because of increasing marginal returns from the variable resource, marginal cost at first declines, so the total cost curve at the outset increases by successively smaller amounts and its slope gets flatter.
2. Because of diminishing marginal returns from the variable resource, marginal cost begins to increase after the ninth unit of output, leading to a steeper and steeper total cost curve.

Keep in mind that economic analysis is marginal analysis. Marginal cost is one of the keys to economic decisions made by firms. The firm operating in the short run has no control over its fixed cost, but it can, by varying the resources employed, vary output. So by varying output in the short run, the firm alters its variable cost and hence its total cost. Marginal cost indicates how much total cost will increase if one more unit is produced or how much total cost will drop if production is reduced by one unit.

Average Cost in the Short Run

Although total cost and marginal cost are of most analytical interest, the average cost per unit of output is also important. There are three average cost measures corresponding to fixed cost, variable cost, and total cost. These average costs are shown in columns (5), (6), and (7) of Exhibit 6.

Average fixed cost Total fixed cost divided by output

Average variable cost Total variable cost divided by output

Average total cost Total cost divided by output; the sum of average fixed cost plus average variable cost

Let's begin with the **average fixed cost**, or *AFC*, which equals total fixed cost divided by output, or $AFC = TFC/q$. In our example the average fixed cost equals the total fixed cost of \$200 divided by the level of output. As the data in column (5) indicate, average fixed cost declines steadily as output increases because \$200 in fixed cost is averaged over more and more units of output. Column (6) lists the **average variable cost**, or *AVC*, which equals total variable cost divided by output, or $AVC = TVC/q$. The final column lists **average total cost**, or *ATC*, which is total cost divided by output, or $ATC = TC/q$. Both average variable cost and average total cost first decline as output expands and then increase.

EXHIBIT 6

Short-Run Cost Data for a Hypothetical Firm

Total Output (q) (1)	Total Variable Cost (TVC) (2)	Total Cost ($TC = TFC + TVC$) (3)	Marginal Cost $\left(MC = \frac{\Delta TC}{\Delta q}\right)$ (4)	Average Fixed Cost $\left(AFC = \frac{TFC}{q}\right)$ (5)	Average Variable Cost $\left(AVC = \frac{TVC}{q}\right)$ (6)	Average Total Cost $\left(ATC = \frac{TC}{q}\right)$ (7)
0	$ 0	$200	$ 0	∞	——	∞
2	100	300	50.00	$100.00	$50.00	$150.00
5	200	400	33.33	40.00	40.00	80.00
9	300	500	25.00	22.22	33.33	55.55
12	400	600	33.33	16.67	33.33	50.00
14	500	700	50.00	14.29	35.71	50.00
15	600	800	100.00	13.33	40.00	53.33

Teaching Tip The relationship between marginal and average values can also be illustrated by considering a baseball star's annual batting averages and lifetime batting average.

The Relation Between Average Cost and Marginal Cost

To understand the relation between marginal cost and average variable cost, perhaps we can begin with an analogy of college grades. Consider a hypothetical example of how your grades for the term, which are your marginal grades, affect your cumulative grade point average, or your average grades. Suppose you do well your first term, starting your college career with a grade point of 3.0. Your grades for the second term slip to 2.4, reducing your average to 2.7. You slip again the third term to 2.1, lowering your average to 2.5. Your grades for the fourth term improve to 2.5, but since your average was already 2.5, it remains unchanged at 2.5. The next term you improve to a 3.0, which pulls up your average to 2.6. Notice that as long as your term grades were below your average grade, your average grade fell. When your term performance improved, your average did not improve until your term grades exceeded your average grades. Think of your term grades as first pulling down your average and then pulling up your average.

Point to Stress Marginal cost can be rising or falling while the average total and average variable cost curves are falling. What is important is whether marginal cost is below the average curves.

In Exhibit 6, marginal cost has the same relation to average cost as your term grades have to your grade point average. Notice the relation between the marginal cost in column (4) and the average variable cost in column (6). Because of increasing marginal returns to the first three workers, the marginal cost falls for the first 9 tons of furniture moved. Since marginal cost is below the average variable cost for the first 9 tons, marginal cost pulls down the average variable cost. The marginal cost of the ninth ton is $25, which is below its average variable cost of $33.33. Diminishing marginal returns set in with the fourth worker, raising the marginal cost of the twelfth ton to $33.33. But because the average variable cost had already been $33.33 for the ninth ton, the average variable cost for the twelfth ton remains unchanged at $33.33. The marginal cost for the fourteenth ton jumps to $50, pulling up the average variable cost to $35.71.

Point to Stress The effects of increasing and diminishing marginal returns are *short-run* phenomena.

The average cost data from Exhibit 6 are graphed as average cost curves in Exhibit 7, along with the marginal cost curve already introduced in Exhibit 5. The average fixed cost curve falls continually as output expands. The average variable and average total cost curves first fall and then, after reaching a low point, rise; overall, each has a U shape. The shape of the average variable cost curve is determined by the shape of the marginal cost curve, and each in turn is shaped by increasing and diminishing marginal returns. At low levels of output, the marginal cost curve declines as output expands because of increasing marginal returns. As long as marginal cost is below average variable cost, average variable cost falls as output expands. The marginal cost curve and the average variable cost curve intersect where output is 12 tons per day and the cost is $33.33 per ton. At higher rates of output marginal cost exceeds average variable cost, so the average variable cost curve starts to rise as output expands—the higher marginal

EXHIBIT 7

Average and Marginal Cost Curves

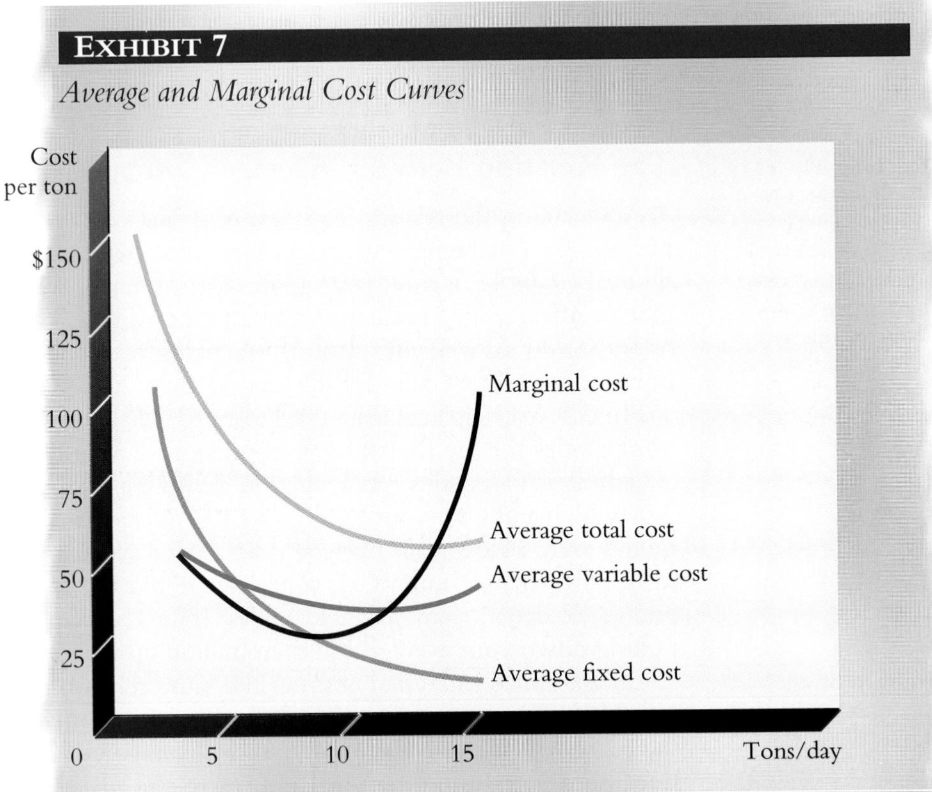

Average fixed cost drops as output expands. Average variable cost and average total cost drop, reach low points, and then rise; overall, they take on U shapes. When marginal cost is below average variable cost, average variable cost is falling. When marginal cost equals average variable cost, average variable cost is at its minimum value. When marginal cost is above average variable cost, average variable cost is increasing. The same relationship holds between marginal cost and average total cost.

cost begins to pull up the average. Thus, the marginal cost curve explains why the average variable cost curve has a U shape.

Teaching Tip Average fixed cost never reaches zero. Therefore, the average variable cost curve never reaches the average total cost curve.

The average total cost curve is the vertical sum of the average fixed cost curve and the average variable cost curve. Therefore, the shape of the average total cost curve reflects the shapes of the underlying average cost curves. Note that as output increases, the average variable cost and the average total cost curves grow closer together because average fixed cost, which is the vertical difference between the two, becomes smaller.

Teaching Tip In Exhibit 6, between the minimum point of average variable cost at 12 units of output and the minimum point of average total cost at 14 units of output, marginal cost is still below average total cost. Therefore, average total cost is still falling. If output expands to 15 units, however, marginal cost is now above average total cost. Note that average variable cost rises by $4.29 and average fixed cost falls by $0.96. Therefore, average total cost rises by $3.33, or $4.29 – $0.96.

The marginal cost curve has the same relation to the average total cost curve as to the average variable cost curve, and for the same reasons. When marginal cost is below average total cost, average total cost declines as output expands. The two curves intersect at 14 units of output. At higher levels of output, marginal cost is above average total cost, so average total cost increases as output expands. Because of these relations, *the rising marginal cost curve intersects both the average variable cost curve and the average total cost curve where these average curves are at a minimum.* Note that the minimum point on the average total cost curve occurs at a greater level of output than does the minimum point on the average variable cost curve because a falling average fixed cost continues to pull the average total cost curve down even after the average variable cost has begun rising.

Summary of Short-Run Cost Curves

The level of the firm's fixed costs, the price of variable inputs, and the law of diminishing marginal returns determine the shape of all the short-run cost curves. The shape of the marginal physical product curve discussed earlier in the chapter determines the shape of the marginal cost curve. And the shape of the marginal physical product curve is determined by the production function, which is the relation between labor and output. Thus, the marginal cost curve depends ultimately on how much each unit of labor produces. When the marginal physical product of labor increases, the marginal cost of output must fall. Conversely, as diminishing marginal returns set in, the marginal cost of output must rise. Thus, the marginal cost curve first falls, then rises. And the marginal cost curve dictates the shapes of the average variable cost and the average total cost curves. When marginal cost is less than average cost, average cost is falling; when marginal cost is above average cost, average cost is rising.

COSTS IN THE LONG RUN

Thus far the analysis has focused on how costs vary as the rate of output expands in the short run for a firm of a given size. In the long run, all inputs that are under the firm's control can be varied, so there are no fixed costs. The long run is not just a succession of short runs. The long run is best thought of as a *planning horizon*; the years into the future for which the firm tries to plan. In the long run the choice of input combinations is flexible, but

Teaching Tip Given factor prices and available technology, the firm in the long run will plan for the lowest cost of producing any given level of output. This behavior maximizes profit. See the appendix for the development of the mathematical equation for cost minimization.

Teaching Tip The average total cost curves move to the right as plant size expands. In order to make its long-run plans, the firm must anticipate its future production needs. Temporarily increased production needs would be met by expanding output within the same plant size, not by increasing the plant size. Consider the increased need for plywood for reconstruction in Florida after Hurricane Andrew in 1992. In contrast, Nissan spent $475 million to double capacity at its Tennessee assembly plant in anticipation of a permanent increase in sales from its new Altima model.

this flexibility is valid only for the firm that has not yet acted on its plans. Firms plan in the long run but they produce in the short run. Once the size of the plant has been selected and resources have been committed, the firm has fixed costs and is once again back in the short run. As we will see, there is a different short-run average total cost curve for each possible plant size. We turn now to the long-run cost curves.

The Long-Run Average Cost Curve

Suppose that, because of the special nature of technology in the industry, a firm's plant can be one of only three possible sizes: small, medium, or large. Exhibit 8 presents this simple case. The short-run average total cost curves for the three plant sizes are SS', MM', and LL'. Which size plant should the firm build to minimize the average cost of production? The appropriate size, or scale, for the plant depends on how much the firm wants to produce. For example, if q is the desired production rate in the long run, the average cost per unit will be lowest with a small plant. If the desired output level is q', the medium plant size ensures the lowest average cost.

EXHIBIT 8

Short-Run Average Cost Curves and the Long-Run Planning Curve

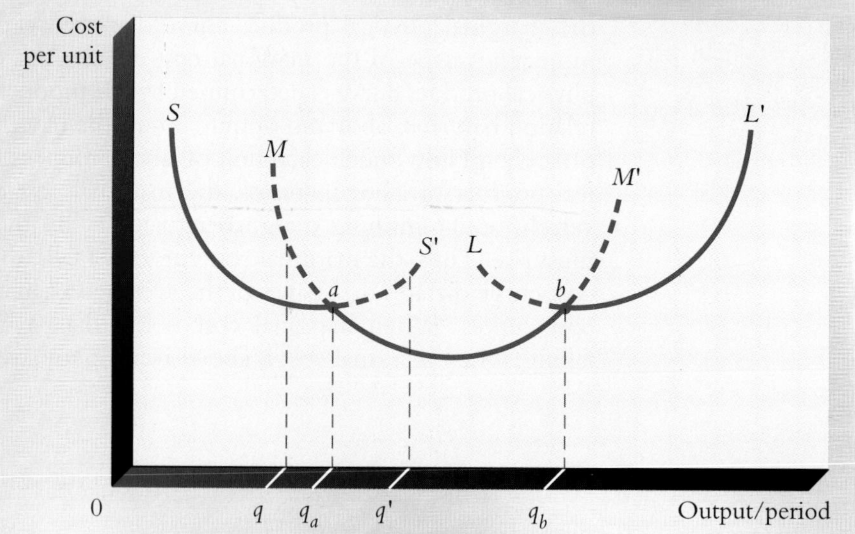

Curves SS', MM', and LL' show short-run average total costs for small, medium, and large plants, respectively. For output less than q_a, average cost is lowest when the plant is small. Between q_a and q_b, cost is lowest with a medium-size plant. If output exceeds q_b, the large plant is best. The long-run average cost curve is $SabL'$.

More generally, for any output less than q_a, the average cost of output is lowest when the plant is small. For output levels between q_a and q_b, the average cost is lowest when the plant is of medium size. And for output levels that exceed q_b, the average cost is lowest when the plant is large. The **long-run average cost curve** connects the points on the three short-run average cost curves that are lowest for each output level. In Exhibit 8, the curve consists of the solid line segments connecting *S*, *a*, *b*, and *L′*.

Long-run average cost curve A curve that indicates the lowest average cost of production at each level of output when the firm's plant size is allowed to vary

Now suppose that the number of possible plant sizes is large. Exhibit 9 presents a sample of possible short-run average total cost curves. The long-run average cost curve is created by connecting the points on the various short-run average cost curves that represent the lowest per-unit cost for each level of output. Each of the short-run cost curves is tangent to the long-run average cost curve, which is sometimes called the firm's *planning curve*, or *envelope curve*. If we could draw enough cost curves, we would have a different plant size for each level of output. These points of tangency represent the least-cost way of producing each particular level of output, given the technology and resource prices. For example, the short-run average cost curve

Teaching Tip Points below the long-run average cost curve are unattainable. Points above the curve are attainable, but points on the curve are attainable only after sufficient time elapses to vary all resources. The movement from point *a* to point *b* in Exhibit 9 represents a short-run adjustment; from point *b* to point *c* is a long-run adjustment. Use the earlier example of the Saturn plant in Tennessee to contrast adding a third shift with building a second plant.

EXHIBIT 9

Family of Many Short-Run Cost Curves Forming a Firm's Long-Run Planning Curve

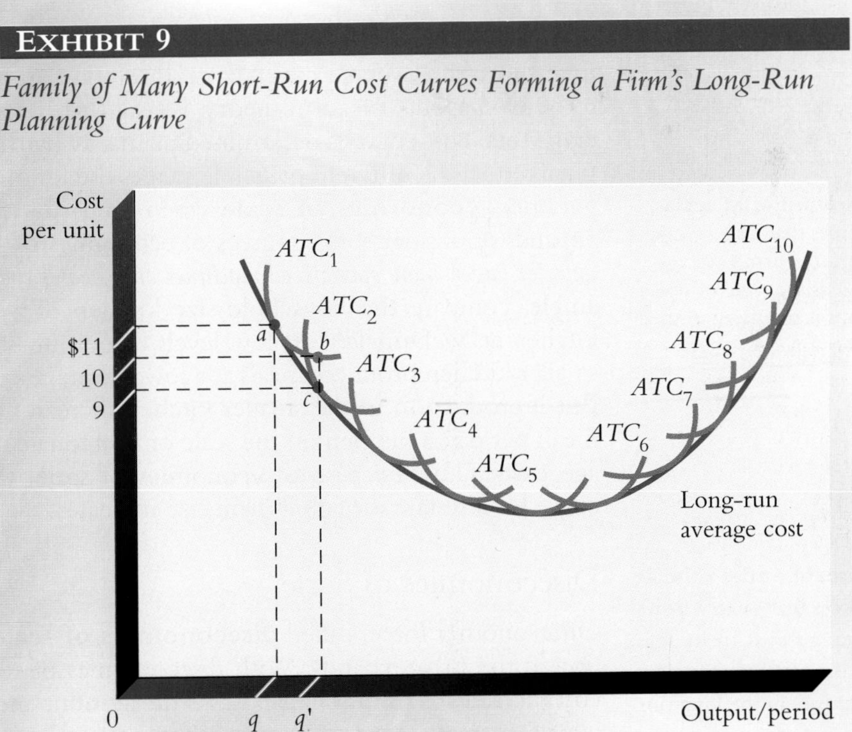

With many possible plant sizes, the long-run average cost curve is the envelope of portions of the short-run average cost curves. Each short-run curve is tangent to the long-run average cost curve, or long-run planning curve. Each point of tangency represents the least-cost way of producing a particular level of output.

ATC_1 is tangent to the planning curve at point *a*, indicating that the least-cost way of producing output level *q* is with the plant size associated with ATC_1. No other size plant would produce output level *q* at as low a cost per unit. Note, however, that other output levels along ATC_1 have a lower average cost of production. In fact, for output level *q′* at point *b*, the average cost per unit is only $10, compared to an average cost per unit of $11 for producing *q* at point *a*. Point *b* depicts the lowest average cost along ATC_1. So although the point of tangency represents the least-cost way of producing a particular level of output, it does not in this case represent a least-cost output level for this particular plant size.

If the firm decides to produce output level *q′* which size plant should it choose to minimize the average cost of production? Output level *q′* could be produced at point *b*, which represents the minimum average cost along ATC_1. However, the firm could achieve a lower average cost with a larger plant. Specifically, if the firm built a plant of the size associated with ATC_2, the average cost of producing *q′* would be minimized at point *c*. *Each point of tangency between a short-run average cost curve and the long-run average cost curve, or planning curve, represents the least-cost way of producing that particular level of output.*

Teaching Tip In Exhibit 9, economies of scale occur as the firm moves from ATC_1 through ATC_5—the average total cost curves get lower as you move to the right.

Economies of Scale

Economies of scale Forces that cause reduction in a firm's average cost as the scale of operations is increased in the long run

Like short-run average cost curves, the long-run average cost curve appears to be U-shaped, at least in theory. Recall that the shape of the short-run average total cost curve is determined primarily by the law of diminishing marginal returns. A different principle shapes the long-run cost curve. A firm experiences **economies of scale** when long-run average cost falls as output expands. Consider some sources of economies of scale. *A larger size often allows for larger, more specialized machines and greater specialization of labor.* For example, compare the household-size kitchen of a small restaurant with the kitchen at McDonald's. At low levels of output, say fifteen meals a day, the smaller kitchen produces meals at a lower average cost than does McDonald's. But if production in the smaller kitchen increases beyond, say, one hundred meals per day, a kitchen on the scale of McDonald's would have a lower average cost. Thus, because of economies of scale, the long-run average cost curve for a restaurant falls as firm size increases.

Diseconomies of Scale

Diseconomies of scale Forces that cause a firm's average cost to increase as the scale of operations increases in the long run

Often another force, called **diseconomies of scale**, is eventually set in motion as the firm expands. With diseconomies of scale, the long-run average cost increases as output expands. As the amount and variety of resources employed increase, so does the management task of coordinating all these inputs. As the work force grows, additional layers of management are needed to monitor production. In the thicket of bureaucracy that develops, communication may become garbled. The top executives have more difficulty keeping in touch with the shop floor because information is distorted as it passes through the chain of command. Indeed, in very large organizations rumors may become a primary source of information, thereby reducing the efficiency of the organization and increasing average cost. For example, in 1988 IBM was

Teaching Tip In Exhibit 9, the average total cost curves start rising as you move to the right beginning with ATC_6—diseconomies of scale set in.

reportedly undertaking a massive restructuring program because the firm was experiencing diseconomies of scale, particularly in management. IBM's solution was to decentralize into six smaller decision-making groups. Note that diseconomies of scale result from a larger firm size, whereas diminishing marginal returns result from using more variable resources in a firm of a given size.

Let's consider economies and diseconomies of scale in commercial shipping. One rule of naval architecture is that larger ships can go faster. Also, the cargo-carrying capacity of a ship increases proportionately more than the increase in the cost of building and operating the ship. Some economies of scale observed in ocean vessels are also found in trucks. For example, hiring a driver for a 50-foot truck costs little more than hiring one for a 25-foot truck. Beyond a certain size of ship or truck, however, diseconomies of scale dominate. Ocean-going vessels may become so large that few ports can handle them. Trucks may become so large that they cannot negotiate some roads.

We assumed at the outset that in the long run the firm could vary all the inputs under its control. Some inputs, however, are not under the firm's control, and the inability to vary these inputs may be a source of diseconomies of scale, as you will see in the following case study, which describes both economies and diseconomies of scale.

CASE STUDY

At the Movies

Consider economies of scale at the movies. A movie theater with one screen needs someone to sell tickets, someone to operate the concession stand, and someone to operate the projector. If another screen is added, the same staff can perform these tasks for both screens. Thus, the ticket seller becomes more productive because tickets are sold to both movies. Furthermore, construction costs per screen are reduced because only one lobby and one set of restrooms are required. This is why we see theater owners adding more and more screens at the same location; they are taking advantage of economies of scale.

Economies of scale clearly result from multiple screens. But why stop at, say, twelve screens? Why not twenty or thirty, particularly in densely populated urban areas, where sufficient demand would warrant such a high level of output? One problem with expanding the number of screens is that the public roads leading to the theaters are a resource that theaters cannot control. The congestion around the theater grows with the number of screens at that location. Also, the supply of popular films may not be sufficient at any one time to fill so many screens.

Finally, time itself is a resource that the firm cannot easily control. Only certain hours are popular with moviegoers. Scheduling becomes more difficult because the manager must space out starting and ending times to avoid having too many customers arrive and depart at once. No more "prime time" can be created. Thus, theater owners' lack control over such inputs as the size of public roads, the supply of films, and the hours in the day, and this lack of control may contribute to an increase in the long-run average cost as output expands, or to diseconomies of scale.

Point to Stress The minimum efficient scale indicates the first output level with the lowest cost per unit.

Example: A study of minimum efficient scales by Joe Bain (*Barriers to New Competition*, Harvard University Press, 1956) showed that the cost of one plant of minimum efficient scale was as high as $665 million in the steel industry and as high as $500 million in the automobile industry.

Example In 1992, General Motors spent nearly $800 more per car in labor costs because the firm had excess capacity. *Time* magazine called GM's size one of its "greatest burdens" (November 9, 1992). GM's chairman and CEO was ousted in 1992 because the board of directors considered that he was acting too slowly to restructure and downsize.

EXHIBIT 10

A Firm's Long-Run Average Cost Curve

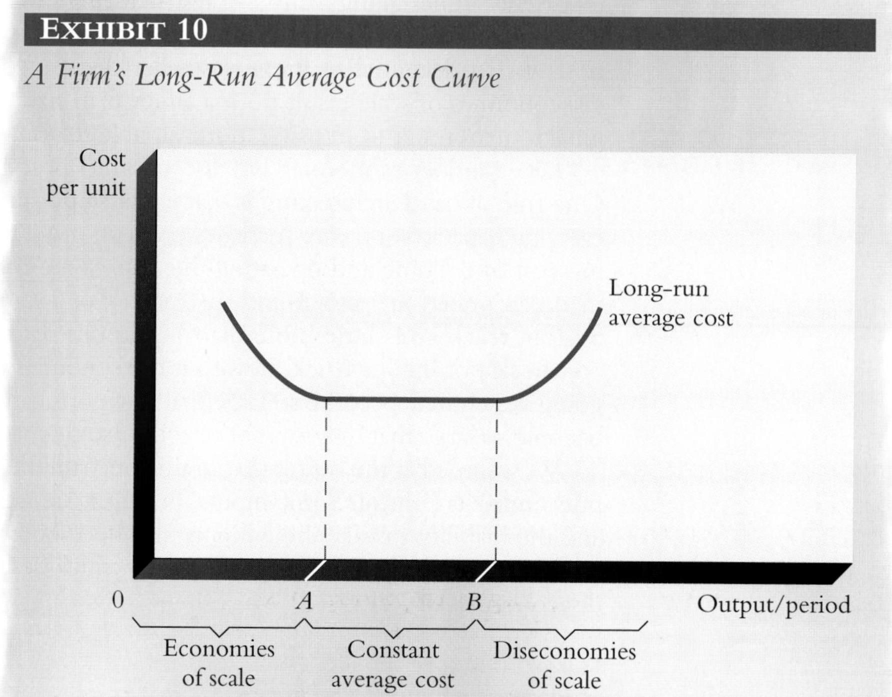

Up to output level *A*, the long-run average cost curve has a negative slope; the firm is experiencing economies of scale. Point *A* is the minimum efficient scale—the lowest rate of output at which the firm takes full advantage of economies of scale. Between *A* and *B*, the average cost is constant. Beyond output level *B*, the long-run average cost curve slopes upward, reflecting diseconomies of scale.

It is possible for average cost to neither increase nor decrease with changes in firm size. If neither economies of scale nor diseconomies of scale are apparent in the production process, the firm experiences *constant average costs*. Perhaps economies and diseconomies of scale exist simultaneously but have offsetting effects.

Exhibit 10 presents a firm's long-run average cost curve, which is divided into segments reflecting economies of scale, constant long-run average cost, and diseconomies of scale. The rate of production would have to reach point *A* for the firm to achieve the **minimum efficient scale**, which is the lowest rate of output at which long-run average cost is at a minimum. From output level *A* to level *B*, average cost is constant. Beyond point *B*, diseconomies of scale increase long-run average cost.

Minimum efficient scale The lowest rate of output at which a firm takes full advantage of economies of scale

Economies and Diseconomies of Scale at the Firm Level

The discussion thus far has usually referred to a particular plant—the size of a movie theater or a restaurant—as opposed to the firm more generally. It is useful, however, to distinguish between economies and diseconomies of scale at the *plant level*—that is, at a particular location—and at the *firm level*. We examine economies and diseconomies of scale at the firm level in the following case study.

CASE STUDY

Billions and Billions of Burgers

McDonald's experiences economies of scale at the plant level because of its specialization of labor and machines, but the company also benefits from economies of scale at the firm level. Operating at many separate locations allows the company to standardize menus and operating procedures, to centralize its management training program at Hamburger University (McDonald's school for restaurant operators), and to spread the cost of its advertising over thousands of individual "plants."

The menu at a local fast-food outlet is the result of intense planning. Every stage of food preparation is timed and evaluated. Each of the major chains calculates how long it takes employees to do everything from flipping burgers to putting pickles on buns. Before any new product is introduced, labor requirements are monitored closely. For example, before Burger King decided to switch from one cola to another, the company spent more than two years on market research. Reportedly, undercover researchers were sent to competitors' sites to track the time required to inform customers who had asked for one cola that only the other was available.

Some diseconomies arise in such large-scale operations. The fact that the menu must be uniform around the country means that if customers in some parts of the country do not like a product, it does not get on the menu regardless of its popularity elsewhere. McDonald's McRib sandwich never quite caught on in some parts of the country and had to be dropped. Wendy's plans for a gourmet hamburger had to be scrapped because most customers in two states were not familiar with such ingredients as alfalfa sprouts and guacamole. Another problem with a uniform national menu is that the ingredients must be available around the country and cannot be subject to droughts or sharp swings in price. One chain decided not to add bacon strips as an option on its burgers because the price of pork bellies was so unstable.

McDonald's now sells in dozens of countries around the world, so menu planning for them has become increasingly complex. For example, when McDonald's went into Russia, the company had to develop supply sources for beef, potatoes, lettuce, and other ingredients. In some cases the company had to train farmers how to grow to specifications. Thus, when a firm expands to multiple firms and to multiple countries, it experiences both economies of scale and diseconomies of scale.

Source: John Koten, "Fast-Food Firms' New Items Undergo Exhaustive Testing," *Wall Street Journal*, 5 January 1984, and "Big MacCurrencies," *The Economist*, 18 April 1992.

CONCLUSION

Teaching Tip The cost curves assume given resource prices and available technology. Increased resource prices shift the entire family of variable and total curves up. Lower resource prices or a technological improvement shift the curves down.

In this chapter, by considering the relation between production and cost, we have developed the foundations of the theory of firm behavior. In the appendix we present an alternative way of determining a firm's most efficient combination of resources. Despite what may appear to be a tangle of short-run and long-run cost curves, *only two relations between resources and outputs underlie all the curves. In the short run, it is increasing and diminishing returns from the variable resource. In the long run, it is economies and diseconomies of scale.* If you understand the sources of these two phenomena, you have grasped the central ideas of this chapter. Our examination of the relation between resource use and the amount produced in both the short run and the long run will in the next chapter help us derive an upward-sloping supply curve.

SUMMARY

1. Explicit costs are payments for the use of resources not owned by the firm. Implicit costs are the opportunity costs of using resources owned by the firm or provided by the firm's owners. A firm is said to be earning a normal profit if total revenue just covers all implicit and explicit costs. Economic profit equals total revenue minus both explicit and implicit costs.

2. Resources that can be easily varied to increase or decrease the output level are called variable resources. Other resources, such as capital, are called fixed resources because of the time required to alter the amount of the resource used. In the short run, at least one resource is fixed. In the long run, all resources are variable.

3. Short-run increases in the variable resource initially may result in increasing marginal returns as the firm takes advantage of increased specialization of the variable resource. The law of diminishing marginal returns indicates that a point is eventually reached where additional units of the variable resource, combined with the fixed resources, yield a smaller and smaller marginal product.

4. The law of diminishing marginal returns is the most important feature of firm production in the short run and is the reason why the marginal cost curve eventually slopes upward as output expands. The law of diminishing marginal returns also explains why the average cost curves eventually increase as output increases in the short run.

5. In the long run, all inputs under the firm's control are variable, so there are no fixed costs. The firm's long-run average cost curve is an envelope formed by a series of short-run average total cost curves. The long run is best thought of as a planning horizon.

6. In the long run, the firm selects the most efficient size for the desired level of output. Once the size of the firm has been selected and resources have been committed, some resources become fixed, so the firm is back in the short run. Thus, the firm plans for the long-run but produces in the short run.

7. In theory, the long-run average cost curve, like the short-run average total cost curve, tends to be U-shaped. As output expands, average cost at first declines because of economies of scale—a larger plant size allows for more specialized machinery and a more extensive division of labor. Eventually, average cost stops falling. Average cost may be constant over some range. As output expands still further, the plant may encounter diseconomies of scale as the cost of coordinating resources grows.

QUESTIONS AND PROBLEMS

1. (Explicit Versus Implicit Costs) Old MacDonald is currently raising corn on his 100-acre farm. He can make an accounting profit of $100 per acre. However, if he raised soybeans, he could make $200 per acre. Is the farmer currently earning an economic profit? Why or why not?

2. (Opportunity Costs) Corporate executives often take jobs with the government for much smaller salaries. What are their opportunity costs? Does your answer depend on whether you take a long-run or a short-run view?

3. (Normal Profits) Why is it reasonable to think of normal profits as a type of cost to the firm?

4. (Diminishing Returns) All commercial jets have a pilot and a copilot. How would you interpret the marginal product of the copilot? Why not have a third or fourth pilot for the same flight?

5. (Diminishing Returns) Suppose that you have some farmland. You must decide how many times during the year you will grow your crops. Also, you must decide how to space each plant (or seedling). Will diminishing returns be a factor in your decision making? Relate your answer to Exhibit 3 in this chapter.

6. (Marginal Cost) Explain why the marginal cost curve must intersect the average total cost and the average variable cost curves at their minimum points.

7. (Average Total Cost and Average Variable Cost) Why must average total cost and average variable cost approach each other as output increases? Will this be true for all cost curves?

8. (Short-Run Costs) Which of the following would shift the short-run marginal cost curve in toward the origin? In which direction might marginal cost shift?
   a. An increase in wage rates
   b. A decrease in property taxes
   c. A rise in the purchase price of new capital
   d. A rise in oil prices (or energy prices)
   e. A sudden change in technology

9. (Long-Run Average Costs) What factors would shift the long-run average cost curve? Would these changes also affect the short-run average cost curves? Why or why not?

10. (Long Run Versus Short Run) What determines the length of the short run? Will this period of time be different for different types of industries?

11. (Marginal Product and Costs) Let *L* equal units of labor, *Q* equal units of output, and *MPP* equal the marginal physical product of labor.
   a. Fill in the table.

L	*Q*	*MPP*	*TVC*	*TC*	*MC*	*ATC*
0	0	___	$0	$12	___	___
1	6	___	3	15	___	___
2	15	___	6	___	___	___
3	21	___	9	___	___	___
4	24	___	12	___	___	___
5	26	___	15	___	___	___
6	27	___	18	___	___	___

   b. At what level of labor do the marginal returns of labor diminish?
   c. What is the implication for marginal cost of the answer to the preceding question?
   d. What is the average variable cost when $Q = 24$?
   e. What is the level of fixed cost?
   f. What is the price of a unit of labor?

12. (Production and Cost) Use the following table to answer the questions below. *C* is units of capital, *L* is units of labor, and *Q* is units of output.

C	*L*	*Q*
5	0	0
5	2	10
5	4	16
5	6	18
5	8	19

Price of labor = $3
TFC = $20

   a. What is the price of capital?
   b. What is the total cost of producing 10 units of *Q*?
   c. What is the average cost of producing 16 units of *Q*?
   d. What is the marginal cost of producing the nineteenth unit of *Q*?

13. (Short- and Long-Run Costs) Suppose that a firm has only three possible scales of production, with the middle scale of production achieving the lowest average cost of any of the three scales. Let the three short-run average total cost curves be U-shaped and intersect each other as shown below.

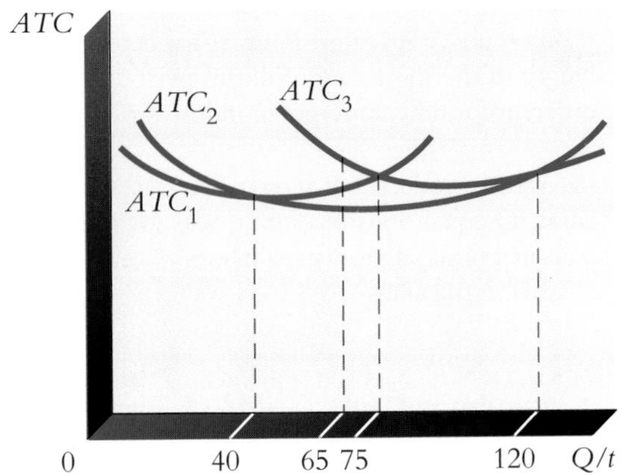

a. Which scale of production is best when $Q = 65$?
b. Which scale of production is best when $Q = 75$?
c. Indicate on the diagram the long-run average cost curve.

14. (Production and Cost) Use the following data to answer the questions below.

L (labor)	0	1	2	3	4	5
Q (output)	0	10	25	35	40	43

a. If the cost of each unit of labor is \$10 and fixed costs are \$50, what is the average cost of output when $Q = 40$? What is the marginal cost of increasing output from 40 to 43 units?
b. Draw a cost diagram showing marginal, average variable, and average total costs for the data in the table.

15. (Diminishing Marginal Product) Explain why the marginal cost of production *must* increase if the marginal physical product of the variable resource is decreasing.

16. (Costs in the Short Run) Suppose that a firm uses 10 units of labor (the variable resource) to produce 25 units of output at a total cost of \$400. If average fixed costs are \$4, what is the price of each unit of labor?

17. (Short-Run Cost) In Exhibit 7, the output level where average total cost is at a minimum is greater than the output level where average variable cost is at a minimum. Why do you suppose that this is true?

18. (Long-Run Cost) Exhibits 8 and 9 illustrate long-run average costs without including long-run marginal costs. Given what you know about the relationship between marginal and average costs, construct a plausible long-run marginal curve for the average cost curve in Exhibit 10.

19. (At the Movies) One fact that may contribute to the ability of movie theater owners to cluster screens is the downsizing of the average size of the seating area for each screen. What reasons can you suggest for such downsizing (ignore congestion problems created by multiple screens)?

20. (At the Movies) According to some movie industry analysts, theater owners break even on their ticket sales and the real source of profits is in the operation of concession stands. If this is true, what are the benefits of staggered movie times, which multiple screens allow?

21. (At the Movies) The most common location for theaters with clustered screens is at shopping malls. Why do you think that is true?

22. (Billions and Billions of Burgers) The hamburger business is an example of a franchise operation, whereby each outlet is purchased and managed—subject to quality control and menu requirements—by individual owners. Is this form of operation related to the economies of scale phenomenon? Explain.

23. (Billions and Billions of Burgers) As noted in the case study, one problem with using a standardized menu is that local supply and demand cannot be incorporated into menu offerings. Yet this standardized menu and operating procedures are used in order to capture economies of scale associated with management training and national supply networks. Can you think of any other reasons for not allowing each franchise operator to offer "individualized" menus?

APPENDIX
A Closer Look at Production and Costs

In this appendix we develop a model for determining how a profit-maximizing firm will combine resources to produce particular amounts of output. The amounts of goods and services that can be produced with a given amount of resources depend on the existing *state of technology*, which is the prevailing knowledge of how resources can be combined. We will therefore begin by considering the technological possibilities available to the firm.

The Production Function and Efficiency

The ways resources can be combined to produce output are summarized by a firm's production function. The *production function* identifies the maximum quantities of a particular good or service that can be produced per time period with various combinations of resources, for a given level of technology. The production function can be presented as an equation, as a graph, or as a table.

The production function summarized in Exhibit 11 reflects, for a hypothetical firm, the output resulting from particular combinations of resources. This firm uses only two resources: capital and labor. The amount of capital used is listed in the left-hand column of the table, and the amount of labor employed is listed across the top. For example, if 1 unit of capital is combined with 7 units of labor, the firm can produce 290 units of output per period.

We assume that those who run the firm are aware of the production function, that the firm produces the maximum possible output given the combination of resources employed, and that the same output could not be produced with fewer resources. Since we assume that the production function combines resources efficiently, 290 units is the most that can be produced with 7 units of labor and 1 unit of capital. Thus, we say that production is **technologically efficient**. The assumption that firms are efficient is linked to our earlier assumption that firms maximize profit. If a firm failed to produce efficiently, the same amount of output could be produced using fewer resources. If fewer resources were used, total cost would be lower. Since a firm's profit equals total revenue minus total cost, its profit would be lower if it failed to produce efficiently. *So the assumption of profit maximization implies that firms produce efficiently.*

EXHIBIT 11

A Firm's Production Function Using Labor and Capital: Production Per Period

Units of Capital Employed per Period	Units of Labor Employed per Period						
	1	2	3	4	5	6	7
1	40	90	150	200	240	270	290
2	90	140	200	250	290	315	335
3	150	195	260	310	345	370	390
4	200	250	310	350	385	415	440
5	240	290	345	385	420	450	475
6	270	320	375	415	450	475	495
7	290	330	390	435	470	495	510

Let's return now to the tabular presentation of the production function. We can examine the effects of adding additional labor to an existing amount of capital by starting with some level of capital and reading across the table. For example, when 1 unit of capital and 1 unit of labor are employed, the firm produces 40 units of output per period. If the amount of labor is increased by 1 unit and the amount of capital employed is held constant, output increases to 90 units, so the marginal physical product of labor is 50 units. If the amount of labor employed increases from 2 to 3 units, other things constant, output goes to 150 units, yielding a marginal physical product of 60 units. By reading across the table, you will discover that the marginal physical product of labor first rises, showing increasing marginal returns from the variable resource (labor), and then declines, showing diminishing marginal returns. Similarly, by holding the amount of labor employed to one unit and following down the column, you will find that the marginal physical product of capital also reflects first increasing marginal returns, then diminishing marginal returns.

EXHIBIT 12

Isoquants

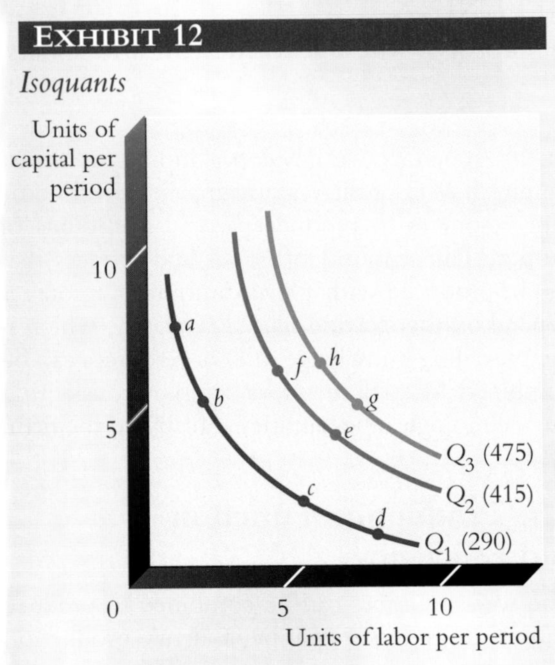

Isoquant Q_1 shows all technically efficient combinations of labor and capital that can be used to produce 290 units of output. Isoquant Q_2 is drawn for 415 units, and Q_3 for 475 units. Each isoquant has a negative slope and is convex to the origin.

Isoquants

Notice from the tabular presentation of the production function in Exhibit 11 that different combinations of resources may yield the same level of output. For example, several combinations of labor and capital yield 290 units of output. The information provided in Exhibit 11 can be presented more clearly in graphical form. In Exhibit 12, the quantity of labor employed is measured along the horizontal axis, and the quantity of capital is measured along the vertical axis. The combinations that yield 290 units of output are presented in Exhibit 12 as points *a*, *b*, *c*, and *d*. These points can be connected to form an *isoquant*, Q_1, which shows all the possible combinations of the two resources that produce 290 units of output. Likewise, Q_2 shows combinations of inputs that yield 415 units of output, and Q_3 shows combinations that yield 475 units of output. (The colors of the isoquants match those of the corresponding entries in the production function table in Exhibit 11.)

An **isoquant**, such as Q_1 in Exhibit 12, is a curve that shows all the technologically efficient combinations of two resources, such as labor and capital, that produce a certain amount of output. *Iso* is from the Greek word meaning *equal*, and *quant* is short for quantity; so *isoquant* means equal quantity. Along a particular isoquant, such as Q_1, the amount of output produced remains constant, in this case 290 units, but the combination of resources varies. To produce a particular level of output, the firm can use resource combinations ranging from much capital and little labor to much labor and little capital. For example, a paving contractor can put in a new driveway with ten workers using shovels and hand rollers; the same job can also be done with only two workers, a road grader, and a paving machine. A Saturday afternoon charity car wash to raise money to send the school band to Disney

World is labor-intensive, involving perhaps a dozen workers per car. In contrast, a professional car wash is fully automated, requiring only one worker to turn on the machine and collect the money. An isoquant shows such alternative combinations of resources that produce the same level of output. Let's consider some properties of isoquants.

Isoquants Farther from the Origin Represent Higher Output Levels. Although we have included only three isoquants in Exhibit 12, there is a different isoquant for every quantity of output depicted in Exhibit 11. Indeed, there is a different isoquant for every output level the firm could possibly produce, with isoquants farther from the origin indicating higher levels of output.

Isoquants Slope Down to the Right. Along a given isoquant, the quantity of labor employed is inversely related to the quantity of capital employed, so isoquants have negative slopes.

Isoquants Do Not Intersect. Since each isoquant refers to a specific level of output, no two isoquants intersect, for such an intersection would indicate that the same combination of resources could with equal efficiency produce two different amounts of output.

Isoquants Are Usually Convex to the Origin. Finally, isoquants are usually convex to the origin, meaning that the slope of the isoquant gets flatter down along the curve. To understand why, keep in mind that the slope of the isoquant measures the ability of additional units of one resource—in this case, labor—to substitute in production for another—in this case, capital. As we said, the isoquant has a negative slope. Take away the minus sign and the slope of the isoquant is the **marginal rate of technical substitution**, ***MRTS***, between two resources. The *MRTS* indicates the rate at which labor can be substituted for capital without affecting output. When much capital and little labor are used, the marginal productivity of labor is relatively great and the marginal productivity of capital is relatively small, so one unit of labor will substitute for a relatively large amount of capital. For example, in moving from point *a* to *b* along isoquant Q_1 in Exhibit 12, we substitute 1 unit of labor for 2 units of capital, so the *MRTS* between points *a* and *b* equals 2. But as more units of labor and fewer units of capital are employed, the marginal product of labor declines and the marginal product of capital increases, so it takes more labor to make up for a reduction in capital. For example, in moving from point *c* to point *d* in Exhibit 12, we substitute 2 units of labor for 1 unit of capital; hence, the *MRTS* between points *c* and *d* equals 1/2.

The extent to which one input can be substituted for another, as measured by the marginal rate of technical substitution, is directly linked to the marginal productivity of each input. For example, between points *a* and *b*, 1 unit of labor replaces 2 units of capital, yet output remains constant. So labor's marginal physical product, MPP_L—that is, the additional output resulting from an additional unit of labor—must be twice as large as capital's marginal physical product, MPP_C. In fact, all along the isoquant, the marginal rate of technical substitution of labor for capital equals the marginal physical product of labor divided by the marginal physical product of capital, which also equals the absolute value of the slope of the isoquant. Thus, we can say that

$$|\textbf{Slope of isoquant}| = MRTS = MPP_L/MPP_C$$

where the lines on either side of "Slope of isoquant" mean the absolute value. For example, between points *a* and *b* the slope equals −2, which has an absolute value of 2, which equals the marginal rate of substitution of labor for capital and the ratio of marginal productivities.

If labor and capital were perfect substitutes in production, the rate at which labor substituted for capital would remain fixed along the isoquant, so the isoquant would be a downward-sloping straight line. Since most resources are *not* perfect substitutes, however, the rate at which one substitutes for another changes along an isoquant. As we move down along an isoquant, more labor is required to offset a decline in capital, so the slope of the isoquant gets flatter, yielding an isoquant that is convex to the origin.

Let's summarize the properties of isoquants.

1. *Isoquants farther from the origin represent greater levels of output.*
2. *Isoquants slope downward.*
3. *Isoquants never intersect.*
4. *Isoquants tend to be bowed toward the origin.*

Isocost Lines

Isoquants graphically illustrate a firm's production function for all quantities of output the firm could possibly produce. Given these isoquants, how much should the firm produce? More specifically, what is the firm's profit-maximizing level of output? The answer depends on the cost of resources and on the amount of money the firm plans to spend.

Suppose a unit of labor costs the firm \$15,000 per year, and the rental price for each unit of capital is \$25,000 per year. The total cost (*TC*) of production is

$$\begin{aligned} TC &= (w \times L) + (r \times C) \\ &= \$15{,}000L + \$25{,}000C \end{aligned}$$

EXHIBIT 13

Firm's Isocost Lines

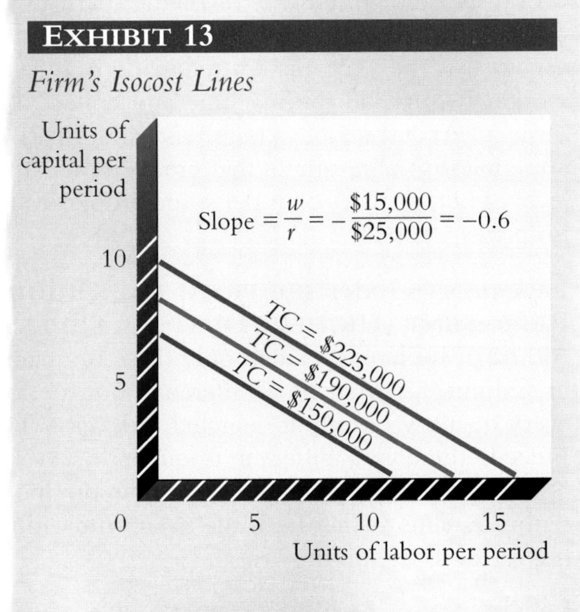

Each isocost line shows combinations of labor and capital that can be purchased for a fixed amount of total cost. The slope of each is equal to minus the wage rate divided by the rental rate of capital. Higher levels of cost are represented by isocost lines farther from the origin.

where *w* is the wage rate, *L* is the quantity of labor employed, *r* is the rental price of capital, and *C* is the quantity of capital employed. An **isocost line** identifies all combinations of capital and labor the firm can hire for a given total cost. Again, *iso* is from the Greek meaning *equal*, so an isocost line is a line representing equal cost. In Exhibit 13, for example, the line *TC* = \$150,000 identifies all combinations of labor and capital that cost a firm a total of \$150,000. If the firm spends the entire \$150,000 on capital, it can rent 6 units per year; if the firm spends the money only on labor, it can hire 10 workers per year; or the firm can employ any combination on the isocost line.

Recall that the slope of any line is the vertical change between two points on the line divided by the corresponding horizontal change. At the point where the isocost line meets the vertical axis, the quantity of capital that can be purchased equals the total cost divided by the price of capital, or *TC*/*r*, where *TC* is total cost and *r* is the rental price of a unit of capital. At the point where the isocost line meets the horizontal axis, the quantity of labor that can be hired equals the firm's total cost divided by the wage, or *TC*/*w*. The slope of any isocost lines in Exhibit 13 can be calculated by considering a movement from the vertical intercept to the horizontal intercept. That is, we divide the vertical change (−*TC*/*r*) by the horizontal change (*TC*/*w*), as follows:

$$\textbf{Slope of isocost line} = -\frac{TC/r}{TC/w} = -\frac{w}{r}$$

The slope of the isocost line equals minus the price of labor divided by the price of capital, or $-w/r$, which indicates the relative prices of the inputs. In our example, the absolute value of the slope of the isocost line equals w/r, or

$$|\textbf{Slope of isocost line}| = w/r = \$15{,}000/\$25{,}000 = 0.6$$

The wage rate of labor is 0.6 of the rental rate of capital, so hiring one more unit of labor, without incurring any additional cost, implies that the firm must employ six-tenths of a unit less capital.

A firm is not confined to a particular isocost line. Thus, a firm's total cost is not constant but varies with the amount it chooses to produce. This is why in Exhibit 13 we include three isocost lines, not just one, each corresponding to a different level of total cost. In fact, there is a different isocost line for every possible budget. *These isocost lines are parallel because each reflects the same relative resource prices.* The prices per unit of resource are assumed to be constant regardless of the amount employed.

The Choice of Input Combinations

We bring the isoquants and the isocost lines together in Exhibit 14. Suppose the firm plans to spend $190,000 to purchase resources; the firm can employ any combination of resources that falls along that line. The profit-maximizing firm will select the combination of resources that yields the greatest output. The firm could choose combination *a*, where 7 units of capital totaling $175,000 and 1 unit of labor at $15,000 exhaust the budget of $190,000. At point *a*, however, only 290 units of output would be produced. By moving to point *e*, the firm produces 415 units of output for the same total cost as at point *a*. At point *e*, the firm employs 4 units of capital, for a total of $100,000, and 6 units of labor, for a total of $90,000, so the total budget of $190,000 is exhausted.

This 415 units is the maximum output that can be produced for a total cost of $190,000. Other isoquants, such as Q_3, lie completely above the isocost line and are thus unattainable at the given total cost. *The firm maximizes output (and profit) for a given total cost by choosing that combination of resources where the isocost line is tangent to the highest attainable isoquant. This level of output also minimizes average total cost.*

EXHIBIT 14

Optimal Combinations of Inputs

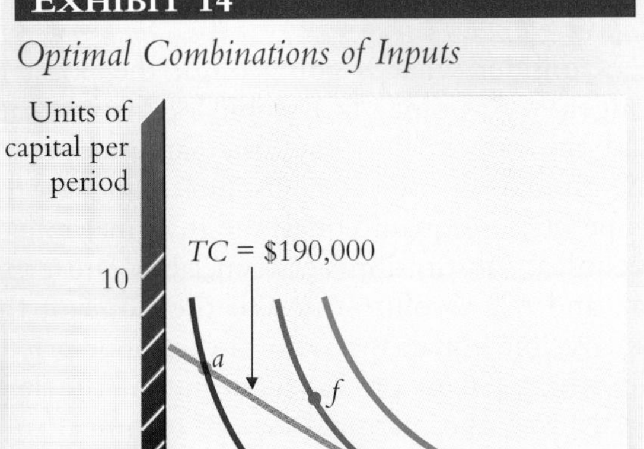

At point *e*, isoquant Q_2 is tangent to the isocost line. The optimal combination of inputs is 6 units of labor and 4 units of capital. The maximum output that can be produced for $190,000 is 415 units. Alternatively, point *e* determines the minimum-cost way of producing 415 units of output.

We have shown that the combination at *e* yields the maximum output that can be produced for $190,000. We could approach the problem differently. Suppose the firm has decided to produce 415 units of output and wants to minimize its total cost. The firm could select point *f*, where 6 units of capital are combined with 4 units of labor. This combination, however, would cost $210,000 at prevailing prices. Since the profit-maximizing firm wants to produce its chosen output at the minimum cost, it tries to find the isocost line closest to the origin that still touches the isoquant. Only at a point of tangency does a movement in either direction along an isoquant shift the firm away from the origin and to a higher cost level. *So the point of tangency between the isocost line and the isoquant shows both the maximum output attainable for a given cost and the minimum cost required to produce a given output.*

Consider what is going on at the point of tangency. At point *e* in Exhibit 14, the isoquant and the isocost line have the same slope. As mentioned already, the absolute value of the slope of an isoquant equals the marginal rate of technical substitution between labor and capital, and the absolute value of the slope of the isocost line equals the ratio of the input prices. So when a firm produces output in the least costly way, the marginal rate of technical substitution must equal the ratio of the resource prices, or

$$MRTS = w/r = \$15,000/\$25,000 = 0.6$$

This equality shows that the firm will adjust its resource use so that the rate at which one input can be substituted for another in production—that is, the marginal rate of technical substitution—will equal the rate at which one resource can be traded for another in resource markets, which is w/r. If this equality does not hold, it means that the firm, by adjusting its input mix, could produce the same output for a lower cost or could produce more output for the same cost.

Recall that the marginal rate of technical substitution equals the ratio of the marginal physical products of the resources. Therefore, we can rewrite the equilibrium condition as

$$MPP_L/MPP_C = w/r$$

This equality can be rearranged to yield

$$MPP_L/w = MPP_C/r$$

This last expression says that the firm should employ resources so that the marginal physical product per dollar's worth of each resource is equal—that is, in equilibrium, the final dollar spent on labor yields the same output as the final dollar spent on capital. This condition holds when the isoquant is tangent to the isocost line. The least-cost combination requires that output cannot be increased by switching spending from labor to capital or vice versa. Incidentally, the above equation can be inverted to show that the wage rate divided by the marginal product of labor equals the rental cost of capital divided by the marginal product of capital. Simply put, the marginal cost of production is equal for each resource.

The Expansion Path

Imagine an isoquant representing each possible level of output. Given the relative cost of resources, we could then draw isocost lines to determine the optimal combination of resources for producing each level of output. The points of tangency in Exhibit 15 show the least-cost input combinations for producing several output levels. For example, output level Q_2 can be produced most cheaply using C units of capital and L units of labor. The line formed by connecting these tangency points is the firm's **expansion path**. If

EXHIBIT 15

The Long-Run Expansion Path

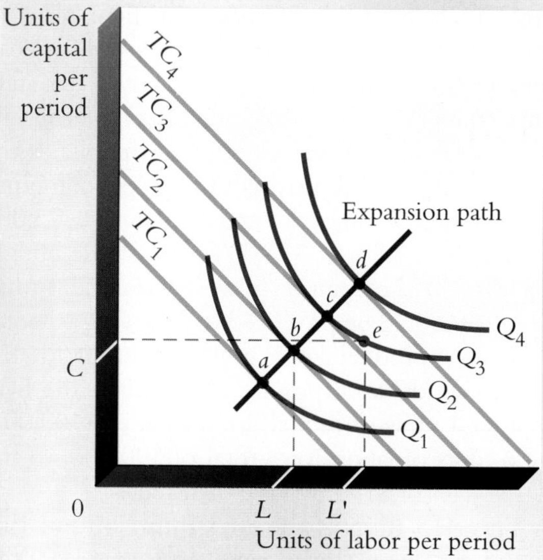

The points of tangency between isoquants and isocost lines each show the least expensive way of producing a particular level of output. Connecting these tangency points gives the firm's expansion path.

the resources are capital and labor, we often refer to this path as the long-run expansion path. The expansion path need not be a straight line, though it will generally slope upward, implying that firms will expand the use of both resources in the long run as output increases. Note that we have assumed that the prices of inputs remain constant as the firm varies output along the expansion path, so the isocost lines at the points of tangency are parallel—that is, they have the same slope.

The expansion path indicates the lowest long-run total cost for each level of output. For example, the firm can produce output level Q_2 for TC_2, output level Q_3 for TC_3, and so on. Similarly, the firm's long-run average cost curve conveys, at each level of output, the total cost divided by the level of output. The firm's expansion path and the firm's long-run average cost curve represent alternative ways of portraying costs in the long run, given resource prices and technology.

We can use Exhibit 15 to distinguish between short-run adjustments in output and long-run adjustments. Let's begin with the firm producing Q_2 at point *b*, which requires C units of capital and L units of labor. Now suppose that in the short run the firm wants to expand output to Q_3. Since capital is fixed in the short run, the only way to expand output to Q_3 is by expanding the quantity of labor employed to L', which requires moving to point *e* in Exhibit 15. Point *e* is not the cheapest way to produce Q_3 in the long run, for it is not a tangency point. In the long run, capital usage is variable, and the firm that wished to produce Q_3 would shift from point *e* to point *c*, thereby minimizing the total cost of producing Q_3.

One final point: If the relative prices of resources change, the least-cost combination of those resources will also change, so the firm's expansion path will change. For example, if the price of labor doubles, capital becomes cheaper relative to labor. The efficient production of any given level of output will therefore call for less labor and more capital. With the cost of labor higher, the firm's total cost for each level of output rises. Such a cost increase could also be reflected by an upward shift in the average total cost curve.

Summary

A firm's *production function* specifies the relation between resource use and output, given prevailing technology. An *isoquant* is a curve that illustrates the possible combinations of resources that will produce a particular level of output. An *isocost* line presents the combinations of resources the firm can employ, given resource prices and the amount of money the firm plans to spend.

For a given budget—that is, for a given isocost line—the firm maximizes output by finding the highest isoquant that just touches, or is tangent to, the isocost line. Alternatively, for a given level of output—that is, for a given isoquant—the firm minimizes its total cost by choosing the lowest isocost line that just touches, or is tangent to, the isoquant. The least-cost combination of resources will depend on the relative cost of resources. So whether the firm's goal is to maximize output for a given level of cost or to minimize cost for a given level of output, the profit-maximizing equilibrium is found where an isocost line is tangent to an isoquant—either the lowest attainable isocost line or the highest attainable isoquant. *In equilibrium, the last dollar spent on each resource yields the same marginal physical product.*

Appendix Question

1. (Choice of Input Combinations) Suppose that a firm's cost of labor is \$10 per unit and its cost of capital is \$40 per unit.
   a. Construct an isocost line such that total cost is constant at \$200.
   b. If this firm is producing efficiently, what is the marginal rate of technical substitution between labor and capital?
   c. Prove your answer to part b using isocost lines and isoquant curves.
   d. Explain how the output level associated with each isoquant can be used to determine whether the firm is facing economies of scale, diseconomies of scale, or constant average costs. (Assume a straight-line expansion path.)

PART 5

Market Structure and Pricing

CHAPTER 21
Perfect Competition

CHAPTER 22
Monopoly

CHAPTER 23
Monopolistic Competition
and Oligopoly

CHAPTER 21

PERFECT COMPETITION

In the previous chapter we examined the cost curves of individual firms in both the short run and the long run. We have not yet addressed how much a firm will produce and what price will be charged. What we can say for sure is that the answer to both questions will be guided by profit maximization. To answer these questions we revisit an old friend: demand. In this chapter we find that, given a firm's cost curves, the amount it produces and the price it charges will depend on the demand for the product. We bring together costs and demand to determine the profit-maximizing levels of price and output. In the next few chapters we will examine how firms respond to their economic environments in deciding what to produce, in what quantities, and at what price. Topics discussed in this chapter include

- Market structure
- Price takers
- Marginal revenue
- Golden rule of profit maximization
- Loss minimization
- Firm's short-run supply curve
- Industry's long-run supply curve
- Competition and efficiency
- Producer surplus

AN INTRODUCTION TO PERFECT COMPETITION

First, a few words about terminology: An industry consists of all firms that supply output to a particular market, such as the market for VCRs or the market for milk. The terms *industry* and *market* are used interchangeably

Market structure The important features of a market, such as the number of firms, uniformity of product across firms, ease of entry, and forms of competition

Teaching Tip The relationship among market structure, firm conduct (such as pricing strategies), and firm performance (such as profits) is summarized in Chapter 29.

throughout the chapter. The decisions a firm makes depend on the structure of the market in which the firm operates. **Market structure** describes the important features of a market, such as the number of firms (are there many or few?), the product's degree of uniformity (do all firms in the market produce identical products or are there differences?), the ease or difficulty with which new firms enter the market (is it easy to break into the industry or is market entry blocked by natural or artificial barriers to entry?), and the forms of competition among firms (do firms compete only through prices or are advertising and product differentiation common as well?). The various features will become clearer as we examine each type of market structure in the next few chapters.

Perfectly Competitive Market Structure

Perfect competition A market structure in which there are large numbers of fully informed buyers and sellers of a homogeneous product and there are no obstacles to entry or exit of firms

We begin with **perfect competition**, in some ways the most basic of market structures. *Perfectly competitive* markets are characterized by the following features: (1) there are many buyers and sellers, each of whom buys or sells only a tiny fraction of the total amount exchanged in the market; (2) firms produce a standardized, or *homogeneous,* product (that is, the product of one firm is identical to those of others in the market); (3) all participants in the market are fully informed about the price and availability of all resources, outputs, and production processes; and (4) firms and resources are freely mobile, with no obstacles, such as patents, licenses, or high capital costs, to prevent new firms from entering or existing firms from leaving a market.

Price takers Firms that face a given market price for their output and whose actions have no effect on the market price

Point to Stress No single buyer or seller is large enough in relation to the entire market to affect prices.

If all these conditions are present in a market, firms in that market are said to be **price takers**. That is, individual firms have no control over the price; they must "take," or accept, whatever price is determined in the market. Price is determined by market supply and demand. A perfectly competitive firm's size is so small relative to the size of the market that the firm's choice of output level has no effect on the market supply or the market price. Recall that market supply is determined by summing the individual firms' supply curves. Once the market price has been determined, each individual firm is free to supply at that price whatever amount will maximize the firm's profit. Thus, *firms in perfectly competitive markets, as price takers, must offer their product for sale at whatever price is established by the market.*

Some markets, such as stock markets and world grain markets, closely approximate perfect competition. Perfect competition is an important benchmark for evaluating the efficiency of production in other types of markets as well. A model of perfect competition allows us to make a large number of predictions that are borne out when we examine the real world.

Point to Stress Since all firms sell identical products, any attempt by one firm to raise its price reduces its sales volume to zero.

Demand Under Perfect Competition

Exhibit 1 presents the relation between the market demand and market supply curves in panel (b) and the demand curve for the output of a perfectly competitive firm in panel (a). The market price of $5 per unit is determined in panel (b) by the intersection of the market demand curve, *D,* and the market

EXHIBIT 1

The Firm's Demand Curve and Market Equilibrium in Perfect Competition

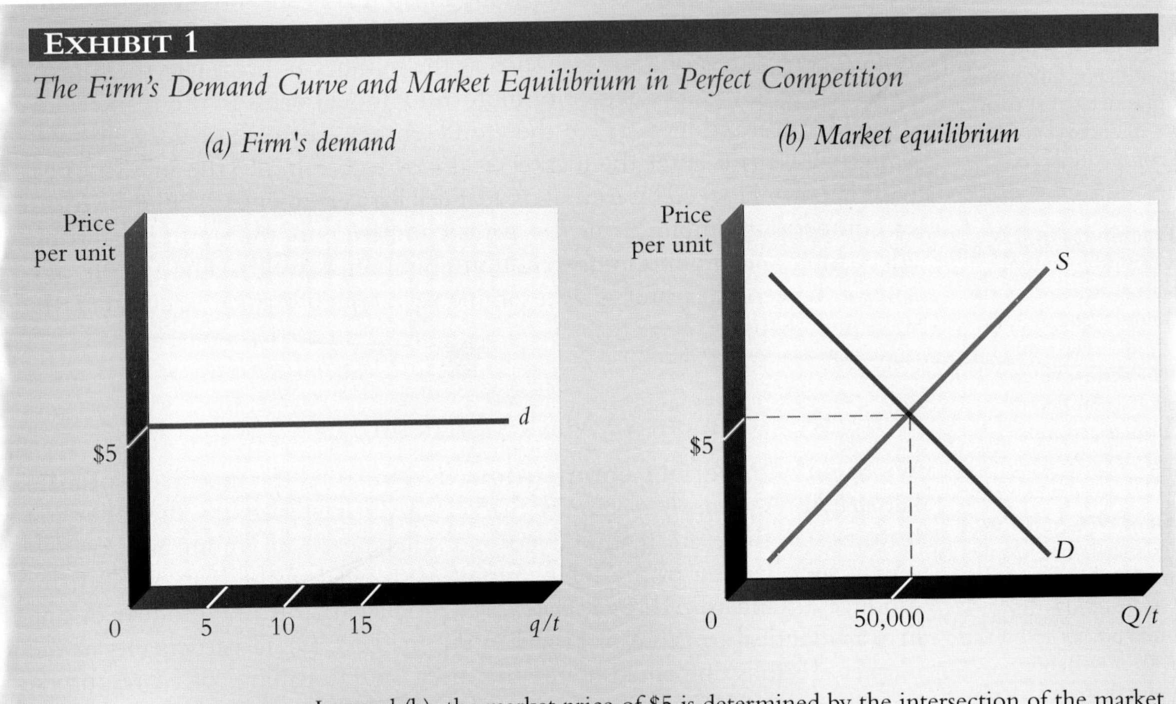

In panel (b), the market price of $5 is determined by the intersection of the market demand and supply curves. The individual perfectly competitive firm can sell any amount at that price. The demand curve facing the competitive firm is horizontal at the market price, as shown by demand curve *d* in panel (a).

Example Kansas, the largest wheat-producing state, generally produces no more than 2.5 percent of the world's total in a given year. There are about 70,000 farms in Kansas.

supply curve, *S*. Once the market price has been established, any firm can sell all it wants at that market price. The demand curve confronted by an individual firm is therefore a horizontal line drawn at the market price. In our example, a firm's demand curve, identified as *d* in panel (a), is drawn at the market price of $5 per unit. This perfectly elastic demand curve indicates that the firm can sell all it wants at the market price. Note that the firm's output is much smaller than the market's. For example, there could be a thousand firms in the market, so any particular firm's output is only a tiny fraction of total output.

Point to Stress The market structure is so competitive (one firm's behavior does not affect another firm's ability to sell) that there is no need for interfirm competitive behavior.

As we have said, each firm is a *price taker* because its output is so small relative to market supply that it has no impact on the market price. Also, because all firms are producing identical goods, no firm charging more than the market price will sell any output. For example, if a farmer charged $5.50 per bushel of grain, customers in this market would simply turn to other suppliers. Any firm is free to charge less than the market price, but why lower the price when any firm can already sell all it wants at the market price? Profit maximizers are not stupid; if they are, they go bankrupt.

It has been said, "In perfect competition there is no competition." Ironically, two neighboring corn farmers in perfect competition are not really competing in the sense of being rivals. The amount that one farmer grows will have no effect on the price the other receives per bushel. They both are free to sell as much corn as they choose at the price determined in the corn market.

SHORT-RUN PROFIT MAXIMIZATION

Teaching Tip The firm controls its rate of output in the short run by varying the amount of its variable resource.

The assumption here and throughout much of this text is that the firm's objective is to maximize economic profit. This is a reasonable assumption because competitive firms that fail to maximize profit will not be around long. The firm's economic profit is equal to its total revenue minus its total cost, (which includes both explicit and implicit costs). Implicit cost, you will recall, is the opportunity cost of resources owned by the firm and includes a normal profit; economic profit is any profit above normal profit. The question is, how do firms maximize profit? As we have said, the perfectly competitive firm has no control over price. What does it control? The firm controls its rate of output. The question then becomes, what rate of output will maximize profit?

Total Revenue Minus Total Cost

The firm maximizes profit by producing the rate of output that maximizes total revenue minus total cost. Columns (3) and (4) in Exhibit 2 list the firm's total revenue and total cost for each rate of output. Remember that total cost already includes a normal profit. Although Exhibit 2 does not distinguish between total fixed cost and total variable cost, total fixed cost must equal $15, since this is the total cost when output is zero. *The fact that the firm incurs a fixed cost indicates that at least one resource must be fixed, so the firm is operating in the short run.*

Point to Stress The firm incurs economic losses even when it may earn accounting profits.

The firm's total revenue per period equals its rate of output multiplied by the market price. The total revenue for a perfectly competitive firm is simply the price per unit ($5 in this example) times the rate of output. Total revenue in column (3) minus total cost in column (4) yields the economic profit or loss per period, which is presented in column (7). As you can see, at very low and very high rates of output, total cost exceeds total revenue, so the firm incurs an *economic loss.* Between 7 units and 14 units of output, total revenue exceeds total cost, so the firm earns an economic profit. Economic profit is maximized at $12 when output is 12 units per period.

These results are presented graphically in panel (a) of Exhibit 3, which shows the total cost and total revenue curves. As output per period increases by 1 unit, total revenue increases by $5. Therefore the firm's total revenue curve is a straight line emanating from the origin, with a slope of 5. The shape of the short-run total cost curve was discussed in the previous chapter. Its backward S shape reflects first increasing marginal returns, then diminishing marginal returns from changes in the variable resource. Total cost therefore increases, first at a decreasing rate and then at an increasing rate.

EXHIBIT 2

Short-Run Costs and Revenues for a Perfectly Competitive Firm

Quantity of Output per period (q) (1)	Marginal Revenue (Price) (p) (2)	Total Revenue ($TR = q \times p$) (3) = (1) × (2)	Total Cost (TC) (4)	Marginal Cost $\left(MC = \frac{\Delta TC}{\Delta q}\right)$ (5)	Average Total Cost $\left(ATC = \frac{TC}{q}\right)$ (6) = (4) ÷ (1)	Economic Profit or Loss = $TR - TC$ (7) = (3) − (4)
0	—	$ 0	$15.00	—	∞	−$15.00
1	$5	5	19.75	$ 4.75	$19.75	−14.75
2	5	10	23.50	3.75	11.75	−13.50
3	5	15	26.50	3.00	8.83	−11.50
4	5	20	29.00	2.50	7.25	−9.00
5	5	25	31.00	2.00	6.20	−6.00
6	5	30	32.50	1.50	5.42	−2.50
7	5	35	33.75	1.25	4.82	1.25
8	5	40	35.25	1.50	4.41	4.75
9	5	45	37.25	2.00	4.14	7.75
10	5	50	40.00	2.75	4.00	10.00
11	5	55	43.25	3.25	3.93	11.75
12	**5**	**60**	**48.00**	**4.75**	**4.00**	**12.00**
13	5	65	54.50	6.50	4.19	10.50
14	5	70	64.00	9.50	4.57	6.00
15	5	75	77.50	13.50	5.17	−2.50
16	5	80	96.00	18.50	6.00	−16.00

At rates of output less than 7 units or greater than 14 units, total cost exceeds total revenue, resulting in an economic loss, which is measured by the vertical distance between the two curves. Total revenue exceeds total cost between output rates of 7 units and 14 units; at these outputs the firm makes an economic profit. *Profit is maximized at the level of output where total revenue exceeds total cost by the greatest amount.* We already know that this distance is greatest when 12 units are produced.

Teaching Tip Marginal revenue is the slope of total revenue in *all market structures.* Only in perfect competition is marginal revenue constant and necessarily equal to the price.

Marginal Cost Equals Marginal Revenue in Equilibrium

Marginal revenue The change in total revenue resulting from a one-unit change in sales

Comparing total cost and total revenue is one way to find the profit-maximizing rate of output. A second and more revealing way is to use marginal revenue and marginal cost. Column (2) of Exhibit 2 presents the firm's marginal revenue. **Marginal revenue** is the change in total revenue divided by the change in output, or $MR = \Delta TR/\Delta q$. In perfect competition the firm is a price taker; if one more unit is sold, total revenue increases by an amount equal to the market price. Thus, *in perfect competition the marginal revenue equals the market price,* an equality that will usually not be true for other market structures. In this example, the marginal revenue is $5.

EXHIBIT 3

Short-Run Profit Maximization

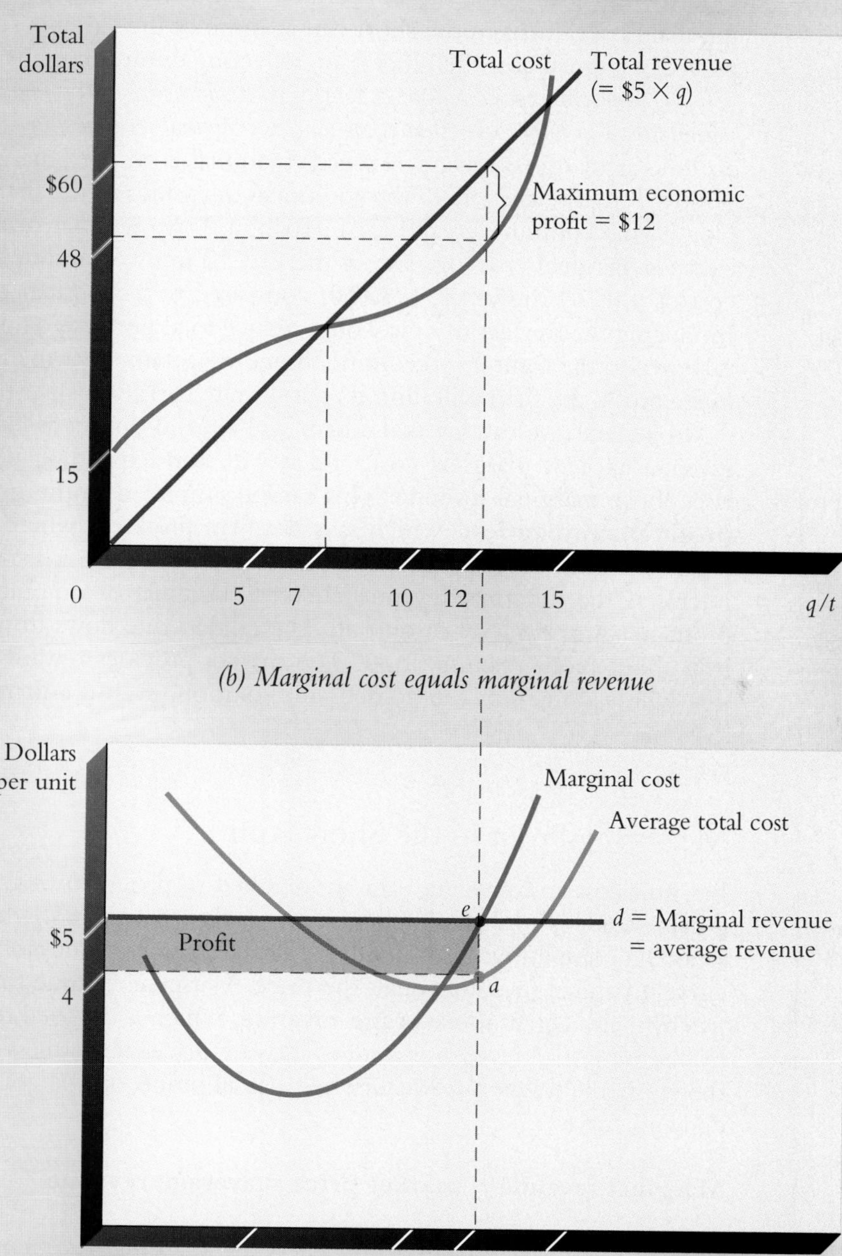

In panel (a), the total revenue curve for a competitive firm is a straight line with a slope equal to the market price of $5. Total cost increases with output, first at a decreasing rate and then at an increasing rate. Profit is maximized at 12 units of output, where total revenue exceeds total cost by the greatest amount. In panel (b), marginal revenue is a horizontal line at the market price of $5. Profit is maximized at 12 units of output, where marginal cost equals marginal revenue (point *e*). Profit is output (12 units) multiplied by the difference between price ($5) and average total cost ($4), as shown by the shaded rectangle.

Teaching Tip The profit-maximization rule applies in *all market structures* for firms producing in the short run. The firm in Exhibits 2 and 3 *neither* maximizes the distance between average revenue and average total cost (profit per unit) *nor* produces at the minimum point of average total cost (both of which are where output is 11 units).

Column (5) presents the firm's marginal cost at each level of output. In the last chapter you learned that *marginal cost* is the change in total cost divided by the change in output. Marginal cost first declines, reflecting increasing marginal returns in the short run as more of the variable resource is employed. Marginal cost then increases, reflecting diminishing marginal returns.

The firm will expand output as long as each additional unit sold adds more to total revenue than to total cost—that is, as long as marginal revenue exceeds marginal cost. As long as marginal revenue exceeds marginal cost, the "marginal" profit is positive—that is, the sale of the additional units adds to the firm's total profit. Comparing columns (2) and (5) in Exhibit 2, we see that marginal revenue exceeds marginal cost for each of the first 12 units of output. The marginal cost of unit 13, however, is $6.50, compared to a marginal revenue of $5. Producing the thirteenth unit would reduce total profit by $1.50. Total profit is shown in the right-hand column. Since we assume that the firm will maximize profit, the firm will limit its output rate to 12 units per period.

Golden rule of profit maximization To maximize profit or minimize loss a firm should produce at the level of output where marginal cost equals marginal revenue

In general, we can say that a firm will expand output as long as marginal revenue exceeds marginal cost, and it will stop expanding if marginal cost rises above marginal revenue. This can be simplified to the **golden rule of profit maximization**, which says the firm produces where marginal cost equals marginal revenue. In panel (b) of Exhibit 3, the marginal cost curve intersects the marginal revenue curve at 12 units of output, which is the profit-maximizing level of output. The golden rule flows from our assumption about profit maximization. The market provides rewards and penalties that will lead firms to the golden-rule solution, even if a firm is unaware of that rule.

Measuring Profit in the Short Run

Average revenue Total revenue divided by output

Per-unit cost and revenue data are graphed in panel (b) of Exhibit 3. Marginal revenue is a horizontal line at the market price of $5, which also represents the competitive firm's demand curve. At any point along the demand curve, marginal revenue equals the price. Marginal revenue for the competitive firm also equals the **average revenue**, which is the total revenue divided by the output. Average revenue is also the price. Regardless of the output, therefore, the following equality holds at all points on the competitive firm's demand curve:

Point to Stress Average revenue equals price in *all market structures.* Average revenue equals marginal revenue only in perfect competition.

Marginal revenue = market price = average revenue

The marginal cost curve intersects the marginal revenue (and demand) curve at point *e*, where 12 units of output are produced. At rates of output to the left of point *e*, marginal revenue exceeds marginal cost, so the firm could increase profit by expanding output. At rates of output to the right of point *e*, marginal cost exceeds marginal revenue, so the firm could increase profit by reducing output. Profit is indicated by the shaded rectangle. The height of that rectangle, *ea*, equals the price (or average revenue), $5, minus the average total cost, $4, at that level of output. Thus, price minus average total cost yields an average profit per unit of $1. Total profit, $12, equals the average profit per unit, $1 denoted by *ea,* times the 12 units produced.

Note that with total cost and total revenue curves, we measure total profit by the vertical *distance* between the two curves. But with per-unit curves, we measure total profit by an *area*—that is, by the two dimensions that result from multiplying the average profit per unit times the number of units sold.

MINIMIZING SHORT-RUN LOSSES

So far the firm has faced the pleasant problem of choosing the rate of output that maximizes short-run economic profit. But, alas, firms are not always so fortunate. Firms in perfect competition have no control over the market price, and sometimes the price is so low that no level of output will yield a profit. Faced with losses at all levels of output, the firm has two options: it can continue to produce at a loss or it can temporarily shut down. Note that even if the firm shuts down, it cannot go out of business in the short run. The short run is a period too short to allow existing firms to leave the industry.

Fixed Costs and Minimizing Losses

Your instincts probably tell you that the firm should temporarily shut down rather than produce at a loss. But it's not that simple. Keep in mind that the firm has two kinds of costs in the short run: fixed cost, which must be paid even if the firm temporarily shuts down, and variable cost, which depends on the level of output. If the firm shuts down, it must still pay property taxes, fire insurance, interest on any loans, and other overhead expenses incurred even when output is zero. At certain rates of output, the short-run loss the firm incurs by operating may be less than the short-run loss suffered by shutting down. *There may be some level of output greater than zero at which the firm's revenue will not only cover its variable cost but also cover some portion of its fixed cost.* Since the firm's short-run objective is to find the level of output that minimizes its loss, it will continue to produce if the revenues thus generated exceed the variable cost of production.

Point to Stress If output is zero, total revenue is zero, and both total cost and the firm's loss equal total fixed cost.

Point to Stress If total revenue exceeds total variable cost at some output levels, the firm's losses are less than total fixed cost if it produces in that output range.

Consider the same cost data presented earlier in Exhibit 2, but now suppose the market price has fallen from $5 to $3. This new situation is presented in Exhibit 4. Because of the lower price, total revenue and total profit have declined at all rates of output. Column (8) indicates that all output rates result in a loss. If the firm produces nothing, its loss is the fixed cost of $15, but if the firm produces between 6 and 12 units per period, the loss is less than $15. From column (8) you can see that the loss is minimized at $10 when 10 units are produced, so the firm minimizes its loss by producing 10 units per period rather than shutting down. The firm's total cost increases from $15 at zero output to $40 when the output rate is 10; so the total cost increases by $25, the variable cost of producing 10 units. Total revenue, however, increases from $0 to $30, so with this revenue the firm is able to pay its variable cost of $25 plus $5 of its fixed cost.

EXHIBIT 4

Minimizing Losses in the Short Run

Quantity of Output per period (q) (1)	Marginal Revenue (Price) (p) (2)	Total Revenue ($TR = q \times p$) (3) = (1) × (2)	Total Cost (TC) (4)	Marginal Cost $\left(MC = \frac{\Delta TC}{\Delta q}\right)$ (5)	Average Total Cost $\left(ATC = \frac{TC}{q}\right)$ (6) = (4) ÷ (1)	Average Variable Cost $\left(AVC = \frac{TVC}{q}\right)$ (7)	Total Profit or Loss = $TR - TC$ (8) = (3) − (4)
0	—	$ 0	$15.00	—	∞	—	−$15.00
1	$3	3	19.75	$ 4.75	$19.75	$4.75	−16.75
2	3	6	23.50	3.75	11.75	4.25	−17.50
3	3	9	26.50	3.00	8.83	3.83	−17.50
4	3	12	29.00	2.50	7.25	3.50	−17.00
5	3	15	31.00	2.00	6.20	3.20	−16.00
6	3	18	32.50	1.50	5.42	2.92	−14.50
7	3	21	33.75	1.25	4.82	2.68	−12.75
8	3	24	35.25	1.50	4.41	2.53	−11.25
9	3	27	37.25	2.00	4.14	2.47	−10.25
10	**3**	**30**	**40.00**	**2.75**	**4.00**	**2.50**	**−10.00**
11	3	33	43.25	3.25	3.93	2.57	−10.25
12	3	36	48.00	4.75	4.00	2.75	−12.00
13	3	39	54.50	6.50	4.19	3.04	−15.50
14	3	42	64.00	9.50	4.57	3.50	−22.00
15	3	45	77.50	13.50	5.17	4.17	−32.50
16	3	48	96.00	18.50	6.00	5.06	−48.00

Producing Where Total Cost Minus Total Revenue Is Minimized

In panel (a) of Exhibit 5, the firm's strategy of minimizing the short-run loss is presented in terms of the total cost and total revenue curves. The drop in price from $5 to $3 per unit changes the slope of the total revenue curve from 5 to 3, so the total revenue curve is now flatter than in Exhibit 3. Since only the price has changed, the total cost curve is the same as in Exhibit 3. Notice that the total cost curve now lies above the total revenue curve at all output rates. The vertical distance between the two curves measures the firm's loss at each level of output. If the firm produces nothing, the loss is its fixed cost of $15. The vertical distance between the two curves is minimized at an output level of 10 units, where the loss is $10.

Marginal Cost Equals Marginal Revenue

Another way to derive the same result is to rely on marginal analysis. The marginal data from Exhibit 4 are presented in panel (b) of Exhibit 5. For the firm to produce rather than shut down, two conditions must be satisfied.

EXHIBIT 5

Minimizing Short-Run Losses

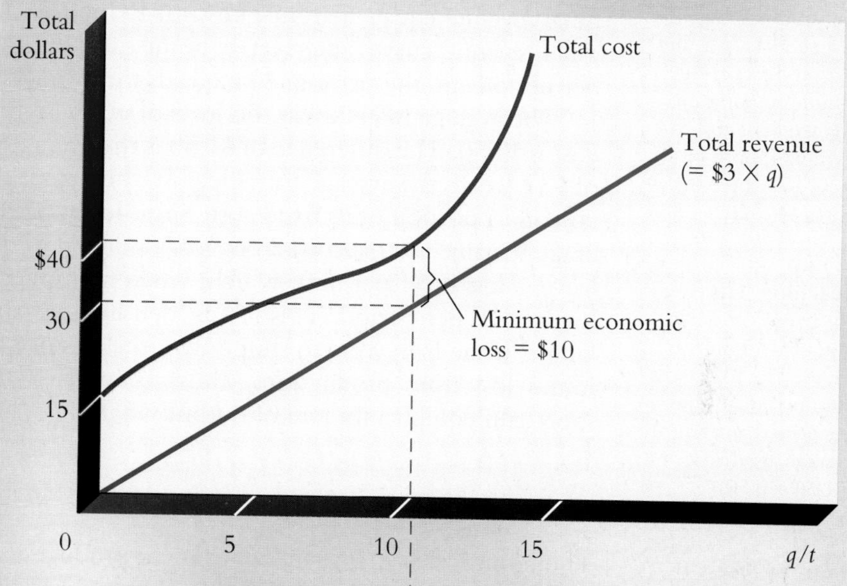

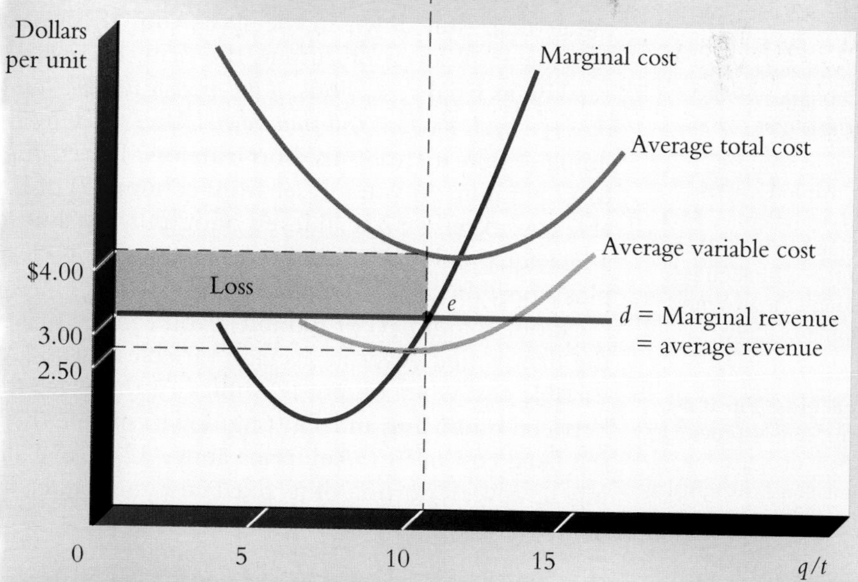

Since total cost always exceeds total revenue in panel (a), the firm suffers a loss at every level of output. The loss is minimized at 10 units of output. Panel (b) shows that marginal cost equals revenue at point *e*. The loss is equal to output (10) multiplied by the difference between average total cost ($4) and price ($3). Since price exceeds average variable cost, the firm is better off continuing to produce in the short run.

Point to Stress The firm neither minimizes average total cost minus average revenue (loss per unit) nor produces at the minimum point of average total cost. In Exhibit 4, both of these are where output is 11 units.

Teaching Tip Average fixed cost when output is 10 units is $1.50. The $1.00 loss per unit equals the uncovered portion of average fixed cost ($1.50 – 0.50).

First, at the level of production where the marginal equality is satisfied, the firm will produce only if the price exceeds the average variable cost. Second, the loss-minimizing level of output is found by expanding output until marginal revenue equals marginal cost. In Exhibit 5, the marginal cost and marginal revenue curves intersect at point *e*, where the output level is 10 units per period and the price of $3 exceeds the average variable cost of $2.50.

The average total cost at this level of output is $4, and the average variable cost is $2.50. The difference of $1.50 is the average fixed cost. Since the price of $3 exceeds the average variable cost, the firm is able to cover all its variable cost and a portion of its fixed cost. Specifically, $2.50 of the price pays the average variable cost, and $0.50 covers a portion of the average fixed cost. This leaves a loss of $1 per unit, which, when multiplied by 10 units, yields a total loss of $10 per period. This loss is identified in panel (b) by the shaded rectangle. If the firm were to shut down, the loss of $15 would exceed the minimum loss from production. Thus, 10 units is the firm's loss-minimizing short-run equilibrium rate of output when the market price is $3 per unit.

Point to Stress Firms in *any market structure* will continue to operate in the short run with losses if they can sell at a price that exceeds minimum average variable cost.

Example General Motors suffered a $4.5 billion loss in 1991 and another $2 billion loss through the first nine months of 1992.

Teaching Tip If the firm were to produce where marginal revenue equals marginal cost (when output is 9 units), total loss would be $19.25—which is greater than the $15 total fixed cost.

Shutting Down in the Short Run

The point is that firms will continue to produce in the short run even if they are losing money if their losses would be even greater if they shut down. You may have read or heard about firms that report a loss. As long as the firm is able to cover all its variable cost and a portion of its fixed cost, it will produce rather than shut down in the short run. If, however, variable cost exceeds revenue at all levels of output, the firm, by operating, will suffer a loss exceeding its fixed cost. Thus, *if the average variable cost of production always exceeds the price level, the firm will shut down.* After all, why should the firm produce if doing so only increases its short-run loss? For example, suppose the price falls to $2 per unit. As you can see from column (7) of Exhibit 4, the average variable cost exceeds $2 at all levels of output. By shutting down, the firm suffers a loss equal only to its fixed cost—a loss that is clearly less than its fixed cost plus a portion of its variable cost.

From column (7) of Exhibit 4 you can see that the lowest price at which the firm would cover its average variable cost is $2.47, which is the average variable cost when output is 9 units. At this price the firm will be indifferent between producing and shutting down, since either way its total loss will be the fixed cost of $15. Any price above $2.47 will allow the firm, by producing, to cover a portion of its fixed cost and reduce its loss.

The Firm and Industry Short-Run Supply Curves

A firm will vary its output as the price changes. If the price allows the firm to cover its average variable cost, the firm will expand output until marginal cost equals marginal revenue. If the price falls below average variable cost, the firm will shut down. The effects of various prices on the firm's output are summarized in Exhibit 6. Points 1, 2, 3, 4, and 5 are all intersections of the firm's marginal cost curve with different marginal revenue curves.

EXHIBIT 6

Summary of Short-Run Output Decisions

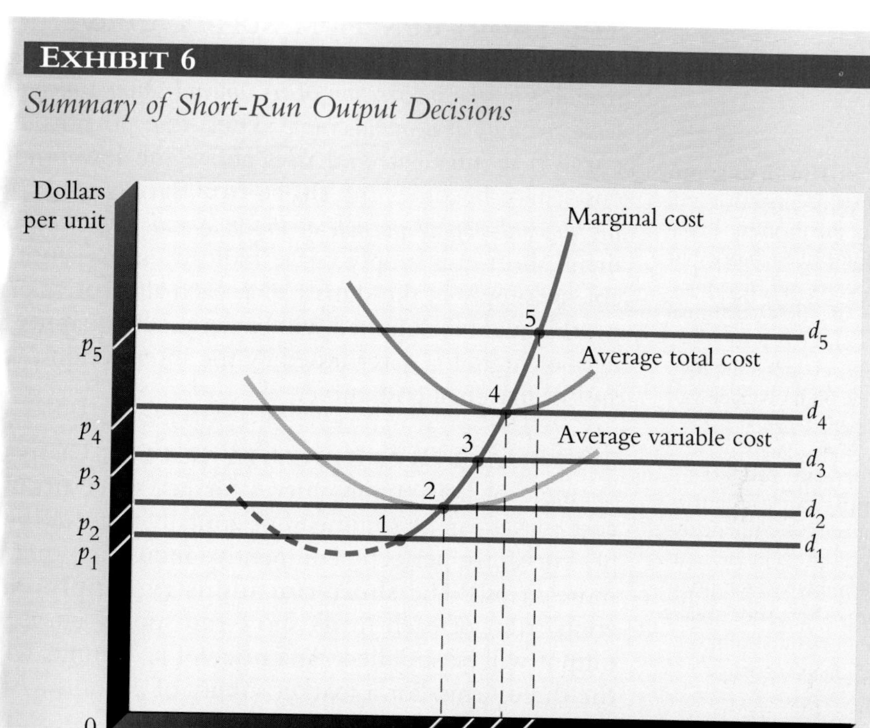

At price p_1, the firm produces nothing because p_1 is less than the firm's average variable cost. At price p_2, the firm is indifferent between shutting down and producing q_2 units of output, because in either case the firm would suffer a loss equal to its fixed cost. At p_3, it produces q_3 units and suffers a loss that is less than its fixed cost. At p_4, the firm produces q_4 and just breaks even, since p_4 equals average total cost. Finally, at p_5, the firm produces q_5 and earns an economic profit. The firm's short-run supply curve is that portion of its marginal cost curve at or rising above the minimum point of average variable cost (point 2).

Teaching Tip If the losses are considered temporary and if the firm can just cover its minimum average variable cost, the decision of whether to shut down may be based on factors such as whether the firm would be able to rehire its skilled labor later if they were laid off now.

(Recall that for perfectly competitive firms, the marginal revenue curve also represents the price, the firm's demand curve, and the firm's average revenue curve.) At a price as low as p_1, the firm will shut down rather than produce at point 1 because no output level generates revenue sufficient to cover average variable cost; so output at price p_1 is zero, or q_1. At a price of p_2, the firm will be indifferent between producing q_2 and shutting down because either way the loss will equal its fixed cost. If the price is p_3, the firm will produce q_3. Although the firm will incur a loss at a price of p_3, that loss is less than what it would face by shutting down. At p_4, the firm will produce q_4 and will just break even since its average total cost equals the price. When it breaks even, the firm earns a normal profit. If the price rises to p_5, the firm will earn an economic profit in the short run by producing q_5.

Short-run firm supply curve A curve that indicates the quantity a firm supplies at each price in the short run; that portion of a firm's marginal cost curve that intersects and rises above the low point on its average variable cost curve

Short-run industry supply curve A curve that indicates the quantity all firms in an industry supply at each price in the short run; usually the horizontal sum of each firm's short-run supply curve

THE SHORT-RUN FIRM SUPPLY CURVE. *As long as the price is high enough to cover the firm's average variable cost, the firm will supply the quantity determined by the intersection of its upward-sloping marginal cost curve and the marginal revenue, or demand, curve.* Thus, that portion of the firm's marginal cost curve that intersects and rises above the low point on its average variable cost curve becomes the **short-run firm supply curve**. *In Exhibit 6, it is the upward-sloping portion of the marginal cost curve, beginning at point 2.* The firm's short-run supply curve indicates the quantity the firm is willing and able to supply in the short run at each alternative price. If the price is below p_2, the quantity supplied will be zero. The quantity supplied when the price is p_2 or higher is determined by the intersection of the firm's demand curve and its marginal cost curve.

THE SHORT-RUN INDUSTRY SUPPLY CURVE. Exhibit 7 presents an example of how supply curves for just three firms with identical marginal cost curves can be summed horizontally to form the short-run industry supply curve. (In perfectly competitive industries, there will obviously be many more firms.) The **short-run industry supply curve** is usually the horizontal sum of each firm's short-run supply curve. At a price below p, no output will be supplied. At a price of p, 10 units will be supplied by each of the three firms, for a market supply of 30 units. At a price above p, say p',

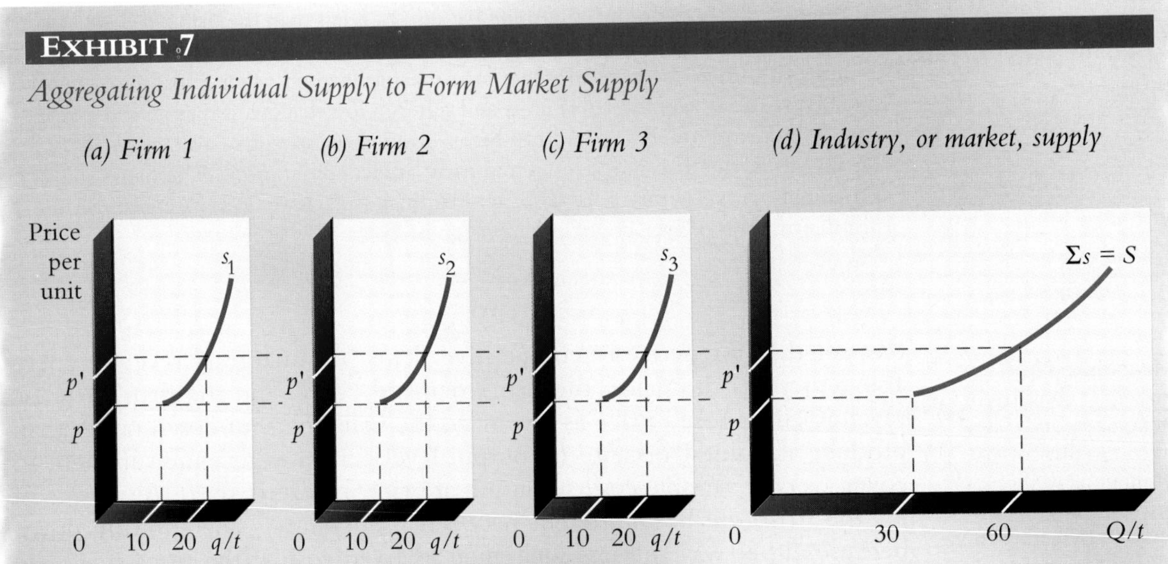

At price p, firms 1, 2, and 3 each supply 10 units of output. Total market supply is 30 units. In general, the market supply curve, panel (d), is the horizontal summation of the individual firm supply curves s_1, s_2, and s_3.

Teaching Tip In perfect competition *only,* the firm produces where price equals marginal cost, as long as variable costs can be covered.

Point to Stress Although no single firm can affect prices, the *collective* action of all firms in an industry determines market supply and thus affects the price.

each firm will supply 20 units, so the quantity supplied to the market will be 60 units.

FIRM SUPPLY AND INDUSTRY EQUILIBRIUM. Exhibit 8 shows the relation between the short-run profit-maximizing output of the individual firm and the market equilibrium price and quantity. We assume that there are 1,000 firms in this industry. The cost conditions of each firm are assumed to be identical. Their individual supply curves (represented by the portion of the marginal cost curve at or rising above the average variable cost) are summed horizontally to yield the market, or industry, supply curve. At a price of $5 per unit, each firm will supply 12 units, for a market supply of 12,000 units. In the short run, each firm is making an economic profit of $12, represented by the shaded rectangle.

In summary, a perfectly competitive firm selects the short-run output level that maximizes profit or minimizes loss. When confronted with a loss, a

EXHIBIT 8

Relation Between Short-Run Profit Maximization and Market Equilibrium

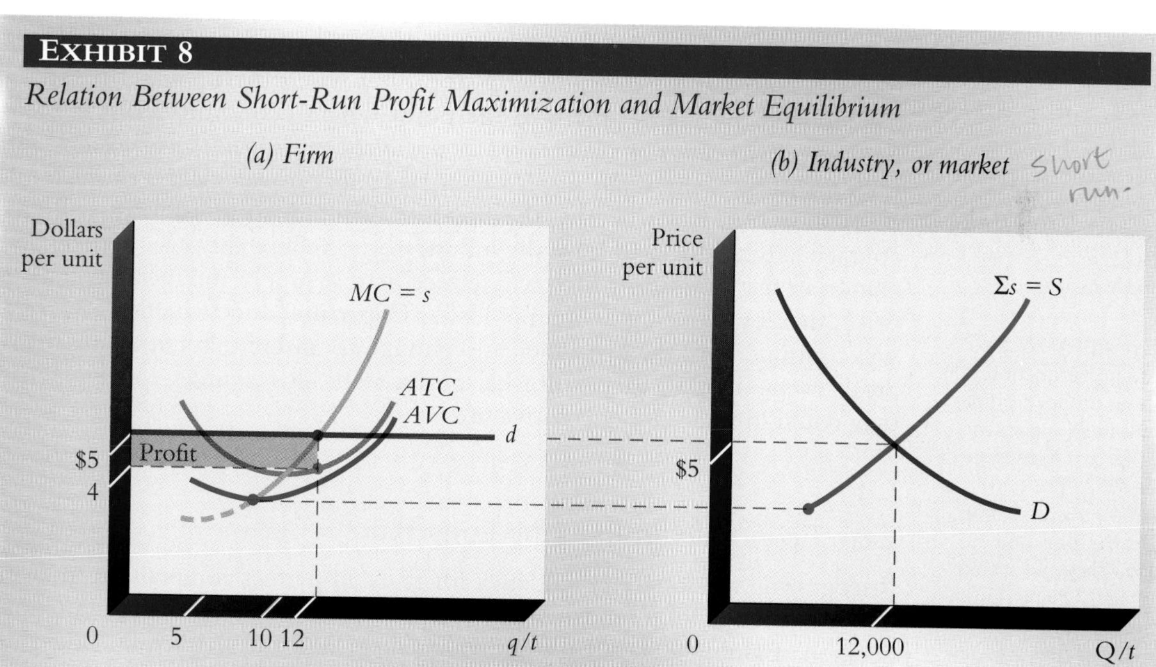

The market supply curve *S* in panel (b) is the horizontal sum of the supply curves of all firms in the industry. The intersection of *S* with the market demand curve *D* determines the market price, $5. That price, in turn, determines the height of the perfectly elastic demand curve facing the individual firm in panel (a). That firm produces 12 units (where marginal cost equals marginal revenue of $5) and earns an economic profit of $1 per unit, or $12 in total.

firm will either produce an output that minimizes its loss or shut down temporarily. So far, so good. Next let's see what happens in the long run.

Perfect Competition in the Long Run

Point to Stress In the short run, an industry has a fixed number of firms, each with a fixed plant size.

Example Chrysler Corp. introduced minivans in 1984. By 1992, minivans were the second-fastest-growing segment of motor vehicle sales in the U.S. market. By then other producers such as Ford, General Motors, and Toyota had joined the minivan market, and models were slated for introduction in late 1992 by Mercury, Nissan, and Volkswagen.

Example U.S. domestic production of shoes dropped from 642 million pairs in 1968 to 176 million in 1992. The two largest manufacturers, Brown Shoe and U.S. Shoe, went from 42 to 17 plants and from 13 to 3 plants, respectively.

Point to Stress Since the firm is producing where marginal revenue equals marginal cost, the normal profit also represents the firm's *maximum* profit.

In the short run, some resources can be varied, but others, which mostly determine firm size, are fixed. In the long run, however, firms are free to come and go and to adjust their size—that is, to adjust the scale of their operations. In the long run there is no distinction between fixed and variable costs because all resources under the firm's control are variable.

Short-run economic profit will, in the long run, attract new entrants and may encourage existing firms to expand the scale of their operations. Short-run economic profit attracts resources from industries where firms earn less profit or are perhaps losing money. Thus, an increase in the number and/or size of firms will expand market supply in the long run. This increase in market supply will lower the market price, thereby reducing economic profits. New firms will continue to enter the industry and existing firms will continue to increase their size as long as economic profit is positive. Entry and expansion will stop only when the increase in supply has reduced the market price to the point where economic profit is zero. *So short-run economic profit will in the long run attract new entrants and may cause existing firms to expand; market supply will expand until economic profit is eliminated.*

A short-run loss will have the opposite effect. A short-run loss will encourage existing firms to leave the industry or to reduce the scale of their operation in the long run, which will reduce market supply and increase market price, thereby reducing economic losses. Departures and reductions in scale will continue until the price increases enough to ensure that remaining firms break even—that is, earn a normal profit, with all resources earning what they could in their best alternative use.

Zero Economic Profit in the Long Run

Recognizing the long-run tendency for firms in perfect competition to earn only a normal profit is fundamental to understanding the long-run production decision. Exhibit 9 shows the individual firm and the market in long-run equilibrium. In the long run, market supply adjusts as firms enter or leave the market or change the scale of their operations; *this process continues until the market supply curve intersects the market demand curve at a price that equals the lowest point on each firm's long-run average cost curve, or LRAC.* Any other price would cause further adjustments in the market supply curve, as firms attempted to increase profits or reduce losses. A higher price would generate economic profit and would therefore attract new entrants. A lower price would result in a loss, causing some firms to leave the industry in the long run.

EXHIBIT 9

Long-Run Equilibrium for the Firm and the Industry

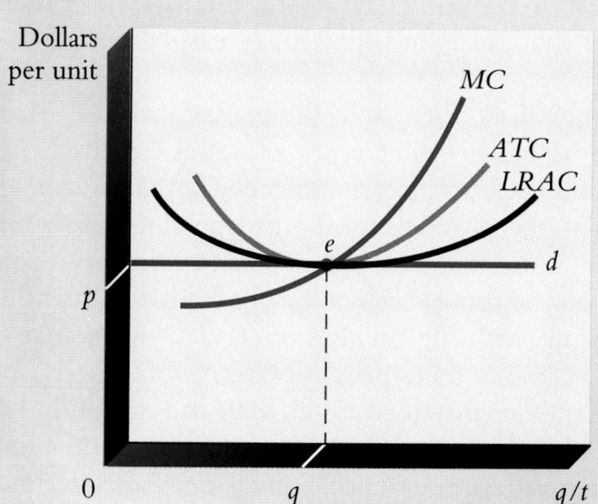

(b) Industry, or market

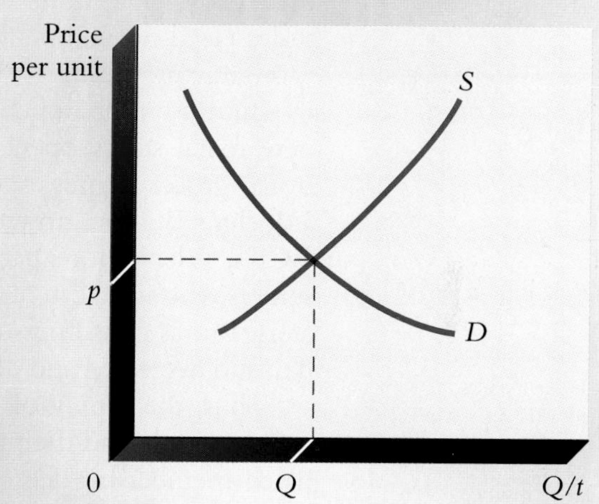

In long-run equilibrium, the firm produces *q* units of output and earns a normal profit. At point *e*, price, marginal cost, short-run average total cost, and long-run average cost are all equal. There is no reason for new firms to enter or for existing firms to leave the market. Thus, the market supply curve, *S*, in panel (b) does not shift. As long as market demand, *D*, is stable, the industry will continue to produce a total of Q units of output at price *p*.

Teaching Tip Firms in perfect competition must be at the minimum efficient scale in the long run. At smaller plant sizes, average total cost drops and profits rise for a given market price if the firm expands. At larger plant sizes, average total cost falls if the firm contracts.

Competition in the long run cuts economic profit to zero. Because the long run is a time period during which all resources under the firm's control are variable and because firms try to maximize profit, *firms in the long run will adjust their scale of operation until their average cost of production is minimized.* Firms that fail to minimize costs will not survive in the long run. At point *e* in Exhibit 9, the firm is in equilibrium, producing *q* units and earning only a normal profit. At point *e,* price, marginal cost, short-run average total cost, and long-run average cost are all equal. No firm in the market has any reason to alter its output and no outside firm has any incentive to enter this industry, since each existing firm in the market is earning normal, but not economic, profit.

One way to understand how short-run economic profit can be competed away by new firms in the long run is to consider the evolution of a newly emerging industry, as the following case study does.

CASE STUDY

Fast Forward

Video recorders are fast becoming standard equipment in the typical home. These recorders have fueled household demand for videotaped movies. The first videotape rental outlets required membership fees of up to $100, rented tapes for as much as $5 per day, and made customers pay a tape deposit. But despite the high prices and high fees, the growing number of VCRs allowed these early rental stores to thrive. In the early days of this industry, most rental stores faced no competition in their area, and they likely earned a short-run economic profit.

But this profit attracted competitors. Entry into the market was easy. Many new rental stores opened for business. Other types of stores—convenience stores, grocery stores, bookstores, even drugstores—also began renting tapes as a sideline. But the growth of new rental outlets soon outstripped the growth in VCRs. What's more, part of the initial surge in rental demand came from consumers who were catching up on old movie classics they had missed at the theaters. But as consumers caught up with the backlog of classics, that source of demand decreased and demand came to focus primarily on new releases.

Thus, the supply of rental movies increased faster than the demand. The greater supply had the predictable effect on market prices. Competition eliminated membership fees and deposit requirements. Rental rates also declined sharply—to as little as 99 cents per night. Some rental stores could not survive at such a low price, and they dropped out of the industry. In fact, so many firms failed that a market developed to buy and resell their tape inventories. The "shakeout" in the industry is still going on, and many existing rental stores will fail. Over the long run, rental stores that remain in business will tend to earn just a normal profit.

The Long-Run Adjustment to a Change in Demand

To explore the long-run adjustment process, let's consider how a firm and an industry respond to an increase in demand. Assume that the costs facing each individual firm do not depend on the number of firms in the industry (this assumption will be explained soon).

Teaching Tip Since the new marginal revenue now exceeds marginal cost at the initial output level q_1, the firm can increase profit by expanding output. Output is expanded along the firm's *short-run* average total cost (plant size has not changed).

EFFECTS OF AN INCREASE IN DEMAND. Exhibit 10 depicts a perfectly competitive market in long-run equilibrium, with the market supply curve intersecting the market demand curve at point *a* in panel (b); the price is *p* and the market-clearing quantity is Q_a. The individual firm supplies *q* at that market price, earning a normal profit. (Remember, a normal profit is built into the firm's average total cost curve.) Now suppose the market demand for this product permanently increases from *D* to *D′*, causing the market price to increase in the short run to *p′*. Each firm responds to the increased demand by expanding output along its short-run supply curve to *q′*, the rate at which the firm's marginal cost equals the new marginal revenue (which is the new price). Because all firms expand production, industry output increases to Q_b, where the change in industry quantity is the sum of the changes of all the individual firms in the industry. Note that in the short run each firm is now earning an economic profit, shown by the shaded rectangle in panel (a).

EXHIBIT 10

Long-Run Adjustment to an Increase in Demand

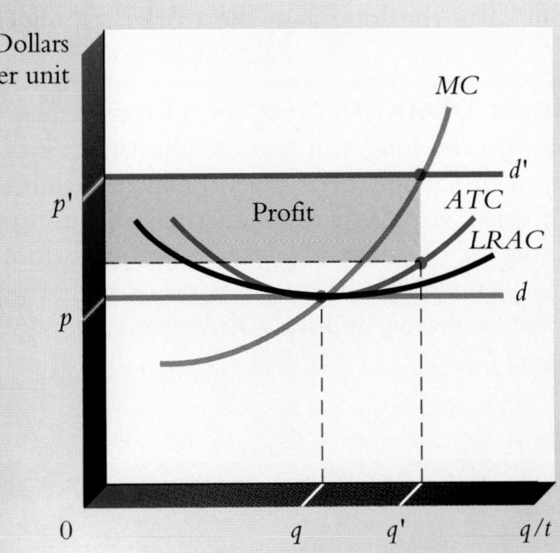

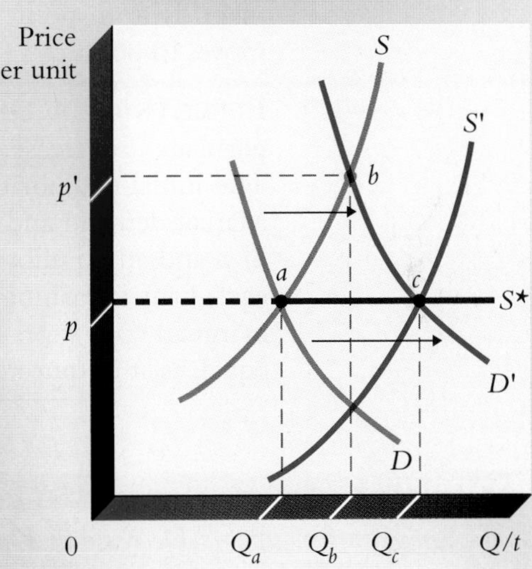

An increase in market demand from D to D' in panel (b) moves the short-run equilibrium point from a to b. Output rises to Q_b and price increases to p'. The rise in market price causes the demand curve facing the firm to rise from d to d' in panel (a). The firm responds by increasing output to q' and earns an economic profit, identified by the shaded rectangle. With existing firms earning economic profits, new firms enter the industry in the long run. Market supply shifts out to S' in panel (b). Output rises further, to Q_c, and price falls back to p. In panel (a), the firm's demand curve shifts back to d, eliminating economic profits. The short-run adjustment is from point a to point b in panel (b), but the long-run adjustment is from point a to point c.

Teaching Tip As long as the market price exceeds minimum average total cost, economic profit is possible. A return to normal profit thus requires that the price fall to minimum average total cost—or the original price if average total cost has neither risen nor fallen.

In the long run, resources are attracted to this industry from markets where profits are lower or where losses are being incurred. The entry of new firms increases supply, causing the market supply curve to shift out and the market price to fall. Firms continue to enter as long as they can earn an economic profit. In the process, the market supply curve shifts out to S', where supply intersects D' at point c, returning the price to its initial equilibrium level, p. Although the market price is back to where it was before the increase in demand, the entry of new firms has increased market quantity to Q_c. Because of the fall in the market price, the demand curve facing the individual firm shifts from d' back down to d. As a result, each firm reduces output from q' back to q and once again each earns just a normal profit. Notice that although industry output increases from Q_a to Q_c, each firm's output returns to q. In our example, the additional output is provided by the new firms

Teaching Tip Assuming they have identical cost structures, the number of firms in Exhibit 10(b) increases from Q_a/q to Q_c/q.

attracted to the industry rather than by an expansion by existing firms. Existing firms could not expand without increasing their long-run average cost.

New firms are attracted to the industry by the short-run economic profits arising from the increase in demand. The resulting increase in market supply, however, drives the profits of new and existing firms down to the normal level. In Exhibit 10(b), the short-run adjustment in response to increased demand is from point *a* to point *b;* in the long run, the market equilibrium moves to point *c*.

EFFECTS OF A DECREASE IN DEMAND. Next consider the effect of a permanent decrease in demand on the long-run market adjustment process. The initial equilibrium situation in Exhibit 11 is the same as in Exhibit 10. Market demand and supply intersect at point *a* to yield an equilibrium price of *p* and an equilibrium quantity of Q_a. This is a long-run equilibrium, so each firm is earning a normal profit by producing at a point where price, marginal cost, short-run average total cost, and long-run average cost are all equal, as at output rate *q* in panel (a).

EXHIBIT 11

Long-Run Adjustment to a Decrease in Demand

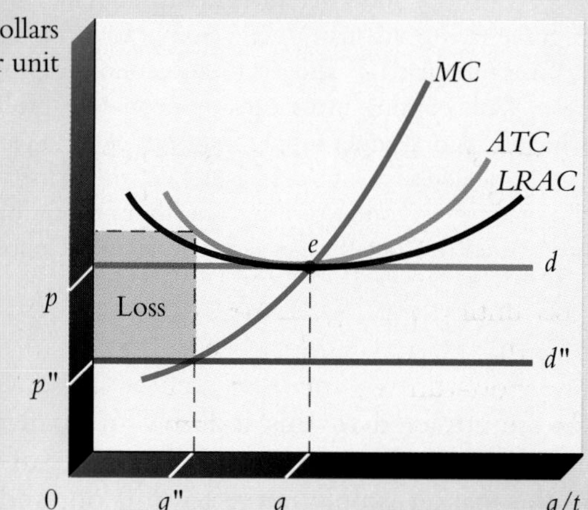

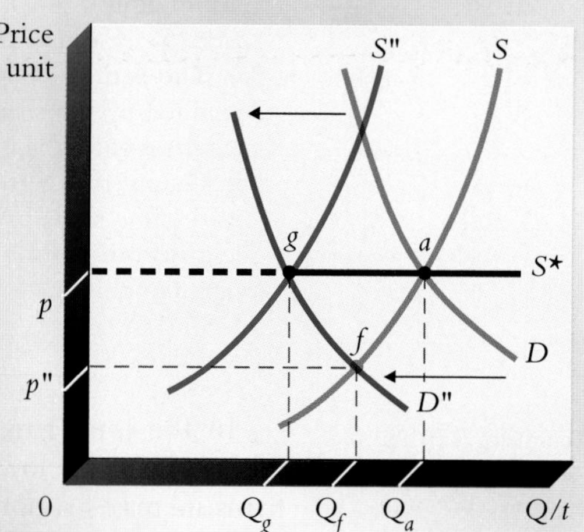

A decrease in demand to D'' in panel (b) disturbs the long-run equilibrium at point *a*. Prices are driven down to p'' in the short run; output falls to Q_f. In panel (a), the firm's demand curve shifts down to d''. The firm reduces its output to q'' and suffers a loss. As firms leave the industry in the long run, the market supply curve shifts left to S''. Market prices rise to *p* as output falls further to Q_g. At price *p*, the remaining firms once again earn zero economic profit. Thus, the short-run adjustment is from point *a* to point *f* in panel (b); the long-run adjustment is from point *a* to point *g*.

Now suppose that the demand for this product declines, as reflected in panel (b) by the shift to the left in the market demand curve, from D to D''. This decline in demand reduces the market price to p'' in the short run. As a result, the demand curve confronting each individual firm drops from d to d''. Each firm responds in the short run by cutting its output to q'', where the marginal cost equals the now lower marginal revenue, or price. Because each firm cuts output, market output falls to Q_f. At the lower price, each firm suffers a loss because the price is below short-run average total cost (the price must still be above average variable cost, however, since each firm continues to produce in the short run rather than shut down). The firm's loss is indicated by the shaded rectangle in panel (a).

Teaching Tip As long as the market price is below minimum average total cost, economic losses occur. A return to normal profit thus requires that the price rise to minimum average total cost—or the original price if average total cost has neither risen nor fallen. Assuming they have identical cost structures, the number of firms in Exhibit 11(b) decreases from Q_a/q to Q_g/q.

In the long run, losses drive some firms out of the industry. As firms leave, market supply shifts to the left, so the market price increases. Firms continue to leave until the market supply curve shifts back to S'', where supply intersects D'' at point g. Output has fallen to Q_g, and price has returned to p. With the price back up to p, the firms still in the industry once again earn a normal profit. At the conclusion of the adjustment process, each firm still in the industry is producing the same rate of output, q, as it did in the initial equilibrium, but market output has fallen from Q_a to Q_g because some firms have left the industry. Note that the adjustment process involves the departure of firms from the industry rather than a reduction in the scale of firms because a reduction in scale would increase long-run average cost.

THE LONG-RUN SUPPLY CURVE

Thus far we have looked at the industry and firm responses to changes in demand, distinguishing between a short-run adjustment and a long-run adjustment. In the short run, firms alter quantity supplied in response to a shift in demand by moving up or down their marginal cost curve (that portion rising above the average variable cost) until the marginal cost equals the marginal revenue, or the price. The long-run adjustment, however, involves the entry or exit of firms until the new short-run market supply curve generates an equilibrium price that provides remaining firms with normal profits. In Exhibits 10 and 11, we identified two long-run equilibrium points generated by the intersection of the shifted demand curve and the shifted short-run market supply curve. In each case the price remained the same in the long run, but industry output increased in Exhibit 10(b) and decreased in Exhibit 11(b). Connecting these long-run equilibrium points yields the long-run industry supply curve, labeled S^* in Exhibits 10 and 11. The long-run supply curve in these exhibits is horizontal, or perfectly elastic, reflecting unchanged production costs per unit as the size of the industry adjusts to changes in demand. Thus, the price of the good in the long run is determined by the minimum point on the firm's long-run average cost curve. More generally, the **long-run industry supply curve** shows the relation between price and quantity supplied once firms have fully adjusted to any short-term economic profit or loss.

Long-run industry supply curve A curve that shows the relation between price and quantity supplied once firms have fully adjusted to any short-run economic profit or loss

Constant-cost industry An industry that can expand or contract without affecting the long-run per-unit cost of production; the long-run industry supply curve is horizontal

Teaching Tip An industry that requires only small percentages of the unskilled labor and unspecialized capital in an area could be a constant-cost industry. This is true of the retail industry in some areas.

Constant-Cost Industries

The industry we have depicted thus far is called a **constant-cost industry** because the short-run cost curves do not shift up or down as industry output changes. Resource prices and other production costs remain constant in the long run as industry output increases or decreases. Recall that at the outset of the discussion of the long run we assumed that each firm's costs do not depend on the number of firms in the market. Because each firm's production costs are assumed to be independent of the number of firms in the industry, per-unit production costs in the long run can remain constant as firms enter or leave the industry. *The long-run supply curve for a constant-cost industry is horizontal,* like those depicted in Exhibits 10 and 11.

A constant-cost industry is most often characterized as one that hires only a small portion of the resources available in the resource market. Firms need not increase the price paid for resources to draw them away from competing uses because firms in this industry hire only a small share of the resources available. For example, producers of pencils can expand industry production without bidding up the prices of wood, graphite, and synthetic rubber since the pencil industry uses such a small share of these resources.

Increasing-cost industry An industry that faces higher per-unit production costs as it expands in the long run; the long-run industry supply curve slopes upward

Teaching Tip Although no single firm is large enough to drive up resource prices, collective action by all firms in the industry can increase the prices of resources heavily employed by them. This is known as a *pecuniary external diseconomy,* which shifts the entire long-run average cost curve.
Example The combined actions of individual firms in the petrochemical industry (including plastics) can affect the price of oil.

Increasing-Cost Industries

Many industries encounter higher per-unit production costs as industry output expands in the long run. These **increasing-cost industries** find that expanding output bids up the prices of some resources or otherwise increases production costs, and these higher production costs cause each firm's cost curves to shift upward. For example, an expansion of the oil industry will bid up the wages of petroleum engineers and geologists, raising average and marginal costs for each oil exploration firm. Likewise, an expansion of the housing-construction industry could bid up the price of lumber.

To illustrate the equilibrium adjustment process for an increasing-cost industry, we again begin in long-run equilibrium in Exhibit 12(b), where the industry demand curve, *D,* intersects the short-run industry supply curve, *S,* at equilibrium point *a* to yield the price p_a and the quantity Q_a. When the price is p_a, the demand (and marginal revenue) curve facing the firm is d_a in panel (a). The firm produces the rate of output at which marginal cost equals marginal revenue, represented by point *a* in panel (a). At the equilibrium rate of output, *q,* the firm is at the low point of its average total cost curve, so the average total cost equals the price and the firm earns no economic profit.

Suppose there is an increase in the demand for this product, reflected by a shift to the right in the demand curve from *D* to *D′* in panel (b). The new demand curve intersects the short-run market supply curve at point *b,* yielding the short-run equilibrium price p_b and quantity Q_b. With an increase in the equilibrium price, each firm's demand curve shifts from d_a up to d_b in panel (a). The new short-run equilibrium occurs at point *b* in panel (a), where marginal cost equals marginal revenue; each firm produces output q_b. In the short run, each firm earns an economic profit equal to q_b times the difference between the price and the average total cost at that rate of output.

EXHIBIT 12

An Increasing-Cost Industry

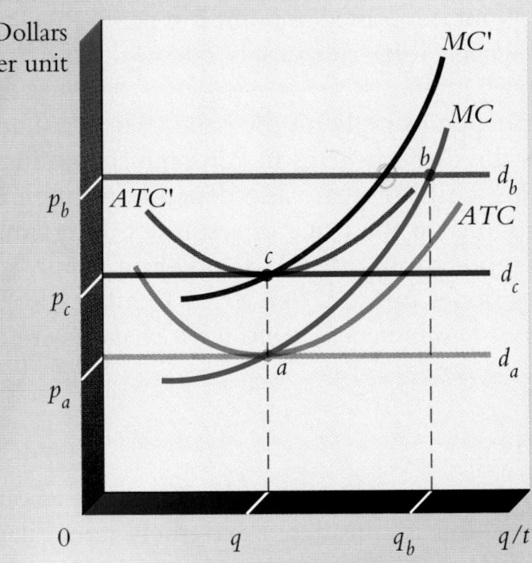

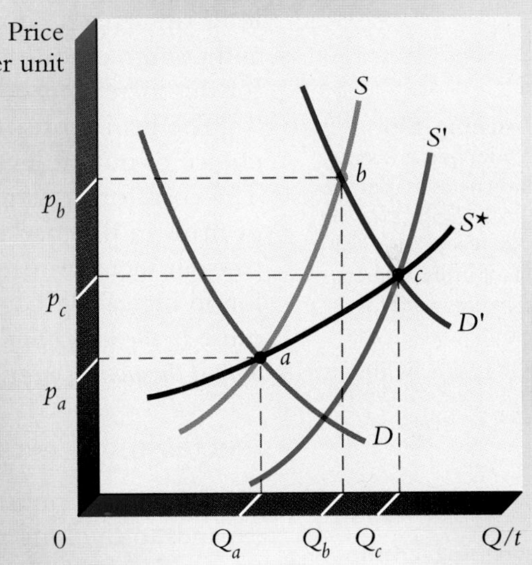

An increase in demand to D' in panel (b) disturbs the initial equilibrium at point *a*. A short-run equilibrium is established at point *b*, where D' intersects the short-run market supply curve, *S*. At the higher price, p_b, the firm's demand curve shifts up to d_b, and its output increases to q_b in panel (a). At point *b*, the firm is earning an economic profit. New firms enter to try to capture some of the profits. As they do so, input prices are bid up, so each firm's marginal and average cost curves rise. The intersection of the new market supply curve, S', with D' determines the market price, p_c. At p_c, individual firms are earning zero economic profit. Point *c* is a point of long-run equilibrium. By connecting long-run equilibrium points *a* and *c* in panel (b), we obtain the upward-sloping long-run market supply curve, S^*, for this increasing-cost industry.

Point to Stress
Since costs have risen, a return to the original price p_a would leave firms with economic losses. The representative firm now has a reduced short-run supply—a higher price is required to justify a given level of output. Market supply has risen only because there are more firms.

The economic profit earned by firms in the industry attracts new entrants in the long run. So far the sequence of events is identical to that for the constant-cost industry. Because this is an increasing-cost industry, however, an expansion of industry output drives up the prices of some of the industry's resources. These higher resource costs raise each firm's marginal and average cost curves, which shift from *MC* and *ATC* up to *MC′* and *ATC′*, as shown in panel (a) of Exhibit 12. Note that for simplicity we are assuming that the new cost curves are parallel to the old curves, so the minimum efficient plant size remains the same, though this need not be the case.

The entry of new firms also shifts the short-run industry supply curve out, thus reducing the market price of the industry's output. *New firms enter the industry until the combination of higher production costs and a lower output price squeezes economic profits to zero.* This occurs when new entry has shifted the short-run industry supply curve out to S', which lowers the price until it equals the minimum on the firm's new average total cost curve. The market price does not fall to the initial equilibrium level because each firm's average total cost curve has increased. The intersection of the new short-run market supply curve, S', and the increased market demand D' determines the new long-run market equilibrium point, identified as point *c* in panel (b). Point *a* and point *c* are on the *upward-sloping* long-run supply curve, denoted as $S^\star$, for this increasing-cost industry.

Teaching Tip Production costs may also rise as a result of a *technological external diseconomy.* For example, if more farmers in a region start irrigating dry soil, the water table drops, increasing everyone's costs to irrigate.

The firm's costs no longer depend simply on the scale of its plant and its choice of output level, as was the case for firms in constant-cost industries. The costs for firms in increasing-cost industries also depend on the number of firms in the market. By bidding up the price of resources, long-run expansion increases each firm's production costs. The long-run supply curve for an increasing-cost industry slopes upward, like $S^\star$ in Exhibit 12(b), because *in the long run firms continue to earn normal profits when production costs rise only if the market price also rises.*

Decreasing-Cost Industries

Decreasing-cost industry The rare case in which an industry faces lower per-unit production costs as it expands in the long run; the long-run industry supply curve slopes downward

Firms in some industries may experience lower production costs as output expands in the long run, though this is considered extremely rare. Firms in **decreasing-cost industries** find that as industry output expands, the cost of production falls, causing a downward shift in each firm's cost curves. For example, in the coal mining industry, a major cost is pumping water out of the mine shafts. As more mines in the same area begin operating pumps, the water table in the area falls, so each mine's pumping costs go down.

An increase in market demand results in a higher price in the short run, so firms earn economic profit. This profit attracts new entrants in the long run, reducing production costs for all firms in the industry. Decreasing-cost industries have long-run supply curves like the one depicted in Exhibit 13, where point *a* is the initial equilibrium, point *b* is the short-run adjustment to an increase in demand, and point *c* is the long-run equilibrium adjustment as new firms are attracted by short-run profits. In the long run, the price, p_c, falls below the initial price, p_a. Entry eliminates economic profit by driving down the price more rapidly than costs.

Example The mine example illustrates a technological external economy. Another example would be if more farmers started draining marshy soil in an area—thus reducing the water on neighbors' lands. A pecuniary external economy occurred in the early years of the U.S. automobile industry when expansion allowed tire manufacturers to develop large-scale production techniques and the price of tires fell for all auto firms.

In summary, firms in perfect competition can earn an economic profit or economic loss in the short run, but in the long run the entry or exit of firms drives economic profit to zero. This is true whether the industry in question exhibits constant costs, increasing costs, or decreasing costs. Notice that regardless of the nature of costs in the industry, the industry supply curve is less elastic in the short run than in the long run. In the long run, firms can adjust all their resources, so they are better able to respond to changes in price.

We mentioned at the outset that perfect competition serves as a useful benchmark for evaluating the efficiency of markets. Next we examine the qualities of perfect competition that make it so useful.

Point to Stress In perfect competition, the minimum point of the long-run average cost curve always determines the long-run price. The minimum point remains unchanged in a constant-cost industry, rises in an increasing-cost industry, and falls in a decreasing-cost industry.

EXHIBIT 13

A Decreasing-Cost Industry

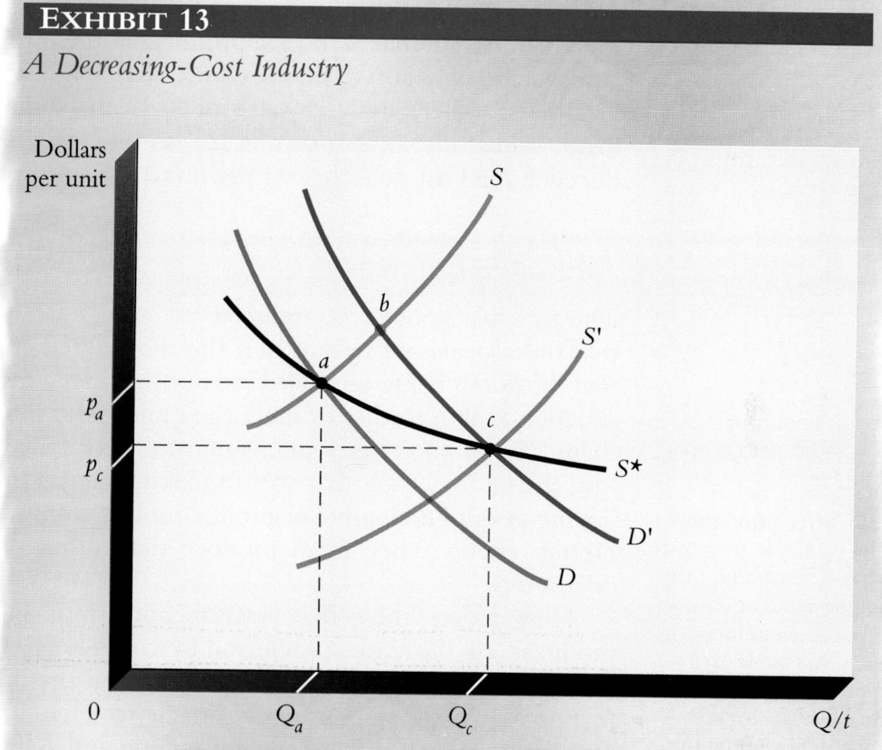

An increase in market demand moves the industry from starting point *a* to short-run equilibrium at point *b*. With each firm earning an economic profit, new firms begin to enter. If entry drives down the average cost of production, long-run equilibrium will be reestablished at point *c*, with a lower price than at point *a*. Connecting long-run equilibrium points *a* and *c* yields the downward-sloping long-run market supply curve, *S**, for this decreasing-cost industry.

PERFECT COMPETITION AND EFFICIENCY

There are two concepts of efficiency used in judging market performance. The first, called *productive efficiency,* refers to the notion of efficiency developed in the production possibilities curve introduced in Chapter 2. The second, called *allocative efficiency,* emphasizes the choice of goods to be produced and the distribution of these goods among consumers.

Productive efficiency The condition that exists when output is produced with the least-cost combination of inputs, given the level of technology

Productive Efficiency

Productive efficiency occurs when the firm produces at the minimum point on its long-run average cost curve. If a firm could produce the same output using fewer resources or could produce more output using the same

Teaching Tip In perfect competition there is a large number of firms because the minimum efficient scale is small relative to the market size.

resources, it is not using resources efficiently. In the long run in perfect competition, the entry and exit of firms and the adjustment in the scale of each firm ensure that each firm produces at the minimum point on its long-run average cost curve. Firms whose size is not at the minimum efficient level must either alter their size or leave the industry to avoid continued losses. Thus, the long-run industry output in perfect competition is produced at the least possible cost per unit.

Allocative Efficiency

Allocative efficiency The condition that exists when firms produce the output that is most preferred by consumers; the marginal cost of each good just equals the marginal benefit that consumers derive from that good

The fact that goods are produced at the least possible cost does not mean that the *allocation* of resources is the most efficient one possible. It may be that the goods being produced are not the ones consumers most prefer. This situation is akin to that of the airline pilot who informs the passengers that there is some good news and some bad news: "The bad news is that we are lost; the good news is that we are making record time!" Firms may be producing goods efficiently yet producing the wrong goods. **Allocative efficiency** occurs when firms produce the output that is most preferred by consumers.

How do we know that perfect competition guarantees that the goods produced are those most preferred by consumers? The answer lies with the demand and supply curves. You'll recall that the demand curve reflects the marginal value that consumers attach to each unit, so the price is the amount of money that people are willing and able to pay for the final unit they consume. We also know that, both in the short run and in the long run, the equilibrium price in perfect competition equals the marginal cost of supplying the last unit sold. Marginal cost measures the opportunity cost of using those resources in their best alternative use. Thus, supply and demand intersect at the combination of price and quantity at which the opportunity cost of the resources employed to produce the last unit of output just equals the marginal value, or the marginal benefit, that consumers attach to that unit of output.

Teaching Tip This discussion assumes that there are no negative externalities (one type of market failure introduced in Chapter 4—the firm's marginal cost matches society's marginal cost.

As long as marginal cost equals marginal benefit, the last unit produced is valued as much as or more than any other good that could have been produced using those same resources. There is no way to reallocate resources to increase the value of output. Thus, there is no way to reallocate resources to increase the total utility or total benefit consumers enjoy from output. When the marginal cost of each good equals the marginal benefit that consumers derive from that good, the economy is allocatively efficient.

Teaching Tip If price exceeds marginal cost, total benefit to consumers increases if output rises. If price is below marginal cost, total benefit increases if output falls.

Gains from Voluntary Exchange Through Competitive Markets

If the marginal cost to firms of supplying the good just equals the marginal benefit to consumers, does this mean that market exchange confers no net benefits on participants? No! Market exchange usually benefits both consumers and producers. Recall that consumers garner a surplus from market exchange because the maximum amount that consumers would be willing to pay for the good exceeds the amount they in fact pay. Exhibit 14 depicts a market in short-run equilibrium. The consumer surplus in this exhibit is represented by the blue shaded area, which is below the demand curve but above the market-clearing price of $10.

Producers in the short run also usually derive a net benefit, or a surplus, from market exchange because the amount they receive for their output exceeds the minimum amount they would require to supply that amount of the good in the short run. Recall that the short-run market supply curve is

EXHIBIT 14

Consumer Surplus and Producer Surplus for a Competitive Market in the Short Run

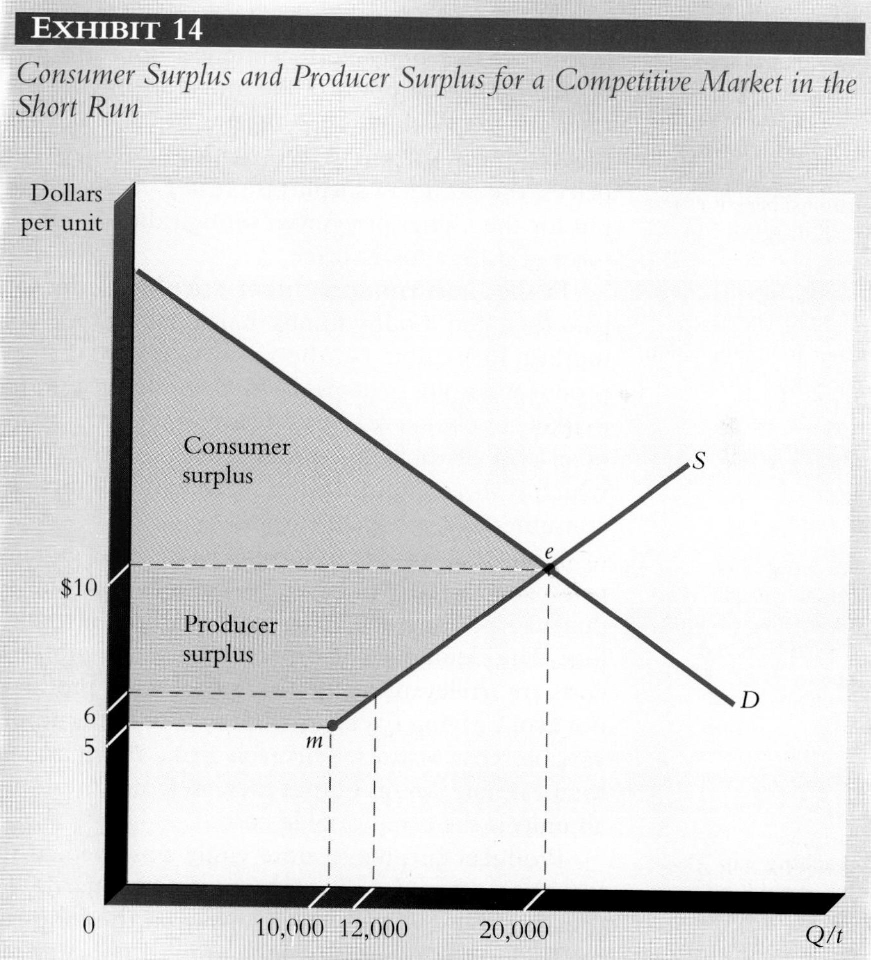

Consumer surplus is represented by the area above the market-clearing price of $10 per unit and below the demand curve; it is shown as a blue triangle. Producer surplus is represented by the area above the short-run market supply curve and below the market-clearing price of $10 per unit; it is shown by the gold shading. At a price of $5 per unit, there is no producer surplus. At a price of $6 per unit, producer surplus is the shaded area between $5 and $6.

the sum of that portion of each firm's marginal cost curve that is at or rising above the minimum point on its average variable cost curve. Point *m* in Exhibit 14 is the minimum point on the market supply curve; it indicates that at a price of $5, firms are willing to supply 10,000 units. At prices below $5, the quantity supplied is zero. At point *m,* firms in this industry gain no net benefit from production in the short run because the total industry revenue derived from selling 10,000 units at $5 each just covers the variable cost incurred by producing that amount of output.

Teaching Tip If output exceeds 20,000 units in Exhibit 14, marginal cost exceeds the price that consumers are willing to pay for the last unit (the marginal benefit). If output is less than 20,000 units, marginal benefit exceeds marginal cost.

If the price increases to $6, firms increase their quantity supplied until their marginal cost equals $6. Market output increases from 10,000 to 12,000 units. Total revenue increases from $50,000 to $72,000. Part of the increased revenue covers the higher marginal cost of production. But the balance of the increased revenue is a bonus to producers, who would have been willing to supply 10,000 units for only $5 each. When the price is $6, they get to sell these 10,000 units for $6 each rather than $5 each. Thus, the producer surplus is the shaded area between $5 and $6. At higher prices, the producer surplus is greater because firms get to sell all their output for the higher price even though they would have been willing to offer most of it for a lower price.

Producer surplus The amount by which total revenue from production exceeds total variable cost

In the short run, **producer surplus** is the total revenue producers are paid for a commodity minus their total variable cost of producing the commodity. In Exhibit 14, the market-clearing price is $10 per unit, and the producer surplus is depicted by the gold area under the price but above the market supply curve. That area represents the market price minus the marginal cost of each unit produced. Allocative efficiency occurs at point *e*, which is the combination of price and quantity that maximizes the sum of consumer and producer surplus.

Teaching Tip Producer surplus represents contributions to fixed costs and then to profit.

Note that producer surplus is not the same as economic profit. Any price that exceeds the average variable cost will result in a short-run producer surplus, even though that price might result in a short-run economic loss. The definition of producer surplus ignores fixed costs because fixed costs are irrelevant to the firm's short-run production decision. Firms cannot avoid paying fixed costs in the short run, no matter what they do. Only variable cost matters. For each firm, the marginal cost is the increase in total variable cost as output increases, and the sum of the marginal costs for all units is the total variable cost.

Teaching Tip The lack of producer surplus in the constant-cost industry is represented by the horizontal long-run supply curve. However, there are still gains from exchange in the form of consumer surplus.

Producer surplus is more easily observed in the short run than in the long run. If producer surplus is defined narrowly as total revenue minus total variable cost, producer surplus in the long run for perfectly competitive industries is zero. In long-run equilibrium, all costs are variable and total cost equals total revenue, so there is no producer surplus. But for increasing-cost industries, the definition of producer surplus is often broadened to include the higher incomes to those resource owners whose pay rates increase when industry demand increases. For example, suppose an increase in the world's demand for grain drives up the rental price of farm acreage. Owners of such land earn more as the rental price increases; they earn a producer surplus.

Conclusion

Point to Stress A single firm can affect neither output prices nor *resource* prices.

Point to Stress The free mobility of resources in response to economic profits and losses ensures the allocation of more resources in markets where demand is expanding and of fewer resources in markets where demand is contracting.

Let's review the characteristics of a perfectly competitive market and see how they relate to ideas developed in this chapter. *First,* there must be a large number of buyers and sellers. This is necessary so that no individual buyer or seller is large enough to influence the price. *Second,* firms must produce a homogeneous product. If consumers could distinguish among the output of different producers, they might prefer the output of one firm even at a higher price, so different producers could sell at different prices. In that case not every firm would be a price taker—that is, the firms' demand curves would no longer be horizontal. *Third,* all market participants must have full information about all prices and all production processes. Otherwise, some producers could charge more than the market price, and some uninformed consumers would pay that higher price. Also, through ignorance, some firms might select outdated technology or fail to recognize the opportunity for short-run economic profits. *Fourth,* all resources must be mobile in the long run, and there must be no obstacles preventing new firms from moving into profitable markets. Otherwise, some firms could earn economic profits in the long run.

Perfect competition is not the form of market structure most commonly observed in the real world. The markets for agricultural products, stocks, commodities such as gold and silver, and foreign exchange come close to being perfect. But even if no single example of perfect competition could be found, the model would be a useful tool for analyzing market behavior. As you will see in the next two chapters, perfect competition provides a valuable benchmark for evaluating the efficiency of other kinds of market structures.

Summary

1. Market structure describes important features of the economic environment in which firms operate. These features include the number of competing firms, the ease or difficulty of entering the market, the similarities or differences in the output produced by each firm, and the forms of competition among firms. As we will see in the next two chapters, there are four types of market structure. This chapter examined perfect competition.

2. Perfectly competitive markets are characterized by (1) a large number of buyers and sellers, (2) production of a homogeneous product, (3) full information about the availability and price of all resources and goods, and (4) free and complete mobility of resources. Firms in such markets are said to be price takers because no individual firm can influence the price. Individual firms can vary only the amount they choose to sell at the market price.

3. The market price in perfect competition is determined by the intersection of the market demand and market supply curves. Each firm then faces a demand curve that is a horizontal line drawn at the market price. Because this demand curve is horizontal, it represents the average revenue and the marginal revenue the firm receives at each level of output.

4. The perfectly competitive firm maximizes profits or minimizes losses by producing where marginal cost equals marginal revenue. That portion of the firm's marginal cost curve at or rising above the average

variable cost curve becomes the firm's short-run supply curve. The horizontal summation of all firms' supply curves forms the market supply curve.

5. Because firms are not free to enter or leave the market in the short run, economic profit or loss is possible in the short run. In the long run, however, firms will adjust their scale of operations, and firms will enter or leave the market until economic profit or loss is driven to zero. In the long run, each firm will produce at the low point on its long-run average cost curve. At this level of output, the price, marginal cost, and average total cost are all equal. Firms that fail to produce at this least-cost combination will not survive in the long run.

6. In the short run, a firm alters quantity supplied in response to a change in price by moving up or down its marginal cost curve. The long-run industry adjustment to a change in demand involves changes in the size of firms and firms' entering or leaving the market until the remaining firms in the industry earn just a normal profit. As the industry expands in the long run, the industry supply curve reflects either increasing costs, constant costs, or decreasing costs.

7. Perfectly competitive markets reflect both productive efficiency, because output is produced using the most efficient combination of resources available, and allocative efficiency, because the goods produced are those most valued by consumers. In equilibrium, perfectly competitive markets allocate goods so that the marginal cost of the last unit produced equals the marginal value that consumers attach to that last unit purchased. Voluntary exchange in competitive markets maximizes consumer surplus and producer surplus.

Questions and Problems

1. (Perfect Competition) Some economists have argued that the U.S. stock market is competitive. Discuss the merits of and flaws in this view. Consider each assumption involved in perfect competition.

2. (Perfect Competition) Do patents and copyrights hinder competition? Should patents be allowed if they do hinder competition? Why or why not?

3. (Perfect Competition) Some people have claimed that there is strong competition in the U.S. auto market. Give some reasons why this market could not be considered perfectly competitive.

4. (Normal Versus Economic Profits) Company A is making millions of dollars in accounting profits. Yet the same company has decided to quit producing its current product. How is this possible?

5. (Competition) Consider Exhibit 3 in this chapter. Explain why the total revenue curve is a straight line from the origin, whereas the slope of the total cost curve changes.

6. (Profit Maximization) Consider Exhibit 3 in this chapter. Why doesn't the firm choose the output that maximizes average profits (i.e., the output for which average cost is the lowest)?

7. (Price and Marginal Revenue) Explain why price and marginal revenue are identical in the perfectly competitive model.

8. (Minimizing Losses) Consider Exhibit 5 in this chapter. The company portrayed is not able to cover its fixed cost by selling its product. However, it is able to cover its variable cost. How might the firm avoid default on its fixed obligations in the short run?

9. (Entry and Exit of Firms) Why is it reasonable that the short-run competitive model does not allow for the entry and exit of firms? Is entry into an industry intrinsically more difficult than exit from an industry?

10. (Long-Run Industry Supply) Why does the long-run industry supply curve for an increasing-cost industry slope upward? What causes the increasing costs in an increasing-cost industry?

11. (Competitive Industry) Draw the short- and long-run cost curves of a competitive firm in long-run equilibrium.

a. Show the firm's short-run response to a reduction in the price of a variable resource.
b. Assuming that the industry is an increasing-cost industry, describe the process by which the industry returns to long-run equilibrium.

12. (Short-Run Competitive Supply) An individual competitive firm's short-run supply curve is the portion of its marginal cost curve that equals or rises above the average variable cost. Explain why this is true.

13. (Short-Run Competitive Supply) Use the following data to answer the questions below.

Q	*TVC*	*Q*	*TVC*
1	$10	5	$31
2	16	6	38
3	20	7	46
4	25	8	55
		9	65

a. Calculate the marginal cost for each level of production.
b. Calculate the average variable cost for each level of production.
c. How much would the firm produce if it could sell its product for $5? for $7? for $10? Explain your answers.
d. Assuming that its fixed cost is $3, calculate the firm's profit at each of the production levels determined in part c.

14. (Long-Run Competitive Behavior) Suppose that a constant-cost industry consists entirely of firms with U-shaped long-run average cost curves. Explain why variation in industry output in response to changes in demand must, in the long run, come from variation in the number of firms rather than from variation in the scale of production by firms in the industry.

15. (Efficiency and Perfect Competition) Use the data below to answer the following questions.

Quantity	*Marginal Cost*	*Marginal Benefit*
0	—	—
1	$ 2	$10
2	3	9
3	4	8
4	5	7
5	6	6
6	8	5
7	10	4
8	12	3
9	15	2
10	18	1

a. Construct a supply-demand diagram for this product and calculate the equilibrium price and quantity.
b. What is the total (short-run) variable cost to producers of producing this equilibrium amount?
c. What is the total benefit to consumers of consuming this equilibrium amount?
d. Compare your answers in parts b and c to the amount that consumers pay (and therefore the revenues producers receive) for this quantity and calculate the amount of consumer and producer surplus associated with this equilibrium quantity.

16. (Time and Industry Demand) Recall from Chapter 19 that to determine the market demand for any particular product, we horizontally sum the individual demand curves for the buyers of the product. Why can't you construct the market demand curve similarly, by summing up the demand curves facing all firms that supply the product?

17. (Profit Maximization) In Exhibit 3, it appears that marginal cost will intersect the marginal revenue curve both at point *e* (where *q*/*t* equals 12 units) and at a production rate below 5 units. Why is point *e* the output level that maximizes total profit rather than the other output level where marginal revenue equals marginal cost?

18. (Long-Run Competitive Equilibrium) Suppose that an industry consisting of a large number of identical firms, each with U-shaped long-run average cost curves, is a decreasing-cost competitive industry. If this industry experiences a reduction in demand, what will happen in the long run to the number of firms in the industry, the price level for the product, the profit level for each firm in the industry, and the per-unit price of resources used in the industry? Illustrate your answer with diagrams of the long-run adjustment process for both the industry and an individual firm.

19. (Competition and Efficiency) Suppose that firms in a competitive industry are able to use a resource (e.g., water) without paying for it. Using the concept of allocative efficiency discussed in this chapter, how would you characterize the output level in this industry? Explain your answer.

20. (Fast Forward) The right to market and rent videotapes comes with a price reflecting the cost in lost movie admission revenues. Yet even though this right has become more expensive as more potential moviegoers have VCRs and hence may participate in the rental market, rental rates for movies have fallen. Aside from increased competition, is there anything in the cost structure for rental movie outlets that would suggest that lower rental rates can still be profitable in the face of rising "rights" costs?

21. (Fast Forward) Video rental stores generally charge different rents for different kinds of tapes. Do you think that the differences reflect differences in cost or demand? What does your answer suggest about how these rate differences might change as competition drives the rate of return toward a normal rate?

CHAPTER 22

MONOPOLY

Teaching Tip Pure monopoly is defined in Chapter 4 as a single producer of a good for which there are no close substitutes.

Monopoly is a Greek word meaning "one seller." Monopolists sell electricity, cable TV service, postage stamps, local phone service, and other products that have no close substitutes. You have heard much about the evils of monopoly. You may have even played the Parker Brothers game Monopoly on a rainy day. Now we will sort out fact from fiction. Pure monopoly, like perfect competition, is not as common as other market structures. Yet a study of the sources of monopoly power and the effects of monopoly on the allocation of resources will convey an understanding not only of this market structure but also of the market structures that lie between pure monopoly and perfect competition. Topics discussed in this chapter include

- Barriers to entry
- Price elasticity and marginal revenue
- Economic profit in the short run and long run
- Welfare cost of monopoly
- Price discrimination

BARRIERS TO ENTRY

Barrier to entry Any impediment that prevents new firms from competing on an equal basis with existing firms in an industry

Perhaps the single most important feature of a monopolized market is that because of barriers to entry new firms cannot profitably enter the market in the long run. **Barriers to entry** are restrictions on the entry of new firms into an industry. We will examine three kinds: legal restrictions, economies of scale, and the monopolist's control of an essential resource.

Legal Restrictions

One way to prevent new firms from entering a market is to make entry illegal. Patents, licenses, and other legal restrictions imposed by the government provide some producers with legal protection against market entry.

Patent A legal barrier to entry that conveys to its holder the exclusive right to supply a product for a certain period of time

Innovation The process of turning an invention into a marketable product

PATENTS AND INVENTION INCENTIVES. In the United States, a **patent** awards to the developer of a new product or production process the exclusive right to production for seventeen years. Originally enacted in 1790, the patent laws encourage inventors to invest the time and money required to make new discoveries. If others could simply copy successful products, inventors would be less inclined to incur the up-front costs of developing new products and bringing them to the market. Patents also provide the stimulus to turn an invention into a marketable product, a process called **innovation**.

Example The Haloid (now Xerox) Corp. held the sole license to develop and market the photocopying process commercially.

LICENSES AND OTHER ENTRY RESTRICTIONS. Governments often confer monopoly status by awarding a single firm the exclusive right to supply particular goods and services. Federal licenses give certain firms the right to broadcast radio and TV signals; state licenses are required to provide services such as medical care, haircuts, and legal assistance. A license is not a monopoly but it does confer the ability to charge a price above what would be the competitive level. Governments confer monopoly rights to sell hot dogs at civic auditoriums, collect garbage, provide bus and cab service in and out of town, and supply services ranging from electricity to cable TV. The government itself may claim the right to provide certain products by outlawing competitors. For example, the U.S. Postal Service has the exclusive right to deliver first class mail, and many states are monopoly sellers of liquor and lottery tickets. The Postal Service monopoly is considered in the following case study.

CASE STUDY

The Mail Monopoly

In 1971 Congress converted the old Post Office Department into an independent agency called the U.S. Postal Service. The Postal Service handles over half a billion pieces of mail a day—nearly half the world's total. It has a legal monopoly in delivering first-class letters; it also has the exclusive right to the use of the space inside people's mailboxes.

The price of a first-class stamp climbed from 6 cents in 1970 to 29 cents by 1991, a price increase that outstripped the rate of inflation in the economy by 132 percent. Telephone rates since 1970 have increased at only one-third the rate of first-class mail, so phone service is now relatively cheaper than it was. Other technologies have also replaced mail delivery, such as fax machines and electronic mail over computer lines. So the Postal Service's monopoly on first-class mail has been eroded by its rising relative cost and by emerging technologies that offer substitutes.

Since the Postal Service does not have a monopoly on other classes of mail, it has lost huge chunks of this other business to private firms offering lower rates and better service. For example, in the last twenty years, the United Parcel Service and others have taken away 95 percent of fourth-class

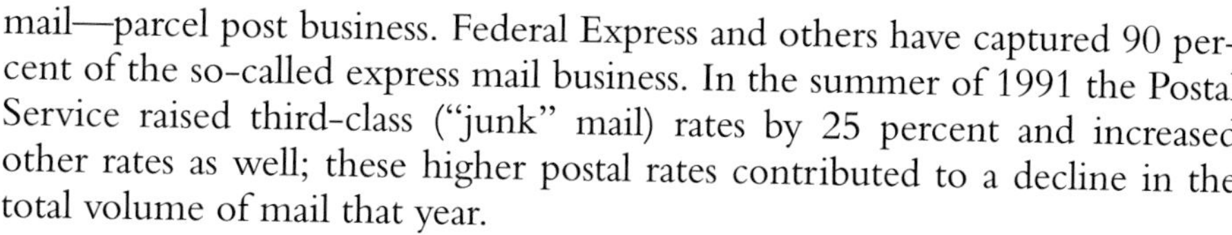

mail—parcel post business. Federal Express and others have captured 90 percent of the so-called express mail business. In the summer of 1991 the Postal Service raised third-class ("junk" mail) rates by 25 percent and increased other rates as well; these higher postal rates contributed to a decline in the total volume of mail that year.

Source: James Cook, "A Mailman's Lot Is Not a Happy One," *Forbes* (April 27, 1992): 82–92.

Economies of Scale

A monopoly sometimes emerges naturally when a firm experiences *economies of scale* and thus a declining average cost over the full range of market demand. When this is the case, a single firm can satisfy the market demand at a lower average cost per unit than could two or more firms operating at smaller levels of output. Thus, a single firm will emerge from the competitive process as the sole seller in the market. Cable TV is an industry that exhibits economies of scale. Once the cable has been strung throughout the community—that is, once the fixed cost has been incurred—the marginal cost of hooking up an additional household is relatively small. Consequently the average cost per household declines as more and more households are tied into the existing system. The average cost per household would be greater if two or more competing companies each strung their own wires throughout the community.

Example Most local public utilities (gas, water, and electricity) are natural monopolies.

Because such a monopoly emerges from the nature of production, it is called a *natural monopoly,* to distinguish it from the artificial monopolies created by government patents, licenses, and other official barriers to entry. A new entrant cannot sell enough output to enjoy the low cost created by the economies of scale experienced by an established natural monopolist, so entry into the market is blocked. We will have more to say about the regulation of natural monopolies in a later chapter, when we examine the government regulation of markets.

Control of Essential Resources

Sometimes the source of monopoly power is a firm's control over some nonreproducible resource that is critical to production. For example, the world's diamond trade is operated primarily by De Beers Consolidated Mines, which produces a substantial portion of all rough diamonds in the world and buys most of the rough diamonds found in other mines. Professional sports leagues try to block the formation of competing leagues by signing the best players to long-term contracts and by seeking the exclusive use of sports stadiums and arenas. Celebrities have a monopoly over the input essential to their success: themselves. Consequently, the most successful stars carefully control their personal appearances to avoid overexposure (this is why big stars seldom appear on TV).

Local monopolies are more common than national or international monopolies. In rural areas monopolies include the only grocery store, movie theater, and restaurant for miles around. But long-lasting monopolies are rare because, as we will see, the economic profit usually earned by a monopolist provides other firms with a powerful incentive to produce close substitutes. Also, over time, technological change tends to break down barriers to entry. For example, the development of wireless transmission of long-distance telephone calls gave rise to competitors for AT&T. Likewise, as noted in the earlier case study, fax machines and electronic mail now compete with the U.S. Postal Service's monopoly on first-class mail.

REVENUE FOR THE MONOPOLIST

Because the monopoly firm supplies the entire market, the demand curve for goods or services produced by a monopolist is also the market demand curve. The demand curve for the firm's output therefore slopes downward, reflecting the law of demand—the inverse relation between price and quantity demanded.

Demand and Marginal Revenue

Point to Stress Average revenue equals the price, and the average revenue curve is the demand curve facing the firm in *all market structures.*

Exhibit 1 offers the downward-sloping market demand curve for a typical monopolist. The monopolist can sell 4 units at a price of $6.75 per unit. That price-quantity combination yields a total revenue of $6.75 × 4, or $27. The total revenue divided by the quantity is the *average revenue per unit,* which in this case is $27/4, or $6.75. Hence the average revenue per unit is equal to the price. (All we have really said is that price times quantity equals total revenue, so total revenue divided by quantity equals the price.)

To sell 5 units, this monopolist must drop the price to $6.50 per unit, for a total revenue of $32.50 and an average revenue of $6.50. Again, the average revenue equals the price for any level of sales, and both can be read from the demand curve. Therefore *the demand curve is also the monopolist's average revenue curve,* just as the perfectly competitive firm's demand curve is also that firm's average revenue curve.

Point to Stress Marginal revenue is less than price after the first unit for all firms facing downward-sloping demand curves except for a perfectly price-discriminating monopolist.

The relation between price and marginal revenue is different in monopoly and perfect competition. Recall that for a perfectly competitive firm, marginal revenue is always equal to the market price because each firm can sell as much as it chooses at that price. Now consider the marginal revenue the monopolist receives from selling a fifth unit of the good. When the price drops from $6.75 to $6.50, total revenue goes from $27 to $32.50. Thus, marginal revenue, which is the change in total revenue resulting from selling one more unit, is $5.50, which is less than the average revenue of $6.50. *For a monopolist, the marginal revenue is less than the price.*

The Gain and Loss from Selling One More Unit

A closer look at Exhibit 1 reveals why marginal revenue will always be less than the price. The monopolist sells the fifth unit for $6.50, as shown by the vertical

EXHIBIT 1

Monopoly Demand: Loss and Gain in Total Revenue from Selling One More Unit

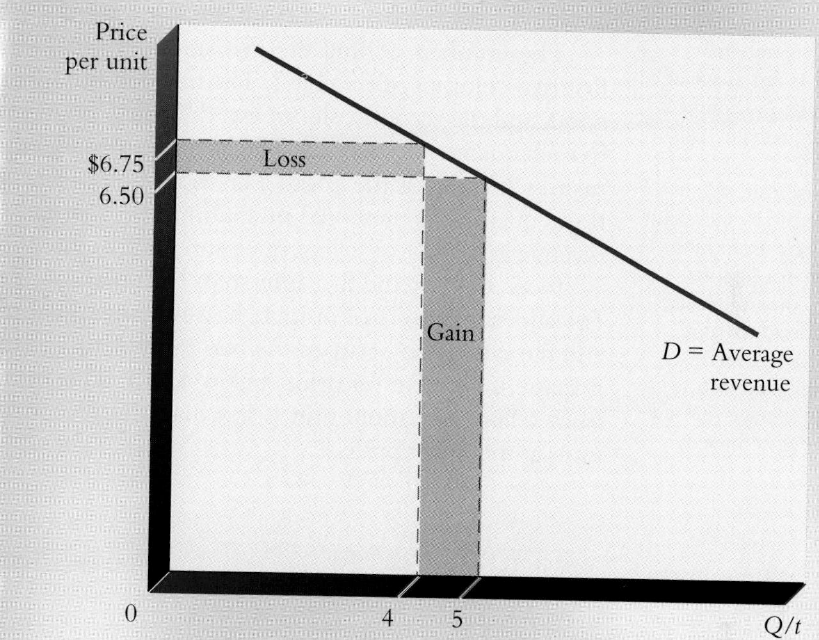

If a monopolist increases production from 4 units to 5, the revenue for the fifth unit sold is $6.50. However, the monopolist loses $1 on the first 4 units, since each unit must now be priced at $6.50, rather than $6.75. Marginal revenue equals the gain minus the loss, or $6.50 – 1.00 = $5.50. Hence, marginal revenue is $5.50 and is less than the price ($6.50).

rectangle marked *Gain*. But to sell a fifth unit, the monopolist must offer *all* five units for $6.50 each. Thus, by selling the fifth unit, the firm sacrifices $0.25 on each of the first four units, which previously could have been sold for $6.75 each. This reduction in revenue from the first four units totals $1.00 ($0.25 × 4) and is identified in Exhibit 1 by the horizontal rectangle marked *Loss.* The net change in total revenue from selling the fifth unit—that is, the marginal revenue from the fifth unit—equals the *Gain* minus the *Loss,* which equals $6.50 minus $1.00, or $5.50. This analysis assumes that all units of the good are sold for the same price; that is, when the price is $6.50, all 5 units must be sold for $6.50 each. Although this is usually true, later in this chapter we will consider some cases in which a monopolist may be able to charge different prices for different units of the good. At that time we will revisit the firm's marginal revenue curve.

To calculate the marginal revenue from selling one more unit of output, we must subtract from the amount received for that additional unit the loss resulting from having to sell all units—not just the marginal unit—at the lower price. As we move down the demand curve, marginal revenue declines for two reasons: (1) the amount received from selling another unit declines (since the price drops), and (2) the revenue forgone by selling all units at this lower price increases (since the quantity that had been sold at a higher price increases). Both factors reduce the marginal revenue as the price falls along a given demand curve.

Teaching Tip
With a *linear* downward-sloping demand curve, marginal revenue falls twice as fast as average revenue. In Exhibit 2, average revenue falls by $0.25 for each additional unit, whereas marginal revenue falls by $0.50. In Exhibit 3, the marginal revenue curve intersects the horizontal axis halfway between 0 and the intersection of the average revenue curve with the axis.

The numbers behind the demand curve in Exhibit 1 are presented in the first two columns of Exhibit 2. The first column lists alternative quantities of the good, and the second column lists the price, or average revenue, corresponding to each quantity demanded. The two columns together are the monopolist's demand schedule for the good. The monopolist's *total revenue,* which equals price times quantity, is presented in column (3). *Marginal revenue,* the change in total revenue as a result of selling one more unit, is listed in column (4).

Note that for the first unit sold, marginal revenue and the price are equal. For additional units of output, however, marginal revenue is below the price, and the difference between the two grows larger as the price declines. Marginal revenue is negative for prices below $3.75. This means that the revenue gained from selling one more unit is less than the revenue lost by selling all previous units at the lower price.

EXHIBIT 2

Revenue for a Monopolist

Quantity per period (Q) (1)	Price (average revenue) (p) (2)	Total Revenue ($TR = Q \times p$) (3) = (1) × (2)	Marginal Revenue $\left(MR = \frac{\Delta TR}{\Delta Q}\right)$ (4)
0	$7.75	$ 0.00	—
1	7.50	7.50	$ 7.50
2	7.25	14.50	7.00
3	7.00	21.00	6.50
4	6.75	27.00	6.00
5	6.50	32.50	5.50
6	6.25	37.50	5.00
7	6.00	42.00	4.50
8	5.75	46.00	4.00
9	5.50	49.50	3.50
10	5.25	52.50	3.00
11	5.00	55.00	2.50
12	4.75	57.00	2.00
13	4.50	58.50	1.50
14	4.25	59.50	1.00
15	4.00	60.00	0.50
16	3.75	60.00	0.00
17	3.50	59.50	−0.50

Revenue Curves

Teaching Tip In Exhibit 2, the value of price elasticity of demand between 1 and 2 units is 19.67, and total revenue rises. Between 16 and 17 units, the value is 0.88, and total revenue drops.

Teaching Tip The exact relationship between marginal revenue and the value of price elasticity of demand is

$MR = p\,(1 - 1/E_D)$,

where E_D is positive. Marginal revenue thus falls as E_D falls, but remains positive as long as E_D exceeds 1. Note that if E_D equals infinity, as in perfect competition, marginal revenue equals the price.

The data in Exhibit 2 are graphed in Exhibit 3, which shows the demand and marginal revenue curves in panel (a) and the total revenue curve in panel (b). Note that the marginal revenue curve is below the demand curve, and that the total revenue curve is at a maximum when marginal revenue is zero. Take a minute to study these relations—they are important.

Total revenue, recall, is price times quantity. What happens to total revenue as the price falls depends on what happens to the percentage change in quantity demanded relative to the percentage change in price. If the percentage increase in quantity demanded more than offsets the percentage decrease in price, then total revenue will increase as the price falls. Earlier you learned that the price elasticity for a straight-line demand curve decreases as you move down the curve. Where demand is elastic—that is, where the percentage increase in quantity demanded more than offsets the percentage decrease in price—a decrease in the price will increase total revenue. On the other hand, where demand is inelastic, the increase in quantity is not enough to make up for the loss in revenue from a lower price, so total revenue will decline if the price falls.

Therefore, *when the demand curve is elastic, marginal revenue is positive so total revenue increases as the price falls.* Demand is of unitary elasticity at the price of $3.75. At that price, marginal revenue is zero and total revenue is at a maximum. (Note that the output at which total revenue is maximized would only by coincidence be the output at which profit is maximized.) From Exhibit 3 you can see that marginal revenue becomes negative if the price drops below $3.75, indicating an inelastic demand at price levels below $3.75. *When the demand curve is inelastic, marginal revenue is negative so total revenue decreases as the price falls.* An understanding of elasticity will be of help later in determining the price and output combination that maximizes the monopolist's profit.

FIRM COSTS AND PROFIT MAXIMIZATION

Point to Stress Although a perfectly competitive firm can sell all it wants at the same price, a price searcher must reduce price in order to sell more.

Price searcher A firm that has some control over the price it charges because its demand curve slopes downward

Given the demand curve, the important question is, how will the monopolist choose among the price-quantity alternatives? We assume that the objective of the monopolist, like that of other firms, is to *maximize economic profit.* In the case of perfect competition, the firm has to choose the profit-maximizing quantity because the price is given to the firm. The perfect competitor is a *price taker.* The monopolist can choose either the price *or* the quantity, but choosing one determines the other. Because the monopolist can select the price that maximizes profit, we say the monopolist is a price searcher. More generally, any firm that has some control over the price it charges is a **price searcher**.

Profit Maximization

What are the profit-maximizing price and output levels for a monopolist? Exhibit 4 repeats the revenue data from Exhibits 2 and 3 and also includes

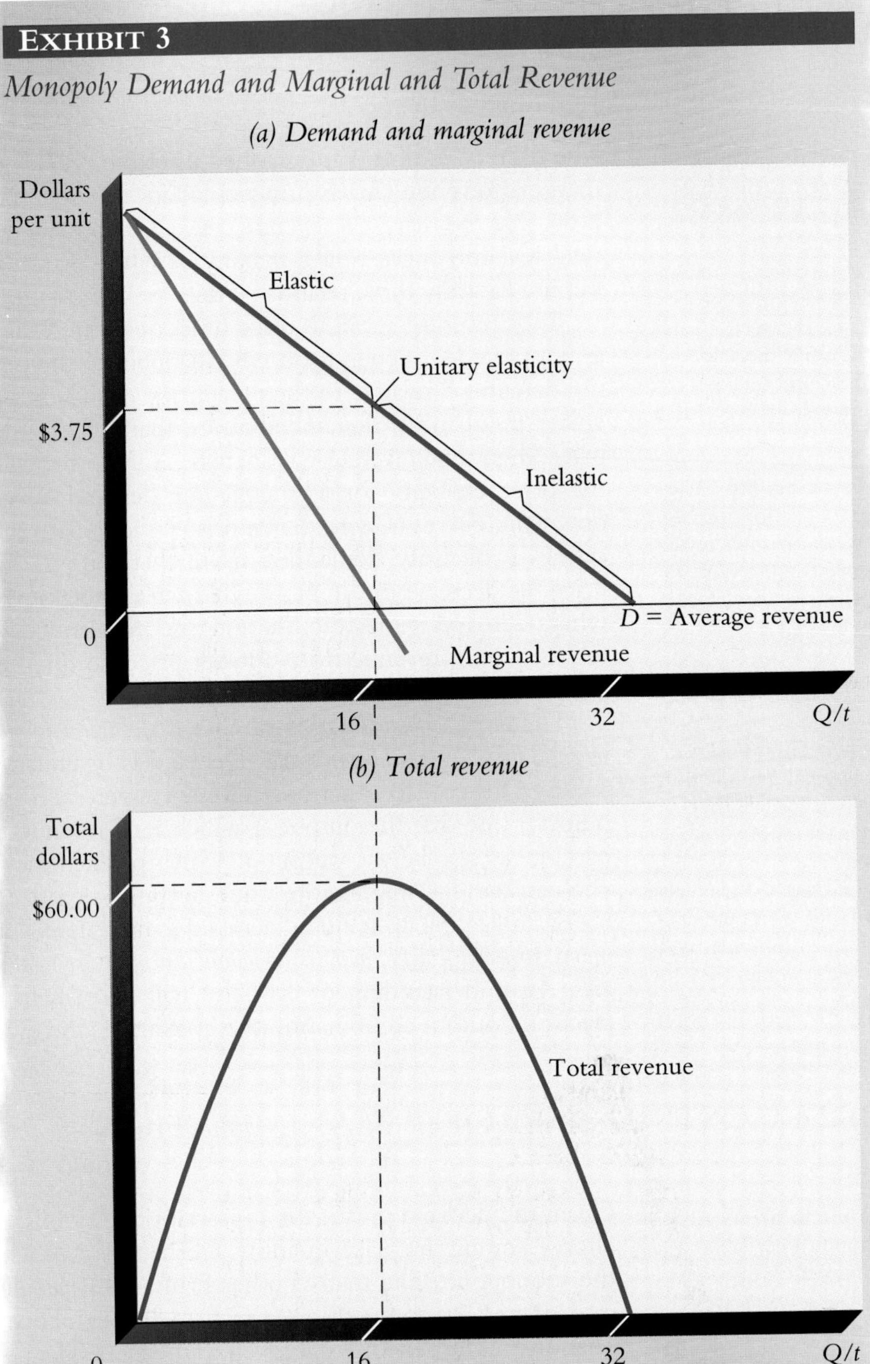

Where demand is price elastic, marginal revenue is positive, so total revenue increases as the price falls and quantity increases. Where demand is price inelastic, marginal revenue is negative, so total revenue decreases as the price falls and quantity increases. Where demand is of unitary elasticity, marginal revenue is zero, so total revenue is at a maximum, neither increasing nor decreasing.

EXHIBIT 4

Short-Run Costs and Revenue for a Monopolist

Quantity per period (Q) (1)	Price (average revenue) (p) (2)	Total Revenue ($TR = Q \times p$) (3) = (1) × (2)	Marginal Revenue $\left(MR = \frac{\Delta TR}{\Delta Q}\right)$ (4)	Total Cost (TC) (5)	Marginal Cost $\left(MC = \frac{\Delta TC}{\Delta Q}\right)$ (6)	Average Total Cost $\left(ATC = \frac{TC}{Q}\right)$ (7)	Total Profit or Loss = $TR - TC$ (8)
0	$7.75	$ 0.00	—	$ 15.00	—	—	−$15.00
1	7.50	7.50	$ 7.50	19.75	$ 4.75	$19.75	−12.25
2	7.25	14.50	7.00	23.50	3.75	11.75	−9.00
3	7.00	21.00	6.50	26.50	3.00	8.83	−5.50
4	6.75	27.00	6.00	29.00	2.50	7.75	−2.00
5	6.50	32.50	5.50	31.00	2.00	6.20	1.50
6	6.25	37.50	5.00	32.50	1.50	5.42	5.00
7	6.00	42.00	4.50	33.75	1.25	4.82	8.25
8	5.75	46.00	4.00	35.25	1.50	4.41	10.75
9	5.50	49.50	3.50	37.25	2.00	4.14	12.25
10	**5.25**	**52.50**	**3.00**	**40.00**	**2.75**	**4.00**	**12.50**
11	5.00	55.00	2.50	43.25	3.25	3.93	11.75
12	4.75	57.00	2.00	48.00	4.75	4.00	9.00
13	4.50	58.50	1.50	54.50	6.50	4.19	4.00
14	4.25	59.50	1.00	64.00	9.50	4.57	−4.50
15	4.00	60.00	0.50	77.50	13.50	5.17	−17.50
16	3.75	60.00	0.00	96.00	18.50	6.00	−36.00
17	3.50	59.50	−0.50	121.00	25.00	7.12	−61.50

the short-run cost data developed in the last chapter. We assume this monopolist faces costs that have the same appearance as those faced by any other firm. For example, since total cost equals $15 when output is zero, fixed cost must equal $15. Given the cost and revenue data, there are two ways to find the price and quantity that maximize profit.

TOTAL REVENUE MINUS TOTAL COST. The profit-maximizing monopolist employs the same decision rule as the competitive firm. The monopolist increases output as long as selling additional output adds more to total revenue than to total cost. *The monopolist must find the production level where total revenue exceeds total cost by the greatest amount.* Economic profit is presented in the right-hand column of Exhibit 4. As you can see, the maximum profit is $12.50, which occurs at an output of 10 units and a price of $5.25. At that level of output, total revenue is $52.50 and total cost is $40.00.

Point to Stress Producing where marginal revenue equals marginal cost assumes that the firm is at least able to cover its variable costs if it produces.

MARGINAL COST EQUALS MARGINAL REVENUE. The profit-maximizing monopolist expands output as long as marginal revenue exceeds marginal cost but must stop before marginal cost exceeds marginal revenue.

Again, profit is maximized at $12.50 when output is 10 units. The marginal revenue for unit 10 is $3.00, and the marginal cost is $2.75. Because unit 11 has a marginal cost of $3.25 but a marginal revenue of only $2.50, producing that unit would lower profit from $12.50 to $11.75. As you can see, at output levels in excess of 10 units, marginal cost exceeds marginal revenue. For simplicity, *we say that profit-maximizing output occurs where marginal cost equals marginal revenue.*

Point to Stress Note that the firm does not attempt to maximize profit per unit. Profit per unit at 9 units is $1.36; it is only $1.25 at the total-profit-maximizing output of 10 units. Nor does the firm attempt to minimize average total cost, which occurs where output is 11 units; at 11 units of output, profit is only $11.75.

Teaching Tip If the firm were producing where marginal revenue is negative, it could increase revenues by *cutting* output. Cutting output would also reduce total cost, so profit would rise.

Point to Stress The firm is not maximizing total revenue (which occurs at output of 16 units).

GRAPHICAL SOLUTION. The cost and revenue data in Exhibit 4 are plotted in Exhibit 5, with per-unit cost and revenue curves in panel (a) and total cost and revenue curves in panel (b). The intersection of the two marginal curves at point *e* in panel (a) indicates that profit is maximized when 10 units are sold. At that level of output, we move up to the demand curve to find the profit-maximizing price. When output equals 10 units, the profit-maximizing price as identified by point *a* is $5.25, which is the highest possible price for which 10 units of output can be sold. The average total cost of $4.00 is identified by point *b*. The average profit per unit sold equals the price, or average revenue, minus the average total cost: $5.25 – $4.00, or $1.25. The total economic profit is the average profit per unit of $1.25 multiplied by the 10 units sold, for a total of $12.50, as identified by the shaded rectangle. So the profit-maximizing level of output is found where the rising marginal cost curve intersects the marginal revenue curve. Because no portion of the marginal cost curve will ever be less than zero, marginal cost will never intersect marginal revenue where marginal revenue is negative. Thus, the monopolist will produce only where the demand curve is elastic.

In the lower panel, the firm's profit or loss is measured by the vertical distance between the total revenue and total cost curves. The profit-maximizing firm will produce at the level of output where total revenue exceeds total cost by the greatest amount. Thus, the firm will expand output as long as the increase in total revenue that results from selling one more unit exceeds the increase in total cost that results from producing that unit. The change in total revenue as a result of a one-unit change in output equals the marginal revenue, or the slope of the total revenue curve. Likewise, the change in total cost resulting from a one-unit change in output equals the marginal cost, or the slope of the total cost curve. *The profit-maximizing quantity can be found by determining where the slopes of the total revenue and total cost curves are equal, which is the same as finding the level of output at which marginal cost equals marginal revenue.* In panel (b), you can see that the slopes are equal where output is 10 units.

One common myth is that the monopolist will charge as high a price as possible. The monopolist, however, is interested in maximizing profit, not price. The amount the monopolist can charge is limited by consumer demand. The monopolist depicted here could have charged a price of $7.50, but only one unit would have been sold at that price. Indeed, the monopolist could have charged $8 per unit, but no product would have been sold. So charging the highest possible price is not consistent with maximizing profit.

EXHIBIT 5

Monopoly Costs and Revenue

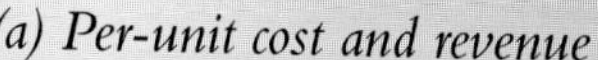

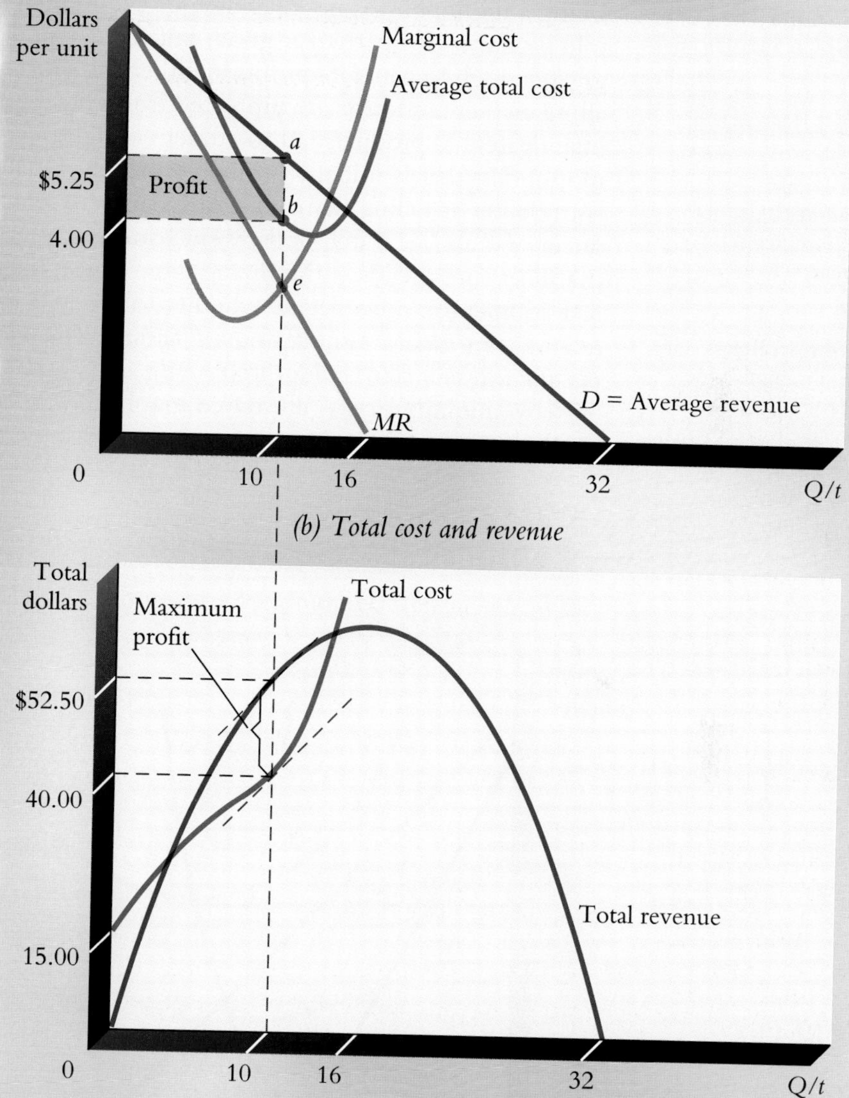

The monopolist produces 10 units of output and charges a price of $5.25. Total profit, shown by the blue rectangle in panel (a), is $12.50, the profit per unit multiplied by the number of units sold. In panel (b), profit is maximized where marginal revenue (the slope of the total revenue curve) equals marginal cost (the slope of the total cost curve), at 10 units of output. Profit is total revenue ($52.50) minus total cost ($40.00), or $12.50.

Short-Run Losses and the Shutdown Decision

Example The Cuisinart Co. introduced the food processor in the early 1980s. By the mid-1980s, the market was crowded with imitations, and Cuisinart filed for bankruptcy shortly thereafter.

Point to Stress The firm minimizes neither loss per unit nor average total cost.

Being a monopolist is no guarantee of economic profit. A monopolist is the sole producer of a particular good, but the demand for that good may not be great enough to generate profits in either the short run or the long run. After all, many new products are protected from direct competition by patents, yet many patented products fail to attract enough buyers to survive. And even a monopolist that is initially profitable may eventually suffer losses because of rising costs or falling demand. For example, Coleco, the original mass producer of Cabbage Patch dolls, went bankrupt after that craze died down. In the short run, the loss-minimizing monopolist, like the loss-minimizing perfect competitor, must decide whether to produce or to shut down. *If the price covers average variable cost, the firm will operate. If no price covers average variable cost, the firm will shut down at least temporarily.*

Loss minimization is illustrated graphically in Exhibit 6, where the marginal cost curve intersects the marginal revenue curve at point *e*. At the

EXHIBIT 6

The Monopolist Minimizes Losses in the Short Run

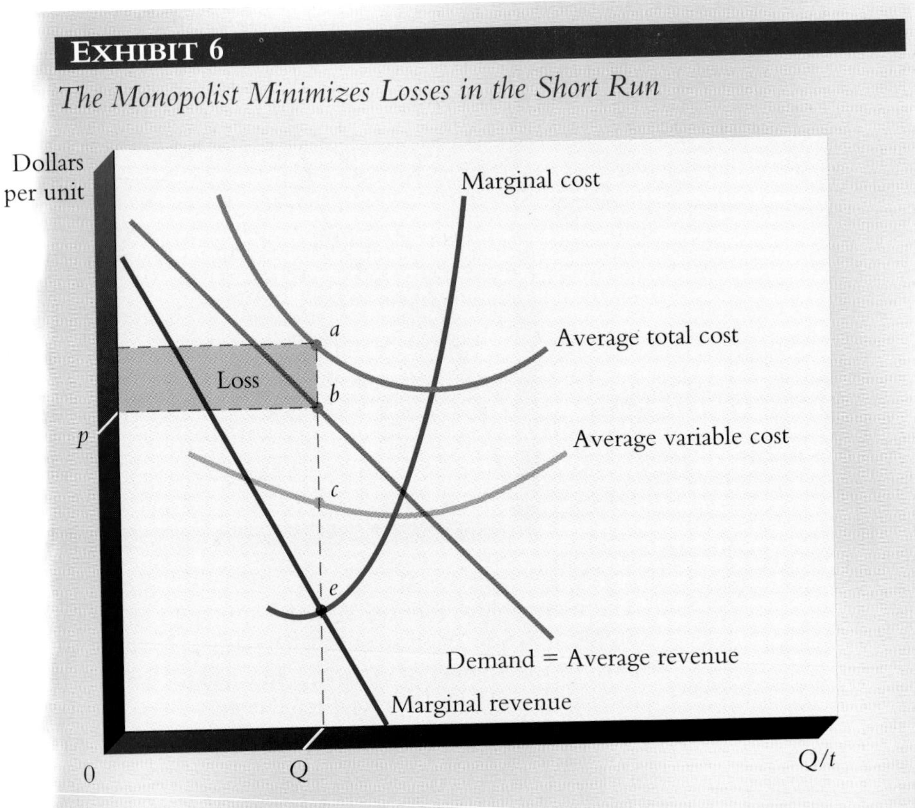

Marginal cost equals marginal revenue at point *e*. At quantity Q, price *p* (at point *b*) is less than average total cost (at point *a*), so the monopolist is suffering a loss. The monopolist will continue to produce in the short run because price is greater than average variable cost (at point *c*).

Point to Stress If the firm operates and cannot cover its variable costs, its loss will equal all fixed costs plus the uncovered portion of variable costs. The minimum loss of fixed costs is only achieved by shutting down.

equilibrium level of output, Q, the price, p (at point *b*), is above the average variable cost (at point *c*) but below the average total cost (at point *a*). Since the firm is able to cover its variable cost and make some contribution to fixed cost, it loses less by producing Q than by shutting down. The firm's loss per unit is *ab,* which is the average total cost minus the average revenue, or price. The total loss, identified by the shaded rectangle, is the average loss per unit, *ab,* times the number of units sold, Q. The firm will shut down if the average variable cost curve is above the demand, or average revenue, curve at all output levels, because at no output can the firm cover its average variable cost.

There Is No Monopolist Supply Curve

For the perfectly competitive firm, the portion of the marginal cost curve that intersects and rises above the average variable cost curve is the supply curve because it reflects the quantity the firm is willing and able to supply at each price. As long as variable costs are covered, the monopolist, like a perfect competitor, maximizes profit or minimizes loss by producing where marginal cost equals marginal revenue. For the monopolist, however, marginal revenue does not equal the price. The price at the profit-maximizing or loss-minimizing level of output is found on the demand curve, which is *above* the marginal revenue and marginal cost curves.

For a monopolist, the profit-maximizing quantity supplied, as determined by the intersection of marginal cost and marginal revenue, may be the same even though demand curves are different. For example, in Exhibit 7, *MC* is that portion of the monopolist's marginal cost curve that rises above the average variable cost curve. Consider first the demand curve *D* and the marginal revenue curve *MR*. The marginal cost curve intersects the marginal revenue curve at point *e,* resulting in an output of Q and a price of p. Suppose that demand increases to D' in such a way that the new marginal revenue curve, MR', also intersects the marginal cost curve at point *e*. The equilibrium quantity remains unchanged, but the equilibrium price increases to p'. Thus, Exhibit 7 indicates that the same equilibrium quantity can be consistent with two different prices. *Since there is no unique relation between price and output, there is no supply curve for the monopolist—no single curve that reflects the amount the monopolist will supply at each price.*

Long-Run Profit Maximization

With perfectly competitive firms, the distinction between the short run and the long run is important. The number and size of firms in perfect competition are fixed in the short run, and these firms may earn economic profits or losses, depending on the demand for the product. In the long run, all resources can vary, so firms in perfect competition will enter or leave the industry until each one is earning just a normal profit, which

EXHIBIT 7

Increased Demand May Not Affect Output

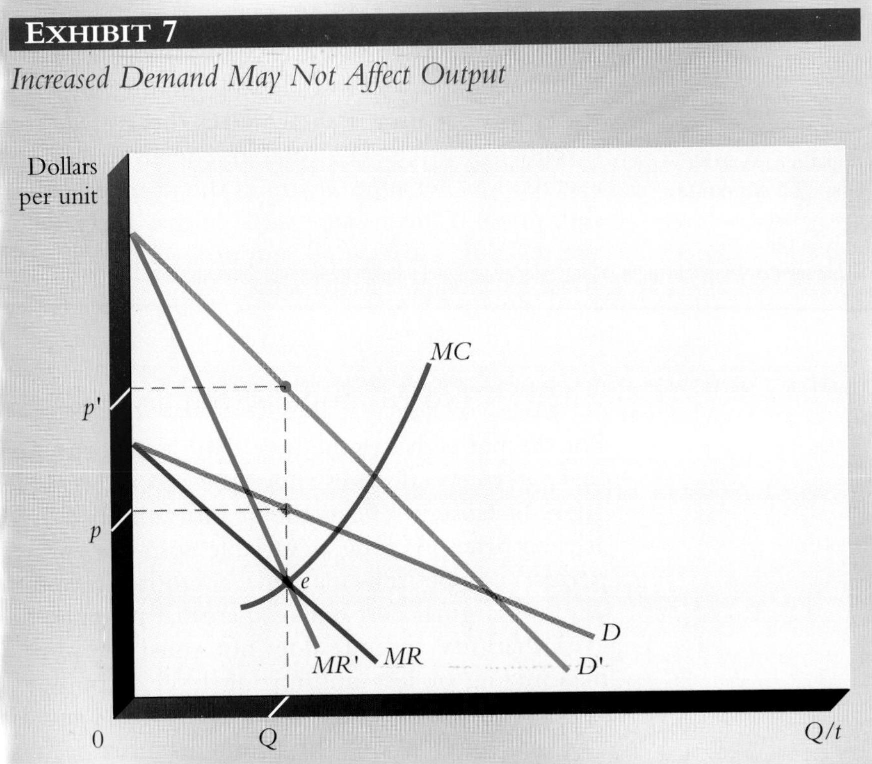

When the demand curve is D, the monopolist maximizes profit by producing Q, the output level for which marginal cost equals marginal revenue. If demand were to increase to D', the marginal revenue curve, MR', would still intersect the marginal cost curve at an output rate of Q. The same equilibrium level of output, Q, could be associated with two different prices, p or p', depending on demand. The exhibit shows that for the monopolist there is no unique relation between the price level and the quantity supplied. Thus, there is no monopolist supply curve.

Teaching Tip There is no guarantee, however, that a firm will retain its monopoly. For example, more than $10 billion worth of brand-name drugs are due to lose patent protection in 1994—including ulcer-fighting Tagamet (SmithKline Beecham) and the antibiotic Ceclor (Eli Lilly). Marion Merrell Dow has set up a subsidiary, Blue Ridge Laboratories, to make generic versions of its brand-name drugs as their patents expire. Patents are also becoming more difficult to protect—patent litigation in the United States soared 52 percent between 1982 and 1992. What's more, some countries do not enforce U.S. patents.

means zero economic profit. For the monopolist, the distinction between the short run and the long run has less significance, because by definition new firms are prevented from entering in the long run. Hence, *since by definition, monopoly means only one seller, there is no tendency for economic profit to be eliminated in the long run by the entry of new firms. Monopoly profit can persist in the long run.*

The monopolist's objective in the long run, like that of the perfectly competitive firm, is to find the scale of production that maximizes profit. A monopolist that earns economic profit in the short run may find that profits can be increased in the long run by adjusting the size of the firm. A monopolist that suffers a loss in the short run may be able to eliminate that loss in the long run by changing the scale of the firm to a more efficient size or by increasing demand for the product. A monopolist that cannot thereby eliminate a loss in the long run will leave the market.

Contestable Markets

The key to monopoly power is barriers to entry and to exit. Even though only one firm may now be serving the market, as long as there are no entry or exit barriers, other firms will enter and "contest" this market if the existing firm charges a price that yields an economic profit. A **contestable market** is one in which the potential entrant can serve the same market and has access to the same technology as the existing firm.

Contestable market One in which potential entrants can serve the same market and have access to the same technology as the existing firm

For example, suppose that you cut grass in your neighborhood during the summer. All you need is the family lawn mower, some gasoline, and some time. If you are the only one in your neighborhood who offers these services, are you a monopolist? Well, you are a monopolist in the sense that you are the only seller of services in this particular market. But you are not necessarily a monopolist in the sense that you have market power. Because no special skills are required and because most homeowners already own lawn mowers, entry into this market is easy.

How high would the price you charge for cutting lawns have to rise to attract rivals? Since the lawn mower in most households is underutilized, its opportunity cost is near zero. Only the opportunity cost of your time is important. Suppose the opportunity cost of your time is the same as that of potential competitors. If demand is such that you can charge a price that yields an economic profit—that is, that pays you more than the opportunity cost of your time—you will be undercut (or mowed down?) by new entrants.

Teaching Tip Irreversible investments make exit costly, so risk in the industry increases.

This market is contestable because entry barriers are relatively low. No irreversible investments need to be made. An investment is said to be *irreversible* if, once made, the asset is dedicated to the production of a particular good and cannot easily be redirected toward producing another good. For example, auto manufacturers and cosmetic surgeons make irreversible investments in capital. Entrepreneurs are less willing to risk entering a market if entry requires irreversible investments. Therefore, whenever irreversible investments in human or physical capital must be made in order to produce in a particular market, that market is not likely to be contestable.

Point to Stress Competitive behavior may occur when there are many *potential* firms, even if the actual number of firms is small.

Let's consider an example of contestability on a larger scale. Suppose only one airline offers passenger service between two cities. If, at the first sign of economic profit, other airlines can easily send planes into that market and reassign the planes to different routes if profits fall, the market is contestable. In summary, the sole producer in a market may not be able to earn economic profit if the market is contestable—that is, if there are no barriers to entry or exit.[1]

1. For an extensive discussion of contestability, see Elizabeth E. Bailey and William J. Baumol, "Deregulation and the Theory of Contestable Markets," *Yale Journal on Regulation* 1, no. 2 (1984): 111–137.

Monopoly and the Allocation of Resources

Teaching Tip Since the demand curve indicates the price at which each quantity can be sold, the intersection of marginal cost with demand at point *e* indicates where price equals marginal cost—which occurs at the profit-maximizing output level in perfect competition.

If monopolists are no more greedy than firms in perfect competition (since both maximize profit), if monopolists do not charge the highest possible price, and if monopolists are not guaranteed a profit, then what, if any, are the problems that arise from monopoly? The clearest way to answer that question is to compare a monopoly to that benchmark established in the previous chapter: perfect competition.

Price and Output Under Perfect Competition

Let's consider first the long-run equilibrium price and output for the perfectly competitive market. Suppose the long-run supply curve in perfect competition is horizontal as shown by S_c in Exhibit 8. Since this is a constant-cost

Exhibit 8

Perfect Competition and Monopoly

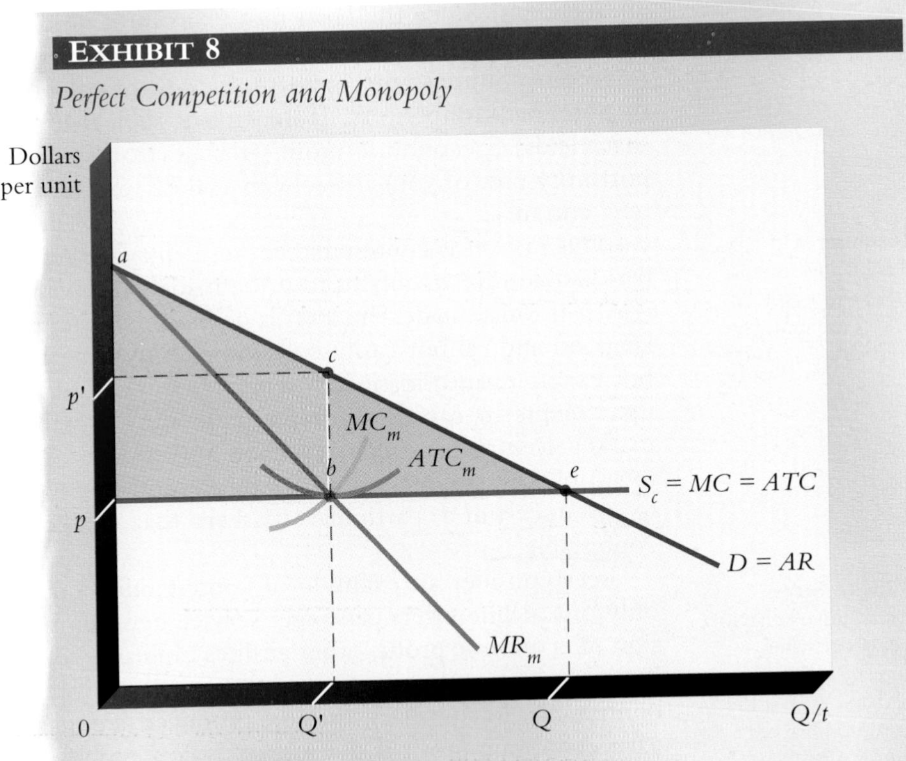

A perfectly competitive industry would produce output Q, determined at the intersection of market demand curve *D* and supply curve S_c. The price would be *p*. A monopoly that could produce output at the same minimum average cost would produce output Q', determined at point *b*, where marginal cost and marginal revenue intersect. It would charge price p'. Hence, output is lower and price is higher under monopoly than under perfect competition.

industry, the horizontal long-run supply curve in perfect competition also equals marginal cost and average total cost at each level of output. The competitive industry is in long-run equilibrium where market demand and market supply intersect at point *e*, yielding price *p* and quantity Q.

Teaching Tip Because price equals marginal cost at point *e*, there is allocative efficiency. There is no producer surplus in the long run in a constant-cost industry, but consumer surplus is maximized.

The demand curve indicates consumers' marginal benefits from each level of output. At the equilibrium combination of price and output, the marginal cost to society of producing the final unit of output (as reflected by the horizontal supply curve) just equals the marginal benefit consumers attach to that unit of the good (as reflected by the market demand curve). Because consumers are able to purchase Q units at price *p*, they enjoy a consumer surplus that is measured by the entire shaded triangle, *aep*. You will recall that consumer surplus represents the dollar value of the net benefits consumers enjoy from purchasing Q units of the good at the market price of *p*. Consumer surplus is a net benefit to society.

Price and Output Under Monopoly

If there is only one firm in the industry, the industry demand curve becomes the monopolist's demand curve, so the price the monopolist can charge depends on how much is sold. Because the monopolist's demand curve slopes downward, its marginal revenue curve also slopes downward, as indicated by MR_m in Exhibit 8. Suppose the monopolist can produce at the same constant long-run average cost as can the competitive industry. The monopolist maximizes profit in the long run by finding the size firm that equates marginal cost with marginal revenue; this firm size is reflected by ATC_m and MC_m in Exhibit 8. Marginal cost equals marginal revenue at point *b;* the monopolist will consequently produce output Q' at a price of p'. At the profit-maximizing level of output, Q', the consumers' marginal benefit, identified as point *c*, exceeds the monopolist's marginal cost, identified as point *b*. Society would be better off if output were expanded beyond Q' because the marginal value consumers attach to additional units exceeds the marginal cost of producing those additional units.

Teaching Tip Since price exceeds marginal cost, the monopolist does not generate allocative efficiency.

Allocative and Distributive Effects

Consider the allocative and distributive effects of monopoly versus perfect competition. In Exhibit 8, the monopolist's reduced output and higher price generate economic profit equal to the rectangle *pbcp'*. Consumer surplus under perfect competition was the large triangle *aep*; under monopoly it's reduced to the smaller triangle *acp'*, which in this example is only one-fourth as large. By comparing the situation under monopoly with that under perfect competition, you can see that monopoly profit comes entirely out of what was consumer surplus under perfect competition.

Notice, however, that consumer surplus has been reduced by more than the gain in monopoly profit. Consumers have lost more than the profit rectangle; they have also lost the triangle *ceb*, which was part of the consumer surplus under perfect competition. Whereas monopoly profit represents

Deadweight loss A loss of consumer surplus that is not transferred to anyone else; it can arise from monopolization of an industry

benefits transferred from consumers to the monopolist, the *ceb* triangle is called the **deadweight loss**, or *welfare loss*, of monopoly because it is a loss to consumers that is not a gain to anyone else. Thus, *if the monopolist can produce output at the same minimum average cost as the competitive firm, the triangle ceb measures the welfare loss arising from the higher price and reduced output of the monopolist*. This triangle is a deadweight loss because it represents consumer surplus forgone on units of output that are no longer produced. Empirical estimates of the annual welfare cost of monopoly have ranged from less than 1 percent to about 5 percent of national income. Applied to 1993 national income data, these estimates imply a welfare cost that could range from $50 billion to $300 billion.

Problems with Estimating the Welfare Cost of Monopoly

Teaching Tip The triangle *ceb* represents the total additional benefit from producing Q′Q (the area under the demand curve) minus the additional cost of producing Q′Q (the area under the marginal cost curve).

Because of forces at work in the economy, the actual cost of monopoly could differ from the welfare loss described in the previous section. We will first consider reasons why the welfare loss of monopoly may be smaller than that measured in Exhibit 8 and then reasons why it might be greater.

Why the Welfare Loss of Monopoly Might Be Lower Than Estimated

If an industry experiences substantial economies of scale, a monopolist may be able to produce output at a lower cost per unit than could perfectly competitive firms. Therefore the price may be less under monopoly than under competition. Even where there are no significant economies of scale, a monopolist may try to keep the price down to discourage new entry and to protect the firm's long-run potential for profits.

Example While Alcoa was the only U.S. aluminum manufacturer, it held prices relatively low in order to discourage imports. Alcoa accounted for 90 percent of sales in the United States; imports made up the other 10 percent. Alcoa's behavior can be interpreted as sacrificing short-run profit in order to maximize long-run profit.

Fear of Potential Rivals. The monopolist may keep the price below the profit-maximizing level because high profits attract potential rivals like a magnet. If the monopolist does not have ironclad protection against new entry, it may keep profits below the profit-maximizing level in order to reduce the chances of attracting new competitors. For example, before World War II Alcoa was the only manufacturer of aluminum in the United States. Some observers claim the company kept prices low to discourage potential rivals from entering the industry.

Fear of Public Intervention. The welfare loss estimated in Exhibit 8 may overstate the true cost of monopoly because monopolists may, in response to public scrutiny and political pressure, keep prices below what the market could bear. We speak here not about government-regulated monopolies, which will be addressed later, but about monopolies that curb their profits to avoid public attention and criticism. Although monopolists would

Teaching Tip Again, the monopolist's behavior can be interpreted as sacrificing short-run profit in order to maximize long-run profit. See Chapter 29 for coverage of government regulation of business.

like to earn as great a profit as possible, they realize that if the public outcry over high profit grows loud enough, some sort of government intervention could reduce or even eliminate profits. For example, because of the increase in oil prices during the middle and late 1970s, Congress increased the taxes on oil companies. Drug companies came under similar scrutiny by President Clinton. Firms may try to avoid such treatment by keeping prices somewhat below the level that would maximize short-run profit.

Why the Welfare Loss of Monopoly Might Be Higher Than Estimated

Example Cable companies must bid for the right to establish service in each municipal area. Then the municipality can impose a franchise fee as high as 5 percent of gross revenues.

Another line of thinking suggests that the welfare loss of monopoly may, in fact, be greater than estimated in our simple diagram.

Monopolists Expend Resources Trying to Secure and Maintain Monopoly Power. If resources must be devoted to securing and maintaining a monopoly position, monopolies may involve more of a welfare loss than simple models suggest. For example, consider radio and TV broadcasting rights, which confer on the recipient the exclusive privilege to use a particular band of the scarce broadcast spectrum. These rights are given away by government agencies to the applicants who are deemed most deserving. Because these rights are so valuable, numerous applicants spend a bundle on lawyers' fees, lobbying expenses, and other costs associated with making themselves appear the most deserving. The efforts devoted to securing and maintaining a monopoly position are largely a social waste because they use up scarce resources but add not one unit to output. Activities undertaken by individuals or firms to influence public policy in a way that will directly or indirectly redistribute income to themselves are referred to as **rent seeking.**

Rent seeking Activities undertaken by individuals or firms to influence public policy in a way that will directly or indirectly redistribute income to themselves

Teaching Tip Rent seeking reduces the monopolist's profit without changing the amount of lost consumer surplus; thus, the deadweight loss increases. In Exhibit 8, *pbcp′* is still lost to consumers, but some of it is no longer redistributed to the firm as profit.

Monopolists May Become Inefficient. The monopolist, insulated from the rigors of competition in the marketplace, may grow fat and lazy—and become inefficient. Since some monopolies would still earn an economic profit even if output were not produced at the least possible cost, corporate executives may employ resources to create a more comfortable life for themselves. Long lunches, afternoon golf, Oriental carpets, and extensive employee benefits may make company life more enjoyable, but these additional expenses also raise the cost of production above what it would be if the firm used the least-cost combination of resources.

Monopolists have also been criticized for being slow to adopt the latest production techniques, being reluctant to develop new products, and generally lacking innovativeness. Because monopolists escape the rigors of competition, they may be content to rest on their oars. As the Nobel Prize–winning British economist J. R. Hicks remarked, "The best of all monopoly profits is a quiet life."

Teaching Tip The organizational slack that results from a lack of competition is known as X-inefficiency.

Not all economists, however, believe that monopolists manage their resources with any less vigilance than do perfect competitors. Professor Joseph Schumpeter, an Austrian who taught at Harvard University, argued that

Example Researchers at AT&T's Bell Laboratories have won seven Nobel Prizes for science. **Teaching Tip** See Chapter 27 for more on the market for corporate control.

because monopolists are protected from rivals, they are in a position to capture the fruits of any innovation and therefore will be more innovative than competitive firms. Some economists argue that if monopolist managers do stray from the path of profit maximization, the value of the firm's stock will be lower than it would be if the firm were more efficient. Lower stock prices provide a strong incentive for outsiders to buy a controlling share of the firm's stock, shape up the operation, and watch profits—as well as the value of the firm's stock—grow. This *market for corporate control* is said to direct even monopolists along the path of efficient production.

Models of Price Discrimination

Price discrimination Selling the same good for different prices to different consumers

The model of monopoly examined thus far is based on the assumption that the monopolist charges all consumers the same price. Under certain conditions, however, the monopolist can increase profit through **price discrimination**, which is the practice of selling output at different prices to different groups of consumers or charging consumers different prices for different amounts of the good for reasons unrelated to cost. The aim is to increase total profit.

Point to Stress Quantity discounts that reflect lower costs per unit are not price discrimination.

Conditions for Price Discrimination

In order for a firm to practice price discrimination, certain conditions must exist. First, the demand curve for the product must slope downward, indicating that the producer has some control over the price—some market power. This condition holds for the monopolist but not for perfect competitors. Second, there must be at least two classes of consumers, each with different price elasticities of demand. Third, the producer must be able, at little cost, to distinguish between the different classes of consumers. Finally, the monopolist must be able to prevent those buyers who pay the lower price from reselling the product to buyers who pay the higher price.

Teaching Tip If the monopolist cannot prevent consumers from reselling the product, it will be unable to sell at its higher price

Examples of Price Discrimination

Let's consider some examples of price discrimination. Because the costs are paid by their companies and are tax deductible, businesspeople tend to be less sensitive to differences in the price of travel and communication than are households. Businesses therefore have a less elastic demand for travel and communication than do households, so airlines and telephone utilities try to maximize profits by charging the two classes of customers different rates. But how do firms distinguish between households and businesses?

Example Two other examples of price discrimination are discounts for children and senior citizens at movie theaters and higher out-of-state tuition rates at state universities.

Telephone companies have been able to sort out their customers by charging different rates based on the time of day. Long-distance charges are higher during normal *business* hours than during evenings and weekends, when households, which presumably have a higher price elasticity of demand, make social calls. The airlines try to distinguish between business customers and household customers based on the terms under which tickets are purchased.

Households plan their vacations well in advance and often stay over Saturday. They have more flexibility about when they travel and are more sensitive to price than are business travelers. Business travel, on the other hand, is more unpredictable and more urgent and seldom involves a weekend stay. The airlines separate business travelers from vacationers by requiring purchasers of "supersaver" fares to buy tickets well in advance and to stay over Saturday.

A Model of Price Discrimination

Exhibit 9 shows the effects of price discrimination. Consumers are divided into two groups with distinctly different demands. The exhibit shows their demand and marginal revenue curves, along with the producer's marginal cost curve. For simplicity, we assume that the monopolist produces at a constant long-run average cost, and that this cost is the same for both groups. Since this is a constant-cost industry, the horizontal long-run average total cost curve also equals marginal cost at each level of output. The consumers in panel (a) generally attach a higher marginal value to each unit of the good than do those in panel (b). In each market the price is determined by finding the level of output that

EXHIBIT 9

Price Discrimination with Two Groups of Consumers

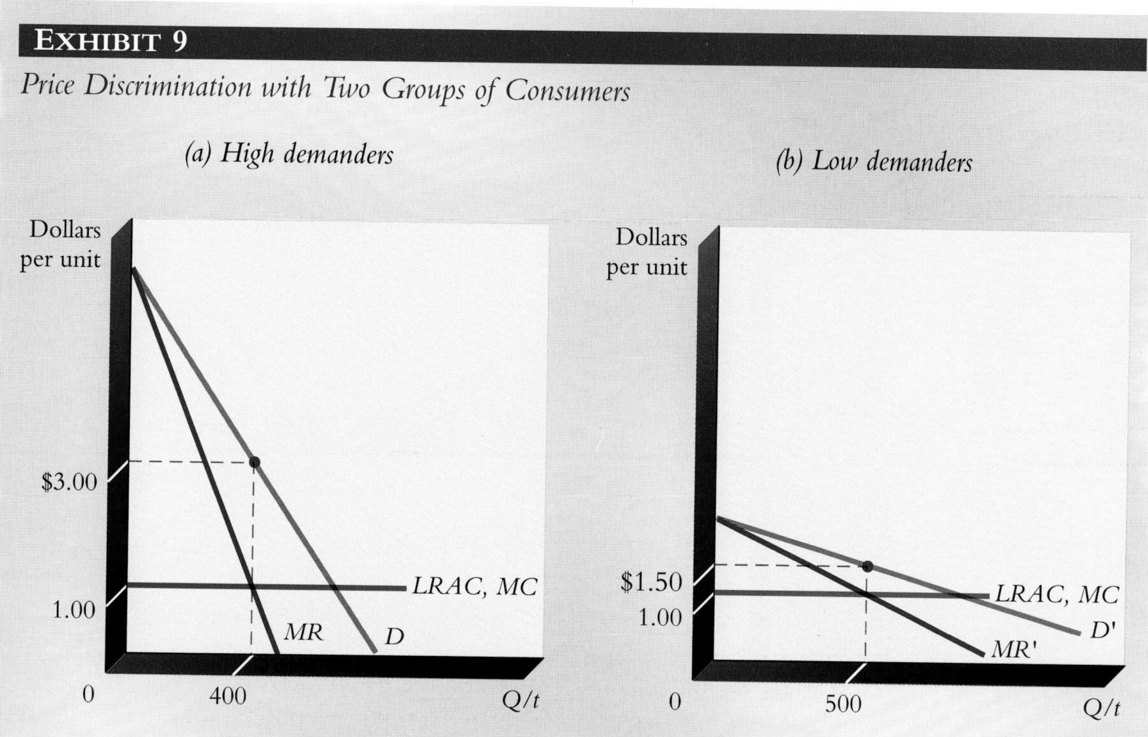

A monopolist that faces two groups of consumers with different demand elasticities may be able to practice price discrimination. With marginal cost the same in both markets, the firm sells 400 units to the high-marginal-value consumers in panel (a) and charges them a price of $3 per unit. It sells 500 units to the low-marginal-value consumers in panel (b) and charges them a price of $1.50.

Point to Stress This is an exception to the general relationship whereby price exceeds marginal revenue whenever a firm faces a downward-sloping demand curve.

equates marginal cost and marginal revenue. At a given price level, the price elasticity of demand in panel (b) is greater than that in panel (a), so consumers in panel (a) are charged a higher price.

Perfect Price Discrimination: The Monopolist's Dream

Perfectly discriminating monopolist A monopolist who charges a different price for each unit of the good

The demand curve conveys the marginal value of each unit consumed. If the monopolist could charge a different price for each unit, a price equal to the consumers' marginal value of each unit consumed, then the firm's marginal revenue from selling one more unit would equal the price of that unit. Thus, the demand curve would become the firm's marginal revenue curve. The **perfectly discriminating monopolist** charges a different price for each unit of the good. How might the firm do this? One way might be to auction off each unit of the good.

To see how this looks refer to Exhibit 10, where the monopolist produces

EXHIBIT 10

Perfect Price Discrimination

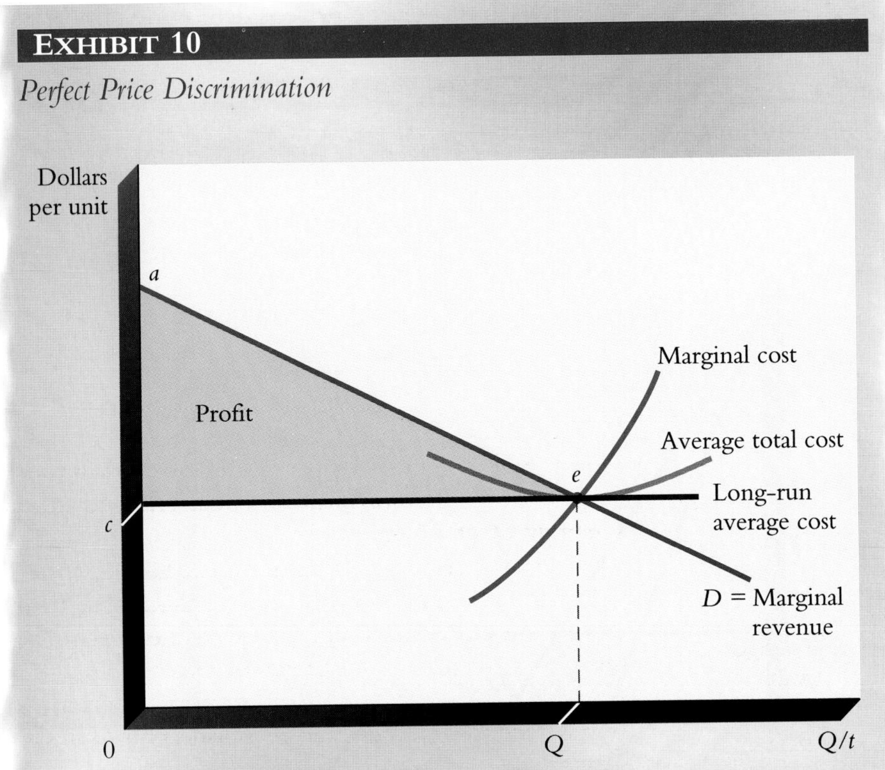

If a monopolist can charge a different price for each unit sold, it may be able to practice perfect price discrimination. By setting the price of each unit equal to the maximum amount consumers are willing to pay for that unit (shown by the height of the demand curve), the monopolist can achieve a profit equal to the area of the shaded triangle. Consumer surplus is zero.

Teaching Tip In Exhibit 10, total revenue equals the area *aeQ0*. As long as average total cost times output is less than or equal to total revenue, the firm can continue operations in the long run.

at a constant average cost in the long run. The perfectly discriminating monopolist expands output as long as marginal revenue exceeds marginal cost and maximizes profit by finding the output level where marginal cost equals marginal revenue, as at point *e* in Exhibit 10. The monopolist's economic profit would be defined by the area of the shaded triangle, *aec*. Price discrimination is a way of increasing firm profit; it could also allow a monopolist to survive in the long run even if its average cost curve lies completely above the demand curve. Put another way, even if no *single* price would cover average cost, charging different prices may cover average cost.

Point to Stress The output of the perfectly discriminating monopolist matches the output that would occur in an equivalent perfectly competitive industry. Output is always higher for a price-discriminating monopolist than for a single-price monopolist.

By charging a different price for each unit of output, the perfectly discriminating monopolist could convert every dollar of consumer surplus into economic profit. Although this might not be the most equitable way to distribute goods, it gets high marks based on allocative efficiency. As in the perfectly competitive outcome, the marginal cost of producing the last unit of output would just equal the marginal benefit consumers attached to that unit. No adjustment in the level of output could make someone better off without reducing monopoly profit. And although consumers would reap no consumer surplus, the total benefits they received from consuming the good would just equal the total price they paid for the good. Note also that because the monopolist would not restrict output, there would be no deadweight loss of monopoly—no welfare triangle. Hence price discrimination enhances social welfare because of the expansion in output relative to the monopolist's output level in the absence of price discrimination.

CONCLUSION

Example In 1991 and 1992, political instability in the former Soviet Union led to diamond smuggling, and instability in Angola led to illegal mining. The De Beers diamond cartel announced a 25-percent dividend cut in 1992, and its stock value dropped 15 percent.

Pure monopoly, like perfect competition, is seldom observed in the real world. Not many firms sell a product for which there are no close substitutes. Economic profit motivates potential rivals to hurdle any barriers to entry. Changing technology works against monopoly in the long run. For example, the U.S. Postal Service's government-granted monopoly on first-class mail delivery has been eroded by competition from express delivery, the fax machine, and electronic mail. Likewise, the monopoly on long-distance phone service has crumbled as microwave technology has replaced copper wire. And cable TV companies may soon lose their monopoly status, since fiber-optics technology makes local phone companies potential suppliers of the service.

Though perfect competition and pure monopoly are relatively rare, our examination of them has produced a framework that will be helpful for viewing market structures that lie between the two extremes. As we will see, many firms have some degree of monopoly power—that is, they face downward-sloping demand curves. In the next chapter we will consider two market structures in which firms have some monopoly power but are not pure monopolies.

Summary

1. A monopolist sells a product with no close substitutes. A monopoly can persist in the long run only if the entry of new firms into the market is blocked. Three barriers to entry are (1) legal restrictions, such as patents and operating licenses; (2) economies of scale, which make it inefficient for more than one firm to produce the good; and (3) control over an essential resource used in production.

2. Because a monopolist is the sole supplier in a market, the market demand curve is also the monopolist's demand curve. Because the monopolist can sell more only if the price falls, the marginal revenue is less than the price. When demand is elastic, marginal revenue is positive, and total revenue increases as the price falls. When demand is inelastic, marginal revenue is negative, and total revenue decreases as the price falls.

3. If, at some positive rate of output, the monopolist can at least cover variable cost, profit is maximized or loss minimized in the short run by finding the price-output combination that equates marginal cost with marginal revenue. Because marginal cost is never less than zero, the monopolist never produces where marginal revenue is negative. To put this another way, the monopolist never produces where demand is inelastic, or where total revenue is declining, since reducing output would both lower total cost and increase total revenue, thereby ensuring that profit increases.

4. In the short run, the monopolist, like the perfect competitor, can earn economic profit but will shut down unless the price is at or above the average variable cost. In the long run, the monopolist, unlike the perfect competitor, can earn economic profits as long as the entry of new firms is blocked. There is no supply curve for the monopolist because there is no unique relation between price and quantity supplied. The sole producer in a market will not earn economic profit in the long run if the market is contestable—that is, if there are no barriers to entry or exit.

5. Resources are not allocated as efficiently under unregulated monopoly as under perfect competition. Monopoly price is higher and monopoly output is lower than under perfect competition. Monopoly usually results in a net welfare loss when compared to perfect competition because the loss in consumer surplus under monopoly exceeds the gain in monopoly profit.

6. To increase profit through price discrimination, the monopolist must have at least two identifiable types of consumers with different elasticities of demand and must be able to prevent those consumers who pay the lower price from reselling to those who pay the higher price. A perfect price discriminator charges a different price for each unit of the good, thereby capturing all consumer surplus as economic profit.

Questions and Problems

1. (Barriers to Entry) What are some barriers to entry into the professional sports industry? For example, why aren't there more professional baseball teams?

2. (Barriers to Entry) In South Korea, ginseng and tobacco distribution are state-owned monopolies. What might motivate a government to impose such a barrier to entry?

3. (Monopoly) Are such wonders of the world as the Grand Canyon and the Great Wall of China monopolies because they are one of a kind? Are there substitutes for such places?

4. (Revenue Maximization) Suppose a UFO crashes in your backyard. Ignoring any costs that may be involved, what price would you charge people to come and view the site? Would you allow photographs? Why or why not?

5. (Monopoly) Only one airline has flights to and from some of the South Sea islands. Would this airline qualify as a monopoly? How would such a company price its flights to the islands to maximize profits? Would it price cargo and mail at the same rate per pound? Why or why not?

6. (Demand and Marginal Revenue) Suppose that at a price of \$3 per unit, the quantity demanded is 10 units. Explain why, when marginal revenue is equal to \$3, quantity demanded must be (roughly) equal to 5 units.

7. (Monopoly) Why is it impossible for a profit-maximizing monopolist to choose any price *and* any quantity it wishes?

8. (Monopoly and Welfare) Why is society worse off under monopoly than under perfect competition? When might monopoly be more efficient?

9. (Price Discrimination) Explain how it may be profitable for Koreans to sell new autos at a cheaper price in the United States than in Korea, even with transportation costs.

10. (Perfect Price Discrimination) Why is the demand curve above marginal cost equal to the marginal revenue curve for the perfectly discriminating monopolist?

11. (Monopoly) Suppose that a certain manufacturer has a monopoly on the sorority and fraternity ring business (a constant-cost industry) because he has persuaded the "Greeks" to give him exclusive rights to their insignia.
    a. Using demand and cost curves, draw a diagram representing the company's profit-maximizing pricing-output decision.
    b. Why is marginal revenue less than price for this company?
    c. On your diagram, show the welfare loss that occurs because the output level is determined by the monopoly situation rather than by a competitive market.
    d. What would happen if the Greeks decided to charge the manufacturer a royalty fee of \$3 per ring?
    e. What would happen if the Greeks charged the manufacturer a franchise fee (unrelated to ring production) instead of the royalty fee?

12. (Discriminating Monopoly) Suppose that do-dads are sold to two types of people and that the long-run production costs are constant at \$1 per do-dad. Use the following data to answer the questions below. Q_1 represents sales to type-1 people; Q_2 is sales to type-2 people.

p	Q_1	Q_2	$Q_1 + Q_2$	*Short-run MC of total Q*
\$10	4	12	16	\$ 1.50
9	6	14	20	2.00
8	8	16	24	3.00
7	10	18	28	7.00
6	12	20	32	12.00
5	14	22	36	20.00
3	18	26	44	40.00
1	22	30	52	80.00

    a. Determine the short-run equilibrium price and quantity for this industry, assuming it is competitive.
    b. Determine the long-run equilibrium price and quantity for this industry, assuming it is competitive.
    c. If do-dads were produced by a nondiscriminating monopolist, what price and quantity would maximize short-run profits? long-run profits?
    d. If this monopolist could practice price discrimination, what would be the long-run profit-maximizing price and quantity for each group of buyers?

13. (Demand and Marginal Revenue) What is marginal revenue when the value of price elasticity of demand is 1? Explain.

14. (Monopoly and Welfare Loss) Suppose that a firm has a monopoly on a good with the following demand schedule.

p	Q	*p*	Q
\$10	0	\$4	6
9	1	3	7
8	2	2	8
7	3	1	9
6	4	0	10
5	5		

    a. Calculate the marginal revenue for each output level.
    b. What is the profit-maximizing output level if the firm faces constant marginal costs of \$3 per unit?
    c. Calculate the dollar value of the welfare loss attributable to the fact that this industry is monopolistic rather than competitive.

15. (Barriers to Entry) According to U.S. patent law, patent holders typically hold exclusive production rights for seventeen years. Do you think that all kinds of products should have the same patent life? How should one determine the "optimal" patent life?

16. (Monopoly and Elasticity) Explain why a monopoly firm would never knowingly produce on the inelastic portion of its demand curve.

17. (Price Discrimination) Suppose that a monopoly firm has been found to be price discriminating among its buyers and is forced instead to charge all consumers the same price. Who gains and who loses by such a change? Explain your answer.

18. (Monopoly Versus Competition) Draw a diagram showing a monopoly firm earning a normal rate of return. If competitive firms could somehow produce output at the same minimum cost as the monopolist, what would a competitive industry produce? What would the deadweight loss be?

19. (Monopoly Versus Competition) Suppose that a constant-cost industry were monopolized, but the monopoly was able to lower production costs by using improved technology while raising the price of the product sold. If average costs both before and after monopolization are independent of the level of output, show on a diagram how you would determine whether society was better off or worse off because of the monopoly.

20. (Mail Monopoly) Suppose that the mail service was completely privatized. What do you think would happen to first-class delivery service? Who would gain? Who would lose?

21. (Mail Monopoly) The postal service offers different services for different prices. Is this an example of price discrimination?

CHAPTER 23

MONOPOLISTIC COMPETITION AND OLIGOPOLY

Teaching Tip Draw a simple spectrum with perfect competition on one end and pure monopoly on the other to show how monopolistic competition and oligopoly compare in terms of the degree of competition.

Perfect competition and pure monopoly represent the two extreme market structures. Perfect competition is characterized by a homogeneous commodity produced by a large number of sellers who in the long run can enter and leave the industry with ease. Monopoly involves only one seller of a product with no close substitutes; competitors are blocked from entering this market by natural or artificial barriers to entry. These polar market structures are logically appealing and are useful in describing the workings of some markets observed in the economy. But most firms are in markets that are not well described by either model. Some firms are in markets that have many sellers producing goods that vary slightly, such as the many radio stations that vie for your attention or the convenience stores that blanket metropolitan areas. Other firms are in markets that consist of a small number of sellers who in some cases produce homogeneous goods, such as oil or steel, and in other cases produce differentiated goods, such as automobiles or breakfast cereals. In this chapter two additional models will be introduced to explain market structures that inhabit the gray area between perfect competition and pure monopoly. Topics discussed in this chapter include

- Monopolistic competition
- Product differentiation
- Oligopoly
- Competing models of oligopoly
- Mergers

Monopolistic Competition

During the 1920s and 1930s, economists began formulating models to fit between perfect competition and pure monopoly. Two models of *monopolistic competition* were developed separately. In 1933 at Harvard University, Edward Chamberlin published *The Theory of Monopolistic Competition*. Across the Atlantic that same year, Cambridge University's Joan Robinson published *The Economics of Imperfect Competition*. Although the theories differed, their underlying principles were similar. We will discuss Chamberlin's approach.

Characteristics of Monopolistic Competition

Monopolistic competition A market structure characterized by a large number of firms selling products that are close substitutes yet different enough that each firm's demand curve slopes downward

The expression **monopolistic competition** is meant to suggest that the market contains elements of both *monopoly* and *competition*. Chamberlin used the expression to describe the structure of a market characterized by many producers offering products that are close substitutes but are not viewed as identical by consumers, such as the many convenience stores that can be found throughout a metropolitan area. Because the products of different producers are not viewed as identical—for example, some convenience stores are closer to you than others—the demand curve for each particular producer is not horizontal but rather slopes downward. Each producer therefore has some power over the price it charges. Thus, the firms that populate this market are not *price takers,* as they would be under perfect competition, but *price searchers*.

Teaching Tip The relations among price, average revenue, and marginal revenue are the same as for a single-price monopoly. Because the products are not identical, firms need not all charge the same price (unlike in perfect competition).

Because barriers to entry are relatively low, firms can enter or leave the market with relative ease. Consequently, there are enough sellers that they behave competitively. There are also enough sellers that each firm tends to get lost in the crowd—that is, each firm is so insignificant relative to the market that its price and output policies will be largely ignored by other firms. For example, in a large metropolitan area, an individual restaurant, gas station, drugstore, dry cleaner, or convenience store is not particularly concerned about how competitors react to any change in its price or output; it tends to act *independently.* In a small town, however, there may be only two or three sellers in each market so they must keep an eye on one another; they act *interdependently.* You will understand the significance of this independent versus interdependent behavior later in the chapter.

Example Jolly Time 100% All Natural Microwave Pop Corn is promoted as grown and processed without chemical pesticides and as the only microwave popcorn using real butter for flavoring. However, the company also attempts to differentiate itself with its two-word spelling of "popcorn."

Product Differentiation

Product differentiation distinguishes monopolistic competition from perfect competition, where the product is viewed as homogeneous. Sellers can differentiate their products in four basic ways.

Physical Differences. The most obvious way products are differentiated is by their physical appearance and their qualities. The ways that products can differ are seemingly endless: size, weight, color, taste, texture, and so on. Shampoos, for example, differ in color, scent, thickness, lathering ability, and bottle design. Particular brands aim at consumers with dandruff, with hair that needs body or is hard to manage, and with hair that is normal, dry, or oily.

Example Banks compete through the number and location of their ATM machines.

LOCATION. The number and variety of locations where a product is available represent another means of differentiation. Some products seem to be available everywhere; finding others requires some search and travel. If you live in a metropolitan area, you are no doubt accustomed to a large number of convenience stores. Each wants to be closest to you when you need that half gallon of milk or bag of Doritos—hence a proliferation of stores. As the name says, these mini grocery stores are selling convenience. Their prices are higher and their selection more limited than those of regular grocery stores, but they are likely to be nearer customers and they often stay open later.

Example In 1992, MasterCard International pursued permission from the major long-distance carriers for its card holders to charge calls with its credit card. It hoped to start the service in late 1993.

SERVICES. Products also differ based on the accompanying services. For example, some pizza sellers deliver; others do not. Some retail stores offer helpful product demonstrations by a well-trained sales staff; other stores are essentially self-service. Some offer a money-back guarantee; others say "no returns."

Example Daimler-Benz maintains limited production of the Mercedes-Benz, despite waiting lists, in order to maintain its special image.

PRODUCT IMAGE. A final way products differ is in the image the producer tries to foster in the mind of the consumer. For example, a clothing manufacturer may try to persuade you that its jeans are special because some celebrity's name is on the back pocket. Particular brand names may suggest high quality by the way they are promoted, the form of packaging, or the kind of stores in which they are sold. Producers try to find a particular niche in the consumer's mind through product promotion and advertising.

Short-Run Profit Maximization or Loss Minimization

Because the monopolistic competitor offers a product that is somewhat differentiated from other products in the industry, each firm has some power to control the price it charges. This *market power* is reflected by a demand curve for the firm's product that slopes downward but is relatively flat when compared to a monopolist's demand curve. Since many firms are producing goods that are close substitutes, any firm that raises its price can expect to lose some customers to rivals. In contrast, a monopolist produces a product with no close substitutes and hence tends to lose relatively fewer customers when the price increases. On the other hand, a firm in perfect competition can expect to lose *all* its customers if it raises its price, since it is producing a product that is identical to those of its competitors. Therefore the demand curve for the output of a monopolistically competitive firm tends to be more elastic than the demand curve for a monopolist and less elastic than the demand curve for the perfectly competitive firm, which is perfectly elastic.

Teaching Tip Product differentiation is an attempt to reduce the price elasticity of demand and gain more price control. Since each firm produces a somewhat different item, defining an industry requires identifying a "product group" of sufficiently similar products.

Recall that the number and similarity of available substitutes for a given product are important determinants of the price elasticity of demand.

Therefore the elasticity of the monopolistically competitive firm's demand curve depends on the number of rival firms that produce a similar product and the firm's ability to differentiate its product from those of its rivals. *A firm's demand curve will be more elastic the greater the number of competing firms and the less differentiated the firm's product.*

MARGINAL COST EQUALS MARGINAL REVENUE. From our analysis of monopoly, we know that the downward-sloping demand curve faced by the firm in monopolistic competition means that the firm's marginal revenue curve also slopes downward and that it lies below the demand curve. Exhibit 1 depicts demand and marginal revenue curves for a firm in monopolistic competition. The exhibit also presents cost curves. Remember that the forces that determine the cost of production are largely independent of the forces that shape demand, so there is nothing special about a monopolistic competitor's cost curves.

EXHIBIT 1

The Firm in Monopolistic Competition in the Short Run

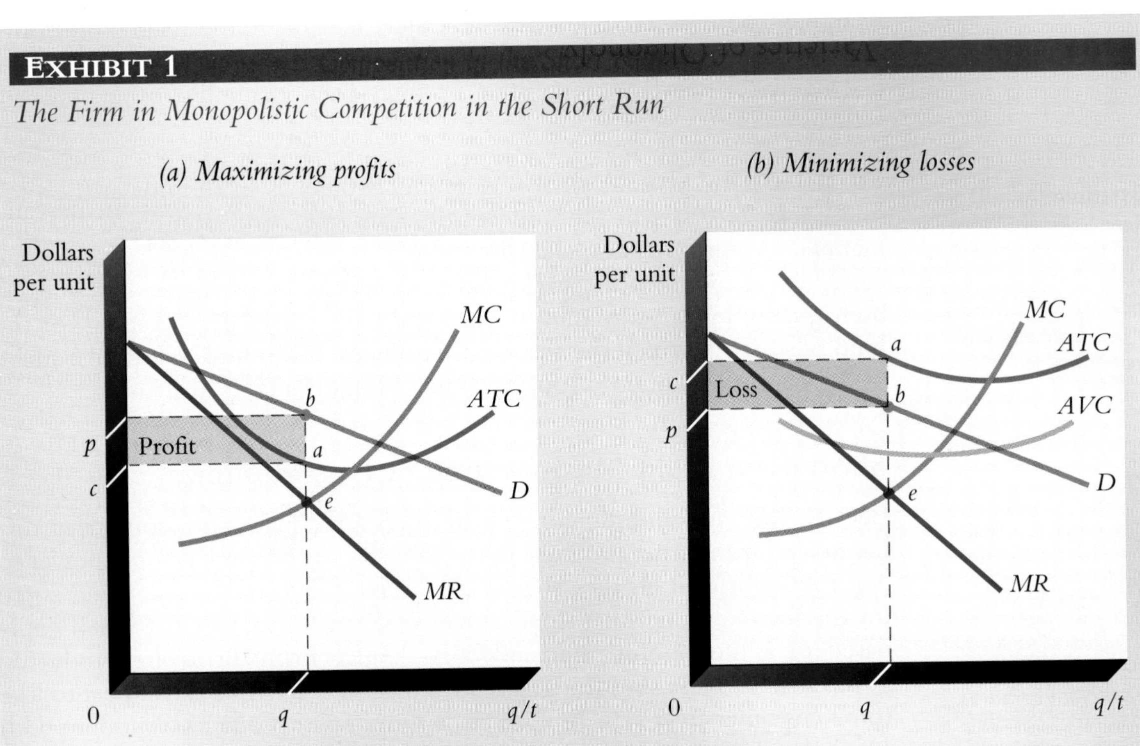

The monopolistically competitive firm produces the level of output at which marginal cost equals marginal revenue (point *e*) and charges the price indicated by point *b* on the downward-sloping demand curve. In panel (a), the firm produces *q* units, sells them at price *p*, and earns a short-run profit equal to $(p - c)$ multiplied by *q* and shown by the blue rectangle. In panel (b), the average total cost exceeds the price at the optimal level of output. Thus, the firm suffers a short-run loss equal to $(c - p)$ multiplied by *q*, represented by the red rectangle.

Point to Stress The perfectly competitive firm determines the profit-maximizing output similarly, but the price is already determined by the market.

If a firm can at least cover its variable cost, it will increase output as long as marginal revenue exceeds marginal cost. Monopolistically competitive firms maximize profit in the short run just as monopolists do: *the profit-maximizing level of output occurs where marginal cost equals marginal revenue; the profit-maximizing price is found on the demand curve at that level of output.* Panels (a) and (b) in Exhibit 1 identify the price and output combinations that, respectively, maximize short-run profit and minimize short-run loss. The intersection of marginal cost and marginal revenue curves is identified as point *e,* the level of output is *q,* the price is *p,* and the average total cost is measured on the vertical axis as *c.*

MAXIMIZING PROFIT OR MINIMIZING LOSS IN THE SHORT RUN. Recall that the short run is a period too short to allow firms to enter or leave the market. The demand and cost conditions depicted in Exhibit 1(a) indicate that this firm will earn an economic profit in the short run. At the firm's profit-maximizing level of output, average total cost, *c,* is below the price, *p.* As noted earlier, the difference between the two is the firm's profit per unit; the profit per unit multiplied by the number of units sold yields the firm's total profit per period, shown by the shaded rectangle in panel (a). Quantity supplied depends on the intersection of the marginal cost and marginal revenue curves, and the price is found on the demand curve at that quantity. Because the demand curve is above the point of intersection, *a monopolistically competitive firm, like a monopolist, has no supply curve*—a change in demand could result in a different price but the same equilibrium level of output.

The monopolistically competitive firm, like other firms, has no guarantee of economic profit. The firm's demand and cost curves could be as depicted in panel (b), where the firm's average total cost curve lies above the demand curve, so no level of output would allow the firm to break even. In such a situation the firm must decide whether to produce or to shut down temporarily. The decision rule here is the same as with perfect competition and monopoly: as long as the price is above the average variable cost, the firm should produce and thereby cover at least a portion of its fixed cost. If the price fails to cover the average variable cost, the firm should shut down. Recall that the halt in production may be only temporary; shutting down is not necessarily the same as going out of business. Firms that expect losses to persist in the long run may leave the industry.

Teaching Tip As new firms enter, the number of substitutes for the products of existing firms rises, so their demand curves also become more price elastic. Note that although product differentiation does not represent an entry barrier in monopolistic competition, it can occur to such an extent that it becomes an entry barrier (as in a differentiated oligopoly).

Zero Economic Profit in the Long Run

In the long run, the monopolistically competitive firm is in the same profit situation as the perfectly competitive firm. Since there are no barriers to entry, economic profit will attract new entrants into the industry. Because new entrants offer a product that is quite similar to those offered by existing firms, new entrants draw many of their customers from existing firms, thereby reducing the demand facing each firm. For example, if a convenience store finds a particular area yields an economic profit in the short run, this economic profit will attract other convenience stores to the area, reducing the demand facing each store until economic profit goes to zero in long-run equilibrium. At that point, there is no incentive for additional firms to enter that market. *Because of the ease of entry, monopolistically competitive firms will in the long run earn no economic profit.*

Teaching Tip As firms leave, the number of substitutes drops for remaining firms, so their demand curves also become less price elastic.

If they incur short-run losses, some firms will leave the industry in the long run, redirecting their resources to activities that are expected to earn at least a normal profit. As firms leave the industry, their customers will switch to the remaining firms, increasing the demand for each remaining firm's product. Firms will continue to leave in the long run until the remaining firms have enough customers to earn a normal profit, but no economic profit.

Exhibit 2 shows the long-run equilibrium for a typical monopolistically competitive firm. In the long run, entry and exit will alter each firm's demand curve until marginal cost equals marginal revenue at a level of output where there is no economic profit. In Exhibit 2, the marginal cost curve intersects the marginal revenue curve at point *a,* and at the equilibrium level of

Point to Stress The market structure generates neither allocative efficiency (because price exceeds marginal revenue) nor productive efficiency (because the firm produces to the left of the minimum point of average total cost) in the long run.

EXHIBIT 2

Long-Run Equilibrium in Monopolistic Competition

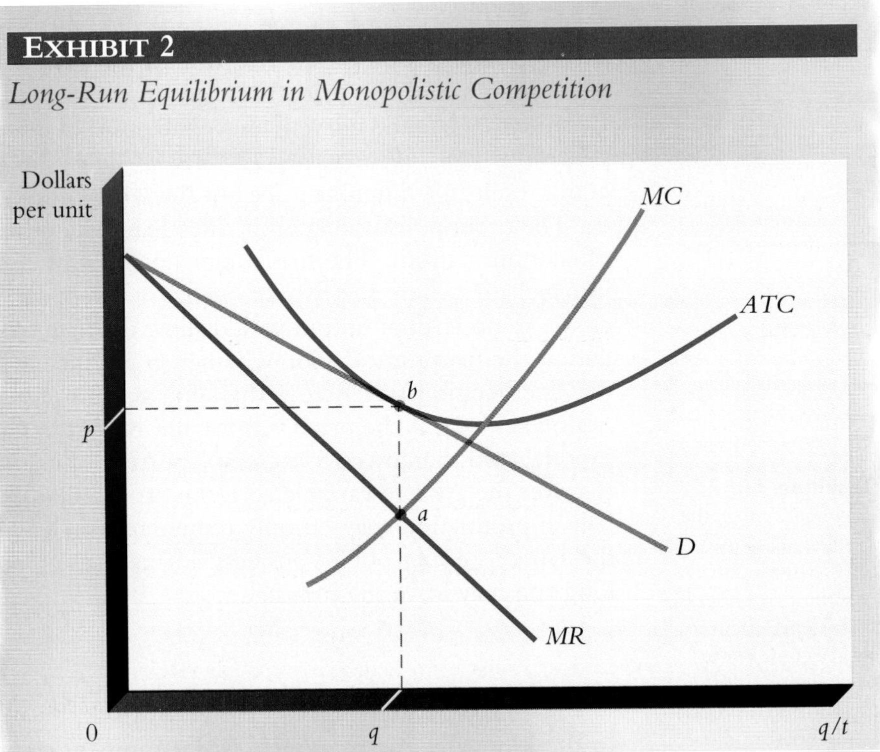

If existing firms are earning economic profits, new firms will enter the industry. The entry of such firms reduces the demand facing each firm. In the long run, demand is reduced until marginal revenue equals marginal cost (point *a*) and the demand curve is tangent to the average total cost curve (point *b*). Profit is zero at output *q*. With zero economic profit, no new firms enter, so the industry is in long-run equilibrium.

output, q, the demand curve at point b is tangent to the average total cost curve. Since the average total cost equals the price, p, the firm earns no economic profit. At all other levels of output, the firm's average total cost is above its demand curve, so the firm would lose money if it reduced or expanded its output.

Thus, if entry is easy and if all firms are selling goods that are close but not perfect substitutes, short-run economic profit will, in the long run, draw new entrants into the industry until that profit disappears. A short-run economic loss will prompt some firms to leave the industry in the long run until remaining firms earn just a normal profit. In summary, *monopolistic competition is like pure monopoly in the sense that firms in each industry face demand curves that slope downward. Monopolistic competition is like perfect competition in the sense that easy entry and exit result in a normal profit in the long run.*

Point to Stress The goal of both the perfectly competitive and the monopolistically competitive firm is to maximize profits. It is simply the different nature of the demand curves that causes the perfectly competitive firm to maximize efficiency while the monopolistically competitive firm does not.

Monopolistic Competition and Perfect Competition Compared

How does monopolistic competition compare with perfect competition in terms of efficiency? In the long run, neither the perfect competitor nor the monopolistic competitor can earn economic profit, so what's the difference? The difference arises because of the different demand curves facing individual firms in each of the two market structures. Exhibit 3 presents the long-run equilibrium price and quantity for firms in each of the two market structures, assuming each firm has identical cost curves. In each case marginal cost intersects marginal revenue at the level of output where the average cost curve is tangent to the demand curve faced by the firm.

Teaching Tip However, promotions that focus on prices and quality can increase competition, make each firm's demand more price elastic, and lead to lower prices. In a 1972 study, for example, Lee Burnham found that the average price of eyeglasses in states that banned advertising was double the average price in states that allowed advertising ("The Effect of Advertising on the Price of Eyeglasses, *The Journal of Law and Economics,* October 1972).

The demand curve for the firm in perfect competition is a horizontal line drawn at the market price, as shown in panel (a). The average cost curve is tangent to this demand curve at the low point of the average total cost curve. Thus, output under perfect competition is produced at the lowest possible average cost. In panel (b), the firm in monopolistic competition faces a downward-sloping demand curve because its product is somewhat differentiated from those produced by other firms. As a result of the entry and exit of other firms in the long run, marginal cost intersects marginal revenue at a level of output where the downward-sloping demand curve is tangent to the firm's average total cost curve. The monopolistic competitor produces at an equilibrium rate of output that lies to the left of the minimum point on its average cost curve. Thus, the price and average cost under monopolistic competition, identified in panel (b) as p', exceed the price and average cost under perfect competition, identified in panel (a) as p. *If firms have the same cost curves, the firm under monopolistic competition tends to produce less and to charge more than the firm under perfect competition.*

Excess capacity The difference between a monopolistic competitor's minimum average cost and its profit-maximizing level of output

Firms in monopolistic competition are not producing at minimum average cost. The firm in monopolistic competition is said to have **excess capacity** since production is short of the level that would achieve the lowest minimum average cost. Excess capacity means that producers could easily serve more customers and as a result could lower the average cost of output

EXHIBIT 3

Monopolistic Competition Versus Perfect Competition

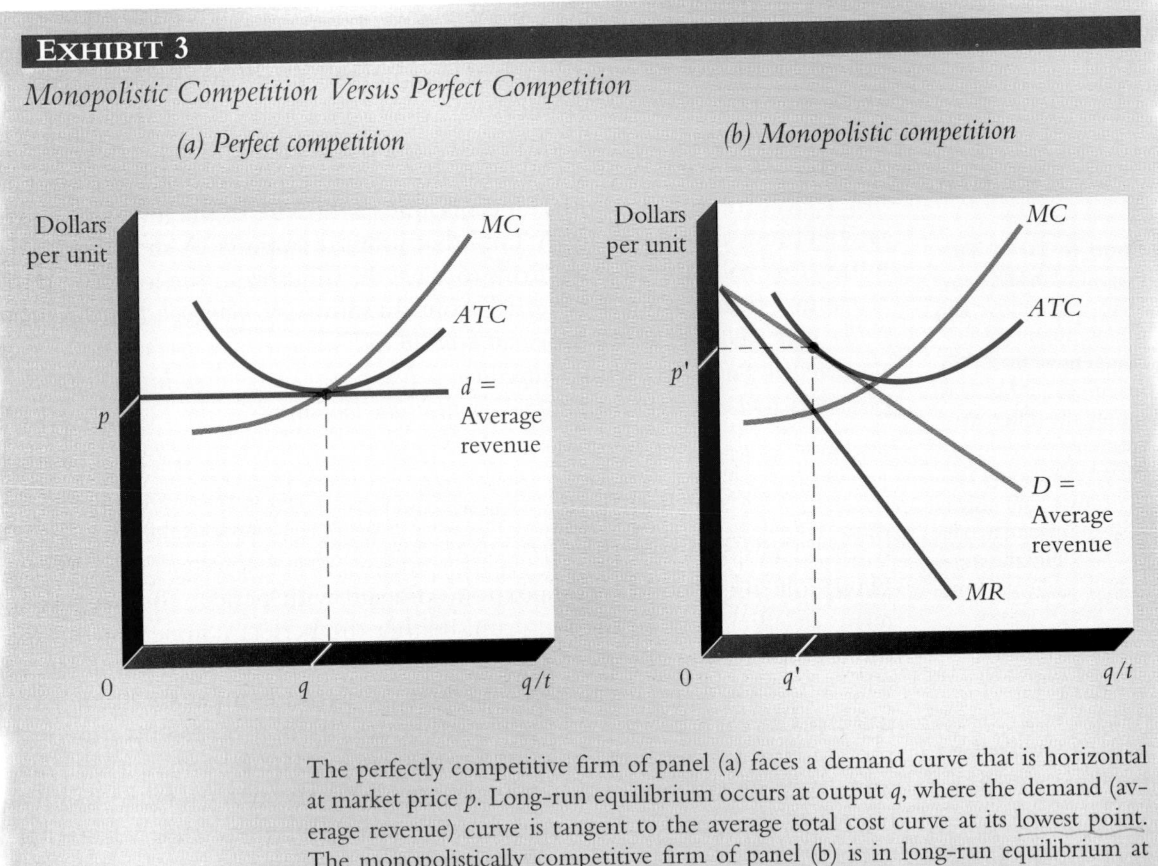

The perfectly competitive firm of panel (a) faces a demand curve that is horizontal at market price p. Long-run equilibrium occurs at output q, where the demand (average revenue) curve is tangent to the average total cost curve at its lowest point. The monopolistically competitive firm of panel (b) is in long-run equilibrium at output q', where demand is tangent to average total cost. However, since the demand curve slopes downward, the tangency does not occur at the minimum point of average total cost. Hence the monopolistically competitive firm produces less output at a higher price than does a perfectly competitive firm facing the same cost conditions.

and increase net social welfare. Such excess capacity can be observed at gas stations, drugstores, convenience stores, restaurants, motels, bookstores, flower shops, and other firms in monopolistic competition. Consider the excess capacity in the funeral-home business. Industry analysts argue that the nation's 22,000 funeral homes could easily handle 4 million funerals a year, but only half that number of people die. So the industry on average operates at only 50 percent of capacity, resulting in a higher average cost per funeral.

There is another difference between perfect competition and monopolistic competition that does not show up in Exhibit 3. Although the cost curves in Exhibit 3 are assumed to be identical, firms in monopolistic competition in fact spend more on advertising and other promotional expenses to differentiate their products than do firms in perfect competition. Thus, monopolistic competitors devote resources to differentiate their products.

Teaching Tip See the chapter's second case study, "The Cost of Variety."

Some economists, including Joan Robinson, have argued that monopolistic competition results in too many suppliers and product differentiation that is often artificial. But Edward Chamberlin, in outlining his theory of monopolistic competition, argued that consumers are willing to pay a higher price for having a greater selection. According to this view, resources are not wasted because consumers are given a wider choice among gas stations, restaurants, convenience stores, clothing stores, drugstores, economics textbooks, and many other goods and services. For example, what if half of the restaurants were closed just so the remaining ones could operate at full capacity? Some consumers would be inconvenienced if their favorite restaurant went out of business.

AN INTRODUCTION TO OLIGOPOLY

Oligopoly A market structure characterized by a small number of firms whose behavior is interdependent

Teaching Tip An oligopoly may have a large number of firms, but the few largest dominate. (For example, there were 121 tire and inner-tube manufacturing companies in the mid-1980s, but the four largest accounted for 70 percent of sales.) The resulting interdependence generates uncertainty about the demand curve facing each firm.

Teaching Tip The two types of oligopolies can be referred to as pure oligopolies (those with a homogeneous product) and differentiated oligopolies.

Another important market structure is **oligopoly**, which is a market dominated by a few sellers—perhaps three or four firms account for more than half the market output. When we think of "big business," we are thinking of oligopoly. Many industries, including steel, automobiles, oil, breakfast cereals, and tobacco, are oligopolistic. But oligopoly also describes the market for groceries in regions where there might be only a few grocery stores, or the market for gasoline in regions where there are only a few gas stations. Perfectly competitive firms and monopolistically competitive firms are so numerous that the actions of each have little effect on the behavior of other firms in the industry. Because there are few firms in an oligopolistic market, however, each firm must weigh the effect of its own policies on rivals' behavior. Consequently, oligopoly involves a few sellers who are *interdependent.*

Varieties of Oligopoly

In some oligopolistic industries, such as steel and oil, the product is homogeneous; in other industries, such as automobiles and tobacco, the product is differentiated. Where the products are homogeneous, there is greater interdependence among the few dominant firms in the industry. For example, the producers of steel ingots are more sensitive to one another's pricing policies than are the producers of autos, because steel ingots are essentially identical, whereas autos differ across producers. A small rise in the price of an ingot will send customers to a rival supplier. Make no mistake, however: auto producers are still sensitive to one another's pricing policies. They are just not as sensitive as steel producers.

Because of this interdependence among firms in an industry, the behavior of a particular firm is difficult to analyze. *Each firm knows that any changes in its product quality, price, output, or advertising policy may prompt a reaction from its rivals. And each firm may react if the behavior of other firms changes.* Whereas monopolistic competition can be likened to a professional golf tournament, where each player is striving for a personal best, oligopoly is more like a tennis match, where one player's actions depend very much on how and where the opponent hits the ball.

Example In 1992, a 5-percent cut and a later 7-percent cut by Procter & Gamble in the prices of its disposable diapers were both matched by Kimberly-Clark Corp.

Why have some industries evolved into an oligopolistic market structure, dominated by only a few firms, whereas other industries have not? Although the reasons are not always clear, *an oligopolistic market structure can often be traced to some form of barrier to entry, such as economies of scale, legal restrictions, brand names built up by years of extensive advertising, or control over an essential resource.* The number of firms is small because new firms find it difficult or unprofitable to break into the industry. In the previous chapter we examined barriers to entry as they applied to monopoly. The same principles apply to oligopoly. In the following case study, we consider some barriers to entry in the airline industry.

CASE STUDY

The Unfriendly Skies

At one time airline routes were straight lines from one city to another. Now they radiate like the spokes of a wagon wheel from the "hub" city. From twenty-nine hub airports across the country, the airlines send out planes along the spokes, then quickly bring them back to the hubs. Key airports are dominated by the major airlines. For example, American Airlines and United Airlines dominate Chicago's O'Hare International, which is a big, centrally located airport. A new airline trying to enter the industry would have to secure a hub as well as landing rights at airports around the country—not an easy task, since all the viable hubs are taken, as are the landing rights at those airports.

Six out of every seven flight reservations are made through travel agents. Another barrier to entry is the computerized reservation systems used by these agents. American Airlines has the Sabre system and United Airlines, the Apollo system. American and United offer their systems free to travel agents, provided the agents make a certain number of reservations with American or United, whichever is providing the system. Entering reservations for other airlines on the system is more complicated, requiring more keystrokes. Thus, travel agents prefer to book with American if they use the Sabre system or with United if they use the Apollo system.

Still another barrier to entry is the frequent-flier mileage programs. The biggest airlines fly more national and international routes so they offer greater opportunities both to accumulate frequent-flier miles and to use the accumulated mileage for free flights. Thus, the biggest airlines have the most attractive programs.

These three factors create barriers to entry into this industry for new entrants and create barriers to expansion for smaller airlines already in the industry. Five airlines now dominate the market. American, United, Delta, USAir, and Northwest handle about 70 percent of all traffic and control 80 percent of the hubs. Eastern and Pan Am are out of business, and Continental, TWA, Midway, and America West may be gone by the time you read this.

Sources: Louis Uchitelle, "Off Course," *New York Times Magazine,* 1 September 1991; and Asra Nomani, "Global Dogfight: World's Major Airlines Scramble to Get Ready for Competitive Battle," *Wall Street Journal,* 1 January 1992.

Economies of Scale

Example Despite the success of Saturn, the GM division was still losing money three years after production began—$700 to $800 million in 1992. GM's initial investment in Saturn was $5 billion. Chrysler spent $1.6 billion to start production of its LH cars introduced in the 1993 model year.

Perhaps the most significant barrier to entry is economies of scale. If the production process requires a relatively large output before minimum efficient scale can be achieved, only a few firms are needed to produce the total output demanded in the market. Perhaps the best example is the auto industry. Recall that the minimum efficient scale is the lowest rate of output at which the firm takes full advantage of economies of scale. Research shows that an automobile plant of minimum efficient scale can produce enough cars to supply nearly 10 percent of the U.S. market demand. If there were one hundred auto plants, each would supply such a tiny portion of the market that the average cost per car would be higher than if only ten plants manufactured autos.

In the automobile industry, economies of scale are a barrier to entry. Any potential entrant into this industry would have to sell enough cars to reach a scale of operation that would reduce the average cost per car to the low level enjoyed by those firms already in the industry. This situation is illustrated in Exhibit 4, which presents the long-run average cost curve for a typical firm

EXHIBIT 4

Economies of Scale as a Barrier to Entry

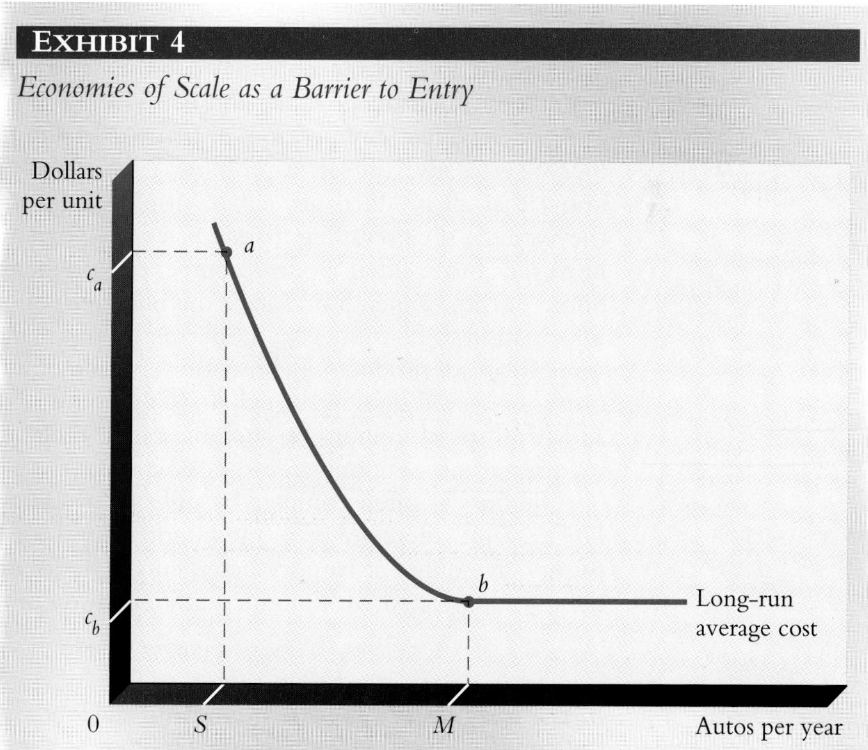

At point b, an existing firm can produce M automobiles at an average cost of c_b. A new entrant that can hope to sell only S automobiles will incur a much higher average cost of c_a at point a. If cars sell for less than c_a, the new entrant will suffer a loss. In this case economies of scale serve as a barrier to entry, protecting the existing firms.

in the industry. Assuming a new entrant can sell only S cars, the average cost per unit for this new entrant, c_a, is much higher than it is for firms that have reached the minimum efficient size, reflected here by output level M. If autos sell for less than c_a, potential entrants can expect to lose money, and this prospect will likely discourage entry. Sometimes there may be only a few producers because the market is small and that is all the market will support. For example, a small town can support only one or two gas stations.

High Cost of Entry

There is another aspect to the problem faced by potential entrants into oligopolistic industries. The total cost of reaching the minimum efficient size is often great. For example, the cost of building a plant of minimum efficient size may be extremely high (an auto plant can cost $1 billion). Or promoting a product enough to compete with established brands may require an enormous initial outlay. High start-up costs and the existence of established name brands can throw up substantial barriers to entry, especially since the fortunes of a new product are so uncertain. An unsuccessful attempt at securing a place in the market could result in huge losses; the prospect of such losses turns away many potential entrants. Consider, for example, what it would cost to challenge Coke and Pepsi in the soft-drink market.

Example Analysts estimate that the cost of establishing a new brand name in the U.S. automobile industry is $200 to $300 million. It took Nissan Motor Co. eight years to rebuild its image after dropping the Datsun name.

Example Procter & Gamble spent $2.15 billion on advertising in 1991.

Example Most of the varieties of bath soaps and laundry detergents are produced by just two firms: Procter & Gamble and Unilever.

Under perfect competition all firms sell identical products. There is no incentive to advertise or to promote a particular product, since consumers know that all products are alike. Moreover, producers already can sell all they want at the prevailing market price, so why advertise? Under oligopoly, however, firms often pour resources into differentiating their products. Some of these expenditures have the beneficial effects of providing valuable information to consumers and offering them a wider array of products. But some forms of product differentiation may be of little value. Little information is conveyed by slogans such as "Gotta have it!" or "Uh huh!" yet Coke and Pepsi spend millions on such messages. Huge expenditures on advertising prevent new entrants into the "cola wars."

Oligopolies often compete by offering a variety of models or products. For example, there are over one hundred kinds of breakfast cereal and over twenty-five different laundry detergents. The following case study explores the costs associated with product differentiation in the auto industry.

CASE STUDY

The Cost of Variety

In the early days, cars were quite similar. Henry Ford's Model Ts were all the same—same style, same color. He used to say that people could choose any color car they wanted, as long as it was black. Since those days, however, car manufacturers have made an effort to follow Alfred Sloan's motto. Sloan, the head of General Motors from 1937 to 1956, wanted to build a car "for every purse and purpose." In recent years the number of choices has proliferated. Considering the possible combinations of engines, transmissions, colors, and other options, there are more than 69,000 versions of the Ford Thunderbird.

Example Overseas carriers are increasingly trying to invest in U.S. airlines in order to gain access to their domestic route networks. In 1992, British Airways offered to buy 44 percent of USAir. Delta, American, United, and Federal Express joined forces to lobby against government approval.

Engineers note that allowing for such variety adds tremendously to the cost of the car. For example, additional costs are necessary to support the sophisticated ordering system and the more complicated factories needed to produce a different car each minute. One study concludes that if the Ford Mustang were introduced today, the price would have to be 25 percent higher just to cover the added costs associated with providing a wider variety of that model.

Because Japanese producers originally shipped their cars halfway around the world, they could not easily fill custom orders. Instead, they concentrated on providing only those features consumers desired the most. The Honda Accord, for example, was offered in only thirty-two varieties, including all the combinations of engine, transmission, and color. Some industry analysts argue that this policy gave Japanese manufacturers a significant cost advantage and allowed them to focus more on quality than on variety. Even after locating plants in the United States, Japanese companies continue to keep their product lines relatively simple.

The point is that although consumers like to select cars that most nearly match their own tastes and preferences, this wider selection increases the average cost of cars. Many items cost more when they are customized to particular tastes. A tailor-made suit, for example, is more expensive than one off the rack. A home built to the buyer's specifications costs more than one built like others in a development. So the wider variety offered by oligopolists is both good and bad. It is good if consumers value the wider choice and are willing to pay the extra cost of variety; it is bad if the marginal cost of product differentiation exceeds the marginal benefit as perceived by consumers. Competition has a way of eliminating frills that are not valued by consumers. U.S. auto manufacturers experienced huge losses in the early 1990s and are now scrambling to survive.

Sources: "General Motors: Shake, Rattle and Roll," *The Economist,* 11 April 1992; and John Koten, "Giving Buyers Wide Choices May Be Hurting Auto Makers," *Wall Street Journal,* 15 December 1983.

MODELS OF OLIGOPOLY

Because oligopolists are interdependent, analyzing the behavior of individual producers under oligopoly is more complicated than analyzing that of producers under market structures where firms behave independently. Since the market opportunities of each firm depend on the actions of rival firms, the demand curve facing the individual firm cannot be specified until the behavior of competing firms has been determined. At one extreme, the firms in the industry may try to coordinate their behavior so they collectively act as a single monopolist, as with the oil cartel, OPEC. At the other extreme, oligopolists may compete so fiercely that price wars erupt, as with the air fare warfare of 1992 and the cigarette war of 1993.

Example In late 1992, the major U.S. steelmakers (U.S. Steel Group, LTV Steel Co., Inland Steel Industries, Bethlehem Steel, and Armco Steel) made a joint attempt to increase prices on flat-rolled steel. At the other extreme, Procter & Gamble reduced the price of Jif peanut butter three times in 1992 in an effort to protect its market share.

Although dozens of theories have been developed to explain oligopoly pricing behavior, we will examine only five of the better-known models: (1) the kinked demand curve, (2) cartels, (3) price leadership, (4) game theory, and (5) cost-plus pricing. Each was developed to explain a different type of behavior observed in oligopolistic markets. As we will see, each model has some relevance, though none is entirely satisfactory as a general theory of oligopoly behavior.

The Kinked Demand Curve

Prices in some oligopolistic industries appear to be stable even during periods when altered cost conditions suggest that a price change would be appropriate. An often-cited case of price stability occurred in the sulfur industry, where the price remained at $18 per ton for a dozen consecutive years despite major shifts in the cost of production. One oligopoly model sheds light on this apparent price stability. That model is based on the simple idea that if a firm cuts its price, other firms will cut theirs as well to avoid losing customers to the price cutter. But if a firm raises its price, other firms will stand pat, hoping to attract customers away from the price raiser. If an oligopolist expects such responses from competitors, the **kinked demand curve** describes the oligopolist's pricing strategy.

Kinked demand curve A curve that illustrates price stickiness; if one firm cuts its prices, other firms in the industry will cut theirs as well, but if the firm raises its prices, other firms will not change theirs

To develop the kinked demand curve model, we start at point *e* in Exhibit 5, with the firm producing *q* units at price *p*. If the firm changes its price, its rivals may choose to imitate the price change or to ignore it. The firm's demand curve will depend on whether other firms follow price moves or ignore them. The firm's demand curve *DD* is based on the assumption that rivals will not follow a change in price. The firm's demand curve *D′D′* is based on the assumption that rivals will match any change in price. As you can see, *DD* is flatter, or more elastic, than *D′D′*. To see why, suppose that General Motors (GM) raises its prices, but other auto producers do not. In this situation GM will lose far more sales than if other producers also raised their prices. Likewise, if GM cuts prices but others do not, GM will pick up more sales than if all producers cut prices. Thus, if rivals do not follow price changes, any price increase will drive away more customers and any price decrease will attract more customers than if rivals matched price changes. Therefore, each oligopolist's demand curve is more elastic when rivals do not follow price changes than when they do.

Example The price of steel rails remained at $28 per ton from 1901 to 1916 despite considerable shifts in demand and costs.

Point to Stress The two potential demand curves intersect at the prevailing price. The kinked demand curve is based on the representative firm's assumption that rivals will imitate price decreases and ignore price increases.

If rivals follow a firm's price decreases but do not match its price increases, the oligopolist's demand curve is *DeD′*. That portion of the demand curve reflecting a price increase, *De*, is flatter than that portion of the demand curve reflecting a price decrease, *eD′*. Because the behavior of rivals is different in the case of a price increase than a price decrease, this oligopolist's demand curve, *DeD′*, has a *kink* at the firm's current price-quantity combination, point *e*.

Marginal Revenue. To find the marginal revenue curve for the kinked demand curve, we simply piece together the relevant portions of the underlying marginal revenue curves. Segment *Da* is the marginal revenue curve

EXHIBIT 5

The Kinked Demand Model of Oligopoly

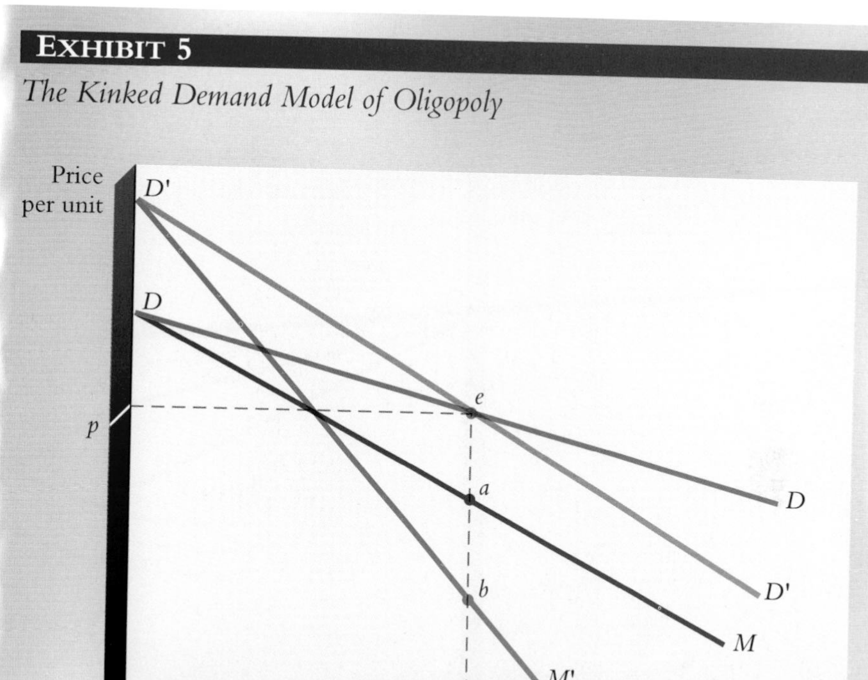

In the initial situation, an oligopolist is at point e, selling q units at price p. The firm's demand curve is DD if its competitors do not match its price changes; its demand curve is $D'D'$ if competitors do match price changes. Assuming that the firm's rivals match price cuts but not price increases, the relevant demand curve is DeD', with a kink at quantity q. $DabM'$ is the associated marginal revenue curve, with a gap at quantity q.

Teaching Tip The upper portion of marginal revenue (Da) is flatter than the lower portion (bM').

applicable to portion De of the kinked demand curve. And segment bM' is the marginal revenue curve associated with the portion eD' of the kinked demand curve. The marginal revenue curve is thus $DabM'$. Because there is a kink in the demand curve, the marginal revenue curve is not a single line; it has a gap at the currently produced quantity, q. The kinked demand curve and the corresponding marginal revenue curve are depicted in Exhibit 6.

Teaching Tip The firm assumes that if it responds to lower costs (within range ab) by reducing its price, rival firms will also reduce prices and the representative firm's profits will drop.

PRICE RIGIDITY. Within the gap in the marginal revenue curve, ab, the firm will not respond to small shifts in the marginal cost curve. Suppose that curve MC in Exhibit 6 is the initial marginal cost curve. The point where MC crosses the gap in the marginal revenue curve identifies equilibrium quantity q and price p. What happens to equilibrium price and quantity if the marginal cost curve drops to MC'? Nothing happens, because profit is still maximized at output level q. The oligopolist can do no better than to offer quantity q at price p. The same holds if marginal cost increases to MC''—

EXHIBIT 6

Demand and Marginal Revenue Curves for the Kinked Demand Model

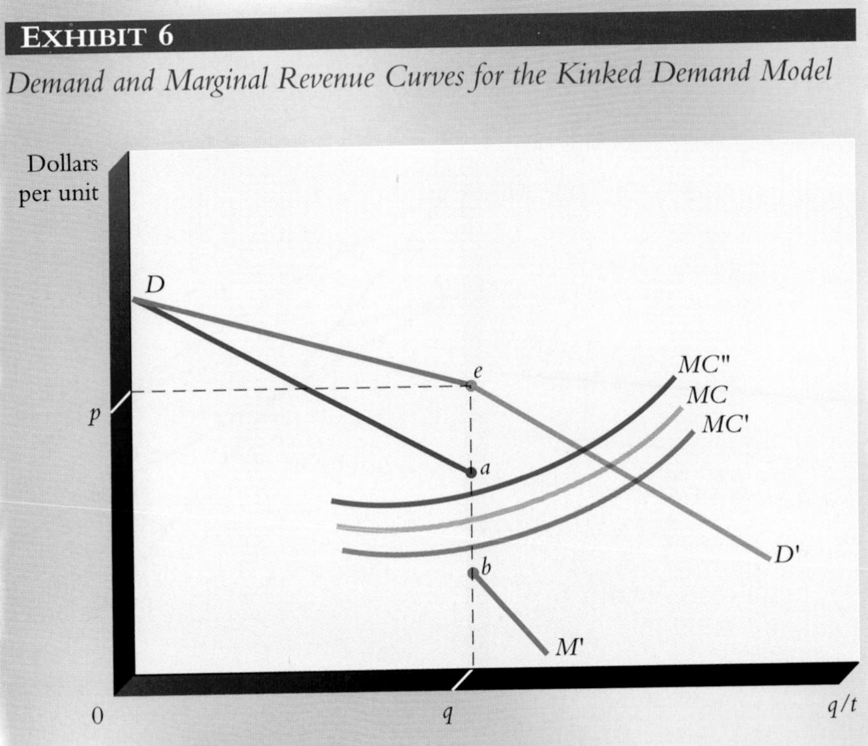

If MC is the initial marginal cost curve, the firm will produce quantity q (where marginal cost equals marginal revenue) at price p. Marginal cost could fall to MC' or increase to MC'' without affecting the quantity produced. Likewise, price p will be rigid if marginal cost for output q varies between a and b.

Teaching Tip Although higher costs reduce profits, the firm assumes that if it responds to higher costs (within range *ab*) by raising its price, rival firms will ignore the price change and the representative firm's profits will drop even further.

again, there is no change in the equilibrium price and quantity. It takes a greater shift in the marginal cost curve to produce a change in equilibrium price and quantity. Specifically, to change the equilibrium price and quantity, the marginal cost curve must intersect the marginal revenue curve above point *a* or below point *b*. *Since the marginal cost curve can fluctuate within the gap in the marginal revenue curve without affecting the equilibrium price, the price tends to be rigid, or stable, in oligopolistic industries if firms behave in the manner described by the kinked demand curve.*

Although the kinked demand theory provides an interesting explanation of those price rigidities that have been observed over the years, two basic criticisms have been leveled at it. First, the theory does not explain how the equilibrium price and quantity are initially determined. The theory simply explains why price, once established, is less likely to change in oligopolistic industries. Second, though there is some evidence supporting price rigidity, other evidence suggests that prices are not as rigid as the theory implies, particularly when it comes to price increases. During the inflationary periods of the 1970s and early 1980s, industries characterized as oligopolistic increased prices frequently. Other evidence comparing the frequency of price changes in oligopolies and monopolies suggests that oligopolies changed prices more often than monopolies did, even though the kinked demand theory would imply just the opposite.

Collusion and Cartels

Cartel A group of firms that agree to coordinate their production and pricing decisions

Point to Stress A cartel refers to collusive arrangements made with formal agreements.

In an oligopolistic market there are few firms, hence they may try to *collude,* or to agree on price and output levels, in order to decrease competition and increase profit. A **cartel** is a group of firms that agree to coordinate their production and pricing decisions so that they act as a single monopolist to earn monopoly profits. Cartels are more likely when the good supplied is homogeneous, as with oil or steel. Cartels can result in many benefits to firms: greater certainty about the behavior of "competitors," an organized effort to block new entry, and, as a result, increased profits.

Colluding firms usually reduce output, increase price, and block the entry of new firms. Consumers suffer because prices are higher, and potential entrants suffer because free enterprise is restricted. Collusion and cartels are illegal in this country. Monopoly profit can be so tempting, however, that firms sometimes break the law. For example, during the 1950s there was evidence of extensive collusion among electrical equipment producers, and some executives went to jail for their participation in the scheme. In many European countries, formal collusion among firms through cartels not only is legal but is sometimes promoted by government. Some cartels are worldwide in scope, such as the now-familiar Organization of Petroleum Exporting Countries (OPEC). Cartels can operate worldwide (even though they are outlawed in some countries) because there are no international laws to stop them.

Teaching Tip If the industry were perfectly competitive, the marginal cost curve would represent supply, and equilibrium price and quantity would occur at the intersection of the marginal cost and demand curves. Thus, for a given cost structure, the cartel produces less and charges a higher price than would occur under competition.

Suppose that the firms in an industry establish a cartel. The industry demand curve is presented as D in Exhibit 7. What price will be charged to maximize the industry's profits, and how will industry output be divided among participating firms? The first task of the cartel is to determine the marginal cost of production for the cartel as a whole. Since the cartel acts as if it were a single monopoly operating many plants, the marginal cost curve in Exhibit 7 represents the horizontal sum of the individual marginal cost curves for all firms in the cartel. The price and total output that maximize the cartel's profits are determined by the intersection of the cartel's marginal cost and marginal revenue curves. This intersection yields price p and industry output Q. So far, so good. Now output must be allocated among members of the cartel. The profit-maximizing solution for the cartel requires that output be allocated so that each firm incurs the same marginal cost on the last unit produced. Problems with maintaining a successful cartel are discussed below.

Teaching Tip If marginal costs are not equalized across producers, the cartel could increase total profits by reallocating production from high-cost to low-cost producers.

Differences in Cost. If all firms have identical costs, output and profit are easily allocated across firms (each firm produces the same output), but if costs differ, problems arise. The greater the differences in average cost across firms, the greater will be the differences in economic profit across firms. For example, a high-cost firm would need to sell more than a low-cost firm to

EXHIBIT 7

Cartel Model Where Firms Act as a Monopolist

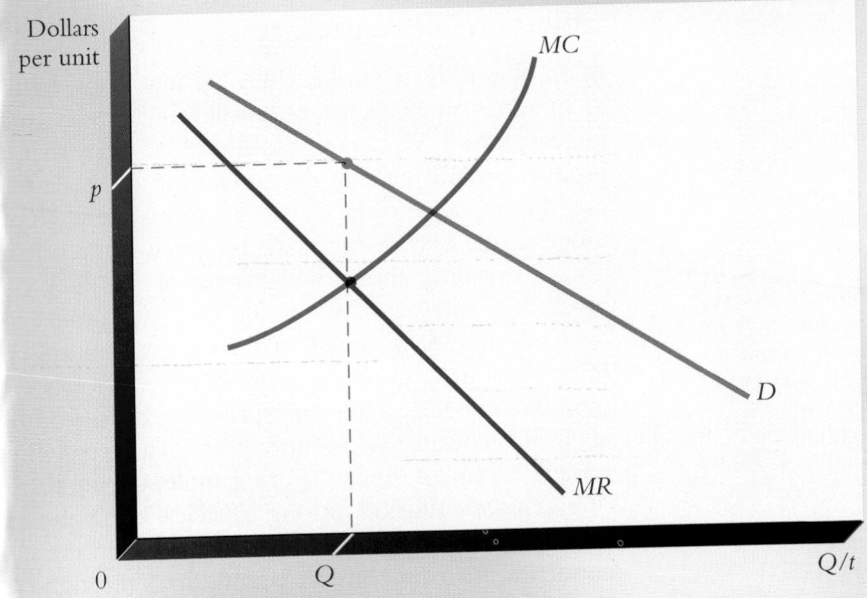

A cartel acts like a monopolist. Here D is the market demand curve, MR the associated marginal revenue curve, and MC the horizontal sum of the marginal cost curves of cartel members. Cartel profits are maximized when the industry produces quantity Q and charges price p.

Example OPEC has also had difficulties dealing with (1) differences in the quality of oil produced in different countries; (2) variable demand resulting from four recessions in the industrialized world since 1973, as well as the increasing price elasticity of demand in the long run as more fuel-efficient cars are developed and natural gas and coal reserves are exploited; and (3) the risk of eroding long-run profit opportunities if prices are set so high as to encourage major investments in nuclear and solar technology.

Teaching Tip Market shares tend to be a constant part of bargaining and are often renegotiated. Consider the highly publicized differences often expressed at the semi-annual OPEC meetings.

earn the same total profit, but this allocation scheme would not be consistent with the goal of maximizing cartel profits. Thus, *if average costs differ across firms, there is a conflict between maximizing the total profits of the cartel and equalizing profits among the participants.* If firms that experience higher costs are allocated too little output, they could drop out of the cartel, thereby undermining it. In reality, the allocation of output is typically the result of haggling among cartel members. Firms that are more influential or more adept at bargaining will get a larger share of output. Allocation schemes are sometimes based simply on the historical division of output among firms, or cartel members may divide up the market along geographical lines.

NUMBER OF FIRMS IN THE CARTEL. The greater the number of firms in the industry, the more difficult it is to negotiate an acceptable allocation of output among them. Consensus is harder to achieve as the cartel grows because the chances increase that at least one member will be dissatisfied.

NEW ENTRY INTO THE INDUSTRY. If a cartel cannot block the entry of new firms into the industry, in the long run new entry will force the price back down to where firms earn just a normal profit. The profits of the cartel attract entry, entry increases market supply, and increased supply forces the price down. A cartel's continued success therefore depends on barriers that block the entry of new firms.

CHEATING. Perhaps a more fundamental problem in keeping the cartel running is that each oligopolist faces a strong temptation to cheat on the agreement. By offering a price slightly below the established price, a firm can usually increase its sales and profit. The urge to cheat is strong, especially during economic slumps. Cartel agreements collapse if cheating becomes widespread.

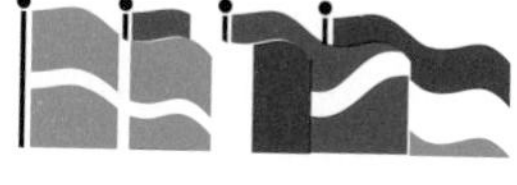

Teaching Tip If other firms maintain the cartel price, the cheating firm's demand curve is very elastic relative to market demand. The cheater can gain many customers. The difficulty is making customers aware of the price cut while keeping it secret from the other cartel members.

OPEC. The problems of establishing and maintaining a cartel are reflected in the spotty history of the Organization of Petroleum Exporting Countries (OPEC). In 1985 the average price of oil reached $34 a barrel. By 1992, the price had dropped to half that, despite the Persian Gulf war. The price fell partly because of competition among the world's oil producers. Many of the OPEC member countries are poor and rely on oil as a major source of revenue, so they argue over the price and their market share. OPEC members also cheat on the cartel. Like other cartels, OPEC has had difficulty with new entrants. The high prices resulting from OPEC's early success attracted new oil suppliers from the North Sea, Mexico, and elsewhere. Most cartel observers doubt that once-powerful OPEC will ever regain its former control. Incidentally, if OPEC ever held a meeting in the United States, its members would probably be arrested for price fixing. Efforts to cartelize the world production of a number of products, including bauxite, copper, and coffee have thus far failed.

More generally, *establishing and maintaining an effective cartel will be more difficult (1) if output is differentiated across firms, (2) if demand is highly variable over time, (3) if average costs vary sharply across firms, (4) if entry barriers are relatively low, or (5) if technology is changing rapidly.*

Price Leadership

Price leader A firm whose price and price changes are followed by the rest of the industry

An informal, or *tacit,* type of collusion occurs in industries that contain **price leaders**, who set the price for the rest of the industry. A single dominant firm or a few firms establish the market price, and other firms in the industry follow that lead. Any changes in the price are initiated by the price-leading firm. By accepting a single price, firms in an industry hope to increase profits by avoiding price competition.

Historically, the steel industry has been a good example of the price-leadership form of oligopoly. Typically, U.S. Steel, the largest firm in the industry, would set the price for various products, and other firms would follow. Congressional investigations of the pricing policy in this industry indicated that smaller steel producers relied on the price schedules of U.S. Steel. Public pressure on U.S. Steel to avoid price increases forced the price leadership role onto smaller producers, resulting in a rotation of the leadership

Point to Stress In contrast to a cartel, price leadership involves no price-fixing agreement. In fact, the participants may never consult each other. In contrast to the kinked demand curve model, the price leader model assumes that *all* price changes will be followed.

Example The highly differentiated breakfast cereal industry divides up the product group, and Kellogg, General Mills, and Post each lead in the areas where they have the best-selling brands.

function among firms. Although the rotating price leadership did reduce price conformity among firms in the industry, particularly during the 1970s, close observers of this industry argue that price levels prevailing in the industry were higher than they would have been with no price leadership.

Like other forms of collusion, price leadership is subject to a variety of obstacles. First, the practice often violates antitrust laws. Second, there is no guarantee that other firms will follow the leader. If other firms in the industry do not follow a price increase, the leading firm must either roll back prices or suffer a loss in sales to lower-priced competitors (recall the results from the kinked demand curve model). Third, the greater the product differentiation across producers, the less effective price leadership will be as a means of organizing oligopolists.

Finally, because oligopolists tend to operate with excess capacity, even if all firms officially follow the price leader, some may cheat on the official price by offering extra services, rebates, or some other deal that lowers the actual price. The incentives to cut prices in order to gain more sales will be particularly strong when the industry is depressed and firms are operating well below capacity. Typically, when production is low, so is the marginal cost of producing more output.

Game Theory

Game theory A model that analyzes oligopolistic behavior as a series of strategic moves and countermoves by rival firms

How will firms act when they recognize their interdependence but either cannot or do not collude? Because oligopoly involves interdependence among a few firms, an analogy has been drawn between interacting firms and the players of games such as cards. This approach to analyzing oligopoly was developed by John von Neumann and Oskar Morgenstern in their classic book, *Theory of Games and Economic Behavior,* published in 1944. **Game theory** examines oligopolistic behavior as a series of strategic moves and countermoves among rival firms. Game theory analyzes the behavior of decision makers, or players, whose decisions affect one another, focusing on the players' incentives to either cooperate or compete.

As an example, consider the market for gasoline in a rural community with only two gas stations. Suppose customers are indifferent between the two brands and consider only the price when choosing between them. Each gas station wants to charge the price that will maximize profits. To keep the analysis manageable, suppose only two prices are possible: a high price or a low price. If both gas stations charge the high price, they split the total quantity demanded and each gas station earns a profit of $70 per day. If they both charge the low price, they also split the market, but profit is only $40 per day. If one gas station charges the high price but the other charges the low price, the low-price station really cleans up, earning a profit of $100 per day. But the high-price station has few customers and loses $20 per day.

Which pricing strategy will be chosen? The answer depends on the assumptions about firm behavior. One common game-theory assumption is that each firm will try to avoid the worst outcome. The worst outcome is to lose $20 per day by being the only station charging the high price. The way to avoid this outcome is to charge the low price. So both gas stations will charge the low price and each will earn $40 per day. Note that this payoff is lower than the $70 each could earn if both charged the high price. If both were charging the high price, however, either one could increase profits to $100 per day by dropping the price.

Avoiding the worst outcome is only one of several behavioral assumptions that could be used to analyze oligopoly markets in terms of game theory. The specific outcome of such an analysis will depend on the rules of the game and on the assumptions that underlie the analysis. Outcomes can be as volatile as the personalities involved. Some players are more conservative than others, and some are more willing to take risks. Price wars sometimes break out among oligopolists. For example, in 1992 American Airlines announced substantial cuts in ticket prices. Within days, most other major airlines followed suit. But TWA announced even deeper price cuts. American then matched the TWA cuts. Despite several attempts at a cease fire, the fare war continued and firms in the industry lost money for the third year in a row.

Cost-Plus Pricing

Cost-plus pricing A method of determining the price of a good by adding a percentage markup to the average variable cost

Point to Stress For cost-plus pricing, the firm must assume a rate of output and set a target rate of profit.

A final model of oligopoly behavior is based on the observation that many oligopolists employ **cost-plus pricing** strategies. Each firm establishes a price by calculating the average variable cost per unit and then adding a percentage, called a *markup.* This markup is designed to cover costs that cannot be allocated to specific units of output and to provide the firm with a profit on its investment. This approach seems to ignore the demand curve, since price is determined as a function of cost, not demand, but more on that later.

Cost-plus pricing appears attractive to producers for several reasons. First, it provides a way of coping with uncertainty about the exact shape and elasticity of the demand curve. Second, the very effort of calculating appropriate prices based on marginal analysis is costly, particularly if the firm produces a variety of products. Adopting a simple markup rule greatly simplifies the pricing process. Third, if firms in the industry have similar costs, their use of the same markup percentage will yield uniform prices across the industry, generating an implicit form of price collusion.

CHOOSING THE TARGET LEVEL OF OUTPUT AND THE MARKUP. Because the average variable cost per unit varies with the level of output, the firm must assume that some target level of output will be sold. For example, the firm may assume that its level of output will be 75 percent of its capacity. A 50-percent markup on an item with an average variable cost of $80 results in a retail price of $120. This markup is designed to cover those elements of cost that do not vary with output, including fixed costs, and other costs that cannot be charged against a particular product, such as outlays for research and development. Some producers also build into the price a target rate of profit. For example, General Motors has employed a markup policy aimed at earning a 15-percent after-tax rate of return on its investment. GM assumed that its output would be 80 percent of its capacity.

Teaching Tip Defenders of the cost-plus approach argue that the "correct" markup is determined through trial and error and eventually approximates pricing that would occur if the firm set marginal revenue equal to marginal cost.

Example A 1980 study found that grocery store markups varied from 10 percent on commonly purchased items with well-publicized prices from competing stores (e.g., coffee) to 55 percent on less commonly purchased items whose prices were less well-known (e.g., light bulbs).

Teaching Tip Mutual interdependence means that a firm cannot estimate its demand curve without projecting rival firms' behavior. All the models describe firms' attempts to deal with the uncertainty of the demand curve and to develop some price stability.

AN ASSESSMENT OF COST-PLUS PRICING. Cost-plus pricing has an appealing simplicity, and it grows more attractive as the variety of products sold by the firm increases. A firm such as General Electric produces hundreds of different products, and GE is hard-pressed to attribute such costs as basic research and overhead to particular products. Or consider the problems faced by a grocery store in trying to assign its various costs of doing business to each of the thousands of products it sells. The store finds it easier to use a percentage markup to determine the price of each product. There is abundant evidence that markup pricing is used extensively, particularly in retailing. Firms do not have to be oligopolistic to adopt a cost-plus pricing policy—firms in other types of industries may employ the policy as well.

Although cost-plus pricing appears at first to be inconsistent with the use of marginal analysis, some observers argue that the cost-plus approach is, in fact, a profit-maximizing response to complicated and uncertain market conditions. When a number of executives were interviewed about their companies' use of cost-plus pricing, most said that they did not believe profits could be increased by any change in pricing procedures.[1] Apparently these executives believed they were charging the prices that maximized profits. Moreover, close scrutiny of actual policies indicates that *firms do not apply the same markup to all their products but vary the markup inversely with the price elasticity of demand for the product.* The greater the elasticity of demand, the lower the markup. This finding suggests that firms do take demand into account and do employ the markup rule in a way that is consistent with profit maximization.

Summary of Models

Each of the oligopoly models we have considered was developed to explain certain phenomena observed in oligopolistic markets. The *kinked demand curve* explains why some oligopoly prices tend to remain unchanged even in the face of changing costs. The *cartel,* or *collusion,* model shows why oligopolists might want to cooperate to determine market price and output; that model also explains how difficult such arrangements are to maintain. The *price leadership* model explains how and why firms may act in unison on prices without actually establishing a formal cartel. *Game theory* models show that, because oligopoly involves firm interdependence, the market outcome can range from cooperation to price wars. Finally, the *cost-plus pricing* model explains why a firm, in the face of complex costs and uncertain market conditions, may attempt to simplify its pricing decision by adding a markup percentage to average variable cost.

Comparison of Oligopoly and Perfect Competition

As we have said, each oligopoly model explains a piece of the oligopoly puzzle. Each model has limitations, however, and at this point none is thought to

1. See, for example, Fritz Machlup, *The Economics of Seller Competition* (Baltimore, MD: Johns Hopkins University Press, 1952), 65.

be a valid depiction of all oligopoly behavior. Consequently, "the" oligopoly model cannot be compared with the competitive model. We might, however, imagine an experiment in which we took the hundreds of firms that populate a competitive industry and, through a series of giant mergers, combined them to form, say, a half dozen firms. We would thereby transform the industry from perfect competition to oligopoly. How would the behavior of firms in this industry before and after the massive mergers differ?

Teaching Tip If the oligopoly exists because of significant economies of scale and if costs are not driven up too far through product differentiation efforts, oligopolists can charge a lower price than would occur in perfect competition.

PRICE IS USUALLY HIGHER UNDER OLIGOPOLY. With fewer competitors, these firms would become more interdependent. Oligopoly models presented in this chapter suggest that the firms could conceivably act in concert in their pricing policies. Even cost-plus pricing could be a tool for tacit price collusion if firms faced similar costs and adopted similar markup rules. *If the oligopolists engaged in some sort of implicit or explicit collusion, industry output would be smaller and the price would be higher under oligopoly than under perfect competition.* Even if oligopolists did not collude but simply operated with excess capacity, the average cost of production in the long run would be greater with oligopoly than with perfect competition.

HIGHER PROFITS UNDER OLIGOPOLY. In the long run, easy entry prevents firms in a perfectly competitive industry from earning more than a normal profit. With oligopoly, however, there are presumably barriers to entry that allow firms in the industry to earn long-run economic profit. The barrier to entry might be economies of scale in production or brand name identification built up through years of advertising. Such barriers could be insurmountable for a new entrant. Therefore, *we should expect profit rates in the long run to be higher with oligopoly than with perfect competition.* Profit rates do in fact appear to be positively correlated with the proportion of industry sales made by the largest firms. Some economists view these higher profit rates as a matter of concern, but not all economists share this view. Harold Demsetz, for example, argues that since it is the largest firms in oligopolistic industries that tend to earn the highest rates of return, higher profit rates in oligopolistic industries stem from the greater efficiency arising from economies of scale in these large firms.[2] Many of these issues will be examined later when we explore government's role in regulating the marketplace.

Teaching Tip In 1992, the trend seemed to tip toward divestiture, with 785 divestitures totalling $31.9 billion occurring during the first nine months. For example, Sears announced a plan to sell off Coldwell Banker Real Estate and Dean Witter Financial Services.

Mergers and Oligopoly

Because large firms are potentially more profitable than small ones, some firms have pursued rapid growth by merging with other firms. In some industries the *merging,* or joining together, of two firms has contributed to the movement toward oligopoly. Over the last century, there have been three major merger waves in this country. The first occurred between 1887 and

2. Harold Demsetz, "Industry Structure, Market Rivalry, and Public Policy," *Journal of Law and Economics* 16 (April 1973): 1–10.

Horizontal merger A merger in which one firm combines with another firm that produces the same product

Vertical merger A merger in which one firm combines with another from which it purchases inputs or to which it sells output

Conglomerate merger A merger involving the combination of firms producing in different industries

1904. Some of today's largest firms, including U.S. Steel and Standard Oil, were formed during this first merger movement. These tended to be **horizontal mergers**, meaning that the merging firms produced the same products. For example, the firm that is today U.S. Steel was formed in 1901 through a billion-dollar merger that involved dozens of individual steel producers and two-thirds of the industry's productive capacity.

The second merger wave took place between 1916 and 1929, when vertical mergers were more common. A **vertical merger** is the merging of one firm with either a firm from which it purchases inputs or a firm to which it sells output. Thus, it is the merging of firms at different stages of the production process. For example, a steel firm might merge with a firm that mines iron ore. **Conglomerate mergers**, which join firms producing in different industries, were also common during the second merger wave.

The third merger wave occurred during the twenty-five years following World War II. In that period many large firms were absorbed by other, usually larger, firms. More than 200 of the 1,000 largest firms in 1950 had disappeared by 1963 as a result of mergers. In recent years corporate takeovers have become more common, and some of the mergers have been huge. But some of the resulting conglomerates have shrunk as the new owners sell off part of the corporation to pay for the purchase. We cannot yet say whether the recent takeover activity forms the basis of a fourth merger wave.

CONCLUSION

Teaching Tip F. M. Scherer, in *Industrial Market Structure and Economic Performance* (2d edition, Houghton Mifflin, 1980), concluded that with as few as ten to twelve evenly matched suppliers, each firm can ignore the others' influence.

This chapter moves us from the extremes of perfect competition and pure monopoly to the gray area inhabited by most firms. Firms in monopolistic competition and firms in oligopoly face a downward-sloping demand for their products. In choosing the profit-maximizing price-output combination, the firm in monopolistic competition is less concerned about the effects of this choice on the behavior of competitors. But oligopolistic firms are interdependent and therefore must consider the effects their pricing and output decisions will have on those of other firms. This interdependence complicates the analysis of oligopoly, leaving open a wide array of possible models.

The analytical results derived in this chapter are not as neat as those derived for the polar cases of perfect competition and pure monopoly, but we can reach some general conclusions, using perfect competition as our benchmark. Given identical cost curves, monopolistic competitors and oligopolists tend to charge higher prices than perfect competitors in part because each operates with excess capacity. In the long run, monopolistic competitors, like perfect competitors, earn only a normal profit because entry barriers are low. But oligopolists can earn economic profits in the long run if new entry is somehow restricted. In a later chapter we will examine how government policy is often aimed at making firms more competitive. *Regardless of the market structure, however, profit maximization prompts firms to produce the output level at which marginal cost equals marginal revenue.*

SUMMARY

1. Whereas the pure monopolist produces output that has no close substitutes, a monopolistic competitor must contend with many rivals offering close substitutes. Because there are some differences among the products offered by different firms, each monopolistically competitive firm faces a downward-sloping demand curve.

2. Sellers in monopolistic competition differentiate their products through (1) physical qualities, (2) sales locations, (3) services provided with the product, and (4) the image of the product established in the consumer's mind.

3. In the short run, monopolistically competitive firms that can at least cover their average variable costs will maximize profits or minimize losses by producing where marginal cost equals marginal revenue. In the long run, free entry and exit of firms ensure that monopolistically competitive firms earn only normal profits, which occurs where the average total cost curve is tangent to the firm's downward-sloping demand curve.

4. An oligopoly is a market dominated by a few sellers, some of which are large enough relative to the entire market to influence price. In some oligopolistic industries, such as steel or oil, the product is homogeneous; in other oligopolistic industries, such as automobiles or tobacco, the product is differentiated.

5. Because an oligopolistic market consists of few firms, each firm may react to another firm's changes in quality, price, output, or advertising policy. Because of this interdependence among oligopolists, the behavior of producers is difficult to analyze. No single model of behavior characterizes oligopolistic markets.

6. In this chapter we considered five possible models of oligopoly behavior: (1) the kinked demand curve, which assumes that a firm's rivals follow price decreases but do not follow price increases; (2) the cartel, through which firms collude to behave like a monopolist; (3) price leadership, whereby one or a few firms set the price for the industry and other firms follow the leaders; (4) game theory, which focuses on each firm's strategy, based on the responses of rivals; and (5) cost-plus pricing, whereby firms determine prices by estimating their average variable cost and adding a percentage markup to cover nonallocated costs and to earn a target rate of profit.

QUESTIONS AND PROBLEMS

1. (Monopolistic Competition) Why would the production of Hollywood movies be an example of a monopolistically competitive industry? What are some of the major firms and how do they differentiate their products?

2. (Monopolistically Competitive Demands) Why does the monopolistically competitive firm's demand curve slope downward in the long run, even after the entry of new firms?

3. (Oligopoly and Technology) How might changes in technology affect whether an industry remains oligopolistic? That is, might some barriers to entry be affected by technological change?

4. (Kinked Demand) How might a kinked demand curve change if the degree of product differentiation within the oligopoly increased? What can you say about the degree of price rigidity before and after an increase in product differentiation?

5. (Oligopoly) Given a kinked demand curve, will oligopolists always experience economic profits, or could they have short-run losses?

6. (Oligopoly) "If the United Auto Workers union bargains for higher wages at Ford, Ford will simply pass on the additional costs to consumers in the form of higher prices." Must this statement be true? Why or why not?

7. (Cartels) Why would each of the following induce some members of OPEC to cheat on their cartel agreement?
   a. Some cartel members are undeveloped countries.
   b. Some members are small countries.
   c. International debts of some members grow.
   d. Expectations grow that some members will cheat.

8. (Price Leadership) Is it reasonable to assume that a price leader will always be the largest producer (that is, the firm with the largest scale)?

9. (Cost-Plus Pricing) How might a firm decide whether its markup was too high or too low? Is this determination governed by market conditions? What is the difference, if any, between sequential markups and profit maximization?

10. (Horizontal Mergers) Why do horizontal mergers seem most likely to occur in those industries that have the potential for substantial economies of scale but have not yet achieved such economies?

11. (Game Theory) Suppose there are only two automobile companies, Ford and Chevy, and Ford believes that Chevy will match any price it sets. Use the following price and profit data to answer the questions below.

If Ford sells for	*and Chevy sells for*	*Ford's profits (millions)*	*Chevy's profits (millions)*
$ 4,000	$ 4,000	$ 8	$ 8
4,000	8,000	12	6
4,000	12,000	14	2
8,000	4,000	6	12
8,000	8,000	10	10
8,000	12,000	12	6
12,000	4,000	2	14
12,000	8,000	6	12
12,000	12,000	7	7

   a. What price will Ford set for its cars?
   b. What price will Chevy set, given Ford's price?
   c. What is Ford's profit after Chevy's response?
   d. If they collaborated to maximize joint profits, what prices would the two companies set?
   e. Given your answer to part d, how could undetected cheating on price increase each car maker's profits?

12. (Price Leadership) Consider an oligopolistic industry in which one dominant firm acts as a price leader. Assume that the dominant firm believes that all other firms will respond to its pricing strategy by maintaining their aggregate market share at 50 percent of the total output demanded at the price set by the price leader. Show what this firm's profit-maximizing strategy should be, using demand and "typical" cost curves.

13. (Monopolistic Competition) In the long run, the monopolistically competitive firm earns zero economic profit, which is exactly what would occur if the industry were perfectly competitive. Assuming that the cost curve for each firm is the same whether the industry is perfectly or monopolistically competitive, answer the following questions.
   a. Why don't perfectly and monopolistically competitive firms produce the same industry output in the long run?
   b. Why is the monopolistically competitive industry said to be economically inefficient?
   c. What benefits might cause us to prefer the monopolistically competitive result over the perfectly competitive result?

14. (Cartel) Suppose that a cartel, knowing the industry demand and cost curves, sets industry output so as to maximize industry profits. Using the cost curves of a "typical" cartel member, show why each member is likely to attempt to increase its allocated share once the profit-maximizing price has been determined, if it is certain its efforts will be undetected by the other firms in the cartel.

15. (Monopolistic Competition) Monopolistically competitive industries tend to be characterized by a lot of advertising. Yet long-run profits are normal. Given this fact, why do firms advertise?

16. (Monopolistic Competition) Suppose that one effect of advertising in a monopolistically competitive industry is to give the firm more flexibility in the price it can charge for its product. What does this imply for the excess capacity argument in the long run?

17. (Advertising) Suppose you are the president of a company and are trying to determine how much advertising to do. Should advertising be regarded as a fixed or a variable cost in terms of the product cost curves you use to determine how much to sell? Explain in terms of a diagram like Exhibit 1 how you would determine the optimal amount of advertising to undertake.

18. (Oligopoly) Many industries that appear to be monopolistically competitive turn out to be oligopolies, because one firm may actually produce many of the differentiated products that compete with each other. Why would firms in an industry pursue such a strategy?

19. (Oligopoly) One of the problems that oligopolistic firms must deal with is uncertainty both with respect to the demand for their product and with respect to the reaction of rival firms to price changes. This leads many firms to react to changes in demand by changing the quantity supplied rather than changing price. If the firm has a choice between a production technology that contributes to a flat average cost curve and one that contributes to a more U-shaped curve, which technology is more attractive? Why would the firm's choice lead to what appears to be a case of cost-plus pricing?

20. (The Unfriendly Skies) One complaint frequently heard about air fares is that flying from a hub city airport is more expensive than flying from a nearby city that is not a hub. Although this may reflect a relative lack of competition in hub city airports, it could also be a form of price discrimination. Discuss.

21. (The Unfriendly Skies) An airline, once its flight schedules, planes, and personnel are in place, would have an incentive to price its flights at the point where the price elasticity of demand is unity. Why?

22. (The Cost of Variety) Generic brands are cheaper and frequently virtually identical to name-brand alternatives. Yet people continue to pay more for these name brands. Are consumers better served by having this "choice" even though the differences may be more perceived than real?

23. (The Cost of Variety) Wine producers, when sitting on big wine inventories, frequently offer a second-label wine that is cheaper and yet very similar to the first-label wine. Why wouldn't they simply reduce the price of the first-label wine and save all the costs of marketing the second-label wine?

PART 6

Resource Markets

CHAPTER 24

RESOURCE MARKETS

Labor Demand.

Why does Charles Schulz, the cartoonist, earn $25 million a year for drawing Peanuts, while Charles Schultze, the economist, earns peanuts, relatively speaking, for drawing conclusions about the economy? Supply and demand. Why does prime Iowa corn acreage cost more than scrubland in the Texas panhandle? Supply and demand. Why are the buildings in downtown Chicago taller than those in the farm towns of southern Illinois? Supply and demand. Why do M.D.s earn more than Ph.D.s? Supply and demand.

You say you've been through supply and demand already? True. But the earlier discussion focused on the product market—that is, the market for final goods and services. Goods and services, however, are produced by resources: land, labor, capital, and entrepreneurial ability. Supply and demand in the resource market determine the price and employment of resources. The distribution of resource ownership then determines the distribution of resource earnings throughout the economy.

Teaching Tip
Recall the three economic questions in Chapter 2: what goods and services will be produced, how will goods and services be produced, and for whom will goods and services be produced. The first is answered in the product market; the second and third are answered in the resource market.

Since your earnings depend on the market value of your resources, resource markets should be of particular interest to you. Certainly one key element in your career decision is the expected income associated with alternative careers. The next several chapters will examine how resource supply and demand interact to establish market prices for various resources. Topics discussed in this chapter include

- Resource markets
- Opportunity cost and economic rent
- Marginal resource cost
- Earnings differentials
- Marginal revenue product
- Elasticity of resource demand
- The functional distribution of income

The Once-Over

You already know a lot more about resource markets than you think. See if you can answer the following questions.

Resource Demand. Consider first the demand for land. A neighbor offers Farmer Jones the opportunity to lease one hundred acres of farmland. Jones figures that farming the extra land would yield $60 per acre in additional revenue but would cost $70 per acre to farm. Should he lease the extra land? Since his additional cost of farming that land exceeds his additional revenue, the answer is no.

Next, consider labor. The manager of Taco Bell knows that hiring one more worker would increase total cost by $400 per week but would increase total revenue by $500 per week. Should the additional worker be hired? Sure. Taco Bell's profit would increase by $100 per week by hiring the additional worker. As long as the additional revenue resulting from employing another worker exceeds the additional cost, the firm should hire that worker.

What about capital? Suppose that you cut lawns during the summer, earning an average of $20 per lawn. With your push mower, you cut about fifteen lawns a week, for a total revenue of $300. You are content until you read about a larger, faster mower—the Lawn Monster—that could cut your time per lawn in half, allowing you to double the number of lawns you mow per week with the same effort. If you can mow thirty lawns per week with the Lawn Monster, your total revenue would double to $600 per week, but you would have to pay an extra $200 per week for the mower. Should you make the switch? Since your total cost would increase by $200 per week but your total revenue would increase by $300 per week, your net revenue would increase by $100 per week, so you should move up to the Monster.

The above examples show that *additional units of a resource will be demanded as long as the marginal revenue generated by the additional units exceeds the marginal cost.*

Point to Stress
This rule is similar to the golden rule of profit maximization developed in Chapter 21 for the firm on the supply side of the product market. Following this rule will cause a firm's profits to rise or losses to fall. However, in this case the firm is on the demand side of the resource market.

Resource Supply. You should also understand the economic logic behind resource supply. Suppose you are deciding between two jobs that are identical except that one pays more than the other. Is there any question which job you will take? Assuming the working conditions of both jobs are equally attractive, you will choose the higher-paying job. Now turn the example around to consider the case in which you must choose between two jobs that pay the same, but one requires you to report for work at 5 A.M., a time of day when your body tends to reject conscious activity; the other is a normal 9-to-5 job. Which job will you choose? Most of you would choose the job that is more in accord with your natural body rhythms. In fact, you likely would be willing to accept less pay for the job with normal hours rather than start at 5 A.M. Put another way, you must be paid more to get up so early. You are interested not only in the wage rate but also in the working conditions; both affect your utility level.

Point to Stress
This rule is similar to the rule for utility maximization developed in Chapter 19 for the consumer on the demand side of the product market.

Resource owners will supply additional resources as long as doing so increases their utility. They will also supply their resources to the highest-paying alternative, other things constant. Since other things are not always constant, however, resource owners must often be paid more to supply their resources to certain uses. In the case of labor, the worker's utility includes both pay and other nonmonetary aspects of the job. Jobs that are dirty, dangerous, exhausting, and of low status are usually less attractive than jobs that are clean, safe, stimulating, and of high status.

The Demand and Supply of Resources

The easiest way to understand resource markets is to draw upon what you already know about the market for final goods and services. In the market for goods and services—that is, in the product market—households are the buyers who determine demand and firms are sellers who determine supply. In the resource market, however, these supply and demand roles are reversed: firms are demanders and households are suppliers. In the product market, households demand the bundle of goods and services that maximizes their utility; in the resource market, firms demand the resources that maximize profit. In the product market, firms supply the goods and services that maximize profit; in the resource market, households supply the resources that maximize their utility.

Teaching Tip
Firms usually compete in the resource market with firms from other product markets as well as with firms in the same product market.

The assumption of profit maximization ensures that each firm will demand the least costly combination of resources available, other things constant. The assumption of utility maximization ensures that each household will supply the bundle of resources that yields the highest income, other things constant. *Any differences between the profit-maximizing goals of firms and the utility-maximizing goals of households are reconciled through voluntary exchange in resource markets.*

Exhibit 1 presents the market for a particular resource, in this case carpenters. This market is characterized by an upward-sloping supply curve and a downward-sloping demand curve. This market will converge to the equilibrium wage rate, or the market price, for this type of labor. *Like the supply and demand for final goods and services, the supply and demand for resources depend on the willingness and the ability of buyers and sellers to participate in market exchange.*

The Market Demand Curve

Derived demand Demand for a resource that is derived from demand for the product the resource helps to produce

Why does a firm employ resources? Resources are used to produce goods and services, which a firm tries to sell for a profit. The firm does not value the resource itself but the resource's ability to produce goods and services. Because the value of any resource depends on the value of what it produces, the demand for a resource is a **derived demand**—derived from the demand for the final product. For example, a carpenter's pay is based on the price of

EXHIBIT 1

Resource Market for Carpenters

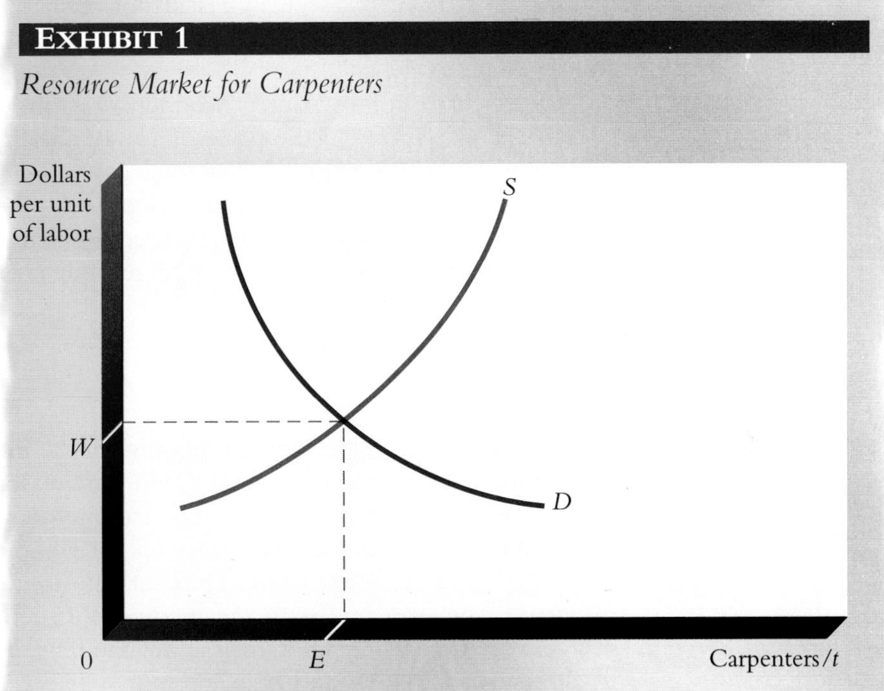

The intersection of the upward-sloping supply curve of carpenters with the downward-sloping demand curve determines the equilibrium wage rate, *W*, and the level of employment, *E*.

new housing; a movie star's pay per movie is based on that star's appeal at the box office; and a professional baseball player's pay is based on his ability to boost ticket sales.

Teaching Tip
Because the production of a good or service requires the cooperation of different resources, the market demand for a resource depends on the quantity and quality of other resources.

The market demand for a resource is the sum of the demands for that resource in all its various uses. For example, the market demand for carpenters is made up of all the various demands for this type of labor in residential and commercial construction, renovations, furniture-making, and so on. Similarly, the market demand for timber consists of its demand in the production of housing, paper products, railway ties, firewood, furniture, toothpicks, pencils, and so on. The demand curve for a resource, like the demand curve for the goods produced by that resource, slopes downward, as depicted in Exhibit 1. As the price of a resource falls, producers are more willing and more able to employ that resource.

Consider first the producer's greater *willingness* to hire resources as the price falls. In constructing the demand curve for a particular resource, we hold constant the prices of other resources. Consequently, if the price of this particular resource falls, it becomes relatively cheaper compared to other resources the firm could use to produce the same output. Hence, as the price of a resource declines, firms are more willing to hire this resource rather than other, now relatively more costly, resources. Thus, we observe *substitution in production*—coal for oil, security alarms for security guards, or plastic tubing for copper tubing, as the relative prices of coal, security alarms, or plastic tubing, respectively, fall.

A lower price for a resource also increases a producer's *ability* to hire that resource. For example, if the price of a resource drops, a producer can produce the same output for a lower total cost or can expand output for the same total cost. The lower resource price makes the firm more able to buy the resource. The amount of the resource the firm actually buys will, as we shall see, depend on how the firm's total revenue changes when more units of the resource are employed.

The Market Supply Curve

Example Held constant along a resource supply curve are prices for that resource in other occupations and nonmonetary aspects of the occupation.

The market supply of a resource is the sum of the individual supply curves of all resource suppliers to that market. The first reason the supply curve for a resource tends to slope upward is the resource owner's greater *willingness* to supply the resource as the price goes up. The higher the market price of a particular resource, other things constant, the more goods and services the resource owner can buy with the income obtained from supplying the resource. Resource prices are signals about the rewards for supplying resources to alternative activities, and higher resource prices will draw resources from lower-valued uses. For example, if the wage for carpenters is relatively low, some will seek other lines of work. As the market wage for carpenters increases, the quantity supplied will increase, as carpenters are attracted from alternative occupations.

Example An increase in starting salaries for holders of master's degrees in business administration in the 1970s and 1980s led to an increase in enrollments in MBA programs.

The second reason for an upward-sloping supply curve is that the resource owners are *able* to supply more of the resource at a higher price. For example, some people may have little natural ability as carpenters but the higher wage justifies the additional training they need to become carpenters. Similarly, when the price of oil increased sharply in the 1970s, oil exploration became economically feasible in less accessible locations, such as the remote jungles of the Amazon and the stormy waters of the North Sea. A higher resource price enables resource suppliers to increase their quantity supplied even though the marginal cost of supply increases as well.

Temporary and Permanent Resource Price Differences

Teaching Tip Even if the nonmonetary aspects of different occupations differ, identical resources will be allocated so that "net benefits" are equal. Also, "wages" should include the value of all employee benefits (for example, General Motors spent $3.4 billion on health care benefits in 1991).

Because *resources tend to flow to their highest-valued use,* the prices paid for identical resources should, over time, tend toward equality. This should be true even if these resources are supplied to different uses as long as there are no differences in the nonmonetary benefits to the resources in the different uses. For example, consider the wages earned by a group of identical workers, such as carpenters, supplying their labor to different uses, such as homebuilding and furniture making. Assume that the nonmonetary benefits of these jobs, such as working conditions, are identical, so we need be concerned only with pay. Suppose the wage offered carpenters employed as homebuilders increases to $25 per hour, which is $5 more than the wage paid carpenters who work as furniture makers.

This difference is shown in Exhibit 2 by a wage of $25 per hour in panel (a) and the wage of $20 per hour in panel (b). As a result of the difference, some carpenters will over time move from furniture making to homebuilding. This shift will reduce the supply of carpenters and increase their wage in furniture making while increasing the supply of carpenters and reducing their wage in homebuilding. Carpenters will move into homebuilding until wages equalize

EXHIBIT 2

Market for Carpenters in Alternative Uses: Homebuilding and Furniture Making

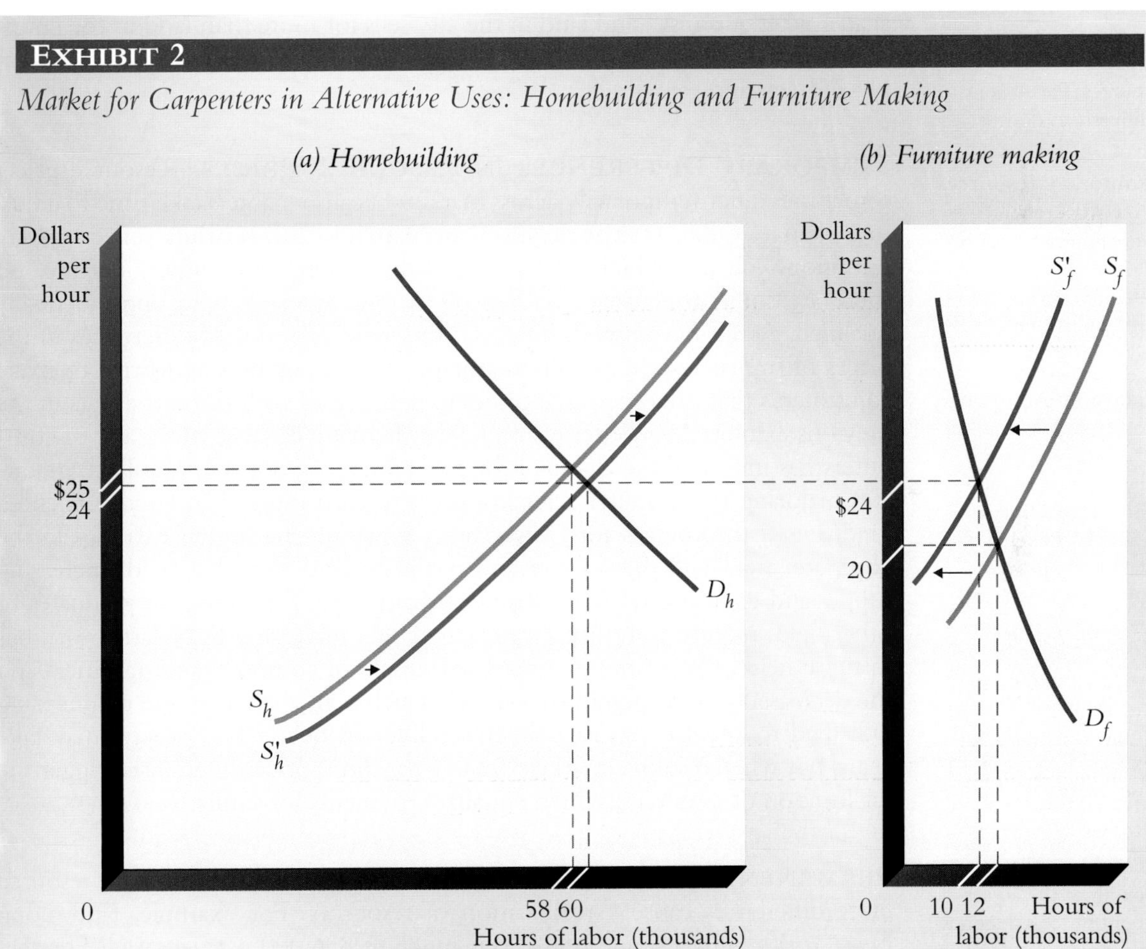

Suppose the wage offered carpenters is $25 per hour in homebuilding but only $20 per hour in furniture making. As a result of the wage differential, some carpenters will shift from furniture making to homebuilding, and this will continue until the wage offered carpenters is identical in each alternative use. In panel (b), the reduction in the supply of carpenters to furniture making increases the equilibrium wage from $20 per hour to $24 per hour. In panel (a), the increase in the supply of carpenters to homebuilding decreases the equilibrium wage from $25 per hour to $24 per hour. A total of 2,000 carpenter hours are shifted from furniture making to homebuilding.

across the different uses of carpenters. In Exhibit 2, supply shifts until a wage of $24 per hour is achieved in both markets. Note that in the adjustment process, two thousand units of labor shifted from furniture making to homebuilding. *As long as the nonmonetary benefits of supplying resources to alternative uses are identical and as long as resources are freely mobile, resources will be paid the same in their alternative uses.*

Point to Stress Temporary differences in resource prices lead to a reallocation of resources. Permanent differences do not.

In practice, we often observe earnings differentials for similar resources across markets. For example, corporate economists on average earn more than academic economists, and land in the city sells for more than land in the country. As you will now see, these differences can be traced to the workings of supply and demand.

Temporary resource price differentials Differences in resource prices that trigger resource reallocation and price adjustments

TEMPORARY DIFFERENCES IN RESOURCE PRICES. Resource prices sometimes differ temporarily across markets because markets take time to adjust to a change. Often **temporary resource price differentials** reflect market transitions, during which certain industries emerge and others decline. So there are sometimes wage differentials among workers who appear equally qualified. As we have noted, however, the mere presence of differences in the prices of similar resources will encourage resource owners and firms to make adjustments that drive resource prices to equality, as with the carpenters in the previous exhibit. As another example, the dramatic increase in the use of computers has increased the demand for programmers. As a result, college graduates majoring in computer science expect to earn more than equally talented graduates with other majors. Over time, however, the higher earnings in the computer field will draw more and more students into that field, increasing supply and lowering relative earnings. Meanwhile, the supply of graduates to other fields requiring similar aptitudes will fall, increasing the relative earnings in those fields. Over time the increased supply of computer programmers and the decreased supply of graduates in fields such as mathematics and engineering will tend to equalize earnings in these different fields. The process may take years, but when resource markets are free to adjust, price differences trigger the reallocation of resources, which equalizes payments for similar resources.

Example According to the American Dental Association, the number of dentists in the United States is expected to start declining later this decade, whereas the general population will increase steadily for another twenty years. The income of dentists is expected therefore to rise sharply.

Teaching Tip The length of the adjustment process depends on the degree of resource mobility.

Permanent resource price differentials Differences in resource prices that do not precipitate resource reallocation or price adjustments

PERMANENT DIFFERENCES IN RESOURCE PRICES. Not all resource price differences cause a reallocation of resources. For example, land along New York's Fifth Avenue sells for as much as $36,000 a *square yard!* For that amount you could buy several acres of farmland in upstate New York. Yet such a differential does not prompt land owners in upstate New York to supply their land to New York City—obviously that's impossible. **Permanent resource price differentials** do not precipitate the reallocation of resources among uses. The price per acre of farmland varies widely, reflecting differences in the land's productivity and location. Such differences do not trigger actions that result in price equality. Similarly, certain wage differentials stem in part from the different costs of acquiring the education and training required to perform particular tasks. This difference explains why brain surgeons earn more than tree surgeons, why opthalmologists earn more than optometrists, and why astronomers earn more than astrologers.

Teaching Tip Other nonmonetary aspects of an occupation that might be considered are occupational expenses (such as a dentist's cost of maintaining an office), the degree of job instability, the cost of living in different regions of the country, and so forth.

Other earnings differentials reflect differences in the nonmonetary aspects of similar jobs. For example, other things constant, most people must be paid more to work in a grimy factory than in a pleasant office. Similarly, corporate economists earn more than academic economists in part because corporate economists typically have less freedom in their daily schedules and in their choices of research topics.

Whereas temporary resource price differentials spark the movement of resources away from lower-paid uses toward higher-paid uses, permanent resource price differentials cause no such reallocations. Permanent resource price differentials are explained by *a lack of resource mobility* (urban land versus rural land), *differences in the inherent quality of the resource* (fertile land versus scrubland), *differences in the time and money involved in developing the necessary skills* (file clerk versus certified public accountant), and *differences in the nonmonetary aspects of the job* (lifeguard at Malibu Beach versus prison guard at San Quentin).

Opportunity Cost and Economic Rent

Example At the beginning of his 1992–1993 rookie year in the NBA, Shaquille O'Neal had signed endorsement contracts expected to total $30 million, in addition to his salary of $40 million over seven years.

According to *Forbes* magazine, Michael Jordan earned $36 million in 1992, mostly from product endorsements.[1] But he would likely be willing to play basketball and endorse products for less. The question is, how much less? What is his best alternative? Suppose his best alternative is becoming a college basketball coach, a job that paid, including endorsements, say, $3 million a year. And assume too that, if it weren't for the pay difference, he would be indifferent between his current position and college coaching, so the nonmonetary aspects of the two jobs balance out. Thus, he must earn at least $3 million to remain a professional player and product endorser. This amount represents his *opportunity cost*—the amount he must be paid to prevent him from supplying his talents to college coaching. The opportunity cost of a resource is what that resource could earn in its best alternative use.

Economic rent The portion of a resource's total earnings above its opportunity cost; earnings above the amount necessary to keep the resource in its present use

The amount Jordan earns in excess of his opportunity cost is called **economic rent.** Economic rent is that portion of a resource's total earnings that is not necessary to keep the resource in its present use; it is, as they say, "pure gravy." In Jordan's case, the economic rent is $36 million minus $3 million, or $33 million. Economic rent is a form of producer surplus earned by resource suppliers. The *division* of resource earnings between economic rent and opportunity cost depends on the resource owner's elasticity of supply. In general, *the less elastic the resource supply, the greater the economic rent as a proportion of total earnings.* To develop a feel for the difference between economic rent and opportunity cost, consider the following three cases.

Teaching Tip Recall (from Chapter 18) that the elasticity of supply tends to increase in the long run. Therefore, economic rent will tend to drop in the long run for some resources.

CASE (A): ALL EARNINGS ARE ECONOMIC RENT. If the supply of a resource to a particular market is perfectly inelastic, this means that resource has no alternative uses. Hence there is no opportunity cost, and all returns are in the form of economic rent. For example, scrubland in the high plains of

1. "Roll, Jordon, Roll," *Forbes*, 23 November 1992.

Montana has no use other than for grazing cattle. The supply of this grazing land is depicted by the vertical line in panel (a) of Exhibit 3, which indicates that the 10 million acres have no alternative use. Since the supply is fixed, the amount paid to use this land for grazing has no effect on the quantity supplied. Since the land has no alternative use, the opportunity cost is zero and all earnings are in the form of economic rent, shown by the blue shaded area. *Here the demand curve determines the equilibrium price of the resource but not the equilibrium quantity; fixed supply determines the equilibrium quantity.*

Teaching Tip An employer must pay an amount for a resource unit *at least* equal to the resource's opportunity cost. The opportunity cost per hour for janitors in Exhibit 3(b) is $10.

CASE (B): ALL EARNINGS EQUAL OPPORTUNITY COSTS. At the other extreme is the case in which a resource can earn as much in its best alternative use as in its present use. This situation is illustrated by the perfectly elastic supply curve in panel (b) of Exhibit 3. Suppose this figure depicts the market for janitors in the local school system. At a wage of $10 per hour, the school system can employ as many janitors as it chooses; here, the system demands 100 units of labor. If the wage offered falls below $10, however, these workers will find employment elsewhere, perhaps in nearby factories, where the wage is $10 per hour. In this case all earnings equal opportunity costs because any reduction in the wage will reduce the quantity of labor supplied to this particular use to zero. *Here the demand curve determines the equilibrium quantity hired but not the equilibrium wage; the equilibrium wage is determined exclusively by the height of the horizontal supply curve—that is, by the wage in an alternative use.*

Point to Stress In cases such as Exhibit 3(c), total resource payments exceed the resource's opportunity costs. The area under a resource's supply curve up to the prevailing quantity equals the total opportunity cost. The area above the supply curve up to the prevailing cost per unit equals the total economic rent.

CASE (C): EARNINGS INCLUDE BOTH ECONOMIC RENT AND OPPORTUNITY COSTS. Whenever a higher price is needed to increase the quantity of a resource supplied—that is, whenever the supply curve slopes upward—resource owners will earn economic rent in addition to their opportunity cost. For example, if the wage for part-time work in your college community increases from $5 to $10 per hour, the quantity of labor supplied will increase, as will the economic rent earned by resource suppliers. This situation is presented in panel (c) of Exhibit 3, where economic rent is indicated by the blue area and the opportunity cost by the red area. If the wage increases from $5 to $10, the quantity supplied will increase by 5,000 units. For those resource suppliers who had been offering their services at a price of $5, the difference between $5 and $10 is additional economic rent. These individuals did not require the higher price to supply their services, but they certainly are not going to turn it down. *In the case of an upward-sloping supply curve and a downward-sloping demand curve, both supply and demand determine the equilibrium price and quantity.*

Note that very specialized resources tend to earn a higher proportion of economic rent than do resources with many alternative uses. Thus, Michael Jordan earns a greater *proportion* of his income as economic rent than does the janitor who sweeps up the Chicago Bulls locker room.

To review: Given a demand curve that slopes downward, when a resource supply curve is vertical (perfectly inelastic), all resource earnings are in the form of economic rent. When resource supply is horizontal (perfectly elastic),

EXHIBIT 3

Opportunity Cost and Economic Rent

(a) All resource returns are economic rent

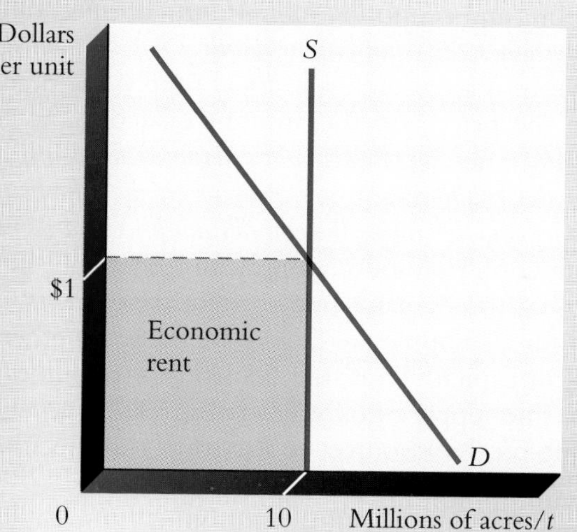

(b) All resource returns are opportunity costs

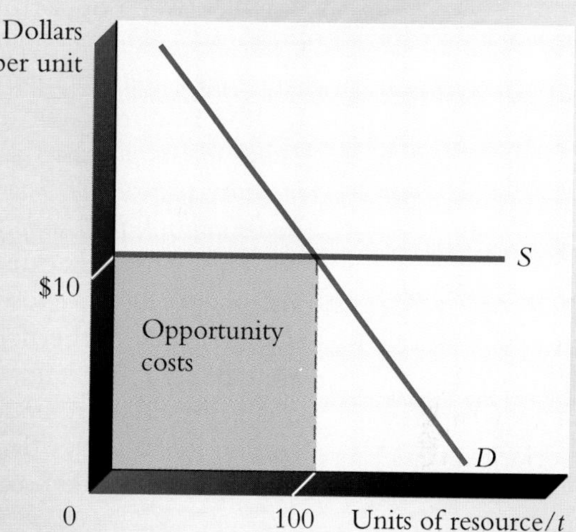

(c) Resource returns are divided between economic rent and transfer earnings

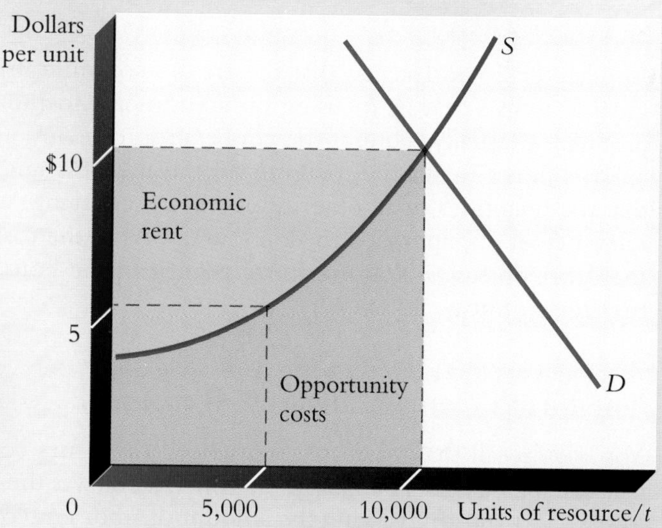

In panel (a), the resource supply curve is vertical, indicating that the resource has no alternative use. The price is demand-determined, and all earnings are in the form of economic rent. In panel (b), the supply curve is horizontal, indicating that the resource can earn as much in its best alternative use. Employment is demand-determined, and all earnings are opportunity costs. Panel (c) shows an upward-sloping supply curve. At the equilibrium price of $10, resource earnings are partly opportunity costs and partly economic rent. Both supply and demand determine the equilibrium price and quantity.

all resource earnings reflect their opportunity costs. And when supply slopes upward (an elasticity greater than zero but less than infinity), earnings are divided between opportunity costs and economic rent. *When the supply curve of a resource is vertical, supply determines the equilibrium quantity but demand determines the equilibrium price.* That is, if a resource is in fixed supply, the demand for the resource will dictate the price and the amount of economic rent. *When the supply curve of a resource is horizontal, demand determines the equilibrium quantity but supply determines the equilibrium price. And when the supply curve slopes upward, both supply and demand determine the equilibrium price and quantity.*

This completes our introduction to resource supply. In the balance of this chapter we take a closer look at the demand side of resource markets. The determinants of the demand for a resource are largely the same whether we are talking about land, labor, or capital. Thus, the demand for resources can be examined more generally. The supply of different resources, however, has certain peculiarities depending on the resource, so the supply of specific resources will be taken up in the next three chapters.

A Closer Look at Resource Demand

Teaching Tip Different market structures occur in resource markets just as in product markets. However, the initial look at resource demand will assume perfect competition in the resource market. In all market structures, the physical productivity of resources combines with consumer valuations of the goods produced to determine resource demand.

Point to Stress In determining the marginal physical product of a resource, all other resources are held constant.

In Chapter 2 you learned that the art of economic reasoning involves marginal analysis—that is, focusing on adjustments to the status quo. Although production usually requires the cooperation of many inputs, we will cut the analysis down to size by focusing on the use of a single resource, assuming that the quantities of all other resources are constant. We will then show the relevance of this approach to all resources. As in the past, we will assume that the firm's objective is to maximize profit and the household's objective is to maximize utility.

The Firm's Demand for One Resource

You may recall that when we introduced the firm's cost, we considered the example of a moving company, for which labor was the only variable resource in the short run. By varying the amount of labor employed, we examined the relation between the quantity of labor employed and the amount of furniture moved per day. The same idea is used in Exhibit 4, where all but one of the firm's inputs are held constant. The first column in the table lists possible employment levels of the variable resource, in this case labor. The second column presents the total output, or total physical product, and the third column presents the marginal physical product. The marginal physical product of labor shows how much additional output is produced by each additional unit of labor. The first unit of labor has a marginal physical product of 10 units, the second unit has a marginal physical product of 9 units, and so on.

The marginal physical product declines as more labor is used, reflecting the law of diminishing marginal returns. Recall that the law of diminishing

EXHIBIT 4

The Marginal Revenue Product When a Firm Sells in a Competitive Market

Units of Variable Resource (1)	Total Physical Product (*TPP*) (2)	Marginal Physical Product (*MPP*) (3)	Product Price (4)	Total Revenue (5) = (2) × (4)	Marginal Revenue Product (*MRP*) (6)
0	0	—	$2	$ 0	—
1	10	10	2	20	$20
2	19	9	2	38	18
3	27	8	2	54	16
4	34	7	2	68	14
5	40	6	2	80	12
6	45	5	2	90	10
7	49	4	2	98	8
8	52	3	2	104	6
9	54	2	2	108	4
10	55	1	2	110	2
11	55	0	2	110	0
12	53	−2	2	106	−4

marginal returns states that as additional units of the variable resource are added, other resources held constant, eventually each additional unit of the variable resource yields a smaller marginal physical product. In Exhibit 4 diminishing marginal returns set in immediately—that is, right after the first unit of labor is employed.

Although labor is used here as the variable resource, we could examine the marginal physical product of any resource. For example, we could consider how many lawns you could cut per week if you varied the quantity of capital employed. You might start off with very little capital—imagine cutting grass with a pair of scissors—and eventually move up from a push mower to the Lawn Monster. By holding labor constant and varying the quantity of capital, we could compute the marginal physical product of capital. Likewise, we could compute the marginal physical product of land by examining crop production for varying amounts of land, holding other inputs, such as the amount of farm labor and capital, constant.

Teaching Tip Marginal revenue measures the change in total revenue from selling one more unit of the firm's output. In contrast, marginal revenue product is the change in total revenue from using one more unit of the resource.

Marginal Revenue Product

The first three columns of Exhibit 4 show what happens to the firm's output as the quantity of labor is increased. For the profit-maximizing firm, however, the important question is, what happens to the firm's *total revenue* as a result of hiring additional labor? The firm is interested in the marginal revenue product of labor, which is how total revenue changes when an additional unit of labor is employed, given that the quantities of other resources are held constant. The **marginal revenue product** (*MRP*) of any resource is the change in total revenue resulting from employment of an additional unit of the resource, other resources constant. You could think of the marginal revenue product as the firm's "marginal benefit" from hiring one more unit of the resource. A resource's marginal revenue product will depend on two factors: (1) the amount of additional output produced and (2) the price at which that output is sold.

Marginal revenue product The change in total revenue when an additional unit of a resource is hired, other things constant

Point to Stress
MRP equals $p \times MPP$ *only* if the firm is a price taker in the product market.

SELLING AS A PRICE TAKER. The calculation of marginal revenue product is simplest when the firm sells its output in a perfectly competitive market, which is the assumption underlying Exhibit 4. Since an individual firm in perfect competition can sell as much as it wants without affecting the product's price, the firm is said to be a *price taker.* The firm must accept, or "take," the market price for its product. The marginal revenue product, listed in column (6), is the change in total revenue that results from changing input usage by one unit. For the competitive firm, the marginal revenue product is simply the price of the product, in this case $2, multiplied by the marginal physical product, or $MRP = p \times MPP$. Because of diminishing returns, the marginal revenue product falls steadily as additional units of the input are employed.

SELLING AS A PRICE SEARCHER. If the firm has some market power in the product market—that is, some ability to set the price—the demand curve for that firm's output slopes downward. To sell more output, the firm must lower its price. The firm, consequently, must search for the price that will maximize its profit. Hence a firm with market power—that is, a firm that faces a downward-sloping demand curve for its product—is often called a *price searcher.* Exhibit 5 reproduces the first two columns of Exhibit 4; the remaining columns reflect the revenue of a firm selling as a price searcher. Together, columns (2) and (3) represent the demand schedule for the product. Total output multiplied by the price at which that output can be sold yields the firm's total revenue, which is presented in column (4). Note that the marginal physical product column has been omitted because it is not directly used in the calculations.

The marginal revenue product of labor, which is the change in total revenue resulting from a one-unit change in the quantity of labor employed, is listed in column (5). For example, the 10 units produced by the first unit of labor can be sold for $4 each, yielding total revenue of $40. The second unit of labor adds 9 more units to the total product, but in order to sell 9 more units, the firm must lower the price of all units from $4 to $3.52. Total revenue increases to $66.88, which yields a marginal revenue product for the second unit of labor of $26.88.

Teaching Tip
For both price takers and price searchers in the product market, *MRP* equals $MR \times MPP$. For a price taker, p equals *MR*, and *MRP* equals $p \times MPP$. For a price searcher, p exceeds *MR*, so $p \times MPP$ exceeds $MR \times MPP$. Therefore, *MRP* falls faster for a price searcher.

The marginal revenue product curve indicates the additional revenue, or the "marginal benefit" to the firm, that results from employing each additional unit of the resource. The profit-maximizing firm should be willing to pay as much as the marginal revenue product for an additional unit of the

EXHIBIT 5

The Marginal Revenue Product When a Firm Sells as a Price Searcher

Units of Variable Resource (1)	Total Physical Product (*TPP*) (2)	Product Price (3)	Total Revenue (4) = (2) × (3)	Marginal Revenue Product (*MRP*) (5)
0	0	—	—	—
1	10	$4.00	$ 40.00	$40.00
2	19	3.52	66.88	26.88
3	27	3.14	84.78	17.90
4	34	2.78	94.52	9.74
5	40	2.50	100.00	5.48
6	45	2.25	101.25	1.25
7	49	2.05	100.45	−0.80
8	52	1.90	98.80	−1.65
9	54	1.80	97.20	−1.60
10	55	1.75	96.25	−0.95
11	55	1.75	96.25	0.00

resource. *Thus, the marginal revenue product curve can be viewed as the firm's demand curve for that resource.*

To review, regardless whether a firm in the product market is a price taker or a price searcher, the marginal revenue product of a resource equals the change in total revenue resulting from a one-unit change in that resource, other things held constant. The marginal revenue product of a resource can be viewed as the demand for the resource—the most that firms would be willing to pay for each unit of the resource. For firms selling as price takers, the marginal revenue product, or the resource demand, equals the marginal physical product times the price. For firms selling as price searchers, this simple formula does not apply because firms can sell more output only if its price falls. *For price takers in the product market, the marginal revenue product declines only because of diminishing marginal returns. For price searchers in the product market, it declines both because of diminishing returns and because additional output can be sold only if the market price declines.*

Teaching Tip A resource price taker faces a horizontal, or perfectly elastic, supply curve. This is similar to the perfectly elastic demand curve for the price taker in the product market.

Marginal Resource Cost

Marginal resource cost The change in total cost when an additional unit of a resource is hired, other things constant

Given the firm's marginal revenue product curve, can we determine how much labor the firm should employ to maximize profit? Not yet, because we know only what marginal revenue the resource generates for the firm. We also need to know how much this resource costs the firm. Specifically, what is the **marginal resource cost**—that is, what is the additional cost to the firm of employing one more unit of the resource? Marginal resource cost is

Resource price taker A firm that faces a given market price for a resource; the firm can buy any amount of the resource without affecting the resource price

Teaching Tip Since *MRP* falls faster for a price searcher in the output market, the firm in Exhibit 6 would hire fewer workers if the *MRP* were based on Exhibit 5 (showing a price searcher) rather than Exhibit 4 (showing a price taker).

simplest to calculate when the firm is a price taker in the resource market. A **resource price taker** hires such a tiny fraction of the available resource that its employment decision has no effect on the market price of the resource. Thus, the resource price taker faces a given market price for the resource and decides only on the quantity to be hired at that price.

For example, if the market wage for factory workers is $10 per hour, the firm's marginal resource cost of this labor is $10 per hour regardless of how much is employed. A marginal resource cost of $10 is represented by the horizontal line drawn at the $10 level in Exhibit 6. Exhibit 6 also shows the marginal revenue product curve, or resource demand curve, based on the schedule presented in Exhibit 4. The marginal revenue product curve indicates the additional revenue the firm receives as a result of employing each additional unit of labor.

Given a marginal resource cost of $10 per hour, how much labor will the profit-maximizing firm purchase? *The firm will hire more labor as long as doing so*

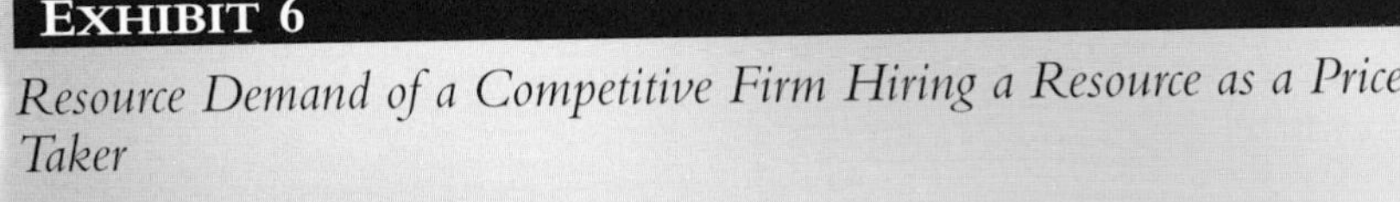

EXHIBIT 6

Resource Demand of a Competitive Firm Hiring a Resource as a Price Taker

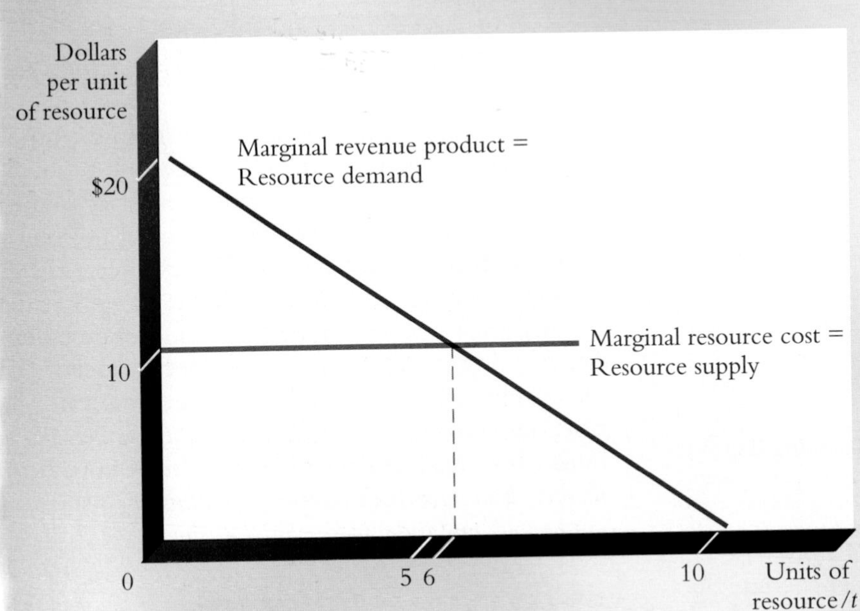

For a competitive firm, the downward-sloping marginal revenue product curve is its demand curve for the resource. If the firm is a price taker in the resource market, it faces a horizontal resource supply curve. It can hire as much of the resource as it desires at a constant marginal resource cost. The firm will hire up to the point where the marginal revenue product equals the marginal resource cost.

adds more to revenue than to cost—that is, as long as the marginal revenue product exceeds the marginal resource cost. The firm will stop hiring labor only when the two are equal. If the marginal resource cost equals $10, the firm will hire 6 units of labor because the marginal revenue product of the sixth worker equals $10. The decision rule of equating marginal cost with marginal revenue applies to all the firm's input decisions, just as it did to the firm's output decisions. Stated more formally, the decision rule of resource utilization is that the firm should hire additional inputs up to the level at which

Marginal resource cost = marginal revenue product

This rule holds for all resources employed. It holds for resource price takers and resource price searchers. It also holds for product price takers and product price searchers. In a competitive labor market, we can say that the profit-maximizing resource use occurs when the market wage equals the marginal revenue product; this reflects the *marginal productivity theory of income distribution.* Based on data presented thus far, we cannot say exactly what the firm's profit will be because we have not presented information about the firm's other costs. We do know, however, that a seventh worker would add $10 to cost but only $8 to revenue, reducing the firm's profit by $2.

Whether the firm sells its output as a price taker or as a price searcher, the profit-maximizing level of employment occurs where the marginal revenue product of labor equals its marginal resource cost. Similarly, the profit-maximizing levels of other resources, such as land and capital, will occur where their respective marginal revenue products equal their marginal resource costs. Regardless of the resource, the firm will hire a resource only if it "pulls its own weight"—only if the resource yields a marginal revenue at least equal to its marginal cost.

In an earlier chapter we developed a rule for determining the profit-maximizing level of output. Profit is maximized when the marginal cost of *output* equals its marginal revenue. Likewise, profit is maximized when the marginal cost of an *input* equals its marginal revenue. Though the first rule focuses on the quantity of output and the second rule focuses on the quantity of input, the two approaches are equivalent ways of deriving the same principle of profit maximization. For example, in Exhibit 6 the firm maximizes profit by hiring 6 units of labor when the wage is $10 per unit. Specifically, the sixth unit of labor produces an additional 5 units of output, which sell for $2 per unit, for a marginal revenue product of $10. The marginal cost of that output is the change in total cost, $10, divided by the change in output, 5 units; so the marginal cost of output is $10/5, or $2. The marginal revenue of that output is simply its price of $2. Thus, in equilibrium the marginal cost of output equals its marginal revenue.

Now that you have some idea of how to derive the demand for a resource, let's consider what could shift resource demand.

Shifts in the Demand for Resources

As we have said, a resource's marginal revenue product consists of two elements: the marginal physical product of the resource and the price at which that product is sold. As we shall see, the marginal physical product will change as a result of a change in other resources employed or a change in technology. And the price at which the final product is sold will change as a result of a change in the demand for the final product.

Other Inputs Employed. Although the analysis thus far has focused on a single input, in practice resources are used in combination with each other. The marginal physical product of any resource depends on the quantity and quality of other resources used in the production process. Sometimes resources are *substitutes.* For example, coal substitutes for oil in the generation of electricity. If resources are substitutes, an increase in the price of one will increase the demand for the other. For example, an increase in the price of oil will increase the demand for coal.

Example Automatic teller machines and tellers are substitute resources.

Example Automatic teller machines and the paper used to print transaction receipts are complements.

Sometimes the resources are *complements,* such as a trucks and truck drivers. If the relationship between resources is complementary, a reduction in the price of one resource will increase the demand for the other. If the price of bigger and better trucks falls, bigger and better trucks will be purchased. An increase in the quantity and quality of trucks will increase the marginal revenue product of truck drivers, so the demand for truck drivers will shift to the right. One reason why a truck driver in the United States usually earns about $15 an hour and a rickshaw driver in the Far East earns only about $0.15 an hour is the truck. The rickshaw driver pulls a cart worth maybe $100; the cart can move only as fast and as far as the driver's legs will take it and can carry only one passenger plus a little baggage. The truck driver is behind the wheel of a $100,000 machine that can haul huge amounts great distances at high speeds. The truck makes the driver more productive.

A valuable resource is one that helps other resources become more productive. In sports, the "most valuable player" is typically a team member who not only contributes a great deal directly but in the process makes other players on the team more productive as well. For example, Michael Jordon is such a great scorer that other teams typically "double team" him—that is, have two players try to prevent him from scoring. This allows him to "assist" other team members who are left open for the shot. *More generally, the greater the quantity and quality of complementary resources used in production, the greater the marginal productivity of the resource in question and the greater the demand for that resource.*

Example A technological improvement can act as a substitute or a complement for labor. The development of computer-controlled milling machines increases the demand for computer-trained machinists but decreases the demand for machinists without computer skills.

Changes in Technology. *Technological improvements can enhance the productivity of some resources and can make other resources obsolete.* The development of fuel-efficient cars has increased the number of miles that can be squeezed out of a gallon of gasoline, so the productivity of gasoline has increased. Word processing programs have increased the productivity of authors and typists. The development of synthetic fibers, such as polyester, has reduced the demand for natural fibers, such as cotton and wool. And the development of fiber optics and satellite communication has reduced the demand for copper wire.

Changes in the Demand for the Final Product. Because the demand for a resource is *derived* from the demand for the final output

Teaching Tip Using the data in Exhibit 4, if the wage is $10, employment will rise from 6 workers when the output price is $2 to 8 workers when the output price is $4.

product produced, any change in the final demand for the final output will change resource demand. For example, an increase in the demand for automobiles will increase their market price and thereby increase the marginal revenue product of labor employed to produce automobiles. In our earlier example, if the price of a good sold in a competitive market doubles from $2 to $4, the marginal revenue product also doubles. The link between derived demand and employment is considered in the following case study.

CASE STUDY

The Derived Demand for Architects

The big drop in real estate prices, particularly commercial real estate, that occurred in the late 1980s and early 1990s caused employment in that industry to shrink. Hard hit were architects, construction workers, building suppliers, real estate agents, and mortgage lenders. In this case study, we consider what happened to the demand for architects.

In New York City the number of classified ads for architectural positions declined from 5,000 in 1987 to 500 in 1991. Similar drops took place in other major cities. For example, employment at one national architecture firm shrank from 1,600 to 700 between 1988 and 1992. One-third of members of the Connecticut Society of Architects were unemployed in 1992. The job loss among entry-level architects was worsened by a change in technology. Drafting jobs have long represented the traditional entry-level positions for new architects, but these positions are now being eliminated by new software—computer-assisted design programs.

The declining demand for architects has had an interesting impact on the demand for higher education in architecture, which itself is a derived demand. Enrollment in undergraduate classes in architecture declined because entry-level positions disappeared, but enrollments in graduate courses remained relatively stable. Apparently, many out-of-work architects decided to pursue graduate degrees since the poor job market reduced their opportunity cost of time. The exception that proves the rule about derived demand is that those architectural firms that specialize in the health-care industry have flourished because health care has been the fastest-growing sector of the economy.

Sources: Maxine Bernstein, "Designs on the Future," *Hartford Courant,* 9 November 1992; and D. W. Dunlap, "Recession Is Ravaging Architects' Firms," *New York Times,* 17 May 1992.

Price Elasticity of Resource Demand

We can examine the price elasticity of demand for a resource, just as we examined the elasticity of demand for final products. The price elasticity of demand for a resource equals the percentage change in the quantity of the resource demanded divided by the percentage change in its price. A variety of forces influence the price elasticity of demand for a resource. Some relate to the derived nature of resource demand; others relate to the productivity of the resource itself.

Teaching Tip If output demand is very elastic and the price of a necessary resource rises, the resulting output price increase (as supply falls) will result in a large drop in the quantity of sales. Therefore, there is a large drop in the demand for the resource.

Teaching Tip The resource price searcher's facing an upward-sloping supply curve in the resource market is equivalent to the output price searcher's facing a downward-sloping demand curve in the product market.

Teaching Tip The ease of substitution is an element held constant in assessing the impact of production cost share on demand elasticity. In the example of electrical wire, there may still be a large drop in quantity demanded if there is a readily available substitute for such wiring.

PRICE ELASTICITY OF DEMAND FOR THE FINAL PRODUCT. Since the demand for a resource is derived from the demand for the final product, the price elasticity of demand for the resource is also derived from the price elasticity of demand for the final product. *The more elastic the demand for the final product, other things constant, the more elastic the demand for the resources used to produce it.*

THE RESOURCE'S SHARE OF PRODUCTION COST. *The greater the resource's share of the total production cost, other things constant, the more elastic the demand for that resource.* For example, because the cost of lumber represents a relatively large share of the cost of housing, an increase in the price of lumber increases the cost of new housing by a relatively large amount, thereby reducing the quantity of housing demanded by a relatively large amount and, in turn, reducing the quantity of lumber demanded by a relatively large amount. On the other hand, the cost of electrical wire makes up only a tiny fraction of the cost of new housing. Therefore a rise in the price of electrical wire will have little impact on the price of housing and, consequently, on the quantity of housing demanded. Since the quantity of housing demanded changes little, neither does the quantity of wire demanded for housing construction. So the demand for electrical wire will be less price elastic than the demand for lumber.

EASE OF SUBSTITUTION. Earlier we mentioned that some resources are substitutes. *The more abundant and the more similar the substitutes are in production, the more easily one resource can be substituted for another and the more elastic the demand for substitute resources.* For example, to the baker, white eggs and brown eggs are virtually identical, so an increase in the relative price of white eggs, holding the price of brown eggs constant, will increase the baker's demand for brown eggs. The demand for white eggs is price elastic, as is the demand for brown eggs. On the other hand, there are no close substitutes for jet fuel, so an increase in its price will not cause airlines to switch to other forms of energy, at least not in the short run. Thus, the demand for jet fuel is relatively inelastic in the short run.

TIME. Finally, as with consumer demand, *the longer the time period under consideration, the greater the elasticity of demand for the resource.* For example, if the price of steel increases, auto manufacturers cannot quickly switch to substitutes. Over time, however, they can change production processes and perhaps redesign cars so that the quantity of steel required for auto production declines. Or consider the nation's experience with oil. Price increases in the 1970s had relatively little effect on the quantity of oil demanded in the short run. In the long run, however, higher oil prices reduced the growth in demand for oil. More fuel-efficient car motors and jet engines were developed, and coal was substituted for oil in electricity generation.

In summary, other things constant, the price elasticity of demand for a resource will be greater (1) the greater the price elasticity of demand for the final product, (2) the greater the resource cost as a fraction of the total cost of the final product, (3) the more substitutes there are for the resource, and (4) the longer the time period under consideration.

Hiring Resources as a Price Searcher

Determining optimal resource use for a price taker in the resource market is quite straightforward because the firm's marginal resource cost is constant and equal to the market price. But what if a firm hires such a large fraction of the available resource that the quantity the firm can hire depends on the resource price. If the quantity of the resource supplied to the firm depends on the price the firm pays, the firm is a **resource price searcher.** A resource price searcher is also called a *monopsonist.* A resource price searcher typically faces an upward-sloping resource supply curve—that is, the quantity of the resource supplied to the firm increases only if the firm pays more for each additional unit of the resource.

Resource price searcher A firm that faces an upward-sloping supply curve for a resource

Example Coca-Cola is the world's largest buyer of sugar. Procter & Gamble and Unilever are both price searchers in the market for soap dies.

Teaching Tip Marginal resource cost rises twice as fast as the resource price. In Exhibit 7, a $1 wage increase leads to a $2 increase in marginal resource cost.

Point to Stress Although the same profit-maximization rule is followed by resource price takers and resource price searchers, the results differ. In Exhibit 7, a market occupied by resource price takers would hire more workers (5 rather than 4) and pay a higher wage ($12 rather than $11), as indicated by the intersection of the resource supply and marginal revenue product curves.

Suppose the firm is an aircraft manufacturer that employs such a large proportion of the total supply of aeronautical engineers that the quantity of labor supplied to the firm depends on the wage the firm offers. The first column in Exhibit 7(a) lists the quantity of labor hired, and the second column shows the wage the firm must pay to attract that quantity of labor to the firm. Together, the first two columns represent the *supply of labor schedule* faced by a firm that is a price searcher in the resource market. This schedule is presented in the form of a *supply of labor curve* in Exhibit 7(b). A hypothetical marginal revenue product schedule is listed in the final column in Exhibit 7(a) and is plotted as the marginal revenue product curve in Exhibit 7(b).

Because the labor supply curve slopes upward, the firm must pay a higher wage in order to increase the quantity supplied. So in order to hire another unit of labor, the firm must increase the wage paid for all units of labor, not just the marginal unit. For example, according to the supply schedule, the firm can hire one unit of labor when the wage is $8 and two units when the wage is $9, so the wage must increase by $1 to hire a second unit of labor. But the total cost increases by $10 when a second unit is hired ($9 for the second unit plus $1 more for the first unit). Thus, the *marginal resource cost* of the second unit is $10, which exceeds the *wage* of $9. *If the firm is a resource price searcher, the marginal resource cost of an additional unit of labor exceeds the wage required to attract that additional unit.*

Likewise, if the firm decides to hire 3 units of labor, it must pay $10 per unit, for a total labor cost of $30, so the marginal resource cost of the third unit is $12. Compare columns (2) and (4) in Exhibit 7(a) and you will see that after the first unit of labor is hired, the marginal resource cost exceeds the wage, and the difference grows as more labor is employed (you could think of the wage as the *average* factor cost). This growing difference is reflected most clearly in Exhibit 7(b) by the growing distance between the marginal resource cost curve and the labor supply curve (which is the average factor cost curve).

The firm maximizes profit by hiring additional units of a resource as long as these marginal units add more to revenue than to cost. Specifically, the

EXHIBIT 7

Resource Demand for a Firm Hiring a Resource as a Price Searcher

(a) MRC and MRP schedules

Units of Variable Resource (1)	Wage (2)	Total Resource Cost (*TRC*) (3)	Marginal Resource Cost (*MRC*) (4)	Hypothetical Marginal Revenue Product (*MRP*) (5)
0	—	$ 0	—	—
1	$ 8	8	$ 8	$20
2	9	18	10	18
3	10	30	12	16
4	11	44	14	14
5	12	60	16	12
6	13	78	18	10
7	14	98	20	8
8	15	120	22	6

(b) MRC and MRP curves

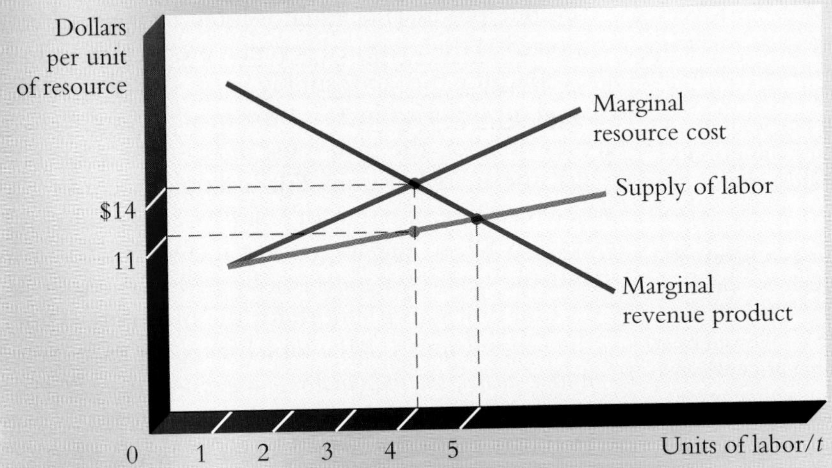

A resource price searcher faces an upward-sloping supply curve. The marginal resource cost lies above that supply curve. The firm will hire the resource up to the point where the marginal revenue product equals the marginal resource cost (4 units) and will pay a wage based on the resource supply curve ($11).

firm hires additional resources until *the marginal resource cost equals the marginal revenue product.* In Exhibit 7, the marginal resource cost curve and the marginal revenue product curve both equal $14 where 4 units of labor are employed. The wage required to call forth that level of employment is $11 per hour. Thus, *for a resource price searcher, the marginal revenue product exceeds the equilibrium resource price.* For a resource price searcher in the labor market, a worker's marginal revenue exceeds the equilibrium wage.

Summarizing Resource Markets

Let's compare a resource price taker and a resource price searcher. A resource price taker is depicted in Exhibit 8(a), where the marginal resource cost curve is a horizontal line drawn at the market-determined resource price. A resource price searcher is depicted in Exhibit 8(b), where the marginal resource cost curve is an upward-sloping line drawn above the resource supply curve. Recall that the resource price-searcher's marginal resource cost curve exceeds the resource supply curve because the firm, in order to attract more units of the resources, must pay *all* units of the resource the higher supply price.

In each panel the firm's marginal revenue product curve equals the change in total revenue divided by the change in the quantity of the resource employed. This holds whether the firm is a price taker or a price searcher in the product market. Regardless of the nature of the resource market or the product market, *the profit-maximizing quantity of the resource is determined where the marginal revenue product curve intersects the marginal resource cost curve.* Note that when the firm is a resource price taker, the equilibrium price of the resource equals the marginal resource cost, but when the firm is a resource price searcher the equilibrium price of the resource is less than the marginal resource cost.

Optimal Use: More than One Resource

As long as the marginal revenue product exceeds the marginal resource cost, the firm can increase profit by employing more of the resource. Regardless of the resource, the firm will increase resource use until the marginal revenue product just equals the marginal resource cost, or

$$MRP = MRC$$

Rearranging terms yields:

$$\frac{MRP}{MRC} = 1$$

EXHIBIT 8

Resource Market Equilibrium Under Alternative Market Conditions

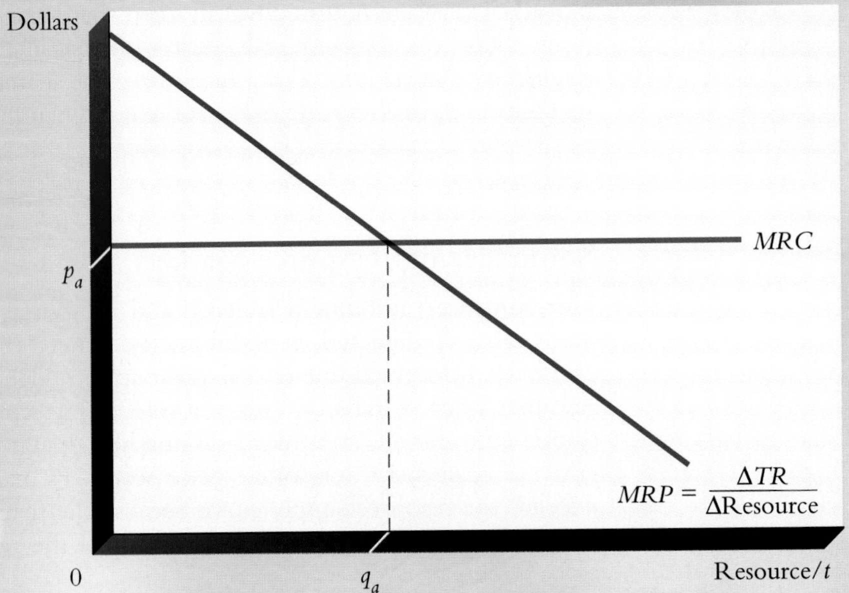

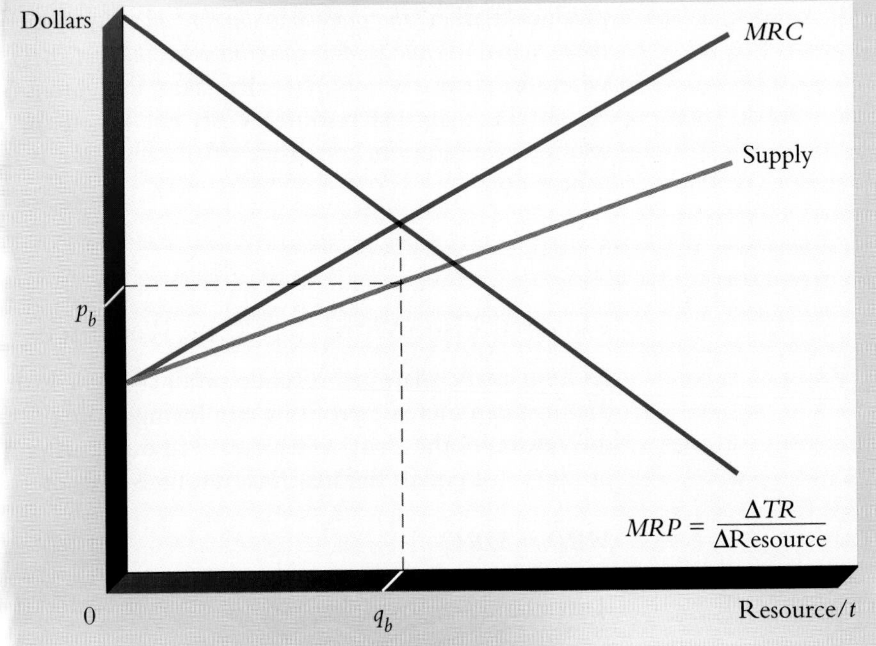

Teaching Tip This analysis addresses the economic question of how goods and services should be produced.

And this holds for each resource employed. Thus, *to maximize profit the firm should employ resources so that the last dollar spent on each resource yields one dollar's worth of marginal revenue product*. In other words, the last dollar spent on each resource should yield the same marginal revenue product. To see the logic of this equality, suppose the marginal revenue product from the last dollar's worth of labor employed exceeds the marginal revenue product from the last dollar's worth of capital employed. Since the marginal productivity of labor exceeds the marginal productivity of capital, the firm's profits could be increased by shifting some spending from capital to labor. Spending will shift from capital to labor until the last dollar spent on each resource yields a dollar's worth of marginal revenue product. Put another way, profit-maximizing employers will hire any resource up to the point at which the last unit hired adds as much to total revenue as it does to total cost.

At the beginning of the chapter, we asked why the buildings at the center of Chicago are taller than those farther out. One rule of optimal resource use is that a firm combines resources in a way that conserves the use of the most expensive resource. Land is more expensive at the center of a large city because of the convenience of the location. Land and capital are to a large extent substitutes in the production of building space. When land is more expensive, builders substitute additional capital for land, building up instead of out. Hence buildings are taller when they are closer to the center of the city and are tallest in cities where the land is relatively most expensive. Buildings in Chicago and New York are taller than buildings in Salt Lake City and Tucson, for example.

The high price of land in metropolitan areas has other implications for the efficient employment of resources. For example, in New York City, as in many large cities, vending carts on street corners specialize in everything from hot dogs to doughnuts. Why are there so many carts? Consider the resources used to supply hot dogs: land, labor, capital, entrepreneurial ability, plus intermediate goods such as hot dogs, buns, and other ingredients. Which of these do you suppose is most expensive in New York City? As we have noted, land there is very costly. Retail space along Fifth Avenue rents for as much as $400 a year per square foot. Since a hot dog cart requires about three square yards to operate, it could cost more than $10,000 a year to rent the required space. Aside from the necessary public permits, however, space on the public sidewalk is free to hot dog vendors. Profit-maximizing street vendors substitute public sidewalk space that is free to them for costly commercial rental space.

Distribution of Resource Earnings

One way to develop an overview of resource markets is to consider how income is distributed among resource owners: what share of the income goes to suppliers of labor and what share goes to suppliers of each of the other resources? In this final section we will examine how the earnings in the United States as a whole are allocated among resource owners.

EXHIBIT 9

Functional Distribution of Income: Percentage Share of Each Source of Income

Time Period	Wages and Salaries (1)	Proprietors' Income (2)	Corporate Profits (3)	Interest (4)	Rent (5)
1900–1909	55.0	23.7	6.8	5.5	9.0
1910–1919	53.6	23.8	9.1	5.4	8.1
1920–1929	60.0	17.5	7.8	6.2	7.7
1930–1939	67.5	14.8	4.0	8.7	5.0
1940–1948	64.6	17.2	11.9	3.1	3.3
1949–1958	67.3	13.9	12.5	2.9	3.4
1959–1970	70.9	10.6	11.7	3.7	3.1
1971–1979	74.6	7.4	9.8	6.3	1.9
1980–1989	73.0	7.9	7.9	10.2	1.0
1990–1992	74.4	8.0	7.9	9.4	0.3

Sources: Irving Kravis, "Income Distribution: Functional Shares," *International Encyclopedia of Social Sciences,* vol. 7 (New York: Macmillan Co. and Free Press, 1968), 134; *Economic Report of the President,* January 1993. Figures after 1970 are not fully consistent with prior figures, but they convey a reasonably accurate picture of income trends.

Teaching Tip This discussion of the *functional distribution of income* in part addresses the economic question of for whom to produce goods and services.

Exhibit 9 shows the proportion of national income that goes to (1) wages and salaries, (2) proprietors' (business owners') income, (3) corporate profits, (4) interest, and (5) rent. Over time, wages and salaries have claimed by far the largest share of national income, accounting most recently for about three-fourths of the total. But this understates the proportion going to labor, because a portion of proprietors' income consists of labor income as well; the proprietor of a corner store typically works long hours, and much of what is counted as the proprietor's income is in fact compensation for the proprietor's labor. Even some profit is a return on entrepreneurial ability, which includes human ingenuity if not labor as such.

Exhibit 9 also shows the sharp decline over time in the share of national income received by proprietors. A generation ago the income received by Mom and Pop from their corner store was counted as proprietors' income; the people who ring up your Pepsi today typically earn salaries and wages as employees of a corporate chain of convenience stores, such as 7-Eleven.

One problem with Exhibit 9 is that the categories and definitions do not neatly match the definitions we have used. We already noted that proprietors' income includes labor income. Additionally, the column headings Corporate Profits, Interest, and Rent do not correspond closely to the terms *profit, interest,* and *economic rent* as they are used by economists. Yet the definitions in Exhibit 9 bear enough similarity to the way economists view the world to make the table of interest to us. *The most important conclusion to draw from Exhibit 9 is that labor's share of total income is relatively large and has grown during this century.* This conclusion still holds even if the definitions of some other income categories do not exactly match our economic definitions.

CONCLUSION

The framework we have developed focuses on the marginal analysis of resource use to determine the equilibrium resource price and quantity. The firm uses each resource up to the point where the marginal revenue product of that resource equals its marginal resource cost. The objective of profit maximization ensures that firms will employ the least-cost combination of resources and will thereby use the economy's resources most efficiently. Using the least-cost combination of resources implies that the last dollar spent on each resource yields a marginal revenue product exactly equal to one dollar. If this were not so, firms could lower their cost by adjusting their resource mix.

Although the focus has been on the marginal productivity of each resource, we should keep in mind that resources combine to produce output, so the marginal productivity of a particular resource will depend in part on what other resources are being employed. For example, a baseball player whose teammates get on base more frequently will have more runs-batted-in during the season and will thereby be considered more productive.

SUMMARY

1. Firms demand resources to maximize profits. Households supply resources to maximize utility. The profit-maximizing goals of firms and the utility-maximizing goals of households are harmonized through voluntary exchange in resource markets.

2. Because the value of any resource depends on the value of what it produces, the demand for a resource is a derived demand—derived from the value of the final product. A resource demand curve slopes downward because firms are more willing and able to increase the quantity demanded as the price of a resource declines. A resource supply curve tends to slope upward because resource owners are more willing and able to increase the quantity supplied as their reward for supplying the resource increases.

3. Differentials in the market prices of similar resources classify them into two broad categories. Some price differentials trigger the reallocation of resources to equalize prices for similar resources. Other price differentials do not precipitate a shift in resources among uses because of a lack of resource mobility, differences in the inherent quality of the resources, differences in the time and money involved in developing the necessary skill, and differences in nonmonetary aspects of the job.

4. Resource earnings can be divided into (1) earnings that reflect the resource's opportunity cost, the amount that must be paid to get a resource owner to supply that resource to a particular use, and (2) economic rent, that portion of a resource's total earnings that exceeds the resource's opportunity cost. If a resource has no alternative uses, earnings consist entirely of economic rent; if a resource has other valuable uses, opportunity cost predominates.

5. A firm's demand for a resource equals the resource's marginal revenue product, which is the change in total revenue that results from each one-unit increase in the amount of the resource employed, other things constant. If a firm sells output in a perfectly competitive market, the marginal revenue product curve declines because of diminishing marginal returns. If a firm has some market power in the product market, the marginal revenue product curve declines both because of diminishing marginal returns and because the product price must fall to sell more output.

6. The demand curve for a resource will shift to the right if there is an increase either in its marginal physical product or in the price of the product produced with the resource. An increase in the use of a complementary resource or a decrease in the use of a substitute resource will increase a resource's marginal productivity.

7. The marginal resource cost is the change in total cost resulting from employing one more unit of the resource. If a firm hires the resources in a competitive resource market, the firm is a resource price taker and has no control over resource prices. If the quantity of the resource supplied to the firm depends on the resource price, the firm is a resource price searcher. Both a resource price taker and a resource price searcher maximize profits by employing each resource to the point where the marginal revenue product equals the marginal resource cost.

8. During this century wages and salaries have grown as a percentage of total resource income, and they now account for about three-quarters of the total. Proprietors' income and rent have fallen as a percentage of the total.

Questions and Problems

1. (Resource Demand) How might the elasticity of demand for a resource depend on the substitutability among resources in the production process?

2. (Supply of Resources) Suppose that worker A speaks only German and worker B speaks only English; otherwise they are identical in their skills. Consider the relative elasticities of supply for their labor in
   a. Germany.
   b. the United States.
   c. all other places.

3. (Resource Demand) Suppose that good A has a perfectly inelastic demand. Would the resources used to produce good A have to have a perfectly inelastic demand? Why or why not?

4. (Opportunity Cost Versus Economic Rent) "If the supply of a resource has unitary elasticity, opportunity cost will be equal to economic rent at every resource price." Evaluate this assertion.

5. (Diminishing Returns) To have diminishing returns, one must add a variable resource to a set of fixed resources. Why must we assume that some fixed resources are being used?

6. (Product Price Taker's Marginal Revenue Product) If a competitive firm hires another full-time worker, total output will increase from 100 units to 110 units per month. Suppose the wage is $200 per week. What market price will allow the additional worker to be hired?

7. (Competitive Resource Market) Explain why a competitive resource market requires that the resource price (that is, the wage rate) be equal to the marginal resource cost to the firm.

8. (Resource Price Searcher) Explain why a price searcher in the product market need not be a price searcher in the resource market. Are all resource price searchers necessarily also product price searchers? Why or why not?

9. (Resource Price Searcher) Why must a resource price searcher pay a higher wage to all of its workers in order to hire an additional worker?

10. (Complements in Production) Many countries are predominantly agrarian. How would the amount of fertilizer available affect the marginal product, and thus the income, of the farmers in such countries?

11. (Resource Demand) Use the following data to answer the questions below.

Units of Labor	*Units of Output*
0	0
1	7
2	13
3	18
4	22
5	25

   a. Calculate the marginal revenue product (*MRP*) for each unit of labor if output sells for $3 per unit.
   b. If labor costs $15 per hour, how much labor will get hired?
   c. Construct the demand curve for labor based on the above data and the $3 per unit output price.
   d. Using your answer to part (b), compare total revenue to the total amount paid to labor. Who gets the difference?
   e. What would happen to your answers to parts (b) and (c) if the price of output increased to $5 per unit?

12. (Economic Rents) Top athletes in baseball, football, basketball, and hockey earn considerably more than a million dollars per year. Yet in many cases their opportunity costs are far lower. Explain the magnitude of their economic rents in terms of the demand for and supply of their services.

13. (Exploitation of Labor) Labor can be said to be exploited if it is not paid what it is worth.
   a. How should "worth" be measured?
   b. Does exploitation occur when labor is hired by a price searcher in the product market? by a resource price searcher? Explain using diagrams of the labor market.

14. (Efficient Resource Use) Earlier you learned that a firm combines resources efficiently by choosing the combination for which the marginal rate of technical substitution between resources equals the price ratio of the resources. Show that this principle is formally equivalent to the efficiency rule presented in this chapter, namely, that each resource should be hired until its marginal revenue product equals its price.

15. (Distribution of Income) How might technological advances affect the functional distribution of income in an economy?

16. (Distribution of Income) Why is land reform essential to bring about a more equitable functional distribution of income in some countries? What dangers exist for countries with very unbalanced distributions?

17. (Resource Demand) The profit-maximizing rule for a competitive firm in the short run is to produce where the product price equals the short-run marginal cost. Show that this rule is formally equivalent to hiring the variable resource (i.e., labor) to the level where its marginal resource cost (i.e., wage) equals its marginal revenue product.

18. (Rents Versus Opportunity Cost) On-the-job work experience typically enhances one's productivity in a particular job. If one's salary increases to reflect this higher productivity, is the increase in opportunity cost or economic rent?

19. (Resource Market Equilibrium) In Chapter 21, you learned about increasing-cost competitive industries. Are firms in such an industry price searchers in the resource markets? Why or why not?

20. (Resource Demand) Suppose that a constant-cost competitive industry experiences an increase in demand for its product.
   a. Show what happens to the market for the variable resource in the short run.
   b. What happens to the mix of resources used in the long run?

21. (Demand for Resources) Fluctuations in demand for industries using specialized resources requiring graduate training (e.g., college professors) will tend to create greater fluctuations in entry-level salaries than would occur in industries that do not use specialized resources. Why?

22. (Demand for Resources) Show, using a diagram of demand for architects, why the reduction in the demand for real estate reduces total income levels for the non-architect resources at architectural firms as well as for architects.

CHAPTER 25

HUMAN RESOURCES: LABOR AND ENTREPRENEURIAL ACTIVITY

Labor Supply

What determines the wage structure in the economy? You don't need a course in economics to figure out why corporate presidents earn more than file clerks, or why heart surgeons earn more than registered nurses. But why do lawyers earn more than accountants and school teachers more than auto mechanics? Will we observe a similar pattern in the year 2000? You can be sure of one thing: supply and demand play a central role in the wage structure.

We have already examined what determines the demand for resources. Demand depends on the resource's marginal revenue product. In the first half of this chapter we will focus more on the supply of labor, then bring supply and demand together to arrive at the market wage. In the second half of the chapter we consider another human resource: entrepreneurial ability. As we will see, entrepreneurial ability is in many ways the most important resource for determining the wealth of nations, but it is also the most elusive. Topics discussed in this chapter include

- Theory of time allocation
- The backward-bending supply curve for labor
- Nonwage factors and labor supply
- Why wages differ
- Entrepreneurial ability and profit
- Theories of profit

LABOR SUPPLY

Teaching Tip Just as the demand curve for a good is derived from the preferences and (income) abilities of households, the supply curve of labor is derived from the preferences and (productive) capabilities of households.

Point to Stress Wage rates are assumed to include employee benefits. The nonmonetary aspects of each labor market are held constant.

You, as a resource supplier, have a labor supply curve for each of the many possible uses of your labor. To some markets your quantity supplied is zero over the realistic range of wages. We say "over the realistic range" because if the wage were high enough, say, $1 million per hour, there might be no activity to which you would not supply labor. In those cases where your quantity supplied is zero over the realistic range of wages, it may be because you are *willing* but *unable* to perform the job (for example, airline pilot, professional golfer, novelist), or it may be because you are *able* but *unwilling* to do so (for example, soldier of fortune, gym teacher, demolition-derby driver).

Therefore you have as many supply curves as there are labor markets, just as you have as many demand curves as there are markets for goods and services. Your labor supply to each market depends, among other things, on your taste for the job in question and the opportunity cost of your time—how much you could earn from other activities. Your supply curve to each particular labor market is developed under the assumption that the wage rates in other markets where you could supply your labor are constant, just as each demand curve is developed under the assumption that prices of related goods are constant.

Labor Supply and Utility Maximization

Recall the definition of economics: it is the study of how individuals choose to use their scarce resources to produce, exchange, and consume products in an attempt to satisfy their unlimited wants. Individuals attempt to use their limited resources so as to maximize their utility. Two sources of utility are of special interest to us in this chapter: the consumption of goods and services and the enjoyment of leisure. The utility derived from consuming goods and services is obvious and serves as the foundation of consumer demand. Leisure time spent relaxing, sleeping, eating, and in recreational activities also represents a valuable source of utility. Leisure can usually be viewed as a normal good that, like other goods, is subject to the law of diminishing marginal utility. Thus, the more leisure time you have, the less you value each additional unit of leisure. Sometimes you may have so much leisure that you "have time on your hands" and are "just killing time." As that sage of the comic page Garfield once lamented, "Spare time would be more fun if I had less to spare."

Teaching Tip Since leisure has diminishing marginal utility, its opposite (work) is subject to *increasing* marginal *dis*utility.

Market work Time sold as labor in return for a money wage

Nonmarket work Time spent producing goods and services in the home or acquiring an education

THREE USES OF TIME. Some of you are at a point in your careers when you possess few resources other than time. Time is the raw material of life. You can use your time in three ways. First, you can undertake **market work**—selling your time in the labor market in return for money. When you offer yourself for employment, you surrender control over the use of your time to the employer in return for a wage. Second, you can undertake what we will call **nonmarket work**—using time to produce your own goods and services. Nonmarket work includes the time you spend doing your laundry, preparing your meals, or typing your term paper. Nonmarket work also includes the time spent acquiring skills and education that enhance your future productivity. Although the time spent attending class, reading, and studying provides little immediate payoff, you are betting that the knowledge and perspective you gain will be rewarded in the future. Third, you can convert time directly into **leisure**—nonwork uses of your time.

Leisure Time spent on nonwork activities

WORK AND UTILITY. Unless you are one of the fortunate few, work is not a pure source of utility, as it often generates some boredom, discomfort, or aggravation. In short, time spent working can be "a real pain," a source of *disutility*—the opposite of utility. You work nonetheless because the pay allows you to afford goods and services. You expect that the utility generated by the goods and services made possible through work will exceed the disutility of that work. Thus, the *net utility of work*—the utility of the consumption made possible through work minus the disutility of the work itself—often makes work an attractive use of your time. In the case of market work, you earn wages, which are used to buy goods and services. In the case of nonmarket work, you either produce goods and services directly, as in making yourself a tuna sandwich, or you invest your time in education with an expectation of higher future earnings and higher future consumption.

Teaching Tip The diminishing marginal utility of consumption combined with the increasing marginal disutility of work leads to diminishing net marginal utility of work.

Teaching Tip If the expected net marginal utility of the last unit of time spent in each activity is not identical, total utility can be increased by reallocating time from the activity with the lower expected net marginal utility to activities with higher expected net marginal utilities.

UTILITY MAXIMIZATION. Within the limits of a twenty-four-hour day, seven days a week, you balance your time among market work, nonmarket work, and leisure so as to maximize utility. As a rational consumer, *you attempt to maximize utility by allocating your time so that the expected marginal utility of the last unit of time spent in each activity is identical.* Thus, in the course of a week, the marginal utility of the last hour of leisure equals the net marginal utility of the last hour of market work, which equals the net marginal utility of the last hour of nonmarket work. In the case of time devoted to acquiring skills, you must consider the marginal utility expected from the future increase in earnings that will result from your enhanced productivity. We will develop a way of analyzing choices involving future production and consumption in a later chapter, when we consider investing in human capital more explicitly.

Perhaps at this point you are saying, "Wait a minute. I don't allocate my time with that sort of precision or logic. I just sort of bump along, doing what feels good." Economists do not claim that you are even aware of making such marginal calculations. But as a rational decision maker, you allocate your scarce time to satisfy your wants, or to maximize utility. And utility maximization, or "doing what feels good," implies that you act "as if" you allocated your time to derive the same expected net marginal utility from the last unit of time spent in each alternative use.

You probably have settled into a rough plan (for meals, work, entertainment, study, sleep, and so on) that fits your overall objectives and appears reasonably rational. This plan is probably in constant flux as you make expected and unexpected adjustments in the use of your time. For example, this morning you may have slept later than you planned because you stayed up late watching television; last weekend you may have failed to crack a book, despite good intentions. Over a week or a month, however, your use of time is roughly in line with an allocation that maximizes utility as you perceive it. Put another way, given the various constraints on your time, money, energy, and other resources, if you could change your use of time to increase your utility, you would do so. Nobody is stopping you. You may emphasize immediate gratification, but that's your choice and you bear the consequences.

This time-allocation process ensures that at the margin the expected utility from the last unit of time spent in each activity is equal. Because information is costly and because the future is uncertain, you sometimes make mistakes in allocating time; you do not always get what you expect. Some mistakes are minor, such as going to see a movie that proves to be a waste of time. But other mistakes can be costly. For example, you may now be preparing for a field of study that will be too crowded by the time you graduate, or you may now be acquiring skills that will become obsolete because of changing technology no bigger than the word "chip."

Example Professional athletes can now compete in many Olympic sports. Allowing pros in the Olympics became necessary in order to encourage the participation of the world's top athletes in sports (such as basketball and tennis) in which a high-paying professional circuit had sharply increased the opportunity cost of maintaining amateur standing long enough to compete in the quadrennial Olympics.

IMPLICATIONS. The model of time allocation that has been described thus far has several implications for individual choice. First, consider the choice between market and nonmarket work. The higher your market wage, other things constant, the greater the opportunity cost of nonmarket work. Hence individuals with a high market wage will spend less time in nonmarket activities, other things constant. High-earning surgeons are less likely to mow their own lawns than are lower-paid butchers. By the same logic, the higher the expected earnings right out of high school, other things constant, the higher the opportunity cost of attending college. Most young, successful movie stars do not go to college, and the most promising college athletes "turn pro" before finishing college.

Alternatively, the more productive people are in nonmarket work, other things constant, the less they will buy from the market. Those who are proficient at preparing meals or who are handy around the house will, other things constant, do more for themselves and hire fewer of these services in the market. And those who find education useful and productive will be more inclined to spend time in school. Conversely, those who find boiling water difficult will eat out more frequently, and those who are all thumbs around the house will hire various services; both will be more inclined to supply their labor to market work rather than to nonmarket work. In summary, *utility maximization implies that individuals will use nonmarket work to produce those goods they can provide more cheaply than the market can.*

Example A reduction in the opportunity cost of nonmarket work makes an individual more likely to allocate time to such activities. Therefore, employees whose employers pay all or part of the cost of tuition are more likely to attend some summer school classes.

Wages and Individual Labor Supply

To breathe life into the time-allocation problem, consider your choices for the summer. If you can afford to, you can take the summer off, spending it entirely on leisure, as perhaps a fitting reward for a rough academic year. Or you can supply your time to market work. Or you can undertake nonmarket work, such as cleaning the basement or attending summer school. As a rational decision maker, you will select that combination of leisure, market work, and nonmarket work that you expect will maximize your utility. And the optimal combination is likely to involve allocating some time to each activity. For example, even if you work during the summer, you might still consider taking one or two summer courses.

Suppose that the only summer job available is some form of unskilled labor, such as working in a fast food restaurant or for the town parks department. For simplicity, let's assume that you view all available jobs to be equally attractive (or unattractive) in terms of their nonmonetary aspects such as working conditions, working hours, and so on. (These nonmonetary aspects will be discussed in the next section.) Since in your view there is no difference among these unskilled jobs, the most important question for you in deciding how much market labor to supply is, what is the market wage for unskilled labor?

Suppose the wage is $5 per hour, just above the minimum wage. At a wage that low, you may decide to work around the house, attend summer school full-time, travel across the country, take a really long nap, or perhaps do some combination of these. In any event, you supply no market labor at such a low wage. The market wage must rise to $6 per hour before you will supply any market labor. Suppose that at a wage of $6 per hour you supply 20 hours per week, perhaps taking fewer summer courses and shorter naps.

Teaching Tip Just as the demand curve for a good measures the marginal value of additional units of consumption, the supply curve of market work measures the value of the marginal disutility of providing labor for market work, or its marginal disvalue. In Exhibit 1, the marginal disvalue of market work has a minimum of $6.

What if the wage increases to $7 per hour, everything else held constant? The higher wage raises the opportunity cost of the time you spend in other activities, so you substitute market work for other uses of your time. You decide to work 30 hours per week, earning a total of $210 a week. At $8 per hour you are willing to cut more into studying or surfing, increasing your quantity of market labor supplied to 40 hours per week, for weekly earnings of $320. At $9 per hour you provide 48 hours of market labor per week, earning $432 per week, and at $10 per hour you increase your quantity supplied to 55 hours, for $550 per week. At a wage of $11 you go to 60 hours per week; you are starting to earn serious money—$660 per week.

If the wage is $12 per hour, a wage you consider to be very attractive indeed, you decide to cut back to 58 hours per week, and you earn $696 per week—more than when the wage was $11 per hour. Finally, if the wage is $13 per hour, you cut your hours supplied to 55 per week and earn $715. To explain why you may eventually reduce your quantity of market labor supplied as the wage rate rises, we must analyze in more detail the impact of wage increases on the utility-maximizing allocation of time among leisure, nonmarket work, and market work.

Teaching Tip See Chapter 3 for a review of substitution and income effects of price changes.

SUBSTITUTION AND INCOME EFFECTS. An increase in the wage rate affects your choice between market work and other uses of your time in two ways. First, at a higher wage, each hour of work buys more goods and services, so a higher wage provides you with an incentive to work more—to substitute work for other activities that now have a higher opportunity cost. This effect is referred to as the *substitution effect* of a wage increase; it encourages you to allocate more time to market work. Something else also happens as the wage rate increases, however. A higher wage means a higher income for the same number of hours, and a higher income means that you demand more of all normal goods. Since leisure is a normal good, a higher income increases your demand for leisure, thereby reducing your allocation of time to market work. The higher wage rate therefore has an income effect, which tends to reduce the quantity of market labor supplied.

Consequently, as the wage goes up, the substitution effect causes you to supply more time to market work and the income effect causes you to supply less time to market work and to demand more leisure time. In the case of your summer job possibilities, the substitution effect exceeds the income effect for wage rates of up to $11 per hour, resulting in a greater quantity of market labor supplied as the wage rises to $11. When the wage hits $12 per hour, however, the income effect exceeds the substitution effect, causing a net reduction in the quantity of labor supplied to market work.

Backward-Bending Labor Supply Curve. The hypothetical market labor supply curve that we have described is presented in Exhibit 1. As you can see, this supply curve slopes upward until a wage of $11 per hour

Exhibit 1

Individual Labor Supply Curve for Market Work

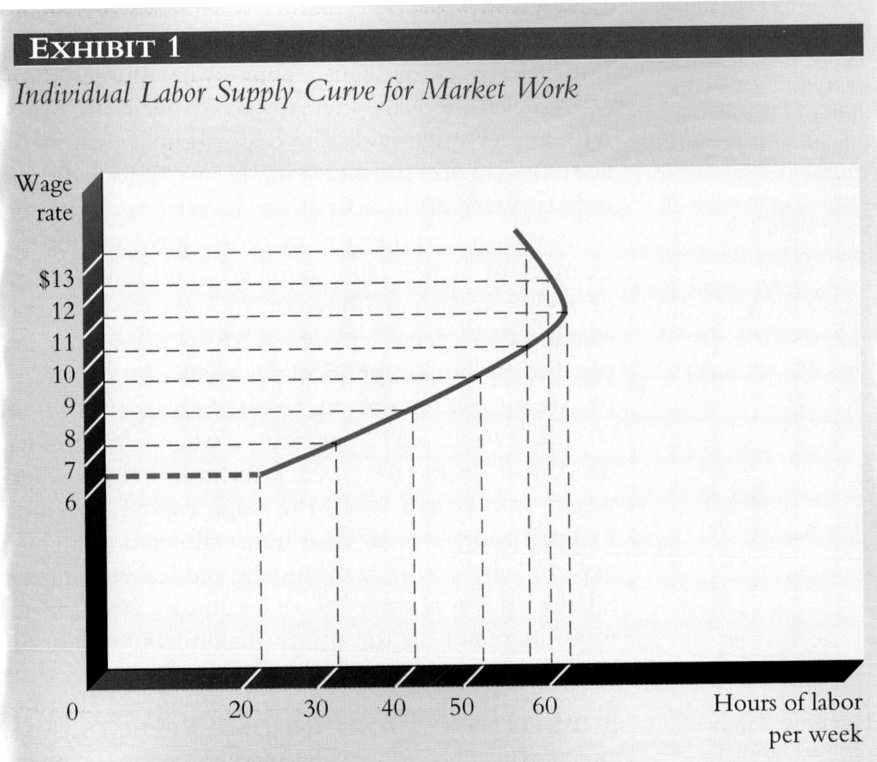

When the substitution effect of a wage increase outweighs the income effect, the quantity of labor supplied increases with the wage rate. At some wage (here, above $11), the income effect dominates. Above that wage, the supply curve bends backward; further increases in the wage rate reduce the quantity of labor supplied.

Backward-bending supply curve of labor Occurs when the income effect of a higher wage dominates the substitution effect of a higher wage

is reached, and then it begins to bend backward. The **backward-bending supply curve** gets its shape from the fact that the income effect of a higher wage eventually dominates the substitution effect, so the quantity of market labor supplied at some point declines with an increase in the wage. We often see evidence of a backward-bending supply curve, particularly among high-wage individuals, who reduce their work and consume more leisure. For example, doctors often play golf on weekday afternoons. Entertainers typically perform less as they become more successful. Unknown bands play hours for hardly anything; famous bands play less for more. In fact, the income effect of rising real wages has been used to explain the declining average work week in the United States. In 1860 the average work week was about 66 hours; today it is less than 40 hours.

Flexibility of Hours Worked. The model we have been describing assumes that workers have some control over the number of hours they work per week. Opportunities for part-time work and overtime allow workers to put together their most preferred quantity of hours (for instance, 30 hours in a restaurant and 15 at the college bookstore). Workers also have some control over the timing and length of their vacations. More generally, individuals can control the length of time they stay in school, when and to what extent they enter the work force, and when they choose to retire. Thus, workers actually have more control over the number of hours worked than you might think if you focused on the standard work week of, say, 40 hours per week.

Example An increase in wages for electrical engineers would lead to a decrease in the supply of civil engineers.

Nonwage Determinants of Labor Supply

The quantity of labor supplied to a particular market depends on a variety of factors other than the wage rate, just as the quantity of a good demanded depends on factors other than the price. As already mentioned, the quantity of labor supplied to a particular market depends on wage levels in other labor markets. The higher the wages in other labor markets, other things constant, the less will be supplied to the labor market in question. So what are the nonwage factors that shape your labor supply for the summer?

Example Polls and other data indicate that most working mothers work out of economic necessity. Fifty-eight percent of households with children in the United States now have two wage earners, versus only 18.6 percent in 1960. During that same period, the annual payments on a house rose from 14 percent of an average thirty-year-old's gross income to 44 percent.

Other Sources of Income. Although some jobs are rewarding in a variety of nonmonetary ways, the primary reason people work is to earn money to buy goods and services. Thus, your willingness to supply your time to the labor market depends on your income from other sources, including savings, borrowing, family support, and scholarships. If you get abundant financial support from your family or if you receive a generous scholarship, you may feel less need to earn additional income during the summer. "In-kind" income is also important. For example, you may live at home, where room and board are provided, or you may drive one of the family cars. The greater these other sources of income, the less inclined you will be to supply your time to market work, other things constant. More generally, wealthy people have less incentive to work. For example, many lottery winners quit their jobs after hitting the jackpot.

NONMONETARY FACTORS IN GENERAL. Labor is a special kind of resource. Unlike capital and land, which can be provided regardless of the whereabouts of the resource owners, time supplied to market work requires the seller of that time to be on the job. Because the individual must be present to supply labor, such *nonmonetary factors* as the difficulty of the job and the quality of the work environment have important effects on the labor supply. For example, deckhands on fishing boats in the winter waters of the Bering Sea off Alaska earn $3,000 for five days' work, but the temperature seldom gets above zero and daily shifts are twenty-one hours long with only three hours for sleep. Thus far we have been able to ignore the role of nonmonetary factors by assuming no difference in them among the unskilled jobs from which you could choose. Now we will look more realistically at these nonmonetary factors.

JOB AMENITIES. Consider the different job amenities you might encounter. For a college student, a library job that allows you to study much of the time is more attractive than a job that affords no study time. A job in the college cafeteria may allow you to eat all you want at no extra charge; you may find this feature attractive. Some jobs have flexible hours; others impose rigid work schedules. Is the workplace air-conditioned or do you have to sweat it out? The more attractive these on-the-job amenities are to you, the more labor you will be willing to supply to that particular market, other things constant.

One job quality that is generally valued is latitude in the use of time on the job. As we said earlier, when you sell your labor in the resource market, you allow the firm to direct your time. The amount and the intensity of this control depend on the kind of job. If you are like most people, the more closely you are monitored and directed, other things constant, the less willing you are to supply labor to that market. Thus, closely monitored workers must be paid more than those whose jobs allow more personal discretion. College professors typically earn less than those with a similar education in private industry because professors earn non-wage income in the form of "academic freedom."

THE VALUE OF JOB EXPERIENCE. You are more inclined to take a job that provides what potential future employers will view as valuable experience; serving as the assistant treasurer for a nearby business looks better on a resumé than serving hash at the college cafeteria. Some people are willing to accept relatively low wages now because of the promise of higher wages later. For example, new lawyers are eager to fill clerkships for judges, though the pay is low and the hours long, because these positions provide experience that will be valued by potential future employers. Some individuals accept relatively low pay to work for certain government agencies because the experience and the personal contacts developed will be valuable later in the private sector, especially to private-sector employers who deal with that particular government agency. Thus, *the greater the investment value of a position in terms of enhancing your future earning possibilities, the more labor you will supply to that market, other things constant.* Because of the greater supply of labor in such positions, these jobs pay less.

Example Athletes who participate in college sports or in baseball's minor leagues are hoping to gain skills and experience leading to employment in the major leagues.

Taste for Work. Just as consumers' tastes for goods and services differ, tastes for work also differ among labor suppliers. Some people like physical labor and avoid any job that would keep them desk-bound. Some people become surgeons; others can't stand the sight of blood. Some become airline pilots; others are afraid to get on a plane. Many struggling writers and artists could earn more elsewhere, but apparently the satisfaction gained from the creative process offsets the low expected pay. In fact, some people evidently have such a strong preference for certain jobs that they are willing to perform those duties for free, such as auxiliary police officers or volunteer fire fighters.

As with the taste for goods and services, economists do not attempt to explain the taste for work. We simply argue that your supply of labor will be greater to those jobs that are more in accord with your tastes. Voluntary sorting based on tastes allocates workers among different jobs in a way that tends to minimize the disutility associated with work. This is not to say that everyone will be perfectly matched to his or her most preferred occupation. The cost of acquiring information about jobs and the cost of changing jobs may prevent some matchups that might otherwise seem desirable. But in the long run people tend to find jobs that suit them. We are not likely, for example, to find tour directors who hate to travel or zoo keepers who are allergic to animals.

Teaching Tip Job mismatches tend to linger longer during recessions when the risk of seeking an alternative occupation rises.

Market Supply of Labor

Teaching Tip Note that individuals A, B, and C enter the labor market at different wages in Exhibit 2, indicating different net marginal utility schedules.

In the previous section we considered those factors, both monetary and nonmonetary, that influence individual supply. *The market supply of labor to a particular market is the horizontal sum of all the individual supply curves.* The horizontal sum means summing the quantities at each particular price level. If an individual supply curve of labor bends backward, does this mean that the market supply curve of labor also bends backward? Not necessarily. Since different individuals have different opportunity costs and different tastes for work, the bend in the supply curve occurs at different wages for different individuals. And for some individuals the labor supply curve may not bend backwards over the realistic range of wages. Exhibit 2 shows how just three individual labor supply curves can be summed to yield a market supply curve that slopes upward over the realistic range of wages.

Why Wages Differ

Teaching Tip These wage differentials do not lead to a reallocation of resources—they are the equivalent of the permanent differences in resource prices introduced in Chapter 24.

Market forces cause the market supply curve and the market demand curve for labor to combine and yield the equilibrium wage and the equilibrium level of employment in the market. Just as both blades of a pair of scissors contribute equally to cutting cloth, both the supply curve and the demand curve determine the market wage rate. Therefore differences in wages across markets can be traced to differences in labor supply, in labor demand, or in both.

In the previous chapter we discussed the elements that influence the demand for resources, and we examined labor in particular. In brief, *a firm is*

EXHIBIT 2

Deriving the Market Labor Supply Curve

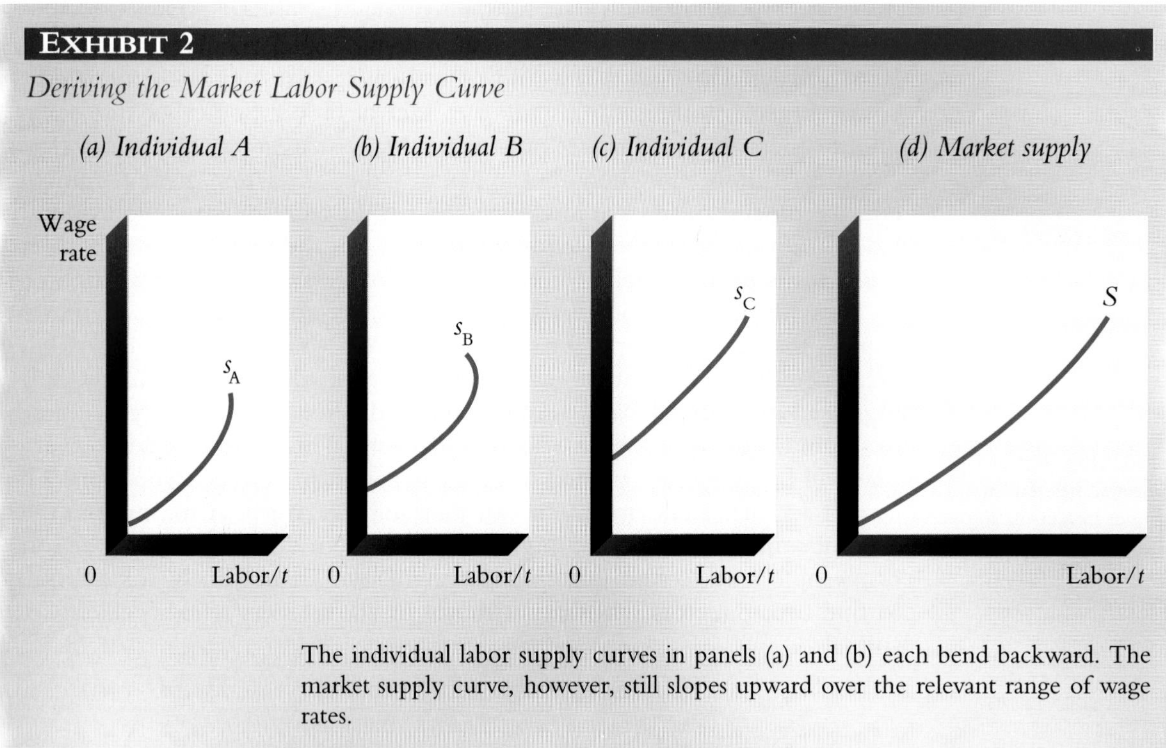

The individual labor supply curves in panels (a) and (b) each bend backward. The market supply curve, however, still slopes upward over the relevant range of wage rates.

willing to hire labor up to the point where labor's marginal revenue product equals its marginal resource cost—that is, where the last unit employed earns the firm just enough to cover its cost. Since we have already discussed the factors that affect the demand for labor, we consider in this section primarily those forces that affect market supply.

DIFFERENCES IN TRAINING, EDUCATION, AND EXPERIENCE. Some jobs pay more than others because they require a long and costly training period. Costly training reduces market supply because fewer individuals are willing to incur such an expense. But the training increases the productivity of each additional unit of labor, thereby increasing the demand for these skills. Reduced supply and increased demand both have a positive effect on the equilibrium wage. Dentists are paid more than dental hygienists primarily because of the great difference in the time and expense required to train for the two jobs. More generally, workers are paid more as they gain job experience if this added experience increases their marginal productivity.

Example After winning two National League most-valuable-player awards in three years and coming in second on the ballots in the middle year, Barry Bonds became a free agent in 1992. He then signed a record six-year $43.75 million contract with the San Francisco Giants.

DIFFERENCES IN ABILITY. Because they are more able and talented, some individuals are paid more than others with identical training and education levels. Two lawyers may have had identical educations, but one earns twice as much as the other because of differences in underlying ability. Most executives have extensive training and business experience, but only a few become chief executives of large corporations. The 1992 pay of major league baseball players ranged from the league minimum of $109,000 a year to $6.1 million earned by Bobby Bonilla of the New York Mets. From lawyers to executives to professional athletes, pay differences reflect differing abilities.

DIFFERENCES IN RISK. Jobs vary in the degree of risk of work-related injury or death. Research indicates that jobs with a higher probability of injury or death, such as coal mining, pay a higher wage, other things constant. Workers are also paid more, other things constant, in fields where the risk of being unemployed is greater, such as construction.

PROBLEMS OF LABOR MOBILITY. Wages are often lower in rural areas than in metropolitan areas in part because there are fewer employers in rural areas and therefore less demand for labor. This difference in wages creates an incentive to migrate to high-wage areas. But some workers are unaware of the higher-paying alternatives or are reluctant to leave their home towns. Generally, however, individuals have a strong incentive to sell their resources in the market where they are valued most. For example, place kickers are drawn to the United States from around the world by the attractive salaries available in the National Football League. Likewise, because physicians are paid more in the United States than elsewhere, more than 10,000 foreign physicians migrate to the United States each year. The flow of labor is not all in one direction: some Americans seek their fortune abroad, such as basketball players who head for the high pay in Europe and baseball players who head for Japan.

DIFFERENCES IN JOB STATUS. Other things constant, employers must pay workers more to perform jobs that are dirty, smelly, noisy, dangerous, boring, irregular, or of low social status. This does not mean that jobs of low social status must pay more than all other jobs. After all, a janitor earns less than a computer programmer. What it means is that, *other things constant,* jobs of lower status must pay more than jobs of higher social status that require the same skills.

JOB DISCRIMINATION. Sometimes individuals are paid different wages because of racial or sexual discrimination in the job market. Although such discrimination is illegal, history shows that certain groups have systematically earned less than others of apparently equal ability. The reasons underlying the differences in average earnings between males and females are discussed in the following case study.

CASE STUDY

Comparable Worth

Despite laws in this country requiring affirmative action and equal pay for equal work, women on average still earn only 71 percent as much as men earn. After adjusting for several factors, such as the tendency of women to interrupt their careers for child rearing, the differential between the sexes shrinks but does not disappear. One explanation for this pay gap is that women have crowded into certain occupations, such as secretarial work, nursing, and retail sales, because other job opportunities have been blocked by discrimination and restrictive sex roles. The increased supply of female labor to these crowded professions has lowered the prevailing wage.

More generally, since 1950 the number of males in the labor force increased by about 60 percent, but the number of women in the labor force increased by more than 200 percent.

Comparable worth The principle that pay should be determined by job characteristics rather than by supply and demand

Some advocates of women's rights have promoted a notion called **comparable worth** as a way of addressing pay differences. The comparable-worth approach calls for evaluating each job based on three criteria: skill required, effort, and responsibility. Pay is then based on this evaluation. Proponents of comparable worth believe that such a system would eliminate situations in which men working in jobs requiring few skills are paid more than women working in occupations requiring greater skills. Pay differences were dramatized in a strike of clerical and technical workers against Yale University. The predominantly female labor union noted that administrative assistants, who were mostly female, performed work that required, in the union's view, at least as much training and experience as the work performed by the university's truck drivers, who were mostly male. But the truck drivers earned 38 percent more than the administrative assistants.

Comparable pay laws have been adopted in more than a dozen states as well as in Australia and Great Britain. Some major employers, such as BankAmerica and AT&T, have also begun to introduce comparable worth into their compensation schemes. In Australia, a decade of comparable worth policies closed the ratio between women's and men's hourly wages from 74 percent to 94 percent. In Washington state, the pay gap among state employees closed from 80 percent to 95 percent in the first four years of the program. These programs have had some unintended consequences. In Australia, the growth rate in female employment slowed somewhat. In Washington state, government pay in some traditionally male fields, such as civil engineering, has fallen so much that government openings are hard to fill.

Teaching Tip Comparable worth can eliminate the temporary resource price differences that lead to resource reallocation (see Chapter 24).

Comparable worth has in some cases also reduced the incentive women have to advance to levels where there are fewer women. For example, in the past an upwardly mobile clerk-typist working for the state of Washington would seek a job as a fiscal technician, a job category in which the proportion of women is smaller. This job could lead to a still bigger promotion to accountant. But the big pay increase for clerk-typists meant that taking a job as fiscal technician would result in a pay cut. So that path of advancement now seems less attractive. Basing pay on comparable worth may provide for more job equity but it reduces the allocative role of the labor market.

Sources: Ronald Ehrenberg and Robert Smith, "Comparable Worth Wage Adjustments and Female Employment in the State and Local Sector," *Journal of Labor Economics* 5 (January 1987): 43–62; Morley Gunderson, "Male-Female Wage Differentials and Policy Responses," *Journal of Economic Literature* (March 1989): 46–72; and Peter Kilborn, "Wage Gap Between Sexes Is Cut in Test, But at a Price," *New York Times*, 31 May 1990.

There remains another human resource to discuss, a resource that in some respects is of critical importance: entrepreneurial ability. Entrepreneurial ability is the wellspring of economic vitality and the source of a rising standard of living.

ENTREPRENEURIAL ABILITY

Though it is difficult to teach, some four hundred colleges now offer courses in it. Though it is difficult to measure, business publications look for it in all the rising stars whose success they track. And though it is difficult to analyze, new books on the topic appear almost daily. What is it? *Entrepreneurial ability.* Perhaps no other economic resource is so poorly understood. There is no market for entrepreneurial ability in the sense in which we usually think of markets. In fact, the reason firms are formed is because entrepreneurs believe they will be better off running their own firms than selling their labor in a market. Entrepreneurs are their own bosses—that is, they hire themselves—because there is no formal market for their special kind of ability.

An *entrepreneur* is a profit-seeking decision maker who organizes an enterprise and assumes the risk of its operation. *An entrepreneur establishes a firm, acquires the right to direct resources in that firm, assumes responsibility for paying these resources, and claims any profit or loss that is left over after all other resources have been paid.* The right to control resources does not necessarily mean that the entrepreneur must manage the firm. But the entrepreneur must have the power to hire and fire the manager; the entrepreneur must have the power to control the manager.

Teaching Tip The problem of assigning the income earned by entrepreneurs when they provide other resources is equivalent to the problem of categorizing proprietor's income, as described in the discussion of income distribution in Chapter 24.

The Entrepreneur Can Supply Other Resources

Recall that accounting profit equals a firm's total revenue minus all explicit costs. Economic profit equals total revenue minus all implicit and explicit costs. Typically, economic profit goes to the entrepreneur as the reward for entrepreneurial ability. To the extent that the entrepreneur provides resources other than entrepreneurial ability, an implicit return should be assigned to these inputs based on what they could earn in resource markets. To arrive at economic profit, we must carefully subtract from accounting profit that portion of the entrepreneur's income that is a return for supplying resources other than entrepreneurial ability.

Example The two owners of a small publishing house in Ohio, Custom Editorial Productions, split managerial and other duties. One owner coordinates the financial, personnel, and marketing decisions of the firm; the other owner oversees the purchase and maintenance of computer equipment and software, deals with authors and clients, and works as senior editor.

For example, economic profit should exclude any salary received by entrepreneurs who also manage their firms. Managers can be viewed as another form of labor, albeit a rather special kind, so the manager's salary should not be confused with profit. The services of managers, like those of teachers and steelworkers, are bought and sold in the labor market. Similarly, any money invested by the entrepreneur in the firm should be assigned an imputed return equal to the return paid on investments involving a comparable degree of risk—what we have referred to as a normal profit. *Economic profit is then the amount over and above all of these imputed payments for resources supplied by the entrepreneur other than entrepreneurial ability.* The net result can be an economic loss rather than an economic profit.

Imagine that a posh new restaurant called the Blue Beagle is opening in your community. Suppose that the founder of the Blue Beagle borrows money from a bank to start the restaurant and selects a manager to hire all other employees and to lease or buy a building, furniture, and everything else the operation requires. The entrepreneur promises to pay all these resource owners at least the market return for putting their resources under the manager's direction. Otherwise, these resources would go elsewhere. In the operation of the Blue Beagle, the entrepreneur, by hiring the manager and agreeing to pay all resource suppliers, supplies no resources other than entrepreneurial ability. The entrepreneur nonetheless controls the restaurant and is liable for its success or failure.

Since all the resources except entrepreneurial ability are either rented or hired, who is the Blue Beagle's owner and what does the owner own? The restaurant's owner is the entrepreneur. *The "firm" owned by the entrepreneur consists of a bundle of contracts or agreements between the entrepreneur and resource suppliers.* The entrepreneur has acquired the right to direct and control these resources in return for a promise to pay their owners a specified amount. At the end of the year, the entrepreneur can consider as economic profit whatever is left after all other resource suppliers have been paid. The entrepreneur is what we referred to earlier as the *residual claimant*—someone who claims the residual left over after all costs, both explicit and implicit, have been subtracted from revenues. If revenues fail to cover outlays, however, the entrepreneur is obliged to make up the shortfall. The entrepreneur is last in line to be paid and is the chief bag-holder should anyone be left holding the bag.

Teaching Tip Highlight the risk-taking role of the entrepreneur.

It is not the management of resources that distinguishes the entrepreneur; it is the control over the decision as to who manages resources. Even if the entrepreneur decided to serve as the restaurant's manager, the entrepreneur as manager would likely still delegate to the chef many decisions about resource use—which assistant chefs to hire, what ingredients to purchase, how to combine these ingredients. In fact, the entrepreneur could serve as the chef, maitre d', cashier, dishwasher, or in whatever capacity was most needed at the time. Therefore, do not think entrepreneurs have to manage (though they often do); *entrepreneurs simply must have the power to appoint or fire the manager and to claim the profit or loss that arises from the manager's decisions.*

As we will see, an entrepreneur is a lot more than a business owner. An entrepreneur is an idea person, an innovator, and a risk taker who sees new opportunities for profit and goes after them. Entrepreneurs are the pioneers of the economy, who drive the engine of growth.

Why Entrepreneurs Often Invest in the Firm

The entrepreneur rarely has the limited role described in the restaurant example. Entrepreneurs usually provide at least a portion of the funds required to start and maintain a business. Since it is not strictly necessary for the entrepreneur to provide resources in addition to entrepreneurial ability, why do entrepreneurs generally provide funds to the firm? In our example the entrepreneur borrowed from the bank the funds necessary to finance the restaurant's operations. In reality a bank would be most reluctant to lend all of the funds required to start a firm, especially one as risky as a new restaurant. Although the entrepreneur would promise to repay the bank, the restaurant could go bankrupt. And, as noted in Chapter 4, under the corporate business structure, an entrepreneur's liability is limited to his or her own investment in the firm. Even if the firm were not incorporated, the entrepreneur, in the face of huge losses, could file for personal bankruptcy.

Teaching Tip Lenders may also require that entrepreneurs maintain cash balances with the institution, put up collateral such as their homes or financial securities, and so forth.

Because of the possibility of bankruptcy and default, lenders typically want entrepreneurs to supply additional resources to the firm. The entrepreneur's supply of funds to the firm reassures wary lenders in at least two ways. First, when the entrepreneur's own assets are tied up in the firm, that individual is likely to exercise greater care and vigilance in shepherding all the firm's resources, including the bank's funds. Second, the entrepreneur's investment in the firm—called *owner's equity*—serves as a buffer, providing lenders and other resource suppliers with some insulation against a default in the event that the firm's costs exceed its revenues in a particular year. Losses can be covered out of owner's equity rather than out of payments due to some other resource owner, such as the bank.

Entrepreneurship and Theories of Profit

Profit plays an important role in a market economy because profit incentives direct the allocation of resources. Profit, therefore, deserves special attention. There is no single theory explaining the source of economic profit in the capitalist system. Rather, there are several theories of profit, each of which focuses on a different role played by the entrepreneur. Here we examine three entrepreneurial roles that represent potential sources of economic profit.

The Entrepreneur as Broker

Perhaps the simplest view of the entrepreneur is that of a broker whose aim is to "buy low and sell high." Entrepreneurs bid against one another for the available resources, and this bidding establishes market prices for the various resources. Entrepreneurs contract with resource suppliers and combine the resources to produce goods and services. The difference between what the entrepreneur pays for resources (including the opportunity cost of other resources supplied by the entrepreneur) and the revenue received from sales equals the entrepreneur's economic profit. Thus, *entrepreneurs earn an economic profit by selling output for more than it costs to produce the output.* At the first sign of economic profit, however, other entrepreneurs will enter this industry. If markets are competitive, economic profit will be driven to zero in the long run, and entrepreneurs will earn just a normal rate of return on resources they supply to the firm, such as investment funds and managerial skills. In order for an entrepreneur to continue to supply entrepreneurial ability, that resource must earn at least its opportunity cost. *As brokers, entrepreneurs direct resources to their highest valued use; thus, entrepreneurs promote economic efficiency in the economy.*

Teaching Tip Resources are allocated to goods and services to which consumers assign values that exceed or equal the opportunity cost of the resources needed to produce them. Thus, profit incentives direct the allocation of resources.

The Entrepreneur as Innovator

Example Presidents Pro-Tem was formed in 1992 to specialize in the temporary placement of presidents, chief executives, and other high-level managers when a company makes an acquisition, expands into new markets, reorganizes, or suffers the departure or illness of a top executive. Only about a dozen such placement firms exist in the United States.

Point to Stress Economic progress requires a continuous succession of new innovations.

A variation of the idea of the entrepreneur as broker is the view that entrepreneurs earn profits arising from successful innovations. If entrepreneurs can make an existing product more cheaply than can competitors or if they can introduce a new product demanded by consumers, they will be able to earn at least short-run economic profits. The possibility of economic profits serves as a powerful motive for innovations. Whether these profits continue in the long run will depend on the ability of other firms to imitate the cost-saving activity or the new product. If the entrepreneur is somehow able to acquire monopoly power, economic profit can be earned in the long run as well.

Profit, said Joseph Schumpeter, an Austrian-born economist who taught at Harvard during the 1930s, is neither a wage nor a reward for bearing risk. Profit, he argued, is a residual: it's what's left over after all the factors of production have been paid. Usually there is no economic profit. But an enterprising individual who creates a new technology, opens a new market, or introduces a cost-saving efficiency generates economic profit—at least for a while, until imitators swarm in to copy the innovation and drive profit back to the normal level. These path-breaking entrepreneurs, as Schumpeter called them, are not simply the source of profit. They are the engine of the entire economic system. Innovations are the wellspring of economic growth, and entrepreneurs are the fountainhead of innovation. Capitalism, Schumpeter said in a famous phrase, is a "perennial gale of creative destruction."

The Entrepreneur as Risk Bearer

Some economists think of the profit earned by entrepreneurs as arising from the risk associated with venturing into a world filled with uncertainty. According to this theory of profit, a portion of the return received by entrepreneurs is a payment for their willingness to bear that risk. But the consideration of risk bearing as a source of economic profit suggests a more general treatment of risk and return for various resource owners. We can speak of two sources of risk for resource owners: (1) the risk of not getting paid after the resource is provided and (2) the risk of a drop in the market value of the resource.

RISK OF NOT GETTING PAID. Despite the entrepreneur's guarantees, resource suppliers, particularly suppliers of loans, often face the possibility of not being paid. If resource owners take a risk by turning the use of their resources over to the entrepreneur, they will require greater compensation than they would if their payment were assured. In this sense, resource suppliers are risk bearers, and they are typically compensated for bearing risk. Consequently, if we define profit as a return for risk bearing, the greater resource payment required for bearing risk can be considered profit. Resource suppliers who do not get paid obviously suffer an economic loss.

Think of the resource suppliers as standing in line waiting to receive the payment guaranteed them by the entrepreneur, not knowing when or if the cashier's window will close. Some suppliers try to get first in line by requiring payment before their resource is supplied, by requiring payment before other resources are paid, or by requiring the entrepreneur to post *collateral*—valued assets that can be claimed by the resource supplier should payment not be forthcoming. Labor suppliers typically are paid weekly or biweekly, so little labor is extended without compensation. Lenders, however, usually extend the entire amount up front and are repaid in installments or when the loan matures; lenders thus often require collateral. If resource suppliers have doubts about getting paid, they will require a higher payment for their services. This additional payment can be considered a return for risk bearing.

Teaching Tip The higher payment required if resource suppliers have doubts about getting paid can be called a risk premium.

RISK OF A DECLINE IN THE VALUE OF THE RESOURCE. The capitalist system is based on the private ownership of resources and the right of resource owners to contract freely for the lease or sale of their resources. An important feature of capitalism is the right of a resource owner to the gain or the loss in the value of that resource. Thus, resource owners bear the risk associated with acquiring or developing resources. Although we typically associate risk bearing with the acquisition of physical capital, investment in human capital is often no more certain.

Right now you are acquiring human capital that you hope will serve you a lifetime. Your decision to specialize in a particular area, such as economics, accounting, chemistry, history, or engineering, involves some risk because you cannot know what return this investment will yield in the future. You can only guess how changes in tastes, in technology, in taxes, and in the supply of resources will shape the future supply and demand for your particular resource. Many college students are understandably tempted to train for that first job; the tendency is to acquire very specific skills, as the students did who studied to be entry-level architects. *The more specific your human capital is, however, the more risk you assume in an uncertain and changing world.* Thus, there is a risk involved in investing in human capital just as there is in investing in physical capital, and a portion of the return on human capital could be identified as an economic profit or an economic loss.

Example An Olympic figure skater who hopes for a professional career assumes more risk than an average high school student. A dentist assumes more risk than a chemist.

Profit and the Supply of Entrepreneurs

The ranks of entrepreneurs are in constant flux, as some emerge from the labor market to form their own enterprises and others return to the labor market after failing with their own firms or selling successful firms. The total supply of entrepreneurial ability is influenced by a variety of forces, such as the pace of technological change, government regulations, the tax laws, and the market return on resources other than entrepreneurial ability.

Example According to the International Labor Organization, women own 25 percent of all businesses in the United States, partly in response to a lack of opportunities for women in the corporate world.

Evidence suggests that most new firms fail within two years. What encourages someone to take on such a risk rather than settle for the predictable salary, vacation time, health benefits, and other amenities that typically come with serving as an employee rather than as an employer? Why do seventeen million people in this country call themselves boss? First, many no doubt prefer the individual freedom that comes from self employment. Some derive satisfaction from the creative process. Some no doubt dream of founding a corporate empire, an empire that can be passed to their children.

One strong economic incentive for founding a firm is that any entrepreneur who can develop a profit-making operation can typically sell the firm for a multiple of the firm's expected profit stream. For example, suppose you put together a company that yields an economic profit of $25,000 per year, a stream that is expected to continue indefinitely. Such a profit stream can be *capitalized* into a much larger number. Capitalization computes a market value to a future stream of profits. Though the derivation will be discussed in a later chapter, for now we can say that such a firm would have a market value of $500,000. Its value would be even higher if profits are expected to grow.

To close our look at entrepreneurs, we offer the following case study of the entrepreneur who developed Lotus 1-2-3.

CASE STUDY

Feasting in the Land of Lotus

Mitch Kapor's background hardly seemed to qualify him for the success that was to come his way. He had held various jobs, ranging from disk jockey to instructor of transcendental meditation. One day he traded his stereo for an Apple computer, and therein lies the tale. He was fascinated by the Apple and soon developed his programming skills to such a level that he reportedly took only two months to write two business applications programs that he sold for more than a million dollars!

With these funds and with additional support, both financial and entrepreneurial, from a *venture capital firm,* he founded the Lotus Development Corporation in 1982. In less than a year, Lotus 1-2-3 became the industry's best-selling business program, with sales of $50 million the first year. In October 1983 the company made its first public offering of stock, making Kapor's stock in the company worth $70 million. In a few short years, Lotus grew out of his basement to become a firm with over 2,200 employees and annual sales exceeding $500 million.

The other side of this success story is about the venture capital firm that invested $2.1 million in Kapor's company in 1982. Venture capitalists shop around, investing in promising new firms. Such investors could be considered entrepreneurs in that, by becoming part owners, they share the responsibility of guaranteeing the payments of the other resources, they share in the control of these resources, and they are residual claimants of any profit or loss. When Lotus made its public offering in 1983, the stock held by the venture capitalists became worth $70 million, or about thirty-three times their investment only a year earlier.

In July 1986 Kapor resigned as chairman of Lotus. Evidently, he did not find the job of managing people as attractive as founding a corporate empire. Since Kapor was viewed as the imaginative force behind Lotus, the day after

he resigned the market price of a share of company stock dropped by 10 percent. Investors apparently believed that Kapor's special skills could not be easily replaced. Over the next five years, however, his successor personally earned over $50 million at Lotus Development, including the appreciation in his stock holdings. Only a half-dozen U.S. executives earned more during that time period. Kapor's initial idea has made a lot of people rich. The same can be said for Steven Jobs at Apple and Bill Gates at Microsoft. Entrepreneurs expand the size of the pie. That's what they do.

Sources: "A Software Whiz Logs Off," *Newsweek,* 21 July 1986; and "What 800 Companies Paid Their Bosses," *Forbes,* 25 May 1992.

CONCLUSION

The first half of this chapter focused on labor supply and on why wages differ both across professions and across individuals within professions. The interaction of the supply and demand for labor determines wage rates and the level of employment. The second half of the chapter dealt with another human resource, entrepreneurial ability. If the skills of the entrepreneur could be learned step by step like the skills of a plumber or an accountant, anyone could complete a course and get rich. Entrepreneurship is a more elusive skill, which is why economic profits are reserved for successful entrepreneurs, and which is why we could not simply draw diagrams to explain it.

Our emphasis has been on competitive markets. To a large extent, we have ignored the influence of institutional forces, such as labor unions and governments. The effect of unions on the labor market is examined in the next chapter.

SUMMARY

1. The supply of labor shows the relation between the wage rate and the quantity of labor workers are willing and able to supply, other things constant. The demand for labor shows the relation between the wage rate and the quantity of labor producers are willing and able to hire, other things constant. The intersection of supply and demand determines the equilibrium wage rate.

2. People allocate their time so as to maximize utility There are three uses of time: market work, nonmarket work, and leisure. The higher the market wage, other things constant, the more goods and services can be purchased with that wage, so a higher wage encourages labor suppliers to substitute market work for other uses of time. But the higher the wage, the higher the income, and as income increases, people

consume more of all normal goods including leisure. The net effect of a higher wage on an individual's quantity of market labor supplied depends on both the substitution effect and the income effect.

3. The quantity of market labor supplied also depends on factors other than the wage, including (1) other sources of income, (2) job amenities, (3) the future value of job experience, (4) the amount of discretion allowed in the use of time while working, and (5) the taste for the work.

4. Market wages differ because of (1) differences in training and education requirements, (2) differences in the skill and ability of workers, (3) differences in the riskiness of the work, both in terms of the workers' safety and the chances of getting laid off, (4) differences in labor mobility, and (5) racial and gender discrimination.

5. An entrepreneur is a profit-seeking decision maker who guarantees payment for the other resources in return for the right to direct these resources in the firm. The entrepreneur is also the residual claimant of any profits or losses of the firm. The entrepreneur need not supply any resource other than entrepreneurial ability, though entrepreneurs usually invest in the firm and often manage the firm.

6. There is no single theory explaining the profit earned by entrepreneurs. Entrepreneurs have been viewed as brokers who earn a profit by selling output for more than they pay resources. They have been viewed as innovators who earn a profit by developing new products and by producing existing products for less. And they have been viewed as risk bearers who earn a profit by taking chances.

Questions and Problems

1. (Utility Maximization) Explain how the consumption of goods, the supplying of labor, and the consumption of leisure affect utility and one another.

2. (Labor Supply) Suppose that the substitution effect of an increase in the wage rate exactly offsets the income effect for all wage levels. What would the market supply of labor look like in this case? Why?

3. (Labor Supply) Many U.S. companies have a problem with worker absenteeism. How is this problem related to market labor supply and, in particular, to the level of wages? What other considerations are there?

4. (Equilibrium Differentials) Suppose that two jobs are exactly the same except that one is performed in an air-conditioned workplace. How might an economist measure the value workers place on such a job amenity?

5. (Labor Supply) What type of education and general skills are needed to improve the productivity of the labor force? Do you believe that high schools and colleges provide such an education? Why or why not?

6. (Risk and Labor Supply) Suppose that you have a choice between a job that involves the death of one worker in a hundred per year and another job that involves no such risk. If the no-risk job pays $20,000 per year, what income would be necessary to induce you to take the risky job?

7. (Equilibrium Wage) Use a labor supply-demand diagram to predict the impact on the equilibrium wage and quantity of market labor of each of the following:
   a. An increase in the income tax
   b. A reduction in labor productivity
   c. An increase in the level of unemployment compensation

8. (Labor Supply and Indifference Curves) Using indifference curves relating leisure to all other goods, show how a backward-bending labor supply curve could be consistent with utility maximization.

9. (Labor Supply) Determine the hourly wage rate necessary to induce you to work this summer. What factors did you take into account in determining this wage rate?

10. (Entrepreneurs) The success and value of entrepreneurship are easiest to identify in small businesses. How would you identify the effect or value of entrepreneurship in large corporations? Give some examples of entrepreneurs in such settings.

11. (Valuing Entrepreneurship) *The Concise Oxford Dictionary* defines the business term *goodwill* as a "privilege granted by the seller of an established business, of trading as the seller's recognized successor; the amount paid for this." How might a company's goodwill be a measure of previous entrepreneurship?

12. (Profits) Some people claim that profits are bad or can be excessive. Support or refute this claim in light of the discussion in this chapter.

13. (Entrepreneurship) Suppose you currently hold a \$30,000-per-year job with an expected rate of salary increase of 5 percent per year. You are considering quitting and starting your own business with expected first-year costs of \$50,000 and first-year revenues of \$60,000. You anticipate that costs will increase annually by 3 percent and revenues will increase annually by 10 percent. If your discount rate is 5 percent and you expect to work for twenty years, show how you would decide whether or not to start your own business. (Ignore all other factors, such as risk.)

14. (Income and Substitution Effects) Suppose that the cost of living increases dramatically and therefore reduces the purchasing power of your income. If your money wage doesn't increase, you may work *more* hours because of this cost-of-living increase. Is this an income or substitution effect response? Explain.

15. (Households and Utility Maximization) In many households, both adults work outside the home and share the work at home. If one household member has a much higher wage rate, does this make sense?

16. (Labor Supply) Is it ever rational to interview for a job for which you are clearly overqualified? Is it rational for the employer to refuse to hire you on that basis?

17. (Risk and Wages) In court cases to determine the economic loss associated with wrongful death, one way to estimate such a loss is to use the wage differential between two kinds of jobs that are identical in every way except for the risk of death. Why are such methods used? What dangers exist in using such differentials?

18. (Entrepreneurship) Economic profit is the amount of revenue left over after all resources (including those supplied by the entrepreneur other than entrepreneurial ability) are paid their explicit or implicit costs. How can you tell if the entrepreneur is earning a normal rate of return?

19. (Comparable Worth) Suppose legislation were passed mandating equal pay for all jobs that require the same skills and training.
    a. What kinds of problems would this create if such jobs had different nonpay attributes?
    b. How might employers respond to the passage of such legislation?

20. (Comparable Worth) Suppose that two organizations that are truly identical in terms of job characteristics and skill requirements offer different pay scales. What would you expect to see in terms of relative numbers of job applications for these two organizations? If one of the organizations predominantly hires women and the other predominantly hires men, how could you determine whether job discrimination exists?

21. (Comparable Worth) Could differences in labor mobility explain patterns of gender-based pay differences? Why or why not?

22. (The Land of Lotus) Are the entrepreneurial returns earned by Kapor, Jobs, and Gates economic rents or opportunity costs?

23. (The Land of Lotus) The 3,300 percent return for venture capitalists in Lotus represents a return on risk of sizable magnitude. What happens to the venture capitalists' risk after the public stock offering?

CHAPTER 26

UNIONS AND COLLECTIVE BARGAINING

Few aspects of the labor market are more in the news than the activities of labor unions. Labor contract negotiations, strikes, picket lines, confrontations between workers and employers—all these fit neatly into TV's "action news" format. Each September, for example, along with another football season we get pictures of striking teachers walking picket lines somewhere in the country. This drama may cause you to miss the real economic significance of unions. Also, you may have developed the mistaken impression that the majority of workers belong to unions and that strikes occur frequently. In this chapter we will step back from the charged rhetoric typically characterizing union-employer relations to review the history of the union movement in the United States, examine more carefully the economic effects of unions, and discuss recent trends in union membership. Topics discussed in this chapter include

- Craft unions
- Industrial unions
- Bilateral monopoly
- Collective bargaining
- Tradeoff between wages and employment
- Union objectives
- Recent trends in union membership

A Brief History of the Labor Movement in the United States

In 1860, before labor unions achieved national prominence, the workday for nonfarm employees averaged about eleven hours, and a six-day work week was normal. Those employed in steel mills, paper mills, and breweries typically worked twelve hours a day, seven days a week. Working conditions were often frightful: estimates from insurance company records indicate that about one out of fifteen workers was seriously injured each year. Mining and metal processing were particularly dangerous. To be compensated for injuries, a worker had to sue the employer and prove the employer's negligence, but most workers did not know how to sue their employers. Child labor was also common. In 1880 a million children between the ages of ten and fifteen were in the work force; this number doubled to two million by 1910, when one-fifth of those between ten and fifteen held full-time jobs. Heavy immigration during the period sent millions of new workers streaming into the labor force, competing for jobs and keeping wages relatively low. *Employers were therefore assured of a ready pool of workers despite the low pay and poor working conditions.*

Example In 1992 child-labor violations were at their highest level since the 1920s. Violations occurred mainly in fast food restaurants, agriculture (among migrant workers), and the garment industry.

Early Labor Organizations

Labor union A group of employees who join together to improve their terms of employment

Craft union A union whose members have a particular skill or work at a particular craft, such as plumbers or carpenters

A **labor union** is a group of employees who join together to improve their terms of employment. The first labor unions in the United States date back to the early days of national independence, when employees in various crafts, such as carpenters, shoemakers, and printers, formed local groups to seek higher wages and shorter hours. Such **craft unions** confined membership to workers with a particular skill, or craft. In the 1850s, because improved transportation systems extended markets beyond the local level, unions in the same trade began widening their membership to regional and even national levels. The National Typographical Union, formed in 1852, was the first national union and was soon followed by several other national craft unions.

Teaching Tip Craft unions were the first to form because the supply of skilled labor was easier to control (by controlling the conditions of apprenticeship) than the supply of unskilled labor. Also, craft workers were close to indispensable to the production process (demand was very inelastic).

Knights of Labor. The first major national labor organization in the United States was the *Knights of Labor,* formed in 1869. Its objectives were generally more political than economic, but the Knights sought an eight-hour workday and the abolition of child labor. Within twenty years the union had over 750,000 members. But the union lacked focus and tried to include as members both skilled and unskilled labor, a combination that proved difficult to organize.

American Federation of Labor The various craft unions that had developed during the nineteenth century did not find the Knights of Labor suited to their interests. Consequently, these craft unions formed their own national organization, called the *American Federation of Labor (AFL).* The AFL was founded in 1886 under the direction of Samuel Gompers, a cigar maker.

It was not a union but rather an organization of national unions, with each retaining its autonomy. By the beginning of World War I, the AFL, still under the direction of Gompers, was viewed as the voice of labor. The Clayton Act of 1914 exempted trade union negotiations from antitrust laws, meaning that *unions in competing companies could join forces in an attempt to raise wages.* Union membership jumped during World War I, but dropped after the war as the government retreated from its support of union efforts. Membership dropped by half between 1920 and 1933.

A New Deal for Labor

Teaching Tip The Great Depression made public opinion openly hostile to big business. Previously, the political climate had been unfavorable to labor unions.

The Great Depression set the stage for a new era in the labor movement. In 1932 Herbert Hoover signed the *Norris-La Guardia Act,* which sharply limited the courts' ability to stop strikes and banned *yellow-dog contracts,* under which workers had to agree not to join a union as a condition of employment.

WAGNER ACT. President Franklin D. Roosevelt took office in 1933 and was a strong supporter of unions as one solution to the huge drop in wages and prices that occurred during the Great Depression. The *Wagner Act* of 1935 required employers to bargain with unions that represented the majority of the workers. The act also made it illegal for employers to interfere with their employees' right to unionize. To investigate unfair labor practices and to oversee union elections, the law established the *National Labor Relations Board.* The act has come to be known as the Magna Carta of the U.S. labor movement.

Teaching Tip The skilled workers represented by the craft unions were often less than the majority of a firm's employees. Therefore, the Wagner Act had more impact on industrial unions.

THE CONGRESS OF INDUSTRIAL ORGANIZATIONS. Such favorable legislation nourished the growth of a new kind of union, organized along industry lines. The *Congress of Industrial Organizations* (*CIO*) was established in 1935 to serve as a national organization of unions in mass-production industries, such as autos and steel. Whereas the AFL had organized workers in particular crafts, such as plumbers and carpenters, the CIO was made up of unions whose membership embraced all workers in a particular industry, including unskilled and semiskilled workers. This **industrial union** approach proved successful, and in 1937 the steelworkers' union joined the CIO, bringing into the organization more than 200,000 members. In 1938 the charismatic leader of the United Mine Workers, John L. Lewis, became president of the CIO. Workers in the auto and rubber industries were able to organize through the use of *sit-down strikes,* in which workers occupied the plants but did not work, thereby paralyzing operations.

Industrial union A union of both skilled and unskilled workers from a particular industry, such as auto workers or steelworkers

Teaching Tip The Taft-Hartley Act allowed states to pass right-to-work laws prohibiting the requirement of union membership as a necessary condition for employment.

The Labor Movement After World War II

After World War II, economic conditions and public sentiment appeared to turn against unions. Postwar inflation seemed to be aggravated by a series of strikes, and in November 1946 the United Mine Workers defied a court order to return to work after a long and bitter strike. In response, Congress in

1947 passed the *Taft-Hartley Act*, which attempted to limit strikes that would affect the public's safety and welfare. The president, by obtaining a court order, could stop a strike for eighty days, during which time the parties could continue to negotiate.

Point to Stress The AFL-CIO is not a single union but a federation of eighty-three autonomous national and international unions designed to provide a united front for organized labor. Seventy-five percent of all union members belong to an AFL-CIO union.

Despite the Taft-Hartley Act, the union movement flourished right after World War II, with membership growing from less than four million, or about 12 percent of the nonfarm work force, in 1930 to more than seventeen million, or about 34 percent, in 1955. The AFL and the CIO merged in 1955. But during the 1950s organized labor suffered from allegations of corruption and misconduct by union leaders. Congressional investigations led to the passage in 1959 of the *Landrum-Griffin Act* to protect the rights of rank-and-file union members against abuses by union leaders. The act regulated union elections, required union officials to file financial reports, and made theft of union funds a federal offense. *The Landrum-Griffin Act has been called the Bill of Rights for union members because it is aimed at guaranteeing each member's right to fair elections and honest union leadership.*

Collective Bargaining and Other Tools of Unionism

Teaching Tip Mediation and arbitration are especially important in the public sector, where strikes are often prohibited.

Now that you have some idea of the labor movement's history, let's consider the tools used by unions to exert some control over wages and working conditions. We begin with a discussion of collective bargaining.

Collective Bargaining

Collective bargaining The process by which union and management negotiate a mutually agreeable labor agreement

Collective bargaining is the process by which representatives from union and management negotiate a mutually agreeable contract specifying wages, employee benefits, and working conditions. The actual contract can run to many pages of fine print written in language only a lawyer could understand. Once an agreement has been reached, union representatives must carry it back to the membership for a vote. If it is rejected, the union can vote to continue negotiations or to strike.

Mediation and Arbitration

Mediator An impartial observer who listens to both sides separately and suggests how each side could adjust its position to resolve differences

Binding arbitration Negotiation in which both parties in a union-management dispute agree to accept an impartial observer's resolution of the dispute

If negotiations over a contract reach an impasse and if the public interest is involved, government officials may ask an independent mediator to step in. A **mediator** is an impartial observer who listens to both sides separately and suggests how each side could adjust its position to resolve differences. If a resolution appears possible, the mediator will bring the parties together to iron out a contract. The mediator has no power to impose a settlement on the parties.

In certain critical sectors, such as police and fire protection, where a strike would seriously harm the public interest, an impasse in negotiations is sometimes settled through **binding arbitration**, whereby a neutral third party evaluates both sides of the dispute and issues a decision that the parties are committed to accept. Some disputes skip the mediation and arbitration steps, going directly from impasse to strike.

The Strike

Strike A union's attempt to withhold labor from a firm

A major source of union power in the bargaining relationship is the threat of a **strike**, which is the union's attempt to withhold labor from the firm. The purpose of a strike is to stop production, thereby forcing the firm to accept the union's position. But a strike imposes significant costs on union members, who forgo pay and benefits for the duration of the strike and risk losing their jobs. Union funds and other sources may provide some support during a strike, but the typical striker's income falls substantially.

Example A 1992 strike at a General Motors fabrication plant in Lordstown, Ohio caused seven assembly plants (including Saturn) with 32,000 workers to shut down because they lacked necessary parts.

Teaching Tip A striking union may also legally use a primary boycott—discouraging purchases of the products of the firm against which they are striking.

Thus, strikes can be very costly. In 1989 a strike at Eastern Airlines forced the company into bankruptcy and cost many union members their jobs as the company attempted to operate with nonunion workers. In 1992, the United Auto Workers ended a long, costly strike against Caterpillar after the company threatened to hire replacement workers. The threat of a strike hangs over labor negotiations and can serve as a real spur to reach an accord. *Although usually neither party wants a strike, both sides usually act as if they could and would endure a strike rather than concede on key points.*

Since the strike's success depends on blocking the supply of labor, firms sometimes respond by hiring nonunion workers. Unions usually picket the targeted employer to prevent or discourage so-called strike-breakers, or "scabs," from working. Not surprisingly, violence occasionally erupts during confrontations between striking and nonstriking workers. Although reports of strikes are often in the news, most bargaining agreements—well over 95 percent—are reached without a strike. And strike activity is way down. For example, during the 1970s there were an average of two hundred strikes a year in the United States involving 1,000 or more workers per strike. By the early 1990s only about forty such strikes were reported per year on average.

The Economic Effects of Unions on Wages and Employment

Union members, like everyone else, have unlimited wants, but no union can regularly get everything it desires. Because resources are scarce, choices must be made. One could prepare a menu of union desires: higher wages, more employee benefits, greater job security, better working conditions, and so on. To keep the analysis manageable, we will focus initially on a single objective: higher wages. We will examine three possible ways of increasing wages: (1) by forming inclusive, or industrial, unions; (2) by forming exclusive, or craft, unions; and (3) by increasing the demand for union labor.

Inclusive, or Industrial, Unions

The first model we will consider describes strong industrial unions, such as the auto and steel unions, which attempt to set an industry-wide wage for each class of labor. In Exhibit 1(b), the market supply and demand for a particular class of labor are presented as *S* and *D*. In the absence of a union, the equilibrium wage is *W* and the equilibrium employment level is *E*. At the market wage, each individual employer faces a horizontal, or perfectly elastic, supply of labor, as reflected by *s* in Exhibit 1(a). Thus, each firm, as a labor price taker, can hire as much labor as it wants at the market wage of *W*. The firm hires labor up to the point where the marginal revenue product, or the firm's demand for labor, equals the marginal resource cost, or the supply of labor to the firm; this amount is represented by quantity *e* in Exhibit 1(a). As we saw earlier, in equilibrium each worker hired is paid a wage just equal to the marginal revenue product.

Point to Stress
Since the firm is a labor price taker, the wage represents the firm's marginal resource cost for labor.

Now suppose that the union is able to negotiate a wage above the market-clearing wage. Specifically, suppose the wage floor negotiated is *W′*,

EXHIBIT 1

Effect of a Union's Wage Floor

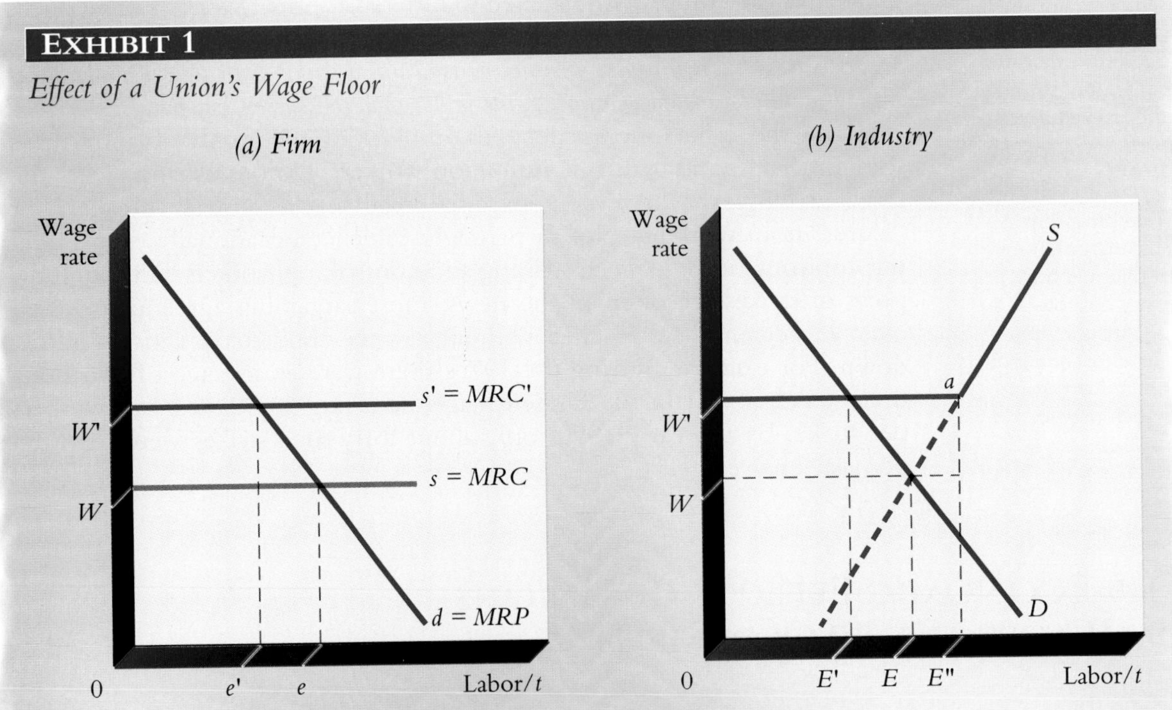

In panel (b), the equilibrium wage rate is *W*. At that wage the individual firm of panel (a) hires labor up to the point where the marginal revenue product equals *W*. Each firm hires quantity *e*; total employment is *E*.

If a union can negotiate a wage *W′* above the equilibrium level, the supply curve facing the firm shifts up to *s′*. The firm hires fewer workers, *e′*, and total employment falls to *E′*. At wage *W′* there is an excess supply of labor equal to $E'' - E'$.

Point to Stress The analysis assumes that the union can strike if the wage offered is lower than W' and can prevent other workers from crossing the picket lines.

meaning that no labor will be supplied at a lower wage, but any amount desired by the firms, up to the quantity identified at point a in Exhibit 1(b), will be supplied at the wage floor. In effect, the supply of union labor is perfectly elastic at the union wage up to point a. If more than a is demanded, however, the wage floor no longer applies; the upward-sloping portion, aS, becomes the relevant part of the labor supply curve. For an industry facing a wage floor of W', the entire labor supply curve is $W'aS$, which has a kink where the wage floor joins the upward-sloping portion of the original supply curve.

Once this wage floor has been established, each individual firm faces a horizontal supply curve for labor at the collectively bargained wage, W'. Since the wage is now higher, the quantity of labor demanded by each employer declines, as reflected by the employment reduction from e to e' in Exhibit 1(a). Consequently, the higher wage leads to a reduction in total employment; the quantity demanded by the industry drops from E to E' in Exhibit 1(b). At wage W' the amount of labor workers would like to supply, E'', exceeds the amount demanded, E'.

In the absence of a union, this excess supply of labor would cause unemployed workers to lower their asking wage. But union members agree *collectively* to a wage, so workers cannot individually offer to work for less, nor can employers hire them at a lower wage. Because the number of union members willing and able to work exceeds the number of jobs available, the union must develop some mechanism for rationing the available jobs, such as awarding jobs based on worker seniority or connections within the union. *With the inclusive, or industrial, union that negotiates with the entire industry, wages are higher and total employment lower than they would be in the absence of a union.*

Teaching Tip The more inelastic the demand for labor, the smaller the wage-employment tradeoff.

Those who cannot find union employment will look for jobs in the nonunion sector. *The increased supply of labor in the nonunion sector drives down the nonunion wage.* So wages are relatively higher in the union sector, first because unions bargain for a wage that exceeds the market-clearing wage and second because those unable to find employment in the union sector supply their labor to the nonunion sector. *Evidence suggests that union wages in the United States are on average about 15 to 20 percent higher than nonunion wages,*[1] though, as we will see later in the chapter, the union advantage is diminishing.

Exclusive, or Craft, Unions

Point to Stress Although the excess supply of labor is avoided, there is still a wage-employment tradeoff.

One way to increase wages while avoiding the excess supply of labor created by the industrial-union approach is for the union to somehow shift the supply curve of labor to the left, as shown in panel (a) of Exhibit 2. Successful supply restrictions of this type require that two conditions be met. First, the union must be able to restrict its membership, and second, the union must be able to force all employers in the industry to hire only union members.

1. A comprehensive discussion of the economic impact of unions is provided by Richard B. Freedman and James L. Medoff in *What Do Unions Do?* (New York: Basic Books, 1984), especially Table 3-1.

EXHIBIT 2

Effect of Reducing Labor Supply or Increasing Labor Demand

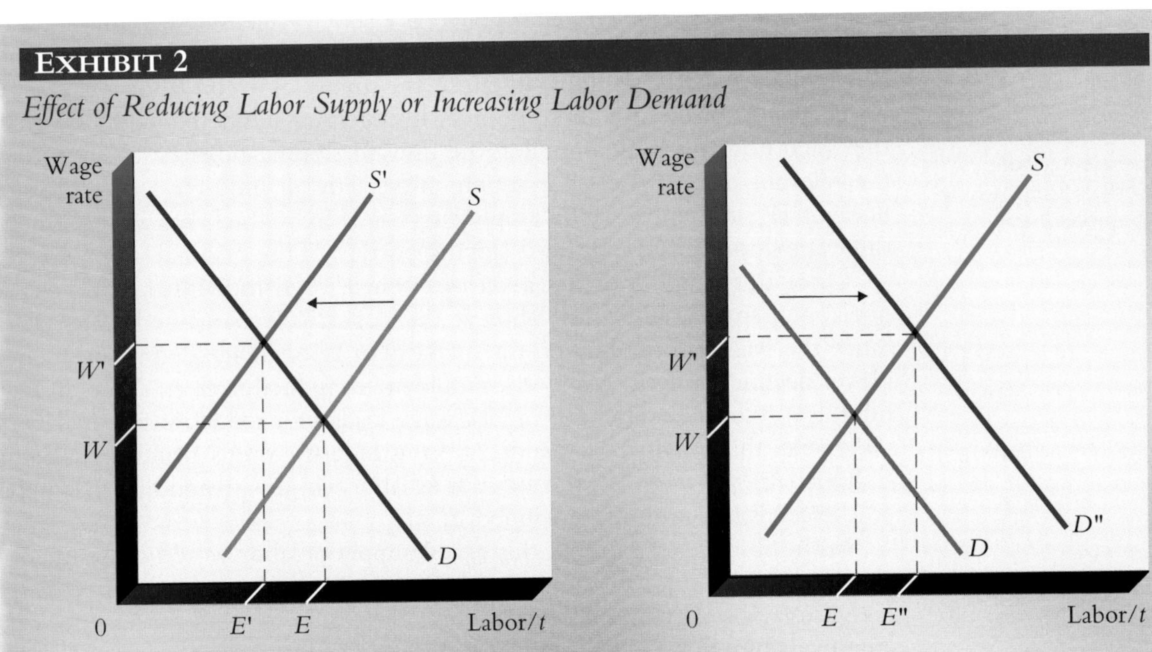

If a union can restrict labor supply to an industry, the supply curve shifts to the left from S to S', as in panel (a). The wage rate rises from W to W' but at the cost of a reduction in employment from E to E'. In panel (b), an increase in labor demand from D to D'' raises both the wage and the level of employment.

The union can restrict its membership with high initiation fees, long apprenticeship periods, difficult qualification exams, restrictive licensing requirements, and other devices designed to slow down or discourage new membership. But, as we will see later, unions have difficulty requiring all firms in the industry to hire only union workers.

Example Employee associations, such as the National Education Association, the American Association of University Professors, and the American Nurses' Association, often behave similarly to craft unions.

Whereas wage setting is more typical of the industrial unions, restricting supply (and employment) is more characteristic of the *craft unions*, such as unions of carpenters, plumbers, and bricklayers. Groups of professionals such as doctors, lawyers, and accountants also impose entry restrictions through education and examination standards. Such restrictions, though usually proposed on the grounds that they protect the public, are often no more than self-serving attempts to increase wages by reducing supply.

Increasing Demand for Union Labor

A third way to increase the wage is to increase the demand for union labor by somehow shifting the labor demand curve outward from D to D'' in panel (b) of Exhibit 2. This approach is an attractive alternative *because it increases both wages and employment,* so there is no need to ration jobs or to restrict union membership. Here are some ways unions try to increase the demand for union labor.

Example In late 1992, the United Food and Commercial Workers Union in Cincinnati, Ohio made plans to picket nonunion grocery stores in the area.

INCREASE DEMAND FOR UNION-MADE GOODS. The demand for union labor may be increased through a direct appeal to consumers to buy only union-made products (as in the familiar refrain "Look for the union label"). Because the demand for labor is a derived demand, an increase in the demand for union-made products will increase the demand for union labor.

RESTRICT SUPPLY OF NONUNION-MADE GOODS. Another way to increase the demand for union labor is to restrict the supply of products that compete with union-made products. Again, this approach relies on the derived nature of labor demand. The United Auto Workers have over the years supported restrictions on imported cars. Fewer imported cars means a greater demand for cars produced by U.S. workers, who are mostly union members. Now that Japanese auto makers also build cars in the United States, the UAW has a trickier problem trying to limit the supply of such cars.

INCREASE PRODUCTIVITY OF UNION LABOR. Some observers claim that the efficiency with which unions organize and monitor the labor-management relationship increases the demand for union labor. According to this theory, unions increase worker productivity by minimizing conflicts, resolving differences, and at times even straightening out workers who are goofing off. In the absence of a union, a dissatisfied worker may simply look for another job, thereby causing job turnover, which is costly to the firm. With a union, however, workers usually have grievance and arbitration channels through which they can more comfortably complain, and the negotiated responses they receive may reduce their urge to leave the firm. Quit rates are in fact significantly lower among union workers (though this may partly be because of the higher pay). If unions increase the productivity of workers in this way, the demand for union labor will increase.

Featherbedding Union efforts to force employers to hire more workers than needed for the task

FEATHERBEDDING. Still another way unions attempt to increase the demand for union labor is by **featherbedding**, which is an attempt to ensure that more union labor is hired than producers would prefer. Featherbedding is often a response to the introduction of labor-saving technology. For example, when the diesel engine replaced the coal-fired engine, locomotives no longer needed someone to shovel coal. For years after the adoption of the diesel engine, however, the railroad unions required such a crew member. Similarly, unions often fight technological developments in electronic composing and typesetting, which have reduced the labor requirements of newspapers; some require that ready-to-use advertising layouts be reset by hand. For the same reason, court transcribers refuse to permit tape recordings of legal proceedings; painters' unions often prohibit the use of spray guns, limiting members to paintbrushes; and musicians object to the use of taped music.

Point to Stress Featherbedding moves the firm to a point to the right of the labor demand curve.

Featherbedding does not create a true increase in demand, in the sense of shifting the demand curve to the right; instead, it forces firms to hire more labor than they really want. The union tries to limit a firm to an all-or-none choice: either hire a certain number of workers or members will strike and you can hire none. Thus, *the union attempts to dictate not only the wage but also the quantity that must be hired at that wage, thereby moving the employers to the right of their demand for labor curve.* An example of featherbedding is considered in the following case study.

CASE STUDY

Featherbedding on Broadway

Broadway producers have long claimed that the restrictive work rules of the theatrical unions are a primary source of the increases in the cost of Broadway tickets. Union contracts specify not only the pay level but also the number of workers required for each position. For example, union rules require a backstage crew of at least four, regardless of the show, and the box office must be staffed by three people. At some theaters union rules require a certain number of musicians, whether or not they are needed in a particular show. (Victor Borge, at the end of his solo piano performance on Broadway, asked musicians whose presence was required by union rules to line up for the curtain call, even though none had played a single note.)

To the extent that these union work rules raise ticket prices, the continued employment of union members depends on the elasticity of demand for theater tickets. With the top price per ticket running as high as $100, there is evidence that the demand has been elastic enough to put many theater employees out of work. Less than half of the theaters on Broadway are operating, and many union members are unemployed. Featherbedding rules require each theater to hire a specified number of employees, but these rules cannot dictate that theaters stay in business.

Because union staffing requirements are based on the number of seats in the theater, new shows have moved to smaller theaters off Broadway, shifting to the larger Broadway theaters only after their success seems assured. Producers have also reduced staffing requirements by reducing the number of seats that can be sold—in some cases by simply blocking off the balcony. In 1991 theater owners and unions agreed on a special arrangement that would allow theaters that had been empty to stage low-budget plays for bargain ticket prices.

Sources: "Unions Are Losing Their Star Billing on Broadway," *Business Week*, 26 November 1984; Robert Lenzner, "Economics Is Dimming the Lights of Broadway," *Boston Globe*, 1 February 1987; and Frank Rich, "The Great Dark Way: Slowly the Lights Are Dimming on Broadway," *New York Times*, 2 June 1991.

We have examined three ways in which unions can attempt to raise members' wages: (1) by negotiating a wage floor above the equilibrium wage for the industry and somehow rationing the limited jobs among union members, (2) by restricting the supply of labor, and (3) by increasing the demand for union labor. Unions can attempt to increase the demand for union labor in several ways: (1) through a direct public appeal to buy only union-made products, (2) by restricting the supply of products made by nonunion labor,

(3) by making union labor more productive through lower turnover costs, and (4) through featherbedding, which forces employers to employ more workers than they would prefer.

Bilateral Monopoly

Thus far we assumed that wages are determined through negotiations between the labor union and the entire industry. Since each firm hires labor as a price taker in the labor market, each firm can hire as much labor as it chooses at the negotiated wage. The model of a union bargaining with the entire industry describes the approach of industrial unions of the past.

More and more, however, negotiations are between a union and an individual employer, such as the UAW's negotiations with Caterpillar. The employer in this case is a price searcher in the labor market, or a **monopsonist**. *A monopsonist faces a labor supply curve that slopes upward.* For simplicity, we begin by examining the situation of this resource price searcher in the absence of a union, as depicted in Exhibit 3. The labor supply curve, *S*, determines the wage the firm must pay at each level of employment. Because the quantity of labor supplied to this firm increases only if the wage increases, the firm's marginal resource cost curve for labor is above the labor supply curve. In the absence of a union, the profit-maximizing firm will hire labor up to the point where labor's marginal resource cost equals its marginal revenue product. In Exhibit 3, the profit-maximizing level of employment is *E*, and the profit-maximizing wage as found at point *m* on the supply curve is *W.*

Monopsonist The sole purchaser of a particular resource

Teaching Tip A common goal of industrial unions that negotiated separately with an individual employer was to achieve wage and benefit provisions at least equal to those provided in other agreements existing within the industry or region. So the United Auto Workers might first bargain with Ford, then GM, then Chrysler. This bargaining style is known as *pattern bargaining.*

Thus, *a profit-maximizing monopsonist pays nonunionized labor a wage below labor's marginal revenue product.* In the absence of a union, workers have little power in dealing with the employer. An individual worker can either work or not for the firm at the wage offered by the employer. Workers whose opportunity cost is at or below *W* will work for the firm; those with a higher opportunity cost will not.

In contrast, the union, as a monopoly supplier of labor to the firm, has some power to negotiate the wage. The union's power rests on its willingness and ability to withhold all labor—to strike—if the employer does not comply. Thus, both sides have some economic power: the firm as the only employer of this type of labor, and the union as the only supplier of this type of labor. The union will try to push wages up, and the profit-maximizing firm will try to pay no more than it has to for a given amount of labor. **Bilateral monopoly** describes the situation in which a single seller, in this case a union, bargains with a single buyer, or monopsonist. Since both sides have some power, the wage will depend on the relative bargaining skills of each side. Economic theory alone cannot predict what the agreed-upon wage will be.

Bilateral monopoly A situation in which a single seller, or monopolist, bargains with a single buyer, or monopsonist

Of special significance in this bargaining model is the fact that the union, by pushing up wages, can initially increase both wages *and* employment. Notice in Exhibit 3 that without unions, workers are initially at point *m* on their supply curve. When the union negotiates a wage floor of *W′*, both the wage and the level of employment increase. The supply curve

EXHIBIT 3

Bilateral Monopoly

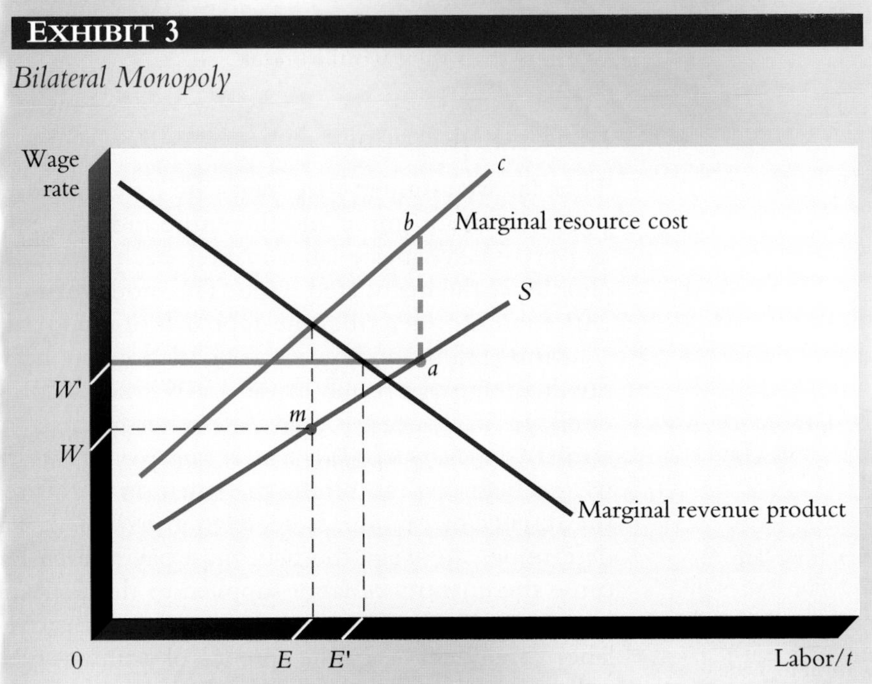

If a monopsonist faces a nonunionized workforce, the profit-maximizing employment level occurs where the marginal resource cost curve intersects the marginal revenue product curve. At that level of employment, *E*, the equilibrium wage, *W*, is found at point *m*, which lies on the labor supply curve, *S*. If the monopsonist faces a unionized workforce and the union can establish a wage floor, such as *W′*, the labor supply curve consists of the horizontal line *W′a* plus the upward-sloping segment *aS* on the labor supply curve. The monopsonist's marginal resource cost curve consists of the line segments *W′a*, *ab*, and *bc*. The monopsonist maximizes profits by operating where the marginal resource cost of labor is equal to its marginal revenue product, which yields an employment level *E′* at the floor wage *W′*.

for union labor now remains horizontal at the bargained wage until supply level *a* is reached. For employment levels greater than *a*, the supply curve is the upward-sloping line segment *aS*. Thus, the union's labor supply curve is *W′aS*, with a kink at point *a*.

Point to Stress
Whenever the supply curve is horizontal, it coincides with the marginal resource cost curve.

Given this kinked supply curve, the monopsonist's marginal resource cost curve for labor consists of two separate segments. For quantities of labor to the left of point *a*, the marginal resource cost curve is the horizontal segment, *W′a*, which is the wage floor. Within this range of employment, the firm can hire more labor at the wage floor, so the marginal resource cost is constant and equal to that wage. For employment levels greater than *a*, the labor supply curve slopes upward, so hiring another unit of labor means paying a higher wage to all workers. Thus, for labor quantities to the right of point *a*, that portion of the marginal resource cost above the supply curve segment *aS* is the relevant segment.

Teaching Tip If the union negotiates a wage above the intersection of the marginal revenue product curve with the original marginal resource cost curve, the level of employment will be lower with the union than without.

The *marginal resource cost curve* is therefore indicated by the line segments *W′a*, *ab*, and *bc*, which put together is *W′abc*. The kink in the labor supply curve, *W′as*, creates a gap in the firm's marginal resource cost curve, as reflected by the dashed line segment, *ab.* In Exhibit 3 the intersection of the firm's marginal resource cost curve for labor and its marginal revenue product curve for labor yields a wage of *W′* and employment of *E′*. In this example, both the wage and level of employment are greater with a union than without.

In summary, when a labor union negotiates with the firm that is the primary employer of that type of labor, a bilateral monopoly exists. The resulting wage will depend on the relative bargaining strength and skills of each side. Both the wage rate and the employment level can be increased over the levels achieved in the absence of a union.

OTHER UNION OBJECTIVES

Thus far we have assumed that unions attempt to maximize wages. Although this appears to be a reasonable assumption, union behavior at times seems to suggest other possible objectives, which we will explore in this section. Keep in mind during this discussion, however, that unions may adopt a variety of goals, depending on the circumstances, so no single model can capture all the variations.

Example The fall, 1992 strike at the GM Lordstown plant was over the loss of jobs, not wages. GM backed down from a plan to move 240 skilled-trade jobs to other plants, agreed to fill an additional 160 vacancies, and added 140 new jobs.

Maximize Employment

Let's turn to the market for a particular type of labor. In Exhibit 4, the industry demand curve is labeled *D* and the supply curve is labeled *S.* Without a union, the competitive market wage is *W* and the equilibrium quantity of labor is *E*. Individual firms in this industry are price takers in the resource market. Now suppose workers in the industry form a union. Consider the alternative wage and employment policies the union could adopt.

The union could attempt to *maximize the number of workers employed in the industry.* In Exhibit 4, employment is maximized at *E* when the competitive wage, *W*, is selected. Any wage higher than *W* lowers employment, since the quantity demanded is reduced, and any wage below *W* lowers employment, since the quantity supplied is reduced. The relevant portions of the supply and demand curves are drawn as solid lines (in contrast to the broken lines for the rest of the curves) to underscore the dominance of what is called the "short side" of the market. Note that at a wage above *W*, the demand curve determines employment, and at a wage below *W*, the supply curve determines employment. *So the competitive wage rate maximizes employment, but the workers do not need a union to achieve this objective.*

Maximize the Wage Bill

Total wage bill Employment multiplied by the average wage rate

Another possible objective for the union is to maximize the **total wage bill**, which is employment multiplied by the wage rate. Union officials may want

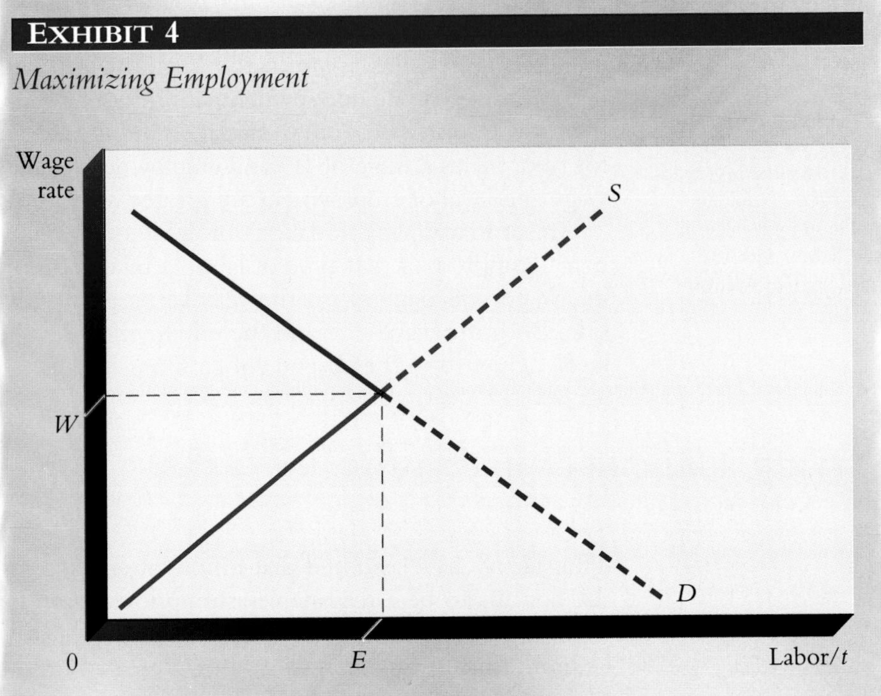

W is the equilibrium wage. At any other wage, employment is either the quantity demanded or the quantity supplied, whichever is less. Employment is maximized at *E* when the wage rate is at equilibrium.

to maximize the wage bill as a way of maximizing union dues, which typically are some percentage of pay. Consider the union as a monopoly seller of labor to firms that are resource price takers. To induce firms to hire additional labor, the union must lower the market wage. But as the union lowers the wage, the wage earned by those workers who were already employed in the industry must also fall. As a result, the union's *marginal revenue* will always be less than the wage.

Teaching Tip Maximizing the wage bill may be opposed by the rank-and-file membership, with eventual negative repercussions for the union leadership.

The union's marginal revenue (*MR*) curve in Exhibit 5 shows how much the total wage bill changes as the wage falls to increase employment. As long as the marginal revenue curve is positive, lower wages will increase the total wage bill. Recall that as long as the elasticity of demand is greater than one, marginal revenue is positive. Therefore, when the demand for labor is elastic, a lower wage will increase the total wage bill. When labor demand is inelastic, however, marginal revenue is negative, so a lower wage will reduce the total wage bill.

Consider the wage that maximizes total wages in this example. *The total wage bill is maximized where marginal revenue is equal to zero,* so a wage floor of W^* will maximize the total wage bill. To put it another way, the total wage bill is maximized where the elasticity of labor demand is equal to one, which is at point *b* on the labor demand curve. But the wage floor that maximizes

EXHIBIT 5

Maximizing the Total Wage Bill

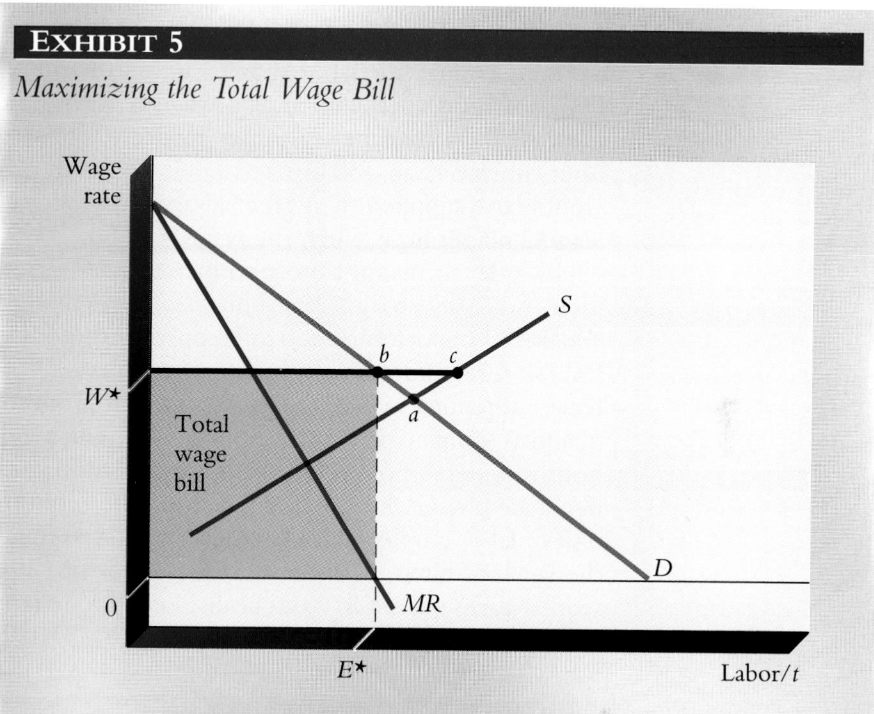

A union that is interested in maximizing the total wage bill paid to its members should negotiate wage W^*. With employment at E^*, the union's marginal revenue is zero. Further increases in employment will cause the wage bill to decrease. Wage W^* is read off the labor demand curve at point *b*. There is an excess quantity of labor supplied at that wage.

Point to Stress W^* is read off the labor demand curve. As long as W^* exceeds *a*, the union will continue to generate a wage-employment tradeoff.

the total wage bill in this example creates an excess supply of labor, identified as *bc*, so jobs must somehow be rationed among union members. Note that in this example the wage that maximizes the total wage bill exceeds the competitive wage, which is the wage associated with the intersection of the supply and demand curves at point *a*. If the labor supply curve intersected the labor demand curve at point *b* in Exhibit 5, the wage that maximized the total wage bill would also be the competitive wage.

Maximize Economic Rent

Some observers have suggested that *union leaders attempt to maximize the difference between the market wage and the opportunity cost of workers' time in its best alternative use*—that is, to maximize the *economic rent* earned by union workers. This approach explicitly takes each member's opportunity cost into account. (Recall that the total earnings of any resource can be divided between opportunity cost and economic rent.) The labor supply curve represents the minimum amount workers must be paid to supply each additional unit of labor to this particular market. The height of the supply curve at each level of

Point to Stress For the first 10,000 hours, workers who are employed have an opportunity cost per hour of $5 or less.

Point to Stress The wage of $20 per hour maximizes total economic rent, not economic rent per unit.

employment represents workers' opportunity cost of providing that marginal unit of employment.

For example, the labor supply curve in Exhibit 6 shows that only 10,000 hours of labor are supplied at a wage of $5 per hour because at that wage most workers have better things to do. If the wage increases to $7.50 per hour, however, an additional 10,000 hours are supplied. All workers who would have supplied their labor at a wage of $5 earn an economic rent of at least $2.50 per hour when the wage is $7.50.

In order to maximize economic rent, the union should expand employment until the marginal revenue from supplying additional units of labor equals the opportunity cost of supplying those additional units of labor. In Exhibit 6 the union's marginal revenue curve and the labor supply curve intersect at point *a*, where the opportunity cost of time is $10 per hour, and the quantity supplied is 30,000 hours. The rent-maximizing wage of $20 per hour is found at point *b* on the labor demand curve. If the union leaders can negotiate a wage floor of $20 per hour, the economic rent earned on the last unit of labor employed is the wage rate of $20 minus the opportunity cost of the last unit hired, $10. So at a wage floor of $20 per hour, each employed worker earns at least $10 per hour in economic rent.

EXHIBIT 6

Maximizing Economic Rent

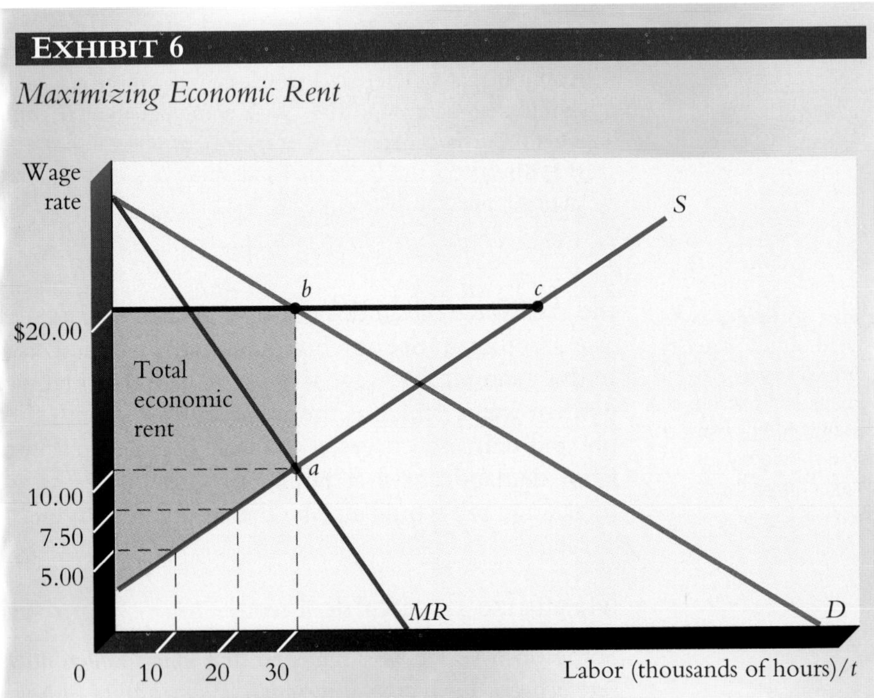

At point *a* the union's marginal revenue curve intersects the labor supply curve. The corresponding employment level (here, 30,000 hours) maximizes economic rent to employed workers. However, there is excess supply at the corresponding wage rate (here, $20 per hour).

The total economic rent is reflected by the blue shaded area above the supply curve but below the wage floor of $20. This economic rent represents "pure gravy" to the workers because it reflects a payment over and above their opportunity cost, the amount required to attract each additional unit of labor to this market.

Point to Stress
Maximizing economic rent also has a wage-employment tradeoff. Without the union, equilibrium would occur at the intersection of supply and demand in Exhibit 6.

There are problems with the rent-maximizing solution, however. Unions are made up of a variety of workers with different backgrounds and different opportunity costs, so it probably would be difficult for a union to pursue such a well-defined objective as rent maximization. And even if rent maximization were achieved, there would be a large excess supply of labor at the wage floor (*bc* in Exhibit 6), which would create much frustration among union members. Nonetheless, the union goal of rent maximization allows us to consider unions as monopoly sellers of labor.

Teaching Tip
Union bargaining over working conditions and safety, although very important during earlier years, became less important with the passage of federal and state legislation dealing with such issues (see the conclusion to this chapter).

Summary of Union Objectives

This section explored several possible union goals other than simply maximizing the wage, including maximizing (1) employment, (2) the total wage bill, and (3) economic rent. A competitive market maximizes employment naturally—without unions. Maximizing the total wage bill is achieved by finding the wage floor that equates the marginal revenue of additional employment to zero. As we've just seen, achieving the third goal—maximizing the economic rent received by union members—requires union leaders to negotiate the wage floor that equates the union's marginal revenue to the opportunity cost of the last unit hired. But achieving either the second or third goal is likely to create excess supply, requiring the union to ration jobs. In reality, unions may adopt a variety of goals, depending on the circumstances.

Some observers believe union officials pursue wage-employment strategies that ensure the survival and growth of the union, keep most union members happy, and keep the leadership in office. Recent empirical work on union goals suggests that whatever their goals, unions appear to be sensitive to the tradeoff between the wage level and the employment level.

Recent Trends in Union Membership and Bargaining Power

In 1955 about one-third of nonfarm wage and salary workers belonged to unions. Union membership as a percentage of the work force has declined since then, so now less than one-sixth of nonfarm wage and salary workers belong to unions. The decline in union membership in recent decades is due in part to structural changes in the economy. Unions have long been more important in the industrial sector than in the service sector. But employment in the industrial sector, including manufacturing, mining, and construction, declined from 37 percent of the nonfarm work force in 1960 to 22 percent today. During the same interval, service employment increased from 63 percent to 78 percent. These days union membership rates are highest among government employees, over one-third of whom are unionized, compared to only one-eighth of the private sector. A typical union member these days is a schoolteacher. Union workers are now more likely brain-workers than brawn-workers.

The bar graph in Exhibit 7 indicates recent U.S. union membership rates by age and gender. The rates for men, indicated by the blue shaded bars, are higher than the rates for women, in part because men tend to be employed more in manufacturing and women more in the service sector, where union membership historically has been lower. The highest membership rates are for middle-aged males. Though the exhibit does not show it, blacks have a higher union membership rate than whites, in part because blacks are more often employed by government and by heavy industries such as autos and steel, where the membership rate tends to be higher.

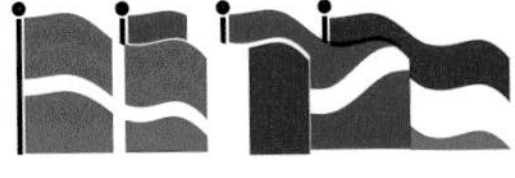

Compared with those of other industrialized countries, the United States' union participation rate is relatively low. Exhibit 8 shows the union participation rate for both 1980 and 1988 for eight leading industrial countries. Notice two points: first, only in Sweden did membership rates increase between

EXHIBIT 7

Union Membership as a Percent of Total Wage and Salary Employment by Age and Gender for 1988

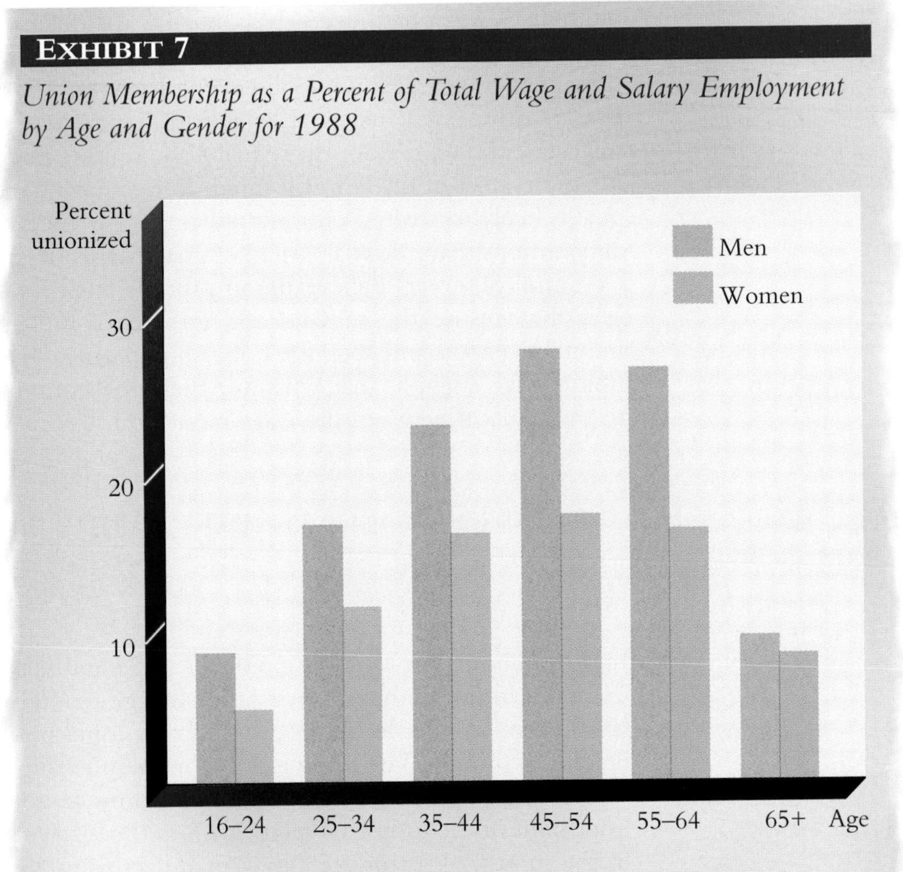

Source: U.S. Department of Labor, Employment and Earnings (Washington, DC: U.S. Government Printing Office, 1989), table 59.

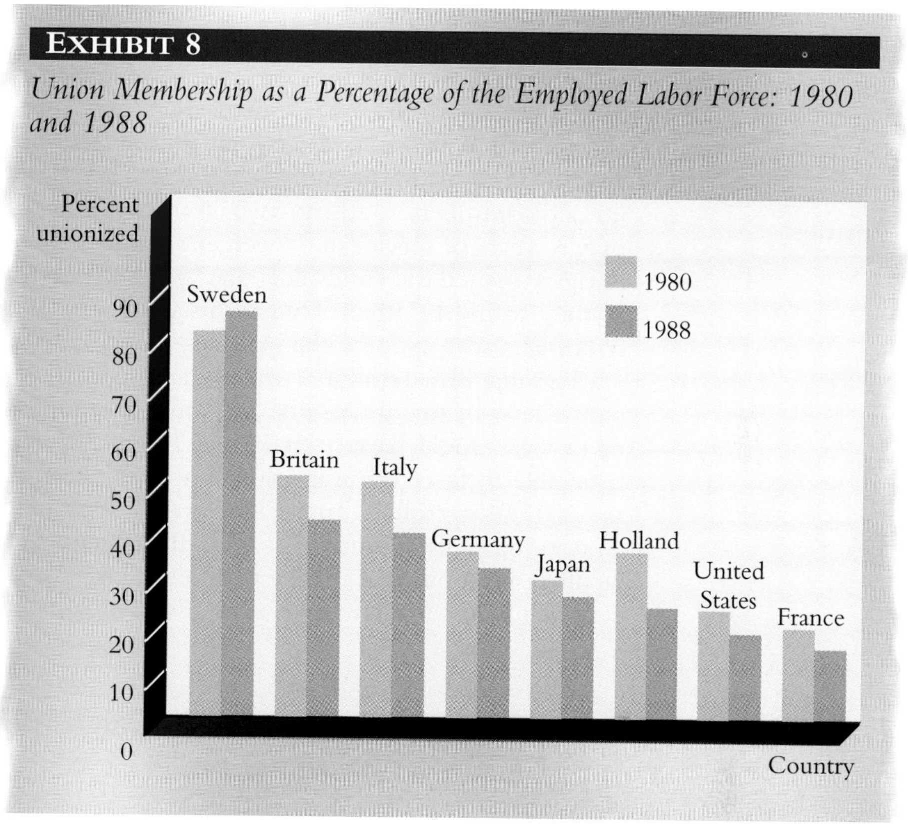

Source: Organization for Economic Cooperation and Development, as reported in *The Economist*, 5 September 1992; figure for the United States is for 1989, not 1988.

1980 and 1988; and second, U.S. union participation rates are lower than in all other countries except France.

Let's examine recent developments that have contributed to current trends in unionization in the United States.

Public Employee Unions

Teaching Tip Executive Order 10988, signed by President Kennedy in 1962, gave the public-sector unions fewer rights than private-sector unions. Most still lack the legal right to strike, although they often do so (note the case of PATCO).

Union membership among public employees (i.e., employees of local, state, and federal government) climbed sharply during the 1970s but leveled off during the 1980s. With increased membership in public employee unions has come the ticklish problem of strikes by such groups. Whereas some consumers suffer modest inconveniences if, say, auto workers go on strike, a strike by police personnel or fire fighters could jeopardize public safety. Most states have laws restricting strikes by public employees.

The issue of public employee strikes was dramatized in 1981, when the Professional Air Traffic Controllers Organization (PATCO) called a strike. As federal employees, they were prohibited by law from striking, and they were fired by President Ronald Reagan. The firings sent a strong signal to other public employee unions. We examine the event more closely in the following case study.

CASE STUDY

PATCO's Billion-Dollar Gamble

On August 3, 1981, PATCO struck for higher wages and better working conditions. PATCO's move was a big gamble because, by undertaking an illegal strike, union members put at risk secure jobs that at the time paid an average of $35,000 per year (which amounts to over $55,000 in 1994 dollars). PATCO made three major demands: a $10,000 across-the-board raise for all controllers, a thirty-two-hour work week, and retirement after twenty years of service at 75 percent of the retiree's highest pay. President Reagan warned the controllers that unless they returned to work by August 5, they would be fired. True to his word, the President fired the 11,345 controllers who ignored the back-to-work ultimatum.

The graph in Exhibit 9 crudely approximates the market for air traffic controllers. In the absence of a union, the equilibrium wage and employment level would have been *W* and *E*, respectively. PATCO, however, had been able to force the wage floor up to an average of $35,000 per year for the 15,000 controllers, an attractive salary for a job that requires no college education. (This amount exceeded the average pay at the time for college faculty—positions that usually require Ph.Ds.) As you can see, there was excess supply at the prevailing wage. Evidence of the excess supply was the

EXHIBIT 9

Labor Market for Air Traffic Controllers

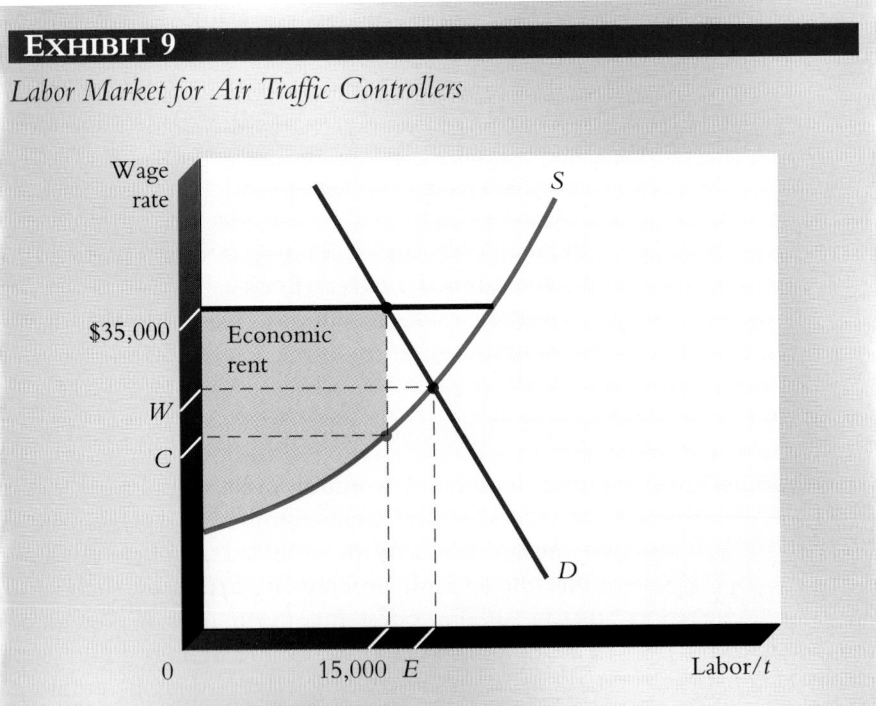

In the absence of a union, the equilibrium wage and employment level would have been *W* and *E*. At the negotiated wage of $35,000 per year, 15,000 PATCO controllers were employed. The corresponding economic rent was about $170 million per year.

overwhelming number of applications from people wishing to replace the striking controllers (over 200,000 people applied for the 11,345 openings).

The supply curve represents the opportunity cost of offering labor services as an air traffic controller. The opportunity cost for the last worker hired, identified as *C* in Exhibit 9, was below the actual wage paid. Given the narrow nature of their job experience and the fact that most controllers had no college degree, their alternatives probably paid much less than a controller's salary. The shaded area is a rough approximation of the economic rent earned by air traffic controllers. Those who were fired lost their share of this economic rent.

Fired workers paid a very high price for their strike. What was their best alternative wage? A survey of 900 former controllers showed that about 60 percent had annual *household* incomes, which include the earnings of spouses, of less than $25,000 three years after the strike. Thus, an optimistic estimate of the average alternative wage in 1981 was about $20,000, implying an average economic rent of at least $15,000 per ex-controller, for a total annual economic rent of $170 million. We will see in the next chapter how to compute the value of a stream of income; for now let's simply say that those who were fired lost a stream of income with a value of about $2 billion, or about $175,000 per fired controller.

There is more to the job than money, however. If the best alternative was an easier, more pleasant job, the dollar difference in pay would have overstated the true economic rent of the job. But most air traffic controllers apparently enjoyed the tension and the prestige associated with the job. As one former controller lamented, "It's hard to get it out of your blood. It's the most exciting thing that most of us will ever do." Many said that guiding airline traffic produced a deep sense of satisfaction. According to one researcher who has tracked many controllers since 1981, most have since found other work, "but they have suffered a substantial drop in income and prestige in occupation."

Source: Roger Lowenstein, "For Fired Air-Traffic Controllers, Life's OK, but Not Like Old Times," *Wall Street Journal*, 1 August 1986.

Competition from Nonunion Suppliers

Example Import competition has also greatly affected union membership in the consumer electronics, clothing, shoe, and textile industries. In addition, union membership has dropped as a result of decertification elections—the unions lost four-fifths of such votes in 1988.

Since the Middle Ages, craft unions have attempted to increase their wages by restricting output. Weavers from a city would sometimes make forays into the countryside to destroy looms and other weaving devices, thereby shutting off these competing sources of labor. Competition from nonunion suppliers is still a major problem facing many unions today. Although unions usually can prevent unionized employers from hiring nonunion workers, they cannot block the entry of new nonunion firms, nor can they always restrict imports. Since 1955, for example, U.S. imports have increased from 5 percent to 12 percent of gross domestic product. The United Auto Workers has lost over one-third of its membership since 1979 to foreign competition. Even more troublesome to the UAW, three Japanese auto producers have established nonunion production facilities in the United States. Unions are now worried about losing jobs to Mexico because of the North American Free Trade Agreement.

Example In late 1992, Caterpillar Inc. decided unilaterally to impose a work schedule of four ten-hour days on its employees. This would allow round-the-clock operation of the expensive machinery purchased in a $2 billion modernization effort.

In competitive markets relatively high-cost producers will not survive. Union membership among construction workers fell sharply over the last decade because many union members were unable to find union jobs. In the face of nonunion competition, these unions have been forced to make concessions over wages and work rules. In some parts of the country, unions are permitting construction contractors to hire a larger proportion of apprentices, who are typically paid only half the union scale, and unions are allowing their members to work on the same jobs as nonunion members, which was unheard of a few years ago. For example, Xerox received union approval to employ more part-time and temporary workers rather than move production of its personal copiers overseas.

Tight times have even caused some union workers to compete among themselves. For example, when General Motors was deciding which plants were to be closed in 1992, they let workers in Arlington, Texas, and Ypsilanti, Michigan, know that only one of the two plants would survive. The 3,200 workers at Texas went all out to make sure they survived, agreeing to allow a three-shift schedule and relaxing other work-rule restrictions. Michigan workers, on the other hand, offered few concessions, so that plant was closed.

Industry Deregulation

Example The Teamsters Union began actively recruiting white-collar workers in the 1990s.

For the last twenty years, the Teamsters Union has negotiated union wages for truckers through a national contract. Government regulations blocked new entry into the industry and prevented existing firms from competing on the basis of price. Thus, trucking regulations provided an environment conducive to union demands. *But the deregulation of several major industries, including trucking, airlines, intercity bus lines, and telecommunications, has reduced the union's negotiating power in these industries.*

Although the Teamsters Union can prevent unionized firms from hiring nonunion drivers, it cannot prevent other firms from entering the industry. Deregulation of the trucking industry dropped the floor that had propped up the rates charged by all companies, both union and nonunion. The demise of regulation set off rate competition, leading to business failures and eliminating nearly one-third of the jobs controlled by the Teamsters. Since deregulation in 1980, more than 10,000 low-cost, nonunion operators have entered the industry, nearly doubling the number of nonunion carriers. The union was obliged to give up its automatic cost-of-living adjustment and to agree to a lower wage for new employees, creating a *two-tiered wage structure.*

Example By the end of 1994, AT&T planned to close thirty-one offices and eliminate up to one-third of long-distance operator jobs by installing computerized voice-recognition systems.

Unionization and Technological Change

Some blue-collar workers, such as members of the United Mine Workers, have lost jobs as a result of automation. With employment stagnant in the so-called smokestack industries, leaders of the union movement looked to emerging high-technology areas as a source of new members. Unions made a special effort in the 1970s and 1980s to organize high-tech workers but were largely unsuccessful. Aside from some defense contractors, the electronics industry remains mostly nonunion. Union organizers could not deal with the high job turnover created by the rapid entry and exit of firms in the high-technology industries. Moreover, progressive managers in many high-tech firms encouraged worker participation and often provided lavish bonuses and perks. For example, stock options made dozens of the original employees at Apple Computer millionaires. The workers in such firms were not good prospects for unionization.

A Fight for Survival

With their membership shrinking, unions have adopted new tactics in an attempt to ensure their survival. One alternative has been to merge with other unions. Mergers can reduce costs per member by spreading out expenses for staff and headquarters, and the larger membership can enhance the union's political clout. Some unions have even resorted to unfriendly takeovers of rival unions. Since 1980 there have been more than thirty union mergers. One problem with the merger solution is that the interests of the resulting organization may be seriously divided. For example, the mismatched marriage between the Pottery Workers Union and the Seafarers International Union lasted only eighteen months before divergent interests caused the parties to split.

Unions are also trying to leverage their thinning ranks by teaming up with other organizations for political support. For example, rather than attack directly the free-trade agreement with Mexico, labor unions such as the Steelworkers and the United Auto Workers encouraged environmental and religious groups to lead the fight. Some U.S. unions have also begun organizing Mexican workers to raise wages and benefits there; the more Mexican workers are paid, the less likely they will take jobs from the United States. And rather than object directly to clothing imports, the Garment Workers Union got help from groups concerned with the destruction of the tropical rain forests. The public responds more readily to environmental appeals than to the special-interest appeals of union workers.

Conclusion

When unions first appeared in our nation's history, working conditions were dreadful. Hours were long, pay was low, and the workplace was hazardous. The last century brought revolutionary improvements in the conditions of the average worker. The real income of workers has increased more than ninefold since 1860, and the average work week has dropped from sixty-six hours to about forty hours. The workplace has also become much safer. We cannot credit all these improvements to the development of organized labor alone, however. Technological change increased labor productivity, which supported higher wages and better benefits. Although union members were always a minority of the work force, never exceeding one-third of the total, just the threat of unionization encouraged some nonunion employers to match benefits available in unionized firms. So the effects of unions spilled over to nonunion firms.

The labor movement also focused attention on the problems of workers and helped develop the political consensus to introduce employee-oriented legislation. In the last thirty years, the federal government has broadened worker protection against unfair dismissal, plant closings, worker injuries, and unemployment. Social Security, medicare, and other government transfer programs buffer workers from the ravages of poor health and old age. *But as government provides a broader menu of social insurance, workers feel less compelled to rely on unions for protection.* Unions to some extent have become victims of their own success.

At one time, because of government regulations, foreign trade restrictions, and the lack of competition from nonunion firms, unions dominated some industries. But deregulation, technological change, the government's replacement of striking air traffic controllers, and growing competition from nonunion firms both here and abroad have seriously challenged union positions in industries such as steel, autos, trucking, airlines, and construction. As global competition intensifies, employers have a harder time passing higher union labor costs along to consumers. In the wake of the PATCO strike, firms have been more aggressive in hiring replacement workers; the threat of losing a job to a replacement worker when well-paying jobs are hard to find has reduced union workers' willingness to strike. Both in the United States and around the world, labor union members represent a diminishing segment of the labor force.

Summary

1. The formation of labor unions in the United States was in part a response to long hours and poor working conditions in the nineteenth and the early twentieth century. Unions received a boost from government during the Great Depression, when several laws were passed to improve unions' legal standing.
2. Unions and employers attempt to negotiate a mutually agreeable labor contract through collective bargaining. A major source of union power is the threat of a strike, which is an attempt to withhold labor from the firm.
3. Inclusive, or industrial, unions attempt to establish a wage floor that exceeds the free market wage. But a wage above the market-clearing level creates an excess supply of labor, so the union must somehow ration jobs among its members. Exclusive, or craft, unions try to raise the wage by restricting the supply of labor. Another way to raise union wages is to increase the demand for union labor.
4. When a labor union negotiates with the only employer of that type of labor, this is a bilateral monopoly. The resulting wage will depend on the relative bargaining strengths and skills of each side. Unions may be able to increase both the wage rate and the employment level beyond the levels the monopsonist would choose if labor were not organized.
5. Unions may pursue goals other than maximizing the wage. The maximization of employment occurs as a result of natural market forces and requires no union. Unions can try to maximize either the total wage bill paid to union members or the total economic rent going to labor, but these policies usually create an excess supply of labor, requiring job rationing. No one goal accounts for all union behavior.
6. Union membership as a percentage of the labor force has been decreasing for decades. Today, less than one-sixth of the nonfarm labor force is unionized, compared to one-third in 1955. Unions' problems have included competition from nonunion workers and imports, deregulation, a greater public safety net, and technological change.

QUESTIONS AND PROBLEMS

1. (Labor History) What historical reasons can be given for the development of labor organizations?

2. (Unions and the Law) Why was the passage of federal laws rather than state or local laws important to the large labor organizations, such as the AFL-CIO?

3. (Strikes) How might a large company protect itself against a protracted strike? Use coal mining as an example in your answer.

4. (Strikes) Why would strikes be most effective in industries where there were very high fixed costs?

5. (Unions and Employee Benefits) Why have past tax laws encouraged unions to ask for higher employee benefits rather than just higher wages?

6. (Union Behavior) Will economic rents for union workers increase if unions are successful in raising the demand for the products the workers produce? Will transfer earnings also increase? Why or why not?

7. (Union Behavior) Show that maximizing the wage bill always leads to greater employment than maximizing economic rent.

8. (Unions and Business) Why might unions and business lobby together in Washington, D.C. to protect the industry from foreign competition? Who would oppose such lobbying?

9. (Wage Bill Maximization) Use the data below to answer the following questions.

Quantity of Labor	*Marginal Revenue Product*
0	——
1	\$50
2	45
3	40
4	33
5	20
6	5
7	0

   a. If the firm's supply of labor is perfectly elastic at \$20, how much labor will get hired?
   b. What labor price would maximize the total wage bill?
   c. Who gains and who loses if a union succeeds in changing the labor price to the level you calculated in part b?

10. (Wage Differentials) Using supply-demand diagrams, show what happens to wage differentials between unionized and nonunionized sectors of the labor force when the union negotiates a wage rate for the unionized sector that is above the labor-market equilibrium.

11. (Union Behavior) Using a supply-demand diagram for labor, compare the effects on wages and employment in a unionized industry of each of the following:
   a. Conducting a "Buy American" plan
   b. Featherbedding
   c. Negotiating a minimum wage above the market-clearing wage

12. (Bilateral Monopoly) What is the marginal resource cost curve for a monopsonist that faces collective bargaining with a union?

13. (Bilateral Monopoly) Refer to Exhibit 3 to answer the following questions.
   a. Show the gains and losses to the employee and the employer if workers receive the union-negotiated wage W' rather than the nonunion wage W.
   b. What wage is the economically efficient wage? Why?

14. (Union Effects) Compare the effects of unions illustrated in Exhibits 1 and 2. What, if any, differences exist in terms of union wage levels and employment? What reason can be suggested for adopting one approach over the other?

15. (Union Effects) If unions are able to increase the industry-wide wage above the competitive market-clearing level, what will happen to the industry price, industry output, labor-capital ratios, and the total payment to nonlabor resources? Explain the basis for your answer.

16. (Union Effects) Compare the economic rents earned by union labor at the market and union wage rate in Exhibit 1. How do you determine which wage yields a greater total economic rent?

17. (Union Effects) Explain how each of the following is likely to affect the impact of a union-backed wage increase on employment in the unionized industry.
    a. The ratio of labor used relative to other resources
    b. The elasticity of product demand
    c. The marginal rate of technical substitution across resources

18. (Maximizing the Wage Bill) If the elasticity of demand for labor exceeds 1 at the competitive wage, forming a union to maximize the wage bill makes no sense. Discuss.

19. (Featherbedding on Broadway) One way to reduce the problems associated with featherbedding on Broadway would be to convince people that there is no substitute for seeing a play on Broadway. What impact would this have on featherbedding?

20. (Featherbedding on Broadway) Broadway show tickets are frequently sold as part of a package that might include transportation, hotel accommodations, and/or other amenities. How would the impact of featherbedding be affected by such package deals?

21. (PATCO) As the text notes, government employees have the highest union membership rates. What reasons can you suggest for this? Why do you think union membership leveled off in the 1980s?

22. (PATCO) PATCO argued that the reduction of the work week to thirty-two hours per week was necessitated by high stress levels associated with traffic control work. What other reason can you suggest for such a demand?

CHAPTER 27

CAPITAL, INTEREST, AND CORPORATE FINANCE

So far the discussion of resources has focused primarily on human resources. This emphasis is appropriate since labor income alone represents more than three-quarters of all resource income. The returns to labor, however, depend in part on the amount and quality of the other resources employed. A farmer driving a huge tractor is more productive than one who scrapes the soil with a stick. In this chapter we discuss the returns to nonhuman resources, particularly capital. We also take a closer look at how firms are financed and the problems that arise when owners do not run the firm.

Teaching Tip See Chapters 1 and 7 to review the two meanings of interest and Chapters 1 and 24 for the two meanings of rent.

One problem that crops up in discussions of resources is that economists sometimes use the same term in slightly different ways. For example, the term *interest* is used to mean both the amount earned for lending money and the return earned by capital as a resource. Another term that can be a source of confusion is *rent*. Earlier we distinguished between opportunity cost, the payment necessary to attract a resource to a particular use, and economic rent, the amount in excess of opportunity cost. Often we refer to the return on land as rent, because land is typically thought to be in fixed supply and the return on a resource in fixed supply consists entirely of economic rent. Topics discussed in this chapter include

- Consumption, production, and time
- Roundabout production
- Optimal investment
- Loanable funds
- Present value and discounting
- Corporate finance
- The separation of ownership from control
- The market for corporate control

THE ROLE OF TIME IN CONSUMPTION AND PRODUCTION

Time plays an important role in both production and consumption. In this section we will first consider the effect of time on the production decision and show why firms are willing to pay for the use of household savings. Next we will consider time in the consumption decision and show why households must be rewarded for saving, or for deferring consumption. Then, bringing together the desires of borrowers and the desires of savers, we will examine the equilibrium rate of interest.

Production, Saving, and Time

Point to Stress Savings are needed whenever current production is not providing for current consumption. This would also include seasons when crops are not being grown.

Point to Stress Jones must compare *present* costs (reduced production and thus consumption) to *future* benefits (increased production and thus consumption).

Teaching Tip Various layers of roundabout production are possible. Capital goods can be used to produce more capital goods rather than consumer goods.

Roundabout production The production of capital goods, which can then be used to produce consumer goods

Suppose Jones is a primitive farmer in a primitive economy. Isolated from any neighbors or markets, he literally scratches out a living on a plot of land, using only crude sticks as farm implements. While a crop is growing, none of it is available for present consumption. Since production takes time, Jones must rely on food saved from prior production to support himself during the time required to grow the crop. The longer the growing season, the more savings required. Thus, even in this simple example, it is clear that *production cannot occur without savings.*

Suppose that with his current resources, consisting of land, labor, seed corn, fertilizer, and some crude sticks, Jones grows about 100 bushels of corn per year. He soon realizes that if he had a plow—a type of investment good, or capital—his productivity would increase. Making a plow in such a crude setting, however, would be time-consuming, keeping him away from the fields for a year. Thus, the plow has an opportunity cost of 100 bushels of corn. Jones will be unable to sustain this temporary drop in production unless he has saved enough food from previous harvests to allow him to forgo the annual crop.

During the time required to produce capital, Jones must rely on his savings from prior production. Should he invest his time in the task of making the plow? The answer depends on the costs and benefits of the plow. We already know that the cost is 100 bushels—the forgone output. The benefit depends on how much the plow will increase crop production and how long it will last. Jones figures that the plow will increase production by 20 bushels per year and will last his lifetime. Suppose he decides the benefit of increasing corn production by 20 bushels per year exceeds the opportunity cost of 100 bushels sacrificed to make the plow.

In making the plow, he will be engaging in **roundabout production**. Roundabout production involves producing capital goods rather than consumer goods. These capital goods are then used to increase output. An increased amount of roundabout production in an economy means that more capital accumulates, so more consumer goods (and capital goods) can be produced in the future. Advanced industrial economies are characterized by much roundabout production and abundant capital accumulation.

We have yet to introduce trade into our discussion of production. Nonetheless, we have demonstrated why production cannot occur without savings. *Production requires savings because both direct and roundabout production require time—time during which goods and services are not available from current production.* Now let's modernize the example by introducing the ability to borrow. Many farmers visit the bank each spring to borrow enough "seed money" to finance production until their crop is grown and sold. Likewise, other businesses often borrow at least a portion of the start-up funds needed to get going. Thus, in a modern economy, production need not rely exclusively on each producer's prior savings. Banks and other financial institutions accept the deposits of savers to lend to borrowers. Financial markets for trading stocks and bonds also help to channel savings to firms.

Teaching Tip The examples given indicate that impatience is a reason for the positive rate of time preference. Another possible reason is uncertainty—if you wait, something may intervene to prevent consumption of the good.

Consumption, Saving, and Time

Did you ever burn the roof of your mouth biting into a slice of pizza before it had cooled sufficiently? Have you done this more than once? Why does such self-mutilation persist? It persists because that bite of pizza is worth more to you now than the same bite five minutes from now. In fact, you are even willing to risk burning your mouth rather than wait until the pizza has lost its destructive properties. In a small way this phenomenon reflects the fact that you and other consumers value *present* consumption more than *future* consumption: you and other consumers have a **positive rate of time preference**.

Positive rate of time preference A characteristic of consumers, who value present consumption more highly than future consumption

Because present consumption is valued more than future consumption, you are willing to pay a higher price to consume something now rather than later. And prices often reflect this greater willingness to pay. Consider the movies. You pay more if you see a movie at a first-run theater than if you wait until it shows up at other theaters. If you are patient, you can wait for the video; if you are extremely patient, you can wait until it shows up on TV. The same is true for books. If you are willing to wait until a new book is available in paperback, you can usually buy it for less than one-third of the hardback price. Photo developers, dry cleaners, fast food restaurants, convenience stores, and other suppliers tout the speed of their services, knowing that consumers are willing to pay more for earlier availability, other things constant. Perhaps this T-shirt slogan captures the point: "Life is uncertain. Eat dessert first."

Point to Stress Future potential consumption includes what can be purchased with all accumulated interest.

Because present consumption is valued more than future consumption, households must be rewarded if they are to postpone consumption; in other words, saving must be rewarded. By saving their money in financial institutions such as banks, households refrain from spending a portion of their income on present consumption in return for the promise of a greater ability to consume in the future. Interest is the reward offered households to forgo present consumption. Specifically, the **interest rate** is the amount of money earned by savers for giving up the use of one dollar for a year. If the interest rate is 5 percent, a saver earns 5 cents per year for each dollar saved in a financial institution.

Interest rate The amount of money paid for the use of a dollar for one year

The greater the interest rate, other things constant, the more consumers are rewarded for saving, so the greater the opportunity cost of present consumption in terms of forgone interest earned and hence future consumption.

For example, at an interest rate of 5 percent, a household can place $100 in a savings account and end up with $105 a year from now. So $100 worth of consumption today has an opportunity cost of $105 in consumption a year from now. At an interest rate of 10 percent, $100 worth of consumption today has an opportunity cost of $110 in consumption a year from now.

Loanable funds market The market in which savers (suppliers of funds) and borrowers (demanders of funds) come together to determine the market rate of interest

Supply of loanable funds The relation between the market rate of interest and the quantity of savings supplied to the economy, other things constant

Consequently, the greater the interest rate offered for saving, other things constant, the greater the amount households are willing to save. Banks are willing to pay interest on consumer savings because the banks can, in turn, lend these savings to those who need credit, such as farmers, home buyers, and firms. The banks play the role of *financial intermediaries* in what is known as the market for loanable funds. The **loanable funds market** brings together savers, or suppliers of loanable funds, and borrowers, or demanders of loanable funds, to determine the market rate of interest. The **supply of loanable funds** reflects the positive relation between the market rate of interest and the quantity of savings, other things constant, as shown by the upward-sloping supply curve in Exhibit 1.

Teaching Tip
Held constant along the supply of loanable funds curve are the rate of time preference (the degree of impatience and uncertainty), the rate of inflation, and tax laws.

EXHIBIT 1

Supply of Loanable Funds

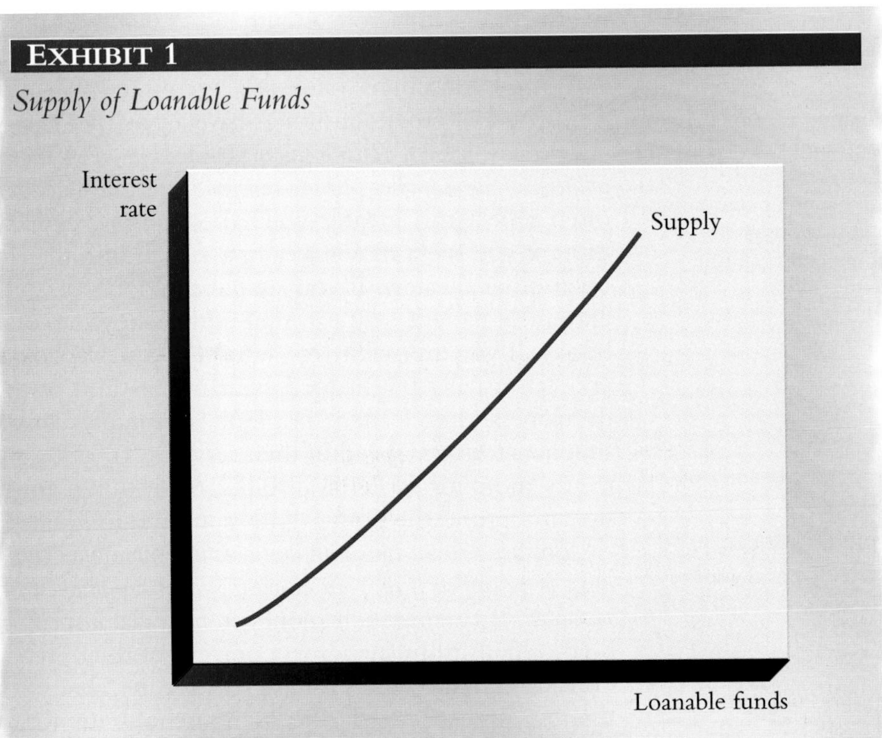

The greater the interest rate, other things constant, the more consumers are rewarded for saving and the greater the cost of present consumption in terms of future consumption. The greater the interest rate, the greater consumers' willingness to save; the supply of loanable funds slopes upward.

Optimal Investment

In a market economy characterized by specialization and exchange, Farmer Jones no longer has to produce his own capital, nor does he need his own savings. He can invest in capital using borrowed funds. Suppose he is interested in buying a tractor. There are many sizes on the market, from the small garden variety to the huge "Terminator." Column (1) of Exhibit 2(a) lists tractor sizes in 40-horsepower increments, beginning with the smallest. The total and marginal physical products of each tractor are listed in columns (2) and (3). Note that other resources are constant (in this case, the farmer's labor, land, seeds, and fertilizer).

Without capital, Jones can grow 100 bushels of corn per year. The smallest tractor will allow him to double production to 200 bushels per year; thus, the smallest size tractor has a marginal physical product of 100 bushels. With the next largest size, total output increases from 200 to 280 bushels, so the marginal physical product of that size tractor is 80 bushels. Note that in this example diminishing marginal returns set in immediately. The marginal physical product continues to decrease as the tractors get larger, dropping to zero for the 240-horsepower tractor. Though the exhibit does not show it, the marginal physical product could turn negative for tractors larger than 240 horsepower. (You might imagine a tractor so large that it would be hard to maneuver on the farmer's relatively small plot.)

Point to Stress Marginal revenue product equals marginal physical product times the product price only if the producer is a price taker in the product market.

Suppose Jones sells corn in a perfectly competitive market, so he is a price taker in the market for corn. He can sell all he wants at the market price of $4 per bushel. This price is multiplied by the marginal physical product from column (3) to yield each tractor's *marginal revenue product* in column (4). The marginal revenue product in this example is the marginal physical product times the price, or the change in total revenue resulting from increasing the tractor size by 40 horsepower. The marginal revenue product is the amount by which an increment in tractor size increases total revenue each year, assuming the price of corn remains unchanged.

Teaching Tip The simplifying assumptions in this example are designed to greatly reduce the complexity of calculating the marginal rate of return on investment.

The purchase price of each tractor is listed in column (5). The smallest tractor sells for $1,000, the next largest for $2,000, and so on, with the price increasing by $1,000 for each 40-horsepower increase in size. Thus, the marginal cost of buying a larger tractor is $1,000, as listed in column (6). Suppose the tractors are so durable that they last indefinitely, that operating expenses are negligible, and that the price of corn is expected to remain at $4 per bushel in the future. The tractor selected will increase revenue not only in the first year but every year into the future. Thus, the tractor yields a flow of marginal productivity now and in the future. Since the tractor costs a sum of money now but yields a stream of revenue now and in the future, the optimal solution requires us to take time into account. We can't simply equate marginal resource cost with marginal revenue product because the marginal resource cost is for a tractor that is expected to last indefinitely but the marginal revenue product is an annual amount now and in the future. As we will see, economists bridge time by use of the interest rate.

EXHIBIT 2

Marginal Rate of Return on Investment

(a) Schedule

Tractor Size (horse-power) (1)	Total Physical Product (bushels) (2)	Marginal Physical Product (*MPP*) (3)	Marginal Revenue Product (*MRP*) (4) = (3) x $4	Total Tractor Cost (5)	Marginal Resource Cost (*MRC*) (6)	Marginal Rate of Return (7) = (4)/(6)
0	100	—	—	$ 0	—	—
40	200	100	$400	1,000	$1,000	40%
80	280	80	320	2,000	1,000	32
120	340	60	240	3,000	1,000	24
160	380	40	160	4,000	1,000	16
200	400	20	80	5,000	1,000	8
240	400	0	0	6,000	1,000	0

(b) Curve

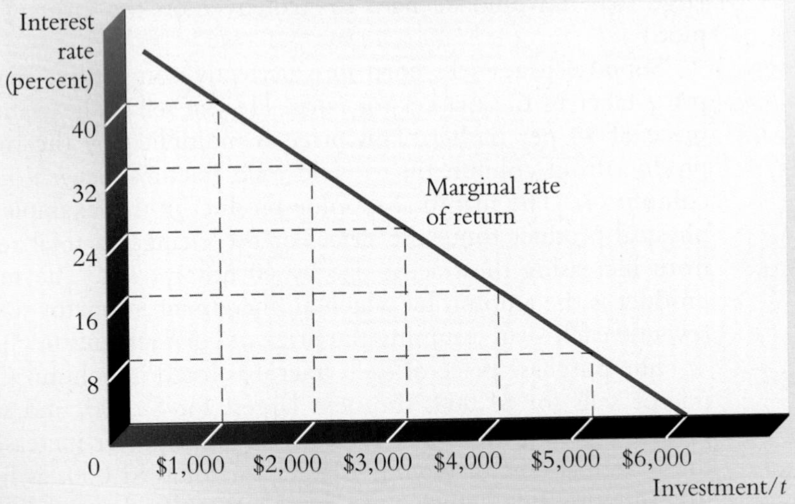

Marginal rate of return on investment The marginal revenue product of capital expressed as a percentage of its marginal cost

Jones must decide how much to invest in a tractor. The first task in determining the optimal investment is to compute the marginal rate of return that could be earned each year by investing in tractors of different sizes. Given the circumstances described thus far, the **marginal rate of return on investment** is equal to the capital's marginal productivity (its marginal revenue product) as a percentage of the marginal expenditure on capital (its marginal resource cost). Since the tractor is expected to last indefinitely, Jones wants to know the marginal rate of return, or the marginal rate of interest, he will earn each year from each size tractor.

The smallest tractor yields a marginal revenue product of $400 per year and has a marginal resource cost of $1,000. Thus, the smallest tractor yields a *marginal rate of return* of $400/$1,000, or 40 percent per year, as shown in column (7) of Exhibit 2(a). The next largest tractor has a marginal revenue product of $320 per year and a marginal cost of $1,000, so the marginal rate of return equals $320/$1,000, or 32 percent per year. By dividing the marginal revenue product of capital in column (4) by the marginal resource cost of that capital in column (6), we get the marginal rate of return on investment in column (7). The data in column (7) are depicted in Exhibit 2(b) as a downward-sloping curve that reflects the marginal rate of return on investing in tractors. This curve slopes downward because of the diminishing marginal productivity of bigger tractors.

Given the marginal rate of return of tractors, how much should Jones invest in order to maximize profits? Suppose he borrows the money. The amount he must pay to borrow depends on the *market rate of interest*, which is the rate of interest determined by the supply and demand for loanable funds. Ideally, Jones would maximize profits by equating the marginal rate of return on tractors with the market rate of interest. But because tractors come in certain sizes, Jones may not be able to equate any of the marginal rates of return on them to the market rate of interest. Instead, he will find the largest tractor size for which the marginal rate of return equals or exceeds the market rate of interest. For example, if the market rate of interest is 20 percent, Jones will invest $3,000 in the 120-horsepower tractor. That size tractor yields a marginal return of 24 percent, a rate exceeding the 20 percent rate of interest on the borrowed funds. Investing another $1,000 in the next largest tractor would yield a marginal return of only 16 percent, a rate below the cost of borrowing. If the market rate of interest dropped to 10 percent, the 160-horsepower tractor would become the most profitable investment. And if the interest rate dropped to 8 percent, Jones would buy the 200-horsepower tractor for $5,000.

Point to Stress The rule about increasing investment as long as the marginal rate of return on investment exceeds the market rate of interest holds even without the example's simplifying assumptions.

Farmer Jones should increase his investment as long as the marginal rate of return on that investment exceeds the market rate of interest. The marginal rate of return curve therefore shows how much will be invested at each interest rate. In other words, the marginal rate of return curve represents the farmer's *demand curve for investment.* This demand curve is a derived demand, based on each tractor's marginal productivity.

Would the example change if Jones already had the money saved and did not need to borrow? Not as long as he can save at the market rate of interest. For example, suppose Jones has $5,000 in savings that is earning the market rate of interest of 10 percent. He should invest $4,000 into a 160-horsepower tractor, which earns a marginal rate of return of 16 percent. Jones should save the remaining $1,000 at the market rate of interest of 10 percent rather than invest in the next largest tractor, which would earn only 8 percent. Thus, as long as he can borrow and save at the same interest rate, Jones ends up with the same size tractor whether he borrows funds or draws on his own savings. *Whether Jones borrows the money or has the savings on hand, the market rate of interest represents his opportunity cost of funds.*

Point to Stress The marginal rate of return on investment equals the marginal revenue product divided by the marginal resource cost only if the example's simplifying assumptions are made.

Let's review the procedure used to determine the optimal amount of investment. First, compute the marginal revenue product of the investment. Next, divide the marginal revenue product by the marginal resource cost to determine the marginal rate of return on the investment. The firm will increase investment until the marginal rate of return on investment equals the market rate of interest. The market rate of interest reflects the opportunity cost of investing either borrowed funds or savings. Finally, the marginal rate of return curve is the firm's demand for investment—that is, it shows the amount invested at each alternative interest rate.

Investing in Human Capital

The tractor has a substantial impact on the farmer's ability to produce. Similarly, education and training that improve the farmer's knowledge of farming also enhance productivity. Jones could invest in his own education—he could invest in human capital. For example, by taking agricultural courses at a nearby college, he could increase his knowledge of plant science, fertilizers, soil drainage, agricultural economics, and other subjects that would make him a more productive farmer. He might read through the course descriptions and decide how valuable each course would be, ranking them from most productive to least productive. The marginal rate of return on each course would equal the marginal revenue product divided by the marginal cost of this investment. (Cost here would include the direct outlays for the course such as tuition and books plus any opportunity cost of time drawn away from production or other valued activities.) How many courses should Jones take? The answer depends on the expected marginal rate of return of each course and the market rate of interest. Investing in human capital can be considered in the same way as investing in physical capital.

Teaching Tip To deal with uncertainty, the potential investor would assign probabilities to future revenues and costs in each year. *Expected* values are found by multiplying each potential future cash flow by its probability and summing for each year.

Note that in our simple model Jones must predict marginal rates of return for tractors and for college courses. To do that, he must predict not only the marginal physical product of these investments but also the price of corn in the future. *Because of technological change and other possible changes in market supply and demand, producers face an uncertain future, so the investment decision is often risky.* In addition, our simple model assumes that Jones can borrow and save at the same interest rate. But financial intermediaries, such as banks, typically charge a higher interest rate to borrowers than they pay to savers. Thus, Jones would likely be charged more interest to borrow than he could earn on savings; consequently, investing with borrowed funds involves a higher opportunity cost. The point is that investment decisions are usually more complicated than those presented here.

The Demand for Loanable Funds

We have now examined why firms are willing to pay interest to borrow money: money gives firms a command over resources that makes roundabout production possible. The simplified principles developed for Farmer Jones can be generalized to other firms. The major demanders of loans are firms that borrow to invest in capital goods, such as machines, trucks, and buildings. At any time each firm has a variety of possible investment opportunities. Each firm ranks its opportunities from highest to lowest based on the expected marginal rates of return on the investments. Firms will finance all investments whose expected rates of return exceed the market rate of interest; they will increase their investment until their expected marginal rate of return just equals the market rate of interest. When other inputs are held constant, as they were on the farm, the demand for investment slopes downward.

Teaching Tip Held constant along the demand for loanable funds curve are the supply of other resources, the level of technology, the rate of inflation, and tax laws.

Firms borrow based on their expectations that they will thereby be able to generate a greater stream of income in the future than they could without borrowing. For the economy as a whole, if the supply of other resources and the level of technology are fixed, diminishing marginal productivity causes the marginal rate of return on investment—the demand for investment—to slope downward. The **demand for loanable funds** is based on the marginal rate of return these borrowed funds yield when invested in capital. Each firm has a downward-sloping demand for loanable funds, reflecting a declining marginal rate of return on investment. With some qualifications, the demand for loanable funds by business firms can be summed horizontally to yield the demand for loanable funds by all firms.

Demand for loanable funds The relation between the market rate of interest and the quantity of loanable funds demanded, other things constant

But firms are not the only demanders of loanable funds. As we have seen, households value present consumption more than future consumption; they are often willing to pay extra to consume now rather than later. One way to ensure that goods and services are available now is to borrow money for present consumption. Mortgages, car loans, college loans, and credit card purchases are examples of household borrowing. The household's demand for loanable funds, like the firm's demand, slopes downward, reflecting consumers' greater ability and greater willingness to borrow at lower interest rates, other things constant. The government sector and the rest of the world may also be demanders of loanable funds. Thus, the market demand curve for loanable funds, presented in Exhibit 3 as D, is the total demand by firms, households, governments, and the rest of the world. The supply of loanable funds has already been introduced and is presented as S in Exhibit 3.

Teaching Tip Firms, the government, and the rest of the world may also be suppliers of loanable funds—although Exhibit 1 was developed by considering only households.

By bringing the supply and demand for loanable funds together, as in Exhibit 3, we can determine the market rate of interest. The equilibrium interest rate of 8 percent is the only rate that will exactly match up the wishes of both borrowers and savers. In this case the equilibrium quantity of loanable funds is $100 billion. Any change in the supply or demand for loanable funds will change the equilibrium rate of interest. For example, some major technological breakthrough might increase the productivity of investment, thereby increasing its marginal rate of return and increasing the demand for loanable funds. In such a case, the demand for loanable funds would shift out to the right, as shown in the movement from D to D' in Exhibit 3. Thus, an increase in the demand for loans would raise the equilibrium rate of interest to 9 percent and increases the quantity of loanable funds to $115 billion.

Point to Stress The quantity supplied of loanable funds rises in response to the higher market rate of interest. Therefore, it is represented as a movement along the given supply curve.

EXHIBIT 3

Market for Loanable Funds

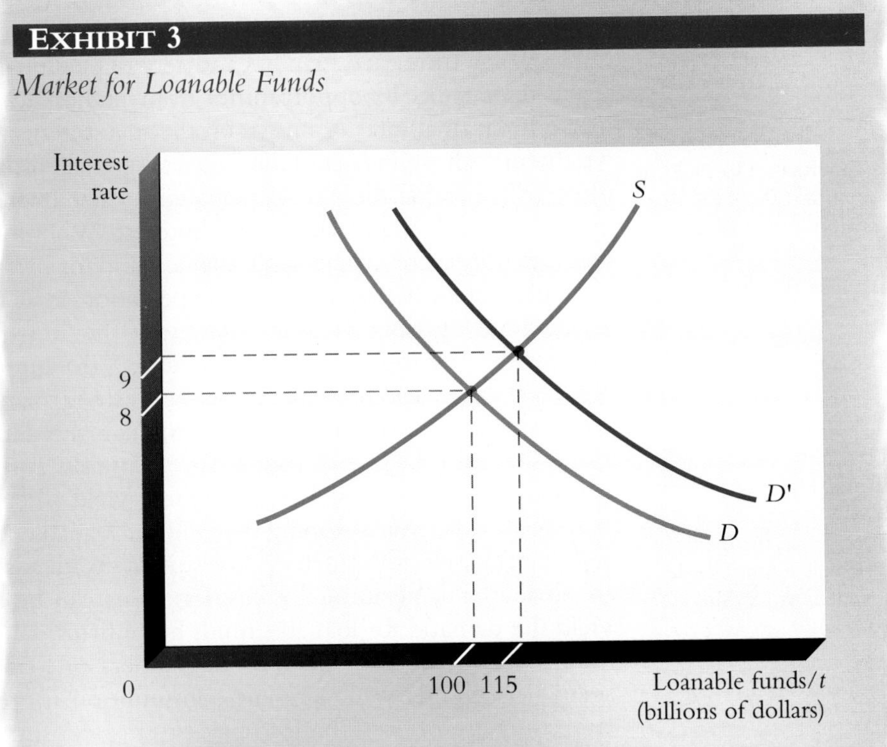

Because of the declining marginal rate of return on capital, the demand for loans is inversely related to the rate of interest. The equilibrium rate of interest, 8 percent, is determined at the intersection of the demand and supply curves for loans. An increase in the demand for loans from D to D' leads to an increase in the equilibrium rate of interest from 8 percent to 9 percent.

Real Versus Nominal Interest Rates

Thus far we have discussed interest rates under the assumption that "other things are constant." One of the factors held constant has been the expected rate of inflation in the economy. *Inflation* is an increase in the average price level in the economy. Thus, the supply and demand curves for loanable funds presented in Exhibit 3 were drawn for a given expected rate of inflation. Our equilibrium interest rate is a nominal interest rate. The **nominal rate of interest** measures the interest rate in terms of the actual dollars paid, even if the value of these dollars has been eroded by inflation. The nominal rate of interest is the rate of interest that appears on the loan agreement, and the interest rate discussed in the media.

Nominal rate of interest The interest rate expressed in current dollars; the interest rate reported in the media

Expected real rate of interest The expected interest rate expressed in dollars of constant value; the nominal interest rate minus the expected inflation rate

Suppose the expected rate of inflation in Exhibit 3 is 5 percent. In this case savers expect to earn and borrowers expect to pay 3 percent interest after adjusting for inflation, so the expected real rate of interest is 3 percent. The **expected real rate of interest** is the nominal rate of interest (in this case 8 percent) minus the expected inflation rate (in this case 5 percent). *Economic decisions are based on the expected real rate of interest, not on the nominal rate of interest.*

Teaching Tip Decision makers can make mistakes. If the actual inflation rate rises above the expected rate, the actual real rate of interest falls short of the expected real rate (and can become negative).

Lenders focus on what the interest they will earn will actually buy in terms of goods and services, and borrowers focus on what the interest rate they will pay will actually cost them in terms of goods and services.

Let's consider how a change in expected inflation affects the market for loanable funds. If the expected rate of inflation increases from 5 percent to 7 percent, savers will be less willing to save at each nominal rate of interest because that nominal interest is expected to buy fewer real goods and services. Specifically, savers will want 2 percent more in nominal interest to compensate them for the expected decline of 2 percent in the real value of the dollars they are to be repaid.

But borrowers will be more willing to pay a higher nominal interest rate since the dollars they pay are expected to buy 2 percent less in terms of real goods and services. Specifically, borrowers will be willing to pay 2 percent more in nominal interest since inflation is expected to be 2 percent higher.

EXHIBIT 4

Effect of Higher Expected Inflation on Nominal Interest Rate

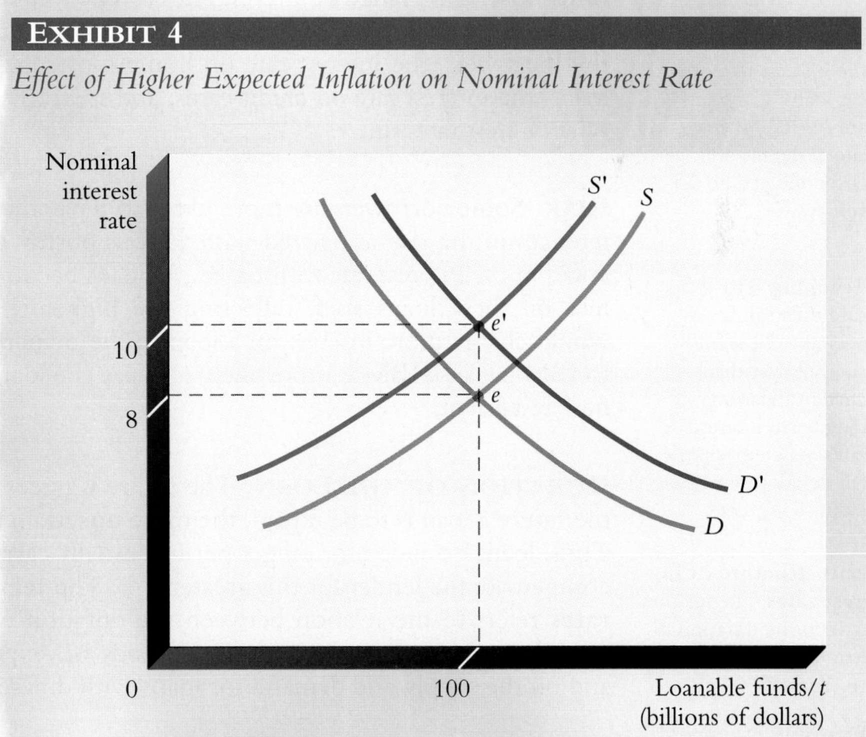

The supply of loanable funds, S, and the demand for loanable funds, D, are based on a given expected rate of inflation (in this case, 5 percent). At the equilibrium identified at point e, the nominal rate of interest is 8 percent. If the expected rate of inflation increases from 5 to 7 percent, both supply and demand shift up by 2 percent. The new equilibrium is point e', at a nominal interest rate of 10 percent. The expected real rate of interest, which equals the nominal interest rate minus the expected rate of inflation, is still 3 percent. Because the expected real rate of interest has not changed, the equilibrium quantity of loanable funds has not changed.

Therefore, an increase in expected inflation in Exhibit 4 decreases the supply of loanable funds from S to S' and increases the demand for loanable funds from D to D'. The supply curve shifts up by 2 percent and the demand curve shifts up by 2 percent. As a result, the equilibrium nominal rate of interest increases from 8 percent to 10 percent. Note that the expected real rate of interest is still 3 percent, or the nominal rate of 10 percent minus the expected inflation rate of 7 percent. Remember that savers and borrowers are interested in the expected real rate of interest not the nominal rate of interest. Since, in equilibrium, the expected real rate of interest has not changed, the equilibrium quantity of loanable funds has not changed.

Why Interest Rates Differ

So far we have been talking about *the* market rate of interest, implying that only one interest rate prevails in the loanable funds market. At any particular time, however, a range of interest rates can be found in the economy. For example, there is the so-called *prime rate*, which is offered to the more trustworthy borrowers, the interest rate on home mortgages, the interest rate on car loans, the interest rate on credit cards, and so on. Let's consider some reasons why interest rates differ.

Example The interest rate on mortgages tends to be lower than the interest rate on car loans. Car loans are riskier—the collateral depreciates faster and can be driven away.

RISK. Some borrowers are more likely to repay their loans than others. Differences in the risk associated with various borrowers are reflected in differences in the interest rate negotiated. As loans become more risky, the interest rate on these loans rises, reflecting the higher risk. For example, a bank would charge more interest on a loan to the owner of a new restaurant than to IBM because IBM is more likely to repay the loan than is the owner of the new restaurant.

Teaching Tip If future inflation is expected to be significantly lower than current inflation, long-term interest rates may temporarily fall below short-term rates.

DURATION OF THE LOAN. The future is uncertain, and the further into the future a loan is to be repaid, the more uncertain that repayment becomes. Thus, loans extended for longer periods usually carry a higher interest rate to compensate the lender for this greater risk. The **term structure of interest rates** refers to the relation between the duration of a loan and the interest rate charged. The term structure depends on expectations about inflation and on the supply and demand for loans with different maturity dates.

Term structure of interest rates The relation between the duration of a loan and the interest rate charged

Example An important consideration in determining administration costs is the number of annual payments. Households loans generally call for monthly payments; large business loans often have less frequent payments.

COST OF ADMINISTRATION. The costs of executing the loan agreement, monitoring the conditions of the loan, and collecting the payments on the loan are called the *administration costs* of the loan. These costs, as a proportion of the total cost of the loan, decrease as the size of the loan increases. For example, the administration costs on a $100,000 loan will be less than ten times greater than the costs on a $10,000 loan. Consequently, that portion of the interest charge reflecting the cost of administering the loan will be smaller for large loans than for small loans. So the larger the loan, the lower the interest rate charged for administration.

Tax Treatment. Differences in the tax treatment of different types of loans will also affect the market rate of interest. For example, the interest earned on funds loaned to state and local governments is not subject to federal income taxes. Since lenders are interested in their after-tax rate of interest, state and local governments can pay lower interest rates than other borrowers.

Present Value and Discounting

Present value The value today of a payment or payments to be received in the future

Because present consumption is valued more than future consumption, present and future consumption cannot be directly compared. A way of standardizing the discussion is to measure all consumption in terms of its present value. **Present value** is the current value of a payment or payments that will be received in the future. For example, how much would you pay now to acquire the right to receive \$100 one year from now? Put another way, what is the *present value* to you of receiving \$100 one year from now?

Present Value of Payment One Year Hence

Suppose that the market interest rate is 10 percent, so you can either lend or borrow money at that rate. One way to determine how much you would pay for the opportunity to receive \$100 one year from now is to ask how much you would have to save, at the market rate of interest, to end up with \$100 one year from now. Here is the problem we are trying to solve: what amount of money, if saved at a rate of 10 percent, will accumulate to \$100 one year from now? We can calculate the answer with a simple formula. Let PV stand for the unknown present value. We can say

$$\mathbf{PV \times 1.10 = \$100}$$

or

$$\mathbf{PV = \frac{\$100}{1.10} = \$90.91}$$

Discounting Determining the present value of a sum of money to be received in the future

Discount rate The interest rate used to convert income to be received in the future into present value

Thus, \$90.91 is the present value of receiving \$100 one year from now; it is the most you would be willing to pay today to receive \$100 one year from now. Rather than pay more than \$90.91, you would simply deposit your \$90.91 at the market rate of interest and end up with \$100 a year from now. The procedure of dividing the future payment by 1 plus the prevailing interest rate in order to express it in today's dollars is called **discounting**. The interest rate that is used to discount future payments is called the **discount rate**.

The present value of \$100 to be received one year from now depends on the interest rate used to discount that payment. *The higher the interest rate, or discount rate, the more the future payment is discounted and the lower its present value*. Put another way, the higher the interest rate, the less you need to save now to yield a given amount in the future. For example, if the interest rate is 15 percent, the present value of receiving \$100 one year from now is \$100/1.15, which equals \$86.96. Conversely, the lower the interest rate, or discount rate, the less the future income is discounted and the greater its present value. A lower interest rate means that you must save more now to yield a given amount in the future. As a general rule, the present value (PV) of receiving M dollars one year from now when the interest rate is i is

$$\mathbf{PV} = \frac{M}{1 + i}$$

For example, when the interest rate is 5 percent, the present value of receiving \$100 one year from now is

$$\mathbf{PV} = \frac{\$100}{1 + 0.05} = \frac{\$100}{1.05} = \$95.24$$

Present Value for Payments in Later Years

Now consider the present value of receiving \$100 two years from now. What amount of money, if deposited at the market rate of interest of 5 percent, would yield \$100 two years from now? Again, let PV represent the unknown amount of money. At the end of the first year, its value would be PV × 1.05, which would then earn the market rate of interest during the second year. At the end of the second year, the deposit would have accumulated to PV × 1.05 × 1.05. Thus, we have the equation

$$\mathbf{PV} \times 1.05 \times 1.05 = \mathbf{PV} \times (1.05)^2 = \$100$$

Solving for PV yields

$$\mathbf{PV} = \frac{\$100}{(1.05)^2} = \frac{\$100}{1.1025} = \$90.70$$

If the \$100 were to be received three years from now, we would discount the payment over three years:

$$\mathbf{PV} = \frac{\$100}{(1.05)^3} = \$86.38$$

More generally, the present value formula for receiving M dollars in year t at interest rate i may be written as

$$\mathbf{PV} = \frac{M}{(1 + i)^t}$$

Point to Stress The further in the future the payment, the more years over which interest can be earned. Therefore, fewer dollars are needed in the present.

Because $1 + i$ is greater than 1, the more times it is multiplied by itself (as determined by t), the greater the denominator will be and the smaller will be the present value. Thus, *the present value of a given payment will diminish the further in the future that payment is to be received.*

Present Value of an Income Stream

The previous method is used to compute the present value of a single sum to be paid at some point in the future. Most investments, however, yield a stream of payments over time. In cases where the payments are to be made over a period of years, the present value of each payment can be computed individually, and then the results can be summed to yield the present value of the entire payment stream. For example, the present value of receiving \$100 next year and \$150 the year after is simply the present value of the first year's payment plus the present value of the second year's payment. If the interest rate is 5 percent, the present value equals

$$\mathbf{PV} = \frac{\$100}{1.05} + \frac{\$150}{(1.05)^2} = \$231.29$$

Present Value of an Annuity

Annuity A given sum of money received each year for a specified number of years

A given sum of money received each year for a specified number of years is called an **annuity**. Such a payment is called a *perpetuity* if it continues indefinitely into the future, as it would in the earlier example of the productivity gain stemming from the purchase of an indestructible tractor. The present value of receiving a certain amount forever seems like a very large sum indeed. But because future payments are valued less the further from the present they are to be received, it turns out that the present value of receiving a particular amount forever is not much more than that of receiving it for, say, twenty years.

To determine the present value of receiving \$100 each year forever, we need only ask how much money must be deposited in a savings account to yield \$100 in interest per year. When the interest rate is 10 percent, a deposit of \$1,000 will earn \$100 per year. Thus, the present value of receiving \$100 a year indefinitely when the interest rate is 10 percent is \$1,000. More generally, we can use the formula $PV = A/i$, where A is the amount received each year and i is the interest rate, or discount rate.

Teaching Tip Without the simplifying assumptions used in the earlier example, the marginal rate of return on investment is the discount rate that makes the present value of all future cash flows plus the salvage value equal to the initial cost.

The concept of present value is useful in making investment decisions. Farmer Jones, by increasing his tractor size from 160 to 200 horsepower, expected to earn \$80 more per year from a marginal investment of \$1,000. Thus, his marginal rate of return was 8 percent. At a market rate of interest of 8 percent, the present value of a cash flow of \$80 discounted at 8 percent would be \$80/0.08, which equals \$1,000. Thus, *at the margin, Jones was willing to invest in capital an amount that would yield a cash stream with a present value just equal to the amount invested.* To develop a better appreciation for present value and discounting, consider the following case study.

CASE STUDY

The Million-Dollar Lottery?

Since New Hampshire introduced the first state-run lottery in 1964, many states have followed suit, and payoffs of millions of dollars are now common. As a winner of a million-dollar lottery, you might expect to be handed a check for a million dollars. Instead, you would typically be paid in installments, such as $50,000 per year for twenty years. Though this adds up to a total of a million dollars, you now know that such a stream has a present value of less than the advertised million. To put this payment schedule in perspective, keep in mind that at a discount rate of 10 percent, the $50,000 received in the twentieth year has a present value of only $7,432. If today you deposited $7,432 in an account earning 10 percent interest, you would wind up with $50,000 in twenty years.

At 10 percent the present value of a $50,000 annuity for the next twenty years is $425,700. Thus, the present value of the actual payment stream is less than half of the promised million, which is the reason lottery officials pay it out in installments. Incidentally, we might consider the present value of receiving $50,000 per year forever. Using the formula $PV = A/i$, where A equals $50,000 and i equals 10 percent, we have $PV = \$50{,}000/0.10 = \$500{,}000$. Since the present value of receiving $50,000 for twenty years is $425,700, continuing the $50,000 annual payment forever adds only $74,300 to the present value. This shows the dramatic effect of discounting on the present value of payments after year twenty.

This discussion of present value and discounting concludes our treatment of capital and interest. We now have the tools to consider how the firms, especially corporations, are financed.

CORPORATE FINANCE

During the Industrial Revolution, labor-saving machinery made large-scale production more profitable, so manufacturing began to require large capital investments. The corporate structure became the easiest way to finance these large investments, and by 1920 corporations accounted for most employment and output in the U.S. economy. In Chapter 4 we examined the pros and cons of the corporate form of business organization, but thus far we have said little about corporate finance.

Teaching Tip Recall the discussion in Chapter 25 of the possibility that creditors may require an entrepreneur to invest in the firm. The entrepreneur may be asked to put up personal assets as collateral even if the business is incorporated.

As was noted in Chapter 4, a corporation is a legal entity, distinct from its shareholders. The corporation may own property, earn a profit, sue or be sued, and incur debt. Stockholders, the owners of the corporation, are liable only to the extent of their investment in the firm. Use of the abbreviation "Inc." or "Corp." in the company name serves as a warning to potential creditors that stockholders will not accept unlimited personal liability for the debts it incurs. *Corporations acquire funds for investment in three ways: by selling stock, by retaining part of their profit, and by borrowing.*

Stocks

Stock A certificate reflecting ownership of a corporation

Corporations *issue stock* to raise money for operations and for new plant and equipment. Suppose you have developed a recipe for a hot, spicy chili that your friends have convinced you will be a best seller. You decide to incorporate and you want to raise $1 million by issuing stock in the company, which you call the Mexican Fire-Drill Chili Corporation. To do this you sell ten thousand shares for $100 per share. A *share* of **stock** represents a claim to a *share* of the company's net assets and earnings, as well as the right to vote on corporate directors and on other important matters. A person who buys 10 percent of the shares issued thereby owns 10 percent of the company and is entitled to 10 percent of any profit and 10 percent of the votes.

Point to Stress Although the stockholder is entitled to 10 percent of any profit, it is management that decides what to do with any profit. The stockholder will receive 10 percent of any dividends paid.

Corporations must pay corporate income taxes on any profits. After-tax profits are either paid as dividends to shareholders or reinvested in the corporation. Reinvested profits, or *retained earnings*, allow the firm to finance expansion. Stockholders expect dividends, but the corporation is not bound by contract to pay dividends. Once shares are issued, their price tends to fluctuate directly with the firm's prospects for profits.

Bonds

Bond A certificate reflecting a firm's promise to pay the holder a periodic interest payment until the date of maturity and a fixed sum of money on the designated maturity date

Another way the corporation can acquire funds is by borrowing. The corporation can go directly to a bank for a loan or can issue bonds. A **bond** is a piece of paper reflecting the corporation's promise to pay the holder a fixed sum of money on the designated *maturity date* plus an annual interest payment, or *coupon*, until the date of maturity. For example, a corporation might sell for $1,000 a bond that promises to pay the holder $1,000 at the end of twenty years plus an annual interest payment, or coupon, of, say, $100.

The payment stream for bonds is more predictable than that for stocks. Unless this corporation goes bankrupt, it is obligated to pay bondholders $100 every year for twenty years and to return the $1,000 at the end of that time. In contrast, stockholders are last in line when resource holders get paid, so bondholders get paid before stockholders. Thus, investors consider bonds less risky than stocks.

Teaching Tip However, bonds are risky because their prices fluctuate inversely in the secondary market with variations in the market rate of interest. If the bond owner wishes to sell the bond early and interest rates have risen, the price received may be well below the price paid for the bond.

Securities Exchanges

Once stocks and bonds have been issued and sold, owners of these securities are free to resell them on *security exchanges.* In the United States there are ten security exchanges registered with the *Securities and Exchange Commission*, or *SEC*, the federal body that regulates securities markets. The New York Stock Exchange is by far the largest, trading the securities of over two thousand major companies and handling over 80 percent of the trades that occur. Nearly all the securities traded each day are *secondhand securities* in the sense that they have already been sold by the issuing company. So the bulk of the transactions do not provide funds to firms in need of investment capital. Most money goes from a securities seller to a securities buyer. *Institutional investors*,

Point to Stress With the sale of existing stock, the company's ownership is being transferred. Bondholders, however, are creditors, not owners.

such as banks, insurance companies, and mutual funds, account for over half the trading volume on the New York Stock Exchange. By providing a *secondary market* for securities, exchanges raise the *liquidity* of these securities—that is, the exchanges make the securities more readily exchangeable for cash.

The secondary markets for stocks also determine the current market value of the corporation. The market value of a firm at any given time can be found by multiplying the share price times the number of shares. For example, if your company's stock price increases from $100 to $200 per share, the market value of the firm equals $200 times the ten thousand outstanding shares, or $2 million. Securities prices give the firm's management some indication of the wisdom of raising new capital through new stock issues or new bond issues. The more profitable the company, other things constant, the higher the value of shares on the stock market and the lower the interest rate that would have to be paid on new bond issues. *Thus, securities markets allocate funds more readily to successful firms than to firms in financial difficulty.* Some firms may be in such poor financial shape that they cannot sell new securities. Securities markets usually promote the survival of the fittest.

Point to Stress The major hypothesis of this section is that managerial control leads to different behavior than does stockholder control.

So one function of securities markets is to allocate investment funds to those firms that appear in a position to make the most efficient use of those funds. Another function performed by securities markets is in the market for corporate control, which we will discuss next.

CORPORATE OWNERSHIP AND CONTROL

Teaching Tip Herbert Simon, who won the Nobel Prize in economics in 1978, hypothesized that a firm's management engages in "satisficing" behavior rather than maximizing behavior. According to this hypothesis, after striving to achieve a target level of profits, management will not work harder to improve those profits.

We have described the entrepreneur as the individual responsible for guaranteeing payment to owners of the other resources in return for the opportunity to direct the use of these resources in the firm and the right to any profit or loss. We said that the entrepreneur need not actually manage the firm's resources as long as the entrepreneur has the power to hire and fire the manager—that is, as long as the entrepreneur controls the manager.

Managerial Behavior in Large Corporations

Up to this point we have assumed that firms attempt to maximize profits. In a small firm there is usually little danger of the hired manager not following the wishes of the owner; the manager and owner are often one and the same. As the modern corporation has evolved, however, its ownership has become widely distributed among many stockholders, leaving no single stockholder with either the incentive or the ability to control the manager. Economists since the days of Adam Smith have been concerned with what is known as the **separation of ownership from control** in the large corporation.

Separation of ownership from control The situation that exists when no single stockholder or unified group of stockholders owns enough shares to control the management of a corporation

Various economists have formulated theoretical models suggesting that, when freed from the control of a dominant stockholding influence, managers attempt to pursue their own selfish goals rather than those of the firm's owners. The alternatives vary from model to model, but emphasis has focused on such goals as maximizing the firm's size or increasing the perquisites and discretionary resources available to the managers, such as attractive surroundings, corporate jets, and other amenities. Managers may pursue firm size because they want to enjoy the power, security, and status associated with a larger firm. As goals other than profit are pursued, so the argument goes, the firm's resources are used less efficiently, resulting in a lower level of profit. Thus, the stockholders—the owners of the firm—suffer because managers are not pursuing the owners' best interests.

Teaching Tip This discussion can be related to Simon's satisficing theory.

Point to Stress The management group usually asks for and receives the proxies of a large enough number of stockholders to elect directors who will reappoint the management team. But recently some boards of directors have exercised real control. For example, after losses in 1990 and 1991 (including a U.S. record $4.45 billion loss in 1991) and an expected loss in 1992, GM's board of directors replaced the chief executive officer, Robert Stempel.

Constraints on Managerial Discretion

Analysts have identified a variety of constraints that can serve as checks on wayward managers. The nature and effectiveness of each constraint will be examined next.

Economics of Natural Selection. Some economists argue that even if managers are freed from the control of a dominant stockholder, the rigors of competition in the product market will force them to maximize profits. The "economics of natural selection" ensures that only the most efficient firms will be able to survive. Other firms simply will not earn enough profit to attract and retain resources and so will eventually go out of business. The problem with this argument is that although pressure to pursue profits may arise when firms sell their product in competitive markets, many large corporations are at least partially insulated from intense product competition. Either because government regulations protect their firms from competition or because the firms enjoy some degree of market power, many managers have a certain amount of discretion in how they use their firms' resources. Such managers could divert corporate resources into activities reflecting their own interests, yet still earn enough profit to ensure their firms' survival.

Example In the early 1980s, managers of what is now Oregon Steel Mills Inc. led a leveraged buyout and extended 100 percent ownership in the company to its employees through an Employee Stock Ownership Plan. In 1988, the firm went public, and its market value soared from $15 million to $400 million. Seventy percent of the employees achieved holdings of over $100,000 and nearly one hundred employees became millionaires.

Managerial Incentives. Other economists have examined the manager's incentive structure. If executive pay is linked closely to the firm's profit, the compensation scheme may encourage the manager to pursue profit even in the absence of a dominant stockholder or competition in the product market. Evidence suggests that at least a portion of the typical manager's compensation is tied to the firm's profitability through some type of bonus pay scheme or stock option plan. But even if the manager's income is tied to profit, the manager will not necessarily attempt to maximize profit. The manager in a large corporation who diverts profit to other ends will simply forgo some income. This profit diversion may be "cheap" in view of the small fraction of the firm's shares typically owned by management. For example, if the manager owns 1 percent of the firm's shares and can divert $10,000 of potential profits to buy an expensive desk, this diversion will cost the manager only $100 in forgone pretax profits. After corporate taxes and personal income taxes, the cost is less than half that amount. Thus, the existence of a link between executive pay and firm profit is not necessarily evidence that managers will attempt to maximize profit; it is only evidence that profit diversion will involve some personal cost, but that cost may be quite small.

Example In the 1960s and 1970s, International Telephone and Telegraph (ITT) specialized in corporate takeovers, acquiring firms such as Avis Car Rental, Continental Baking, Sheraton Hotels, and Hartford Life Insurance. Operating profits increased significantly for each company after the takeover.

Example In 1992, many conglomerates announced the divestiture of firms that had been taken over in the 1980s but whose performance had not met expectations: Sears sold Dean Witter Financial Services, Xerox sold the Van Kampen Merrit money management firm, DuPont unloaded its electronic divisions, and so forth.

STOCKHOLDER VOTING. Each year stockholders have an opportunity to attend the company meeting and elect the board of directors. Couldn't stockholders join forces to oust an inefficient manager? What about that "corporate democracy" so often heralded on Wall Street? In fact, chances of an effective stockholder revolt are slim. The average stockholder does not have the information, the resources, or the incentive to challenge management. Most shareholders either ignore the voting altogether or dutifully pass their votes to the managers.

Dissatisfied stockholders, however, do have one very important alternative. Stockholders can "fire" the manager and the firm simply by selling their shares in the corporation. As dissatisfied stockholders sell their holdings, the share price drops and the firm becomes more attractive as a target for a reform-minded capitalist. A so-called *corporate raider* can buy a controlling interest in the firm at a relatively low price, reform or replace the management, and then get rich when the firm's rising profits lead to an appreciation in the value of shares. The effects of this market discipline will be examined next.

The Market for Corporate Control

The market for corporate control has been championed by many economists as an efficient mechanism for allocating and reallocating corporate assets to those who value them most highly. If the firm's assets are undervalued in the stock market, some entrepreneur has an incentive to "buy low and sell high"—that is, to buy firms that are selling for less than they should be and take measures to increase their value. The effectiveness of this market in checking managerial abuses depends on the existence of someone with (1) the ability to identify firms that are performing below potential, (2) access to the resources necessary to carry off a successful takeover, and (3) the savvy to improve the firm's performance. There are a variety of reasons why this market may not operate perfectly.

One problem with the market for corporate control is that outsiders have difficulty determining whether a firm is being run efficiently. Often when a firm performs poorly, it is unclear whether the management is poor or the assets of the firm are not what they seem. Management is likely to be better informed than a potential corporate raider. Some types of information are more public than others, however. For example, the value of an oil firm's reserves tends to be widely known in that industry. Thus, when an oil firm's market value falls significantly below the underlying value of the firm's assets, we expect a takeover to be attempted, as happened frequently in the oil industry during the 1980s.

Other problems arise during a takeover attempt. Although the corporate raider would prefer to quietly buy up a controlling interest in the firm, such a major purchase would not go unnoticed in the stock market. Moreover, a single party who buys 5 percent or more of a firm must register that fact with the SEC, so the information becomes public.

Tender offer An offer to buy a controlling number (i.e., more than half) of a firm's shares

A corporate raider usually attempts to acquire a controlling interest (more than half) through a public **tender offer** to buy shares. For example, a raider may offer to pay $25 per share for stock that had been trading at $20 per share prior to the takeover attempt. If a controlling number of shares are "tendered" by shareholders, the raider will purchase them and the takeover will be successful. If too few shareholders agree to sell, however, the deal will fall through and the tender offer will be withdrawn or amended.

Leveraged buyout The purchase of controlling interest in a corporation using borrowed funds

A **leveraged buyout** is a corporate takeover that is financed mostly by debt. A firm's financial *leverage* is measured by the ratio of its debt to its net worth; net worth equals the amount originally invested in the firm plus retained earnings. The higher this ratio, the more the firm is said to be *leveraged*, or dependent on debt. Corporate acquisitions that are financed primarily by debt result in firms that are highly leveraged, so debt-financed acquisitions are called leveraged buyouts. The debt resulting from a leveraged buyout is often repaid by selling off parts of the acquired company. Leveraged buyouts allow a corporate raider with little personal wealth to acquire a large corporation by using debt secured with the assets and potential profits of the acquired firm. The gamble, if successful, can yield a huge payoff to the raider. Debt is all the more attractive because interest payments on that debt are tax deductible for the corporation. Not all leveraged buyouts succeed, however, and some of the leveraged buyouts of the 1980s have become financial casualties in the 1990s. One recent failure is discussed in this closing case study.

CASE STUDY

Too Much Leverage

In April 1988, Robert Campeau, a Canadian real estate developer, paid $6.6 billion to acquire Federated Department Stores. A year earlier, he had purchased Allied Stores for $3.7 billion. Both acquisitions were financed by borrowed funds, and thus the deals were leveraged buyouts. As collateral, Campeau pledged the assets and earnings of the newly acquired companies. To help pay the huge debt, he planned to cut operating costs and sell off parts of the vast retailing empire the two companies comprised. Over ten thousand employees were laid off, and retail chains, such as Bonwit Teller, Brooks Brothers, and I. Magnin, were sold. But proceeds from these sales were less than expected, and the remaining stores faced substantial debt costs, which drained the cash needed to pay other bills. By the summer of 1989, store suppliers were reluctant to provide goods on credit to Campeau's remaining stores since suppliers were unsure of payment.

To reduce the debt, Campeau attempted to sell the crown jewel of his acquisitions, Bloomingdale's. But nobody was willing to pay what Campeau thought the chain was worth. Federated and Allied were left in an impossible position since their debt service requirements far outstripped their expected cash flow. On January 15, 1990, after failing to make scheduled interest payments on $2.3 billion in debt, Federated and Allied filed for bankruptcy protection. The filing affected more than 100,000 employees at 258 stores, about 300,000 suppliers, plus bondholders and other creditors. Negotiations with creditors and subsequent debt restructuring permitted Federated to emerge from bankruptcy in February 1992.

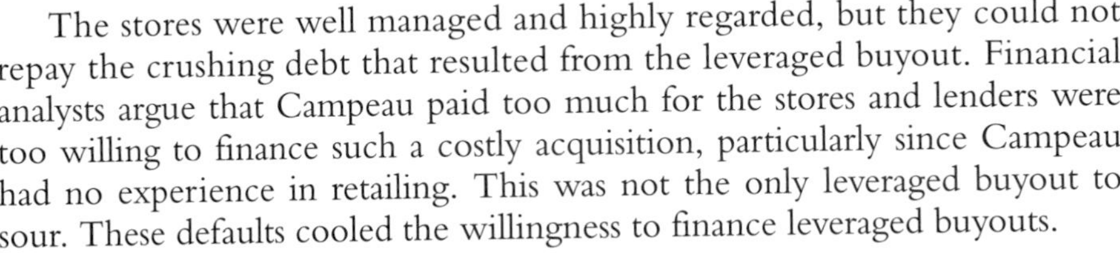

The stores were well managed and highly regarded, but they could not repay the crushing debt that resulted from the leveraged buyout. Financial analysts argue that Campeau paid too much for the stores and lenders were too willing to finance such a costly acquisition, particularly since Campeau had no experience in retailing. This was not the only leveraged buyout to sour. These defaults cooled the willingness to finance leveraged buyouts.

Sources: "An Extra $500 Million Paid for Federated Got Campeau in Trouble," *Wall Street Journal*, 11 January 1990; "Campeau Bankers Are Posing Some $2.3 Billion Questions," *New York Times*, 14 January 1990; and "KKR in Peril: The Fight to Save RJR," *Wall Street Journal*, 6 April 1992.

CONCLUSION

This chapter introduced you to capital, interest, and corporate finance. Capital is the physical asset involved in roundabout production and corporate finance describes how firms acquire the funds to buy capital and keep going. Capital is a more complicated resource than this chapter has conveyed. For example, the demand curve for investment looks more like a moving target than like the stable relation drawn in Exhibit 2. An accurate depiction of the investment demand curve calls for knowledge of the marginal physical product of capital and the price of output in the future. But the marginal physical product changes from period to period with changes in technology and in the employment of other resources. And the future price of the product can vary widely. Consider, for example, the dilemma of someone considering investing in oil wells during the 1980s, when oil prices were fluctuating between $10 and $36 per barrel. Although the real world of investment and finance is more complicated than we have let on, this chapter still conveys a reasonable introduction to these topics.

SUMMARY

1. Production cannot occur without savings because both direct production and roundabout production require time—time during which the resources required for production must be paid. Because present consumption is valued more than future consumption, consumers must be rewarded if they are to defer consumption. Interest is the reward paid to savers for forgoing present consumption and is the cost paid by borrowers to increase present consumption.

2. Choosing the profit-maximizing level of capital is complicated because capital purchased today yields a stream of benefit for years into the future. The marginal rate of return of a capital investment equals the marginal revenue product of capital as a percentage of the marginal resource cost of capital. The profit-maximizing firm invests up to the point where its marginal rate of return on capital equals the market rate of interest, which is the opportunity cost of investing borrowed funds or savings.

3. The nominal rate of interest measures the interest rate in terms of the actual dollars paid, even if these dollars have lost purchasing power because of inflation. The expected real rate of interest equals the nominal rate of interest minus the expected inflation rate.

Savers and borrowers are interested in the expected real rate of interest, not the nominal rate of interest. At any given time, market rates of interest may differ because of differences in risk, maturity, administrative costs, and tax treatment.

4. Corporations secure investment capital from three sources: stock issues, retained earnings, and borrowing (either directly from a lender or by issuing bonds). Once new stocks and bonds are issued, these securities are bought and sold on securities exchanges. Stock prices tend to vary directly with the firm's expected profitability.

5. The ownership of a large corporation is typically fragmented among many stockholders, with no stockholder owning a dominant share. The fact that a poorly performing firm can be bought at a bargain price, shaped up, and sold for a profit is said to keep management behavior in accord with stockholders' interests.

Questions and Problems

1. (Capital in Production) Why would seed also be considered part of Jones' savings? Should seed be considered part of the capital stock? Why or why not?

2. (Marginal Efficiency of Capital) Consider Exhibit 2 in this chapter. If the marginal resource cost rose to $2,400, what would be the optimum stock of capital? If the interest rate then rose to 16.6 percent, what would be the optimum stock of capital?

3. (Real Interest Rates) Is it possible for the realized real rate of interest to be negative? If so, what would cause this?

4. (Taxes and Investment) How does the tax deductibility of mortgage interest payments affect the demand for housing and building construction?

5. (Present Value) How would the present value of an investment project change if interest rates rose?

6. (Bond Prices) Why is $10,000 a reasonably close approximation of the price of a bond paying $1,000 each year for thirty years at 10 percent interest?

7. (Present Value) Suppose you are hired by your state government to determine the profitability of a lottery offering a grand prize of $10 million paid out in equal installments over twenty years. Show *how* you calculate the cost to the state of paying out such a prize.

8. (Loanable Funds Market) Using a supply-demand diagram for loanable funds, show the effect of each of the following on (nominal) interest rates:

   a. An increase in the expected rate of inflation
   b. An increase in the productivity of capital
   c. A decrease in the tax rate on savings

9. (Human Capital) Suppose you are considering enrolling in a graduate school program costing a total of $40,000. You expect that the graduate degree will increase your annual income by $5,000. Calculate the interest rate that would make such an investment in human capital a good one.

10. (Corporate Finance) When a firm needs to raise capital, it can do so by issuing stocks or bonds. What are some of the factors management must take into account in determining which method to use?

11. (Managerial Behavior) Why might separation of ownership from control lead to lower profitability for the firm?

12. (Managerial Behavior) How might the objectives of stockholders and the objectives of a growth-oriented management conflict?

13. (Corporate Takeovers) Who stands to gain and who stands to lose in a corporate takeover? Is the economy helped by such takeovers?

14. (Corporate Indebtedness) Why do corporate takeovers frequently lead to a rise in corporate indebtedness? Does corporate indebtedness benefit the economy? Why or why not?

15. (Financial Intermediaries) The financial intermediary can, in effect, get the supply of loanable funds to

shift to the right relative to what it would be in a direct financial market (i.e., one without the intermediary). Why do you think this occurs?

16. (Present Value and Risk) Suppose that the interest rate (discount rate) is not known with certainty, but is expected to fluctuate between 10 percent and 20 percent. Calculate the present value of a $1,000 payment one year in the future at each interest rate. Do the same for a $1,000 payment two years in the future. Which is more risky?

17. (Nominal Versus Real Interest Rate) It is easy to understand why suppliers of loanable funds require an inflation premium to be added to the real interest rate they receive to compensate them for the loss in future purchasing power due to the expected inflation. Why are borrowers willing to pay the higher rate?

18. (Present Value) Suppose the market rate of interest is 10 percent. Would you be willing to loan out $10,000 if you were guaranteed to receive $1,000 for the next twelve years plus a $5,000 payment in fifteen years? Why or why not?

19. (Consumption and Time) You value consumption today twice as much as consumption five years from now. Would you be willing to borrow at 15 percent a year to move consumption forward in time?

20. (State Lottery) Suppose that a state running a lottery like that described in the case study offers to pay back in prizes an amount guaranteed to equal the total amount of dollars raised by lottery ticket sales. (Typically states pay out far less than this.) Would this mean the lottery would raise no money for the state?

21. (State Lottery) Typically, a lottery prize can be awarded either as a cash stream over twenty years or as a lump-sum, one-time payment. If you win the lottery, which way would you prefer to receive your winnings?

22. (Leverage) It sounds like there were only losers in the Allied-Federated debacle. Were there any winners?

23. (Leverage) A leveraged buyout theoretically is paid for by stripping the purchased corporation of cash flow and/or assets to repay the junk bonds used to finance the stock purchase in the first place. If the result is a valueless stock in a valueless corporation, what are the incentives to carry out such a maneuver?

CHAPTER 28

IMPERFECT INFORMATION, TRANSACTION COSTS, AND MARKET BEHAVIOR

Point to Stress
Transaction costs and information costs are frequently associated with problems that lead to inefficiency.

The firm has been viewed thus far as a "black box" that hires resources on the basis of their marginal products, combines these resources efficiently to produce the profit-maximizing level of output, and sells this output for the profit-maximizing price. We have assumed that those who run the firm know what resources to employ and in what quantities. We have also assumed that the firm's operators are aware of the latest technology, the price, quality, and availability of all resources, and the demand for its product. We have said little about the internal structure of the firm because our objective has been to understand how the price system coordinates the allocation of resources through markets, not to understand the internal workings of the firm. In the first half of this chapter we will step inside the factory gate to reconsider some assumptions about the firm and its behavior.

Turning now to consumers, thus far we have assumed that consumers have all the information they need to make informed choices, including knowledge of the price, availability, and quality of the goods and services they demand. As we will see in the second half of the chapter, participants in most markets do not operate with complete information about the variables that matter most, such as price and quality. To complicate markets further, sometimes sellers know more than buyers about the quality of the product; sometimes it's the other way around. Sometimes the quality of a product becomes obvious only after it has been purchased. In the second half of this chapter, we examine how imperfect information affects the behavior of the market participants and shapes the market outcome. Overall, this chapter should help you develop a deeper understanding of market behavior. Topics discussed in this chapter include

- Transaction costs and the firm
- Vertical integration
- Economies of scope
- Optimal search
- Winner's curse
- Asymmetric information
- Adverse selection
- Signaling and screening
- Principal-agent problems

THE RATIONALE FOR THE FIRM AND THE SCOPE OF ITS OPERATION

The competitive model assumes that all participants in the market are fully informed about the price and availability of all inputs, outputs, and production processes. Perfect competition assumes that the firm is headed by a decision maker with a computer-like ability to calculate all the marginal productivities of alternative resources. This individual knows everything necessary to solve complex production and pricing problems. But if everyone had easy access to all the information required to make decisions, there would be little need for entrepreneurs.

The irony is that if the black-box characterization of the firm were accurate—that is, if the marginal products of all inputs could be easily measured and if prices for all inputs could be determined without cost—then there would be little reason for production to take place in firms. In a world characterized by perfect competition, perfect information, constant returns to scale, and frictionless exchange, the consumer could bypass the firm, purchasing inputs in the appropriate amounts and paying each resource owner accordingly. Someone who wanted a table could buy timber, have it milled, contract with a carpenter, contract with a painter, and end up with a finished product. The consumer could carry out transactions directly with each resource supplier.

Teaching Tip The development of the firm as a response to transaction costs was introduced in Chapter 4.

The Firm Reduces Transaction Costs

Point to Stress Market exchange directs resources to various uses through the forces of supply and demand—through the decentralized actions of individual decision makers.

In this section we explore why production is carried out within the firm. The theory we examine argues that the firm is a response to the transaction costs of using the market directly. Over fifty years ago, in a classic article entitled "The Nature of the Firm," 1991 Nobel Prize winner Ronald Coase asked the fundamental question "Why do firms exist?"[1] Why do people organize in the hierarchical structure of the firm and coordinate their decisions through a central authority rather than simply relying on market exchange? Coase's answer would not surprise today's students of economics: *organizing activities through the hierarchy of the firm is often more efficient than market exchange because production requires the coordination of many transactions among many resource owners.* The costs

1. *Economica* 4 (November 1937): 386–405.

of transacting business through market relations are, according to Coase, often higher than those of undertaking the same activities within the firm.

Coase's major insight was that economic activity is best understood in terms of the transaction costs involved in any system of exchange between individuals. The exchange relation between individuals is contractual in nature. When you buy any product, such as a leather jacket, you agree to pay a certain amount—a contract is implicit. With major purchases, such as homes or cars, you actually sign a contract. Many resource owners, such as employees ranging from auto workers to professional athletes, sign contracts specifying the terms of supply. Thus, contractual relations abound.

The firm itself is most easily understood in terms of a particular kind of contractual relation, called the *authority relation.* The entrepreneur agrees to pay the resource owner a specified amount in return for the authority to direct the use of that resource in the firm. The owner therefore sells the right to control the resource to the entrepreneur, who may do the managing or may hire a manager. In the market, resources are allocated based on prices, but in the firm, resources are guided by the decisions of managers. *Coase argues that firms emerge when the transaction costs involved in using the price system exceed the costs of organizing those same activities through direct managerial controls within a firm.*

Teaching Tip Managerial controls organize activities within a firm; market exchange organizes activities between firms and their customers.

Consider again the example of the consumer purchasing a table by contracting directly with all the different resource suppliers, from the grower of timber to the individual who paints the table. Using resource markets directly involves (1) the cost of determining what inputs are needed and how they are combined and (2) the cost of negotiating a separate agreement with each resource owner for each specific contribution to production *over and above* the direct costs of the timber, nails, machinery, and labor required to make the table. Where inputs are easily identified, measured, priced, and hired, production can be carried out through a "do-it-yourself" approach rather than within the firm. For example, getting your house painted is a relatively simple production task: you can buy the paint and brushes and hire painters by the hour. In this case you, the consumer, become your own painting contractor, hiring inputs in the market and combining these inputs to do the job.

Where the costs of determining inputs and negotiating a contract for each specific contribution are high, the consumer minimizes transaction costs by purchasing the finished product from a firm rather than hiring all the inputs directly through markets. For example, although some people serve as their own general contractor when it comes to painting a house, few do so when it comes to building a house; most hire general contractors. The more complicated the task, the greater the ability to economize on transaction costs through specialization and centralized control. For example, attempting to buy a car by contracting with the hundreds of resource suppliers required to put one together would be time-consuming and costly. What type of skilled labor should be hired and at what wages? How much steel, aluminum, and other materials should be purchased? How should the resources be combined and in what proportions? The task is impossible for someone who lacks specialized engineering knowledge of car production. Consequently, it is more efficient for a consumer to buy a car produced by a firm than to contract separately with each resource supplier.

Teaching Tip Firms also choose to purchase from other firms rather than contracting with all resource owners themselves—for example, an automobile manufacturer buys steel rather than producing its own. See the chapter's later discussion of the boundaries of the firm.

At the margin there will be some activities that could go either way, with some consumers using firms and some hiring resources directly in the markets. The choice will depend on the skill and opportunity cost of time of each consumer. For example, some people may not want to be troubled with hiring all the inputs to get their house painted; instead, they will simply contract with a firm to do the entire job for an agreed-upon price—they will hire a contractor. As we will see later in the chapter, however, hiring a contractor may give rise to other problems of quality control.

Example A specialized asset may include a unique machine or production process to which the firm controls the patent rights—as was the case for both Alcoa Aluminum and U.S. Shoe during the early 1900s.

The Firm As Owner of Specialized Assets

Sometimes specialized assets create problems for the smooth functioning of markets. Here is why. Someone who plays a unique part in a specialized and complex production process can threaten to pull out unless the other parties involved agree to transfer more of the gains of production to that person. For example, suppose the individual who owns the paving machine used by a paving contractor threatens not to show up on an important job unless the rental payment increases. This possibility creates friction in the marketplace. But if one party—the firm—owns all the unique machines and other specialized assets used in production, there is no longer a threat of a holdout.

Example After 1909, Alcoa Aluminum controlled the U.S. aluminum market by controlling the supply of bauxite ore. U.S. Steel owned iron ore mines.

The Boundaries of the Firm

Vertical integration The expansion of a firm into stages of production earlier or later than those in which it has specialized

We have explained why firms exist: firms minimize both the transaction costs and the production costs of economic activity. Next we ask, what is the efficient scope of the firm? The theory of the firm described in earlier chapters has been largely silent on questions concerning the boundaries of the firm—that is, on the appropriate degree of vertical integration. **Vertical integration** is the expansion of a firm into stages of production earlier or later than those in which the firm has specialized. For example, a steel company may decide to mine its own ore or to form its steel into various components. A large manufacturer employs an amazing variety of production processes, but on average about half of the cost of production goes to purchasing inputs from other firms. For example, General Motors spends over $50 billion a year on parts and raw materials, an amount that exceeds the total output of most countries.

Point to Stress Different firms within the same industry may choose different levels of vertical integration, depending on factors such as the skill and opportunity cost of time of the managerial team and the firm's ability to achieve an efficient scale in the input production.

What determines which activities the firm will undertake and which it will purchase from other firms? Should IBM manufacture its own computer chips or buy them from another firm? The answer depends on a comparison of the costs and benefits of internal production versus market purchases. The point bears repeating: *internal production and markets are alternative ways of organizing transactions.* The choice will depend on which form of organization is the more efficient way to carry out the transaction in question. Keep in mind that market prices coordinate transactions *between* firms, whereas managers coordinate activities *within* firms. The market coordinates resources by integrating the independent plans of separate decision makers, but a firm coordinates resources through the conscious direction of the manager.

The usual assumption is that transactions will be organized by market exchange unless markets present problems. Sometimes, for example, it is difficult to use markets because the item in question is not standardized or the exact performance requirements are hard to specify. Consider, for example, trying to contract with another firm to supply research and development services. The amount of uncertainty involved in the purchase of such a nonspecific service makes it difficult to write, execute, and enforce contracts covering all possible circumstances that could arise. Many contingencies cannot be addressed adequately during contract negotiations, so events not covered in the contract inevitably occur. For example, what if the R&D service, in the course of product development, makes a valuable discovery for an application in an unrelated field? Who has the right to that new application, the firm or the R&D service? Since incomplete contracts create a potentially troublesome situation, conducting research and development *within the firm* often involves a lower transaction cost than purchasing it in the market. Coase's analysis of transaction costs helps explain why production often can be carried out more efficiently inside the firm than through market transactions between the firm and others. His analysis also suggests the appropriate amount of vertical integration in the firm.

Example In late 1992, Procter & Gamble announced a worldwide project to review its work process and organizational structure. The review was in response to P&G's dramatic growth since the early 1980s—its acquisition of more than forty businesses, its entry into twenty-nine more countries, and its move into twenty new business categories.

At this point it will be useful to discuss specific criteria the firm considers in deciding whether to purchase a particular input from the market or produce it internally.

BOUNDED RATIONALITY OF MANAGERS. To direct and coordinate activity in a conscious way in the firm, the manager must comprehend how all the pieces of the puzzle fit together. As the firm takes on more and more activities, however, the manager starts losing track of things and the quality of managerial decisions suffers. The larger the firm, the longer the lines of communication between the manager and the production worker who must implement the decision. One limit to the extent of vertical integration is the manager's **bounded rationality**, which limits the amount of information the manager can comprehend about the firm's operation. When the firm takes on additional functions, it can experience diseconomies similar to those it experiences when it expands output beyond the efficient scale of production. Even if the manager understands what's going on, communication to others over long lines becomes difficult. (As an example of the way communications become garbled, think of an experiment you may have been part of in a psychology class, in which the instructor whispers into a student's ear a sentence that is passed in whispers from student to student around the class and then reported by the last in line. The sentence that emerges is usually quite different from the original.)

Bounded rationality The notion that there is a limit on the amount of information an economic agent, such as a manager, can comprehend

MINIMUM EFFICIENT SCALE. In the long run, the average cost of production is minimized when the firm achieves its minimum efficient scale—that is, the minimum level of output at which economies of scale have been fully exploited. For example, suppose that economies of scale in the production of dishwashers are exhausted when the production rate reaches 100,000 units per year, as shown by the average cost curve in panel (a) of Exhibit 1,

Teaching Tip The concept of minimum efficient scale was introduced in Chapter 20.

EXHIBIT 1

Minimum Efficient Scale and Vertical Integration

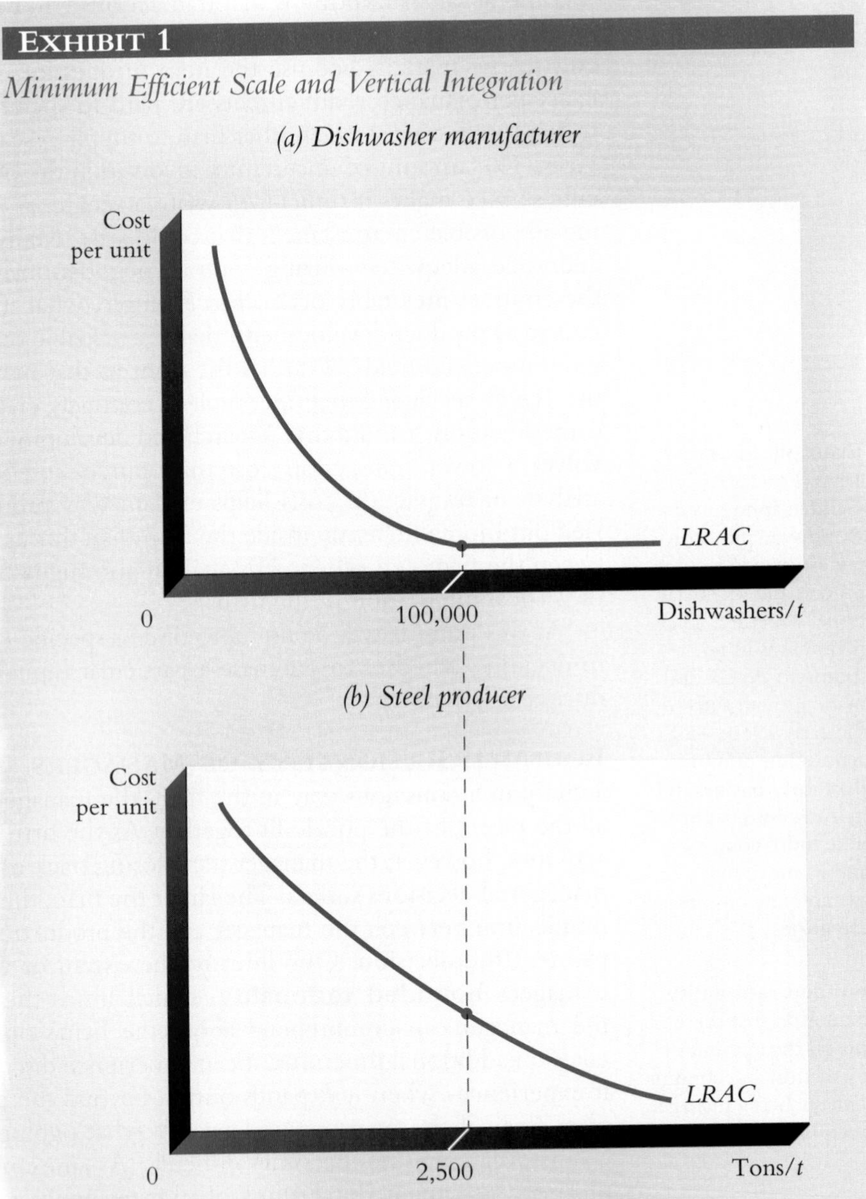

The dishwasher manufacturer of panel (a) is producing at the minimum efficient scale of 100,000 units per period. That level of production requires 2,500 tons of steel. If the manufacturer produced its own steel, the cost would be much higher than if it purchased steel from a steel producer operating on a much larger scale. As panel (b) shows, at 2,500 tons, economies of scale in steel production are far from exhausted.

and this turns out to be the amount the firm wants to produce to maximize profit. Since steel is an important component in dishwashers, should the dishwasher manufacturer integrate backward into steel production? Suppose that economies of scale in steel production are not exhausted until production reaches a rate of one million tons per year. If each dishwasher requires 50 pounds of steel, the dishwasher manufacturer needs only 2,500 tons of steel per year—a tiny fraction of the amount produced at the minimum efficient scale for steel plants. As you can see in panel (b) of Exhibit 1, if only 2,500 tons of steel were produced per year, the cost per ton would be very high relative to the cost that could be achieved at minimum efficient size. The dishwasher manufacturer therefore minimizes production costs by buying steel from a steel firm of optimal size rather than trying to produce steel. More generally, *other things constant, firms should buy an input in the resource market when the cost is lower than it would be if the input were internally produced.*

EASILY OBSERVABLE QUALITY. If an input is well defined and its quality is easily determined at the time of purchase, it is more apt to be purchased in the market than produced internally, other things constant. For example, a flour mill will typically buy its wheat in the market rather than grow its own, as the quality of the wheat can be easily assessed upon inspection. In contrast, the quality of certain inputs can be determined only during the production process. Firms whose reputations depend on the operation of a key component are likely to produce that component, especially if the quality of that component cannot be easily observed by inspection and varies widely across producers and time. For example, suppose that the manufacturer of a sensitive measuring instrument requires a crucial gauge, the quality of which can be observed only as the gauge is assembled. If the firm produces the gauge itself, it can closely monitor quality.

Example The McDonald's Corp. produces its own beef.

Another reason why producers sometimes integrate backward is so they can offer consumers a guarantee about the quality of the components or ingredients in a product. For example, Frank Perdue can talk about the health and quality of the chickens he sells because he raises his own. Kentucky Fried Chicken does not discuss the family background of its chickens because the company makes no claim about raising them. Instead their ads focus on such things as the secret ingredients used to fry the chicken or the fact that by specializing in cooking only chicken ("We do chicken right!"), the company does a better job than other fast-food franchises that sell much more besides chicken.

NUMBER OF SUPPLIERS. A firm wants an uninterrupted source of component parts. When there are many interchangeable suppliers of a particular input, a firm is more likely to purchase that input in the market rather than produce it internally, other things constant. Not only does the existence of many suppliers ensure a dependable source of components, but competition among the many suppliers keeps the component price down. If the resource market is so unstable that the firm cannot rely on a consistent supply of the component, the firm may produce the item to insulate itself from the vagaries of that market.

In summary, the extent to which a firm integrates vertically is limited by the bounded rationality of managers. Other things equal, the firm is more likely to buy a component part rather than produce it if (1) the item can be purchased for less than the firm would have to pay to produce it, (2) the item is well defined and its quality is easily observable, or (3) there are many interchangeable suppliers.

Economies of Scope

Economies of scope Forces that make it cheaper for a firm to produce two or more different products than just one

Example Blockbuster Entertainment, the video-rental firm, acquired Sound Warehouse and Music Plus in 1992 in order to move into the compact disk market. The company also unveiled plans for Family Entertainment Centers—mini-amusement parks with movie theaters, miniature golf courses, pinball arcades, and so forth.

Thus far we have considered issues affecting the optimal degree of vertical integration. Sometimes firms branch out into product lines that do not have a vertical relation. **Economies of scope** exist when it is cheaper to combine two or more product lines in one firm than to produce them separately. Outlays for buildings, research and development, advertising, and product distribution can be minimized when spread over different products. For example, General Electric produces hundreds of products ranging from toasters to jet engines. General Motors sells cars, provides financing for those cars, and even offers a credit card that rebates 5 percent of purchases toward a new GM car. Farmers often grow a variety of crops and raise different kinds of farm animals, animals that often recycle damaged crops and food scraps into useful fertilizer. With economies of scale, the cost per unit of output falls as the scale of the firm increases; *with economies of scope, per-unit production costs fall as the firm produces additional types of product.* The cost of some fixed resources, such as specialized knowledge, can be spread out across product lines.

Thus far we have considered why firms exist, why they often integrate vertically, and why they often produce a whole range of products. These steps toward greater realism move us beyond the simple depiction of the firm employed earlier. In the balance of the chapter we challenge some other simplifying assumptions, in this case assumptions about how much information is available to market participants.

Market Behavior with Imperfect Information

Point to Stress Searching for and acquiring information (such as data on prices, resource and product availability, and resource and product quality) are major parts of the cost of many transactions.

For the most part, our analysis of market behavior has assumed that market participants have full information about products and resources. For consumers, full information reflects knowledge about product prices, quality, and availability. For firms, full information reflects knowledge about the marginal productivity of various resources, about the appropriate technology for combining them, and about the demand for the firm's product. In reality, *reliable information is costly for both consumers and producers.* What's more, in some markets one side of a transaction often has better information about the product being sold than does the other side of the transaction. In this section we examine the impact of less-than-perfect information on market behavior.

Optimal Search with Imperfect Information

Suppose you want to buy a new computer. You need information about the quality and features of each model and the prices of each model at various retail outlets and mail-order firms. To learn about your choices, you may read advertisements, promotional brochures, and computer publications; you may also talk with those with more expertise than you have.

Teaching Tip The new computer is an example of a product sold in a decentralized market—it is available at a large number of different physical locations. Items such as stocks, bonds, and commodities are sold in centralized markets—all transactions occur in one location.

Once you narrow your choice down to one or two models, you may price shop by going from store to store or by letting your fingers do the walking through the yellow pages, computer catalogues, newspaper ads, and the like. The point is that searching for the best product at the lowest price involves a cost. The primary cost of gathering information is usually the opportunity cost of your time. This cost will obviously vary from individual to individual and from item to item. Some people actually enjoy shopping, but this "shop-'til-you-drop" attitude does not necessarily carry over to all items. *For most of us, the process of gathering consumer information can be considered nonmarket work.*

Point to Stress Information costs involve elements such as checking credentials, monitoring honesty, reading ads and consumer reports, telephoning, shopping, and so forth.

MARGINAL COST OF SEARCH. In your quest for product information, you gather the easy and obvious information first, such as the types of products on the market and where these products are sold. For example, you may check on the price and availability at the few computer stores at the mall. But as your search widens, the *marginal cost* of acquiring additional information increases, both because you may have to travel greater distances to check prices and services and because the opportunity cost of your time increases as you spend more time acquiring information—that is, as you spend more time searching, your time must be drawn away from alternative uses that grow increasingly more attractive. Consequently, the marginal cost curve for additional information slopes upward, as shown in Exhibit 2. Note the assumption in Exhibit 2 is that a certain amount of information, I_f, is simply common knowledge and is freely available.

MARGINAL BENEFIT OF SEARCH. The *marginal benefit* from acquiring additional information is any improvement in quality and any reduction in price that you are able to uncover because of that additional unit of information. The marginal benefit is relatively large at first, but as you gather more information and grow more acquainted with the market, additional information yields less and less additional benefit. For example, the likelihood of finding a lower price or a higher quality at the twentieth store visited is lower than that of finding a lower price or a higher quality at the second store visited. The marginal benefit of additional information slopes downward, as shown in Exhibit 2.

OPTIMAL SEARCH. Whether we are talking about a consumer attempting to maximize utility or a firm attempting to maximize profit, market participants will continue to gather information as long as the marginal benefit of additional information exceeds its marginal cost. *Optimal search occurs where the marginal benefit just equals the marginal cost,* which in Exhibit 2 occurs where

EXHIBIT 2

Optimal Search with Imperfect Information

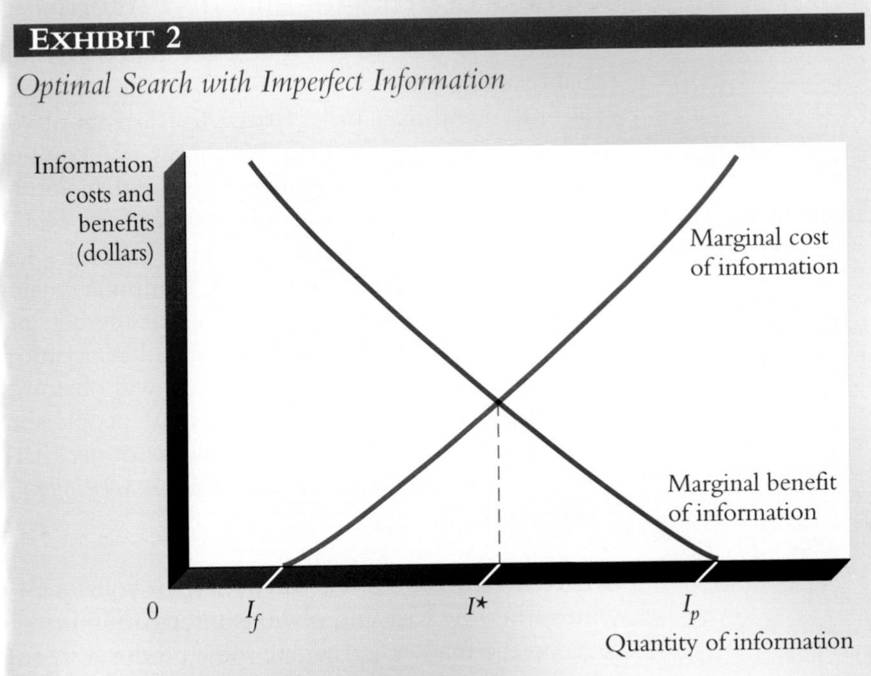

When information is costly, additional information is acquired as long as its marginal benefit exceeds its marginal cost. Equilibrium, or optimal search, occurs where marginal benefit equals marginal cost.

Teaching Tip The more decentralized the market in which a product is sold, other things constant, the higher the marginal cost of achieving perfect information. Therefore, it is more likely that prices will vary across sellers.

the two curves intersect. Note that at search levels exceeding the equilibrium amount, the marginal benefit of additional information is still positive, but it's below the marginal cost. Note also that full and complete information, what we might call *perfect information,* would occur at level I_p, where the marginal benefit of more information is zero. The high marginal cost of acquiring I_p, however, makes it impractical to become fully informed. Thus, firms and consumers, by gathering the optimal amount of information, I^*, have less than perfect knowledge about the price, availability, and quality of products and resources.

IMPLICATIONS. The search model we have presented was developed by George Stigler, winner of the Nobel Prize in 1982. Over three decades ago, he showed that the price of a product can differ across sellers because some consumers are unaware of lower prices offered by some sellers.[2] Thus, *search costs result in price dispersion, or different prices, for the same product.* Some sellers call attention to price dispersions by claiming to have the lowest prices around and by promising to match any competitor's price. Likewise, *search costs lead to quality differences across sellers even for identically priced products.*

2. George Stigler, "The Economics of Information," *Journal of Political Economy* (June 1961): 213–225.

Example Stigler found that prices were less widely dispersed for identical makes of automobiles than for identical makes of washing machines.

There are other implications of Stigler's search model. As the market wage of the consumer rises, the opportunity cost of the consumer's time increases. This shifts the marginal cost of additional information up, resulting in less search and more price dispersion in the market. On the other hand, any change in technology that lowers the marginal cost of information, such as a computerized search program, will lead to more search and less price dispersion. Finally, the marginal benefits of search are likely to be higher for expensive items, such as a house or a car, than for small ones, such as an alarm clock or Odor Eaters. So the more expensive a product, other things constant, the more information will be gathered by consumers and the less price dispersion there will be.

The Winner's Curse

In the early 1970s oil companies were invited to bid on oil leases in the Gulf of Mexico. At the time, they had little experience with such leases. Each company submitted bids indicating the most it would bid for each lease. Suppose the average of these bids across companies for a particular lease was $10 million, with some companies bidding more and others less. The winning bid was from the company that attached the greatest value to the lease. Suppose the winning bid was $18 million. The problem is that the winning bid frequently exceeded the actual value of the oil lease. How come?

Winner's curse The plight of the winning bidder for an asset of uncertain value who has overestimated the asset's true value

The winner often lost money because the lease's actual value was unknown and could only be estimated. The problem is that the winning bid is not the average bid in the group, which is likely the most unbiased estimate of the lease's true value, but the highest bid, which is the most optimistic estimate from among all bidders. Winners of such bids are said to experience the **winner's curse** because they often lose money by winning the bid. Oil companies have blamed the winner's curse for the poor earnings performance on their offshore tracts. The winner's curse applies to all cases of bidding in which the true value is unknown at the outset. For example, movie companies often bid up the price of screenplays to what many argue are unrealistic ranges. Likewise, publishers get into bidding wars over book manuscripts and even book proposals that are little more than titles. Television networks often overbid for the rights to broadcast the Olympics. And sports team owners bid for free agents and often overpay.

If there were perfect information about the market value of a resource, potential buyers would never bid more than the market value. But when competitive bidding is coupled with imperfect information, the winning bidder may lose money on the deal. Once bidders realize that the winning bid will tend to be too high, they may try to scale down their bids. If all bids are scaled down by the same amount or by the same proportion, the winning bid should be lower, though the winning bidder should be the same. But such self-restraint is difficult, particularly if a bidder truly believes the resource is worth more.

Market Behavior with Asymmetric Information

Asymmetric information A situation in which one side of the market has more reliable information than does the other side

Hidden characteristics A type of asymmetric information problem in which one side of the market knows more than the other side about characteristics that are important to the transaction

Hidden actions A type of asymmetric information problem in which one side of an economic relation can take a relevant action that the other side cannot observe

Thus far we have considered the effects of costly information and limited information on market behavior. The problem gets more complicated when one side of the market has more reliable information than does the other side, a situation in which there is **asymmetric information**. In this section we examine several examples of asymmetric information and its effect on market efficiency.

We can identify two types of information that a market participant may want but lack. First, one side of the market may know about *characteristics* of the product for sale that the other side does not know. For example, the seller of a used car knows more about that car's record of reliability than does the buyer. Likewise, the buyer of a health insurance policy knows more about his or her general state of health than does the insurance company. When one side of the market knows more than the other side about characteristics that are important in the transaction, the asymmetric information problem involves **hidden characteristics**.

A second type of asymmetric information problem occurs when one side of a transaction can pursue an *action* that affects the other side even though the other side cannot directly observe that action. For example, the mechanic you hire to check out that strange noise under your car's hood may undertake unneeded repairs, charging you for three hours' work even though the job should have taken only ten minutes. Whenever one side of an economic relationship can take a relevant action that the other side cannot observe, the situation is described as one of **hidden actions**.

Hidden Characteristics: The "Lemon" Problem

One type of hidden characteristic model occurs when sellers know more about the quality of the product than do the buyers. Consider the market for used cars. The seller of a used car normally has had abundant experience with important *characteristics* of that car: the record of breakdowns, accidents, gas mileage, miles driven, and so on. A prospective buyer can only guess at these based on the car's appearance and perhaps a test drive. The buyer cannot really know how good a car it is without owning it for several months. So buyers of used cars have less information than sellers.

To simplify the problem, suppose there are only two types of used cars for sale: good ones and bad ones, or "lemons." Again, only the seller knows which type is for sale. Suppose that if buyers were certain about a car's type, they would be willing on average to pay $10,000 for good cars but only $4,000 for lemons. If buyers believed that half the used cars on the market were good ones and half were lemons, buyers would be willing to pay, say, $7,000 for a car of unknown type (since buyers believe this to be the average value of cars on the market). Would $7,000 be the equilibrium price of used cars?

So far we have ignored the actions of the potential sellers, who know

Point to Stress As the mix shifts toward lemons, the average value of available used cars falls.

Teaching Tip Established dealers who were seen to act as certifiers of quality would be able to place good used cars on the market.

Teaching Tip The revolution in digital technology is predicted to reduce employees' potential for hidden actions, thus reducing the principal-agent problem. Employers will use the new technology to monitor workers and measure their productivity to the tiniest detail—such as the number of keystrokes made every hour by data-entry clerks. A new badge system would allow employers to instantly locate and talk with any employee.

which type of cars they have. If potential sellers can get only $7,000 for a car that they know to be worth $10,000 on average, then many will choose not to sell their cars or will sell them to friends or relatives. But owners of lemons will find $7,000 an attractive price since their cars are worth only $4,000 on average. As a result, the proportion of good cars on the market will fall and the proportion of lemons will increase.

As buyers come to realize that the mix has shifted toward lemons, they will reduce the amount they are willing to pay for a car of unknown quality. As the market price of used cars falls, potential sellers of good cars become even more reluctant to sell at such a low price, so the proportion of lemons increases, leading to lower prices still. The process could continue until there were few good cars sold on the open market. More generally, *when sellers have more information about a product's quality than buyers do, lower-quality products tend to dominate the market.*

Hidden Actions: The Principal-Agent Problem

In this age of specialization, there are many tasks we do not do for ourselves because others do them better and because others have a lower opportunity cost of time. Suppose your objective is to get your car repaired, but you have little knowledge of cars. The mechanic you hire may have other objectives, such as maximizing on-the-job leisure or maximizing the garage's revenue. But the mechanic's actions are hidden from you. Even though your car may have only a loose wire, the mechanic could inflate the bill by charging you for services you did not really need or for services that were not performed. This asymmetric information problem occurs because one side of a transaction can pursue *hidden actions* that affect the other side. When buyers have difficulty monitoring and evaluating the quality of goods or services purchased, some suppliers may tend to substitute poor quality resources or to exercise less diligence in providing the service.

Principal-agent problem Occurs when the agent's objectives differ from those of the principal and the agent can pursue hidden actions

Principal A person who enters into a contractual agreement with an agent in the expectation that the agent will act on behalf of the principal

Agent A person who performs work or provides a service on behalf of another person, the principal

The problem that arises from hidden actions is called the **principal-agent problem**, which describes a relation in which one party, known as the **principal**, makes a contractual agreement with another party, known as the **agent**, in the expectation that the agent will act on behalf of the principal. *The problem arises when the goals of the agent are incompatible with those of the principal and when the agent can pursue hidden actions.* You could confront a principal-agent problem when you deal with a doctor, lawyer, TV repairer, or financial advisor, to name a few. More generally, any employer-employee relation is a principal-agent relation and could potentially be a source of a principal-agent problem. The owners of a corporation are the principals and the managers are the agents. Again, the problem arises because the agent's objectives are not the same as the principal's *and* because the agent's actions are hidden. Note that not all principal-agent relations pose a problem. For example, when you get your hair cut, there are no hidden actions, and you have the ability to judge the result; thus, you can tip accordingly.

Adverse Selection

Adverse selection A situation in which those on the informed side of the market self-select in a way that harms the uninformed side of the market

When those on the informed side of the market self-select in a way that harms the uninformed side of the market, the problem is one of **adverse selection**. In our earlier example, car sellers, the informed parties, self-select—that is, decide whether to offer their cars for sale—in a way that harms buyers. Because of this adverse selection, car buyers, the uninformed side of the market, end up trading primarily with owners of lemons—exactly the group buyers do not want to deal with.

Point to Stress With adverse selection, a buyer or seller enters into a disadvantageous contract on the basis of incomplete or inaccurate information.

Adverse selection also creates problems in insurance markets. For example, from an insurance company's point of view, ideal candidates for health insurance are those who lead long, healthy lives, then die peacefully in their sleep. But many people are poor risks for health insurers because of hidden characteristics (bad genes) or hidden actions (smoking and drinking excessively, getting exercise only on trips to the refrigerator, and thinking a seven-course meal consists of beef jerky and a six-pack of beer). In the insurance market, it is the buyers, not the sellers, who have more information about characteristics and actions that predict their likely need for insurance in the future.

Teaching Tip Adverse selection is used as an argument for a universal, national health insurance program.

If the insurance company has no way of discriminating among applicants, it must charge the same insurance rate to both those who are poor health risks and those who are good health risks. This average rate is attractive to those in poor health, but the rate will seem too high to healthy people, some of whom will choose to self-insure. As the number of healthy people who self-insure increases, the insurance pool becomes less healthy on average, so rates must rise, making insurance even less attractive to healthy people. Because of adverse selection, people who are poor health risks will become the dominant group of insurance buyers.

Moral Hazard

Teaching Tip Moral hazard may also arise not because one party is *unable* to monitor the other party's post-contractual behavior, but because doing so is too costly.

The insurance problem is compounded by the fact that, once people buy insurance, their behavior may change in a way that increases the probability that a claim will be made. Some people with health insurance may take less care of their health than people without it. This same behavioral problem affects other types of insurance such as fire, auto, and theft insurance. For example, after buying theft insurance, people may take less care of their valuables. This incentive problem is referred to as moral hazard. **Moral hazard** occurs when an individual's behavior changes in a way that increases the likelihood of an unfavorable outcome.

Moral hazard A situation in which one party to a contract has an incentive after the contract is made to alter behavior in a way that harms the other party to the contract

More generally, *moral hazard results when those on one side of the transaction have an incentive to shirk their responsibilities because the other side is unable to observe them.* The responsibility could be to repair a car or to safeguard valuables. Both the mechanic and the policy buyer take advantage of the ignorant party. In the car-repair problem, the mechanic is the agent; in the insurance example, the policy buyer is the principal. Thus, moral hazard arises on the part of the party that can undertake hidden action; this could be either the agent or the principal, depending on the circumstance.

Coping with Asymmetric Information

There are ways of reducing the consequences of asymmetric information. An incentive structure or an information-revealing system can be developed to reduce the problems associated with the lopsided availability of information. For example, some auto-repair garages provide written estimates before a job is done and return the defective parts to the customer as evidence that the repair was necessary and was completed. Consumers often get multiple estimates for major expenditures and may seek second and third opinions on medical procedures. And several states have passed "lemon laws" that offer compensation to buyers of new or used cars that turn out to be lemons.

Insurance companies deal with adverse selection and moral hazard in a variety of ways. Most require applicants to complete a lengthy form with questions about the applicant's medical history plus take a physical exam. A policy often covers all those in a group, such as all company employees, not just those who would otherwise self-select. Such group policies avoid the problem of adverse selection. Insurers reduce moral hazard by making the policyholder pay, say, the first $250 of a claim as a "deductible" and by requiring the policyholder to pay a certain percentage of a claim. Also the premiums on some policies go up as more claims are filed.

Asymmetric Information in Labor Markets

In our market analysis of the supply and demand for particular kinds of labor, we typically assumed that workers are identical. In equilibrium, each worker in a particular labor market is assumed to be paid the same wage, a wage that for resource price takers is equal to the marginal revenue product of the last unit of labor hired. Here we talk about the problems arising from differences in the ability of workers.

Differences in the ability of workers present no particular problem as long as the effect of these differences on the workers' productivity can be readily observed by the buyers of labor. If the productivity of each particular worker is easily quantified through a measure such as the quantity of oranges picked, the number of shoes stitched, or the number of papers typed, that measure itself can and does serve as the basis for pay. But because production often takes place through the coordinated efforts of several workers, it is usually easier to pay workers by the hour rather than try to keep a detailed account of each worker's contribution to total output.

Often the pay is some combination of an hourly rate and incentive pay linked to a measure of productivity. For example, a sales representative typically receives a base salary plus a commission tied to the amount sold. At times the task of evaluating performance is left to the consumer rather than to the firm. Workers who provide personal services, such as waiters and waitresses, barbers and beauticians, and bellhops, get paid partly in tips. Since these services are by definition "personal," customers are in the best position to judge the quality of service and to tip accordingly.

Adverse Selection Problems in Labor Markets

Teaching Tip In the early 1990s, the leasing of employees (especially professional and technical staff) grew 30 percent per year. According to the National Staff Leasing Association, employees gain better benefits through the leasing company and the business gains better quality employees.

An adverse selection problem arises in the labor market when labor suppliers have better information about their productivities than employers do, because the abilities of workers are not observable before employment. Before the individual is hired, that worker's true abilities—motivation, work habits, skills, ability to get along with others, and the like—are *hidden characteristics.* A given wage tends to attract the least productive workers available in the labor pool; the most productive workers view the given wage as below the value of their marginal productivity.

Example The use of brand names is a form of signaling to consumers. Soundesign Corp. leases the Zenith name for modestly priced home, car, and portable audio equipment and for telephone products.

Suppose an employer wants to hire a program coordinator for a new project, a job that calls for imagination, organizational skills, and the ability to work independently. The employer would like to attract the most qualified person in the market, but the qualities demanded are not directly observable. The pay level advertised for the position is not the marginal revenue product of the best person in the market; it is more likely the "average" marginal revenue product of all those in the market. (Just as the market price of used cars was an average of good cars and lemons.) Individual workers have a good idea of their own intelligence and creativity and are able to evaluate this wage in view of their own abilities and opportunitities. Talented people will find that the salary offered is below the true value of their abilities and will be less inclined to apply for the job. Less talented individuals, however, will find that the offered wage exceeds their marginal productivity, so they will be more likely to seek the job. Because of adverse selection, the employer ends up with a pool of applicants of below average ability. In a labor market with hidden characteristics, employers might be better off offering a higher wage. The higher the wage, the more attractive the market is to more qualified workers. Paying higher wages to improve the productivity of the work force is called paying **efficiency wages**, an idea also discussed in macroeconomics.

Efficiency wage theory The idea that offering high wages attracts a more talented labor pool

Signaling

The side of the market with hidden characteristics and hidden actions has an incentive to say the right thing. For example, a job applicant might say, "Hire me because I am hard-working, reliable, prompt, highly motivated, and just an all-around great employee." Or a producer might say, "At Ford, quality is job one." But such direct claims of quality appear self-serving and therefore are not necessarily believable. Yet both sides of the market have an incentive to develop credible ways of communicating reliable information. This leads us to signaling.

Signaling Using a proxy measure to communicate information about unobservable characteristics

Adverse selection may give rise to **signaling**, which is the attempt by the informed side of the market to communicate information that the other side would find valuable. Consider signaling in the job market. Because the true requirements for many jobs are qualities that are unobservable on a resumé or in an interview, the job applicant offers evidence of the unobservable features by relying on proxy measures, such as educational attainment. A job-seeker tries to "look good on paper." A proxy measure is called a *signal,* which is an observable indicator of some hidden characteristic.

A signal is sent by the informed side of the market to the uninformed side and may serve as a useful way of sorting out applicants as long as the signal is a true indicator of the hidden characteristic of interest.

Screening The process used by employers to select the most qualified workers based on readily observable characteristics, such as level of education.

In order to identify the best workers, employers try to *screen* applicants. **Screening** is the attempt by the uninformed side of the market to uncover the relevant but hidden characteristics of the informed party. An initial screen might be to check each resumé for spelling and typographical errors. Although not important in themselves, such errors indicate a lack of attention to detail. The uninformed party must find signals that less productive individuals will have more difficulty acquiring. A signal that can be acquired with equal ease or difficulty by all workers, regardless of their productivity, does not provide a useful way of screening applicants. But if, for example, more productive workers find it easier to succeed in college than do less productive workers, a good college record is a signal worth using to distinguish among workers. In this case education may be important not so much because of its effects on a worker's productivity but because it enables employers to distinguish among workers.

Example Potential employers may also require particular college majors or set minimum grade point averages.

Reputation as a Hostage

As we said, buyers cannot always inspect an item thoroughly before buying it. Sellers who believe they offer a high-quality product try to signal this quality to buyers. If buyers can't recognize quality, producers of high-quality products cannot sell the product for enough to cover the added cost associated with the high quality. One response to asymmetric information—one way sellers can signal quality—is to offer warranties or money-back guarantees if the buyer is not completely satisfied.

A more general signal for a seller is to develop a reputation for quality. Companies often present their long history as evidence of their ability to satisfy customers over the years, as in "Over a century of service" or "A market leader since 1864." Many producers try to sell an image of quality and dependability, as reflected by the lonely, underemployed Maytag repairman. In a sense, a firm's reputation for high quality is offered as a *hostage* to the consumer. The seller is in effect saying: "If we fail to live up to high standards, then you can hurt us by not buying from us anymore and by berating our product with your friends and relatives." Thus, the firm loses its good reputation if it lets the customer down. For this threat of lost reputation to be credible to the buyer, the buyer must believe that the firm cannot profit in the long run by selling a poor product today. That is, this one transaction must not represent an opportunity to take advantage of a reputation.

Example A firm may also offer a variety of levels of quality under different brand names. Soundesign Corp., for example, a producer of audio and telephone equipment, uses Jensen for its top-of-the-line brand, Zenith for its moderately priced line, and Soundesign for its lowest line.

The potential loss of reputation becomes more costly and therefore more effective as an advertising tool if the seller offers a range of products. Sears, for example, sells a full line of house brands ranging from appliances to paint. Sears knows that if you get stuck with a poorly functioning appliance, you may be less likely to buy anything else there. *Thus, multiproduct firms have more incentive to offer quality products on a consistent basis because any poor performance harms the reputation of all other products they sell.*

The success of major franchise operations can be explained by reputation effects. For example, McDonald's has over ten thousand restaurants and is opening more than five hundred a year. The secret to their success is that customers can count on product consistency whether they are buying a Big Mac in Anchorage, Moscow, or Singapore. The problem for the McDonald's Corporation is that any particular McDonald's franchise could increase profits by temporarily reducing cost by lowering quality—for example, by using lower-quality meat and stale buns. To prevent franchises from taking advantage of the reputation of the brand name, the McDonald's Corporation must make sure it attracts the right kind of franchises and that these franchises face the optimal incentives and constraints. This balancing act is discussed in the following case study.

CASE STUDY

The Reputation of a Big Mac

Since its founding in 1955, McDonald's has been able to grow so fast because it relies primarily on local people to purchase franchises in its restaurants. To avoid adverse selection, McDonald's never advertises for franchises. Still, each year there are more than ten applications for each new franchise. Even to be granted an interview, the applicant must show sufficient financial resources and adequate business experience. An applicant who gets past the two-hour interview is then required to work fifty hours, after which there is another interview and evaluation. If the applicant survives these, there is a preliminary training period lasting six to nine months, followed by testing and more evaluation.

Those who are selected after all this must make a security deposit and complete the twelve- to eighteen-month formal training program involving twenty hours per week of unpaid work at an established McDonald's plus more time in the classroom. During this time the individual is paid nothing, not even expenses. After completing the program to the satisfaction of the corporation, applicants may wait up to three years to open their own restaurants. Once the restaurant opens, a franchisee is required to work full time in its daily operation.

Franchisees make a huge commitment of time and of money. About \$160,000 toward the \$400,000 cost of a new franchise must come from the franchisee's own resources, not from borrowed funds. The franchisee cannot sell the restaurant without prior approval and the company retains the right of first refusal. Any buyer must have company approval and must complete the same training program as all other franchisees.

Example McDonald's Founder Ray Kroc and other members of top management became legendary for personally inspecting stores and assessing their quality, service, and cleanliness.

Since each franchisee gets a large share of the restaurant's operating profit, there is a strong incentive to be efficient. As a further reward, successful operators may apply for and get additional restaurants. If all goes well, the franchise is valid for twenty years and renewable after that, but it can be cancelled *at any time* if the restaurant fails the company's standards of quality, pricing, cleanliness, hours of operation, and so on. Thus, the franchisee is bound to the company by highly specific investments in physical capital and in human capital. In most cases, the loss of a franchise would represent the loss of the individual's life savings. In selecting and monitoring franchises, McDonald's has successfully addressed problems stemming from hidden characteristics and hidden actions.

Source: D. L. Noren, "The Economics of the Golden Arches," *American Economist* (Fall 1990), pp. 60–64.

Conclusion

The firm has evolved through a natural selection process as the form of organization that minimizes both transaction and production costs. According to this theory of natural selection, those forms of organization that are most efficient will be selected by the economic system for survival. Attributes that yield an economic profit will thrive, and those that do not will fall by the wayside. The form of organization selected may not be optimal in the sense that it cannot be improved upon, but it will be the most efficient form among those that have been tried. If there is a way to organize production that is more efficient than the firm, some entrepreneur will stumble upon it one day and will be rewarded with greater profit. Thus, the improvement may not be the result of any conscious design. Once a more efficient way of organizing production is uncovered, others will imitate the successful innovation.

Problems created by asymmetric information are not reflected in the simple account of how markets work. In conventional supply and demand analysis, trades occur in impersonal markets, and the buyer has no special concern about who is on the selling side. But with asymmetric information, the mix and characteristics of the other side of the market become important. When the problem of adverse selection is severe enough, markets may cease to function. There may be no price that will clear the market. Market participants try to overcome the limitations of asymmetric information by signaling, screening, and trying to be quite explicit about the terms of the transaction.

Summary

1. According to Coase, firms exist because production often can be accomplished more efficiently through the hierarchy of the firm than through transactions carried out independently by consumers in markets. Because production requires the extensive coordination of transactions among many resource owners, all this activity can be carried out better under the direction of a manager in a firm than by consumers' specifying detailed performance contracts with many separate suppliers.

2. The extent to which a firm integrates vertically will depend on both the transaction and the production costs of economic activity. Other things equal, the firm is more likely to buy a component part rather than produce it if (1) the item can be purchased for less than it would cost the firm to produce it, (2) the item is well defined and its quality is easily observable, or (3) there are a large number of interchangeable suppliers of the item. Economies of scope exist when it is cheaper to combine two or more kinds of product in one firm than to produce them separately.

3. A buyer acquires additional information as long as its marginal benefit in the form of a lower price or higher quality exceeds the marginal cost of searching for that information. In equilibrium, the marginal cost of information equals its marginal benefit. Because price and quality information are costly, the same good may sell for different prices across sellers.

4. Asymmetric information occurs when one side of the market is better informed about the quality of a product than the other side. The uninformed party may not know about hidden characteristics or about hidden actions. Because of the problem of adverse selection, those on the uninformed side of the market find they are dealing with exactly the wrong people.

5. When the productivity of potential employees is not directly observable, employers sometimes try to screen workers based on some signal that appears to be related to productivity, such as education. This system of screening applicants is effective as long as more productive workers find it easier to send the correct signal than less productive workers do.

Questions and Problems

1. (Adverse Selection and Signaling) Suppose that you were charged with the responsibility of recruiting for a major corporation. What signals would you use to reduce the problem of adverse selection? How might these signals be faulty indicators of productivity?

2. (Principal and Agent) Export management companies help firms market their products in foreign countries. Are such export management companies principals or agents? What skills must employees of such companies possess to be successful?

3. (Internal Production Versus the Market) What economic factors determine whether a firm has its own legal staff or retains an outside law firm to handle its litigation?

4. (Internal Production Versus the Market) Ashland Oil, Inc. is an oil refiner that buys its crude oil in the marketplace. Larger oil companies, such as Texaco, have their own crude oil production facilities. How would you explain this situation?

5. (Contracting) Department stores, among other enterprises, often contract with janitorial services to clean the stores every night. Why don't the stores simply hire their own janitors?

6. (Contracting) When you deposit money in a bank, you are really lending the money to firms and home purchasers who borrow from the bank. The bank typically makes a profit on this transaction. What is it doing for you? That is, what keeps you from lending your money directly to the borrowers without paying the "middleman"?

7. (Production and Information) How does the technology of information processing influence both economies of scale and economies of scope?

8. (Management Services) If you are planning to remodel your home, you typically hire a contractor to handle the job. The contractor, in turn, frequently hires subcontractors to do the actual work. If you hire the subcontractors directly, it is usually cheaper. Which should you do?

9. (Information) Fifty years ago, people often shopped by mail using catalogues from large mail-order houses. In the last few years, catalogue shopping has again become a widely used method of buying. What reasons can you suggest for the resurgence of this form of shopping?

10. (Signaling) Give an example of signaling for each of the following situations involving information asymmetry.
    a. Choosing a doctor
    b Buying a home
    c. Applying to graduate school

11. (Economies of Scope) What are some reasons firms produce different product lines that relate to economies of scope? Can you think of any reasons *unrelated* to production costs to produce different products?

12. (Moral Hazard) Insurance companies frequently give discounts for certain kinds of activities. Examples include discounts on homeowner's insurance for installing smoke detectors and discounts on automobile insurance for maintaining a history of safe driving. Obviously these behaviors affect the insurance company's expected payments on the policy, but they also affect the moral hazard problem. How?

13. (McDonald's Franchise) Explain how the time and financial requirements involved in obtaining a McDonald's franchise bear on the hidden characteristics problem.

14. (McDonald's Franchise) Each franchise owner has a vested interest not only in his or her franchise, but also in the maintenance of application standards for new franchise owners. Why?

PART 7

Market Failure and Public Policy

CHAPTER 29

REGULATION, DEREGULATION, AND ANTITRUST ACTIVITY

It has been said that businesspeople praise competition but love monopoly. They praise competition because it harnesses the diverse and often conflicting objectives of various market participants and channels them into the efficient production of goods and services. And competition does this "as if by an invisible hand." They love monopoly because it provides the surest path to economic profit in the long run—and, after all, profit is the firm's objective. The fruits of monopoly are so great they can tempt firms to try to eliminate or to conspire with competitors. As Adam Smith remarked more than two hundred years ago, "People of the same trade seldom meet together, even for merriment or diversion, but the conversation ends in a conspiracy against the public, or in some contrivance to raise prices."

The tendency of firms to seek monopolistic advantage is understandable, but the pursuit of monopoly is often at odds with achieving the most efficient use of the economy's scarce resources. Public policy plays a role by attempting to promote competition in those markets where competition seems desirable and to reduce the harmful consequences of monopolistic behavior in those markets where the output can be most efficiently produced by one or a few firms. This chapter discusses the ways in which government regulates business. As you will see, there is some disagreement about what government is doing and what it should be doing. Topics discussed in this chapter include

Teaching Tip Methods of coordinating activity to approximate the behavior of a monopoly are discussed in Chapter 23.

- Market power
- Regulating natural monopolies
- Theories of economic regulation
- Deregulation
- Antitrust activity
- Competitive trends of the economy

Business Behavior and Public Policy

Market power The ability of one or more firms to maintain a price above the competitive level

Teaching Tip The welfare costs of a monopoly are discussed in detail in Chapter 22.

You'll recall that a monopolist supplies a product with no close substitutes and so can charge a higher price than would prevail if the market were more competitive. When a few firms account for most of the sales in a market, those firms are sometimes able to coordinate their actions, either explicitly or implicitly, to approximate the behavior of a monopolist. This ability of one or more firms to maintain a price above the competitive level is termed **market power**. The presumption is that a monopoly or firms acting together as a monopoly will restrict output and charge a higher price than competitive firms. With output restrictions, the marginal benefit of the final unit produced exceeds its marginal cost, so social welfare could be increased by expanding output. By failing to expand output to the point where marginal benefit and marginal cost are equal, monopoly misallocates resources. Other distortions have also been associated with monopolies. Because monopolies are insulated from competition, many critics argue that they are not as innovative as aggressive competitors would be. Moreover, because of their size and economic importance, monopolies have been said to exert a disproportionate influence on the political system, influence used to protect and even strengthen their monopoly power.

Industrial organization A branch of economics that examines the relation between the structure of a market and the conduct and performance of firms in that market

Market Structure, Conduct, and Performance

Economists have developed a branch of economic analysis called **industrial organization** to trace the relationship between the structure of a market and the performance of firms in that market. The *structure* of a particular market, such as the market for steel or personal computers, can be measured by observable characteristics such as the number and size of firms, the extent of product differentiation, and the effectiveness of barriers to entry. Market structure affects the *conduct* of firms in the market—that is, market structure affects how firms behave in such areas as price competition, research and development activity, advertising strategy, and investment policy. And the conduct of firms, in turn, affects their *performance* in the market, as measured by the efficiency of production, the extent of innovative activity in the industry, and the level of profit. Therefore *market structure and market conduct shape market performance.*

Example In 1992, Procter & Gamble started reviewing its less popular sizes and flavors with the intention of eliminating 15 to 25 percent of some brands' versions—a change in product differentiation (a measure of structure). At the same time, P&G announced a movement toward fewer coupons and more everyday low prices (a change in conduct). P&G was hoping in part to protect its market share (a measure of performance) in certain markets.

When used to analyze public policies, industrial organization focuses on how to bring about the market structure and market conduct that will lead to the most desirable market performance. More specifically, it focuses on *how public policy can enhance social welfare by harnessing the benefits of economies of scale where production by only one or a few firms seems most efficient and by promoting competition where competition is appropriate.*

Government Regulation of Business

There are two kinds of government policies designed to alter or control the market structure and market conduct of firms: economic regulation and

Economic regulation Government measures aimed at controlling prices, output, market entry and exit, and product quality in situations in which, because of economies of scale, average production costs are lowest when the market is served by only one or a few firms

Antitrust activity Government activity aimed at preventing monopoly and fostering competition

antitrust activity. **Economic regulation** is concerned with controlling the price, the output, the entry of new firms, and the quality of service *in industries in which monopoly appears inevitable or even desirable.* The regulation of natural monopolies, such as electrical utilities, is an example of this type of regulation. Several other industries such as land and air transportation have also been regulated, for reasons that will be discussed later in this chapter. Economic regulation is carried out by various regulatory bodies at the federal, state, and local levels. **Antitrust activity** attempts to prohibit firm behavior aimed at monopolizing or cartelizing markets where competition is desirable. Antitrust activity is pursued in court by government attorneys and by individual firms that charge other firms with violations of antitrust laws. Both economic regulation and antitrust activity will be examined in this chapter. Federal spending on economic regulation and antitrust activity has increased at an annual rate of 7.4 percent since 1970, after adjusting for inflation.[1] The first type of economic regulation we consider is the regulation of natural monopolies.

REGULATING NATURAL MONOPOLIES

Example Under the cable regulatory act passed in 1992, the Federal Communications Commission sets rate guidelines, which are monitored by city or state governments. Cable franchises are typically acquired from municipal governments.

Because of economies of scale, natural monopolies have a downward-sloping long-run average cost curve over the entire range of market demand. This means that the lowest average total cost is achieved if one firm serves the entire market. As mentioned earlier, electricity is an example of a good provided by a natural monopoly. The cost per household is lowest when a single company "wires" the community. If four electric companies all strung their own wires through town, the average cost per household would be higher.

Unregulated Profit Maximization

Teaching Tip Antitrust violations may be tried as either criminal or civil cases. For example, the 1990s saw a spate of private lawsuits against doctors and hospitals by non-physician health care providers (such as nurse midwives).

Exhibit 1 shows the demand and cost conditions for a natural monopoly. A natural monopoly usually faces large capital costs, such as those associated with laying the tracks for a railroad, putting a satellite in orbit, building a nuclear power plant, installing a natural gas pipeline, or stringing the wires to transmit electricity, local phone service, or cable TV signals. Because of the heavy capital outlays, the average cost tends to fall as production increases, so the average cost curve slopes downward over a broad range of output. In this situation the average cost of production is minimized by having only one producer.

We know that a monopolist, if unregulated, will choose the price-quantity combination that maximizes profit. In Exhibit 1, the monopolist maximizes profit by producing where marginal cost equals marginal revenue, which occurs at output level Q. The monopolist will charge price p and earn

1. Computed based on budget data compiled in Melinda Warren and James Lis, "Regulatory Standstill: Analysis of the 1993 Federal Budget," Center for the Study of American Business, Occasional Paper 105.

EXHIBIT 1

Regulating the Natural Monopoly

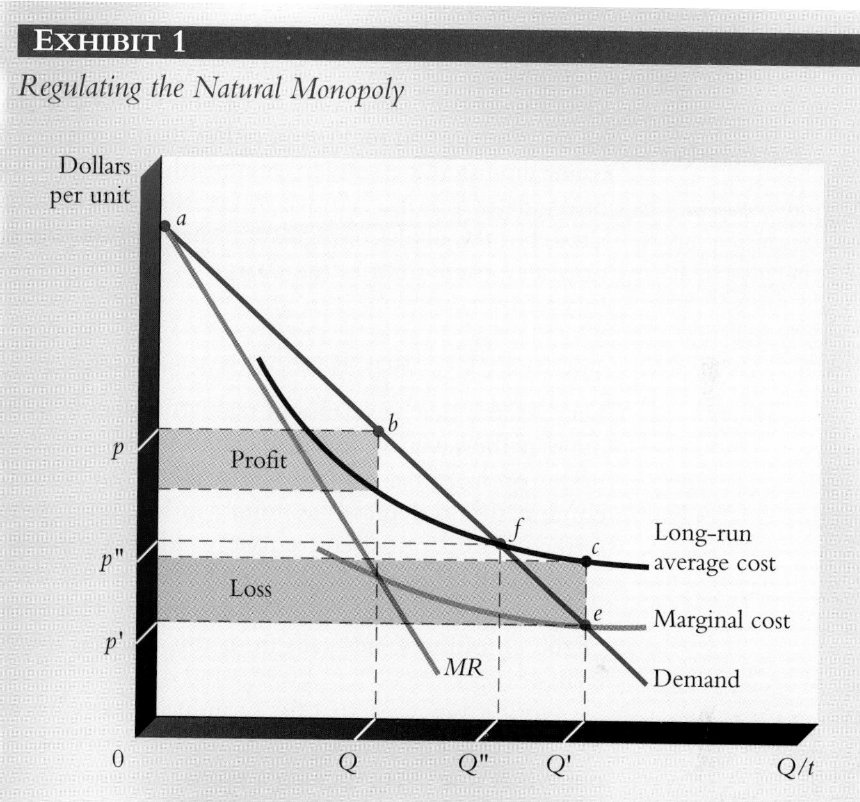

In a natural monopoly, the long-run average cost curve slopes downward at its point of intersection with the market demand curve. The unregulated firm produces output Q (where marginal cost equals marginal revenue) and charges price p. This situation is inefficient because price exceeds marginal cost. To obtain the efficient level of output, government could regulate the monopolist's price. At price p', the monopoly would produce output Q'—an efficient solution. However, at that price and quantity, the firm would suffer a loss and require a subsidy. As an alternative, the government could set a price of p''. The monopoly would produce output Q''—an inefficient level. Since p'' equals the average cost, the firm would earn a normal profit and no subsidy would be required.

Teaching Tip A high ratio of capital to other resources causes a high ratio of fixed to variable costs. Output expansion spreads the fixed costs over more and more units, so average cost falls.

Teaching Tip Recall from Chapter 22 that the monopolist's profits come at the expense of lower consumer surplus relative to the competitive outcome. The loss in surplus exceeds the gain in profits.

the economic profit indicated by the blue-shaded rectangle. The problem is that the monopolist's choice of price and output is inefficient in terms of social welfare: consumers pay a price that is higher than the marginal cost of producing the good. Because the price, which is consumers' marginal valuation of output, exceeds the marginal cost, there is an underallocation of resources to the production of this good. Economic welfare would improve if output were to expand because at present the marginal valuation of additional output exceeds the marginal cost of that output.

The government has three options for dealing with natural monopolies. First, the government can do nothing. If left alone, monopolists will maximize profits, as at price p in Exhibit 1. Second, the government can own and

Teaching Tip Economic regulation at the federal level in the United States began with the establishment of the Interstate Commerce Commission (ICC) in 1887. However, few regulatory commissions, including the ICC, now deal with economic regulation.

operate monopolies, as it does the Tennessee Valley Authority and many urban transit systems. Third, the government can regulate privately operated monopolies, as it does most electrical utilities and local phone services. Regulated industries have come to be known as *public utilities.* The focus here will be on government regulation rather than government ownership, though the issues discussed are similar whether the government operates as a monopoly or regulates a monopoly. Many facets of natural monopolies have been regulated, but the object of regulation that captures the most attention is the rates, or prices, these utilities can charge.

Setting Price Equal to Marginal Cost

Let's assume that government regulators decide to make the monopolist produce at the level of output dictated by allocative efficiency—that is, where price, or marginal valuation, equals marginal cost. That price and output combination is depicted as point *e* in Exhibit 1, where the demand curve intersects the marginal cost curve, yielding a price p' and quantity Q'. Consumers will clearly prefer this outcome because the price is lower than when the monopolist is free to maximize profit. The consumer surplus, a measure of the consumers' net gain from this market, increases from triangle *abp* to triangle *aep*′.

Point to Stress Recall that average cost falls as long as marginal cost is *below* average cost. Therefore, for the natural monopolist, the intersection of marginal cost with the demand curve must occur below the average cost curve, and the firm must be suffering a loss. In contrast to the unregulated situation, part of the gain in consumer surplus now comes at the expense of losses to the firm.

Notice, however, that the monopolist now has a problem. At output level Q', the regulated price, p', is below the firm's average total cost, identified as point *c*. Rather than earning a profit, the monopolist now suffers a loss identified by the red rectangle. *Forcing the natural monopolist to produce where marginal cost equals price results in an economic loss.* In the long run the monopolist would go out of business rather than suffer such losses.

Subsidizing the Natural Monopolist

How can regulators encourage the monopolist to stay in business and to produce where marginal cost equals price? One way is for the government to compensate the monopolist for the losses—to subsidize the firm so that it earns a normal profit. Bus and subway fares are typically set below the average cost of providing the service; the difference is made up through a subsidy. For example, the Washington, D.C. subway system receives over $200 million per year in subsidies from the federal government; Amtrak also receives substantial federal subsidies. One problem with the subsidy solution is that, to provide the subsidy, the government must raise taxes, borrow more, or forgo spending in some other area.

Setting Price Equal to Average Cost

Although some public utilities are subsidized, most are not. Instead, the regulators attempt to establish a price that will provide the monopolist with a "fair return." Recall that the average total cost curve includes a normal profit. Thus, setting *price equal to average total cost* provides a normal, or "fair," profit

Teaching Tip Many commissions use a pricing formula that sets price equal to average *operating* cost (exclusive of normal profit) plus a fair (or normal) rate of return on capital. Use of this formula makes defining rules of allowable costing and supervising costs important functions of regulatory agencies. They must also set *rate bases,* the value of capital on which the fair rate of return on capital is calculated. A third problem area is establishing permitted rates of return.

Teaching Tip The Supreme Court has advised regulators to allow a "fair return upon . . . the fair value of the property being used."

for the monopolist. In Exhibit 1, the demand curve and the average cost curve intersect at point *f,* yielding a price of p'' and a quantity of Q''. Incidentally, setting price equal to average total cost does enhance economic welfare relative to the unregulated situation. But the regulated monopolist would rather earn an economic profit. If given no choice, however, the monopolist will continue to operate with a normal profit, since that is what could be earned if the resources were redirected to their most profitable alternative use. But the marginal value that consumers attach to output level Q'' exceeds the marginal cost of that output level. Therefore, social welfare could be enhanced by expanding output until consumers' marginal value equals the marginal cost of production.

The Regulatory Dilemma

Setting price equal to marginal cost yields the *socially optimal* allocation of resources *because the marginal cost of producing the last unit sold equals the consumers' marginal value of that last unit.* Under this pricing rule, however, the monopolist will face recurring losses unless a subsidy is provided. These losses disappear when price is set equal to average cost, thereby ensuring the monopolist a normal profit. But this solution only partially corrects the monopolist's tendency to restrict output; output is still less than would be socially optimal. Thus, the dilemma facing regulators is whether to subsidize the firm and have the monopolist charge the socially optimal price or to allow for a normal profit by setting a price that is higher than is socially optimal. There is no right answer. Compared to the outcome without regulation, either approach reduces price, increases output, increases consumer surplus, and eliminates economic profit.

A problem not yet mentioned is discovering the relevant demand curve and cost curves. Although Exhibit 1 neatly lays out the options, regulators usually do not have such a clear picture of things. Demand and costs can only be estimated and the regulated firm may not always be completely forthcoming with the information. For example, a utility may overstate its costs so it can charge a higher price.

Alternative Theories of Economic Regulation

Why does government regulate certain markets? Why not allow market forces to allocate resources? There are two views of government regulation. The first view has been implicit in the discussion thus far—namely, that economic regulation is in the public interest. Economic regulation is designed to promote social welfare by controlling the price and output when the market is most efficiently served by one or just a few firms. A second view of economic regulation is that it is not in the public, or consumer, interest but rather in the special interest of producers. According to this view, *well-organized producer groups expect to profit from economic regulation and are able to persuade public officials to*

Teaching Tip Without precise knowledge of demand and cost information, regulatory commissions may rely on profit information. Price increases are permitted when profits fall below "fair" levels, and price reductions are required when profits rise above "fair" levels.

impose the desired restrictions, such as limiting entry into the industry or preventing competition among existing firms. Individual producers have more to gain or lose from regulation than do individual consumers; producers typically are also better organized than consumers and therefore better able to bring about regulations that are favorable to them.

Producers Have a Special Interest in Economic Regulation

To understand how producer interests could influence public regulation, consider the last time you had your hair cut. Whoever cut your hair probably cuts hair for a living. Most states regulate the training and licensing of hair professionals. If any new regulations affecting the profession are proposed, such as entry restrictions or training requirements, who has more interest in the outcome of that legislation, you or the person who cuts hair for a living? *Producers have a strong interest in matters that affect their specialized source of income, so they play a disproportionately large role in trying to influence such legislation.* If there are public hearings on haircut regulations, the industry will provide expert witnesses while consumers ignore the proceedings.

Point to Stress The larger the portion of consumers' incomes that is spent on an item, the greater the interest they take in regulatory hearings. Thus, hearings for utility rate increases receive more media coverage than haircut regulations.

As a consumer, you do not specialize in getting haircuts. You purchase haircuts, socks, soft drinks, notebooks, and thousands of other goods and services. You have no *special interest* in legislation affecting hair cutting. Some critics argue that because of this asymmetry in the interests of producers and consumers, business regulations often favor producer interests rather than consumer interests. Well-organized producer groups, as squeaky wheels in the legislative system, receive the most grease in the form of favorable regulations.

Legislation favoring producer groups is usually introduced under the guise of the advancement of consumer interests. Producer groups may argue that unbridled competition in their industry would lead to results that were undesirable for consumers. For example, the alleged problem of "cutthroat" competition among taxi drivers has led to regulations fixing rates and limiting the number of taxis in most large metropolitan areas. Or, regulation may appear under the guise of quality control, as in the case of state control of professional groups such as barbers, doctors, and lawyers, in which case regulations are viewed as necessary to keep unlicensed "quacks" out of the professions.

Example A federal probe of the generic drug industry that began in the late 1980s uncovered corruption in the Food and Drug Administration and fraud among drug companies. The FDA had to reorganize the generic drug division, hire more reviewers, issue new ethics policies, and establish new procedures for reviewing drug applications.

The special interest theory may be valid even when the initial intent of the legislation is in the consumer interest. Over time, the regulatory machinery may begin to act more in accord with the special interests of producers, because producers' political power and strong stake in the regulatory outcome lead them, in effect, to "capture" the regulating agency and prevail upon it to serve producers. This capture theory of regulation was best explained by George Stigler, a Nobel Prize winner formerly at the University of Chicago, who argued that "as a general rule, regulation is acquired by the industry and is designed and operated for its benefit."[2]

2. George Stigler, "The Theory of Economic Regulation," *The Bell Journal of Economics and Management Science* (Spring 1971): 3.

Example The Miller-Tydings Act of 1937 allowed manufacturers to establish and enforce minimum prices for their products. The legislation was designed to protect small retailers from price competition by chain stores and discount firms.

A more complex variant of the capture theory emphasizes the idea that industry members may not all be of one mind regarding the most favorable kind of regulation. For example, small retail stores might support measures that would be opposed by large retail stores; major trucking companies might choose different regulations than independent truckers would. Competing interest groups jockey with one another for the most favorable regulations. Thus, it is not simply a question of consumer interests versus producer interests but rather of one producer's interest versus another producer's interest.[3]

Perhaps it would be useful at this point to discuss in some detail the direction that economic regulation and, more recently, deregulation have taken in particular industries. We will consider two extensive case studies of regulation and deregulation. The first examines the role of the Interstate Commerce Commission as a regulator of the railroads and trucking.

CASE STUDY

Rail and Truck Regulation and Deregulation

Point to Stress The ICC became the protector of the railroads, as predicted by Stigler's capture theory.

The *Interstate Commerce Commission* (ICC), established in 1887 to regulate the railroads, was the first federal regulatory agency in this country. The major railroads supported formation of the ICC as a way to stabilize rates and reduce "cutthroat" competition by allocating business among the railroads. The ICC was also supposed to ensure that even small towns would receive railroad service. Thus, at the outset, railroad regulations had several objectives. In the 1930s the railroads began to face vigorous competition from the emerging trucking industry. The railroads wanted to avoid competition with trucks, and in 1935 Congress authorized the ICC to regulate trucking. The intent of the regulation was to equalize the prices of the two kinds of transportation, so that the two would not compete directly on the basis of price.

Regulating Entry and Rates. The ICC was able to control the structure of the so-called ground transportation industry by regulating new entry, price competition, and shipping conditions. To control entry, the ICC decreed that no carrier could operate without a license, and it would not issue a new license unless the applicant could show that such entry was "necessary for the public convenience." Existing shippers had a strong interest in presenting evidence to the contrary, so few new licenses were granted. Recall that *the ability to exclude new entrants from a market is a prerequisite for, though not a guarantee of, long-run economic profit*. The ICC had control over shipping rates, but much of this power was relegated to rate-setting committees drawn from the rail and trucking industries, an arrangement that allowed industry members to fix prices legally. Any competitor that wished to charge a lower price had to receive ICC permission. Because such rulings required hearings and often took up to a year to settle, the system discouraged price competition.

3. But just as producer groups may not represent a single interest, consumer groups may not either. For example, major users of electricity prefer rates that decline as usage increases, whereas smaller users do not because they fear that their rates might be higher on average with a declining rate structure. Residents of small rural communities view train service differently from residents in major metropolitan areas.

Regulating Trucking Services. The ICC also regulated the conditions of trucking services, including the kinds of products that could be hauled, the routes that could be taken, and even the number of cities that could be served along the way. The idea was to limit the versatility of trucks by treating them as if they ran on tracks, thereby reducing any advantage trucks had over the railroads. Truck routes operated on the "gateway" system, similar to railroad junction points. For example, a trucking firm with a license to ship between points A and B and between points B and C could haul from A to C only if it passed through point B first. Other rules allowed trucks to haul from A to B but not from B to A. So a truck could haul a load from St. Louis to Chicago but could not carry a return load. Such restrictions often required trucks to go hundreds of miles out of their way or to travel empty part of the time. Of course, all this added to trucking costs. Despite the higher cost of shipping created by regulation, *the ability of truckers to fix their prices and restrict entry generally ensured their profitability, because transportation services were much in demand and there were no close substitutes except for railroads*. In fact, "shipping rights," or the authority to haul particular goods between cities, became valuable and were bought and sold.

Teaching Tip The ICC could have captured some or all of these rents by auctioning off available rights to the highest bidders.

Resulting Inefficiencies. Scholars who examined the issue concluded that regulation kept trucking rates higher than the competitive level. As we have seen, the higher rates resulted in part from the production inefficiency caused by the regulations. Regulation also cultivated higher wages in the industry, particularly for the members of the truckers' union, the International Brotherhood of Teamsters. Because regulation strictly limited the entry of new firms and prohibited price competition between particular locations, trucking firms could comply with union demands for higher wages without fear of losing business to rivals charging lower prices. Unionized truck drivers thereby captured some of the producer surplus that resulted from regulation.

Deregulation. During the 1970s support grew for deregulation in a variety of industries. The Motor Carriers Act of 1980 began the deregulation of trucking. Not only was new entry allowed, but the restrictions on routes, commodities, and the like were reduced. The elimination of "gateways," one-way shipping, and other vestiges of a system aimed at treating trucks as if they were trains reduced duplication and waste. During the first three years after deregulation, an estimated ten thousand small new trucking firms entered the industry. During the same interval, trucking rates dropped substantially in many categories. For example, the average rate per mile for a full truckload of machinery dropped from $1.55 to $1.11, a 28-percent decline.

Point to Stress Recall the discussion in Chapter 26 of deregulation as one source of the decline in union power.

Winners and Losers. Although consumers benefited from falling prices, deregulation also created some losers. More than three hundred trucking firms, some of them very large, went bankrupt, and nearly one-third of the nation's three hundred thousand unionized truck drivers lost unionized jobs. In the wake of deregulation, Teamsters union members were often forced to accept labor contracts that called for wage cuts. Another predictable effect of deregulation was a decline in the value of shipping rights. When shipping certificates were closely regulated, they had an estimated aggregate value of $750 million. When entry restrictions were eliminated, however, their value disappeared almost overnight.

Despite the clear efficiency gains from deregulation, the concentrated allocation of the losses to well-identified groups meant deregulation measures would be resisted. The losers (owners of shipping rights, unionized truck drivers) are concentrated in groups and know they are losers; the winners (purchasers of trucking services, consumers) are widely dispersed and often do not even know that they are winners. As a result, the ICC chairman, supported by the Teamsters union, was slow to push deregulation. In fact, there was so much internal strife on the ICC that the commission met infrequently during the 1980s. In the early 1990s, the Teamsters union was the biggest contributor to Congressional campaigns. Despite foot-dragging by the ICC bureaucracy, the efficiency gains resulting from deregulation have been impressive.

The Railroads and Cross-Subsidization. Deregulation may have promoted thriving competition in trucking, but the railroads faced bigger problems. Despite the setting of minimum rates, the restriction of competition along rail routes, subsidies, and other measures designed to prop up this ailing industry, some railroads had become too inefficient to survive in a more competitive environment. One problem that railroads had was that regulations required them to provide service to remote and rural locations that might not otherwise receive service based on market demand. The railroads were not allowed to drop unprofitable routes or services, so revenue from profitable routes was used to subsidize operations on unprofitable routes, a policy called **cross-subsidization**. This cross-subsidy from profitable to unprofitable routes contributed to the bankruptcy of some lines.

Example Urban transit systems face the same problem of providing service to locations where demand is insufficient to cover variable costs.

Cross-subsidization A firm's use of revenues from profitable activities to subsidize unprofitable activities

After several railroads in the Northeast went bankrupt, deregulation was introduced in 1980 to promote efficiency and stability in the industry. Railroads were allowed to abandon unprofitable routes, and as a result route mileage fell by 29 percent. The number of major railroads dropped from 37 to 14, employment declined by 52 percent, and labor productivity nearly doubled. For example, Conrail was formed in 1976 from the bankrupt Penn Central Railroad and other ailing Northeast railroads. Conrail went from one hundred thousand employees in 1976 to only twenty-five thousand in 1992. Because of a greater ability to eliminate unprofitable routes and more aggressive efforts to reduce payroll costs, railroads have become more profitable. And despite the drop in the number of railroad companies, competition among remaining firms has forced down shipping rates in real terms.

Sources: A. F. Friedlaender, E. R. Berndt, and G. McCullough, "Governance Structure, Managerial Characteristics, and Firm Performance in the Deregulated Rail Industry," *Brookings Papers on Economic Activity: Microeconomics,* 1992: 95–186; and Daniel Machalaba, "After Sharp Cost Cuts, Conrail Is Resembling a Growth Company," *Wall Street Journal,* 20 November 1992.

The next case study examines regulation and deregulation as they shaped the airline industry.

CASE STUDY

Airline Regulation and Deregulation

The interstate airline business was closely regulated by the *Civil Aeronautics Board* (CAB), established in 1938. Any potential entrant interested in serving an interstate route had to persuade the CAB that the route needed another airline, a task that proved impossible. During the forty years prior to deregulation, more than 150 applications for long-distance routes were submitted by potential entrants, *but not a single new interstate airline was allowed.* The CAB also forced strict compliance with regulated prices. A request to lower prices on any route would result in a rate hearing, during which the request was scrutinized by both the CAB and competitors. In effect, the CAB had created a cartel among the ten existing airlines.

Although the CAB prohibited price competition in the industry, *nonprice competition was abundant.* Airlines competed on the basis of the frequency of flights, the quality of meals, the width of the seats, even the friendliness of the staff. Such competition, particularly in the area of the frequency of flights, increased operating costs. Frequent flights meant more empty seats; before deregulation, flights on average were nearly half empty. In addition, firms in the industry spent more on promotion, which also raised the average cost of providing airline service. Costs rose until the firms in the industry earned only a normal rate of return. Thus, *air fares set above competitive levels plus entry restrictions are no guarantee of economic profit as long as there are no restrictions on nonprice competition or on the number of flights each airline can offer.* The CAB did not regulate airlines that flew *intrastate* airlines. The record shows that the fares on intrastate airlines were about 50 percent below the fares on identical routes flown by regulated airlines. So regulated airlines were quite inefficient.

Point to Stress Recall that a cartel controls output as well as price in order to earn monopoly profits.

Airline Deregulation. In 1978, despite opposition from the major airlines and their labor unions, Congress passed the Airline Deregulation Act, which reduced restrictions on price competition and on new entry. The biggest change brought on by deregulation was in the number of new entrants: between 1978 and 1983, fourteen new airlines entered the industry. During the first year of deregulation, the average fare fell by 20 percent. By the end of the 1980s, air fares were lower than they had been at the beginning of the decade. The fall in fares predictably led to a near-doubling of passenger miles flown. One study found that during the first decade of deregulation air travelers had saved $100 billion from lower fares. In early 1992 a price war broke out among the major airlines, driving fares down still more. Some major airlines such as Braniff and Eastern went bankrupt.

The insulation from price competition provided by regulation had allowed firms to pay higher wages than they would have in a more competitive industry. The Air Line Pilots Association, the union that represented pilots for all the major airlines prior to deregulation, had been able to negotiate extremely attractive wages for its members over the years. In the

Example TWA's employees all accepted a 15-percent pay cut in 1992 in an attempt to keep the bankrupt airline flying. After layoffs of three thousand workers in July 1992, Delta announced in late 1992 a 5-percent salary cut for nonunion employees and a 20-percent pay cut for its directors.

early 1980s, a senior pilot, who typically worked less than two weeks a month, earned as much as $150,000 per year. Just how attractive a pilot's position was became apparent after deregulation. America West Airlines, a nonunion employer that sprouted from deregulation, paid its pilots only $32,000 a year and required them to work forty hours a week, performing dispatch and marketing tasks when they were not flying. Yet America West received some *four thousand* applications for its twenty-nine pilot vacancies.

Some critics of deregulation were concerned that the government would lose the control it had, under regulation, over the quality and safety of airline service. Despite the demise of the CAB, however, the Federal Aviation Administration (FAA) still regulates the safety and quality of air service. Research indicates that since deregulation neither accident rates nor fatality rates have increased. Another concern was that smaller communities would no longer be served by a deregulated industry. This has not been a problem; commuter airlines have replaced major airlines in servicing smaller communities.

Airport Capacity Has Restricted Competition. Yet competitive trends in the airline industry in recent years raise some troubling questions. Though airline traffic nearly doubled during the 1980s, no new airports were opened and the air traffic control system did not expand. Airports and air traffic control are provided by government. Thus, *the government did not follow up deregulation with an expansion of airport capacity.* Consequently, departure gates and landing rights became the scarce resources in the industry. Those airlines unable to secure such facilities at major airports went out of business. Some argue that the major airlines have not pushed for an expansion of airport facilities because this additional capacity could encourage new entry and greater competition. Before deregulation the five largest airlines controlled 63 percent of the passenger business. Deregulation initially promoted a wave of new entry by such upstarts as People Express and New York Air. By the early 1990s, however, most of the new entrants had disappeared or had been absorbed by larger airlines. *New entrants could not acquire the necessary departure gates and landing rights at key airports.* The market share of the five largest airlines had climbed from 63 percent before deregulation to 70 percent by the early 1990s, and most key airports came to be dominated by a single airline, such as American Airlines at Dallas/Fort Worth and USAir at Pittsburgh.

Example European airlines eager to enter the large U.S. market gain landing rights and gates by purchasing portions of U.S. airlines. For example, KLM Royal Dutch owns 20 percent of Northwest; both Lufthansa and Air Canada were bidding for Continental in 1992.

Sources: Nancy Rose, "Fear of Flying? Economic Analyses of Airline Safety," *Journal of Economic Perspectives,* Vol. 6 (Spring 1992): 75–94; and Victor F. Zohana, "End of Glamorous Life Looms for U.S. Pilots As Competition Grows," *Wall Street Journal,* 2 November 1983.

The course of regulation and deregulation raises some interesting questions about the true objective of regulation. Recall the competing views of regulation: one view holds that regulation is in the public, or consumer, interest; the second view holds that regulation is in the special, or producer, interest. In the ground transportation and airline industries, regulation appeared more in accord with producer interests, and producer groups fought deregulation.

This concludes our discussion of economic regulation, which tries to reduce the harmful consequences of monopolistic behavior in those markets where the output can be most efficiently produced by one or a few firms. We now turn to antitrust activity, which tries to promote competition in those markets where competition seems desirable.

ANTITRUST LAWS

Although competition typically ensures the most efficient use of the nation's resources, an individual firm would prefer to operate in a business climate that is more akin to monopoly. If left alone, some competing firms might try to create a monopolistic environment by driving competitors out of business, merging with competitors, or colluding with competitors. In the United States, *antitrust policy* is an attempt to curb these anticompetitive tendencies. Antitrust policy works in two ways. First, it is aimed at promoting the sort of market structure that will lead to greater competition. Second, it is aimed at controlling market conduct so as to reduce or eliminate anticompetitive behavior. Thus, *antitrust laws represent an attempt to shape market structure and control market conduct in ways that will promote socially desirable market performance.*

Point to Stress Although antitrust policy affects market structure and conduct directly, its impact on market performance tends to be indirect. Economic regulation, in contrast, can have direct influences on performance, especially efficiency and profits.

Origins of Antitrust Policy

A variety of economic events that occurred in the last half of the nineteenth century created a political climate supportive of antitrust legislation. Perhaps the two most important factors were (1) technological breakthroughs that led to more extensive use of capital and a larger optimal plant size in many manufacturing industries, and (2) the rapid growth of the railroads, which lowered the cost of transporting manufactured goods. *Economies of scale in production and cheaper transportation extended the geographical boundaries of markets.* So firms grew larger and reached wider markets.

Declines in the national economy in 1873 and 1883, however, caused a panic among these large manufacturers, who were now committed to the heavy fixed costs associated with large-scale production. Their defensive reaction was to lower prices in an attempt to stimulate sales. Price wars erupted, creating economic chaos. Firms desperately sought ways to stabilize their markets. One solution was for competing firms to form a **trust**, either by merging to form a single enterprise or by simply agreeing on a uniform pricing policy. Early trusts were formed in the sugar, tobacco, and oil industries. Although the activity of these early trusts is still a matter of debate today, they allegedly pursued anticompetitive practices to develop and maintain a dominant market position.

Trust A merger of or collusive agreement among competing firms

These practices provoked widespread criticism and earned promoters of trusts the derisive title of "robber barons." Public sentiment lay on the side of the smaller competitors. Farmers, especially, resented the higher prices of manufactured goods, which resulted from the trusts' activity, particularly since the prices farmers were receiving for their own products were declining through the latter part of the nineteenth century. Public dissatisfaction with trusts led eighteen states in the 1880s to enact *antitrust* laws, which prohibited the formation of trusts. State antitrust laws, however, were largely ineffective because the trusts could move across state lines to avoid them.

SHERMAN ANTITRUST ACT OF 1890. In 1888 the major political parties put antitrust planks in their platforms. This consensus culminated in the passage of the *Sherman Antitrust Act* of 1890, the first national legislation against monopoly in the world. The law contains two main sections:

Teaching Tip The Sherman Act left it unclear whether only market conduct leading to a monopoly is illegal or whether the market structure of monopoly itself is also illegal.

> Section 1: Every contract, combination in the form of trust or otherwise, or conspiracy in restraint of trade or commerce among the several states or with foreign nations is hereby declared illegal.
> Section 2: Every person who shall monopolize, or attempt to monopolize, or combine or conspire with any other person or persons to monopolize any part of the trade or commerce among the several states, or with foreign nations, shall be guilty of a misdemeanor.

Point to Stress The Sherman Act does not specify what constitutes "restraint of trade" or "monopolize." The Clayton Act was an attempt to be more specific and to allow the government to stop a potential monopoly before it developed. The Clayton Act exempts labor unions from monopolization charges.

Current penalties for violations include fines of up to $1 million plus possible jail terms. During the first ten years after its passage, enforcement of the law was hampered by a lack of funds and the absence of a forceful attorney general. Not until President Theodore Roosevelt took office in 1901 was a special Antitrust Division established in the Department of Justice to prosecute offenders. The laws on the books were stiffened in 1914 by additional legislation.

THE CLAYTON ACT OF 1914. Some ambiguous language in the Sherman Act let much anticompetitive activity slip by. Therefore the *Clayton Act* of 1914 was passed to outlaw certain practices not prohibited by the Sherman Act. Section 2 of the Clayton Act prohibits *price discrimination* when this practice tends to create a monopoly. You'll recall that price discrimination is charging different customers different prices for the same good or charging the same customer different prices for different quantities of the good. Price discrimination is permitted when the firm can show that it does not reduce competition or when differences in selling costs justify the different prices. For example, your local convenience store can legally charge more per can for one Pepsi than for a six-pack.

Tying contract An arrangement in which a seller of one good requires buyers to purchase other goods as well

Exclusive dealing The situation that occurs when a producer prohibits customers from purchasing from other sellers

Section 3 of the Clayton Act prohibits tying contracts and exclusive dealing if they substantially lessen competition. **Tying contracts** require the buyer of one good to purchase another good as well. For example, a seller of a patented machine might require customers to purchase unpatented supplies as part of the deal. **Exclusive dealing** occurs when a producer will sell a product only if the buyer agrees not to purchase from other manufacturers.

Interlocking directorate An arrangement whereby one individual serves on the boards of directors of competing firms

For example, a computer chip maker might sell chips to a computer maker only if the computer maker agrees not to purchase chips elsewhere. The law also prohibits **interlocking directorates**, whereby the same individual serves on the boards of directors of competing firms. Finally, *mergers* through the acquisition of the stock of a competing firm are outlawed in cases in which the merger would substantially lessen competition. More on that later.

Teaching Tip Although FTC cases are initially tried before the commission, any appeals go to the federal court system.

Federal Trade Commission Act of 1914. To facilitate antitrust enforcement, the *Federal Trade Commission* (FTC) was established in 1914 to investigate and prosecute what the Federal Trade Commission Act termed "unfair methods of competition." The commission consists of five full-time commissioners appointed by the president for seven-year terms and assisted by a professional staff. A 1919 Supreme Court decision ruled that only the courts could interpret the laws to determine what practices were "unfair," thus limiting the role of the FTC. In 1938 the *Wheeler-Lea Act* gave the FTC the responsibility for prohibiting "deceptive acts or practices in commerce," so the FTC took on the role of policing untrue and deceptive advertising. For example, in recent years the FTC has cracked down on deceptive advertising practices by promoters of liquid diet programs, travel clubs, and telemarketing sales schemes.

The Sherman, Clayton, and FTC acts provided the antitrust framework, a framework that has been clarified and embellished by subsequent amendments. Specifically, the 1936 *Robinson-Patman Act* prohibits firms from selling "at unreasonably low prices" when the intent is to reduce competition. This act was aimed at keeping small merchants in business by preventing manufacturers from giving a price break to large department stores.

Teaching Tip The major impetus for passage of the Celler-Kefauver Act was the Justice Department's inability to stop a horizontal merger between U.S. Steel and Continental Steel. Between 1914 and 1950, the government dissolved only fifteen mergers.

A loophole in the Clayton Act was closed in 1950 with the passage of the *Celler-Kefauver Anti-Merger Act,* which prevents one firm from buying the *assets* of another firm if the effect is to reduce competition. This law prohibits both horizontal mergers and vertical mergers when these mergers would tend to reduce competition in a particular industry. For example, a merger of Coke and Pepsi would most likely be prohibited.

Antitrust Law Enforcement

Consent decree A legal agreement through which the accused party, without admitting guilt, agrees to refrain in the future from certain illegal activity if the government drops the charges

Any law's effectiveness depends on the vigor and vigilance of enforcement. The pattern of antitrust enforcement goes something like this. Either the Antitrust Division of the Justice Department or the Federal Trade Commission charges a firm or group of firms with breaking the law. These government agencies are often acting on a complaint by a customer or a competitor. At that point, those charged with the wrongdoing may be able, without admitting guilt, to sign a **consent decree** whereby they agree not to continue doing whatever they had been charged with. If the charges are contested, evidence from both sides is presented in a court trial, and a decision is rendered by a judge. Certain decisions may be appealed all the way to the Supreme Court, and in such cases the high court may render new interpretations of existing law.

Example A class-action lawsuit against the six largest airlines was settled for $458 million in 1992. More than one thousand private cases are initiated per year; the government initiates only fifty or so.

Parties that can show injury by firms that have violated antitrust laws can sue the offending company and recover three times the amount of the damages sustained. These so-called *treble damage* suits increased after World War II; more than one thousand cases are initiated each year. Courts have been relatively generous to those claiming to have been wronged. The potential liability for treble damages makes firms more wary of violating antitrust laws.

Since these cases often start with the Justice Department, antitrust law enforcement is affected by the attorney general's inclination to file charges. The vigor of this enforcement varies with the political party in power and with the judicial climate. Antitrust laws were not enforced aggressively until after World War II. Most other industrial countries take a more tolerant view of market power. United States antitrust laws seem to have prevented U.S. firms from adopting many restrictive and predatory practices tolerated elsewhere.

Per Se Illegality and the Rule of Reason

Per se illegality A category of illegality in antitrust law, applied to business practices that are deemed illegal regardless of their economic rationale or their consequences

Rule of reason A principle used by a court to examine the reasons for certain business practices and their effects on competition before ruling on their legality

Predatory pricing Pricing tactics employed by a dominant firm to drive competitors out of business, such as temporarily selling below cost and dropping the price only in certain markets

The courts have interpreted the antitrust laws in essentially two ways. One set of practices has been declared illegal **per se**—that is, without regard to economic rationale or consequences. For example, under the Sherman Act, all formal agreements among competing firms to fix prices, restrict output, or otherwise restrain the forces of competition are viewed as illegal *per se.* Under a *per se* rule, in order for the defendant to be found guilty, the government need only show that the offending practice took place; thus, the government need only examine the firm's conduct.

Another set of practices falls under the **rule of reason**. Here the courts engage in a broader inquiry into the facts surrounding the particular offense—namely, the reasons why the offending practices were adopted and the effect of these practices on competition. The rule of reason was first set forth in 1911, when the Supreme Court held that the Standard Oil Company had illegally monopolized the petroleum refining industry. Standard Oil allegedly had come to dominate 90 percent of the market by acquiring more than 120 former rivals and by implementing **predatory pricing** tactics to drive remaining rivals out of business, such as temporarily selling below cost or dropping the price only in certain markets. In finding Standard Oil guilty, the Court focused on both its market *conduct* and the market *structure* that resulted from Standard Oil's activity, and the Court found that Standard Oil had behaved *unreasonably.*

Point to Stress Under the rule of reason, conduct is emphasized over structure.

But, using the rule of reason, the Court in 1920 found U.S. Steel not guilty of monopolization. In that case the Court ruled that not every contract or combination in restraint of trade was illegal—only those that "unreasonably" restrain trade violate antitrust laws. The Court said that mere size was not an offense. Although U.S. Steel clearly possessed market power, the company was not in violation of antitrust laws because it had not unreasonably used that power. The Court changed that view twenty-five years later in reviewing the charges against the Aluminum Company of America (Alcoa). In a 1945 decision, the Supreme Court held that although a firm's conduct might be reasonable and legal, the mere possession of market power—Alcoa controlled 90 percent of the aluminum ingot market—violated the antitrust laws. Here the Court was using market *structure* rather than market *conduct* as the test of legality.

Example In 1992, MIT was found guilty of price fixing in the form of sharing financial aid information with Ivy League colleges. The schools involved used the information to put together similar aid offers to students. The other schools settled out of court.

Problems with Enforcement of Antitrust Legislation

There is growing doubt about the economic value of some of the lengthy antitrust cases pursued in the past. One case against Exxon was in the courts seventeen years before the company was cleared of charges in 1992.[4] Another case began in 1969 when IBM, with nearly 70 percent of domestic sales of electronic data processing equipment, was accused of monopolizing that market. IBM was also charged with introducing its 360 line of computers so as to eliminate competition. IBM responded that its large market share was based on its innovative products and on its economies of scale. The trial began in 1975, and the government took nearly three years to present its case. Litigation persisted for years. In the meantime many other computer manufacturers emerged both in this country and abroad to challenge IBM's dominance. In 1982 the Reagan administration dropped the case, noting that the threat of monopoly had diminished enough that the case was "without merit."

Point to Stress The government sometimes errs on the side of protecting *competitors* rather than protecting *competition*.

Too Much Emphasis on the Competitive Model. Joseph Schumpeter argued half a century ago that competition should be viewed as a dynamic process, one of "creative destruction." Firms are continually in flux—introducing new products, phasing out old products, trying to compete for the consumer's dollar in a variety of ways. In light of this, antitrust policy should not necessarily be aimed at increasing the number of firms in each industry. In some cases firms will grow large because they are more efficient than rivals at offering what consumers want. Accordingly, firm size should not be the primary concern. Moreover, the theory of contestable markets, discussed in the chapter on monopoly, argues that competition can occur even when there is only one or a few firms in the industry as long as entry and exit barriers are low. Finally, economists have shown through market experiments that most of the desirable properties of perfect competition can be achieved with a small number of firms.[5]

Example A major issue in any case is often the definition of the firm's market. For example, substitutes for aluminum were not considered in the Alcoa case. However, DuPont, with 75 percent of the cellophane market (Saran Wrap) in 1956, was ruled to be without monopoly power because the court also considered aluminum foil, wax paper, and so forth.

Growing Importance of International Markets. One yardstick for measuring the market power of a firm is its share of the market. With the growth of international trade, however, the local or even the national market share becomes less relevant. General Motors may dominate U.S. auto manufacturing, accounting for over half of sales in the United States by domestically owned firms in 1992. But when sales by Japanese and European producers are

4. As reported in Allanna Sullivan, "Exxon Is Cleared of Antitrust Charges in Alleged Plot to Fix Prices in the 1970s," *Wall Street Journal,* 11 May 1992.
5. Vernon Smith, "Markets as Economizers of Information: Experimental Examination of the 'Hayek Hypothesis'," *Economic Inquiry* 20 (1982).

Teaching Tip Vertical mergers are challenged if a buyer merges with a supplier and thus limits the access of other buyers to the supplier or if there is a transfer of significant market power. DuPont—an important supplier to General Motors—was forced in 1957 to sell its 23-percent share in GM.

included, GM's share of the U.S. auto market falls to about one-third. GM's share of world production has declined steadily since the mid-1950s. *Where markets are open to foreign competition, antitrust enforcement that focuses on domestic production share makes less economic sense.*

Mergers and Public Policy

Concentration ratio A measure of the market share of the largest firms in an industry

The Justice Department has been sensitive to some of its critics, and in 1982 and 1984 issued long-awaited guidelines on mergers. Perhaps the most significant feature of the guidelines is the redefinition of market share. In determining the possible detrimental effects a merger might have on competition, one important factor to consider is the effect of the merger on the level of concentration in that market. The measure of concentration employed until 1982 by the Justice Department was the four-firm **concentration ratio**, which is the sum of the percentage market shares of the top four firms in the market. Suppose that forty-four firms supply a market. Also suppose that the top four firms account for 23 percent, 18 percent, 13 percent, and 6 percent, respectively, of the total market sales, and the remaining forty firms account for 1 percent each. The four-firm concentration ratio is the sum of the shares of the top four firms in the market, which in this case is 60 percent. Though definitions are somewhat arbitrary, in markets where the four-firm concentration ratio is above 50 percent, that market may be oligopolistic.

Example In 1992, Nabisco planned to sell its cereal business to General Mills. The deal was called off because it would have pushed General Mills's market share over 30 percent and led to a "lengthy and prolonged review . . . by regulatory authorities. . . ."

One problem with the concentration ratio is that it says nothing about the distribution of market share among the four firms. For example, the four-firm concentration ratio is 60 percent if the top four firms each have 15 percent of the market share or if one firm has 57 percent of the market and the next three have 1 percent each. Yet clearly an industry in which one firm captures over half the market is less competitive than an industry with four firms of identical size.

Herfindahl index The sum of the squared percentage market shares of all firms in an industry; a measure of the level of concentration in that industry

To remedy this lack of precision, the Justice Department's new merger guidelines call for the use of the **Herfindahl index**, which is calculated by squaring the percentage market share of each firm in the market and then adding those squares. For example, if the industry consists of one hundred firms of equal size, the Herfindahl index is 100 [$100 \times (1)^2$]. If the industry is a pure monopoly, the index is 10,000 [$1 \times (100)^2$]. The index is smaller the more firms there are in the industry and the more equal in size the firms are.

The Herfindahl index provides more information than the four-firm concentration ratio because it gives greater weight to firms with a larger market share. The Herfindahl index for each of the three examples (where the four-firm concentration ratio is 60 percent) is calculated in Exhibit 2. Although each example has the same four-firm concentration ratio, each yields a different Herfindahl index. Note that the index for Industry III is nearly triple that for the two other industries.

The Justice Department's new guidelines also sort all mergers into two bins: horizontal mergers, which involve firms in the same market, and

EXHIBIT 2

Computation of the Herfindahl Index Based on Market Share in Three Hypothetical Industries

	Industry I		Industry II		Industry III	
Firm	**Market Share (percent)**	**Market Share Squared**	**Market Share (percent)**	**Market Share Squared**	**Market Share (percent)**	**Market Share Squared**
A	23	529	15	225	57	3,249
B	18	324	15	225	1	1
C	13	169	15	225	1	1
D	6	36	15	225	1	1
Remaining forty firms (at 1 percent each)	1 each	40	1 each	40	1 each	40
Four-firm concentration ratio	60		60		60	
Herfindahl index		1,098		940		3,292

nonhorizontal mergers, which include all others. Of most interest for antitrust purposes are horizontal mergers, such as a merger between competing oil companies. The Justice Department generally challenges any merger in an industry where two conditions are met: (1) the post-merger Herfindahl index would exceed 1,800 and (2) the merger would increase the index by more than 100 points. Mergers in an industry that would have a post-merger index of less than 1,000 are seldom challenged. Other factors, such as the ease of entry into the market, are considered for intermediate cases.

COMPETITIVE TRENDS IN THE U.S. ECONOMY

For years there has been concern about the sheer size of some firms because of the real or potential power these firms might exercise in both the economic and the political arenas. One way to measure the power of the largest corporations is to calculate the share of the nation's corporate assets controlled by the one hundred largest firms. What percentage of the nation's manufacturing assets do the top one hundred manufacturing companies own, and how has this share changed over time?

The largest one hundred firms control about half of all manufacturing assets in the United States, up from a 40 percent share after World War II. We

Example Procter & Gamble controls 45 percent of the disposable diaper market; Kimberly-Clark controls 30 percent. However, they compete vigorously with each other in terms of pricing and product innovation.

should recognize, however, that size alone is not synonymous with market power. A very big firm, such as a large oil company, may face stiff competition from other very big oil companies; on the other hand, the only movie theater in an isolated community may be able to raise its price with less concern about competition.

Market Competition over Time

More important than the size of the largest firms in the nation is the market structure in each industry. Various studies have examined the level of competition and change in industry structure over the years. All have used some variation of the four-firm concentration ratio or the Herfindahl index as a point of departure, sometimes supplementing this measure with data from the specific industry about barriers to entry and other evidence suggesting whether the largest firms can control prices. Among the most comprehensive of these studies is the research of William Shepherd, who relied on many sources to determine the competitiveness of each industry in the U.S. economy.[6]

Shepherd sorted industries into four groups: (1) pure monopoly, in which a single firm controlled the entire market and was able to block entry; (2) dominant firm, in which a single firm had over half the market share and had no close rival; (3) tight oligopoly, in which the top four firms supplied more than 60 percent of the market, with stable market shares and evidence of cooperation; and (4) effective competition, in which firms in the industry exhibited low concentration, low entry barriers, and little or no collusion.

Exhibit 3 presents Shepherd's breakdown of all U.S. industries into the four categories for the years 1939, 1958, and 1980. The table shows a modest

EXHIBIT 3

Trends of Competition in the U.S. Economy, 1939–1980

	Percentage Income Share of Each Category		
Competitive Group	**1939**	**1958**	**1980**
Pure monopoly	6.2	3.1	2.5
Dominant firm	5.0	5.0	2.8
Tight oligopoly	36.4	35.6	18.0
Effectively competitive industries	52.4	56.3	76.7
	100.0	100.0	100.0

Source: William G. Shepherd, "Causes of Increased Competition in the U.S. Economy, 1939–1980," *Review of Economics and Statistics* 64 (November 1982): 618, Table 2. The income share is the percentage of national income generated by industries in each competitive group.

6. William G. Shepherd, "Causes of Increased Competition in the U.S. Economy, 1939–1980," *Review of Economics and Statistics* 64 (November 1982).

trend toward increased competition between 1939 and 1958, with the percentage of those industries rated as "effectively competitive" growing from 52.4 percent to 56.3 percent of all industries. Between 1958 and 1980, however, there was a clear increase in competitiveness in the economy, with the percentage of effectively competitive industries jumping from 56.3 percent to 76.7 percent.

Exhibit 4 presents Shepherd's findings in greater detail, with the economy broken down into eight broad industrial sectors. The left column lists the sectors. To provide some idea of the relative importance of each sector, the second column lists the income generated by that sector in 1978. The remaining columns list the percentage of industries in each sector that were rated "effectively competitive." The table shows a modest but widespread increase in competition between 1939 and 1958, with increases in seven of the eight industrial sectors. Between 1958 and 1980, according to Shepherd, there were solid gains in the economy's competitiveness, with all sectors showing greater competition. He notes, however, that though competition

EXHIBIT 4

Competitive Trends in the U.S. Economy, 1939–1980, by Industry Sector

Sectors of Economy	**National Income Arising from Each Sector in 1978 (billions of dollars)**	**Percentage of Each Sector Rated as Effectively Competitive**		
		1939	**1958**	**1980**
Agriculture, forestry, and fishing	54.7	91.6	85.0	86.4
Mining	24.5	87.1	92.2	95.8
Construction	87.6	27.9	55.9	80.2
Manufacturing	459.5	51.5	55.9	69.0
Transportation and public utilities	162.3	8.7	26.1	39.1
Wholesale and retail	261.8	57.8	60.5	93.4
Finance, insurance, and real estate	210.7	61.5	63.8	94.1
Services	245.3	53.9	54.3	77.9
Totals	1,506.4	52.4	56.3	76.7

Source: William G. Shepherd, "Causes of Increased Competition," 618, Table 2.

blossomed, market power remained high in many manufacturing industries, such as drugs, as well as among utilities.

According to Shepherd, the growth in competition from 1958 to 1980 can be traced to three primary causes: *imports, deregulation, and antitrust activity.* Foreign imports between 1958 and 1980 resulted in increased competition in thirteen major industries, including autos, tires, and steel. According to Shepherd, the growth in imports accounted for one-sixth of the increase in competition. Imports were attractive to consumers because of their superior quality and lower price. Because they were competing with U.S. producers that often had been tightly knit domestic oligopolies, foreign competitors found these U.S. markets relatively easy to penetrate. Finding themselves at a cost and technological disadvantage, domestic producers initially responded by seeking trade barriers, such as quotas and tariffs, to reduce foreign competition.

Trucking, airlines, and telecommunications were among the industries deregulated between 1958 and 1980. We have already discussed some of the effects of this deregulation, particularly in reducing barriers to entry and in eliminating uniform pricing schedules. According to Shepherd's study, the deregulation movement accounted for one-fifth of the increase in competition.

Although it is difficult to attribute an increase in competition to specific antitrust activity, Shepherd concludes that about two-fifths of the increase in competition between 1958 and 1980 can be credited to the effects of antitrust activity. He argues that although imports and deregulation were also important, their benefits could be quickly reversed by a shift toward protectionism and a return to regulation. In contrast, the effects of antitrust legislation are more permanent, and a reversal would require a much greater reversal in both legislation and judicial opinion.

CONCLUSION

Teaching Tip The application of antitrust legislation to conglomerate mergers has had mixed results. The first substantial challenge (in 1963) disallowed the purchase of Clorox by Procter & Gamble on the grounds that P&G's huge resources could be used to harm Clorox's competitors. However, conglomerate mergers (such as U.S. Steel's purchase of Marathon Oil) have generally been allowed since 1973.

If we look at all large corporations, we see evidence that the share of corporate assets controlled by the largest firms has been increasing over time, but if we focus on particular industries, the overall degree of competition in the U.S. economy appears to be increasing. How can this paradox be resolved? Many mergers in the years since World War II have been conglomerate mergers, which join firms operating in unrelated markets. If two giant firms from different industries merge, the assets held by the top one hundred firms increase, yet there is no effect on the competitiveness of particular industries.

Shepherd's data go through 1980. What has been the trend in competition since then? On the antitrust front, the trial against American Telephone and Telegraph Company, which began in 1974, was settled in 1982 with AT&T divesting itself of twenty-two companies that provide most of the country's local phone service. As a result, long distance rates are now more competitive. More generally, however, antitrust policy during the decade was not forceful, particularly with regard to the big story during the 1980s: corporate takeovers. Even after adjusting for inflation, the dollar value of corporate acquisitions during the 1980s was more than double that during the post-World War II merger

Teaching Tip The trend in the early 1990s was toward divestiture as flagging profitability led firms to retreat to their core businesses.

wave. These corporate takeovers could benefit the economy to the extent that more efficient managers replace less efficient managers, but the merging of large firms in the same industry could have negative effects on competition.

Since 1980, growing world trade increased competition in the U.S. economy, but some U.S. industries such as auto makers continue to pressure the government for trade protection to reduce competition. Some deregulation has also run into snags. Airlines are now more concentrated than they were before deregulation. And the bankruptcy of many savings and loan institutions has been blamed in part on banking deregulation. The enthusiasm for deregulation thus has waned in the United States. In short, since 1980 international competition has increased, deregulation has continued, and antitrust activity has been relatively quiet; the competitive record since 1980 has been a mixed one.

SUMMARY

1. In this chapter we examined two forms of government regulation of business: (1) economic regulation, such as the regulation of natural monopolies and (2) antitrust activity, which promotes competition and prohibits efforts to monopolize or to cartelize an industry.

2. Natural monopolies are regulated by government so that output is greater and prices are lower than they would be if the monopolist were allowed to maximize profits. One problem with regulation is that the price that maximizes social welfare creates an economic loss, whereas the price that allows the firm to earn a normal profit does not maximize social welfare.

3. There are two views of economic regulation. The first is that economic regulation is in the public interest because it controls natural monopolies where monopoly is most efficient and promotes competition where competition is most efficient. A second view is that regulation is not in the public, or consumer, interest, but is more in the special interest of producers.

4. Both the ground transportation and the airline industry were regulated for much of this century. Regulation had the effect of restricting entry and fixing prices. Both industries underwent deregulation in the early 1980s, which stimulated new entry and reduced prices overall.

5. Antitrust laws are aimed at promoting competition and prohibiting efforts to cartelize or monopolize an industry. The Sherman, Clayton, and FTC acts provided the basic framework for antitrust enforcement, a framework that has been clarified and embellished by subsequent amendments.

6. Research indicates that competition in U.S. industries has been increasing since World War II. Three reasons for the growth in competition are foreign trade, deregulation, and antitrust activity.

QUESTIONS AND PROBLEMS

1. (Trucking Regulations) "The trucking industry has an unfair advantage over other transportation industries such as the railroads, since it uses the public highways, which were not built exclusively by the trucking companies. Therefore the trucking industry should be regulated." Comment on this assertion.

2. (Regulation) Why might some industries prefer to be regulated rather than face an unregulated environment?

3. (Utility Regulation) It has often been noted that utility stocks tend to go up more slowly and to fall more slowly than the stock market as a whole. Is the stability of utility stocks a result of the regulation of the industry? Why or why not?

4. (Antitrust) Why might a company plead guilty to charges of anticompetitive behavior even though it knew such charges were unjustified? Would this plea depend on how large the company was?

5. (Antitrust) "The existence of only three or four big auto manufacturers in the United States is prima facie evidence that the market structure is anticompetitive and that antitrust laws are being broken." Evaluate this assertion.

6. (Antitrust) Why might the Herfindahl index be an indication of the relative success of certain firms in an industry rather than a measure of the anticompetitive structure of the industry?

7. (Monopoly Regulation) Compare the impacts of the following policies on the profit level and economic inefficiency of a natural monopoly.
   a. Enacting an excise (sales) tax
   b. Enacting a franchise (lump-sum) tax
   c. Setting a price ceiling where marginal cost intersects the demand curve
   d. Setting a price ceiling where average cost intersects the demand curve
   e. Allowing price discrimination in the form of "peak load" pricing

8. (Natural Monopoly) For a natural monopoly, a price equal to marginal cost is economically efficient in the sense that it produces the greatest net benefits to consumers, even though at such a price, the costs of production are not being covered. Explain why this isn't a contradiction.

9. (Discriminating Monopoly) Using demand and cost curves, show why regulation that forces a perfectly discriminating monopolist to charge everyone the same price could lead to a decrease in economic efficiency.

10. (Patents and Deregulation) Discuss whether patents, by restricting access to information and product design, have the effect of decreasing competition.

11. (Antitrust) A relatively recent development in the theory of economic regulation is the idea of "contestable markets" in which industries with few firms may behave as if they were competitive because of the potential for outside entry. What problems does this create for regulators using, say, concentration ratio information as a basis for determining whether an antitrust action is warranted?

12. (Antitrust) When the Clayton Act is applied in price discrimination cases, the burden of proof in establishing differential selling costs as the basis for differential pricing falls on the firm. Some analysts have argued that placing the burden of proof on the firm in this way actually causes rather than limits price discrimination. Comment.

13. (Antitrust) One of the most vexing issues in antitrust cases is dealing with the possibility that harm to competition and harm to competitors are not necessarily the same thing. Why do you suppose that this distinction is of such importance?

14. (Mergers) Conglomerate mergers, i.e., mergers of firms in different industries, are sometimes subject to antitrust regulation. Can you think of reasons why such mergers might be attractive for firms producing different products? Why should they be subject to regulation?

15. (Regulation) Regulating quality in consumer products is generally the most controversial form of regulation in business. Using motor vehicle air bag regulations as an example, discuss some reasons for the controversial nature of such regulation.

16. (ICC) Regulating entry on the basis of whether there is a need for a firm, as has been done in granting licenses to carriers as well as granting charters to banks, makes it difficult for potential entrants to "make their case." Discuss.

17. (ICC) Have any consumers been hurt by the deregulation of the trucking and rail service industries? Explain.

18. (CAB) Do you think that price deregulation will continue to be effective in the face of increased concentration levels at many individual airports?

19. (CAB) Is there anything about the airline industry that suggests that the "contestable markets" idea is appropriate for analyzing airline competition?

CHAPTER 30

PUBLIC CHOICE

The effects of government are all around us. The clothes you put on this morning were manufactured according to government regulations about everything from the working conditions of textile employees to the label providing washing instructions. Your breakfast cereal was made from grain grown on subsidized farms; the milk and sugar you put on your cereal were also subject to government price supports. The condition of the vehicle in which you rode to campus was regulated by government, as were the driver's speed and sobriety. Your education has been subsidized in a variety of ways by government. Government has a pervasive influence on all aspects of your life and on the economy. Yes, government is big business. The federal government alone spends over $1,500,000,000,000.00 per year—over $1.5 *trillion*—including more than $1 million just on paper clips. In addition to federal spending, state and local governments raise and spend nearly $1 trillion on their own.

Teaching Tip
Shortcomings in the private market mean that the unrestricted workings of the market do not achieve efficiency in the allocation of society's resources or fail to address social goals other than efficiency (such as a more equal income distribution).

In Chapter 4 we introduced the roles government plays in the economy, and in the previous chapter we considered the government regulation of business. For the most part, we have assumed that government makes optimal decisions in response to the shortcomings of the private market—that is, when confronted with a failure in the private market, government adopts and implements the appropriate program to address the problem. But this is easier said than done. There are limits to the effectiveness of government activity, just as there are limits to the effectiveness of market activity. Sometimes a government "solution" may be worse than the market failure.

In this chapter we will trace the government decision-making process and explore problems that arise in this process. Beginning with the problem of majority rule in direct democracy, we proceed to complications that arise when public choices are delegated to elected representatives, who, in turn, delegate the implementation of these choices to government bureaus. Topics discussed in this chapter include

- The economy as a game
- Median voter model
- Cyclical majority
- Representative democracy
- Rational ignorance
- Special-interest legislation
- Rent seeking
- Underground economy
- Bureaucratic behavior

The Economy as a Game

One useful way of understanding the role of government is to think of the economy as a kind of game, which initially involves two major groups of players: consumers and producers. The players pursue their own self-interests: consumers attempt to maximize utility, and producers attempt to maximize profit. Economic coordination in a market economy hinges on players' ability to secure the rights and obligations of property as well as to enforce contracts. From time to time disagreements arise about property rights or the interpretations of contracts. For example, a consumer may not want to pay for a roofing job that seems of poor quality. Or an insurance company may not want to pay a fire claim because of the claimant's negligence in starting the fire.

Point to Stress Government rules ban or require certain private behaviors or establish the acceptable limits for behavior.

Players can either police themselves, as they do in card games, or hire an umpire or referee, as they do in most sports. A market economy often requires some third party (government) to resolve disputes, protect the rights to resources, and enforce contracts. Also, government may provide public goods and services, control activities that involve externalities in production or consumption, and redistribute income—topics addressed in this and subsequent chapters.

Fairness of the Game

Teaching Tip The discussion of a game's fairness may be easily applied to antitrust activity or income distribution.

Participants in a game often attach a value to the fairness of the game. Fairness can be viewed from two perspectives. First, are the rules of the game fair to all participants—that is, is the *process* fair? A game may not be fair because the cards are marked, one player can see another's hand, or a group of players conspires against one player. Fairness can also be viewed in terms of the results of the game. Is the *outcome* of the game fair? Suppose a few skilled or lucky players win all the chips. Some argue that if the rules are fair, then the outcome must by definition be fair, even if there are big winners and losers. Others argue that even fair rules will not result in a fair outcome if the players are not on equal footing at the outset. For example, what if certain players begin the game with fewer chips than the others? Or what if some players lack the skill to play well? Do these differences among players make the game less fair? If by fairness we mean that every player has an equal opportunity to win, differences in the initial endowment of chips or in the ability to play the game need to be taken into account. If players believe it is important that the *result* be fair, the rules can be changed to bring about what is viewed as a fairer outcome.

Kinds of Games

Positive-sum game A game in which total winnings exceed total losses

Zero-sum game A game in which total winnings just equal total losses

Negative-sum game A game in which total losses exceed total winnings

Example A monopolist gains profit at the expense of consumer surplus, relative to the perfectly competitive outcome, but the consumer still receives some surplus.

By comparing the total amount of winnings and losses, we can classify games into three categories. If the winnings exceed the losses, the game is a **positive-sum game**; if the winnings are just offset by the losses, the game is a **zero-sum game**; and if the losses exceed the winnings, the game is a **negative-sum game**. Poker is a zero-sum game because the total amount of the winnings just equals the total amount of the losses. Most gambling activities, such as horse racing and state lotteries, are negative-sum games because the "house" or the government takes a cut of the amount wagered.

Many people mistakenly think of market activity as a zero-sum game. Intuition suggests that the gains from one side of the market must come at the expense of the other side. But a key feature of market activity ensures that most exchanges will yield positive gains. Because market exchange is *voluntary*, participants expect to be at least as well off after engaging in market exchange as before. Product demanders expect consumer surplus, and resource suppliers typically expect producer surplus or profit. Thus, market exchange is usually a positive-sum game.

Rules and Behavior

Teaching Tip The impact of pollution controls is analyzed in detail in Chapter 32. Income redistribution and the incentive effects of welfare programs are discussed in Chapter 31.

Rules and rule changes can affect either the way the game is played or the distribution of winnings when the game is over. Laws such as those governing minimum wages, pollution controls, import restrictions, affirmative action, and farm price supports affect the conditions of market production and exchange. They influence what resources are used, in what quantities, and often at what price. These rules thereby have a direct effect on how the game is played.

Another set of rules redistributes the winnings when the game is over. Taxes and transfers redistribute earnings after production and exchange have taken place. The problem is that the way the winnings are reallocated can also influence the way the game is played. For example, what if all the winnings were divided equally among the players when the game was over? What effect do you suppose this would have on the intensity and quality of play? It's likely that players would not accord the same attention to the game as they would if it were "for keeps." Likewise, each individual's incentives to work, to invest, and to take risks will be affected by the redistribution of earnings.

Teaching Tip A player can also devote resources to finding loopholes in existing rules; the government then devotes resources to counteracting rule evasion.

Allowing changes in the rules can introduce other distortions that affect the efficiency and fairness of the game. A player can either devote resources toward winning under the existing rules (sharpening game skills or playing with greater intensity) or spend time trying to change the rules to his or her

Pareto optimal A change in the status quo that makes at least one person better off while making no one else worse off

Example A recent study showed that a nationwide workplace smoking ban could cost cigarette manufacturers $4 billion per year in lost sales.

advantage. Some rule changes can be of the positive-sum variety, actually helping players by making the game more efficient. Rule changes are known as **Pareto optimal** if at least one player is made better off and none is made worse off. Changes in the rules that help one player or class of players, however, often harm other players. In fact, rule changes may in the aggregate result in more harm to the losers than gain to the winners; such changes thus have a negative sum.

As you can see, the introduction of rules and rule changes can affect the economy in a variety of ways. Choices about the rules of the game are typically *public choices*—choices that are made collectively by voters, either directly or indirectly. We turn now to a closer examination of the public choice process.

PUBLIC CHOICE IN DIRECT DEMOCRACY

Government decisions about the supply of public goods and services and the collection of revenues are public choices. In a democracy public choices usually require approval by a majority of the voters. As it turns out, we can frequently explain the choice of the electorate by focusing on the preferences of the median voter.

Median Voter Model

Median voter model Under certain conditions the preference of the median, or middle, voter will dominate other public choices.

The **median voter model** predicts that under certain conditions the preference of the median, or middle, voter will dominate other choices. Consider the logic behind the median voter model. Suppose you and two roommates have just moved into an apartment, and the three of you must decide on furnishings. You all agree that the common costs will be divided equally among the three of you and that majority rule will prevail, with one vote per person. The issue at hand is whether to buy a TV and, if so, of what size. The problem is that you each have different preferences. The more studious of your roommates considers a TV to be an annoying distraction. Your other roommate, a real TV fan, prefers the 36-inch screens often seen in bars and other cultural centers. Although by no means a TV addict, you enjoy watching TV as a relief from the rigors of academe; you think a 19-inch screen would be just fine. What to do, what to do?

Exhibit 1 illustrates your preferences and those of your roommates. The horizontal axis specifies the size of the TV screen; we focus on three possibilities: no TV, a 19-inch TV, and a 36-inch TV. The vertical axis indicates, for the different size TVs, a ranking of preferences, from most preferred to least preferred. Your studious roommate's preference is shown by the blue line, S; the TV fan's preference is shown by the gold line, F; and your preference is shown by the red line, Y. Your studious roommate, S, most prefers the option of no TV, has medium preference for the 19-inch TV, and least prefers the 36-inch TV. The order of preferences of the TV fan, F, are just the opposite. You,

EXHIBIT 1

Preferences for Size of TV Screen

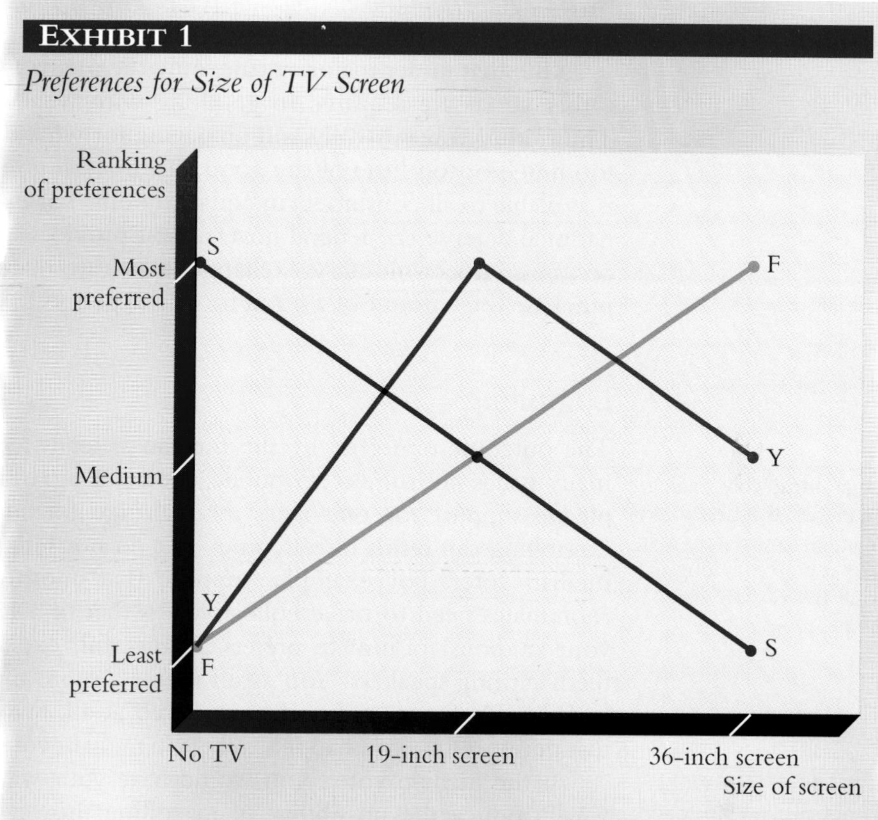

S prefers no TV most and a 36-inch screen least. F prefers just the opposite. The median voter, Y, prefers a 19-inch screen most and no TV least. In this case the 19-inch screen will be selected because there are more votes for it than for either of the other two options. The median voter's preference prevails.

Y, most prefer the 19-inch screen but would rather have the 36-inch TV than no TV at all. Spend a moment becoming familiar with the figure.

You all agree to make the decision by voting on two alternatives at a time, then pairing the winning alternative against the remaining alternative until one choice dominates the others. When a motion for no TV is paired with a motion to buy the 19-inch set, the 19-inch set gains majority support because this option gets both your vote and the TV fan's vote. When a motion for the 36-inch screen is then paired with the motion for the 19-inch screen, the 19-inch screen wins a majority again, this time because your studious roommate sides with you rather than voting for the super screen.

Example Studies of public school funding in Michigan and New York have found that the actual level of spending per pupil roughly equals the level preferred by the median voter.

Majority voting in effect delegates the public choice to the person whose preference is the median for the group. You, as the median voter in this case, can have your way; if you had wanted a 12-inch screen, you could have received majority support for that size. Similarly, *the median voter in an electorate often determines public choices. Political candidates try to get elected by appealing to the median voter.* This is one reason why there often appears to be little difference among candidates.

Note that under majority rule, only the median voter gets his or her way. Other voters are required to go along with what the median voter wants. Thus, other voters usually end up paying for what they consider to be either too much or too little of the good. With *public* goods the amount provided is available to all consumers in equal amount. For example, whatever level of national defense the federal government provides is available to all of us. In contrast, under voluntary exchange in private markets, each consumer can purchase the amount of a good he or she prefers.

Logrolling

Logrolling Vote trading on preferred issues; voter A agrees to vote for voter B's pet project as long as voter B votes for voter A's pet project

The outcome preferred by the median voter is less likely to prevail when many issues are subject to public choice. **Logrolling** occurs when voters pledge support for one issue in exchange for support on another issue. Logrolling can result in outcomes that do not reflect the preferences of the median voter. For example, suppose that another choice you and your roommates need to make collectively is that of a stereo system. In this case your studious roommate prefers a powerful, expensive system—one with teeth-rattling speakers. You again prefer a more moderately priced system, and the TV fan would prefer no stereo at all, favoring MTV and VH1 to just music. Thus, you happen to be the median voter in this decision as well.

Teaching Tip Without logrolling, majority voting does not reflect the relative intensity of preferences. The vote of the studious roommate (who is perhaps marginally opposed to the 36-inch screen TV) is given a weight equal to the vote of the TV fan (who is passionately in favor of the large screen). However, if the studious roommate is passionately in favor of a large stereo and the TV fan is marginally against it, they become more likely to trade votes under logrolling.

As the median voter, you would have your way under majority rule. If we introduce the possibility of logrolling, however, your choice may no longer dominate. Your two roommates realize that they are not getting their first choices in either decision. Suppose that the studious roommate agrees to vote for the super TV screen in return for the TV fan's vote for the expensive stereo. By trading votes, or logrolling, they each get a first choice in one of the two decisions. You, as the median voter, no longer cast the deciding vote. This exchange of support usually results in greater outlays for the two items than would have been the case without such logrolling.

Cyclical Majority

Even without logrolling, a clear majority choice may not emerge. Suppose, for example, that the TV fan, as a purist, prefers having no TV to having any TV smaller than the super size. F's preference is shown by the gold line in Exhibit 2; preferences of S and Y are the same as before. If under these circumstances the 19-inch screen is up for a vote against the giant screen, the 19-inch screen will win a majority, as before. If the option for the 19-inch screen is then paired with the option of no TV, however, the no-TV alternative will gain a majority, winning both the studious roommate's vote and the TV fan's vote. If the no-TV option is then paired with the motion for a 36-inch screen, the large screen will win your vote and the TV fan's vote, thereby gaining a majority.

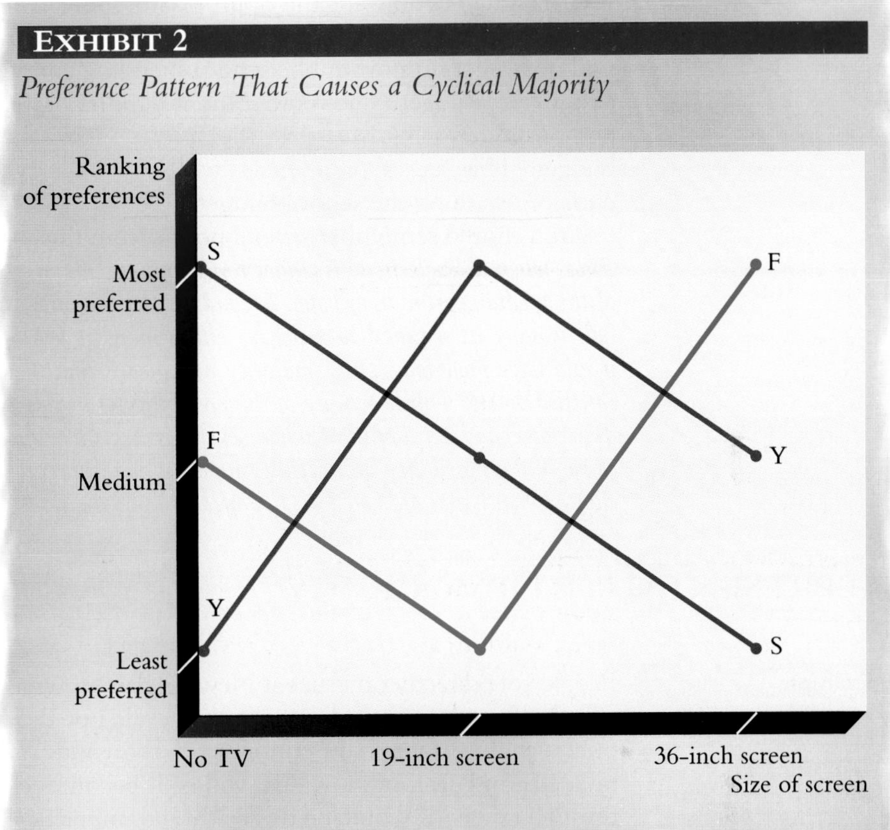

If voter F prefers a 36-inch screen to no TV and no TV to a 19-inch screen, a cyclical majority results. No matter which option is proposed, some other option will be preferred by a majority of voters.

There is no dominant choice in this case. Although the 19-inch option defeats the 36-inch option, the no-TV option defeats the 19-inch option, and then the 36-inch option defeats the no-TV option. No matter which alternative wins in a particular pairing, there is always another option that can beat that winner. Instead of a clear majority, there is a **cyclical majority**, with the outcome depending on the order of voting. What causes this cycle is that the TV fan prefers no TV to any TV smaller than the giant one. Thus, the TV fan's ordering does not rank TV size from highest to lowest in a direct way.

Cyclical majority A situation in which no choice dominates all others, and the outcome of a vote depends on the order in which issues are considered

Perhaps an application to public finance will clarify the notion of a cyclical majority. Consider the preferences for education in your home town. Suppose that high-income families prefer that the public schools be first-rate. Families of middle income and below are not able to afford the taxes needed to pay for a top-quality school system and so prefer a moderate budget. High-income voters believe that if the schools are not going to be first-rate, then private schools are the appropriate choice for their children. If high-income families feel obliged to send their children to private schools, they will no longer support public school spending and will prefer a low budget to a moderate budget. The most affluent families prefer the highest school budget, but if they can't have that, they prefer a low school budget to a moderate budget. This set of preferences will lead to a cyclical majority in public choices regarding the school budget.

You should remember several points from this discussion of majority rule. *First, when a single issue is under consideration, majority rule often reflects the views of the median, or middle, voter. Second, under majority rule all but the median voter will usually be required to purchase either more or less of the public good than they would have preferred. Thus, majority rule means that there are likely to be many dissatisfied voters. Third, because of the possibility of logrolling, the preferences of the median voter may not dominate when several issues are being considered. And fourth, because of the possibility of a cyclical majority, majority rule may result in no dominant choice when issues are voted on two at a time.*

Representative Democracy

Example The state and local issues often listed on November ballots are types of referenda. They tend to deal with items such as property tax levies and state constitutional amendments.

People vote directly on issues at New England town meetings and on the occasional referendum, but direct democracy is not the most common means of public choice. When you consider the thousands of public choices that must be made on behalf of individual voters, it becomes clear that direct democracy through referenda would be unwieldy and impractical. Rather than make myriad decisions by direct referenda, voters typically elect representatives, who, in turn, make public choices to reflect constituents' views.

In our federal system each voter helps choose representatives at a minimum of three levels of government: federal, state, and local. Logrolling is more common with representative democracy than with direct voting. For example, members of Congress agree to trade votes on one another's pet projects, and the result is *pork barrel* legislation, such as an over-supply of military bases. Logrolling is more likely when the voting is public and not by secret ballot.

Direct and representative democracy have several properties in common. For example, under certain conditions the resulting public choices reflect the preferences of the median voter. The question of representation, however, raises a special set of issues. For example, each candidate elected to office reflects a bundle of positions on a variety of issues. The most important of these positions likely match the preferences of the median voters, but the candidate's positions on the remaining issues may not. Thus, some public policy decisions may not match the preferences of the median voters. Other problems of representative democracy will be explored next.

Goals of the Participants

We assume that consumers maximize utility and firms maximize profit, but what about governments? As noted in Chapter 4, there is no common agreement about what governments maximize or, more precisely, what elected officials maximize. One theory that appears to parallel the rational self-interest employed in private choices is that elected officials attempt to *maximize their political support*. Political support can take the form not only of votes but also of campaign contributions and in-kind support, such as the efforts of campaign workers.

Point to Stress If politicians are catering to special interests, they may pass legislation that imposes net costs on society and not pass legislation that provides net benefits.

When representative democracy replaces direct democracy, there is a greater possibility that elected representatives will cater to special interests rather than serve the interests of the majority. The problem arises because of the asymmetry between special interests and the common interest. Let's consider only one of the thousands of decisions that are made each year by elected representatives: funding of an obscure federal program that subsidizes U.S. wool production. Under the wool subsidy program, the federal government establishes and guarantees a floor price to be paid to sheep farmers for each pound of wool they produce. The guaranteed price was $1.53 per pound at a time when the world market price was $0.61 per pound, thereby providing wool producers with a subsidy of $0.92 per pound.[1] During deliberations to renew the subsidy program, the only person to testify before Congress was a representative of the National Wool Growers Association, who claimed that the subsidy was vital to the nation's economic welfare. The federal subsidy costs taxpayers over $75 million per year. Why didn't a single representative of taxpayer interests testify against the subsidy? Why were sheep farmers able to pull the wool over the taxpayers' eyes?

Teaching Tip Recall from Chapter 28 that a consumer will gather information up to the point at which the marginal benefit equals the marginal cost. In public choices, where consumers' interests are dispersed, marginal benefits tend to be low. Even in private markets, consumers will be less likely to search for information about items that represent a small portion of their budget.

Rational Ignorance

Households consume so many different public and private goods and services that they have neither the time nor the incentive to understand the effects of public choices on every one of these products. Voters realize that each has but a tiny possibility of influencing the outcome of public choices. Moreover, even if an individual voter is somehow able to affect the outcome, the impact of the chosen policy on that voter is likely to be small. For example, even if a taxpayer could successfully stage a grass-roots campaign to eliminate the wool subsidy, the taxpayer would save on average less than $1 per year in federal income taxes. Therefore, unless voters have concentrated interests, they adopt a policy of **rational ignorance**, which means that they remain largely oblivious to the costs and benefits of the thousands of proposals considered by elected officials. The costs of acquiring and acting on such information are typically greater than any expected benefits.

Rational ignorance A stance adopted by voters when they find that the costs of understanding and voting on a particular issue exceed the expected benefits of doing so

In contrast, consumers have a greater incentive to gather and act upon information about decisions they make in private markets because they benefit directly from the knowledge acquired. *In a world where information and the time required to acquire and digest it are scarce, consumers concentrate on private choices*

1. The prices quoted are for 1983, as noted by James Bovard in "A Subsidy Both Wooly-Headed and Mammoth," *Wall Street Journal,* 17 April 1985.

rather than public choices because the payoff in making wise private choices is usually more immediate and more direct. The consumer in the market for a new car has an incentive to examine the performance records of different models rather than get stuck with a lemon. That consumer can then choose from among the various models. But the same individual has less incentive to examine the performance records of candidates for public office because that single voter has virtually no chance of deciding the election. What's more, political candidates, who aim to please the median voter, will often take positions that are quite similar anyway.

Example A U.S. tariff on imported automobiles benefits hundreds of thousands of people: stockholders in U.S. automobile firms, U.S. auto workers, property owners and retail business owners in cities with auto plants, and so forth. However, the interests of a large part of this group are served by just four organizations: General Motors, Ford, Chrysler, and the UAW. Therefore, the benefits are best described as concentrated.

Distribution of Costs and Benefits

The costs imposed by a particular legislative measure may be either narrowly or widely distributed over the population, depending on the issue. Likewise, the benefits may be conferred on only a small group or on much of the population. The more widespread the costs or benefits of a legislative measure, the less they will affect any individual. Alternatively, the more concentrated the costs or benefits, the more important they become to those affected. The possible combinations of costs and benefits yield four alternative types of distributions: (1) widespread costs and widespread benefits, (2) widespread costs and concentrated benefits, (3) concentrated costs and concentrated benefits, and (4) concentrated costs and widespread benefits.

Traditional public goods, such as national defense and a system of justice, have widespread costs and benefits—nearly everyone pays and nearly everyone benefits from this category of distribution. Traditional public goods are often a positive-sum game because the benefits outweigh the costs. With **special-interest legislation**, benefits are concentrated but costs are widespread. For example, if some special-interest group, such as the wool producers, can get Congress to adopt legislation that fleeces just $1 from each taxpayer and transfers it to the wool producers, this yields that special interest over $100 million. Legislation that caters to special interests is often a negative-sum game.

Special-interest legislation Legislation that generates concentrated benefits but imposes widespread costs

Competing-interest legislation Legislation that imposes concentrated costs on one group and provides concentrated benefits to another group

Competing-interest legislation involves both concentrated costs and concentrated benefits. Consider, for example, how a tariff affects importers of shoes versus domestic manufacturers of shoes. Though resolving a competing-interest issue may appear to be a zero-sum game because the gains and losses of the competing interests seem to offset each other, it will be a negative-sum game if the resolution generates economic inefficiencies.

When legislators try to impose costs in a concentrated way so as to confer benefits widely, the group getting hit with the concentrated costs will object strenuously. Meanwhile, those who will benefit remain rationally ignorant of the proposed legislation, so they will provide little political support for such a measure. For example, whenever Congress considers imposing a tax on a particular industry, that industry floods Washington with lobbyists and mail, usually noting how the tax will lead to economic ruin, not to mention the decline of Western civilization as we know it today. Thus, legislation that imposes costs on a small group but confers benefits widely has less chance of being passed than do measures that confer benefits narrowly but spread costs widely.

In the following case study, we consider the redistributive and efficiency effects of a specific example of special interest legislation: farm subsidy programs.

CASE STUDY

Farm Subsidies: A Negative-Sum Game

The Agricultural Marketing Agreement Act became law in 1937 to prevent what had been viewed as "ruinous competition" among farmers. In the years since, the government has introduced a variety of policies to set floor prices for a wide range of farm products. The federal government spends over $10 billion a year to support higher farm prices on products ranging from wool to peanuts.

Let's see how price supports work in the dairy industry. Exhibit 3 depicts a simplified view of the market for milk. Suppose that in the absence of government intervention, the market price of milk is $2 per gallon and the equilibrium quantity is 100 million gallons per month. In long-run equilibrium, dairy farmers earn a normal rate of return. Consumers as a group capture the consumer surplus shown by the blue-shaded area. Recall that consumer surplus is the difference between the most that consumers would have been willing to pay for each unit of the good and the amount actually paid.

Teaching Tip The concentrated benefits of dairy price supports are especially obvious when you consider that one-third of the cows are owned by just 6 percent of the dairy farmers, who receive the largest portion of the benefits.

But suppose that dairy farmers persuade Congress that the free-market price is too low, so legislation establishes a price floor for milk of, say, $3 per gallon. The higher price floor provides farmers with an incentive to increase the quantity supplied to 150 million gallons per month. In response to the higher price, however, consumers reduce their quantity demanded to 75 million gallons per month. To make the higher price stick, the government must buy the 75 million gallons of "surplus" milk generated by the floor price or somehow get dairy farmers to restrict their output to 75 million gallons per month. For example, the government may pay dairy farmers not to produce or may buy cows from farmers to reduce production.

Consumers end up paying dearly to subsidize the farmers. First, the price per gallon increases by $1. Second, taxpayers must pay for the surplus milk or otherwise pay farmers not to produce the surplus milk. And third, if the government buys the surplus milk, taxpayers must then pay for storage. Consider the price the typical consumer-taxpayer now pays for a gallon of milk. The consumer pays $3 per gallon for milk purchased on the market; the consumer as an average taxpayer pays another $3 for the gallon the government buys, plus, say, an extra $0.50 per gallon to convert that surplus milk into powder and to store it. Instead of paying just $2 for a gallon of milk, which is the price in the absence of government price supports, the typical consumer-taxpayer in our example is milked for a total of $6.50 per gallon, or an extra outlay of $4.50 per gallon of milk consumed.

Point to Stress The higher price is just offset by higher production costs if the farmers increase production to 150 million gallons.

How do the farmers make out? Each farmer receives an extra $1 per gallon in additional revenue over the price that would have prevailed in a free market. As farmers increase their output, however, the marginal cost of production increases; at the margin, the higher price the farmer receives is just offset by higher production costs. Still, farmers gain an increase in producer surplus because of the subsidy program, identified in Exhibit 3 by the area

EXHIBIT 3

Effects of Milk Price Supports

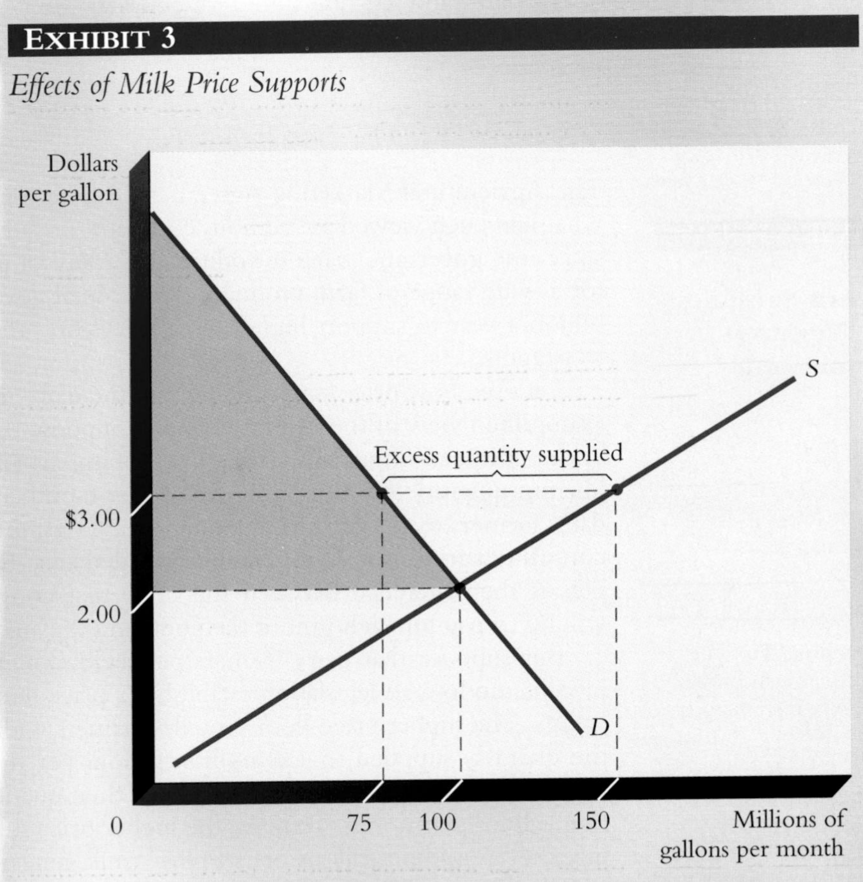

In the absence of government intervention, the market price of milk is $2 per gallon and 100 million gallons are sold per month. If Congress establishes a floor price of $3 per gallon, then the quantity supplied will increase and the quantity demanded will decrease. To maintain the higher price, the government must buy up the excess quantity at $3 per gallon.

Consumers are worse off as a result of this policy. In addition to paying an extra $1 per gallon, they must pay for government purchases of surplus milk as well as for storing that milk. In the long run, farmers are no better off, since the policy drives up the prices of resources specialized to dairy farming.

above the supply curve that is between the market price of $2 and the floor price of $3.

The subsidy will increase the value of resources specialized to dairy farming, such as cows and grazing land, and farmers who owned these resources when the subsidy program started will benefit. Farmers who purchase these resources after the subsidy has been introduced will pay more and will end up earning just a normal rate of return. So with free entry into the dairy industry, most farmers in the long run earn just a normal rate of return despite the billions of dollars spent on farm subsidies.

If the extra $1 per gallon that farmers receive for milk were pure profit, farm profits would increase by $150 million per month. But consumer-taxpayer costs per month would increase by $337.5 million: $75 million for the higher price of each of the 75 million gallons consumers purchase, plus $225 million in higher taxes for the 75 million surplus gallons purchased by the government, plus $37.5 million to store the 75 million surplus gallons. Thus, consumer-taxpayer costs are more than double the farmers' maximum possible gain of $150 million. The government subsidy program is therefore a negative-sum game, as the sum of all the gains and losses is less than zero. This does not mean that nobody gains—those who owned specialized resources gained when the subsidy was first introduced. But once the price of farm resources increases, new farmers must pay more to get in a position to reap the subsidies. Everyone would be better off if the government made a direct transfer payment to farmers, a payment not tied to milk production or price.

In practice the milk program combines purchasing surplus milk products with paying dairy farmers not to produce and with even buying cows from farmers. By the mid-1980s dairy herds had expanded so much that the government spent more than $1 billion to reduce herd size (herds are now growing again). The dairy industry is supported in other ways. Since 1980 U.S. milk prices have been double or triple the average price on world markets, yet imports are restricted. Regulations also limit farmers in one part of the country from selling their milk in another part of the country. Some state programs support even higher prices. Other laws promote the consumption of dairy products. For example, laws in many states prohibit restaurants from serving margarine unless customers specifically request it instead of butter.

Point to Stress Despite the high total cost of dairy price subsidies, the cost per household is low. Because of rational ignorance, few households are aware of the existence or costs of the program.

Experts conclude that the so-called "farm problem" disappeared during the decades following World War II, yet government intervention increased and became more complicated. The 1990 Farm Bill was twice the length of its 1985 predecessor. Explaining the intricacies of milk-price supports takes up three volumes of the *Code of Federal Regulation*. (For example, the minimum milk prices in each region around the country are determined by a complicated formula based on the distance from Eau Claire, Wisconsin!) Just to shuffle the paperwork for the program costs the federal government about $1,000 per year for each commercial farm.

Although a direct transfer payment to dairy farmers would be more efficient, such a transparent special-interest proposal could attract the public's attention and be doomed. Special-interest legislation is often promoted under the cover of some greater good. The ostensible goal of farm subsidies, for example, is to save the family farm, but farm households on average earn a higher income than non-farm households and are wealthier (the average farmer has assets valued at more than $1 million). The federal government spent about the same amount in 1990 to subsidize 4.5 million farmers as it spent on the 11.4 million poor recipients of Aid to Families with Dependent Children.

Sources: Bruce L. Gardner, "Changing Economic Perspectives on the Farm Problem," *Journal of Economic Literature* 30 (March 1992): 62–101; and Scott Kilman, "Market Maze: Why the Price of Milk Depends on Distance from Eau Claire, Wis.," *Wall Street Journal,* 20 May 91.

Rent Seeking

Teaching Tip The concept of rent seeking was introduced in Chapter 22 in the discussion of monopoly.

An important feature of representative democracy is the incentive and political power it offers participants to employ legislation to increase their wealth, either through direct transfers or through favorable public expenditures and regulations. Special-interest groups, such as farmers, try to persuade elected officials to approve measures that provide the special interest with some market advantage or some outright transfer or subsidy. Such benefits are sometimes called *rents.* The term in this context implies that the government transfer or subsidy constitutes a payment to the resource owner that is over and above the earnings necessary to call forth that resource—a payment exceeding opportunity cost. The activity that interest groups undertake to elicit these special favors from government is called **rent seeking**.

Rent seeking Any effort by individuals or firms to obtain favorable treatment from government

The government frequently bestows some special advantage on a producer or group of producers, and abundant resources are expended to secure these rights. For example, *political action committees*, known more popularly as PACs, contribute millions to congressional campaigns. In the early 1990s, the top contributors included the Teamsters union, the American Trial Lawyers Association, the Electrical Workers union, and the American Bankers Association. All these groups are special interests with actions before the Congress. For example, the Teamsters union would like trucking to be reregulated.

Teaching Tip Rent seeking serves to reduce any producer surplus generated by special-interest legislation.

To the extent that special-interest groups engage in rent-seeking activities, they shift resources from productive endeavors that create income to activities that focus more on transferring income. *Resources that are employed in an attempt to get government to redistribute income or wealth are largely unproductive because they do nothing to increase output and usually end up reducing it.* And often many firms compete for the same government advantage, thereby wasting still more resources. If the special advantage conferred by government to some special-interest group requires all taxpayers to pay more, the net return individuals expect from working and investing will fall, so less work and less investment may occur. If this happens, potential income will go unearned.

Competition among groups to obtain rents has been of growing concern among public finance economists. As a firm's profitability becomes more and more dependent on decisions made in Washington, resources are diverted from productive activity to rent seeking, or lobbying. One firm may thrive because it secured some special advantage at a critical time; another firm may fail because its managers were more concerned with productive efficiency than with rent seeking.

As economist Mancur Olson of the University of Maryland notes, special-interest groups typically have little incentive to make the economy more efficient.[2] In fact, special-interest groups will usually support legislation transferring wealth to them even if the measure reduces the economy's overall efficiency. For example, suppose that the American Trial Lawyers Association is able to push through a measure that has the effect of increasing lawyers' incomes by a total of $1 billion per year, or about $1,900 for each

2. Mancur Olson, *The Rise and Decline of Nations* (New Haven, CT: Yale University Press, 1982).

lawyer in private practice. Suppose too that, as a result of this measure, litigation increases, thus driving up insurance premiums and raising the total cost of production by, say, $5 billion. Lawyers themselves will have to bear part of this higher cost, but since they account for only about 1 percent of the spending in the economy, they will bear only about 1 percent of the $5 billion in higher costs, or a total of $50 million, which amounts to about $100 per lawyer. Thus, the legislation is a bargain for lawyers because it increases each lawyer's income by $1,900 but increases each lawyer's costs by only $100.

Example Through logrolling, some unrelated special interests may work together. For example, the government's dairy-support legislation in the mid-1980s was endorsed by key politicians in tobacco-growing states in exchange for dairy-state endorsement of tobacco-support legislation.

There are hundreds of special-interest groups representing farmers, physicians, lawyers, teachers, manufacturers, barbers, and so on. Since there are many competing groups, the situation becomes, in Olson's words, "like a china shop filled with wrestlers battling over the china, and breaking far more than they carry away."[3] Some of the country's best minds are occupied with devising schemes to avoid taxes and engaging in other practices that transfer income to favored groups at the expense of market efficiency. For example, the pursuit of tax loopholes fills up the days of some of the best and the brightest lawyers and accountants.

Think of the economy's output in a particular period as depicted by a pie. The pie is the total value of goods and services produced. In deciding on answers to the "what," "how," and "for whom" questions introduced in Chapter 2, rule makers have three alternatives: (1) they can introduce changes that will yield a bigger pie (that is, positive-sum changes), (2) they can decide simply to carve up the existing pie differently (zero-sum changes), or (3) they can start fighting over the pie, causing some of it to end up on the floor (negative-sum changes). Much special-interest legislation involves a negative sum.

THE UNDERGROUND ECONOMY

A government subsidy promotes production, as we saw in the case study on milk price supports. Conversely, a tax on output discourages production. Perhaps it would be more accurate to say that when government taxes production, less production is *reported.* If you worked as a waiter or waitress, did you faithfully report all your tips to the Internal Revenue Service? To the extent that you did not, your income became part of the underground economy. The **underground economy** is a term used for all market activity that goes unreported to the government either to avoid taxes or because the activity is illegal. Thus, income arising in the underground economy ranges from unreported tips to the earnings of a drug dealer.

Underground economy All economic activity not reported to the government

The introduction of a tax has two effects. First, resource owners may supply less of the taxed resource because the tax reduces the net return expected from supplying the resource. Second, in an attempt to evade taxes, some

3. Mancur Olson, "What We Lose When the Rich Go on the Dole," *The Washington Monthly* (January 1984): 49.

market participants will divert their economic activity from the formal, reported economy to an underground, "off-the-books" economy. Thus, when the government taxes market exchange or the income arising from that exchange, less market activity is reported. For example, a plumber and an accountant may barter services to evade taxes, rather than paying each other in money that would have to be reported and taxed as income.

We should take care to distinguish between tax *avoidance* and tax *evasion.* Tax avoidance is a legal attempt to arrange one's economic affairs so as to pay the least tax possible, such as buying municipal bonds because of their tax-free interest. Tax evasion is illegal; it takes the form of either failing to file a tax return or filing a fraudulent return by understating income or overstating deductions.

Although there are no official figures on the size of the underground economy, federal agencies try to make inferences based on other data. The Census Bureau estimates that its official figures capture only 90 percent of U.S. income. An Internal Revenue Service survey estimated that only 87 percent of tax liabilities are paid. These studies suggest a value of between $600 billion and $800 billion for the underground economy in 1993.

Teaching Tip If the value of recorded economic activity rose proportionately more than the decrease in the tax rate, tax revenues from former underground activities increased.

One motive for lowering the rates on personal income taxes in 1986 was to encourage those in the underground economy to join the mainstream of recorded economic activity. A lower marginal tax rate reduces the benefit of tax evasion. Prior to the 1986 tax reform, the top marginal tax rate of 50 percent meant that a person who went underground evaded a maximum of $0.50 in taxes for each $1 earned. But after 1986, the highest marginal rate fell to 33 percent, so the tax evader saved at most only $0.33 in federal income taxes for each $1 of income not reported.

Those who pursue rent-seeking activity and those involved in the underground economy view government from opposite perspectives. Rent seekers want government to become actively involved in transferring wealth to them, but those in the underground economy want to evade any government contact. *Subsidies and other advantages bestowed by government draw some groups closer to government; taxes encourage others to go underground.*

BUREAUCRACY AND REPRESENTATIVE DEMOCRACY

Bureaus Government agencies charged with implementing legislation and financed by appropriations from legislative bodies

Elected representatives approve legislation, but the task of implementing that legislation is typically left to various government departments and agencies. The organizations charged with implementing legislation are usually referred to as **bureaus**; bureaus are government agencies whose activities are financed by appropriations from legislative bodies.

Point to Stress Bureaucrats are non-elected government officials.

Ownership and Funding of Bureaus

We can get a better feel for government bureaus by comparing them to corporations. Ownership of a corporation is based on the proportion of shares owned by each stockholder. Stockholders are the residual claimants of any profits or losses arising from the firm's operations. Ownership in the firm is *transferable*; the shares can be sold in the stock market. In contrast, taxpayers, by dint of their citizenship, are in a sense the "owners" of government bureaus in the jurisdiction in which they live. If the bureau earns a "profit," taxes will be reduced; if the bureau operates at a "loss," as most do, this loss must be covered by taxes. Each taxpayer has just one vote, regardless of the taxes paid. Ownership in the bureau is surrendered only if the taxpayer dies or moves out of the relevant jurisdiction; it is not transferable—it cannot be bought and sold directly.

Teaching Tip Although most bureaus rely on appropriations from legislatures (and thus deal only indirectly with taxpayers), a few (such as school boards and county libraries) rely on funds raised through taxes passed by voters specifically for those purposes.

Whereas firms derive their revenue when customers voluntarily purchase their products, bureaus are typically financed by a budget appropriation from the legislature. Most of this budget comes from taxpayers. On occasion bureaus will earn revenue through user charges, such as admission fees at state parks or tuition at state colleges, but supplementary funds often come from budget appropriations. Because of these differences in the forms of ownership and in the sources of revenue, bureaus have different incentives than do profit-making firms, so we are likely to observe different behavior in the two organizations.

Ownership and Organizational Behavior

A central assumption of economics is that people behave rationally and respond to economic incentives. The more compensation is linked to individual incentives, the more people will behave in accord with those incentives. If a letter carrier's pay is based on the customers' satisfaction, the letter carrier will make a greater effort to deliver mail promptly and intact.

The firm has a steady stream of consumer feedback when its product is sold in free markets. If the price is too high or too low to clear the market, the firm will know as surpluses or shortages develop. Not only is consumer feedback abundant, but the firm's owners have a profit incentive to act on that information in an attempt to satisfy consumer wants. The promise of profits also creates incentives to produce the output at minimum cost. Thus, the firm's owners stand to gain from any improvement in customer satisfaction or in production efficiency.

Since public goods and services are not sold in free markets, government bureaus receive less consumer feedback. There are no prices and no obvious shortages or surpluses. For example, how would you know whether there was a shortage or a surplus of police protection in your community? (Would gangs of police officers hanging around the doughnut shop indicate a surplus?) Not only do bureaus receive less consumer feedback than do firms, they also have less incentive to act on the information available. Because any "profits" or "losses" arising in the bureau are spread among all taxpayers and because there is no transferability of ownership, bureaus have less incentive to satisfy customers or to produce their output using the least-cost combination of resources. (Laws prevent bureaucrats from taking home any "profit.")

Point to Stress Both elected representatives, who must deal with a number of different bureaus, and voters find it rational to remain ignorant of the bureaus' cost functions.

Some pressure for customer satisfaction and cost minimization may be communicated by voters to their elected representatives and thereby to the bureaus. But this discipline is less precise than that operating in the firm, particularly since any gains or losses in efficiency are diffused among all taxpayers. For example, suppose that you are a citizen in a state with a million taxpayers and you become aware of some inefficiency that is costing taxpayers a million dollars a year. If you undertake measures that succeed in correcting the shortcoming, you save yourself about a dollar per year in taxes.

At the state or local level, those dissatisfied with their government can move to another jurisdiction; if enough people moved, this could stimulate government to be more responsive. In a sense, state and local governments compete for households and for firms by trying to offer an attractive bundle of taxes and public services. Yet this mechanism whereby people "vote with their feet" by moving to a more responsive jurisdiction is a rather crude way to approximate voter satisfaction. And of course at the federal level one cannot move to another jurisdiction without leaving the country.

Example At one time in the United Kingdom, marginal income tax rates were as high as 85 percent at moderate levels of income. This led to a brain drain in many professional, scientific, and managerial fields as workers moved to other English-speaking countries.

Because of differences between public and private organizations—in the owners' ability both to transfer ownership and to appropriate profits—we expect bureaus to be less concerned with satisfying consumer demand and minimizing costs than private firms are. A variety of empirical studies have attempted to compare costs for products that are provided by both public bureaus and private firms, such as garbage collection. Of those studies that show a difference, some find public bureaus to be more efficient, but the majority find private firms to be more efficient.

Bureaucratic Objectives

Assuming that bureaus are not simply at the beck and call of the legislature—that is, assuming that bureaucrats have some autonomy—what sort of objectives will they pursue? The traditional view is that bureaucrats are "public servants" who try to serve the public as best they can. No doubt many public employees do just that, but some observers wonder whether this is a realistic assumption about the behavior of bureaucrats more generally. Why should we assume self-sacrificing behavior by public-sector employees when we make no such assumption about private-sector employees?

Teaching Tip This theory also assumes that bureaus know their own cost functions but the legislatures do not. The bureaus can lie to the legislature about the cost of alternative levels of output.

One widely discussed alternative theory of bureaucratic behavior has been put forth by William Niskanen. Niskanen argues that bureaus attempt to *maximize their budgets*, for along with a big budget comes size, prestige, amenities, and staff, which are valued by bureaucrats.[4] How do bureaucrats maximize the bureau's budget? According to Niskanen, bureaus supply their output to the legislature as monopolists. Rather than charge a price per unit, bureaus offer the legislature the entire amount as a package deal in return for the requested appropriation. According to this theory, the legislature has little

4. William A. Niskanen, Jr., *Bureaucracy and Representative Government* (Chicago, IL: Aldine-Atherton, 1971).

ability to dig into the budget and cut particular items (no line-item veto). If the legislature proposes cuts in the bureau's budget, the bureau will threaten to make those cuts as painful to the legislature and its constituents as possible. For example, if town officials attempt to reduce the school budget, school bureaucrats, rather than increasing teaching loads, may threaten to eliminate kindergarten, eliminate the high school football team, or disband the school band. If such threats are effective in forcing the legislature to back off from any cuts, the government budget turns out to be larger than taxpayers would prefer. *Budget maximization results in a budget higher than that desired by the median voter.*

Private Versus Public Production

Simply because public goods and services are financed by the government does not mean that they must be produced by the government. Profit-making firms have government contracts to provide everything from fire protection to prisons to local education. The mix of firms and bureaus varies over time and across jurisdictions. Elected officials may contract directly with private firms to produce public output. For example, a city council may contract with a firm to handle garbage-collection services for the city. Elected officials may also use some combination of bureaus and firms to produce desired output. For example, the Pentagon, a giant bureau, hires and trains military personnel, yet contracts with private firms to develop and produce various weapon systems. State governments typically hire private contractors to build roads but maintain them with state employees.

Teaching Tip Similarly, as discussed in Chapter 28, the firm may choose to produce through a combination of managerial coordination and market exchange.

When governments produce public goods and services, they are using *the internal organization of the government*—the bureaucracy—to supply the product. When governments contract with private firms to produce public goods and services, they are using *the market* to supply the product. Legislators might prefer dealing with bureaus rather than with firms for two reasons. First, in situations where it is difficult to specify a contract that clearly spells out all the possible contingencies, the internal organization of the bureau may be more responsive to the legislature's concerns than the manager of a firm would be. Second, to the extent that legislators view bureaus as a vehicle for political patronage and discretion, they may prefer bureaus because bureaus provide more opportunities to reward friends and supporters with jobs than private firms would.

Using market competition to supply services that are not well defined, such as the guidance provided by a social worker, may lead to poor service. A private firm that wins the contract might be tempted to shade on quality, particularly if the quality of the service can be determined only by direct observation when the service is provided. For example, suppose that government put social work out for bid, selected the lowest bidder, then attempted to monitor the quality of the service through direct observation. The government would find direct monitoring quite costly. These services thus might best be provided by a government bureau. Because the bureau is less concerned with minimizing costs, it has less reason to lower the quality to reduce cost.

Conclusion

Teaching Tip The public-choice issue likely to be in the forefront in the mid-1990s is universal health care. The competing interest groups involved in this issue are consumers, businesses, hospitals, doctors, non-physician health care providers, insurers, and government.

This chapter examined how individual preferences are reflected in public choices. We began with direct voting based on majority rule, moved on to problems arising from representative democracy, and finally examined bureaus, the organizations that usually implement public choices. We also considered indirect income transfers, which arise because of changes in the rules governing economic activity in the private sector. Price supports, import restrictions, and other indirect transfers are not reflected fully in the government budget but often have profound effects on the economy. Whenever governments become involved in the workings of the economy to favor one group over another, some resources are shifted from productive activity to rent-seeking activity—that is, efforts to persuade the government to confer benefits on certain groups. Individual incentives may also be distorted in a way that reduces the economy's real output. In the next chapter we focus on the direct redistribution of income through transfer payments to poor people.

Governments attempt to address market failures in the private economy. But simply turning problems of perceived market failure over to government may not always be the best solution, because government has failings of its own. Participation in markets is based on voluntary exchange. Governments, however, have the legal power to enforce public choices. We should employ at least as high a standard in judging the performance of government, where allocations have the force of law, as we do in judging the private market, where allocations are decided by voluntary exchange between consenting parties.

Summary

1. Under certain conditions public choice under majority rule reflects the preferences of the median voter, often requiring other taxpayers to buy either more or less of the public good than they would prefer. Logrolling, or vote trading, produces public choices that may represent the preferences of a minority of voters rather than those of the median voter. When a cyclical majority arises, no clear public choice emerges.

2. Producers have an abiding interest in any legislation that affects their livelihood. Consumers, however, purchase thousands of different products and have no special interest in legislation affecting any particular product. Consumers are said to adopt a posture of rational ignorance about producer-oriented legislation because the costs of keeping up with special-interest issues outweigh the expected benefits.

3. The intense interest that producer groups express in relevant legislation, coupled with rational ignorance of voters on most issues, leaves government vulnerable to rent seeking by special interests. Elected officials interested in maximizing their political support may have a tendency to serve producer interests rather than consumer interests—that is, to serve special interests rather than the public interest.

4. Much of the redistribution of wealth that occurs through the process of public choice is not from rich to poor but from all taxpayers to some special-interest groups. The harm special-interest groups inflict on the economy often outweighs the benefits they reap, so this type of redistribution is a negative-sum game.

5. Bureaus differ from firms in the amount of consumer feedback they receive, in their incentive to minimize costs, and in the transferability of their ownership. Because of these differences, bureaus may not be as efficient or as sensitive to consumer preferences as firms are.

Questions and Problems

1. (Median Voter) In a single-issue vote, such as the television example in the chapter, will the median voter necessarily always get his or her most preferred outcome? If not, how would you alter the preferences in Exhibit 1 to show this?

2. (Majority Vote) We often hear that in the United States we are governed by the principle of majority rule. Is it true that there must always be a majority?

3. (Representative Government) What would guide a senator in deciding how to vote on an issue that did not directly affect his or her constituency? Is logrolling an important consideration here? Why or why not?

4. (Party Affiliation) Why might it be important to a person running for office to have a party affiliation? Does the existence of political parties reduce the transaction costs involved in voting?

5. (Consumer Interest Lobbies) Why might consumer interest groups in Washington be less effective than producer lobbies?

6. (Voting) Why does 50 percent of the U.S. voting population consistently fail to vote?

7. (Logrolling) Is it possible for lobbies to engage in a type of logrolling? How?

8. (Political Action Committees) How might the emergence of political action committees have contributed to the soaring costs of running a political campaign? Why are seats in the government, which pay relatively poorly, becoming so expensive to obtain?

9. (Underground Economy) Why is it important to reduce the size of the underground economy? How might the government do so?

10. (Efficiency and Price Supports) Suppose that the government decides to guarantee an above-market price for a good by buying up any surplus at that above-market price. Using a conventional supply-demand diagram, illustrate the following gains and losses from a price support:
    a. The loss of consumer surplus
    b. The gain of producer surplus in the short run
    c. The tax cost of running the government program (assuming no storage costs)
    d. The net efficiency loss, assuming that the government-purchased products are distributed to consumers. (Hint: This loss is caused purely by overproduction of the good.)

11. (Median Voter) The text describes circumstances under which the outcome of a vote will be the one desired by the median voter. Using a single-issue example with three voters, answer the following questions:
    a. Why did the vote result in the outcome it did?
    b. Would the outcome have been different if non-median voters' feelings about the preferred choice had been stronger or less strong?
    c. Is the outcome likely to be the economically efficient one? Why or why not?

12. (Representative Government) Political parties typically produce "middle of the road" platforms rather than taking extreme positions. Is this consistent with the concepts of the median voter and rational ignorance discussed in the text?

13. (Cyclical Majority) Compare the preferences shown in Exhibits 1 and 2. What is the key difference between them that leads to a cyclical majority in Exhibit 2? Does such a pattern of preferences necessarily lead to a cyclical majority?

14. (Majority Voting) Deciding an issue on the basis of majority vote assumes that everyone has an equal say in the outcome. How does this differ from using markets to allocate resources in private good production? What are the implications of these differences?

15. (Public Goods) One characteristic of many goods provided by the government is that they are nonrival in consumption, which means that they can be consumed simultaneously by all people in the consuming group (for example, national defense). Using efficiency as your criterion, what rule can you suggest for determining the optimal level of such goods to provide?

16. (Logrolling) Suppose that coalitions of people who vote for each other's projects do so because the combined benefit accruing to each coalition exceeds the tax costs to each. If the benefits on the margin to the winning coalition equal the costs on the margin to that same coalition, on what basis would you conclude that spending exceeded the level that is socially optimal?

17. (Lobbying) The largest blocs of individuals affected by legislation are frequently the least represented in the lobbying process. Why do you suppose that this is true?

18. (Farm Subsidies) "To subsidize the price of milk or other agricultural products is not very expensive considering how many consumers there are in the United States. Therefore, there is little harmful effect from such subsidies." Evaluate this point of view.

19. (Farm Subsidies) Farm subsidy programs are likely to have a number of secondary or side effects in addition to the direct effect on dairy prices. What impact do you suppose such subsidies are likely to have on the following?
    a. Housing prices
    b. Technological change in the dairy industry
    c. The price of dairy product substitutes

20. (Farm Subsidies) Farming is often subsidized in other ways in addition to price supports. For example, land used for farming is frequently subject to a lower tax rate than it would be in some other use. The rationale offered is that farmers can't afford, on a cash-flow basis, to pay taxes on their land if it is valued at true market value for tax purposes. What's wrong with this argument? Could you devise a tax system that wouldn't hurt a farmer's cash flow?

CHAPTER 31

EXTERNALITIES AND THE ENVIRONMENT

Example Ranked according to the amount of trash produced per person, the world's five top trash-producing cities are all in the United States: Los Angeles, Washington, D.C., Seattle, New York, and Cincinnati.

Toilets in Athens, Greece, flush directly into the Aegean Sea. The river at the port of Bilbao, Spain, is fouled from raw sewage and from 110 waste dumps. Breathing the air in Bombay, India, is reportedly equivalent to smoking ten cigarettes a day. In Mexico City those who can afford it buy oxygen in tanks to breathe in their homes. The air in Paris has more lead and carbon monoxide than that of any other major city in the world. The air in some U.S. cities is also dangerous, and in some areas the ground has been poisoned with toxic waste. The market revolution in Eastern Europe has uncovered the deplorable environmental conditions in many of those countries. In Poland, for example, half the bodies of water are reportedly too polluted even for industrial use, and what had been East Germany has been called an environmental disaster area. What does all this have to do with economics? Plenty.

Market prices can efficiently direct the allocation of resources only as long as property rights are well defined and can be easily enforced. But property rights to clean water, air, and soil, to peace and quiet, and to scenic vistas are hard to establish and enforce. This chapter will examine why it is difficult to assign property rights to some key resources, and why a lack of property rights results in inefficient use of these resources. The focus will be on how externalities affect resource allocation and on public policies to promote greater efficiency. As we know from Chapter 4, externalities may be either negative—for example, air pollution—or positive—for example, the general improvement in the civic climate that results from better education. This chapter will concentrate primarily on negative externalities. Topics discussed in this chapter include

- Private property rights
- Open-access resources
- The common pool problem
- Negative and positive externalities
- Marginal social cost and marginal social benefit
- The greenhouse effect
- The market for pollution permits
- The Coase theorem

Externalities and the Common Pool Problem

Private property rights The right of an owner to use or to exchange property

In an economic system that allows for private property rights, specific individuals own the rights to a resource and have an abiding interest in using that resource efficiently. For example, you own your clothes, your compact disk player, and your time. **Private property rights** allow individuals to control the use of certain resources now and in the future and to charge others for their use. Property rights are defined and enforced by government, by informal social actions, and by ethical norms. But not all resources are owned as private property, because specifying and enforcing some property rights is quite costly. For example, how could specific individuals claim and enforce a right to the air, to fish in the ocean, or to migrating birds? There are usually no individual property rights to such resources because an individual cannot easily exclude others from using the resource and cannot easily capture the value of the resource by "consuming" it all or selling it all. Thus, some resources are both *nonexcludable*—preventing someone from using the resource is extremely costly if not impossible—and *nonappropriable*—no individual can easily capture the value of the resource.

Renewable Resources

Renewable resource A resource that can regenerate itself and so can be used periodically for an indefinite length of time

A resource may be defined as **renewable** if periodic use of it can be continued indefinitely. Thus, fish are a renewable resource if the amount taken does not jeopardize each species's ability to sustain itself. Timber is a renewable resource because felled trees can be replanted at rates that provide a steady supply. The atmosphere and rivers are renewable resources to the extent that they can absorb pollutants and/or neutralize them. More generally, biological resources such as fish, game, forests, rivers, grasslands, and agricultural soil are renewable if they are shepherded appropriately.

Open-access resource A type of resource that is difficult or costly to exclude individuals from using

Common pool problem The problem that unrestricted access to a resource results in overuse until the net marginal value of additional use drops to zero

Some renewable resources are **open-access resources**, meaning that it is difficult or costly to exclude individuals from using the resource. Open-access resources are often subject to the **common pool problem**: open-access resources tend to be overused or overharvested. Because the atmosphere is an open-access resource, producers tend to use the air as a dump for gases that are unwanted by-products of their production processes. Air pollution is a negative externality imposed by polluters on society. As noted in Chapter 4, *negative externalities* are unpriced by-products of production or consumption that impose costs on other consumers or other firms. For example, some spray cans release fluorocarbons into the atmosphere; these gases

Example Preventing poaching of wild animals in the United States is very expensive (that is, wild animals are a nonexcludable resource). Poaching is second only to the drug trade in illegal profits. Property rights to clean air are much harder to capture than property rights to land—land does not move, air does.

Point to Stress However, being renewable does not guarantee that a resource will be shepherded appropriately. The Worldwatch Institute estimates that air pollution cuts annual crop production in the United States by 5 to 10 percent.

are said to cause thinning of the ozone layer that protects us from the sun's ultraviolet rays. Carbon dioxide emissions and other gases are said to form a blanket that is trapping the sun's heat and causing global warming. And some scientists claim that the sulfur dioxide emitted from coal-fired power plants located primarily in the Midwest is responsible for the acid rain that is killing lakes and trees in the Northeast (though other scientists aren't so sure).

Pollution and other negative externalities arise because there are no practical, enforceable, private property rights to open-access resources, such as the air. Market prices usually fail to reflect the costs that negative externalities impose on society. For example, the cost of a can of hairspray powered by fluorocarbons does not reflect the effect of gas emissions on the ozone layer. The price you pay for gasoline does not reflect the costs imposed by the dirtier air and the traffic congestion your driving creates. And electric rates in the Midwest do not reflect the negative externalities, or *external costs*, that sulfur dioxide emissions impose on those downwind from power plants. Let's take a closer look at externalities and the production of electricity.

External Costs with Fixed Technology

Suppose the demand for electricity in the Midwest is depicted by *D* in Exhibit 1. Recall that demand reflects consumers' marginal benefit for each level of consumption. The horizontal curve reflects the *marginal private cost* of production incurred by electricity producers. If producers base their pricing and output decisions on their private marginal costs, the equilibrium quantity of electricity used per month is 50 million kilowatt hours and the equilibrium price is $0.10 per kilowatt hour. At that price and output level, the marginal private cost of production just equals the marginal benefit enjoyed by consumers of electricity.

But research suggests (though the issue is far from resolved) that the sulfur dioxide emitted by coal-fired power plants during the production of electricity mixes with moisture in the air to form sulfuric acid, which is carried by the prevailing winds and falls elsewhere as acid rain. Many argue that acid rain has killed lakes and forests and has corroded buildings, bridges, and other capital. Electricity production, therefore, involves not only the private marginal cost of the resources employed but also the external cost of using the atmosphere as a gas dump. Suppose that the marginal external cost imposed on the environment by the generation of electricity is $0.04 per kilowatt hour. If the only way of reducing the emission of sulfur is by reducing the output of electricity, then the relation between the production of electricity and the production of pollution is a fixed one. Thus, we say that pollution occurs with **fixed-production technology**.

Fixed-production technology Technology for which the relation between output and the generation of an externality is a fixed one; the only way to reduce the externality is to reduce the output

Marginal social cost The total of the marginal private cost and the marginal external cost of production or consumption

The marginal external cost of $0.04 per kilowatt hour is reflected by the vertical distance between the marginal private cost curve and the marginal social cost curve in Exhibit 1. The **marginal social cost** includes both the marginal private cost and the marginal external cost that production imposes on society. Because the marginal external cost is assumed to be constant, the two cost curves are parallel. Notice that at the private-sector equilibrium

Example The extreme mobility of the American buffalo made it impossible to assign enforceable private property rights, leading to the near-extinction of the species. Small herds of buffalo have been saved by fencing in their remaining range.

Point to Stress Consumption may also involve external costs—consider the creation of second-hand smoke by cigarette smokers or the impact on the fetus of the mother's use of drugs.

Point to Stress The relationship between marginal benefit and the demand curve was introduced in Chapter 19. The horizontal marginal cost curves indicate a constant-cost industry.

Teaching Tip Acid rain has been blamed more on coal-burning plants in the Midwest because the coal mined in that area has a higher sulfur content than coal mined and used in other areas in the United States. However, some scientists blame acid rain on nitrogen oxide, which comes from sources other than coal. The issue of acid rain has also caused controversy between the governments of Canada and the United States.

EXHIBIT 1

Negative Externalities: The Market for Electricity in the Midwest

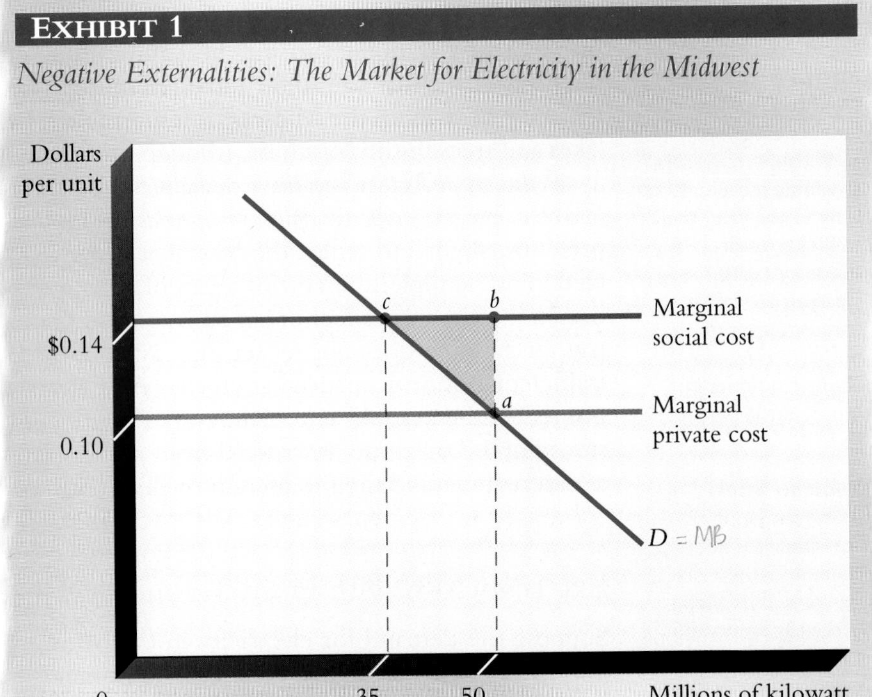

If producers base their output decisions on marginal private cost, 50 million kilowatt hours of electricity are produced per month. The marginal external cost of electricity production reflects the cost of pollution imposed on society. The marginal social cost curve includes both the marginal private cost and the marginal external cost. If producers base their output decisions on marginal social cost, only 35 million kilowatt hours are produced, which is the optimal level of output. The total social gain from basing production on marginal social cost is reflected by the blue triangle.

MC to Society > MB

output level of 50 million kilowatts, the marginal social cost, identified at point *b*, exceeds society's marginal benefit from that unit of electricity, identified at point *a* on the demand curve. The last kilowatt hour of electricity produced costs society $0.14 to produce but has a marginal benefit of only $0.10. Because the marginal cost to society exceeds the marginal benefit, the firm's choice of output results in a *market failure.* Too much electricity is produced.

The efficient level of output from society's point of view is where the demand, or marginal benefit, curve intersects the marginal social cost curve—a point identified as *c* in Exhibit 1. How could output be restricted to the socially efficient level of 35 million kilowatts? If government policy makers knew the demand curve and the marginal cost curves, they could simply require electric utilities to produce no more than the optimal level. Or they could impose on each unit of output a *pollution tax* equal to the marginal external cost of generating electricity. If correctly determined, such a tax would

Teaching Tip The marginal external cost always equals the vertical distance at each output level between the marginal private cost curve and the marginal social cost curve. If external costs rise as production rises, the vertical distance increases as output increases.

raise the industry supply curve up to the marginal social cost curve, so the marginal private cost of electricity would equal the marginal social cost. The externality would, in effect, be internalized.

With the appropriate tax, the equilibrium combination of price and output moves from point *a* to point *c*. The price rises from $0.10 to $0.14 per kilowatt hour, and output falls to 35 million kilowatts. Setting the tax equal to the marginal external cost results in a level of output that is socially efficient; at point *c*, the marginal social cost of production equals the marginal benefit.

Teaching Tip A market failure also occurs if at equilibrium the marginal benefit to society exceeds the marginal cost—see the discussion of positive externalities later in this chapter.

Notice that pollution is not eliminated at point *c*, but the utilities no longer generate electricity whose marginal social cost exceeds its marginal benefit. The total social gain from reducing production to the socially optimal level of output is shown by the blue triangle in Exhibit 1. This triangle also measures the total social cost of ignoring the negative externalities in the production decision; it reflects the total amount by which the social cost exceeds the benefit of the good if 50 million kilowatts are produced. Though Exhibit 1 offers a tidy solution, the external costs of pollution often cannot be easily calculated or taxed. At times government intervention may result in more or less production than the optimal solution calls for.

External Costs with Variable Technology

Variable technology A technology whose externality can be reduced by altering the production process rather than simply by altering the rate of output

The above example assumes that the only way to reduce the total amount of pollution is to reduce output. But power companies can usually change their resource mixes to reduce emissions, particularly in the long run. Because pollution can be reduced by altering the way electricity is produced rather than simply altering the rate of output, these externalities are said to be produced under **variable technology**. To examine the optimal amount of pollution under variable technology, consider Exhibit 2. The horizontal axis measures the air quality. If all firms made their production decisions based simply on their marginal private cost, then little or no efforts to reduce air pollution would be undertaken, so air quality would be poor. Alternatively, if somehow all air pollution could be eliminated, air quality would be excellent.

On the cost side, air quality can be improved by adopting cleaner production technology. For example, coal-burning plants can be fitted with smoke "scrubbers" to reduce toxic emissions. But the production of cleaner air, like the production of other goods, is subject to increasing marginal cost. For example, cutting emissions of the largest particles may involve simply putting a screen over the smokestack, but eliminating successively finer particles requires more sophisticated and more expensive processes. Thus, the marginal social cost of cleaner air slopes upward, as shown in Exhibit 2.

Marginal social benefit The sum of the marginal private benefit and the marginal external benefit of production or consumption

The **marginal social benefit** curve reflects all the benefits society derives from improvements in air quality. When air quality is poor, an improvement can save lives and will be valued by society more than when air quality is good. Cleaner air, like other goods, has a declining marginal benefit to society. The marginal social benefit curve from cleaner air therefore slopes downward, as shown in Exhibit 2. The optimal level of air quality is found at

Example Because of problems associated with estimating the efficient tax and monitoring pollution, taxes have seldom been attempted. Although it also involved a small change in technology in the form of an additive, a situation involving what amounted to a tax occurred during the winter of 1992–1993. The EPA required service stations in thirty-nine urban areas that didn't meet carbon monoxide health standards to sell only a cleaner-burning gasoline that cost consumers more.

Teaching Tip If production is reduced below 35 million kilowatts, and therefore more pollution is eliminated, there would be unproduced units of electricity whose marginal benefit exceeded the marginal social cost.

Teaching Tip The total social cost of moving from A to A' is the area under the marginal social cost curve, or $acA'A$. The total social benefit is the area under the marginal social benefit curve, or $abA'A$.

EXHIBIT 2

The Optimal Level of Air Quality

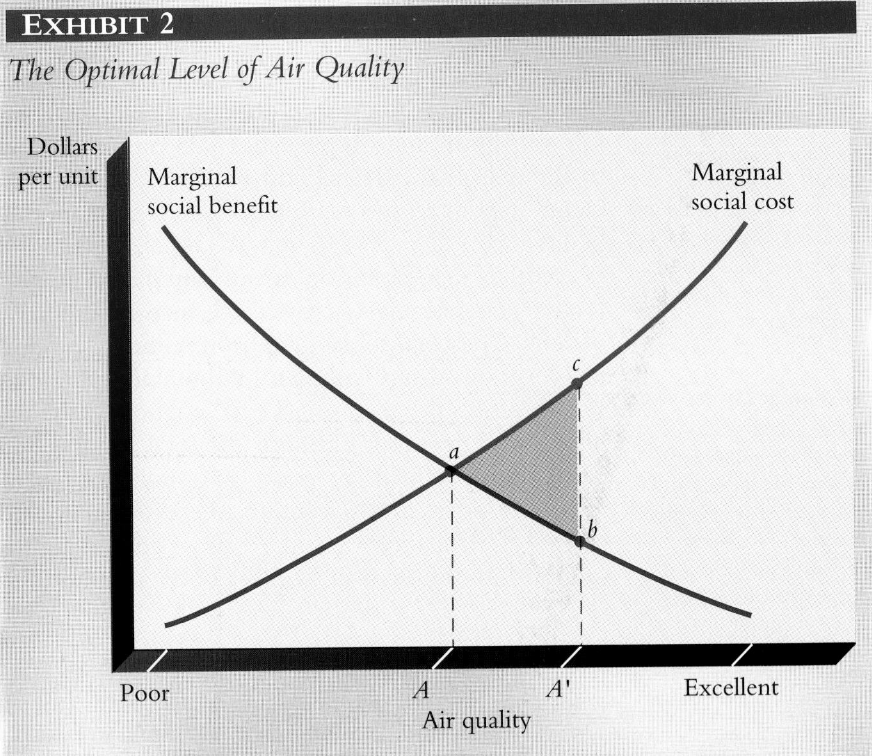

The optimal level of air quality is found at point *a*, where the marginal social cost of cleaner air equals its marginal social benefit. If some higher level of air quality were dictated by the government, the marginal social cost would exceed the marginal social benefit, and social waste would result. The total social waste resulting from a higher-than-optimal air quality is indicated by the red triangle.

point *a*, where the marginal social cost of cleaner air equals the marginal social benefit of that cleaner air. In this example the optimal level of air quality is A.

What if the government decreed that the level of air quality should exceed A? For example, suppose a law were passed setting A' as the minimum acceptable level. The marginal social cost, *c*, of achieving that level of air quality exceeds the marginal social benefit, identified as *b*. The total social waste associated with dictating a higher-than-optimal level of air quality is represented by the red triangle, *abc*. This is the total amount by which the social costs of cleaner air (associated with a move from A to A') exceed the social benefits.

The idea that all pollution should be eliminated is a popular misconception. If pollution occurs with fixed technology, completely eliminating that pollution would require that output be reduced to zero. Completely eliminating carbon dioxide emissions would require that everyone stop breathing. Even with variable technology, some pollution is consistent with efficiency. *Improving air quality benefits society as a whole as long as the marginal benefit of cleaner air exceeds its marginal cost.*

Example As many infections, such as tuberculosis, become resistant to existing antibiotics, researchers are turning to microorganisms in the sea as a new source for drugs to fight infections and cancer—research that increases the potential benefit of reducing ocean pollution.

Consider what would happen to the optimal level of air quality if either the marginal cost or the marginal benefit of cleaner air changed. Suppose, for example, that some technological breakthrough allowed producers to remove harmful emissions from the air more cheaply. As shown in panel (a) of Exhibit 3, the marginal cost of reducing pollution would fall to MSC' thereby increasing the optimal level of air quality from A to A'. The simple logic is that *the lower the cost of reducing pollution, other things constant, the greater the optimal level of air quality.*

An increase in the marginal benefit of air quality would have a similar effect. For example, what if we discovered that cleaner air reduced the incidence of certain types of cancer? The marginal benefit of cleaner air would increase, as reflected in panel (b) of Exhibit 3 by a shift up in the marginal benefit curve to MSB'. As a result, the optimal level of air quality would increase. *The greater the benefit of cleaner air, other things constant, the greater the optimal level of air quality.* We actually know very little about the health effects of various types of pollution. As medical science advances and our knowledge of pollution effects grows clearer, the perceived marginal benefits of pollution reduction will shift accordingly.

Resolving the Common Pool Problem

Because property rights do not attach to open-access resources, individual exploiters of fresh air, clean water, wildlife, and other open-access renewable resources tend to ignore the effects of their activities on the resources' ability to renew themselves. As stocks diminish from overuse or overharvesting, a resource grows more scarce. For example, lack of regulation in the fishing industry allowed years of massive harvesting of the ocean's bounty, which has depleted the stock of fish.

Example In 1992, a chemist at the University of Wyoming announced the development of a high-frequency microwave technology to transform sulfur dioxide into by-products that could be used to treat waste water and clean toxic gases. It was expected to cost $250 per kilowatt to install this microwave technology in a 1-megawatt plant (that is, $250,000 versus the millions of dollars required to install conventional smokestack scrubbers) and the new technology was expected to eliminate a significantly greater percentage of the sulfur dioxide.

The common pool problem of resource exploitation can be reduced if some central authority imposes restrictions on resource use. By imposing an appropriate removal, or depletion, tax or by restricting output, a regulatory authority can force competitive firms to use the resource at a rate that is socially optimal. For example, in the face of the tendency to overfish and to catch fish before they are sufficiently mature, the government has imposed a variety of restrictions on the fishing industry. There are limits on the total amount of the catch, on the size of fish that can be caught, on the duration of the fishing season, on the kind of equipment used, and on other aspects of the business.

More generally, *when imposing and enforcing private property rights would be too costly, government regulations may improve allocative efficency.* For example, stop signs allocate the scarce road space at a traffic intersection, minimum-size restrictions control lobster fishing, hunting seasons control the stock of game, and official study hours may calm the din in the dormitory during certain hours.

But not all regulations are equally efficient. For example, to prevent the extinction of fishing regions, fishing authorities sometimes limit the *total* industry catch and allow all firms to fish until that total is reached. Consequently, when the fishing season opens, there is a mad scramble to catch as much as possible before the industry limit is reached. Firms make no effort to

EXHIBIT 3

Effect of Changes in Costs and Benefits on the Optimal Level of Air Quality

(a) Lower cost of air quality

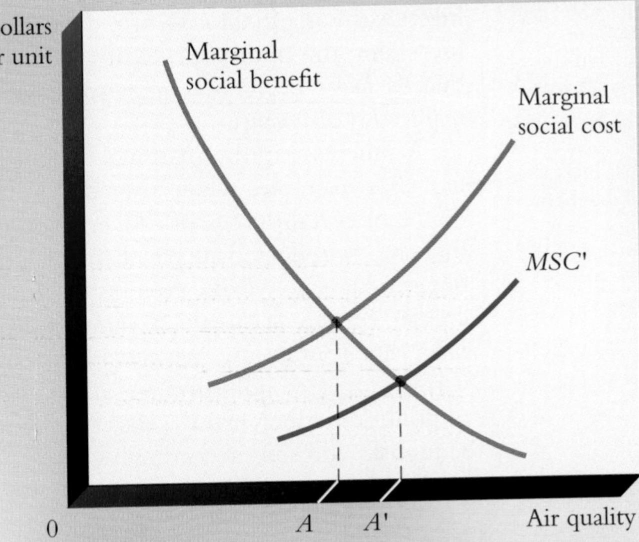

(b) Higher benefits of air quality

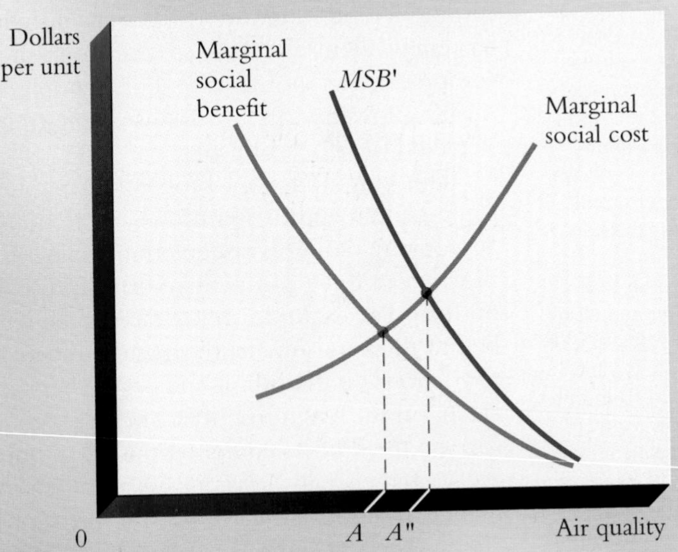

Either a reduction in the marginal social cost of cleaner air, as shown in panel (a), or an increase in the marginal social benefit of cleaner air, as shown in panel (b), will increase the optimal level of air quality.

fish selectively, since time is of the essence. And the catch reaches processors all at once, creating a problem for all segments of the industry. Also, each firm has an incentive to expand its fishing fleet to catch more in those few weeks. Thus, large fleets of technologically efficient fishing vessels sit in port for most of the year, except during the beginning of the fishing season. Each firm is acting rationally, but the collective effect of the regulation is grossly inefficient in terms of social welfare. Fishing authorities are gradually moving to a quota system that promotes a more efficient allocation of resources.

The Greenhouse Effect

As we have said, the difficulty of preventing use of open-access resources encourages polluters to use the air, water, and land as waste dumps. For example, the carbon dioxide content of the atmosphere is on the rise, primarily as the result of burning fossil fuels in power plants, homes, and automobiles. Worldwide, carbon dioxide emissions from burning fossil fuels average about one ton per person per year. In the United States, the figure is about five tons per person per year.

Carbon dioxide and other gases form a blanket around the globe, preventing solar heat from escaping and thus causing heat to build up. The gases act like the glass in a greenhouse—hence the expression **greenhouse effect**. The greenhouse effect is said to be causing the earth's atmospheric temperature to rise. Although the issue is still hotly debated, some experts believe that the earth's overall temperature will rise 3 to 8 degrees Fahrenheit by the middle of the next century. Because of the resulting expansion of the ocean as temperatures rise, sea levels will rise to flood coastlines. Ocean currents that dictate weather patterns will grow stronger. Thus, such a temperature rise could have a significant impact on weather systems and plant life.

Greenhouse effect The formation of a blanket of carbon dioxide and other gases around the earth, causing heat buildup

The atmosphere has the ability to cleanse itself of a certain level of emissions, but other global events have reduced this ability, as we see in the following case study.

CASE STUDY

Destruction of the Tropical Rain Forests

The tropical rain forests have been called "the lungs of the world" because they naturally recycle carbon dioxide by transforming it into oxygen and wood, thus helping to maintain the world's atmospheric balance. But the world's demand for timber products has caused loggers to cut down much of the tropical forest. Worse yet, farmers burn down these forests to create pastures and farmland. Burning the world's forests has a double-barreled effect. The loss of trees reduces the atmosphere's ability to cleanse itself, and the burning adds yet more harmful gases to the atmosphere. So both the loss of trees and the burning of forests contribute to the greenhouse effect. But the atmosphere is a common pool, so the costs of deforestation are imposed on people around the world.

Forest acreage throughout the world has declined by 15 percent over the last decade, and the rate of decline is now accelerating. The amount of Amazon jungle that has been cleared in the last decade is equal to an area the size of

Example There are a few examples in history of situations in which assigning private property rights eliminated the common pool problem. Commonly held grazing pastures in sixteenth-century England were generally overgrazed until the enclosure movement, during which authorities fenced in the pastures and established private property rights so owners could prevent overgrazing.

Teaching Tip According to the Organization for Economic Cooperation and Development, the United States is twice as energy-intensive as Japan or Germany.

Example The anti-cancer chemical taxol is extracted from the bark of Pacific yew trees. Prostratin, a compound that may be able to protect cells against the AIDS virus, comes from trees in the rain forest of Western Samoa.

France. In Central America the forests have been cleared for cattle ranches. Haiti is now a treeless wasteland, and once-lush El Salvador is a semi-desert. At current rates of destruction, no forests will be left in Central America by 1995. Commercial logging has been so extensive in the African countries of Ghana and the Ivory Coast that the business is already winding down, leaving behind poverty and devastation. According to the World Bank, two-thirds of the countries that export tropical forest products will be out of trees in a decade.

The loss of the tropical forests causes other negative externalities as well. As long as the tropical forest has its canopy of trees, it remains a rich, genetically diverse ecosystem. Tropical forests cover only 6 percent of the earth's land surface (down from 12 percent fifty years ago), but they contain *half* of the world's species of plants and animals, thus representing an abundant source of fruits, crops, and medicines. One-fourth of the prescription drugs used in the United States are derived from tropical plants. Scientists recently discovered that the seeds of a certain tropical plant may help cure some types of cancer. Biologists estimate that 50,000 species are condemned to eventual extinction each year because of deforestation. Yet most tropical plants have not yet been tested for their medicinal properties.

Small-time farmers and wood gatherers and big-time lumber companies are stripping the tropical forests. Once the forests are cut down, the tropical soil is eroded by rains and baked by the sun and soon runs out of nutrients. Once the nutrients are lost, the system is not very resilient. It takes a century for a clearcut forest to return to its original state. The policy of cutting down everything in sight is of benefit only to loggers, who usually do not own the land and thus have little interest in its future.

The world's rain forests are located in countries that tend to be relatively poor: Brazil, Zaire, Peru, Indonesia, and the Philippines. Environmental quality is a normal good, meaning that as incomes rise the demand for it increases. In very poor countries the priority is not environmental quality but food and shelter. Brazil and other developing countries are destroying their forests to provide jobs. But since the soil quickly loses its nutrients to erosion and the sun, few settlers have become successful farmers.

Sources: "Exotic Herb May Speed Colon Cancer Detection," *Wall Street Journal,* 27 July 1989; "Playing with Fire," *Time,* 18 September 1989, pp. 76–85; and Vernon Loeb, "The Lungs of the Earth Are Dying," *Orlando Sentinel,* 2 June 1992.

Example The Worldwatch Institute estimates that the world's farmers are losing about 24 billion tons of topsoil per year.

The tropical rain forests, by serving as lungs of the world, confer benefits around the globe. But the positive effects that the trees have on the atmosphere tend to be ignored in the decision to clear the land. Worse yet, the taking of timber is often "first come, first served," and government investment programs often subsidize the harvesting of timber. *It is not the greed of peasants and timber companies that leads to inefficient, or wasteful, uses of resource, but the fact that the atmosphere is an open access resource that can be degraded at little personal cost to those who clear the forests.* Government programs that encouraged selective cutting and replanting would allow the forest to remain an air filter and a renewable source of forest products.

The Coase Analysis of Externalities

In the traditional analysis of externalities, it is assumed that market failures arise because people ignore the external effects of their actions. Suppose a laboratory that tests delicate equipment is located next to a manufacturer of heavy machinery, and the vibrations caused by the manufacturing process throw off the delicate machinery in the lab next door. Professor Ronald Coase, who won the Nobel Prize in 1991, would point out that the negative externality in this case is not imposed by the machinery producer on the testing lab—rather, it *arises from the incompatible activities of the two parties.* The externality is the result both of vibrations created by the factory *and* of the location of the testing lab next door. One efficient solution to this externality problem might be to modify the machines in the factory; others might be to make the equipment in the testing lab more shock resistant or to move the lab elsewhere.

Teaching Tip Similarly, the controversial acid rain externality results from a conflict between the activities of power-generating plants in the Midwest that use high-sulfur-content coal and the fact that people live in the Northeast.

According to Coase, the most efficient solution to an externality problem depends on which party can avoid the problem at the lower cost. Suppose the factory has determined that it would cost $2 million to reduce vibrations enough to allow the lab to function normally. For its part, the testing lab has concluded that it cannot alter its equipment to reduce the effects of the vibrations (it has fixed technology), so its only recourse would be to move the lab elsewhere at a cost of $1 million. Based on these costs, the efficient resolution to the externality problem is for the testing lab to relocate.

Teaching Tip The pollution tax example used earlier can be seen as a special case of the Coase theorem applied when the least-cost avoider of the problem is already known—it costs less to control emissions from power generators in the Midwest than to evacuate the Northeast. The solution does not result from a voluntary agreement, but it does internalize the external cost just as an agreement would.

Coase argued that if the government assigns property rights to one party or another, the two parties will agree on the efficient solution to an externality problem as long as transaction costs are low and as long as the income effects associated with the assignment of property rights are relatively small. This efficient solution will be achieved regardless of which party is assigned the property right. Suppose the government awarded the testing lab the right to operate free of vibrations from next door, so the testing lab had the right to ask the factory to reduce its vibration. Rather than cut vibrations at a cost of $2 million, the factory could offer to pay the lab to relocate. Any payment by the factory that was greater than $1 million but less than $2 million would make both firms better off, since the lab would receive more than its moving cost and the factory would pay less than its cost of reducing vibrations. Thus, the lab would move, which is the efficient outcome.

Alternatively, suppose the factory was awarded the right to generate vibrations in its production process. For the factory, this would mean business as usual. The lab might consider paying the factory to alter its production method, but since the minimum payment the factory would accept would be $2 million, the lab would rather move at a cost of $1 million. Thus, whether property rights were awarded to the lab or to the factory, the lab would move, which is the efficient outcome. The **Coase theorem** argues that as long as bargaining costs and income effects are small the assignment of property rights will generate an efficient solution to an externality problem regardless of which party is assigned the property rights. A particular assignment of property rights determines only who incurs the externality costs, not the efficient outcome.

Coase theorem The theory that as long as bargaining costs are small, an efficient solution to the problem of externalities will be achieved by assigning property rights

Inefficient outcomes do occur, however, when the transaction costs of arriving at a solution are high. For example, an airport located in a populated area may have difficulty negotiating with all the surrounding residents about noise levels. Or a power plant emitting sulfur dioxide would have trouble negotiating with the millions of people scattered across the downwind states. Or a would-be farmer contemplating clearing a portion of the tropical rain forest cannot negotiate with the millions of people affected by that decision. When the number of parties involved in the transaction gets large, the chance for a voluntary agreement grows small.

A Market for Pollution Rights

According to Coase, the assignment of property rights is often sufficient to resolve the market failure typically associated with externalities; further government intervention is not necessary. If pollution can be easily monitored and polluters easily identified, the government may be able to achieve an efficient solution to the problem of pollution simply by assigning the right to pollute. For example, firms that dump *effluents* into a river evidently value the ability to discharge their waste matter in this way; for them the river provides an inexpensive outlet for effluents that otherwise would have to be disposed of at greater cost. In fact, the river provides services just like other resources, and the demand for this effluent transportation system slopes downward, just like the demand for other resources.

The demand for the river as a discharge system is presented as D in Exhibit 4. The horizontal axis measures the amount of effluent dumped into the river per day, and the vertical axis measures firms' marginal benefits of disposing of their effluent in this way. The demand curve measures the marginal revenue product that comes from dumping in the river. With no restrictions on pollution—that is, if all are free to discharge their wastes into the river—the daily discharge rate can be found where the marginal benefit of discharging effluents goes to zero—that is, where the demand curve hits the horizontal axis, which is at output level Q in Exhibit 4. Dumping will continue as long as it yields some private marginal benefit. Thus, if dumping remains unregulated, the river must carry away whatever polluters choose to dump there.

Example Water experts claim that each country needs about 725 gallons a day of replenishable water supply per person.

The river, like the atmosphere and the soil, can absorb and neutralize a certain amount of pollution each day without deteriorating in quality. Suppose voters in the jurisdiction that encompasses the river make the public choice that the river should be clean enough for swimming and fishing. The maximum level of effluent discharge that is consistent with this quality is Q^* in Exhibit 4. Hence, if the river is to be preserved at the specified level of quality, the "supply" of the river as a discharge resource is fixed at S.

If polluters can be easily identified and monitored, government regulators can somehow allocate an amount of pollution permits equal to Q^*. If polluters are simply given these permits (that is, if the price of permits is zero), there is excess demand for them, since the quantity supplied is Q^* but the quantity demanded at a price of zero is Q. An alternative is to *sell* the speci-

EXHIBIT 4

Optimal Allocation of Pollution Rights

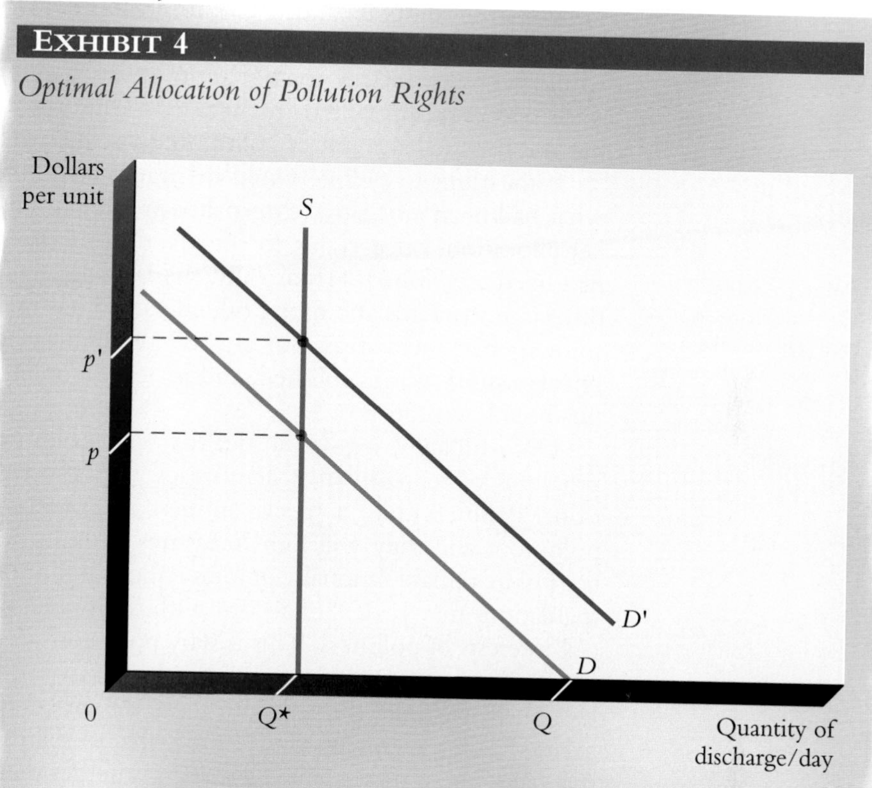

Suppose the demand for a river as an outlet for pollution is *D*. In the absence of any environmental controls, pollution will occur up to point *Q*, where the marginal benefit of further pollution equals zero. If regulatory authorities establish *Q** as the maximum allowable level of pollution and then sell the rights to pollution, the market for these pollution rights will clear at price *p*. If the demand for pollution rights increases to *D*′, the market-clearing price will rise to *p*′.

fied quantity of pollution permits at the market-clearing price. The intersection of the supply curve, *S*, and the demand curve, *D*, yields a permit price, *p*, which is the the marginal value of dumping quantity *Q** into the river each day. Selling the permits ensures that they go to the firms that value them most highly.

Teaching Tip Like the pollution tax and the voluntary agreements in the Coase theorem, the effluent fee causes the firm to internalize the external cost.

The beauty of this system is that only those producers that value the discharge rights the most will ultimately end up with them. Producers that attach a lower marginal value to river dumping obviously have cheaper ways of resolving their effluent problems, including changing their production functions to reduce their pollution. What's more, if conservation groups wished to maintain a higher river quality than was implied by the government's standard, they could purchase pollution permits but not exercise them.

What if new firms located along the river and wanted to discharge effluents? This additional demand for discharge rights is reflected in Exhibit 4 by the higher level of demand, D'. This greater demand would bid up the market price of pollution permits to p'. Regardless of the comings and goings of would-be polluters, the total quantity of discharge rights is restricted to $Q^\star$, so the river's quality will be maintained. Thus, the value of pollution permits, but not the total amount of pollution, may fluctuate over time.

Point to Stress The use of discharge standards fails to take into account that the costs of reducing discharges tends to vary widely among producers.

If the right to pollute could be granted, monitored, and enforced, then what had been a negative externality problem could be solved through market allocation, once rights to the river as an effluent transportation system had been established. Historically, the U.S. government has relied on setting discharge standards and fining offenders and has used pollution rights only in some metropolitan areas. But in 1989 a pollution rights market for fluorocarbon emissions was established, and in 1990 a pollution rights market for sulfur dioxide was proposed.[1]

Unfortunately, legislation dealing with pollution is affected by the same problems of representative democracy that affect other public policy questions. Polluters have a special interest in government proposals relating to pollution, and they will fight measures to limit pollution. But members of the public remain rationally ignorant about pollution legislation. So pollution regulations may be less in accord with the public interest than with the special interests of polluters. This is why pollution permits are usually given free to existing firms. Because firms thereby receive something of value, they are less likely to fight the institution of the program. Once the permits are granted, some recipients find it profitable to sell their permits to other firms that value them more. Thus, a market emerges that leads to an efficient allocation of pollution permits.

Positive Externalities

Example The activities of beekeepers and the owners of apple orchards have mutual positive externalities. The production of honey is stimulated by the apple blossoms; the pollination of apple blossoms is performed by the bees.

Until now we have considered only negative externalities. Externalities can sometimes be positive, or beneficial. *Positive externalities* are created when the unpriced by-product of consumption or production benefits other consumers or other firms. For example, people who get innoculated against a disease reduce their own likelihood of contracting the disease, but they also reduce the chance of transmitting the disease to others. Innoculations thus provide *external benefits* to others. Education also confers external benefits on society as a whole because those who acquire more education become better citizens, are better able to support themselves and their families, are more able to read road signs, and are less likely to require public assistance or to resort to crime for income.

The effect of external benefits on the optimal level of consumption is illustrated in Exhibit 5, which presents the supply and demand for education. The demand curve, D, represents the private demand for education, which reflects the *marginal private benefit* obtained by those who acquire the education. More education is demanded at a lower price than at a higher price.

1. See Dick Thompson, "Giving Greed a Chance," *Time,* 12 February 1990.

Teaching Tip The total increase in social benefit in moving from E to E' is the area under the marginal social benefit curve. The total increase in cost is the area under the supply curve. The blue triangle represents the difference between the two areas.

EXHIBIT 5

Education and Positive Externalities

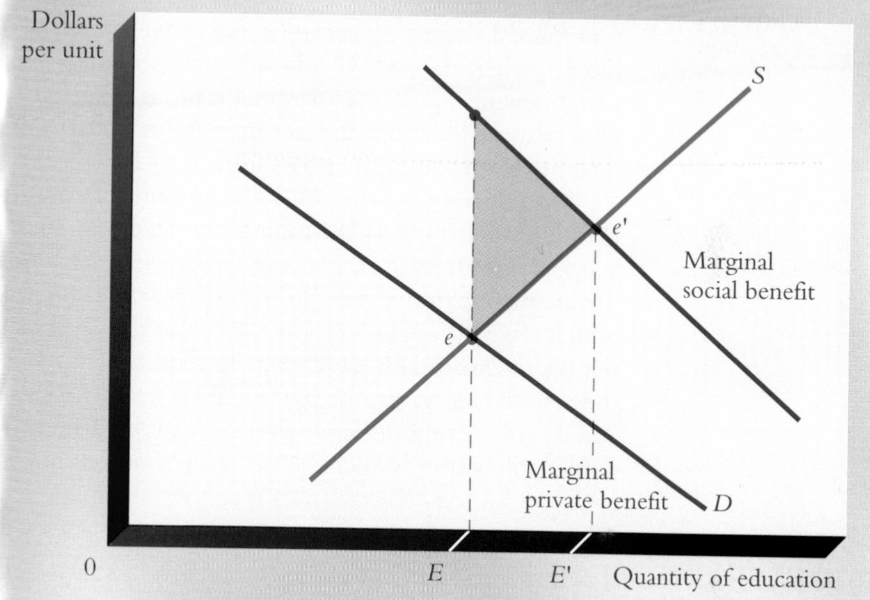

In the absence of government intervention, the quantity of education demanded is E, at which the marginal cost equals the marginal private benefit of education. However, education also conveys a positive externality on the rest of society, so the marginal social benefit exceeds the private benefit. At quantity E, the marginal social benefit exceeds the marginal cost, so more education is in society's best interest. In such a situation, government will try to encourage an increase in the quantity of education to E', at which point the marginal cost equals the marginal social benefit.

Point to Stress The marginal external benefit at each consumption level equals the vertical distance between the private demand curve and the marginal social benefit curve.

The benefits of education, however, spill over to others in society. If we add these positive externalities, or the *marginal external benefit*, to the marginal private benefit of education, we get the marginal social benefit of education. The marginal social benefit includes all the benefit society derives from education. The marginal social benefit curve appears above the private demand curve in Exhibit 5. At each level of education, the marginal social benefit exceeds the marginal private benefit by the marginal external benefit generated by that particular unit of education.

If determining how much education to acquire were a strictly private decision, the amount purchased would be determined by the intersection of the private demand curve, D, with the supply curve, S. The supply curve reflects the marginal cost of producing each unit of the good. This intersection, identified as point e in Exhibit 5, yields education level E, where the marginal cost of education equals the marginal private benefit.

Teaching Tip In perfect competition, the supply curve equals the marginal cost curve rising above the average variable cost curve.

But is E the optimal level of education from the society's point of view? What if one more unit of education were produced? The marginal social benefit of producing an additional unit of education exceeds the marginal cost, so net social welfare increases when education is expanded beyond E. *As long as the marginal social benefit of education exceeds its marginal cost, social welfare is increased by expanding education.* Social welfare is maximized at point e' in Exhibit 5, where E' units of education are provided—that is, where the marginal social benefit equals the marginal cost, as reflected by the supply curve. The blue triangle identifies the net increase in social welfare that results when the quantity of education increases from E to E'.

Thus, society is better off if the amount of education provided exceeds the private equilibrium. *When positive externalities are present, decisions based on private marginal benefits result in less than the socially optimal quantity of the good.* Hence, like negative externalities, positive externalities typically point to *market failure*, which is why government often gets into the act. For example, government attempts to encourage education by requiring students to stay in school until they are sixteen years old, by providing free primary and secondary education, and by subsidizing public higher education. When there are external benefits, public policy tries to increase the level of output beyond the private optimum.

Environmental Protection in the United States

Federal efforts to clean up the environment are coordinated by the *Environmental Protection Agency* (*EPA*). Four federal laws and subsequent amendments underpin federal efforts to protect the environment: the Clean Air Act of 1970, the Clean Water Act of 1972, the Resource Conservation and Recovery Act of 1976, which governs solid waste disposal, and the *Superfund* law, a 1980 law focusing on toxic waste dumps. In 1970, EPA had about 4,000 employees and a budget of $200 million. By 1992, EPA had about 18,000 employees and a budget of $4.5 billion.

According to EPA estimates, compliance with pollution-control regulations cost U.S. producers and consumers $115 billion in 1990, or 2 percent of GDP.[2] We can divide pollution abatement spending into three main categories: spending for air pollution abatement, spending for water pollution abatement, and spending for solid waste disposal. About 40 percent of the pollution abatement expenditures in the United States go toward cleaner air, another 40 percent go toward cleaner water, and 20 percent go toward disposing of solid waste. In this section we will consider, in turn, air pollution, water pollution, Superfund activities, and disposing of solid waste.

2. Other research estimates that clean air and clean water regulations reduced GDP in 1990 by about 6 percent below what it would have been in the absence of such regulations. See Michael Hazilla and Raymond Kopp, "Social Cost of Environmental Quality Regulations: A General Equilibrium Analysis," *Journal of Political Economy* 98 (August 1990): 544–551.

Point to Stress Note that currently our GDP statistics include the cost of pollution control, but they do not include the value of a cleaner environment. Pollution controls lower our standard of living only if the marginal cost of the improved environment exceeds the marginal benefit.

Example State and federal regulations classify dry cleaning fluid as hazardous and require its proper disposal. The Clean Air Act also required dry cleaners to reduce the parts per million of solvent emissions, so they installed new and expensive equipment.

Air Pollution

In the Clean Air Act of 1970 and subsequent amendments, Congress set national standards for the amount of pollution that could be emitted into the atmosphere. Congress thereby recognized air as an economic resource, which, like other resources, has alternative uses. The air can be used, for example, as a source of life-giving oxygen, as a prism for viewing breathtaking vistas, or as a dump for carrying away unwanted soot and gases. The 1970 act gave Americans the right to breathe air of a certain quality and at the same time gave producers the right to emit certain specified pollutants into the air.

Smog is the most visible form of air pollution. Automobile emissions account for 40 percent of smog. Another 40 percent comes from consumer products, such as paint thinner and fluorocarbon sprays, dry cleaning solvents, and baker's yeast by-products. Only 15 percent comes from manufacturing. The 1970 Clean Air Act mandated a reduction of 90 percent in auto emissions, leaving it to the auto industry to achieve this target. At the time, auto manufacturers complained that the objective was impossible, but between 1970 and 1990 average emissions of lead fell 97 percent, carbon monoxide emissions fell 41 percent, and sulfur oxide emissions fell 25 percent. The 1990 amendment to the Clean Air Act requires a ten-million-ton reduction in sulfur emissions aimed at reducing acid rain. Although air pollution is still a problem, U.S. pollution levels are down on average since the 1970s. And U.S. air quality is relatively good compared to the air in some parts of the world, as discussed in the following case study.

CASE STUDY

City in the Clouds

Mexico City has a metropolitan population of twenty-one million, ranking it the second-largest city in the world. The population is expected to grow to thirty million by the end of the decade. With so many people, pollution problems abound. Many sewer pipes run directly into rivers; worse yet, about one-third of the population has no sewerage service at all. As a result, every day the air is polluted with about 600 tons of fecal dust. Moreover, the city's 3.5 million vehicles and tens of thousands of small, poorly regulated businesses add substantially to air pollution. For example, brick makers fire their kilns with sawdust soaked in fuel oil and old rubber tires—fuels that generate black, acrid smoke. In all, 12,000 tons of pollutants are released into the atmosphere each day. In 1992 the air quality was often in the range termed "very dangerous."

Mexico City's pollution problems are compounded by its geography and altitude. It is surrounded on three sides by mountains, so the wind that blows in from the north (the open side) traps pollution over the city. Even worse, the city's high altitude reduces the oxygen content of the atmosphere by about one-quarter. The combination of high pollution and low oxygen makes for unhealthy air. On average, the city's air pollution exceeds acceptable levels on four out of five days. Winter smog sends thousands to the city's hospitals with respiratory problems. Foreign countries advise their diplomats not to have babies while stationed there. Some foreigners who are stationed in Mexico City by their employers earn a 10-percent premium as hardship pay.

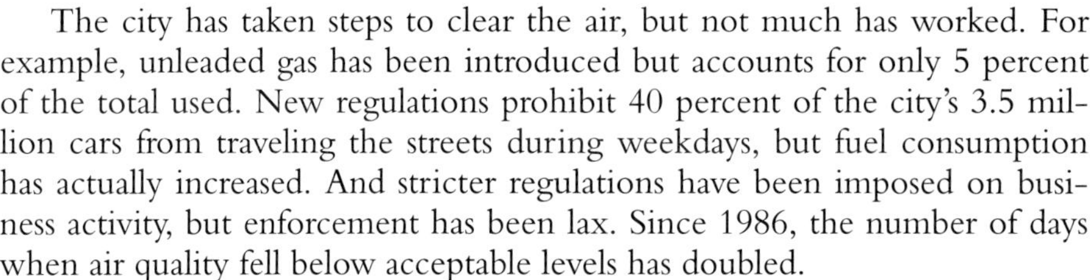

The city has taken steps to clear the air, but not much has worked. For example, unleaded gas has been introduced but accounts for only 5 percent of the total used. New regulations prohibit 40 percent of the city's 3.5 million cars from traveling the streets during weekdays, but fuel consumption has actually increased. And stricter regulations have been imposed on business activity, but enforcement has been lax. Since 1986, the number of days when air quality fell below acceptable levels has doubled.

Sources: Mark Uhlig, "Mexico City: The World's Foulest Air Grows Worse," *New York Times* 12 May 1991; and "Under a Cloud," *The Economist,* 4 April 1992.

Water Pollution

Two major sources of water pollution are sewage and chemicals. For many decades U.S. cities had an economic incentive to dump their sewage directly into waterways rather than incur the expense of cleaning it up first. Frequently, the current or tides would carry the effluent away to become someone else's problem. Although each community found it rational, based on a narrow view of the situation, to dump into the river or sea, the combined effect of these individual choices was polluted waterways. Thus, water pollution is a negative externality imposed by one community on other communities.

Most of the EPA's money over the years has gone to build sewage treatment plants. Real progress has been made in lessening sewage-related water pollution. Hundreds of once-polluted waterways have been cleaned up enough to permit swimming and fishing. The majority of U.S. cities now have modern sewage control. Notable exceptions include Boston, which still dumps sewage directly into Boston Harbor, and New York City, which teams up with New Jersey to dump raw sewage into the Atlantic Ocean, using a discharge point 106 miles off Cape May, New Jersey. At a huge cost, Boston is in the process of cleaning up its harbor. The typical residential water and sewer bill in Boston is projected to rise from $360 per year in 1990 to $1,620 per year in 2000.[3]

Example Recent studies of caves have shown that about 20 percent of the U.S. fresh water supply flows through the myriad cavities and pores of limestone karst, making the containment of a toxic spill almost impossible. Garbage that is dumped in a sinkhole can contaminate groundwater miles away.

Chemicals are another source of water pollution. Chemical pollution may conjure up an image of a chemical company dumping in the river, but only about 10 percent of water pollution comes from *point* pollution, which means pollution from factories and other fixed industrial sites. About two-thirds of the chemical pollutants in water come from what is called *nonpoint* pollution, derived mostly from runoff of pesticides and fertilizer from agriculture. Congress has been reluctant to limit the use of pesticides, though pesticides pollute water and contaminate food. Industrial America seems an easier target than Old MacDonald's farm.

3. See David Stipp, "Poor Pay a Big Price to Drink Clean Water," *Wall Street Journal,* 15 January 1992.

Teaching Tip Recall the capture theory of government regulation discussed in Chapter 29.

In 1970 Congress shifted control of pesticides from the U.S. Department of Agriculture to the newly formed EPA. But the EPA already had its hands full administering the Clean Water Act, so it turned pesticide regulation over to the states. Most states turned the job over to their departments of agriculture. But these state agencies tend to promote the interests of farmers, not to restrict what farmers can do. The EPA now reports that in most states pesticides have fouled the ground water. The EPA also argues that pesticide residues on food pose more health problems than do toxic waste dumps or air pollution. Though the facts remain in dispute, according to EPA estimates, some six thousand cancer deaths a year are caused by just one-third of the *approved* pesticides that have been tested. Over fifty thousand pesticides on the market today have never been tested for their long-term health effects.

Hazardous Waste and the Superfund

The U.S. synthetic chemical industry has flourished in the last forty years, and about fifty-five thousand chemicals are in common use. Some have harmful effects on humans and other living creatures. These chemicals can pose risks at every stage of their production, use, and disposal. New Jersey manufactures more toxic chemicals than any other state and, not surprisingly, has the worst toxic waste burden. Prior to 1980 the disposal of toxic waste created get-rich-quick opportunities for anyone who could rent or buy a few acres of land to open a toxic waste dump. One site in New Jersey took in 71 million gallons of hazardous chemicals between 1973 and 1976.[4]

Prior to 1980, once a company paid someone to haul away its hazardous waste, the company was no longer responsible. The Comprehensive Environmental Response, Compensation and Liability Act of 1980, known more popularly as the *Superfund* law, requires any company that generates, stores, *or* transports hazardous wastes to pay to clean up any wastes that are improperly disposed of. A producer or hauler that is the source of even one barrel of pollution dumped at a site can be held responsible for cleaning up the entire site.

Teaching Tip As seen in the analysis of a sales tax in Chapter 18, at least a portion of this tax on manufacturers will ultimately appear in the price of their products.

The Superfund law gives the federal government authority over sites contaminated with toxins. But to get an offending company to comply with its edicts, the EPA frequently must sue the company. So the process is slow, and over 80 percent of the Superfund budget, which is financed by a tax on manufacturers, has been spent on court costs and consultants' fees rather than on site cleanups. As of 1992, only 84 of the 1,245 sites designated for cleanup under the Superfund law had actually been cleaned up, though $11 billion has been spent. The law does not require that benefits exceed costs or even that such calculations be attempted.[5] A General Accounting Office study says that the number of cleanup sites could reach four thousand and the cost could

4. See Jason Zweig, "Real-Life Horror Story," *Forbes,* 12 December 1988.
5. For a fuller discussion of the costs and benefits of environmental protection, see Maureen L. Cropper and Wallace E. Oates, "Environmental Economics: A Survey," *Journal of Economic Literature* 30 (June 1992): 675–740.

reach $39 billion. An Office of Technology Assessment study suggests the site count could reach ten thousand and the cost could climb to $100 billion.

A recent EPA study concludes that the health hazards of Superfund sites have been vastly exaggerated. Chemicals in the ground often move very slowly, sometimes taking years to travel a few feet, so any possible health threat may be narrowly limited. In contrast, air pollution represents a more widespread threat because the air is so mobile and polluted air is taken into the lungs. Those who are neighbors of toxic waste sites know it and can exert political pressure to get something done. But those who may in the future develop some disease from air or water pollution do not know it now; thus, most people see no reason to press their elected officials for legislation that mandates clean air and clean water. Because of their greater media appeal and political urgency, toxic waste dumps tend to receive more attention than air or water pollution.

Solid Waste

Islip, Long Island, with little space left in its municipal landfill, piled 3,186 tons of garbage on a barge, hoping to dump it elsewhere. The barge wandered from port to port, but nowhere did people want the garbage in their backyard. After traveling six thousand miles, the barge returned to New York, where the garbage was burned and buried. The "barge to nowhere" illustrates another major environmental problem in the United States: how to dispose of the 200 million tons of garbage generated in this country each year. We generate about 4.3 pounds of garbage per resident per day in this country—more than double the quantity produced in 1960 and the largest amount per capita in the world. Much of our solid waste is packaging.

Example Paper makes up the biggest percentage of material contributed to landfills. About 39 percent of the paper and paperboard going into landfills and incinerators in 1992 came from packaging. Companies such as Unilever and Procter & Gamble reacted to the environmental movement by introducing superconcentrated versions of their laundry detergents that require smaller boxes.

Advanced economies produce more, so there is more to throw away. And because of higher incomes in advanced economies, the opportunity cost of time is higher, so there is a tendency to throw away items rather than fix or recycle them. A toaster that goes on the fritz, for example, is more likely to be sent to the dump than to the repair shop. It's cheaper to buy a new toaster for $30 than to pay up to $40 per hour to have it repaired, assuming you can find a repair shop. (Look up "Small Appliance Repair" in the Yellow Pages and see if you can find even one such repair shop in your area.)

About 75 percent of the nation's garbage is bulldozed and covered with soil in landfills. Not only are landfills an unsightly mess, but toxic materials deposited in landfills may leach into the soil, contaminating wells and aquifers. Therefore the prevailing attitude is NIMBY (Not In My Back Yard): everybody wants their garbage picked up but nobody wants it put down anywhere nearby.

As the cost of solid waste disposal accelerates, state and local governments are instituting economizing measures, such as requiring households to sort their trash, charging households by the pound for trash pickups, and requiring deposits on bottles. The number of recycling programs grew from 600 in 1989 to 3,500 in 1992. Only about 35 million of the 200 million tons of garbage generated annually in the United States is recycled. Seventy percent

Example In 1992, the EPA estimated the annual cost of disposing of solid waste in the United States at $30 billion and expected it to reach $75 billion by the year 2000.

of the recycled material consists of corrugated boxes, newspapers, and office paper. Much of the paper product is shipped to Korea and Taiwan, where it becomes packaging material for U.S. imports such as VCRs and compact disk players. About two out of three aluminun cans now get recycled.

Governments have tried to stimulate demand for recycled material, for example, by requiring newspapers to use a certain amount of recycled newsprint. Still, the increased supply of recycled material has outstripped the demand, so market prices in some cases have fallen. In fact, some recycled products have become worthless and must be hauled to the dump.[6]

About 15 million tons of garbage are burned each year, most in trash-to-energy plants, which generate electricity using the heat from incineration. Until recently such plants looked like the wave of the future, but a decline in energy prices, less favorable tax treatment in the 1986 tax reform act, and environmental concerns over the siting of incinerators have taken the steam out of the trash-to-energy movement.

Example A program started in Germany in 1992 will require manufacturers to collect 80 percent of their packaging waste by mid-1995.

So about 75 percent of our garbage goes to landfills, and only 25 percent is incinerated or recycled. In contrast, the Japanese recycle 40 percent of their waste and incinerate 33 percent, leaving only 27 percent to be deposited in landfills. Japanese households sort their trash into as many as twenty-one categories. Because land is more scarce in Japan—we know this because it costs relatively more there—it is not surprising that the Japanese deposit a smaller share of their garbage in landfills.

CONCLUSION

Over 5.5 billion people inhabit the globe, and the population increases by ninety million each year. The population is projected to double during the first half of the next century; 90 percent of this growth will occur in less developed countries, where most people barely eke out a living. Growing population pressure coupled with a lack of incentives to shepherd open-access resources results in denuded forests, dwindling fish stocks, and polluted air, land, and water.

Example In 1992, the Worldwatch Institute predicted that water scarcity would become the major environmental crisis of the 1990s.

Ironically, because of tighter pollution controls, developed countries tend to be less polluted than developing countries, where there is more pollution from what little industry there is. The air in places such as Mexico City and Lagos, Nigeria, is dangerous. Visitors to China's cities report rarely seeing the sun through the smoke and smog. People there cover their mouths with masks when the smog is especially thick. Farmers in Central America douse their crops with pesticides long banned in the United States. Most develop-

6. Frank Allen, "As Recycling Surges, Market for Materials Is Slow to Develop," *Wall Street Journal,* 17 January 1992.

ing countries have such profound economic problems that environmental quality is not high on their list of priorities.

Market prices can direct the allocation of resources only as long as property rights are well defined and can be enforced at low cost. Pollution of air, land, and water arises not so much from the greed of producers and consumers as from the fact that these open-access resources are subject to the common pool problem.

Summary

1. Private choices will result in too little output when positive externalities exist and too much output when negative externalities exist. Public policy should subsidize or otherwise promote the production of goods generating positive externalities and should tax or otherwise discourage the production of goods generating negative externalities.

2. The optimal amount of environmental quality occurs where the marginal social cost of higher quality equals its marginal social benefit. A decrease in the marginal cost or an increase in the marginal benefit of environmental quality increases the optimal level of environmental quality.

3. Some experts argue that the thermal blanket of carbon dioxide and other gases building up in the atmosphere causes the greenhouse effect. The world's tropical rain forests have served to recycle noxious gases and convert them into oxygen and wood; the destruction of these forests reduces the environment's ability to cleanse itself.

4. The Coase theorem argues that as long as bargaining costs and income effects are small, assigning property rights to one party leads to an efficient solution to the problem of externalities. An example of the Coase theorem in action is the market for pollution permits.

5. In the last two decades, progress has been made in cleaning up the nation's air and waterways. The air is cleaner because of stricter emissions standards for motor vehicles; the water is cleaner because of billions spent on sewage treatment facilities. Though much of the federal attention and federal budget goes toward cleaning up toxic waste dumps, this pollution source does not pose as great a health threat to the population as a whole as other forms of pollution such as smog and pesticides.

Questions and Problems

1. (Positive Externalities) Consider the situation illustrated in Exhibit 5, which generates external benefits. Show on the diagram the welfare (deadweight) loss associated with producing at the point where marginal private benefit equals supply instead of where marginal social benefit equals supply.

2. (Negative Externalities) Consider the situation illustrated in Exhibit 1, which generates a negative externality. If the government simply sets the price of electricity at the optimal level (that is, where the marginal social cost equals the demand), why is the net gain equal to triangle *abc* even though consumers now pay a higher price for electricity?

3. (Externalities) When students rent local housing, they often drive up rents in the neighborhood, causing a loss of utility to existing residents. Is this an externality? Explain.

4. (Coase Theorem) Suppose a firm pollutes a stream that has recreational value only when it is unpolluted. Why does the assignment of property rights to the stream lead to the same (efficient) level of pollution whether the firm or the recreational users own the stream?

5. (Efficiency Costs of Externalities) Use the data below to answer the following questions.

Quantity	*Marginal Private Benefit (Demand)*	*Marginal Private Cost (Supply)*	*Marginal Social Cost*
0	——	$ 0	$ 0
1	$10	2	4
2	9	3	5
3	8	4	6
4	7	5	7
5	6	6	8
6	5	7	9
7	4	8	10
8	3	9	11
9	2	10	12
10	1	11	13

a. What is the external cost per unit of production?
b. At what level will the economy produce if there is no regulation of the externality?
c. At what level should the economy produce to achieve economic efficiency?
d. Calculate the dollar value of the net gain to society from correcting the externality.

6. (Externalities and Economic Efficiency) Describe the specific externality, if any, created by each of the following, and discuss the implications of each for economic efficiency:
a. Crabbing in the Chesapeake Bay
b. Airport runway noise
c. Cloud seeding
d. Smoking on airplanes

7. (Education and Positive Externalities) Discuss the following proposition: "Education should be subsidized because society is better off when education consumption increases."

8. (Negative Externalities) Show why, in general, the optimal amount of a negative externality is not zero.

9. (Reduction of Negative Externalities) Suppose you wish to reduce a negative externality by imposing a tax on the activity that creates the externality. If the amount of the externality produced per unit of output increases as output increases, show how to determine the correct tax by using a supply-demand diagram.

10. (Public Goods) In a sense, a public good (one that, once produced, is available for all whether or not they pay) is an example of an externality. Explain.

11. (External Cost) Suppose that a factory locates in a residential neighborhood and creates an environment that is so unattractive that everyone leaves and the area around the factory is unoccupied. Since no one is around to bear the cost of the nuisance the factory produces, is there no longer any negative externality? Would your answer be different if the factory located in an area where no one lived to begin with?

12. (Correcting an Externality) In Exhibit 1, correction of the negative externality creates a *net* gain of area *abc*. If the correction is achieved by imposing a tax of 4 cents per kilowatt hour and the tax revenues are rebated back to electricity users, show the gains and losses (if any) that occur as a result of this correction. Can you think of any reason to rebate the tax revenues to those who bear the costs of the pollution (e.g., recreational lake and stream users in the eastern parts of the United States)?

13. (Open-Access Resources) Could sunlight be considered an example of an open-access resource? Why or why not?

14. (Externality) You and I may benefit from the existence of Yosemite National Park even if we never actually visit it. Is the benefit we reap therefore a positive externality?

15. (Air Quality Regulation) In amending the Clean Air Act in 1990, Congress outlined national air quality standards that were to be established by the Environmental Protection Agency without regard to cost considerations. What implicit assumption about benefits is being made by such a regulatory approach? Do the 1990 amendments mandating changes in the gasoline sold in the nation's nine smoggiest cities represent a change in thinking by federal government regulators?

16. (Tropical Rain Forests) Although the atmosphere is clearly an example of an open-access resource, trees are not. Why don't countries that have tropical rain forests simply establish and enforce property rights over their rain forests?

17. (Tropical Rain Forests) Why does a solution involving reduction in the demand for tropical forest lumber require some form of international cooperation?

18. (City in the Clouds) Which is more visible to the typical citizen of Mexico City, the benefits or costs associated with sources of air pollution?

19. (City in the Clouds) Although reduced life expectancy may be a consequence of the poor air quality in Mexico City, could it also contribute to the reluctance to set and enforce corrective regulatory action?

CHAPTER 32

INCOME DISTRIBUTION AND POVERTY

Income in a market economy depends primarily on the productivity of the household's resources. The problem with allocating income according to productivity is that some people have difficulty earning income. Those born with mental or physical disabilities tend to be less productive and may be unable to earn a living. Others may face limited job choices and reduced wages because of advanced age, a poor education, or discrimination in the marketplace. Still others may be unable to seek employment because they must care for small children.

In this chapter we will first examine the distribution of income in the United States, paying special attention to poverty in recent years. We will then discuss and evaluate the "social safety net"—public policies aimed at helping the poor. We will also consider the impact of the changing family structure on the incidence of poverty, focusing in particular on the increase in female householders. We will explore the effects of discrimination on the distribution of income and close the chapter by examining recent welfare reforms. Topics discussed in this chapter include

- Personal distribution of income
- Lorenz curve
- Official poverty level
- Public policy and poverty
- The feminization of poverty
- Poverty and discrimination
- Negative income tax
- Recent welfare reforms

THE DISTRIBUTION OF FAMILY INCOME

Point to Stress Each group represents 20 percent of all families, with the first group the poorest and the last group the richest. Cash transfers considered include items such as Aid to Families with Dependent Children.

The best way to consider the distribution of income in the economy is to focus on the family as an economic unit. After dividing the total number of families into five groups of equal size, ranked according to income, we can examine what percentage of income is received by each group. *Income is measured after cash transfer payments have been received but before taxes have been paid.* Such a division is presented in Exhibit 1 for various years since 1929. Take a moment to look this exhibit over. Notice that in 1929 families in the lowest, or poorest, fifth of the population received only 3.5 percent of the income, whereas families in the highest, or richest, fifth received 54.4 percent of the income. Thus, the richest 20 percent of the families received over half the income.

Notice also that the richest group's share of income dropped from 54.4 percent in 1929 to 43.0 percent in 1947. What caused this drop in the amount going to the top group? The Great Depression erased many personal fortunes, and World War II brought more people into the labor force and increased the average wage. Beginning with 1947 the data display a remarkable stability over the next three decades, with the share going to the lowest fifth hovering around 5 percent and the share to the highest fifth around 41 percent.

But data in recent years show a rising share of income going to the top fifth and a dwindling share to the bottom fifth. Specifically, in 1991, 44.2 percent of the money income went to the top fifth of families and 4.5 percent went to the bottom fifth. Thus, in 1991 the top fifth received nearly ten times more income than the bottom fifth. Again, income is measured after

EXHIBIT 1

The Distribution of Money Income Among Families for Selected Years Since 1929

	Percentage Share				
Year	**Lowest Fifth**	**Second-Lowest Fifth**	**Middle Fifth**	**Second-Highest Fifth**	**Highest Fifth**
1929	3.5%	9.0%	13.8%	19.3%	54.4%
1947	5.0	11.9	17.0	23.1	43.0
1957	5.1	12.7	18.1	23.8	40.4
1967	5.5	12.4	17.9	23.9	40.4
1977	5.2	11.6	17.5	24.2	41.5
1987	4.6	10.8	16.9	24.1	43.7
1991	4.5	10.7	16.6	24.1	44.2

Source: U.S. Bureau of the Census, *Current Population Reports,* series P-60, no. 180 (Washington, D.C.: U.S. Government Printing Office, 1992), Table B-7.

cash transfer payments are received but before taxes are paid. To give you some idea of the levels of income involved, the upper limit for families in the poorest 20 percent was $17,000 in 1991. The lower limit for families in the top 20 percent was $62,991—so many families in the top group would not be considered wealthy.

Other evidence tends to support the conclusion that the income going to those who were at the top increased during the 1980s. For example, a study by the Federal Reserve System found that the share of *wealth* held by the top 1 percent of families increased from 31 percent in 1983 to 37 percent in 1989. And the Census Bureau reported that the percentage of full-time workers whose wages would be below the poverty level (for a family of four) increased from 12 percent in 1979 to 18 percent in 1990.[1]

Why did income, when measured before taxes but after cash transfer payments, become more unevenly distributed during the 1980s? One possible explanation is that 1981 and 1986 reductions in marginal tax rates on personal income reduced the amount of income at the top that had been "hidden" or "sheltered." According to this argument, a reduction in the top marginal tax rate simply brought more income to the surface that had been there all along. Another possible explanation is that technological advances increased the returns to higher education during the 1980s. For example, half those in the top 20 percent based on income in 1991 had at least a college degree; in contrast, half of those in the poorest 20 percent had less than a ninth grade education. The returns to higher education did increase during the 1980s.

Example Harvard economist Lawrence Katz, after studying the results of a recent study, concluded that students can increase future income by 10 to 16 percent for each year they stay in school. Past estimates have been in the range of 9 to 11 percent.

Note that it is not necessarily the same families who remain rich or poor over time. Some families drop out of high income ranks and are replaced by others; likewise, some families work their way out of poverty to be replaced, for example, by a young unmarried woman who has a child. So we are not talking about the same families getting richer or poorer over time. Later in the chapter we will look more closely at the income dynamics over time and across families.

The distribution of income in the United States is similar to that in other developed countries throughout the world, including Canada, France, Germany, Great Britain, Japan, Italy, and Australia. Income in many developing countries, such as India, Brazil, Turkey, Mexico, and the Philippines, tends to be more unevenly distributed, with half or more of all income going to the richest 20 percent of the population.

Teaching Tip Income distribution in developing countries is discussed in more detail in Chapter 35.

The Lorenz Curve

The Lorenz curve is another way of picturing the distribution of income in an economy. As shown in Exhibit 2, the cumulative percentage of families is measured along the horizontal axis, and the cumulative percentage of income

1. Bureau of the Census, *Workers with Low Earnings: 1964 to 1990*, U.S. Dept. of Commerce, Current Population Reports, Series P-120, No. 178, 1992.

EXHIBIT 2

Lorenz Curves, 1929 and 1990

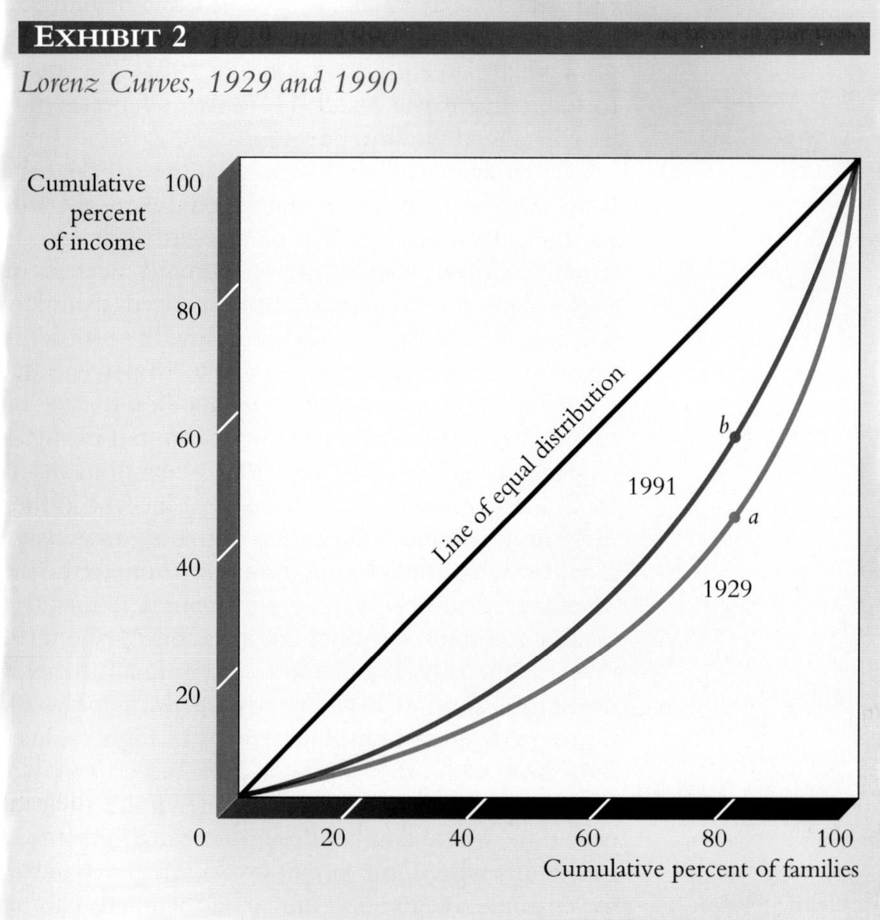

Teaching Tip At point *a* in Exhibit 2, for example, the cumulative percentage of income for the bottom 80 percent of households is

3.5%
9.0
13.8
+19.3
45.6%

according to the data in Exhibit 1.

Lorenz curve A curve showing the percentage of total income received by a given percentage of recipients whose incomes are arranged from smallest to largest

is measured along the vertical axis. The **Lorenz curve** shows the percentage of total income received by any given percentage of recipients when incomes are arrayed from smallest to largest.

Any given distribution of income can be compared to an equal distribution of income among families. If income were evenly distributed, the poorest 20 percent of the population would receive 20 percent of the total income, the poorest 40 percent of the population would receive 40 percent of the income, and so on. The Lorenz curve in this case would be a straight line with a slope equal to 1.0, as shown in Exhibit 2.

As the distribution becomes more uneven, the Lorenz curve is pulled down and to the right, away from the line of equal distribution. The Lorenz curves in Exhibit 2 were calculated for 1929 and 1991, based on the data in Exhibit 1. As a point of reference, point *a* on the 1929 Lorenz curve indicates that in that year the bottom 80 percent of families had 45.6 percent of the income and the top 20 percent had 54.4 percent of the income. Point *b* on the 1991 Lorenz curve shows that in that year the bottom 80 percent had 55.8 percent of the income; the income share of the top 20 percent was down to 44.2 percent. The Lorenz curve for 1991 is closer to

Teaching Tip The inequality of income may also be measured through the Gini coefficient. The Gini coefficient is the area between the equal-distribution line and the Lorenz curve divided by the area of the entire triangle under the equal-distribution line. If income is distributed with perfect equality, the Lorenz curve coincides with the equal-distribution line, and the coefficient is zero. If one family has all the income, the Lorenz curve coincides with the bottom horizontal and right vertical axes (the triangle), and the coefficient is one. The more equal the distribution, the smaller the coefficient.

Example The Heritage Foundation calculates that in-kind welfare transfers come to about $10,500 per family per year. Free public education is also an example of an in-kind transfer.

Median income The middle income in a series of incomes ranked from smallest to largest

Example After adjustment for inflation, median household income fell 3.5 percent between 1990 and 1991.

the center than the one for 1929; the shift indicates that the distribution of income among families has become more even.

One problem with examining income distributions is that there is no objective standard for evaluating them. The inference thus far is that a more equal distribution of income is more desirable, but is a perfectly even distribution most preferred? If not, then how uneven should the distribution be? For example, among major league baseball players, about 54 percent of the pay in 1992 went to 20 percent of the players.[2] So income among major league baseball players is more unevenly distributed than family income in the economy. Does this mean the economy as a whole is "fairer" than professional baseball?

Families receive income from two primary sources: resource earnings and transfer payments from the government. Exhibits 1 and 2 measure money income after cash transfers but before taxes. Thus, the distributions shown in Exhibits 1 and 2 omit the effects of taxes and of in-kind transfers, such as food stamps and free medical care for poor families. The tax system as a whole tends to be mildly progressive, so families with higher incomes pay a larger fraction of their incomes in taxes. In-kind transfers benefit the lowest-income groups the most. Consequently, if the representations of the distribution of income in Exhibits 1 and 2 incorporated the effects of taxes and in-kind transfers, the share of income going to the lower groups would increase, the share going to the higher groups would decrease, and income would be more evenly distributed.

Finally, the income distribution figures include only reported sources of income. If people receive payment "under the table" to evade taxes, or if they earn money through illegal activities, their actual income will exceed their reported income. The omission of unreported income will distort the data in the first two exhibits only if the unreported income as a percentage of total family income differs across income levels. For example, if people who appear to be poor based on official reports actually earn significant amounts of income they do not report, then the distribution of income will be more even than the official data indicate.

Why Do Family Incomes Differ?

The **median income** of all families is the middle income when incomes are ranked from lowest to highest. In any given year, half the families are above the median income and half are below it. In 1991 the median income among the 67.2 million families in the United States was $35,939. Since most income comes from selling labor, variations in family income stem primarily from differences in the number of workers in each family. Thus, *one reason family incomes differ is that the number of family members who are working differs.* For example, the median income for families with two

2. This statistic was computed by the author based on data on all salaries provided in Hal Bodley, "Baseball Salaries: Mets Are Leaders of Pact, *USA Today*, 2 April 1992.

earners is about 68 percent higher than for families with only one earner and nearly *three times* higher than for families with no earners.

Teaching Tip The nation's loss of high-paying manufacturing jobs has hurt the earnings of men without much education. According to the Urban Institute, achieving the middle-class dream now requires two wage earners in the family.

Incomes also differ for all the reasons labor income differs, such as differences in education, ability, job experience, and so on. Exhibit 3 links *education* and *age* to the year-round *median income* of males aged twenty-five years or older who worked full time in 1991. Age is measured on the horizontal axis and median money income on the vertical axis. The bottom, middle, and top lines reflect the median money income of those with less than a ninth grade education, with a high school diploma, and with a college education or more, respectively.

The relation between income and education is clear. At every age, those with more education earn more, on average. Age itself also has an important effect on income. As workers mature, they acquire valuable job experience, get promoted, and earn more. But unless a worker has a college degree or more, his income falls off between age sixty and seventy. Note in Exhibit 3 that the additional earnings from higher education are large at the outset and grow even larger as the workers get older. This suggests that college graduates, who are more likely doing mental work, are rewarded more for their job experience than are others, who are more likely doing physical work. And college graduates who continue to work remain productive even at age seventy.

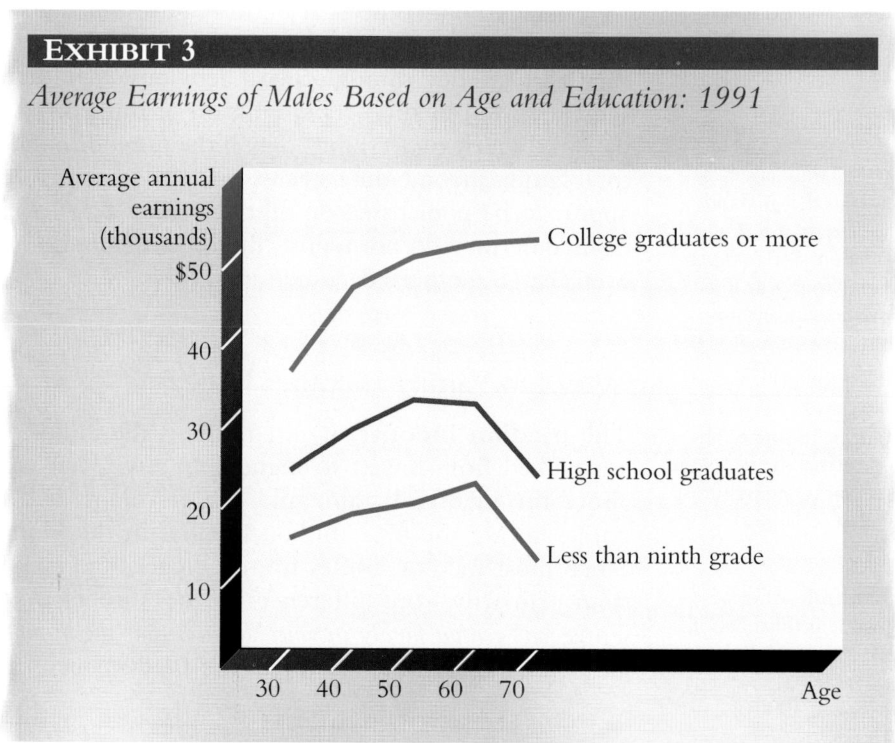

Source: U.S. Bureau of the Census, Current Population Reports, series P-60, no. 159 (Washington, D.C.: U.S. Government Printing Office, 1992).

Teaching Tip A U.S. Lorenz curve in which the distribution of income is adjusted for differences in age shows less inequality than the ordinary U.S. Lorenz curve.

Differences in earnings based on age and education reflect the normal *life-cycle* pattern of income. In fact, most income differences across households reflect the normal workings of resource markets, whereby workers are rewarded according to their marginal productivity. High-income families often consist of well-educated couples and both spouses are employed. Low-income families tend to be headed by single parents who are young, female, poorly educated, and not working. Low incomes are a matter of public concern, especially when children are involved, as we will see in the next section.

Poverty and the Poor

Since poverty is such a relative concept, how do we measure it objectively and how do we ensure that our measure can be applied with equal relevance over time? The federal government has developed a method for calculating an official poverty level; this level has become the benchmark for poverty analysis in the United States.

Official Poverty Level

To derive the official poverty level, the U.S. Department of Agriculture first estimates the cost of minimum food consumption requirements. Then, based on the assumption that the poor spend about one-third of their income on food, the official poverty level is calculated by multiplying these food costs by three. Adjustments are made for family size and for inflation over time. The official poverty threshold of money income for a family of four was $13,924 in 1991; families of four at or below that income threshold were regarded as living in poverty. Poverty thresholds in 1991 ranged from $6,932 for a person living alone to $27,942 for a family of nine or more members. The poverty definition is based on pre-tax money income, including cash transfers, but it does not include the value of noncash transfers such as food stamps, Medicaid, subsidized housing, or employer-provided health insurance.

Teaching Tip The definition of poverty also ignores holdings of personal property such as automobiles, homes, and household furniture.

Each year the Census Bureau conducts a survey comparing individual families' annual cash incomes to the annual poverty threshold applicable to that family. The percentage of the U.S. population below the official poverty level since 1959 is shown in Exhibit 4. The biggest decline in the rate of poverty came prior to 1970; *the poverty rate dropped from 22.4 percent in 1959 to 12.1 percent in 1969* (between points *a* and *b* in Exhibit 4). During that period the number of poor people as measured by the official government definition dropped from about 40 million to 24 million. The poverty rate bottomed out at 11.1 percent in 1973, fluctuated between 1973 and 1979, then rose between 1979 and 1983. After a six-year decline since 1983, the rate turned up in 1990 and was 14.2 percent in 1991. The 35.7 million people in

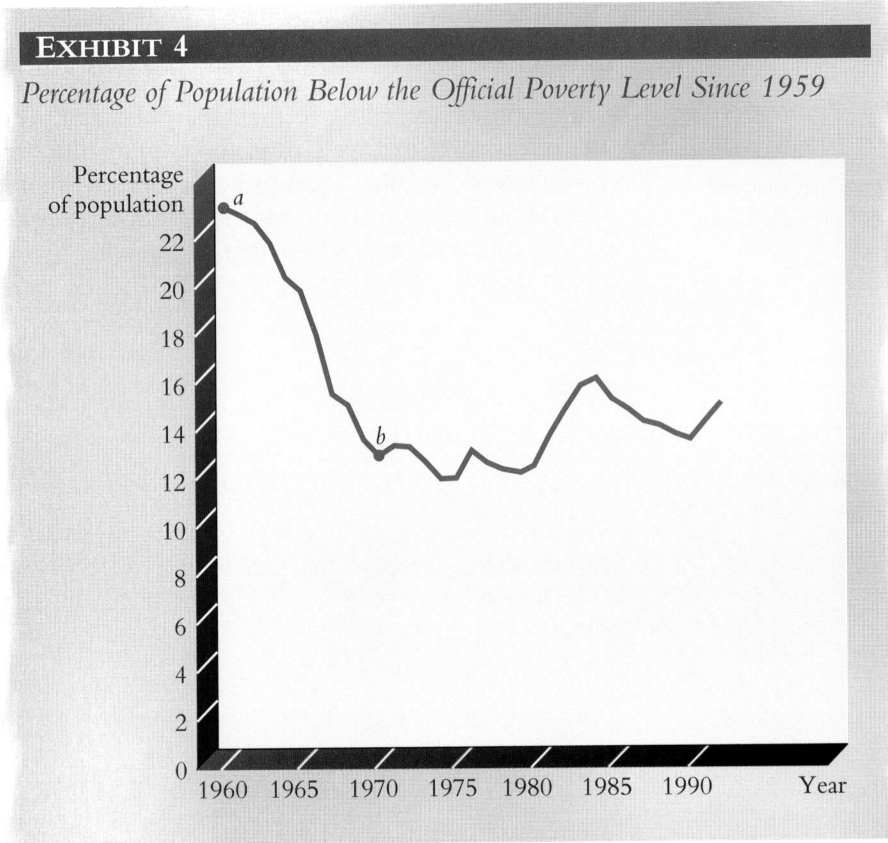

EXHIBIT 4

Percentage of Population Below the Official Poverty Level Since 1959

Source: U.S. Bureau of the Census, Current Population Reports, series P-60, no. 175 (Washington, D.C.: U.S. Government Printing Office, 1992).

Example According to the Heritage Foundation, the poor in the United States eat much more meat and have much more living space than the average-income person in Europe and Japan. Only 1.8 percent of U.S. poor lack an indoor toilet compared to 17 percent of average-income French and 54 percent of average-income Japanese.

poverty in 1991 represent the greatest number of poor in the United States since 1964.

Poverty is a relative term. If we examined the distribution of income across the countries of the world, we would find huge gaps between rich and poor nations. For example, the official U.S. poverty level of income is many times greater than the average income for three-fourths of the world's population.[3] Also, an income at the U.S. poverty level today provides a standard of living that would have been considered attractive by most people who lived in the United States at the turn of the century, when only 15 percent of families had flush toilets, only 3 percent had electricity, and only 1 percent had central heating.

---

3. See the World Bank, *World Development Report 1992* (New York: Oxford University Press, 1992), Table 1.

Public Policy and Poverty

Example In 1991 only 9 percent of the poor had year-round, full-time jobs.

What should the government's response to poverty be? Families with a full-time worker are nine times more likely to escape poverty than are families without any worker. Thus, the government's first line of defense in fighting poverty is to promote a healthy economy and to provide the education and training that enhance job opportunities. Yet even when the unemployment rate is relatively low, some people may remain poor because they lack marketable skills, must care for small children, or face discrimination in the labor market.

Programs to Help the Poor

Teaching Tip Lyndon Johnson's Great Society War on Poverty was declared in 1964.

Although some government programs to help the poor involve direct market intervention, such as minimum wage laws, the most visible programs redistribute income after the market has provided an initial distribution. Since the mid-1960s, social welfare expenditures at all levels of government have increased significantly. We can divide social welfare programs into two major categories: social insurance and income assistance.

SOCIAL INSURANCE. The social insurance system is designed to replace the lost income of those who worked but are now retired, temporarily unemployed, or unable to work because of total disability or work-related injury. By far the major social insurance program is *Social Security*, established during the Great Depression of the 1930s to provide retirement income to those with a work history and a record of contributing to the program. Medicare, another social insurance program, provides health insurance for short-term medical care for those aged sixty-five and older, regardless of income. Other social insurance programs include unemployment insurance and worker's compensation, both of which require beneficiaries to have a prior record of employment.

Teaching Tip Social Security benefits have risen automatically each year since 1975, keeping pace with the annual inflation rate. The annual increase for 1992 was 3.0 percent.

The social insurance system deducts what may be thought of as insurance premiums from workers' pay to provide retirement benefits, disability, or unemployment. These programs protect some families from poverty, particularly the elderly receiving Social Security, but they are aimed more at those with a work history. Still, the social insurance system tends to redistribute income from rich to poor and from young to old. Most Social Security beneficiaries receive far more in benefits than they paid into the program, especially those with a work history of low wages.

Means-tested program A benefit program that requires that recipients' incomes and/or assets be less than specified levels

INCOME ASSISTANCE. Income assistance programs—what we usually call "welfare"—provide money and in-kind assistance to the poor. Unlike social insurance programs, income assistance programs do not require the recipient to have worked or to have contributed to the program. Income assistance programs are means tested. In a **means-tested program**, a household's income and/or assets must be below a certain level to qualify for ben-

EXHIBIT 5

Antipoverty Expenditures by Program and by Level of Government: 1990 (billions of dollars)

	Source			
Program	**Federal**	**State and Local**	**Total**	**Percent of Expenditures**
Cash Transfers	**$ 26.0**	**$16.4**	**$ 42.4**	**26.5%**
AFDC	10.1	9.7	19.8	12.4
SSI	11.5	3.6	15.1	9.4
Earned Income Tax Credit	4.4	—	4.4	2.7
General Assistance	—	3.1	3.1	2.0
Medical Care	**41.1**	**35.7**	**76.8**	**48.0**
Medicaid	41.1	31.0	72.1	45.1
General Assistance	—	4.7	4.7	2.9
Food Assistance	**22.2**	**1.2**	**23.4**	**14.6**
Food Stamps	15.0	1.2	16.2	10.1
School lunch program	5.0	—	5.0	3.1
Other food programs	2.2	—	2.2	1.4
Housing Assistance	**15.9**	**—**	**15.9**	**9.9**
Energy Assistance	**1.3**	**0.1**	**1.4**	**1.0**
Total Expenditures	**106.5**	**53.4**	**159.9**	**100.0**
Percent of spending by government level	66.6%	33.4%	100.0%	

Source: Developed from data found in *Economic Report of the President,* February, 1992, Table 4-1.

efits. People who qualify for assistance are *entitled* to the program; hence these programs are sometimes called *entitlement programs.* The major cash transfer and in-kind transfer programs are listed in Exhibit 5. As you can see, the federal government funds two-thirds of welfare spending and state and local governments one-third. Nearly half of all welfare spending goes for medical care.

Example According to the Congressional Research Service of the Library of Congress, the government has spent an inflation-adjusted $3.6 trillion on poverty programs since 1966.

The two primary *cash transfer* programs are *Aid to Families with Dependent Children* (*AFDC*), which provides cash to poor families with dependent children, and *Supplemental Security Income* (*SSI*), which provides cash to the indigent elderly and the totally disabled. Cash transfers vary inversely with family income from other sources. AFDC began during the Great Depression and was originally aimed at providing support for widows with young children. The cost is divided between the state and federal governments, with the federal government paying a higher fraction of the total in poorer states. In 1990, 12.2 million people received monthly AFDC transfers averaging $396 per family. Because benefit levels are set by each state, they vary widely. For example, benefit levels in California are over five times larger, on average, than those in Alabama. Such differences may encourage some poor people to migrate to states where benefit levels are more attractive.

Teaching Tip As with Social Security benefits, SSI payments increase each year by an amount matching inflation. 1992 payments rose 3.0 percent.

The Supplemental Security Income program provides support for elderly and disabled poor. The federal portion of this program is uniform across states, but states can supplement federal aid. Monthly benefits averaged $279 per person in 1990 for the 4.8 million recipients. Benefit levels in California average nearly twice those in Alabama. Most states offer modest *General Assistance* aid to those who are poor but do not qualify for AFDC or SSI. The federal government also provides an *earned income tax credit* to the working poor with one or more children; the maximum amount available in 1990 was $953 per year. That year about 12 million workers received an earned income tax credit.

In addition to cash transfer programs, a variety of *in-kind transfer* programs provide health care (through Medicaid), food stamps, and housing assistance to the poor. *Medicaid* is by far the largest welfare program, costing nearly twice as much as all cash transfer programs combined. Medicaid has grown more than any other poverty program since 1980. It pays for medical care for those with incomes below a certain level who are aged, blind, disabled, or in families with dependent children. The qualifying level of income is set by each state, and some states are very strict. Therefore the proportion of poor covered by Medicaid varies greatly across states. In 1990 about twenty-five million individuals received Medicaid; payments averaged about $2,570 per person. Spending on the 3.2 million beneficiaries age sixty-five and older averages $6,720 per year; for many elderly, Medicaid pays for long-term nursing care. Some states also offer General Assistance to provide health care coverage to those who are poor but not eligible for Medicaid. Despite that fact that half the welfare budget goes for health care, about thirty-five million people had no health insurance in 1991. President Clinton promised during the presidential campaign to address health care problems.

Example According to the House Select Committee on Hunger, the average allotment of food stamps per meal is $0.70 per person. Public-assistance programs have failed to keep pace with a 50-percent increase in hunger in the United States since the mid-1980s. In reaction, an estimated fifty thousand food banks and soup kitchens now serve twenty million people per month, according to Bread for the World.

Food stamps are vouchers that can be redeemed for food. The program is aimed at reducing hunger and providing for proper nutrition in poor families. The cost is paid by the federal government, and benefits are uniform across states. In 1990, twenty million people received benefits in an average month, benefits that averaged $257 per month for a family of four. By 1992, because of sluggish economy and Hurricane Andrew, the number of recipients increased to twenty-six million; one in ten Americans was on food stamps.

Housing assistance programs include direct assistance for rental payments and subsidized low-income housing. Spending for housing assistance has more than doubled since 1980. During 1990, about ten million people received some form of housing assistance.[4] Other in-kind programs listed in Exhibit 5 include the *school lunch program* for poor children, supplemental food vouchers for pregnant women, infants, and children (i.e., WIC), and *energy assistance* to help pay the energy bills of poor families. Not shown in Exhibit 5 are education and training assistance for poor families, such as Head Start, Pell grants, and the Job Training Partnership Act.

---

4. This number is an increase of about 50 percent over the number receiving benefits in 1980. About 60 percent of families in public housing in 1990 had incomes below the poverty level.

EXHIBIT 6

Federal Expenditures Aimed Specifically at Poor People Since 1960 (in 1990 constant dollars)

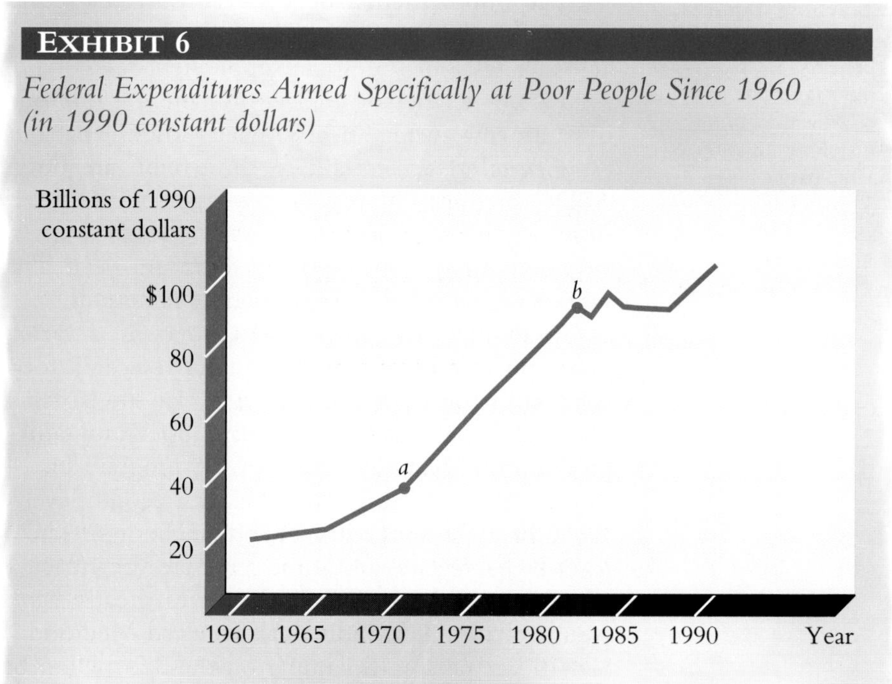

Source: *Budget of the United States Government* (Washington, D.C.: U.S. Government Printing Office, various years).

Expenditures and the Rate of Poverty

Teaching Tip Two other programs not considered are the Pension Benefit Guaranty Corporation that insures private pension plans and the federal government's own pension obligations. The PBGC had liabilities in 1991 of $51 billion. In addition, military and civil service retirees cost the federal government tens of billions of dollars per year.

Social insurance programs and income assistance programs at all levels of government cost about $600 billion in 1990, or about 11 percent of GDP. Most of the funding went to social insurance programs rather than to programs aimed more specifically at the poor. Income assistance programs—what we typically think of as welfare programs—amounted to only about 4 percent of GDP.

Exhibit 6 indicates what happened since 1960 to federal expenditures aimed specifically at assisting poor people—the cash and in-kind transfer programs listed in Exhibit 5. Expenditures are measured in dollars of constant purchasing power, so outlays are in real terms. The most rapid growth occurred between 1970 and 1981 (points *a* and *b*), when real expenditures nearly tripled, growing by an average of 9.6 percent per year. Since 1981 real spending has fluctuated but has shown a modest trend upward.

If you compare Exhibit 6 with Exhibit 4, which presents the poverty rate since 1959, you will notice that the decline in the poverty level ceased just when federal outlays for the poor showed their greatest increase. What happened?

EXCLUSION OF IN-KIND TRANSFERS. One reason official poverty statistics seem unaffected by the greater welfare spending between 1970 and 1981 is that the Census Bureau includes only *money transfers* in the definition

Teaching Tip According to the University of Colorado, some families are at high risk for hunger because they have never experienced economic trouble before. They do not understand the system of eligibility and applying for aid.

of income. It ignores the value of in-kind transfer programs, such as Medicaid, food stamps, and housing assistance. When official poverty statistics were first collected in the 1960s, in-kind transfers were minimal, so neglecting these transfers did not seem to matter. But in-kind programs expanded during the 1970s and most recently accounted for about three-fourths of all welfare spending. Ignoring in-kind transfers in the definition of income biases the poverty statistics, making the official figures higher than the actual values. When poverty data are reestimated to include the value of in-kind transfers, the poverty rate drops by about one-fifth.

Despite the growth in in-kind benefit programs, many of the poor still do not receive them, though some families above the poverty line do. Often the poor do not receive benefits because they fail to apply for them, but just as often coverage is limited because of long waiting lists (such as for public housing) or because some states establish eligibility requirements (such as for Medicaid) that allow only the poorest of the poor to qualify.

SLOWER ECONOMIC GROWTH. For another explanation of why the war on poverty has stalled since 1973, we must look beyond welfare programs to the health of the underlying economy. "A rising tide lifts all boats"—so goes the old saying about the relation between a thriving economy and rising individual fortunes. A healthy economy can reduce poverty. Between 1959 and 1969, the period during which poverty dropped the most, the economy showed the strongest growth; real family income grew on average by more than one-third. Between 1969 and 1979, however, economic growth slowed. Twice as many people were unemployed in 1979 as in 1969. The effect of the growth in transfer spending during the 1970s may have been to compensate in part for a flat economy, with the result that poverty rates remained relatively unchanged. Poverty rates climbed in the early 1980s because the economy was weakening, then began to fall after 1983 as the economy improved. The poverty rates climbed again in 1990 with the onset of a recession.

Teaching Tip The Center on Budget and Public Priorities pinpoints declining wages for low-skilled work and a weakening of labor unions as major factors in the rising poverty level.

Perhaps more important than the effect of the economy on poverty has been the change in the family structure. To develop a fuller understanding of the extent and composition of poverty over time, we must look behind the totals and examine the change in the composition of the family.

WHO ARE THE POOR?

Who are the poor, and how has the composition of this group changed over time? We will slice poverty statistics in several ways to examine the makeup of the group. Keep in mind that we are relying on official poverty estimates, which ignore the value of in-kind transfers and so to some extent overstate the problem.

EXHIBIT 7

Official Poverty Rate of Families by Age of Household Head for Selected Years Since 1959

Age of Household Head	1959	1968	1970	1975	1980	1991
All families	18.5%	10.0%	10.1%	9.7%	10.3%	11.5%
Under 25	26.9	13.2	15.5	21.0	21.8	34.9
25–44	16.5	9.3	9.5	10.3	11.8	13.9
45–54	15.0	7.0	6.6	6.6	7.6	7.1
65 and over	30.0	17.0	16.5	8.9	9.1	6.5

Source: U.S. Bureau of the Census, *Current Population Reports,* series P-60, no. 181 (Washington, D.C.: U.S. Government Printing Office, 1992), Table 5.

Poverty Growth Among Young Families

Point to Stress The figures in the first row of Exhibit 7 do not match the figures used to develop Exhibit 4 because Exhibit 7 considers the percentage of families and Exhibit 4 considers the percentage of the total population.

Earlier we looked at the poverty rate of the entire population. Now we will focus on poverty in families. The poverty rate since 1959, based on the age of the head of the family, or householder, is presented in Exhibit 7. The first row lists the poverty rate for all families regardless of age. The largest reduction in the overall rate occurred between 1959 and 1968, when the poverty rate declined from 18.5 percent to 10.0 percent. However, there has been no general improvement since 1968.

Poverty is highest in families where the householder is under twenty-five years old. Older householders have a lower poverty rate, especially in more recent years. Although earnings tend to be lowest for those just entering the labor market, the data show more than a simple age-wage effect, as *the poverty rate among young families has more than doubled since 1968.* In 1968 the poverty rate for families headed by someone under twenty-five was only one-third greater than the rate for all families, but by 1991 these younger families had a poverty rate more than *triple* the average.

The most dramatic reversal of poverty has occurred among families in which the householder is sixty-five or over. In 1959 elderly families were the poorest, with a poverty rate of 30 percent. Since then elderly poverty has fallen steadily, and by 1991 the poverty rate for elderly families dropped to 6.5 percent, the lowest rates of any age group. This reduction in poverty among elderly families can be attributed to a tremendous growth in Social Security and Medicare spending, which grew from $49 billion in 1959 to over $375 billion in 1991, measured in 1991 dollars. In 1991, Social Security and Medicare spending was triple what the federal government spent on income assistance, or welfare, programs. Social Security has been credited with lifting fifteen million Americans above the poverty line. *Though not welfare programs in a strict sense, Social Security and Medicare have been extremely successful in reducing poverty among the elderly.*

Example According to Census Bureau data, Social Security and other retirement benefits are the primary sources of income for most elderly people. Adjusting for inflation, income levels for the elderly have more than doubled since 1957.

Poverty and Public Choice

In a democratic country such as ours, public policies depend very much on the political power of the interest groups involved. In recent years the elderly have become a strong political force. Unlike most interest groups, the elderly are a group we all expect to join one day. The elderly actually are represented by four constituencies: (1) the elderly themselves, (2) those under sixty-five who are concerned about the current benefits to their parents or other elderly relatives, (3) those under sixty-five who are concerned about their own benefits in the future, and (4) those who earn their living by caring for the elderly, such as doctors and nursing home operators.

Moreover, the voter participation rate of those sixty-five and over tends to be higher than that of other age groups. Specifically, those between sixty-five and seventy-four vote at more than twice the rate of those under thirty-four. The political muscle of the elderly has been flexed whenever a question of Social Security benefits has come up. In 1985, for example, at a time when Congress was seeking ways to address a huge federal deficit, a proposal to delay for several months a cost-of-living increase in Social Security benefits was defeated amid much furor among members of Congress about how the country could not solve the deficit at the expense of the elderly. Yet as we have seen, the poverty rate among elderly families is now lower than among all other age groups.

Teaching Tip Social Security payments were skipped for a six-month period in 1983 to help alleviate a crisis in the system.

Poverty and Gender

As we noted, one way of classifying the incidence of poverty is by the age of the family head, or householder. We saw that since 1969, poverty rates have climbed among young families and have dropped among elderly families. Another way to examine the incidence of poverty is based on the gender of the householder. Female householders have a poverty rate that averages about 33 percent—five times higher than the average rate among other householders.

Though the poverty rates among female householders are high, these rates have increased little since 1969. What has increased is the number of female householders in the economy. The percentage of births to unmarried mothers is five times greater today than in 1960. Since the father in such cases typically assumes little responsibility for child support, children born outside marriage are likely to be poorer than other children. Also, since 1960 the divorce rate doubled. Because of the higher divorce rate, even children born to married couples now face a greater likelihood of living in a one-parent household before they grow up. Divorce usually reduces the resources available for the children. *Children of female householders are five times more likely to live in poverty than are other children.*

Example Census findings indicate that 40 percent of the poor in 1991 were children.

The increase in the number of unwed mothers and in the divorce rate has doubled the number of female householders since 1969. With a doubling in the number of householders came a doubling in the number of poor people

Example A Census Bureau study indicated that the median family income in a black household when both husband and wife work is more than double that of other black households.

from such families. Thus, even though the poverty *rate* among such families has remained relatively constant since 1969 at about 33 percent, the *number* of poor in families of female householders has increased because the *number* of female householders has increased. Whereas the number of female householders doubled since 1969, the number of other types of families grew by only 20 percent, and the poverty rate of these other types of families declined from 6.9 percent to 6.4 percent.

Poor female householders represented 86 percent of the 2.7 million additional poor families between 1969 and 1991. Thus, *the growth in the number of poor families since 1969 resulted overwhelmingly from the growth in the number of female householders.* Since 1969 the U.S. economy has generated about forty million new jobs. Married couples were in the best position to take advantage of this job growth because they typically had one more potential wage earner than did single female householders. Young single motherhood is a recipe for instant poverty. Often the young mother drops out of school, which reduces her future earning possibilities when and if she seeks work outside the home. Even a strong economy is little aid to households with nobody in the labor force.

Example Census data indicate that households headed by single black mothers now make up 60 percent of poor families with children, compared to 28 percent in 1959.

Poverty has therefore become increasingly feminized, mostly because female householders have become more common in the population as a whole. Because the number of female householders has grown more rapidly among blacks, the feminization of poverty has been more dramatic in black households. About two-thirds of all black births in 1989 were to unmarried women, compared to one-third of all births among those of Hispanic origin and one-fifth of births among whites.[5] (Keep in mind that those of Hispanic origin may be of any race.)

Much black poverty occurs in the poorest areas of central cities, where crime, gangs, and drug abuse compound the problem of poverty, creating a group of poor called the *underclass.* The underclass must cope not only with poverty but also with the daily horror of crime and drug addiction in the neighborhood. Poor job prospects among unskilled young black men in some cases leads to crime and drug addiction—activities that may result in prison or even death. Thus, marriage prospects of young black females are limited by a shortage of eligible black males.[6]

Some children are born to drug-addicted mothers.[7] The expression "no-parent" households can be used to reflect the sad circumstances of such children. According to one study, six million children in 1990 were living in

5. These figures are from *Statistical Abstract of the United States 1992*, U.S. Bureau of the Census (Washington D.C.: U.S. Government Printing Office, 1992), Table 87.
6. For an interesting examination of the relationship between welfare dependency and the marriage pool of eligible males, see Mwangi S. Kimenyi, "Rational Choice, Culture of Poverty, and the Intergenerational Transmission of Welfare Dependency," *Southern Economic Journal* 57 (April 1991): 947–960.
7. In 1989, for example, an estimated ten thousand babies were born in New York City to substance-abusing mothers. See "Crack Mothers, Crack Babies and Hope," *New York Times*, 31 December 1989.

households without either parent.[8] In one inner-city school, half the students lived with neither a mother nor a father. Some schools are trying to adapt to the needs of children from no-parent households by providing more social services such as health care at school. Washington, D.C. is even considering operating a boarding school for such children. For a description over time of the relations among poverty, gender, race, and Hispanic origin, see the section entitled "A Closer Look," which appears at the end of the chapter.

The high poverty rate among female householders and the poor job prospects for unskilled black males raise the question of whether discrimination exists either in the job market or in the availability of transfer payments. In an earlier chapter we considered discrimination against women and examined the issue of comparable worth. In the next section we consider racial discrimination.

Poverty and Discrimination

Example In 1991, census data showed that blacks had a poverty rate of 32.7 percent; the rate among Hispanics was 28.7 percent; Asians and Pacific Islanders had a 13.8 percent rate; and 10.7 percent of whites were poor.

Family income comes from two primary sources: resource earnings—typically labor—and transfer income. The question we ask is this: are the lower family income and greater incidence of poverty among blacks the result of discrimination in job markets or discrimination in the availability of transfer programs, or are there other explanations?

We should note that discrimination can occur in many ways: in school funding, in housing, in employment, in career advancement. Also, discrimination in one area can affect opportunities in another. For example, housing discrimination may reduce job opportunities because the black family cannot move within commuting distance of the best employers. Moreover, the legacy of discrimination can affect career choices long after discrimination has ceased. A black man whose father and grandfather found job avenues blocked may be less inclined to pursue an education or to accept a job that requires a long training program. Thus, discrimination is a complex topic, and we cannot do it justice in this brief section.

Discrimination in the Job Market?

Job market discrimination can take many forms. An employer may fail to hire a black job applicant because the applicant lacks training. But this lack of training may arise from discrimination in the schools, in union apprenticeship programs, or in training programs run by employers. For example, evi-

8. As reported in Jane Gross, "Collapse of Inner City Families Creates America's New Orphans," *New York Times*, 29 March 1992.

Teaching Tip Without adjustments for other factors, Census Bureau data indicate that black households in which both husband and wife work earned only 85 percent of what a two-earner white couple earned in 1991. Black men and women were almost twice as likely to work in low-paying service jobs. Black families in general had median incomes equal to only 57 percent of white median incomes. In one out of five black families, no one is earning any money.

dence suggests that black workers receive less on-the-job training than otherwise similar white workers.

We will first consider the difference between the earnings of nonwhite and white workers. After adjusting for a variety of factors that could affect the wage, such as education, work experience, and so on, research shows that whites earn more than blacks, but the wage gap between the two narrowed between 1940 and 1976 to the point where blacks earned only 7 percent less than white workers. However, the gap has since widened again so that by 1990, black workers earned 12 percent less than white workers.[9]

Could other explanations besides job discrimination account for the wage gap? Though the data adjust for the *years* of schooling, some research suggests that black workers received a lower *quality* of schooling than white workers.[10] For example, black students were less likely to use computers in school. Inner-city schools may have more problems with classroom discipline, which takes time away from instruction. Such quality differences could account for at least a portion of the remaining difference in standardized wages. Although any differences attributable to a poorer quality education would not necessarily reflect job discrimination, they might well reflect discrimination in the funding of schools.

Affirmative Action

The Equal Employment Opportunity Commission, established by the Civil Rights Act of 1964, monitors cases involving unequal pay for equal work and unequal access to promotion. Executive Order 11246, signed by President Lyndon Johnson, required all companies doing business with the federal government to set numerical hiring, promotion, and training goals. The objective was to ensure that these firms did not discriminate in hiring on the basis of race, sex, religion, or national origin. Today that executive order governs employment practices in firms that account for one-third of all jobs. Attention has been focused on hiring practices and equality of opportunity at the state level as well. The federal focus on employment practices appears to have improved employment opportunities for blacks. Black employment increased sharply in those firms required to file affirmative action plans.[11] In the U.S. economy, the percentage of the black labor force employed in white-collar jobs increased from 16.5 percent in 1960 to 40.5 percent in 1981—an increase that greatly exceeded the growth of white-collar jobs in the labor force as a whole.

---

9. See the evidence in M. Boozer, A. Krueger, and S. Wolkon, "Race and School Quality Since *Brown v. Board of Education*," *Brookings Papers on Economic Activity: Microeconomics*, 1992: 269–326.
10. See Finis Welch, "Black-White Differences in Returns to Schooling," *American Economic Review* 63 (September 1973): 893–907.
11. See the evidence provided in James Smith and Finis Welch, "Black Economic Progress After Myrdal," *Journal of Economic Literature* 27 (June 1989): 519–563.

EXHIBIT 8

Percentage of Families and Unrelated Individuals Who Received Cash Transfers

	Families		Unrelated Individuals	
	Black	**White**	**Black**	**White**
All income levels	56.0%	42.5%	45.5%	43.9%
Below the poverty level	75.3%	57.5%	63.5%	53.5%

Source: U.S. Bureau of the Census, *Statistical Abstract of the United States* (Washington, D.C.: U.S. Government Printing Office, 1984), Table 766, 459. Data are for 1982.

Discrimination in Transfer Programs?

Teaching Tip Census Bureau data show that, in general, only 73 percent of those classified as poor receive public assistance.

Market-related earnings represent the primary source of income for most households, but many households rely on government transfers. Are the lower family income and higher incidence of poverty among blacks linked to unequal treatment of blacks in the welfare system? Are blacks more likely than whites to fall through the safety net provided by social service programs? For example, blacks living in rural areas of the South must often travel to the county seat to apply for welfare; does this affect their participation rate?

Exhibit 8 presents the percentage, by race, of families and unrelated individuals who received federal cash transfers. The exhibit also provides a separate breakdown for those below the poverty line. No matter which group we examine, there is no evidence that blacks participate any less than whites in the cash transfer system.

Teaching Tip See Chapter 7 for a review of differences in unemployment rates. In addition, note that from 1989 to 1991, non-Hispanic white unemployment rates increased faster than minority unemployment rates, according to the Center on Budget and Policy Priorities. Therefore, U.S. poverty has increased fastest among non-Hispanic whites in recent years.

In summary, evidence presented in this section suggests that blacks earn less than whites after adjusting for other factors that could affect the wage, such as education and job experience. Part of this wage gap may reflect differences in the quality of education, differences that could themselves be the result of discrimination. There is no evidence that blacks have less access to government transfer programs. Keep in mind that unemployment rates are twice as high among blacks as among whites and are higher still among black teenagers, the group most in need of job skills and job experience.

We should also note that black families are not a homogeneous group. In fact, the distribution of income is more uneven among black families than it is among the population as a whole. We have already discussed the sad circumstances facing many black households in the inner city. The good news is that there is a growing middle class among black households. The percentage of black families earning more than $35,000, adjusted for inflation, increased from 16 percent in 1982 to 25 percent in 1990. Some of the progress among blacks stems from their steady advances in education. In 1970 the percentage of young blacks without a high school diploma was nearly twice that of whites. By 1990, the percentage of young blacks without diplomas had fallen by half and was nearly identical to that of whites.[12] In 1960 the average black adult had only a junior high school education; by 1990 a high school education was the average. In 1980 only 7 percent of middle-aged blacks had a college degree; by 1990 that figure had jumped to 17 percent. More generally, since 1970, the number of black doctors, nurses, college teachers, and newspaper reporters has more than doubled, the number of black engineers, lawyers, computer programmers, accountants, managers, and administrators has more than tripled, and the number of black elected officials has quadrupled.

Some Undesirable Consequences of Income Assistance

On the plus side, antipoverty programs increase the consumption possibilities of poor families, and this is critical, especially since children are the largest poverty group. But programs to assist the poor may have secondary effects that limit their ability to reduce poverty. Here we consider some secondary effects.

Work Disincentives

Society, through government, tries to provide families with an adequate standard of living, but society also wants to ensure that only those in need receive benefits. As we have seen, income assistance consists of a bundle of cash and in-kind programs. Because these programs are designed to help the poor and only the poor, the level of benefits is inversely related to income from other sources. This results in a system in which benefits are reduced sharply as earned income increases, in effect imposing a high marginal tax rate on that earned income. Any increase in earnings may cause a decline in benefits received from AFDC, Medicaid, food stamps, housing assistance, energy assistance, and other programs. If a bite is taken from each program as earned income increases, working may result in little or no increase in total income. In fact, over certain income ranges the welfare recipient may lose well over $1 in benefits for each $1 increase in earnings. The *marginal tax rate* on earned income could exceed 100 percent.

Since holding even a part-time job involves additional expenses, such as transportation and child care costs, not to mention the loss of free time, such a system of perverse incentives can frustrate those who would like to work their way off welfare. *This high marginal tax rate could discourage employment and self-sufficiency*. In many cases, the value of welfare benefits exceeds the disposable income resulting from full-time employment. For example, consider the welfare-versus-work choice facing a welfare mother with two children living

12. See Jason DeParle, "Without Fanfare, Blacks March to Greater High School Success," *New York Times*, 9 June 1991.

in Pennsylvania, as of 1989.[13] If she does not work and collects welfare, she has a disposable income of $8,590 in AFDC transfers, food stamps, and Medicaid. If, however, she takes a full-time job paying $4.80 an hour, or $10,000 a year, what happens to her disposable income? On the plus side, she receives $910 as an earned-income tax credit, the bonus the tax system pays the working poor. On the minus side, she must pay $751 in Social Security taxes and $210 in state income taxes, so her net taxes are $51. If she takes the job, her food stamp allowance is cut by one-third, she loses all her AFDC benefits, and, after one year, she loses all her Medicaid benefits. The main effect of working is a loss of welfare benefits and an increase in work-related expenses. Her net income from working would be $8,144, which is less than her net income from not working. The welfare option becomes even more attractive if she receives other welfare benefits for housing, energy assistance, and school lunches.

Example In 1992, the Connecticut Supreme Court ordered a New Haven welfare recipient to give back almost $10,000 in AFDC payments because two of her children had saved enough money from their after-school jobs to put the family's financial assets above the $10,000 limit. A sixteen-year-old daughter had saved $5,000 toward college, and her brother had saved almost $1,000, but they were forced to spend it on items such as clothing in order to reduce the family's assets.

Just how much the higher marginal tax rates reduce the incentive to work remains unclear. We do know that only about one of every twenty persons receiving AFDC is employed. Twice as many welfare recipients worked in the mid-1970s. These high marginal tax rates also encourage welfare recipients to conceal earned income; some may work "off the books" for cash or may become involved in illegal activities.

Suppose the high marginal tax rates do discourage recipients from working—is this a problem? The longer people are out of the labor force, the more their job skills deteriorate, so when they do seek employment, their marginal product and their pay are lower than when they were last employed. This lowers their expected wage and makes work less attractive. Some economists argue that in this way welfare benefits can lead to long-term dependency. What seems to be a rational choice in the short run has an unfavorable long-term outcome.

Does Welfare Cause Dependency?

Does the system of incentives created by high marginal tax rates create dependency among welfare recipients? How could we examine such a question? High turnover among welfare recipients would be evidence of little dependency. If, however, the same families were found to be poor year after year, this would be a matter of concern.

To explore the possibility of welfare dependency in the United States, a University of Michigan study tracked five thousand families over a number of years, paying particular attention to economic mobility both from year to year and from one generation to the next.[14] The study first examined

13. Most of this example was developed by the Committee on Ways and Means, U.S. House of Representatives, *Background Material and Data on Programs Within the Jurisdiction of the Committee on Ways and Means* (Washington, D.C.: U.S. Government Printing Office, 1989).
14. Greg J. Duncan, Richard D. Coe, and others, *Years of Poverty, Years of Plenty* (Ann Arbor: University of Michigan Press, 1984).

Teaching Tip Studies show that human-capital investments explain much of differences in income levels among households. Empirical research has had varying results, but some studies indicate that family background has a substantial impact on schooling and training and thus income.

poverty from year to year, or dependency within a generation. It found that most recipients received welfare for less than a year, but about 30 percent of all welfare recipients remained on welfare for at least eight years. Thus, there is a core of long-term recipients. The second and more serious concern was, do the children of the poor end up in poverty as well? Is there a cycle of poverty? To answer this question, the Michigan study examined the relation between the income of one generation and that of the next generation. The results indicate that less than half of those who grow up in welfare homes become dependent on welfare as adults.

One way to look at the cycle-of-poverty question more generally is to examine how much mobility there is in the income distribution from one generation to the next. In the Michigan study, parents were divided into five equal groups based on income; their grown children were also placed in five groups according to income. The point was to see if the children of poor parents also tended to be poor. Exhibit 9 presents data on mobility between generations for the sample tracked by the University of Michigan study. The five groups of parents, from poorest to richest, are listed in the left-hand column; the five groups of children, also ranked from poorest to richest, are listed across the top.

The first row of the table indicates how the children of the poorest parents fared with respect to income. A total of 44 percent of the children of the poorest parents were themselves among the poorest fifth of their generation; 27 percent moved up to the next highest fifth, 18 percent jumped to the middle fifth, and so on. In contrast, among children of the wealthiest parents, only 9 percent found themselves among the poorest fifth, 13 percent in the next poorest, and so on. Although having poor parents does not doom one to be poor, those with parents in the poorest group were five times more likely to be in the bottom group than those with parents in the wealthiest

EXHIBIT 9

Intergenerational Mobility

	Young Adults Forming Households				
Parents	**Poorest Fifth**	**Second-Lowest Fifth**	**Middle Fifth**	**Second-Highest Fifth**	**Highest Fifth**
Poorest fifth	44%	27%	18%	9%	2%
Second-lowest fifth	23	24	19	19	15
Middle fifth	11	23	23	26	17
Second-highest fifth	10	17	22	26	25
Highest fifth	9	13	19	23	36

Source: Computed based on Greg J. Duncan, Richard D. Coe, and others, *Years of Poverty, Years of Plenty* (Ann Arbor, MI: University of Michigan Press, 1984).

group. Conversely, the chances of ending up in the wealthiest group were eighteen times greater if one's parents were in that group than if they came from the poorest group. If the children of all income groups had an equal opportunity of joining the highest group, the children of the poor would be just as likely to end up rich as poor.

WELFARE REFORM

There is much dissatisfaction with the welfare system, both among those who pay for the programs and among direct beneficiaries. A variety of welfare reforms has been suggested in recent years, ranging from dismantling many federal programs to increasing federal control so as to ensure more uniform benefits across states. One possible reform, introduction of the so-called negative income tax, was the subject of a massive social experiment.

Negative Income Tax

Negative income tax A cash transfer program in which cash transfers are reduced as earnings rise

A **negative income tax** (NIT) gives cash transfers to poor families, providing them with a guaranteed minimum income and allowing them to keep a portion of any earnings. The program is called a negative income tax because the cash transfer is reduced as the family's earnings rise. Let's see how the NIT works.

Point to Stress Under the negative income tax system, total after-tax income for families *below the break-even point* equals earned income plus cash transfers. Because the tax rate is less than zero, a family with a wage earner is better off than a family with no earned income.

Suppose that the program guarantees a family of four at least $8,000 per year regardless of the family's earnings. If the family has no earnings, it will receive $8,000 in transfers. The cash transfer decreases as the family's earned income increases; the amount by which transfers are reduced depends on the negative income tax rate. For example, if the negative income tax rate is 40 percent, transfers will be cut by $0.40 for each $1 earned. If the family earns $6,000, its $8,000 cash transfer will be reduced by $6,000 × 0.40, or $2,400. Thus, the family's total income will be $6,000 in earnings plus $5,600 in transfers, for a total of $11,600.

As the family's earned income increases, the tax rate (or benefit-reduction rate) on these earnings reduces the family's net cash transfer. If the family earns $20,000, its income tax is $8,000 (that is, $20,000 × 0.40), which reduces the transfer to zero. Such a family is at the *break-even point*, which is where the tax and the subsidy cancel out. Thus, we can specify three components to the negative income tax: the guaranteed minimum, G, the negative tax rate, r, and the break-even point, B. They are related as follows: $B = G/r$. If you know the value of any two variables, you can solve for the third. The higher the guaranteed minimum, given the negative tax rate, the higher the break-even point and the larger the government budget required to finance the program.

The important question for the researchers was whether the guaranteed minimum reduced work effort. Studies in the 1970s of NIT programs in Seattle and Denver suggest that it did. In the Seattle and Denver experiments,

Example If the guaranteed minimum in the example rises from $8,000 to $10,000 and the negative tax rate remains at 40 percent, the break-even point rises to $25,000. Note that families with earned incomes above the break-even point pay income taxes.

the number of hours worked fell on average by 9 percent for husbands and by 20 percent for wives. The greatest effect appeared to be among young males not yet heading households, who reduced their work effort by 43 percent. This latter outcome is troubling, because young workers must work to develop the skills and job discipline required to establish themselves in the work force.

Another concern of experimenters was the effect of the NIT on the stability of the family. There is some indication that a guaranteed income had a destabilizing effect on the family, as divorce rates were above average among participants in the experiment, particularly among households with no children. The results concerning work effort and family stability have been interpreted differently by different researchers, but the net effect of the experiments has been to deflate enthusiasm for a negative income tax as a solution to the problem of poverty.

Recent Reforms

Point to Stress Recall that income in a market economy depends primarily on the productivity of the household's resources.

Few women on welfare are in the labor force. Some analysts believe that one way to reduce poverty is to provide welfare recipients with job skills and to find jobs for those who are able to work. Some sort of "workfare" component for welfare recipients has been introduced in over thirty-five states. In such states, as a condition of receiving AFDC, the head of the household must agree to search for work, participate in education and training programs, or take some form of paid or unpaid position. The idea is to acquaint those on welfare with the job market so that they need not depend on welfare. Evidence from various states indicates that programs involving mandatory job searches, short-term unpaid work, and training can be operated at low cost and do increase employment.

Reforms at the state level set the stage for federal reform. Federal welfare reform was debated for nearly two years before a bill was finally passed, the *Family Support Act* of 1988, the first substantial welfare reform since 1935. To increase the incentive to work, welfare recipients are assured one year of day care assistance and Medicaid after they work their way off the AFDC program. The reform is aimed at smoothing the transition from welfare dependency for some of the 3.5 million single mothers on welfare. By providing day care and Medicaid for a year, the measure reduces the marginal tax rate associated with employment.

To encourage spouses to stay together, the Family Support Act requires all states to provide benefits for families with dependent children even if an unemployed father is present. (Half the states already provided such coverage.) Another provision requires that in two-parent welfare families where neither parent is employed, one parent should work at least sixteen hours a week in unpaid community service. The objective is to help people develop job skills and make a social contribution. The measure also calls for deducting from the paycheck of the absent parent child support payments that are legally due. But half of the children receiving AFDC were born outside marriage, and in most such cases the whereabouts of the father is unknown. Also, since AFDC aid is reduced by child support payments, the mother has little economic incentive to identify the father for support. Whether the 1988 measure will have any real impact on poverty remains to be seen. The poverty rate among families with female householders was higher in 1991 than in 1988, but the economy was in recession in 1991, so we cannot really judge the effect of the program. Though state governments endorse the reforms, the act has attracted little public attention or support.

Example According to the U.S. Conference of Mayors, requests for emergency food assistance increased 26 percent in major U.S. cities in 1991. Public-assistance programs failed to keep pace with increased hunger.

Much of the action lately has been at the state level, where tight state budgets have forced some states to cut welfare benefit levels, particularly for able-bodied adults. Benefit levels have also come to depend more on the behavior of the recipients. In Ohio and Wisconsin, for example, welfare benefits can be withheld if recipients or their children fail to attend school regularly. New Jersey no longer provides higher benefits to those on welfare who have more children, but those who marry or go to work find their benefit package enhanced.

We close this chapter by considering the profound problems confronted by a group not yet discussed: the homeless.

CASE STUDY

The Homeless

According to the U.S. Bureau of the Census, during the early morning of March 21, 1990, there were 228,621 homeless people sleeping in shelters, doorways, boxes, or in other makeshift quarters. From that number, the Census Bureau estimated there were 400,000 homeless people in the United States. Some critics argue that census count was much too low. A lawsuit has charged that the census takers did not check rooftops, bushes, trees, cars, and dumpsters.

Although some homeless are people who became unemployed and could not find a job, most homeless people fall into one of three groups: (1) discharged mental patients, (2) young women who are "runaways" or young mothers with children who have moved into a shelter, and (3) men who are addicted to drugs or alcohol or who are mentally ill but who have never received any in-patient treatment.

Most studies report that up to one-third of the homeless are deinstitutionalized mental patients. In the mid-1950s the nation's mental hospitals began releasing patients on a large scale. Newly developed miracle drugs effective in treating mental illness were supposed to follow these patients into society, helping them lead productive lives. Some former patients made successful transitions, but many ended up homeless and on the streets. Fewer than one-fourth of those discharged are in any kind of mental health program.

Teaching Tip According to *A Nation in Denial: The Truth about Homelessness*, very poor families may be fiscally poorer than the homeless. However, the homeless have used up "network resources"—church, family, neighbors, and friends.

Women and young children make up about one-third of the homeless. Research suggests that homeless families consist mainly of young, single women with children who were receiving AFDC and had received it longer than other welfare families.

Homeless families often stay in shelters or in government-funded "hotels" while waiting for a home. Because the homeless tend to have no permanent address, they are less likely to register to vote, so they tend to be underrepresented in the political process. Though some homeless receive welfare benefits, especially women with families, those without dependent children may not qualify for much support. There is episodic support, most of it in-kind, from shelters, soup kitchens, and hospital emergency rooms, but coverage varies widely across regions. Many homeless feel safer on the streets even when shelters are available.

Some cities fear that the more support they offer the homeless, the more homeless they will attract from other areas. As a way to encourage homeless people to move on, several cities in Southern California prohibit camping in public places. Santa Monica has tried to restrict outdoor meal programs. The constitutionality of these ordinances is being challenged in the courts.

Homelessness appears to be more prevalent in cities with strong rent control laws and other housing restrictions. Because the supply of housing is restricted, people who might otherwise move into better housing instead stay put. There is thus little turnover of housing, and less "filtering down" of housing to the low end of the housing market. Affordable housing is therefore more scarce in cities with greater housing restrictions, such as New York and Boston, than in cities with fewer housing restrictions, such as Kansas City and Pittsburgh.

Sources: "Census Bureau Sued Over Homeless Count," *New York Times*, 11 October 1992; David Tucker, *The Excluded Americans: Homelessness and Housing Policy* (Washington, D.C.: Regency Gateway, 1990); and "The Homeless Sharply Split Santa Monica," *New York Times*, 29 November 1992.

Conclusion

Government redistribution programs have been most successful at reducing poverty among the elderly. But poverty rates among children have increased in recent years because of the growth in the number of female householders. We might ask why transfer programs have reduced poverty rates among the elderly but not among female householders. Transfer programs do not encourage people to get old; that process occurs naturally and is independent of the level of transfers. But the level and availability of transfer programs may, at the margin, influence some young unmarried women as they are deciding whether to have a child and may, at the margin, influence a married mother's decision to get divorced.

Most transfers in the economy are not from the government but rather are in-kind transfers within the family, from parents to children. Thus, any change in a family's capacity to earn income has serious consequences for dependent children. Family structure appears to be a primary determinant of family income. The poorest income group, the underclass, consists primarily of minority female householders concentrated in the poorest sections of our central cities. The problem of poverty in the central cities is compounded by the crime and drug addiction that can make daily life there terrifying. Those who suffer most are the children. One-fifth of the children in the United States live in poverty—some thirteen million in 1991. Children are the innocent victims of the changing family structure.

The section at the end of the chapter entitled "A Closer Look" examines poverty rates over time based on the householders' gender, race, and Hispanic origin. The findings show that regardless of race or Hispanic origin, children with two parents at home are much less likely to be poor than children in families headed by a single mother.

Summary

1. Money income (before taxes but after cash transfers) in the United States became more evenly distributed across households between 1929 and 1947, remained relatively stable between 1947 and 1977, and has become somewhat less evenly distributed since then.

2. During the 1960s the economy boomed and the poverty rate fell, reaching a low of 11.1 percent in 1973. Between 1973 and 1979, the rate of poverty fluctuated but showed no substantial decline. Between 1979 and 1983 the rate of poverty increased, then declined for the next six years, before rising with the recession of the early 1990s.

3. Families with a head of household under twenty-five were the only group to experience an increase in the poverty rate since 1959. Since 1959 poverty rates have dropped the most among elderly families. The growth in the number of poor families has been the result of the growth in the number of female householders.

4. The wage gap between blacks and whites narrowed between 1940 and 1975, but has increased since then. Affirmative action provisions seem to have increased employment opportunities among blacks. There is no evidence that blacks have less access to cash transfer programs. Two groups of black households have been growing: (1) a black underclass consisting primarily of female householders living in the poorest part of the inner city and (2) an emerging black middle class employed in professional positions and living in the suburbs.

5. Among the undesirable effects of income assistance is a high marginal tax rate on earned income, which may discourage employment and encourage welfare dependency. According to one survey, about 30 percent of families on welfare remain there for eight years or more.

6. The results of experiments with a negative income tax suggest that providing families a guaranteed income through cash transfers may reduce the incentive to work. Welfare reforms introduced by the states set the stage for federal welfare reforms aimed at promoting the transition from welfare to work. The states are now experimenting with different systems aimed at promoting greater personal responsibility.

Questions and Problems

1. (Depressions and the Rich) "The only people who benefit from a depression are the rich, who can adequately protect themselves." Evaluate this statement in light of Exhibit 1.

2. (Lorenz Curve) Construct a Lorenz curve using the following hypothetical income data for a country with only five households: H1, $10,000; H2, $4,000; H3, $3,000; H4, $2,000; H5, $1,000.

3. (Poverty in the United States) How would you explain the drop in Exhibit 4 in the percentage of the population below the official poverty level during the 1960s? Why did the percentage rise during the early 1980s? Are these statistics deceptive?

4. (Poverty in the United States) Should the U.S. government attempt to completely eliminate poverty? Why or why not?

5. (Economic Growth and Poverty) "Economic growth is more effective than welfare programs in reducing poverty in the United States." Evaluate this statement.

6. (Poverty and Age) Why has poverty been rising dramatically among younger households and falling dramatically among elderly households?

7. (Poverty and Gender) Why are female-headed households more vulnerable to poverty than male-headed households?

8. (Discrimination and Earnings) What types of discrimination can drive a wedge between what whites earn and what nonwhites earn? Consider discrimination in schooling, for example. How could you detect such discrimination?

9. (Welfare and the Underground Economy) How might the implicit tax on earned income (in the form of the loss of benefits from government assistance programs) affect the underground economy? How might some people avoid the implicit tax?

10. (Negative Income Tax) Give some reasons why the experiment with a negative income tax, as discussed in the chapter, might have led to a reduction in work effort. How could adjustments be made to reduce this loss of incentives?

11. (Indifference Curve Analysis) Using an indifference curve diagram that relates food to "all other goods," show the impact on utility of an in-kind transfer of food. (Hint: Such a transfer would allow the consumer to increase his or her consumption by the amount of the transfer, but not change the prices of the goods.) Compare the result to that of a pure cash transfer of equal dollar value.

12. (Impact of Transfer Programs) Suppose that cash transfers tend to decrease work effort. How would this affect your interpretation of before- and after-transfer income distributions as a measure of the impact of the cash transfer program?

13. (Charitable Contributions) Suggest a reason why people who voluntarily give money to charities tend to give less than they give through government.

14. (Income Distribution) Suppose the data in Exhibit 3 yield the following income-age relationships:

Age	*Income (average)*
22–31	$25,000
32–41	35,000
42–51	43,000
52–61	48,000
62–71	35,000

Calculate a Lorenz curve for each of the following age distributions:q

	22–31	*32–41*	*42–51*	*52–61*	*62–71*
a.	20%	20%	20%	20%	20%
b.	15%	25%	25%	20%	15%
c.	15%	20%	30%	25%	10%

15. (Lorenz Curve) A perfectly even income distribution would most certainly mean that each individual would be worse off than those at the bottom end of a more unevenly allocated income distribution. Discuss.

16. (Transfer Programs) Some forms of in-kind transfer programs do not allow you to supplement consumption of the subsidized good with additional units purchased privately. Examples include higher education at state universities and public housing. Could such programs actually reduce the recipients' consumption of the subsidized good below the level they would have purchased without assistance?

17. (Negative Income Tax) Suppose you wished to run a negative income tax program in which the guaranteed minimum income level is $10,000 and the cash transfers are uniformly phased out over earned income levels up to $20,000. What is the marginal tax rate on earned income? Why does reducing the tax rate mean lowering the base level or increasing the number of people being assisted? How could you decide what option is best?

18. (Income Distribution) When you look at people's earning patterns over their lifetimes, they tend to be poor when they are young and when they are old and relatively well-off in between. How should this observation affect income assistance programs designed to help the poor?

19. (The Homeless) Some cities have enacted anti-panhandling ordinances. What impact would you expect such ordinances to have on homelessness?

20. (The Homeless) Does it make sense for policies to assist the homeless to be made at the municipal level or should such policies be made at the state or federal level?

A CLOSER LOOK

Poverty, Marital Status, Race, and Hispanic Origin

Earlier we examined the poverty rates among families and found the greatest improvement between 1959 and 1973, when the average rate declined from 18.5 percent to 8.8 percent. One way we classified the incidence of poverty was by the age of the householder. Between 1959 and 1973, younger families showed the least improvement and older families, the greatest improvement. A more comprehensive way of examining the incidence of poverty among families is based on the marital status, gender, race, and Hispanic origin of householders. This breakdown is shown in the series of overlays presented as part of Exhibit 10. When you turn the page, you will find Exhibit 10 on the right-hand page and an explanation on the left-hand page. Please turn the page.

Poverty Rates Among Married Couples We begin with poverty rates among married couples, which are shown in the Base Page of Exhibit 10. (To see the Base Page, lift the transparencies and keep them in your hand.) The Base Page shows the poverty rates among married couples since 1974. Shading is used to indicate periods of recession. As you can see, the poverty rate has been lowest among white married couples, identified by the red line along the bottom, and highest among married couples of Hispanic origin, identified by the gold line along the top. (Keep in mind that those of Hispanic origin may be of any race.) The blue line in the middle shows the poverty rate for black married couples. During the period considered, the poverty rate among white couples was only about half that of black couples and only about one-third that of Hispanic couples.

Poverty Rates Among Male Householders We now consider the poverty rates among families other than married couples. The First Overlay adds to the picture the poverty rates for families with male householders. (Place the First Overlay over the Base Page.) Again, white families are identified by the red line, black families by the blue line, and Hispanic families by the gold line. Note that among black families and white families, poverty rates for male householders are about twice the rates for married couples. Married couples have two possible workers versus only one for families with male householders. Curiously, for Hispanic families, there is little difference in poverty rates between male householders and married couples; this may reflect a lower labor participation rate among Hispanic couples. Note also that for the last decade poverty rates have been highest among black male householders and lowest among white male householders.

Poverty Rates Among Female Householders Next we consider poverty rates among families with female householders. The Second Overlay shows that poverty rates are sharply higher among these families than among other families. (Add the Second Overlay to the exhibit.) This high poverty rate stems from the fact that families with a female householder are less likely than other families to have anybody in the labor force. During the years under consideration, about half of the black and Hispanic families with female householders lived in poverty, compared to about one-fourth of such families with a white householder. For whites and for blacks, the poverty rates among families with female householders are about five times higher than poverty rates among married couples.

In summary, since 1974 rates for the nine groups have fluctuated, especially between 1974 and 1984, but there has been little long-term trend up or down. The lowest poverty rates have been for married couples. The highest poverty rates have been for families with female householders. Overall, poverty rates among white families have been about half those of black and Hispanic families.

EXHIBIT 10

Percent of Families in Poverty

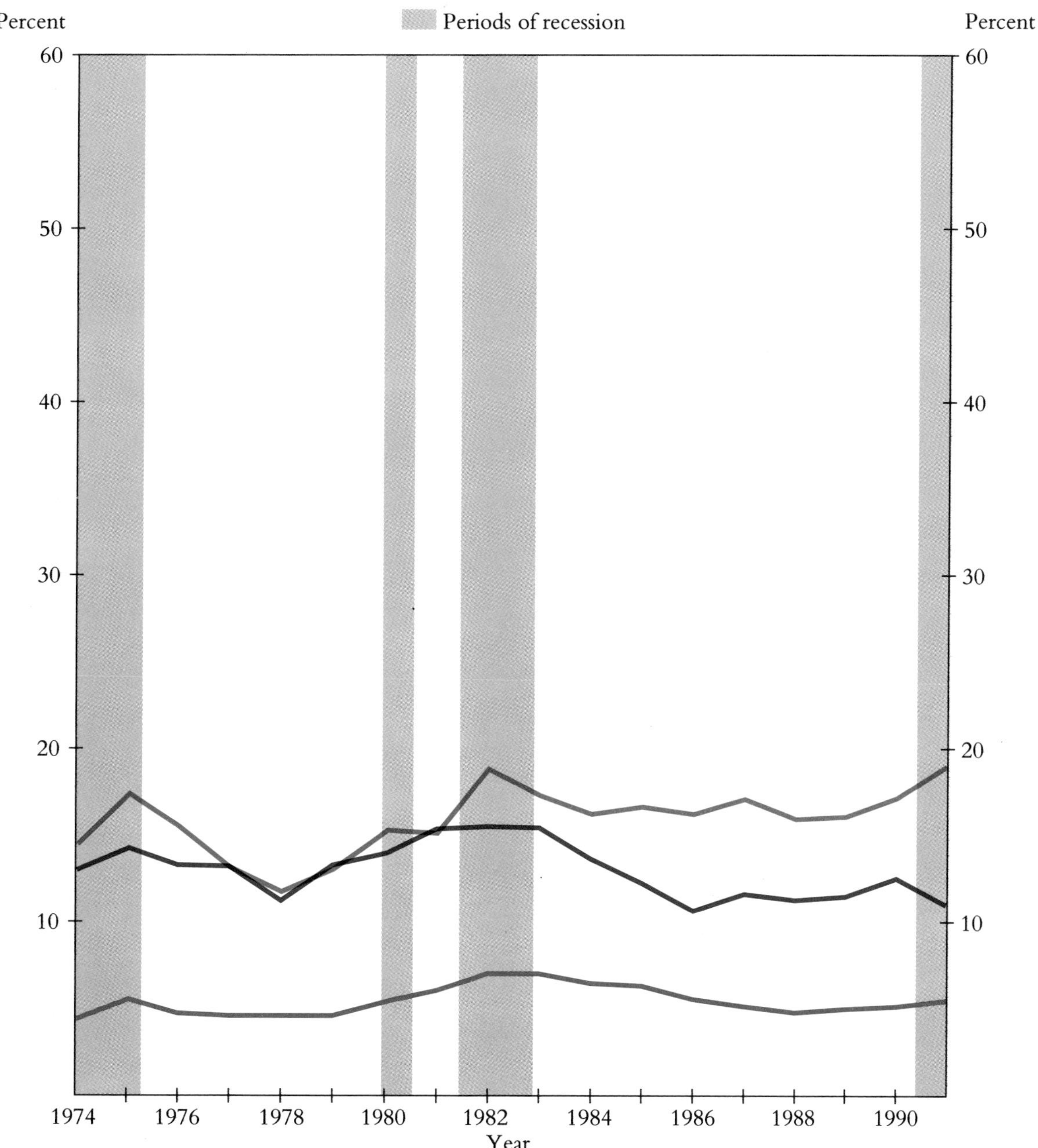

Source: U.S. Bureau of the Census, *Current Population Reports*, series P-60, no. 181 (Washington, DC: U.S. Government Printing Office, 1992), Table 4.

PART 8

The International Setting

CHAPTER 33

INTERNATIONAL TRADE

This morning you put on your Jordache jeans from Taiwan, laced up your Nikes from Korea, and pulled on your Benetton sweater from Italy. After a breakfast that included ham from Poland and coffee from Brazil, you climbed into your Japanese Toyota fueled by Saudi Arabian oil and headed for a lecture by a visiting professor from England. Americans buy Japanese cars, French wine, Swiss clocks, foreign trips, and thousands of other goods and services from around the globe. The world is a giant shopping mall, and Americans are big spenders. But foreigners spend a lot on American products as well—on grain, personal computers, aircraft, trips to Disney World, and thousands of other goods and services. In this chapter we will examine the gains from international trade and the effects of trade and trade restrictions on the allocation of resources. We will base the analysis primarily on the familiar concepts of supply and demand. Topics discussed in this chapter include

- Gains from international trade
- Absolute and comparative advantage
- Tariffs
- Import quotas
- Welfare loss from trade restrictions
- Arguments for trade restrictions

THE GAINS FROM TRADE

A family from Georgia that sits down for a meal of Kansas prime rib, Idaho potatoes, and California string beans has been involved in interstate trade. You likely have little difficulty understanding why the the residents of one

Teaching Tip Unlike interstate trade, international trade is complicated by the existence of different currencies. Currency systems are discussed in Chapter 34.

state trade with those of another. Back in Chapter 2 we looked at the gains arising from specialization and exchange. You may recall the discussion of how you and your roommate could maximize output by specializing in typing and ironing. Just as individuals benefit from specialization and exchange, so do states and, indeed, nations. To reap the gains that arise from specialized production, countries engage in international trade. *With trade, each country can concentrate on producing those goods and services that involve the least opportunity cost.*

A Profile of Imports and Exports

Example In 1991, North America (the United States, Canada, and Mexico) accounted for 16 percent of total world exports; the twelve nations of the European Community accounted for 38 percent.

Some nations are more involved in international trade than others, just as some states are more involved in interstate trade than others. For example, exports account for about half of the gross domestic product (GDP) in the Netherlands; about one-third of the GDP in Germany, Sweden, and Switzerland; and about a quarter of the GDP in Canada and the United Kingdom. Despite the perception that Japan has a giant export sector, only about 13 percent of Japanese production is exported.

In the United States, foreign trade amounts to about 11 percent of GDP. Though small relative to GDP, foreign trade plays a vital role in the economy and it has increased significantly in the last three decades. The four main types of U.S. exports are (1) high-technology manufactured products, such as computers, aircraft, and telecommunication equipment, (2) industrial supplies and materials, (3) agricultural products, especially corn and soybeans, and (4) entertainment products, such as movies and recorded music.

The United States depends on imports for some key inputs. For example, most of the bauxite used in this country to produce aluminum is imported; importing vast amounts of bauxite allows the United States to be the world's largest producer of aluminum. Most of the platinum and chromium and all of the manganese, mica, diamonds, and nickel are imported. Two-thirds of U.S. imports are (1) manufactured consumer goods, such as automobiles from Japan and color TVs from Taiwan and (2) capital goods, such as specialty machines.

Example The U.S.–Canada trade relationship has been the world's largest for years: imports plus exports totalled $176 billion in 1991.

The primary change in U.S. exports over the last two decades has been a growth in the dollar value of machinery exports; nearly half of the capital goods produced in the United States are exported. The primary change in U.S. imports over the last two decades has been the marked increase in spending on foreign oil. Canada is the United States's largest trading partner; Japan is the next largest. Other important trading partners include Mexico, Germany, Great Britain, South Korea, France, Hong Kong, Italy, and Brazil.

Production Possibilities Without Trade

Teaching Tip The consumption possibilities schedule shows the *maximum* combinations of food and clothing that each country can consume. Without trade, no country can consume more than it can produce—its production possibilities.

The rationale behind some international trade is obvious. The United States grows no coffee beans because our climate is not suited for coffee. It is more revealing, however, to examine the gains from trade where the cost advantage is not quite so obvious. Suppose that just two goods—food and clothing—are produced and consumed and that there are only two countries in the world—the United States, with a labor force of 100 million workers, and the mythical country of Izodia, with 200 million workers. The conclusions we derive from our simple model will have general relevance to the pattern of international trade.

Exhibit 1 presents each country's production possibilities schedule *in the absence of trade*, based on the size of the labor force and the productivity of workers in each country. We assume a given technology and that labor is fully and efficiently employed. Since no trade occurs between countries, Exhibit 1 presents each country's **consumption possibilities schedule** as well, which reflects the country's consumption alternatives.

Consumption possibilities schedule A schedule reflecting the alternative consumption alternatives available in an economy; in the absence of trade, the consumption possibilities schedule is the same as the production possibilities schedule

The production numbers imply that each worker in the United States can produce either 6 units of food or 3 units of clothing per day. If all 100 million U.S. workers produce food, 600 million units can be produced per day, as reflected by combination U_1 in part (a) of Exhibit 1. If all U.S. workers produce clothing, the United States can produce 300 million units per day, as reflected by combination U_6. Combinations in between represent alternative mixes of output if some workers produce food and some produce clothing. Because a U.S. worker can produce either 6 units of food or 3 units of clothing, the opportunity cost of producing 1 more unit of food is 0.5 unit of clothing.

In Izodia workers are less educated, work with less capital, and farm less fertile land than in the United States. So each Izodian worker is less productive than each U.S. worker and can produce only 1 unit of food or 2 units of

EXHIBIT 1

Production Possibilities Schedules for the United States and Izodia

(a) United States

	Units Produced (per worker per day)	Production Possibilities with 100 Million Workers (millions of units per day)					
		U_1	U_2	U_3	U_4	U_5	U_6
Food	6	600	480	360	240	120	0
Clothing	3	0	60	120	180	240	300

(b) Izodia

	Units Produced (per worker per day)	Production Possibilities with 200 Million Workers (millions of units per day)					
		I_1	I_2	I_3	I_4	I_5	I_6
Food	1	200	160	120	80	40	0
Clothing	2	0	80	160	240	320	400

Teaching Tip At combination U_2, for example, in order to produce 60 million units of clothing, the clothing industry would need 60/3, or 20 million, workers. This leaves 80 million workers for the food industry; those workers can produce 80 times 6, or 480 million, units of food.

clothing per day. If all 200 million Izodian workers specialize in food production, they can produce 200 million units of food per day, as reflected by combination I_1 in part (b) of Exhibit 1. If all Izodian workers produce clothing, they can produce 400 million units of clothing per day, as reflected by combination I_6. Some intermediate production possibilities are also listed in the exhibit. Because an Izodian worker can produce either 1 unit of food or 2 units of clothing, the opportunity cost of producing 1 more unit of food is 2 units of clothing.

We can convert the data in Exhibit 1 to a production possibilities frontier for each country, as shown in Exhibit 2. In each diagram the amount of food produced is measured on the vertical axis and the amount of clothing produced is on the horizontal axis. Production combinations for the United States are designated in panel (a) by U_1, U_2, and so on; production combinations in Izodia are designated in panel (b) by I_1, I_2, and so on. Because we assume that each country's resources are perfectly adaptable to the production of each commodity, each production possibilities curve is a straight line.

Exhibit 2 illustrates the possible combinations of food and clothing that residents of each country can produce and consume if all resources are fully

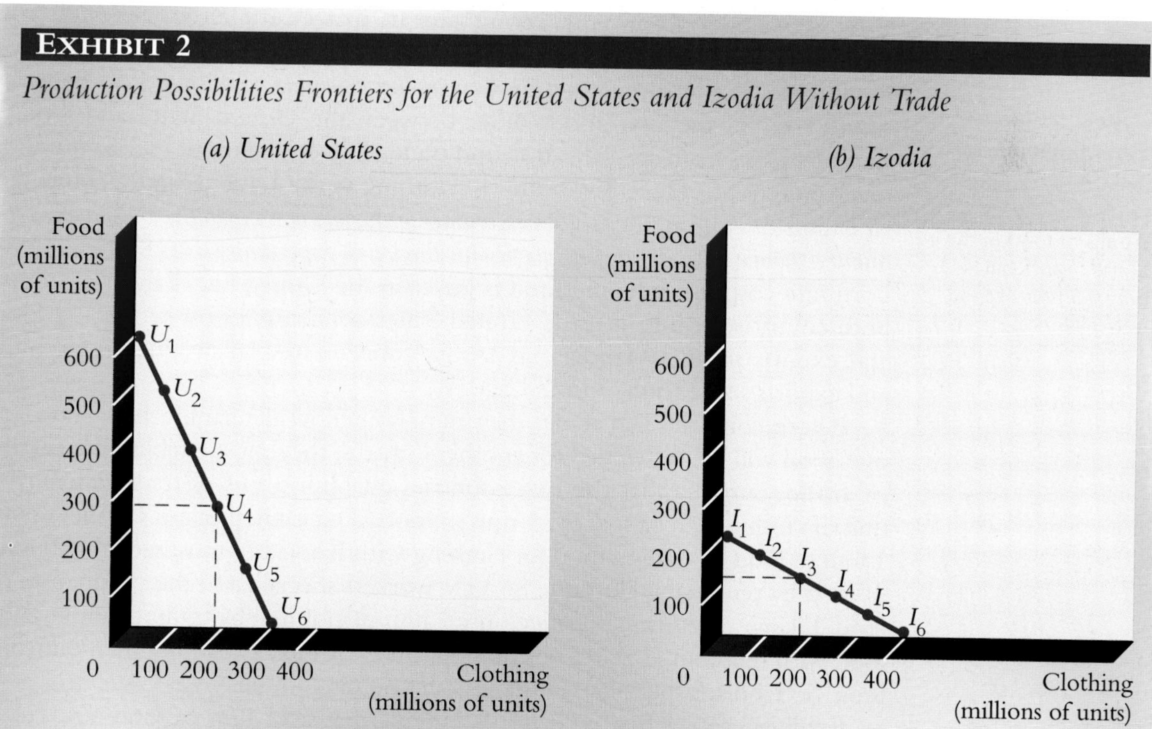

Panel (a) shows the U.S. production possibilities curve; its slope indicates that the opportunity cost of an additional unit of clothing is 2 units of food. Panel (b) shows production possibilities in Izodia; an additional unit of clothing costs 0.5 unit of food. Clothing is relatively cheaper to produce in Izodia.

and efficiently employed and there is no trade between the two countries. **Autarky** is the term that describes the situation of national self-sufficiency, in which there is no economic interaction with foreigners. Suppose that U.S. producers maximize profit and U.S. consumers maximize utility with the combination of 240 million units of food and 180 million units of clothing—combination U_4. This combination will be called the *autarky equilibrium*. Suppose also that Izodians have an autarky equilibrium, identified as combination I_3, of 120 million units of food and 160 million units of clothing.

Autarky A situation of national self-sufficiency in which there is no economic interaction with foreigners

Teaching Tip Assuming perfect resource adaptability results in constant opportunity costs. Increasing costs occur when resources are not perfectly adaptable (see Chapter 2).

Consumption Possibilities Based on Comparative Advantage

In our example, each U.S. worker can produce both more clothing and more food per day than can each Izodian worker. U.S. workers have an *absolute advantage* in the production of both goods because a U.S. worker can produce each good in less time than can an Izodian worker. With an absolute advantage in the production of both commodities, should the U.S. economy remain an autarky—that is, self-sufficient in both food and clothing—or are there gains from trade?

We learned the answer in Chapter 2, when we observed the gains from trade between you and your roommate. In that example, even though you were better at both typing and ironing than your roommate, you each benefited from specialization based on *comparative advantage*. As long as the opportunity costs of the two goods differ between the United States and Izodia, there are gains from specialization and trade. The opportunity cost of producing 1 more unit of food is 0.5 unit of clothing in the United States, compared to 2 units of clothing in Izodia. *According to the law of comparative advantage, each country should specialize in the good with the lower opportunity cost.* Since the opportunity cost of producing food is lower in the United States than in Izodia, both countries will gain if the United States concentrates on producing food and exports some to Izodia and Izodia concentrates on producing clothing and exports some to the United States.

Teaching Tip The opportunity cost of producing clothing is 2 units of food in the United States but only 0.5 unit of food in Izodia.

Before countries can trade, they must somehow determine how much of one good will be exchanged for another—that is, they must establish the **terms of trade**. Suppose that the two countries establish terms of trade whereby 1 unit of clothing exchanges for 1 unit of food. The United States sacrifices only 1 unit of food by trading food for clothing with Izodia but must sacrifice 2 units of food by producing clothing. So U.S. workers specialize in the production of food. Likewise, Izodians sacrifice only 1 unit of clothing by trading clothing for food with the United States but must sacrifice 2 units of clothing by producing food. So Izodians specialize in the production of clothing.

Terms of trade An indication of how much of one good will be exchanged for a unit of another good

Exhibit 3 shows that with terms of trade that set 1 unit of food equal to 1 unit of clothing, Americans and Izodians can consume anywhere along or below their blue consumption possibilities frontiers. (Note that the consumption possibilities curve for the United States does not extend to the right of 400 million units of clothing because that is the most the Izodians can produce.) The amount each country actually consumes will depend on its relative preferences for food and clothing. Suppose Americans select point U in panel (a) and

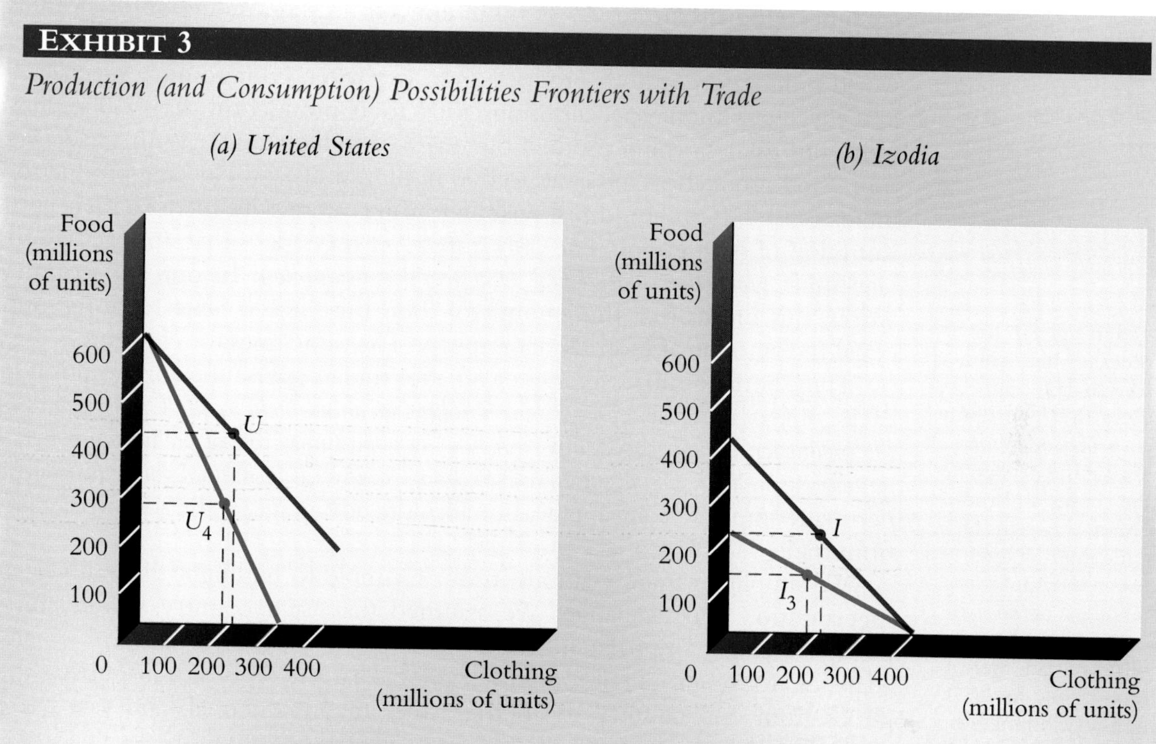

If Izodia and the United States can trade at the rate of 1 unit of clothing for 1 unit of food, both can benefit. Consumption possibilities at those terms of trade are shown by the blue lines. The United States was previously producing and consuming combination U_4. By trading with Izodia, it can produce only food and still consume combination U—a combination that contains more food and more clothing than combination U_4 does. Likewise, Izodia can attain the preferred combination I by trading its clothing for U.S. food. Both countries are better off as a result of international trade.

Teaching Tip The terms of trade are affected by the forces of supply and demand for food and clothing. They determine the slopes of the consumption possibilities frontiers. The United States produces where its production possibilities frontier intersects the vertical axis; Izodia produces where its production possibilities frontier intersects its horizontal axis.

Izodians select point *I* in panel (b).

Without trade, the United States produced and consumed 240 million units of food and 180 million units of clothing. With trade, the United States specializes in food by producing 600 million units; Americans eat 400 million units and exchange the remaining 200 million for 200 million units of Izodian clothing. This consumption combination is reflected by point *U* in panel (a). Through exchange, Americans are able to increase their consumption of both food and clothing.

Without trade, Izodians produced and consumed 120 million units of food and 160 million units of clothing. With trade, Izodians specialize in clothing by producing 400 million units; Izodians wear 200 million units of clothing and exchange the remaining 200 million units for 200 million units of food. This consumption combination is reflected by point *I* in panel (b). Izodians, like Americans, are able to increase their consumption of both food and clothing through trade. How is this possible?

Point to Stress Specialization according to comparative advantage and exchange allows each country to consume combinations outside its production possibilities frontier.

Since Izodians are relatively more efficient in the production of clothing and Americans relatively more efficient in the production of food, total world production of both products increases when each country specializes. Specifically, without specialization, total food production was 360 million units and total clothing production was 340 million units. With specialization, food production increases to 600 million units and clothing production increases to 400 million units, enabling both countries to increase their consumption of both goods. The only constraint on trade is that, for each good, *total world production must equal total world consumption*. In our two-country world, this means that the amount of food the United States exports must equal the amount of food Izodia imports. The same goes for clothing.

Teaching Tip In order for both countries to gain from trade, the opportunity costs of production must differ between the countries. In addition, the terms of trade must be between the opportunity costs of the two countries. If the terms of trade were 1 unit of food for 2 units of clothing, for example, Izodia's consumption possibilities would simply match its production possibilities, as in the autarky situation.

Thus, both countries are better off after trade because the consumption in each country increases. *Despite the absolute advantage held by the United States in the production of both goods, differences in the opportunity cost of production between nations ensure that specialization and exchange can result in mutual gains.* Remember that comparative advantage, not absolute advantage, is the source of gains from trade.

We simplified trade relations in our example to highlight the gains from specialization and exchange. We assumed that each country would completely specialize in producing a particular good, that resources were equally adaptable to the production of either good, that the costs of transporting the goods from one country to another were inconsequential, and that there were no problems in arriving at the terms of trade.

Consumer and Producer Surplus

Teaching Tip At the extreme, each pound of chicken could be sold for a different price. See Chapter 19 for a detailed development of consumer surplus.

Point to Stress In perfect competition, the firm's supply curve is the portion of the marginal cost curve rising above the average variable cost curve. See Chapter 21 for a detailed development of producer surplus.

Before we move on to a model of world trade, we will consider a way of describing the benefits that consumers and producers derive from exchange. To do this we discuss the hypothetical market for chicken shown in Exhibit 4. The height of the demand curve for chicken reflects the amount that consumers are willing and able to pay for each additional pound of chicken. In effect, the height of the demand curve shows the *marginal benefit* consumers expect to derive from each pound of chicken. For example, the demand curve indicates that some consumers are willing to pay $1.50 or more per pound for the first few pounds of chicken. But all consumers get to buy chicken at the market-clearing price, which in Exhibit 4 is only $0.50 per pound. The blue triangle below the demand curve and above the market price reflects the *consumer surplus*, which is the difference between the maximum sum of money consumers would pay for the amount of chicken traded and the actual sum they do pay. Consumers thus get a bonus, or a surplus, from market exchange. We all enjoy a consumer surplus from most products we consume.

There is a similar surplus on the producer side. The height of the supply curve reflects the minimum amount that producers are willing and able to accept for each additional pound of chicken. In effect, the height of the supply curve shows the *marginal cost* producers incur in supplying each additional pound of chicken. For example, the supply curve indicates that some

EXHIBIT 4

Consumer Surplus and Producer Surplus

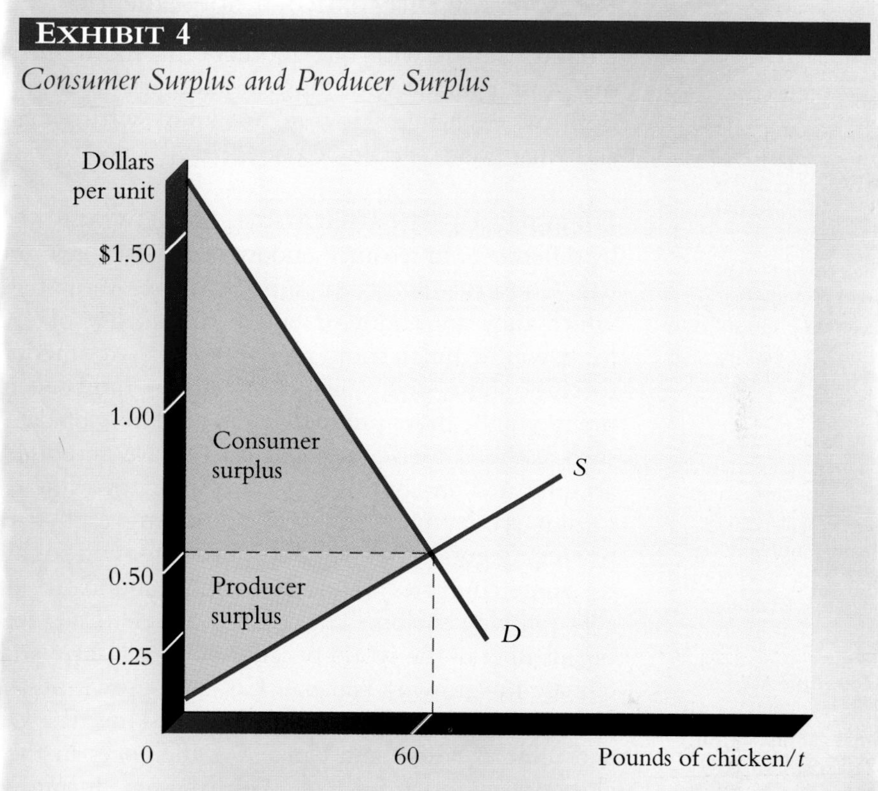

Consumer surplus, shown by the blue triangle, shows the net benefits consumers reap by being able to purchase 60 pounds of chicken at $0.50 per pound. Some consumers would have been willing to pay $1.50 or more per pound for the first few pounds. Consumer surplus measures the difference between the maximum sum of money consumers would pay for 60 pounds of chicken and the actual sum they pay. Producer surplus, shown by the gold triangle, shows the net benefits producers reap by being able to sell 60 pounds of chicken at $0.50 per pound. Some producers would have been willing to supply chicken for $0.25 per pound or less. Producer surplus measures the difference between the actual sum of money producers receive for 60 pounds of chicken and the minimum amount they would accept for this amount of chicken.

producers would have been willing to accept $0.25 or less per pound for supplying the first few pounds of chicken. But all producers get to sell chicken for the market-clearing price—in this case, $0.50 per pound. The gold triangle above the supply curve and below the market price reflects the *producer surplus*, which is the difference between the actual sum of money producers receive for the quantity traded and the minimum sum they would accept for the quantity traded.

The point is that market exchange usually yields a surplus, or a bonus, to both producers and consumers. In the balance of the chapter, we focus on how consumer surplus and producer surplus are affected by international trade.

Reasons for International Specialization

Example Apple Computer has formed an alliance with Toshiba to manufacture a CD-ROM player and one with Sharp to manufacture a personal display digital assistant. Apple will provide R&D expertise and software know-how; the Japanese electronics firms will provide manufacturing experience and certain key components. Each firm appears to be contributing along the lines of its comparative advantage.

Countries trade with one another—or, more precisely, people and firms in one country trade with those in another—because each side expects to gain from the exchange. How do we know what each country should produce and what goods should be traded?

DIFFERENCES IN RESOURCE ENDOWMENTS. Trade is often prompted by differences in resource endowments. Two key resources are labor and capital. Countries differ not simply in the amount of labor and capital with which they are endowed but in the quality of each. A well-trained labor force will be much more productive than an uneducated and unskilled labor force. Sophisticated capital reflecting the most recent technological developments will be more productive than old, out-of-date capital. Some countries, such as the United States and Japan, have an educated labor force and have accumulated an abundant stock of modern capital. Both resources result in greater productivity per worker, making each nation very competitive in producing goods that require skilled labor and sophisticated capital.

Example Western Europe relies on natural gas piped from Russia through Ukraine for a quarter of its energy needs. Finland buys all its gas from Russia, and Austria about 75 percent.

Some countries are blessed with an abundance of fertile land and a favorable growing season. The United States, for example, has been called the breadbasket of the world because of its rich farmland. Honduras has the ideal climate for growing bananas. Coffee is grown best in the climate and elevation of Colombia, Brazil, and Jamaica. Thus, the United States exports corn and imports coffee and bananas. Differences in the seasons across countries also serve as a basis for trade. For example, during winter months Americans import fruit from Chile and Canadian tourists travel to Florida for sun and fun. During summer months Americans export fruit and American tourists travel to Canada for fishing and camping.

Teaching Tip Differences in tastes and preferences, by affecting demand, affect the prices of imported and exported goods. The domestic price of a highly preferred good will rise relative to foreign prices, leading consumers to import the good. Note, however, that gains from trade will not continue if the production possibilities frontier is a straight line and the terms of trade rise to match the opportunity cost.

Mineral resources are often concentrated in particular countries: oil in Saudi Arabia, bauxite in Jamaica, diamonds in South Africa, coal in the United States. The United States has abundant coal supplies but not enough oil to satisfy domestic demand. Thus, the United States exports coal and imports oil. More generally, countries export those products that they can produce more cheaply in return for those that are unavailable domestically or are more costly to produce than to buy from other countries.

DIFFERENCES IN TASTES. Even if all countries had identical resource endowments and combined those resources with equal efficiency, each country would still gain from trade as long as tastes and preferences differed among countries. Differences in taste across countries lead to trade, and trade in turn leads to specialization if a country chooses to exploit its comparative advantage. Consumption patterns do appear to differ, often because of custom or religion. For example, the per-capita consumption of beer in Germany is more than double that in Portugal or Sweden. The French drink three times as much wine as the Danes. The Danes consume twice as much pork as do Americans. Americans consume twice as much chicken as do Hungarians. Soft drinks are four times more popular in the United States than in Western Europe. The English like tea; Americans, coffee. Algeria has an ideal climate for growing grapes, but it also has a large Moslem population that abstains from alcohol. Thus, Algeria exports wine.

Example The commercial aircraft industry is subject to substantial economies of scale. U.S. dominance of this world industry is due in part to its early start in manufacturing such aircraft.

ECONOMIES OF SCALE. If production is subject to *economies of scale*—that is, if the average cost per unit falls as output expands—countries can gain from trade if each nation specializes in one product. Such specialization allows each nation to produce at a higher output level, which reduces average production costs. The primary reason for establishing the Single Integrated Market by 1993 in Western Europe is to offer European producers a very large open market of over 320 million consumers so that producers can increase production, experience economies of scale, and in the process become more competitive in international markets.

TRADING ON THE WORLD MARKET

World price The price at which a good or service is traded internationally; it is determined by the world supply and demand for a product

So far we have analyzed the case in which each country fully specializes in the production of a particular good. How does international trade affect prices and output in domestic markets when two countries both produce a certain good? In this section we will rely on supply and demand analysis to develop an understanding of international markets. The **world price** is the price determined by the world supply and world demand for a product. It is the price at which any supplier can sell output on the world market and at which any demander can purchase output on the world market. Let's consider the market for a particular product: steel.

What If World Price Is Above Domestic Equilibrium Price?

Point to Stress The intersections of the domestic demand and supply curves in Exhibit 5(a) and point *e* in Exhibit 5(b) both represent the U.S. autarky equilibrium in the steel market.

Exhibit 5(a) shows hypothetical curves reflecting the supply and demand for steel in the United States. The U.S. demand curve for steel intersects the U.S. producers' supply curve at a price of $150 per ton. Therefore a price of $150 per ton is the market-clearing price that would prevail in the United States without international trade. Notice that the world price per ton of steel is measured on the vertical axis in Exhibit 5(a). What if the world price of steel is $200 per ton—a price *above* the $150 per ton price that would prevail in the United States in the absence of trade? If international trade is prohibited, the world price is irrelevant, and only the price determined in the United States matters. But if U.S. producers can easily export steel to the rest of the world, they will increase the quantity supplied whenever the world price rises above $150 per ton. You can see from the supply curve in panel (a) that when the world price is $200 per ton, the quantity of U.S. steel produced increases to 130 million tons per month. Because U.S. demanders now face the higher price of $200 per ton, they reduce the quantity they demand to 70 million tons per month.

The amount by which the quantity supplied by U.S. producers exceeds the quantity demanded in the United States equals the amount of steel exported by U.S. producers.

EXHIBIT 5

The Domestic Market and World Market for Steel

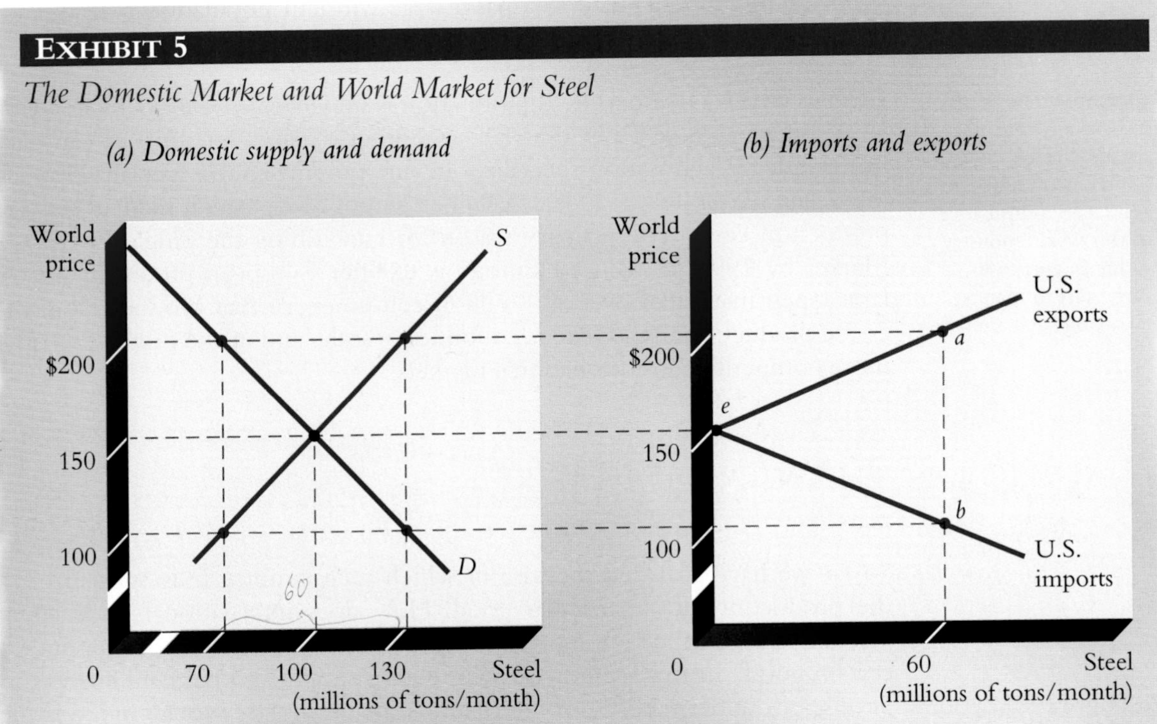

Panel (a) shows the domestic supply and demand for steel in the United States. At a world price of $150 per ton, U.S. consumers demand all that U.S. producers supply. Panel (b) shows that no U.S. steel is exported or imported at that price.

At world prices above $150 per ton, U.S. producers supply more than enough to satisfy domestic quantity demanded. The excess is exported. The U.S. export line in panel (b) shows the volume of exports at prices above $150. If the world price is below $150, domestic quantity demanded exceeds domestic quantity supplied. The difference is made up by imports.

Point to Stress The export line is a *supply curve*, representing the amounts that U.S. manufacturers are willing and able to export at various prices, other things constant. It is determined by comparing quantity supplied to quantity demanded at each price above the autarky price.

Thus, when the world price equals $200 per ton, 60 million tons of steel are exported from the United States. U.S. exports and imports as a function of the world price are illustrated in panel (b) of Exhibit 5. In that panel the vertical axis again presents the world price of steel, but the horizontal axis measures the amount of steel that is imported or exported based on the world price. At point *e* on the horizontal axis of panel (b), the world price is $150 per ton, so imports and exports equal zero. When the world price is $200, the United States exports 60 million tons of steel, a combination identified as point *a* in panel (b). By connecting points *e* and *a*, we form an upward-sloping *export line*. At each point on this export line, the quantity exported by the United States is equal to the difference in panel (a) between the U.S. quantity supplied and the U.S. quantity demanded at that price.

What If World Price Is Below the Domestic Equilibrium Price?

What if the world price is below $150 per ton? If U.S. steel buyers cannot buy from abroad, the world price of steel is irrelevant. If, however, U.S. buyers can purchase foreign output at the world price, the United States will become an importer of steel whenever the world price falls below $150 per ton. The quantity demanded in the United States at a price below $150 per ton exceeds the quantity supplied by U.S. producers, so *the excess quantity demanded in U.S. markets is satisfied by purchases from foreign producers*. Suppose the world price is $100 per ton. In Exhibit 5(a) you can see that when the price is $100 per ton, the amount U.S. producers are willing to supply drops to 70 million tons, but the U.S. quantity demanded increases to 130 million tons. At that price 60 million tons of steel are purchased on the world market.

Point to Stress The import line is a *demand curve*, representing the amounts that U.S. consumers are willing and able to import at various prices, other things constant. It is determined by comparing quantity supplied to quantity demanded at each price below the world price.

The quantity of steel imported by the United States when the price is $100 per ton is shown by point *b* in panel (b). At any prices below $150 per ton, the quantity of imports is equal to the excess of U.S. quantity demanded over the quantity supplied by U.S. steel producers, shown in panel (a); with these quantities we can construct the *import line* in panel (b), which starts at a price of $150 (point *e*) and slopes down to the right.

To summarize: When the world price of steel is $150 per ton, the quantity of steel demanded in the United States equals the quantity supplied by U.S. producers, so steel is neither imported nor exported. When the world price is above $150, the quantity of steel supplied by U.S. producers exceeds the quantity demanded by U.S. buyers, so steel is exported. And when the world price is below $150, the quantity demanded by U.S. buyers exceeds the quantity supplied by U.S. producers, so steel is imported. The world price therefore determines whether the United States is an importer, an exporter, or neither.

Teaching Tip The role of the world price as the determinant of the trading position of a country is altered by barriers to trade, discussed later in the chapter.

The Rest of the World

To simplify our analysis, let's suppose that there is just one other country in the "rest of the world": Japan, a major producer and user of steel. To keep the accounting simple, we'll convert all Japanese prices into U.S. dollars. Japan's domestic supply and demand for steel, along with its supply of exports and demand for imports, are presented in Exhibit 6. As you can see from panel (a), when the world price of steel is $100 per ton, the quantity supplied by Japanese producers just equals the quantity demanded in Japan. In panel (b), therefore, there are no imports or exports when the world price is $100 per ton. But at a world price above $100 per ton, Japanese producers supply more steel than is demanded in Japan, so the difference is exported to the world market, as shown in panel (b). The reverse is true for world prices below $100; in that case the quantity demanded in Japan exceeds the quantity Japanese producers supply, and the difference becomes Japan's imports, as shown in panel (b).

EXHIBIT 6

The Domestic Japanese Market and the World Market for Steel

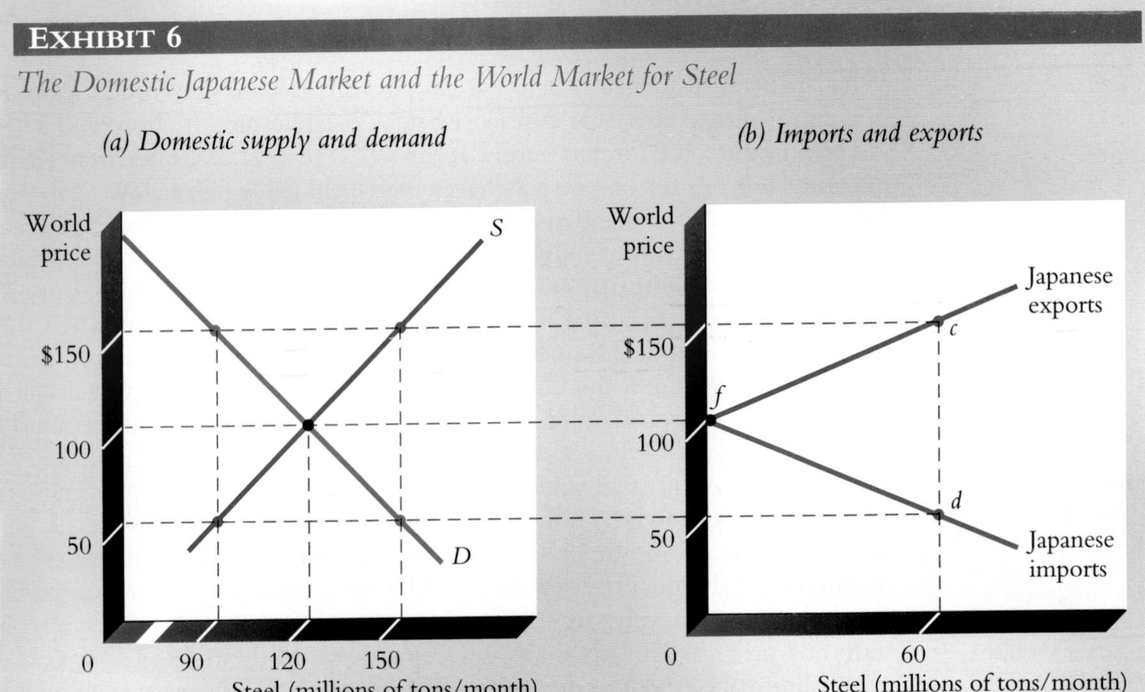

At a world price of $100 per ton, Japan neither exports nor imports steel. At prices higher than $100, Japan exports the amount by which domestic production exceeds domestic quantity demanded. At prices below $100, Japan imports steel.

Determining the World Price

Teaching Tip In order for world quantity demanded to match world quantity supplied, imports must match exports. In our example, world prices above $150 would cause both countries to try to export, so the price would fall. World prices below $100 would cause both countries to try to import, so the price would rise. One country must be exporting, the other importing.

The world price of steel is determined by international supply and demand. In our simplified two-country model, *the world price is found where the exports of one country equal the imports of the other country.* To determine the world price of steel, we combine elements of Exhibits 5 and 6. Panel (a) of Exhibit 7 again presents the supply and demand for steel in the United States, and panel (c) presents the same information for Japan.

The U.S. *import* line and the Japanese *export* line are shown in panel (b). The U.S. export line and the Japanese import line are not shown because, given the supply and demand conditions, the United States will not export steel and Japan will not import it. But at a price above $100 per ton, Japanese producers are willing to export, and at a price below $150 per ton, U.S. buyers are willing to import. International trade will therefore occur at a world price between $100 and $150 per ton. Specifically, the intersection of the Japanese export line with the U.S. import line yields the world equilibrium price of steel. (Again, we are assuming that the world market consists of only these two countries.) Given the supply and demand for steel in the two countries, the equilibrium world price will be $125 per ton. At that price Japan will export 30 million tons of steel per month to the United States.

EXHIBIT 7

Determination of the World Price

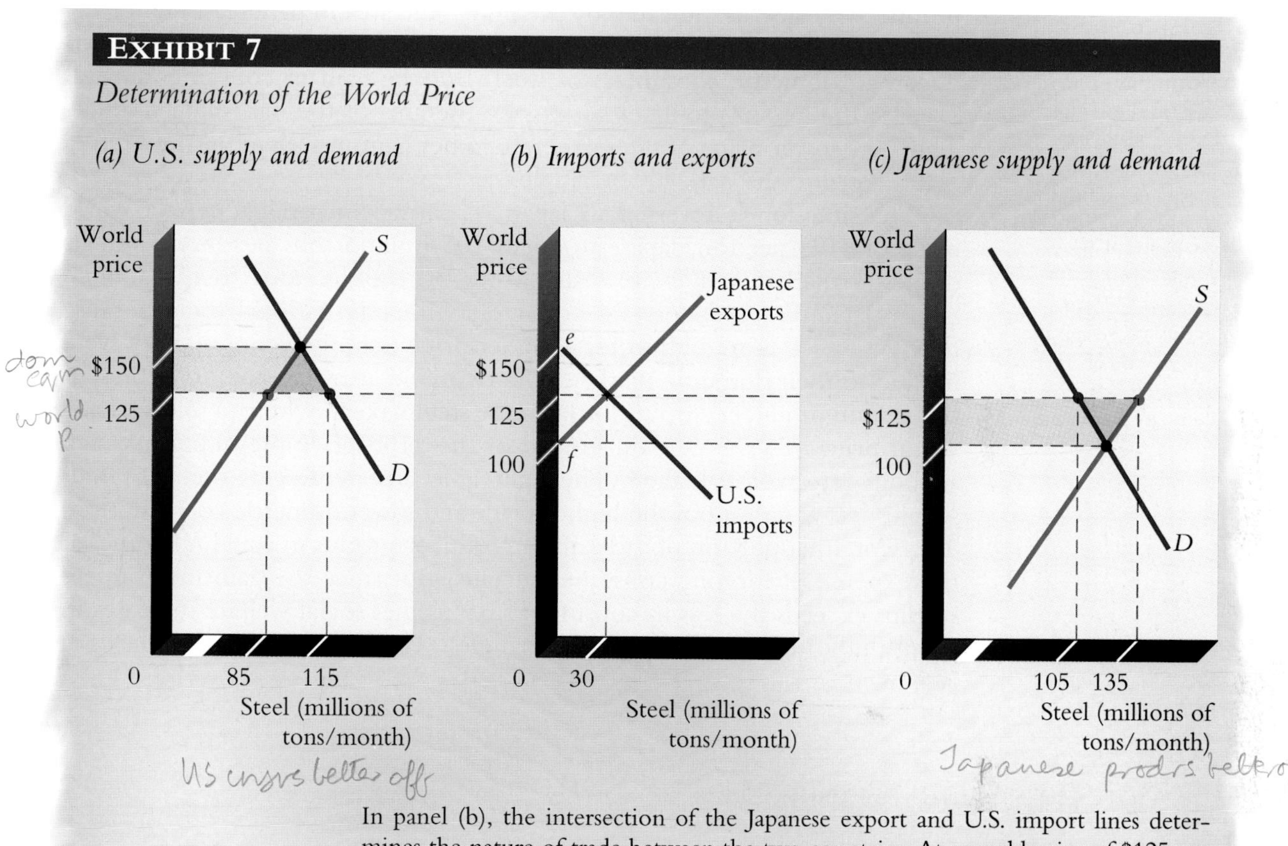

In panel (b), the intersection of the Japanese export and U.S. import lines determines the nature of trade between the two countries. At a world price of $125 per ton, Japan exports 30 million tons of steel to the United States. In the United States prices are lower and the quantity consumed is greater as a result of trade. The blue areas reflect the gain in consumer surplus. In Japan prices are higher and the quantity produced is greater. The gold areas indicate the gain in producer surplus. The net gains in the two countries are shown by the darker shaded triangles in panels (a) and (c).

The Net Effect of Trade on Social Welfare

Teaching Tip Just as in the chapter's earlier discussion on opportunity costs, which pointed out that the terms of trade must be between the countries' opportunity costs, the world price must be between the no-trade prices in the two countries.

Let's consider the gains from trade in each country. *The net change in social welfare is determined by summing the net changes in consumer and producer surpluses.* In panel (a) of Exhibit 7, you can see that at a price of $125 per ton, 115 million tons per month are demanded in the United States. At that price 85 million tons are supplied by U.S. producers and 30 million tons are imported from Japan. In the United States the price is lower and the quantity consumed is greater than would be the case without trade. U.S. consumers in effect enjoy a bonus, or a consumer surplus, resulting from the lower world price.

The two blue areas in panel (a) reflect the gain in U.S. consumer surplus resulting from the lower world price. But the lower price also means that U.S. producers receive a lower price for their output and thus forgo some

Point to Stress In the importing industry (in this example, steel in the United States), trade causes the price to fall, domestic consumption to rise, domestic production to fall, consumer surplus to rise, and producer surplus to fall. Although the country on average is better off, some residents are worse off.

producer surplus, as indicated by the light-blue area in panel (a). Hence the light-blue area represents the surplus transferred from domestic steel producers to domestic consumers of steel. But the gain in consumer surplus exceeds the loss in producer surplus by the area of the dark-blue triangle. Thus, the lower price of steel generates a net gain in welfare in the United States equal to the dark-blue triangle.

The situation is reversed in Japan, as shown in panel (c). At a world price of $125 per ton, Japan produces 105 million tons per month for its domestic market and exports the other 30 million tons to the United States. Japanese producers are better off with international trade because they get to sell more output for a higher price than they could if they were limited to their domestic market. The two gold areas in panel (c) represent the gain in producer surplus for Japanese steelmakers, who can sell steel at a world price of $125 per ton instead of the $100 price prevailing in Japan without international trade. The light-gold area represents the consumer surplus lost as a result of the higher price and lower domestic consumption. Therefore that portion of the gain in producer surplus in panel (c) comes at the expense of forgone consumer surplus. But since the gain in producer surplus exceeds the loss in consumer surplus, net social welfare increases in Japan (indicated by the dark-gold triangle). Thus, *trade confers net benefits in both countries.*

TRADE RESTRICTIONS

Point to Stress In the exporting industry (steel in Japan), trade causes the price to rise, domestic consumption to fall, domestic production to rise, consumer surplus to fall, and producer surplus to rise. Although the country on average is better off, some residents are worse off.

Despite the benefits of international trade, nearly all countries at one time or another erect barriers to impede or block free trade among nations. The trade restrictions usually benefit domestic producers, but harm domestic consumers. In this section we will consider the effects of restrictions and the reasons they are imposed.

Tariffs

A *tariff*, a term first introduced in Chapter 4, is a tax on imports. (Tariffs can also be applied to exports, but we will focus on import tariffs.) A tariff can be either *specific*, such as a tariff of $5 per barrel of oil, or *ad valorem*, a percentage of the price of imports at the port of entry. Let's consider the effects of a specific tariff on a particular good. In Exhibit 8, D is the domestic demand for sugar and S is the supply provided by domestic producers. Suppose that the world price of sugar is $0.10 per pound. With free trade, domestic consumers can buy any amount desired at the world price, so the quantity demanded is 70 million pounds per month, of which 20 million pounds are supplied by domestic producers and 50 million pounds are imported. Domestic producers cannot charge more than the world price, since domestic buyers can purchase as much sugar as they want at $0.10 per pound in the world market.

EXHIBIT 8

Effect of a Tariff

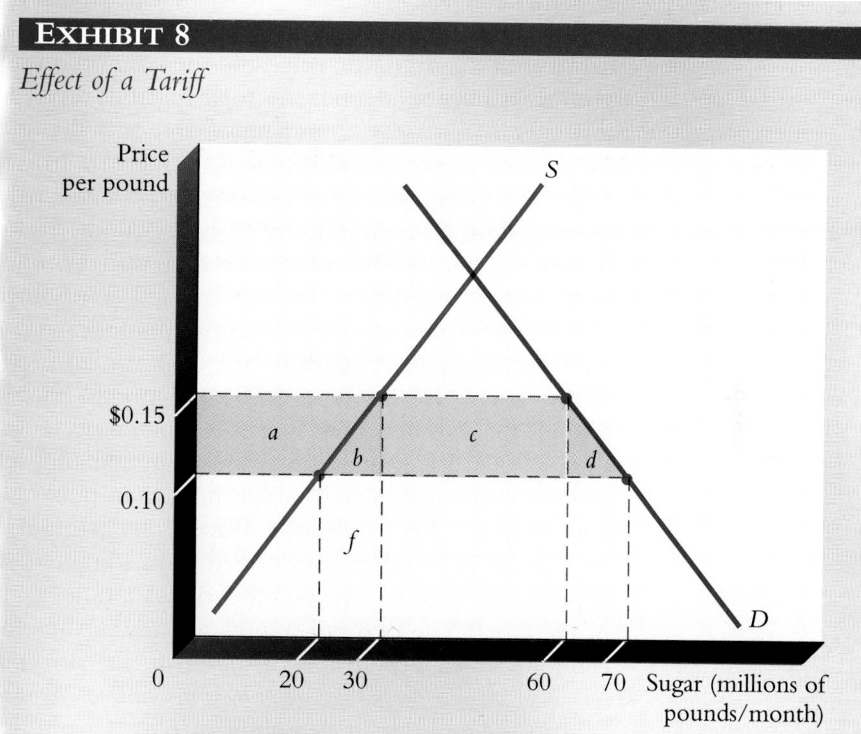

At a world price of $0.10 per pound, domestic consumers demand 70 million pounds per month and domestic producers supply 20 million pounds per month; the difference is imported. With the imposition of a $0.05 per pound tariff, the domestic price rises to $0.15 per pound, domestic producers increase production to 30 million pounds, and domestic consumers cut back to 60 million pounds. Imports fall to 30 million pounds. At the higher domestic price, consumers are worse off; their loss of consumer surplus is the sum of areas *a*, *b*, *c*, and *d*. Area *a* represents an increase in producer surplus: a transfer from consumers to producers. Areas *b* and *f* reflect the portion of additional revenues to producers that is just offset by the higher production costs of expanding domestic output by 10 million pounds. Area *c* shows government revenue from the tariff. The net welfare loss to society is the sum of area *d*, which reflects the loss of consumer surplus resulting from the drop in consumption, and area *b*, which reflects the higher marginal cost of producing domestically output that could have been produced more cheaply abroad.

Example The North American Free Trade Agreement (NAFTA) is designed to roll back twenty thousand separate tariffs among Mexico, the United States, and Canada over a ten- to fifteen-year period. During 1992, when NAFTA was being negotiated, tariffs were averaging nearly 11 percent in Mexico, 5 percent in Canada, and less than 4 percent in the United States.

Teaching Tip The country in Exhibit 8 has imports so small relative to total world demand for sugar that its consumers face a perfectly elastic world supply of sugar.

Teaching Tip With a specific tariff, the new price equals the free trade price plus the amount of the tariff. Exhibit 8 shows a *nonprohibitive* tariff, whereby some imports continue despite the tariff.

Now suppose that a specific tariff of $0.05 is imposed on each pound of sugar imported, raising the price of imported sugar from $0.10 to $0.15 per pound. Domestic producers can therefore raise their price to $0.15 per pound as well without losing sales to imports. With the higher price, the quantity supplied by domestic producers increases to 30 million pounds per month, but the quantity demanded by domestic consumers declines to 60 million pounds per month. Because the quantity demanded has declined and the quantity supplied by domestic producers has increased, imports decline from 50 million to 30 million pounds per month.

Since the price is higher after the tariff, consumers are worse off. The loss in consumer surplus is identified in Exhibit 8 by the blue and red areas. Because both the domestic price and the quantity of sugar supplied by domestic producers have increased, the total revenue received by domestic producers increases by the areas *a* plus *b* plus *f*. But only the light-blue area, *a*, represents an increase in producer surplus. The increase in revenue represented by the area *b* plus *f* just offsets the higher marginal cost of expanding domestic production from 20 million to 30 million pounds. The red triangle, *b*, represents part of the net welfare loss to the domestic economy, because those 10 million pounds could have been purchased from abroad for $0.10 per pound rather than produced domestically at a higher marginal cost.

Government revenue from the tariff is identified by the light-blue area, *c*, which equals the tariff of $0.05 per pound multiplied by the 30 million pounds that are imported. Tariff revenue represents a loss to consumers, but since the tariff is revenue to the government, this loss can potentially be offset by a reduction in taxes or an increase in public services. The red triangle, *d*, represents a loss in consumer surplus reflecting the 10-million-pound drop in quantity demanded that resulted from a higher price. This loss is not redistributed as a gain to anyone else, so area *d* reflects part of the net welfare loss of the tariff. The two red triangles, *b* and *d*, therefore measure the domestic economy's net welfare loss of the tariff; the *two triangles measure a net loss in consumer surplus that is not offset by a net gain to anyone else.*

Teaching Tip Since free trade and trade restrictions have opposite effects on consumers, the impact of a country's trade policy on an individual consumer will depend on the industry in which the consumer earns the major part of his or her income and the mixture of goods that he or she purchases.

Of the total loss in consumer surplus (areas *a*, *b*, c, and *d*) resulting from the tariff, area *a* is redistributed from consumers to domestic producers (and suppliers of resources specific to the industry), area *c* becomes tariff revenue for the government, and the two red areas, *b* and *d*, reflect a net loss in social welfare because of the tariff.

Import Quotas

An *import quota* is a legal limit on the quantity of a particular commodity that can be imported per year. Quotas often target exports from certain countries. For example, a quota may limit the number of autos that can be imported from Japan or the number of pairs of shoes that can be imported from Brazil. To have an impact on the market, or to be *effective*, a quota must limit imports to less than would be imported under free trade.

Example For example, the United States has quotas on dairy, steel, and cotton products. Voluntary export quotas are also negotiated by the United States with major textile-exporting countries, for example, under the threat of imposing tariffs or import quotas. Similarly, Japan prohibits the importation of almost all rice.

Let's consider the impact of a quota on the domestic market for sugar. In panel (a) of Exhibit 9, the domestic supply of sugar is *S* and the domestic demand is *D*. Suppose that the world price of sugar is $0.10 per pound. With free trade, that price would prevail in the domestic market, and 70 million pounds per month would be demanded. Domestic producers would supply 20 million pounds and importers 50 million pounds. With a quota of 50 million pounds or more per month, the domestic price would be the same as the world price of $0.10 per pound, and domestic sales would be 70 million pounds per month. Any more stringent quota, however, would reduce the supply of imports, which, as we will see, would raise the domestic price.

EXHIBIT 9

Effect of a Quota

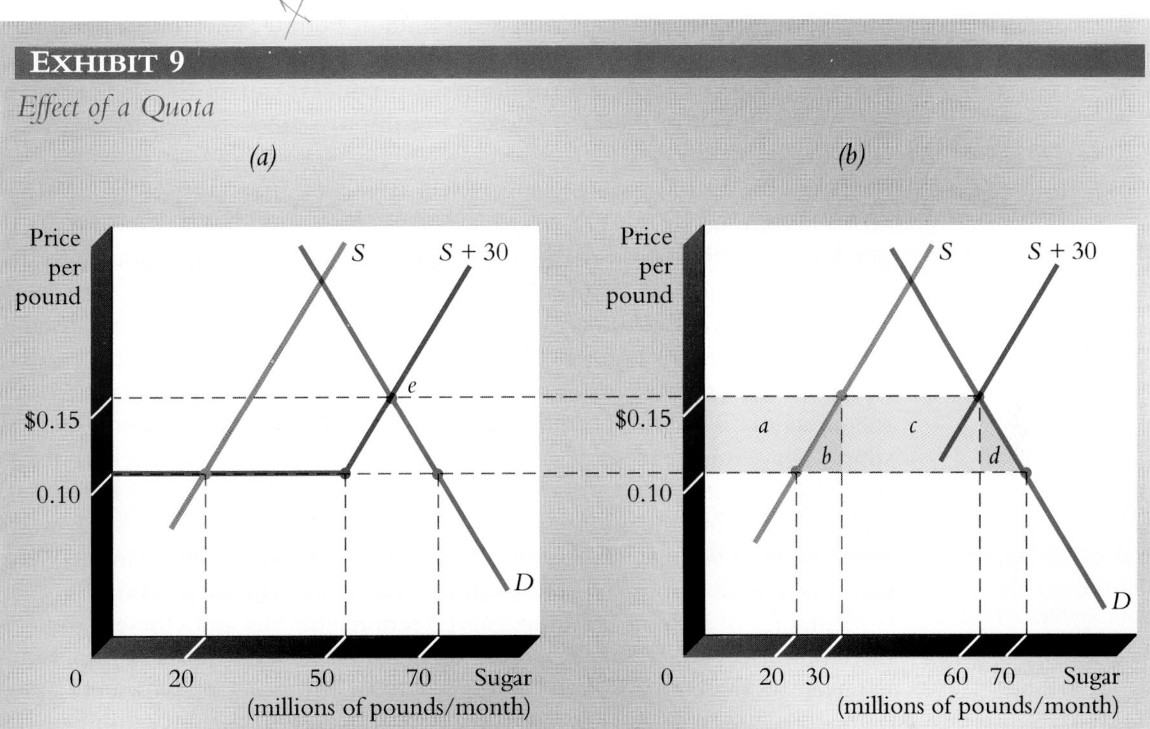

In panel (a), *D* is the domestic demand curve and *S* is the domestic supply curve. When the government establishes a sugar quota of 30 million pounds per year, the supply curve from both domestic production and imports becomes horizontal at the world price of $0.10 per pound and remains horizontal until the supply reaches 50 million pounds. For higher prices, the supply curve equals the horizontal sum of the domestic supply curve, *S*, and the quota. The new domestic price, $0.15 per pound, is determined by the intersection of the new supply curve, *S* + 30, with the domestic demand curve, *D*. Panel (b) shows the welfare effect of the quota. As a result of the higher domestic price, consumer surplus is reduced by the amount of the shaded area. Area *a* represents a transfer from domestic consumers to domestic producers. Rectangular area *c* shows the gain to those who can import sugar at the world price and sell it at the higher domestic price. Triangular area *b* reflects a net loss; it represents the amount by which the cost of producing an extra 10 million pounds of sugar in the United States exceeds the cost of buying it from abroad. Area *d* also reflects a net loss—a reduction in consumer surplus as consumption falls. Thus, the blue areas illustrate the loss in consumer surplus that is captured by domestic producers and those who are permitted to fulfill the quota, and the red triangles illustrate the minimum net welfare cost.

Suppose that a quota of 30 million pounds per month is established. As long as the price in the U.S. market is at or above the world price of $0.10 per pound, foreign producers supply 30 million pounds to the U.S. market. So at price levels at or above $0.10 per pound, the total supply of sugar to the domestic market is found by adding 30 million pounds of sugar to the amount supplied by domestic producers. At the world price of $0.10 per pound, domestic producers supply 20 million pounds, and importers supply the limit of 30 million pounds, for a total quantity supplied of 50 million pounds. At prices above $0.10, domestic producers can and do expand their quantity supplied in the U.S. market, but imports are restricted by the quota to 30 million pounds.

Domestic and foreign producers will never sell their output for less than $0.10 per pound in the U.S. market because they can always sell it for $0.10 per pound on the world market. Thus, the supply curve that sums both domestic production and imports becomes horizontal at the world price of $0.10 per pound and remains horizontal until the quantity supplied reaches 50 million pounds. For prices above $0.10 per pound, the supply curve equals the horizontal sum of the supply curve of domestic producers, *S*, and the quota of 30 million pounds. The domestic price is found where this new supply curve intersects the domestic demand curve, which in panel (a) of Exhibit 9 occurs at point *e*. *An effective quota, by limiting imports, raises the domestic price of sugar above the world price and makes the quantity demanded lower than it would be under free trade.* Note that by design the quota in this example yields the same equilibrium price and quantity as did the tariff we examined earlier.

Teaching Tip A quota that yields the same equilibrium price and quantity as a tariff is termed an *equivalent* quota—in this example, the quota is set at the import level that develops when the tariff is set at $0.05.

Panel (b) of Exhibit 9 focuses on the redistributional and efficiency effects of the quota. The decline in consumer surplus after the quota is imposed is depicted by the blue and red areas. The loss in consumer surplus represented by the blue area *a* is converted into the gain in producer surplus resulting from the higher price. Because the value of area *a* is simply transferred from domestic consumers to domestic producers, area *a* involves no loss in domestic welfare. The blue rectangle *c* shows the gain to those permitted by the quota to sell 30 million pounds per month at the domestic price of $0.15 per pound. To the extent that the gains from the quota go to foreign exporters rather than to domestic importers, area *c* reflects a net loss in domestic welfare.

Teaching Tip The government can regain all or part of area *c* by selling the quota rights.

The red triangle *b* shows the amount by which the marginal cost of producing another 10 million pounds in the United States exceeds the world price of the good. This triangular area represents a welfare loss to the domestic economy, because sugar could have been purchased for $0.10 per pound from abroad and the domestic resources employed to increase sugar production could have been used more efficiently in the production of other goods. The red triangle *d* also represents a welfare loss, because it reflects a reduction in consumer surplus (resulting from the fact that less sugar is consumed because of the higher price) with no offsetting gain to anyone. Thus, the two red triangles in panel (b) of Exhibit 9 measure the minimum welfare cost imposed on the domestic economy by an effective quota. To the extent the profits of quota rights (area *c*) accrue to foreigners, the welfare loss imposed on the domestic economy is greater.

Teaching Tip See the chapter's conclusion for further discussion of the effects of trade restrictions.

Comparison of Tariffs and Quotas

Consider the similarities and differences between the quota and the tariff we have discussed, both of which raised the domestic price of sugar by the same amount. Since the tariff and the quota had identical effects on the price, they reflected the same change in quantity demanded. In both cases domestic consumers suffered the same loss in consumer surplus and domestic producers gained the same amount of producer surplus. The primary difference between the two restrictive policies is that the revenue resulting from the tariff goes to the domestic government, whereas the revenue resulting from the quota goes to whomever is awarded the right to sell foreign goods in the domestic market. If the quota rights accrue to foreigners, then the domestic economy is worse off with a quota than with a tariff.

Mindful of the welfare loss from trade restrictions, the United States, after World War II, invited its trading partners to negotiate less stringent restrictions. The result was the **General Agreement on Tariffs and Trade (GATT)**, which was an international trade treaty adopted in 1947 by twenty-three countries, including the United States. Each member of GATT agreed to (1) treat all member nations equally with respect to trade, (2) reduce tariff rates through multinational negotiations, and (3) reduce import quotas. The agreement resulted in thousands of tariff reductions; the number of signers has since grown to nearly one hundred. International trade increased in the 1950s and 1960s, partly in response to a lowering of tariffs. On average tariffs fell from about 40 percent of the value of tariffed products during the 1930s to about 5 percent since 1980. About one-third of imports face no tariff at all.

General Agreement on Tariffs and Trade (GATT) An international tariff-reduction treaty adopted in 1947 by the United States and twenty-three other countries; there are nearly one hundred treaty signers today

Teaching Tip GATT headquarters are in Geneva, Switzerland. The most recent round of negotiations were instituted in Uruguay and thus were termed the Uruguay Round.

Point to Stress The expenditure of resources on such rent seeking by quota supporters increases the welfare losses resulting from quotas.

GATT has become a permanent international agreement. Members of GATT agree to honor the *most-favored nation clause*, which means that tariff reductions granted to one country are extended to other trading members of GATT. Multilateral negotiations since 1947 have focused primarily on reducing tariffs. As a result, nontariff barriers such as quotas have grown.

Currently the United States grants quotas to specific countries. These countries, in turn, award these rights to their exporters through a variety of means. The value of these export rights has been estimated recently to exceed $7 billion, with more than half of this amount due to quotas on textiles and apparel.[1] *By rewarding domestic producers with higher prices and foreign producers with the right to sell goods to the United States, the quota system creates two groups intent on securing and perpetuating these quotas.* Lobbyists for foreign producers work the halls of Congress seeking the right to export to the United States. This strong support from producers, coupled with a lack of opposition from consumers (who remain largely unaware of all this), results in quotas that have lasted for decades. Steel quotas have been in effect for over twenty years, apparel quotas for over thirty years, and sugar quotas for over fifty years.

Some economists have argued that if quotas are to be used, the United States should auction off quota allocations to foreign producers, thereby capturing the difference between the world price and the U.S. price. Auctioning off quotas would not only increase federal revenue but also reduce the attractiveness of quotas to foreign exporters to the United States and thereby reduce pressure on Washington to perpetuate quotas.

1. See C. Fred Bergsten, "Reform Trade Policy with Auction Quotas," *Challenge* (May/June 1987): 5.

Other Trade Restrictions

Example In fall 1992, the U.S. government provided credit guarantees to eighteen countries to help them buy U.S. farm products. NAFTA negotiations resulted in a requirement that at least 62.5 percent of parts for light trucks and cars sold tariff-free in any of the three countries involved should come from North America.

Besides tariffs and quotas, there are a variety of other restrictions on free trade. A country may provide *export subsidies* to encourage firms to export or *low-interest loans* to foreign buyers to promote exports of large capital goods. Some countries impose *domestic content requirements* specifying that a certain percentage of a final good's value must be produced domestically. Other requirements concerning health, safety, or technical standards often discriminate against foreign goods. For example, European countries prohibit imports of beef from hormone-fed cattle, a measure aimed at U.S. beef producers. Purity laws in Germany bar the importation of many non-German beers. Until uniform standards are adopted by members of the European Community, differing technical standards force manufacturers to make seven different models of the same TV for this market. The point is that tariffs and quotas are only two of many devices aimed at restricting imports.

Common Markets

Teaching Tip The European Community was to begin negotiating membership with Austria, Sweden, and Finland in 1993.

Some countries have considered the success of the U.S. economy, with its free trade within the fifty states, and have developed free-trade pacts. The largest and best known is the European Community, which began in 1958 with a half-dozen countries and has now expanded to twelve. The idea was to create a barrier-free European market like the United States in which goods, services, people, and capital were free to flow to their highest-valued use without restrictions. Another trading bloc has formed among the newly industrialized countries of East Asia. And most recently, the United States, Canada, and Mexico have developed a free-trade agreement, as discussed in the following case study.

CASE STUDY

The North American Free Trade Agreement

In 1992 trade officials were working out the final details of a U.S.–Canada–Mexico pact called the North American Free Trade Agreement, or NAFTA for short. Across the Atlantic another set of trade negotiators was involved with the latest round of GATT talks in Geneva, Switzerland. Regional trading bloc agreements such as NAFTA and the European Community, or EC, require an exception to GATT rules because bloc members can make special deals among themselves and can then discriminate against outsiders. Recall that under GATT rules any trade concession granted one country must be given to *all other* GATT members.

Through NAFTA, Mexico hopes to increase U.S. investment in Mexico by guaranteeing to those who build manufacturing plants in Mexico duty-free access to U.S. markets, which is where over two-thirds of Mexico's exports go. From a trade point of view, building a plant in Mexico would be equivalent to building one in the United States. But labor costs are much cheaper in Mexico. (In 1992 U.S. manufacturing wages were about seven times higher than Mexican wages.) The United States is interested in NAFTA because Mexico's eighty-five million people represent an attractive export

Example In late 1992, Zenith Electronics closed its Asian assembly plant and moved many of its operations from Taiwan to Mexico. Zenith estimated that if it had been unable to move to Mexico, the company would have been forced to close U.S. plants in Chicago and Missouri.

market for U.S. producers, and Mexico's huge oil reserves could ease U.S. energy problems. The United States would also like to bolster Mexico's move toward a more market-oriented economy, as reflected, for example, by Mexico's recent privatization of its phone system and banks.

Canada does not trade much with Mexico but joined the talks partly in self-defense to ensure that the agreement did not undermine an existing U.S.–Canada trade accord. (Canada is the leading trading partner of the United States.) In the negotiation of NAFTA, many special side deals were made that violate the spirit of free trade. For example, negotiators have devised a complicated formula to favor General Motors at the expense of Toyota and Honda. General Motors claims to need protection because its factories are less efficient. In countries such as Venezuela and Colombia, where import restrictions have been lifted, GM faces competition from all over the world—even from the Russian-made Lada, whose price is less than half that of a GM car.

Among other things, the two-thousand-page NAFTA agreement abolishes a U.S. quota imposed on Mexican textiles. But since Mexico never exported many textiles to the United States anyway, the quota was irrelevant. Since NAFTA did not threaten U.S. textile manufacturers, they supported it, but they were against GATT negotiations that called for a worldwide end to textile quotas. In fact, U.S. textile manufacturers tried to broaden NAFTA to include Central America in return for support from Central American countries to weaken the GATT textile proposals in Geneva. Whenever trade negotiations take place, the bazaar in trade concessions and restrictions is open and everything is up for grabs.

Source: Bob Davis, "Pending Trade Pact with Mexico, Canada, Has Protectionist Air," *Wall Street Journal*, 12 July 1992.

Arguments for Trade Restrictions

In view of their distributional effects and the welfare loss they can cause, trade restrictions often appear to be little more than welfare programs for the protected domestic industries. Given the welfare loss that results from these restrictions, it would be more efficient simply to transfer money from domestic consumers to domestic producers. But such a blatant transfer would probably be politically unpopular. Arguments for trade restrictions avoid mention of transfers to domestic producers and instead cite loftier concerns. As we shall now see, some of these arguments have more validity than others.

National Defense Argument

Certain industries are said to be in need of protection from import competition because they produce output that becomes vital in time of war. Because of their strategic importance, industries such as weapons manufacturing are sometimes insulated from foreign competition by trade restrictions. Thus, national defense considerations outweigh concerns about efficiency and equity.

How valid is this argument? Trade restrictions may shelter the defense industry, but other methods of sheltering it, such as government subsidies to U.S. producers, might be more efficient. Or the government could stockpile basic military hardware so that maintaining an ongoing productive capacity would become less essential, though technological change soon makes some weapons obsolete. Since nearly all industries can make some claim on national defense grounds, instituting trade restrictions on this basis can get out of hand. For example, one reason domestic wool producers benefit from protective policies is that wool is said to be critical to the production of military uniforms.

Infant Industry Argument

The infant industry argument was formulated as a rationale for protecting emerging domestic industry from foreign competition. According to this argument, in industries where a firm's average cost per unit falls as production expands, new domestic firms may need to be insulated from mature foreign competitors until the domestic firms reach sufficient size to be competitive. Trade restrictions are thus viewed as temporary devices for allowing domestic firms to achieve sufficient economies of scale to compete with established foreign producers.

Example The French government used the infant industry argument to foster development of the Concorde supersonic jet. Revenues have yet to cover the jet's actual operating costs. If the potential for eventual profits exists in a new industry, private financial markets will provide the necessary funding to cover losses during the initial years.

The first problem with this argument is that it is more relevant to developing economies, such as those of Eastern Europe, Africa, and South America, than to industrial economies, such as the United States, Germany, and Great Britain. Another problem is how to identify which industries merit protection. Finally, when do domestic firms become old enough to look after themselves? The very existence of protection may foster production inefficiencies that firms may not be able to outgrow. The immediate cost of such restrictions is the net welfare loss from higher domestic prices. These costs may become permanent if the industry never realizes the expected economies of scale and thus never becomes competitive. As with the national defense argument, policy makers should be careful in adopting trade restrictions based on the infant industry argument. Here again, production subsidies are more efficient than import restrictions.

Antidumping Argument

Dumping Selling a commodity abroad at a price that is below its cost of production or below the price charged in the domestic market

Dumping is selling a commodity abroad at a price that is below its cost of production or below the price charged in the home market. Exporters may be able to sell the good for less overseas because of export subsidies, or firms may simply find it profitable to charge lower prices in foreign markets, where there are more competitors. Critics of dumping recommend applying a tariff to raise the price of dumped goods.

What's wrong with foreign producers selling goods for less in the United States than in their own countries? Why should U.S. consumers be prevented from buying products for as little as possible even if these low prices are the result of a foreign subsidy? If the dumping is *persistent*, the lower price may increase consumer surplus by an amount that will more than offset losses to domestic producers. *Thus, there is no good reason why consumers should not be allowed to buy imports for a persistently lower price.*

An alternative form of dumping, termed *predatory dumping*, is the *temporary* sale of a product at a lower price abroad in order to drive out competing producers. Once the competition has been eliminated, so the story goes, the exporting firm can raise the price. Predatory dumping may also be a way to discourage the development of domestic production of a good. Domestic firms would not find entry into this industry attractive because they would not be able to sell at the low price that results from dumping. By driving out established firms or by discouraging domestic entry, the dumpers try to monopolize the market. The trouble with this argument is (1) it would be difficult to block entry from around the world, and (2) if dumpers try to take advantage of their monopoly position by sharply increasing the price, then other firms may enter the market and sell for less. There are very few documented cases of predatory dumping.

Teaching Tip A tariff to offset dumping is termed a *countervailing duty*. Rebates of sales taxes or value-added taxes have not been considered dumping since the Trade Agreements Act of 1979.

Sometimes dumping may be *sporadic*, as firms occasionally sell at a discount to unload excess inventories. Sporadic dumping can be unsettling for domestic industry, but the economic impact is not a matter of great public concern. Regardless, all dumping is prohibited in the United States by the Trade Agreements Act of 1979, which calls for the imposition of tariffs when a good is sold for less in the United States than in its home market. In addition, GATT allows for the imposition of offsetting tariffs when products are sold for "less than fair value" and when there is "material injury" to domestic producers. The U.S. producers of lumber and beer have recently accused their Canadian counterparts of dumping.

Jobs and Income Argument

Example During NAFTA negotiations, labor leaders argued that tens of thousands of U.S. jobs would be lost as firms shifted production to Mexico to take advantage of low wages.

Example Both Honda and Toyota ship automobiles from their U.S. plants for sale in Japan.

One rationale for trade restrictions that is commonly heard in the United States today is that they protect U.S. jobs and wage levels. Using trade restrictions to protect domestic jobs is a strategy that dates back for centuries. One problem with such a policy is that other countries will likely retaliate by restricting *their* imports to save *their* jobs, so international trade is reduced, jobs are lost in export industries, and potential gains from trade are not realized.

Wages in other countries, especially developing countries, are often a small fraction of wages in the United States. Looking simply at differences in the wage rate narrows the focus too much, however. Wages represent just one component of the total production cost and may not necessarily be the most important. Employers are interested in the labor cost per unit of output, which depends on both the wage rate and labor productivity.

The high wage rate in the United States exists in part because of the high marginal productivity of U.S. workers. U.S. labor productivity remains the highest in the world. This high productivity can be traced to education and training and to the abundant machines and other physical capital that make workers more productive. Workers in the United States also benefit from a business climate that is relatively stable and that offers appropriate incentives to produce.

But how about the lower wages in many competing countries? These low wages can often be linked to workers' lack of education and training, the meager amount of physical capital that accompanies each worker, and a business climate that is less stable and less attractive. In areas where higher U.S. wages are supported by higher U.S. output per worker, the labor cost per unit of output may be as low, if not lower, in the United States than in many countries with low wages and low productivity. For example, although total hourly compensation is more than twice as high at Birmingham Steel, a U.S. corporation, than at South Korean steel plants, Birmingham's labor productivity is four times greater, so the labor cost per ton of steel is lower for Birmingham.[2]

Once multinational firms build plants and provide technological know-how in developing countries, however, U.S. workers lose some of their competitive edge, and their relatively high wages could price some U.S. products out of the world market. This has already happened in the stereo and consumer electronics industries. Over time, as labor productivity in developing countries increases, wage differentials among countries will narrow, much as wage differentials between Northern states and Southern states have narrowed. As technology and capital spread, U.S. workers cannot expect to maintain wage levels that are far above those in other countries. The U.S. government may promote research and development to keep U.S. producers on the cutting edge of technological developments. Staying ahead of the technological game is a constant battle.

Domestic producers do not like to compete with foreign producers whose costs are lower, so they often push for trade restrictions. But if restrictions negate any cost advantage a foreign producer might have, the law of comparative advantage becomes inoperative and domestic consumers are denied access to the lower-priced goods.

Teaching Tip Similarly, where a reciprocal trade agreement (such as occurs under GATT) threatens or causes serious harm to a domestic industry, the U.S. President can use an "escape clause" to prevent reducing the tariff. Increased imports must be a substantial cause of the serious injury to the import-competing industry. The escape clause is used sparingly.

Declining Industries Argument

Where an established domestic industry is in jeopardy of being displaced by lower-priced imports, there could be a rationale for *temporary* import restrictions to allow the orderly adjustment of the domestic industry. After all, domestic producers employ many industry-specific resources—both specialized machines and specialized labor. This physical and human capital is worth less in its next best alternative use. If the extinction of the domestic industry is forestalled through trade restrictions, specialized machines can be allowed to wear out naturally and specialized workers can retire voluntarily or can gradually pursue more promising careers.

2. Dana Milbank, "U.S. Productivity Gains Cut Costs, Close Gap with Low-Wage Overseas Firms," *Wall Street Journal*, 23 December 1992.

Thus, in the case of declining domestic industries, trade protection is viewed as a temporary measure to help lessen shocks to the economy and to allow for an orderly transition to a new industrial mix. But the protection offered should not be so generous as to encourage continued investment in the industry. Protection should be of specific duration and should be phased out over that period.

The clothing industry is an example of a declining U.S. industry. The 22,000 U.S. jobs saved as a result of trade restrictions pay an average of about $18,000 per year. But a recent Congressional Budget Office study estimates that because of higher domestic prices, U.S. consumers pay between $39,000 and $74,000 per year for each textile and apparel job saved. What's more, because tariffs and quotas are relatively higher on low-priced products, poor people pay proportionately more for these trade restrictions.

Example BMW and Audi were building plants in the United States in the early 1990s.

Although particular workers suffer in the short run as imports displace U.S. workers, jobs are also created by the export sector. And even where foreign competition appears to have displaced U.S. workers, many foreign companies have built plants in the United States and employ U.S. workers. For example, a dozen foreign television manufacturers and all major Japanese automobile manufacturers have plants in the United States. In fact, a U.S. consumer who buys a Honda Accord is more likely to be getting a car produced in the United States than is a U.S. consumer who buys a Pontiac Le Mans.

Since 1960 the number of jobs in the United States has grown by fifty-five million, nearly doubling the 1960 figure. To recognize this job growth is not to deny the problems facing those workers who are displaced by imports. Some displaced workers, particularly those in blue-collar jobs in steel and other unionized industries, are not apt to find jobs that will pay as well as the jobs they lost. As with infant industries, however, the problems posed by declining industries need not be solved by trade restrictions. To support the affected industry, the government could offer wage subsidies or special tax breaks that decline over time. The government could also fund programs to retrain workers for jobs that are in more demand.

Problems with Protection

Trade restrictions raise a number of problems in addition to the ones already mentioned. First, protecting one stage of production often requires protecting downstream stages of production. Protecting the U.S. textile industry from foreign competition, for example, raises the cost of cloth to U.S. clothing manufacturers, reducing their competitiveness. Thus, if the government protects domestic textile manufacturers, it must also protect the domestic garment industry. Otherwise, foreign garment manufacturers will fashion lower-priced foreign textiles into garments for export to the United States, where they will sell for less than U.S.-made garments made from higher-priced U.S. textiles.

Second, the cost of protection includes not only the welfare loss arising from the higher domestic price but also the cost of the resources used by domestic producers and groups to secure the favored protection. The cost of *rent seeking*—lobbying fees, propaganda, legal actions—can amount to as much as or more than the direct welfare loss from restrictions. A final problem with restrictions is policing and enforcing the myriad quotas, tariffs, and other restrictions. Consider the following case study.

CASE STUDY

Enforcing Trade Restrictions

The United States is the richest, most attractive market in the world. Trade restrictions often make U.S. markets even more appealing to foreign producers because U.S. prices exceed world prices. With 8,753 different tariff classifications and with tariffs ranging from zero to 458 percent, the U.S. Customs Service has difficulty keeping things straight. We should not be surprised that some U.S. importers try to skirt trade restrictions, either avoiding tariffs or illegally importing goods that are restricted by quotas. A diverse array of goods is imported in violation of quotas, including clothing, sugar, coffee, gems, and steel pipes. It has been estimated that more than 10 percent of all imports are illegal.

Restrictions affect not only the quantity of imports but also the quality. Nearly all schemes to import clothing illegally involve fraudulent documents intended to misrepresent the clothing so that it fits into some quota or qualifies for a lower tariff. Sometimes the garments are altered to evade detection. For example, because imports of men's running shorts are controlled by a quota, the shorts in one shipment reportedly had a flimsy inner lining so they would pass for swimming trunks, which face no quotas.

Because the United States allows some countries more generous quotas than others, exporters in a country under tight control sometimes ship their goods through a country with a liberal ceiling. For example, Japan typically makes so little clothing for export that the United States imposes no clothing quota for imports from Japan. As a result, clothing made in Korea is often shipped through Japan to evade U.S. quotas on Korean goods. Similarly, because Nepal is not subject to a clothing quota but India is, India ships clothing to the United States through Nepal.

Higher tariffs are often imposed on lower-priced products. Foreign steel companies have been accused of falsely inflating the price of steel to avoid import duties on low-priced steel. Allegedly, part of the higher price paid by importers was secretly rebated by steel producers through a variety of schemes. Producers of other steel products have mislabeled and falsely weighed them to avoid certain restrictions.

Some foreign producers and U.S. importers are said to engage in "port shopping," or testing various ports to see where inspections are most lax. Documents are often forged. U.S. Customs inspectors are responsible for policing all this activity. These inspectors must remain alert because of thousands of tariffs, quotas, and other trade restrictions in effect and the myriad ways to get around them.

Sources: Anthony De Stefano, "Customs Agents Fight Often Losing Battle Against Illegal Imports," *Wall Street Journal*, 26 January 1986; and James Bovard, "The Customs Service's Fickle Philosophers," *Wall Street Journal*, 31 July 1991.

Conclusion

Comparative advantage, specialization, and trade allow people to use their scarce resources most efficiently to satisfy their unlimited wants. International trade arises from voluntary exchange among buyers and sellers pursuing their self-interest. Despite the clear gains from free trade, restrictions on international trade date back hundreds of years.

Those who benefit from trade restrictions are the domestic producers (and their resource suppliers) who are able to sell their output for a higher price because of the restrictions. Protection insulates an industry from the rigors of global competition, in the process stifling innovation and leaving the industry vulnerable to technological change in other countries. Under a system of quotas, the winners also include those who have secured the right to import the good at the world price and sell it at the domestic price.

Example Consider the competitive positions of two of the most highly protected industries in the United States: automobiles and steel.

Consumers who must pay higher prices for protected goods suffer from trade restrictions, as do the domestic producers who use imported resources. Other losers are U.S. exporters, who face higher trade barriers if foreigners retaliate. Even if other countries do not retaliate, U.S. trade restrictions reduce the gains from comparative advantage and thereby reduce world income. With world income lower, U.S. exporters find that their foreign markets have shrunk. Some of these losers may go out of business; other firms may never even start producing. To the extent that protected industries expand and thereby drive up resource prices, other producers using these same resources are losers.

Trade restrictions are often imposed gradually over a period of years. Because the domestic adjustments to them are slow and because the losers are scattered throughout the economy, the losers frequently do not know that they are losers or they fail to connect their troubles with trade policy. On the other hand, those who benefit from trade restrictions are usually a well-defined group who can clearly identify the source of their gains. *One reason trade restrictions exist is that most losers do not know they are losers, whereas winners know what is at stake.* Producers have an abiding interest in trade legislation, but consumers remain largely ignorant. Consumers purchase thousands of different goods and thus have no special interest in the effects of trade policy on any particular good. Congress tends to support the group that makes the most noise, so trade restrictions persist, despite the clear gains from free trade.

Summary

1. Even if a country has an absolute advantage in producing all goods, that country should specialize in producing the good for which it has a comparative advantage—that is, the good for which its opportunity cost of production is lower than that of other countries. If each country specializes and trades according to the law of comparative advantage, all countries will be better off.

2. Tariffs and effective import quotas raise prices in domestic markets. The primary difference between a tariff and a quota is in the distribution of the gains resulting from higher domestic prices.

3. Tariff revenues go to the government and could be used to lower taxes; quotas confer benefits on those with the right to buy the good at the world price and sell it at the higher domestic price. Both restrictions harm domestic consumers more than they help domestic producers, though tariffs at least yield domestic government revenue.

4. Despite the gains from free trade and the net welfare losses arising from tariffs and quotas, trade restrictions have been a part of trade policy for hundreds of years. Some of the reasons given for instituting trade restrictions include promoting national defense, giving infant industries time to grow, preventing foreign producers from dumping goods in domestic markets, protecting domestic jobs, and allowing declining industries time to phase out.

QUESTIONS AND PROBLEMS

1. (Resources and Trade) Malaysia exports tin and rubber. Why have these resources become progressively less important to the world economy? Explain why the decline in the importance of these resources could hinder the growth of the Malaysian economy.

2. (U.S. Trade) What reasons would you give for the rise in importance of international trade to the U.S. economy? Will these reasons continue to have an influence in the future?

3. (Differences in Tastes and Trade) What products might the U.S. Virgin Islands trade with the Bahamas, which were formerly British, and Martinique, which is French? Is trade possible among islands that are so much alike?

4. (Absolute and Comparative Advantage) Suppose that each worker in the United States can produce 8 units of food or 2 units of clothing. In Izodia, which has the same number of workers, each worker can produce 7 units of food or 1 unit of clothing. Why does the United States have an absolute advantage in both goods? Which country enjoys a comparative advantage in food? Why?

5. (Specialization and Consumer Welfare) Why do economists believe that consumers are better off when countries specialize in the goods for which they have a comparative advantage and then trade with each other?

6. (World Equilibrium Price) Diagram the domestic supply and demand for steel, assuming that the world equilibrium price is the same as the domestic equilibrium price. If there is an increase in foreign supply, what will happen in the domestic market for steel?

7. (Tariffs) Very high tariffs usually cause black markets and smuggling. How is government revenue reduced by such activity? Relate your answer to the graph in Exhibit 8 in this chapter. Does smuggling have any social benefits?

8. (Voluntary Quotas or Restraints) The United States tried to limit Japanese exports to the United States by way of voluntary restraints. Why did the U.S. government opt to lose revenues by adopting this approach rather than using tariffs?

9. (Quotas) The Immigration Service in the United States allows only a certain number of individuals to apply each year for U.S. citizenship. Quotas are set for each country. How might the Immigration Service allocate such privileges among so many applicants?

10. (Efficiency and Production Possibilities) The data from the production possibilities tables in Exhibit 1 can be used to construct a world production possibilities frontier.
    a. Draw a graph illustrating this joint production possibilities curve. (Hint: Start with all resources producing food and then gradually switch resources into clothing as efficiently as possible.)
    b. Why does this curve have a kink in it?
    c. Explain why it is necessary for one or both countries to specialize in production in order to be on the joint production possibilities curve.
    d. Why does the trading rate between the countries have to fall between 0.5 and 2 units of food per unit of clothing?
    e. How do the relative gains from trade between the two countries depend on what terms of trade are established?

11. (Absolute Versus Comparative Advantage) Explain why the potential gains from trade depend on relative rather than absolute resource costs for the goods produced.

12. (Restricting Trade) Suppose that the world price for steel is below the U.S. domestic price, but the government requires that all steel used in the United States be domestically produced.
    a. Use a diagram like the one in Exhibit 9 to show who gains and who loses from such a policy.
    b. How could you estimate the net welfare loss (deadweight loss) from such a diagram?
    c. What kind of response to such a policy would you expect from industries (like automobile producers) that use U.S. steel?

13. (Restricting Trade) Industries hurt by cheap imports typically argue that restricting trade will save U.S. jobs. What's wrong with this argument? Are there ever any reasons to support such an argument?

14. (Terms of Trade) The consumption possibilities frontiers shown in Exhibit 3 assume terms of trade of 1 unit of clothing for 1 unit of food. What would the consumption possibilities frontiers look like if the terms of trade were 1 unit of clothing for 2 units of food? 3 units of food? $\frac{1}{2}$ unit of food?

15. (Determining World Price) Suppose that there is an increase in the U.S. demand for steel. Using Exhibit 7 to illustrate your analysis, show what would happen to the level of world trade and the world price of steel.

16. (Restricting Trade) Exhibits 8 and 9 show net losses to the domestic economy of the country imposing tariffs or quotas on imported sugar. What kinds of gains and losses would occur to the economies of countries exporting sugar?

17. (Restricting Trade) What kinds of gains and losses are created in importing and exporting countries from export subsidies? From domestic content requirements?

18. (Anti-Dumping Efforts) Industries arguing that foreign manufacturers are dumping their products in U.S. markets are frequently unsuccessful in making their case to the International Trade Commission. Is there anything about the definition of dumping that might explain this difficulty?

19. (NAFTA) A number of lobbying groups, including organized labor and environmental groups, have argued against ratifying NAFTA. They argue that it will be bad for Mexico. Proponents of NAFTA argue that Mexico will be helped because jobs will be created. Who's right?

20. (NAFTA) According to the case study, U.S. manufacturing wages are seven times higher than Mexican wages. In the next chapter we will discuss the exchange rate, the rate at which one currency is traded for another. How would changes in the exchange rate affect the relative cost of U.S. and Mexican labor?

21. (Enforcing Trade Restrictions) Increasingly, goods are manufactured using a variety of domestic and imported parts and/or resources. What problem does this create in enforcing trade restrictions?

22. (Enforcing Trade Restrictions) What effect do you think U.S. trade restrictions are likely to have on the world prices of restricted products?

CHAPTER 34

INTERNATIONAL FINANCE

A U.S. firm that plans to buy a machine from a British manufacturer will be quoted a price in British pounds. Suppose that machine costs 10,000 pounds. How many dollars will it cost? The cost in dollars will depend on the current exchange rate. When buyers and sellers from two countries trade, two national currencies are almost always involved. Supporting the flows of goods and services are flows of currencies that connect all international transactions. The exchange rate between two currencies—the price of one in terms of the other—is the means by which the price of a good in one country is translated into the price to the buyer in another country. The willingness of buyers and sellers to strike deals therefore depends on the rate of exchange between currencies. In this chapter we will examine the international transactions that determine the relative value of the dollar. Topics discussed in this chapter include

- Balance of payments
- Trade deficits and surpluses
- Foreign exchange markets
- Floating exchange rates
- Purchasing power parity
- Fixed exchange rates
- The international monetary system
- Managed float

BALANCE OF PAYMENTS

A country's gross domestic product conveys an idea of the flow of economic activity that occurs within that country during a given period. To account for their dealings abroad, countries keep track of their international transactions.

A country's *balance of payments*, as introduced in Chapter 4, is a summary statement reflecting all economic transactions that occur during a given time period between residents of that country and residents of other countries. *Residents* include individuals, firms, and governments.

International Economic Transactions

Point to Stress An economic transaction occurs whenever the ownership of a good or asset changes hands, a service is rendered, or a transfer payment is made.

Balance of payments statements measure economic transactions that occur between countries, whether they involve goods and services, real or financial assets, or transfer payments. Because the balance of payments reflects the volume of transactions that occur during a particular time period, usually a year, the balance of payments measures a *flow*.

Some transactions included in the balance of payments account do not involve payments of money. For example, if *Time* magazine ships a new printing press to its Australian subsidiary, no money payment occurs, yet an economic transaction involving another country has taken place and must be included in the balance of payments account. Similarly, if you send money to friends or relatives abroad, if CARE sends food to Africa, or if the Pentagon sends military assistance to Bosnia, these transactions must be captured in the balance of payments. So remember that although we speak of the balance of *payments*, a more descriptive phrase would be the *balance of economic transactions*.

Balance of payments accounts are maintained according to the principles of double-entry bookkeeping, in which one side of the ledger reflects liabilities, or debits, and the other side reflects assets, or credits. Each transaction gives rise to both a credit and a debit entry, so the sum of the credits must always equal the sum of the debits. As we will see, the balance of payments accounts are made up of several individual accounts; a deficit in one or more accounts must be offset by a surplus in the other accounts. Thus, the total debits must be in balance with, or equal to, the total credits—hence the name *balance* of payments. The balance of payments involves a comparison during a given time period, such as a year, between the outflow of payments to the rest of the world, which are entered as debits, and the inflow of receipts from the rest of the world, which are entered as credits.

Point to Stress Although the balance of payments always balances, the different individual accounts need not balance.

International trade statistics were the first commercial data compiled on a regular basis. Until the nineteenth century, *tariffs*—or taxes—on imports were an important source of government revenue, so governments kept records about the amount and kind of imports. Tariffs on imports remained an important source of government revenue in the nineteenth and early twentieth centuries in many countries. Countries tried to export more than they imported, so records were kept on exports too. In fact, *for many countries data on international trade were often more reliable than data on domestic trade.* The next sections describe the major accounts in the balance of payments.

Teaching Tip The media's description of trade balances as "favorable" or "unfavorable" is a modern remnant of this mercantilist doctrine.

Merchandise Trade Balance

The *merchandise trade balance*, a term first introduced in Chapter 4, equals the value of merchandise exported minus the value of merchandise imported.

Teaching Tip Credit entries involve either a decrease in a country's assets (for example, merchandise leaves the country) or an increase in its liabilities (for example, a foreigner's bank account increases). Debit entries involve either an increase in a country's assets or a decrease in its liabilities.

Point to Stress With a trade surplus, total credits in the merchandise trade balance exceed total debits. With a trade deficit, total debits exceed total credits.

The merchandise account reflects trade in tangible products, such as French wine and U.S. computers, and is often referred to simply as the *trade balance.* The value of U.S. merchandise exports is listed as a credit in the U.S. balance of payments account because U.S. residents must *be paid* for the exported goods. The value of U.S. merchandise imports is listed as a debit in the balance of payments account because U.S. residents must *pay* for the imported goods.

If the value of merchandise exports exceeds the value of merchandise imports, there is a *surplus* in the merchandise trade balance, or, more simply, a *trade surplus*. If the value of merchandise imports exceeds the value of merchandise exports, there is a *deficit* in the merchandise trade balance, or a *trade deficit*. The merchandise trade balance is reported on a monthly basis; this report influences the stock market and other financial markets. The trade balance depends on a variety of factors, including the relative strength of the domestic economy compared to other economies and the relative value of the domestic currency compared to other currencies.

The U.S. merchandise trade balance since 1979 is presented in Exhibit 1. Because imports have exceeded exports nearly every year, the balance has been in deficit, as reflected by the bottom line. Note that during recessions,

EXHIBIT 1

Merchandise Trade Balance (billions of 1987 dollars)

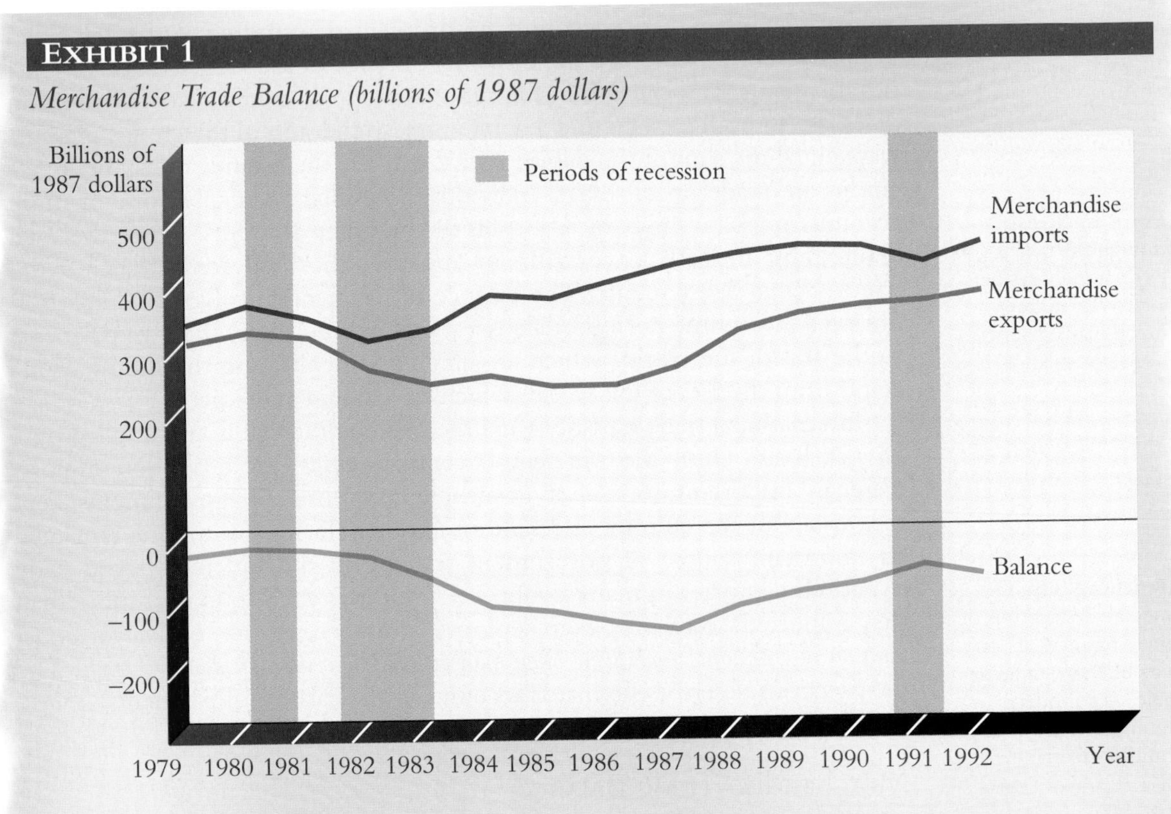

Source: Department of Commerce, Bureau of Economic Analysis, National Income and Product Accounts.

which are indicated by shading, imports were relatively flat, as was the overall trade deficit. Between 1983 and 1990, the U.S. economy expanded. *When the economy expands, the demand for all goods increases, so imports tend to increase.*

Balance on Goods and Services

The merchandise trade balance focuses on the flow of goods, but services are also traded internationally. *Services* are intangibles, such as transportation, insurance and banking services, military transactions, and tourist expenditures. For example, a Connecticut insurance company may send its claim forms and other paperwork by overnight courier to Ireland, where the data are entered on a computer and then wired back to Connecticut. Services also include the income earned from foreign investments less the income earned by foreigners from their investment in the domestic economy. Services are often called the "invisibles," because they are not tangible. The value of U.S. service exports, such as when an Irish tourist visits New York City, is listed as a credit in the U.S. balance of payments account because U.S. residents receive payments for these services. The value of U.S. service imports, such as when an Irish computer specialist enters claim form information for a Connecticut insurer, is listed as a debit in the balance of payments account because U.S. residents must pay for the imported services.

Balance on goods and services A section of a country's balance of payments account that measures the difference in value between a country's exports of goods and services and its imports of goods and services

The **balance on goods and services** is the difference between the value of exports of goods and services and the value of imports of goods and services. Currently produced goods and services that are sold or otherwise provided to foreigners form part of the nation's output. The production of these goods and services generates income during the current period. Conversely, imports of goods and services form part of the nation's current expenditures—part of consumption, investment, and government expenditures. Allocating imports to each of the major expenditure components is an accounting nightmare, so we usually just subtract imports from exports to yield *net exports*. Thus, the U.S. gross domestic product in a given year equals total expenditures for consumption, investment, and government, plus net exports.

Teaching Tip With a surplus in the balance on goods and services, net exports are positive. With a deficit in the balance on goods and services, net exports are negative.

Unilateral Transfers

Net unilateral transfers The unilateral transfers (gifts and grants) received from abroad by residents of a country minus the unilateral transfers these residents send to foreign residents

Unilateral transfers consist of government transfers to foreign residents, foreign aid, personal gifts to friends and relatives abroad, personal and institutional charitable donations, and the like. For example, money sent abroad by a U.S. resident to friends or relatives would be included in U.S. unilateral transfers and would be a debit in the balance of payments account. U.S. **net unilateral transfers** equal the unilateral transfers received from abroad by U.S. residents minus the unilateral transfers sent to foreign residents. U.S. net unilateral transfers have been negative each year since World War II, except for 1991, when the U.S. government received sizable transfers from foreign governments to support the Persian Gulf war.

The United States places no restrictions on money sent out of the country.[1] Other countries, particularly developing countries, strictly limit the amount of money that may be sent abroad. More generally, developing countries often restrict the convertibility of their currencies into another country's currency.

When we add net unilateral transfers to the exports of goods and services minus the imports of goods and services, we get the **balance on current account**. Thus, *the current account includes all transactions in currently produced goods and services plus net unilateral transfers*. It can be negative, reflecting a current account deficit; positive, reflecting a current account surplus; or zero.

Balance on current account A section of a country's balance of payments account that measures the sum of the country's net unilateral transfers and its balance on goods and services

Capital Account

Whereas the current account records international transactions involving goods, services, and transfers, the **capital account** records international transactions involving purchases or sales of investments. U.S. investors purchase foreign assets in order to earn a higher rate of return and to diversify their portfolios. When economists talk about capital, they usually mean the physical and human resources employed to produce goods and services. But sometimes *capital* is used as another word for *money*—money used to acquire financial assets, such as stocks, bonds, and bank balances, and money used to make direct investments in foreign plants and equipment. U.S. capital outflows result when Americans purchase foreign assets. U.S. capital inflows result from foreign purchases of U.S. assets.

Capital account The record of a country's international transactions involving purchases or sales of financial and real assets

Between 1917 and 1982, the United States was a net capital exporter, and the net return of all this foreign investment over the years improved our balance on current account. In 1983, high real interest rates in the United States (relative to those in the rest of the world) resulted in a net inflow of capital, for the first time in sixty-five years. Since then, U.S. imports of capital have exceeded exports of capital nearly every year, meaning that Americans owe foreigners more and more. *The United States is now the world's largest debtor nation*. This is not as bad as it sounds, since foreign investment in the United States adds to America's productive capacity and promotes employment. But the return on foreign investment in the United States flows to foreigners, not to Americans. During the early 1990s, low real U.S. interest rates (relative to Germany in particular) made U.S. investments less attractive and reduced the inflow of foreign capital.

The **official reserve transactions account** indicates the net amount of international reserves that shift among central banks to settle international transactions. (Many government publications show this not as a separate account but as part of the capital account.) International reserves consist of gold, dollars, other major currencies, and a special-purpose reserve currency called Special Drawing Rights, or SDRs, which will be discussed in more detail later.

Official reserve transactions account A section of a country's balance of payments that reflects the flow of gold, Special Drawing Rights, and currencies among central banks; the sum of the current account and the capital account

1. Federal authorities do, however, require reporting of the source of cash exports of $10,000 or more. This measure is aimed at reducing money laundering overseas.

Point to Stress The value of capital outflows are debit entries in the balance of payments; the value of capital inflows are credit entries.

Example In late August 1992, the federal funds rate in the United States stood at 3.5 percent. The equivalent German rate was 10 percent.

Teaching Tip Official reserve transactions are often used for the purpose of stabilizing the international value of a country's currency.

Point to Stress The sum of the current account, the capital account, the official reserve transactions account, and the statistical discrepancy must equal zero.

Point to Stress With double-entry bookkeeping, all transactions are recorded with two entries. For example, an exported good paid for with a deposit in a foreign bank account has a credit entry for the exported good and a debit entry for the capital outflow.

Statistical Discrepancy

As we have said, the U.S. balance of payments is a record of all transactions between U.S. residents and foreign residents over a specified period. It is easier to describe this record than to compile it. Despite efforts to capture all international transactions, some go unreported. Yet, as the name *balance of payments* clearly states, debits must equal credits—the entire balance of payments account must be in balance. To ensure that the accounts balance, a residual account called the *statistical discrepancy* was created. An excess of credits in all other accounts is offset by an equivalent debit in the statistical discrepancy account, or an excess of debits in all other accounts is offset by an equivalent credit in the discrepancy account.

The statistical discrepancy provides analysts with both a measure of the net error in the balance of payments data and a means of satisfying the double-entry bookkeeping requirement that total debits must equal total credits. The United States's positive statistical discrepancy during most years since 1980 may reflect large, secret money flows into the country. Wealthy people from countries with unstable governments or with high taxes may secretly purchase U.S. financial assets to shelter their wealth.

Deficits and Surpluses

Nations, like households, operate under a cash-flow constraint. Expenditures cannot exceed income plus cash on hand and borrowed funds. We have distinguished between *current* transactions, which are the income and expenditures from exports, imports, and unilateral transfers, and *capital* transactions, which are international investments and borrowing. Any surplus or deficit in the one account must be balanced by other changes in the balance of payments accounts. The current account has been in deficit since 1982, meaning that the sum of U.S. imports and unilateral transfers to foreigners has exceeded the sum spent by foreigners on our exports and sent as unilateral transfers to us.

Exhibit 2 presents the U.S. balance of payments statement for 1992. All payments from foreigners to U.S. residents are entered in the credits column using a plus sign (+), because they result in a flow of funds to U.S. residents. All payments to foreigners from U.S. residents are entered in the debits column using a minus sign (−), because they result in a flow of funds to foreign residents. As you can see, deficits in the current account and in the official reserve transactions account were offset by surpluses in the capital account and in the statistical discrepancy.

If a country runs a deficit in its current account, it is because the amount of foreign currency a country gets from exporting goods and services and from receipts of unilateral transfers falls short of the amount of foreign currency needed to pay for its imports and to make unilateral transfers. The additional foreign currency required must be provided by a net capital inflow (international borrowing, foreign purchases of domestic stocks and bonds, and so forth) or through official government transactions in foreign currency. If a country runs a current account surplus, the foreign

EXHIBIT 2

U.S. Balance of Payments: 1992 (billions of dollars)

Item	Debits	Credits	Balance
Current Account			
1. Merchandise exports		+439.3	
2. Merchandise imports	−535.5		
3. Trade balance (1 + 2)			−96.2
4. Service exports		+287.7	
5. Service imports	−222.5		
6. Goods and services balance (3 + 4 + 5)			−31.0
7. Net unilateral transfers	− 31.4		
8. Current account balance (6 + 7)			−62.4
Capital Account			
9. Outflow of U.S. capital	− 48.8		
10. Inflow of foreign capital		+ 80.1	
11. Capital account balance (9 + 10)			+31.3
Official Reserve Transactions Account			
12. Decrease in U.S. official assets abroad		+ 3.9	
13. Increase in foreign official assets in U.S.		+ 40.3	
14. Official reserve balance (12 + 13)			+44.2
15. Statistical discrepancy	− 13.1		
TOTAL (8 + 11 + 14 + 15)			**0.0**

Source: *Survey of Current Business*, U.S. Dept. of Commerce, March 1993.

exchange received from exports and from unilateral transfers exceeds the amount required to pay for imports and to make unilateral transfers. This excess foreign exchange could be held in a bank account, converted to the domestic currency, or used to purchase foreign stocks and bonds.

When all transactions are considered, the balance of payments always balances, though specific accounts may not be in balance. A deficit in a particular account should not necessarily be viewed as a source of concern, nor should a surplus be viewed as a reason for elation. The deficit in the U.S. current account in recent years has been offset by a net inflow of capital from abroad. As a result of the net inflow of capital, foreigners are acquiring larger claims on U.S. assets.

Some developing countries have had particular problems repaying their loans to industrialized countries. We close this section with a case study of Brazil's foreign debt problems.

CASE STUDY

Brazil Gets Bailed Out

On the morning of Friday, February 20, 1987, Brazil's finance minister notified seven hundred banks around the world that Brazil was suspending interest payments on $67 billion in bank loans. Brazil was beset with staggering economic problems, including a 600 percent inflation rate. In 1989 inflation jumped to over 1,700 percent per year. Brazil was one of the world's largest debtor nations, with a total debt at the time of the moratorium of $108 billion, the largest of any developing country. Interest alone was about $10 billion per year, or 4 percent of the country's GDP. Some say that Brazil's announcement to stop paying interest was aimed at forcing lenders to renegotiate the terms of their loans to Brazil's advantage. Brazil had already stopped paying the principal on its foreign debt in 1982. Rather than forgo interest altogether, so the argument goes, lenders might be willing to settle for some smaller amount.

The largest holder of Brazilian debt was Citibank, which held $4.6 billion worth of debt at the time the moratorium on interest payments was declared. Chase Manhattan and Bank of America each held an estimated $2.7 billion. After Brazil's declaration, the stock prices of these banks fell. In 1989 Brazilian debt was selling for only 33 percent of its redemption value, implying that lenders expected to get back only one-third of what they had lent Brazil.

In July 1992, with help from the U.S. government, Brazil worked out an agreement with foreign lenders to restructure its foreign loans. In essence foreign banks agreed to cancel much of the debt in return for a U.S. guarantee that the rest would be paid. Not only was Brazil's foreign debt restructured to reduce debt-service requirements, but the United States also announced plans to write off about 20 percent of its loans to sixteen of the poorest African nations, which also had huge foreign debts. All told, between 1987 and 1991, the top fifty U.S. banks ended up losing $26.1 billion in developing-country loans that were not repaid.

Brazil and the African countries experienced clear benefits by having a portion of their debts canceled. In the long run, however, these countries may have more difficulty attracting borrowing from abroad. Since lenders realize that future loans can be canceled as well, they may be less willing to lend or may lend only at interest rates that reflect the greater risk of default.

Sources: William Rhodes, "An Insider's Reflection on the Brazilian Debt Package," *Wall Street Journal*, 14 October 1988; "How Latin America's Economies Look After a Decade's Decline," *New York Times*, 11 February 1990; and Steven Lipin, "Banks Escape the Latin Debt Crisis with Little Damage," *Wall Street Journal*, 16 July 1992.

FOREIGN EXCHANGE RATES AND MARKETS

Now that you have some idea about the international flow of products and capital, we can take a closer look at the forces that determine the underlying value of the currencies involved in these transactions. We begin by looking at exchange rates and the market for foreign exchange.

Foreign Exchange

Exchange rate The price of one country's currency measured in terms of another country's currency

Teaching Tip The text's initial discussion of foreign exchange rates assumes that exchange rates are flexible.

The **exchange rate** is the price of one country's currency measured in terms of another country's currency. Exchange rates are determined by the interaction of the households, firms, private financial institutions, and central banks that buy and sell foreign currencies. The exchange rate fluctuates to equate the quantity of foreign currency demanded with the quantity of foreign currency supplied. The market in which the currencies are traded is called the foreign exchange market. *Foreign exchange* is the currency of another country that is needed to carry out international transactions. Typically, foreign exchange is made up of bank deposits denominated in the foreign currency. When foreign travel is involved, foreign exchange may consist of foreign paper money.

The foreign exchange market incorporates all the arrangements used to buy and sell foreign exchange. The foreign exchange market is not so much a physical place as it is a network of telephones and telex systems connecting large banks all over the world. Perhaps you have seen pictures of foreign exchange traders in New York, London, or Tokyo amid a tangle of telephones. The foreign exchange market is like an all-night diner—it never closes. Some trading center is always open somewhere in the world.

Currency depreciation An increase in the number of units of a particular currency needed to purchase one unit of another currency

Currency appreciation A decrease in the number of units of a particular currency needed to purchase one unit of another currency

Consider the market for pounds in terms of dollars. The price, or exchange rate, is specified in terms of the number of dollars required to purchase one British pound. An increase in the number of dollars needed to purchase a pound indicates a weakening, or a **depreciation**, of the dollar. A decrease in the number of dollars needed to purchase a pound indicates a strengthening, or an **appreciation**, of the dollar. Put another way, a decrease in the number of pounds needed to purchase a dollar is a depreciation of the dollar, and an increase in the number of pounds needed to purchase a dollar is an appreciation of the dollar.

Since the exchange rate is a price, we can explain its determination using the conventional tools of supply and demand: the equilibrium price of foreign exchange is the one that equates quantity demanded with quantity supplied. To simplify the analysis, let's suppose that the United States and Great Britain are the only two countries in the world, so the supply and demand for British pounds in the United States is the supply and demand for foreign exchange from the U.S. perspective.

Point to Stress The media often express exchange rates as the foreign currency price of the dollar. Therefore, a depreciation of the dollar is a drop in the exchange rate and an appreciation is a rise in the exchange rate.

Demand for Foreign Exchange

U.S. residents need pounds to pay British residents for goods and services, to invest in British assets, to make loans in Great Britain, or simply to send cash gifts to British friends or relatives. Whenever U.S. residents need pounds, they must buy pounds in the foreign exchange market, paying for them with dollars.

Exhibit 3 depicts a hypothetical market for foreign exchange, in this case British pounds. The horizontal axis identifies the quantity of foreign exchange, measured here as millions of pounds per day. The vertical axis identifies the price per unit of foreign exchange, measured here as the number of

EXHIBIT 3

The Foreign Exchange Market

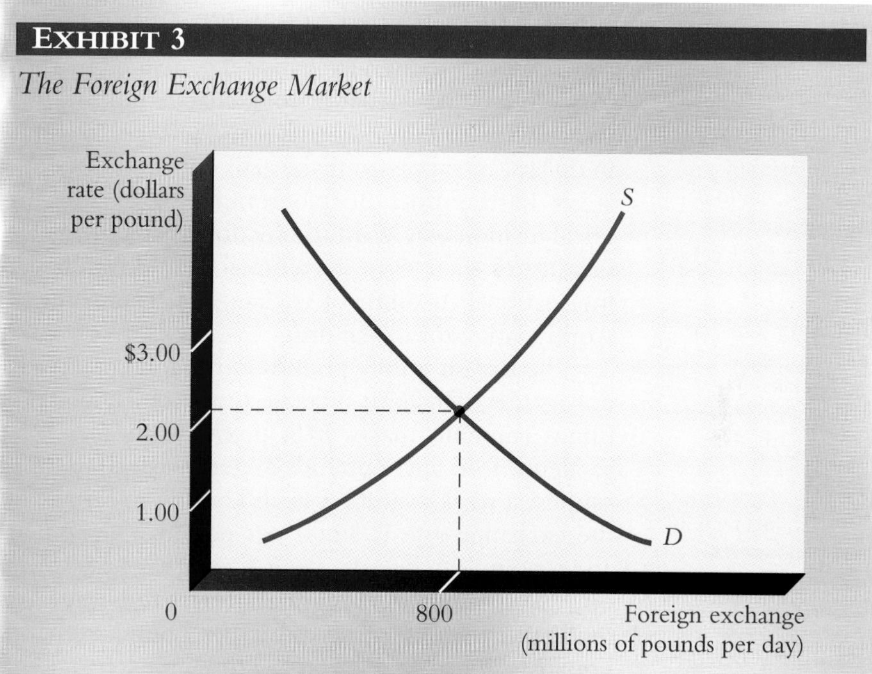

The fewer dollars needed to purchase one unit of foreign exchange, the lower the price of foreign goods and the greater the quantity of foreign goods demanded. The greater the demand for foreign goods, the greater the amount of foreign exchange demanded. The demand curve for foreign exchange slopes downward. An increase in the exchange rate makes U.S. products cheaper for foreigners. The increased demand for U.S. goods implies an increase in the quantity of foreign exchange supplied. The supply curve of foreign exchange slopes upward.

Teaching Tip The quantity demanded of foreign currency is determined by debit entries in the U.S. balance of payments (imports of goods and services, unilateral outflows, and capital outflows).

Example In early September 1992, the dollar depreciated to its record lowest value since World War II. In London, the cost of a room in a moderately priced hotel soared to $450, and an average breakfast cost $35.

dollars required to purchase each pound. The demand curve for foreign exchange, identified as *D*, shows the inverse relation between the dollar price of pounds and the quantity of pounds demanded, other things constant. Some of the factors held constant along the demand curve are the incomes of U.S. consumers, the expected inflation rates in the United States and Britain, the pound prices of British goods, the preferences of U.S. consumers, and interest rates in the United States and Britain. People have many different reasons for demanding foreign exchange, but in the aggregate the lower the dollar price of foreign exchange, the greater the quantity demanded.

A drop in the dollar price of foreign exchange, in this case the pound, means that fewer dollars are needed to purchase each pound, so the dollar prices of British goods, which have price tags listed in pounds, become cheaper. The cheaper it is to buy pounds, the lower the dollar price of British goods and the larger the quantity of British goods demanded by U.S. residents, so the greater the quantity of pounds demanded by U.S. residents, other things constant.

Point to Stress If the exchange rate is expressed as the dollar price of foreign exchange, multiply the foreign price by the exchange rate to determine the U.S. price.

Teaching Tip The quantity supplied of foreign currency is determined by credit entries in the U.S. balance of payments (exports of goods and services, unilateral inflows, and capital inflows).

Example When the dollar depreciated to a post-war record in early September 1992, Sicilian tourists found the cost of perfumes and cosmetics at New York's Bloomingdale's to be half the price of the same items in Sicily. On flights home, their bags bulged with American-bought goods.

Point to Stress If the exchange rate is expressed as the dollar price of foreign exchange, divide the U.S. price by the exchange rate to determine the foreign price.

Supply of Foreign Exchange

The supply of foreign exchange is generated by the desire of foreign residents to acquire dollars—that is, to exchange pounds for dollars. Foreign residents want dollars to buy U.S. goods and services, to buy U.S. assets, to make loans in dollars, or simply to make cash gifts in dollars to their U.S. friends and relatives. Furthermore, people from countries suffering from economic and political turmoil may want to buy dollars as a hedge against the inflation and instability of their own currencies. The dollar has long been accepted as an international medium of exchange. It is also the currency of choice in the world market for illegal drugs.

The British supply pounds in the foreign exchange market to acquire the dollars they need. An increase in the dollar-per-pound exchange rate, other things constant, makes U.S. products cheaper for foreigners, since foreign residents need fewer pounds to get the same number of dollars. For example, suppose a week's vacation from London to Disney World costs $2,000. When the exchange rate is $2.00 per pound, that vacation costs a British tourist 1,000 pounds; when the exchange rate is $2.50 per pound, the vacation costs only 800 pounds. The number of trips to Disney World demanded by British residents increases as the dollar-per-pound exchange rate increases, so more pounds will be supplied on the foreign exchange market to buy dollars.[2]

More generally, the higher the dollar-per-pound exchange rate, other things constant, the greater the quantity of pounds supplied per day to the foreign exchange market. The positive relation between the dollar-per-pound exchange rate and the quantity of pounds supplied on the foreign exchange market is expressed in Exhibit 3 by the upward-sloping supply curve for foreign exchange (again, pounds in our example). The supply curve is drawn holding other things constant, including British incomes and preferences, expectations about the rates of inflation in Britain and the United States, and interest rates in Britain and the United States.

Determining the Exchange Rate

Exhibit 3 brings together the supply and demand for foreign exchange to determine the exchange rate. At an exchange rate of $2.00 per pound, the quantity of pounds demanded equals the quantity of pounds supplied—in our example, 800 million pounds per day. Once achieved, this equilibrium rate of exchange remains constant until a change occurs in one of the factors that affect supply or demand. When the exchange rate is allowed to adjust

2. As the exchange rate rises, the British have a greater incentive to buy more U.S. goods and services since their prices in terms of pounds have decreased. As more is bought at lower prices, however, the total expenditure of British pounds rises only if the percentage increase in quantities of U.S. products demanded by the British exceeds the percentage decrease in their prices in terms of pounds. If the percentage increase in quantities demanded is less than the percentage decrease in the price in terms of pounds, the supply curve of British pounds will slope downward.

freely, or to *float*, in response to market forces, market rate will clear continually, as the quantities of foreign exchange demanded and supplied are equated.

What if the initial equilibrium is upset by a change in one of the underlying forces that affect supply or demand? For example, suppose an increase in U.S. income causes Americans to increase their demand for all normal goods, including products imported from Britain. An increase in income will shift the demand curve for foreign exchange to the right, as Americans seek more pounds to buy more cashmere sweaters, Jaguars, trips to London, and British securities.

This increased demand for pounds is shown in Exhibit 4 by a shift to the right in the demand curve for foreign exchange. The supply curve does not change. The shift in the demand curve from D to D' leads to an increase in the exchange rate from \$2.00 per pound to \$2.05 per pound. Thus, the pound increases in value, or appreciates, while the dollar falls in value, or depreciates. The higher exchange value of the pound prompts British residents to increase the quantity of pounds supplied on the foreign exchange market

EXHIBIT 4

Effect on the Foreign Exchange Market of an Increase in Demand

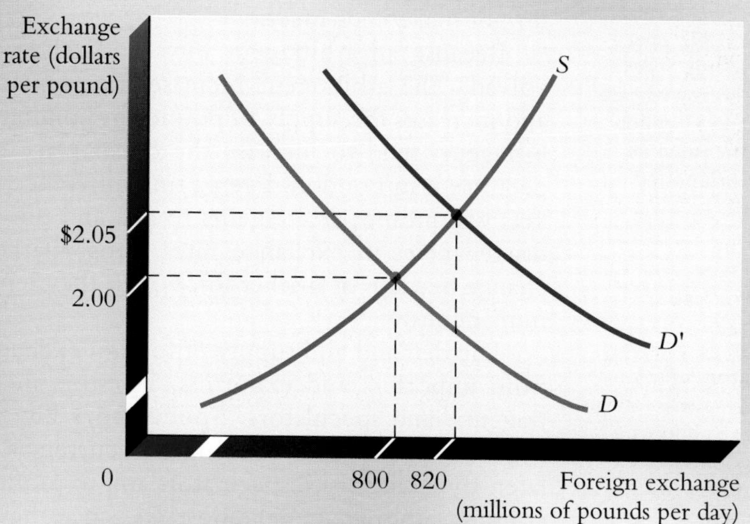

The intersection of supply curve S and demand curve D determines the exchange rate. At an exchange rate of \$2.00 per pound, the quantity of pounds demanded equals the quantity supplied. An increase in the demand for pounds from D to D' leads to an increase in the exchange rate from \$2.00 to \$2.05 per pound.

Teaching Tip A dollar depreciation caused by a decrease in supply makes British goods more expensive to U.S. consumers. U.S. imports drop, as does the quantity of pounds demanded. In contrast to the impact of an increase in demand for foreign exchange, the equilibrium quantity decreases.

Teaching Tip Arbitrage may require operations in two currencies (bilateral), three currencies (trilateral), or more than three (multilateral). Many arbitrageurs and speculators are large commercial banks that serve as dealers in foreign exchange.

to purchase more American products, which are now cheaper in terms of the pound. In our example, the equilibrium quantity increases from 800 million to 820 million pounds per day.

Any increase in the demand for foreign exchange or any decrease in its supply, other things constant, causes an increase in the number of dollars required to purchase one unit of foreign exchange, which is a depreciation of the dollar. On the other hand, any decrease in the demand for foreign exchange or any increase in its supply, other things constant, causes a reduction in the number of dollars required to purchase one unit of foreign exchange, which is an appreciation of the dollar.

Arbitrageurs and Speculators

Arbitrageur A person who takes advantage of temporary geographic differences in the exchange rate by simultaneously purchasing foreign exchange in one market and selling it in another market

Exchange rates between specific currencies are nearly identical at any given time in the different markets around the world. For example, the price of a dollar in terms of the pound is the same in New York, Tokyo, London, Zurich, Istanbul, and other financial centers. This equality is ensured by **arbitrageurs**—dealers who take advantage of any temporary difference in exchange rates across markets by buying low and selling high. Their actions tend to equalize exchange rates across markets. For example, if one pound cost $1.99 in New York and $2.00 in London, an arbitrageur could buy, say, $10,000,000 worth of pounds in New York and at the same time sell these pounds in London for $10,050,251.26, thereby earning $50,251.26 minus the transactions costs of executing the trades. Because exchange rate differences tend to be very small and because of transactions costs, an arbitrageur has to trade huge amounts to make enough profit to survive. Many do not make ends meet.

Example During a European currency crisis in 1992, speculator George Soros staked borrowed cash and made $1 billion when the value of the British pound tumbled.

Because an arbitrageur buys and sells simultaneously, no risk is involved. The arbitrageur increases the demand for pounds in New York and increases the supply of pounds in London. Therefore the actions of arbitrageurs tend to increase the dollar price of pounds in New York and decrease it in London. Even a tiny difference in exchange rates across markets will prompt arbitrageurs to act, and this action will quickly eliminate discrepancies in exchange rates across markets. Exchange rates may still change because of market forces, but they tend to change in all markets simultaneously.

Speculator A person who buys or sells foreign exchange in hopes of profiting from fluctuations in the exchange rate over time

The demand and supply of foreign exchange arises from many sources: from importers and exporters, investors in foreign assets, tourists, arbitrageurs, and speculators. **Speculators** buy and sell foreign exchange in hopes of profiting by trading the currency at a different exchange rate later. By taking risks, speculators aim to profit from market fluctuations. In contrast, arbitrageurs take no risks, since they *simultaneously* buy and sell a currency in different markets.

Purchasing power parity theory Exchange rates between two countries will adjust in the long run to reflect price level differences between the countries

Purchasing Power Parity

As long as trade across borders is unrestricted and as long as exchange rates are allowed to adjust freely, the **purchasing power parity theory** predicts that exchange rates between two national currencies will adjust in the long run to reflect the price level differences in the two countries. *A given basket of internationally traded goods should therefore sell for similar amounts in different countries (except for differences reflecting transportation costs and the like).* Suppose a given basket of internationally traded commodities that costs $1,500 in the United States costs 750 pounds in Great Britain. According to the purchasing power parity theory, the equilibrium exchange rate between the United States and Great Britain should be $2 per pound. If this were not the case—if the exchange rate were, say, $1.50 per pound—then the basket of goods could be purchased in Great Britain for 750 pounds and sold in the United States for $1,500. The $1,500 could then be exchanged for 1,000 pounds, yielding a profit of 250 pounds (minus any transactions costs). Selling dollars and buying pounds drives up the dollar price of pounds.

Point to Stress Recall that expected inflation rates were listed as determinants of both the demand and supply of foreign exchange in the dollar-pound market.

The purchasing power parity theory is more a predictor of the long-run tendency than of the day-to-day relationship between changes in the price level and the exchange rate. For example, a country's currency generally appreciates when its inflation rate is lower than the rest of the world's and depreciates when its inflation rate is higher. Likewise, a country's currency generally appreciates when its real interest rates are higher than the rest of the world and depreciates when its real interest rates are lower. As a case in point, the dollar appreciated during the first half of the 1980s, when real U.S. interest rates were relatively high, and depreciated in the early 1990s, when real U.S. interest rates were relatively low.

Example The depreciation of the U.S. dollar to a post-war record in early September 1992 was due in large part to high real interest rates in Germany (with low inflation but high nominal rates) versus relatively low real interest rates in the United States.

Because of trade barriers, central bank intervention in exchange markets, and the fact that some products are not traded or are not comparable across countries, the purchasing power parity theory may not explain exchange rates at a particular point in time, but the theory is still helpful in explaining long-run trends.

Flexible exchange rates Rates determined by the forces of supply and demand without government intervention

Flexible Exchange Rates

What we have been describing thus far is a system of **flexible exchange rates**, in which the exchange rate is determined by the forces of supply and demand. Flexible, or *floating*, exchange rates adjust continually to the myriad forces that buffet the foreign exchange market. Consider how the exchange rate is linked to the balance of payments accounts. Debit entries in the current and capital accounts increase the demand for foreign exchange, and credit entries in these accounts increase the supply of foreign exchange. If planned debit transactions exceed planned credit transactions, the domestic currency depreciates; if planned credit transactions exceed planned debit transactions, it appreciates.

Example Flexible exchange rates are used by the United States, Japan, and Canada, as well as about twenty other countries such as Australia. As discussed later, the European Monetary System establishes fixed rates among the members, but exchange rates float against nonmembers.

The wild swings in exchange rates that sometimes occur with flexible exchange rates have forced policy makers to consider alternatives, such as some combination of flexible and fixed exchange rates. Let's look now at how fixed rates work.

Fixed Exchange Rates

Fixed exchange rates Rates pegged within a narrow range of values by central banks' ongoing purchases and sales of currencies

When exchange rates are flexible, government officials have little direct role in the foreign exchange market. If government officials try to set, or fix, exchange rates, however, active central bank intervention is necessary to establish and maintain these **fixed exchange rates**. Suppose that monetary officials select what they think is an appropriate rate of exchange between the dollar and the pound. They undertake to *fix*, or to "peg," the exchange rate within a narrow band around the particular value selected. Let's assume that the exchange rate is set at $2.00 per British pound, with a permitted margin of fluctuation of 1 percent on either side of the pegged rate. Therefore dollars per pound can vary from $1.98 to $2.02. But monetary authorities will not permit the rate to stray outside this narrow band.

To explore the mechanics of fixed exchange rates, let's begin with a situation in which the equilibrium exchange rate is exactly $2.00 per pound, as indicated in Exhibit 5 by point *e*, the intersection of *D* and *S*. Since the fixed rate equals the equilibrium rate, monetary authorities need not intervene in the foreign exchange market.

EXHIBIT 5

Central Bank Intervention to Maintain an Exchange Rate Ceiling

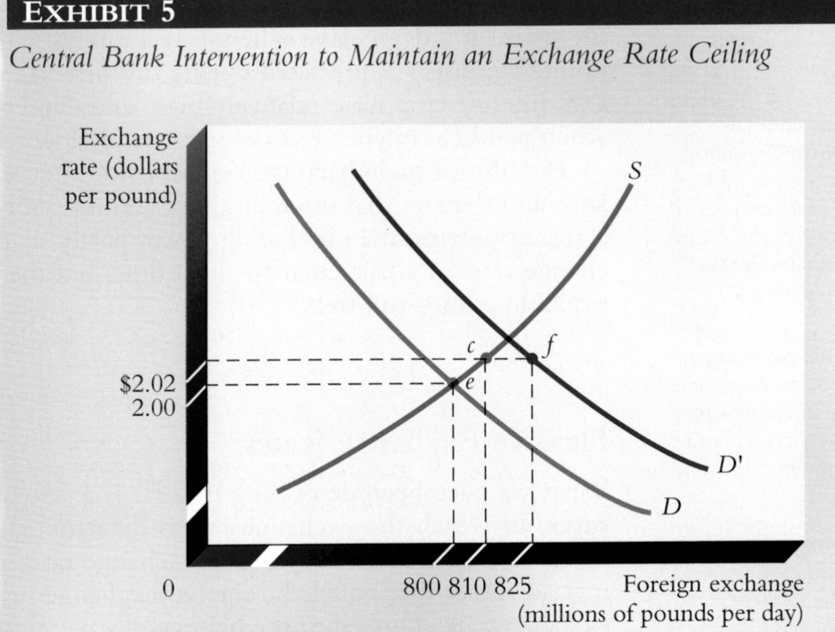

Point *e*, the intersection of demand curve *D* and supply curve *S*, determines an exchange rate within a band of 1 percent on either side of $2 per pound. An increase in the demand for foreign exchange from *D* to *D′* would drive the exchange rate above the permitted margin of fluctuation. To maintain the exchange rate within the band, monetary authorities must sell pounds for dollars at an exchange rate of $2.02 per pound. That is, the Federal Reserve must sell 15 million pounds per day to maintain an exchange rate of $2.02 per pound.

Enforcing a Rate Ceiling

Suppose the U.S. economy surges, increasing consumer income and causing the demand curve for foreign exchange to shift to the right as U.S. consumer demand for imports rises. If the resulting increase in the equilibrium exchange rate is within the limits set by the government, the increase in demand will prompt no action by monetary authorities. But if the increase in demand is large enough to increase the equilibrium price above $2.02 per pound, monetary authorities will intervene.

Example When the dollar weakened to a post-war record low in early September 1992, its value against the German mark changed at what was considered an extraordinarily rapid rate of 4 percent in four days.

The shift to the right from D to D' in Exhibit 5 would result in an equilibrium exchange rate *above* $2.02. At the ceiling exchange rate of $2.02, 825 million pounds per day are demanded and 810 million pounds per day are supplied. Thus, the quantity demanded exceeds the quantity supplied by 15 million pounds per day. To keep the dollar-per-pound rate from rising above $2.02, monetary authorities must therefore sell 15 million pounds per day at $2.02 per pound in the foreign exchange market. As long as the foreign exchange market has a ready supply of pounds at this ceiling rate, traders will be willing to exchange pounds for dollars at that rate. *By supplying pounds at $2.02, monetary authorities, such as the Federal Reserve in this example, can prevent the exchange rate from rising above the designated rate.* As long as the Federal Reserve is willing to sell pounds at the ceiling price of $2.02, the supply of foreign exchange in effect becomes horizontal where the upward-sloping supply curve reaches $2.02—that is, to the right of point *c*.

Teaching Tip Alternatively, the Bank of England could buy dollars for pounds, which also would provide pounds to the foreign exchange market.

Example In 1992, the wide variation in the performance of the economies in the European Monetary System put massive pressure on the British, Italian, and Spanish fixed exchange rates. Germany had high interest rates and slow growth; both Britain and Italy were hard hit by recession; Spain was receiving aid from the other members of the European Community.

Enforcing a Rate Floor

What if the exchange rate is in danger of falling below the floor rate established by monetary authorities? Suppose that high inflation in Britain makes British goods more expensive, decreasing the U.S. demand for pounds, reflected in Exhibit 6 by the shift to the left from D to D''. At the floor price of $1.98, the quantity of pounds supplied by the market, 785 million pounds per day, exceeds the quantity demanded by the market, 760 million pounds per day. Without central bank intervention, this excess supply of pounds at the floor price would force the equilibrium exchange rate lower, to the point where supply and demand intersect. To prevent the value of the pound from slipping below the floor rate, monetary authorities, in this case the U.S. Federal Reserve, must be willing to buy the excess supply of pounds at the floor rate. As long as there is a ready demand for pounds at the floor rate, other traders will be unwilling to exchange pounds for dollars at less than that rate. Since the central bank buys, or demands, any excess pounds at the floor rate, then to the right of point *h* the demand curve becomes horizontal at the floor price.

Teaching Tip Alternatively, the Bank of England could sell dollars for pounds, which also would take excess pounds off the foreign exchange market.

Through such intervention in the foreign exchange market, monetary authorities can stabilize the exchange rate, keeping it within the specified band. In sum, the situation under fixed exchange rates around a narrow band is as follows: (1) at the exchange rate ceiling, the supply curve is

EXHIBIT 6

Central Bank Intervention to Maintain an Exchange Rate Floor

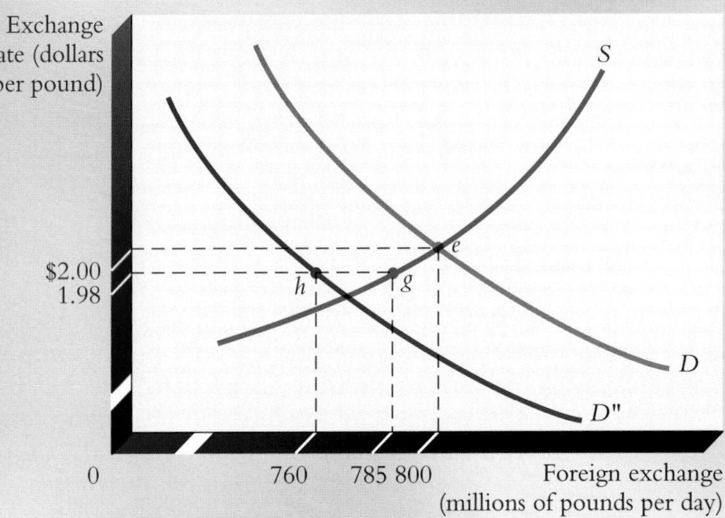

Point *e*, the intersection of demand curve *D* and supply curve *S*, determines an exchange rate within a band of 1 percent on either side of $2 per pound. A decrease in the demand for foreign exchange from *D* to *D''* would drive the exchange rate below the permitted margin of fluctuation. To maintain the exchange rate within the band, monetary authorities must sell pounds for dollars at an exchange rate of $1.98 per pound. That is, the Federal Reserve must buy 25 million pounds per day to maintain an exchange rate of $1.98 per pound.

Point to Stress Depreciation and appreciation occur under flexible exchange rates—due only to shifts in supply and/or demand. Devaluation and revaluation occur under fixed exchange rates—requiring government action.

horizontal, since the central bank supplies any excess quantity demanded; (2) within the permitted margin of exchange rate fluctuations, the supply curve slopes upward and the demand curve slopes downward; and (3) at the exchange rate floor, the demand curve is horizontal, since the central bank demands any excess quantity supplied. Government transactions to enforce the fixed exchange rate are recorded as part of the official reserve transactions account of the balance of payments.[3]

3. Currency transactions by the central bank will affect a country's money supply unless the bank tries to offset, or "sterilize," the transactions by buying or selling other central bank assets. An official reserve transactions surplus increases the money supply; a deficit decreases the money supply.

If the equilibrium exchange rate is sometimes above and other times below the floor, the central bank will be alternatively selling and buying foreign exchange. Its reserves may therefore fluctuate around a constant average level. The possibility of reserve depletion arises if the equilibrium exchange rate remains continually above the pegged rate on a long-term basis. When this occurs, the government has several options for eliminating the exchange rate disequilibrium. Suppose there is excess demand for foreign exchange at the ceiling rate, as was the case back in Exhibit 5. First, the pegged exchange rate can be increased, which is a **devaluation** of the domestic currency. (A decrease in the pegged exchange rate is called a **revaluation**.) Second, the government can impose restrictions on imports or on capital outflows in an attempt to reduce the demand for foreign exchange directly. Third, the government can adopt contractionary fiscal or monetary policies that reduce the country's income level, increase interest rates, or reduce inflation relative to that of the country's trading partners, thereby indirectly decreasing the demand for foreign exchange. Finally, the government can allow the disequilibrium to persist and ration the available foreign currency through some form of foreign exchange control.

Currency devaluation An increase in the official pegged price of foreign currency in terms of the domestic currency

Currency revaluation A reduction in the official pegged price of foreign currency in terms of the domestic currency

We have now concluded an introduction to international finance in theory. We next examine how international finance works in practice.

HISTORY AND DEVELOPMENT OF THE INTERNATIONAL MONETARY SYSTEM

From 1879 to 1914, the international financial system operated under a **gold standard**, whereby the major currencies were convertible into gold at a fixed rate. For example, the U.S. dollar could be redeemed at the U.S. Treasury for one-twentieth of an ounce of gold. The British pound could be redeemed at the British Exchequer, or treasury, for one-fourth of an ounce of gold. Since each pound could buy five times as much gold as each dollar, one pound exchanged for $5.

Gold standard An arrangement whereby the currencies of most countries are convertible into gold at a fixed rate

Teaching Tip The costs of transporting gold between the two countries may have allowed the exchange rate to differ very slightly from the ratio of gold redemption rates.

The gold standard provided a predictable exchange rate, one that did not vary as long as currency could be redeemed for gold at the announced rate. But the money supply in each country was determined in part by the flow of gold between countries, so each country's monetary policy was influenced by the supply of gold. A balance of payments deficit resulted in a loss of gold, which theoretically caused a country's money supply to drop. A balance of payments surplus resulted in an increase in gold, which theoretically caused a country's money supply to rise. Also, the supply of money throughout the world depended to some extent on the vagaries of gold discoveries. When gold production was slow and the money supply did not keep pace with the growth in economic activity, the result was a drop in the price level, or *deflation*. When gold

Teaching Tip According to David Hume, writing in 1752, as the money supplies changed, the deficit country's price level fell while the surplus country's price level rose. These price level changes increased net exports in the deficit country and decreased net exports in the surplus country until both the deficit and surplus were eliminated.

production was up and the growth of the money supply exceeded the growth in economic activity, the result was a rise in the price level, or *inflation*. For example, gold discoveries in Alaska and South Africa in the late 1890s expanded the U.S. money supply, leading to inflation.

The Bretton Woods Agreement

During World War I, many countries could no longer convert their currencies to gold, and the gold standard eventually collapsed, disrupting international trade during the 1920s and 1930s. Once an Allied victory in World War II appeared certain, the Allies met in Bretton Woods, New Hampshire, in July of 1944 to formulate a new international monetary system. Because the United States was not ravaged by World War II and had a strong economy, the dollar was selected as the key reserve currency in the new international monetary system. All exchange rates were fixed in terms of the dollar, and the United States, which held most of the world's gold reserves, stood ready to convert foreign holdings of dollars into gold at a fixed rate of $35 per ounce. Even though exchange rates were fixed by the Bretton Woods accord, *other* countries could adjust *their* exchange rates relative to the U.S. dollar if there was a fundamental disequilibrium in their balance of payments—that is, if there was a large and persistent deficit or surplus.

Special Drawing Right (SDR) A form of international reserve currency created by the International Monetary Fund; its value is a weighted average of the values of the major national currencies

The Bretton Woods agreement also created the International Monetary Fund (IMF) to set rules for maintaining the international monetary system and to make loans to countries with temporary balance of payments problems. The IMF, which today has more than 150 member countries, also standardized financial reporting for international trade and finance. The IMF now issues paper substitutes for gold called **Special Drawing Rights**, or **SDRs**, which function as international reserves. The value of a unit of SDR is a weighted average of the values of the major national currencies. Whereas the supply of gold depends on discoveries and the cost of production, SDRs can be created by the IMF to satisfy the world's demand for international reserves. Within limits, each central bank can exchange its own currency for SDRs. Note that SDRs are used exclusively to make settlements between central banks.

Teaching Tip The dollar was the only currency directly convertible into gold for official monetary purposes. As European countries began to develop reserve surpluses in the early 1950s, the central banks chose to hold those reserves in dollar assets which, unlike gold, paid interest. If necessary, the dollar assets could be exchanged for gold.

Demise of the Bretton Woods System

During the latter part of the 1960s, inflation began heating up in the United States, and the higher U.S. prices meant that the dollar did not buy as much as it used to. So those exchanging foreign currencies for dollars at the official exchange rates found these dollars bought less in U.S. goods and services. Because of U.S. inflation, the dollar had become *overvalued* at the official exchange rate, meaning that the gold value of the dollar exceeded the exchange value of the dollar. With the dollar overvalued, foreigners redeemed more dollars for gold. To stop this outflow of gold, something had to give. On August 15, 1971, President Richard Nixon closed the "gold window," refusing to exchange gold

Teaching Tip The IMF accumulates funds for lending by requiring each member to submit a gold and currency subscription. A country's subscription determines its voting rights in the IMF and the amount that it can borrow from the Fund.

Teaching Tip From 1958 through 1971, U.S. gold reserves fell from $22.9 billion to $10.2 billion. Gold coverage of dollar holdings by foreign central banks fell to 55 percent by 1970.

for dollars. In December 1971 the ten richest countries of the world met in Washington and devalued the dollar by 8 percent. The hope at the time was that this devaluation would put the dollar on firmer footing and would save the "dollar standard." With inflation rising at different rates around the world, however, an international monetary system based on fixed exchange rates was doomed.

In 1971 U.S. merchandise imports exceeded merchandise exports for the first time since World War II. When the trade deficit tripled in 1972, it became clear that the dollar was still overvalued. In early 1973 the dollar was devalued another 10 percent, but this did not quiet foreign exchange markets. The dollar, for twenty-five years the anchor of the international monetary system, suddenly became a hot potato, and speculators began betting the dollar would fall even more. Dollars were exchanged for German marks because the mark appeared to be the most stable currency. Monetary officials at the Bundesbank, Germany's central bank, exchanged marks for dollars to defend the official exchange rate and to prevent an appreciation of the mark. Why didn't Germany want the mark to appreciate? Appreciation of the mark would make their goods more expensive abroad and foreign goods cheaper in Germany. But after selling $10 billion worth of marks, the German central bank quit defending the dollar. As soon as the value of the dollar was allowed to float against the mark, the Bretton Woods system, already on shaky ground, collapsed.

The Current System: Managed Float

Managed float system An exchange rate system that combines features of freely floating rates with intervention by central banks

The Bretton Woods system has been replaced by a **managed float system**, which combines features of a freely floating exchange rate with occasional intervention by central banks as a way of moderating exchange rate fluctuations among the world's major currencies. Most smaller countries, particularly developing countries, peg their currencies to one of the major currencies (such as the U.S. dollar or the French franc), to Special Drawing Rights, or to a "basket" of major currencies. What's more, in developing countries, private international borrowing and lending are severely restricted; governments may allow residents to purchase foreign exchange only for certain purposes. In some countries, different exchange rates apply to different categories of transactions.

Example The European Monetary System does not face an easy task in developing the common currency by 1999. In the fall of 1992, three adjustments in exchange rates were required in less than two months, and Ireland and Denmark were still battling market forces threatening to push their exchange rates outside the permitted margins.

Western European countries in 1979 formed the European Monetary System, through which they are attempting to align the values of their respective currencies. The members have agreed to fix exchange rates among themselves in an attempt to increase the economic integration among member countries. Members of the European Monetary System have even developed a new monetary unit called the European Currency Unit, or ECU, which they hope will one day become one of the world's key currencies, perhaps replacing the dollar in international transactions.

Exchange rates between the German mark, the Japanese yen, and the U.S. dollar are relatively unstable, particularly because of international speculation about official efforts to stabilize exchange rates. Major criticisms of flexible exchange rates are that (1) they are inflationary, since they free

Teaching Tip In a system of *currency areas,* a currency is pegged to either a major currency, SDRs, or a basket of currencies.

Teaching Tip The proposed development of a common currency in Europe by 1999 would reduce currency speculation on the continent and therefore lessen the swings in the values of the dollar and the yen.

monetary authorities to pursue expansionary policies, and (2) they have very often been volatile, especially since the late 1970s. This volatility creates much uncertainty and risk for importers and exporters, increasing the cost of international trade and thus reducing its volume. Furthermore, exchange rate volatility can lead to wrenching changes in the competitiveness of a country's export sector and of those domestic producers who must compete with imports. These changes in competitiveness cause swings in employment, resulting in calls for import restrictions.

Policy makers are always on the lookout for an international monetary system that will perform better than the current managed float system with its fluctuating currency values. *Their ideal is a system that will foster international trade, lower inflation, and promote a more stable world economy.* International finance ministers have acknowledged that the world must find an international standard and establish a more stable exchange rate.

Conclusion

At one time the United States was largely self-sufficient. A technological lead over the rest of the world, an abundance of natural resources, a well-trained work force, a modern and extensive capital stock, and the ability to convert its currency into gold made the United States the envy of the world. The dollar was the world's premier international currency—readily accepted and prized.

The situation has changed. The United States is now very much a part of the world economy, not only as the largest exporter but also as the largest importer in the world. Multinational corporations have spread advanced technology around the world. As a result of the spread of technology and capital, U.S. workers now face stiff competition from abroad. Americans have borrowed billions from abroad; we are now the world's largest debtor nation.

As a result of chronic balance of payments deficits, enormous numbers of dollars circulate in the world markets. Although the dollar remains the unit of transaction in many international settlements—OPEC, for example, still states oil prices in dollars—the wild gyrations of exchange rates have made those involved in international finance wary of putting all their eggs in one basket. Traders therefore hedge against a decline in the dollar. The international monetary system is now going through a difficult adjustment period as it gropes for a new source of stability after the collapse of the Bretton Woods agreement.

Summary

1. The balance of payments reflects all economic transactions across national borders. The current account measures the flow of (1) merchandise, (2) services, including investment income, military transactions,

and tourism, and (3) unilateral transfers, or public and private transfer payments to foreign residents. The capital account reflects international flows involving purchases or sales of investment assets.

2. Currencies support the flow of goods and services across international borders. The intersection of the supply and demand for currency on the foreign exchange market determines the equilibrium exchange rate.

3. Under a system of fluctuating, or floating, exchange rates, the value of the dollar relative to foreign exchange varies over time. An increase in the demand for foreign exchange or a reduction in its supply, other things constant, will cause an increase in the value of foreign exchange relative to the dollar, which is a depreciation of the dollar. Conversely, a reduction in the demand for foreign exchange or an increase in its supply will cause a decrease in the value of foreign exchange relative to the dollar, which is an appreciation of the dollar.

4. Under a system of fixed exchange rates, monetary authorities usually try to stabilize the exchange rate, keeping it between a specified ceiling and floor. At the exchange rate ceiling, the supply of foreign exchange is horizontal, since the central bank supplies any excess quantity demanded. Within the permitted margin of exchange rate fluctuations, the supply curve for foreign exchange slopes upward and the demand curve slopes downward. And at the exchange rate floor, the demand curve for foreign exchange is horizontal, since the central bank demands any excess quantity supplied.

5. For much of this century the international monetary system was based on fixed exchange rates. A managed float has been in effect for the major currencies since the demise of the Bretton Woods system in the early 1970s. Although central banks have often tried to stabilize exchange rates, recent swings in exchange rates have troubled policy makers.

Questions and Problems

1. (The Versatility of the Dollar) In general, an American cannot use U.S. currency to buy products in Rome or London. However, businesses in some places, especially border towns such as Windsor, Ontario, and Nuevo Laredo, Mexico, do accept U.S. dollars. Why do businesses in border towns engage in this practice? Why would we expect the practice in countries that have exchange controls, which give rise to black markets?

2. (The Demand for Money and Dollars) What is the difference between the demand for the U.S. dollar and the U.S. domestic demand for money?

3. (Current and Capital Accounts) An important debate in international finance is whether, under flexible exchange rates, changes in the current account are caused by movements in the capital account or vice versa. Choose one side and argue your point.

4. (Balance of Payments Accounting) Explain which entry in the U.S. balance of payments is relevant to each of the following:
   a. A Hong Kong financier buys some U.S. corporate stock.
   b. A U.S. tourist in Paris buys some perfume.
   c. IBM-Japan sells computers to a pineapple company in Hawaii.
   d. U.S. farmers make a gift of food to starving children in Ethiopia.
   e. The U.S. Treasury sells a thirty-year bond to a Saudi Arabian prince.
   f. A West German student buys a U.S. textbook in France.
   g. A U.S. company deposits dollars in a Eurodollar account in Hong Kong.

5. (Recessions and the Trade Balance) Explain why recessions in the United States (which are not currently world recessions) tend to reduce the U.S. trade deficit.

6. (Flexible Exchange Rates) Why must the balance on capital account and the balance on current account sum to zero (on average) when exchange rates are flexible?

7. (Flexible Exchange Rates) Explain why, under flexible exchange rates, if the price of the dollar is above its equilibrium level, the balance of payments will be in deficit.

8. (Trade Balances) Why is it unreasonable to expect all countries, regardless of their level of development, to have balanced trade (that is, exports equal to imports)?

9. (The European Currency Unit) Of what value would it be to the members of the European Monetary System to have their own currency?

10. (Developing Countries' Debt) John Maynard Keynes is credited with saying that if you borrow $1,000 from a bank and can't pay it back, then it's your problem, but if you borrow $1,000 million from a bank and can't pay it back, it's the bank's problem. How does Keynes's humorous remark relate to the problem of the debt of developing countries?

11. (Trade Deficits) Suppose the United States ran a balance on goods and services surplus by exporting goods and services while importing nothing.
    a. How would such a surplus be offset elsewhere in the balance of payments accounts?
    b. If the level of U.S. production does not depend on the balance on goods and services, how does running this surplus affect our *current* standard of living?
    c. How will such a surplus probably affect our *future* standard of living?

12. (Exchange Rate Determination) Using a supply-demand diagram for foreign exchange (for example, the pound or yen) against dollars, determine the likely impact of each of the following on the strength of the dollar against foreign exchange, other things constant.
    a. An increase in U.S. interest rates
    b. An increase in the U.S. money supply
    c. An increase in U.S. productivity
    d. An increase in U.S. citizens' preferences for imported goods

13. (Exchange Rate Determination) Use the data below to answer the following questions:

Price of pounds (in $)	Q_D *(of pounds)*	Q_S *(of pounds)*
$4.00	50	100
3.00	75	75
2.00	100	50

    a. Construct the supply and demand curves for pounds, and determine the equilibrium exchange rate (dollars per pound).
    b. Construct the supply and demand curves for dollars, and determine the equilibrium exchange rate (pounds per dollar).

14. (Purchasing Power Parity) According to the theory of purchasing power parity, what will happen to the value of the dollar (against foreign currencies) if the U.S. price level doubles and price levels in other countries stay constant? Why is the theory more suitable to analyzing events in the long run?

15. (Fixed Versus Floating Exchange Rates) Compare the adjustment processes necessary to eliminate trade imbalances under the fixed and the floating exchange rate models.
    a. By what means do central banks and governments maintain fixed exchange rates?
    b. What are the benefits and costs of each model?

16. (Exchange Rate Determination) Floating exchange rates move whenever imbalances in the supply and demand for foreign exchange occurs. Yet the balance of payments is always balanced. Does this mean that exchange rates are always stable?

17. (Gold Standard) Explain why, under the gold standard, a high inflation rate in the United States (relative to rates in other countries) put pressure on the United States to devalue the dollar in terms of its price in gold.

18. (Balance of Trade) According to Exhibit 2, the United States ran a large deficit on its current account, which was largely offset by a surplus in its capital account. Is there any reason to think that the recent reduction in real interest rates here affected these numbers? Explain.

19. (Merchandise Trade Balance) If the value of the dollar drops in foreign exchange markets, this should

improve our merchandise trade balance as imports to the United States become more expensive and our exports become cheaper. Can you think of any reason why a lower-valued dollar could lead to a *worsening* of the merchandise trade balance even though imports are more expensive and exports are cheaper?

20. (Free Trade and Exchange Rates) The previous chapter described a new treaty, NAFTA, which will reduce trade barriers in North America. Some organized labor groups have opposed NAFTA, arguing that U.S. jobs will be lost to cheap Mexican labor. If they are right, what would you anticipate would happen to the value of the dollar against the Mexican peso? How would this affect the "cheap Mexican labor" argument?

21. (Brazil Gets Bailed Out) Explain why inflation like that experienced by Brazil hinders a country's ability to repay foreign bank loans.

22. (Brazil Gets Bailed Out) Why do you suppose that the U.S. government guaranteed the remaining Brazilian obligation to U.S. banks?

CHAPTER 35

PROBLEMS OF DEVELOPING COUNTRIES

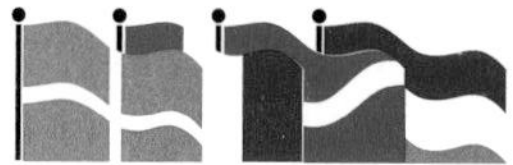

Teaching Tip The 1992 edition of the National Geographic Society's world atlas includes 193 countries, 20 more than the 1990 edition. The atlas did not include the division of Czechoslovakia into two nations.

Teaching Tip The definition of development economics expands somewhat on the traditional definition of economics in Chapter 1. Development economics is also concerned with structural and institutional changes necessary to generate large-scale improvement in standards of living for broad segments of the population.

The sun rises around the world, but people face the day under very different circumstances. Many Americans arise from a comfortable bed in a nice home, select the day's clothing from a diverse wardrobe, choose from a variety of foods for breakfast, and drive to school or to work in one of the family's personal automobiles. But most of the 5.6 billion people on earth do not have spacious homes, closets full of clothes, or pantries full of food. They own no automobile, and many have no formal job. Their health is poor, as is their education. Many cannot read or write.

So far this book has focused on the United States, one of the richest countries on earth. In this chapter we turn to problems confronting developing countries. We should acknowledge at the outset that no single theory of economic development has gained general acceptance, so this chapter will focus less on a theory of economic development than on the differences between developed and developing countries. Thus, the chapter will be more descriptive than theoretical. Topics discussed in this chapter include

- Third World economies
- Developing countries
- Absolute poverty level
- Productivity and development
- Obstacles to development
- Foreign aid
- Third World debt problems

Worlds Apart

Countries are classified in a variety of ways based on their level of economic development. The *First World* is the name given to the economically advanced capitalist countries of Western Europe, North America, Australia, New Zealand, and Japan. First World countries were the first to experience long-term economic growth during the nineteenth century. These countries are more commonly called *industrial market countries* and *developed countries*. The *Second World* is the name given to economically advanced socialist countries, though the ranks of these are thinning as countries become more market oriented. The *Third World* consists of about 140 developing countries in Asia, Africa, and Latin America. Third World economies may be capitalist, socialist, or a mix. These countries tend to have a low level of per capita income, a low standard of living, a high rate of population growth, and they rely on First and Second World countries for technology. But differences in the level of economic development are actually greater among Third World countries than among industrial countries. Third World countries are also called **developing countries** and less-developed countries, or LDCs. In this chapter we will refer to them as developing countries.

Example In 1800, the now economically advanced nations accounted for 56 percent of total world production. Relatively rapid growth in these advanced nations caused their share of production to rise to 81 percent by 1900.

Developing countries Nations typified by high rates of illiteracy, high unemployment, rapid population growth, and exports of primary products

Developing Countries

The term *developing countries* is an expression adopted by the United Nations to describe countries with high rates of illiteracy, high unemployment, extensive underemployment, rapid population growth, and exports consisting primarily of agricultural products and raw materials. Typically, more than half the labor force in developing countries is in agriculture. Because farming methods are relatively primitive, farm productivity is low and most people are barely subsisting.

Point to Stress Note that a low level of per capita income is not listed as a necessary characteristic for a developing country. A nation such as the United Arab Emirates may have a high level of per capita income because of its oil revenues yet still be considered a developing country.

The differences in economic activity across countries are profound. For example, the United States, with its 260 million people, has a gross domestic product that exceeds by one-third the *combined* gross domestic products of three billion people from over sixty countries, including China and India. Thus, only 5 percent of the world's population produces more than does about 60 percent of the world's population put together.

To get a general feel for the differences between developed and developing countries, consider the following comparison. A typical family of four in the United States, though by no means rich, has a comfortable standard of living. Each of the two children has a bedroom. The children will finish high school and will probably go to college. Compare this with a typical extended family in rural Asia. The Asian household is likely to be much larger, including grandparents, aunts, and uncles. The family lives in a one-room shack without electricity, running water, or sanitation. Family members work the land as tenant farmers. Of the four school-age children, only one attends school regularly, and that child can expect to get through only three or four grades. The family eats only one meal a day—a meal that does not change and is never enough to ward off hunger. Family members are frequently ill, but health care often is not available, as most of the doctors are located in urban areas, where higher-income families reside.

Classification of Economies

The developing nations vary greatly, ranging from the tragically poor economies of sub-Saharan Africa to the booming economies of the Far East—Taiwan, South Korea, Singapore, and Malaysia (the so-called newly industrialized countries, or NICs). It is helpful therefore to draw finer distinctions among developing countries.

Teaching Tip An organization called the Overseas Development Council supplements per capita income data with the Physical Quality of Life Index (PQLI). The PQLI is an index of infant mortality, life expectancy at age one, and literacy. A country must meet specified per capita income and PQLI minima in order to be classified as developed.

The yardstick used most often to compare living standards across nations is per capita gross domestic product. We caution that making intercountry comparisons of GDP is tricky, because countries employ different national income accounting procedures and all measures must be translated into comparable accounting formats and into a common currency. One problem with international comparisons is determining the appropriate exchange rate for putting different countries' GDP statistics on common footing. The exchange rate problem is compounded when some countries produce a significant amount of output that is not traded across international boundaries. Furthermore, although official international comparisons based on per capita GDP usually include an estimate of the value of food produced and consumed by the farm households, other nonmarket activities are not always captured by GDP. So international comparisons that compare only GDP per capita tend to underestimate the quantity of goods and services available per person in developing countries, which have more nonmarket production than do industrial nations.

The World Bank, an economic development institution affiliated with the United Nations, attempts to estimate comparable GDP per capita figures for all reporting countries and then uses these figures to classify these economies. The World Bank divides reporting countries into three major groups based on their per capita GDP. In 1990 there were (1) fifty-one low-income economies, (2) eighty-four middle-income economies, and (3) forty-seven high-income economies. The low- and middle-income countries are often referred to as *developing* countries, and the high-income countries are often referred to as *industrial market* countries (though some of the high-income countries have income based primarily on oil and are considered to be still developing). A few, primarily socialist, countries such as Cuba and North Korea do not report data on their economic status and consequently are classified by the World Bank as *nonreporting economies*.

Point to Stress The purchasing-power approach to per capita GDP yields much larger values for the low-income and middle-income economies than the exchange rate conversion method.

Data on total population, GDP per capita, and average growth in real GDP per capita are summarized in Exhibit 1 for all reporting countries with a population of one million or more. The GDP per capita figures have been adjusted by the United Nations to reflect the actual purchasing power of the native currency in its respective economy. The idea is to measure for each country what per capita GDP will in fact buy. The per capita GDP figures reported are for the median country within each classification. For example, the per capita GDP for the median country among the fifty-one low-

EXHIBIT 1

Population, GDP Per Capita, and Annual Growth Rate(for countries with a population of 1 million or more)

		Real GDP per Capita	
Classification	**Population, mid-1990 (millions)**	**Median 1990 Dollars**	**Annual Growth Rate, 1965–1990 (percent)**
1. Low-income economies	3,058.3	950	2.9
China	1,133.7	1,950	5.8
India	849.5	1,150	1.9
2. Middle-income economies	1,087.5	4,680	2.2
3. High-income economies	816.4	15,620	2.4
4. Nonreporting economies	321.7	Not reported	

Source: Based on data presented by the World Bank in *World Development Report 1992* (New York: Oxford University Press, 1992), Tables 1 and 30.

income economies was $950 in 1990 (with twenty-five countries below that figure and twenty-five countries above it). Low income economies make up fifty-eight percent of the world's population.

The per capita GDP for the median country among the eighty-four middle-income economies was $4,680 in 1990. Middle-income economies make up about 20 percent of the world's population. Developing countries (low- and middle-income economies plus a few high-income countries) account for about 80 percent of the world's population. The per capita GDP for the median country among the forty-seven high-income economies was $15,620 in 1990. The median real GDP per capita income among high-income economies was about *sixteen times* the median among the low-income economies—quite a difference.

Example One of every five births in the world is in India, which is expected to replace China as the most populous nation early in the next century.

The two giants among the poorest countries are China and India, which are shown separately in Exhibit 1. Together they account for more than a third of the world's population. China's GDP per capita of $1,950 was more than double the median of all low-income economies, and its annual growth rate since 1965 of 5.8 percent was double the average growth rate for low-income economies. India's GDP per capita was above the median of low-income economies but its growth rate was below the average.

Exhibit 2 presents GDP per capita for selected countries, arranged from left to right in descending order. Switzerland, the top-ranked country in 1990, had a GDP per capita that was about nine times that of the Philippines. But GDP per capita in the Philippines, in turn, was over seven times that of Ethiopia, the poorest country in the world. Residents of the Philippines likely feel poor relative to industrialized nations, but they appear well off compared to the poorest developing countries. Per capita GDP in Switzerland was

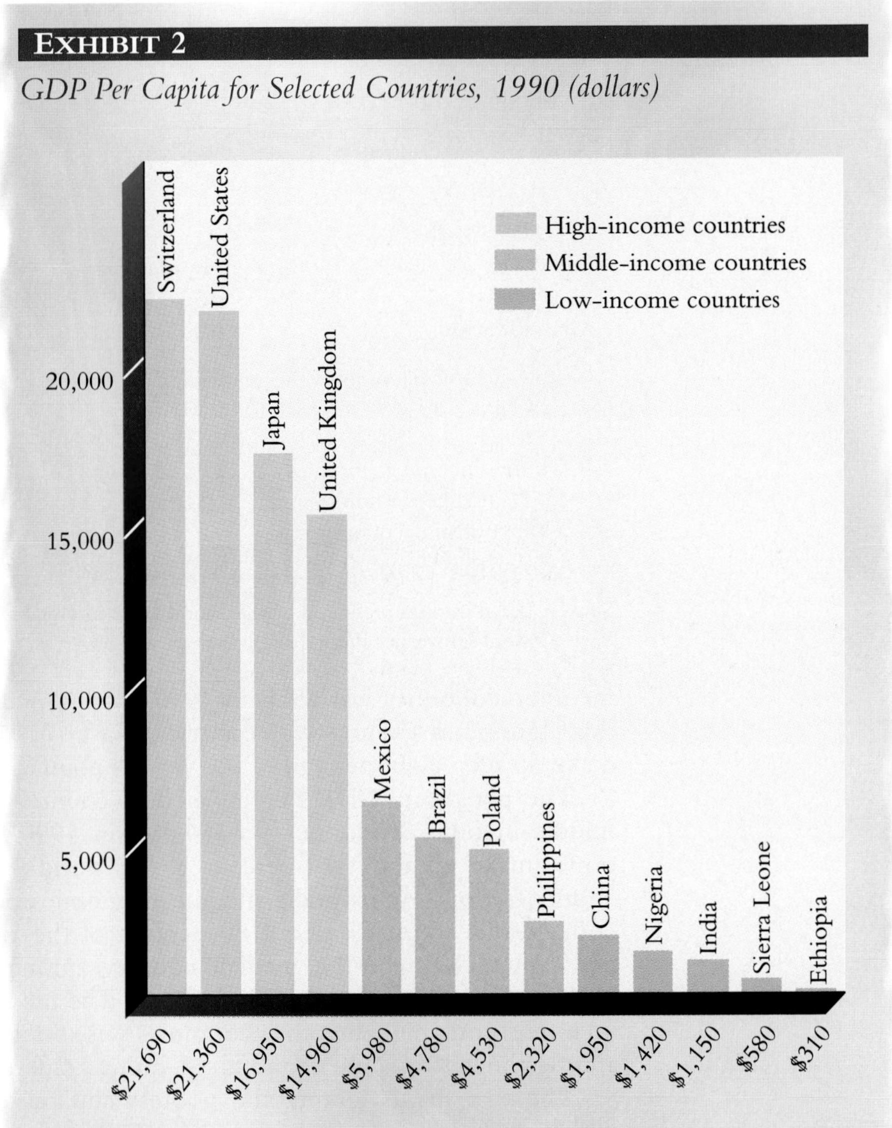

Source: Based on data presented by the World Bank in *World Development Report 1992* (New York: Oxford University Press, 1992), Table 30.

seventy times greater than in Ethiopia. Thus, there is a tremendous range of productive performance around the world.

Health and Nutrition

Differences in stages of development among countries are reflected in a number of ways besides per capita income levels. For example, many people of the Third World suffer from poor health as a result of malnutrition and disease. AIDS is also having a devastating impact on some developing countries, particularly those in central and east Africa. Life expectancy in the least-developed African countries averaged forty-eight years in 1990, compared with sixty-four years in other developing economies and seventy-seven years in industrial economies. The average life expectancy at birth worldwide ranged from forty years in the African country of Chad to eighty years in Japan.

Example During the famine in Somalia in the early 1990s, measles and diarrhea claimed at least as many lives as famine. Hardest hit by the diseases were children under five, who died at twice the rate of adults.

INFANT MORTALITY RATES. Health differences among countries are reflected by infant mortality rates. In 1990, among the least-developed African countries, the probability that a newborn infant would die before its fifth birthday was 180 of every 1,000 males and 160 of every 1,000 females. These mortality rates were about fifteen times higher than those in high-income countries. Mortality rates for selected countries are presented in Exhibit 3. Countries with the longest life expectancies in the world also have the lowest infant mortality rates. Similarly, the countries with the shortest life expectancies have the highest infant mortality rates.

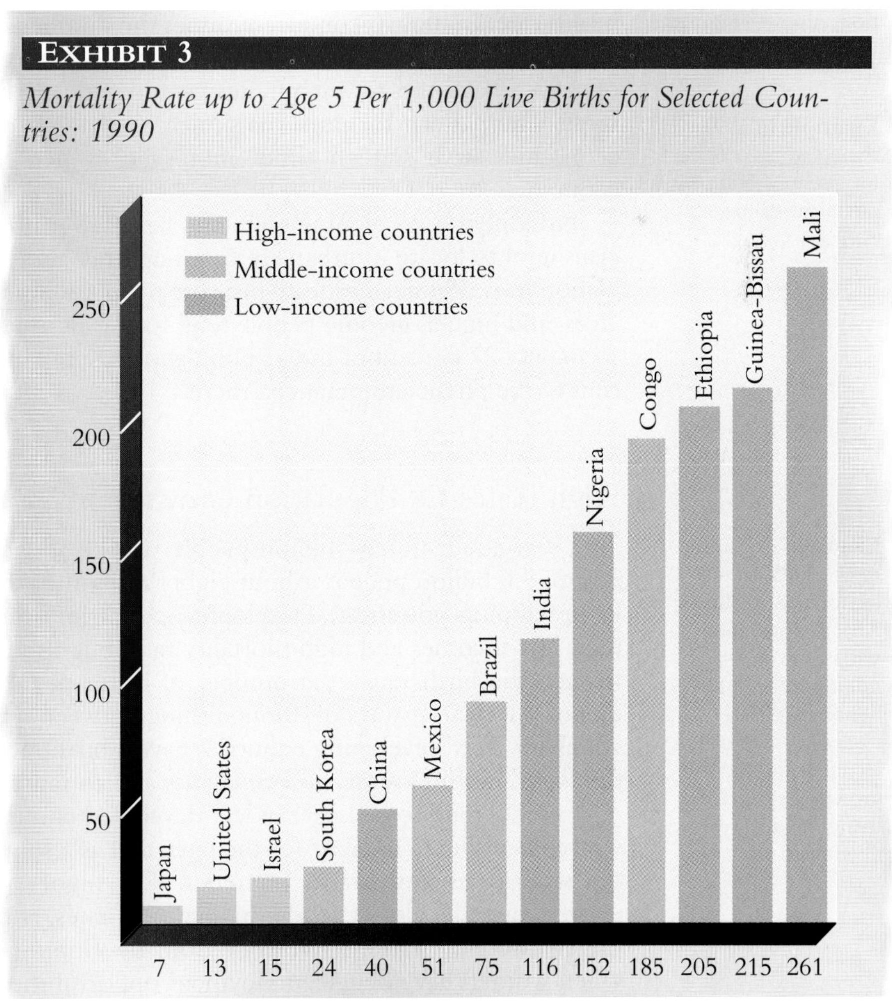

Source: Based on data presented by the World Bank in *World Development Report 1992* (New York: Oxford University Press, 1992), Table 32.

MALNUTRITION. People living in much of Africa, South Asia, and the Indian subcontinent often do not have enough food to maintain good health. Those in the very poorest countries consume only half the calories of those in high-income countries. Even if an infant survives the first year, malnutrition can turn normal childhood diseases, such as measles, into life-threatening events. Malnutrition is a primary or contributing factor in more than half of all deaths among children under five in low-income countries. Diseases that are well controlled in the industrial countries—malaria, whooping cough, polio, dysentery, typhoid, and cholera—become epidemics in poor countries. Many of these diseases are water borne, and residents of urban areas in less-developed countries are often unable to obtain safe drinking water.

Example Food production in sub-Saharan Africa was 20 percent lower in 1992 than in 1970. In addition, only 37 percent of the population had access to clean drinking water. The United Nations estimated that 53 million Africans were at immediate risk of starvation, disease, and malnutrition.

AVAILABILITY OF PHYSICIANS. Life expectancy and infant mortality rates are a reflection, in part, of how well the health care system operates. The number of physicians in a country is one measure of the availability of health care. In high-income economies the number of physicians per capita is twelve times greater than in low-income economies. The poorest countries of Africa have the fewest physicians and industrialized countries have the most. The pattern for nurses is similar to that for physicians. High-income economies have sixteen times more nurses per capita than low-income economies.

Example In 1992, there was one doctor for every 24,500 people in sub-Saharan Africa.

Not only do developing countries have fewer physicians, but these physicians tend to locate in urban areas, where only about one-fourth of the population lives. Physicians locate near the people who can most afford their services, and higher-income people tend to live in urban areas. For example, in 1990 only 27 percent of India's population resided in urban areas, but 80 percent of the physicians practiced there.

High Rates Of Population Growth

This year about ninety million people will be added to the world's population of 5.6 billion people. About eighty million of these people will be born in developing countries. Developing countries are identified not only by their low incomes and high mortality rates but also by their high birth rates. In fact, the birth rate—the number of births per one thousand people—is one of the clearest ways of distinguishing between developed and developing countries. Few developing countries have a birth rate of less than twenty per thousand, but no industrial country has a birth rate above that level.

Example According to World Bank projections, sub-Saharan Africa's population will rise from 548 million in 1992 to 2.9 billion by 2050, negating any projected economic growth and forcing living standards ever downward.

Families tend to be larger in less-developed countries because children are viewed as a source of labor for the farm and as a source of economic and social security as the parents get older. The higher infant mortality rates in poorer countries also engender higher birth rates, as parents strive to ensure a sufficiently large family. Evidence from developing countries indicates that when women have better employment opportunities outside the home, fertility rates decline. As women become better educated, they tend to earn more and have fewer children.

Much international aid to developing countries has taken the form of medical care and programs to improve hygiene. These advances have allowed people in developing countries to live longer, but increased longevity has placed a greater strain on the limited resources in those economies. Therefore improved health does little to avert poverty, at least in the short run. For example, in Sri Lanka modern medicine has eliminated malaria and has doubled the population growth rate. Other major diseases have also been wiped out. With 40 percent of the population in developing countries already living in absolute poverty, a greater survival rate is a mixed blessing in the short run. Over the long run, however, improved health leads to increased labor productivity and thus to higher income levels.

Despite improvements in medical care, death rates are still higher in developing countries than in developed countries. But these higher death rates are not great enough to offset the higher birth rates. Thus, since 1980 the population in developing countries has grown by an average of 2.0 percent per year, more than triple the 0.6 percent growth rate in industrial countries. The annual population growth rates since 1965 for major groupings of countries are presented in Exhibit 4, along with projections to the year 2000. For all classifications except sub-Saharan Africa, the growth rate has been slower since 1980 than it was between 1965 and 1980.

Example In 1990, the combined income of the countries of sub-Saharan Africa was roughly equal to that of Belgium, yet sub-Saharan Africa's population was fifty-three times larger than Belgium's.

Sub-Saharan African countries are the poorest in the world and have the fastest-growing populations. Because of the high birth rates there, children under fifteen make up almost half the total population in developing countries. In industrial countries children are only about a quarter of the population. In some developing countries the growth rate in population has exceeded the growth rate in real GDP, so the standard of living as measured by per capita GDP has been falling. Still, even in the poorest of countries, attitudes are changing about family size. For example, surveys of Kenyan women in late 1970s showed that they thought the ideal

EXHIBIT 4

Average Annual Population Growth Rate (percent)

Classification	1965–1980	1980–1990	1990–2000 (projected)
1. Low-income economies	2.3	2.0	1.8
China and India	2.2	1.7	1.5
Other	2.5	2.6	2.5
Sub-Saharan Africa	2.7	3.1	3.0
2. Middle-income economies	2.3	2.0	1.9
3. High-income economies	0.9	0.6	0.5

Source: Based on data presented by the World Bank in *World Development Report 1992* (New York: Oxford University Press, 1992), Table 26.

family had more than seven children. A 1992 Kenyan survey found between four and five children to be the most preferred family size.[1]

Women in Developing Countries

Throughout the world, poverty is greater among women, particularly women who head households. Because women often must work in the home as well as in the labor market, poverty can impose a special hardship on them. In many cultures women's responsibilities include gathering firewood and carrying water, tasks that are especially burdensome if firewood is scarce and water is far from home. The percentage of households headed by women varies from country to country, but exceeds 40 percent in some areas of the Caribbean and Africa.

Women in developing countries tend to be less educated than men. In the countries of sub-Saharan Africa and South Asia, for example, only half as many women as men complete high school. Women have fewer employment opportunities and earn lower wages than men do. For example, the Sudan's Muslim fundamentalist government bans women from working in public places after 5 P.M.[2] Women are often on the fringes of the labor market, working long hours in agriculture. They also have less access to other resources, such as land, capital, and technology.

Intracountry Income Distribution

Teaching Tip This method was described in detail in Chapter 32 in the discussion of income distribution in the United States.

Teaching Tip Many African nations have a large "informal sector" not captured by official statistics. The U.N. International Labor Organization estimates that the informal sector employs 59 percent of sub-Saharan Africa's urban labor force.

Per capita income differs not only across countries but also across households within countries. A standard procedure for measuring the distribution of household income is to group households from poorest to richest. After dividing the total number of households into five groups of equal size, or quintiles, we can examine what percentage of income is received by each quintile. Income distribution studies have been conducted for various countries around the world, and some of the results are presented in Exhibit 5. Countries are classified as developing, industrial, or economies of Eastern Europe that are in transition between socialism and capitalism. The figures are not strictly comparable because data for most of the developing countries reflect per capita *spending* rather than income. For a given country, per capita spending tends to be more evenly distributed than income.

All countries show some degree of income inequality. The pattern between developing and industrial countries is not clear-cut. On the one hand, the rich seem relatively richer in the developing countries. For example, on average the top 20 percent of households in the sample of

1. As reported in "More Choice, Fewer Babies," *The Economist*, 11 July 1992.
2. "World Wire," *Wall Street Journal*, 20 November 1992.

EXHIBIT 5

Percentage Share of Household Income or Spending by Groups of Households for Selected Countries

Country	Year	Lowest Fifth	Second-lowest Fifth	Middle Fifth	Second-highest Fifth	Highest Fifth
Developing Countries						
Bangladesh*	1985–86	10.0	13.7	17.2	21.9	37.2
India*	1983	8.1	12.3	16.3	22.0	41.4
Pakistan*	1984–85	7.8	11.2	15.0	20.6	45.6
Sri Lanka	1985–86	4.8	8.5	12.1	18.4	56.1
Indonesia*	1987	8.8	12.4	16.0	21.5	41.3
Brazil	1983	2.5	5.7	10.7	18.6	62.6
Transition Economies						
Hungary	1987–89	10.9	14.8	17.8	22.0	34.5
Poland	1987	9.7	14.2	18.0	22.9	35.2
Industrial Countries						
Canada	1987	5.7	11.8	17.7	24.6	40.2
Italy	1986	6.8	12.0	16.7	23.5	41.0
Australia	1985	4.4	11.1	17.5	24.8	42.2
United States	1985	4.7	11.0	17.4	25.0	41.9

*Indicates distribution of per capita spending

Source: Based on data presented by the World Bank in *World Development Report 1992* (New York: Oxford University Press, 1992), Table 30.

developing countries received 47 percent of the income, compared to only 41 percent for industrial countries. On the other hand, the poor seem relatively not quite as poor in the developing countries. For example, the bottom 20 percent in the developing countries earned on average 7 percent of the income versus 5 percent in the industrial countries.

In developing countries about two-thirds of the very poor scratch out a living as subsistence farmers or as farm workers. Although poverty is primarily a rural phenomenon, most government spending in developing countries occurs in urban areas, perhaps because urban poverty is more visible and because government officials who make budget decisions live in urban areas. Economist Simon Kuznets, who won the Nobel Prize for economics in 1971, has suggested that during the early stages of economic development, income tends to be unevenly distributed, but as an economy develops, the distribution of income tends to become more equal. The data in Exhibit 5 offer mixed support for his hypothesis.

Productivity and Development

We have examined some of the symptoms of poverty in developing countries, but not why poor countries are poor. At the risk of appearing too simplistic, we might say that poor countries are poor because they do not produce many goods and services. In this section we will examine why some developing countries experience such low productivity.

Low Labor Productivity

Teaching Tip Simon Kuznets has argued that technological progress achieved through the upgrading of capital and human resources accounts for most of the economic growth of the developed countries.

Labor productivity, measured in terms of output per worker, is very low in low-income countries. Why? Labor productivity depends on both the quality of the labor and on the amount of capital, land, and other resources that are combined with labor. For example, with respect to the quality of labor, one certified public accountant can sort out a company's finances more quickly and more accurately than a dozen clerks with only high school educations. Also, the greater the quality and amount of other resources, the greater the productivity of labor. A worker digging a ditch with an excavation machine is much more productive than one using only a shovel.

Example In 1992, wealthy Nigerians were estimated to have more than $36 billion in foreign personal deposits—enough to pay off the country's entire foreign debt.

One way to raise productivity is to invest more in human and physical capital. This investment must be financed by either domestic savings or foreign funds. Income per capita is often too low in developing countries to permit extensive investments to be financed with internal funds. In poor countries with unstable governments, the wealthy minority may invest in more stable foreign economies. There are thus few domestic funds available for investment in either human or physical capital, and without sufficient capital workers are less productive.

Technology and Education

Teaching Tip The empirical work of development economists Irma Adelman and Cynthia Morris concluded that one of the three most important factors determining a country's level of development is its "degree of modernization of outlook."

What exactly is the contribution of education to the process of economic development? Richard Easterlin of the University of Southern California argues that the spread of technology underlying modern economic growth depended largely on the acquisition of skills and motivation through formal schooling.[3] Education makes people more receptive to new ideas and methods. Thus, the nations with the most advanced educational systems were also the first to develop. In this century the leader in schooling and in economic development has been the United States. In Latin America, Argentina was the most advanced nation educationally a hundred years ago and is one of the most developed Latin American nations today. The growth of education in Japan during the nineteenth century contributed to a ready acceptance of technology and thus to Japan's remarkable economic growth in the twentieth century.

3. Richard Easterlin, "Why Isn't the Whole World Developed?" *Journal of Economic History,* 61 (March 1981): 1–17.

Knowledge is a resource, and the lack of knowledge can diminish the productivity of other resources. If knowledge is insufficient, other resources may not be used efficiently. For example, a country may be endowed with fertile land, but the land may be subdivided into such small parcels that farmers cannot take advantage of economies of scale. Or a poor country may have adequate land but may lack knowledge of irrigation and fertilization techniques. Or farmers may lack the know-how to rotate crops so as to avoid soil depletion.

In the least-developed countries 40 percent of the adult population is illiterate. Among developed countries only 4 percent of the adult population is illiterate. The percentage of the population enrolled in school at various levels differs sharply across countries. In high-income economies an average of 40 percent of those aged twenty to twenty-four are enrolled in post-secondary education, compared with 17 percent in middle-income economies and only 4 percent in low-income economies. Post-secondary enrollment percentages for selected countries are presented in Exhibit 6.

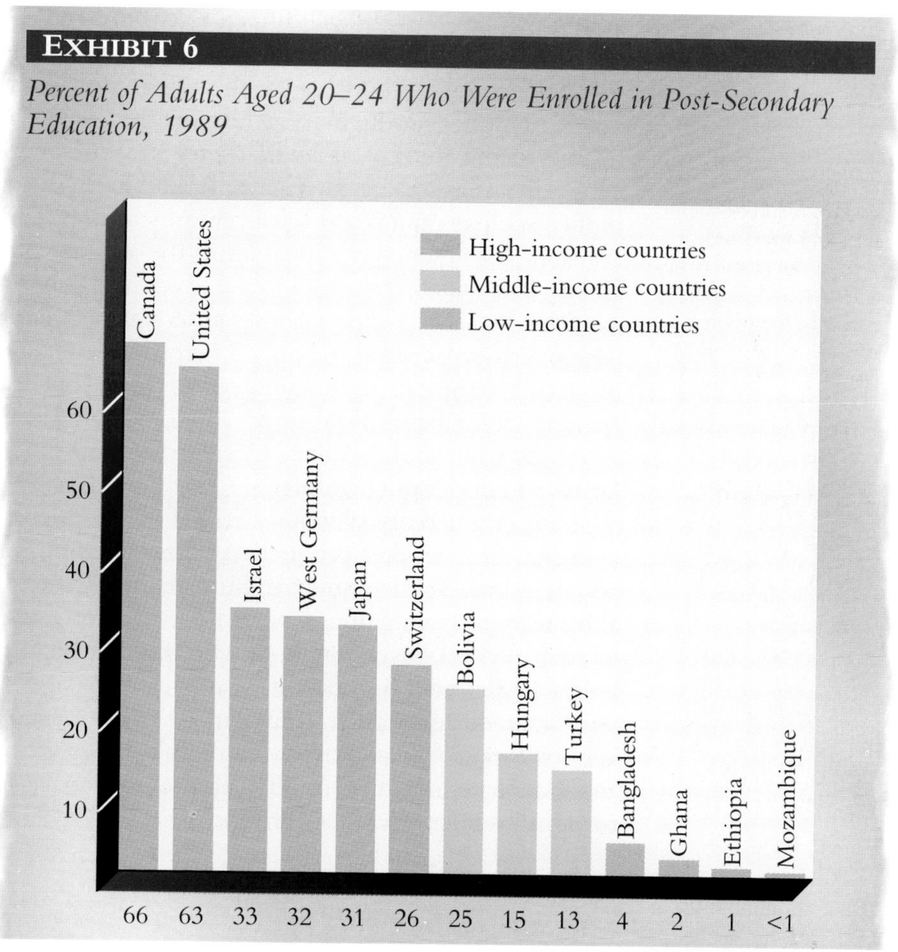

Source: Based on data presented by the World Bank in *World Development Report 1992* (New York: Oxford University Press, 1992), Table 29.

Canada and the United States are the leaders by far, each with over 60 percent in post-secondary education. Among the poorest countries, less than 1 percent of the relevant population pursues higher education.

Teaching Tip Unemployment and underemployment problems are often aggravated by government policies designed to keep food prices low. Investment in agriculture is thus discouraged, and large portions of the population move to the cities where few formal jobs exist.

Poor Use of Labor

Another feature of developing countries is that they use labor less efficiently than developed nations. Poor use of labor results from both unemployment and underemployment. *Underemployment* occurs when people are working less than they would like to—a worker seeking full-time employment may find only a part-time job, or a highly skilled worker may be employed in a low-skill job. *Unemployment* occurs when those who are willing and able to work cannot find jobs.

Unemployment is measured primarily in urban areas, because in rural areas farm work is usually an outlet for labor even if most workers are underemployed there. The unemployment rate in developing nations on average is about 10 to 15 percent of the urban labor force. Unemployment among young workers—those aged fifteen to twenty-four—is typically twice that of older workers. In developing nations about 30 percent of the combined urban and rural work forces is either unemployed or underemployed.

Example When Zambia gained independence from Britain in 1964, it was the richest black country south of the Sahara, with large mineral resources and immense expanses of fertile farmland. Today, unemployment is high, only 5 percent of the arable land is in use, and Zambia is one of the poorest nations in the world.

Agricultural productivity is low because of the large number of farmers relative to the amount of land farmed. In some developing countries the average farm is as small as two acres. Productivity is low also because few other inputs, such as capital and fertilizer, are employed. Even where more land is available, the absence of capital limits the amount of land that can be farmed. *Although two-thirds of the labor force in developing countries works in agriculture, only one-third of GDP in these countries arises from agriculture.* In the United States, where farmers account for only 3 percent of the labor force, a farmer with a modern tractor can farm hundreds of acres, but in developing countries a farmer with a hand plow or an ox-drawn plow can farm maybe 10 to 20 acres. As you would expect, U.S. farmers are much more productive than farmers in developing countries.

Example Businesses previously anxious to build plants in Africa to take advantage of cheap labor are now finding that because of unreliable infrastructures and bad government policies, capital and operating costs are 50 percent to 100 percent higher in Africa than in South Asia. Return on investment is now nine times higher in South Asia; twenty-five years ago returns on investment in the two regions were even.

Low productivity obviously results in low income, but low income can, in turn, affect worker productivity. Low income means less saving and less saving means less investment in human and physical capital. Low income can also mean poor nutrition during the formative years, which can retard mental and physical development. These difficult beginnings may be aggravated by poor diet and insufficient health care in later life, making the worker poorly suited for regular employment. Thus, *low income and low productivity may reinforce each other.* Poverty can result in less saving, less capital formation, an inadequate diet, and insufficient attention to health care—all of which, in turn, can reduce a worker's productive ability.

Capital Infrastructure

Some development economists believe that the single most important ingredient in economic development is the political organization and the administrative competence of the government. Production and exchange often rely on an infrastructure of communication and transportation networks provided by the public sector. Roads, bridges, airports, harbors, and other transportation facilities are vital to commercial activity. Reliable mail service, telephone communication, and a steady supply of water and electricity are also essential for advanced production techniques. Imagine how difficult it would be to run even a personal computer if the supply of electricity were continually interrupted, as is often the case in developing countries. Many developing countries tend to have serious deficiencies in their infrastructures. And some of the poorest countries in Africa have been ravaged by internal strife. For example, Mozambique has been caught up in a bloody civil war since 1975, and the anarchy and resulting hunger in Somalia has resulted in intervention by the United Nations involving U.S. troops.

Teaching Tip Chapter 4 discussed the role of the government in providing such a system of property rights in the United States.

Teaching Tip Gunnar Myrdal, Nobel Prize winner in economics, argued that cultural reform and attitudinal changes are necessary in developing countries before the free market approach to economics can work.

Example As a result of collapsing coffee and cocoa prices, the Ivory Coast's export earnings fell from $3.2 billion in 1986 to $2.5 billion in 1989. Falling export prices in combination with rising oil prices caused total foreign debt to rise from 37 percent of GDP in 1979 to 130 percent in 1991.

Institutions and Economic Incentives[4]

Institutions are constraints that structure political, economic, and social interaction. They consist of (1) formal rules of behavior, such as a constitution, laws, and property rights, and (2) informal constraints on behavior, such as sanctions, manners, customs, traditions, and codes of conduct. Throughout history, institutions have been devised by human beings to, among other things, create order and reduce uncertainty in exchange. Thus, underlying the surface of market behavior lies a grid of informal, often unconscious, habits, customs, and norms, that make the functioning of markets possible. *A reliable system of property rights and enforceable contracts are prerequisites for creating incentives that could support a healthy market economy.*

Together with the standard constraints of economics, such as income, resource availability, and prices, institutions shape the incentive structure of an economy. As the incentive structure evolves, it can direct economic change toward growth, stagnation, or decline. Economic history is largely a story of economies that have failed to produce a set of economic rules of the game that lead to sustained economic growth. After all, three-quarters of the nations of the world are still trying to develop.

Customs and conventions can sometimes be obstacles to development. In developed market economies, resource owners tend to supply their resources where they are most valued, but in developing countries links to the family or clan may be the most important consideration. For example, in some cultures children are expected to remain in the father's occupation even if they are better suited to some other line of work. Family businesses may resist growth because such growth would involve hiring people from outside the family.

4. In preparing this section the author benefited from two articles by Douglas C. North: "Institutions," *Journal of Economic Perspectives*, 5 (Winter 1991): 97–112; and "Institutions, Ideology, and Economic Performance," *Cato Journal*, 11 (Winter 1992): 477–488.

Problems with International Trade

Developing countries need to trade with developed countries in order to acquire the capital and technology that will increase labor productivity both on the farm and in the factory. To import capital and technology, developing countries must first acquire the funds, or foreign exchange, needed to pay for imports. Exports usually generate more than half of the annual flow of foreign exchange in developing countries. Foreign aid and private investment make up the rest.

Example In the 1970s, world copper prices slumped, with disastrous results for Zambia, which relied on copper exports for at least 90 percent of its foreign exchange earnings. The subsequent underinvestment in the copper industry forced Zambian manufacturers to continue to use old and inefficient equipment, which in turn caused copper production to fall from 700,000 tons in 1964 to 450,000 tons in 1992.

Primary products, such as agricultural goods and other raw materials, make up the bulk of exports from developing countries, just as manufactured goods make up the bulk of exports from developed countries. One problem with exporting primary products rather than finished goods is that primary products are worth a small amount relative to finished products. Consequently, developing countries must export a large amount of raw materials in order to buy back the finished products made from these same materials. A second problem is that the prices of primary products, such as coffee, cocoa, sugar, and rubber, fluctuate more widely than the prices of finished goods, because crop production fluctuates with the weather.

Another problem of developing countries has been their deteriorating trade position. In recent years the prices of raw materials have fallen as demand has softened and as substitutes have been developed for products such as rubber. Since the prices of manufactured imported goods have not dropped, developing countries have received less money from exports than they have spent on imports, resulting in trade deficits. To reduce these deficits, developing countries have tried to restrict imports. Because imported food often is critical to survival, developing countries were more likely to cut back on imports of capital goods—the very items needed to promote long-term growth and productivity. So many developing countries cannot afford the modern machinery that will help them become more productive.

Example Farm subsidies have been the major stumbling block toward the free trade promoted by GATT since its founding in 1947. Japan bans virtually all imports of rice. The United States has export subsidies for wheat and heavy protection for sugar.

Developing countries often must also confront industrial countries' trade restrictions, such as tariffs and quotas, which often discriminate against primary products. Developing countries' share of world trade has been falling since 1950. But some of the obstacles to international trade are imposed from within, as reflected in the following case study.

CASE STUDY

A Hard Sell in Egypt

The conditions seemed right in Egypt for Mohammed Marzouk to develop a business that made cotton underwear for export. After all, Egypt grows the best cotton in the world. Quality cotton combined with low labor costs seemed like a sure winner. So why is Egyptian underwear too costly to compete on the world market? As developing countries grow desperate for exports, why can't Egypt compete?

The thin cotton yarn used to weave the cloth is produced by government-owned spinning companies. These companies have a monopoly in the production of yarn from raw cotton, and yarn prices tripled in seven years. To protect the state monopoly, a tariff of 65 percent is imposed on imported yarn. But the government-produced yarn tends to be inferior and breaks easily. So although Egyptian cotton is of fine quality, the production chain is only as strong as its weakest link, and yarn spinning is the weak link.

Although wages are low in Egypt, total labor costs are high because labor productivity is low as well. Since the yarn breaks so easily, workers must rewind and wax it before knitting can begin. The objective is to detect irregularities in the yarn that could damage machinery or produce holes in fabric. Because there is little modern machinery, much other work must be done by hand as well. For example, each finished article is pressed with a hand iron. When steam is needed, the presser sips water and spits.

Egypt, like many Third World countries, is plagued by bureaucratic snarls and petty corruption that gum up the wheels of commerce. Mr. Marzouk employs workers whose primary job is to run interference with the government bureaucracy. As many as thirty-four government signatures are needed to ship an order for export. At each step along the way, someone's palm must be greased with *baksheesh*, or a bribe, to move the paperwork along.

One of Mr. Marzouk's biggest problems is the apparently arbitrary treatment he receives from the government. His factory was started under an investment law that conferred a five-year income tax break. But because of this tax break, another government agency decided that he should pay more for electricity, so he pays triple the rate charged most other customers. Because of the uncertainty created by the arbitrary nature of government regulations, Marzouk is reluctant to expand, even though he has $1 million worth of crated machinery plus fourteen acres of land on which to build. Regulations and trade restrictions have recently been eased a bit, so investments may become somewhat more attractive in Egypt.

Sources: Barbara Rosewicz, "Factory Owner Joins Egypt's Exports Push but Runs into Hurdles," *Wall Street Journal*, 11 November 1985; and "Egypt: Killing the Dinosaur," *The Economist*, 25 July 1992.

Import Substitution Versus Export Promotion

Import substitution A development strategy that emphasizes manufacturing products that are currently imported

Teaching Tip See Chapter 33 for a discussion of the infant industry argument for trade protection.

Economic development frequently involves a shift from the production of raw materials and agricultural products to manufacturing. If a country is fortunate, this transformation occurs gradually through natural market forces. Sometimes the shift is pushed along by government. Many developing countries, including Argentina and India, have pursued a policy called **import substitution**, whereby the country manufactures products that until then had been imported. To insulate domestic producers from foreign competition, the government imposes tariffs and quotas on imports. This development strategy is popular for several reasons. First, demand already exists for these products, so the "What to produce" question is answered. Second, by reducing imports, the approach addresses the balance-of-payments problem so common among developing countries. Third, import substitution nurtures infant industries, providing them the market and the protection to grow. Finally, import substitution is popular with those who supply capital, labor, and other resources to the favored domestic industries.

The problem is that like all protection measures, import substitution bypasses the gains from specialization and comparative advantage among countries. Often the developing country replaces low-cost foreign goods with high-cost domestic goods. And domestic producers insulated from foreign competition may never become efficient. Even the balance-of-payments picture may not improve because other countries often retaliate with their own trade restrictions.

Critics of the import-substitution approach claim that export promotion is a surer path to economic development. **Export promotion** is a development strategy that concentrates on producing for the export market. This approach begins with relatively simple products, such as textiles. As a developing country builds its technological and educational base, producers can begin exporting more complex products. Economists tend to favor export promotion over import substitution because the emphasis is on trade expansion rather than trade restriction. Export promotion also forces producers to be more efficient in order to compete on world markets. What's more, export promotion requires less bureaucratic intervention into the market than does import substitution.

Export promotion A development strategy that concentrates on producing for the export market

Teaching Tip A study of import substitution industries in seven countries found that the effective rate of protection or subsidy ranged from 25 to more than 200 percent.

Export promotion has been the more successful development strategy. Developing countries with the highest rate of export growth have also tended to experience the highest growth of real GDP per capita. For example, export-promoting countries such as China, South Korea, and Hong Kong have in recent decades grown much more quickly than import-substituting countries such as Argentina, India, and Peru. The export-promotion approach is not without its critics, but it has gained support from economic success stories, such as the newly industrialized countries of East Asia.

Point to Stress As with import substitution, countries that pursue export promotion must not choose to invest in industries in which they have a long-term comparative disadvantage. Furthermore, they must devote resources to development of an infrastructure and overcoming social and cultural barriers to efficient production.

Migration and the Brain Drain

Migration plays an important role in the economies of developing countries. A major source of foreign exchange in some countries is the money sent home by migrants who find jobs in industrial countries. Thus, migration provides a valuable safety valve for poor countries. But there is a negative aspect as well. Often the best and the brightest professionals, such as doctors, nurses, and engineers, migrate to developed countries after they have been trained at great expense to the developing country. Since human capital is such a key resource, this "brain drain" can have devastating effects on the developing economy.

Point to Stress Exhibit 1 indicates a real GDP per capita growth rate since 1965 of 5.8 percent for China versus 1.9 percent for India.

Natural Resources

Some countries are richer than others because they are blessed with natural resources. The difference is most striking when we compare countries with oil reserves and those without. Some developing countries of the Middle East are classified as high-income economies because they are lucky enough to be sitting atop major oil reserves. But oil-rich countries are the exception.

Example Despite the fact that some countries on the continent have rich endowments of natural resources (Zambia, for example), most countries in Africa lack a class of entrepreneurs. Thus, Africa's share of the world's total output fell from 1.9 percent in 1960 to 1.2 percent in 1989.

Teaching Tip Consider the case study on wild inflation in Bolivia in Chapter 7.

Many developing countries, such as Chad and Ethiopia, have little in the way of natural resources. Developing countries without oil reserves were in trouble during the 1970s, when oil prices rose. Oil had to be imported, and these imports drained the oil-poor countries of precious foreign exchange. But a few countries, such as Japan and South Korea, have managed to do very well despite their lack of natural resources.

Financial Institutions

Another requirement for development is an adequate and trusted system of financial institutions. An important source of funds for investment is the savings of households and firms. People in developing countries often have little confidence in their currency because the government tends to finance a large fraction of public outlays by printing money. This practice results in high inflation on average and sometimes very high inflation, or hyperinflation. High and unpredictable inflation discourages saving.

Developing countries have special problems because banks are often not held in high regard. At the first sign of economic problems, many depositors withdraw their funds. Since banks cannot consequently rely on a continuous supply of deposits, they cannot make loans for extended periods. Another problem banks in developing countries face in making loans is that potential borrowers often lack the collateral, or valued assets, that banks desire as security for loans. Also, governments often impose ceilings on the interest rates that lenders can charge, forcing lenders to ration credit among borrowers. Investment is critical to growth. If financial institutions fail to serve as intermediaries between borrowers and lenders, the lack of funds for investment becomes an obstacle to growth.

Entrepreneurial Ability

Teaching Tip The lack of entrepreneurial ability is also a problem in the former Soviet Union and Eastern Europe.

A country can have abundant supplies of land, labor, and capital, but without entrepreneurial ability the other resources will not be combined efficiently to produce goods and services. Unless a country has a class of entrepreneurs who are able to bring together resources and take the risk of profit or loss, development may never begin. Many developing countries were until recently under colonial rule, a system of government that offered the local population little opportunity to develop entrepreneurial skills.

Example After independence in Zambia, the state came to own and manage 80 percent of the formal economy. Senior managers were appointed for political reasons involving tribalism, provincialism, and nepotism.

Government Monopolies

Government officials often decide that local, private sector entrepreneurs are unable to generate the kind of economic growth the country needs. State enterprises are therefore created to do what government believes the free market cannot do. State-owned enterprises, however, may have multiple objectives other than producing goods efficiently—objectives that could include maximizing employment and providing jobs for friends and relatives of government officials. Economies may be less productive if people respond not to the normal market incentives but to opportunities for some special market advantage from the government. Consider the government's role in the following case study.

CASE STUDY

All in the Family

Indonesia is a country of 190 million people spread across more than thirteen thousand islands in the Indian Ocean. The country is rich in natural resources, including oil, yet economic development has been hampered by bureaucratic red tape and corruption. At the center is President Suharto, who has ruled Indonesia since 1965. Over the years, he has conferred monopoly privileges on his family and friends. For example, friends and relatives hold the exclusive rights to import steel, plastic, tin, cotton, industrial machinery, and other key resources.

Based on the strength of government-granted monopolies, President Suharto's children have been able to build an economic empire. One of the president's sons has an interest in more than fifty companies that make products ranging from baby food to petroleum. Another son is the sole distributor of several key petrochemicals produced by the state oil company. Most of these businesses started with lucrative government contracts, government decrees, or government licenses conferring the right to import or to produce the goods and services in question. Forms of government intervention have included (1) awarding import licenses, often to a single company; (2) imposing quotas to control imports; (3) designating "approved traders" to restrict the number of firms that may distribute a product; and (4) licensing investment to block the new entry of firms.

Because of government-imposed monopolies, the prices of products in Indonesia are higher than those prevailing on the world market. All imported plastic must flow through a company controlled by Suharto's children, an arrangement that is said to add 15 to 20 percent to the domestic price of plastics. A family monopoly on the importing of cold-rolled sheet steel—a key input in products ranging from appliances to automobiles—has raised the price of steel 25 to 45 percent above the world price. All tin must be purchased from a tin monopoly, an arrangement that is said to raise the domestic price of tin by 60 to 70 percent. The domestic cement industry is protected from imports, and domestic cement costs twice as much as cement sold on the world market. Indocement, the nation's largest cement producer, is owned by Suharto's business partner, who has become one of the richest people in the world (according to *Forbes* 1992 list of billionaires).

The higher domestic prices for resources impose a burden on Indonesian consumers and also raise the prices of goods produced with these resources, making Indonesian products less competitive on world markets. The consequent reduction in exports limits the foreign exchange available for purchasing modern machinery from abroad and for making other investments that could advance the Indonesian economy.

Thus, these monopolies reduce competition, increase costs to consumers, and hinder the development of an export sector that can compete on the world market. In this environment, political connections become more important than ability or expertise; free enterprise is thereby discouraged. Businesses are

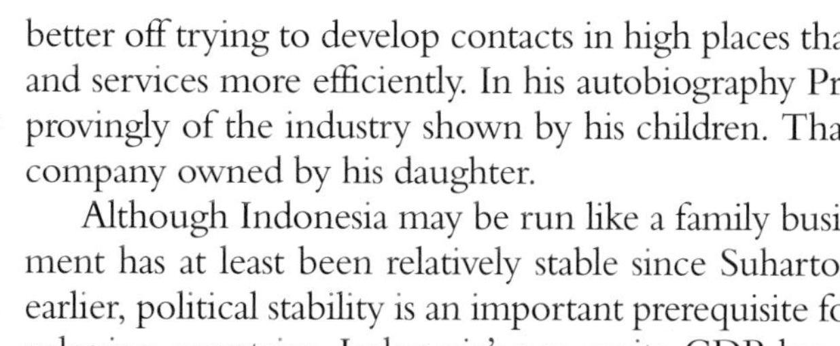

better off trying to develop contacts in high places than trying to produce goods and services more efficiently. In his autobiography President Suharto speaks approvingly of the industry shown by his children. That book was published by a company owned by his daughter.

Although Indonesia may be run like a family business, the political environment has at least been relatively stable since Suharto took over. And, as noted earlier, political stability is an important prerequisite for economic growth in developing countries. Indonesia's per capita GDP has grown by 4.5 percent per year since 1965, compared to only 2.9 percent among other low-income countries. In recent years, trade restrictions on some imports have been lifted and some regulations have been eased.

Sources: Steven Jones and Raphael Pura, "Indonesian Decrees Help Suharto's Friends and Relatives Prosper," *Wall Street Journal*, 24 November 1986; Barry Wain, "An Indonesian of Few Words Spills the Beans," *Wall Street Journal*, 25 March 1989; and "The World's Billionaires," *Forbes*, 20 July 1992.

Teaching Tip For a detailed discussion of widespread versus concentrated costs and benefits, see Chapter 30.

Though most people would benefit from freer markets, some would be significantly worse off in the short run. Consequently, governments in some developing countries have difficulty pursuing policies conducive to development. Often the gains from economic development are widespread, but the beneficiaries, such as consumers, do not recognize their potential gains. On the other hand, the losers tend to be concentrated, such as producers in an industry that had been sheltered from foreign competition, and they know quite well the source of their losses. So the government has difficulty removing the impediments to development, because the potential losers fight reforms that might affect their livelihood while the potential winners remain largely unaware of what's at stake. What's more, consumers have a difficult time organizing even if they become aware of what's going on. A recent study by the World Bank suggests a strong correlation in Africa between governments that cater to special-interest groups and low rates of economic growth.

Example In part as a result of the freeing of markets in Mexico, U.S.–Mexico trade more than doubled to $43 billion over the five-year period before the negotiation of the North American Free Trade Agreement.

Nonetheless, many developing countries have been opening their borders to freer trade. People around the world have been exposed to information about the opportunities and goods available in more successful countries at world prices. A country can no longer allow its own goods to sell for some multiple of the world price. So consumers want the goods that are available abroad and firms want the technology and inputs, such as capital, available abroad. Both groups want government to ease trade restrictions. Studies by the World Bank and others have underscored the successes of countries that have adopted trade liberalization policies.

Foreign Aid and Economic Development

We have already seen that because poor countries do not generate enough savings to fund an adequate level of investment, these countries often rely on

Teaching Tip African nations owe the bulk of their debt to governments of developed nations, the IMF, and the World Bank. Other heavily indebted countries owe most of their debt to commercial banks and other private creditors.

foreign capital. Private international borrowing and lending are heavily restricted by the governments of developing countries. Governments may allow residents to purchase foreign exchange only for certain purposes. In some developing countries different exchange rates apply to different categories of transactions. Thus, the local currency is not easily convertible into other currencies. Some developing countries also require foreign investors to find a local partner who must be granted controlling interest. All these restrictions discourage foreign investment. In this section we will look primarily at foreign aid and its link to economic development.

Foreign Aid

Foreign aid An international transfer made on especially favorable terms for the purpose of promoting economic development

Foreign aid is any international transfer made on concessional (that is, especially favorable) terms for the purposes of promoting economic development. Foreign aid includes both grants that need not be repaid and loans extended on more favorable repayment terms than the recipient could secure in normal markets. Concessional loans have lower interest rates, longer repayment periods, or grace periods during which payments are reduced or waived. Foreign aid may be provided not only as money but as capital goods, technical assistance, food, and so forth.

Some foreign aid is from a specific country, such as the United States, to a specific country, such as the Philippines. Country-to-country aid is called *bilateral* assistance. Other aid is through international bodies such as the World Bank, which was established in 1946 as an affiliate of the United Nations. Assistance provided by organizations that use funds from a number of countries is called *multilateral.* For example, the World Bank provides loans and grants to support activities that are viewed as prerequisites for development, such as health and education programs or basic development projects like dams, roads, and communications networks.

The World Bank gets its money through contributions from member nations and through bond issues in private capital markets. Loans must be used for specifically approved projects. Most World Bank loans are not made unless there is reasonable assurance that the borrower can service and repay the loan. But the World Bank also lends to countries that are poor credit risks. Such loans usually include terms considered more favorable to the developing countries—that is, lower interest rates and longer repayment periods.

Teaching Tip The International Bank for Reconstruction and Development is the department of the World Bank Group that requires that borrowers have a reasonable chance of servicing and repaying the loan. Loans to poor credit risks are made by the International Development Association.

During the last four decades, the United States has provided the developing world with over $400 billion in aid. Since 1961 most foreign aid by the United States has been coordinated by the U.S. Agency for International Development (AID), which is part of the U.S. Department of State. This agency concentrates primarily on health, education, and agriculture, providing both technical assistance and loans. AID emphasizes long-range plans to meet the basic needs of the poor and to promote self-sufficiency. Foreign aid is a controversial, though relatively small, part of the federal budget. Official U.S. aid in recent years has amounted to only one-quarter of one percent of U.S. GDP—a lower percentage than for many other industrial countries.

Does Foreign Aid Promote Economic Development?

In general, foreign aid provides additional purchasing power and thus the possibility of increasing investment, capital imports, or consumption. But it is unclear whether foreign aid *supplements* domestic saving, thus increasing investment, or simply *substitutes for* domestic saving, thereby increasing consumption rather than investment. What is clear is that foreign aid often becomes a source of discretionary funds that benefit not the poor but their leaders. More than 90 percent of the funds distributed by AID go to governments, whose leaders assume responsibility for distributing these funds.

Much bilateral funding is tied to purchases of goods and services from the donor nation, and such programs can sometimes be counterproductive. For example, in the 1950s the United States began the "Food for Peace" program, which helped U.S. farmers, but some governments sold the food to finance poorly conceived projects. What's more, the availability of low-priced food drove down food prices, hurting farmers in the countries that received the aid.

Teaching Tip A 1989 World Bank publication, *Sub-Saharan Africa: From Crisis to Sustainable Growth*, indicated that Africa stagnated in the 1970s and declined in the 1980s. The report made it clear that the World Bank, the IMF, and the major donor countries want to steer African nations away from thinking of foreign aid as a permanent fact of life. The lenders want to encourage government policies based on better economic fundamentals—not ineptness or corruption financed through donations.

Much hope has been held out that foreign aid will provide a spur to development. Foreign aid may have raised the standard of living in some developing countries, but it has not increased their ability to become self-supporting at that higher standard of living. Many countries that receive aid are doing less of what they had done well. Their agricultural sectors have suffered. For example, though we should be careful about drawing conclusions about causality, per capita food production in Africa has fallen since 1960. Outside aid has often insulated government officials from the troubles of their own economies. No country receiving U.S. aid in the past twenty years has moved up in status from less developed to developed. Most countries today that have achieved the status of "industrial country" did so without foreign aid.

Third World Debt Problems

As we have said, economic development usually requires that developing countries receive capital, or investment funds, from abroad because they do not generate enough domestic saving to meet their investment needs. When an economy is at or below subsistence productivity, the only way people can save is to eat even less. The oil price increases of 1973 were a major shock to the development process. Most developing countries are oil importers, so they soon experienced deficits in their trade balances. To offset these trade deficits, many countries borrowed in international capital markets. At the time their economies seemed relatively healthy, so foreign banks were willing to lend them money to get through the period of high oil prices.

Teaching Tip The commercial banks were willing to make the loans in part because the oil-exporting nations had a large increase in deposits at the banks. See Chapter 13 for a discussion of the banking issues of profitability versus liquidity.

Some developing countries, such as South Korea and Taiwan, immediately began adjusting to the new economics of higher oil prices, and by the late 1970s these countries were growing again at a robust rate. But some other developing countries borrowed and borrowed as long as anyone would lend them money. Rising interest rates during the 1970s increased the cost of borrowing. Countries continued to import more than they exported and did little to address the fundamental imbalances in their economies, in part because any belt-tightening would have been politically unpopular. Their debts mounted.

The worldwide recession in the early 1980s was a crippling blow to many developing nations. The recession was followed by high real interest rates, declining prices for the agricultural products that developing countries export, and a cutoff of private lending to most developing countries. These shocks hit developing countries hard. The value of their commodity exports was falling, making debt service more difficult and further credit unavailable. Net investment in these countries consequently fell during the 1980s, as did per capita incomes.

Example Loans to Brazil, Mexico, and Venezuela in the mid-1980s by three major U.S. banks—Citibank, Chase Manhattan, and Manufacturer's Hanover—amounted to almost double the net worth of the three banks.

Some countries, such as Brazil, defaulted on their foreign debts. (See the case study on Brazil in the previous chapter.)

As noted earlier, not all developing countries had trouble repaying their foreign debts. South Korea had one of the highest levels of external debt per capita in the world, but this borrowed money has been invested and managed wisely—for example, to purchase technologically efficient machines—so South Korea has had little difficulty servicing its debt. Taiwan has also employed its borrowed funds efficiently. Thus, foreign borrowing, if employed wisely, can help promote economic development.

CONCLUSION

As we said at the outset, because no single theory of economic development has become widely accepted, the emphasis in this chapter has been more descriptive than theoretical. We can readily define the features that distinguish developing and industrial economies, but we are less sure how to foster growth and development. As noted earlier, economic history is largely a story of economies that have failed to produce a set of economic rules of the game that lead to sustained economic growth. After all, three-quarters of the nations of the world are still trying to develop. In conclusion, we underscore some important prerequisites to development.

Perhaps the most elusive ingredients for development are the formal and informal institutions that promote market activity: the laws, customs, conventions, and other institutional elements that encourage people to undertake productive activity. A stable political environment with well-defined property rights is important. Little private sector investment will occur if potential investors believe their capital might be appropriated by government, destroyed by civil unrest, or stolen by thieves. Education is also key to development, both because of its direct effect on productivity and because those who are more educated tend to be more receptive to new ideas. A physical infrastructure of transportation and communication systems and utilities is needed to link economic actors. And trusted financial institutions are needed to link savers and borrowers. Finally, a country needs entrepreneurs with the vision to move the economy forward. The newly emerging industrial countries of South Korea, Taiwan, Singapore, and Malaysia prove that economic development is achievable, though not necessarily easy.

SUMMARY

1. Developing countries are distinguished by low levels of real GDP per capita, poor health and nutrition, high birth rates, low levels of education, and saving rates that are too low to finance sufficient investment.

2. Worker productivity is low in developing countries because the stocks of physical and human capital are low, technological advances are not widely diffused throughout the economy, natural resources and entrepreneurial ability are scarce, financial markets are not well developed, some talented professionals migrate to high-income countries, formal and informal institutions do not provide individual incentives for market activity, and governments may serve the interests of the group in power rather than the public interest.

3. The secret to growth and a rising standard of living is increased productivity. To foster productivity, developing nations must stimulate investment, support education and training programs, and provide the infrastructure necessary to support economic development. Economic development often involves government planning, foreign technical assistance, and foreign aid.

4. Increases in productivity do not occur without prior saving, but most people in developing countries have such low incomes that there is little opportunity to save. Also, even if some people had the money to save, financial institutions in developing countries are not well developed, and savings are often sent abroad, where there is a more stable investment climate.

5. Foreign aid has been a mixed blessing for most developing countries. In some cases that aid has helped countries build the roads, bridges, schools, and other capital infrastructure necessary for development. In other cases foreign aid has simply increased consumption, while having little impact on the country's productive capability. Worse still, cheap food from abroad has undermined domestic agriculture.

QUESTIONS AND PROBLEMS

1. (Developing Countries) How would you explain why agricultural production in developing countries is usually low? Is the law of diminishing returns important to your answer? Why?

2. (Per Capita Real Income) What arguments are there for using real per capita GDP to compare living standards between countries? What weakness does this measure have?

3. (Developing Countries) Why is a higher survival rate a mixed blessing for developing countries? That is, what problems does a developing country face when life expectancy increases?

4. (Developing Countries and Trade) How might a country that is predominantly agricultural grow into an industrial economy? Is saving an important feature of growth? What about import substitution, whereby imported products are replaced by domestically produced goods?

5. (Growth and Foreign Exchange) How does a country that wants to import more productive capital and technology get the foreign exchange to do so?

6. (Political Stability and Development) Why is political stability a key element in a country's ability to grow? Consider the effect of political instability on capital.

7. (Growth and Fixed Exchange) In an effort to spur growth, governments in developing countries often fix the price of their currency at low levels. How might fixing the rate in this way help stimulate growth? What problems might it cause?

8. (Low Wages and Growth) Sometimes it is argued that low wages for labor are essential for growth. How is this argument dependent on exchange rates?

9. (Domestic Aggregate Demand) Why is it important to develop a strong domestic economy if the economy as a whole is to continue to grow?

10. (Heavy Industry and Growth) Policy makers in many developing countries believe the country must produce steel and autos in order to experience fast economic growth. Why is this policy usually misguided? Consider the issue of comparative advantage.

11. (Per Capita Real Income) How do differences in each of the following affect the usefulness of per capita real income as a means of comparing living standards across countries?
    a. Income distribution
    b. The level of nonmarket activity using resources
    c. The level of externalities generated by income production
    d. The amount of leisure consumption

12. (Developing Versus Industrial Market Economies) Compare developing and industrial market economies on the basis of each of the following general economic characteristics, and relate the differences to the process of development:
    a. Diversity of the industrial base
    b. Distribution of resource ownership
    c. Educational level of the labor force

13. (Economic Growth) Countries that need new capital and technology often institute "austerity programs" centered around increasing exports. What is the purpose of such programs and why do they often create political instability?

14. (Foreign Aid) Foreign aid, if it is to be successful in enhancing economic development, must lead to a more productive resource base. Describe some of the problems in achieving such an objective through foreign aid.

15. (Impediments to Growth) Among the problems that hinder growth in the developing economies of the world are poor infrastructure, lack of financial institutions and a sound money supply, low savings rate, poor capital base, and lack of foreign exchange. Explain how these problems are interconnected.

16. (Import Substitution Versus Export Promotion) Although export promotion is often regarded as a better approach than import substitution to enhancing economic growth in developing economies, there are clearly dangers to this approach that are similar to those associated with import substitution. Explain.

17. (Foreign Aid) It is widely recognized that aid that promotes productivity in developing economies is superior to merely shipping products like food to these countries. Yet the latter is the approach frequently taken. Why do you think this is the case?

18. (Developing Economies and the Production Possibilities Frontier) Growth may be thought of as a shift of the production possibilities frontier outward. Yet in many developing economies, a major problem is simply getting to the frontier in the first place. Explain.

19. (Developing Countries and the Environment) The global conference on the environment that took place in Rio de Janeiro in 1990 was widely seen as pitting the interests of developing nations against those of the developed world. Why do you think this conflict of interest exists?

20. (A Hard Sell in Egypt) To some extent this case study reflects the problems associated with using import substitution as opposed to export promotion to foster growth. Explain.

21. (A Hard Sell in Egypt) How might a devaluation of the Egyptian currency, the Egyptian pound, affect Mr. Marzouk's ability to compete in world markets?

22. (All in the Family) Many of the restrictions on imports to Indonesia take the form of import quotas rather than tariffs. What difference, if any, would it make if tariffs were used instead?

23. (All in the Family) By keeping domestic prices above world prices, President Suharto has created both gainers and losers. How do we know that the losers lose more than the gainers gain?

CHAPTER 36

ECONOMIES IN TRANSITION: FROM CENTRAL PLANNING TO COMPETITIVE MARKETS

On one Sunday in February of 1990, in more than thirty cities from Siberia to the southern republic of Georgia, hundreds of thousands of Soviet citizens rallied for democracy, in the first nationwide protest in the Soviet Union since the Revolution of 1917. That same month the Communist Party agreed to surrender its monopoly on government control. On Christmas Day 1991, President Mikhail Gorbachev announced his immediate resignation. Moments later the Soviet hammer and sickle flying above the Kremlin was replaced by the flag of Russia. Russia thus became a sovereign country. Russia and the other former Soviet republics are currently undergoing their most dramatic revolution since 1917.

Around the world, the demise of central planning has been stunning and pervasive. In Eastern Europe, communist leaders in one country after another have been toppled. And other communist states, such as China, Vietnam, and Laos, have been introducing market incentives. The past and present economic problems of these emerging market economies have tremendous significance for those who study economics. Like geologists, economists must rely primarily on natural experiments to figure out how things work. *The attempt to create a centrally planned economy and the subsequent replacement of central planning by the market are two of the greatest economic experiments in history*. In the study of geology, these events would be comparable to a huge earthquake.

Teaching Tip The Communist Party in China appears to be focusing on economic restructuring but not on changing political ideology. The all-powerful Politburo Standing Committee, unlike the party in Russia, does not appear to be in danger of losing control.

In this chapter we will try to learn what we can from these rich experiments—these works in progress. We first consider how central planning is supposed to work; we then see how it has worked in practice; finally we examine the bumpy transition to a market economy. The focus will be on the former Soviet Union and the succeeding independent states, especially Russia. Since we are trying to describe unfolding developments, we cannot know at this point how it will all work out. No doubt there are more surprises in store. But we can outline the problems these emerging market economies must deal with. Topics discussed in this chapter include

- Planned socialism
- Market socialism
- Bureaucratic coordination
- Material balance system
- The Soviet elite
- *Perestroika*
- Privatization

INTRODUCTION TO ALTERNATIVE ECONOMIC SYSTEMS

In Chapter 2 we considered the three questions that every economic system must answer: what is to be produced, how is it to be produced, and for whom is it to be produced. Laws regarding resource ownership and the role of government in resource allocation determine the "rules of the game"—the incentives and constraints that guide the behavior of individual decision makers. This book has focused on the role of market forces in primarily capitalist economies, such as the United States, Canada, Germany, France, or Great Britain. Although government has an important role in the U.S. economy, other economies rely on government more extensively. Some countries, such as Cuba and Vietnam, carefully limit the private ownership of resources such as land and capital. Each country employs a slightly different system of resource ownership, resource allocation, and individual incentives to answer the three economic questions.

Teaching Tip The U.S. Peace Corps is now sending experienced business people as volunteers to several former republics of the Soviet Union to help fledging entrepreneurs and inexperienced local governments learn to deal better with market forces.

Under pure capitalism the rules of the game include private ownership of resources and the coordination of economic activity by price signals generated by competitive markets; market coordination answers the three questions. Under a command economy the rules of the game include government ownership of resources and the allocation of resources through central planning rather than through market forces. No country exhibits either capitalism or a command economy in its pure form.

Teaching Tip See Chapter 2 for a review of the various basic forms of economic systems.

Planned and Market Socialism

Example Although the Chinese government did not own labor even before the recent reforms, the government did choose most workers' careers and assign their jobs, which became lifetime jobs that did not depend on performance.

An *economic system* is the set of mechanisms and institutions that resolve the what, how, and for whom questions. Several criteria are used to distinguish among economic systems: who owns the resources, what decision-making process is used to allocate resources, and what type of incentives guide activities. *Capitalism* means private ownership of most resources; *communism* means state ownership of most resources, including labor. Thus, under pure communism a worker has no claim to labor earnings. Workers provide their labor in service to the state. No country practices communism in its pure form. The countries that are typically referred to as communist are, in fact, socialist. *Socialism* means state ownership of all resources other than labor.

Planned socialism An economic system in which the state owns all resources other than labor and directs them by means of economic plans and central decision making

Market socialism An economic system in which the state owns all resources other than labor, but uses market forces to allocate the resources

Under **planned socialism** the state directs these resources by means of economic plans and central decision making. The state attempts to motivate labor through both philosophical and economic incentives. Under **market socialism** incentives are largely economic, planning is decentralized, and market forces are used to allocate economic resources.

Just as capitalism and communism represent polar cases not found in the real world, planned socialism and market socialism are not found in their pure form either. Until recent market reforms, China was best described as a planned socialist economy, as resources other than labor were publicly owned, resource allocation was by plan, and decision making was centralized. Now even China is pursuing a two-track course with a command economy mixed with more and more market incentives. Until its recent fragmentation, Yugoslavia's economy had been the best example of market socialism. Once-socialist countries of Eastern Europe, including Poland, Hungary, and Romania, have become more market oriented, and in 1991 socialist East Germany reunited with capitalist West Germany, thereby becoming a market economy.

Kinds of Coordination

Market coordination A type of economic coordination whereby price signals in competitive markets direct the activities of economic actors; from a legal perspective, buyers and sellers are on equal footing

Bureaucratic coordination A type of economic coordination whereby an administrative hierarchy directs the activities of economic actors

An economic system coordinates the activities and interaction of individuals and organizations. We distinguish between two types of coordination: market coordination and bureaucratic coordination. In **market coordination** the relation between buyers and sellers is horizontal; that is, from a legal perspective, buyers and sellers are on equal footing. Both are motivated by self-interest. Their self-interests are coordinated by means of agreed-upon prices. Transactions occur because each party hopes to benefit, not because one side has the power to coerce the other. *Exchange is voluntary*.

In **bureaucratic coordination** control is exercised through an administrative hierarchy. The coordinating relation is vertical, from the higher level of the organization to the lower level. Administrative pressure and legal restraints force individuals and organizations to accept orders and restrictions from above. The transactions among levels in the bureaucracy need not involve money, but when they do, the lower level of the organization depends on the higher level for its finances. The decision makers in the bureaucracy control the allocation of resources as well as the distribution of income.

Point to Stress In most cases, market coordination generates both consumer surplus and producer surplus.

Teaching Tip Bureaucracy in a representative democracy is discussed in detail in Chapter 30.

Governments in planned economies rely primarily on *central plans* rather than on market signals to answer the three economic questions. Bureaucratic coordination rather than market coordination determines the method of producing goods and services. Decisions about how to produce goods and services are based on historical experience and technological know-how. To ensure that the directions of the central planners are followed, the government relies on moral, material, and physical (coercion) incentives.

Why would a country want a planned economy? The leaders can establish whatever priorities they believe are best for the economy and can pursue these objectives using the full authority of the state. For example, leaders can direct the capital formation required for growth and development. The

Example Before the government of Margaret Thatcher, even Great Britain had several times in the twentieth century elected Labor governments sufficiently committed to socialism to nationalize key industries: railroads, steel, coal, gas, electricity, atomic power, postal services, telephones, telegraphs, airlines, and some trucking—although Parliament exerted very little control over their operations.

problem of unemployment can appear to be solved by creating enough enterprises to hire all those seeking employment and by subsidizing enterprises to be sure they stay in business.

Communism, Socialism, and the Birth of the Soviet Union

According to Karl Marx (1818–1883), capitalism was doomed because of its alleged long-run tendency toward declining profits, increased unemployment, subsistence wages, and successively more severe economic crises. Communists believe that modern industrial economies will eventually achieve communism, but only after a long period of socialism. During the socialist stage of evolution, the state will own and operate the means of production, distribution, and exchange, but workers will have a right to their labor and each person will be paid based on the work performed. After the economy's productive capacity has developed enough to provide for everyone, the state will wither away and pure communism will arise. *People will work according to their ability and receive according to their needs.* Thus, socialism is a transitory economic system, a step on the road to communism.

The writings of Marx inspired the Russian Revolution of 1917, which overthrew the czarist form of government. The Soviet Union was formed in 1922, and from 1928 to its dissolution on December 25, 1991, it was guided by a series of one-year and five-year central plans. The economy was based on "socialist ownership of the means of production." With limited exceptions, the central government owned all the land, natural resources, and capital goods, as well as nearly all businesses and most urban housing. Virtually all the industrial sector was owned by the state.

Point to Stress Marxists argued that communism would eventually alter human motivations. They believed that people would cease to respond in predictable, traditional ways to personal costs and benefits. In other words, Marxists argued against the rational self-interest assumption introduced in Chapter 1. However, experiences in countries such as the former Soviet Union produced little support for this view.

Prior to its dissolution, the Soviet Union consisted of fifteen republics with 280 million people living on a land area almost two and a half times that of the United States. The Soviet Union had the world's longest frontier and was ethnically diverse. Since the borders were established as recently as the end of World War II, ethnic feelings ran deep among the fifteen republics, and some of the republics sought independence long before the final dissolution.

Central Planning

Leaders of the Soviet Communist Party believed that central planning could direct resources better, or at least more fairly, than could market coordination. Party leaders established priorities and presented them to the State Planning Agency, called *Gosplan*, which developed long-term economic and social plans and generally supervised their execution. Gosplan was a relatively new agency that established specific aggregate output targets to reflect the Communist Party's preferences. These targets were then passed down to the ministries, which disaggregated them into specific products and assigned targets to enterprises. The enterprises would then tell the ministries what resources would be necessary to comply with the plan. Ministry officials would aggregate these orders and provide them to Gosplan. At this point Gosplan

Example Between 1929 and 1935, the Soviet government forced 94 percent of its peasants to join state-owned collective farms.

would undertake "material balancing" and would communicate the availability of resources to the ministries, which then assigned resources to the enterprises. Included in these orders governing the production of intermediate and final goods were the kinds and amounts of commodities that the industrial plant should produce, the wages to be paid, the prices to be charged, and the surplus revenue that should go to the state. *Thus, Gosplan personnel and others involved in the planning process translated the priorities established by the Communist Party into specific directives for each enterprise.*

Point to Stress Gosplan faced an enormous coordination problem, since the output of one industry is often the input of another industry.

Point to Stress The Communist Party established the economic policy objectives, and Gosplan was then directly responsible to the Communist Party officials.

Individual plants were operated by *directors*, or plant managers, appointed by the government with the approval of the local Communist Party. Although they were far from entrepreneurs, plant directors had some discretion over how to combine resources to meet the output objectives established by the planning hierarchy. Household income in the Soviet Union consisted almost exclusively of labor earnings: wages and salaries paid to employees of government enterprises and bureaus. Since the state owned nearly all resources except labor, any return on resources other than labor was government revenue from state-owned enterprises.

Teaching Tip Farmers on state-controlled collective and cooperative farms did not receive wages, but shared in the income of the farm.

Supply and Demand

How did central planning coordinate hundreds of different resources in thousands of different enterprises? The type of central planning developed in the former Soviet Union during the 1930s was called the **material balance system**. Under this system central authorities controlled only the most important industrial output, leaving decisions about less important output to the lower levels of the planning hierarchy. For example, Gosplan in Moscow planned the production of steel, energy, motor vehicles, and machine tools. Lower-level planners guided the production of shoes, clothing, and household services. Items of still lower priority were not planned for at all and were sometimes left to market coordination

Material balance system A system of central planning designed to ensure a balance of supply and demand for important types of industrial output

The planning machinery tried to achieve a material balance of quantity supplied and quantity demanded. For example, based on past experience, the planning agency projected how much steel would be required to meet output targets for motor vehicles, machine tools, construction, and other uses. Gosplan would select a target to equate the quantity of steel produced with the anticipated quantity required, thereby achieving a *material balance* through bureaucratic coordination rather than through market coordination. Gosplan would follow the same approach for other critical commodities, as well as for labor, machinery, and finance.

Example In the first five-year plan, 1928–1933, consumer goods were a residual sector, in which output could be produced only after all other priorities had been met. The emphasis was first on heavy industry and second on light industry.

Each five-year plan for the economy was actually the result of bargaining among several planning elements: Gosplan, Communist Party officials, the various ministries, and the plant managers. After much haggling up and down the hierarchy, a final plan was prepared and submitted to the central government for approval. Once approved, the economic plan became law, determining how many employees each enterprise could hire, what resources it could expect through supply channels, and how much bank credit would be made available. The plan was broken down by week, month, quarter, and year.

Example The one-year plans provide the more than two hundred thousand enterprises with a document outlining what to produce, the amounts of labor and raw materials to use, the new machinery to install, the timing of available credit, and other operational details.

So the planning system appeared to rely on law. In reality there was much give and take once the plan was set in motion. In fact, each enterprise employed an "expeditor" who did nothing but develop and maintain informal relations with other organizations and enterprises so the firm could get needed supplies, particularly in an emergency situation. Within the socialist bureaucracy, subordinates would often make large personal gifts to superiors as an "investment" in a long-term relationship. Superiors thereby gained tribute and bribes from their discretionary authority.

Enterprises and Soft Budget Constraints

Soft budget constraint The budget condition faced by socialist enterprises that lose money and then are subsidized

In the socialist system, enterprises that earned a "profit" would see that profit appropriated by the state. Firms that ended up with a loss would find that loss covered by a state subsidy. Thus, socialist enterprises faced what has been called a **soft budget constraint**. This led to inefficiency, a lack of response to changes in supply or demand, and poor investment decisions. Quality was also a problem under central planning because plant managers would rather meet production quotas than satisfy consumer demands—plant managers did not score extra bureaucratic points by producing garments that were in style and in popular sizes. Tales of shoddy products abound.

Example In the early 1990s, Russian President Yeltsin's major opposition came from a party consisting mainly of former state-enterprise managers who objected to the proposed ending of subsidies to the country's aging and inefficient mills.

Capitalist economies equate quantity supplied with quantity demanded through the invisible hand of market coordination; centrally planned economies use the visible hand of bureaucratic coordination assisted by taxes and subsidies. If quantity supplied and quantity demanded are not in balance, something has to give. In a capitalist system what gives is the price. In a centrally planned economy what usually gives is the plan itself. A common problem in the Soviet system was that the amount produced often fell short of planned production. When the quantity supplied fell below the planned amount, Gosplan reduced the amount supplied to each sector, cutting critical sectors such as heavy industry and the military the least and lower-priority sectors such as consumer products the most. When a shortage occurred, consumers often paid a higher "price" in terms of more shortages and more time spent waiting in line.

Productivity and Technological Change

How did central planning perform based on the standards typically used to evaluate an economic system? Abram Bergson of Harvard University, an expert on the Soviet economy, concluded that when Gorbachev took office, output per worker ranked the former Soviet Union substantially below that of major capitalist economies.[1] Output per worker was only slightly above that of Turkey, which is considered a Third World country, or a developing economy.

1. Abram Bergson, "The USSR Before the Fall: How Poor and Why," *Journal of Economic Perspectives* 5 (Fall 1991): 29–44.

Point to Stress Military expenditures were given top priority in the Gosplan directives and allocated the prime scientific and technical talent. The problem of obsolete capital developed despite the fact that investment was also a high priority in the Gosplan directives—for many years, the Soviet investment rate was one of the highest in the world.

Except for military and space applications, the former Soviet Union lagged behind in the development of technology, including computers and software, and this lag contributed to a lower level of labor productivity. Other problems included obsolete capital, poor labor morale, collapsing government credibility, and the allocation of 15 percent of total output to military expenditures (compared to about 5 percent in the United States).

To supplement their own technological developments, Soviet officials would buy, borrow, or steal technology from capitalist countries. Yet *the problem in the Soviet Union was not so much that the latest technology was not available but that it was not diffused throughout the economy*. Bureaucracies are not geared to technological change because change tends to destabilize rigid hierarchical relations. For example, the modern computer would seem to be the ideal tool for central planners, who could then solve complex resource allocation problems. But computers never really became part of the planning system, in part because enterprise directors had little incentive to provide detailed information to higher authorities. Bureaucrats who made significant investments in long-run personal relationships within the chain of command were understandably wary of any disruptions from new technologies and other changes.

Point to Stress According to the Soviet Union's own Nobel Prize–winning physicist, A. K. Sakharov, who was for many years subject to internal exile, a highly centralized economy has a stultifying effect on invention and innovation.

There were really three economies in the former Soviet Union: (1) the official economy, where things were done by the book, according to orders from on high; (2) the so-called second economy, the Soviet version of the underground economy, or black market, where individuals bought and sold to promote their self-interest; and (3) the "informal economy," where Soviet managers pursued official objectives by skirting the official rules. In the following case study we examine the informal economy.

CASE STUDY

The Informal Economy

Teaching Tip The related concept of vertical integration in a market economy was discussed in detail in Chapter 28.

The resource distribution system in the Soviet economy was not the well-oiled operation envisioned by central planners. For example, enterprises often failed to receive critical resources and were sent resources they could not use. Because of the chronic problem of inadequate and late resources, factory workers sometimes had little to do. The pace of the work was therefore uneven, with workers idle for days, then frantically trying to meet production quotas once the required supplies or replacement parts finally arrived.

To alleviate these problems, managers frequently bartered with other enterprises for critical resources or bought resources on the black market. More importantly, rather than depend on a sporadic supply system, *the enterprise frequently manufactured its own replacement parts*. For example, in the Soviet Union only about 4 percent of standard metalworking products were produced in specialized plants. The rest were produced by the enterprises that used the machines. In contrast, in the United States 70 percent of these products are produced by specialized firms.

Thus, Soviet enterprises tried to reduce the risk of interrupted supplies by bringing activities inside the firm. Plants of all sizes often designed and produced equipment for their own use. An automobile plant might make its own robots, a shoe plant its own machines and glue, and a computer center might develop its own computer programs. If an enterprise wanted to

Point to Stress This practice varies substantially from efforts to take advantage of economies of scope, discussed in Chapter 28, whereby the firm produces more than one line of goods because it is efficient to do so.

expand, it might use its own workers to put up a new building. And in areas where electricity was frequently interrupted, some enterprises would build their own power generators.

Self-reliance was not directed solely toward providing industrial resources. Because many consumer goods were scarce, *enterprises also produced goods and services for employee consumption*. For example, many industrial firms raised crops and livestock on the side. The resources needed to produce these other products were siphoned from official channels, acquired through barter, or purchased on the black market.

Thus, self-service was the implicit motto of Soviet enterprise. Because the transaction costs of relying on the bureaucratic hierarchy as a source of supply were high, more and more activities were brought inside the enterprise. Plant directors, rather than being simply underlings who carried out orders in the chain of command, tried to satisfy their production quotas while providing employees with goods and services that were hard to get on the market.

But this intramural activity violated one of the principles of efficiency: the division of labor. As an individual enterprise expanded into more and more activities, workers were spread thinner, so they performed all jobs less efficiently. Each worker became a jack-of-all-trades but a master of none. The plant director's attention span was strained, and the coordination of resources became a problem. Many studies in the Soviet Union showed that in-house production cost more than production in specialized plants. Soviet planning officials were understandably concerned about the loss of production as enterprises sought self-sufficiency.

Sources: V. Kontorovich and V. Shlapentokh, "Soviet Industry Grows Its Own Potatoes," *Wall Street Journal*, 11 January 1985; and Richard Ericson, "The Classical Soviet-Type Economy: Nature of the System and Implications for Reform," *Journal of Economic Perspectives* 5 (Fall 1991): 11–28.

Prices, Shortages, and Consumer Satisfaction

Teaching Tip Consumer prices were made up of two parts: a portion initially based on the cost of production and a turnover tax. The turnover tax was based on what planners thought consumers should be encouraged to purchase or discouraged from purchasing.

As we've said, most prices in the Soviet system were determined not by market forces but by central planners. As a result, consumers had little to say about what was produced. Once set, prices tended to be inflexible. For example, the price of a cabbage slicer was stamped on the metal at the factory. In the spirit of equity, Soviet planners priced most consumer goods below the market-clearing level, so shortages (or "interruptions in supply," as they were called) were common. The price of bread had not changed since 1954 and, by 1990, the price amounted to only 7 percent of its production cost. Meat prices had not changed since 1962. Rents had not changed in sixty years.

To see how the system worked, suppose the planning process called for 200 million pounds of chicken per month, to be sold for 15 rubles per pound. The quantity supplied depended not on how much consumers would be willing to pay but on the priority that chicken held in the larger scheme of the economy. Thus, the supply of chicken was fixed by central planners, as shown by the supply curve, *S*, in Exhibit 1. Also presented in Exhibit 1 is the

EXHIBIT 1

Supply and Demand for Chicken

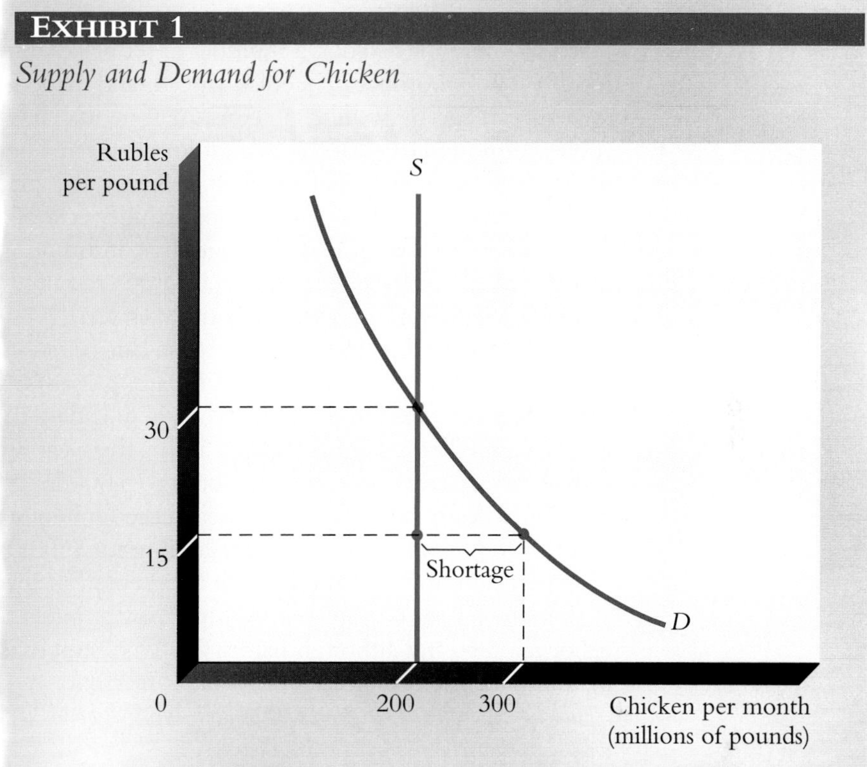

Under central planning, the amount of chicken produced is 200 million pounds per month. A price of 30 rubles per pound would equate quantities supplied and demanded. However, the price is usually held below the market-clearing level. A price of 15 rubles per pound results in a shortage.

demand curve for chicken, *D*. A price of 30 rubles per pound would equate quantity demanded and quantity supplied.

Example The prices of goods purchased extensively by the poor were often set relatively low—with a very low turnover tax—so as to create a more equal distribution of purchasing power. Prices of other goods may have been set initially at a level designed to almost equate the quantity demanded with the quantity supplied.

But as we have seen, the prices of chicken and many other consumer goods were established by bureaucrats, not by markets, and prices were often set below the market-clearing level. Once set, prices tended to be inflexible. In Exhibit 1, a price of 15 rubles per pound resulted in a shortage of 100 million pounds of chicken per month. Necessities such as housing, electricity, and basic food were cheap, but because their prices were set below the market-clearing level, they were also in short supply. Probably the scarcest good in the Soviet Union over the years was housing. Couples often would wait years for an apartment. Food was rationed in most of the fifteen Soviet republics. *Necessities were scarce because the price was set below the market-clearing level.*

Evidence of shortages included long waiting lines at retail stores, empty store shelves, the "tips," or bribes, shop operators expected for supplying scarce consumer goods, and the higher price for the goods on the black market. Shoppers would sometimes wait in line all night and into the next day.

Consumers often relied on "connections" through acquaintances to obtain most goods and services. Scarce goods were frequently diverted to the black market, where they sold at a multiple of set prices. Shortages of medicine, soap, toothbrushes, toothpaste, needles, thread, and diapers were especially common. As you can see in Exhibit 1, consumers would have been willing to pay 30 rubles per pound to clear the market for chicken. The effect of waiting in line is to raise the total price of chicken, because the price includes not only the money price of 15 rubles but the opportunity cost of the waiting time.

Soviet officials tried to discourage the consumption of luxuries such as automobiles by allocating few of the economy's resources to their production. For example, relatively few Soviet automobiles were produced and those produced were of poor quality by U.S. standards. But because automobiles were scarce, their prices were relatively high and waiting lists for them were long. For the typical Soviet worker, the purchase of a new Lada—the Soviet version of a 1965 Fiat—required seven years' wages and a five-year wait. Even used cars were scarce. A four-year-old Lada cost about $15,000 in 1990—one and a half times the typical yearly household income. In the United States this would be equivalent to a four-year-old Ford Escort's selling for $50,000.

Many consumer products taken for granted in the West were not produced at all in the Soviet Union. For example, Soviet industry did not make dishwashers or toasters, and although hair dryers were supposedly produced, none could be found for sale. *Compared to U.S. prices, necessities were relatively cheap and luxuries relatively expensive. But shortages of both types of goods would often occur because prices were set below the market-clearing level.*

Problems with Agriculture

Most agricultural output in the former Soviet Union was produced on state-owned farms or on cooperatives that were closely controlled by the state. The remainder was produced by cooperative members permitted to farm private plots in their spare time. Those who worked on cooperative farms did not receive wages but shared in the income of the farm. State policy, however, was aimed at keeping farm prices low, which kept farm incomes low as well. Bureaucracies were the key to central planning, and the agricultural sector had its share of them. For example, the details of how teams of farmers were to be paid were worked out by a long list of agencies. In the Ministry of Agriculture alone there were three million bureaucrats—more than in the entire U.S. government.

Farm equipment was a constant problem. Soviet industry produced huge tractors but without the threshers, reapers, and other implements required to take advantage of their size. Tractors were left to rust in the freezing winters because there were no sheds. Farm machinery was scrapped at a much higher rate in the Soviet Union than elsewhere because spare parts and trained mechanics were both scarce.[2] Enough mechanics were trained, but Soviet planners had

2. These examples are found in Gale Johnson and K. M. Brooks, *Prospects for Soviet Agriculture in the 1980s* (Bloomington, IN: Indiana University Press, 1984).

Example Most of the Soviet Union's once-affluent peasants, the kulaks, were deported or died during the collectivization of 1929 to 1935.

difficulty keeping them down on the farm because they could earn much more in urban areas.

Once the world's largest grain exporter, the Soviet Union became the world's largest grain importer. Yet Soviet agriculture employed 20 percent of the labor force—far more than the 3 percent figure for the United States. In summary, poor morale, low farm prices, unreliable equipment, transportation problems, and interrupted supplies of key inputs combined to dampen work incentives on the farm and reduce farm productivity.

Secondary Effects of Socialist Ownership of Property

Because in a socialist economy everyone owns state property, nobody in particular owns it. Since those who allocate and use resources do not immediately benefit from that use, resources are sometimes wasted. For example, about one-third of the Soviet harvest reportedly deteriorated before it reached retailers.[3] Likewise, to meet planning goals, oil producers often pumped large pools of oil reserves so quickly that remaining oil became inaccessible. Soviet workers usually had little regard for equipment that belonged to the state. New trucks or tractors might be dismantled for parts, or working equipment might be sent to a scrap plant. Pilfering of state-owned property, though considered a serious crime, was a high art and a favorite sport.

Teaching Tip Consider the similarity between the problem of socialist ownership of property and the negative externality problems arising with common pool resources, as discussed in Chapter 32.

A narrow focus on meeting plan objectives also imposed a high cost on the environment. The Aral Sea, which is about the size of Lake Michigan, has been called "a salinated cesspool." Thousands of barrels of nuclear waste were dumped into Soviet rivers and seas. The 1986 Chernobyl reactor meltdown still poses a threat of nuclear contamination; nineteen similar reactors still supply energy to Russia, Ukraine, and Lithuania. In a drive for military supremacy, the Soviet government set off 125 nuclear explosions above ground. The resulting bomb craters later filled up with water, forming contaminated lakes.

In contrast, individual Soviet citizens took extremely good care of their personal property. For example, personal cars would run for twenty years or more on average—twice the official projected automobile life. The incentives of private ownership were also evident on the farm. Each farmer on the collective was allowed a small plot of land on which to cultivate crops for personal consumption or for sale at prices determined in unregulated markets. Despite the small size of the plots and the taxes on earnings from these plots, farmers produced a disproportionate share of output on private plots. Privately farmed plots constituted only 3 percent of the Soviet Union's farmland, but they supplied 30 percent of all meat, milk, and vegetables and 60 percent of all potatoes. *The point is that the personal incentives provided by private property promote the efficient use of that property.*

3. These examples are provided in Vladimir Shlapentokh, "Soviet Ideas on Private Property Invite Abuse of Capital Stock," *Wall Street Journal*, 20 March 1986.

The Distribution of Income and Consumption

Point to Stress Note the contrast to Marx's ideal of people working according to their abilities and receiving according to their needs.

Under socialism, the state owns all resources other than labor. Except during times of war, most Soviet workers had some discretion in their choice of occupation and place of work. The manager of an enterprise also had some discretion over whom to hire. Central planners would frequently set relative wages to reflect market realities, the plans of the state, and the nature of the work performed—its complexity, the responsibility involved, and other relevant features. Other things constant, those involved in more arduous or unhealthy work—coal miners and metalworkers, for example—earned more than other industrial workers. Thus, wage differentials were not that different from those observed in capitalist markets.

Wages, bonuses, housing availability, and other amenities were tied explicitly to length of employment in a particular job. University graduates and others with specialized training received administrative assignments to particular jobs and were expected to hold these jobs for several years. More generally, movement into large cities was restricted through a system of internal passports. Housing availability also limited mobility.

Income Distribution

As we saw, output per worker in the former Soviet Union was far below that in industrial market economies. The average household income in the Soviet Union in 1990 was only about one-third the level in the United States. Another way of evaluating the performance of an economic system is in terms of equity. How evenly were the fruits of production distributed among Soviet households? Wage and salary inequality across households was less than that found in other industrial countries, though the difference was not substantial. But money income had less significance in the Soviet Union because most goods were in short supply and could not be purchased without waiting in line or having an inside connection. The Soviet Union had a well-defined class structure, and not all people were created equal, as we will see next.

The Soviet Elite

Socialist dogma called for a "withering away" of the state as classless communism emerged, but Joseph Stalin, head of the Soviet Union from 1924 to 1953, held that in the meantime special rewards were required to call forth productive capabilities. Thus, Stalin fostered social stratification, and the Soviet elite flourished. Although there are no exact definitions or reliable statistics, the Soviet ruling class, or *nomenklatura*, had about 250,000 members. Counting family members, this ruling class made up less than 1 percent of the population. Exhibit 2 provides some idea of the Soviet elite by occupation. Note that only 7.5 percent of the elite were enterprise directors (only a fraction of all directors qualified for elite status). Salaries of the elite in academic and research positions averaged about four times that of the average

EXHIBIT 2

Elite Personnel by Occupation During the 1970s

Occupation	Percentage
Enterprise directors	7.5
Intelligentsia (academicians, artists, editors)	17.6
Government and trade union officials	26.5
Military, police, and diplomats	13.2
Communist party officials	35.2

Source: Based on data presented in Abram Bergson, "Income Inequality Under Soviet Socialism," *Journal of Economic Literature* 22 (September 1984), Table 10.

Teaching Tip Personal services was another area besides privately owned farm plots in which private enterprise was permitted. Soviet professionals such as physicians and teachers could sell their services to consumers as well as working for a state enterprise. (Craft laborers such as tailors could also sell their services.)

worker.[4] As we will see, rank had its privilege not only in pay but in virtually every aspect of Soviet life.

CONSUMPTION. Ordinary citizens of Moscow might spend hours in line trying to buy meat, but members of the elite could shop at the famous Kremlin canteen. This shop, which stocked the best food available at the lowest prices anywhere, accepted payment only in *kemliovka* coupons. Members of the *nomenklatura* received part of their pay in *kemliovka*. The Central Committee building in Moscow had three dining rooms on different floors, each serving a different category of official. The food was said to be as good as in the best restaurants, but the prices were considerably lower. The most select restaurant had a military guard at the door.

HOUSING. Housing was heavily subsidized and in short supply. The best housing went to top Communist Party officials, who were also entitled to second homes—country retreats called *dachas*. Housing assignments were based on rank, as could be observed in one research facility: a Soviet academy member—the cream of academe—was provided a separate cottage. In that same complex, a family of four headed by a professor rated only 604 square feet of living space—about the size of an efficiency apartment. A service worker's family had to make do with only half that space—about the size of a bedroom.[5]

When bureaucratic coordination replaces market coordination, some nonmarket system of rationing must be used to deal with excess quantity demanded. Bribes replaced long lines and actually could be more efficient, though not necessarily more equitable. Interviews with thousands of emigrants from Russia attest to the widespread use of bribery to obtain first jobs and university positions.

4. Abram Bergson, "Income Inequality Under Soviet Socialism," *Journal of Economic Literature* 22 (September 1984), Table 10.
5. This example is found in Abram Bergson, "Income Inequality," p. 1059.

Social Mobility

Point to Stress Even under Soviet reform, many of the new elite are former members of the elite of the old regime. In order to keep their country operating, democratic leaders must rely on those who ran the communist system—and often resist the reforms that would dilute their power.

In the United States wealth and power are passed from one generation to another through genes, family life, education, and inheritance. The same was true in the Soviet Union. Since most resources were owned by the state, private wealth was limited primarily to savings deposits, government bonds, and other personal possessions. Interest rates in the Soviet Union were fixed at a low level, but there was little or no inheritance tax, so large sums could be passed along to the next generation.

How did one join the elite? The surest way was to be born into it. Children of the elite had a much better chance of being accepted into the right schools. Young men from elite families were routinely appointed to *nomenklatura* positions, and their sisters married those who held such positions. (Women from elite families usually did not seek employment.) For an outsider, the best route was to join the Communist Party and get noticed.

TOWARD A MARKET ECONOMY

Teaching Tip Reform in the former Soviet Union was motivated by a substantial slowing in its economic growth rate, a string of disastrous agricultural harvests, the increasing burdens of military spending, and the rising strain of using the cumbersome bureaucratic coordination to organize the economy.

The word *reform* means different things in different countries. In the United States reform often implies greater bureaucratic intervention because of a perceived market failure, such as reform of the way hazardous waste is handled or the way health care is provided. In the Soviet Union, however, reform was more a reaction to bureaucratic failure, and the solution was to decentralize decisions and to introduce more market mechanisms.

Gorbachev's Reforms

Glasnost The greater willingness of what had been the Soviet government to allow the Soviet people and the rest of the world know what was going on in the Soviet Union

Perestroika The "restructuring" of what had been the Soviet economy to promote more decentralization, less bureaucracy, and greater individual incentives

Economic reform in the Soviet Union had a checkered past. Soviet President Mikhail Gorbachev introduced major reforms in 1986 with *glasnost* and *perestroika*. **Glasnost** referred to the new openness in Soviet affairs: a greater willingness to let the Soviet people and the rest of the world know what was going on in the Soviet Union. Because of *glasnost*, Soviet intellectuals had more freedom to think, to speak, and to write. **Perestroika** was a restructuring of the economy to promote more decentralization, less bureaucracy, and greater individual incentives. Many bureaucrats who were afraid of losing their jobs resisted *perestroika*.

Gorbachev's economic experiment was to give plant managers a freer hand in solving problems, in regulating the size of their workforce, and in negotiating wages and prices. Gorbachev also tried to promote a more efficient use of capital resources by allowing enterprises to retain more of their profits so that only the most efficient firms would expand. To deal with the question of quality, central planners changed their pricing system to pay producers less for lower-quality goods and more—up to 30 percent more—for higher-quality goods.

Earlier we discussed the greater agricultural productivity on private plots. Although the country clearly benefited from the greater output, this example of capitalism had long irritated Communist officials. In 1961 the Party

Example Gorbachev's economic experiment included a reduction in the number of targets a plant manager must meet from forty to eight.

Congress called for the elimination of private plots by 1980. But this decree was reversed by Mikhail Gorbachev, and in early 1990, Soviet citizens could lease land (at prices set by the government) and bequeath these leases to their children.

A five-year plan devised in May 1990 was aimed at shifting from a centrally planned economy to a "regulated market economy." The plan was to raise consumer prices sharply, close inefficient factories, establish a modern banking system, and allow for private ownership of what had been state enterprises. Announcements of the proposed reforms caused panic buying of consumer staples throughout the Soviet Union. Consider the soap opera related in the following case study.

CASE STUDY

No Soap

Since prices in Russia and other Soviet republics were set below the market-clearing level, consumers had an excess demand for goods on average, which implied they had an excess supply of money, in this case rubles. This excess supply of rubles accumulated as a form of forced savings. So rubles piled up just waiting for goods to become available. This forced savings was called a *monetary overhang.*

In early 1989, a rumor began that soap was in particularly short supply. Spurred by the rumor, and armed with more rubles than they could spend, consumers bought up all the soap available in the shops, leaving the shelves bare. From that point on, the rumor became a reality. Throughout 1989 soap could not be found for sale, even though soap production had increased that year when compared to the year earlier. The combination of artificially low prices and a monetary overhang proved to be an explosive mix.

Soap was not the only item people stocked up on. By the second half of 1991 hoarding took on epic proportions. The hoarding mindset was reinforced by announcements that prices would increase sharply when they were set free on January 1, 1992. In the cold of January, outside almost every window, residents had hung bundles of food wrapped in cloth, evidence of hoarding during the weeks leading up to the price increases. Food was hung outside because refrigerators were already stuffed with the results of many search efforts.

Sources: Fred Hiatt, "New Prices Leave Russians Cold," *Cincinnati Enquirer*, 2 January 1992; and Martin L. Weitzman, "Price Distortion and Shortage Deformation, or What Happened to the Soap?" *American Economic Review* 81 (June 1991): 401–414.

The success of Gorbachev's reforms depended on the support of the elite. But centralized planning was a comfortable habit for the elite. Private production represented competition for the state monopoly. A Communist Party official's wife was quoted in *Pravda* as challenging Gorbachev: "We are the elite, and you will not pull us down. You don't have the strength. We'll rip the flimsy sails of your restructuring."[6] But the exalted position of the

6. As reported in "Gorbachev's Opposition," *Newsweek* (18 May 1987): 48.

Example Gorbachev proposed that the co-operative farms turn a fixed amount of their harvests over to the state and then sell the balance at market prices. The government later announced that it would pay the farmers in foreign currency for wheat and other crop production in excess of their early 1980s average.

Example Russian President Boris Yeltsin banned the Communist Party in 1991. The Constitutional Court was holding hearings in 1993 to determine the legality of Yeltsin's decree.

Teaching Tip For political reasons, Yeltsin has had to name the former head of the Soviet state bank (Gosbank) to head the Russian central bank.

Soviet elite, especially the Communist Party leadership, began showing signs of erosion. In 1990 members of the Communist Party's ruling body lost their country dachas, and upon retirement, they lost the three household workers and the cars provided by the government.[7]

The market system is not an expression of the "anarchy of production," as communists claimed, but a sophisticated feedback mechanism that offers producers a detailed picture of consumer demand and the relative value of resources used in production. Central planning without feedback results in allocative inefficiency. And selling products for less than the cost of production required huge government subsidies, which climbed from 2.5 percent of GDP in 1985 to 20 percent of GDP in 1991. *Perestroika* under Gorbachev was unable to deliver the goods to consumers. The Communist Party broke up and the Soviet Union dissolved into its fifteen republics.

Some argue that Gorbachev was not committed to the creation of a free market system, for he apparently realized that such a change would end socialism and his political power. Gorbachev wanted the market *plus* socialism—but he could not have both. He wanted what he called "regulated markets." This is one of several reasons why his economic restructuring, or *perestroika*, failed. Still, his policy of *glasnost*, or political openness, helped open up the communist state and formed the basis for a more radical reform. This openness allowed people to see for themselves the huge gap between a planned and a free society. This openness and the open debate that ensued set the stage for the intellectual revolution in the Soviet Union as well as in East Bloc countries that ultimately led to the collapse of communism.

After the dissolution of the Soviet Union on Christmas Day, 1991, Boris Yeltsin, who had been elected president of Russia, the largest of the Soviet republics, tried to reform Russia with bolder strokes. On January 2, 1992, price controls on 90 percent of goods were abolished. The next day prices rose by an average of 250 percent. But Russia and the other newly independent republics continued to subsidize money-losing industries. Deficits were financed by simply printing more money. Between July and October of 1992 the money supply tripled. The combination of a flood of rubles and prices set free for the first time in seven decades resulted in hyperinflation. Overall, the annual rate of inflation in Russia jumped from 150 percent for 1991 to 1,400 percent during the first half of 1992 and 2,200 percent in the second half. Let's look more closely at how Yeltsin planned to transform the economy.

The 1992 Privatization Plan for Russia

Privatization The process of turning public enterprises into private enterprises

Privatization is the process of turning public enterprises into private enterprises. It is the opposite of nationalization. Russian privatization began in April 1992 with the sale of municipally owned shops. The government also decreed that state and collective farms must convert into joint-stock companies owned by the workforce and must sell plots of land to anyone who

7. "No More Dachas," *Wall Street Journal*, 21 February 1990.

Teaching Tip The Russian government recommended that people pool their vouchers to purchase small stores or buy into investment funds to purchase shares in large enterprises.

wanted to farm privately. In October 1992, the Russian government began issuing each of the 150 million citizens a voucher worth 10,000 rubles. In late 1990 those rubles would have been worth about $5,000, but because of inflation, by May 1993, 10,000 rubles were worth only about $12—not much to stir the imagination of a new era of capitalism. State property such as trucks, hotels, and shops were sold for vouchers at auction. According to the plan, by the end of 1993 about two thousand medium and large firms and one hundred thousand shops and small firms would be transferred from the state to private hands. And by the end of 1994 another four thousand large firms were to be sold. One problem with the plan was that many enterprises had been so inefficient for so long, who would want to buy them? What's more, Yeltsin's privatization plan faced stiff opposition because the Russian economy seemed to be coming apart, with hyperinflation, falling industrial production, and a growth in organized crime.

Example Industrial production in the Russian economy was projected to drop 20 to 22 percent in 1992.

Transition Problems

Although most property in a socialist economy is nominally owned by the state, it often remained unclear who had the authority to sell the property and who was to receive the proceeds. This ambiguity resulted in cases in which the same property was purchased from different officials by different buyers. Yet, *there was no clear legal process for resolving title disputes*. Worse still, some enterprises were stripped of their assets by self-serving managers, a process that came to be called derisively "spontaneous" privatization. The necessarily complex process of privatization will be undermined if the general population perceives the process of privatization to be unfair.

Russia and the other former Soviet republics face difficulties of transition even more profound than other socialist countries. To begin with, their economies had been run from Moscow, so they had no internal agencies that had such an encompassing responsibility. Since Moscow is located in Russia, Russia would seem to have an advantage over the other former republics, but Russia must dismantle a huge bureaucracy and build its own operation. Trade, currency, and legal relations among the republics are in flux. The ruble was initially used, but some republics in the newly formed Commonwealth of Independent States introduced their own currencies.

Example Six members of the Commonwealth of Independent States signed an agreement in October 1992 to create a single monetary system, or ruble zone. However, hyperinflation threatened the convertibility of the ruble into other currencies.

Privatization requires the development of modern accounting and other information systems, the training of competent managers, and the installation of adequate facilities for telecommunication, computing, travel, and transportation. This transformation cannot be accomplished overnight. Consider just the accounting problem. A market economy depends on financial accounting rules as well as on an independent system for auditing financial reports. The information needed shows up in a company's balance sheet and income statement. Prospective buyers of enterprises need such information, as do banks and other lenders. By all reports, the accounting systems of socialist firms are almost worthless. For decades data had been aimed more at central planners, who wanted to know about physical flows, than at someone who wanted to know about the efficiency and financial promise of the firm.

Example A machinery factory measures output in tons of machinery.

So there is much information but little that is relevant. Incidentally, the major advantage of the market economy is that it minimizes the need for the kind of resource-flow data that had been reported under central planning. Prices convey most of the information necessary to coordinate economic activity among firms.

THE ROLE OF ECONOMIC INSTITUTIONS IN PRIVATIZATION[8]

As noted in the previous chapter, the institutions that shape the economy consist of (1) formal rules of behavior, such as constitutions, laws, and property rights, and (2) informal constraints on behavior, such as sanctions, manners, customs, traditions, and codes of conduct. Underlying the surface of market behavior lies a grid of informal, often unconscious, habits, customs, and norms, which make the functioning of impersonal markets possible.

Institutions and Economic Development

Institutions shape the incentive structure of an economy, but most countries in the world have failed to produce a set of economic rules of the game that lead to sustained economic growth. Although political and judicial decisions may change formal rules overnight, informal constraints embodied in customs, traditions, and codes of conduct are more immune to deliberate policies. Respect for the law cannot be legislated but relies on the beliefs of the population.

Prior to the market reforms, widespread corruption and a lack of faith in formal institutions were woven into the social fabric of nearly all Soviet-type economies. Subordinates bribed their superiors to get relief from an economic plan's requirements or to get vital resources. Workers bribed officials to get good jobs. And consumers bribed clerks to get desired products. Bribery became a way of life, a way of dealing with the distortions that arise when prices are not allowed to allocate resources efficiently.

Example Moscow city officials refused to issue to Alexander Panikin, owner of a T-shirt factory in Moscow, the necessary permits to expand his factory. He simply lacked the connections with the bureaucrats.

In centrally planned economies the exchange relation was typically *personal*, based as it was on bureaucratic ties on the production side and inside connections on the consumption side. But in the United States and other developed market economies, successful institutional evolution permits the complex *impersonal* exchange that is necessary to capture the potential economic benefits of specialization and modern technology. Impersonal exchange allows for a far greater division of labor, but it requires a richer and more stable institutional setting.

8. In preparing this section the author benefited from two articles by Douglas C. North: "Institutions," *Journal of Economic Perspectives* 5 (Winter 1991): 97–112, and "Institutions, Ideology, and Economic Performance," *Cato Journal* 11 (Winter 1992): 477–488.

Capitalism and Institutions

Teaching Tip Similarly, centuries of restrictions on free movement in Russia started during czarist times.

The shift from central planning to competitive markets involves more than privatization within a price system. Simply loosening constraints to create private property may not be enough for successful reform. The pattern of communal ownership that prevailed in Russia before the recent reforms existed long before the Russian Revolution of 1917. The development of institutions is essential in economic reform, but *there is no unified economic theory on how to construct the institutions that are central to the success of capitalism.*

Most so called "economists" employed in Soviet-type systems did not understand even the basics of how markets work. They had been trained to regard the alleged "anarchy" of the market as a primary defect of capitalism.[9] Thus, Gorbachev's reforms called for "regulated markets" to avoid what he perceived to be market chaos. A more fundamental problem is that though Western economic theory focuses on the operation of efficient markets, *even market economists usually do not understand the institutional requirements of efficient markets.* Market economists simply take the necessary institutions for granted. Those involved in the transition must develop a deeper appreciation for the institutions that nurture and support impersonal market activity.

The "Big Bang" Versus Gradualism

The Hungarian economist Janos Kornai of Harvard University believes that a market order should be grown from the bottom up.[10] First, small-scale capitalism in farming, trade, light manufacturing, and services thrives under the evolving rules of "just conduct." The resulting spontaneous order can take hold at the grass-roots level and serve as a foundation for the privatization of larger industrial sectors. Large industrial enterprises should quickly find the market-clearing price so that input and output decisions are consistent with market preferences. But, according to Kornai, their ownership structure and way of doing business cannot be reformed overnight by legislative mandates. In the meantime state-owned enterprises should be run more like businesses in which state directors attempt to maximize profit. Money-losing enterprises should be phased out. This "bottom-up" approach proposed by Kornai could be termed *gradualism*, which can be contrasted with a *big-bang* approach, whereby the transition would take place in a matter of months.

Teaching Tip In the early 1990s, China was experimenting with market reforms in southern provinces such as Shanghai. A securities exchange opened in late 1990, a metals exchange is now operating, and foreign investment is rapidly expanding.

One example of gradualism is taking place in China. In 1978 the government began dismantling agricultural communes in favor of a "household-responsibility" system of small-farm agriculture. Land was assigned to a family, which could keep any excess production after meeting specific state-imposed

9. For a discussion of the education of Soviet economists, see M. Alexeev, C. Gaddy, and J. Leitzel, "Economics in the Former Soviet Union," *Journal of Economic Perspectives* 6 (Spring 1992): 137–148.
10. Janos Kornai, "The Postsocial Transition and the State: Reflections in the Light of Hungarian Fiscal Problems," *American Economic Review* 82 (May 1992): 1–21.

Example In November 1992, Russia issued property rights to about one hundred million people—for millions of small country land plots held by urban dwellers and almost all workers of the state-run farms.

goals. Initially the system was to be applied only to the poorest 20 percent of the rural areas. Once the positive effects became apparent, however, the system spread on its own. Eventually farmers were to establish their own wholesale and retail marketing systems and were allowed to sell directly to urban areas at market-clearing prices. This gave rise to a market for truckers to buy, transport, and resell farm products. Over the next seven years agricultural output increased by an impressive 8 to 10 percent per year. Based in part on China's success, in 1991 Russia began carving up state-owned farms and giving parts to individual farmers. By mid-1992 some seventy thousand family farms were operating.[11]

In structuring the transition from central planning to a market system, economists are feeling their way. Nobel Prize winner Friedrich von Hayek argued that a fundamental flaw of central planning is that, unlike competitive markets, it provides no way to discover and process localized information about supply and demand. And the more rigid prices become, the less information they convey. Hayek believed that *government's role is to support the dynamic market order by identifying and codifying the conventions of trade and by protecting property rights.* According to Hayek, competition generates market-clearing prices in a discovery process. But the determination of the rules of "just conduct" for supporting market order is also a discovery process for lawmakers. Both discovery processes are especially difficult for transitional economies that have no history of market interaction and no established record of codified law or rules of conduct for market participants.

Conclusion

Lifting the bonds of state control has unleashed some pent-up forces. The fall of communism has been relatively peaceful in some countries but has resulted in the fragmentation of other countries. The fifteen former republics of the Soviet Union are now independent nations; ten are held together in a loose organization called the Commonwealth of Independent States. Some Eastern European countries in transition were on the verge of collapse, with high inflation and a collapsing industrial output. Czechoslovakia split in two after its peaceful "velvet" revolution because the Slovaks wanted to move more slowly to a market economy than did the Czechs. But the regions of what had been Yugoslavia erupted in a separatist revolt. Poland was trying to establish a privatized system through which shares of stock in state-owned firms would be sold to Polish citizens, with a fund of these shares run by foreign fund managers. After a bumpy start, Poland in the latter half of 1992 became the first transitional economy in Eastern Europe to experience economic growth. China continued on a gradual path to a market economy, using its farms and southern provinces as testing grounds. From Africa to

11. "Russian Farming: The Least Likely Agricultural Miracle," *The Economist*, 11 April 1992.

Mongolia the trend around the world has been toward more use of market incentives and less reliance on bureaucratic coordination.

Some may look at the initial instability that resulted from the dismantling of communist states and argue that the move toward markets has been a failure. But in the former Soviet Union, for example, the state dismantled central controls before institutions such as property rights, customs, codes of conduct, and a legal system were in place. For example, the personal income tax in Russia jumped from a graduated rate topping out at 13 percent to a flat rate of 60 percent and then to a graduated rate topping at 40 percent. As long as taxes seem so arbitrary and capricious, people have less incentive to work, to save, to invest, and more generally to go about the business of building an economy. Some monopoly state enterprises used the relaxation of pricing restrictions as an excuse to jack up prices and then to raise wages to soak up the resulting profit. Firms that failed to cover costs at the higher price were subsidized by the state, resulting in huge deficits. Worse yet, some enterprise insiders, such as directors, stripped enterprises of their assets, which they sold. The corruption drifted down to the store clerks who channeled valued goods to the black market.

Example Business executives in Moscow complain of contracts signed and simply ignored, of money paid and goods never delivered. Car theft is one of Moscow's most thriving businesses. Cynics claim that organized crime is one of the few sectors in Russia that is growing, because crime was already privatized.

So the jury is still out on the transition to markets. Lessons about the nature of economic processes will likely emerge from the analysis of these transitions. The course of economic reform will provide insights into both the potential and the limits of economics itself.

SUMMARY

1. Economic systems can be classified based on the ownership of resources, the way these resources are allocated to produce goods and services, and the incentives used to motivate people. In capitalist systems resources are owned by individuals and are allocated through market coordination. In socialist economies resources other than labor are owned by the state. Under planned socialism resources are directed by bureaucratic coordination. Under market socialism resources are directed by market coordination.

2. Gosplan was the Soviet Union's state agency that developed the central plan for production targets in major industrial sectors. Production decisions for less important commodities were relegated to a lower level of the planning bureaucracy or in some cases were left to the market. Because prices for most goods and services were set by the state below their market-clearing level, the quantity demanded exceeded the quantity supplied, resulting in long lines and at times panic buying.

3. There were three economies in the Soviet Union: (1) the official economy, established by the central plan; (2) the "second economy," which was the Soviet version of the underground economy; and (3) the "informal economy," through which Soviet managers pursued official objectives by skirting the official rules. The second economy and the informal economy evolved in response to shortcomings of the official economy.

4. Under Gorbachev, *perestroika* did not result in greater availability, better quality, or more variety in consumer goods. It only heightened consumer expectations. Ironically, *glasnost*, the policy of greater openness, made people more aware of nationwide shortages of consumer goods. Because of *glasnost*, consumer shortages were publicly admitted, and public grievances were aired for the first time since the Russian Revolution.

5. Major reforms have been introduced in recent years to decentralize decision making, to provide greater

production incentives to the workers, and to introduce private markets. But central controls were dismantled before the institutional framework had developed to support a market economy, and the initial result has been opportunistic behavior by bureaucratic insiders, growing government debt to subsidize money-losing enterprises, high inflation, falling output, and the spread of organized crime.

Questions and Problems

1. (Socialism) Is there any reason why socialist economies couldn't have as much diversity in the production of goods as capitalist economies do? Does your answer depend on how much central planning is undertaken by the government?

2. (Capitalism) Many socialists stress the fact that in market economies there is much waste resulting from the production of useless luxuries for the rich. Also, they claim that consumers are often fooled into buying products they do not really want through advertising ploys. How would you respond to such claims?

3. (Ownership of Resources) Socialists argue that no person is responsible for creating the natural resources found in a country. Therefore these resources should be publicly owned. Do you see problems with this line of reasoning? Consider also the efficiency of private ownership.

4. (Material Balance System) Would the Soviet method of material balance planning necessarily lead to a burdensome expansion of the bureaucracy? How might lags in decision making cause problems?

5. (Internal Passports) Why might the authorities in centrally planned economies attempt to prevent migration through the use of internal passports?

6. (China and Socialism) One of the periods of greatest economic growth in China was shortly after the communist revolution of 1949. How might you explain this short-term economic success of central planning?

7. (Specialization) Explain why central planning in the former Soviet Union led many companies to abandon specialization of production in favor of self-reliance and independence of production.

8. (Rationing Without Prices) The price in Exhibit 1 is set in such a way that there is a shortage of chicken.
   a. Do any consumers lose out compared to the situation in which the price clears the market?
   b. Is a "black market" for chicken likely to develop? Why?

9. (Rationing Without Prices) In China there are "friendship stores," which typically carry imported goods that can be purchased only with foreign exchange certificates, not with domestic currency. Can you suggest any reasons for having such stores?

10. (Centrally Owned Resources) In an economy in which the state owns resources like land and capital, such resources are often wasted. Can you explain such waste in terms of the "common pool problem" discussed in the chapter on externalities and the environment?

11. (Rationing With or Without Markets) One of the questions every economic system must answer is for whom are products produced. How is the answer determined in a market system as compared to a centrally planned system? Which is fairer?

12. (Productivity and Technology) As the chapter notes, one impediment to productivity growth in a command economy is the lack of diffusion of technology. Why is diffusion difficult in such an economy? How does knowledge of new technology spread in a market system?

13. (Price and Shortages) Setting prices of consumer goods below cost need not, in and of itself, lead to shortages. However, to avoid shortages or surpluses, one needs to know what the demand curves look like and to be able to control supply. Explain. Can you set price below cost for all goods and avoid shortages?

14. (Reform in Russia) Obviously the conversion to a market-based system of resource allocation, particularly in an economy like that in Russia where consumer goods were priced below production cost, is difficult, and Yeltsin has a large array of opponents to such change. Who would gain from the conversion?

15. (Transition Problems) Explain why a system of well-defined and enforceable property rights is crucial when converting to a market-based system of resource allocation.

16. (The Informal Economy) Because the system for distributing critical resources to various industries in the Soviet Union was so ineffective, firms tended to produce many such resources internally. In agriculture, for example, a farmer needed to be a "jack-of-all-trades," maintaining everything from buildings to farm equipment and animals. Explain how such a system creates inefficiency.

17. (The Informal Economy) Explain how paying resources at rates reflective of their opportunity cost would alter this situation.

18. (No Soap) The situation in the Soviet soap market, where speculation became reality, is similar to what often happens in foreign exchange markets when rates are flexible. Explain.

19. (No Soap) When products like soap and food are hoarded and prices (both official and unofficial) increase, what does holding onto these goods actually cost those who hoard them?

GLOSSARY

A

absolute advantage The ability to produce something with fewer resources than other producers would use to produce the same thing

accounting profit A firm's total revenue minus its explicit cost

activists Those who consider the private sector to be relatively unstable and able to absorb economic shocks only with the aid of discretionary government policy

actual investment The amount of investment actually undertaken during a year; equals planned investment plus unplanned changes in inventories

adverse selection A situation in which those on the informed side of the market self-select in a way that harms the uninformed side of the market

adverse supply shocks Unexpected events that reduce aggregate supply, sometimes only temporarily

agent A person who performs work or provides a service on behalf of another person, the principal

aggregate demand The relation between the price level in the economy and the quantity of aggregate output demanded

aggregate demand curve A curve representing the relation between the economy's price level and the amount of aggregate output demanded per period of time, other things held constant

aggregate expenditure Total spending on final goods and services at a given price level during a given time period

aggregate expenditure function A relationship showing, for a given price level, the amount of planned spending for each level of income; the total of $C + I + NX$

aggregate income The sum of all income earned by resource suppliers in an economy during a given time period

aggregate output The total quantity of final goods and services produced in an economy during a given time period

aggregate supply curve A curve representing the relation between the economy's price level and the amount of aggregate output supplied per period of time, other things held constant

allocative efficiency The condition that exists when firms produce the output that is most preferred by consumers; an industry is operating with allocative efficiency when the marginal cost of each good just equals the marginal benefit that consumers derive from that good

alternative goods Other goods that use some of the same type of resources used to produce the good in question

annually balanced budget Budget philosophy prior to the Great Depression; aimed at equating revenues with expenditures, except during times of war

annuity A given sum of money received each year for a specified number of years

antitrust activity Government activity aimed at preventing monopoly and fostering competition

applied research Research that seeks to answer particular questions or to apply scientific discoveries to the development of specific products

arbitrageur A person who takes advantage of temporary geographic differences in the exchange rate by simultaneously purchasing foreign exchange in one market and selling it in another market

asset Anything of value that is owned

association-causation fallacy The incorrect idea that if two variables are associated in time, one must necessarily cause the other

asymmetric information An inequality in the information known by each party to a transaction; or, a situation in which one side of the market has more reliable information than does the other side

autarky A situation of national self-sufficiency in which there is no economic interaction with foreigners

automatic stabilizers Structural features of government spending and taxation that smooth fluctuations in disposable income over the business cycle

autonomous A term that means "independent"; autonomous investment is independent of the level of income

autonomous government purchases Government purchases that do not vary with the level of real GDP

autonomous net taxes Taxes minus transfers, independent of the level of real GDP

average fixed cost Total fixed cost divided by output

average revenue Total revenue divided by output

average total cost Total cost divided by output; the sum of average fixed cost plus average variable cost

average variable cost Total variable cost divided by output

B

backward-bending supply curve of labor Occurs when the income effect of a higher wage dominates the substitution effect of a higher wage

balance of payments A record of all economic transactions between residents of one country and residents of the rest of the world during a given time period

balance on current account A section of a country's balance of payments account that measures the sum of the country's net unilateral transfers and its balance on goods and services

balance on goods and services A section of a country's balance of payments account that measures the difference in value between a country's exports of goods and services and its imports of goods and services

balance sheet A financial statement that shows assets, liabilities, and net worth at a given point in time

balanced budget amendment Proposed amendment to the U.S. Constitution requiring a balanced federal budget

balanced budget multiplier A factor that shows that identical changes in government purchases and net taxes change equilibrium real GDP demanded by that same amount

bank holding company A corporation that owns banks

bank notes Papers promising a specific amount of money in gold to bearers who presented them to issuing banks for redemption; an early type of money

barrier to entry Any impediment that prevents new firms from competing on an equal basis with existing firms in an industry

barter The direct exchange of one good for another without the use of money

base year A reference year against which other years are measured

basic research The search for knowledge without regard to how that knowledge will be used; a first step toward technological advancement

behavioral assumption An assumption that describes the expected behavior of economic actors

beneficial supply shocks Unexpected events that increase aggregate supply, sometimes only temporarily

bilateral monopoly A situation in which a single seller, or monopolist, bargains with a single buyer, or monopsonist

binding arbitration Negotiation in which both parties in a union-management dispute agree to accept an impartial observer's resolution of the dispute

bond A certificate reflecting a firm's promise to pay the holder a periodic interest payment until the date of maturity and a fixed sum of money on the designated maturity date

bounded rationality The notion that there is a limit on the amount of information an economic agent, such as a manager, can comprehend

budget deficit Amount by which government spending during the year exceeds government revenues

budget line A line showing all combinations of two goods that can be purchased at given prices with a fixed amount of income

bureaucratic coordination A type of economic coordination whereby an administrative hierarchy directs the activities of economic actors

bureaus Government agencies charged with implementing legislation and financed by appropriations from legislative bodies

business cycle The rise and fall of economic activity relative to the long-term growth trend of the economy

C

capital All buildings, equipment, and human skill used to produce goods and services

capital account The record of a country's international transactions involving purchases or sales of financial and real assets

cartel A group of firms that agree to coordinate their production and pricing decisions

change in demand A shift in a given demand curve caused by a change in one of the determinants of demand for the good

change in quantity demanded A movement along the demand curve for a good in response to a change in the price of the good

change in quantity supplied A movement along the supply curve for a good in response to a change in the price of the good

change in supply A shift in a given supply curve caused by a change in one of the determinants of the supply of the good

checkable deposits Deposits in financial institutions against which checks can be written

classical economists A group of eighteenth- and nineteenth-century British economists who criticized mercantilism and believed that self-interest and competition promoted economic development

Coase theorem The theory that as long as bargaining costs are small, an efficient solution to the problem of externalities will be achieved by assigning property rights

cold turkey The announcement and execution of tough measures to reduce high inflation

collective bargaining The process by which union and management negotiate a mutually agreeable labor agreement

command economy An economic system characterized by centralized economic planning and public ownership of resources

commercial banks Depository institutions that make short-term loans primarily to businesses

commodity money Anything that serves both as money and as a commodity

common pool problem The problem that unrestricted access to a resource results in overuse until the net marginal value of additional use drops to zero

comparable worth The principle that pay should be determined by job characteristics rather than by supply and demand

comparative advantage The ability to produce something at a lower opportunity cost than other producers face

competing-interest legislation Legislation that imposes concentrated costs on one group and provides concentrated benefits to another group

complements Goods that are related in such a way that an increase in the price of one leads to a decrease in the demand for the other

concentration ratio A measure of the market share of the largest firms in an industry

conglomerate merger A merger involving the combination of firms producing in different industries

consent decree A legal agreement through which the accused party, without admitting guilt, agrees to refrain in the future from certain illegal activity if the government drops the charges

constant-cost industry An industry that can expand or contract without affecting the long-run per-unit cost of production; the long-run industry supply curve is horizontal

constant elasticity of demand The type of demand that exists when price elasticity is the same everywhere along the curve; the elasticity value is constant

consumer equilibrium The condition in which an individual consumer's budget is completely exhausted and the last dollar spent on each good yields the same marginal utility

consumer price index (CPI) A measure over time of the cost of a fixed "market basket" of consumer goods and services

consumer surplus The difference between the maximum amount that a consumer is willing to pay for a given quantity of a good and what the consumer actually pays

consumption All household purchases of final goods and services

consumption function The relation between the level of income in an economy and the amount households spend on consumption, other things constant

consumption possibilities schedule A schedule reflecting the alternative consumption possibilities available in an economy; in the absence of trade, the consumption possibilities schedule is the same as the production possibilities schedule

contestable market One in which potential entrants can serve the same market and have access to the same technology as the existing firm

continuing resolution Budget agreements that allow agencies, in the absence of an approved budget, to spend at the rate of the previous year's budget

contractionary gap The amount by which actual output in the short run falls below the economy's potential output

convergence A theory that economies around the world will grow more alike over time, with poorer countries catching up with richer countries

corporate profits A component of the government measure of national income; the net revenues received by incorporated business before corporate income taxes are subtracted

corporation A legal entity owned by stockholders whose liability is limited to the value of their stock

cost-plus pricing A method of determining the price of a good by adding a percentage markup to the average variable cost

cost-push inflation A continuous rise in the price level caused by reductions in aggregate supply

craft union A union whose members have a particular skill or work at a particular craft, such as plumbers or carpenters

cross-price elasticity of demand The percentage change in the quantity demanded of one good (holding the price constant) divided by the percentage change in the price of another good

cross-subsidization A firm's use of revenues from profitable activities to subsidize unprofitable activities

crowding in The potential for government spending to stimulate private investment in an otherwise sluggish economy

crowding out The displacement of interest-sensitive private investment that occurs when increased government spending drives up interest rates

currency appreciation A decrease in the number of units of a particular currency needed to purchase one unit of another currency

currency depreciation An increase in the number of units of a particular currency needed to purchase one unit of another currency

currency devaluation An increase in the official pegged price of foreign currency in terms of the domestic currency

currency revaluation A reduction in the official pegged price of foreign currency in terms of the domestic currency

current dollar value The value of dollars that are actually paid or received at the time of a transaction; nominal dollar values of national output

cyclical majority A situation in which no choice dominates all others, and the outcome of a vote depends on the order in which issues are considered

cyclical unemployment Unemployment that occurs because of declines in the economy's aggregate output during recessions

cyclically balanced budget Budget philosophy calling for budget deficits during recessions to be financed by budget surpluses during expansions

D

deadweight loss A loss of consumer surplus that is not transferred to anyone else; it can arise from monopolization of an industry

decision-making lag The time needed

to decide what changes to make in government policy after a macroeconomic problem is identified

decreasing-cost industry The rare case in which an industry faces lower per-unit production costs as it expands in the long run; the long-run industry supply curve slopes downward

deflation A sustained and continuous decrease in the price level

demand A relation showing how much of a good consumers are willing and able to buy at each possible price during a given period of time, other things constant

demand curve A curve showing the quantity of a commodity demanded at various possible prices, other things constant

demand deposits Accounts at financial institutions that pay no interest and on which depositors can write checks to obtain their deposits at any time

demand for loanable funds The relation between the market rate of interest and the quantity of loanable funds demanded, other things constant

demand-pull inflation A continuous rise in the price level caused by increases in aggregate demand

demand-side economics Macroeconomic policy that focuses on changes in aggregate demand as a way of promoting full employment and price stability

dependent variable A variable whose value is affected by the value(s) of some other variable(s)

depository institutions Commercial banks and other financial institutions that accept deposits from the public

depreciation The value of capital stock used up during a year in producing GDP

depression A severe reduction in an economy's total production accompanied by high unemployment lasting several years

derived demand Demand for a resource that is derived from demand for the product the resource helps to produce

developing countries Nations typified by high rates of illiteracy, high unemployment, rapid population growth, and exports of primary products

discount rate The interest rate the Federal Reserve charges banks for discount loans; also, the interest rate used to convert income to be received in the future into present value

discounting Determining the present value of a sum of money to be received in the future

discouraged worker A person who has dropped out of the labor force because of lack of success in finding a job

discretionary fiscal policy The deliberate manipulation of government spending or taxation in order to promote full employment and price stability

diseconomies of scale Forces that cause a firm's average cost to increase as the scale of operations increases in the long run

disinflation A reduction in the rate of inflation

disposable income The income households have available to spend or save after paying taxes and receiving transfer payments

division of labor The organization of production of a single good into separate tasks in which people specialize

double coincidence of wants A situation in which two traders are willing to exchange their products directly

dumping Selling a commodity abroad at a price that is below its cost of production or below the price charged in the domestic market

E

economic profit A firm's total revenue minus its explicit and implicit costs

economic regulation Government measures aimed at controlling prices, output, market entry and exit, and product quality in situations in which, because of economies of scale, average production costs are lowest when the market is served by only one or a few firms

economic rent The portion of a resource's total earnings above its opportunity cost; earnings above the amount necessary to keep the resource in its present use

economic system The set of mechanisms and institutions that resolve the what, how, and for whom questions

economic theory or model A simplification of reality designed to capture the important elements of the relationship under consideration

economics The study of how people choose to use their scarce resources in an attempt to satisfy unlimited wants

economies of scale Forces that cause reductions in a firm's average cost as the scale of operations is increased in the long run

economies of scope Forces that make it cheaper for a firm to produce two or more different products than just one

effectiveness lag The time necessary for changes in monetary or fiscal policy to have an effect on the economy

efficiency The condition that exists when there is no way resources can be reallocated to increase the production of one good without decreasing the production of another

efficiency wage theory The idea that keeping wages above the level required to attract a sufficient pool of workers makes workers compete to keep their jobs and results in greater productivity

elastic demand The type of demand that exists when a change in price has a relatively large effect on quantity demanded; the percentage change in quantity demanded exceeds the percentage change in price

employee compensation A component of the government measure of national income made up of wages and salaries plus payments by employers to cover Social Security taxes, medical insurance, and other fringe benefits

entrepreneurial ability Managerial and organization skills combined with the willingness to take risks

equation of exchange The quantity of money, *M,* multiplied by its velocity, *V,* equals nominal income, which is the product of the price level, *P,* and real GDP, *Y*

equilibrium The condition that exists in a market when the plans of buyers match the plans of sellers

excess capacity The difference between a monopolistic competitor's minimum average cost and its profit-maximizing level of output

excess reserves Reserves held by depository institutions in excess of required reserves

exchange rate The price of one country's currency measured in terms of another country's currency

exclusive dealing The situation that occurs when a producer prohibits customers from purchasing from other sellers

expansion An increase in the economy's total production lasting six months or longer

expansionary gap The amount by which actual output in the short run exceeds the economy's potential output

expected real rate of interest The expected interest rate expressed in dollars of constant value; the nominal interest rate minus the expected inflation rate

expenditure approach A method of calculating GDP that involves adding up expenditures on all final goods and services produced during the year

explicit cost Opportunity cost of a firm's resources that takes the form of actual cash payments

export promotion A development strategy that concentrates on producing for the export market

externality A cost or a benefit that falls on a third party and is therefore ignored by those who take part in the transaction

F

fallacy of composition The incorrect belief that what is true for the individual or part must necessarily be true for the group or whole

featherbedding Union efforts to force employers to hire more workers than needed for the task

federal funds market A market for day-to-day lending and borrowing of reserves among financial institutions

federal funds rate The interest rate prevailing in the federal funds market

Federal Reserve System The central bank and monetary authority of the United States, known as "the Fed"

fiat money Money not redeemable for any commodity; its status as money is conferred by the government

final goods and services Goods and services sold to final, or ultimate, users

financial intermediaries Institutions that serve as go-betweens, accepting funds from savers and lending those funds to borrowers

financial markets Banks and other institutions that facilitate the flow of funds from savers to borrowers

firms Economic units, formed by profit-seeking entrepreneurs, that hire resources to produce goods and services for sale

fiscal policy The use of government purchases, taxes, and borrowing to influence aggregate economic activity

fixed cost Any production cost that is independent of the firm's rate of output

fixed exchange rates Rates pegged within a narrow range of values by central banks' ongoing purchases and sales of currencies

fixed-production technology Technology for which the relation between output and the generation of an externality is a fixed one; the only way to reduce the externality is to reduce the output

fixed resource Any resource that cannot be varied in the short run

flexible exchange rates Rates determined by the forces of supply and demand without government intervention

flow A variable that measures the amount of something over an interval of time, such as the amount you spend on food per week

foreign aid An international transfer made on especially favorable terms for the purpose of promoting economic development

foreign exchange The currency of another country needed to carry out international transactions

fractional reserve banking system A banking system in which only a portion of deposits in the depository institutions are backed up by reserves

frictional unemployment Unemployment that arises because of the time needed to match qualified job seekers with available job openings

full employment The level of employment when there is no cyclical unemployment

functional finance Budget philosophy aiming fiscal policy at achieving potential GDP rather than balancing budgets either annually or over the business cycle

functional relation A relation between two variables in which the value of one variable depends on the value of the other variable

G

game theory A model that analyzes oligopolistic behavior as a series of strategic moves and countermoves by rival firms

GDP implicit price deflator A comprehensive price index of all goods and services included in the gross domestic product

General Agreement on Tariffs and Trade (GATT) An international tariff-reduction treaty adopted in 1947 by the United States and twenty-three other countries; there are nearly one hundred treaty signers today

glasnost The greater willingness of what had been the Soviet government to allow the Soviet people and the rest of the world know what was going on in the Soviet Union

gold standard An arrangement whereby the currencies of most countries are convertible into gold at a fixed rate

golden rule of profit maximization To maximize profit or minimize loss a firm should produce at the level of output where marginal cost equals marginal revenue

good A tangible item that is used to satisfy wants

government budget A plan for government expenditures and revenues for a specified period, usually a year

government budget deficit A flow variable measuring, for a particular time period, the amount by which one flow variable, total government outlays, exceeds another flow variable, total government revenues

government debt A stock variable measuring, at a particular point in time, the net accumulation of all prior budget deficits

government purchases Spending for goods and services by all levels of government

government subsidies Government transfers to businesses

graph A diagram that shows the relationship between one variable and another

greenhouse effect The formation of a blanket of carbon dioxide and other gases around the earth, causing heat buildup

Gresham's Law People tend to trade away inferior money and hoard the best

gross domestic product (GDP) The market value of all final goods and services produced by resources located in the United States, regardless of who owns those resources

gross investment The value of all investment during a period, including investment required to replace capital used up during the production process

gross national product (GNP) The market value of all final goods and services produced by resources supplied by U.S. residents and firms, regardless of location

gross product The market value of final goods and services produced in a particular geographical region during a given time period, usually one year

H

Herfindahl index The sum of the squared percentage market shares of all firms in an industry; a measure of the level of concentration in that industry

hidden actions A type of asymmetric information problem in which one side of an economic relation can take a relevant action that the other side cannot observe

hidden characteristics A type of asymmetric information problem in which one side of the market knows more than the other side about characteristics that are important to the transaction

horizontal axis The base line of a graph; sometimes called the *x*-axis

horizontal merger A merger in which one firm combines with another firm that produces the same product

hyperinflation A very high rate of inflation

hypothesis A statement about relationships among key variables

hysteresis The theory that a sustained period of high (or low) unemployment can increase (or decrease) the natural rate of unemployment

I

implementation lag The time needed to introduce a change in monetary or fiscal policy

implicit cost A firm's opportunity cost of using its own resources or those provided by its owners without a corresponding cash payment

import substitution A development strategy that emphasizes manufacturing products that are currently imported

income approach A method of calculating GDP that involves adding up all payments to owners of resources used to produce output during the year

income effect A fall in the price of a good increases consumers' real income, making them more able to purchase all normal goods, so the quantity demanded increases

income elasticity of demand The percentage change in quantity demanded (holding the price constant) divided by the percentage change in income

income-expenditure model A graph that measures real income on the horizontal axis and aggregate spending on the vertical axis to determine the equilibrium quantity of aggregate output demanded

increasing-cost industry An industry that faces higher per-unit production costs as it expands in the long run; the long-run industry supply curve slopes upward

increasing marginal returns Marginal physical product increases experienced by a firm when another unit of a particular resource is employed, other resources constant

independent variable A variable whose value affects, but is not affected by, the value(s) of some other variable(s)

indifference curve A curve showing all combinations of two goods that provide a consumer the same level of total utility

indifference map A set of indifference curves representing each possible level of total utility that can be derived by a particular consumer from the consumption of two goods

indirect business taxes Federal, state, and local business taxes that are partially or entirely shifted to other taxpayers; taxes on sales and on property are examples

industrial organization A branch of economics that examines the relation between the structure of a market and the conduct and performance of firms in that market

industrial policy The view that government, using taxes, subsidies, and regulations, should nurture the industries and technologies of the future to give domestic industries an advantage over foreign competition

industrial union A union of both skilled and unskilled workers from a particular industry, such as auto workers or steelworkers

inelastic demand The type of demand that exists when a change in price has relatively little effect on quantity demanded; demand is inelastic when the percentage change in quantity demanded is less than the percentage change in price

inferior good A good for which demand decreases as consumer income rises

inflation A sustained and continuous increase in the price level

inflation rate The annual percentage change in the price level

injection Any payment of income other than by firms or any spending other than by domestic households; includes investment, government purchases, transfer payments, and exports

innovation The process of turning an invention into a marketable product

intercept The point where a line or curve in a graph crosses the horizontal or vertical axis

interest The payment resource owners receive for the use of their capital

interest rate The amount of money paid for the use of a dollar for one year

interlocking directorate An arrangement whereby one individual serves on the boards of directors of competing firms

intermediate goods and services Goods and services purchased for further processing and resale

inventories Producers' stocks of finished or in-process goods

investment Purchases of output produced during a year but not used for current consumption

investment demand curve The relation between the market rate of interest and the quantity of investment demanded in the economy, other things constant

investment function The relation between planned investment and the level of income, other things constant

K

kinked demand curve A curve that illustrates price stickiness; if one firm cuts its prices, other firms in the industry will cut theirs as well, but if the firm raises its prices, other firms will not change theirs

L

labor The physical and mental effort of humans

labor force All noninstitutionalized individuals sixteen years of age and older who are either working or actively looking for work

labor force participation rate The ratio of the number in the labor force to the population of working age

labor union A group of employees who join together to improve their terms of employment

land Plots of ground and other natural resources used in the production of goods and services

law of comparative advantage The individual or country with the lowest opportunity cost of producing a particular good should specialize in producing that good

law of demand The quantity of a good demanded is inversely related to its price, other things constant

law of diminishing marginal rate of substitution The amount of good A a consumer is willing to give up to get one additional unit of good B declines as the consumption of B increases

law of diminishing marginal returns When more and more of a variable resource is added to a given amount of a fixed resource, the resulting changes in output will eventually diminish

law of diminishing marginal utility The more of a good consumed per period, the smaller the increase in total utility from consuming one more unit, other things constant

law of increasing opportunity cost As more of a particular good is produced, larger and larger quantities of an alternative good must be sacrificed if the economy's resources are already being used fully and efficiently

law of supply The quantity of product supplied in a given time period is usually directly related to its price, other things constant

leading economic indicators Economic statistics, such as housing starts, stock prices, and consumer expectations, that foreshadow future changes in economic activity

leakage Any diversion of aggregate income from the domestic spending stream; includes saving, taxes, and imports

legal tender Anything that creditors are required to accept as payment for debts

leisure Time spent on nonwork activities

leveraged buyout The purchase of controlling interest in a corporation using borrowed funds

liability Anything that is owed to another individual or institution

line-item veto A provision to allow the president to reject particular portions of the budget rather than simply accept or reject the entire budget

linear demand curve A straight-line demand curve

liquidity A measure of the ease with which an asset can be converted into money without significant loss in its value

loanable funds market The market in which savers (suppliers of funds) and borrowers (demanders of funds) come together to determine the market rate of interest

logrolling Vote trading on preferred issues; voter A agrees to vote for voter B's pet project as long as voter B votes for voter A's pet project

long run A period during which all the firm's resources are variable; also, a period during which previous wage contracts and resource price agreements can be renegotiated

long-run aggregate supply (*LRAS*) curve The vertical line drawn at potential output

long-run average cost curve A curve that indicates the lowest average cost of production at each level of output when the firm's plant size is allowed to vary

long-run industry supply curve A curve that shows the relation between price and quantity supplied once firms have fully adjusted to any short-run economic profit or loss

long-run Phillips curve A vertical line drawn at the economy's natural rate of unemployment that traces equilibrium points that can occur when employers and workers have the time and the ability to adjust fully to any unexpected change in aggregate demand

Lorenz curve A curve showing the percentage of total income received by a given percentage of recipients whose incomes are arranged from smallest to largest

M

M1 A measure of the money supply consisting of currency and coin held by the nonbank public, checkable deposits, and traveler's checks

M2 A monetary aggregate consisting of M1 plus savings deposits, small time deposits, and money market mutual funds

M3 A monetary aggregate consisting of M2 plus negotiable certificates of deposit

macroeconomics The study of the behavior of entire economies

managed float system An exchange rate system that combines features of freely floating rates with intervention by central banks

marginal A term meaning "incremental" or "decremental," used to describe a change in an economic variable

marginal cost The change in total cost divided by the change in output; the change in total cost resulting from a one-unit change in output

marginal physical product The change in total physical product that occurs when the usage of a particular resource increases by one unit, all other resources constant

marginal propensity to consume The fraction of a change in disposable income that is spent on consumption; the change in consumption spending divided by the change in disposable income that caused it

marginal propensity to import The fraction of a change in income that is spent on imported goods and services; the change in total spending on imports divided by the change in income that caused it

marginal propensity to save The fraction of a change in disposable income that is saved; a change in saving divided by the change in disposable income that caused it

marginal rate of return on investment The marginal revenue product of capital expressed as a percentage of its marginal cost

marginal rate of substitution (MRS) A measure of how much of one good a consumer would give up to get one more unit of another good while remaining equally satisfied

marginal resource cost The change in total cost when an additional unit of a resource is hired, other things constant

marginal revenue The change in total revenue resulting from a one-unit change in sales

marginal revenue product The change in total revenue when an additional unit of a resource is hired, other things constant

marginal social benefit The sum of the marginal private benefit and the marginal external benefit of production or consumption

marginal social cost The total of the marginal private cost and the marginal external cost of production or consumption

marginal utility The change in total utility derived from a one-unit change in consumption of a good

marginal valuation The dollar value of the marginal utility derived from consuming each additional unit of a good

market A set of arrangements through which buyers and sellers carry out exchange at mutually agreeable terms

market coordination A type of economic coordination whereby price signals in competitive markets direct the activities of economic actors; from a legal perspective, buyers and sellers are on equal footing

market failure A condition that arises when unrestrained operation of markets yields socially undesirable results

market power The ability of one or more firms to maintain a price above the competitive level

market socialism An economic system in which the state owns all resources other than labor but uses market forces to allocate the resources

market structure The important features of a market, such as the number of firms, uniformity of product across firms, ease of entry, and forms of competition

market work Time sold as labor in return for a money wage

material balance system A system of central planning designed to ensure a balance of supply and demand for important types of industrial output

means-tested program A benefit program that requires that recipients' incomes and/or assets be less than specified levels

median income The middle income in a series of incomes ranked from smallest to largest

median voter model Under certain conditions the preference of the median, or middle, voter will dominate other public choices

mediator An impartial observer who listens to both sides separately and suggests how each side could adjust its position to resolve differences

medium of exchange Anything that facilitates trade by being generally accepted by all parties in payment for goods or services

mercantilism A theory that viewed the accumulation of precious metals as the source of a nation's economic vitality; nations that followed the theory tried to promote exports and restrict imports

merchandise trade balance The value of a country's merchandise exports minus the value of its merchandise imports during a given time period

microeconomics The study of the economic behavior of decision makers

midpoint elasticity formula Computes the percentage change by using the average quantity and the average price as bases rather than the initial price and the initial quantity

minimum efficient scale The lowest rate of output at which a firm takes full advantage of economies of scale

monetarism A school of thought that attaches great significance to variations in the money supply as a primary determinant of aggregate demand

monetary aggregates Measures of the economy's money supply

monetary policy Regulation of the money supply by the Fed in order to influence aggregate economic activity; the Fed's role in supplying money to the economy

monetary theory The study of the effect of money on the economy

money A medium that circulates throughout the economy, facilitating the exchange of resources and products among individual economic units; also, anything that is generally acceptable in exchange for goods and services

money market mutual fund A collection of short-term interest-earning assets purchased with funds collected from many shareholders

money multiplier The multiple by which the money supply increases as a result of an increase in excess reserves in the banking system

monopolistic competition A market structure characterized by a large number of firms selling products that are close substitutes yet different enough that each firm's demand curve slopes downward

monopoly A sole producer of a product for which there are no good substitutes

monopsonist The sole purchaser of a particular resource

moral hazard A situation in which one party to a contract has an incentive after the contract is made to alter behavior in a way that harms the other party to the contract

multiplier The ratio of a change in equilibrium income to the initial change in expenditure that brought it about

N

national debt The net accumulation of federal budget deficits

national income The amount of aggregate income earned by suppliers of resources employed to produce GNP; net national product plus government subsidies minus indirect business taxes

natural monopoly When one firm can serve a market more cheaply than two or more firms can, the firm is called a natural monopoly

natural rate hypothesis The natural rate of unemployment is largely independent of the stimulus provided by monetary or fiscal policy

natural rate of unemployment The unemployment rate that occurs when the economy is producing its potential level of output

near moneys Financial assets that are like money but that do not serve as mediums of exchange

negative income tax A cash transfer program in which cash tranfers are reduced as earnings rise

negative (inverse) relation A relation between two variables such that an increase in the value of one causes a decrease in the value of the other

negative-sum game A game in which total losses exceed total winnings

net export function The relation between net exports and the level of income in the economy, other things constant

net exports The value of a country's products purchased by foreigners minus the value of foreign products purchased by a country's residents

net interest A component of the government measure of national income made up of the interest received by individuals, excluding interest paid by consumers to businesses and interest paid by government

net investment Gross investment minus depreciation

net national product GNP minus depreciation; a measure of the value of aggregate output available for use

net taxes *(NT)* Taxes minus transfer payments

net unilateral transfers The unilateral transfers (gifts and grants) received from abroad by residents of a country minus the unilateral transfers these residents send to foreign residents

net wealth The value of a household's assets minus its liabilities

net worth The difference between the values of an institution's assets and liabilities

nominal rate of interest The interest rate expressed in current dollars; the interest rate reported in the media

nominal value Value measured in current-year dollars

nominal wage The wage measured in terms of current dollars; the dollars received in the pay envelope

nonactivists Those who consider the private sector to be relatively stable and able to absorb economic shocks without discretionary government policy

nonmarket work Time spent producing goods and services in the home or acquiring an education

normal good A good for which demand increases as consumer income rises

normal profit The accounting profit required to induce a firm's owners to employ their resources in the firm; the accounting profit earned when all resources used by the firm are earning their opportunity cost

normative economic statement A statement that represents an opinion, which cannot be proved or disproved

O

official reserve transactions account A section of a country's balance of payments that reflects the flow of gold, Special Drawing Rights, and currencies among central banks; the sum of the current account and the capital account

oligopoly A market structure characterized by a small number of firms whose behavior is interdependent

open-access resource A type of resource that is difficult or costly to exclude individuals from using

open-market operations Purchases and sales of government securities by the Federal Reserve in an effort to change the money supply

opportunity cost The benefit expected from the best alternative forgone when an item or activity is chosen

origin The intersection of the horizontal and vertical axes

other-things-constant assumption The assumption, when focusing on key economic variables, that other variables remain unchanged

P

Pareto optimal A change in the status quo that makes at least one person better off while making no one else worse off

partnership A firm with multiple owners who share the firm's profits and who each bear unlimited liability for the firm's debts

patent A legal barrier to entry that conveys to its holder the exclusive right to supply a product for a certain period of time

per se illegality A category of illegality in antitrust law, applied to business practices that are deemed illegal regardless of their economic rationale or their consequences

per-worker production function The relation between the amount of capital per worker in the economy and the output per worker

perestroika The "restructuring" of what had been the Soviet economy to promote more decentralization, less bureaucracy, and greater individual incentives

perfect competition A market structure in which there are large numbers of fully informed buyers and sellers of a homogeneous product and there are no obstacles to entry or exit of firms

perfectly discriminating monopolist A monopolist who charges a different price for each unit of the good

perfectly elastic demand curve A horizontal line reflecting the fact that any price increase reduces quantity demanded to zero; the elasticity value is infinity

perfectly elastic supply curve A horizontal line reflecting the fact that any price decrease reduces the quantity supplied to zero; the elasticity value is infinity

perfectly inelastic demand curve A vertical line reflecting the fact that a price change has no effect on the quantity demanded; the elasticity value is zero

perfectly inelastic supply curve A vertical line reflecting the fact that a price change has no effect on the quantity supplied; the elasticity value is zero

permanent income Income that individuals expect to receive on average over the long term

permanent resource price differentials Differences in resource prices that do not precipitate resource reallocation or price adjustments

personal income The amount of before-tax income received by households; national income less income earned but not received plus income received but not earned

Phillips curve A curve showing possible combinations of the inflation rate and the unemployment rate, given the expected price level

physical capital Manufactured items used to produce goods and services

planned investment The amount of investment firms plan to undertake during a year

planned socialism An economic system in which the state owns all resources other than labor and directs them by means of economic plans and central decision making

political business cycles Business cycles that result when discretionary policy is manipulated for political gain

positive economic statement A statement that can be proved or disproved by reference to facts

positive rate of time preference A characteristic of consumers, who value present consumption more highly than future consumption

positive (direct) relation A relation between two variables such that an increase in the value of one causes an increase in the value of the other

positive-sum game A game in which total winnings exceed total losses

potential output The economy's maximum sustainable output level, given the supply of resources, the state of technology, and the underlying economic institutions; the output level when there are no surprises about the price level

predatory pricing Pricing tactics employed by a dominant firm to drive competitors out of business, such as temporarily selling below cost and dropping the price only in certain markets

present value The value today of a payment or payments to be received in the future

price ceiling A maximum legal price above which a good or service cannot be sold

price discrimination Selling the same good for different prices to different consumers

price elasticity of demand A measure of the responsiveness of quantity demanded to a price change; the percentage change in quantity demanded divided by the percentage change in price

price elasticity of supply A measure of the responsiveness of quantity supplied to a price change; the percentage change in quantity supplied divided by the percentage change in price

price floor A minimum legal price below which a good or service cannot be sold

price leader A firm whose price and price changes are followed by the rest of the industry

price level A composite measure reflecting the prices of all goods and services in the economy

price searcher A firm that has some control over the price it charges because its demand curve slopes downward

price takers Firms that face a given market price for their output and whose actions have no effect on the market price

principal A person who enters into a contractual agreement with an agent in the expectation that the agent will act on behalf of the principal

principal-agent problem Occurs when the agent's objectives differ from those of the principal and the agent can pursue hidden actions

private property rights The right of an owner to use or to exchange property

privatization The process of turning public enterprises into private enterprises

producer surplus The amount by which total revenue from production exceeds total variable cost

product market A market in which goods and services are exchanged

production possibilities frontier A curve showing all alternative combinations of goods that can be produced when available resources are used fully and efficiently

productive efficiency The condition that exists when output is produced with the least-cost combination of inputs, given the level of technology

productivity The ratio of a specific measure of output to a specific measure of input

profit The return resource owners receive for their entrepreneurial ability

proportional income tax Taxes calculated as a percentage of real GDP that remains constant as real GDP increases

proprietors' income A component of the government measure of national income made up of the earnings of farmers and other incorporated businesses

public good A good that is available for all to consume, regardless of who pays and who does not

purchasing power parity theory Exchange rates between two countries will adjust in the long run to reflect price level differences between the countries

pure capitalism An economic system characterized by private ownership of resources and the use of prices to coordinate economic activity in free, competitive markets

Q

quantity theory of money The theory that the velocity of money is predictable, so changes in the money supply have predictable effects on nominal income

quota A legal limit on the quantity of a particular product that can be imported or exported

R

rational expectations A school of thought that claims people form expectations based on all available information, including the probable future actions of government policy makers

rational ignorance A stance adopted by voters when they find that the costs of understanding and voting on a particular issue exceed the expected benefits of doing so

ray A straight line from the origin; that is, a straight line from the intersection of the horizontal and vertical axes

real GDP The value of GDP measured in terms of dollars of fixed purchasing power

real income Income measured in terms of the goods and services it can buy

real rate of interest The nominal rate of interest minus the inflation rate

real wage The wage measured in terms of dollars of constant purchasing power; hence, the wage measured in terms of the quantity of goods and services it will purchase

recession A decline in an economy's total production lasting six months or longer

recognition lag The time needed to identify a macroeconomic problem and assess its seriousness

relevant resources Resources used to produce the good in question

renewable resource A resource that can regenerate itself and so can be used periodically for an indefinite length of time

rent seeking Activities undertaken by individuals or firms to influence public policy in a way that will directly or indirectly redistribute income to themselves; any effort by individuals or firms to obtain favorable treatment from government

rent The payment resource owners receive for the use of their land

rental income of persons A component of the government measure of national income consisting mainly of the imputed rental value of owner-occupied housing

required reserve ratio The proportion of deposits a depository institution is legally required to hold in the form of reserves

required reserves The dollar amount of reserves a depository institution is legally required to hold

reserves Funds that banks use to satisfy the cash demands of their customers; reserves consist of deposits at the Fed plus currency that is physically held by banks

resource market A market in which resources are exchanged

resource price searcher A firm that faces an upward-sloping supply curve for a resource

resource price taker A firm that faces a given market price for a resource; the firm can buy any amount of the resource without affecting the resource price

roundabout production The production of capital goods, which can then be used to produce consumer goods

rule of reason A principle used by a court to examine the reasons for certain business practices and their effects on competition before ruling on their legality

S

saving function The relation between saving and level of income in the economy, other things constant

savings deposits Deposits that earn interest but have no specific maturity date

Say's Law People produce because they want to spend, so the supply of a given quantity of aggregate output generates an equivalent quantity demanded

scarce The amount people desire exceeds the amount that is freely available

screening The process used by employers to select the most qualified workers based on readily observable characteristics, such as level of education

seasonal unemployment Unemployment caused by seasonal shifts in labor supply and demand

secondary effects Unintended consequences of economic actions that develop slowly over time as people react to events

seigniorage The difference between the face value of money and the cost of supplying it; the "profit" from issuing money

separation of ownership from control The situation that exists when no single stockholder or unified group of stockholders owns enough shares to control the management of a corporation

service An intangible activity that is used to satisfy wants

short run A period during which at least one of a firm's resources cannot be varied; also, a period during which some resource prices, especially those for labor, are fixed by agreement

short-run aggregate supply (*SRAS*) curve A curve that shows the direct relation between the price level and the quantity of aggregate output supplied, other things constant

short-run firm supply curve A curve that indicates the quantity a firm supplies at each price in the short run; that portion of a firm's marginal cost curve that rises above the low point on its average variable cost curve

short-run industry supply curve A curve that indicates the quantity all firms in an industry supply at each price in the short run; usually the horizontal sum of each firm's short-run supply curve

short-run Phillips curve A curve that, based on an expected price level, reflects an inverse relation between the inflation rate and the level of unemployment

shortage An excess of quantity demanded over quantity supplied at a given price

signaling Using a proxy measure to communicate information about unobservable characteristics

simple money multiplier The reciprocal of the required reserve ratio, or $1/r$

slope A measure of the steepness of a line, expressed as the ratio of the change in the value measured along the vertical axis to the change in the value measured along the horizontal axis

soft budget constraint The budget condition faced by socialist enterprises that lose money and then are subsidized

sole proprietorship A firm with a single owner who has the right to all profits and who bears unlimited liability for the firm's debts

Special Drawing Right (SDR) A form of international reserve currency created by the International Monetary Fund; its value is a weighted average of the values of the major national currencies

special-interest legislation Legislation that generates concentrated benefits but imposes widespread costs

specialization of labor Focusing an individual's efforts on a particular product or a single task

speculator A person who buys or sells foreign exchange in hopes of profiting from fluctuations in the exchange rate over time

stagflation A contraction of a nation's output accompanied by inflation

standard of value A common unit for measuring the value of every good or service

stock A certificate reflecting ownership of a corporation; also, a variable that measures the amount of something at a particular point in time, such as the amount of money you have right now

store of wealth Anything that retains its purchasing power over time

strike A union's attempt to withhold labor from a firm

strong version of the natural rate hypothesis The short-run gains in employment resulting from monetary or fiscal surprises diminish as the public comes to expect as much

structural deficit A measure of what the federal budget deficit would be if the economy were producing its potential level of output

structural unemployment Unemployment that arises because the skills demanded by employers do not match the skills of the unemployed or because the unemployed do not live where the jobs are located

substitutes Goods that are related in such a way that an increase in the price of one leads to an increase in demand for the other

substitution effect When the price of a good falls, consumers will substitute it for other goods, which are now relatively more expensive

sunk cost A cost that cannot be recovered and that is therefore irrelevant when an economic choice is being made

supply A relation showing how much of a good producers are willing and able to sell at various prices during a given time period, other things constant

supply curve A curve showing the quantity of a good supplied at various prices, other things constant

supply of loanable funds The relation between the market rate of interest and the quantity of savings supplied to the economy, other things constant

supply shocks Unexpected events that affect aggregate supply; sometimes the effect is only temporary

supply-side economics Macroeconomic policy that focuses on use of tax cuts to stimulate production so as to increase aggregate supply

surplus An excess of quantity supplied over quantity demanded at a given price

T

tariff A tax on imports or exports

tastes A consumer's attitudes toward and preferences for different goods and services

tax incidence A description of who actually bears the burden of a tax

temporary resource price differentials Differences in resource prices that trigger resource reallocation and price adjustments

tender offer An offer to buy a controlling number (i.e., more than half) of a firm's shares

term structure of interest rates The relation between the duration of a loan and the interest rate charged

terms of trade An indication of how much of one good will be exchanged for a unit of another good

thrift institutions, or thrifts Depository institutions that make long-term loans primarily to households

time deposits Deposits that earn a fixed rate of interest if they are held for the specified period, which can range anywhere from thirty days to several years

time inconsistency problem The problem that arises when policy makers have an incentive to announce one policy to influence expectations but then pursue a different policy once those expectations have been formed and acted upon

time-series graph A graph showing the behavior of one or more variables over time

token money The name given to money whose face value exceeds the value of the material from which it is made

total cost The sum of fixed cost and variable cost

total physical product The total output produced by a firm

total revenue Price multiplied by the quantity sold at that price

total utility The total satisfaction a consumer derives from consumption

total wage bill Employment multiplied by the average wage rate

transaction costs The costs of time and information required to carry out an exchange

transactions demand for money The demand for money to support the exchange of goods and services

transfer payments Cash or in-kind benefits given to individuals as outright grants from the government

trust A merger of or collusive agreement among competing firms

tying contract An arrangement in which a seller of one good requires buyers to purchase other goods as well

U

underemployment A situation in which workers are overqualified for their jobs or work fewer hours than they would prefer

underground economy An expression used to describe all market exchange that goes unreported either because it is illegal or because those involved want to evade taxes

unemployment insurance Temporary income provided to unemployed workers who actively seek employment and who meet other qualifications

unemployment rate The number of unemployed individuals expressed as a percentage of the labor force

unitary elastic demand The type of demand that exists when a percentage change in price causes an equal percentage change in quantity demanded; the elasticity value is one

unitary elastic supply A percentage change in price causes an equal percentage change in quantity supplied; depicted by a supply curve that is a ray from the origin; the elasticity value is one

utility The satisfaction received from consuming a good or service

V

value added The difference at each stage of production between the value of a product and the cost of materials needed to make it

variable A measure, such as price or quantity, that can take on different possible values

variable cost Any production cost that increases as output increases

variable resource Any resource that can be quickly varied in the short run to increase or decrease the level of output

variable technology A technology whose externality can be reduced by altering the production process rather than simply by altering the rate of output

velocity of money The average number of times per year a dollar is used to purchase final goods and services

vertical axis The line drawn perpendicular to the base line of a graph; sometimes called the *y*-axis

vertical integration The expansion of a firm into stages of production earlier or later than those in which it has specialized

vertical merger A merger in which one firm combines with another from which it purchases inputs or to which it sells output

W

wages The payment resource owners receive for their labor

weak version of the natural rate hypothesis Policy makers can influence the tradeoff between unemployment and inflation in the short run but not in the long run

winner's curse The plight of the winning bidder for an asset of uncertain value who has overestimated the asset's true value

world price The price at which a good or service is traded internationally;

it is determined by the world supply and demand for a product

Z

zero-sum game A game in which total winnings just equal total losses

INDEX

Marginal definitions and their page numbers are indicated in boldface type.

N

TABLE C U.S. MONEY SUPPLY AND INTEREST RATES

Year	M1	M2	M3	Three-Month T-Bill Rate	Prime Rate	Federal Funds Rate
	Billions of Dollars			*Percent*		
1969	204.0	589.6	615.1	6.7%	8.0%	8.2%
1970	214.5	628.1	677.4	6.5%	7.9%	7.2%
1971	228.4	712.7	776.2	4.3%	5.7%	4.7%
1972	249.3	805.2	886.0	4.1%	5.3%	4.4%
1973	262.9	861.0	985.0	7.0%	8.0%	8.7%
1974	274.4	908.6	1,070.4	7.9%	10.8%	10.5%
1975	287.6	1,023.3	1,172.3	5.8%	7.9%	5.8%
1976	306.4	1,163.7	1,311.8	5.0%	6.8%	5.0%
1977	331.3	1,286.7	1,472.6	5.3%	6.8%	5.5%
1978	358.5	1,389.0	1,646.6	7.2%	9.1%	7.9%
1979	382.9	1,497.1	1,803.2	10.0%	12.7%	11.2%
1980	408.9	1,629.9	1,987.5	11.5%	15.3%	13.4%
1981	436.5	1,793.5	2,234.2	14.0%	18.9%	16.4%
1982	474.5	1,953.1	2,441.9	10.7%	14.9%	12.3%
1983	521.2	2,186.5	2,693.4	8.6%	10.8%	9.1%
1984	552.1	2,371.6	2,982.8	9.6%	12.0%	10.2%
1985	620.1	2,570.6	3,202.1	7.5%	9.9%	8.1%
1986	724.7	2,814.2	3,494.5	6.0%	8.3%	6.8%
1987	750.4	2,913.2	3,678.7	5.8%	8.2%	6.7%
1988	787.5	3,072.4	3,918.3	6.7%	9.3%	7.6%
1989	794.1	3,227.3	4,059.8	8.1%	10.9%	9.2%
1990	826.1	3,339.0	4,114.6	7.5%	10.0%	8.1%
1991	899.3	3,445.8	4,168.1	5.4%	8.5%	5.7%
1992	1,026.6	3,497.3	4,167.1	3.5%	6.3%	3.5%

TABLE D LABOR MARKET DATA

Year	Civilian Labor Force	Civilian Employment	Unemployment	Civilian Unemployment Rate	Civilian Labor Force Participation Rate	Output per Hour (1982=100)
	Millions of Persons			*Percent*		*Index Number*
1969	80.7	77.9	2.8	3.5%	60.1%	86.5
1970	82.8	78.7	4.1	4.9%	60.4%	87.3
1971	84.4	79.4	5.0	5.9%	60.2%	90.1
1972	87.0	82.2	4.9	5.6%	60.4%	92.8
1973	89.4	85.1	4.4	4.9%	60.8%	95.0
1974	91.9	86.8	5.2	5.6%	61.3%	93.2
1975	93.8	85.8	7.9	8.5%	61.2%	95.1
1976	96.2	88.8	7.4	7.7%	61.6%	97.9
1977	99.0	92.0	7.0	7.1%	62.3%	99.7
1978	102.3	96.0	6.2	6.1%	63.2%	100.6
1979	105.0	98.8	6.1	5.8%	63.7%	99.5
1980	106.9	99.3	7.6	7.1%	63.8%	99.2
1981	108.7	100.4	8.3	7.6%	63.9%	100.7
1982	110.2	99.5	10.7	9.7%	64.0%	100.0
1983	111.6	100.8	10.7	9.6%	64.0%	102.3
1984	113.5	105.0	8.5	7.5%	64.4%	104.9
1985	115.5	107.2	8.3	7.2%	64.8%	106.1
1986	117.8	109.6	8.2	7.0%	65.3%	108.3
1987	119.9	112.4	7.4	6.2%	65.6%	109.4
1988	121.7	115.0	6.7	5.5%	65.9%	110.4
1989	123.9	117.3	6.5	5.3%	66.5%	109.5
1990	124.8	117.9	6.9	5.5%	66.4%	109.7
1991	125.3	116.9	8.4	6.7%	66.0%	110.1
1992	127.0	117.6	9.4	7.4%	66.3%	113.3

SOURCE: *Economic Report of the President,* January, 1993.